SIXTH EDITION

Programming iOS 9

Matt Neuburg

Beijing · Boston · Farnham · Sebastopol · Tokyo

Programming iOS 9, Sixth Edition

by Matt Neuburg

Copyright © 2016 Matt Neuburg. All rights reserved.

Printed in the United States of America.

Published by O'Reilly Media, Inc., 1005 Gravenstein Highway North, Sebastopol, CA 95472.

O'Reilly books may be purchased for educational, business, or sales promotional use. Online editions are also available for most titles (*http://safaribooksonline.com*). For more information, contact our corporate/institutional sales department: (800) 998-9938 or *corporate@oreilly.com*.

Editor: Rachel Roumeliotis
Production Editor: Kristen Brown
Proofreader: O'Reilly Production Services
Indexer: Matt Neuburg

Cover Designer: Randy Comer
Interior Designer: David Futato
Illustrator: Matt Neuburg

May 2011:	First Edition
March 2012:	Second Edition
March 2013:	Third Edition
December 2013:	Fourth Edition
December 2014:	Fifth Edition
November 2015:	Sixth Edition

Revision History for the Sixth Edition:

2015-11-05:   First release

See *http://oreilly.com/catalog/errata.csp?isbn=9781491936856* for release details.

ISBN: 978-1-491-93685-6

[LSI]

Table of Contents

Part II. Interface

Part III.   Some Frameworks

Part IV.   Final Topics

Preface

Aut lego vel scribo; doceo scrutorve sophian.

—Sedulius Scottus

On June 2, 2014, Apple's WWDC keynote address ended with a shocking announcement: "We have a new programming language." This came as a huge surprise to the developer community, which was accustomed to Objective-C, warts and all, and doubted that Apple could ever possibly relieve them from the weight of its venerable legacy. The developer community, it appeared, had been wrong.

Having picked themselves up off the floor, developers immediately began to examine this new language — Swift — studying it, critiquing it, and deciding whether to use it. My own first move was to translate all my existing iOS apps into Swift; this was enough to convince me that, for all its faults, Swift deserved to be adopted by new students of iOS programming, and that my books, therefore, should henceforth assume that readers are using Swift.

Therefore, Swift is the programming language used throughout this book. Nevertheless, the reader will also need some awareness of Objective-C (including C). The Foundation and Cocoa APIs, the built-in commands with which your code must interact in order to make anything happen on an iOS device, are still written in C and Objective-C. In order to interact with them, you have to know what those languages would expect. For example, in order to pass a Swift array where an Objective-C NSArray is expected, you need to know what consitutes an object acceptable as an element of an Objective-C NSArray.

If you don't already know the Swift language and how it interacts with Objective-C, you'll want to start with my other book, *iOS 9 Programming Fundamentals with Swift*. It is both an introduction and a companion to *Programming iOS 9*. Like Homer's *Iliad*, *Programming iOS 9* begins in the middle of the story, with the reader jumping with all four feet into views and view controllers, and with a knowledge of the language and the Xcode IDE already presupposed. Discussion of the programming language, as well as the Xcode IDE (including the nature of nibs, outlets, and actions, and the mechanics of nib loading), plus the fundamental conventions, classes, and architectures of the Cocoa Touch framework (including delegation, the responder chain, key–value coding, memory management, and so on) — material that constituted Chapters 1–13 in the early editions of this book, but whose presence was eventually deemed to be making the book unwieldy in size and scope — has now been relegated to *iOS 9 Programming Fundamentals with Swift*.

So if something appears to be missing from this book, that's why! If you start reading *Programming iOS 9* and wonder about such unexplained matters as Swift language basics, the UIApplicationMain function, the nib-loading mechanism, Cocoa patterns of delegation and notification, and retain cycles, wonder no longer — I don't explain them here because I have already explained them in *iOS 9 Programming Fundamentals with Swift*. If you're not sufficiently conversant with those topics, I'd suggest that you might want to read that book first; you will then be completely ready for this one.

The Scope of This Book

To a large extent, iOS 9 represents a pause in the steady march of revisions, often quite radical, that Apple has felt free to introduce with every major system update since iOS 3. In my opinion, this is all to the good. iOS 9, for the most part, is not terribly different from iOS 8. Instead, it consists mostly of fairly small but valuable rationalizations of iOS 8, giving the system's growth and development a chance to catch up with itself. For example:

- iOS 9 introduces a new notation for describing a layout constraint.
- iOS 9 expands the power of UIKit dynamics.
- iOS 9 implements unwind segues in such a way that they actually work.

In addition, many small bugs are fixed; these fixes do nothing for those who want their apps to run under iOS 8, but they are welcome nonetheless. To cite just one instance, UIProgressView custom progress images, which stopped working in iOS 7, are working once again in iOS 9.

iOS 9 also brings some important linguistic improvements. A major issue that had to be worked around in the previous edition of this book, covering iOS 8 and Swift 1.2, was that not every C and Objective-C API could be called from Swift, necessitating the frequent use of Objective-C "helper" methods. But in iOS 9 and Swift 2.0, this is no longer the case; I'm happy to say that no Objective-C code appears in this edition.

iOS 9 does introduce a few grand sweeping innovations, such as App Transport Security and iPad multitasking; I am less happy with these, but of course I do document them nonetheless.

Here's a summary of this book's major sections:

- Part I describes *views*, the fundamental units of an iOS app's interface. Views are what the user can see and touch in an iOS app. To make something appear before the user's eyes, you need a view. To let the user interact with your app, you need a view. This part of the book explains how views are created, arranged, drawn, layered, animated, and touched.

- Part II starts by discussing *view controllers*. Perhaps the most remarkable and important feature of iOS programming, view controllers enable views to come and go coherently within the interface, thus allowing a single-windowed app running on what may be a tiny screen to contain multiple screens of material. This part of the book talks about all the ways in which view controllers can be manipulated in order to make their views appear. It also describes *every kind of view* provided by the Cocoa framework — the built-in building blocks with which you'll construct an app's interface.

- Part III surveys the most important secondary *frameworks* provided by iOS. These are clumps of code, sometimes with built-in interface, that are not part of your app by default, but are there for the asking if you need them, allowing you to work with such things as sound, video, user libraries, mail, maps, and the device's sensors.

- Part IV wraps up the book with some miscellaneous but important topics: files, networking, threading, and how to implement undo.

- Appendix A summarizes the most important lifetime event messages sent to your app delegate.

- Appendix B catalogs some useful Swift utility functions. You should keep an eye on this appendix, consulting it whenever a mysterious method name appears. For instance, my example code frequently uses my `delay` function, which embraces `dispatch_after` with a convenient shorthand; when I use `delay` and you don't know what it is, consult this appendix.

Someone who has read this book (and who, it goes without saying, is conversant with the material in *iOS 9 Programming Fundamentals with Swift*) will, I believe, be capable of writing a real-life iOS app, with a clear understanding of what he or she is doing and where the app is going as it grows and develops. The book itself doesn't show how to write any particularly interesting iOS apps; but it is backed by dozens of example projects that you can download from my GitHub site, *http://github.com/mattneub/ Programming-iOS-Book-Examples*, and it constantly uses my own real apps and real programming situations to illustrate and motivate its explanations.

Just as important, this book is intended to prepare you for your own further explorations. In the case of some topics, especially in Parts III and IV, I guide you past the initial barrier of no knowledge to reach an understanding of the topic, its concepts, its capabilities, and its documentation, along with some code examples; but the topic itself may be so huge that there is room only to introduce it here. Your feet, nevertheless, will now be set firmly on the path, and you will know enough that you can now proceed further down that path on your own whenever the need or interest arises.

Indeed, there is *always* more to learn about iOS. iOS is vast! It is all too easy to find areas of iOS that have had to be ruled outside the scope of this book. In Part IV, for example, I peek at Core Data, and demonstrate its use in code, but a true study of Core Data would require an entire book of its own (and such books exist); so, having opened the door, I quickly close it again, lest this book suddenly double in size. By the same token, many areas of iOS are not treated at all in this book:

OpenGL

An open source C library for drawing, including 3D drawing, that takes full advantage of graphics hardware. This is often the most efficient way to draw, especially when animation is involved. iOS incorporates a simplified version of OpenGL called OpenGL ES. See Apple's *OpenGL Programming Guide for iOS*. Open GL interface configuration, texture loading, shading, and calculation are simplified by the GLKit framework; see the *GLKit Framework Reference*. The Metal and (new in iOS 9) Metal Kit and Model I/O classes allow you to increase efficiency and performance.

Sprite Kit

Sprite Kit provides a built-in framework for designing 2D animated games.

Scene Kit

Ported from OS X, this framework makes it much easier to create 3D games and interactive graphics.

Gameplay Kit

New in iOS 9, this framework provides architectural underpinnings for writing a game app.

Accelerate

Certain computation-intensive processes will benefit from the vector-based Accelerate framework. See the *vDSP Programming Guide*.

Game Kit

The Game Kit framework covers three areas that can enhance your user's game experience: Wireless or Bluetooth communication directly between devices (peer-to-peer); voice communication across an existing network connection; and Game Center, which facilitates these and many other aspects of interplayer communication, such as posting and viewing high scores and setting up competitions. See the *Game Kit Programming Guide*. New in iOS 9, users can even make screencasts of their own game play for sharing with one another; see the *ReplayKit Framework Reference*.

Advertising

The iAD framework lets your free app attempt to make money by displaying advertisements provided by Apple. See the *iAD Programming Guide*.

Newsstand

Your app may represent a subscription to something like a newspaper or magazine. See the *Newsstand Kit Framework Reference.*

Printing

See the "Printing" chapter of the *Drawing and Printing Guide for iOS.*

Security

This book does not discuss security topics such as keychains, certificates, and encryption. See the *Security Overview* and the Security framework.

Accessibility

VoiceOver assists visually impaired users by describing the interface aloud. To participate, views must be configured to describe themselves usefully. Built-in views already do this to a large extent, and you can extend this functionality. See the *Accessibility Programming Guide for iOS.*

Telephone

The Core Telephony framework lets your app get information about a particular cellular carrier and call.

Pass Kit

The Pass Kit framework allows creation of downloadable passes to go into the user's Passbook app. See the *Passbook Programming Guide.*

Health Kit

The Health Kit framework lets your app obtain, store, share, and present data and statistics related to body activity and exercise. See the *HealthKit Framework Reference.*

External accessories

The user can attach an external accessory to the device, either directly via USB or wirelessly via Bluetooth. Your app can communicate with such an accessory. See *External Accessory Programming Topics.* The Home Kit framework lets the user communicate with devices in the physical world, such as light switches and door locks. See the *HomeKit Framework Reference.*

Handoff

Handoff permits your app to post to the user's iCloud account a record of what the user is doing, so that the user can switch to another copy of your app on another device and resume doing the same thing. See the *Handoff Programming Guide.*

Spotlight

New in iOS 9, the user's Spotlight search results can include data supplied by your app. See the *Core Spotlight Framework Reference.*

Some Swift Conventions

I have had to settle on some conventions for presenting and describing code. The most important question has been how to state the name of a method. My solution, if this method is defined originally through an Objective-C API (that is, through Cocoa), is to give *the method's Objective-C name*. As an example, what is the name of the method that you call when you set a value using key–value coding? The actual call, in Swift, would be something like this:

```
someObject.setValue(someValue, forKey:"someKey")
```

But when I *give the name* of the method being called here, that name is `setValue:for-Key:`. This choice has several advantages:

- It is clear, compact, and predictable, being formed according to perfectly consistent and well-established rules.

- For those who have been programming in Objective-C all these years, it's what we're used to. The way Objective-C methods are named is a thoroughly entrenched convention; even Swift programmers must accommodate themselves to seeing Objective-C method names plastered all over the Internet and Apple's own documentation.

- That name *is* in fact its name as far as Objective-C and the Cocoa APIs are concerned, and even in Swift you would need to know this. For example, if you wanted to specify this method when providing its name as a selector parameter (or as a string representing a selector), it is the Objective-C name that you would have to provide.

- The translation from the Objective-C name into practical Swift syntax is mechanical and unambiguous — the first colon is replaced by parentheses embracing the first parameter plus the names and values of any remaining parameters — and is something that every Swift programmer needs to know how to do.

Similarly, I will speak of the `setValue:` parameter, even though, in an actual Swift method call, the name of that parameter appears before the parentheses, with no colon.

Apple has its own convention for saying the name of a Swift function, but, in this edition at least, I don't use it. For example, Apple's name for `setValue:forKey:` *as a Swift function* is `setValue(_:forKey:)`. This has the advantage that it works even for Swift functions that don't obey the Objective-C conventions for method names. But Apple's own application of this convention is inconsistent — for example, the `__FUNCTION__` literal sometimes obeys it and sometimes doesn't — and it doesn't help with the question of how to write a selector. My convention is about the names of *Objective-C* methods, so I give them Objective-C names.

My treatment of *initializer* names, however, is closer to Apple's convention. Here, the difference between Objective-C and Swift is greater than a simple shorthand can readily encompass, so I give the initializer's name *as you would implement it.* For example, in Objective-C, the default initializer for a UIView is `initWithFrame:`. In this book, I will call that initializer `init(frame:)`. The same thing applies to what in Objective-C would be class factory methods with a corresponding initializer: when I want to mention what in Objective-C would be the UIImage class factory method `imageNamed:`, I'll call it `init(named:)`.

This treatment of initializer names has the great virtue that the name clarifies instantly that such a method *is* an initializer. Swift effectively abolishes class factory methods and brings such methods into the fold of formal initializers; my treatment of their names is a way of supporting and adopting that innovation.

Again, this convention requires some mental translation on the reader's part, because in Swift the way you would name an initializer when you *implement* it is not the same as the way you would usually name it when you *call* it. If you were to override this method in a UIView subclass, you'd override `init(frame:)`; but if you were to *call* it to create a new UIView, you'd say `UIView(frame:)`. This mental translation, however, is hardly objectionable, as it is a practical fact to which every Swift user is already habituated.

Versions

This book was written using iOS 9 and Xcode 7, including Swift 2.0. (Just before publication, Apple released iOS 9.1, Xcode 7.1, and Swift 2.1, but this did not entail any changes in the book's content.) In general, only very minimal attention is given to earlier versions of iOS and Xcode (and none at all to earlier versions of Swift). It is not my intention to embrace in this book any detailed knowledge about earlier versions of the software, which is, after all, readily and compendiously available in my earlier books. The book does contain, nevertheless, a few words of advice about backward compatibility, and now and then I will call out a particularly noteworthy change from earlier system versions, especially where your existing iOS 8 code is likely to break or behave differently when compiled against iOS 9.

Please bear in mind that Apple continues to make adjustments to the Swift language and to the way the Objective-C APIs are bridged to it. I have tried to keep my code up-to-date, but if, at some future time, a new version of Xcode is released along with a new version of Swift, some of the code in this book might be slightly incorrect. Please make allowances, and be prepared to compensate, for the possibility that my examples may contain slight occasional impedance mismatches, such as the lack of a needed Optional unwrap or the presence of a superfluous one.

Screenshots of Xcode were taken using Xcode 7 under OS X 10.10 Yosemite. I have *not* upgraded my machine to OS X 10.11 El Capitan, because at the time of this writing it was too new to be trusted with mission-critical work. If you are braver than I am and are running El Capitan, your interface may naturally look slightly different from the screenshots, but this difference will be minimal and shouldn't cause any confusion.

Acknowledgments

My thanks go first and foremost to the people at O'Reilly Media who have made writing a book so delightfully easy: Rachel Roumeliotis, Sarah Schneider, Kristen Brown, Dan Fauxsmith, Adam Witwer, and Sanders Kleinfeld come particularly to mind. And let's not forget my first and long-standing editor, Brian Jepson, who had nothing whatever to do with this edition, but whose influence is present throughout.

As in the past, I have been greatly aided by some fantastic software, whose excellences I have appreciated at every moment of the process of writing this book. I should like to mention, in particular:

- git (*http://git-scm.com*)
- SourceTree (*http://www.sourcetreeapp.com*)
- TextMate (*http://macromates.com*)
- AsciiDoc (*http://www.methods.co.nz/asciidoc*)
- BBEdit (*http://barebones.com/products/bbedit/*)
- EasyFind (*http://www.devontechnologies.com/products/freeware.html*)
- Snapz Pro X (*http://www.ambrosiasw.com*)
- GraphicConverter (*http://www.lemkesoft.com*)
- OmniGraffle (*http://www.omnigroup.com*)

The book was typed and edited entirely on my faithful Unicomp Model M keyboard (*http://pckeyboard.com*), without which I could never have done so much writing over so long a period so painlessly. For more about my physical work environment, see *http://matt.neuburg.usesthis.com*.

From the Programming iOS 4 Preface

A programming framework has a kind of personality, an overall flavor that provides an insight into the goals and mindset of those who created it. When I first encountered Cocoa Touch, my assessment of its personality was: "Wow, the people who wrote this are really clever!" On the one hand, the number of built-in interface objects was severely and deliberately limited; on the other hand, the power and flexibility of some of those objects, especially such things as UITableView, was greatly enhanced over their OS X counterparts. Even more important, Apple created a particularly brilliant way (UIView-Controller) to help the programmer make entire blocks of interface come and go and supplant one another in a controlled, hierarchical manner, thus allowing that tiny iPhone display to unfold virtually into multiple interface worlds within a single app without the user becoming lost or confused.

The popularity of the iPhone, with its largely free or very inexpensive apps, and the subsequent popularity of the iPad, have brought and will continue to bring into the fold many new programmers who see programming for these devices as worthwhile and doable, even though they may not have felt the same way about OS X. Apple's own annual WWDC developer conventions have reflected this trend, with their emphasis shifted from OS X to iOS instruction.

The widespread eagerness to program iOS, however, though delightful on the one hand, has also fostered a certain tendency to try to run without first learning to walk. iOS gives the programmer mighty powers that can seem as limitless as imagination itself, but it also has fundamentals. I often see questions online from programmers who are evidently deep into the creation of some interesting app, but who are stymied in a way that reveals quite clearly that they are unfamiliar with the basics of the very world in which they are so happily cavorting.

It is this state of affairs that has motivated me to write this book, which is intended to ground the reader in the fundamentals of iOS. I love Cocoa and have long wished to write about it, but it is iOS and its popularity that has given me a proximate excuse to do so. Here I have attempted to marshal and expound, in what I hope is a pedagogically helpful and instructive yet ruthlessly Euclidean and logical order, the principles and elements on which sound iOS programming rests. My hope, as with my previous books, is that you will both read this book cover to cover (learning something new often enough to keep you turning the pages) and keep it by you as a handy reference.

This book is not intended to disparage Apple's own documentation and example projects. They are wonderful resources and have become more wonderful as time goes on. I have depended heavily on them in the preparation of this book. But I also find that they don't fulfill the same function as a reasoned, ordered presentation of the facts. The online documentation must make assumptions as to how much you already know; it can't guarantee that you'll approach it in a given order. And online documentation is more suitable to reference than to instruction. A fully written example, no matter how well commented, is difficult to follow; it demonstrates, but it does not teach.

A book, on the other hand, has numbered chapters and sequential pages; I can assume you know views before you know view controllers for the simple reason that Part I precedes Part II. And along with facts, I also bring to the table a degree of experience, which I try to communicate to you. Throughout this book you'll find me referring to "common beginner mistakes"; in most cases, these are mistakes that I have made myself, in addition to seeing others make them. I try to tell you what the pitfalls are because I assume that, in the course of things, you will otherwise fall into them just as naturally as I did as I was learning. You'll also see me construct many examples piece by piece or extract and explain just one tiny portion of a larger app. It is not a massive finished program that teaches programming, but an exposition of the thought process that developed that program. It is this thought process, more than anything else, that I hope you will gain from reading this book.

Conventions Used in This Book

The following typographical conventions are used in this book:

Italic
> Indicates new terms, URLs, email addresses, filenames, and file extensions.

`Constant width`
> Used for program listings, as well as within paragraphs to refer to program elements such as variable or function names, databases, data types, environment variables, statements, and keywords.

`Constant width bold`
> Shows commands or other text that should be typed literally by the user.

`Constant width italic`
> Shows text that should be replaced with user-supplied values or by values determined by context.

 This element signifies a tip or suggestion.

 This element signifies a general note.

 This element indicates a warning or caution.

Using Code Examples

Supplemental material (code examples, exercises, etc.) is available for download at *https://github.com/mattneub/Programming-iOS-Book-Examples*.

This book is here to help you get your job done. In general, if example code is offered with this book, you may use it in your programs and documentation. You do not need to contact us for permission unless you're reproducing a significant portion of the code. For example, writing a program that uses several chunks of code from this book does not require permission. Selling or distributing a CD-ROM of examples from O'Reilly books does require permission. Answering a question by citing this book and quoting example code does not require permission. Incorporating a significant amount of example code from this book into your product's documentation does require permission.

We appreciate, but do not require, attribution. An attribution usually includes the title, author, publisher, and ISBN. For example: "*Programming iOS 9* by Matt Neuburg (O'Reilly). Copyright 2016 Matt Neuburg, 978-1-491-93685-6."

If you feel your use of code examples falls outside fair use or the permission given above, feel free to contact us at *permissions@oreilly.com*.

Safari® Books Online

 *Safari Books Online* is an on-demand digital library that delivers expert content in both book and video form from the world's leading authors in technology and business.

Technology professionals, software developers, web designers, and business and creative professionals use Safari Books Online as their primary resource for research, problem solving, learning, and certification training.

Safari Books Online offers a range of plans and pricing for enterprise, government, education, and individuals.

Members have access to thousands of books, training videos, and prepublication manuscripts in one fully searchable database from publishers like O'Reilly Media, Prentice Hall Professional, Addison-Wesley Professional, Microsoft Press, Sams, Que, Peachpit Press, Focal Press, Cisco Press, John Wiley & Sons, Syngress, Morgan Kaufmann, IBM Redbooks, Packt, Adobe Press, FT Press, Apress, Manning, New Riders, McGraw-Hill, Jones & Bartlett, Course Technology, and hundreds more. For more information about Safari Books Online, please visit us online.

How to Contact Us

Please address comments and questions concerning this book to the publisher:

O'Reilly Media, Inc.
1005 Gravenstein Highway North
Sebastopol, CA 95472
800-998-9938 (in the United States or Canada)
707-829-0515 (international or local)
707-829-0104 (fax)

We have a web page for this book, where we list errata, examples, and any additional information. You can access this page at *http://bit.ly/programming_iOS9*.

To comment or ask technical questions about this book, send email to *bookquestions@oreilly.com*.

For more information about our books, courses, conferences, and news, see our website at *http://www.oreilly.com*.

Find us on Facebook: *http://facebook.com/oreilly*

Follow us on Twitter: *http://twitter.com/oreillymedia*

Watch us on YouTube: *http://www.youtube.com/oreillymedia*

PART I

Views

The things that appear in your app's interface are, ultimately, *views*. A view is a unit of your app that knows how to draw itself. A view also knows how to sense that the user has touched it. Views are what your user sees on the screen, and what your user interacts with by touching the screen. Thus, views are the primary constituent of an app's visible, touchable manifestation. They *are* your app's interface. So it's going to be crucial to know how views work.

- Chapter 1 discusses views in their most general aspect — their hierarchy, visibility, and position, including an explanation of autolayout.

- Chapter 2 is about drawing. A view knows how to draw itself; this chapter explains how to tell a view what you want it to draw, from displaying an existing image to constructing a drawing in code.

- Chapter 3 explains about layers. The drawing power of a view comes ultimately from its layer. To put it another way, a layer is effectively the aspect of a view that knows how to draw — with even more power.

- Chapter 4 tells about animation. An iOS app's interface isn't generally static; it's lively. Much of that liveliness comes from animation. iOS gives you great power to animate your interface with remarkable ease; that power, it turns out, resides ultimately in layers.

- Chapter 5 is about touches. A view knows how to sense that the user is touching it. This chapter explains the iOS view-based mechanisms for sensing and responding to touches, with details on how touches are routed to the appropriate view and how you can customize that routing.

CHAPTER 1

Views

A *view* (an object whose class is UIView or a subclass of UIView) knows how to draw itself into a rectangular area of the interface. Your app has a visible interface thanks to views. Creating and configuring a view can be extremely simple: "Set it and forget it." For example, you can drag an interface object, such as a UIButton, into a view in the nib editor; when the app runs, the button appears, and works properly. But you can also manipulate views in powerful ways, in real time. Your code can do some or all of the view's drawing of itself (Chapter 2); it can make the view appear and disappear, move, resize itself, and display many other physical changes, possibly with animation (Chapter 4).

A view is also a responder (UIView is a subclass of UIResponder). This means that a view is subject to user interactions, such as taps and swipes. Thus, views are the basis not only of the interface that the user sees, but also of the interface that the user touches (Chapter 5). Organizing your views so that the correct view reacts to a given touch allows you to allocate your code neatly and efficiently.

The *view hierarchy* is the chief mode of view organization. A view can have subviews; a subview has exactly one immediate superview. Thus there is a tree of views. This hierarchy allows views to come and go together. If a view is removed from the interface, its subviews are removed; if a view is hidden (made invisible), its subviews are hidden; if a view is moved, its subviews move with it; and other changes in a view are likewise shared with its subviews. The view hierarchy is also the basis of, though it is not identical to, the responder chain.

A view may come from a nib, or you can create it in code. On balance, neither approach is to be preferred over the other; it depends on your needs and inclinations and on the overall architecture of your app.

The Window

The top of the view hierarchy is the app's window. It is an instance of UIWindow (or your own subclass thereof), which is a UIView subclass. Your app should have *exactly one main window*. It is created at launch time and is never destroyed or replaced. It forms the background to, and is the ultimate superview of, all your other visible views. Other views are visible by virtue of being subviews, at some depth, of your app's window.

 If your app can display views on an external screen, you'll create an additional UIWindow to contain those views; but in this chapter I'll behave as if there were just one screen, the device's own screen, and just one window.

The app's window must initially fill the device's screen. This is ensured by setting the window's frame to the screen's bounds as the window is instantiated. (I'll explain later in this chapter what "frame" and "bounds" are.) If you're using a main storyboard, that's taken care of for you automatically behind the scenes by the UIApplicationMain function as the app launches; but an app without a main storyboard is possible, and in that case you'd need to create the window and set its frame yourself, very early in the app's lifetime, like this:

```
let w = UIWindow(frame: UIScreen.mainScreen().bounds)
```

New in iOS 9, it's sufficient to instantiate UIWindow with *no* frame; the screen's bounds will be assigned to the window's frame for you:

```
let w = UIWindow()
```

The window must also persist for the lifetime of the app. To make this happen, the app delegate class has a window property with a strong retain policy. As the app launches, the UIApplicationMain function instantiates the app delegate class and retains the resulting instance. This is the app delegate instance; it is never released, so it persists for the lifetime of the app. The window instance is then assigned to the app delegate instance's window property; therefore it, too, persists for the lifetime of the app.

You will typically not put any view content manually and directly inside your main window. Instead, you'll obtain a view controller and assign it to the main window's root-ViewController property. Once again, if you're using a main storyboard, this is done automatically behind the scenes; the view controller in question will be your storyboard's initial view controller.

When a view controller becomes the main window's rootViewController, its main view (its view) is made the one and only immediate subview of your main window — the main window's *root view*. All other views in your main window will be subviews of the root view. Thus, the root view is the highest object in the view hierarchy that the user will usually see. There might be just a chance, under certain circumstances, that the user will catch a glimpse of the window, behind the root view; for this reason, you may want to assign the main window a reasonable backgroundColor. But this seems unlikely, and in general you'll have no reason to change anything about the window itself.

Your app's interface is not visible until the window, which contains it, is made the app's key window. This is done by calling the UIWindow instance method makeKeyAndVisible.

Let's summarize how the initial creation, configuration, and display of the main window happens. There are two cases to consider:

App with a main storyboard

> If your app has a main storyboard, as specified by its *Info.plist* key "Main storyboard file base name" (UIMainStoryboardFile) — the default for all Xcode 7 app templates — then UIApplicationMain instantiates UIWindow, sets its frame correctly, and assigns that instance to the app delegate's window property. In addition, it instantiates the storyboard's initial view controller, and assigns that instance to the window's rootViewController property. All of that happens *before* the app delegate's application:didFinishLaunchingWithOptions: is called (Appendix A).
>
> Finally, UIApplicationMain calls makeKeyAndVisible on the window, to display your app's interface. This in turn automatically causes the root view controller to obtain its main view (typically by loading it from a nib), which the window adds as its own root view. That happens *after* application:didFinishLaunchingWithOptions: is called.

App without a main storyboard

> If your app has no main storyboard, then creation and configuration of the window must be done in some other way. Typically, it is done in code. No Xcode 7 app template lacks a main storyboard, but if you start with, say, the Single View Application template, you can experiment as follows:
>
> 1. Edit the target. In the General pane, select "Main" in the Main Interface field and delete it (and press Tab to set this change).
>
> 2. Delete *Main.storyboard* and *ViewController.swift* from the project.
>
> 3. Delete the entire content of *AppDelegate.swift*.
>
> You now have a project with an app target but no storyboard and no code. To make a minimal working app, you need to edit *AppDelegate.swift* in such a way as to recreate the AppDelegate class with just enough code to create and show the window at launch time, as demonstrated in Example 1-1.

Example 1-1. An App Delegate class with no storyboard

```
import UIKit
@UIApplicationMain
class AppDelegate : UIResponder, UIApplicationDelegate {
    var window : UIWindow?
    func application(application: UIApplication,
        didFinishLaunchingWithOptions launchOptions: [NSObject: AnyObject]?)
        -> Bool {
            self.window = UIWindow()
            self.window!.rootViewController = UIViewController()
            self.window!.backgroundColor = UIColor.whiteColor()
            self.window!.makeKeyAndVisible()
            return true
    }
}
```

The result of implementing Example 1-1 is a minimal working app with an empty white window; you can prove to yourself that your code is creating the window by changing its backgroundColor to something else (such as UIColor.redColor()) and running the app again. The app is extremely simple and rather inflexible because its root view controller is a generic UIViewController, but it's a legal working app and is sufficient for some basic experimentation with views; in real life, you'd set the window's rootViewController to a new instance of your own custom UIViewController subclass (and I'll talk more about that in Chapter 6).

It is extremely improbable that you would ever need to subclass UIWindow. If, however, you wanted to create a UIWindow subclass and make an instance of that subclass your app's main window, then how you proceed depends on how the window is instantiated in the first place:

App with a main storyboard

As the app launches, after UIApplicationMain has instantiated the app delegate, it asks the app delegate instance for the value of its window property. If that value is nil, UIApplicationMain instantiates UIWindow and assigns that instance to the app delegate's window property. If that value is *not* nil, UIApplicationMain leaves it alone and uses it as the app's main window. Therefore, to make your app's main window be an instance of your UIWindow subclass, you'll make that instance the default value for the app delegate's window property, like this:

```
lazy var window : UIWindow? = {
    return MyWindow()
}()
```

App without a main storyboard

You're already instantiating UIWindow and assigning that instance to the app delegate's self.window property, in code (Example 1-1). So instantiate your UIWindow subclass instead:

```
// ...
self.window = MyWindow()
// ...
```

Once the app is running, there are various ways to refer to the window:

- If a UIView is in the interface, it automatically has a reference to the window through its own `window` property.

  You can also use a UIView's `window` property as a way of asking whether it is ultimately embedded in the window; if it isn't, its `window` property is `nil`. A UIView whose `window` property is `nil` cannot be visible to the user.

- The app delegate instance maintains a reference to the window through its `window` property. You can get a reference to the app delegate from elsewhere through the shared application's `delegate` property, and through it you can refer to the window:

  ```
  let w = UIApplication.sharedApplication().delegate!.window!!
  ```

  If you prefer something less generic (and requiring less extreme unwrapping of Optionals), cast the `delegate` explicitly to your app delegate class:

  ```
  let w = (UIApplication.sharedApplication().delegate as! AppDelegate).window!
  ```

- The shared application maintains a reference to the window through its `keyWindow` property:

  ```
  let w = UIApplication.sharedApplication().keyWindow!
  ```

  That reference, however, is slightly volatile, because the system can create temporary windows and interpose them as the application's key window.

Experimenting With Views

In the course of this and subsequent chapters, you may want to experiment with views in a project of your own. Since view controllers aren't formally explained until Chapter 6, I'll just outline two simple approaches.

Single View Application template

 If you start your project with the Single View Application template, it gives you a main storyboard containing one scene containing one view controller instance containing its own main view; when the app runs, that view controller will become the app's main window's `rootViewController`, and its main view will become the window's root view.

 You will now want some subviews of the main view, to experiment with. In the nib editor, you can drag a view from the Object library into the main view as a subview, and it will be instantiated in the interface when the app runs. Alternatively, you can write code to create views and add them to the interface; the simplest place to do this, for now, is the view controller's `viewDidLoad` method, which has a reference to the view controller's main view as `self.view`. For example:

```
override func viewDidLoad() {
    super.viewDidLoad()
    let mainview = self.view
    let v = UIView(frame:CGRectMake(100,100,50,50))
    v.backgroundColor = UIColor.redColor() // small red square
    mainview.addSubview(v) // add it to main view
}
```

App without a main storyboard

If you start with the empty application without a storyboard that I described in Example 1-1, it has no *.xib* or *.storyboard* file, so your views will have to be created entirely in code. Our root view controller is a purely generic UIViewController, so we have no `viewDidLoad` override, but we can access its main view through its `view` property. For example:

```
func application(application: UIApplication,
    didFinishLaunchingWithOptions launchOptions: [NSObject: AnyObject]?)
    -> Bool {
        self.window = UIWindow()
        self.window!.rootViewController = UIViewController()
        // here we can add subviews
        let mainview = self.window!.rootViewController!.view
        let v = UIView(frame:CGRectMake(100,100,50,50))
        v.backgroundColor = UIColor.redColor() // small red square
        mainview.addSubview(v) // add it to main view
        // and the rest is as before...
        self.window!.backgroundColor = UIColor.whiteColor()
        self.window!.makeKeyAndVisible()
        return true
}
```

Subview and Superview

Once upon a time, and not so very long ago, a view owned precisely its own rectangular area. No part of any view that was not a subview of this view could appear inside it, because when this view redrew its rectangle, it would erase the overlapping portion of the other view. No part of any subview of this view could appear outside it, because the view took responsibility for its own rectangle and no more.

Those rules, however, were gradually relaxed, and starting in OS X 10.5, Apple introduced an entirely new architecture for view drawing that lifted those restrictions completely. iOS view drawing is based on this revised architecture. In iOS, some or all of a subview can appear outside its superview, and a view can overlap another view and can be drawn partially or totally in front of it without being its subview.

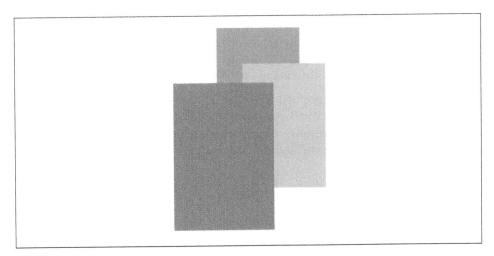

Figure 1-1. Overlapping views

Figure 1-2. A view hierarchy as displayed in the nib editor

For example, Figure 1-1 shows three overlapping views. All three views have a background color, so each is completely represented by a colored rectangle. You have no way of knowing, from this visual representation, exactly how the views are related within the view hierarchy. In actual fact, the view in the middle (horizontally) is a sibling view of the view on the left (they are both direct subviews of the root view), and the view on the right is a subview of the middle view.

When views are created in the nib, you can examine the view hierarchy in the nib editor's document outline to learn their actual relationship (Figure 1-2). When views are created in code, you know their hierarchical relationship because you created that hierarchy. But the visible interface doesn't tell you, because view overlapping is so flexible.

Nevertheless, a view's position within the view hierarchy is extremely significant. For one thing, the view hierarchy dictates the *order* in which views are drawn. Sibling subviews of the same superview have a definite order: one is drawn before the other, so if they overlap, it will appear to be behind its sibling. Similarly, a superview is drawn before its subviews, so if they overlap it, it will appear to be behind them.

You can see this illustrated in Figure 1-1. The view on the right is a subview of the view in the middle and is drawn on top of it. The view on the left is a sibling of the view in the middle, but it is a later sibling, so it is drawn on top of the view in the middle and on top of the view on the right. The view on the left *cannot* appear behind the view on the right but in front of the view in the middle, because those two views are subview and superview and are drawn together — both are drawn either before or after the view on the left, depending on the ordering of the siblings.

This layering order can be governed in the nib editor by arranging the views in the document outline. (If you click in the canvas, you may be able to use the menu items of the Editor → Arrange menu instead — Send to Front, Send to Back, Send Forward, Send Backward.) In code, there are methods for arranging the sibling order of views, which we'll come to in a moment.

Here are some other effects of the view hierarchy:

- If a view is removed from or moved within its superview, its subviews go with it.
- A view's degree of transparency is inherited by its subviews.
- A view can optionally limit the drawing of its subviews so that any parts of them outside the view are not shown. This is called *clipping* and is set with the view's `clipsToBounds` property.
- A superview *owns* its subviews, in the memory-management sense, much as an array owns its elements; it retains them and is responsible for releasing a subview when that subview ceases to be its subview (it is removed from the collection of this view's subviews) or when it itself goes out of existence.
- If a view's size is changed, its subviews can be resized automatically (and I'll have much more to say about that later in this chapter).

A UIView has a `superview` property (a UIView) and a `subviews` property (an array of UIView objects, in back-to-front order), allowing you to trace the view hierarchy in code. There is also a method `isDescendantOfView:` letting you check whether one view is a subview of another at any depth. If you need a reference to a particular view, you will probably arrange this beforehand as a property, perhaps through an outlet. Alternatively, a view can have a numeric tag (its `tag` property), and can then be referred to by sending any view higher up the view hierarchy the `viewWithTag:` message. Seeing that all tags of interest are unique within their region of the hierarchy is up to you.

Manipulating the view hierarchy in code is easy. This is part of what gives iOS apps their dynamic quality, and it compensates for the fact that there is basically just a single window. It is perfectly reasonable for your code to rip an entire hierarchy of views out of the superview and substitute another! You can do this directly; you can combine it with animation (Chapter 4); you can govern it through view controllers (Chapter 6).

The method `addSubview:` makes one view a subview of another; `removeFrom-Superview` takes a subview out of its superview's view hierarchy. In both cases, if the superview is part of the visible interface, the subview will appear or disappear; and of course this view may itself have subviews that accompany it. Just remember that removing a subview from its superview releases it; if you intend to reuse that subview later on, you will wish to retain it first. This is often taken care of by assignment to a property.

Events inform a view of these dynamic changes. To respond to these events requires subclassing. Then you'll be able to override any of these methods:

- `didAddSubview:`, `willRemoveSubview:`
- `didMoveToSuperview`, `willMoveToSuperview`
- `didMoveToWindow`, `willMoveToWindow:`

When `addSubview:` is called, the view is placed last among its superview's subviews; thus it is drawn last, meaning that it appears frontmost. A view's subviews are indexed, starting at 0, which is rearmost. There are additional methods for inserting a subview at a given index, or below (behind) or above (in front of) a specific view; for swapping two sibling views by index; and for moving a subview all the way to the front or back among its siblings:

- `insertSubview:atIndex:`
- `insertSubview:belowSubview:`, `insertSubview:aboveSubview:`
- `exchangeSubviewAtIndex:withSubviewAtIndex:`
- `bringSubviewToFront:`, `sendSubviewToBack:`

Oddly, there is no command for removing all of a view's subviews at once. However, a view's `subviews` array is an immutable copy of the internal list of subviews, so it is legal to cycle through it and remove each subview one at a time:

```
myView.subviews.forEach {$0.removeFromSuperview()}
```

Visibility and Opacity

A view can be made invisible by setting its `hidden` property to `true`, and visible again by setting it to `false`. Hiding a view takes it (and its subviews, of course) out of the visible interface without the overhead of actually removing it from the view hierarchy. A hidden view does not (normally) receive touch events, so to the user it really is as if the view weren't there. But it is there, so it can still be manipulated in code.

A view can be assigned a background color through its `backgroundColor` property. A color is a UIColor; this is not a difficult class to use, and I'm not going to go into details. A view whose background color is `nil` (the default) has a transparent background. It is perfectly reasonable for a view to have a transparent background and to do no additional drawing of its own, just so that it can act as a convenient superview to other views, making them behave together.

A view can be made partially or completely transparent through its alpha property: 1.0 means opaque, 0.0 means transparent, and a value may be anywhere between them, inclusive. This affects subviews: if a superview has an alpha of 0.5, none of its subviews can have an *apparent* opacity of more than 0.5, because whatever alpha value they have will be drawn relative to 0.5. (Just to make matters more complicated, colors have an alpha value as well. So, for example, a view can have an alpha of 1.0 but still have a transparent background because its backgroundColor has an alpha less than 1.0.) A view that is completely transparent (or very close to it) is like a view whose hidden is true: it is invisible, along with its subviews, and cannot (normally) be touched.

A view's alpha property value affects both the apparent transparency of its background color and the apparent transparency of its contents. For example, if a view displays an image and has a background color and its alpha is less than 1, the background color will seep through the image (and whatever is behind the view will seep through both).

A view's opaque property, on the other hand, is a horse of a different color; changing it has no effect on the view's appearance. Rather, this property is a hint to the drawing system. If a view completely fills its bounds with ultimately opaque material and its alpha is 1.0, so that the view has no effective transparency, then it can be drawn more efficiently (with less drag on performance) if you inform the drawing system of this fact by setting its opaque to true. Otherwise, you should set its opaque to false. The opaque value is *not* changed for you when you set a view's backgroundColor or alpha! Setting it correctly is entirely up to you; the default, perhaps surprisingly, is true.

Frame

A view's frame property, a CGRect, is the position of its rectangle within its superview, *in the superview's coordinate system*. By default, the superview's coordinate system will have the origin at its top left, with the x-coordinate growing positively rightward and the y-coordinate growing positively downward.

Setting a view's frame to a different CGRect value repositions the view, or resizes it, or both. If the view is visible, this change will be visibly reflected in the interface. On the other hand, you can also set a view's frame when the view is not visible — for example, when you create the view in code. In that case, the frame describes where the view *will* be positioned within its superview when it is given a superview. UIView's designated initializer is init(frame:), and you'll often assign a frame this way, especially because the default frame might otherwise be CGRectZero, which is rarely what you want.

Forgetting to assign a view a frame when creating it in code, and then wondering why it isn't appearing when added to a superview, is a common beginner mistake. A view with a zero-size frame is effectively invisible. If a view has a standard size that you want it to adopt, especially in relation to its contents (like a UIButton in relation to its title), an alternative is to call its sizeToFit method.

We are now in a position to generate programmatically the interface displayed in Figure 1-1:

```
let v1 = UIView(frame:CGRectMake(113, 111, 132, 194))
v1.backgroundColor = UIColor(red: 1, green: 0.4, blue: 1, alpha: 1)
let v2 = UIView(frame:CGRectMake(41, 56, 132, 194))
v2.backgroundColor = UIColor(red: 0.5, green: 1, blue: 0, alpha: 1)
let v3 = UIView(frame:CGRectMake(43, 197, 160, 230))
v3.backgroundColor = UIColor(red: 1, green: 0, blue: 0, alpha: 1)
mainview.addSubview(v1)
v1.addSubview(v2)
mainview.addSubview(v3)
```

In that code, we determined the layering order of v1 and v3 (the middle and left views, which are siblings) by the order in which we inserted them into the view hierarchy with addSubview:.

Bounds and Center

Suppose we have a superview and a subview, and the subview is to appear inset by 10 points, as in Figure 1-3. The Foundation utility function CGRectInset and the Swift CGRect method insetBy make it easy to derive one rectangle as an inset from another, so we'll use one of them to determine the subview's frame. But *what* rectangle should this be inset from? Not the superview's frame; the frame represents a view's position within *its* superview, and in that superview's coordinates. What we're after is a CGRect describing our superview's rectangle in its *own* coordinates, because those are the coordinates in which the subview's frame is to be expressed. The CGRect that describes a view's rectangle in its own coordinates is the view's bounds property.

So, the code to generate Figure 1-3 looks like this:

```
let v1 = UIView(frame:CGRectMake(113, 111, 132, 194))
v1.backgroundColor = UIColor(red: 1, green: 0.4, blue: 1, alpha: 1)
let v2 = UIView(frame:v1.bounds.insetBy(dx: 10, dy: 10))
v2.backgroundColor = UIColor(red: 0.5, green: 1, blue: 0, alpha: 1)
mainview.addSubview(v1)
v1.addSubview(v2)
```

You'll very often use a view's bounds in this way. When you need coordinates for positioning content inside a view, whether drawing manually or placing a subview, you'll often refer to the view's bounds.

Figure 1-3. A subview inset from its superview

Figure 1-4. A subview exactly covering its superview

Interesting things happen when you set a view's bounds. If you change a view's bounds *size*, you change its *frame*. The change in the view's frame takes place around its *center*, which remains unchanged. So, for example:

```
let v1 = UIView(frame:CGRectMake(113, 111, 132, 194))
v1.backgroundColor = UIColor(red: 1, green: 0.4, blue: 1, alpha: 1)
let v2 = UIView(frame:v1.bounds.insetBy(dx: 10, dy: 10))
v2.backgroundColor = UIColor(red: 0.5, green: 1, blue: 0, alpha: 1)
mainview.addSubview(v1)
v1.addSubview(v2)
v2.bounds.size.height += 20
v2.bounds.size.width += 20
```

What appears is a single rectangle; the subview completely and exactly covers its superview, its frame being the same as the superview's bounds. The call to `insetBy` started with the superview's bounds and shaved 10 points off the left, right, top, and bottom to set the subview's frame (Figure 1-3). But then we added 20 points to the subview's bounds height and width, and thus added 20 points to the subview's frame height and width as well (Figure 1-4). The center didn't move, so we effectively put the 10 points back onto the left, right, top, and bottom of the subview's frame.

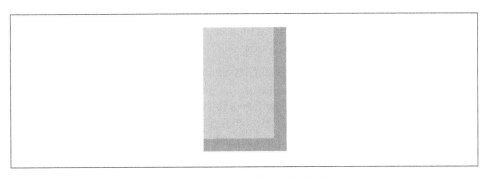

Figure 1-5. The superview's bounds origin has been shifted

When you create a UIView, its bounds coordinate system's zero point (0.0,0.0) is at its top left. If you change a view's bounds *origin*, you move the *origin of its internal coordinate system*. Because a subview is positioned in its superview with respect to its superview's coordinate system, a change in the bounds origin of the superview will change the apparent position of a subview. To illustrate, we start once again with our subview inset evenly within its superview, and then change the bounds origin of the superview:

```
let v1 = UIView(frame:CGRectMake(113, 111, 132, 194))
v1.backgroundColor = UIColor(red: 1, green: 0.4, blue: 1, alpha: 1)
let v2 = UIView(frame:v1.bounds.insetBy(dx: 10, dy: 10))
v2.backgroundColor = UIColor(red: 0.5, green: 1, blue: 0, alpha: 1)
mainview.addSubview(v1)
v1.addSubview(v2)
v1.bounds.origin.x += 10
v1.bounds.origin.y += 10
```

Nothing happens to the superview's size or position. But the subview has moved up and to the left so that it is flush with its superview's top-left corner (Figure 1-5). Basically, what we've done is to say to the superview, "Instead of calling the point at your upper left (0.0,0.0), call that point (10.0,10.0)." Because the subview's frame origin is itself at (10.0,10.0), the subview now touches the superview's top-left corner. The effect of changing a view's bounds origin may seem directionally backward — we increased the superview's origin in the positive direction, but the subview moved in the negative direction — but think of it this way: a view's bounds origin point coincides with its frame's top left.

We have seen that changing a view's bounds size affects its frame size. The converse is also true: changing a view's frame size affects its bounds size. What is *not* affected by changing a view's bounds size is the view's center. This property, like the frame property, represents a subview's position within its superview, in the superview's coordinates; in particular, it is the position within the superview of the subview's bounds center, the point derived from the bounds like this:

```
let c = CGPointMake(theView.bounds.midX, theView.bounds.midY)
```

A view's center is thus a single point establishing the positional relationship between the view's bounds and its superview's bounds.

Changing a view's bounds does not change its center; changing a view's center does not change its bounds. Thus, a view's bounds and center are orthogonal (independent), and describe (among other things) both the view's size and its position within its superview. The view's frame is therefore superfluous! In fact, the `frame` property is merely a convenient expression of the `center` and `bounds` values. In most cases, this won't matter to you; you'll use the `frame` property anyway. When you first create a view from scratch, the designated initializer is `init(frame:)`. You can change the frame, and the bounds size and center will change to match. You can change the bounds size or the center, and the frame will change to match. Nevertheless, the proper and most reliable way to position and size a view within its superview is to use its bounds and center, not its frame; there are some situations in which the frame is meaningless (or will at least behave very oddly), but the bounds and center will always work.

We have seen that every view has its own coordinate system, expressed by its `bounds`, and that a view's coordinate system has a clear relationship to its superview's coordinate system, expressed by its `center`. This is true of every view in a window, so it is possible to convert between the coordinates of any two views in the same window. Convenience methods are supplied to perform this conversion both for a CGPoint and for a CGRect:

- `convertPoint:fromView:`, `convertPoint:toView:`
- `convertRect:fromView:`, `convertRect:toView:`

If the second parameter is `nil`, it is taken to be the window.

For example, if `v2` is a subview of `v1`, then to center `v2` within `v1` you could say:

```
v2.center = v1.convertPoint(v1.center, fromView:v1.superview)
```

 When setting a view's position by setting its center, if the height or width of the view is not an integer (or, on a single-resolution screen, not an even integer), the view can end up *misaligned*: its point values in one or both dimensions are located between the screen pixels. This can cause the view to be displayed incorrectly; for example, if the view contains text, the text may be blurry. You can detect this situation in the Simulator by checking Debug → Color Misaligned Images. A simple solution is to set the view's frame, after positioning it, to the `CGRectIntegral` of its frame, or (in Swift) to call `makeIntegralInPlace` on the view's frame.

Window Coordinates and Screen Coordinates

The device screen has no frame, but it has bounds. The main window has no superview, but its frame is set with respect to the screen's bounds, as I showed earlier:

```
let w = UIWindow(frame: UIScreen.mainScreen().bounds)
```

In iOS 9, you can omit the `frame` parameter, as a shortcut, but the effect is exactly the same:

```
let w = UIWindow()
```

The window thus starts out life filling the screen, and generally continues to fill the screen, and so, for the most part, *window coordinates are screen coordinates.* (However, new in iOS 9, there are circumstances under which that won't be the case; I'll discuss them in Chapter 9.)

In iOS 7 and before, the screen's coordinates were invariant, regardless of the orientation of the device and of the rotation of the app to compensate. iOS 8 introduced a major change in this coordinate system: when the app rotates to compensate for the rotation of the device, the screen (and therefore the window) is what rotates. This change is expressed in part as a transposition of the size components of the bounds of the screen and window (and the frame of the window): in portrait orientation, the size is taller than wide, but in landscape orientation, the size is wider than tall.

Nevertheless, you might still want to obtain device coordinates, independent of the rotation of the app. Therefore, the screen reports its coordinates through two different properties; their values are typed as UICoordinateSpace, a protocol (also adopted by UIView) that provides a `bounds` property:

UIScreen's `coordinateSpace` *property*
> This coordinate space rotates, so that its `bounds` height and width are transposed when the app rotates to compensate for a change in the orientation of the device; its (`0.0,0.0`) point is at the app's top left.

UIScreen's `fixedCoordinateSpace` *property*
> This coordinate space is invariant, meaning that its `bounds` top left represents the physical top left of the device *qua* physical device; its (`0.0,0.0`) point thus might be in any corner (from the user's perspective).

To help you convert between coordinate spaces, UICoordinateSpace also provides four methods parallel to the coordinate-conversion methods I listed in the previous section:

- `convertPoint:fromCoordinateSpace:`, `convertPoint:toCoordinateSpace:`
- `convertRect:fromCoordinateSpace:`, `convertRect:toCoordinateSpace:`

So, for example, suppose we have a UIView v in our interface, and we wish to learn its position in fixed device coordinates. We could do it like this:

```
let r = v.superview!.convertRect(
    v.frame, toCoordinateSpace: UIScreen.mainScreen().fixedCoordinateSpace)
```

Occasions where you need such information, however, will be rare. Indeed, my experience is that it is rare even to worry about window coordinates. All of your app's visible action takes place within your root view controller's main view, and the bounds of that view, which are adjusted for you automatically when the app rotates to compensate for a change in device orientation, are probably the highest coordinate system that will interest you.

Transform

A view's transform property alters how the view is drawn — it may, for example, change the view's perceived size and orientation — without affecting its bounds and center. A transformed view continues to behave correctly: a rotated button, for example, is still a button, and can be tapped in its apparent location and orientation.

A transform value is a CGAffineTransform, which is a struct representing six of the nine values of a 3×3 transformation matrix (the other three values are constants, so there's no need to represent them in the struct). You may have forgotten your high-school linear algebra, so you may not recall what a transformation matrix is. For the details, which are quite simple really, see the "Transforms" chapter of Apple's *Quartz 2D Programming Guide*, especially the section called "The Math Behind the Matrices." But you don't really need to know those details, because convenience functions, whose names start with CGAffineTransformMake..., are provided for creating three of the basic types of transform: rotation, scaling, and translation (i.e., changing the view's apparent position). A fourth basic transform type, skewing or shearing, has no convenience function.

By default, a view's transformation matrix is CGAffineTransformIdentity, the identity transform. It has no visible effect, so you're unaware of it. Any transform that you do apply takes place around the view's center, which is held constant.

Here's some code to illustrate use of a transform:

```
let v1 = UIView(frame:CGRectMake(113, 111, 132, 194))
v1.backgroundColor = UIColor(red: 1, green: 0.4, blue: 1, alpha: 1)
let v2 = UIView(frame:v1.bounds.insetBy(dx: 10, dy: 10))
v2.backgroundColor = UIColor(red: 0.5, green: 1, blue: 0, alpha: 1)
mainview.addSubview(v1)
v1.addSubview(v2)
v1.transform = CGAffineTransformMakeRotation(45 * CGFloat(M_PI)/180.0)
```

The transform property of the view v1 is set to a rotation transform. The result (Figure 1-6) is that the view appears to be rocked 45 degrees clockwise. (I think in

Figure 1-6. A rotation transform

degrees, but Core Graphics thinks in radians, so my code has to convert.) Observe that the view's `center` property is unaffected, so that the rotation seems to have occurred around the view's center. Moreover, the view's `bounds` property is unaffected; the internal coordinate system is unchanged, so the subview is drawn in the same place relative to its superview. The view's `frame`, however, is now useless, as no mere rectangle can describe the region of the superview apparently occupied by the view; the frame's actual value, roughly (`63.7,92.7,230.5,230.5`), describes the minimal bounding rectangle surrounding the view's apparent position. The rule is that if a view's `transform` is not the identity transform, you should not set its `frame`; also, automatic resizing of a subview, discussed later in this chapter, requires that the superview's transform be the identity transform.

Suppose, instead of `CGAffineTransformMakeRotation`, we call `CGAffineTransform-MakeScale`, like this:

```
v1.transform = CGAffineTransformMakeScale(1.8, 1)
```

The `bounds` property of the view `v1` is still unaffected, so the subview is still drawn in the same place relative to its superview; this means that the two views seem to have stretched horizontally together (Figure 1-7). No bounds or centers were harmed by the application of this transform!

Transformation matrices can be chained. There are convenience functions for applying one transform to another. Their names do *not* contain `Make`. These functions are not commutative; that is, order matters. (That high school math is starting to come back to you now, isn't it?) If you start with a transform that translates a view to the right and then apply a rotation of 45 degrees, the rotated view appears to the right of its original position; on the other hand, if you start with a transform that rotates a view 45 degrees and then apply a translation to the right, the meaning of "right" has changed, so the rotated view appears 45 degrees down from its original position. To demonstrate the difference, I'll start with a subview that exactly overlaps its superview:

Figure 1-7. A scale transform

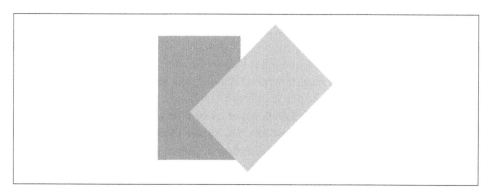

Figure 1-8. Translation, then rotation

```
let v1 = UIView(frame:CGRectMake(20, 111, 132, 194))
v1.backgroundColor = UIColor(red: 1, green: 0.4, blue: 1, alpha: 1)
let v2 = UIView(frame:v1.bounds)
v2.backgroundColor = UIColor(red: 0.5, green: 1, blue: 0, alpha: 1)
mainview.addSubview(v1)
v1.addSubview(v2)
```

Then I'll apply two successive transforms to the subview, leaving the superview to show where the subview was originally. In this example, I translate and then rotate (Figure 1-8):

```
v2.transform = CGAffineTransformMakeTranslation(100, 0)
v2.transform = CGAffineTransformRotate(v2.transform, 45 * CGFloat(M_PI)/180.0)
```

In this example, I rotate and then translate (Figure 1-9):

```
v2.transform = CGAffineTransformMakeRotation(45 * CGFloat(M_PI)/180.0)
v2.transform = CGAffineTransformTranslate(v2.transform, 100, 0)
```

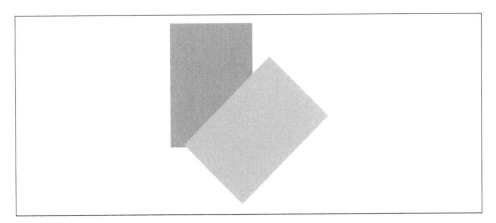

Figure 1-9. Rotation, then translation

The function `CGAffineTransformConcat` concatenates two transform matrices using matrix multiplication. Again, this operation is not commutative. The order is the *opposite* of the order when using convenience functions for applying one transform to another. For example, this gives the same result as Figure 1-9:

```
let r = CGAffineTransformMakeRotation(45 * CGFloat(M_PI)/180.0)
let t = CGAffineTransformMakeTranslation(100, 0)
v2.transform = CGAffineTransformConcat(t,r) // not r,t
```

To remove a transform from a combination of transforms, apply its inverse. A convenience function lets you obtain the inverse of a given affine transform. Again, order matters. In this example, I rotate the subview and shift it to its "right," and then remove the rotation (Figure 1-10):

```
let r = CGAffineTransformMakeRotation(45 * CGFloat(M_PI)/180.0)
let t = CGAffineTransformMakeTranslation(100, 0)
v2.transform = CGAffineTransformConcat(t,r)
v2.transform = CGAffineTransformConcat(
    CGAffineTransformInvert(r), v2.transform)
```

Finally, as there are no convenience methods for creating a skew (shear) transform, I'll illustrate by creating one manually, without further explanation (Figure 1-11):

```
v1.transform = CGAffineTransformMake(1, 0, -0.2, 1, 0, 0)
```

Transforms are useful particularly as temporary visual indicators. For example, you might call attention to a view by applying a transform that scales it up slightly, and then applying the identity transform to restore it to its original size, and animating those changes (Chapter 4).

In iOS 7 and before, the `transform` property lay at the heart of an iOS app's ability to rotate its interface: the window's frame and bounds were invariant, locked to the screen,

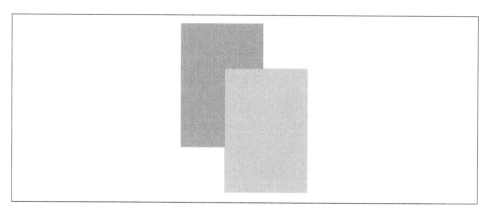

Figure 1-10. Rotation, then translation, then inversion of the rotation

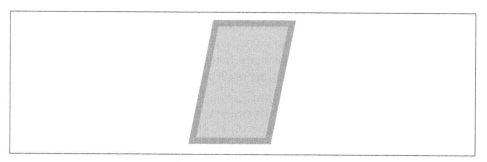

Figure 1-11. Skew (shear)

and an app's interface rotated to compensate for a change in device orientation by applying a rotation transform to the root view, so that its (0.0,0.0) point moved to what the user now saw as the top left of the view.

In iOS 8 and later, as I've already mentioned, this is no longer the case. The screen's coordinate space is effectively rotated, but a coordinate space doesn't have a `transform` property, so the rotation transform applied to that coordinate space is fictitious: you can work out what has happened, if you really want to, by comparing the screen's `coordinateSpace` with its `fixedCoordinateSpace`, but none of the views in the story — neither the window, nor the root view, nor any of its subviews — receives a rotation transform when the app's interface rotates.

Instead, you are expected to concentrate on the *dimensions* of the window, the root view, and so forth. This might mean their absolute dimensions, but it will often mean their dimensions as embodied in a set of *size classes* which are vended by a view's `trait-Collection` property as a UITraitCollection object. I'll discuss trait collections and size classes further in the next section.

You can thus treat app rotation as effectively nothing more than a change in the interface's *proportions*: when the app rotates, the long dimension (of the root view, the window, and the screen's coordinate space bounds) becomes its short dimension and *vice versa*. This, after all, is what your interface needs to take into account in order to keep working when the app rotates.

Consider, for example, a subview of the root view, located at the bottom right of the screen when the device is in portrait orientation. If the root view's bounds width and bounds height are effectively transposed, then that poor old subview will now be outside the bounds height, and therefore off the screen — unless your app responds in some way to this change to reposition it. Such a response is called *layout*, a subject that will occupy most of the rest of this chapter. The point, however, is that what you're responding *to* is just a change in the window's proportions; the fact that this change stems from rotation of the app's interface is all but irrelevant.

Trait Collections and Size Classes

Every view in the interface, from the window on down, as well as any view controller whose view is part of the interface, inherits from the environment the value of its `trait-Collection` property, which it has by virtue of implementing the UITraitEnvironment protocol. The `traitCollection` is a UITraitCollection, a value class consisting of four properties:

`displayScale`
> The scale inherited from the current screen, typically 1 or 2 for a single- or double-resolution screen respectively — or 3 for the iPhone 6 Plus. (This will be the same, by default, as the UIScreen `scale` property.)

`userInterfaceIdiom`
> A UserInterfaceIdiom value, either `.Phone` or `.Pad`, stating generically what kind of device we're running on. (This will be the same, by default, as the UIDevice `user-InterfaceIdiom` property.)

`horizontalSizeClass`, `verticalSizeClass`
> A UIUserInterfaceSizeClass value, either `.Regular` or `.Compact`. These are called *size classes*. The size classes, in combination, have the following meanings:
>
> *Both the vertical and horizontal size classes are* `.Regular`
> > We're running on an iPad.
>
> *The vertical size class is* `.Regular`, *but the horizontal size class is* `.Compact`
> > We're running on an iPhone with the app in portrait orientation. (Alternatively, we might be running on an iPad in a splitscreen iPad multitasking configuration; see Chapter 9.)

Both the vertical and horizontal size classes are `.Compact`
We're running on an iPhone (except an iPhone 6 Plus) with the app in landscape orientation.

The vertical size class is `.Compact`, *but the horizontal size class is* `.Regular`
We're running on an iPhone 6 Plus with the app in landscape orientation.

The trait collection properties can differ from one run of an app to another. For example, if you write a universal app, one that runs natively on different device types (iPhone and iPad), you will probably want your interface to differ depending on which device type we're running on; trait collections are the way to detect that.

Moreover, some trait collection properties can change while the app is running. For example, the size classes on an iPhone reflect the orientation of the app — which can change as the app rotates in response to a change in the orientation of the device.

Therefore, both at app launch time and, thereafter, if the trait collection changes while the app is running, the `traitCollectionDidChange:` message is propagated down the hierarchy of UITraitEnvironments (meaning primarily, for our purposes, view controllers and views); the old trait collection (if any) is provided as the parameter, and the new trait collection can be retrieved as `self.traitCollection`.

It is also possible to create a trait collection yourself. (It may not be immediately obvious why this would be a useful thing to do; I'll give an example in the next chapter.) Oddly, however, you can't set any trait collection properties directly; instead, you form a trait collection through an initializer that determines just *one* property, and if you want to add further property settings, you have to combine trait collections by calling `init(traitsFromCollections:)`. For example:

```
let tcdisp = UITraitCollection(displayScale: 2.0)
let tcphone = UITraitCollection(userInterfaceIdiom: .Phone)
let tcreg = UITraitCollection(verticalSizeClass: .Regular)
let tc = UITraitCollection(traitsFromCollections: [tcdisp, tcphone, tcreg])
```

When combining trait collections with `init(traitsFromCollections:)`, an *ordered intersection* is performed. If two trait collections are combined, and one sets a property and the other doesn't (the property isn't set or its value isn't yet known), the one that sets the property wins; if they both set the property, the winner is the trait collection that appears later in the array.

Similarly, if you create a trait collection and you don't specify a property, this means that the value for that property is to be inherited if the trait collection finds itself in the inheritance hierarchy.

To compare trait collections, call `containsTraitsInCollection:`. This returns `true` if the value of every *specified* property of the second trait collection (the argument) matches that of the first trait collection (the target of the message).

You cannot insert a trait collection directly into the inheritance hierarchy simply by setting a view's trait collection; `traitCollection` isn't a settable property. Instead, you'll call a special `setOverrideTraitCollection:...` method; I'll give an example in Chapter 6.

Layout

We have seen that a subview moves when its superview's bounds *origin* is changed. But what happens to a subview when its superview's bounds (or frame) *size* is changed?

Of its own accord, nothing happens. The subview's bounds and center haven't changed, and the superview's bounds origin hasn't moved, so the subview stays in the same position relative to the top left of its superview. In real life, however, that often won't be what you want. You'll want subviews to be resized and repositioned when their superview's bounds size is changed. This is called *layout*.

Here are some ways in which a superview might be resized dynamically:

- Your app might compensate for the user rotating the device 90 degrees by rotating itself so that its top moves to the new top of the screen, matching its new orientation — and, as a consequence, transposing its bounds width and height values.
- An iPhone app might launch on screens with different aspect ratios: for example, the screen of the iPhone 4s is relatively shorter than the screen of later iPhone models, and the app's interface may need to adapt to this difference.
- A universal app might launch on an iPad or on an iPhone. The app's interface may need to adapt to the size of the screen on which it finds itself running.
- A view instantiated from a nib, such as a view controller's main view or a table view cell, might be resized to fit the interface into which it is placed.
- A view might respond to a change in its surrounding views. For example, when a navigation bar is shown or hidden dynamically, the remaining interface might shrink or grow to compensate, filling the available space.
- New in iOS 9, the user might alter the width of your app's window on an iPad, as part of the iPad multitasking interface.

In any of those situations, and others, layout will probably be needed.

Layout is performed in three primary ways:

Manual layout
> The superview is sent the `layoutSubviews` message whenever it is resized; so, to lay out subviews manually, provide your own subclass and override `layout-Subviews`. Clearly this could turn out to be a lot of work, but it means you can do anything you like.

Autoresizing

>Autoresizing is the pre-iOS 6 way of performing layout automatically. When its superview is resized, a subview will respond in accordance with the rules prescribed by its own `autoresizingMask` property value.

Autolayout

>Autolayout, introduced in iOS 6, depends on the *constraints* of views. A constraint (an instance of NSLayoutConstraint) is a full-fledged object with numeric values describing some aspect of the size or position of a view, often in terms of some other view; it is much more sophisticated, descriptive, and powerful than the `autoresizingMask`. Multiple constraints can apply to an individual view, and they can describe a relationship between *any* two views (not just a subview and its superview). Autolayout is implemented behind the scenes in `layoutSubviews`; in effect, constraints allow you to write sophisticated `layoutSubviews` functionality without code.

Your layout strategy can involve any combination of these. The need for manual layout is rare, but it's there if you need it. Autoresizing is used automatically unless you deliberately turn it off by setting a superview's `autoresizesSubviews` property to `false`, or unless a view uses autolayout instead. Autolayout is an opt-in technology, and can be used for whatever areas of your interface you find appropriate; a view that uses autolayout can live side by side with a view that uses autoresizing.

One of the chief places where you opt in to autolayout is the nib file, and in Xcode 7 all new *.storyboard* and *.xib* files do opt in — they have autolayout turned on, by default. To see this, select the file in the Project navigator, show the File inspector, and examine the "Use Auto Layout" checkbox. On the other hand, a view that your code creates and adds to the interface, by default, uses autoresizing, not autolayout.

Autoresizing

Autoresizing is a matter of conceptually assigning a subview "springs and struts." A spring can stretch; a strut can't. Springs and struts can be assigned internally or externally, horizontally or vertically. Thus you can specify (using internal springs and struts) whether and how the view can be resized, and (using external springs and struts) whether and how the view can be repositioned. For example:

• Imagine a subview that is centered in its superview and is to stay centered, but is to resize itself as the superview is resized. It would have struts externally and springs internally.

• Imagine a subview that is centered in its superview and is to stay centered, and is *not* to resize itself as the superview is resized. It would have springs externally and struts internally.

- Imagine an OK button that is to stay in the lower right of its superview. It would have struts internally, struts externally to its right and bottom, and springs externally to its top and left.
- Imagine a text field that is to stay at the top of its superview. It is to widen as the superview widens. It would have struts externally, but a spring to its bottom; internally it would have a vertical strut and a horizontal spring.

In code, a combination of springs and struts is set through a view's autoresizing-Mask property, which is a bitmask so that you can combine options. The options, members of the UIViewAutoresizing struct, represent springs; whatever isn't specified is a strut. The default is .None, apparently meaning all struts — but of course it can't really be *all* struts, because if the superview is resized, *something* needs to change; in reality, .None is the same as .FlexibleRightMargin together with .FlexibleBottom-Margin.

 In debugging, when you log a UIView to the console, its autoresizingMask is reported using the word "autoresize" and a list of the springs. The margins are LM, RM, TM, and BM; the internal dimensions are W and H. For example, autoresize = LM +TM means that what's flexible is the left and top margins; autoresize = W+BM means that what's flexible is the width and the bottom margin.

To demonstrate autoresizing, I'll start with a view and two subviews, one stretched across the top, the other confined to the lower right (Figure 1-12):

```
let v1 = UIView(frame:CGRectMake(100, 111, 132, 194))
v1.backgroundColor = UIColor(red: 1, green: 0.4, blue: 1, alpha: 1)
let v2 = UIView(frame:CGRectMake(0, 0, 132, 10))
v2.backgroundColor = UIColor(red: 0.5, green: 1, blue: 0, alpha: 1)
let v3 = UIView(frame:CGRectMake(
    v1.bounds.width-20, v1.bounds.height-20, 20, 20))
v3.backgroundColor = UIColor(red: 1, green: 0, blue: 0, alpha: 1)
mainview.addSubview(v1)
v1.addSubview(v2)
v1.addSubview(v3)
```

To that example, I'll add code applying springs and struts to the two subviews to make them behave like the text field and the OK button I was hypothesizing earlier:

```
v2.autoresizingMask = .FlexibleWidth
v3.autoresizingMask = [.FlexibleTopMargin, .FlexibleLeftMargin]
```

Now I'll resize the superview, thus bringing autoresizing into play; as you can see (Figure 1-13), the subviews remain pinned in their correct relative positions:

```
v1.bounds.size.width += 40
v1.bounds.size.height -= 50
```

Figure 1-12. Before autoresizing

Figure 1-13. After autoresizing

That example shows exactly what autoresizing is about, but it's a little artificial; in real life, the superview is more likely to be resized, not because you resize it in code, but because of automatic behavior, such as compensatory resizing of the interface when the device is rotated. To see this, you might modify the previous example to pin the size of v1 to the size of the root view, and then run the app and rotate the device. Thus you might initially configure v1 like this:

```
v1.frame = mainview.bounds
v1.autoresizingMask = [.FlexibleHeight, .FlexibleWidth]
```

Now run the app and rotate the device (in the Simulator, repeatedly choose Hardware → Rotate Left). The view v1 now fills the screen as the interface rotates, and its subviews stay pinned in their correct relative positions.

Autoresizing is effective but simple — sometimes too simple. The only relationship it describes is between a subview and its superview; it can't help you do such things as space a row of views evenly across the screen relative to one another. Before autolayout, the way to achieve more sophisticated goals of that sort was to combine autoresizing with manual layout in layoutSubviews. Autoresizing happens before layout-Subviews is called, so your layoutSubviews code is free to come marching in and tidy up whatever autoresizing didn't get quite right. Nowadays, though, autolayout is the norm.

Autolayout

Autolayout is an opt-in technology, at the level of each individual view. A view may opt in to autolayout in any of three ways:

- Your code adds an autolayout constraint to a view. The views involved in this constraint use autolayout.
- Your app loads a nib for which "Use Auto Layout" is checked. *Every* view instantiated from that nib uses autolayout.
- A view in the interface, which would be an instance of a custom UIView subclass of yours, returns true from the class method requiresConstraintBasedLayout. That view uses autolayout.

  The reason for this third approach to opting in to autolayout is that you might need autolayout to be switched on in order to add autolayout constraints in code. A common place to create constraints in code is in a view's updateConstraints implementation (discussed later in this chapter). However, if autolayout isn't switched on, updateConstraints won't be called. So requiresConstraintBased-Layout provides a way of switching it on.

One sibling view can use autolayout while another sibling view does not, and a superview can use autolayout while some or all of its subviews do not. However, autolayout is implemented through the superview chain, so if a view uses autolayout, then automatically so do all its superviews; and if (as will almost certainly be the case) one of those views is the main view of a view controller, that view controller receives autolayout-related events that it would not have received otherwise.

 You can't turn off autolayout for just part of a nib. Either all views instantiated from a nib use autolayout or they all use autoresizing. To generate different parts of your interface from nibs, one part with autoresizing, another part with autolayout, separate those parts into different nibs (different *.storyboard* or *.xib* files) and then load and combine them at runtime.

Constraints

An autolayout constraint, or simply *constraint*, is an NSLayoutConstraint instance, and describes either the absolute width or height of a view or a relationship between an attribute of one view and an attribute of another view. In the latter case, the attributes don't have to be the same attribute, and the two views don't have to be siblings (subviews of the same superview) or parent and child (superview and subview) — the only requirement is that they share a common ancestor (a superview somewhere up the view hierarchy).

Here are the chief properties of an NSLayoutConstraint:

`firstItem`, `firstAttribute`, `secondItem`, `secondAttribute`
> The two views and their respective attributes (NSLayoutAttribute) involved in this constraint. If the constraint is describing a view's absolute height or width, the second view will be `nil` and the second attribute will be `.NotAnAttribute`. Additional NSLayoutAttribute values are:
>
> - `.Top`, `.Bottom`
> - `.Left`, `.Right`, `.Leading`, `.Trailing`
> - `.Width`, `.Height`
> - `.CenterX`, `.CenterY`
> - `.FirstBaseline`, `.LastBaseline`
>
> `.FirstBaseline` applies primarily to multiline labels, and is some distance down from the top of the label (Chapter 10); `.LastBaseline` is some distance up from the bottom of the label.
>
> The meanings of the other attributes are intuitively obvious, except that you might wonder what "leading" and "trailing" mean: they are the international equivalent of "left" and "right," automatically reversing their meaning on systems for which your app is localized and whose language is written right-to-left. New in iOS 9, the *entire* interface is automatically reversed on such systems — but that will work properly only if you've used "leading" and "trailing" constraints throughout.

`multiplier`, `constant`
> These numbers will be applied to the second attribute's value to determine the first attribute's value. The `multiplier` is multiplied by the second attribute's value; the `constant` is added to that product. The first attribute is set to the result. (The name *constant* is a very poor choice, as this value isn't constant; have the Apple folks never heard the term *addend*?) Basically, you're writing an equation $a_1 = ma_2 + c$, where a_1 and a_2 are the two attributes, and m and c are the multiplier and the constant. Thus, in the degenerate case where the first attribute's value is to equal the second attribute's value, the multiplier will be 1 and the constant will be 0. If you're describing a view's width or height absolutely, the multiplier will be 1 and the constant will be the width or height value.

`relation`
> An NSLayoutRelation stating how the two attribute values are to be related to one another, as modified by the `multiplier` and the `constant`. This is the operator that goes in the spot where I put the equal sign in the equation in the preceding paragraph. It might be an equal sign (`.Equal`), but inequalities are also permitted (`.LessThanOrEqual`, `.GreaterThanOrEqual`).

`priority`

Priority values range from 1000 (required) down to 1, and certain standard behaviors have standard priorities. Constraints can have different priorities, determining the order in which they are applied.

A constraint belongs to a view. A view can have many constraints: a UIView has a `constraints` property, along with these instance methods:

- `addConstraint:`, `addConstraints:`
- `removeConstraint:`, `removeConstraints:`

The question then is *which* view a given constraint will belong to. The answer is: the view that is closest up the view hierarchy from both views involved in the constraint. If possible, it should *be* one of those views. Thus, for example, if the constraint dictates a view's absolute width, it belongs to that view; if it sets the top of a view in relation to the top of its superview, it belongs to that superview; if it aligns the tops of two sibling views, it belongs to their common superview.

Starting in iOS 8, however, instead of adding a constraint to a particular view explicitly, you can *activate* the constraint using the NSLayoutConstraint class method `activateConstraints:`, which takes an array of constraints. The activated constraints are *added to the correct view automatically*, relieving the programmer from having to determine what view that would be. There is also a method `deactivateConstraints:` which removes constraints from their view. And a constraint has an `active` property; you can set it to activate or deactivate a single constraint, plus it tells you whether a given constraint is part of the interface at this moment.

NSLayoutConstraint properties are read-only, except for `priority` and `constant`. If you want to change anything else about an existing constraint, you must remove the constraint and add a new one.

 Once you are using explicit constraints to position and size a view, *do not set its frame* (or bounds and center) subsequently; use constraints alone. Otherwise, when `layoutSubviews` is called, the view will jump back to where its constraints position it. (The exception is that you *may* set a view's frame if you are *in* `layoutSubviews`, as I'll explain later.)

Autoresizing constraints

The mechanism whereby individual views can opt in to autolayout can suddenly involve other views in autolayout, even though those other views were not using autolayout previously. Therefore, there needs to be a way, when such a view becomes involved in autolayout, to determine that view's position and layout through constraints in the same way they were previously being determined through its frame and its `autoresizing-Mask`. The runtime takes care of this for you: it translates the view's frame and `autoresizingMask` settings into constraints. The result is a set of implicit constraints, of class NSAutoresizingMaskLayoutConstraint, affecting this view (though they may be attached to a different view). Thanks to these implicit constraints, the layout dictated by the view's `autoresizingMask` continues to work.

For example, suppose I have a UILabel whose frame is (`20.0,20.0,42.0,22.0`), and whose `autoresizingMask` is `.None`. If this label were suddenly to come under autolayout, then its superview would acquire four implicit constraints setting its width and height at 42 and 22 and its center x and y at 41 and 31.

This conversion is performed only if the view in question has its `translates-AutoresizingMaskIntoConstraints` property set to `true`. That is, in fact, the default if the view came into existence either in code or by instantiation from a nib where "Use Auto Layout" is not checked. The assumption is that if a view came into existence in either of those ways, you want its frame and `autoresizingMask` to act as its constraints if it becomes involved in autolayout.

That's a sensible rule, but it means that if you intend to apply any explicit constraints of your own to such a view, you'll probably want to remember to turn off this automatic behavior by setting the view's `translatesAutoresizingMaskIntoConstraints` property to `false`. If you don't, you're going to end up with both implicit constraints and explicit constraints affecting this view, and it's unlikely that you would want that. Typically, that sort of situation will result in a conflict between constraints, as I'll explain a little later; indeed, what usually happens to me is that I *don't* remember to set the view's `translatesAutoresizingMaskIntoConstraints` property to `false`, and am reminded to do so only when I *do* get a conflict between constraints.

Creating constraints in code

We are now ready to write some code involving constraints! I'll start by using the NSLayoutConstraint initializer `init(item:attribute:relatedBy:toItem:attribute:multiplier:constant:)`, which sets every property of the constraint as I described them a moment ago (except the `priority`, which defaults to 1000 and can be set later if necessary).

I'll generate the same views and subviews and layout behavior as in Figures 1-12 and 1-13, but using constraints. Observe that I don't bother to assign the subviews v2 and v3 explicit frames as I create them, because constraints will take care of positioning them, and that I remember (for once) to set their `translatesAutoresizingMaskInto-Constraints` properties to `false`:

```
let v1 = UIView(frame:CGRectMake(100, 111, 132, 194))
v1.backgroundColor = UIColor(red: 1, green: 0.4, blue: 1, alpha: 1)
let v2 = UIView()
v2.backgroundColor = UIColor(red: 0.5, green: 1, blue: 0, alpha: 1)
let v3 = UIView()
v3.backgroundColor = UIColor(red: 1, green: 0, blue: 0, alpha: 1)
mainview.addSubview(v1)
v1.addSubview(v2)
v1.addSubview(v3)
v2.translatesAutoresizingMaskIntoConstraints = false
v3.translatesAutoresizingMaskIntoConstraints = false
v1.addConstraint(
    NSLayoutConstraint(item: v2,
        attribute: .Leading,
        relatedBy: .Equal,
        toItem: v1,
        attribute: .Leading,
        multiplier: 1, constant: 0)
)
v1.addConstraint(
    NSLayoutConstraint(item: v2,
        attribute: .Trailing,
        relatedBy: .Equal,
        toItem: v1,
        attribute: .Trailing,
        multiplier: 1, constant: 0)
)
v1.addConstraint(
    NSLayoutConstraint(item: v2,
        attribute: .Top,
        relatedBy: .Equal,
        toItem: v1,
        attribute: .Top,
        multiplier: 1, constant: 0)
)
v2.addConstraint(
    NSLayoutConstraint(item: v2,
        attribute: .Height,
        relatedBy: .Equal,
        toItem: nil,
        attribute: .NotAnAttribute,
        multiplier: 1, constant: 10)
)
v3.addConstraint(
    NSLayoutConstraint(item: v3,
        attribute: .Width,
        relatedBy: .Equal,
        toItem: nil,
        attribute: .NotAnAttribute,
        multiplier: 1, constant: 20)
)
v3.addConstraint(
```

```
        NSLayoutConstraint(item: v3,
            attribute: .Height,
            relatedBy: .Equal,
            toItem: nil,
            attribute: .NotAnAttribute,
            multiplier: 1, constant: 20)
    )
    v1.addConstraint(
        NSLayoutConstraint(item: v3,
            attribute: .Trailing,
            relatedBy: .Equal,
            toItem: v1,
            attribute: .Trailing,
            multiplier: 1, constant: 0)
    )
    v1.addConstraint(
        NSLayoutConstraint(item: v3,
            attribute: .Bottom,
            relatedBy: .Equal,
            toItem: v1,
            attribute: .Bottom,
            multiplier: 1, constant: 0)
    )
```

Now, I know what you're thinking. You're thinking: "What are you, nuts? That is a boatload of code!" (Except that you probably used another four-letter word instead of "boat.") But that's something of an illusion. I'd argue that what we're doing here is actually *simpler* than the code with which we created Figure 1-12 using explicit frames and autoresizing.

After all, we merely create eight constraints in eight simple commands. (I've broken each command into multiple lines, but that's just a matter of formatting.) They're verbose, but they are the same command repeated with different parameters, so creating them is just a matter of copy-and-paste. Moreover, our eight constraints determine the *position, size, and layout behavior* of our two subviews, so we're getting a lot of bang for our buck.

Even more telling, these constraints are a far clearer expression of what's supposed to happen than setting a frame and `autoresizingMask`. The position of our subviews is described once and for all, both as they will initially appear and as they will appear if their superview is resized. And it is described meaningfully; we don't have to use arbitrary math. Recall what we had to say before:

```
let v3 = UIView(frame:CGRectMake(
    v1.bounds.width-20, v1.bounds.height-20, 20, 20))
```

That business of subtracting the view's height and width from its superview's bounds height and width in order to position the view is confusing and error-prone. With constraints, we can speak the truth directly; our constraints say, plainly and simply, "v3 is 20 points wide and 20 points high and flush with the bottom-right corner of v1."

In addition, of course, constraints can express things that autoresizing can't. For example, instead of applying an absolute height to v2, we could require that its height be exactly one-tenth of v1's height, regardless of how v1 is resized. To do that without constraints, you'd have to implement layoutSubviews and enforce it manually, in code.

Anchor notation

New in iOS 9, it's possible to do everything I just did, making exactly the same eight constraints and adding them to the same views, using a much more compact notation. The old notation has the virtue of singularity: one NSLayoutConstraint initializer method can create any constraint. The new notation takes the opposite approach: it concentrates on brevity but sacrifices singularity. To do so, instead of focusing on the constraint, it focuses on the attributes to which the constraint relates. These attributes are expressed as *anchor* properties of a UIView:

- topAnchor, bottomAnchor
- leftAnchor, rightAnchor, leadingAnchor, trailingAnchor
- centerXAnchor, centerYAnchor
- firstBaselineAnchor, lastBaselineAnchor

The anchor values are all NSLayoutAnchor instances (some are instances of NSLayout-Anchor subclasses). The constraint-forming methods are then NSLayoutAnchor instance methods, and there are a lot of them, with your choice depending on whether your constraint needs to specify just another anchor (with the constant and the multiplier defaulting to 0 and 1), a constant or a multiplier or both, and upon your choice of relation:

- constraintEqualToConstant:
- constraintGreaterThanOrEqualToConstant:
- constraintLessThanOrEqualToConstant:
- constraintEqualToAnchor:
- constraintGreaterThanOrEqualToAnchor:
- constraintLessThanOrEqualToAnchor:
- constraintEqualToAnchor:constant:
- constraintGreaterThanOrEqualToAnchor:constant:
- constraintLessThanOrEqualToAnchor:constant:
- constraintEqualToAnchor:multiplier:
- constraintGreaterThanOrEqualToAnchor:multiplier:

- `constraintLessThanOrEqualToAnchor:multiplier:`

- `constraintEqualToAnchor:multiplier:constant:`

- `constraintGreaterThanOrEqualToAnchor:multiplier:constant:`

- `constraintLessThanOrEqualToAnchor:multiplier:constant:`

All of that may sound very elaborate when I describe it, but when you see it in action, you will appreciate immediately the benefit of this compact notation: it's easy to write (especially thanks to Xcode's code completion), easy to read, and easy to maintain. The new notation is particularly convenient in connection with `activateConstraints:`, as we don't have to worry about specifying what view each constraint should be added to:

```
NSLayoutConstraint.activateConstraints([
    v2.leadingAnchor.constraintEqualToAnchor(v1.leadingAnchor),
    v2.trailingAnchor.constraintEqualToAnchor(v1.trailingAnchor),
    v2.topAnchor.constraintEqualToAnchor(v1.topAnchor),
    v2.heightAnchor.constraintEqualToConstant(10),
    v3.widthAnchor.constraintEqualToConstant(20),
    v3.heightAnchor.constraintEqualToConstant(20),
    v3.trailingAnchor.constraintEqualToAnchor(v1.trailingAnchor),
    v3.bottomAnchor.constraintEqualToAnchor(v1.bottomAnchor)
])
```

That's eight constraints in eight lines of code — plus the surrounding `activate-Constraints` call to put those constraints into our interface. It isn't strictly necessary to activate all one's constraints at once, but it's best to try to do so.

Visual format notation

Another way to abbreviate your creation of constraints is to use a sort of text-based shorthand, called a *visual format*. This has the advantage of allowing you to describe multiple constraints simultaneously, and is appropriate particularly when you're arranging a series of views horizontally or vertically. I'll start with a simple example:

```
"V:|[v2(10)]"
```

In that expression, `V:` means that the vertical dimension is under discussion; the alternative is `H:`, which is also the default (so it is permitted to specify no dimension). A view's name appears in square brackets, and a pipe (`|`) signifies the superview, so here we're portraying v2's top edge as butting up against its superview's top edge. Numeric dimensions appear in parentheses, and a numeric dimension accompanying a view's name sets that dimension of that view, so here we're also setting v2's height to 10.

To use a visual format, you have to provide a dictionary mapping the string name of each view mentioned to the actual view. For example, the dictionary accompanying the preceding expression might be `["v2":v2]`. So here's another way of expressing of the preceding code example, using the visual format shorthand throughout:

```
let d = ["v2":v2,"v3":v3]
NSLayoutConstraint.activateConstraints([
    NSLayoutConstraint.constraintsWithVisualFormat(
        "H:|[v2]|", options: [], metrics: nil, views: d),
    NSLayoutConstraint.constraintsWithVisualFormat(
        "V:|[v2(10)]|", options: [], metrics: nil, views: d),
    NSLayoutConstraint.constraintsWithVisualFormat(
        "H:[v3(20)]|", options: [], metrics: nil, views: d),
    NSLayoutConstraint.constraintsWithVisualFormat(
        "V:[v3(20)]|", options: [], metrics: nil, views: d)
].flatten().map{$0})
```

That example creates the same constraints as the previous example, but in four commands instead of eight. (The constraintsWithVisualFormat: method yields an array of constraints, so my literal array is an array of arrays of constraints. But activateConstraints expects an array of constraints, so I flatten my literal array.)

The visual format syntax shows itself to best advantage when multiple views are laid out in relation to one another along the same dimension; in that situation, you get a lot of bang for your buck (many constraints generated by one visual format string). The syntax, however, is somewhat limited in what constraints it can readily express; it conceals the number and exact nature of the constraints that it produces; and personally I find it easier to make a mistake with the visual format syntax than with the complete expression of each constraint. Still, you'll want to become familiar with the visual format syntax, not least because console messages describing a constraint sometimes use it.

Here are some further things to know when generating constraints with the visual format syntax:

- The metrics: parameter is a dictionary with numeric values. This lets you use a name in the visual format string where a numeric value needs to go.

- The options: parameter is a bitmask (NSLayoutFormatOptions) chiefly letting you do things like add alignments. The alignments you specify are applied to all the views mentioned in the visual format string.

- To specify the distance between two successive views, use hyphens surrounding the numeric value, like this: "[v1]-20-[v2]". The numeric value may optionally be surrounded by parentheses.

- A numeric value in parentheses may be preceded by an equality or inequality operator, and may be followed by an at sign with a priority. Multiple numeric values, separated by comma, may appear in parentheses together. For example: "[v1(>=20@400,<=30)]".

For formal details of the visual format syntax, see the "Visual Format Syntax" chapter of Apple's *Auto Layout Guide*.

In Objective-C, you can form a dictionary for mapping view names to view references more or less automatically, thanks to the `NSDictionaryOfVariableBindings` macro; for example, `NSDictionaryOfVariableBindings(v2,v3)` yields the Objective-C equivalent of the dictionary `["v2":v2,"v3":v3]` that we formed manually in the preceding code. But Swift lacks macros; there's no preprocessor, so the textual transformation needed to generate a literal dictionary from a literal list of view variable names is impossible. For an alternative, see the `dictionaryOfNames` utility function in Appendix B.

Constraints as objects

Although the examples so far have involved creating constraints and adding them directly to the interface — and then forgetting about them — it is frequently useful to form constraints and keep them on hand for future use (typically in a property). A common use case is where you intend, at some future time, to change the interface in some radical way, such as by inserting or removing a view; you'll probably find it convenient to keep multiple sets of constraints on hand, each set being appropriate to a particular configuration of the interface. It is then trivial to swap constraints out of and into the interface along with views that they affect.

In this example, we create within our main view (`mainview`) three views, v1, v2, and v3, which are red, yellow, and blue rectangles respectively. We keep strong references (as properties) to all three views. For some reason, we will later want to remove the yellow view (v2) dynamically as the app runs, moving the blue view to where the yellow view was; and then, still later, we will want to insert the yellow view once again (Figure 1-14). So we have two alternating view configurations. Therefore we create *two* sets of constraints, one describing the positions of v1, v2, and v3 when all three are present, the other describing the positions of v1 and v3 when v2 is absent. For purposes of maintaining these sets of constraints, we have already prepared two properties, `constraintsWith` and `constraintsWithout`, initialized as empty arrays of NSLayoutConstraint:

```
var constraintsWith = [NSLayoutConstraint]()
var constraintsWithout = [NSLayoutConstraint]()
```

Here's the code for creating the views and the two sets of constraints. We start with v2 present, so it is the first set of constraints that we initially make active:

```
let v1 = UIView()
v1.backgroundColor = UIColor.redColor()
v1.translatesAutoresizingMaskIntoConstraints = false
let v2 = UIView()
v2.backgroundColor = UIColor.yellowColor()
v2.translatesAutoresizingMaskIntoConstraints = false
let v3 = UIView()
v3.backgroundColor = UIColor.blueColor()
```

Figure 1-14. Alternate sets of views and constraints

```
v3.translatesAutoresizingMaskIntoConstraints = false
mainview.addSubview(v1)
mainview.addSubview(v2)
mainview.addSubview(v3)
self.v1 = v1
self.v2 = v2
self.v3 = v3
// construct constraints
let c1 = NSLayoutConstraint.constraintsWithVisualFormat(
    "H:|-(20)-[v(100)]", options: [], metrics: nil, views: ["v":v1])
let c2 = NSLayoutConstraint.constraintsWithVisualFormat(
    "H:|-(20)-[v(100)]", options: [], metrics: nil, views: ["v":v2])
let c3 = NSLayoutConstraint.constraintsWithVisualFormat(
    "H:|-(20)-[v(100)]", options: [], metrics: nil, views: ["v":v3])
let c4 = NSLayoutConstraint.constraintsWithVisualFormat(
    "V:|-(100)-[v(20)]", options: [], metrics: nil, views: ["v":v1])
let c5with = NSLayoutConstraint.constraintsWithVisualFormat(
    "V:[v1]-(20)-[v2(20)]-(20)-[v3(20)]", options: [], metrics: nil,
    views: ["v1":v1, "v2":v2, "v3":v3])
let c5without = NSLayoutConstraint.constraintsWithVisualFormat(
    "V:[v1]-(20)-[v3(20)]", options: [], metrics: nil,
    views: ["v1":v1, "v3":v3])
// first set of constraints
self.constraintsWith.appendContentsOf(c1)
self.constraintsWith.appendContentsOf(c2)
self.constraintsWith.appendContentsOf(c3)
self.constraintsWith.appendContentsOf(c4)
self.constraintsWith.appendContentsOf(c5with)
// second set of constraints
self.constraintsWithout.appendContentsOf(c1)
self.constraintsWithout.appendContentsOf(c3)
self.constraintsWithout.appendContentsOf(c4)
self.constraintsWithout.appendContentsOf(c5without)
// apply first set
NSLayoutConstraint.activateConstraints(self.constraintsWith)
```

All that preparation may seem extraordinarily elaborate, but the result is that when the time comes to swap v2 out of or into the interface, swapping the appropriate constraints is trivial:

```
    if self.v2.superview != nil {
        self.v2.removeFromSuperview()
        NSLayoutConstraint.deactivateConstraints(self.constraintsWith)
        NSLayoutConstraint.activateConstraints(self.constraintsWithout)
    } else {
        mainview.addSubview(v2)
        NSLayoutConstraint.deactivateConstraints(self.constraintsWithout)
        NSLayoutConstraint.activateConstraints(self.constraintsWith)
    }
```

Guides and margins

So far, I've been assuming that the attributes (anchors) between which you want to create constraints are, for the most part, the exact edges and centers of views, and that these will stay put. But that's not always the case. Sometimes, you want a view to vend some *other* anchor, a kind of *secondary* anchor, to which another view can be constrained. It is even possible that you'll want this anchor to be able to move, and thus move the constrained view along with it. This notion of a secondary anchor has evolved by accretion over the past several iterations of iOS, so that now it is expressed in several different ways.

Consider, to begin with, the business of pinning your subviews to the bottom and (especially) the top of a view controller's main view. The top and bottom of the interface are often occupied by a bar (status bar, navigation bar, toolbar, tab bar — see Chapter 12). Your layout of subviews will typically occupy the region *between* these bars. Since iOS 7, however, the main view can extend vertically to the edges of the window *behind* those bars. Moreover, such bars can come and go dynamically, and can change their heights; for example, since iOS 8 the default behavior has been for the status bar to vanish when an iPhone app is in landscape orientation, and a navigation bar is taller when an iPhone app is in portrait orientation than when the same app is in landscape orientation.

Therefore, you need something else, other than the *literal* top and bottom of a view controller's main view, to which to anchor the vertical constraints that position its subviews — something that will move vertically to reflect the current location of the bars. Otherwise, an interface that looks right under some circumstances will look wrong in others.

For example, consider a view whose top is literally constrained to the top of the view controller's main view, which is its superview:

```
let arr = NSLayoutConstraint.constraintsWithVisualFormat(
    "V:|-0-[v]", options: [], metrics: nil, views: ["v":v])
```

When the app is in landscape orientation, with the status bar removed by default, this view will be right up against the top of the screen, which is fine. But in portrait orientation, this view will *still* be right up against the top of the screen — which looks bad because the status bar reappears and overlaps it.

To solve this problem, UIViewController supplies and maintains two invisible views, the *top layout guide* and the *bottom layout guide*, which it injects as subviews into the view hierarchy of its main view. Your topmost and bottommost vertical constraints will usually not be between a subview and the top or bottom of the main view, but between a subview and the bottom of the top layout guide, or a subview and the top of the bottom layout guide. The bottom of the top layout guide matches the bottom of the lowest top bar, or the top of the main view if there is no top bar; the top of the bottom layout guide matches the top of the bottom bar, or the bottom of the main view if there is no bottom bar. Most important, these layout guides change their size as the situation changes — the top or bottom bar changes its height, or vanishes entirely — and so your views constrained to them move to track the edges of the main view's visible area.

You can access these layout guides programmatically through the UIViewController properties topLayoutGuide and bottomLayoutGuide. For example (this code is in a view controller, so the top layout guide is self.topLayoutGuide):

```
let arr = NSLayoutConstraint.constraintsWithVisualFormat(
    "V:[tlg]-0-[v]", options: [], metrics: nil,
    views: ["tlg":self.topLayoutGuide, "v":v])
```

In iOS 9, the topLayoutGuide has a bottomAnchor and the bottomLayoutGuide has a topAnchor:

```
let tlg = self.topLayoutGuide
let c = v.topAnchor.constraintEqualToAnchor(tlg.bottomAnchor)
```

In iOS 8, views acquired *margins*. These are things you can constrain to that are *inset* from the edge of a UIView. The main idea, clearly, is that you might want subviews to keep a minimum standard distance from the edge of the superview. Thus, a UIView has a layoutMargins property which is a UIEdgeInsets, a struct consisting of four floats representing inset values starting at the top and proceeding counterclockwise — top, left, bottom, right. The default for a view controller's main view is a top and bottom margin of 0 and a right and left margin of 16; for any other view, it's 8 for all four margins.

You can constrain things to these margins. A visual format string that pins a subview's edge to its superview's edge, expressed as a pipe character (|), using *a single hyphen with no explicit distance value*, is interpreted as a constraint to the superview's margin. Thus, for example, here's a view that's butting up against its superview's left margin:

```
let arr = NSLayoutConstraint.constraintsWithVisualFormat(
    "H:|-[v]", options: [], metrics: nil, views: ["v":v])
```

As an NSLayoutAttribute value, a view's margin is expressed as one of the following:

- .TopMargin, .BottomMargin
- .LeftMargin, .RightMargin, .LeadingMargin, .TrailingMargin

- `.CenterXWithinMargins`, `.CenterYWithinMargins`

So here's another way to form the same constraint, with a view placed against its super-view's left margin:

```
let c = NSLayoutConstraint(item: v,
    attribute: .Leading,
    relatedBy: .Equal,
    toItem: mainview,
    attribute: .LeadingMargin,
    multiplier: 1, constant: 0)
```

In the compact anchor notation, use the view's `layoutMarginsGuide` property (new in iOS 9). It is a UILayoutGuide object (another iOS 9 innovation), which itself has anchors just like a UIView. So here's the same constraint once more:

```
let c = v.leadingAnchor.constraintEqualToAnchor(
    mainview.layoutMarginsGuide.leadingAnchor)
```

An additional UIView property, `preservesSuperviewLayoutMargins`, if `true`, causes a view to adopt as its `layoutMargins` the intersection of its own and its superview's `layout-Margins`. To put it another way, the superview's `layoutMargins` are allowed to supervene if the subview overlaps them. For example, suppose the view v has default layout margins {8,8,8,8}. And suppose its superview, `mainview`, is the view controller's main view, and has the default layout margins {0,16,0,16}. And suppose v is constrained exactly to the literal edges of its superview `mainview` — it covers it completely. Then if v's `preservesSuperviewLayoutMargins` is `true`, its effective layout margins are {8,16,8,16}.

iOS 9 introduces a second set of margins, a UIView's `readableContentGuide` (a UILayoutGuide), which you cannot change. The idea is that a subview consisting of text should not be allowed to grow as wide as an iPad in landscape, because that's too wide to read easily. By constraining such a subview horizontally to its superview's `readableContentGuide`, you ensure that that won't happen.

Finally, we come to a major iOS 9 innovation: it permits you to add your own custom UILayoutGuide objects to a view. They constitute a view's `layoutGuides` array, and are managed by calling `addLayoutGuide:` or `removeLayoutGuide:`. Such custom layout guide objects must be configured entirely using constraints. A UILayoutGuide has anchors, but that's effectively all it has. Thus, it can participate in layout as if it were a subview, but it is *not* a subview, and therefore it avoids all the overhead and complexity that a UIView would have.

Why is that useful? Well, consider the question of how to distribute views equally within their superview. This is easy to arrange initially, but it is not obvious how to design evenly spaced views that will remain evenly spaced when their superview is resized. The problem is that constraints describe relationships between *views*, not between *con-*

straints; there is no way to constrain the spacing constraints between views to remain equal to one another automatically as the superview is resized.

You can, on the other hand, constrain the heights or widths of *views* to remain equal to one another. The traditional solution, therefore, has been to resort to spacer views with their hidden set to true. But spacer views are views; hidden or not, they add overhead with respect to drawing, memory, touch detection, and more. Custom UILayoutGuides solve the problem; they can serve the same purpose as spacer views, but they are *not* views.

Suppose, for example, that I have four views that are to remain equally distributed vertically. I constrain their left and right edges, their heights, and the top of the first view and the bottom of the last view. This leaves open the question of how we will determine the vertical position of the two middle views; they must move in such a way that they are always equidistant from their vertical neighbors.

To solve the problem, I introduce three UILayoutGuide objects between my real views. A custom UILayoutGuide object is added to a UIView, so I'll add mine to the superview of my four real views:

```
let guides = [UILayoutGuide(), UILayoutGuide(), UILayoutGuide()]
for guide in guides {
    mainview.addLayoutGuide(guide)
}
```

I then involve my three layout guides in the layout. Remember, they must be configured entirely using constraints (the three layout guides are referenced through my guides array, and the four views are referenced through another array, views):

```
NSLayoutConstraint.activateConstraints([
    // guide left is arbitrary, let's say superview margin ❶
    guides[0].leadingAnchor.constraintEqualToAnchor(mainview.leadingAnchor),
    guides[1].leadingAnchor.constraintEqualToAnchor(mainview.leadingAnchor),
    guides[2].leadingAnchor.constraintEqualToAnchor(mainview.leadingAnchor),
    // guide widths are arbitrary, let's say 10
    guides[0].widthAnchor.constraintEqualToConstant(10),
    guides[1].widthAnchor.constraintEqualToConstant(10),
    guides[2].widthAnchor.constraintEqualToConstant(10),
    // bottom of each view is top of following guide ❷
    views[0].bottomAnchor.constraintEqualToAnchor(guides[0].topAnchor),
    views[1].bottomAnchor.constraintEqualToAnchor(guides[1].topAnchor),
    views[2].bottomAnchor.constraintEqualToAnchor(guides[2].topAnchor),
    // top of each view is bottom of preceding guide
    views[1].topAnchor.constraintEqualToAnchor(guides[0].bottomAnchor),
    views[2].topAnchor.constraintEqualToAnchor(guides[1].bottomAnchor),
    views[3].topAnchor.constraintEqualToAnchor(guides[2].bottomAnchor),
    // guide heights are equal! ❸
    guides[1].heightAnchor.constraintEqualToAnchor(guides[0].heightAnchor),
    guides[2].heightAnchor.constraintEqualToAnchor(guides[0].heightAnchor),
])
```

➊ I constrain the leading edges of the layout guides (arbitrarily, to the leading edge of their superview) and their widths (arbitrarily).

➋ I constrain each layout guide to the bottom of the view above it and the top of the view below it.

➌ Finally, our whole purpose is to distribute our views *equally*, so the heights of our layout guides must be *equal to one another*.

In that code, I clearly could have (and should have) generated each group of constraints as a loop, thus making this approach suitable for any number of distributed views; I have deliberately unrolled those loops for the sake of the example.

 In real life, you are unlikely to use this technique directly, because you will use a UIStackView instead, and let the UIStackView generate all of that code — as I will explain a little later.

Intrinsic content size and alignment rects

Some built-in interface objects, when using autolayout, have an inherent size in one or both dimensions. For example:

- A UIButton, by default, has a standard height, and its width is determined by its title.
- A UIImageView, by default, adopts the size of the image it is displaying.
- A UILabel, by default, if it consists of multiple lines and if its width is constrained, adopts a height sufficient to display all of its text.

This inherent size is the object's *intrinsic content size*. The intrinsic content size is used to generate constraints implicitly (of class NSContentSizeLayoutConstraint).

A change in the characteristics or content of a built-in interface object — a button's title, an image view's image, a label's text or font, and so forth — may thus cause its intrinsic content size to change. This, in turn, may alter your layout. You will want to configure your autolayout constraints so that your interface responds gracefully to such changes.

You do not have to supply explicit constraints configuring a dimension of a view whose intrinsic content size configures that dimension. But you might! And when you do, the tendency of an interface object to size itself to its intrinsic content size must not be allowed to conflict with its tendency to obey your explicit constraints. Therefore the constraints generated from a view's intrinsic content size have a lowered priority, and come into force only if no constraint of a higher priority prevents them. The following methods allow you to access these priorities (the parameter is a UILayoutConstraint-Axis, either .Horizontal or .Vertical):

`contentHuggingPriorityForAxis:`

A view's resistance to growing larger than its intrinsic size in this dimension. In effect, there is an inequality constraint saying that the view's size in this dimension should be less than or equal to its intrinsic size. The default prority is usually 250 (the same as `UILayoutPriorityDefaultLow`), though some interface classes will default to 251 if initialized in a nib.

`contentCompressionResistancePriorityForAxis:`

A view's resistance to shrinking smaller than its intrinsic size in this dimension. In effect, there is an inequality constraint saying that the view's size in this dimension should be greater than or equal to its intrinsic size. The default priority is usually 750 (the same as `UILayoutPriorityDefaultHigh`).

Those methods are getters; there are corresponding setters. Situations where you would need to change the priorities of these tendencies are few, but they do exist. For example, here are the visual formats configuring two adjacent labels (`lab1` and `lab2`) pinned to the superview and to one another:

```
"V:|-20-[lab1]"
"V:|-20-[lab2]"
"H:|-20-[lab1]"
"H:[lab2]-20-|"
"H:[lab1(>=100)]-(>=20)-[lab2(>=100)]"
```

The inequalities ensure that as the superview becomes narrower or the text of the labels becomes longer, a reasonable amount of text will remain visible in both labels. At the same time, one label will be squeezed down to 100 points width, while the other label will be allowed to grow to fill the remaining horizontal space. The question is: which label is which? You need to answer that question. To do so, it suffices to raise the compression resistance priority of one of the labels by a single point above that of the other:

```
let p = lab2.contentCompressionResistancePriorityForAxis(.Horizontal)
lab1.setContentCompressionResistancePriority(p+1, forAxis: .Horizontal)
```

You can supply an intrinsic size in your own custom UIView subclass by implementing `intrinsicContentSize`. Obviously you should do this only if your view's size depends on its contents. If you need the runtime to call `intrinsicContentSize` again, because that size has changed and the view needs to be laid out afresh, it's up to you to call your view's `invalidateIntrinsicContentSize` method.

Another question with which your custom UIView subclass might be concerned is what it should mean for another view to be aligned with it. It might mean aligned with your view's frame edges, but then again it might not. A possible example is a view that draws, internally, a rectangle with a shadow; you probably want to align things with that drawn rectangle, not with the outside of the shadow. To determine this, you can override your view's `alignmentRectInsets` method (or, more elaborately, its `alignmentRectForFrame:` and `frameForAlignmentRect:` methods).

By the same token, you may want to be able to align your custom UIView with another view by their baselines. The assumption here is that your view has a subview containing text and, therefore, possessing a baseline. Your custom view will return that subview in its implementation of `viewForFirstBaselineLayout` or `viewForLastBaselineLayout`.

Stack views

A stack view (UIStackView), new in iOS 9, is a view whose primary task is to generate constraints for some or all of its subviews. These are its *arranged subviews*. In particular, a stack view solves the problem of providing constraints when subviews are to be configured linearly in a horizontal row or a vertical column. In practice, it turns out that the vast majority of complex layouts can be expressed as an arrangement, possibly nested, of simple rows and columns of subviews. Thus, you are likely to resort to stack views to make your layout easier to construct and maintain.

Configuration of a stack view is extremely simple and yet remarkably powerful. First, you supply it with arranged subviews, usually by calling its initializer `init(arranged-Subviews:)`. The arranged subviews become the stack view's `arrangedSubviews` read-only property. You can also manage the arranged subviews with these methods:

- `addArrangedSubview:`
- `insertArrangedSubview:atIndex:`
- `removeArrangedSubview:`

The `arrangedSubviews` is different from, but is a subset of, the stack view's `subviews`. To put it another way, it's perfectly fine for the stack view to have subviews that are *not* arranged (and which you'll have to provide with constraints yourself), but any subview that *is* arranged must in fact be a subview plain and simple as well, and if you set a view as an arranged subview and it is *not* already a subview, the stack view will adopt it as a subview at that moment. The *order* of the `arrangedSubviews` is independent of the order of the `subviews`; the `subviews` order, you remember, determines the order in which the subviews are drawn, but the `arrangedSubviews` order determines how the stack view will *position* those subviews.

You will also want to set the following properties of the stack view:

axis
> Which way should the arranged subviews be arranged? Your choices are:
>
> - `.Horizontal`
> - `.Vertical`

distribution
> How should the arranged subviews be positioned along the `axis`? Your choices are:

- `.Fill`
- `.FillEqually`
- `.FillProportionally`
- `.EqualSpacing`
- `.EqualCentering`

Except for `.FillEqually`, the exact interpretation of your instructions may depend upon the intrinsic content sizes of the views. For example, `.FillProportionally` fills the full `axis` dimension, sizing the views in proportion to their intrinsic content sizes in this dimension. The stack view's `spacing` property determines the spacing (or minimum spacing) between the views.

`alignment`

This describes how the arranged subviews should be laid out with respect to the *other* dimension. Your choices are:

- `Fill`
- `Leading` (or `Top`)
- `Center`
- `Trailing` (or `Bottom`)
- `FirstBaseline` or `LastBaseline` (if the `axis` is `.Horizontal`)

Again, except in the case of `.Fill`, the interpretation here will depend upon the views having intrinsic content size (or baselines). If the `axis` is `.Vertical`, you can still involve the subviews' baselines in their spacing by setting the stack view's `baselineRelativeArrangement` to `true`.

`layoutMarginsRelativeArrangement`

If `true`, the stack view's internal `layoutMargins` are involved in the constraints of its arranged subviews. If `false` (the default), the stack view's literal edges are used.

Finally, note that although you will not have to constrain the arranged views — it is exactly the job of the stack view to do that — you *will* have to constrain the stack view *itself* (though of course this, too, might be done automatically because the stack view is an arranged view of a containing stack view).

To illustrate, I'll rewrite the code from earlier in this chapter. I have four views, with height constraints. I want to distribute them vertically in my main view. This time, I'll have a stack view do all the work for me:

```
// give the stack view arranged subviews
let sv = UIStackView(arrangedSubviews: views)
// configure the stack view
sv.axis = .Vertical
sv.alignment = .Fill
sv.distribution = .EqualSpacing
// constrain the stack view
sv.translatesAutoresizingMaskIntoConstraints = false
mainview.addSubview(sv)
NSLayoutConstraint.activateConstraints([
    sv.topAnchor.constraintEqualToAnchor(self.topLayoutGuide.bottomAnchor),
    sv.leadingAnchor.constraintEqualToAnchor(mainview.leadingAnchor),
    sv.trailingAnchor.constraintEqualToAnchor(mainview.trailingAnchor),
    sv.bottomAnchor.constraintEqualToAnchor(mainview.bottomAnchor),
])
```

Inspecting the resulting constraints, you can see that the stack view is doing for us effectively just what we did earlier (generating UILayoutGuide objects and using them as spacers). But letting the stack view do it is a lot easier!

Another nice feature of UIStackView is that it responds intelligently to changes. For example, if we were to make one of our arranged subviews invisible (set its hidden to true), the stack view would respond by distributing the remaining subviews evenly, as if the hidden subview didn't exist. Similarly, we can change properties of the stack view itself in real time. (Moreover, all such changes are animatable, as I'll explain in Chapter 4.)

Internationalization

New in iOS 9, the entire interface and its behavior are reversed when the app runs on a system for which the app is localized and whose language is right-to-left. Wherever you use leading and trailing constraints instead of left and right constraints, or if your constraints are constructed using the visual format language, your app's layout will participate in this reversal more or less automatically.

There may, however, be exceptions. Apple gives the example of a horizontal row of transport controls that mimic the buttons on a CD player: you wouldn't want the Rewind button and the Fast Forward button to be reversed just because the user's language reads right-to-left. Therefore, a UIView is endowed with a semanticContentAttribute property stating whether it should be flipped; the default is .Unspecified, but a value of .Playback or .Spatial will prevent flipping.

If you are constructing a view's subviews in code in real time, you can feed a subview's semanticContentAttribute value to the UIView class method userInterfaceLayout-DirectionForSemanticContentAttribute: to find out whether directionality is .Left-ToRight or .RightToLeft.

Mistakes with constraints

Creating constraints manually, as I've been doing so far in this chapter, is an invitation to make a mistake. Your totality of constraints constitute instructions for view layout, and it is all too easy, as soon as more than one or two views are involved, to generate faulty instructions. You can (and will) make two major kinds of mistake with constraints:

Conflict
> You have applied constraints that can't be satisfied simultaneously. This will be reported in the console (at great length).

Underdetermination (ambiguity)
> A view uses autolayout, but you haven't supplied sufficient information to determine its size and position. This is a far more insidious problem, because nothing bad may seem to happen, so you might not discover it until much later. If you're lucky, the view will at least fail to appear, or will appear in an undesirable place, alerting you to the problem.

Only required constraints (priority 1000) can contribute to a conflict, as the runtime is free to ignore lower-priority constraints that it can't satisfy. Constraints with different priorities do not conflict with one another. Nonrequired constraints with the same priority can contribute to ambiguity.

Let's start by generating a conflict. In this example, we return to our small red square in the lower right corner of a big purple square (Figure 1-12) and append a contradictory constraint:

```
NSLayoutConstraint.activateConstraints([
    // ...
    NSLayoutConstraint.constraintsWithVisualFormat(
        "H:[v3(20)]|", options: [], metrics: nil, views: d),
    NSLayoutConstraint.constraintsWithVisualFormat(
        "V:[v3(20)]|", options: [], metrics: nil, views: d),
    NSLayoutConstraint.constraintsWithVisualFormat(
        "V:[v3(10)]|", options: [], metrics: nil, views: d), // *
].flatten().map{$0})
```

The height of v3 can't be both 10 and 20. The runtime reports the conflict, and tells you which constraints are causing it:

```
Unable to simultaneously satisfy constraints. Probably at least one of the
constraints in the following list is one you don't want...

    "<NSLayoutConstraint:0x7f7fabc10750 V:[UIView:0x7f7fabc059d0(20)]>",
    "<NSLayoutConstraint:0x7f7fabc10d10 V:[UIView:0x7f7fabc059d0(10)]>"
```

 You can assign a constraint (or a UILayoutGuide) an `identifier` string; this can make it easier to determine which constraint in a conflict report is which.

Now we'll generate an ambiguity. Here, we neglect to give our small red square a height:

```
NSLayoutConstraint.activateConstraints([
    // ...
    NSLayoutConstraint.constraintsWithVisualFormat(
        "H:[v3(20)]|", options: [], metrics: nil, views: d),
].flatten().map{$0})
```

No console message alerts us to our mistake. Fortunately, however, v3 fails to appear in the interface, so we know something's wrong. *If your views fail to appear, suspect ambiguity.* In a less fortunate case, the view might appear, but (if we're lucky) in the wrong place. In a truly unfortunate case, the view might appear in the right place, but not consistently.

Suspecting ambiguity is one thing; tracking it down and proving it is another. A useful trick is to pause in the debugger and give the following mystical command in the console:

```
(lldb) expr -l objc++ -O -- [[UIWindow keyWindow] _autolayoutTrace]
```

The result is a graphical tree describing the view hierarchy and marking any ambiguously laid out views:

```
UIWindow:0x7fe8d0d9dbd0
|   •UIView:0x7fe8d0c2bf00
|   |   +UIView:0x7fe8d0c2c290
|   |   |   *UIView:0x7fe8d0c2c7e0
|   |   |   *UIView:0x7fe8d0c2c9e0- AMBIGUOUS LAYOUT
```

UIView also has a hasAmbiguousLayout method; I find it useful to set up a utility method that lets me check a view and all its subviews at any depth for ambiguity:

```
extension NSLayoutConstraint {
    class func reportAmbiguity (var v:UIView?) {
        if v == nil {
            v = UIApplication.sharedApplication().keyWindow
        }
        for vv in v!.subviews {
            print("\(vv) \(vv.hasAmbiguousLayout())")
            if vv.subviews.count > 0 {
                self.reportAmbiguity(vv)
            }
        }
    }
}
```

You can call that method in your code, or while paused in the debugger:

```
(lldb) expr NSLayoutConstraint.reportAmbiguity(nil)
```

To get a full list of the constraints responsible for positioning a particular view within its superview, log the results of calling the UIView instance method constraintsAffectingLayoutForAxis:. These constraints do not necessarily belong to this view (and the output doesn't tell you what view they do belong to). Your choices of axis

(UILayoutConstraintAxis) are .Horizontal and .Vertical. If a view doesn't participate in autolayout, the result will be an empty array. Again, a utility method can come in handy:

```
extension NSLayoutConstraint {
    class func listConstraints (var v:UIView?) {
        if v == nil {
            v = UIApplication.sharedApplication().keyWindow
        }
        for vv in v!.subviews {
            let arr1 = vv.constraintsAffectingLayoutForAxis(.Horizontal)
            let arr2 = vv.constraintsAffectingLayoutForAxis(.Vertical)
            NSLog("\n\n%@\nH: %@\nV:%@", vv, arr1, arr2)
            if vv.subviews.count > 0 {
                self.listConstraints(vv)
            }
        }
    }
}
```

And here's how to call it from the debugger:

```
(lldb) expr NSLayoutConstraint.listConstraints(nil)
```

Xcode's view debugging feature can also be a great help (Figure 1-15). With the app running, choose Debug → View Debugging → Capture View Hierarchy, or click the Debug View Hierarchy button in the debug toolbar. At the left, the Debug navigator lists your window and all its views hierarchically, along with their constraints. What's more, when a view is selected in this list or in the canvas, the Size inspector at the right lists its bounds and all the constraints that determine those bounds. This, along with the layered graphical display of your views and constraints in the canvas, is very likely to help you penetrate to the cause of any constraint-related difficulties.

Given the notions of conflict and ambiguity, we can understand what priorities are for. Imagine that all constraints have been placed in boxes, where each box is a priority value, in descending order. The first box (1000) contains all the required constraints, so all required constraints are obeyed first. (If they conflict, that's bad, and a report appears in the log; meanwhile, the system implicitly lowers the priority of one of the conflicting constraints, so that it doesn't have to obey it and can continue with layout by satisfying the remaining required constraints.) If there still isn't enough information to perform unambiguous layout given the required priorities alone, we pull the constraints out of the next box and try to obey them. If we can, consistently with what we've already done, fine; if we can't, or if ambiguity remains, we look in the *next* box — and so on. For a box after the first, we don't care about obeying exactly the constraints it contains; if an ambiguity remains, we can use a lower-priority constraint value to give us something to aim at, resolving the ambiguity, without fully obeying the lower-priority constraint's desires. For example, an inequality is an ambiguity, because an infinite number of values

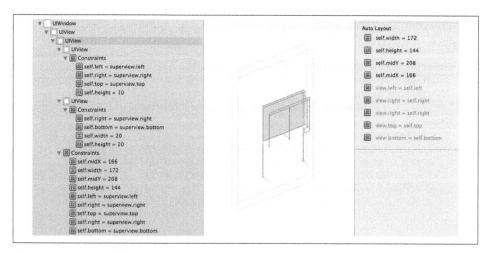

Figure 1-15. View debugging

will satisfy it; a lower-priority equality can tell us what value to prefer, resolving the ambiguity, but there's no conflict even if we can't fully achieve that preferred value.

Configuring Layout in the Nib

The focus of the discussion so far has been on configuring layout in code. This, however, will often be unnecessary; instead, you'll set up your layout (autoresizing or autolayout) in the nib, using the nib editor (Interface Builder). It would not be strictly true to say that you can do absolutely anything in the nib that you could do in code, but the nib editor is certainly a remarkably powerful way of configuring layout (and where it falls short, you can always supplement it with some code in addition).

Autoresizing in the nib

To configure autoresizing in the nib editor, you'll need to ensure that autolayout is turned off for the *.storyboard* or *.xib* file you're editing. To do so, select that file in the Project navigator and show the File inspector: uncheck "Use Auto Layout."

When editing a nib file with autolayout turned off, you can assign a view springs and struts in the Size inspector. A solid line externally represents a strut; a solid line internally represents a spring. A helpful animation shows you the effect on your view's position as its superview is resized.

Constraints in the nib

In a *.xib* or *.storyboard* file where "Use Auto Layout" is checked, a vast array of tools springs to life in the nib editor to help you create constraints that will be instantiated

---

from the nib along with the views. What's more, the nib editor will help prevent you from ending up with conflicting or ambiguous constraints.

Even in a nib with "Use Auto Layout" checked, the nib editor *doesn't generate any constraints* unless you ask it to. However, it doesn't want the app to run with ambiguous layout, because then you might not see any views at all; you wouldn't be able to test your app until you'd fully worked out all the constraints throughout the interface. Therefore, if your views lack needed constraints, the nib supplies them implicitly behind the scenes so that they are present at runtime:

No constraints
> If a view is affected by no constraints at all, it is given constraints tagged in the debugger as "IB auto generated at build time for view with fixed frame."

Ambiguous constraints
> If a view is affected by some constraints but not enough to disambiguate fully, it is given additional constraints tagged in the debugger as "IB auto generated at build time for view with ambiguity."

The nib editor also *doesn't change any constraints* unless you ask it to. If you create constraints and then move or resize a view affected by those constraints, the constraints are *not* automatically changed. This means that the constraints no longer match the way the view is portrayed; if the constraints were to position the view, they wouldn't put it where you've put it. The nib editor will alert you to this situation (a Misplaced Views issue), and can readily resolve it for you, but it won't do so unless you explicitly ask it to.

Creating a constraint

The nib editor provides two primary ways to create a constraint:

- Control-drag from one view to another. A HUD appears, listing constraints that you can create (Figure 1-16). Either view can be in the canvas or in the document outline. To create an internal width or height constraint, control-drag from a view to itself! When you control-drag within the canvas, the direction of the drag is used to winnow the options presented in the HUD; for example, if you control-drag horizontally within a view in the canvas, the HUD lists Width but not Height.
- Choose from the Editor → Align or Editor → Pin hierarchical menus, or click the Align or Pin button at the right end of the layout bar below the canvas.

The buttons in the layout bar are very powerful! They present little popover dialogs where you can choose multiple constraints to create (possibly for multiple views, if that's what you've selected beforehand) and provide them with numeric values (Figure 1-17). Constraints are not actually added until you click Add Constraints at the bottom. Before clicking Add Constraints, think about the Update Frames pop-up menu; if you don't

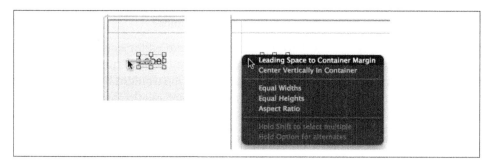

Figure 1-16. Creating a constraint by control-dragging

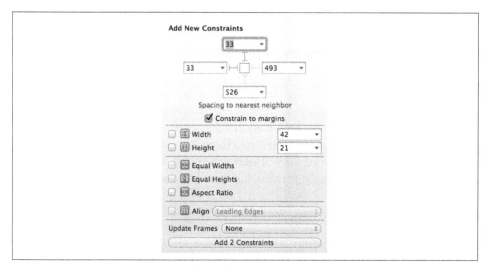

Figure 1-17. Creating constraints from the layout bar

update frames, the views may end up being drawn in the canvas differently from how the constraints describe them (a Misplaced Views issue).

The nib editor displays layout margins as faint lines in the canvas. (The faint vertical line at the left of Figure 1-16 is a margin.) When you Control-drag to form a constraint from a view to its superview, you might want to toggle the Option key to see some alternatives; for example, this might make the difference between an edge-based constraint and a margin-based constraint. Similarly, the popover dialog from the Pin button in the layout bar has a "Constrain to margins" checkbox (Figure 1-17). Finally, when editing a constraint (as I describe in the next section), the First Item and Second Item pop-up menus have a "Relative to margin" option.

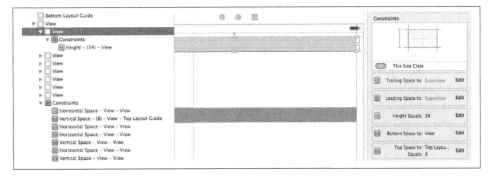

Figure 1-18. A view's constraints displayed in the nib

To set a view's layout margins explicitly, switch to the Size inspector and change the Layout Margins pop-up menu to Explicit. To make a view's layout margins behave as `readableContentGuide` margins, check Follow Readable Width.

 In Xcode 7, it is possible to create a constraint in the nib editor between a subview and the *literal* top or bottom of a view controller's main view — something that was absolutely impossible in earlier versions of Xcode. When Control-dragging from a subview to the main view, the default is a constraint to the top layout guide or the bottom layout guide, but holding Option lets you make a constraint to the margin. You can then edit the resulting constraint to switch off "Relative to margin."

Viewing and editing constraints

Constraints in the nib are full-fledged objects. They can be selected, edited, and deleted. Moreover, you can create an outlet to a constraint (and there are reasons why you might want to do so).

Constraints in the nib are visible in three places (Figure 1-18):

In the document outline
Constraints are listed in a special category, "Constraints," under the view to which they belong. (You'll have a much easier time distinguishing these constraints if you give your views meaningful labels!)

In the canvas
Constraints appear graphically as dimension lines when you select a view that they affect.

In the Size inspector
When a view affected by constraints is selected, the Size inspector lists those constraints, and a Constraints grid displays the view's constraints graphically.

When you select a constraint in the document outline or the canvas, you can view and edit its values in the Attributes or Size inspector. The inspector gives you access to almost all of a constraint's features: both anchors involved in the constraint, the relation, the constant and multiplier, and the priority. You can also set the identifier here (useful when debugging, as I mentioned earlier).

Alternatively, for simple editing of a constraint's constant, relation, and priority, double-click the constraint in the canvas to summon a little popover dialog. Similarly, when a constraint is listed in a view's Size inspector, double-click it to edit it in its own inspector, or click its Edit button to summon the little popover dialog.

A view's Size inspector also provides access to its content hugging and content compression resistance priority settings. Beneath these, there's an Intrinsic Size pop-up menu. The idea here is that your custom view might have an intrinsic size, but the nib editor doesn't know this, so it will report an ambiguity when you fail to provide (say) a width constraint that you know isn't actually needed; choose Placeholder to supply an intrinsic size and relieve the nib editor's worries (and to prevent the missing constraints from being generated automatically at runtime).

In a constraint's Attributes or Size inspector, there is a Placeholder checkbox ("Remove at build time"). If you check this checkbox, the constraint you're editing *won't* be instantiated when the nib is loaded, and it will *not* be replaced by an automatically generated constraint: in effect, you are deliberately generating ambiguous layout when the views and constraints are instantiated from the nib. Why might you want to do such a thing? One reason might be that you intend to substitute, in code, a constraint that you weren't quite able to configure in the nib. You need *some* constraint in the nib, because otherwise the nib editor will complain of ambiguity and will generate a constraint anyway at load time.

Problems with constraints

I've already said that generating constraints manually, in code, is error-prone. The nib editor, however, knows whether it contains problematic constraints. If a view is affected by any constraints, the Xcode nib editor will permit them to be ambiguous or conflicting, but it will also complain helpfully. You should pay attention to such complaints! The nib editor will bring the situation to your attention in various places:

Canvas
    Constraints drawn in the canvas when you select a view that they affect use color coding to express their status:

    Satisfactory constraints
        Drawn in blue.

    Problematic constraints
        Drawn in red.

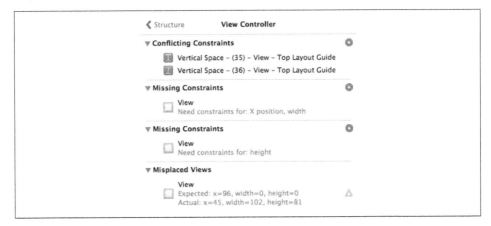

Figure 1-19. Layout issues in the document outline

Misplacement constraints
> Drawn in orange; these constraints are valid, but they are inconsistent with the frame you have imposed upon the view. I'll discuss misplaced views in the next paragraph.

Document outline
> If there are layout issues, the document outline displays a right arrow in a red or orange circle. Click it to see a detailed list of the issues (Figure 1-19). Hover the mouse over a title to see an Info button which you can click to learn more about the nature of this issue. The icons at the right are buttons: click one for a list of things the nib editor is offering to do to fix the issue for you. The chief issues are:

Conflicting Constraints
> A conflict between constraints.

Missing Constraints
> Ambiguous layout.

Misplaced Views
> If you manually change the frame of a view that is affected by constraints (including its intrinsic size), then the nib editor canvas may be displaying that view differently from how it would really appear if the current constraints were obeyed. A Misplaced Views situation is also reflected in the canvas:

> - The constraints in the canvas, drawn in orange, display the numeric *difference* between their values and the view's frame.

> - A dotted outline in the canvas may show where the view would be drawn if the existing constraints were obeyed.

A hierarchical menu, Editor → Resolve Auto Layout Issues, also available from the Resolve Auto Layout Issues button in the layout bar, proposes five large-scale moves involving *all* the constraints affecting selected views or all views:

Update Frames

Changes the way the view is drawn in the canvas, to show how it would really appear in the running app under the constraints as they stand. Be careful: if constraints are ambiguous, *this can cause a view to disappear.*

Alternatively, if you have resized a view with intrinsic size constraints, such as a button or a label, and you want it to resume the size it would have according to those intrinsic size constraints, select the view and choose Editor → Size to Fit Content.

Update Constraints

Choose this menu item to change numerically all the existing constraints affecting a view to match the way the canvas is currently drawing the view's frame.

Add Missing Constraints

Create new constraints so that the view has sufficient constraints to describe its frame unambiguously. The added constraints correspond to the way the canvas is currently drawing the view's frame.

Not everything that this command does may be what you ultimately want; you should regard it as a starting point. For example, the nib editor doesn't know whether you think a certain view's width should be determined by an internal width constraint or by pinning it to the left and right of its superview; and it may generate alignment constraints with other views that you never intended.

Reset to Suggested Constraints

This is as if you chose Clear Constraints followed by Add Missing Constraints: it removes all constraints affecting the view, and replaces them with a complete set of automatically generated constraints describing the way the canvas is currently drawing the view's frame.

Clear Constraints

Removes all constraints affecting the view.

Conditional constraints

Constraints and views can be made conditional in the nib editor. The conditions on which they depend are the size classes that I discussed earlier. This means that you can design your interface's constraints, and even the presence or absence of views, to depend on the size of the screen. In effect, the interface detects `traitCollectionDidChange:` and responds to it. Thus:

- You can design directly into your interface a complex rearrangement of that interface when an iPhone app rotates to compensate for a change in device orientation.
- A single *.storyboard* or *.xib* file can be used to design the interface of a universal app, even though the iPad interface and the iPhone interface may be quite different from one another.

Use of conditional constraints is an opt-in feature of the nib editor. You have opted in if "Use Size Classes" is checked in the File inspector for this *.storyboard* or *.xib*. In that case, the following nib editor interface features are present:

- The main view in the canvas, by default, is portrayed as a square, to suggest the dimension-agnostic nature of the design process.
- The center of the layout bar, below the canvas, acquires a pop-up menu where you can choose any combination of size classes. Your choices are Compact, Regular, and (between them) Any, so the choice is represented as a 3×3 grid.

The idea is that you design your interface initially for the general case (Any width, Any height, which is the default). You then use the pop-up grid to switch to a specific case — *the layout bar turns blue* to indicate that you're in specific-case mode — and modify the design for that case. Do *not* impulsively start moving interface items around! Instead, use the inspectors:

- Use a view's Attributes inspector to determine whether that view is present for a particular size class combination. Note the Installed checkbox! Initially, it applies to the general case. Click the Plus button, at its left, to add *another* Installed checkbox applicable to a particular set of size classes. Now you can check or uncheck Installed checkboxes so that this view is present for some size class combinations but removed for others.
- Use a constraint's Attributes or Size inspector to determine:
  - Whether that constraint is present for a particular size class combination. There is an Installed checkbox, which works just like the Installed checkbox for a view.
  - The value of that constraint's constant for a particular size class combination. The Constant field has a Plus button, at its left, just like the Installed checkbox; click it to add *another* Constant field applicable to a particular set of size classes.

A constraint or view that is not installed for the set of size classes you're looking at is listed in gray in the document outline.

In Xcode 7, other features of a view can be conditional on the size class. For example, the font of a button, label, or text field, and *every* feature of a stack view, can be different for different size classes. Keep your eyes peeled for that telltale Plus button in the Attributes or Size inspector.

View Debugging, Previewing, and Designing

Xcode has several features for helping you visualize and understand your view hierarchy and the effect of your constraints. This section calls attention to some of these.

View debugger

To enter the view debugger, choose Debug → View Debugging → Capture View Hierarchy, or click the Debug View Hierarchy button in the debug bar. The result is that your app's current view hierarchy is analyzed and displayed (Figure 1-15):

- On the left, in the Debug navigator, the views and their constraints are listed hierarchically.

- At the top, the jump bar shows the same hierarchy in a different way, and helps you navigate it.

- In the center, in the canvas, the views and their constraints are displayed graphically. The window starts out facing front, much as if you were looking at the screen with the app running; but if you swipe sideways a little in the canvas, the window rotates and its subviews are displayed in front of it, in layers. The slider at the lower left changes the distance between these layers. The double-slider at the lower right lets you eliminate the display of views from the front or back of the layering order (or both). You can switch to wireframe mode. You can display constraints for the currently selected view.

- On the right, the Object inspector and the Size inspector tell you details about the currently selected object (view or constraint).

Previewing your interface

When you're displaying the nib editor in Xcode, the assistant pane's Tracking menu (the first component in its jump bar, Control-4) includes the Preview option. Choose it to see a preview of the currently selected view controller's view (or, in a *.xib* file, the top-level view). The Plus button at the lower left lets you add previews for different devices and device sizes. At the bottom of each preview, a Rotate button lets you switch this preview to the other orientation.

The previews take account of constraints, including conditional constraints. At the lower right, a language pop-up menu lets you switch your app's text (buttons and labels) to another language for which you have localized your app, or to an artificial "double-length" language.

Designable views and inspectable properties

Your view can appear more or less correctly in the nib editor canvas and preview *even if it is configured in code*. To take advantage of this feature, you need a UIView subclass declared @IBDesignable:

```
@IBDesignable class MyView: UIView {
    // ... your code goes here ...
}
```

If an instance of this UIView subclass appears in the nib, then its self-configuration methods, such as init(coder:) and willMoveToSuperview:, will be compiled and run as the nib editor prepares to portray your view. For example, if your view's init(coder:) method adds a UILabel as a subview of this view, then the nib editor will show that label.

In addition, your view can implement prepareForInterfaceBuilder to perform visual configurations aimed specifically at how it will be portrayed in the nib editor. For example, if your view contains a UILabel that is created and configured empty but will eventually contain text, you could implement prepareForInterfaceBuilder to give the label some sample text to be displayed in the nib editor.

In Figure 1-20, the nib editor displays a MyView instance; the green and red subviews come from MyView's initializer, and the purple background is added in prepareForInterfaceBuilder.

You can also configure custom view properties directly in the nib editor. If your UIView subclass has a property whose value type is understood by the nib editor, and if this property is declared @IBInspectable, then if an instance of this UIView subclass appears in the nib, that property will get a field of its own at the top of the view's Attributes inspector. Thus, when a custom UIView subclass is to be instantiated from the nib, its custom properties can be set in the nib editor rather than having to be set in code. (This feature is actually a convenient equivalent of setting a nib object's User Defined Runtime Attributes in the Identity inspector.)

Inspectable property types are: Bool, number, String, CGRect, CGPoint, CGSize, UIColor, or UIImage — or an Optional wrapping any of these. You can assign a default value in code; Interface Builder won't portray this value as the default, but you can tell Interface Builder to use the default by leaving the field empty (or, if you've entered a value, by deleting that value).

In Figure 1-20, the nib editor displays MyView's custom name property.

@IBDesignable and @IBInspectable are unrelated, but the former is aware of the latter. Thus, you can use an inspectable property to change the nib editor's display of your

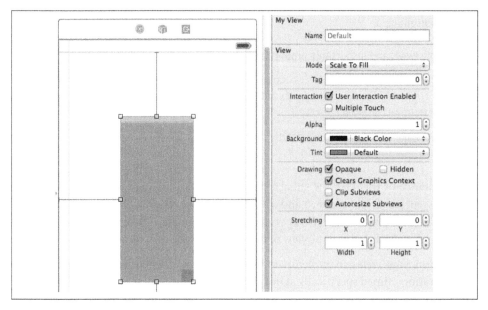

Figure 1-20. A designable view with an inspectable property

interface in real time. For example, if my view is @IBDesignable, and if its prepareFor-
InterfaceBuilder creates and adds to the interface a label whose text is its name prop-
erty, and if name is @IBInspectable, then if I change the name property in the nib editor
(Figure 1-20), the label's text changes in the nib editor canvas or preview.

View Events Related to Layout

This section summarizes the chief UIView events related to layout. These are events that
you can receive and respond to by overriding them in your UIView subclass. You might
want to do this in situations where layout is complex — for example, when you need to
supplement autoresizing or autolayout with manual layout in code, or when your
autoresizing or autolayout configuration itself needs to change in response to changing
conditions.

These UIView events are not the same as the layout-related events you can receive
and respond to in a UIViewController. I'll discuss those in Chapter 6.

At launch time, and if the environment's trait collection changes thereafter, the trait-
CollectionDidChange: message is propagated *down* the hierarchy of UITrait-
Environments.

Thus, if your interface needs to respond to a change in the trait collection — by changing constraints, adding or removing subviews, or what have you — an override of `trait-CollectionDidChange:` is the place to do it. For example, earlier in this chapter I showed some code for swapping a view into or out of the interface together with the entire set of constraints laying out that interface. But I left open the matter of the conditions under which we wanted such swapping to occur; `traitCollectionDidChange:` might be an appropriate moment.

If your interface involves autolayout and constraints, then `updateConstraints` is propagated *up* the hierarchy, starting at the deepest subview. This event may be omitted for a view if its constraints have not changed, but it will certainly be called for the view at the top of the hierarchy.

You might override `updateConstraints` in a UIView subclass if your subclass is capable of altering its own constraints and you need a signal that now is the time to do so. You must call `super` or the app will crash (with a helpful error message).

You should never call `updateConstraints` directly. To trigger an immediate call to `updateConstraints`, send a view the `updateConstraintsIfNeeded` message. But `updateConstraints` may still not be sent unless constraints have changed or the view is at the top of the hierarchy. To force `updateConstraints` to be sent to a view, send it the `setNeedsUpdateConstraints` message.

Finally, we come to layout itself. Layout can be triggered even if the trait collection didn't change; for example, perhaps a constraint was changed, or the text of a label was changed, or a superview's size changed. The `layoutSubviews` message is propagated *down* the hierarchy, starting at the top (typically the root view) and working down to the deepest subview.

You can override `layoutSubviews` in a UIView subclass in order to take a hand in the layout process. If you're not using autolayout, `layoutSubviews` does nothing by default; `layoutSubviews` is your opportunity to perform manual layout after autoresizing has taken place. If you are using autolayout, you must call `super` or the app will crash (with a helpful error message).

You should never call `layoutSubviews` directly; to trigger an immediate call to `layout-Subviews`, send a view the `layoutIfNeeded` message (which may cause layout of the entire view tree, not only below but also above this view), or send `setNeedsLayout` to trigger a call to `layoutSubviews` later on, after your code finishes running, when layout would normally take place.

When you're using autolayout, what happens in `layoutSubviews`? The runtime examines all the constraints affecting this view's subviews, works out values for their center and bounds, and assigns those views those center and bounds values. In other words, `layoutSubviews` performs manual layout! The constraints are merely instructions attached to the views; layoutSubviews reads them and responds accordingly, sizing and positioning views in the good old-fashioned way, by setting their frames, bounds, and centers. (Thus, layoutSubviews is a place where it is legal — and indeed necessary — to set the size and position of a view governed by explicit constraints.)

Knowing this, you might override layoutSubviews when you're using autolayout, in order to tweak the outcome. A typical structure is: first you call super, causing all the subviews to adopt their new frames; then you examine those frames; if you don't like the outcome, you can change things; and finally you call super *again*, to get a new layout outcome. Keep in mind, however, that you are cooperating with an elaborate existing layout operation that is already in train. Do not call setNeedsUpdateConstraints (that moment has passed), and do not stray beyond the subviews *of this view*.

It is also possible to *simulate* layout of a view in accordance with its constraints and those of its subviews. This is useful for discovering ahead of time what a view's size would be if layout were performed at this moment. Send the view the systemLayout-SizeFittingSize: message. The system will attempt to reach or at least approach the size you specify, at a very low priority; mostly likely you'll specify either UILayout-FittingCompressedSize or UILayoutFittingExpandedSize, depending on whether what you're after is the smallest or largest size the view can legally attain. You can dictate the individual axis priorities explicitly (systemLayoutSizeFittingSize:with-HorizontalFittingPriority:verticalFittingPriority:). I'll show an example in Chapter 7.

 Unless you explicitly demand immediate layout, layout isn't performed until your code finishes running (and then only if needed). Moreover, ambiguous layout isn't ambiguous until layout actually takes place. Thus, for example, it's perfectly reasonable to cause an ambiguous layout temporarily, provided you resolve the ambiguity before layoutSubviews is called. On the other hand, a conflicting constraint conflicts the instant it is added.

CHAPTER 2

Drawing

The views illustrated in Chapter 1 were mostly colored rectangles; they had a backgroundColor and no more. But that, of course, is not what a real iOS program looks like. Everything the user sees is a UIView, and what the user sees is a lot more than a bunch of colored rectangles. That's because the views that the user sees have *content*. They contain *drawing*.

Many UIView subclasses, such as a UIButton or a UILabel, know how to draw themselves. Sooner or later, you're also going to want to do some drawing of your own. You can prepare your drawing as an image file beforehand. You can draw an image as your app runs, in code. You can display an image in your interface in a UIView subclass that knows how to show an image, such as a UIImageView or a UIButton. A pure UIView is all about drawing, and it leaves that drawing largely up to you; your code determines what the view draws, and hence what it looks like in your interface.

This chapter discusses the mechanics of drawing. Don't be afraid to write drawing code of your own! It isn't difficult, and it's often the best way to make your app look the way you want it to. (For how to draw text, see Chapter 10.)

Images and Image Views

The basic general UIKit image class is UIImage. UIImage can read a file from disk, so if an image does not need to be created dynamically, but has already been created before your app runs, then drawing may be as simple as providing an image file as a resource in your app's bundle. The system knows how to work with many standard image file types, such as TIFF, JPEG, GIF, and PNG; when an image file is to be included in your app bundle, iOS has a special affinity for PNG files, and you should prefer them whenever possible. You can also obtain image data in some other way, such as by downloading it, and transform this into a UIImage. Conversely, your code can construct a UIImage for display in your interface or for saving to disk (image file output is discussed in Chapter 23).

Image Files

A pre-existing image file in your app's bundle can be obtained through the UIImage initializer init(named:). This method looks in two places for the image:

Asset catalog
> We look in the asset catalog for an image set with the supplied name. The name is case-sensitive.

Top level of app bundle
> We look at the top level of the app's bundle for an image file with the supplied name. The name is case-sensitive and should include the file extension; if it doesn't include a file extension, *.png* is assumed.

When calling init(named:), an asset catalog is searched before the top level of the app's bundle. If there are multiple asset catalogs, they are all searched, but the search order is indeterminate and cannot be specified, so avoid image sets with the same name.

A nice thing about init(named:) is that the image data may be cached in memory, and if you ask for the same image by calling init(named:) again later, the cached data may be supplied immediately. Alternatively, you can read an image file from anywhere in your app's bundle directly and without caching, using init(contentsOfFile:), which expects a pathname string; you can get a reference to your app's bundle with NSBundle.mainBundle(), and NSBundle then provides instance methods for getting the pathname of a file within the bundle, such as pathForResource:ofType:.

Methods that specify a resource in the app bundle, such as init(named:) and pathForResource:ofType:, respond to suffixes in the name of an actual resource file. On a device with a double-resolution screen, when an image is obtained by name from the app bundle, a file with the same name extended by @2x, if there is one, will be used automatically, with the resulting UIImage marked as double-resolution by assigning it a scale property value of 2.0. Similarly, if there is a file with the same name extended by @3x, it will be used on the triple-resolution screen of the iPhone 6 Plus, with a scale property value of 3.0.

In this way, your app can contain multiple versions of an image file at different resolutions. Thanks to the scale property, a high-resolution version of an image is drawn at the same size as the single-resolution image. Thus, on a high-resolution screen, your code continues to work without change, but your images look sharper.

Similarly, a file with the same name extended by ~ipad will automatically be used if the app is running natively on an iPad. You can use this in a universal app to supply different images automatically depending on whether the app runs on an iPhone or iPod touch, on the one hand, or on an iPad, on the other. (This is true not just for images but for *any* resource obtained by name from the bundle. See Apple's *Resource Programming Guide.*)

One of the great benefits of an asset catalog, though, is that you can forget all about those name suffix conventions. An asset catalog knows when to use an alternate image within an image set, not from its name, but from its place in the catalog. Put the single-, double-, and triple-resolution alternatives into the slots marked "1x," "2x," and "3x" respectively. For a distinct iPad version of an image, check iPhone and iPad in the Attributes inspector for the image set; separate slots for those device types will appear in the asset catalog.

An asset catalog can also distinguish between versions of an image intended for different size class situations. (See the discussion of size classes and trait collections in Chapter 1.) In the Attributes inspector for your image set, use the Width and Height pop-up menus to specify which size class possibilities you want to distinguish. Thus, for example, if we're on an iPhone with the app rotated to landscape orientation, and if there's both an Any height and a Compact height alternative in the image set, the Compact height version is used. These features are live as the app runs; if the app rotates from landscape to portrait, and there's both an Any height and a Compact height alternative in the image set, the Compact height version is replaced with the Any height version in your interface, automatically.

The way an asset catalog performs all this magic is through trait collections and the UIImageAsset class. When an image is extracted from an asset catalog through `init(named:)` and the name of its image set, its `imageAsset` property is a UIImageAsset. All the images in that image set are available through the UIImageAsset; each image has a trait collection associated with it (its `traitCollection`), and you can ask an image's `imageAsset` for the image from the same image set appropriate to a particular trait collection, by calling `imageWithTraitCollection:`.

A built-in interface object that displays an image is automatically trait collection–aware; it receives the `traitCollectionDidChange:` message and responds accordingly. We can imagine how this works under the hood by building a UIView with an `image` property that does the same thing:

```
class MyView: UIView {
    var image : UIImage!
    override func traitCollectionDidChange(previous: UITraitCollection?) {
        self.setNeedsDisplay() // causes drawRect to be called
    }
    override func drawRect(rect: CGRect) {
        if var im = self.image {
            if let asset = self.image.imageAsset {
                let tc = self.traitCollection
                im = asset.imageWithTraitCollection(tc)
            }
```

```
            im.drawAtPoint(CGPointZero)
        }
    }
}
```

Moreover, your code can combine images into a UIImageAsset — the code equivalent of an image set in an asset catalog, but *without* an asset catalog. Thus you could create images in real time (as I'll describe later in this chapter), or fetch images out of your app bundle, and configure them so that one is used when an iPhone app is in portrait orientation and the other is used when the app is in landscape orientation, *automatically*. For example:

```
let tcdisp = UITraitCollection(displayScale: UIScreen.mainScreen().scale)
let tcphone = UITraitCollection(userInterfaceIdiom: .Phone)
let tcreg = UITraitCollection(verticalSizeClass: .Regular)
let tc1 = UITraitCollection(traitsFromCollections: [tcdisp, tcphone, tcreg])
let tccom = UITraitCollection(verticalSizeClass: .Compact)
let tc2 = UITraitCollection(traitsFromCollections: [tcdisp, tcphone, tccom])
let moods = UIImageAsset()
let frowney = UIImage(named:"frowney")!
let smiley = UIImage(named:"smiley")!
moods.registerImage(frowney, withTraitCollection: tc1)
moods.registerImage(smiley, withTraitCollection: tc2)
```

After that, if frowney is placed into the interface — for example, by handing it over to a UIImageView as its image, as I'll explain in a moment — it automatically alternates with smiley when the app changes orientation. The remarkable thing is that this works even though there is no persistent reference to frowney, smiley, or the UIImageAsset (moods). The reason is that frowney and smiley are cached by the system (because of the call to init(named:)), and they each maintain a strong reference to the UIImage-Asset with which they are registered.

You can also specify a target trait collection while fetching an image from the asset catalog or from your app bundle, by calling init(named:inBundle:compatibleWith-TraitCollection:). The bundle specified will usually be nil, meaning the app's main bundle.

Image Views

Many built-in Cocoa interface objects will accept a UIImage as part of how they draw themselves; for example, a UIButton can display an image, and a UINavigationBar or a UITabBar can have a background image. I'll discuss those in Chapter 12. But when you simply want an image to appear in your interface, you'll probably hand it to an image view — a UIImageView — which has the most knowledge and flexibility with regard to displaying images and is intended for this purpose.

The nib editor supplies some shortcuts in this regard: the Attributes inspector of an interface object that can have an image will have a pop-up menu listing known images in your project, and such images are also listed in the Media library (Command-Option-Control-4). Media library images can often be dragged onto an interface object in the canvas to assign them, and if you drag a Media library image into a plain view, it is transformed into a UIImageView displaying that image.

A UIImageView can actually have *two* images, one assigned to its `image` property and the other assigned to its `highlightedImage` property; the value of the UIImageView's `highlighted` property dictates which of the two is displayed at any given moment. A UIImageView does not automatically highlight itself merely because the user taps it, the way a button does. However, there are certain situations where a UIImageView will respond to the highlighting of its surroundings; for example, within a table view cell, a UIImageView will show its highlighted image when the cell is highlighted (Chapter 8).

A UIImageView is a UIView, so it can have a background color in addition to its image, it can have an alpha (transparency) value, and so forth (see Chapter 1). An image may have areas that are transparent, and a UIImageView will respect this; thus an image of any shape can appear. A UIImageView without a background color is invisible except for its image, so the image simply appears in the interface, without the user being aware that it resides in a rectangular host. A UIImageView without an image and without a background color is invisible, so you could start with an empty UIImageView in the place where you will later need an image and subsequently assign the image in code. You can assign a new image to substitute one image for another, or set the image view's `image` property to `nil` to remove it.

How a UIImageView draws its image depends upon the setting of its `contentMode` property (UIViewContentMode). (The `contentMode` property is inherited from UIView; I'll discuss its more general purpose later in this chapter.) For example, `.Scale-ToFill` means the image's width and height are set to the width and height of the view, thus filling the view completely even if this alters the image's aspect ratio; `.Center` means the image is drawn centered in the view without altering its size. The best way to get a feel for the meanings of the various `contentMode` settings is to assign a UIImageView a small image in a nib and then, in the Attributes inspector, change the Mode pop-up menu, and see where and how the image draws itself.

You should also pay attention to a UIImageView's `clipsToBounds` property; if it is `false`, its image, even if it is larger than the image view and even if it is not scaled down by the `contentMode`, may be displayed in its entirety, extending beyond the image view itself.

When creating a UIImageView in code, you can take advantage of a convenience initializer, `init(image:)` (or `init(image:highlightedImage:)`). The default `content-Mode` is `.ScaleToFill`, but the image is not initially scaled; rather, *the view itself is sized to match the image.* You will still probably need to position the UIImageView correctly

Figure 2-1. Mars appears in my interface

in its superview. In this example, I'll put a picture of the planet Mars in the center of the app's interface (Figure 2-1; for the CGRect `center` property, see Appendix B):

```
let iv = UIImageView(image:UIImage(named:"Mars")) // asset catalog
mainview.addSubview(iv)
iv.center = iv.superview!.bounds.center
iv.frame.makeIntegralInPlace()
```

What happens to the size of an existing UIImageView when you assign an image to it depends on whether the image view is using autolayout. If it isn't, or if its size is constrained absolutely, the image view's size doesn't change. But under autolayout, the size of the new image becomes the image view's new `intrinsicContentSize`, so the image view will adopt the image's size unless other constraints prevent.

An image view automatically acquires its `alignmentRectInsets` from its image's `alignmentRectInsets`. Thus, if you're going to be aligning the image view to some other object using autolayout, you can attach appropriate `alignmentRectInsets` to the image that the image view will display, and the image view will do the right thing. To do so, derive a new image by calling the original image's `imageWithAlignmentRectInsets:`.

 In theory, you should be able to set an image's `alignmentRectInsets` in an asset catalog. As of this writing, however, this feature is not working correctly.

Resizable Images

Certain places in the interface require a resizable image; for example, a custom image that serves as the track of a slider or progress view (Chapter 12) must be resizable, so that it can fill a space of any length. And there can frequently be other situations where you want to fill a background by tiling or stretching an existing image.

To make a resizable image, start with a normal image and call its `resizableImageWith-CapInsets:resizingMode:` method. The `capInsets:` argument is a UIEdgeInsets, whose components represent distances inward from the edges of the image. In a context larger than the image, a resizable image can behave in one of two ways, depending on the `resizingMode:` value (UIImageResizingMode):

Figure 2-2. Tiling the entire image of Mars

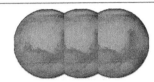

Figure 2-3. Tiling the interior of Mars

`.Tile`
> The interior rectangle of the inset area is tiled (repeated) in the interior; each edge is formed by tiling the corresponding edge rectangle outside the inset area. The four corner rectangles outside the inset area are drawn unchanged.

`.Stretch`
> The interior rectangle of the inset area is stretched *once* to fill the interior; each edge is formed by stretching the corresponding edge rectangle outside the inset area *once*. The four corner rectangles outside the inset area are drawn unchanged.

In these examples, assume that `self.iv` is a UIImageView with absolute height and width (so that it won't adopt the size of its image) and with a `contentMode` of `.ScaleToFill` (so that the image will exhibit resizing behavior). First, I'll illustrate tiling an entire image (Figure 2-2); note that the `capInsets:` is `UIEdgeInsetsZero`:

```
let mars = UIImage(named:"Mars")!
let marsTiled = mars.resizableImageWithCapInsets(
    UIEdgeInsetsZero, resizingMode: .Tile)
self.iv.image = marsTiled
```

Now we'll tile the interior of the image, changing the `capInsets:` argument from the previous code (Figure 2-3):

```
let marsTiled = mars.resizableImageWithCapInsets(
    UIEdgeInsetsMake(
        mars.size.height / 4.0,
        mars.size.width / 4.0,
        mars.size.height / 4.0,
        mars.size.width / 4.0
    ), resizingMode: .Tile)
```

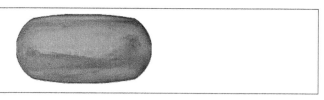

Figure 2-4. Stretching the interior of Mars

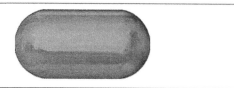

Figure 2-5. Stretching a few pixels at the interior of Mars

Next, I'll illustrate stretching. We'll start by changing just the `resizingMode:` from the previous code (Figure 2-4):

```
let marsTiled = mars.resizableImageWithCapInsets(
    UIEdgeInsetsMake(
        mars.size.height / 4.0,
        mars.size.width / 4.0,
        mars.size.height / 4.0,
        mars.size.width / 4.0
    ), resizingMode: .Stretch)
```

A common stretching strategy is to make almost half the original image serve as a cap inset, leaving just a pixel or two in the center to fill the entire interior of the resulting image (Figure 2-5):

```
let marsTiled = mars.resizableImageWithCapInsets(
    UIEdgeInsetsMake(
        mars.size.height / 2.0 - 1,
        mars.size.width / 2.0 - 1,
        mars.size.height / 2.0 - 1,
        mars.size.width / 2.0 - 1
    ), resizingMode: .Stretch)
```

You should also experiment with different scaling `contentMode` settings. In the preceding example, if the image view's `contentMode` is `.ScaleAspectFill`, and if the image view's `clipsToBounds` is `true`, we get a sort of gradient effect, because the top and bottom of the stretched image are outside the image view and aren't drawn (Figure 2-6).

Alternatively, you can configure a resizable image without code, in the project's asset catalog. It is often the case that a particular image will be used in your app chiefly as a resizable image, and always with the same `capInsets:` and `resizingMode:`, so it makes

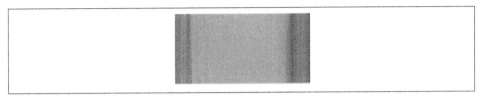

Figure 2-6. Mars, stretched and clipped

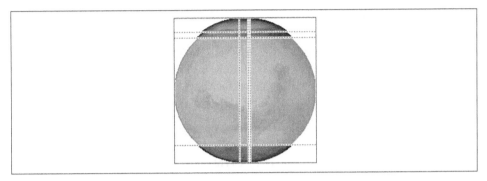

Figure 2-7. Mars, sliced in the asset catalog

sense to configure this image once rather than having to repeat the same code. And even if an image is configured in the asset catalog to be resizable, it can appear in your interface as a normal image as well — for example, if you assign it to an image view that resizes itself to fit its image, or that doesn't scale its image.

To configure an image in an asset catalog as a resizable image, select the image and, in the Slicing section of the Attributes inspector, change the Slices pop-up menu to Horizontal, Vertical, or Horizontal and Vertical. When you do this, additional interface appears. You can specify the `resizingMode` with another pop-up menu. You can work numerically, or click Show Slicing at the lower right of the canvas and work graphically. The graphical editor is zoomable, so zoom in to work comfortably.

This feature is actually even more powerful than `resizableImageWithCap-Insets:resizingMode:`. It lets you specify the end caps *separately* from the tiled or stretched region, with the rest of the image being sliced out. In Figure 2-7, for example, the dark areas at the top left, top right, bottom left, and bottom right will be drawn as is. The narrow bands will be stretched, and the small rectangle at the top center will be stretched to fill most of the interior. But the rest of the image, the large central area covered by a sort of gauze curtain, will be omitted entirely. The result is shown in Figure 2-8.

Figure 2-8. Mars, sliced and stretched

Image Rendering Mode

Several places in an iOS app's interface automatically treat an image as a *transparency mask*, also known as a *template*. This means that the image color values are ignored, and only the transparency (alpha) values of each pixel matter. The image shown on the screen is formed by combining the image's transparency values with a single tint color. Such, for example, is the behavior of a tab bar item's image.

The way an image will be treated is a property of the image, its `renderingMode`. This property is read-only; to change it, start with an image and generate a new image with a different rendering mode, by calling `imageWithRenderingMode:`. The rendering mode values (UIImageRenderingMode) are:

- `.Automatic`
- `.AlwaysOriginal`
- `.AlwaysTemplate`

The default is `.Automatic`, which means that the image is drawn normally everywhere except in certain limited contexts, where it is used as a transparency mask.

With the `renderingMode` property, you can *force* an image to be drawn normally, even in a context that would usually treat it as a transparency mask. You can also do the opposite: you can *force* an image to be treated as a transparency mask, even in a context that would otherwise treat it normally.

To accompany this feature, iOS gives every UIView a `tintColor`, which will be used to tint any template images it contains. Moreover, this `tintColor` by default is inherited down the view hierarchy, and indeed throughout the entire app, starting with the window (Chapter 1). Thus, assigning your app's main window a tint color is probably one of the few changes you'll make to the window; otherwise, your app adopts the system's blue tint color. (Alternatively, if you're using a main storyboard, set the Global Tint color in its File inspector.) Individual views can be assigned their own tint color, which is inherited by their subviews. Figure 2-9 shows two buttons displaying the same background image, one in normal rendering mode, the other in template rendering mode,

Figure 2-9. One image in two rendering modes

in an app whose window tint color is red. (I'll say more about template images and tint-Color in Chapter 12.)

An asset catalog can assign an image a rendering mode. Select the image set in the asset catalog, and use the Render As pop-up menu in the Attributes inspector to set the rendering mode to Default (.Automatic), Original Image (.AlwaysOriginal), or Template Image (.AlwaysTemplate). This is an excellent approach whenever you have an image that you will use primarily in a specific rendering mode, because it saves you from having to remember to set that rendering mode in code every time you fetch the image. Instead, any time you call init(named:), this image arrives with the rendering mode already set.

Reversible Images

New in iOS 9, the entire interface is automatically reversed when your app runs on a system for which your app is localized if the system language is right-to-left. In general, this probably won't affect your images. The runtime assumes that you *don't* want images to be reversed when the interface is reversed, so its default behavior is to leave them alone.

Nevertheless, you *might* want an image reversed when the interface is reversed. For example, suppose you've drawn an arrow pointing in the direction from which new interface will arrive when the user taps a button. If the button pushes a view controller onto a navigation interface, that direction is from the right on a left-to-right system, but from the left on a right-to-left system. This image has directional meaning within the app's own interface; it needs to flip horizontally when the interface is reversed.

To make this possible, call the image's imageFlippedForRightToLeftLayout-Direction and use the resulting image in your interface. On a left-to-right system, the normal image will be used; on a right-to-left system, a reversed version of the image will be created and used automatically. You can override this behavior, even if the image is reversible, for a particular UIView displaying the image, such as a UIImageView, by setting that view's semanticContentAttribute to prevent mirroring.

Unfortunately, there's no way to designate an image as reversible in an asset catalog. Thus, if your image appears in the interface automatically — because of the way a view, such as an image view, is configured in the nib editor — you'll have to intervene in code.

In this example, my view controller's `viewDidLoad` pulls the image out of an image view (`self.iv`) and replaces its with a reversible version of itself:

```
override func viewDidLoad() {
    super.viewDidLoad()
    self.iv.image =
        self.iv.image?.imageFlippedForRightToLeftLayoutDirection()
}
```

Graphics Contexts

Instead of plopping an existing image file directly into your interface, you may want to create some drawing yourself, in code. To do so, you will need a *graphics context*.

A graphics context is basically a place you can draw. Conversely, you can't draw in code unless you've got a graphics context. There are several ways in which you might obtain a graphics context; in this chapter I will concentrate on two, which have proven in my experience to be far and away the most common:

You create an image context
> The function `UIGraphicsBeginImageContextWithOptions` creates a graphics context suitable for use as an image. You then draw into this context to generate the image. When you've done that, you call `UIGraphicsGetImageFromCurrentImageContext` to turn the context into a UIImage, and then `UIGraphicsEndImageContext` to dismiss the context. Now you have a UIImage that you can display in your interface or draw into some other graphics context or save as a file.

Cocoa hands you a graphics context
> You subclass UIView and implement `drawRect:`. At the time your `drawRect:` implementation is called, Cocoa has already created a graphics context and is asking you to draw into it, right now; whatever you draw is what the UIView will display.
>
> A slight variant of this situation is that you subclass CALayer and implement `drawInContext:`, or else implement `drawLayer:inContext:` in the layer's delegate; layers are discussed in Chapter 3.

Moreover, at any given moment there either is or is not a *current graphics context*:

- `UIGraphicsBeginImageContextWithOptions` not only creates an image context, it also makes that context the current graphics context.
- When `drawRect:` is called, the UIView's drawing context is already the current graphics context.
- Callbacks with a `context:` parameter have *not* made any context the current graphics context; rather, that parameter is a reference to a graphics context into which

you are invited to draw, but if you need to make it current so that you *can* draw into it, doing so is up to you.

What beginners find most confusing about drawing is that there are two sets of tools for drawing, which take different attitudes toward the context in which they will draw. One set needs a current context; the other just needs a context:

UIKit

Various Cocoa classes know how to draw themselves; these include UIImage, NSString (for drawing text), UIBezierPath (for drawing shapes), and UIColor. Some of these classes provide convenience methods with limited abilities; others are extremely powerful. In many cases, UIKit will be all you'll need.

With UIKit, you can draw *only into the current context*. So if you're in a `UIGraphics-BeginImageContextWithOptions` or `drawRect:` situation, you can use the UIKit convenience methods directly; there is a current context and it's the one you want to draw into. If you've been handed a `context:` parameter, on the other hand, then if you want to use the UIKit convenience methods, you'll have to make that context the current context; you do this by calling `UIGraphicsPushContext` (and be sure to restore things with `UIGraphicsPopContext` later).

Core Graphics

This is the full drawing API. Core Graphics, often referred to as Quartz, or Quartz 2D, is the drawing system that underlies all iOS drawing — UIKit drawing is built on top of it — so it is low-level and consists of C functions. There are a lot of them! This chapter will familiarize you with the fundamentals; for complete information, you'll want to study Apple's *Quartz 2D Programming Guide*.

With Core Graphics, you must *specify a graphics context* (a CGContext) to draw into, explicitly, in every function call. If you've been handed a `context:` parameter, then that's probably the graphics context you want to draw into. But in a `UIGraphics-BeginImageContextWithOptions` or `drawRect:` situation, you have no reference to a context; to use Core Graphics, you need to get such a reference. Since the context you want to draw into is the current graphics context, you call `UIGraphicsGet-CurrentContext` to get the needed reference.

 You don't have to use UIKit or Core Graphics *exclusively*. On the contrary, you can intermingle UIKit calls and Core Graphics calls in the same chunk of code to operate on the same graphics context. They merely represent two different ways of telling a graphics context what to do.

So we have two sets of tools and three ways in which a context might be supplied; that makes six ways of drawing. I'll now demonstrate all six of them! Without worrying just yet about the actual drawing commands, focus your attention on how the context is specified and on whether we're using UIKit or Core Graphics. First, I'll draw a blue circle by implementing a UIView subclass's `drawRect:`, using UIKit to draw into the current context, which Cocoa has already prepared for me:

```
override func drawRect(rect: CGRect) {
    let p = UIBezierPath(ovalInRect: CGRectMake(0,0,100,100))
    UIColor.blueColor().setFill()
    p.fill()
}
```

Now I'll do the same thing with Core Graphics; this will require that I first get a reference to the current context:

```
override func drawRect(rect: CGRect) {
    let con = UIGraphicsGetCurrentContext()!
    CGContextAddEllipseInRect(con, CGRectMake(0,0,100,100))
    CGContextSetFillColorWithColor(con, UIColor.blueColor().CGColor)
    CGContextFillPath(con)
}
```

Next, I'll implement a UIView subclass's `drawLayer:inContext:`. In this case, we're handed a reference to a context, but it isn't the current context. So I have to make it the current context in order to use UIKit:

```
override func drawLayer(layer: CALayer, inContext con: CGContext) {
    UIGraphicsPushContext(con)
    let p = UIBezierPath(ovalInRect: CGRectMake(0,0,100,100))
    UIColor.blueColor().setFill()
    p.fill()
    UIGraphicsPopContext()
}
```

To use Core Graphics in `drawLayer:inContext:`, I simply keep referring to the context I was handed:

```
override func drawLayer(layer: CALayer, inContext con: CGContext) {
    CGContextAddEllipseInRect(con, CGRectMake(0,0,100,100))
    CGContextSetFillColorWithColor(con, UIColor.blueColor().CGColor)
    CGContextFillPath(con)
}
```

Finally, I'll make a UIImage of a blue circle. We can do this at any time (we don't need to wait for some particular method to be called) and in any class (we don't need to be in a UIView subclass). The resulting UIImage (here called `im`) is suitable anywhere you would use a UIImage. For instance, you could hand it over to a visible UIImageView as its `image`, thus causing the image to appear onscreen. Or you could save it as a file. Or, as I'll explain in the next section, you could use it in another drawing.

First, I'll draw my image using UIKit:

```
UIGraphicsBeginImageContextWithOptions(CGSizeMake(100,100), false, 0)
let p = UIBezierPath(ovalInRect: CGRectMake(0,0,100,100))
UIColor.blueColor().setFill()
p.fill()
let im = UIGraphicsGetImageFromCurrentImageContext()
UIGraphicsEndImageContext()
// im is the blue circle image, do something with it here ...
```

Here's the same thing using Core Graphics:

```
UIGraphicsBeginImageContextWithOptions(CGSizeMake(100,100), false, 0)
let con = UIGraphicsGetCurrentContext()!
CGContextAddEllipseInRect(con, CGRectMake(0,0,100,100))
CGContextSetFillColorWithColor(con, UIColor.blueColor().CGColor)
CGContextFillPath(con)
let im = UIGraphicsGetImageFromCurrentImageContext()
UIGraphicsEndImageContext()
// im is the blue circle image, do something with it here ...
```

You may be wondering about the arguments to UIGraphicsBeginImageContextWith-Options. The first argument is obviously the size of the image to be created. The second argument declares whether the image should be opaque; if I had passed true instead of false here, my image would have a black background, which I don't want. The third argument specifies the image scale, corresponding to the UIImage scale property I discussed earlier; by passing 0, I'm telling the system to set the scale for me in accordance with the main screen resolution, so my image will look good on both single-resolution and high-resolution devices.

 The dance required to begin an image context, draw into it, extract the image, and end the context, is a bit tedious and error-prone. A utility function that I provide in Appendix B has the advantage that you provide just the drawing instructions, and the utility function does the dance and returns the image.

UIImage Drawing

A UIImage provides methods for drawing itself into the current context. We know how to obtain a UIImage, and we know how to obtain a graphics context and make it the current context, so we can experiment with these methods.

Here, I'll make a UIImage consisting of two pictures of Mars side by side (Figure 2-10):

```
let mars = UIImage(named:"Mars")!
let sz = mars.size
UIGraphicsBeginImageContextWithOptions(
    CGSizeMake(sz.width*2, sz.height), false, 0)
```

Figure 2-10. Two images of Mars combined side by side

```
mars.drawAtPoint(CGPointMake(0,0))
mars.drawAtPoint(CGPointMake(sz.width,0))
let im = UIGraphicsGetImageFromCurrentImageContext()
UIGraphicsEndImageContext()
```

Observe that image scaling works perfectly in that example. If we have multiple resolution versions of our original Mars image, the correct one for the current device is used, and is assigned the correct `scale` value. Our call to `UIGraphicsBeginImageContextWith-Options` has a third argument of 0, so the image context that we are drawing into also has the correct `scale`. And the image that results from calling `UIGraphicsGetImage-FromCurrentImageContext` has the correct `scale` as well. Thus, this same code produces an image that looks correct on the current device, whatever its screen resolution may be.

Additional UIImage methods let you scale an image into a desired rectangle as you draw, and specify the compositing (blend) mode whereby the image should combine with whatever is already present. To illustrate, I'll create an image showing Mars centered in another image of Mars that's twice as large, using the `.Multiply` blend mode (Figure 2-11):

```
let mars = UIImage(named:"Mars")!
let sz = mars.size
UIGraphicsBeginImageContextWithOptions(
    CGSizeMake(sz.width*2, sz.height*2), false, 0)
mars.drawInRect(CGRectMake(0,0,sz.width*2, sz.height*2))
mars.drawInRect(
    CGRectMake(sz.width/2.0, sz.height/2.0, sz.width, sz.height),
    blendMode: .Multiply, alpha: 1.0)
let im = UIGraphicsGetImageFromCurrentImageContext()
UIGraphicsEndImageContext()
```

There is no UIImage drawing method for specifying the source rectangle — that is, for times when you want to extract a smaller region of the original image. You can work around this by creating a smaller graphics context and positioning the image drawing so that the desired region falls into it. For example, to obtain an image of the right half of Mars, you'd make a graphics context half the width of the `mars` image, and then draw `mars` shifted left, so that only its right half intersects the graphics context. There is no

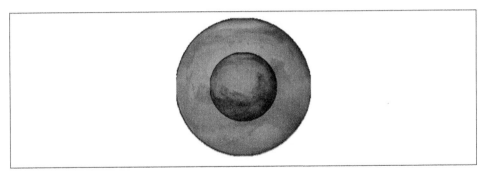

Figure 2-11. Two images of Mars in different sizes, composited

Figure 2-12. Half the original image of Mars

harm in doing this, and it's a perfectly standard strategy; the left half of `mars` simply isn't drawn (Figure 2-12):

```
let mars = UIImage(named:"Mars")!
let sz = mars.size
UIGraphicsBeginImageContextWithOptions(
    CGSizeMake(sz.width/2.0, sz.height), false, 0)
mars.drawAtPoint(CGPointMake(-sz.width/2.0,0))
let im = UIGraphicsGetImageFromCurrentImageContext()
UIGraphicsEndImageContext()
```

CGImage Drawing

The Core Graphics version of UIImage is CGImage. They are easily converted to one another: a UIImage has a `CGImage` property that accesses its Quartz image data, and you can make a UIImage from a CGImage using `init(CGImage:)` or its more configurable sibling, `init(CGImage:scale:orientation:)`.

A CGImage lets you create a new image directly from a rectangular region of the original image, which you can't do with UIImage. (A CGImage has other powers a UIImage doesn't have; for example, you can apply an image mask to a CGImage.) I'll demonstrate by splitting the image of Mars in half and drawing the two halves separately (Figure 2-13):

Figure 2-13. Image of Mars split in half (and flipped)

```
let mars = UIImage(named:"Mars")!
// extract each half as CGImage
let marsCG = mars.CGImage
let sz = mars.size
let marsLeft = CGImageCreateWithImageInRect(
    marsCG,
    CGRectMake(0,0,sz.width/2.0,sz.height))
let marsRight = CGImageCreateWithImageInRect(
    marsCG,
    CGRectMake(sz.width/2.0,0,sz.width/2.0,sz.height))
// draw each CGImage
UIGraphicsBeginImageContextWithOptions(
    CGSizeMake(sz.width*1.5, sz.height), false, 0)
let con = UIGraphicsGetCurrentContext()!
CGContextDrawImage(con,
    CGRectMake(0,0,sz.width/2.0,sz.height), marsLeft)
CGContextDrawImage(con,
    CGRectMake(sz.width,0,sz.width/2.0,sz.height), marsRight)
let im = UIGraphicsGetImageFromCurrentImageContext()
UIGraphicsEndImageContext()
```

But there's a problem with that example: the drawing is upside-down! It isn't rotated; it's mirrored top to bottom, or, to use the technical term, *flipped*. This phenomenon can arise when you create a CGImage and then draw it with CGContextDrawImage, and is due to a mismatch in the native coordinate systems of the source and target contexts.

There are various ways of compensating for this mismatch between the coordinate systems. One is to draw the CGImage into an intermediate UIImage and extract *another* CGImage from that. Example 2-1 presents a utility function for doing this.

Example 2-1. Utility for flipping an image drawing

```
func flip (im: CGImage) -> CGImage {
    let sz = CGSizeMake(
        CGFloat(CGImageGetWidth(im)),
        CGFloat(CGImageGetHeight(im)))
    UIGraphicsBeginImageContextWithOptions(sz, false, 0)
    CGContextDrawImage(UIGraphicsGetCurrentContext()!,
        CGRectMake(0, 0, sz.width, sz.height), im)
```

```
let result = UIGraphicsGetImageFromCurrentImageContext().CGImage
UIGraphicsEndImageContext()
return result!
}
```

Armed with the utility function from Example 2-1, we can fix our calls to `CGContext-DrawImage` in the previous example so that they draw the halves of Mars the right way up:

```
CGContextDrawImage(con,
    CGRectMake(0,0,sz.width/2.0,sz.height), flip(marsLeft!))
CGContextDrawImage(con,
    CGRectMake(sz.width,0,sz.width/2.0,sz.height), flip(marsRight!))
```

However, we've *still* got a problem: on a high-resolution device, if there is a high-resolution variant of our image file, the drawing comes out all wrong. The reason is that we are obtaining our initial Mars image using UIImage's `init(named:)`, which returns a UIImage that compensates for the increased size of a high-resolution image by setting its own `scale` property to match. But a CGImage doesn't have a `scale` property, and knows nothing of the fact that the image dimensions are increased! Therefore, on a high-resolution device, the CGImage that we extract from our Mars UIImage as `mars.CGImage` is larger (in each dimension) than `mars.size`, and all our calculations after that are wrong.

The best solution for dealing a CGImage, therefore, is to wrap it in a UIImage and draw the UIImage instead of the CGImage. The UIImage can be formed in such a way as to compensate for scale: call `init(CGImage:scale:orientation:)` as you form the UIImage from the CGImage. Moreover, by drawing a UIImage instead of a CGImage, we avoid the flipping problem! So here's an approach that deals with both flipping and scale, with no need for the `flip` utility:

```
let mars = UIImage(named:"Mars")!
let sz = mars.size
let marsCG = mars.CGImage
let szCG = CGSizeMake(
    CGFloat(CGImageGetWidth(marsCG)),
    CGFloat(CGImageGetHeight(marsCG)))
let marsLeft =
    CGImageCreateWithImageInRect(
        marsCG, CGRectMake(0,0,szCG.width/2.0,szCG.height))
let marsRight =
    CGImageCreateWithImageInRect(
        marsCG, CGRectMake(szCG.width/2.0,0,szCG.width/2.0,szCG.height))
UIGraphicsBeginImageContextWithOptions(
    CGSizeMake(sz.width*1.5, sz.height), false, 0)
// instead of calling flip, pass through UIImage
UIImage(CGImage: marsLeft!, scale: mars.scale,
    orientation: mars.imageOrientation)
    .drawAtPoint(CGPointMake(0,0))
```

```
UIImage(CGImage: marsRight!, scale: mars.scale,
    orientation: mars.imageOrientation)
    .drawAtPoint(CGPointMake(sz.width,0))
let im = UIGraphicsGetImageFromCurrentImageContext()
UIGraphicsEndImageContext()
```

Yet another solution to flipping is to apply a transform to the graphics context before drawing the CGImage, effectively flipping the context's internal coordinate system. This is elegant, but can be confusing if there are other transforms in play. I'll talk more about graphics context transforms later in this chapter.

Snapshots

An entire view — anything from a single button to your whole interface, complete with its contained hierarchy of views — can be drawn into the current graphics context by calling the UIView instance method drawViewHierarchyInRect:afterScreen-Updates:. (This method is much faster than the CALayer method renderInContext:; nevertheless, renderInContext: does still come in handy, as I'll show in Chapter 5.) The result is a *snapshot* of the original view: it looks like the original view, but it's basically just a bitmap image of it, a lightweight visual duplicate.

An even faster way to obtain a snapshot of a view is to use the UIView (or UIScreen) instance method snapshotViewAfterScreenUpdates:. The result is a UIView, not a UIImage; it's rather like a UIImageView that knows how to draw only one image, namely the snapshot. Such a snapshot view will typically be used as is, but you can enlarge its bounds and the snapshot image will stretch. If you want the stretched snapshot to behave like a resizable image, call resizableSnapshotViewFromRect:afterScreen-Updates:withCapInsets: instead. It is perfectly reasonable to make a snapshot view from a snapshot view.

Snapshots are useful because of the dynamic nature of the iOS interface. For example, you might place a snapshot of a view in your interface in front of the real view to hide what's happening, or use it during an animation to present the illusion of a view moving when in fact it's just a snapshot.

Here's an example from one of my apps. It's a card game, and its views portray cards. I want to animate the removal of all those cards from the board, flying away to an offscreen point. But I don't want to animate the views themselves! They need to stay put, to portray future cards. So I make a snapshot view of each of the card views; I then make the card views invisible, put the snapshot views in their place, and animate the snapshot views. This code will mean more to you after you've read Chapter 4, but the strategy is evident:

```
for v in views {
    let snapshot = v.snapshotViewAfterScreenUpdates(false)
    let snap = MySnapBehavior(item:snapshot, snapToPoint:CGPointMake(
        self.anim.referenceView!.bounds.midX,
        -self.anim.referenceView!.bounds.height))
    self.snaps.append(snapshot) // keep a list so we can remove them later
    snapshot.frame = v.frame
    v.hidden = true
    self.anim.referenceView!.addSubview(snapshot)
    self.anim.addBehavior(snap)
}
```

CIFilter and CIImage

The "CI" in CIFilter and CIImage stands for Core Image, a technology for transforming images through mathematical filters. Core Image started life on the desktop (OS X), and when it was migrated into iOS, some of the filters available on the desktop were not available in iOS (presumably because they were too intensive mathematically for a mobile device). Over the years, however, more and more OS X filters were added to the iOS repertory, and now, new in iOS 9, the two have complete parity: *all* OS X filters are available in iOS, and the two platforms have nearly identical APIs.

A filter is a CIFilter. The available filters fall naturally into several broad categories:

Patterns and gradients
These filters create CIImages that can then be combined with other CIImages, such as a single color, a checkerboard, stripes, or a gradient.

Compositing
These filters combine one image with another, using compositing blend modes familiar from image processing programs such as Photoshop.

Color
These filters adjust or otherwise modify the colors of an image. Thus you can alter an image's saturation, hue, brightness, contrast, gamma and white point, exposure, shadows and highlights, and so on.

Geometric

These filters perform basic geometric transformations on an image, such as scaling, rotation, and cropping.

Transformation

These filters distort, blur, or stylize an image.

Transition

These filters provide a frame of a transition between one image and another; by asking for frames in sequence, you can animate the transition (I'll demonstrate in Chapter 4).

Special purpose

These filters perform highly specialized operations such as face detection and generation of QR codes.

The basic use of a CIFilter is quite simple:

- You specify what filter you want by supplying its string name; to learn what these names are, consult Apple's *Core Image Filter Reference*, or call the CIFilter class method `filterNamesInCategories:` with a `nil` argument.

- Each filter has a small number of keys and values that determine its behavior (as if a filter were a kind of dictionary). You can learn about these keys entirely in code, but typically you'll consult the documentation. For each key that you're interested in, you supply a key–value pair. In supplying values, a number must be wrapped up as an NSNumber (Swift will take care of this for you), and there are a few supporting classes such as CIVector (like CGPoint and CGRect combined) and CIColor, whose use is easy to grasp.

Among a CIFilter's keys are the input image or images on which the filter is to operate; such an image must be a CIImage. You can obtain this CIImage from a CGImage with `init(CGImage:)` or from a UIImage with `init(image:)`.

 Do not attempt, as a shortcut, to obtain a CIImage directly from a UIImage through the UIImage's `CIImage` property. This property does *not* transform a UIImage into a CIImage! It merely points to the CIImage that *already* backs the UIImage, if the UIImage *is* backed by a CIImage; but your images are *not* backed by a CIImage, but rather by a CGImage. I'll explain where a CIImage-backed UIImage comes from in just a moment.

Alternatively, you can obtain a CIImage as the output of a filter — which means that *filters can be chained together.*

There are three ways to describe and use a filter:

- Create the filter with CIFilter's `init(name:)`. Now append the keys and values by calling `setValue:forKey:` repeatedly, or by calling `setValuesForKeysWith-Dictionary:`. Obtain the output CIImage as the filter's `outputImage`.

- Create the filter and supply the keys and values in a single move, by calling CIFilter's `init(name:withInputParameters:)`. Obtain the output CIImage as the filter's `outputImage`.

- If a CIFilter requires an input image and you already have a CIImage to fulfill this role, specify the filter and supply the keys and values, *and receive the output CIImage as a result*, all in a single move, by calling the CIImage instance method `imageBy-ApplyingFilter:withInputParameters:`.

As you build a chain of filters, nothing actually happens. The only calculation-intensive move comes at the very end, when you transform the final CIImage in the chain into a bitmap drawing. This is called *rendering* the image. There are two main ways to do this:

With a CIContext
Create a CIContext (by calling `init(options:)`) and then call `create-CGImage:fromRect:`, handing it the final CIImage as the first argument. This renders the image. The only mildly tricky thing here is that a CIImage doesn't have a frame or bounds; it has an `extent`. You will often use this as the second argument to `createCGImage:fromRect:`. The final output CGImage is ready for any purpose, such as for display in your app, for transformation into a UIImage, or for use in further drawing.

This approach has the advantage of giving you full control over the moment when rendering takes place. But be warned: creating a CIContext is expensive! Wherever possible, create your CIContext once, beforehand — preferably, once per app — and reuse it each time you render.

With a UIImage
Create a UIImage directly from the final CIImage by calling `init(CIImage:)` or `init(CIImage:scale:orientation:)`. You can then draw the UIImage into some graphics context. At the moment of drawing, the image is rendered.

 Apple claims that you can simply hand a UIImage created by calling `init(CIImage:)` to a UIImageView, as its `image`, and that the UIImageView will render the image. In my experience, this is *not true*. You must draw the image *explicitly* in order to render it.

(Other ways to render a CIImage involve things like GLKView or CAEAGLLayer, which are not discussed in this book. They have the advantage of being very fast and suitable for animated or rapid rendering.)

Figure 2-14. A photo of me, vignetted

To illustrate, I'll start with an ordinary photo of myself (it's true I'm wearing a motorcycle helmet, but it's still ordinary) and create a circular vignette effect (Figure 2-14). We derive from the image of me (moi) a CIImage (moici). We use a CIFilter (grad) to form a radial gradient between the default colors of white and black. Then we use a second CIFilter that treats the radial gradient as a mask for blending between the photo of me and a default clear background: where the radial gradient is white (everything inside the gradient's inner radius) we see just me, and where the radial gradient is black (everything outside the gradient's outer radius) we see just the clear color, with a gradation in between, so that the image fades away in the circular band between the gradient's radii. The code illustrates two different ways of configuring a CIFilter:

```
let moi = UIImage(named:"Moi")!
let moici = CIImage(image:moi)!
let moiextent = moici.extent
let center = CIVector(x: moiextent.width/2.0, y: moiextent.height/2.0)
let smallerDimension = min(moiextent.width, moiextent.height)
let largerDimension = max(moiextent.width, moiextent.height)
// first filter
let grad = CIFilter(name: "CIRadialGradient")!
grad.setValue(center, forKey:"inputCenter")
grad.setValue(smallerDimension/2.0 * 0.85, forKey:"inputRadius0")
grad.setValue(largerDimension/2.0, forKey:"inputRadius1")
let gradimage = grad.outputImage!
// second filter
let blendimage = moici.imageByApplyingFilter(
    "CIBlendWithMask", withInputParameters: [
        "inputMaskImage":gradimage
    ])
```

We now have the final CIImage in the chain (blendimage); remember, the processor has not yet performed any rendering. Now, however, we want to generate the final bitmap and display it. Let's say we're going to display it as the image of a UIImageView. We can do it in two different ways. We can create a CGImage by passing the CIImage through a CIContext which we have prepared beforehand as a property, self.context, by calling CIContext(options: nil):

```
let moicg = self.context.createCGImage(blendimage, fromRect: moiextent)
self.iv.image = UIImage(CGImage: moicg)
```

Alternatively, we can capture our final CIImage as a UIImage and then draw with it in order to generate the bitmap output of the filter chain:

```
UIGraphicsBeginImageContextWithOptions(moiextent.size, false, 0)
UIImage(CIImage: blendimage).drawInRect(moiextent)
let im = UIGraphicsGetImageFromCurrentImageContext()
UIGraphicsEndImageContext()
self.iv.image = im
```

A filter chain can be encapsulated into a single custom filter by subclassing CIFilter. Your subclass just needs to override the outputImage property (and possibly other methods such as setDefaults), with additional properties to make it key–value coding compliant for any input keys. Here's our vignette filter as a simple CIFilter subclass, where the input keys are the input image and a percentage that adjusts the gradient's smaller radius:

```
class MyVignetteFilter : CIFilter {
    var inputImage : CIImage?
    var inputPercentage : NSNumber? = 1.0
    override var outputImage : CIImage? {
        return self.makeOutputImage()
    }
    private func makeOutputImage () -> CIImage? {
        guard let inputImage = self.inputImage else {return nil}
        guard let inputPercentage = self.inputPercentage else {return nil}
        let extent = inputImage.extent
        let grad = CIFilter(name: "CIRadialGradient")!
        let center = CIVector(x: extent.width/2.0, y: extent.height/2.0)
        let smallerDimension = min(extent.width, extent.height)
        let largerDimension = max(extent.width, extent.height)
        grad.setValue(center, forKey:"inputCenter")
        grad.setValue(smallerDimension/2.0 * CGFloat(inputPercentage),
            forKey:"inputRadius0")
        grad.setValue(largerDimension/2.0, forKey:"inputRadius1")
        let blend = CIFilter(name: "CIBlendWithMask")!
        blend.setValue(inputImage, forKey: "inputImage")
        blend.setValue(grad.outputImage, forKey: "inputMaskImage")
        return blend.outputImage
    }
}
```

And here's how to use our CIFilter subclass and display its output:

```
let vig = MyVignetteFilter()
let moici = CIImage(image: UIImage(named:"Moi")!)!
vig.setValuesForKeysWithDictionary([
    "inputImage":moici,
    "inputPercentage":0.7
])
let outim = vig.outputImage!
let outimcg = self.context.createCGImage(outim, fromRect: outim.extent)
self.iv.image = UIImage(CGImage: outimcg)
```

 You can also create your own CIFilter from scratch — not by combining existing filters, but by coding the actual mathematics of the filter. The details are outside the scope of this book; you'll want to look at the CIKernel class.

Blur and Vibrancy Views

Certain views on iOS, such as navigation bars and the control center, are translucent and display a blurred rendition of what's behind them. To help you imitate this effect, iOS provides the UIVisualEffectView class. You can place other views in front of a UIVisualEffectView, but any subviews should be placed inside its contentView. To tint what's seen through a UIVisualEffectView, set the backgroundColor of its contentView.

To use a UIVisualEffectView, create it with init(effect:); the effect: argument will be an instance of a UIVisualEffect subclass:

UIBlurEffect
> To initialize a UIBlurEffect, call init(style:); the styles (UIBlurEffectStyle) are .Dark, .Light, and .ExtraLight. (.ExtraLight is suitable particularly for pieces of interface that function like a navigation bar or toolbar.) For example:
>
> ```
> let fuzzy = UIVisualEffectView(effect:(UIBlurEffect(style:.Light)))
> ```

UIVibrancyEffect
> To initialize a UIVibrancyEffect, call init(forBlurEffect:). Vibrancy tints a view so as to make it harmonize with the blurred colors underneath it. The intention here is that the vibrancy effect view should sit in front of a blur effect view, typically in its contentView, adding vibrancy to a single UIView that's inside its *own* content-View; you tell the vibrancy effect what the underlying blur effect is, so that they harmonize. You can fetch a visual effect view's blur effect as its effect property, but that's a UIVisualEffect — the superclass — so you'll have to cast to a UIBlurEffect in order to hand it to init(forBlurEffect:).

Here's an example of a blur effect view covering and blurring the interface (mainview), and containing a UILabel wrapped in a vibrancy effect view (Figure 2-15):

Figure 2-15. A blurred background and a vibrant label

```
let blur = UIVisualEffectView(effect: UIBlurEffect(style: .ExtraLight))
blur.frame = mainview.bounds
blur.autoresizingMask = [.FlexibleWidth, .FlexibleHeight]
let vib = UIVisualEffectView(effect: UIVibrancyEffect(
    forBlurEffect: blur.effect as! UIBlurEffect))
let lab = UILabel()
lab.text = "Hello, world!"
lab.sizeToFit()
vib.frame = lab.frame
vib.contentView.addSubview(lab)
vib.center = CGPointMake(blur.bounds.midX, blur.bounds.midY)
vib.autoresizingMask = [.FlexibleTopMargin, .FlexibleBottomMargin,
    .FlexibleLeftMargin, .FlexibleRightMargin]
blur.contentView.addSubview(vib)
mainview.addSubview(blur)
```

Apple seems to think that vibrancy makes a view more legible in conjunction with the underlying blur, but I'm not persuaded. The vibrant view's color is made to harmonize with the blurred color behind it, but harmony implies similarity, which can make the vibrant view *less* legible. You'll have to experiment. With the particular interface I'm blurring, the vibrant label in Figure 2-15 looks okay with a `.Dark` or `.ExtraLight` blur effect view, but is very hard to see with a `.Light` blur effect view.

There are a lot of useful additional notes, well worth consulting, in the *UIVisualEffect-View.h* header. For example, the header points out that an image displayed in an image view needs to be a template image in order to receive the benefit of a vibrancy effect view.

Observe that both a blur effect view and a blur effect view with an embedded vibrancy effect view are available as built-in objects in the nib editor.

Drawing a UIView

The examples of drawing so far in this chapter have mostly produced UIImage objects, chiefly by calling `UIGraphicsBeginImageContextWithOptions` to obtain a graphics context, suitable for display by a UIImageView or any other interface object that knows how to display an image. But, as I've already explained, a UIView provides a graphics context; whatever you draw into that graphics context will appear in that view. The technique here is to subclass UIView and implement the subclass's drawRect: method.

So, for example, let's say we have a UIView subclass called MyView. You would then instantiate this class and get the instance into the view hierarchy. One way to do this would be to drag a UIView into a view in the nib editor and set its class to MyView in the Identity inspector; another would be to create the MyView instance and put it into the interface in code.

The result is that, from time to time, MyView's drawRect: will be called. This is your subclass, so you get to write the code that runs at that moment. Whatever you draw will appear inside the MyView instance. There will usually be no need to call super, since UIView's own implementation of drawRect: does nothing. At the time that drawRect: is called, the current graphics context has already been set to the view's own graphics context. You can use Core Graphics functions or UIKit convenience methods to draw into that context. I gave some basic examples earlier in this chapter ("Graphics Contexts" on page 76).

 You should *never* call drawRect: yourself! If a view needs updating and you want its drawRect: called, send the view the setNeedsDisplay message. This will cause drawRect: to be called at the next proper moment. Also, don't override drawRect: unless you are assured that this is legal. For example, it is not legal to override draw-Rect: in a subclass of UIImageView; you cannot combine your drawing with that of the UIImageView.

The need to draw in real time, on demand, surprises some beginners, who worry that drawing may be a time-consuming operation. This can indeed be a reasonable consideration, and where the same drawing will be used in many places in your interface, it may well make sense to construct a UIImage instead, once, and then reuse that UIImage by drawing it in a view's drawRect:. In general, however, you should not optimize prematurely. The code for a drawing operation may appear verbose and yet be extremely fast. Moreover, the iOS drawing system is efficient; it doesn't call drawRect: unless it has to (or is told to, through a call to setNeedsDisplay), and once a view has drawn itself, the result is cached so that the cached drawing can be reused instead of repeating the drawing operation from scratch. (Apple refers to this cached drawing as the view's *bitmap backing store.*) You can readily satisfy yourself of this fact with some caveman debugging, logging in your drawRect: implementation; you may be amazed to discover that your custom UIView's drawRect: code is called only once in the entire lifetime of the app! In fact, moving code to drawRect: is commonly a way to *increase* efficiency. This is because it is more efficient for the drawing engine to render directly onto the screen than for it to render offscreen and then copy those pixels onto the screen.

Where drawing is extensive and can be compartmentalized into sections, you may be able to gain some additional efficiency by paying attention to the rect parameter passed into drawRect:. It designates the region of the view's bounds that needs refreshing. Normally, this is the view's entire bounds; but if you call setNeedsDisplayInRect:, it will be the CGRect that you passed in as argument. You could respond by drawing only what goes into those bounds; but even if you don't, your drawing will be clipped to those bounds, so, while you may not spend less time drawing, the system will draw more efficiently.

When creating a custom UIView subclass instance in code, you may be surprised (and annoyed) to find that the view has a black background:

```
let mv = MyView(frame:CGRectMake(20,20,150,100))
self.view.addSubview(mv)
```

This can be frustrating if what you expected and wanted was a transparent background, and it's a source of considerable confusion among beginners. The black background arises when two things are true:

- The view's backgroundColor is nil.
- The view's opaque is true.

Unfortunately, when creating a UIView in code, both those things *are* true by default! So if you don't want the black background, you must do something about one or the other of them (or both). If a view isn't going to be opaque, its opaque should be set to false anyway, so that's probably the cleanest solution:

```
let mv = MyView(frame:CGRectMake(20,20,150,100))
self.view.addSubview(mv)
mv.opaque = false
```

Alternatively, this being your own UIView subclass, you could implement its init(frame:) (the designated initializer) to have the view set its *own* opaque to false:

```
override init(frame: CGRect) {
    super.init(frame:frame)
    self.opaque = false
}
```

With a UIView created in the nib, on the other hand, the black background problem doesn't arise. This is because such a UIView's backgroundColor is not nil. The nib assigns it *some* actual background color, even if that color is UIColor.clearColor().

Of course, if a view fills its rectangle with opaque drawing or has an opaque background color, you can leave opaque set to true and gain some drawing efficiency (see Chapter 1).

Graphics Context Settings

As you draw in a graphics context, the drawing obeys the context's current settings. Thus, the procedure is always to configure the context's settings first, and then draw. For example, to draw a red line followed by a blue line, you would first set the context's line color to red, and then draw the first line; then you'd set the context's line color to blue, and then draw the second line. To the eye, it appears that the redness and blueness are properties of the individual lines, but in fact, at the time you draw each line, line color is a feature of the entire graphics context. This is true regardless of whether you use UIKit methods or Core Graphics functions.

A graphics context thus has, at every moment, a *state*, which is the sum total of all its settings; the way a piece of drawing looks is the result of what the graphics context's state was at the moment that piece of drawing was performed. To help you manipulate entire states, the graphics context provides a *stack* for holding states. Every time you call CGContextSaveGState, the context pushes the entire current state onto the stack; every time you call CGContextRestoreGState, the context retrieves the state from the top of the stack (the state that was most recently pushed) and sets itself to that state.

Thus, a common pattern is:

1. Call CGContextSaveGState.
2. Manipulate the context's settings, thus changing its state.
3. Draw.
4. Call CGContextRestoreGState to restore the state and the settings to what they were before you manipulated them.

You do not have to do this before *every* manipulation of a context's settings, however, because settings don't necessarily conflict with one another or with past settings. You can set the context's line color to red and then later to blue without any difficulty. But in certain situations you do want your manipulation of settings to be undoable, and I'll point out several such situations later in this chapter.

Many of the settings that constitute a graphics context's state, and that determine the behavior and appearance of drawing performed at that moment, are similar to those of any drawing application. Here are some of them, along with some of the commands that determine them. I list Core Graphics functions, followed by some UIKit convenience methods that call them:

Line thickness and dash style
CGContextSetLineWidth, CGContextSetLineDash (and UIBezierPath lineWidth, setLineDash:count:phase:)

Line end-cap style and join style

`CGContextSetLineCap`, `CGContextSetLineJoin`, `CGContextSetMiterLimit` (and UIBezierPath `lineCapStyle`, `lineJoinStyle`, `miterLimit`)

Line color or pattern

`CGContextSetRGBStrokeColor`, `CGContextSetGrayStrokeColor`, `CGContextSet-StrokeColorWithColor`, `CGContextSetStrokePattern` (and UIColor `setStroke`)

Fill color or pattern

`CGContextSetRGBFillColor`, `CGContextSetGrayFillColor`, `CGContextSetFill-ColorWithColor`, `CGContextSetFillPattern` (and UIColor `setFill`)

Shadow

`CGContextSetShadow`, `CGContextSetShadowWithColor`

Overall transparency and compositing

`CGContextSetAlpha`, `CGContextSetBlendMode`

Anti-aliasing

`CGContextSetShouldAntialias`

Additional settings include:

Clipping area

Drawing outside the clipping area is not physically drawn.

Transform (or "CTM," for "current transform matrix")

Changes how points that you specify in subsequent drawing commands are mapped onto the physical space of the canvas.

Many of these settings will be illustrated by examples later in this chapter.

Paths and Shapes

By issuing a series of instructions for moving an imaginary pen, you construct a *path*, tracing it out from point to point. You must first tell the pen where to position itself, setting the current point; after that, you issue a series of commands telling it how to trace out each subsequent piece of the path. Each additional piece of the path starts at the current point; its end becomes the new current point.

Note that a path, in and of itself, does *not* constitute drawing! First you provide a path; *then* you draw. Drawing can mean stroking the path or filling the path, or both. Again, this should be a familiar notion from certain drawing applications.

Here are some path-drawing commands you're likely to give:

Position the current point

`CGContextMoveToPoint`

Trace a line
    CGContextAddLineToPoint, CGContextAddLines

Trace a rectangle
    CGContextAddRect, CGContextAddRects

Trace an ellipse or circle
    CGContextAddEllipseInRect

Trace an arc
    CGContextAddArcToPoint, CGContextAddArc

Trace a Bezier curve with one or two control points
    CGContextAddQuadCurveToPoint, CGContextAddCurveToPoint

Close the current path
    CGContextClosePath. This appends a line from the last point of the path to the first point. There's no need to do this if you're about to fill the path, since it's done for you.

Stroke or fill the current path
    CGContextStrokePath, CGContextFillPath, CGContextEOFillPath, CGContext-DrawPath. Stroking or filling the current path *clears the path*. Use CGContextDraw-Path if you want both to fill and to stroke the path in a single command, because if you merely stroke it first with CGContextStrokePath, the path is cleared and you can no longer fill it. There are also a lot of convenience functions that create a path and stroke or fill it all in a single move:

- CGContextStrokeLineSegments
- CGContextStrokeRect
- CGContextStrokeRectWithWidth
- CGContextFillRect
- CGContextFillRects
- CGContextStrokeEllipseInRect
- CGContextFillEllipseInRect

A path can be compound, meaning that it consists of multiple independent pieces. For example, a single path might consist of two separate closed shapes: a rectangle and a circle. When you call CGContextMoveToPoint in the middle of constructing a path (that is, after tracing out a path and without clearing it by filling or stroking it), you pick up the imaginary pen and move it to a new location without tracing a segment, thus preparing to start an independent piece of the same path. If you're worried, as you begin to trace out a path, that there might be an existing path and that your new path might

Figure 2-16. A simple path drawing

be seen as a compound part of that existing path, you can call `CGContextBeginPath` to specify that this is a different path; many of Apple's examples do this, but in practice I usually do not find it necessary.

To illustrate the typical use of path-drawing commands, I'll generate the up-pointing arrow shown in Figure 2-16. This might not be the best way to create the arrow, and I'm deliberately avoiding use of the convenience functions, but it's clear and shows a nice basic variety of typical commands:

```
// obtain the current graphics context
let con = UIGraphicsGetCurrentContext()!
// draw a black (by default) vertical line, the shaft of the arrow
CGContextMoveToPoint(con, 100, 100)
CGContextAddLineToPoint(con, 100, 19)
CGContextSetLineWidth(con, 20)
CGContextStrokePath(con)
// draw a red triangle, the point of the arrow
CGContextSetFillColorWithColor(con, UIColor.redColor().CGColor)
CGContextMoveToPoint(con, 80, 25)
CGContextAddLineToPoint(con, 100, 0)
CGContextAddLineToPoint(con, 120, 25)
CGContextFillPath(con)
// snip a triangle out of the shaft by drawing in Clear blend mode
CGContextMoveToPoint(con, 90, 101)
CGContextAddLineToPoint(con, 100, 90)
CGContextAddLineToPoint(con, 110, 101)
CGContextSetBlendMode(con, .Clear)
CGContextFillPath(con)
```

If a path needs to be reused or shared, you can encapsulate it as a CGPath. You can copy the graphics context's current path using `CGContextCopyPath`. Even without a graphics context, you can create a new CGMutablePath (with `CGPathCreateMutable`, for example) and construct the path using various CGPath functions that parallel the CGContext path-construction functions. Also, there are a number of CGPath functions for creating a path based on simple geometry or based on an existing path:

- `CGPathCreateWithRect`
- `CGPathCreateWithEllipseInRect`

- CGPathCreateWithRoundedRect

- CGPathCreateCopyByStrokingPath

- CGPathCreateCopyByDashingPath

- CGPathCreateCopyByTransformingPath

The UIKit class UIBezierPath wraps CGPath (in its CGPath property); it provides methods parallel to the CGContext and CGPath functions for constructing a path, such as:

- init(rect:)

- init(ovalInRect:)

- init(roundedRect:cornerRadius:)

- moveToPoint:

- addLineToPoint:

- addArcWithCenter:radius:startAngle:endAngle:clockwise:

- addQuadCurveToPoint:controlPoint:

- addCurveToPoint:controlPoint1:controlPoint2:

- closePath

When you call the UIBezierPath instance method fill or stroke (or fillWithBlend-Mode:alpha: or strokeWithBlendMode:alpha:), the current graphics context settings are saved, the wrapped CGPath is made the current graphics context's path and stroked or filled, and the current graphics context settings are restored.

Thus, using UIBezierPath together with UIColor, we could rewrite our arrow-drawing routine entirely with UIKit methods:

```
let p = UIBezierPath()
// shaft
p.moveToPoint(CGPointMake(100,100))
p.addLineToPoint(CGPointMake(100, 19))
p.lineWidth = 20
p.stroke()
// point
UIColor.redColor().set()
p.removeAllPoints()
p.moveToPoint(CGPointMake(80,25))
p.addLineToPoint(CGPointMake(100, 0))
p.addLineToPoint(CGPointMake(120, 25))
p.fill()
// snip
p.removeAllPoints()
```

```
p.moveToPoint(CGPointMake(90,101))
p.addLineToPoint(CGPointMake(100, 90))
p.addLineToPoint(CGPointMake(110, 101))
p.fillWithBlendMode(.Clear, alpha:1.0)
```

There's no savings of code here over calling Core Graphics functions, so your choice of Core Graphics or UIKit is a matter of taste. UIBezierPath is also useful when you want to capture a CGPath and pass it around as an object; an example appears in Chapter 21. See also the discussion in Chapter 3 of CAShapeLayer, which takes a CGPath that you've constructed and draws it for you within its own bounds.

Clipping

Instead of drawing a path by stroking or filling, you might use a path to mask out areas, protecting them from future drawing. This is called *clipping*. By default, a graphics context's clipping region is the entire graphics context: you can draw anywhere within the context.

The clipping area is a feature of the context as a whole, and any new clipping area is applied by intersecting it with the existing clipping area; so if you apply your own clipping region, the way to remove it from the graphics context later is to plan ahead and wrap things with calls to `CGContextSaveGState` and `CGContextRestoreGState`.

To illustrate, I'll rewrite the code that generated our original arrow (Figure 2-16) to use clipping instead of a blend mode to "punch out" the triangular notch in the tail of the arrow. This is a little tricky, because what we want to clip to is not the region inside the triangle but the region outside it. To express this, we'll use a compound path consisting of more than one closed area — the triangle, and the drawing area as a whole (which we can obtain with `CGContextGetClipBoundingBox`).

Both when filling a compound path and when using it to express a clipping region, the system follows one of two rules:

Winding rule
    The fill or clipping area is denoted by an alternation in the direction (clockwise or counterclockwise) of the path demarcating each region.

Even-odd rule (EO)
    The fill or clipping area is denoted by a simple count of the paths demarcating each region.

Our situation is extremely simple, so it's easier to use the even-odd rule. So we set up the clipping area using `CGContextEOClip` and then draw the arrow:

```
// obtain the current graphics context
let con = UIGraphicsGetCurrentContext()!
// punch triangular hole in context clipping region
CGContextMoveToPoint(con, 90, 100)
```

```
CGContextAddLineToPoint(con, 100, 90)
CGContextAddLineToPoint(con, 110, 100)
CGContextClosePath(con)
CGContextAddRect(con, CGContextGetClipBoundingBox(con))
CGContextEOClip(con)
// draw the vertical line
CGContextMoveToPoint(con, 100, 100)
CGContextAddLineToPoint(con, 100, 19)
CGContextSetLineWidth(con, 20)
CGContextStrokePath(con)
// draw the red triangle, the point of the arrow
CGContextSetFillColorWithColor(con, UIColor.redColor().CGColor)
CGContextMoveToPoint(con, 80, 25)
CGContextAddLineToPoint(con, 100, 0)
CGContextAddLineToPoint(con, 120, 25)
CGContextFillPath(con)
```

The UIBezierPath clipping commands are usesEvenOddFillRule and addClip.

Gradients

Gradients can range from the simple to the complex. A simple gradient (which is all I'll describe here) is determined by a color at one endpoint along with a color at the other endpoint, plus (optionally) colors at intermediate points; the gradient is then painted either linearly between two points or radially between two circles.

You can't use a gradient as a path's fill color, but you can restrict a gradient to a path's shape by clipping, which amounts to the same thing.

To illustrate, I'll redraw our arrow, using a linear gradient as the "shaft" of the arrow (Figure 2-17):

```
// obtain the current graphics context
let con = UIGraphicsGetCurrentContext()!
CGContextSaveGState(con)
// punch triangular hole in context clipping region
CGContextMoveToPoint(con, 90, 100)
CGContextAddLineToPoint(con, 100, 90)
```

Figure 2-17. Drawing with a gradient

```
CGContextAddLineToPoint(con, 110, 100)
CGContextClosePath(con)
CGContextAddRect(con, CGContextGetClipBoundingBox(con))
CGContextEOClip(con)
// draw the vertical line, add its shape to the clipping region
CGContextMoveToPoint(con, 100, 100)
CGContextAddLineToPoint(con, 100, 19)
CGContextSetLineWidth(con, 20)
CGContextReplacePathWithStrokedPath(con)
CGContextClip(con)
// draw the gradient
let locs : [CGFloat] = [ 0.0, 0.5, 1.0 ]
let colors : [CGFloat] = [
    0.8, 0.4, // starting color, transparent light gray
    0.1, 0.5, // intermediate color, darker less transparent gray
    0.8, 0.4, // ending color, transparent light gray
]
let sp = CGColorSpaceCreateDeviceGray()
let grad =
    CGGradientCreateWithColorComponents (sp, colors, locs, 3)
CGContextDrawLinearGradient (
    con, grad, CGPointMake(89,0), CGPointMake(111,0), [])
// done clipping
CGContextRestoreGState(con)
// draw the red triangle, the point of the arrow
CGContextSetFillColorWithColor(con, UIColor.redColor().CGColor)
CGContextMoveToPoint(con, 80, 25)
CGContextAddLineToPoint(con, 100, 0)
CGContextAddLineToPoint(con, 120, 25)
CGContextFillPath(con)
```

The call to `CGContextReplacePathWithStrokedPath` pretends to stroke the current path, using the current line width and other line-related context state settings, but then creates a new path representing the outside of that stroked path. Thus, instead of a thick line we have a rectangular region that we can use as the clip region.

We then create the gradient and paint it. The procedure is verbose but simple; everything is boilerplate. We describe the gradient as an array of locations on the continuum between one endpoint (`0.0`) and the other endpoint (`1.0`), along with the color components of the colors corresponding to each location; in this case, I want the gradient

Figure 2-18. A patterned fill

to be lighter at the edges and darker in the middle, so I use three locations, with the dark one at 0.5. We must also supply a color space; this will tell the gradient how to interpret our color components. Finally, we create the gradient and paint it into place.

(There are also gradient CIFilters, as I demonstrated earlier in this chapter; for yet another way to create a simple gradient, see the discussion of CAGradientLayer in the next chapter.)

Colors and Patterns

A color is a CGColor. CGColor is not difficult to work with, and can be converted to and from a UIColor through UIColor's init(CGColor:) and CGColor methods.

A pattern is also a kind of color. You can create a pattern color and stroke or fill with it. The simplest way is to draw a minimal tile of the pattern into a UIImage and create the color by calling UIColor's init(patternImage:). To illustrate, I'll create a pattern of horizontal stripes and use it to paint the point of the arrow instead of a solid red color (Figure 2-18):

```
// CGContextSetFillColorWithColor(con, UIColor.redColor().CGColor)
// not any more, we're going to paint with a pattern instead of red!
// create the pattern image tile
UIGraphicsBeginImageContextWithOptions(CGSizeMake(4,4), false, 0)
let imcon = UIGraphicsGetCurrentContext()!
CGContextSetFillColorWithColor(imcon, UIColor.redColor().CGColor)
CGContextFillRect(imcon, CGRectMake(0,0,4,4))
CGContextSetFillColorWithColor(imcon, UIColor.blueColor().CGColor)
CGContextFillRect(imcon, CGRectMake(0,0,4,2))
let stripes = UIGraphicsGetImageFromCurrentImageContext()
UIGraphicsEndImageContext()
// paint the point of the arrow with it
let stripesPattern = UIColor(patternImage:stripes)
stripesPattern.setFill()
let p = UIBezierPath()
p.moveToPoint(CGPointMake(80,25))
p.addLineToPoint(CGPointMake(100,0))
p.addLineToPoint(CGPointMake(120,25))
p.fill()
```

The Core Graphics equivalent, CGPattern, is considerably more powerful, but also much more elaborate:

```
let sp2 = CGColorSpaceCreatePattern(nil)
CGContextSetFillColorSpace(con, sp2)
let drawStripes : CGPatternDrawPatternCallback = {
    _, con in
    CGContextSetFillColorWithColor(con!, UIColor.redColor().CGColor)
    CGContextFillRect(con!, CGRectMake(0,0,4,4))
    CGContextSetFillColorWithColor(con!, UIColor.blueColor().CGColor)
    CGContextFillRect(con!, CGRectMake(0,0,4,2))
}
var callbacks = CGPatternCallbacks(
    version: 0, drawPattern: drawStripes, releaseInfo: nil)
let patt = CGPatternCreate(nil, CGRectMake(0,0,4,4),
    CGAffineTransformIdentity, 4, 4,
    .ConstantSpacingMinimalDistortion,
    true, &callbacks)
var alph : CGFloat = 1.0
CGContextSetFillPattern(con, patt, &alph)
CGContextMoveToPoint(con, 80, 25)
CGContextAddLineToPoint(con, 100, 0)
CGContextAddLineToPoint(con, 120, 25)
CGContextFillPath(con)
```

To understand that code, it helps to read it backwards. Everything revolves around the call to CGPatternCreate. A pattern is a drawing in a rectangular "cell"; we have to state both the size of the cell (the second argument) and the spacing between origin points of cells (the fourth and fifth arguments). In this case, the cell is 4×4, and every cell exactly touches its neighbors both horizontally and vertically. We have to supply a transform to be applied to the cell (the third argument); in this case, we're not doing anything with this transform, so we supply the identity transform. We supply a tiling rule (the sixth argument). We have to state whether this is a color pattern or a stencil pattern; it's a color pattern, so the seventh argument is true. And we have to supply a pointer to a callback function that actually draws the pattern into its cell (the eighth argument).

Except that that's *not* what we have to supply as the eighth argument. What we actually have to supply here is a pointer to a CGPatternCallbacks struct. This struct consists of the number 0 and pointers to *two* functions, one called to draw the pattern into its cell, the other called when the pattern is released. We're not specifying the second function, however; it is for memory management, and we don't need it in this simple example.

As you can see, the actual pattern-drawing code (drawStripes) is very simple. The only tricky issue is that the call to CGPatternCreate must be in agreement with the pattern-drawing function as to the size of a cell, or the pattern won't come out the way you expect. We know in this case that the cell is 4×4. So we fill it with red, and then fill its lower half with blue. When these cells are tiled touching each other horizontally and vertically, we get the stripes that you see in Figure 2-18.

Having generated the CGPattern with `CGPatternCreate`, we call `CGContextSetFill-Pattern`; instead of setting a fill color, we're setting a fill pattern, to be used the next time we fill a path (in this case, the triangular arrowhead). The third parameter to `CGContextSetFillPattern` is a pointer to a CGFloat, so we have to set up the CGFloat itself beforehand. The second parameter is the CGPattern.

The only thing left to explain is the first two lines of that code. It turns out that before you can call `CGContextSetFillPattern` with a colored pattern, you have to set the context's fill color space to a pattern color space. If you neglect to do this, you'll get an error when you call `CGContextSetFillPattern`. This means that the code as presented has left the graphics context in an undesirable state, with its fill color space set to a pattern color space. This would cause trouble if we were later to try to set the fill color to a normal color. The solution, as usual, is to wrap the code in calls to `CGContextSave-GState` and `CGContextRestoreGState`.

You may have observed in Figure 2-18 that the stripes do not fit neatly inside the triangle of the arrowhead: the bottommost stripe is something like half a blue stripe. This is because a pattern is positioned not with respect to the shape you are filling (or stroking), but with respect to the graphics context as a whole. We could shift the pattern position by calling `CGContextSetPatternPhase` before drawing.

Graphics Context Transforms

Just as a UIView can have a transform, so can a graphics context. However, applying a transform to a graphics context has no effect on the drawing that's already in it; it affects only the drawing that takes place after it is applied, altering the way the coordinates you provide are mapped onto the graphics context's area. A graphics context's transform is called its CTM, for "current transform matrix."

It is quite usual to take full advantage of a graphics context's CTM to save yourself from performing even simple calculations. You can multiply the current transform by any CGAffineTransform using `CGContextConcatCTM`; there are also convenience functions for applying a translate, scale, or rotate transform to the current transform.

The base transform for a graphics context is already set for you when you obtain the context; this is how the system is able to map context drawing coordinates onto screen coordinates. Whatever transforms you apply are applied to the current transform, so the base transform remains in effect and drawing continues to work. You can return to the base transform after applying your own transforms by wrapping your code in calls to `CGContextSaveGState` and `CGContextRestoreGState`.

For example, we have hitherto been drawing our upward-pointing arrow with code that knows how to place that arrow at only one location: the top left of its rectangle is hard-coded at (`80,0`). This is silly. It makes the code hard to understand, as well as inflexible and difficult to reuse. Surely the sensible thing would be to draw the arrow at (0,0), by subtracting 80 from all the x-values in our existing code. Now it is easy to draw the arrow at *any* position, simply by applying a translate transform beforehand, mapping (0,0) to the desired top-left corner of the arrow. So, to draw it at (80,0), we would say:

```
CGContextTranslateCTM(con, 80, 0)
// now draw the arrow at (0,0)
```

A rotate transform is particularly useful, allowing you to draw in a rotated orientation without any nasty trigonometry. However, it's a bit tricky because the point around which the rotation takes place is the origin. This is rarely what you want, so you have to apply a translate transform first, to map the origin to the point around which you really want to rotate. But then, after rotating, in order to figure out where to draw you will probably have to reverse your translate transform.

To illustrate, here's code to draw our arrow repeatedly at several angles, pivoting around the end of its tail (Figure 2-19). Since the arrow will be drawn multiple times, I'll start by encapsulating the drawing of the arrow as a UIImage. This is not merely to reduce repetition and make drawing more efficient; it's also because we want the entire arrow to pivot, including the pattern stripes, and this is the simplest way to achieve that:

```
func arrowImage () -> UIImage {
    UIGraphicsBeginImageContextWithOptions(CGSizeMake(40,100), false, 0.0)
    // obtain the current graphics context
    let con = UIGraphicsGetCurrentContext()!
    // draw the arrow into the image context
    // draw it at (0,0)! adjust all x-values by subtracting 80
    // ... actual code omitted ...
    let im = UIGraphicsGetImageFromCurrentImageContext()
    UIGraphicsEndImageContext()
    return im
}
```

We produce the arrow image once and store it somewhere — I'll use a property accessed as self.arrow. In our drawRect: implementation, we draw the arrow image multiple times:

```
override func drawRect(rect: CGRect) {
    let con = UIGraphicsGetCurrentContext()!
    self.arrow.drawAtPoint(CGPointMake(0,0))
    for _ in 0..<3 {
        CGContextTranslateCTM(con, 20, 100)
        CGContextRotateCTM(con, 30 * CGFloat(M_PI)/180.0)
        CGContextTranslateCTM(con, -20, -100)
        self.arrow.drawAtPoint(CGPointMake(0,0))
    }
}
```

A transform is also one more solution for the "flip" problem we encountered earlier with CGContextDrawImage. Instead of reversing the drawing, we can reverse the context

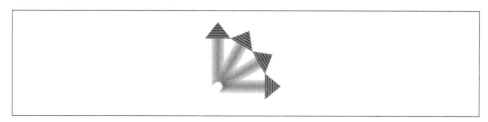

Figure 2-19. Drawing rotated with a CTM

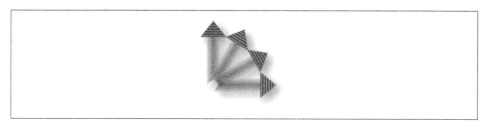

Figure 2-20. Drawing with a shadow

into which we draw it. Essentially, we apply a "flip" transform to the context's coordinate system. You move the context's top downward, and then reverse the direction of the y-coordinate by applying a scale transform whose y-multiplier is `-1`:

```
CGContextTranslateCTM(con, 0, theHeight)
CGContextScaleCTM(con, 1.0, -1.0)
```

How far down you move the context's top (`theHeight`) depends on how you intend to draw the image.

Shadows

To add a shadow to a drawing, give the context a shadow value before drawing. The shadow position is expressed as a CGSize, where the positive direction for both values indicates down and to the right. The blur value is an open-ended positive number; Apple doesn't explain how the scale works, but experimentation shows that 12 is nice and blurry, 99 is so blurry as to be shapeless, and higher values become problematic.

Figure 2-20 shows the result of the same code that generated Figure 2-19, except that before we start drawing the arrow repeatedly, we give the context a shadow:

```
let con = UIGraphicsGetCurrentContext()!
CGContextSetShadow(con, CGSizeMake(7, 7), 12)
self.arrow.drawAtPoint(CGPointMake(0,0)) // ... and so on
```

It may not be evident from Figure 2-20, but we are adding a shadow each time we draw. Thus the arrows are able to cast shadows on one another. Suppose, however, that we want all the arrows to cast a single shadow collectively. The way to achieve this is with a *transparency layer*; this is basically a subcontext that accumulates all drawing and then adds the shadow. Our code for drawing the shadowed arrows now looks like this:

```
let con = UIGraphicsGetCurrentContext()!
CGContextSetShadow(con, CGSizeMake(7, 7), 12)
CGContextBeginTransparencyLayer(con, nil)
self.arrow.drawAtPoint(CGPointMake(0,0))
for _ in 0..<3 {
    CGContextTranslateCTM(con, 20, 100)
    CGContextRotateCTM(con, 30 * CGFloat(M_PI)/180.0)
    CGContextTranslateCTM(con, -20, -100)
    self.arrow.drawAtPoint(CGPointMake(0,0))
}
CGContextEndTransparencyLayer(con)
```

Erasing

The function CGContextClearRect erases all existing drawing in a rectangle; combined with clipping, it can erase an area of any shape. The result can "punch a hole" through all existing drawing.

The behavior of CGContextClearRect depends on whether the context is transparent or opaque. This is particularly obvious and intuitive when drawing into an image context. If the image context is transparent — the second argument to UIGraphicsBegin-ImageContextWithOptions is false — CGContextClearRect erases to transparent; otherwise it erases to black.

When drawing directly into a view (as with drawRect: or drawLayer:inContext:), if the view's background color is nil or a color with even a tiny bit of transparency, the result of CGContextClearRect will appear to be transparent, punching a hole right through the view including its background color; if the background color is completely opaque, the result of CGContextClearRect will be black. This is because the view's background color determines whether the view's graphics context is transparent or opaque; thus, this is essentially the same behavior that I described in the preceding paragraph.

Figure 2-21 illustrates; the blue square on the left has been partly cut away to black, while the blue square on the right has been partly cut away to transparency. Yet these are instances of the same UIView subclass, drawn with exactly the same code! The UIView subclass's drawRect: looks like this:

```
let con = UIGraphicsGetCurrentContext()!
CGContextSetFillColorWithColor(con, UIColor.blueColor().CGColor)
CGContextFillRect(con, rect)
CGContextClearRect(con, CGRectMake(0,0,30,30))
```

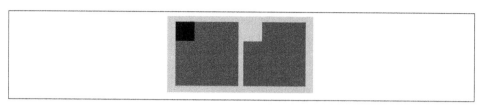

Figure 2-21. The very strange behavior of CGContextClearRect

The difference between the views in Figure 2-21 is that the backgroundColor of the first view is solid red with an alpha of 1, while the backgroundColor of the second view is solid red with an alpha of 0.99. This difference is utterly imperceptible to the eye (not to mention that the red color never appears, as it is covered with a blue fill), but it completely changes the effect of CGContextClearRect.

Points and Pixels

A point is a dimensionless location described by an x-coordinate and a y-coordinate. When you draw in a graphics context, you specify the points at which to draw, and this works regardless of the device's resolution, because Core Graphics maps your drawing nicely onto the physical output using the base CTM and anti-aliasing. Therefore, throughout this chapter I've concerned myself with graphics context points, disregarding their relationship to screen pixels.

However, pixels do exist. A pixel is a physical, integral, dimensioned unit of display in the real world. Whole-numbered points effectively lie between pixels, and this can matter if you're fussy, especially on a single-resolution device. For example, if a vertical path with whole-number coordinates is stroked with a line width of 1, half the line falls on each side of the path, and the drawn line on the screen of a single-resolution device will seem to be 2 pixels wide (because the device can't illuminate half a pixel).

You will sometimes encounter advice suggesting that if this effect is objectionable, you should try shifting the line's position by 0.5, to center it in its pixels. This advice may appear to work, but it makes some simpleminded assumptions. A more sophisticated approach is to obtain the UIView's contentScaleFactor property. You can divide by this value to convert from pixels to points. Consider also that the most accurate way to draw a vertical or horizontal line is not to stroke a path but to fill a rectangle. So this UIView subclass code will draw a perfect 1-pixel-wide vertical line on any device (con is the current graphics context):

```
CGContextFillRect(con, CGRectMake(100,0,1.0/self.contentScaleFactor,100))
```

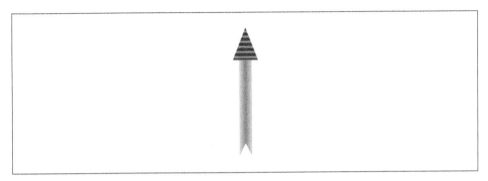

Figure 2-22. Automatic stretching of content

Content Mode

A view that draws something within itself, as opposed to merely having a background color and subviews (as in the previous chapter), has *content*. This means that its content-Mode property becomes important whenever the view is resized. As I mentioned earlier, the drawing system will avoid asking a view to redraw itself from scratch if possible; instead, it will use the cached result of the previous drawing operation (the bitmap backing store). So, if the view is resized, the system may simply stretch or shrink or reposition the cached drawing, if your contentMode setting instructs it to do so.

It's a little tricky to illustrate this point when the view's content is coming from draw-Rect:, because I have to arrange for the view to obtain its content (from drawRect:) and then cause it to be resized without also causing it to be redrawn (that is, without drawRect: being called *again*). Here's how I'll do that. As the app starts up, I'll create an instance of a UIView subclass, MyView, that knows how to draw our arrow. Then I'll use delayed performance to resize the instance after the window has shown and the interface has been initially displayed (for the delay utility function, see Appendix B):

```
delay(0.1) {
    mv.bounds.size.height *= 2 // mv is the MyView instance
}
```

We double the height of the view without causing drawRect: to be called. The result is that the view's drawing appears at double its correct height. For example, if our view's drawRect: code is the same as the code that generated Figure 2-17, we get Figure 2-22.

Sooner or later, however, drawRect: will be called, and the drawing will be refreshed in accordance with our code. Our code doesn't say to draw the arrow at a height that is relative to the height of the view's bounds; it draws the arrow at a fixed height. Thus, the arrow will snap back to its original size.

A view's contentMode property should therefore usually be in agreement with how the view draws itself. Our drawRect: code dictates the size and position of the arrow relative to the view's bounds origin, its top left; so we could set its contentMode to .TopLeft. Alternatively, we could set it to .Redraw; this will cause automatic scaling of the cached content to be turned off — instead, when the view is resized, its setNeedsDisplay method will be called, ultimately triggering drawRect: to redraw the content.

CHAPTER 3

Layers

The tale told in Chapters 1 and 2 of how a UIView works and how it draws itself is only half the story. A UIView has a partner called its *layer*, a CALayer. A UIView does not actually draw itself onto the screen; it draws itself into its layer, and it is the layer that is portrayed on the screen. As I've already mentioned, a view is not redrawn frequently; instead, its drawing is cached, and the cached version of the drawing (the bitmap backing store) is used where possible. The cached version is, in fact, the layer. What I spoke of in Chapter 2 as the view's graphics context is actually the layer's graphics context.

This might seem to be a mere implementation detail, but layers are important and interesting. To understand layers is to understand views more deeply; layers extend the power of views. In particular:

Layers have properties that affect drawing.
> Layers have drawing-related properties beyond those of a UIView. Because a layer is the recipient and presenter of a view's drawing, you can modify how a view is drawn on the screen by accessing the layer's properties. In other words, by reaching down to the level of its layer, you can make a view do things you can't do through UIView methods alone.

Layers can be combined within a single view.
> A UIView's partner layer can contain additional layers. Since the purpose of layers is to draw, portraying visible material on the screen, this allows a UIView's drawing to be composited of multiple distinct pieces. This can make drawing easier, with the constituents of a drawing being treated as objects.

Layers are the basis of animation.
> Animation allows you to add clarity, emphasis, and just plain coolness to your interface. Layers are made to be animated; the "CA" in "CALayer" stands for "Core Animation." Animation is the subject of Chapter 4.

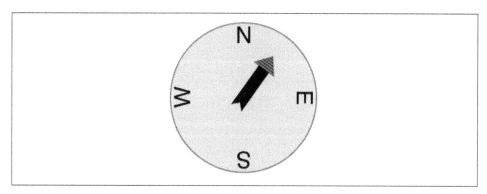

Figure 3-1. A compass, composed of layers

For example, suppose we want to add a compass indicator to our app's interface. Figure 3-1 portrays a simple version of such a compass. It takes advantage of the arrow that we figured out how to draw in Chapter 2; the arrow is drawn into a layer of its own. The other parts of the compass are layers too: the circle is a layer, and each of the cardinal point letters is a layer. The drawing is thus easy to composite in code (and later in this chapter, that's exactly what we'll do); even more intriguing, the pieces can be repositioned and animated separately, so it's easy to rotate the arrow without moving the circle (and in Chapter 4, that's exactly what we'll do).

The documentation discusses layers chiefly in connection with animation (in particular, in the *Core Animation Programming Guide*). This categorization gives the impression that layers are of interest only if you intend to animate. That's misleading. Layers are the basis of animation, but they are also the basis of view drawing, and are useful and important even if you don't use them for animation.

View and Layer

A UIView instance has an accompanying CALayer instance, accessible as the view's layer property. This layer has a special status: it is partnered with this view to embody all of the view's drawing. The layer has no corresponding view property, but the view is the layer's delegate. The documentation sometimes speaks of this layer as the view's *underlying layer*.

By default, when a UIView is instantiated, its layer is an instance of CALayer. If you subclass UIView and you want your subclass's underlying layer to be an instance of a CALayer subclass (built-in or your own), implement the UIView subclass's layer-Class class method to return that CALayer subclass.

That, for example, is how the compass in Figure 3-1 is created. We have a UIView subclass, CompassView, and a CALayer subclass, CompassLayer. Here is Compass-View's implementation:

```
class CompassView : UIView {
    override class func layerClass() -> AnyClass {
        return CompassLayer.self
    }
}
```

Thus, when CompassView is instantiated, its underlying layer is a CompassLayer. In this example, there is no drawing in CompassView; its job — in this case, its *only* job — is to give CompassLayer a place in the visible interface, because a layer cannot appear without a view.

Because every view has an underlying layer, there is a tight integration between the two. The layer portrays all the view's drawing; if the view draws, it does so by contributing to the layer's drawing. The view is the layer's delegate. And the view's properties are often merely a convenience for accessing the layer's properties. For example, when you set the view's backgroundColor, you are really setting the layer's backgroundColor, and if you set the layer's backgroundColor directly, the view's backgroundColor is set to match. Similarly, the view's frame is really the layer's frame and *vice versa*.

 A CALayer's delegate property is settable, and can be an instance of any NSObject-based class (CALayerDelegate is an informal protocol, a category injected into NSObject). But a UIView and its underlying layer have a special relationship. A UIView *must* be the delegate of its underlying layer; moreover, it must *not* be the delegate of any *other* layer. *Don't do anything to mess this up.* If you do, drawing will stop working correctly.

The view draws into its layer, and the layer caches that drawing; the layer can then be manipulated, changing the view's appearance, without necessarily asking the view to redraw itself. This is a source of great efficiency in the drawing system. It also explains such phenomena as the content stretching that we encountered in the last section of Chapter 2: when the view's bounds size changes, the drawing system, by default, simply stretches or repositions the cached layer image, until such time as the view is told to draw freshly (drawRect:), replacing the layer's content.

Layers and Sublayers

A layer can have sublayers, and a layer has at most one superlayer. Thus there is a tree of layers. This is similar and parallel to the tree of views (Chapter 1). In fact, so tight is the integration between a view and its underlying layer that these hierarchies are effectively the same hierarchy. Given a view and its underlying layer, that layer's superlayer

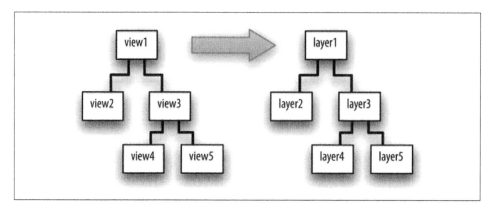

Figure 3-2. A hierarchy of views and the hierarchy of layers underlying it

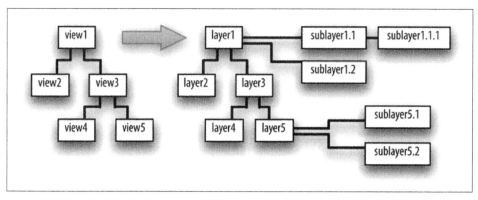

Figure 3-3. Layers that have sublayers of their own

is the view's superview's underlying layer, and that layer has as sublayers all the underlying layers of all the view's subviews. Indeed, because the layers are how the views actually get drawn, one might say that the view hierarchy really *is* a layer hierarchy (Figure 3-2).

At the same time, the layer hierarchy can go beyond the view hierarchy. A view has exactly one underlying layer, but a layer can have sublayers that are not the underlying layers of any view. So the hierarchy of layers that underlie views exactly matches the hierarchy of views, but the total layer tree may be a superset of that hierarchy. In Figure 3-3, we see the same view-and-layer hierarchy as in Figure 3-2, but two of the layers have additional sublayers that are theirs alone (that is, sublayers that are not any view's underlying layers).

From a visual standpoint, there may be nothing to distinguish a hierarchy of views from a hierarchy of layers. For example, in Chapter 1 we drew three overlapping rectangles

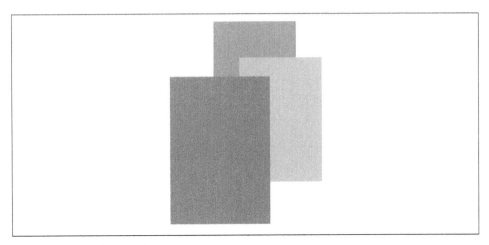

Figure 3-4. Overlapping layers

using a hierarchy of views (Figure 1-1). This code gives exactly the same visible display by manipulating layers (Figure 3-4):

```
let lay1 = CALayer()
lay1.backgroundColor = UIColor(red: 1, green: 0.4, blue: 1, alpha: 1).CGColor
lay1.frame = CGRectMake(113, 111, 132, 194)
mainview.layer.addSublayer(lay1)
let lay2 = CALayer()
lay2.backgroundColor = UIColor(red: 0.5, green: 1, blue: 0, alpha: 1).CGColor
lay2.frame = CGRectMake(41, 56, 132, 194)
lay1.addSublayer(lay2)
let lay3 = CALayer()
lay3.backgroundColor = UIColor(red: 1, green: 0, blue: 0, alpha: 1).CGColor
lay3.frame = CGRectMake(43, 197, 160, 230)
mainview.layer.addSublayer(lay3)
```

A view's subview's underlying layer is a sublayer of that view's underlaying layer, just like any other sublayers of that view's underlying layer. Therefore, it can be positioned anywhere among them in the drawing order. The fact that a view can be interspersed among the sublayers of its superview's underlying layer is surprising to beginners. For example, let's construct Figure 3-4 again, but between adding lay2 and lay3 to the interface, we'll add a subview:

```
// ...
lay1.addSublayer(lay2)
let iv = UIImageView(image:UIImage(named:"smiley"))
mainview.addSubview(iv)
iv.frame.origin = CGPointMake(180,180)
let lay3 = CALayer() // the red rectangle
// ...
```

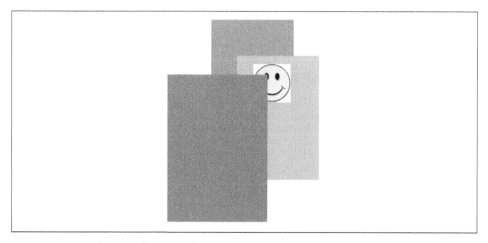

Figure 3-5. Overlapping layers and a view

The result is Figure 3-5. The smiley face was added to the interface before the red (left) rectangle, so it appears behind that rectangle. By reversing the order in which the red rectangle (lay3) and the smiley face (iv) are added to the interface, the smiley face can be made to appear in front of that rectangle. The smiley face is a *view*, whereas the rectangle is just a *layer*; so they are not siblings as views, since the rectangle is not a view. But the smiley face is both a view and its layer; as layers, the smiley face and the rectangle *are* siblings, since they have the same superlayer, so either one can be made to appear in front of the other.

Whether a layer displays regions of its sublayers that lie outside that layer's own bounds depends upon the value of its masksToBounds property. This is parallel to a view's clipsToBounds property, and indeed, for a layer that is its view's underlying layer, they are the same thing. In Figures 3-4 and 3-5, the layers all have clipsToBounds set to false (the default); that's why the right layer is visible beyond the bounds of the middle layer, which is its superlayer.

Like a UIView, a CALayer has a hidden property that can be set to take it and its sublayers out of the visible interface without actually removing it from its superlayer.

Manipulating the Layer Hierarchy

Layers come with a full set of methods for reading and manipulating the layer hierarchy, parallel to the methods for reading and manipulating the view hierarchy. A layer has a superlayer property and a sublayers property, along with these methods:

- addSublayer:
- insertSublayer:atIndex:

- `insertSublayer:below:`, `insertSublayer:above:`
- `replaceSublayer:with:`
- `removeFromSuperlayer`

Unlike a view's `subviews` property, a layer's `sublayers` property is writable; thus, you can give a layer multiple sublayers in a single move, by assigning to its `sublayers` property. To remove all of a layer's sublayers, set its `sublayers` property to `nil`.

Although a layer's sublayers have an order, reflected in the `sublayers` order and regulated with the methods I've just mentioned, this is not necessarily the same as their back-to-front drawing order. By default, it is, but a layer also has a `zPosition` property, a CGFloat, and this also determines drawing order. The rule is that all sublayers with the same `zPosition` are drawn in the order they are listed among their `sublayers` siblings, but lower `zPosition` siblings are drawn before higher `zPosition` siblings. (The default `zPosition` is `0.0`.)

Sometimes, the `zPosition` property is a more convenient way of dictating drawing order than sibling order is. For example, if layers represent playing cards laid out in a solitaire game, it will likely be a lot easier and more flexible to determine how the cards overlap by setting their `zPosition` than by rearranging their sibling order. Moreover, a subview's layer is itself just a layer, so you can rearrange the drawing order of subviews by setting the `zPosition` of their underlying layers. In our code constructing Figure 3-5, if we assign the image view's underlying layer a `zPosition` of 1, it is drawn in front of the red (left) rectangle:

```
mainview.addSubview(iv)
iv.layer.zPosition = 1
```

Methods are also provided for converting between the coordinate systems of layers within the same layer hierarchy:

- `convertPoint:fromLayer:`, `convertPoint:toLayer:`
- `convertRect:fromLayer:`, `convertRect:toLayer:`

Positioning a Sublayer

Layer coordinate systems and positioning are similar to those of views. A layer's own internal coordinate system is expressed by its bounds, just like a view; its size is its bounds size, and its bounds origin is the internal coordinate at its top left.

However, a sublayer's position within its superlayer is not described by its center, like a view; a layer does not have a center. Instead, a sublayer's position within its superlayer is defined by a combination of two properties:

`position`
> A point expressed in the superlayer's coordinate system.

`anchorPoint`
> Where the `position` point is located, with respect to the layer's own bounds. It is a CGPoint describing a fraction (or multiple) of the layer's own bounds width and bounds height. Thus, for example, (0.0,0.0) is the top left of the layer's bounds, and (1.0,1.0) is the bottom right of the layer's bounds.

Here's an analogy; I didn't make it up, but it's pretty apt. Think of the sublayer as pinned to its superlayer; then you have to say both where the pin passes through the sublayer (the `anchorPoint`) and where it passes through the superlayer (the `position`).

If the `anchorPoint` is (0.5,0.5) (the default), the `position` property works like a view's `center` property. A view's `center` is thus a special case of a layer's `position`. This is quite typical of the relationship between view properties and layer properties; the view properties are often a simpler — but less powerful — version of the layer properties.

A layer's `position` and `anchorPoint` are orthogonal (independent); changing one does not change the other. Therefore, changing either of them without changing the other changes where the layer is drawn within its superlayer.

For example, in Figure 3-1, the most important point in the circle is its center; all the other objects need to be positioned with respect to it. Therefore they all have the same `position`: the center of the circle. But they differ in their `anchorPoint`. For example, the arrow's `anchorPoint` is (0.5,0.8), the middle of the shaft, near the tail. On the other hand, the `anchorPoint` of a cardinal point letter is (0.5,3.0), well outside the letter's bounds, so as to place the letter near the edge of the circle.

A layer's `frame` is a purely derived property. When you get the `frame`, it is calculated from the bounds size along with the `position` and `anchorPoint`. When you set the `frame`, you set the bounds size and `position`. In general, you should regard the `frame` as a convenient façade and no more. Nevertheless, it is convenient! For example, to position a sublayer so that it exactly overlaps its superlayer, you can just set the sublayer's `frame` to the superlayer's bounds.

 A layer created in code (as opposed to a view's underlying layer) has a `frame` and bounds of (0.0,0.0,0.0,0.0) and will not be visible on the screen even when you add it to a superlayer that is on the screen. Be sure to give your layer a nonzero width and height if you want to be able to see it. Creating a layer and adding it to a superlayer and then wondering why it isn't appearing in the interface is a common beginner error.

CAScrollLayer

If you're going to be moving a layer's bounds origin as a way of repositioning its sublayers *en masse*, you might like to make the layer a CAScrollLayer, a CALayer subclass that provides convenience methods for this sort of thing. (Despite the name, a CAScrollLayer provides no scrolling interface; the user can't scroll it by dragging, for example.) By default, a CAScrollLayer's `masksToBounds` property is `true`; thus, the CAScrollLayer acts like a window through which you see can only what is within its bounds. (You can set its `masksToBounds` to `false`, but this would be an odd thing to do, as it somewhat defeats the purpose.)

To move the CAScrollLayer's bounds, you can talk either to it or to a sublayer (at any depth):

Talking to the CAScrollLayer
`scrollToPoint:`
> Changes the CAScrollLayer's bounds origin to that point.

`scrollToRect:`
> Changes the CAScrollLayer's bounds origin minimally so that the given portion of the bounds rect is visible.

Talking to a sublayer
`scrollPoint:`
> Changes the CAScrollLayer's bounds origin so that the given point *of the sublayer* is at the top left of the CAScrollLayer.

`scrollRectToVisible:`
> Changes the CAScrollLayer's bounds origin so that the given rect *of the sublayer's bounds* is within the CAScrollLayer's bounds area. You can also ask the sublayer for its `visibleRect`, the part of this sublayer now within the CAScrollLayer's bounds.

Layout of Sublayers

The view hierarchy is actually a layer hierarchy (Figure 3-2). The positioning of a view within its superview is actually the positioning of its layer within its superlayer (the superview's layer). A view can be repositioned and resized automatically in accordance with its `autoresizingMask` or through autolayout based on its constraints. Thus, there is automatic layout for layers *if they are the underlying layers of views*. Otherwise, there is *no* automatic layout for layers in iOS. The only option for layout of sublayers that are not the underlying layers of views is manual layout that you perform in code.

When a layer needs layout, either because its bounds have changed or because you called `setNeedsLayout`, you can respond in either of two ways:

- The layer's `layoutSublayers` method is called; to respond, override `layout-Sublayers` in your CALayer subclass.

- Alternatively, implement `layoutSublayersOfLayer:` in the layer's delegate. (Remember, if the layer is a view's underlying layer, the view is its delegate.)

To do effective manual layout of sublayers, you'll probably need a way to identify or refer to the sublayers. There is no layer equivalent of `viewWithTag:`, so such identification and reference is entirely up to you. Key–value coding can be helpful here; layers implement key–value coding in a special way, discussed at the end of this chapter.

For a view's underlying layer, `layoutSublayers` or `layoutSublayersOfLayer:` is called after the view's `layoutSubviews`. Under autolayout, you must call `super` or else autolayout will break. Moreover, these methods may be called more than once during the course of autolayout; if you're looking for an automatically generated signal that it's time to do manual layout of sublayers, a view layout event might be a better choice (see "View Events Related to Layout" on page 62).

Drawing in a Layer

The simplest way to make something appear in a layer is through its `contents` property. This is parallel to the `image` in a UIImageView (Chapter 2). It is expected to be a CGImage (or `nil`, signifying no image). So, for example, here's how we might modify the code that generated Figure 3-5 in such a way as to generate the smiley face as a layer rather than a view:

```
let lay4 = CALayer()
let im = UIImage(named:"smiley")!
lay4.frame = CGRect(origin:CGPointMake(180,180), size:im.size)
lay4.contents = im.CGImage
mainview.layer.addSublayer(lay4)
```

 Setting a layer's contents to a UIImage, rather than a CGImage, will *fail silently* — the image doesn't appear, but there is no error either. This is absolutely maddening, and I wish I had a nickel for every time I've done it and then wasted hours figuring out why my layer isn't appearing.

There are also four methods that can be implemented to provide or draw a layer's content on demand, similar to a UIView's `drawRect:`. A layer is very conservative about calling these methods (and you must not call any of them directly). When a layer *does* call these methods, I will say that the layer *redisplays itself*. Here is how a layer can be caused to redisplay itself:

- If the layer's `needsDisplayOnBoundsChange` property is `false` (the default), then the only way to cause the layer to redisplay itself is by calling `setNeedsDisplay` (or `setNeedsDisplayInRect:`). Even this might not cause the layer to redisplay itself right away; if that's crucial, then you will also call `displayIfNeeded`.

- If the layer's `needsDisplayOnBoundsChange` property is `true`, then the layer will also redisplay itself when the layer's bounds change (rather like a view's `.Redraw` content mode).

Here are the four methods that can be called when a layer redisplays itself; pick one to implement (don't try to combine them, you'll just confuse things):

`display` *in a subclass*
> Your CALayer subclass can override `display`. There's no graphics context at this point, so `display` is pretty much limited to setting the `contents` image.

`displayLayer:` *in the delegate*
> You can set the CALayer's `delegate` property and implement `displayLayer:` in the delegate. As with `display`, there's no graphics context, so you'll just be setting the `contents` image.

`drawInContext:` *in a subclass*
> Your CALayer subclass can override `drawInContext:`. The parameter is a graphics context into which you can draw directly; it is *not* automatically made the current context.

`drawLayer:inContext:` *in the delegate*
> You can set the CALayer's `delegate` property and implement `drawLayer:in-Context:`. The second parameter is a graphics context into which you can draw directly; it is *not* automatically made the current context.

Assigning a layer a `contents` image and drawing directly into the layer are, in effect, mutually exclusive. So:

- If a layer's `contents` is assigned an image, this image is shown immediately and replaces whatever drawing may have been displayed in the layer.

- If a layer redisplays itself and `drawInContext:` or `drawLayer:inContext:` draws into the layer, the drawing replaces whatever image may have been displayed in the layer.

- If a layer redisplays itself and none of the four methods provides any content, the layer will be empty.

If a layer is a view's underlying layer, you usually won't use any of the four methods to draw into the layer: you'll use the view's `drawRect:`. However, you *can* use these methods

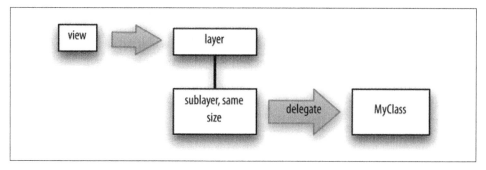

Figure 3-6. A view and a layer delegate that draws into it

if you really want to. In that case, you will probably want to implement `drawRect:` anyway, leaving that implementation empty. The reason is that this causes the layer to redisplay itself at appropriate moments. When a view is sent `setNeedsDisplay` — including when the view first appears — the view's underlying layer is also sent `setNeedsDisplay`, *unless the view has no drawRect: implementation* (because in that case, it is assumed that the view never needs redrawing). So, if you're drawing a view entirely by drawing to its underlying layer directly, and if you want the underlying layer to be redisplayed automatically when the view is told to redraw itself, you should implement `drawRect:` to do nothing. (This technique has no effect on sublayers of the underlying layer.)

Thus, these are legitimate (but unusual) techniques for drawing into a view:

- The view subclass implements an empty `drawRect:`, along with either `displayLayer:` or `drawLayer:inContext:`.
- The view subclass implements an empty `drawRect:` plus `layerClass`, to give the view a custom layer subclass — and the custom layer subclass implements either `display` or `drawInContext:`.

Remember, you must not set the `delegate` property of a view's underlying layer! The view is its delegate and must remain its delegate. A useful architecture for drawing into a layer through a delegate of your choosing is to treat a view as a *layer-hosting* view: the view and its underlying layer do nothing except to serve as a host to a sublayer of the view's underlying layer, which is where the drawing occurs (Figure 3-6).

A layer has a scale, its `contentsScale`, which maps point distances in the layer's graphics context to pixel distances on the device. A layer that's managed by Cocoa, if it has contents, will adjust its `contentsScale` automatically as needed; for example, if a view implements `drawRect:`, then on a device with a double-resolution screen its underlying layer is assigned a `contentsScale` of 2. A layer that you are creating and managing yourself, however, has no such automatic behavior; it's up to you, if you plan to draw into the layer, to set its contentsScale appropriately. Content drawn into a layer with a contentsScale of 1 may appear pixellated or fuzzy on a high-resolution screen. And when you're starting with a UIImage and assigning its CGImage as a layer's contents, if there's a mismatch between the UIImage's scale and the layer's contentsScale, then the image may be displayed at the wrong size.

Three layer properties strongly affect what the layer displays, in ways that can be baffling to beginners:

backgroundColor
> Equivalent to a view's backgroundColor (and if this layer is a view's underlying layer, it *is* the view's backgroundColor). Changing the backgroundColor takes effect immediately. Think of the backgroundColor as separate from the layer's own drawing, and as painted *behind* the layer's own drawing.

opacity
> Affects the overall apparent transparency of the layer. It is equivalent to a view's alpha (and if this layer is a view's underlying layer, it *is* the view's alpha). It affects the apparent transparency of the layer's sublayers as well. It affects the apparent transparency of the background color and the apparent transparency of the layer's content separately (just as with a view's alpha). Changing the opacity property takes effect immediately.

opaque
> Determines whether the layer's graphics context is opaque. An opaque graphics context is black; you can draw on top of that blackness, but the blackness is still there. A non-opaque graphics context is clear; where no drawing is, it is completely transparent. Changing the opaque property has no effect until the layer redisplays itself. A view's underlying layer's opaque property is independent of the view's opaque property; they are unrelated and do entirely different things.

 If a layer is the underlying layer of a view that implements drawRect:, then setting the view's backgroundColor changes the layer's opaque — setting it to true if the new background color is opaque (alpha component of 1), to false otherwise. This is the reason behind the strange behavior of CGContextClearRect described in Chapter 2.

Also, when drawing directly into a *layer*, the behavior of GCContextClearRect differs from what was described in Chapter 2 for drawing into a *view*: instead of punching a hole through the background color, it effectively paints with the layer's background color. (This can have curious side effects.)

I regard all this as deeply weird.

Content Resizing and Positioning

A layer's content is stored (cached) as a bitmap which is then treated like an image and drawn in relation to the layer's bounds in accordance with various layer properties:

- If the content came from setting the layer's `contents` property to an image, the cached content is that image; its size is the point size of the CGImage we started with.

- If the content came from drawing directly into the layer's graphics context (`drawIn-Context:`, `drawLayer:inContext:`), the cached content is the layer's entire graphics context; its size is the point size of the layer itself at the time the drawing was performed.

The layer properties in question cause the cached content to be resized, repositioned, cropped, and so on, as it is displayed. The properties are:

`contentsGravity`

> This property, a string, is parallel to a UIView's `contentMode` property, and describes how the content should be positioned or stretched in relation to the bounds. For example, `kCAGravityCenter` means the content is centered in the bounds without resizing; `kCAGravityResize` (the default) means the content is sized to fit the bounds, even if this means distorting its aspect; and so forth.

 For historical reasons, the terms `Bottom` and `Top` in the names of the `contents-Gravity` settings have the opposite of their expected meanings.

`contentsRect`

> A CGRect expressing the proportion of the content that is to be displayed. The default is (`0.0,0.0,1.0,1.0`), meaning the entire content is displayed. The specified part of the content is sized and positioned in relation to the bounds in accordance with the `contentsGravity`. Thus, for example, by setting the `contentsRect`, you can scale up part of the content to fill the bounds, or slide part of a larger image into view without redrawing or changing the `contents` image.

> You can also use the `contentsRect` to scale down the content, by specifying a larger `contentsRect` such as (`-0.5,-0.5,1.5,1.5`); but any content pixels that touch the edge of the `contentsRect` will then be extended outward to the edge of the layer (to prevent this, make sure that the outermost pixels of the content are all empty).

`contentsCenter`

> A CGRect, structured like `contentsRect`, expressing the central region of nine rectangular regions of the `contentsRect` that are variously allowed to stretch if the

contentsGravity calls for stretching. The central region (the actual value of the contentsCenter) stretches in both directions. Of the other eight regions (inferred from the value you provide), the four corner regions don't stretch, and the four side regions stretch in one direction. (This should remind you of how a resizable image stretches! See Chapter 2.)

If a layer's content comes from drawing directly into its graphics context, then the layer's contentsGravity, of itself, has no effect, because the size of the graphics context, by definition, fits the size of the layer exactly; there is nothing to stretch or reposition. But the contentsGravity *will* have an effect on such a layer if its contentsRect is not (0.0,0.0,1.0,1.0), because now we're specifying a rectangle of some *other* size; the contentsGravity describes how to fit that rectangle into the layer.

Again, if a layer's content comes from drawing directly into its graphics context, then when the layer is resized, if the layer is asked to display itself again, the drawing is performed again, and once more the layer's content fits the size of the layer exactly. But if the layer's bounds are resized when needsDisplayOnBoundsChange is false, then the layer does *not* redisplay itself, so its cached content no longer fits the layer, and the contentsGravity matters.

By a judicious combination of settings, you can get the layer to perform some clever drawing for you that might be difficult to perform directly. For example, Figure 3-7 shows the result of the following settings:

```
arrow.needsDisplayOnBoundsChange = false
arrow.contentsCenter = CGRectMake(0.0, 0.4, 1.0, 0.6)
arrow.contentsGravity = kCAGravityResizeAspect
arrow.bounds.insetInPlace(dx: -20, dy: -20)
```

Because needsDisplayOnBoundsChange is false, the content is not redisplayed when the arrow's bounds are increased; instead, the cached content is used. The contents-Gravity setting tells us to resize proportionally; therefore, the arrow is both longer and wider than in Figure 3-1, but not in such a way as to distort its proportions. However, notice that although the triangular arrowhead is wider, it is not longer; the increase in length is due entirely to the stretching of the arrow's shaft. That's because the contents-Center region is within the shaft.

A layer's masksToBounds property has the same effect on its content that it has on its sublayers. If it is false, the whole content is displayed, even if that content (after taking account of the contentsGravity and contentsRect) is larger then the layer. If it is true, only the part of the content within the layer's bounds will be displayed.

 The value of a layer's bounds origin does not affect where its content is drawn. It affects only where its sublayers are drawn.

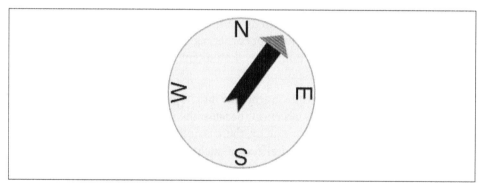

Figure 3-7. One way of resizing the compass arrow

Layers that Draw Themselves

A few built-in CALayer subclasses provide some basic but extremely helpful self-drawing ability:

CATextLayer

A CATextLayer has a `string` property, which can be an NSString or NSAttributed-String, along with other text formatting properties, somewhat like a simplified UILabel; it draws its `string`. The default text color, the `foregroundColor` property, is white, which is unlikely to be what you want. The text is different from the `contents` and is mutually exclusive with it: either the contents image or the text will be drawn, but not both, so in general you should not give a CATextLayer any contents image. In Figures 3-1 and 3-7, the cardinal point letters are CATextLayer instances.

CAShapeLayer

A CAShapeLayer has a `path` property, which is a CGPath. It fills or strokes this path, or both, depending on its `fillColor` and `strokeColor` values, and displays the result; the default is a `fillColor` of black and no `strokeColor`. It has properties for line thickness, dash style, end-cap style, and join style, similar to a graphics context; it also has the remarkable ability to draw only part of its path (`strokeStart` and `strokeEnd`), making it very easy, for example, to draw an arc of an ellipse. A CAShapeLayer may also have `contents`; the shape is displayed on top of the contents image, but there is no property permitting you to specify a compositing mode. In Figures 3-1 and 3-7, the background circle is a CAShapeLayer instance, stroked with gray and filled with a lighter, slightly transparent gray.

CAGradientLayer

A CAGradientLayer covers its background with a simple linear gradient; thus, it's an easy way to draw a gradient in your interface (and if you need something more

Figure 3-8. A gradient drawn behind the compass

elaborate you can always draw with Core Graphics instead). The gradient is defined much as in the Core Graphics gradient example in Chapter 2, an array of locations and an array of corresponding colors, along with a start and end point. To clip the gradient's shape, you can add a mask to the CAGradientLayer (masks are discussed later in this chapter). A CAGradientLayer's contents are not displayed.

Figure 3-8 shows our compass drawn with an extra CAGradientLayer behind it.

Transforms

The way a layer is drawn on the screen can be modified though a transform. This is not surprising, because a view can have a transform (see Chapter 1), and a view is drawn on the screen by its layer. But a layer's transform is more powerful than a view's transform; you can use it to accomplish things that you can't accomplish with a view's transform alone.

In the simplest case, when a transform is two-dimensional, you can access a layer's transform through the affineTransform method (and the corresponding setter, setAffineTransform:). The value is a CGAffineTransform, familiar from Chapters 1 and 2. The transform is applied around the anchorPoint. (Thus, the anchorPoint has a second purpose that I didn't tell you about when discussing it earlier.)

You now know everything needed to understand the code that generated Figure 3-8, so here it is. In this code, self is the CompassLayer; it does no drawing of its own, but merely assembles and configures its sublayers. The four cardinal point letters are each drawn by a CATextLayer; they are drawn at the same coordinates, but they have different rotation transforms, and are anchored so that their rotation is centered at the center of the circle. To generate the arrow, we make ourselves the arrow layer's delegate and call setNeedsDisplay; this causes drawLayer:inContext: to be called in CompassLayer (that code is just the same code we developed for drawing the arrow in Chapter 2, and is not repeated here). The arrow layer is positioned by an `anchorPoint` pinning its tail to the center of the circle, and rotated around that pin by a transform:

```
// the gradient
let g = CAGradientLayer()
g.contentsScale = UIScreen.mainScreen().scale
g.frame = self.bounds
g.colors = [
    UIColor.blackColor().CGColor,
    UIColor.redColor().CGColor
]
g.locations = [0.0,1.0]
self.addSublayer(g)
// the circle
let circle = CAShapeLayer()
circle.contentsScale = UIScreen.mainScreen().scale
circle.lineWidth = 2.0
circle.fillColor = UIColor(red:0.9, green:0.95, blue:0.93, alpha:0.9).CGColor
circle.strokeColor = UIColor.grayColor().CGColor
let p = CGPathCreateMutable()
CGPathAddEllipseInRect(p, nil, CGRectInset(self.bounds, 3, 3))
circle.path = p
self.addSublayer(circle)
circle.bounds = self.bounds
circle.position = self.bounds.center
// the four cardinal points
let pts = "NESW"
for (ix,c) in pts.characters.enumerate() {
    let t = CATextLayer()
    t.contentsScale = UIScreen.mainScreen().scale
    t.string = String(c)
    t.bounds = CGRectMake(0,0,40,40)
    t.position = circle.bounds.center
    let vert = circle.bounds.midY / t.bounds.height
    t.anchorPoint = CGPointMake(0.5, vert)
    t.alignmentMode = kCAAlignmentCenter
    t.foregroundColor = UIColor.blackColor().CGColor
    t.setAffineTransform(
        CGAffineTransformMakeRotation(CGFloat(ix)*CGFloat(M_PI)/2.0))
    circle.addSublayer(t)
}
// the arrow
let arrow = CALayer()
arrow.contentsScale = UIScreen.mainScreen().scale
arrow.bounds = CGRectMake(0, 0, 40, 100)
arrow.position = self.bounds.center
arrow.anchorPoint = CGPointMake(0.5, 0.8)
arrow.delegate = self // we will draw the arrow in the delegate method
arrow.setAffineTransform(CGAffineTransformMakeRotation(CGFloat(M_PI)/5.0))
self.addSublayer(arrow)
arrow.setNeedsDisplay() // draw, please
```

A full-fledged layer transform, the value of the `transform` property, takes place in three-dimensional space; its description includes a z-axis, perpendicular to both the x-axis and y-axis. (By default, the positive z-axis points out of the screen, toward the viewer's face.) Layers do not magically give you realistic three-dimensional rendering — for that you would use OpenGL, which is beyond the scope of this discussion. Layers are two-dimensional objects, and they are designed for speed and simplicity. Nevertheless, they do operate in three dimensions, quite sufficiently to give a cartoonish but effective sense of reality, especially when performing an animation. We've all seen the screen image flip like turning over a piece of paper to reveal what's on the back; that's a rotation in three dimensions.

A three-dimensional transform takes place around a three-dimensional extension of the `anchorPoint`, whose z-component is supplied by the `anchorPointZ` property. Thus, in the reduced default case where `anchorPointZ` is `0.0`, the `anchorPoint` is sufficient, as we've already seen in using CGAffineTransform.

The transform itself is described mathematically by a struct called a CATransform3D. The *Core Animation Function Reference* lists the functions for working with these transforms. They are a lot like the CGAffineTransform functions, except they've got a third dimension. For example, the function for making a 2D scale transform, `CGAffine-TransformMakeScale`, takes two parameters; the function for making a 3D scale transform, `CATransform3DMakeScale`, takes three parameters.

The rotation 3D transform is a little more complicated. In addition to the angle, you also have to supply three coordinates describing the vector around which the rotation is to take place. Perhaps you've forgotten from your high-school math what a vector is, or perhaps trying to visualize three dimensions boggles your mind, so think of it this way.

Pretend for purposes of discussion that the anchor point is the origin, (`0.0,0.0,0.0`). Now imagine an arrow emanating from the anchor point; its other end, the pointy end, is described by the three coordinates you provide. Now imagine a plane that intersects the anchor point, perpendicular to the arrow. That is the plane in which the rotation will take place; a positive angle is a clockwise rotation, as seen from the side of the plane with the arrow (Figure 3-9). In effect, the three coordinates you supply describe (relative to the anchor point) where your eye would have to be to see this rotation as an old-fashioned two-dimensional rotation.

A vector specifies a direction, not a point. Thus it makes no difference on what scale you give the coordinates: (`1.0,1.0,1.0`) means the same thing as (`10.0,10.0,10.0`). If the three values are (`0.0,0.0,1.0`), with all other things being equal, the case is collapsed to a simple CGAffineTransform, because the rotational plane is the screen. If the three values are (`0.0,0.0,-1.0`), it's a backward CGAffineTransform, so that a

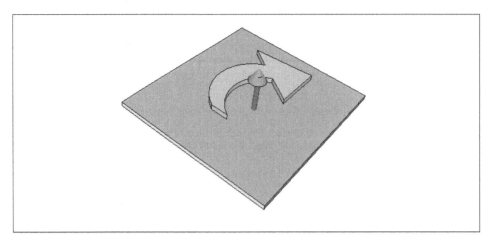

Figure 3-9. An anchor point plus a vector defines a rotation plane

positive angle looks counterclockwise (because we are looking at the "back side" of the rotational plane).

A layer can itself be rotated in such a way that its "back" is showing. For example, the following rotation flips a layer around its y-axis:

```
someLayer.transform = CATransform3DMakeRotation(CGFloat(M_PI), 0, 1, 0)
```

By default, the layer is considered double-sided, so when it is flipped to show its "back," what's drawn is an appropriately reversed version of the content of the layer (along with its sublayers, which by default are still drawn in front of the layer, but reversed and positioned in accordance with the layer's transformed coordinate system). But if the layer's doubleSided property is false, then when it is flipped to show its "back," the layer disappears (along with its sublayers); its "back" is transparent and empty.

Depth

There are two ways to place layers at different nominal depths with respect to their siblings. One is through the z-component of their position, which is the zPosition property. (Thus the zPosition, too, has a second purpose that I didn't tell you about earlier.) The other is to apply a transform that translates the layer's position in the z-direction. These two values, the z-component of a layer's position and the z-component of its translation transform, are related; in some sense, the zPosition is a shorthand for a translation transform in the z-direction. (If you provide both a zPosition and a z-direction translation, you can rapidly confuse yourself.)

In the real world, changing an object's zPosition would make it appear larger or smaller, as it is positioned closer or further away; but this, by default, is not the case in the world

Figure 3-10. A disappointing page-turn rotation

of layer drawing. There is no attempt to portray perspective; the layer planes are drawn at their actual size and flattened onto one another, with no illusion of distance. (This is called *orthographic projection*, and is the way blueprints are often drawn to display an object from one side.)

However, there's a widely used trick for introducing a quality of perspective into the way layers are drawn: make them sublayers of a layer whose `sublayerTransform` property maps all points onto a "distant" plane. (This is probably just about the only thing the `sublayerTransform` property is ever used for.) Combined with orthographic projection, the effect is to apply one-point perspective to the drawing, so that things do get perceptibly smaller in the negative z-direction.

For example, let's try applying a sort of "page-turn" rotation to our compass: we'll anchor it at its right side and then rotate it around the y-axis. Here, the sublayer we're rotating (accessed through a property, `rotationLayer`) is the gradient layer, and the circle and arrow are its sublayers so that they rotate with it:

```
self.rotationLayer.anchorPoint = CGPointMake(1,0.5)
self.rotationLayer.position = CGPointMake(
    self.bounds.maxX, self.bounds.midY)
self.rotationLayer.transform = CATransform3DMakeRotation(
    CGFloat(M_PI)/4.0, 0, 1, 0)
```

The results are disappointing (Figure 3-10); the compass looks more squashed than rotated. Now, however, we'll also apply the distance-mapping transform. The superlayer here is `self`:

```
var transform = CATransform3DIdentity
transform.m34 = -1.0/1000.0
self.sublayerTransform = transform
```

Figure 3-11. A dramatic page-turn rotation

The results (shown in Figure 3-11) are better, and you can experiment with values to replace 1000.0; for example, 500.0 gives an even more exaggerated effect. Also, the zPosition of the rotationLayer will now affect how large it is.

Another way to draw layers with depth is to use CATransformLayer. This CALayer subclass doesn't do any drawing of its own; it is intended solely as a host for other layers. It has the remarkable feature that you can apply a transform to it and it will maintain the depth relationships among its own sublayers. For example:

```
// lay1 is a layer, f is a CGRect
let lay2 = CALayer()
lay2.frame = f
lay2.backgroundColor = UIColor.blueColor().CGColor
lay1.addSublayer(lay2)
let lay3 = CALayer()
lay3.frame = f.offsetBy(dx: 20, dy: 30)
lay3.backgroundColor = UIColor.greenColor().CGColor
lay3.zPosition = 10
lay1.addSublayer(lay3)
lay1.transform = CATransform3DMakeRotation(CGFloat(M_PI), 0, 1, 0)
```

In that code, the superlayer lay1 has two sublayers, lay2 and lay3. The sublayers are added in that order, so lay3 is drawn in front of lay2. Then lay1 is flipped like a page being turned by setting its transform. If lay1 is a normal CALayer, the sublayer drawing order doesn't change; lay3 is *still* drawn in front of lay2, even after the transform is applied. But if lay1 is a CATransformLayer, lay3 is drawn *behind* lay2 after the transform; they are both sublayers of lay1, so their depth relationship is maintained.

Figure 3-12 shows our page-turn rotation yet again, still with the sublayerTransform applied to self, but this time the only sublayer of self is a CATransformLayer:

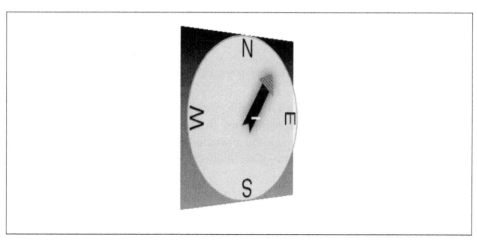

Figure 3-12. Page-turn rotation applied to a CATransformLayer

```
var transform = CATransform3DIdentity
transform.m34 = -1.0/1000.0
self.sublayerTransform = transform
let master = CATransformLayer()
master.frame = self.bounds
self.addSublayer(master)
self.rotationLayer = master
```

The CATransformLayer, to which the page-turn transform is applied, holds the gradient layer, the circle layer, and the arrow layer. Those three layers are at different depths (using different zPosition settings), and I've tried to emphasize the arrow's separation from the circle by adding a shadow (discussed in the next section):

```
circle.zPosition = 10
arrow.shadowOpacity = 1.0
arrow.shadowRadius = 10
arrow.zPosition = 20
```

You can see from its apparent offset that the circle layer floats in front of the gradient layer, but I wish you could see this page-turn as an animation, which makes the circle jump right out from the gradient as the rotation proceeds.

Even more remarkable, I've added a little white peg sticking through the arrow and running into the circle! It is a CAShapeLayer, rotated to be perpendicular to the CATransformLayer (I'll explain the rotation code later in this chapter):

```
let peg = CAShapeLayer()
peg.contentsScale = UIScreen.mainScreen().scale
peg.bounds = CGRectMake(0,0,3.5,50)
let p2 = CGPathCreateMutable()
CGPathAddRect(p2, nil, peg.bounds)
peg.path = p2
```

```
peg.fillColor = UIColor(red:1.0, green:0.95, blue:1.0, alpha:0.95).CGColor
peg.anchorPoint = CGPointMake(0.5,0.5)
peg.position = master.bounds.center
master.addSublayer(peg)
peg.setValue(M_PI/2, forKeyPath:"transform.rotation.x")
peg.setValue(M_PI/2, forKeyPath:"transform.rotation.z")
peg.zPosition = 15
```

In that code, the peg runs straight out of the circle toward the viewer, so it is initially seen end-on, and because a layer has no thickness, it is invisible. But as the CATransformLayer pivots in our page-turn rotation, the peg maintains its orientation relative to the circle, and comes into view. In effect, the drawing portrays a 3D model constructed entirely out of layers.

There is, I think, a slight additional gain in realism if the same sublayerTransform is applied also to the CATransformLayer, but I have not done so here.

Shadows, Borders, and Masks

A CALayer has many additional properties that affect details of how it is drawn. Since these drawing details can be applied to a UIView's underlying layer, they are effectively view features as well.

A CALayer can have a shadow, defined by its shadowColor, shadowOpacity, shadow-Radius, and shadowOffset properties. To make the layer draw a shadow, set the shadowOpacity to a nonzero value. The shadow is normally based on the shape of the layer's nontransparent region, but deriving this shape can be calculation-intensive (so much so that in early versions of iOS, layer shadows weren't implemented). You can vastly improve performance by defining the shape yourself and assigning this shape as a CGPath to the shadowPath property.

 If a layer's masksToBounds is true, no part of its shadow lying outside its bounds is drawn. (This includes the underlying layer of a view whose clipsToBounds is true.) Wondering why the shadow isn't appearing for a layer that masks to its bounds is a common beginner quandary.

A CALayer can have a border (borderWidth, borderColor); the borderWidth is drawn inward from the bounds, potentially covering some of the content unless you compensate.

A CALayer can be bounded by a rounded rectangle, by giving it a cornerRadius greater than zero. If the layer has a border, the border has rounded corners too. If the layer has a backgroundColor, that background is clipped to the shape of the rounded rectangle.

Figure 3-13. A layer with a mask

If the layer's masksToBounds is true, the layer's content and its sublayers are clipped by the rounded corners.

A CALayer can have a mask. This is itself a layer, whose content must be provided somehow. The transparency of the mask's content in a particular spot becomes (all other things being equal) the transparency of the layer at that spot. The mask's colors (hues) are irrelevant; only transparency matters. To position the mask, pretend it's a sublayer.

For example, Figure 3-13 shows our arrow layer, with the gray circle layer behind it, and a mask applied to the arrow layer. The mask is silly, but it illustrates very well how masks work: it's an ellipse, with an opaque fill and a thick, semitransparent stroke. Here's the code that generates and applies the mask:

```
let mask = CAShapeLayer()
mask.frame = arrow.bounds
let path = CGPathCreateMutable()
CGPathAddEllipseInRect(path, nil, CGRectInset(mask.bounds, 10, 10))
mask.strokeColor = UIColor(white:0.0, alpha:0.5).CGColor
mask.lineWidth = 20
mask.path = path
arrow.mask = mask
```

Using a mask, we can do manually and in a more general way what the cornerRadius and masksToBounds properties do. For example, here's a utility method that generates a CALayer suitable for use as a rounded rectangle mask:

```
func maskOfSize(sz:CGSize, roundingCorners rad:CGFloat) -> CALayer {
    let r = CGRect(origin:CGPointZero, size:sz)
    UIGraphicsBeginImageContextWithOptions(r.size, false, 0)
    let con = UIGraphicsGetCurrentContext()!
    CGContextSetFillColorWithColor(
        con, UIColor(white:0, alpha:0).CGColor)
    CGContextFillRect(con, r)
    CGContextSetFillColorWithColor(
        con, UIColor(white:0, alpha:1).CGColor)
    let p = UIBezierPath(roundedRect:r, cornerRadius:rad)
    p.fill()
    let im = UIGraphicsGetImageFromCurrentImageContext()
    UIGraphicsEndImageContext()
    let mask = CALayer()
```

```
            mask.frame = r
            mask.contents = im.CGImage
            return mask
    }
```

The CALayer returned from that method can be placed as a mask anywhere in a layer by adjusting its frame origin and assigning it as the layer's mask. The result is that all of that layer's content drawing and its sublayers (including, if this layer is a view's underlying layer, the view's subviews) are clipped to the rounded rectangle shape; everything outside that shape is not drawn. That's just one example of the sort of thing you can do with a mask. A mask can have values between opaque and transparent, and it can be any shape. And the transparent region doesn't have to be on the outside of the mask; you can use a mask that's opaque on the outside and transparent on the inside to punch a hole in a layer (or a view).

Alternatively, you can apply a mask as a view directly to another view through its maskView property, rather than having to drop down to the level of layers. This may be a notational convenience, but it is not functionally distinct from applying the mask view's layer to the view's layer; under the hood, in fact, it *is* applying the mask view's layer to the view's layer. Thus, for example, it does nothing to solve the problem that the mask is not automatically resized along with the view.

Layer Efficiency

By now, you're probably envisioning all sorts of compositing fun, with layers masking sublayers and laid semitransparently over other layers. There's nothing wrong with that, but when an iOS device is asked to shift its drawing from place to place, the movement may stutter because the device lacks the necessary computing power to composite repeatedly and rapidly. This sort of issue is likely to emerge particularly when your code performs an animation (Chapter 4) or when the user is able to animate drawing through touch, as when scrolling a table view (Chapter 8). You may be able to detect these problems by eye, and you can quantify them on a device by using the Core Animation template in Instruments, which shows the frame rate achieved during animation. Also, both the Core Animation template and the Simulator's Debug menu let you summon colored overlays that provide clues as to possible sources of inefficient drawing which can lead to such problems.

In general, opaque drawing is most efficient. (Nonopaque drawing is what Instruments marks in red as "blended layers.") If a layer will always be shown over a background consisting of a single color, you can give the layer its own background of that same color; when additional layer content is supplied, the visual effect will be the same as if that additional layer content were composited over a transparent background. For example, instead of an image masked to a rounded rectangle (with a layer's cornerRadius or mask property), you could use Core Graphics to clip the drawing of that image to a rounded rectangle shape within the graphics context of a layer whose background color is the same as that of the destination in front of which the drawing will be shown.

Another way to gain some efficiency is by "freezing" the entirety of the layer's drawing as a bitmap. In effect, you're drawing everything in the layer to a secondary cache and using the cache to draw to the screen. Copying from a cache is less efficient than drawing directly to the screen, but this inefficiency may be compensated for, if there's a deep or complex layer tree, by not having to composite that tree every time we render. To do this, set the layer's `shouldRasterize` to `true` and its `rasterizationScale` to some sensible value (probably `UIScreen.mainScreen().scale`). You can always turn rasterization off again by setting `shouldRasterize` to `false`, so it's easy to rasterize just before some massive or sluggish rearrangement of the screen and then unrasterize afterward.

In addition, there's a layer property `drawsAsynchronously`. The default is `false`. If set to `true`, the layer's graphics context accumulates drawing commands and obeys them later on a background thread. Thus, your drawing commands run very quickly, because they are not in fact being obeyed at the time you issue them. I haven't had occasion to use this, but presumably there could be situations where it keeps your app responsive when drawing would otherwise be time-consuming.

Layers and Key–Value Coding

All of a layer's properties are accessible through key–value coding by way of keys with the same name as the property. Thus, to apply a mask to a layer, instead of saying this:

```
layer.mask = mask
```

we could have said:

```
layer.setValue(mask, forKey: "mask")
```

In addition, CATransform3D and CGAffineTransform values can be expressed through key–value coding and key paths. For example, instead of writing this:

```
self.rotationLayer.transform = CATransform3DMakeRotation(
    CGFloat(M_PI)/4.0, 0, 1, 0)
```

we can write this:

```
self.rotationLayer.setValue(M_PI/4, forKeyPath:"transform.rotation.y")
```

This notation is possible because CATransform3D is key–value coding compliant for a repertoire of keys and key paths. These are not properties, however; a CATransform3D doesn't have a `rotation` property. It doesn't have *any* properties, because it isn't even an object. You cannot say:

```
self.rotationLayer.transform.rotation.y = //... No, sorry
```

The transform key paths you'll use most often are:

- `"rotation.x"`, `"rotation.y"`, `"rotation.z"`
- `"rotation"` (same as `"rotation.z"`)
- `"scale.x"`, `"scale.y"`, `"scale.z"`
- `"translation.x"`, `"translation.y"`, `"translation.z"`
- `"translation"` (two-dimensional, a CGSize)

The Quartz Core framework also injects KVC compliance into CGPoint, CGSize, and CGRect, allowing you to use keys and key paths matching their struct component names. For a complete list of KVC compliant classes related to CALayer, along with the keys and key paths they implement, plus rules for how to wrap nonobject values as objects, see "Core Animation Extensions to Key-Value Coding" in Apple's *Core Animation Programming Guide*.

Moreover, you can treat a CALayer as a kind of dictionary, and get and set the value for *any* key. This means you can attach arbitrary information to an individual layer instance and retrieve it later. For example, earlier I mentioned that to apply manual layout to a layer's sublayers, you will need a way of identifying those sublayers. This feature could provide a way of doing that. For example:

```
myLayer1.setValue("Manny", forKey:"name")
myLayer2.setValue("Moe", forKey:"name")
```

A layer doesn't have a `name` property; the `"name"` key is something I'm attaching to these layers arbitrarily. Now I can identify these layers later by getting the value of their respective `"name"` keys.

Also, CALayer has a `defaultValueForKey:` class method; to implement it, you'll need to subclass and override. In the case of keys whose value you want to provide a default for, return that value; otherwise, return the value that comes from calling `super`. Thus, even if a value for a particular key has never been explicitly provided, it can have a non-`nil` value.

The truth is that this feature, though delightful (and I often wish that all classes behaved like this), is not put there for your convenience and enjoyment. It's there to serve as the basis for animation, which is the subject of the next chapter.

CHAPTER 4

Animation

Animation is the visible change of an attribute over time. The changing attribute might be positional: something moves or changes size. But other kinds of attribute can animate as well. For example, a view's background color might change from red to green, not instantly, but perceptibly fading from one to the other. Or a view might change from opaque to transparent, not instantly, but perceptibly fading away.

Without help, most of us would find animation beyond our reach. There are just too many complications — complications of calculation, of timing, of screen refresh, of threading, and many more. Fortunately, help is provided. You don't perform an animation yourself; you describe it, you order it, and it is performed for you. You get *animation on demand*.

Asking for an animation can be as simple as setting a property value; under some circumstances, a single line of code will result in animation:

```
myLayer.backgroundColor = UIColor.redColor().CGColor // animate to red
```

And this is no coincidence. Apple wants to facilitate your use of animation. Animation is crucial to the character of the iOS interface. It isn't just cool and fun; it clarifies that something is changing or responding. For example, one of my first apps was based on an OS X game in which the user clicks cards to select them. In the OS X version, a card was highlighted to show it was selected, and the computer would beep to indicate a click on an ineligible card. On iOS, these indications were insufficient: the highlighting felt weak, and you can't use a sound warning in an environment where the user might have the volume turned off or be listening to music. So in the iOS version, animation is the indicator for card selection (a selected card waggles eagerly) and for tapping on an ineligible card (the whole interface shudders, as if to shrug off the tap).

(If you're looking to create a complete constantly running animated world, as for certain types of game, look into Sprite Kit. This book doesn't discuss Sprite Kit, but an understanding of the concepts in this chapter will prepare you very well for Sprite Kit.)

The Simulator's Debug → Toggle Slow Animations menu item helps you inspect animations by making them run more slowly.

Drawing, Animation, and Threading

When you change a visible view property, that change does *not* visibly take place there and then. Rather, the system records that this is a change you would like to make, and marks the view as needing to be redrawn. Later, when all your code has run to completion and the system has, as it were, a free moment, then it redraws all views that need redrawing, applying their new visible property features. Let's call this the *redraw moment*. (I'll explain what the redraw moment really is later in this chapter.)

You can see that this is true simply by changing some visible aspect of a view and changing it back again, in the same code: on the screen, nothing happens. For example, suppose a view's background color is green, and that your code changes it to red, and then later changes it back to green:

```
// view starts out green
view.backgroundColor = UIColor.redColor()
// ... time-consuming code goes here ...
view.backgroundColor = UIColor.greenColor()
// code ends, redraw moment arrives
```

The system accumulates all the desired changes until the redraw moment happens, and the redraw moment doesn't happen until after your code has finished, so when the redraw moment does happen, the last accumulated change in the view's color is to green — which is its color already. Thus, no matter how much time-consuming code lies between the color changes, the user won't see any color change at all.

Animation works the same way, and is part of the same process. When you ask for an animation to be performed, the animation doesn't start happening on the screen until the next redraw moment. (You can force an animation to start immediately, but this is unusual.)

The animation mechanism itself is an ingenious illusion. Think of the animation as a kind of movie, a cartoon, interposed between the user and the "real" screen. While the animation lasts, this movie is superimposed onto the screen. When the animation is finished, the movie is removed, revealing the state of the "real" screen behind it. The user is unaware of all this, because (if you've done things correctly) at the time that it starts, the movie's first frame looks just like the state of the "real" screen at that moment, and at the time that it ends, the movie's last frame looks just like the state of the "real" screen at *that* moment.

So, when you animate a view's movement from position 1 to position 2, you can envision a typical sequence of events like this:

1. You reposition the view. The view is now set to position 2, but there has been no redraw moment, so it is still portrayed at position 1.

2. You order an animation of the view from position 1 to position 2.

3. The rest of your code runs to completion.

4. The redraw moment arrives. If there were no animation, the view would now suddenly be portrayed at position 2. But there *is* an animation, and so the "animation movie" appears. It starts with the view portrayed at position 1, so that is still what the user sees.

5. The animation proceeds, portraying the view at intermediate positions between position 1 and position 2. (The documentation describes the animation as now *in-flight*.)

6. The animation ends, portraying the view ending up at position 2.

7. The "animation movie" is removed, revealing the view indeed at position 2 — where you put it in the first step.

Realizing that the "animation movie" is different from what happens to the *real* view is key to configuring an animation correctly. A frequent complaint of beginners is that a position animation is performed as expected, but then, at the end, the view "jumps" to some other position. This happens because you set up the animation but failed to move the view to match its final position in the "animation movie"; the "jump" happens because, when the "movie" is whipped away at the end of the animation, the real situation that's revealed doesn't match the last frame of the "movie."

There isn't really an "animation movie" in front of the screen — but it's a good analogy, and the effect is much the same. In reality, it is not a layer itself that is portrayed on the screen; it's a derived layer called the *presentation layer*. Thus, when you animate the change of a view's position or a layer's position from position 1 to position 2, its nominal position changes immediately; meanwhile, the presentation layer's position remains unchanged until the redraw moment, and then changes over time, and because that's what's actually drawn on the screen, that's what the user sees.

(A layer's presentation layer can be accessed through its `presentationLayer` method — and the layer itself may be accessed through the presentation layer's `modelLayer` method. I'll give examples, in this chapter and the next, of situations where accessing the presentation layer is a useful thing to do.)

Like a real movie (especially an old-fashioned animated cartoon), an "animation movie" has "frames." An animated value does not change smoothly and continuously; it changes in small, individual increments that give the *illusion* of smooth, continuous change. This illusion works because the device itself undergoes a periodic, rapid, more or less regular screen refresh, and the incremental changes are made to fall between these refreshes. Apple calls the system component responsible for this the *animation server*.

The animation server operates on an independent thread. You don't have to worry about the details (thank heavens, because multithreading is generally rather tricky and complicated), but you can't ignore it either. Your code runs independently of and possibly simultaneously with the animation — that's what multithreading means — so communication between the animation and your code can require some planning.

Arranging for your code to be notified when an animation ends is a common need. Most of the animation APIs provide a way to set up such a notification. One use of an "animation ended" notification might be to chain animations together: one animation ends and then another begins, in sequence. Another use is to perform some sort of cleanup. A very frequent kind of cleanup has to do with handling of touches: while an animation is in-flight, if your code is not running, the interface by default is responsive to the user's touches, which might cause all kinds of havoc as your views try to respond while the animation is still happening and the screen presentation doesn't match reality. To take care of this, it's common practice to turn off your app's responsiveness to touches as you set up an animation and then turn it back on when you're notified that the animation is over.

Since your code can run even after you've set up an animation, or might start running while an animation is in-flight, you need to be careful about setting up conflicting animations. Multiple animations can be set up (and performed) simultaneously, but trying to animate or change a property that's already in the middle of being animated may be an incoherency. You'll want to take care not to let your animations step on each other's feet accidentally.

Outside forces can interrupt your animations. The user might click the Home button to send your app to the background, or an incoming phone call might arrive while an animation is in-flight. The system deals coherently with this situation by simply canceling all in-flight animations when an app is backgrounded; you've already arranged *before* the animation for your views to assume the final states they will have *after* the animation, so no harm is done — when your app resumes, everything is in that final state you arranged beforehand. But if you wanted your app to resume an animation in the middle, where it left off when it was interrupted, that would require some canny coding on your part.

Image View and Image Animation

UIImageView provides a form of animation so simple as to be scarcely deserving of the name; still, sometimes it might be all you need. You supply the UIImageView with an array of UIImages, as the value of its `animationImages` or `highlightedAnimation-Images` property. This array represents the "frames" of a simple cartoon; when you send the `startAnimating` message, the images are displayed in turn, at a frame rate determined by the `animationDuration` property, repeating as many times as specified by the `animationRepeatCount` property (the default is 0, meaning to repeat forever), or until the stopAnimating message is received. Before and after the animation, the image view continues displaying its image (or highlightedImage).

For example, suppose we want an image of Mars to appear out of nowhere and flash three times on the screen. This might seem to require some sort of NSTimer-based solution, but it's far simpler to use an animating UIImageView:

```
let mars = UIImage(named: "Mars")!
UIGraphicsBeginImageContextWithOptions(mars.size, false, 0)
let empty = UIGraphicsGetImageFromCurrentImageContext()!
UIGraphicsEndImageContext()
let arr = [mars, empty, mars, empty, mars]
let iv = UIImageView(image:empty)
iv.frame.origin = CGPointMake(100,100)
self.view.addSubview(iv)
iv.animationImages = arr
iv.animationDuration = 2
iv.animationRepeatCount = 1
iv.startAnimating()
```

You can combine UIImageView animation with other kinds of animation. For example, you could flash the image of Mars while at the same time sliding the UIImageView rightward, using view animation as described in the next section.

UIImage supplies a form of animation parallel to that of UIImageView: an image can itself be an *animated image*. Just as with UIImageView, this really means that you've prepared multiple images that form a sequence serving as the "frames" of a simple cartoon. You can create an animated image with one of these UIImage class methods:

animatedImageWithImages:duration:
> As with UIImageView's animationImages, you supply an array of UIImages. You also supply the duration for the whole animation.

animatedImageNamed:duration:
> You supply the name of a single image file, as with init(named:), with no file extension. The runtime appends "0" (or, if that fails, "1") to the name you supply and makes *that* image file the first image in the animation sequence. Then it increments the appended number, gathering images and adding them to the sequence (until there are no more, or we reach "1024").

animatedResizableImageNamed:capInsets:resizingMode:duration:
> Combines an animated image with a resizable image (Chapter 2).

You do not tell an animated image to start animating, nor are you able to tell it how long you want the animation to repeat. Rather, an animated image is *always animating*, repeating its sequence once every duration seconds, so long as it appears in your interface; to control the animation, add the image to your interface or remove it from the interface, possibly exchanging it for a similar image that isn't animated.

An animated image can appear in the interface anywhere a UIImage can appear as a property of some interface object. In this example, I construct a sequence of red circles of different sizes, in code, and build an animated image which I then display in a UIButton:

```
var arr = [UIImage]()
let w : CGFloat = 18
for i in 0 ..< 6 {
    UIGraphicsBeginImageContextWithOptions(CGSizeMake(w,w), false, 0)
    let con = UIGraphicsGetCurrentContext()!
    CGContextSetFillColorWithColor(con, UIColor.redColor().CGColor)
    let ii = CGFloat(i)
    CGContextAddEllipseInRect(con, CGRectMake(0+ii,0+ii,w-ii*2,w-ii*2))
    CGContextFillPath(con)
    let im = UIGraphicsGetImageFromCurrentImageContext()
    UIGraphicsEndImageContext()
    arr += [im]
}
let im = UIImage.animatedImageWithImages(arr, duration:0.5)
b.setImage(im, forState:.Normal) // b is a button in the interface
```

View Animation

All animation is ultimately layer animation, which I'll discuss later in this chapter. However, for a limited range of properties, you can animate a UIView directly: these are its alpha, bounds, center, frame, transform, and (if the view doesn't implement drawRect:) backgroundColor. You can also animate a UIView's change of contents. This list of animatable features, despite its brevity, will often prove quite sufficient.

The syntax for animating a UIView involves calling a UIView class method and expressing the desired animation in a function that you pass as an argument. Such a function corresponds to an Objective-C *block*, so the documentation refers to this as *block-based animation*, and I will use phrases such as "animation block" or "animations: block" even though "block" is not the official Swift term for such a construct.

For example, suppose we have a UIView self.v in the interface, with a yellow background color, and we want to animate that view's change of background color to red. This will do it:

```
UIView.animateWithDuration(0.4, animations: {
    self.v.backgroundColor = UIColor.redColor()
})
```

Any animatable change made within an animations: block will be animated, so we can animate a change both in the view's color and in its position simultaneously:

```
UIView.animateWithDuration(0.4, animations: {
    self.v.backgroundColor = UIColor.redColor()
    self.v.center.y += 100
})
```

We can also animate changes to multiple views within the same animations: block. For example, suppose we want to make one view dissolve into another. We start with the second view present in the view hierarchy, but with an alpha of 0, so that it is invisible. Then we animate the change of the first view's alpha to 0 and the second view's alpha to 1.

In that case, we might like to place the second view in the view hierarchy just before the animation starts (invisibly, because its alpha starts at 0) and remove the first view just after the animation ends (invisibly, because its alpha ends at 0). An additional parameter, completion:, lets us specify what should happen after the animation ends:

```
let v2 = // ... create and configure new view here ...
v2.alpha = 0
self.v.superview!.addSubview(v2)
UIView.animateWithDuration(0.4, animations: {
    self.v.alpha = 0
    v2.alpha = 1
    }, completion: {
        _ in
        self.v.removeFromSuperview()
})
```

 Another way to remove a view from the view hierarchy with animation is to call performSystemAnimation:onViews:options:animations:completion: with a first argument .Delete (the only possible first argument). This causes the view to blur, shrink, and fade, and sends it removeFromSuperview() afterward.

Code that isn't about animatable view properties can appear in an animations: block with no problem, but we must be careful to keep any changes to animatable properties that we do *not* want animated out of the animations: block. In the preceding example, in setting v2.alpha to 0, I just want to set it right now, instantly; I don't want that change to be animated. So I've put that line before the animations: block.

Sometimes, though, that's not so easy; perhaps, within the animations: block, we must call a method that might perform animatable changes. The performWithoutAnimation: method solves the problem; it goes inside an animations: block, but whatever happens in *its* block is *not* animated. In this rather artificial example, the view jumps to its new position and then slowly turns red:

```
UIView.animateWithDuration(0.4, animations: {
    self.v.backgroundColor = UIColor.redColor()
    UIView.performWithoutAnimation {
        self.v.center.y += 100
    }
})
```

The material inside an `animations:` block (but not inside a `performWithoutAnimation:` block) *orders* the animation — that is, it gives instructions for what the animation will be when the redraw moment comes. If you change an animatable view property as part of the animation, you should not change that property again afterward; the results can be confusing. This code, for example, is essentially incoherent:

```
UIView.animateWithDuration(2, animations: {
    self.v.center.y += 100
})
self.v.center.y += 300
```

What actually happens is that the view *jumps* 300 points down and then *animates* 100 points further down. That's probably not what you intended. After you've ordered an animatable view property to be animated inside an `animations:` block, *don't change that view property's value again* until after the animation is over.

On the other hand, this code does a smooth single animation to a position 400 points further down:

```
UIView.animateWithDuration(2, animations: {
    self.v.center.y += 100
    self.v.center.y += 300
})
```

That's because basic positional view animations are *additive* by default (in iOS 8 and later). This means that the second animation is run simultaneously with the first, and is blended with it.

 New in iOS 9, a UIVisualEffectView is animatable in the same ways as a regular UIView. What's more, setting a UIVisualEffectView's `effect` is animatable! Thus, for example, you can blur with animation by starting with a UIVisualEffectView whose `effect` is `nil` and then setting its `effect` to a UIBlurEffect inside an `animations:` block.

View Animation Options

The UIView class methods `animateWithDuration:` and `animateWithDuration:completion:` are both reduced forms. The full form of this method, which you should use whenever you need the maximum in flexibility and power, is `animateWithDuration:delay:options:animations:completion:`. The parameters are:

duration

The duration of the animation: how long it takes (in seconds) to run from start to finish. You can also think of this as the animation's speed. Obviously, if two views are told to move different distances in the same time, the one that must move further must move faster.

delay

The delay before the animation starts. The default is no delay. A delay is *not* the same as applying the animation using delayed performance; the animation is applied immediately, but when it starts running it spins its wheels, with no visible change, until the delay time has elapsed.

options

A bitmask combining additional options.

animations

The block containing view property changes to be animated.

completion

The block to run when the animation ends (or nil). It takes one Bool parameter indicating whether the animation ran to completion. The block is called, with a parameter indicating true, even if nothing in the animations: block triggers any animations. It's fine for this block to order a further animation, thus chaining animations.

Here are some of the chief options: values (UIViewAnimationOptions) that you might wish to use:

Animation curve

An animation curve describes how the animation changes speed during its course. The term "ease" means that there is a gradual acceleration or deceleration between the animation's central speed and the zero speed at its start or end. Specify one at most:

- .CurveEaseInOut (the default)
- .CurveEaseIn
- .CurveEaseOut
- .CurveLinear (constant speed throughout)

.Repeat

If included, the animation will repeat indefinitely. There is no way, as part of this command, to specify a certain number of repetitions; you ask either to repeat forever or not at all. This feels like an oversight (a serious oversight); I'll suggest a workaround in a moment.

.Autoreverse

> If included, the animation will run from start to finish (in the given duration time), and will then run from finish to start (also in the given duration time). The documentation's claim that you can autoreverse only if you also repeat is incorrect; you can use either or both (or neither).

When using .Autoreverse, you will want to clean up at the end so that the view is back in its original position when the animation is over. To see what I mean, consider this code:

```
let opts = UIViewAnimationOptions.Autoreverse
UIView.animateWithDuration(1, delay: 0, options: opts, animations: {
    self.v.center.x += 100
    }, completion: nil)
```

The view animates 100 points to the right and then animates 100 points back to its original position — and then *jumps* 100 points *back to the right*. The reason is that the last actual value we assigned to the view's center x is 100 points to the right, so when the animation is over and the "animation movie" is whipped away, the view is revealed still sitting 100 points to the right. The solution is to move the view back to its original position in the completion: handler:

```
let opts = UIViewAnimationOptions.Autoreverse
let xorig = self.v.center.x
UIView.animateWithDuration(1, delay: 0, options: opts, animations: {
    self.v.center.x += 100
    }, completion: {
        _ in
        self.v.center.x = xorig
})
```

Working around the inability to specify a finite number of repetitions is tricky. One solution is to resort to an outmoded animation syntax:

```
let count = 3
UIView.animateWithDuration(1, delay: 0, options: opts, animations: {
    UIView.setAnimationRepeatCount(Float(count)) // *
    self.v.center.x += 100
    }, completion: {
        _ in
        self.v.center.x = xorig
})
```

I regard this as unfortunate. The setAnimationRepeatCount method is part of a completely different animation syntax — the "begin/commit" syntax — which was superseded by the block-based syntax back in iOS 4, and whose use Apple has subsequently discouraged (which is why I don't discuss it in this book). Yet Apple also treats it as the official way to order a limited number of view animation repetitions. It would have been better to add a repeat count parameter, and in Appendix B I extend UIView with a class method that does exactly that.

There are also some options saying what should happen if another animation is already ordered or in-flight:

.BeginFromCurrentState
> If this animation animates a property already being animated by an animation that is previously ordered or in-flight, then instead of canceling the previous animation (completing the requested change instantly), if that is what would normally happen, this animation will use the presentation layer to decide where to start, and, if possible, will "blend" its animation with the previous animation.

.OverrideInheritedDuration
> Prevents inheriting the duration from a surrounding or in-flight animation (the default is to inherit it).

.OverrideInheritedCurve
> Prevents inheriting the animation curve from a surrounding or in-flight animation (the default is to inherit it).

You will have less need for .BeginFromCurrentState than in iOS 7 and before, because, as I've already said, simple view animations are additive by default in iOS 8 and later. This code, for example, caused a jump in iOS 7 unless you used .BeginFromCurrent-State (because we're ordering two conflicting animations of the view's position), but is a single smooth diagonal animation in iOS 8 and later:

```
UIView.animateWithDuration(1, animations: {
    self.v.center.x += 100
})
UIView.animateWithDuration(1, animations: {
    self.v.center.y += 100
})
```

To see what it means for animations to be additive, try this code:

```
UIView.animateWithDuration(2, animations: {
    self.v.center.x += 100
})
delay(1) {
    let opts = UIViewAnimationOptions.BeginFromCurrentState
    UIView.animateWithDuration(1, delay: 0, options: opts,
        animations: {
            self.v.center.y += 100
        }, completion: nil)
}
```

The second animation launches under delayed performance halfway through the first animation. When the second animation starts, the view turns the corner in a gentle curve, with some residual horizontal motion from the first animation.

Canceling a View Animation

Once a view animation is in-flight, how can you cancel it? To illustrate the problem, I'll start with a simple unidirectional positional animation, with a long duration so that we can interrupt it in midflight. To facilitate the explanation, I'll conserve both the view's original position and its final position in properties:

```
self.pOrig = self.v.center
self.pFinal = self.v.center
self.pFinal.x += 100
UIView.animateWithDuration(4, animations: {
    self.v.center = self.pFinal
})
```

Now imagine that we have a button that we can tap during that animation, and that this button is supposed to cancel the animation. How can we do that?

One possibility is to reach down to the CALayer level and call `removeAllAnimations`. (If the layer has more than one animation and you want to cancel only one of them, you can call `removeAnimationForKey:`; I'll talk later in this chapter about how to distinguish layer animations by key.) This has the advantage of simplicity, but the disadvantage that it simply stops the animation dead: the "animation movie" is whipped away instantly, "jumping" the view to its final position, effectively doing what the system does automatically when the app goes into the background:

```
self.v.layer.removeAllAnimations()
```

Now let's try to devise a more subtle form of cancellation: the view should hurry to its final position. This is not easy to arrange in iOS 8 and later, because animations are additive. We cannot merely impose another animation that moves the view to its final position with a short duration, because this doesn't cancel the existing animation. Therefore we must remove the first animation manually. We already know how to do that: call `removeAllAnimations`. But we also know that if we do that, the view will jump to its final position; we want it to remain, for the moment, at its current position — meaning *the animation's* current position. That position is where the presentation layer currently is. Therefore we reposition the view at the location of its presentation layer, and *then* remove the animation, and *then* perform the final "hurry home" animation:

```
self.v.layer.position =
    (self.v.layer.presentationLayer() as! CALayer).position
self.v.layer.removeAllAnimations()
UIView.animateWithDuration(0.1, animations: {
    self.v.center = self.pFinal
})
```

If cancellation means returning the view to its original position, set the view's `center` to `self.pOrig` instead of `self.pFinal`. If it means just stopping wherever we happen to be, then omit the final animation.

Now let's suppose that the animation we want to cancel is an infinitely repeating autoreversing animation:

```
self.pOrig = self.v.center
let opts : UIViewAnimationOptions = [.Autoreverse, .Repeat]
UIView.animateWithDuration(1, delay: 0, options: opts,
    animations: {
        self.v.center.x += 100
    }, completion: nil)
```

In that case, it *is* sufficient to impose another animation, because the new animation is *not* additive with the first one. Only *simple* view animations are additive; I have not elaborated on what "simple" means, but one thing it means is "not repeating." Thus, the second animation cancels the first. Here's how to cancel that animation by returning it rapidly to its original position:

```
UIView.animateWithDuration(0.1, delay:0,
    options:.BeginFromCurrentState,
    animations: {
        self.v.center = self.pOrig
    }, completion:nil)
```

This is a situation where the `.BeginFromCurrentState` option is useful! It is needed to prevent the view from jumping momentarily to the "final" position, 100 points to the right, to which we set it to initiate the repeating animation.

(If you object that storage of the view's original or final position as a view controller property is not a very encapsulated solution, then consider storing it instead in the view's layer using key–value coding. The implementation is left as an exercise for the reader. Hint: a CGPoint will need to be wrapped in an NSValue.)

Custom Animatable View Properties

You can define your own custom view property that can be animated by changing it in an animation block, provided the custom view property itself changes an animatable view property.

For example, imagine a UIView subclass, MyView, which has a Bool `swing` property. All this does is reposition the view: when `swing` is set to `true`, the view's center x value is increased by 100; when `swing` is set to `false`, the view's center x value is decreased by 100. A view's `center` is animatable, so we can make a MyView's `swing` property *itself* be animatable.

The trick (which I had never thought of it until an Apple WWDC 2014 video suggested it) is to implement MyView's `swing` setter with a zero-duration animation block. This basically means that there is no animation by default, but if we happen to be inside an animation block already when the `swing` property is set, the setter's animation block inherits the duration of the surrounding animation block — because such inheritance is, as I mentioned earlier, the default:

```
class MyView : UIView {
    var swing : Bool = false {
        didSet {
            var p = self.center
            p.x = self.swing ? p.x + 100 : p.x - 100
            UIView.animateWithDuration(0, animations: {
                self.center = p
                })
        }
    }
}
```

If we now change a MyView's swing directly, the view jumps to its new position. But if we change it in an animation block, the change in position is animated, with the specified duration:

```
UIView.animateWithDuration(1, animations: {
    self.v.swing = !self.v.swing // "animatable" Bool property
})
```

Springing View Animation

A springing view animation has an animation curve with a very fast ease-in and a very slow ease-out; the animation can even oscillate for a while around its final value, as if it were being snapped into place by a spring. To use it, call animateWithDuration:delay: usingSpringWithDamping:initialSpringVelocity:.... For example:

```
UIView.animateWithDuration(0.8, delay: 0,
    usingSpringWithDamping: 0.7,
    initialSpringVelocity: 20,
    options: [],
    animations: {
        self.v.center.y += 100
    }, completion: nil)
```

The damping: and initialSpringVelocity: parameters modify the behavior of the animation curve. If the damping is less than 1, there's a waggle as the animated view assumes its final position; this waggle becomes quite pronounced at values less than about 0.7, and at values like 0.3 there are several waggles before the view settles into place.

The initial spring velocity gives the view an initial "kick," speeding up the initial ease-in and increasing the tendency of the view to overshoot its final position on its first approach. Depending on the duration and damping amount, it may need to be quite large to make an appreciable difference. You can have a lot of waggly fun with smaller damping values and larger initial spring velocity values. Conversely, a small initial spring velocity (about 10 or less) and a high damping (1.0 or close to it) gives a normal animation that wouldn't particularly remind anyone of a spring, but that does have a pleasingly rapid beginning and slow ending; many of Apple's own system animations are actually spring animations of that type (consider, for example, the way folders open in the springboard).

Keyframe View Animation

A view animation can be described as a set of keyframes. This means that, instead of a simple beginning and end point, you specify multiple stages in the animation and those stages are joined together for you. You call animateKeyframesWithDuration:...; it has an animations: block, and inside that block you call addKeyframeWithRelativeStart-Time:relativeDuration:animations: multiple times to specify each stage. Each keyframe's start time and duration is between 0 and 1, *relative to the animation as a whole*. (Giving a keyframe's start time and duration in seconds is a common beginner mistake.)

For example, here I'll waggle a view back and forth horizontally while moving it down the screen vertically:

```
var p = self.v.center
let dur = 0.25
var start = 0.0
let dx : CGFloat = 100
let dy : CGFloat = 50
var dir : CGFloat = 1
UIView.animateKeyframesWithDuration(4,
    delay: 0, options: [],
    animations: {
        UIView.addKeyframeWithRelativeStartTime(start,
            relativeDuration: dur,
            animations: {
                p.x += dx*dir; p.y += dy
                self.v.center = p
        })
        start += dur; dir *= -1
        UIView.addKeyframeWithRelativeStartTime(start,
            relativeDuration: dur,
            animations: {
                p.x += dx*dir; p.y += dy
                self.v.center = p
        })
        start += dur; dir *= -1
        UIView.addKeyframeWithRelativeStartTime(start,
            relativeDuration: dur,
            animations: {
                p.x += dx*dir; p.y += dy
                self.v.center = p
        })
```

```
        start += dur; dir *= -1
        UIView.addKeyframeWithRelativeStartTime(start,
            relativeDuration: dur,
            animations: {
                p.x += dx*dir; p.y += dy
                self.v.center = p
        })
}, completion: nil)
```

In that code, there are four keyframes, evenly spaced: each is 0.25 in duration (one-fourth of the whole animation) and each starts 0.25 later than the previous one (as soon as the previous one ends). In each keyframe, the view's center x value increases or decreases by 100, alternately, while its center y value keeps increasing by 50.

The keyframe values are points in space and time; the actual animation interpolates between them. How this interpolation is done depends upon the options:, which are UIKeyframeAnimationOptions values whose names start with CalculationMode. The default is .CalculationModeLinear. In our example, this means that the path followed by the view is a sharp zig-zag, the view seeming to bounce off invisible walls at the right and left. But if the setting is .CalculationModeCubic, our view describes a smooth S-curve, starting at the view's initial position and ending at the last keyframe point, and passing through the three other keyframe points like the maxima and minima of a sine wave.

Because my keyframes are perfectly even, I could achieve the same effects by using .CalculationModePaced and .CalculationModeCubicPaced, respectively. The Paced options simply ignore the relative start time and relative duration values of the keyframes; you might as well pass 0 for all of them. Instead, they divide up the times and durations evenly, exactly as my code has done.

Finally, .CalculationModeDiscrete means that the changed animatable properties don't animate: the animation jumps to each keyframe.

The outer animations: block can contain other changes to animatable view properties, as long as they don't conflict with the keyframe animations:; these are animated over the total duration. For example:

```
UIView.animateKeyframesWithDuration(4,
    delay: 0, options: [],
    animations: {
        self.v.alpha = 0
        // ...
```

The result is that as the view zigzags back and forth down the screen, it also gradually fades away.

It is also legal and meaningful to supply an animation curve as part of the options: argument. Unfortunately, the documentation fails to make this clear; and Swift's obsessive-compulsive attitude towards data types resists folding a UIViewAnimation-Options animation curve directly into a value typed as a UIViewKeyframeAnimation-Options. Yet if you don't do it, the default is `.CurveEaseInOut`, which may not be what you want. Here's how to combine `.CalculationModeLinear` with `.CurveLinear`:

```
var opts : UIViewKeyframeAnimationOptions = .CalculationModeLinear
let opt2 : UIViewAnimationOptions = .CurveLinear
opts.insert(UIViewKeyframeAnimationOptions(rawValue:opt2.rawValue))
```

That's two different senses of `Linear`. The first means that the path described by the moving view is a sequence of straight lines. The second means that the moving view's speed along that path is steady.

Transitions

A transition is an animation that emphasizes a view's change of content. Transitions are ordered using one of two UIView class methods:

- `transitionWithView:duration:options:animations:completion:`
- `transitionFromView:toView:duration:options:completion:`

The transition animation types are expressed as part of the `options:` bitmask:

- `.TransitionFlipFromLeft`, `.TransitionFlipFromRight`
- `.TransitionCurlUp`, `.TransitionCurlDown`
- `.TransitionFlipFromBottom`, `.TransitionFlipFromTop`
- `.TransitionCrossDissolve`

`transitionWithView:...` performs the transition animation on that view. In this example, a UIImageView containing an image of Mars flips over as its image changes to a smiley face; it looks as if the image view were two-sided, with Mars on one side and the smiley face on the other:

```
let opts : UIViewAnimationOptions = .TransitionFlipFromLeft
UIView.transitionWithView(self.iv, duration: 0.8, options: opts,
    animations: {
        self.iv.image = UIImage(named:"Smiley")
    }, completion: nil)
```

In that example, I've put the content change inside the `animations:` block. That's conventional but misleading; the truth is that if all that's changing is the content, *nothing* needs to go into the `animations:` block. The change of content can be anywhere, before or even after this entire line of code. It's the flip that's being animated. You might use the `animations:` block here to order additional animations, such as a change in a view's center.

You can do the same sort of thing with a custom view that does its own drawing. Let's say that I have a UIView subclass, MyView, that draws either a rectangle or an ellipse depending on the value of its Bool reverse property:

```
class MyView : UIView {
    var reverse = false
    override func drawRect(rect: CGRect)  {
        let f = self.bounds.insetBy(dx: 10, dy: 10)
        let con = UIGraphicsGetCurrentContext()!
        if self.reverse {
            CGContextStrokeEllipseInRect(con, f)
        } else {
            CGContextStrokeRect(con, f)
        }
    }
}
```

This code flips a MyView instance while changing its drawing from a rectangle to an ellipse or *vice versa*:

```
let opts : UIViewAnimationOptions = .TransitionFlipFromLeft
self.v.reverse = !self.v.reverse
UIView.transitionWithView(self.v, duration: 1, options: opts,
    animations: {
        self.v.setNeedsDisplay()
    }, completion: nil)
```

By default, if a view has subviews whose layout changes as part of a transition animation, that change in layout is *not* animated: the layout changes directly to its final appearance when the transition ends. If you want to display a subview of the transitioning view being animated as it assumes its final state, use .AllowAnimatedContent in the options bitmask.

transitionFromView:toView:... names two views; the first is *replaced* by the second, while *their superview* undergoes the transition animation. There are two possible configurations, depending on the options you provide:

Remove one subview, add the other

If .ShowHideTransitionViews is *not* one of the options, then the second subview is not in the view hierarchy when we start; the transition removes the first subview from its superview and adds the second subview to that same superview.

Hide one subview, show the other

If .ShowHideTransitionViews *is* one of the options, then both subviews are in the view hierarchy when we start; the hidden of the first is false, the hidden of the second is true, and the transition reverses those values.

In this example, a label `self.lab` is already in the interface. The animation causes the superview of `self.lab` to flip over, while at the same time a different label, `lab2`, is substituted for the existing label:

```
let lab2 = UILabel(frame:self.lab.frame)
lab2.text = self.lab.text == "Hello" ? "Howdy" : "Hello"
lab2.sizeToFit()
UIView.transitionFromView(self.lab, toView: lab2,
    duration: 0.8, options: .TransitionFlipFromLeft,
    completion: {
        _ in
        self.lab = lab2
})
```

It's up to you to make sure beforehand that the second view (`toView:`) has the desired position, so that it will appear in the right place in its superview.

Implicit Layer Animation

Animating a layer can be as simple as setting a property. A change in what the documentation calls an *animatable property* is *automatically* interpreted as a request to animate that change. In other words, animation of layer property changes is the default! Multiple property changes are considered part of the same animation. This mechanism is called *implicit animation*.

You may be wondering: if implicit animation is the default, why didn't we notice it happening in any of the layer examples in Chapter 3? It's because there are two common situations where implicit layer animation *doesn't* happen:

- Implicit layer animation doesn't operate on a UIView's underlying layer. You can animate a UIView's underlying layer directly, but you must use explicit layer animation (discussed later in this chapter).

- Implicit layer animation doesn't affect a layer as it is being created, configured, and added to the interface. Implicit animation comes into play when you change an animatable property of a layer that is *already* present in the interface.

In Chapter 3 we constructed a compass out of layers. The compass itself is a Compass-View that does no drawing of its own; its underlying layer is a CompassLayer that also does no drawing, serving only as a superlayer for the layers that constitute the drawing. None of the layers that constitute the actual drawing is the underlying layer of a view, so a property change to any of them, once they are established in the interface, is animated automatically.

So, presume that we *have* established all our compass layers in the interface. And suppose we have a reference to the arrow layer (`arrow`). If we rotate the arrow layer simply by changing its `transform` property, *the arrow rotation is animated:*

```
// an implicit animation
arrow.transform = CATransform3DRotate(
    arrow.transform, CGFloat(M_PI)/4.0, 0, 0, 1)
```

CALayer properties listed in the documentation as animatable in this way are anchor-Point and anchorPointZ, backgroundColor, borderColor, borderWidth, bounds, contents, contentsCenter, contentsRect, cornerRadius, doubleSided, hidden, masksToBounds, opacity, position and zPosition, rasterizationScale and should-Rasterize, shadowColor, shadowOffset, shadowOpacity, shadowRadius, and sublayerTransform and transform.

In addition, a CAShapeLayer's path, strokeStart, strokeEnd, fillColor, stroke-Color, lineWidth, lineDashPhase, and miterLimit are animatable; so are a CAText-Layer's fontSize and foregroundColor, and a CAGradientLayer's colors, locations, and endPoint.

Basically, a property is animatable because there's some sensible way to interpolate the intermediate values between one value and another. The nature of the animation attached to each property is therefore generally just what you would intuitively expect. When you change a layer's hidden property, it fades out of view (or into view). When you change a layer's contents, the old contents are dissolved into the new contents. And so forth.

(The fact that a CAShapeLayer's path can be animated is particularly intriguing, and I'll give an example later in this chapter.)

Animation Transactions

Animation operates with respect to a *transaction* (a CATransaction), which collects all animation requests and hands them over to the animation server in a single batch. Every animation request takes place in the context of some transaction. You can make this explicit by wrapping your animation requests in calls to the CATransaction class methods begin and commit; the result is a *transaction block*. Additionally, there is always an *implicit transaction* surrounding your code, and you can operate on this implicit transaction without any begin and commit.

To modify the characteristics of an implicit animation, you modify the transaction that surrounds it. Typically, you'll use these CATransaction class methods:

setAnimationDuration:
> The duration of the animation.

setAnimationTimingFunction:
> A CAMediaTimingFunction; timing functions are discussed in the next section.

setDisableActions:
> Toggles implicit animations for this transaction.

`setCompletionBlock:`
> A block to be called when the animation ends. The block takes no parameters. The block is called even if no animation is triggered during this transaction.

CATransaction also implements KVC to allow you to set and retrieve a value for an arbitrary key, similar to CALayer.

By nesting transaction blocks, you can apply different animation characteristics to different elements of an animation. You can also use transaction commands outside of any transaction block to modify the implicit transaction. So, in our previous example, we could slow down the animation of the arrow like this:

```
CATransaction.setAnimationDuration(0.8)
arrow.transform = CATransform3DRotate(
    arrow.transform, CGFloat(M_PI)/4.0, 0, 0, 1)
```

An important use of transactions is to turn implicit animation *off*. This is valuable because implicit animation is the default, and can be unwanted (and a performance drag). To turn off implicit animation, call `setDisableActions:` with argument `true`. There are other ways to turn off implicit animation (discussed later in this chapter), but this is the simplest.

`setCompletionBlock:` is an extraordinarily useful and probably underutilized tool. The transaction's completion block signals the end, not only of the implicit layer property animations you yourself have ordered as part of this transaction, but of *all* animations ordered during this transaction, including Cocoa's own animations. Thus, it's a way to be notified when any and all animations come to an end.

The "redraw moment" that I've spoken of in connection with drawing, layout, layer property settings, and animation is actually the end of the current transaction. Thus, for example:

- You set a view's background color; the displayed color of the background is changed when the transaction ends.
- You call `setNeedsDisplay`; `drawRect:` is called when the transaction ends.
- You call `setNeedsLayout`; layout happens when the transaction ends.
- You order an animation; the animation starts when the transaction ends.

What's really happening is this. Your code runs within an implicit transaction. Your code comes to an end, and the transaction commits itself. It is then, as part of the transaction commit procedure, that the screen is updated: first layout, then drawing, then obedience to layer property changes, then the start of any animations. The transaction then continues on a background thread, under the guidance of the animation server, while any animations are performed, and finally calls its completion block, if any, when the animations are over.

An explicit transaction block that orders an animation to a layer, if the block is *not preceded by any other changes to the layer*, can cause animation to begin immediately when the CATransaction class method `commit` is called, without waiting for the redraw moment, while your code continues running. In my experience, this can cause trouble (animation delegate messages cannot arrive, and the presentation layer can't be queried properly) and should be avoided.

Media Timing Functions

The CATransaction class method `setAnimationTimingFunction:` takes as its parameter a media timing function (CAMediaTimingFunction). This class is the general expression of the animation curves we have already met (ease-in-out, ease-in, ease-out, and linear), and you can use it with those very same predefined curves, by calling the CAMediaTimingFunction initializer `init(name:)` with one of these parameters:

- `kCAMediaTimingFunctionLinear`
- `kCAMediaTimingFunctionEaseIn`
- `kCAMediaTimingFunctionEaseOut`
- `kCAMediaTimingFunctionEaseInEaseOut`
- `kCAMediaTimingFunctionDefault`

A media timing function is a Bézier curve defined by two points. The curve graphs the fraction of the animation's time that has elapsed (the x-axis) against the fraction of the animation's change that has occurred (the y-axis); its endpoints are therefore at `(0.0,0.0)` and `(1.0,1.0)`, because at the beginning of the animation there has been no elapsed time and no change, and at the end of the animation all the time has elapsed and all the change has occurred.

The curve's defining points are its endpoints, and each endpoint needs only one Bézier control point to define the tangent to the curve. And because the curve's endpoints are known, defining the two control points is sufficient to describe the entire curve. And because a point is a pair of floating-point values, a media timing function can be expressed as four floating-point values. That is, in fact, how it is expressed.

So, for example, the ease-in-out timing function is expressed as the four values `0.42`, `0.0`, `0.58`, `1.0`. That defines a Bézier curve with one endpoint at `(0.0,0.0)`, whose control point is `(0.42,0.0)`, and the other endpoint at `(1.0,1.0)`, whose control point is `(0.58,1.0)` (Figure 4-1).

To define your own media timing function, supply the coordinates of the two control points by calling `init(controlPoints:)`. (It helps to design the curve in a standard drawing program first so that you can visualize how the placement of the control points

---

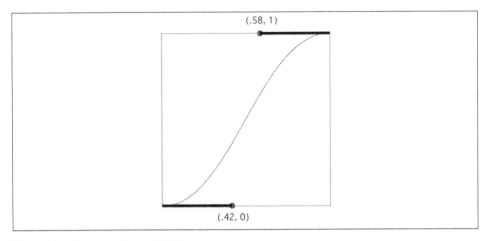

Figure 4-1. An ease-in-out Bézier curve

shapes the curve.) For example, here's a media timing function that starts out quite slowly and then whips quickly into place after about two-thirds of the time has elapsed. I call this the "clunk" timing function, and it looks great with the compass arrow:

```
let clunk = CAMediaTimingFunction(controlPoints: 0.9, 0.1, 0.7, 0.9)
CATransaction.setAnimationTimingFunction(clunk)
arrow.transform = CATransform3DRotate(
    arrow.transform, CGFloat(M_PI)/4.0, 0, 0, 1)
```

Core Animation

Core Animation is the fundamental underlying iOS animation technology. View animation and implicit layer animation are merely convenient façades for Core Animation. Core Animation is *explicit layer animation,* and revolves primarily around the CA Animation class and its subclasses, which allow you to create far more elaborate specifications of an animation than anything we've encountered so far.

You may never program at the level of Core Animation, but you should read this section anyway, if only to learn how animation really works and to get a sense of its mighty powers. In particular:

- Core Animation works even on a view's underlying layer. Thus, Core Animation is the *only* way to apply full-on layer property animation to a view.
- Core Animation permits fine control over the intermediate values and timing of an animation.
- Core Animation allows animations to be grouped into complex combinations.

- Core Animation provides transition animation effects that aren't available otherwise, such as new content "pushing" the previous content out of a layer.

 Animating a view's underlying layer with Core Animation is layer animation, not view animation — so you don't get any automatic layout of that view's subviews. This can be a reason for preferring view animation.

CABasicAnimation and Its Inheritance

The simplest way to animate a property with Core Animation is with a CABasicAnimation object. CABasicAnimation derives much of its power through its inheritance, so I'll describe that inheritance along with CABasicAnimation itself. You will readily see that all the property animation features we have met so far are embodied in a CABasicAnimation instance.

CAAnimation

>   CAAnimation is an abstract class, meaning that you'll only ever use a subclass of it. Some of CAAnimation's powers come from its implementation of the CAMedia-Timing protocol.

`delegate`

>   The delegate messages are `animationDidStart:` and `animationDidStop: finished:`.
>
>   A CAAnimation instance *retains its delegate*; this is very unusual behavior and can cause trouble if you're not conscious of it (I'm speaking from experience). Alternatively, don't set a delegate; to make your code run after the animation ends, call the CATransaction class method `setCompletionBlock:` before configuring the animation.

`duration, timingFunction`

>   The length of the animation, and its timing function (a CAMediaTiming-Function). A duration of 0 (the default) means 0.25 seconds unless overridden by the transaction.

`autoreverses, repeatCount, repeatDuration, cumulative`

>   For an infinite `repeatCount` (in Swift), use `Float.infinity`. The `repeat-Duration` property is a different way to govern repetition, specifying how long the repetition should continue rather than how many repetitions should occur; don't specify both a `repeatCount` and a `repeatDuration`. If `cumulative` is `true`, a repeating animation starts each repetition where the previous repetition ended (rather than jumping back to the start value).

beginTime

> The delay before the animation starts. To delay an animation with respect to now, call CACurrentMediaTime and add the desired delay in seconds. The delay does not eat into the animation's duration.

timeOffset

> A shift in the animation's overall timing; looked at another way, specifies the starting frame of the "animation movie," which is treated as a loop. For example, an animation with a duration of 8 and a time offset of 4 plays its second half followed by its first half.

CAAnimation, along with all its subclasses, implements KVC to allow you to set and retrieve a value for an arbitrary key, similar to CALayer (Chapter 3) and CATransaction.

CAPropertyAnimation

> CAPropertyAnimation is a subclass of CAAnimation. It too is abstract, and adds the following:

keyPath

> The all-important string specifying the CALayer key that is to be animated. Recall from Chapter 3 that CALayer properties are accessible through KVC keys; now we are using those keys! The convenience initializer init(keyPath:) creates the instance and assigns it a keyPath.

additive

> If true, the values supplied by the animation are added to the current presentation layer value.

valueFunction

> Converts a simple scalar value that you supply into a transform.

 There is no animatable CALayer key called "frame". To animate a layer's frame using explicit layer animation, if both its position and bounds are to change, you must animate both. Similarly, you cannot use explicit layer animation to animate a layer's affineTransform property, because affineTransform is not a property (it's a pair of convenience methods); you must animate its transform instead. Attempting to form an animation with a key path of "frame" or "affineTransform" is a common beginner error.

CABasicAnimation

> CABasicAnimation is a subclass (not abstract!) of CAPropertyAnimation. It adds the following:

fromValue, toValue

> The starting and ending values for the animation. These values must be Objective-C objects, so numbers and structs will have to be wrapped accordingly, using NSNumber and NSValue (Swift will automatically take care of the former but not the latter). If neither fromValue nor toValue is provided, the former and current values of the property are used. If just one of fromValue or toValue is provided, the other uses the current value of the property.

byValue

> Expresses one of the endpoint values as a *difference* from the other rather than in absolute terms. So you would supply a byValue instead of a fromValue or instead of a toValue, and the actual fromValue or toValue would be calculated for you by subtraction or addition with respect to the other value. If you supply *only* a byValue, the fromValue is the property's current value.

Using a CABasicAnimation

Having constructed and configured a CABasicAnimation, the way you order it to be performed is to *add it to a layer*. This is done with the CALayer instance method addAnimation:forKey:. (I'll discuss the purpose of the forKey: parameter later; it's fine to ignore it and use nil, as I do in the examples that follow.)

However, there's a slight twist. A CAAnimation is *merely* an animation; all it does is describe the hoops that the presentation layer is to jump through, the "animation movie" that is to be presented. It has no effect on the layer *itself*. Thus, if you naively create a CABasicAnimation and add it to a layer with addAnimation:forKey:, the animation happens and then the "animation movie" is whipped away to reveal the layer sitting there in exactly the same state as before. It is up to *you* to change the layer to match what the animation will ultimately portray.

This requirement may seem odd, but keep in mind that we are now in a much more fundamental, flexible world than the automatic, convenient worlds of view animation and implicit layer animation. Using explicit animation is more work, but you get more power. The converse, of course, is that you *don't* have to change the layer if it *doesn't* change as a result of the animation.

To ensure good results, start by taking a plodding, formulaic approach to the use of CABasicAnimation, like this:

1. Capture the start and end values for the layer property you're going to change, because you're likely to need these values in what follows.

2. Change the layer property to its end value, first calling setDisableActions: if necessary to prevent implicit animation.

---

3. Construct the explicit animation, using the start and end values you captured earlier, and with its `keyPath` corresponding to the layer property you just changed.

4. Add the explicit animation to the layer.

 The explicit animation is *copied* when it is added to the layer. Therefore the animation must be configured first and added to the layer later. Configuring an animation after it has been added to a layer will have no effect on how that layer is animated, because the animation that has been added to the layer is no longer the animation you are configuring.

Here's how you'd use this approach to animate our compass arrow rotation:

```
// capture the start and end values
let startValue = arrow.transform
let endValue = CATransform3DRotate(
    startValue, CGFloat(M_PI)/4.0, 0, 0, 1)
// change the layer, without implicit animation
CATransaction.setDisableActions(true)
arrow.transform = endValue
// construct the explicit animation
let anim = CABasicAnimation(keyPath:"transform")
anim.duration = 0.8
let clunk = CAMediaTimingFunction(controlPoints:0.9, 0.1, 0.7, 0.9)
anim.timingFunction = clunk
anim.fromValue = NSValue(CATransform3D:startValue)
anim.toValue = NSValue(CATransform3D:endValue)
// ask for the explicit animation
arrow.addAnimation(anim, forKey:nil)
```

Once you're comfortable with the full form, you will find that in many cases it can be condensed. For example, when the `fromValue` and `toValue` are not set, the former and current values of the property are used automatically. (This magic is possible because, at the time the CABasicAnimation is added to the layer, the presentation layer still has the former value of the property, while the layer itself has the new value; thus, the CABasicAnimation is able to retrieve them.) In our example, therefore, there is no need to set the `fromValue` and `toValue`, and no need to capture the start and end values beforehand. Here's the condensed version:

```
CATransaction.setDisableActions(true)
arrow.transform = CATransform3DRotate(
    arrow.transform, CGFloat(M_PI)/4.0, 0, 0, 1)
let anim = CABasicAnimation(keyPath:"transform")
anim.duration = 0.8
let clunk = CAMediaTimingFunction(controlPoints:0.9, 0.1, 0.7, 0.9)
anim.timingFunction = clunk
arrow.addAnimation(anim, forKey:nil)
```

As I mentioned earlier, you will omit changing the layer if it doesn't change as a result of the animation. For example, let's make the compass arrow appear to vibrate rapidly, without ultimately changing its current orientation. To do this, we'll waggle it back and forth, using a repeated animation, between slightly clockwise from its current position and slightly counterclockwise from its current position. The "animation movie" neither starts nor stops at the current position of the arrow, but for this animation it doesn't matter, because it all happens so quickly as to appear perfectly natural:

```
// capture the start and end values
let nowValue = arrow.transform
let startValue = CATransform3DRotate(
    nowValue, CGFloat(M_PI)/40.0, 0, 0, 1)
let endValue = CATransform3DRotate(
    nowValue, CGFloat(-M_PI)/40.0, 0, 0, 1)
// construct the explicit animation
let anim = CABasicAnimation(keyPath:"transform")
anim.duration = 0.05
anim.timingFunction = CAMediaTimingFunction(
    name:kCAMediaTimingFunctionLinear)
anim.repeatCount = 3
anim.autoreverses = true
anim.fromValue = NSValue(CATransform3D:startValue)
anim.toValue = NSValue(CATransform3D:endValue)
// ask for the explicit animation
arrow.addAnimation(anim, forKey:nil)
```

That code, too, can be shortened considerably from its full form. We can eliminate the need to calculate the new rotation values based on the arrow's current transform by setting our animation's `additive` property to `true`; this means that the animation's property values are added to the existing property value for us, so that they are relative, not absolute. For a transform, "added" means "matrix-multiplied," so we can describe the waggle without any reference to the arrow's current rotation. Moreover, because our rotation is so simple (around a cardinal axis), we can take advantage of CAProperty-Animation's `valueFunction`; the animation's property values can then be simple scalars (in this case, angles), because the `valueFunction` tells the animation to interpret these as rotations around the z-axis:

```
let anim = CABasicAnimation(keyPath:"transform")
anim.duration = 0.05
anim.timingFunction = CAMediaTimingFunction(
    name:kCAMediaTimingFunctionLinear)
anim.repeatCount = 3
anim.autoreverses = true
anim.additive = true
anim.valueFunction = CAValueFunction(
    name:kCAValueFunctionRotateZ)
anim.fromValue = M_PI/40
anim.toValue = -M_PI/40
arrow.addAnimation(anim, forKey:nil)
```

Instead of using a valueFunction, we could have set the animation's key path to "transform.rotation.z" to achieve the same effect. However, Apple advises against this, as it can result in mathematical trouble when there is more than one rotation.

Let's return once more to our arrow "clunk" rotation for one final alternative implementation using the additive and valueFunction properties. We set the arrow layer to its final transform at the outset, so when the time comes to configure the animation, its toValue, in additive terms, will be 0; the fromValue will be its current value expressed *negatively*, like this:

```
let rot = CGFloat(M_PI)/4.0
CATransaction.setDisableActions(true)
arrow.transform = CATransform3DRotate(arrow.transform, rot, 0, 0, 1)
// construct animation additively
let anim = CABasicAnimation(keyPath:"transform")
anim.duration = 0.8
let clunk = CAMediaTimingFunction(controlPoints:0.9, 0.1, 0.7, 0.9)
anim.timingFunction = clunk
anim.fromValue = -rot
anim.toValue = 0
anim.additive = true
anim.valueFunction = CAValueFunction(name:kCAValueFunctionRotateZ)
arrow.addAnimation(anim, forKey:nil)
```

This is an interesting way of describing the animation; in effect, it expresses the animation in reverse, regarding the final position as correct and the current position as an aberration to be corrected. It also happens to be how additive view animations are rewritten behind the scenes, and explains their behavior.

Springing Animation

New in iOS 9, springing animation is exposed at the Core Animation level, through the CASpringAnimation class (a CABasicAnimation subclass). As might be expected, it has more options than its corresponding view animation API. Here's a rough equivalent of the springing view animation from earlier in this chapter; the mass and stiffness values were arrived at experimentally:

```
CATransaction.setDisableActions(true)
self.v.layer.position.y += 100
let anim = CASpringAnimation(keyPath: "position")
anim.damping = 0.7
anim.initialVelocity = 20
anim.mass = 0.04
anim.stiffness = 4
anim.duration = 0.8
self.v.layer.addAnimation(anim, forKey: nil)
```

A very nice feature of CASpringAnimation is that its `settlingDuration` property will tell you, even without running the animation, how long it will take the animation as currently configured to come to rest.

Keyframe Animation

Keyframe animation (CAKeyframeAnimation) is an alternative to basic animation (CABasicAnimation); they are both subclasses of CAPropertyAnimation and they are used in identical ways. The difference is that a keyframe animation, in addition to specifying a starting and ending value, also specifies multiple values through which the animation should pass on the way, the stages (*keyframes*) of the animation. This can be as simple as setting the animation's `values` array.

Here's a more sophisticated version of our animation for waggling the compass arrow: the stages include the start and end states and eight alternating waggles in between, with the degree of waggle becoming progressively smaller:

```
var values = [0.0]
for (var i = 20, direction = 1.0; i < 60; i += 5, direction *= -1) {
    values.append( direction * M_PI / Double(i) )
}
values.append(0.0)
let anim = CAKeyframeAnimation(keyPath:"transform")
anim.values = values
anim.additive = true
anim.valueFunction = CAValueFunction(name: kCAValueFunctionRotateZ)
arrow.addAnimation(anim, forKey:nil)
```

Here are some CAKeyframeAnimation properties:

`values`
The array of values the animation is to adopt, including the starting and ending value.

`timingFunctions`
An array of timing functions, one for each stage of the animation (so that this array will be one element shorter than the `values` array).

`keyTimes`
An array of times to accompany the array of values, defining when each value should be reached. The times start at 0 and are expressed as increasing fractions of 1, ending at 1.

`calculationMode`
Describes how the `values` are treated to create *all* the values through which the animation must pass:

- The default is `kCAAnimationLinear`, a simple straight-line interpolation from value to value.

- `kCAAnimationCubic` constructs a single smooth curve passing through all the values (and additional advanced properties, `tensionValues`, `continuity-Values`, and `biasValues`, allow you to refine the curve).

- `kCAAnimationPaced` and `kCAAnimationCubicPaced` means the timing functions and key times are ignored, and the velocity is made constant through the whole animation.

- `kCAAnimationDiscrete` means no interpolation: we jump directly to each value at the corresponding key time.

`path`

When you're animating a property whose values are pairs of floats (CGPoints), this is an alternative way of describing the values; instead of a `values` array, which must be interpolated to arrive at the intermediate values along the way, you supply the entire interpolation as a single CGPath. The points used to draw the path are the keyframe values, so you can still apply timing functions and key times. If you're animating a position, the `rotationMode` property lets you ask the animated object to rotate so as to remain perpendicular to the path.

In this example, the `values` array is a sequence of five images to be presented successively and repeatedly in a layer's `contents`, like the frames in a movie; the effect is similar to image animation, discussed earlier in this chapter:

```
let anim = CAKeyframeAnimation(keyPath:"contents")
// self.images is an array of UIImage
anim.values = self.images.map {$0.CGImage!}
anim.keyTimes = [0.0, 0.25, 0.5, 0.75, 1.0]
anim.calculationMode = kCAAnimationDiscrete
anim.duration = 1.5
anim.repeatCount = Float.infinity
// self.sprite is a CALayer
self.sprite.addAnimation(anim, forKey:nil)
```

Making a Property Animatable

So far, we've been animating built-in animatable properties. If you define your own property on a CALayer subclass, you can easily make that property animatable through a CAPropertyAnimation (a CABasicAnimation or a CAKeyframeAnimation). For example, here we animate the increase or decrease in a CALayer subclass property called `thickness`, using essentially the pattern for explicit animation that we've already developed:

```
let lay = self.v.layer as! MyLayer
let cur = lay.thickness
let val : CGFloat = cur == 10 ? 0 : 10
lay.thickness = val
let ba = CABasicAnimation(keyPath:"thickness")
ba.fromValue = cur
lay.addAnimation(ba, forKey:nil)
```

To make our layer responsive to such a command, it needs a thickness property (obviously) and it must return true from the class method needsDisplayForKey:, where the
key is the string name of the property:

```
class MyLayer : CALayer {
    var thickness : CGFloat = 0
    override class func needsDisplayForKey(key: String) -> Bool {
        if key == "thickness" {
            return true
        }
        return super.needsDisplayForKey(key)
    }
}
```

Returning true from needsDisplayForKey: causes this layer to be redisplayed repeatedly as the thickness property changes. So if we want to *see* the animation, this layer
also needs to draw itself in some way that depends on the thickness property. Here, I'll
implement the layer's drawInContext: to make thickness the thickness of the black
border around a red rectangle:

```
override func drawInContext(con: CGContext) {
    let r = self.bounds.insetBy(dx:20, dy:20)
    CGContextSetFillColorWithColor(con, UIColor.redColor().CGColor)
    CGContextFillRect(con, r)
    CGContextSetLineWidth(con, self.thickness)
    CGContextStrokeRect(con, r)
}
```

At every frame of the animation, drawInContext: is called, and because the thickness
value differs at each step, it appears animated.

We have made MyLayer's thickness property animatable when using explicit layer
animation, but it would be even cooler to make it animatable when using implicit layer
animation (that is, when setting lay.thickness directly). Later in this chapter, I'll show
how to do that.

 No law says that you *have* to draw in response to animated changes in a layer
property. Consider layer animation more abstractly as a way of getting the runtime
to calculate and send you timed interpolated value changes! The possibilities are
limitless.

Grouped Animations

A grouped animation (CAAnimationGroup) combines multiple animations into one, by means of its animations property (an array of animations). By delaying and timing the various component animations, complex effects can be achieved.

A CAAnimationGroup is itself an animation; it is a CAAnimation subclass, so it has a duration and other animation features. Think of the CAAnimationGroup as the parent, and its animations as its children. Then *the children inherit default property values from their parent*. Thus, for example, if you don't set a child's duration explicitly, it will inherit the parent's duration.

Let's use a grouped animation to construct a sequence where the compass arrow rotates and then waggles. This requires very little modification of code we've already written. We express the first animation in its full form, with explicit fromValue and toValue. We postpone the second animation using its beginTime property; notice that we express this in relative terms, as a number of seconds into the parent's duration, not with respect to CACurrentMediaTime. Finally, we set the overall parent duration to the sum of the child durations, so that it can embrace both of them (failing to do this, and then wondering why some child animations never occur, is a common beginner error):

```
// capture current value, set final value
let rot = M_PI/4.0
CATransaction.setDisableActions(true)
let current = arrow.valueForKeyPath("transform.rotation.z") as! Double
arrow.setValue(current + rot, forKeyPath:"transform.rotation.z")
// first animation (rotate and clunk)
let anim1 = CABasicAnimation(keyPath:"transform")
anim1.duration = 0.8
let clunk = CAMediaTimingFunction(controlPoints:0.9, 0.1, 0.7, 0.9)
anim1.timingFunction = clunk
anim1.fromValue = current
anim1.toValue = current + rot
anim1.valueFunction = CAValueFunction(name:kCAValueFunctionRotateZ)
// second animation (waggle)
var values = [0.0]
for (var i = 20, direction = 1.0; i < 60; i += 5, direction *= -1) {
    values.append( direction * M_PI / Double(i) )
}
values.append(0.0)
let anim2 = CAKeyframeAnimation(keyPath:"transform")
anim2.values = values
anim2.duration = 0.25
anim2.additive = true
anim2.beginTime = anim1.duration - 0.1
anim2.valueFunction = CAValueFunction(name: kCAValueFunctionRotateZ)
// group
```

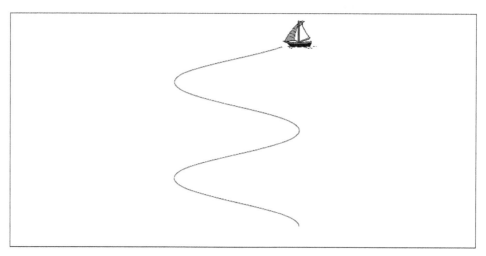

Figure 4-2. A boat and the course she'll sail

```
let group = CAAnimationGroup()
group.animations = [anim1, anim2]
group.duration = anim1.duration + anim2.duration
arrow.addAnimation(group, forKey:nil)
```

In that example, I grouped two animations that animated the same property sequentially. Now let's go to the other extreme and group some animations that animate different properties simultaneously. I have a small view (self.v), located near the top-right corner of the screen, whose layer contents are a picture of a sailboat facing to the left. I'll "sail" the boat in a curving path, both down the screen and left and right across the screen, like an extended letter "S" (Figure 4-2). Each time the boat comes to a vertex of the curve, changing direction across the screen, I'll turn the boat picture so that it faces the way it's about to move. At the same time, I'll constantly rock the boat, so that it always appears to be pitching a little on the waves.

Here's the first animation, the movement of the boat along its curving path. It illustrates the use of a CAKeyframeAnimation with a CGPath; the calculationMode of kCAAnimationPaced ensures an even speed over the whole path. We don't set an explicit duration because we want to adopt the duration of the group:

```
let h : CGFloat = 200
let v : CGFloat = 75
let path = CGPathCreateMutable()
var leftright : CGFloat = 1
var next : CGPoint = self.v.layer.position
var pos : CGPoint
CGPathMoveToPoint(path, nil, next.x, next.y)
for _ in 0 ..< 4 {
    pos = next
```

```
        leftright *= -1
        next = CGPointMake(pos.x+h*leftright, pos.y+v)
        CGPathAddCurveToPoint(path, nil,
            pos.x, pos.y+30,
            next.x, next.y-30,
            next.x, next.y)
    }
    let anim1 = CAKeyframeAnimation(keyPath:"position")
    anim1.path = path
    anim1.calculationMode = kCAAnimationPaced
```

Here's the second animation, the reversal of the direction the boat is facing. This is simply a rotation around the y-axis. It's another CAKeyframeAnimation, but we make no attempt at visually animating this reversal: the calculationMode is kCAAnimation-Discrete, so that the boat image reversal is a sudden change, as in our earlier "sprite" example. There is one less value than the number of points in our first animation's path, and the first animation has an even speed, so the reversals take place at each curve apex with no further effort on our part. (If the pacing were more complicated, we could give both the first and the second animation identical keyTimes arrays, to coordinate them.) Once again, we don't set an explicit duration:

```
    let revs = [0.0, M_PI, 0.0, M_PI]
    let anim2 = CAKeyframeAnimation(keyPath:"transform")
    anim2.values = revs
    anim2.valueFunction = CAValueFunction(name:kCAValueFunctionRotateY)
    anim2.calculationMode = kCAAnimationDiscrete
```

Here's the third animation, the rocking of the boat. It has a short duration, and repeats indefinitely:

```
    let pitches = [0.0, M_PI/60.0, 0.0, -M_PI/60.0, 0.0]
    let anim3 = CAKeyframeAnimation(keyPath:"transform")
    anim3.values = pitches
    anim3.repeatCount = Float.infinity
    anim3.duration = 0.5
    anim3.additive = true
    anim3.valueFunction = CAValueFunction(name:kCAValueFunctionRotateZ)
```

Finally, we combine the three animations, assigning the group an explicit duration that will be adopted by the first two animations. As we hand the animation over to the layer displaying the boat, we also change the layer's position to match the final position from the first animation, so that the boat won't jump back to its original position afterward:

```
    let group = CAAnimationGroup()
    group.animations = [anim1, anim2, anim3]
    group.duration = 8
    self.v.layer.addAnimation(group, forKey:nil)
    CATransaction.setDisableActions(true)
    self.v.layer.position = next
```

Here are some further CAAnimation properties (from the CAMediaTiming protocol) that come into play especially when animations are grouped:

speed

> The ratio between a child's timescale and the parent's timescale. For example, if a parent and child have the same duration, but the child's speed is 1.5, its animation runs one-and-a-half times as fast as the parent.

fillMode

> Suppose the child animation begins after the parent animation, or ends before the parent animation, or both. What should happen to the appearance of the property being animated, outside the child animation's boundaries? The answer depends on the child's fillMode:
>
> - kCAFillModeRemoved means the child animation is removed, revealing the layer property at its actual current value whenever the child is not running.
>
> - kCAFillModeForwards means the final presentation layer value of the child animation remains afterward.
>
> - kCAFillModeBackwards means the initial presentation layer value of the child animation appears right from the start.
>
> - kCAFillModeBoth combines the previous two.

Freezing an Animation

CALayer adopts the CAMediaTiming protocol. Thus, a layer can have a speed. This will affect any animation attached to it. A CALayer with a speed of 2 will play a 10-second animation in 5 seconds. A layer can also have a timeOffset.

One remarkably powerful way to take advantage of this feature of CALayer is to assign a layer a speed of 0. This effectively "freezes" any animation attached to the layer. You can then change the layer's timeOffset to display any single frame of the animation. In effect, the frozen animation has given you a whole slew of interpolated states "for free," any of which you can select by setting the layer's timeOffset.

To illustrate, let's explore the animatable path property of a CAShapeLayer. Consider a layer that can display a rectangle or an ellipse *or any of the intermediate shapes between them*. I can't imagine what the notion of an intermediate shape between a rectangle or an ellipse may mean, let alone how to draw such an intermediate shape; but thanks to frozen animations, I don't have to. Here, I'll construct the CAShapeLayer, add it to the interface, give it an animation from a rectangle to an ellipse, and keep a reference to it as a property:

```
let shape = CAShapeLayer()
shape.frame = v.bounds
v.layer.addSublayer(shape)
shape.fillColor = UIColor.clearColor().CGColor
shape.strokeColor = UIColor.redColor().CGColor
let path = CGPathCreateWithRect(shape.bounds, nil)
shape.path = path
let path2 = CGPathCreateWithEllipseInRect(shape.bounds, nil)
let ba = CABasicAnimation(keyPath: "path")
ba.duration = 1
ba.fromValue = path
ba.toValue = path2
shape.speed = 0
shape.timeOffset = 0
shape.addAnimation(ba, forKey: nil)
self.shape = shape
```

I've added the animation to the layer, but because the layer's speed is 0, no animation takes place; the rectangle is displayed and that's all. There's also a UISlider in the interface. I'll respond to the user changing the value of the slider by setting the frame of the animation:

```
@IBAction func doSlider(sender: AnyObject) { // slider action
    let slider = sender as! UISlider
    self.shape.timeOffset = Double(slider.value)
}
```

This astonishing feature of layers and animations can be used in many powerful ways. It lies at the heart of interactive view controller transition animations (Chapter 6), and is probably used in unsuspected places throughout the iPhone and iPad interface.

Transitions

A layer transition is an animation involving two "copies" of a single layer, in which the second "copy" appears to replace the first. It is described by an instance of CATransition (a CAAnimation subclass), which has these chief properties describing the animation:

type
　　Your choices are:

- kCATransitionFade
- kCATransitionMoveIn
- kCATransitionPush
- kCATransitionReveal

subtype
　　If the type is not kCATransitionFade, your choices are:

Figure 4-3. A push transition

- kCATransitionFromRight
- kCATransitionFromLeft
- kCATransitionFromTop
- kCATransitionFromBottom

> For historical reasons, the terms Bottom and Top in the names of the subtype settings have the opposite of their expected meanings.

To understand a layer transition, first implement one without changing anything else about the layer:

```
let t = CATransition()
t.type = kCATransitionPush
t.subtype = kCATransitionFromBottom
t.duration = 2
lay.addAnimation(t, forKey: nil)
```

The entire layer exits moving down from its original place while fading away, and another copy of the very same layer enters moving down from above while fading in. If, at the same time, we change something about the layer's contents, then the old contents will appear to exit downward while the new contents appear to enter from above:

```
// ... configure the transition as before ...
CATransaction.setDisableActions(true)
lay.contents = UIImage(named: "Smiley")!.CGImage
lay.addAnimation(t, forKey: nil)
```

A common device is for the layer that is to be transitioned to be inside a superlayer that is exactly the same size and whose masksToBounds is true. This confines the visible transition to the bounds of the layer itself. Otherwise, the entering and exiting versions of the layer are visible outside the layer. In Figure 4-3, which shows a smiley face pushing an image of Mars out of the layer, I've emphasized this arrangement by giving the superlayer a border as well.

A transition on a superlayer can happen simultaneously with animation of a sublayer. The animation will be seen to occur on the second "copy" of the layer as it moves into position. This is analogous to the .AllowAnimatedContent option for view animation.

Animations List

The method that asks for an explicit animation to happen is CALayer's add-Animation:forKey:. To understand how this method actually works (and what the "key" is), you need to know about a layer's *animations list*.

An animation is an object (a CAAnimation) that modifies how a layer is drawn. It does this merely by being attached to the layer; the layer's drawing mechanism does the rest. A layer maintains a list of animations that are currently in force. To add an animation to this list, you call addAnimation:forKey:. When the time comes to draw itself, the layer looks through its animations list and draws itself in accordance with whatever animations it finds there. (The list of things the layer must do in order to draw itself is sometimes referred to by the documentation as the *render tree*.) The order in which animations were added to the list is the order in which they are applied.

The animations list is maintained in a curious way. The list is not exactly a dictionary, but it behaves somewhat like a dictionary. An animation has a key — the forKey: parameter in addAnimation:forKey:. If an animation with a certain key is added to the list, and an animation with that key is already in the list, the one that is already in the list is removed. Thus a rule is maintained that *only one animation with a given key* can be in the list at a time — the *exclusivity rule*. This explains why sometimes ordering an animation can cancel an animation already ordered or in-flight: the two animations had the same key, so the first one was removed. (In iOS 8 and later, additive view animations affecting the same property work around this limitation simply by giving the additional animations a *different key name* — for example, "position" and "position-2".)

It is also possible to add an animation with *no key* (the key is nil); it is then *not* subject to the exclusivity rule (that is, there can be more than one animation in the list with no key).

The forKey: parameter in addAnimation:forKey: is thus *not a property name*. It *could* be a property name, but it can be any arbitrary value. Its purpose is to enforce the exclusivity rule. It does *not* have any meaning with regard to what property a CAPropertyAnimation animates; that is the job of the animation's keyPath. (Apple's use of the term "key" in addAnimation:forKey: is thus unfortunate and misleading; I wish they had named this method addAnimation:withIdentifier: or something like that.)

However, there *is* a relationship between the "key" in addAnimation:forKey: and a CAPropertyAnimation's keyPath — if a CAPropertyAnimation's keyPath is nil at the time that it is added to a layer with addAnimation:forKey:, *that keyPath is set to the forKey: value.* Thus, you can *misuse* the forKey: parameter in addAnimation:forKey: as a way of specifying what keyPath an animation animates. (Implicit layer animation crucially depends on this fact.)

 I have seen many prominent but misleading examples that use this technique, apparently in the mistaken belief that the "key" in addAnimation:forKey: is the way you are *supposed* to specify what property to animate. *This is wrong.* Set the CAPropertyAnimation's keyPath explicitly (as do all my examples); that's what it's for.

You can use the exclusivity rule to your own advantage, to keep your code from stepping on its own feet. Some code of yours might add an animation to the list using a certain key; then later, some other code might come along and correct this, removing that animation and replacing it with another. By using the same key, the second code is easily able to override the first: "You may have been given some other animation with this key, but throw it away; play this one instead."

In some cases, the key you supply is ignored and a different key is substituted. In particular, the key with which a CATransition is added to the list is always kCATransition (which happens to be "transition"); thus there can be only one transition animation in the list.

You can think of an animation in a layer's animations list as being the "animation movie" I spoke of at the start of this chapter. As long as an animation is in the list, the movie is present, either waiting to be played or actually playing. An animation that has finished playing is, in general, pointless; the animation should now be removed from the list, as its presence serves no purpose and it imposes an extra burden on the render tree. Therefore, an animation has a removedOnCompletion property, which defaults to true: when the "movie" is over, the animation removes itself from the list.

 You may encounter examples that set removedOnCompletion to false and set the animation's fillMode to kCAFillModeForwards or kCAFillModeBoth, as a way of causing the layer to keep the appearance of the last frame of the "animation movie" even after the animation is over, and preventing a property from apparently jumping back to its initial value when the animation ends. *This is wrong.* The correct approach, as I have explained, is to change the property value to match the final frame of the animation. The proper use of kCAFillModeForwards is in connection with a child animation within a grouped animation.

You can't access the entire animations list directly. You can access the key names of the animations in the list, with animationKeys; and you can obtain or remove an animation with a certain key, with animationForKey: and removeAnimationForKey:; but animations with a `nil` key are inaccessible. You can, however, remove all animations, including animations with a `nil` key, using `removeAllAnimations`. When your app is suspended, `removeAllAnimations` is called on all layers for you; that is why it is possible to suspend an app coherently in the middle of an animation.

If an animation is in-flight when you remove it from the animations list manually, by calling `removeAllAnimations` or `removeAnimationForKey:`, it will stop; however, that doesn't happen until the next redraw moment. You might be able to work around this, if you need an animation to be removed immediately, by wrapping the `remove...` call in an explicit transaction block.

Actions

For the sake of completeness, I will now explain how implicit animation really works — that is, how implicit animation is turned into explicit animation behind the scenes. The basis of implicit animation is the *action mechanism*. Feel free to skip this section if you don't want to get into the under-the-hood nitty-gritty of implicit animation.

What an Action Is

An *action* is an object that adopts the CAAction protocol. This means simply that it implements `runActionForKey:object:arguments:`. The action object could do *anything* in response to this message. The notion of an action is completely general. The only class that adopts the CAAction protocol is CAAnimation, but in fact the action object doesn't have to be an animation — it doesn't even have to perform an animation.

You would never send `runActionForKey:object:arguments:` to an animation directly. Rather, this message is sent to an action object for you, as the basis of implicit animation. The key is the property that was set, and the `object` is the layer whose property was set.

What an animation does when it receives `runActionForKey:object:arguments:` is to assume that the second parameter, the `object:`, is a layer, and to add itself to that layer's animations list. Thus, for an animation, receiving the `runActionForKey:object:arguments:` message is like being told: "Play yourself!"

This is where the rule comes into play, which I mentioned earlier, that if an animation's `keyPath` is `nil`, the key by which the animation is assigned to a layer's animations list is used as the `keyPath`. When an animation is sent `runActionForKey:object:arguments:`, it calls `addAnimation:forKey:` to add itself to the layer's animation's list, *using the name of the property as the key*. The animation's `keyPath` for an implicit layer animation is usually `nil`, so the animation's `keyPath` winds up being set to the same key! That is how the property that you set ends up being the property that is animated.

Action Search

When you set a property of a layer and trigger an implicit animation, you are actually triggering the *action search*: the layer *searches* for an action object (a CAAction) to which it can send the `runActionForKey:object:arguments:` message. The procedure by which the layer searches for this object is quite elaborate.

The search for an action object begins when something causes the layer to be sent the `actionForKey:` message. Three sorts of event can cause this to happen:

- A specially marked CALayer property is set — by calling the setter method explicitly, by setting the property itself, or by means of `setValue:forKey:`. All animatable properties, and indeed most (or all) other CALayer properties, are marked in this special way. (You can mark a custom property in this same way by designating it as `@NSManaged`, as I'll demonstrate later in this chapter.)

    Setting a layer's `frame` property sets its `position` and `bounds` and calls `actionForKey:` for the `"position"` and `"bounds"` keys. Calling a layer's `setAffineTransform:` method sets its `transform` and calls `actionForKey:` for the `"transform"` key.

- The layer is sent `setValue:forKey:` with a key that is *not* a property. This is because CALayer's `setValue:forUndefinedKey:`, by default, calls `actionForKey:`.

- Various other miscellaneous types of event take place, such as the layer being added to the interface. I'll give some examples later in this chapter.

 CATransaction's `setDisableActions:`, with an argument of `true`, prevents the `actionForKey:` message from being sent. That's how it actually works behind the scenes.

At each stage of the action search, the following rules are obeyed regarding what is returned from that stage of the search:

An action object
  If an action object is produced, that is the end of the search. The action mechanism sends that action object the `runActionForKey:object:arguments:` message; if this an animation, the animation responds by adding itself to the layer's animations list.

`NSNull()`
  If `NSNull()` is produced, that is the end of the search. There will be no implicit animation; `NSNull()` means, "Do nothing and stop searching."

`nil`
  If `nil` is produced, the search continues to the next stage.

The action search proceeds by stages, as follows:

1. The layer's `actionForKey:` might terminate the search before it even starts. The layer will do this if it is the underlying layer of a view, or if the layer is not part of a window's layer hierarchy. In such a case, there should be no implicit animation, so the whole mechanism is nipped in the bud. (This stage is special in that a returned value of `nil` ends the search and no animation takes place.)

2. If the layer has a delegate that implements `actionForLayer:forKey:`, that message is sent to the delegate, with this layer as the layer and the property name as the key. If an action object or `NSNull()` is returned, the search ends.

3. The layer has a property called `actions`, which is a dictionary. If there is an entry in this dictionary with the given key, that value is used, and the search ends.

4. The layer has a property called `style`, which is a dictionary. If there is an entry in this dictionary with the key `actions`, it is assumed to be a dictionary; if this `actions` dictionary has an entry with the given key, that value is used, and the search ends. Otherwise, if there is an entry in the `style` dictionary called `style`, the same search is performed within it, and so on recursively until either an `actions` entry with the given key is found (the search ends) or there are no more `style` entries (the search continues).

   (If the `style` dictionary sounds profoundly weird, that's because it is profoundly weird. It is actually a special case of a larger, separate mechanism, which is also profoundly weird, having to do not with actions, but with a CALayer's implementation of KVC. When you call `valueForKey:` on a layer, if the key is undefined by the layer itself, the `style` dictionary is consulted. I have never written or seen code that uses this mechanism for anything, and I'll say no more about it.)

5. The layer's class is sent `defaultActionForKey:`, with the property name as the key. If an action object or `NSNull()` is returned, the search ends.

6. If the search reaches this last stage, a default animation is supplied, as appropriate. For a property animation, this is a plain vanilla CABasicAnimation.

Hooking Into the Action Search

You can affect the action search at any of its various stages to modify what happens when the search is triggered.

For example, you can turn off implicit animation for some particular property. One way would be to return `nil` from `actionForKey:` itself, in a CALayer subclass. Here's the code from a CALayer subclass that doesn't animate its `position` property (but does animate its other properties normally):

```
override func actionForKey(key: String) -> CAAction? {
    if key == "position" {
        return nil
    }
    return super.actionForKey(key)
}
```

For more flexibility, we can take advantage of the fact that a CALayer acts like a dictionary (allowing us to set an arbitrary key's value) — we'll embed a switch in our CALayer subclass that we can use to turn implicit position animation on and off at will:

```
override func actionForKey(key: String) -> CAAction? {
    if key == "position" {
        if self.valueForKey("suppressPositionAnimation") != nil {
            return nil
        }
    }
    return super.actionForKey(key)
}
```

To turn off implicit position animation for an instance of this layer, we set its "suppress-PositionAnimation" key to a non-nil value:

```
layer.setValue(true, forKey:"suppressPositionAnimation")
```

Another possibility is to cause some stage of the search to produce an action object of your own. You would then be affecting how implicit animation behaves.

Let's say we want a certain layer's duration for an implicit position animation to be 5 seconds. We can achieve this with a minimally configured animation, like this:

```
let ba = CABasicAnimation()
ba.duration = 5
```

The idea now is to situate this animation where it will be produced by the action search for the "position" key. We could, for instance, put it into the layer's actions dictionary:

```
layer.actions = ["position": ba]
```

The only property of this animation that we have set is its duration; that setting, however, is final. Although animation properties that you don't set can be set through CATransaction, in the usual manner for implicit property animation, animation properties that you *do* set can *not* be overridden through CATransaction. Thus, when we set this layer's position, if an implicit animation results, its duration is 5 seconds, even if we try to change it through CATransaction:

```
CATransaction.setAnimationDuration(1.5) // won't work
layer.position = CGPointMake(100,100)
```

Storing an animation in the actions dictionary, however, is a somewhat inflexible way to hook into the action search. If we have to write our animation beforehand, we know nothing about the layer's starting and ending values for the changed property. A much more powerful approach is to make our action object a custom CAAction object — because in that case, it will be sent runActionForKey:..., and we can construct and run an animation *now*, when we are in direct contact with the layer to be animated. Here's a barebones version of such an object:

```
class MyAction : NSObject, CAAction {
    func runActionForKey(event: String, object anObject: AnyObject,
        arguments dict: [NSObject : AnyObject]?) {
            let anim = CABasicAnimation(keyPath: event)
            anim.duration = 5
            let lay = anObject as! CALayer
            let newP = lay.valueForKey(event)
            let oldP = (lay.presentationLayer() as! CALayer)
                .valueForKey(event)
            lay.addAnimation(anim, forKey:nil)
    }
}
```

The idea is that this would then be the action object that we store in the actions dictionary:

```
layer.actions = ["position": MyAction()]
```

Our custom CAAction object, MyAction, doesn't do anything very interesting — but it could. That's the point. As the code demonstrates, we have access to the name of the animated property (event), the old value of that property (from the layer's presentation layer), and the new value of that property (from the layer itself). We are thus free to configure the animation in all sorts of ways. In fact, we can add more than one animation to the layer, or a group animation. We don't even have to add an animation to the layer! We are free to interpret the setting of this property in any way we like.

Here's a modification of our MyAction object that creates and runs a keyframe animation that "waggles" as it goes from the start value to the end value:

```
class MyWagglePositionAction : NSObject, CAAction {
    func runActionForKey(event: String, object anObject: AnyObject,
        arguments dict: [NSObject : AnyObject]?) {
            let lay = anObject as! CALayer
            let newP = (lay.valueForKey(event) as! NSValue).CGPointValue()
            let oldP = ((lay.presentationLayer() as! CALayer)
                .valueForKey(event) as! NSValue).CGPointValue()
            let d = sqrt(pow(oldP.x - newP.x, 2) + pow(oldP.y - newP.y, 2))
            let r = Double(d/3.0)
            let theta = Double(atan2(newP.y - oldP.y, newP.x - oldP.x))
            let wag = 10*M_PI/180.0
            let p1 = CGPointMake(
                oldP.x + CGFloat(r*cos(theta+wag)),
                oldP.y + CGFloat(r*sin(theta+wag)))
            let p2 = CGPointMake(
                oldP.x + CGFloat(r*2*cos(theta-wag)),
                oldP.y + CGFloat(r*2*sin(theta-wag)))
```

```
        let anim = CAKeyframeAnimation(keyPath: event)
        anim.values = [oldP,p1,p2,newP].map{NSValue(CGPoint:$0)}
        anim.calculationMode = kCAAnimationCubic
        lay.addAnimation(anim, forKey:nil)
    }
}
```

By adding this CAAction object to a layer's `actions` dictionary under the `"position"` key, we have created a CALayer that waggles when its position is set. Our CAAction doesn't set the animation's `duration`, so our own call to CATransaction's `setAnimation-Duration:` works. The power of this mechanism is simply staggering. We can modify *any* layer in this way — even one that doesn't belong to us.

Instead of modifying the layer's `actions` dictionary, we could hook into the action search by setting the layer's delegate to an instance that responds to `actionForLayer:for-Key:`. This has the advantage of serving as a single locus that can do different things depending on what the layer is and what the key is. Here's an implementation that does exactly what the `actions` dictionary did — it returns an instance of our custom CAAction object, so that setting the layer's position waggles it into place:

```
override func actionForLayer(layer: CALayer,
    forKey key: String) -> CAAction? {
        if key == "position" {
            return MyWagglePositionAction()
        }
        return nil
}
```

Finally, I'll demonstrate overriding `defaultActionForKey:`. This code would go into a CALayer subclass; setting this layer's `contents` will automatically trigger a push transition from the left:

```
override class func defaultActionForKey(key: String) -> CAAction? {
    if key == "contents" {
        let tr = CATransition()
        tr.type = kCATransitionPush
        tr.subtype = kCATransitionFromLeft
        return tr
    }
    return super.defaultActionForKey(key)
}
```

 Both the delegate's `actionForLayer:forKey:` and the subclass's `defaultActionFor-Key:` are declared as returning a CAAction. Therefore, to return `NSNull()` from your implemention of one of these methods, you'll need to typecast it to `CAAction` to quiet the compiler; you're lying (NSNull does not adopt the CAAction protocol), but it doesn't matter.

Making a Custom Property Implicitly Animatable

Earlier in this chapter, we made a custom layer's `thickness` property animatable through explicit layer animation. Now that we know how implicit layer animation works, we can make our layer's `thickness` property animatable through implicit animation as well. Thus, we will be able to animate our layer's thickness with code like this:

```
let lay = self.v.layer as! MyLayer
let cur = lay.thickness
let val : CGFloat = cur == 10 ? 0 : 10
lay.thickness = val // implicit animation
```

We have already implemented `needsDisplayForKey:` to return `true` for the `"thickness"` key, and we have provided an appropriate `drawInContext:` implementation. Now we'll add two further pieces of the puzzle. As we now know, to make our MyLayer class respond to direct setting of a property, we need to hook into the action search and return a CAAction. The obvious place to do this is in the layer itself, at the very start of the action search, in an `actionForKey:` implementation:

```
override func actionForKey(key: String) -> CAAction? {
    if key == "thickness" {
        let ba = CABasicAnimation(keyPath: key)
        ba.fromValue =
            (self.presentationLayer() as! CALayer).valueForKey(key)
        return ba
    }
    return super.actionForKey(key)
}
```

Finally, we must declare MyLayer's `thickness` property @NSManaged. Otherwise, `action-ForKey:` won't be called in the first place (the action search will never happen):

```
class MyLayer : CALayer {
    @NSManaged var thickness : CGFloat
    // ...
}
```

 The @NSManaged declaration invites Cocoa to generate and dynamically inject getter and setter accessors into our layer class; it is the equivalent of Objective-C's @dynamic (and is completely different from Swift's `dynamic`).

Nonproperty Actions

An action search is also triggered when a layer is added to a superlayer (key `kCAOnOrder-In`) and when a layer's sublayers are changed by adding or removing a sublayer (key `"sublayers"`).

These triggers and their keys are incorrectly described in Apple's documentation (and headers).

In this example, we use our layer's delegate so that when our layer is added to a superlayer, it will "pop" into view:

```
let layer = CALayer()
// ... configure layer here ...
layer.delegate = self
self.view.layer.addSublayer(layer)
```

In the layer's delegate (`self`), we implement the actual animation as a group animation, fading the layer quickly in from an opacity of 0 and at the same time scaling its transform to make it momentarily appear a little larger:

```
override func actionForLayer(layer: CALayer,
    forKey key: String) -> CAAction? {
        if key == kCAOnOrderIn {
            let anim1 = CABasicAnimation(keyPath:"opacity")
            anim1.fromValue = 0.0
            anim1.toValue = layer.opacity
            let anim2 = CABasicAnimation(keyPath:"transform")
            anim2.toValue = NSValue(CATransform3D:
                CATransform3DScale(layer.transform, 1.2, 1.2, 1.0))
            anim2.autoreverses = true
            anim2.duration = 0.1
            let group = CAAnimationGroup()
            group.animations = [anim1, anim2]
            group.duration = 0.2
            return group
        }
}
```

The documentation says that when a layer is removed from a superlayer, an action is sought under the key kCAOnOrderOut. This is true but useless, because by the time the action is sought, the layer has already been removed from the superlayer, so returning an animation has no visible effect. A possible workaround is to trigger the animation in some other way (and remove the layer afterward, if desired).

Recall, for example, that an action search is triggered when an arbitrary key is set on a layer. Let's implement the key "farewell" so that it shrinks and fades the layer and then removes it from its superlayer:

```
layer.delegate = self
layer.setValue("", forKey:"farewell")
```

The supplier of the action object — in this case, the layer's delegate — returns the shrink-and-fade animation; it also sets itself as that animation's delegate, and removes the layer when the animation ends:

```
override func actionForLayer(layer: CALayer,
    forKey key: String) -> CAAction? {
        if key == "farewell" {
            let anim1 = CABasicAnimation(keyPath:"opacity")
            anim1.fromValue = layer.opacity
            anim1.toValue = 0.0
            let anim2 = CABasicAnimation(keyPath:"transform")
            anim2.toValue = NSValue(CATransform3D:
                CATransform3DScale(layer.transform, 0.1, 0.1, 1.0))
            let group = CAAnimationGroup()
            group.animations = [anim1, anim2]
            group.duration = 0.2
            group.delegate = self // animationDidStop will be called
            group.setValue(layer, forKey:"remove") // identifier
            layer.opacity = 0
            return group
        }
    }
    override func animationDidStop(anim: CAAnimation, finished flag: Bool) {
        if let layer = anim.valueForKey("remove") as? CALayer {
            layer.removeFromSuperlayer()
        }
    }
}
```

Emitter Layers

Emitter layers (CAEmitterLayer) are, to some extent, on a par with animated images: once you've set up an emitter layer, it just sits there animating all by itself. The nature of this animation is rather narrow: an emitter layer emits particles, which are CAEmitterCell instances. However, by clever setting of the properties of an emitter layer and its emitter cells, you can achieve some astonishing effects. Moreover, the animation is itself animatable using Core Animation.

Here are some useful basic properties of a CAEmitterCell:

contents, contentsRect
> These are modeled after the eponymous CALayer properties, although CAEmitter-Cell is not a CALayer subclass; so, respectively, an image (a CGImage) and a CGRect specifying a region of that image. They define the image that a cell will portray.

birthrate, lifetime
> How many cells per second should be emitted, and how many seconds each cell should live before vanishing, respectively.

velocity
> The speed at which a cell moves. The unit of measurement is not documented; perhaps it's points per second.

`emissionLatitude`, `emissionLongitude`

> The angle at which the cell is emitted from the emitter, as a variation from the perpendicular. Longitude is an angle within the plane; latitude is an angle out of the plane.

So, here's code to create a very elementary emitter cell:

```
// make a gray circle image
UIGraphicsBeginImageContextWithOptions(CGSizeMake(10,10), false, 1)
let con = UIGraphicsGetCurrentContext()!
CGContextAddEllipseInRect(con, CGRectMake(0,0,10,10))
CGContextSetFillColorWithColor(con, UIColor.grayColor().CGColor)
CGContextFillPath(con)
let im = UIGraphicsGetImageFromCurrentImageContext()
UIGraphicsEndImageContext()
// make a cell with that image
let cell = CAEmitterCell()
cell.birthRate = 5
cell.lifetime = 1
cell.velocity = 100
cell.contents = im.CGImage
```

(In the first line, we deliberately keep the scale at 1, even on a high-resolution screen, because a CAEmitterCell has no `contentsScale`, as a CALayer does; we're going to derive a CGImage from this image, and we don't want its size doubled.)

The result is that little gray circles should be emitted slowly and steadily, five per second, each one vanishing in one second. Now we need an emitter layer from which these circles are to be emitted. Here are some basic CAEmitterLayer properties (beyond those it inherits from CALayer); these define an imaginary object, an emitter, that will be producing the emitter cells:

`emitterPosition`

> The point at which the emitter should be located, in superlayer coordinates. You can optionally add a third dimension to this point, `emitterZPosition`.

`emitterSize`

> The size of the emitter.

`emitterShape`

> The shape of the emitter. The dimensions of the shape depend on the emitter's size; the cuboid shape depends also on a third size dimension, `emitterDepth`. Your choices are:
>
> - `kCAEmitterLayerPoint`
> - `kCAEmitterLayerLine`
> - `kCAEmitterLayerRectangle`
> - `kCAEmitterLayerCuboid`

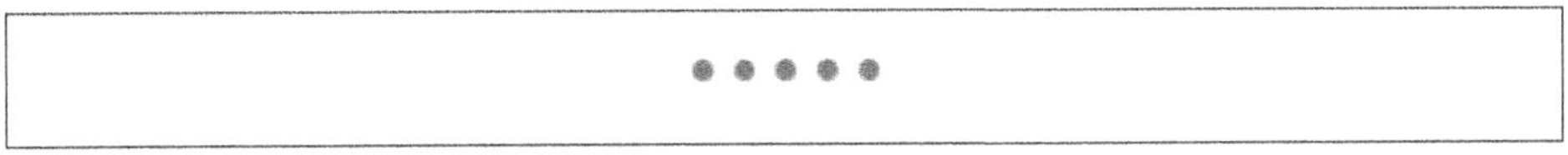

Figure 4-4. A really boring emitter layer

- kCAEmitterLayerCircle
- kCAEmitterLayerSphere

emitterMode
The region of the shape from which cells should be emitted. Your choices are:

- kCAEmitterLayerPoints
- kCAEmitterLayerOutline
- kCAEmitterLayerSurface
- kCAEmitterLayerVolume

Let's start with the simplest possible case, a single point emitter:

```
let emit = CAEmitterLayer()
emit.emitterPosition = CGPointMake(30,100)
emit.emitterShape = kCAEmitterLayerPoint
emit.emitterMode = kCAEmitterLayerPoints
```

We tell the emitter what types of cell to emit by assigning those cells to its emitter-Cells property (an array of CAEmitterCell). We then add the emitter to our interface, and presto, it starts emitting:

```
emit.emitterCells = [cell]
self.view.layer.addSublayer(emit)
```

The result is a constant stream of gray circles emitted from the point (30.0,100.0), each circle marching steadily to the right and vanishing after one second (Figure 4-4).

Now that we've succeeded in creating a boring emitter layer, we can start to vary some parameters. The emissionRange defines a cone in which cells will be emitted; if we increase the birthRate and widen the emissionRange, we get something that looks like a stream shooting from a water hose:

```
cell.birthRate = 100
cell.lifetime = 1.5
cell.velocity = 100
cell.emissionRange = CGFloat(M_PI)/5.0
```

In addition, as the cell moves, it can be made to accelerate (or decelerate) in each dimension, using its xAcceleration, yAcceleration, and zAcceleration properties. Here, we turn the stream into a falling cascade, like a waterfall coming from the left:

```
cell.xAcceleration = -40
cell.yAcceleration = 200
```

All aspects of cell behavior can be made to vary randomly, using the following CAEmitterCell properties:

lifetimeRange, velocityRange

> How much the lifetime and velocity values are allowed to vary randomly for different cells.

scale

scaleRange, scaleSpeed

> The scale alters the size of the cell; the range and speed determine how far and how rapidly this size alteration is allowed to change over the lifetime of each cell.

color

redRange, greenRange, blueRange, alphaRange

redSpeed, greenSpeed, blueSpeed, alphaSpeed

> The color is painted in accordance with the opacity of the cell's contents image; it combines with the image's color, so if we want the color stated here to appear in full purity, our contents image should use only white. The range and speed determine how far and how rapidly each color component is to change.

spin

spinRange

> The spin is a rotational speed (in radians per second); its range determines how far this speed is allowed to change over the lifetime of each cell.

Here we add some variation so that the circles behave a little more independently of one another. Some live longer than others, some come out of the emitter faster than others. And they all start out a shade of blue, but change to a shade of green about half-way through the stream (Figure 4-5):

```
cell.lifetimeRange = 0.4
cell.velocityRange = 20
cell.scaleRange = 0.2
cell.scaleSpeed = 0.2
cell.color = UIColor.blueColor().CGColor
cell.greenRange = 0.5
cell.greenSpeed = 0.75
```

Once the emitter layer is in place and animating, you can change its parameters and the parameters of its emitter cells through key–value coding on the emitter layer. You can access the emitter cells through the emitter layer's "emitterCells" key path; to specify a cell type, use its name property (which you'll have to have assigned earlier) as the next piece of the key path. For example, suppose we've set cell.name to "circle"; now we'll change the cell's greenSpeed so that each cell changes from blue to green much earlier in its lifetime:

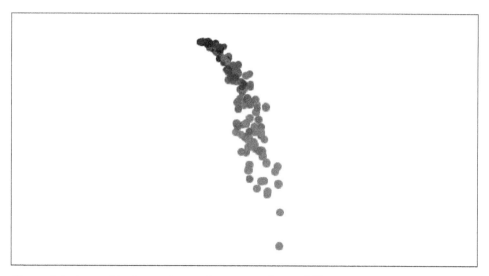

Figure 4-5. An emitter layer that makes a sort of waterfall

```
emit.setValue(3.0, forKeyPath:"emitterCells.circle.greenSpeed")
```

The significance of this is that such changes can themselves be animated! Here, we'll attach to the emitter layer a repeating animation that causes our cell's greenSpeed to move slowly back and forth between two values. The result is that the stream varies, over time, between being mostly blue and mostly green:

```
let key = "emitterCells.circle.greenSpeed"
let ba = CABasicAnimation(keyPath:key)
ba.fromValue = -1.0
ba.toValue = 3.0
ba.duration = 4
ba.autoreverses = true
ba.repeatCount = Float.infinity
emit.addAnimation(ba, forKey:nil)
```

A CAEmitterCell can itself function as an emitter — that is, it can have cells of its own. Both CAEmitterLayer and CAEmitterCell conform to the CAMediaTiming protocol, and their beginTime and duration properties can be used to govern their times of operation, much as in a grouped animation. For example, this code causes our existing waterfall to spray tiny droplets in the region of the "nozzle" (the emitter):

```
let cell2 = CAEmitterCell()
cell.emitterCells = [cell2]
cell2.contents = im.CGImage
cell2.emissionRange = CGFloat(M_PI)
cell2.birthRate = 200
cell2.lifetime = 0.4
```

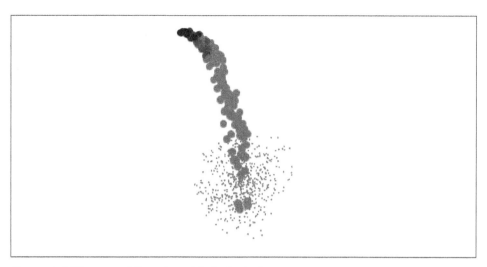

Figure 4-6. The waterfall makes a kind of splash

```
cell2.velocity = 200
cell2.scale = 0.2
cell2.beginTime = 0.04
cell2.duration = 0.2
```

But if we change the beginTime to be larger (hence later), the tiny droplets happen near the bottom of the cascade. We must also increase the duration, or stop setting it altogether, since if the duration is less than the beginTime, no emission takes place at all (Figure 4-6):

```
cell2.beginTime = 1.4
cell2.duration = 0.4
```

We can also alter the picture by changing the behavior of the emitter itself. This change turns the emitter into a line, so that our cascade becomes broader (more like Niagara Falls):

```
emit.emitterPosition = CGPointMake(100,25)
emit.emitterSize = CGSizeMake(100,100)
emit.emitterShape = kCAEmitterLayerLine
emit.emitterMode = kCAEmitterLayerOutline
cell.emissionLongitude = 3*CGFloat(M_PI)/4
```

There's more to know about emitter layers and emitter cells, but at this point you know enough to understand Apple's sample code simulating such things as fire and smoke and pyrotechnics, and you can explore further on your own.

Figure 4-7. Midway through a starburst transition

CIFilter Transitions

Core Image filters (Chapter 2) include transitions. You supply two images and a frame time between 0 and 1; the filter supplies the corresponding frame of a one-second animation transitioning from the first image to the second. For example, Figure 4-7 shows the frame at frame time 0.75 for a starburst transition from a solid red image to a photo of me. (You don't see the photo of me, because this transition, by default, "explodes" the first image to white first, and then quickly fades to the second image.)

Animating a Core Image transition filter is up to you. Thus we need a way of rapidly calling the same method repeatedly; in that method, we'll request and draw each frame of the transition. This could be a job for an NSTimer, but a better way is to use a *display link* (CADisplayLink), a form of timer that's highly efficient, especially when repeated drawing is involved, because it is linked directly to the refreshing of the display (hence the name). The display refresh rate is typically about one-sixtieth of a second; the actual value is given as the display link's duration, and will undergo slight fluctuations. Like a timer, the display link calls a designated method of ours every time it fires. We can slow the rate of calls by an integral amount by setting the display link's frame-Interval; for example, a display link with a frameInterval of 2 will call us about every one-thirtieth of a second. We can learn the exact time when the display link last fired by querying its timestamp.

In this example, I'll display the animation in a view's layer. We initialize ahead of time, in properties, everything we'll need later to obtain an output image for a given frame of the transition — the CIFilter, the image's extent, and the CIContext. We also have a timestamp property, which we initialize as well:

```
let moi = CIImage(image:UIImage(named:"moi")!)!
self.moiextent = moi.extent
let col = CIFilter(name:"CIConstantColorGenerator")!
let cicol = CIColor(color:UIColor.redColor())
```

```
col.setValue(cicol, forKey:"inputColor")
let colorimage = col.valueForKey("outputImage") as! CIImage
let tran = CIFilter(name:"CIFlashTransition")!
tran.setValue(colorimage, forKey:"inputImage")
tran.setValue(moi, forKey:"inputTargetImage")
let center = CIVector(x:self.moiextent.width/2.0, y:self.moiextent.height/2.0)
tran.setValue(center, forKey:"inputCenter")
self.tran = tran
self.context = CIContext(options:nil)
self.timestamp = 0.0
```

We create the display link, setting it to call into our nextFrame: method, and set it going by adding it to the run loop, which retains it:

```
let link = CADisplayLink(target:self, selector:"nextFrame:")
link.addToRunLoop(NSRunLoop.mainRunLoop(), forMode:NSDefaultRunLoopMode)
```

Our nextFrame: method is called with the display link as parameter (sender). We store the initial timestamp in a property, and use the difference between that and each successive timestamp value to calculate our desired frame. We ask the filter for the corresponding image and display it. When the frame value exceeds 1, the animation is over and we invalidate the display link (just like a repeating timer), which releases it from the run loop:

```
let SCALE = 1.0
func nextFrame(sender:CADisplayLink) {
    if self.timestamp < 0.01 { // pick up and store first timestamp
        self.timestamp = sender.timestamp
        self.frame = 0.0
    } else { // calculate frame
        self.frame = (sender.timestamp - self.timestamp) * SCALE
    }
    sender.paused = true // defend against frame loss
    self.tran.setValue(self.frame, forKey:"inputTime")
    let moi = self.context.createCGImage(
        tran.outputImage!, fromRect:self.moiextent)
    CATransaction.setDisableActions(true)
    self.v.layer.contents = moi
    if self.frame > 1.0 {
        sender.invalidate()
    }
    sender.paused = false
}
```

I have surrounded the time-consuming calculation and drawing of the image with calls to the display link's paused property, in case the calculation time exceeds the time between screen refreshes; perhaps this isn't necessary, but it can't hurt. Our animation occupies one second; changing that value is merely a matter of multiplying by a different scale value when we set our frame property.

If you experiment with this code, run on the device, as display links do not work well in the Simulator.

UIKit Dynamics

The term *UIKit dynamics* refers to a suite of classes that supplies a convenient API for animating views in a manner reminiscent of real-world physical behavior. For example, views can be subjected to gravity, collisions, bouncing, and momentary forces, with effects that would otherwise be difficult to achieve.

UIKit dynamics should not be treated as a game engine. It is deliberately quite cartoony and simple, animating only the position (`center`) and rotation transform of views within a flat two-dimensional space. UIKit dynamics relies on CADisplayLink, and the calculation of each frame takes place on the main thread (not on the animation server's background thread). There's no "animation movie" and no distinct presentation layer; the views really are being repositioned in real time. Thus, UIKit Dynamics is not intended for extended use; it is a way of momentarily emphasizing or clarifying functional transformations of your interface.

The Dynamics Stack

Implementing UIKit dynamics involves configuring a "stack" of three things:

A dynamic animator
> A dynamic animator, a UIDynamicAnimator instance, is the ruler of the physics world you are creating. It has a reference view, whose bounds define the coordinate system of the animator's world. A view to be animated must be a subview of the reference view (though it does not have to be within the reference view's bounds). Retaining the animator is up to you, typically with an instance property. It's fine for an animator to sit empty until you need it; an animator whose world is empty (or at rest) is not running, and occupies no processor time.

A behavior
> A UIDynamicBehavior is a rule describing how a view should behave. You'll typically use a built-in subclass, such as UIGravityBehavior or UICollisionBehavior. You configure the behavior and add it to the animator; an animator has methods and properties for managing its behaviors, such as `addBehavior:`, `behaviors`, `removeBehavior:`, and `removeAllBehaviors`. A behavior's configuration can be changed, and behaviors can be added to and removed from an animator, even while an animation is in progress.

An item

An item is any object that implements the UIDynamicItem protocol. A UIView is such an object! You add a UIView (one that's a subview of your animator's reference view) to a behavior (one that belongs to that animator) — and at that moment, the view comes under the influence of that behavior. If this behavior is one that causes motion, and if no other behaviors prevent, the view will now move (the animator is running).

Some behaviors can accept multiple items, and have methods and properties such as addItem:, items, and removeItem:. Others can have just one or two items and must be initialized with these from the outset.

New in iOS 9, a UIDynamicItemGroup is a way of combining multiple items to form a single item. Its only property is its items. You apply behaviors to the resulting grouped item, not to the subitems that it comprises. Those subitems maintain their physical relationship to one another. For purposes of collisions, the boundaries of the individual subitems are respected.

That's sufficient to get started, so let's try it! I'll start by creating my animator and storing it in a property:

```
self.anim = UIDynamicAnimator(referenceView: self.view)
```

Now I'll cause an existing subview of self.view (a UIImageView, self.iv) to drop off the screen, under the influence of gravity. I create a UIGravityBehavior, add it to the animator, and add self.iv to it:

```
let grav = UIGravityBehavior()
self.anim.addBehavior(grav)
grav.addItem(self.iv)
```

As a result, self.iv comes under the influence of gravity and is now animated downward off the screen. (A UIGravityBehavior object has properties configuring the strength and direction of gravity, but I've left them here at their defaults.)

An immediate concern is that our view falls forever. This is a serious waste of memory and processing power. If we no longer need the view after it has left the screen, we should take it out of the influence of UIKit dynamics by removing it from any behaviors to which it belongs (and we can also remove it from its superview). One way to do this is by removing from the animator any behaviors that are no longer needed. In our simple example, where the animator's entire world contains just this one item, it will be sufficient to call removeAllBehaviors.

But how will we know when the view is off the screen? A UIDynamicBehavior can be assigned an action function, which is called repeatedly as the animator drives the animation. I'll configure our gravity behavior's action function to check whether self.iv is still within the bounds of the reference view, by calling the animator's `itemsInRect:` method. Here's my first attempt:

```
grav.action = {
    let items = self.anim.itemsInRect(self.view.bounds) as! [UIView]
    let ix = items.indexOf(self.iv)
    if ix == nil {
        self.anim.removeAllBehaviors()
        self.iv.removeFromSuperview()
    }
}
```

This works in the sense that, after the image view leaves the screen, the image view is removed from the window and the animation stops. Unfortunately, there is also a memory leak: neither the image view nor the gravity behavior has been released. One solution is, in `grav.action`, to set `self.anim` (the animator property) to `nil`, thus breaking the retain cycle. This is a perfectly appropriate solution if, as here, we no longer need the animator for anything; a UIDynamicAnimator is a lightweight object and can very reasonably come into existence only for as long as we need to run an animation. Another possibility is to use delayed performance; even a delay of 0 solves the problem, presumably because the behavior's `action` function is no longer running at the time we remove the behavior:

```
grav.action = {
    let items = self.anim.itemsInRect(self.view.bounds) as! [UIView]
    let ix = items.indexOf(self.iv)
    if ix == nil {
        delay(0) {
            self.anim.removeAllBehaviors()
            self.iv.removeFromSuperview()
        }
    }
}
```

Now let's add some further behaviors. If falling straight down is too boring, we can add a UIPushBehavior to create a slight rightward impulse to be applied to the view as it begins to fall:

```
let push = UIPushBehavior(items:[self.iv], mode:.Instantaneous)
push.pushDirection = CGVectorMake(1, 0)
self.anim.addBehavior(push)
```

The view now falls in a parabola to the right. Next, let's add a UICollisionBehavior to make our view strike the "floor" of the screen:

```
let coll = UICollisionBehavior()
coll.collisionMode = .Boundaries
coll.addBoundaryWithIdentifier("floor",
    fromPoint:CGPointMake(0, self.view.bounds.maxY),
    toPoint:CGPointMake(self.view.bounds.maxX, self.view.bounds.maxY))
self.anim.addBehavior(coll)
coll.addItem(self.iv)
```

The view now falls in a parabola onto the floor of the screen, bounces a tiny bit, and comes to rest. It would be nice if the view bounced a bit more. Characteristics internal to a dynamic item's physics, such as bounciness (elasticity), are configured by assigning it to a UIDynamicItemBehavior:

```
let bounce = UIDynamicItemBehavior()
bounce.elasticity = 0.8
self.anim.addBehavior(bounce)
bounce.addItem(self.iv)
```

Our view now bounces higher; nevertheless, when it hits the floor, it stops moving to the right, so it just bounces repeatedly, less and less, and ends up at rest on the floor. I'd prefer that, after it bounces, it should roll to the right, so that it eventually leaves the screen. Part of the problem here is that, in the mind of the physics engine, our view is *not round*. New in iOS 9, we can change that. We'll have to subclass our view class (UIImageView), and make sure our view is an instance of this subclass:

```
class MyImageView : UIImageView {
    override var collisionBoundsType: UIDynamicItemCollisionBoundsType {
        return .Ellipse
    }
}
```

Our image view now has the ability to roll. If the image view is portraying a circular image, the effect is quite realistic: the image itself appears to roll to the right after it bounces. However, it isn't rolling very fast (because we didn't initially push it very hard). To remedy that, I'll add some rotational velocity as part of the first bounce. A UICollisionBehavior has a delegate to which it sends messages when a collision occurs. I'll make self the collision behavior's delegate, and when the delegate message arrives, I'll add rotational velocity to the existing dynamic item bounce behavior, so that our view starts spinning clockwise:

```
func collisionBehavior(behavior: UICollisionBehavior,
    beganContactForItem item: UIDynamicItem,
    withBoundaryIdentifier identifier: NSCopying?,
    atPoint p: CGPoint) {
        // look for the dynamic item behavior
        let b = self.anim.behaviors
        if let ix = b.indexOf({$0 is UIDynamicItemBehavior}) {
            let bounce = b[ix] as! UIDynamicItemBehavior
            let v = bounce.angularVelocityForItem(item)
            if v <= 6 {
```

```
            bounce.addAngularVelocity(6, forItem:item)
            }
        }
    }
```

The view now falls in a parabola to the right, strikes the floor, spins clockwise, and bounces off the floor and continues bouncing its way off the right side of the screen.

Custom Behaviors

You will commonly find yourself composing a complex behavior out of a combination of several built-in UIDynamicBehavior subclass instances. For neatness, clarity, maintainability, and reusability, it might make sense to express that combination as a single custom UIDynamicBehavior subclass.

To illustrate, I'll turn the behavior from the previous section into a custom UIDynamicBehavior subclass. Let's call it MyDropBounceAndRollBehavior. Now we can apply this behavior to our view, self.iv, very simply:

```
self.anim.addBehavior(MyDropBounceAndRollBehavior(view:self.iv))
```

All the work is now done by the MyDropBounceAndRollBehavior instance. I've designed it to affect just one view, so its initializer looks like this:

```
init(view v:UIView) {
    self.v = v
    super.init()
}
```

A UIDynamicBehavior receives a reference to its dynamic animator just before being added to it, by implementing willMoveToAnimator:, and can refer to it subsequently as self.dynamicAnimator. To incorporate actual behaviors into itself, our custom UIDynamicBehavior subclass creates and configures them, and calls addChild-Behavior:; it can refer to the array of its child behaviors as self.childBehaviors. When our custom behavior is added to or removed from the dynamic animator, the effect is the same as if its child behaviors themselves were added or removed.

Here is the rest of MyDropBounceAndRollBehavior. Our precautions in the gravity behavior's action block not to cause a retain cycle are simpler than before; it suffices to designate self as an unowned reference and remove self from the animator explicitly:

```
override func willMoveToAnimator(anim: UIDynamicAnimator?) {
    guard let anim = anim else { return }
    let sup = self.v.superview!
    let grav = UIGravityBehavior()
    grav.action = {
        [unowned self] in
        let items = anim.itemsInRect(sup.bounds) as! [UIView]
        if items.indexOf(self.v) == nil {
            anim.removeBehavior(self)
```

```
                    self.v.removeFromSuperview()
            }
        }
        self.addChildBehavior(grav)
        grav.addItem(self.v)
        let push = UIPushBehavior(items:[self.v], mode:.Instantaneous)
        push.pushDirection = CGVectorMake(1, 0)
        self.addChildBehavior(push)
        let coll = UICollisionBehavior()
        coll.collisionMode = .Boundaries
        coll.collisionDelegate = self
        coll.addBoundaryWithIdentifier("floor",
            fromPoint:CGPointMake(0, sup.bounds.maxY),
            toPoint:CGPointMake(sup.bounds.maxX, sup.bounds.maxY))
        self.addChildBehavior(coll)
        coll.addItem(self.v)
        let bounce = UIDynamicItemBehavior()
        bounce.elasticity = 0.8
        self.addChildBehavior(bounce)
        bounce.addItem(self.v)
    }
    func collisionBehavior(behavior: UICollisionBehavior,
        beganContactForItem item: UIDynamicItem,
        withBoundaryIdentifier identifier: NSCopying?,
        atPoint p: CGPoint) {
            let b = self.childBehaviors
            if let ix = b.indexOf({$0 is UIDynamicItemBehavior}) {
                let bounce = b[ix] as! UIDynamicItemBehavior
                let v = bounce.angularVelocityForItem(item)
                if v <= 6 {
                    bounce.addAngularVelocity(6, forItem:item)
                }
            }
        }
}
```

Animator and Behaviors

Here are some further UIDynamicAnimator methods and properties:

delegate

> The delegate (UIDynamicAnimatorDelegate) is sent messages dynamicAnimator-
> DidPause: and dynamicAnimatorWillResume:. The animator is paused when it has
> nothing to do: it has no dynamic items, or all its dynamic items are at rest.

running

> If true, the animator is not paused; some dynamic item is being animated.

elapsedTime

> The total time during which this animator has been running since it first started
> running. The elapsedTime does not increase while the animator is paused, nor is

it reset. You might use this in a delegate method or `action` method to decide that the animation is over.

`updateItemUsingCurrentState:`
Once a dynamic item has come under the influence of the animator, the animator is responsible for positioning that dynamic item. If your code manually changes the dynamic item's position or other relevant attributes, call this method so that the animator can take account of those changes.

 New in iOS 9, you can turn on a display that reveals visually what the animator is doing, showing its field vectors, attachment lines, and so forth; assuming that `self.anim` refers to the dynamic animator, you would say:

```
self.anim.performSelector("setDebugEnabled:", withObject:true)
```

The rest of this section surveys the various built-in UIDynamicBehavior subclasses.

UIDynamicItemBehavior

A UIDynamicItemBehavior doesn't apply any force or velocity; instead, it is a way of endowing items with internal physical characteristics that will affect how they respond to other dynamic behaviors. Here are some of them:

`density`
Changes the impulse-resisting mass in relation to size. In other words, when we speak of an item's mass, we mean a combination of its size and its `density`.

`elasticity`
The item's tendency to bounce on collision.

`friction`
The item's tendency to be slowed by sliding past another item.

`anchored`
New in iOS 9. An anchored item is not affected by forces that would make an item move; thus it remains stationary. This gives you something with friction and elasticity off of which you can bounce and slide other items.

`resistance, angularResistance, allowsRotation`
The item's tendency to come to rest unless forces are actively applied. `allows-Rotation` prevents the item from acquiring any angular velocity at all.

`charge`
New in iOS 9; meaningful only with respect to magnetic and electric fields, which I'll get to in a moment.

```
addLinearVelocity:forItem:, linearVelocityForItem
addAngularVelocity:forItem:, angularVelocityForItem
```
Methods for tweaking linear and angular velocity.

UIGravityBehavior

UIGravityBehavior imposes an acceleration on its dynamic items. By default, this acceleration is downward with a magnitude of 1 (arbitrarily defined as 1000 points per second per second). You can customize gravity by changing its `gravityDirection` (a CGVector) or its `angle` and `magnitude`.

In iOS 9, UIGravityBehavior is effectively a specialization of a new class of behavior, UIFieldBehavior.

UIFieldBehavior

UIFieldBehavior, new in iOS 9, is a generalization of UIGravityBehavior. A field affects any of its `items` for as long as they are within its `region`. A region (a UIRegion, also new in iOS 9) has a shape, which is a circle, a rectangle, or the union, intersection, or difference of two regions, or the inverse of a region. An infinite region is legal, and is the default. The shape defines the region's size; the region's location within the reference view is defined by the field behavior's `position`, which is the region's effective *center*. The default `position` is `CGPointZero`, the reference view's top left corner.

A field has a `strength` property (which can be negative to reverse the directionality of its forces) as well as a `falloff` defining a change in strength proportional to distance from the center, and a `minimumRadius` that specifies a central circle in which there is no field effect. Other properties (`direction`, `smoothness`, and `animationSpeed`) are applicable only to those built-in field types that define them.

The built-in field types are obtained by calling a class factory method:

`linearGravityFieldWithVector:`
Like UIGravityBehavior. Accelerates the item in the direction of a vector that you define, proportionally to its mass, the length of the vector, and the `strength` of the field. The vector is the field's `direction`, and can be changed.

`velocityFieldWithVector:`
Like UIGravityBehavior, but it doesn't apply an acceleration (a force) — instead, it applies a constant velocity.

`radialGravityFieldWithPosition:`
Like a point-oriented version of UIGravityBehavior. Accelerates the item towards, or pushes it away from, the field's designated central point (its `position`).

springField

Behaves as if there were a spring stretching from the item to the center, so that the item oscillates back and forth across the center until it settles there.

electricField

Behaves like an electric field emanating from the center. A negatively charged item is attracted to the center but repelled as it reaches it.

magneticField

Behaves like a magnetic field emanating from the center. A moving charged item's path is bent away from the center.

vortexField

Accelerates the item sideways with respect to the center.

dragField

Reduces the item's speed.

noiseFieldWithSmoothness:animationSpeed:

Adds random disturbance to the position of the item. The smoothness is between 0 (noisy) and 1 (smooth). The animationSpeed is how many times per second the field should change randomly. Both can be changed in real time.

turbulenceFieldWithSmoothness:animationSpeed:

Like noiseField..., but takes the item's velocity into account.

Think of a field as an infinite grid of CGVectors, with the potential to affect the speed and direction (that is, the velocity) of an item within its borders; these CGVectors are interactive, in the sense that at every instant of time the vector applicable to a particular item can be recalculated. You can write a custom field by calling the UIFieldBehavior class method fieldWithEvaluationBlock: with a function that takes the item's position, velocity, mass, and charge, along with the animator's elapsed time, and returns a CGVector.

In this (silly) example, we create a delayed drag field: for the first quarter second it does nothing, but then it suddenly switches on and applies the brakes to its items, bringing them to a standstill if they don't already have enough velocity to escape the region's boundaries:

```
let b = UIFieldBehavior.fieldWithEvaluationBlock {
    (beh, pt, v, m, c, t) -> CGVector in
    if t > 0.25 {
        return CGVectorMake(-v.dx, -v.dy)
    }
    return CGVectorMake(0,0)
}
```

The evaluation function receives the behavior itself as a parameter, so it can consult the behavior's properties in real time. You can define your own properties by subclassing UIFieldBehavior. If you're going to do that, you might as well also define your own class function to configure and return the custom field. To illustrate, I'll turn the hard-coded 0.25 delay from the previous example into a property:

```
class MyDelayedFieldBehavior : UIFieldBehavior {
    var delay = 0.0
    class func dragFieldWithDelay(del:Double) -> Self {
        let f = self.fieldWithEvaluationBlock {
            (beh, pt, v, m, c, t) -> CGVector in
            if t > (beh as! MyDelayedFieldBehavior).delay {
                return CGVectorMake(-v.dx, -v.dy)
            }
            return CGVectorMake(0,0)
        }
        f.delay = del
        return f
    }
}
```

Here's an example of creating and configuring our delayed drag field:

```
let b = MyDelayedFieldBehavior.dragFieldWithDelay(0.25)
b.region = UIRegion(size: self.view.bounds.size)
b.position = CGPointMake(self.view.bounds.midX, self.view.bounds.midY)
b.addItem(v)
self.anim.addBehavior(b)
```

UIPushBehavior

UIPushBehavior applies a force either instantaneously or continuously (mode), the latter constituting an acceleration. How this force affects an object depends in part upon the object's mass. The effect of a push behavior can be toggled with the active property; an instantaneous push is repeated each time the active property is set to true.

To configure a push behavior, set its pushDirection or angle and magnitude. In addition, a push may be applied at an offset from the center of an item. This will apply an additional angular acceleration. Thus, in my earlier example, I could have started the view spinning clockwise by means of its initial push, like this:

```
push.setTargetOffsetFromCenter(UIOffsetMake(0, -200), forItem:self.v)
```

UICollisionBehavior

UICollisionBehavior watches for collisions either between items belonging to this same behavior or between an item and a boundary (mode). One collision behavior can have multiple items and multiple boundaries. A boundary may be described as a line between two points or as a UIBezierPath, or you can turn the reference view's bounds into boundaries (setTranslatesReferenceBoundsIntoBoundaryWithInsets:). Boundaries that you create can have an identifier. The collisionDelegate (UICollision-BehaviorDelegate) is called when a collision begins and again when it ends.

How a given collision affects the item(s) involved depends on the physical characteristics of the item(s), which may be configured through a UIDynamicItemBehavior.

New in iOS 9, a dynamic item, such as a UIView, can have a customized collision boundary, rather than its collision boundary being merely the edges of its frame (as in iOS 8 and before). You can have a rectangle dictated by the frame, an ellipse dictated by the frame, or a custom shape — a convex counterclockwise simple closed UIBezierPath. The relevant properties, collisionBoundsType and (for a custom shape) collision-BoundingPath, are read-only, so you will have to subclass, as I did in my earlier example.

UISnapBehavior

UISnapBehavior causes one item to snap to one point as if pulled by a spring. Its damping describes how much the item should oscillate as its settles into that point. This is a very simple behavior: the snap occurs immediately when the behavior is added to the animator, and there's no notification when it's over.

New in iOS 9, the snap behavior's snapPoint is a settable property. Thus, having performed a snap, you can subsequently change the snapPoint and cause another snap to take place.

UIAttachmentBehavior

UIAttachmentBehavior attaches an item to another item or to a point in the reference view, depending on how you initialize it:

- init(item:attachedToItem:)
- init(item:attachedToAnchor:)

The attachment point is, by default, the item's center; to change that, there's a different pair of initializers:

- init(item:offsetFromCenter:attachedToItem:offsetFromCenter:)
- init(item:offsetFromCenter:attachedToAnchor:)

The attaching medium's physics are governed by the behavior's length, frequency, and damping. If the frequency is 0 (the default), the attachment is like a bar; otherwise, and especially if the damping is very small, it is like a spring.

You can subsequently move the anchorPoint (if the attachment is to an anchor). As the other item or the anchorPoint moves, this item moves with it, in accordance with the physics of the attaching medium. An `anchorPoint` is particularly useful for implementing a draggable view within an animator world, as I'll demonstrate in the next chapter.

New in iOS 9, there are several more varieties of attachment:

Limit attachment
> A limit attachment is created with this class method:
>
> - `limitAttachmentWithItem:offsetFromCenter:attachedToItem:offset-FromCenter:`
>
> It's like a rope running between two items. Each item can move freely and independently until the `length` is reached, at which point the moving item drags the other item along.

Fixed attachment
> A fixed attachment is created with this class method:
>
> - `fixedAttachmentWithItem:attachedToItem:attachmentAnchor:`
>
> It's like two rods, each with an item at one end, and welded together at the other end, which is at the anchor point. If one item moves, it must remain at a fixed distance from the anchor, and will tend to rotate around it while pulling it along, at the same time making the other item rotate around the anchor.

Pin attachment
> A pin attachment is created with this class method:
>
> - `pinAttachmentWithItem:attachedToItem:attachmentAnchor:`
>
> A pin attachment is like a fixed attachment, but instead of the rods being welded together, they are hinged together. Each item is thus free to rotate around the anchor point, at a fixed distance from it, *independently*, subject to the pin attachment's `frictionTorque` which injects resistance into the hinge.

Sliding attachment
> A sliding attachment can involve one or two items, and is created with one of these class methods:
>
> - `slidingAttachmentWithItem:attachmentAnchor:axisOfTranslation:`
> - `slidingAttachmentWithItem:attachedToItem:attachmentAnchor:axisOf-Translation:`
>
> Imagine a channel running through the anchor point, its direction defined by the axis of translation (a CGVector). Then an item is attached to a rod whose other end slots into that channel and is free to slide up and down it, but whose angle relative to the channel is fixed by its initial definition (given the item's position, the anchor's position, and the channel axis) and cannot change.

The channel is infinite by default, but you can add end caps that define the limits of sliding, by specifying the attachment's `attachmentRange`, whose type is a UIFloatRange, which has a `minimum` and a `maximum`, plus you can use constants `UIFloatRangeZero` and `UIFloatRangeInfinite` (and there's a convenience function `UIFloatRangeIsEqualToRange:`). The anchor point is 0, and you are defining the `minimum` and `maximum` with respect to that; thus, a float range (`-100.0,100.0`) provides freedom of movement up to 100 points away from the initial anchor point. It can take some experimentation to discover whether the end cap along a given direction of the channel is the `minimum` or the `maximum`.

If there is one item, the anchor is fixed. If there are two items, they can slide independently, and the anchor is free to follow along if one of the items pulls it.

Here's an example of a sliding attachment. We start with a black square and a red square, sitting on the same horizontal, and attached to an anchor midway between them:

```
// first view
let v = UIView(frame:CGRectMake(0,0,50,50))
v.backgroundColor = UIColor.blackColor()
self.view.addSubview(v)
// second view
let v2 = UIView(frame:CGRectMake(200,0,50,50))
v2.backgroundColor = UIColor.redColor()
self.view.addSubview(v2)
// sliding attachment
let a = UIAttachmentBehavior.slidingAttachmentWithItem(v,
    attachedToItem: v2, attachmentAnchor: CGPointMake(125,25),
    axisOfTranslation: CGVectorMake(0,1))
a.attachmentRange = UIFloatRangeMake(-200,200)
self.anim.addBehavior(a)
```

The axis through the anchor point is vertical, and we have permitted a `maximum` of 200. We now apply a slight vertical downward push to the black square:

```
let p = UIPushBehavior(items: [v], mode: .Instantaneous)
p.pushDirection = CGVectorMake(0,0.1)
self.anim.addBehavior(p)
```

The black square moves slowly downward, absolutely vertical, with its rod sliding down the channel, until its rod hits the `maximum` end cap at 200. At that point, the anchor breaks free and begins to move, dragging the red square with it, the two of them continuing downward and slowly rotating round their connection of two rods and the channel (Figure 4-8).

Motion Effects

A view can respond in real time to the way the user tilts the device. Typically, the view's response will be to shift its position slightly. This is used in various parts of the interface,

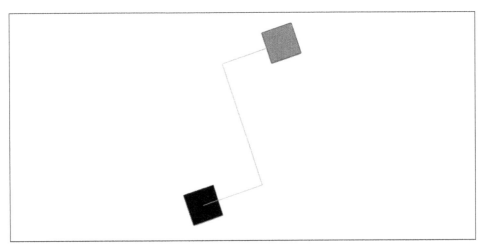

Figure 4-8. A sliding attachment

to give a sense of the interface's being layered (parallax). When an alert is present, for example, if the user tilts the device, the alert shifts its position; the effect is subtle, but sufficient to suggest subconsciously that the alert is floating slightly in front of everything else on the screen.

Your own views can behave in the same way. A view will respond to shifts in the position of the device if it has one or more motion effects (UIMotionEffect). A view's motion effects are managed with methods addMotionEffect: and removeMotionEffect:, and the motionEffects property.

The UIMotionEffect class is abstract. The chief subclass provided is UIInterpolating-MotionEffect. Every UIInterpolatingMotionEffect has a single key path, which uses key–value coding to specify the property of its view that it affects. It also has a type, specifying which axis of the device's tilting (horizontal tilt or vertical tilt) is to affect this property. Finally, it has a maximum and minimum relative value, the furthest distance that the affected property of the view is to be permitted to wander from its actual value as the user tilts the device.

Related motion effects should be combined into a UIMotionEffectGroup (a UIMotion-Effect subclass), and the group added to the view. So, for example:

```
let m1 = UIInterpolatingMotionEffect(
    keyPath:"center.x", type:.TiltAlongHorizontalAxis)
m1.maximumRelativeValue = 10.0
m1.minimumRelativeValue = -10.0
let m2 = UIInterpolatingMotionEffect(
    keyPath:"center.y", type:.TiltAlongVerticalAxis)
m2.maximumRelativeValue = 10.0
```

```
m2.minimumRelativeValue = -10.0
let g = UIMotionEffectGroup()
g.motionEffects = [m1,m2]
v.addMotionEffect(g)
```

You can write your own UIMotionEffect subclass by implementing a single method, keyPathsAndRelativeValuesForViewerOffset:, but this will rarely be necessary.

Animation and Autolayout

The interplay between animation and autolayout can be tricky. As part of an animation, you may be changing a view's frame (or bounds, or center). You're really not supposed to do that when you're using autolayout. If you do, an animation may not work correctly. Or, it may appear to work perfectly, because no layout has happened; however, it is entirely possible that layout *will* happen, and that it will be accompanied by undesirable effects. As I explained in Chapter 1, when layout takes place under autolayout, what matters are a view's constraints. If the constraints affecting a view don't resolve to the size and position that the view has at the moment of layout, the view will jump as the constraints are obeyed. This is almost certainly not what you want.

To persuade yourself that this can be a problem, just animate a view's position and then ask for immediate layout, like this:

```
UIView.animateWithDuration(1, animations:{
    self.v.center.x += 100
    }, completion: {
        _ in
        self.v.superview!.setNeedsLayout()
        self.v.superview!.layoutIfNeeded()
})
```

If we're using autolayout, the view slides to the right and then jumps back to the left. This is bad. It's up to us to keep the constraints synchronized with the reality, so that when layout comes along in the natural course of things, our views don't jump into undesirable states.

One option is to revise the violated constraints to match the new reality. If we've planned far ahead, we may have armed ourselves in advance with a reference to those constraints; in that case, our code can now remove and replace them — or, if the only thing that needs changing is the constant value of a constraint, we can change that value in place. Otherwise, discovering what constraints are now violated, and getting a reference to them, is not at all easy.

Alternatively, instead of performing the animation first and then revising the constraints, we can change the constraints first and then *animate the act of layout*. Again, this assumes that we have a reference to the constraints in question. For example, if we are animating a view 100 points rightward, and if we have a reference to the constraint whose constant positions that view horizontally, we would say this:

```
let con = self.v_horizontalPositionConstraint
con.constant += 100
UIView.animateWithDuration(1, animations:{
    self.v.superview!.layoutIfNeeded()
})
```

This technique is not limited to a simple change of constant. You can overhaul the constraints quite dramatically and still animate the resulting change of layout. In this example, I animate a view (v) from one side of its superview (self.view) to the other by removing its leading constraint and replacing it with a trailing constraint:

```
let c = self.oldConstraint.constant
NSLayoutConstraint.deactivateConstraints([self.oldConstraint])
let newConstraint = v.trailingAnchor.constraintEqualToAnchor(
    self.view.layoutMarginsGuide.trailingAnchor, constant:-c)
NSLayoutConstraint.activateConstraints([newConstraint])
UIView.animateWithDuration(0.4) {
    v.superview!.layoutIfNeeded()
}
```

Another possibility is to use a snapshot of the original view (Chapter 1). Add the snapshot temporarily to the interface — without using autolayout, and perhaps hiding the original view — and animate the snapshot:

```
let snap = self.v.snapshotViewAfterScreenUpdates(false)
snap.frame = self.v.frame
self.v.superview!.addSubview(snap)
self.v.hidden = true
UIView.animateWithDuration(1, animations:{
    snap.center.x += 100
})
```

That works because the snapshot view is not under the influence of autolayout, so it stays where we put it even if layout takes place. If, however, we need to remove the snapshot view and reveal the real view, and if the nature of the animation is such that the real view ultimately needs to be shifted to a new permanent position, then its constraints will still have to be revised.

Still another possibility is to remove the animated view *itself* from the influence of autolayout by setting its translatesAutoresizingMaskIntoConstraints to true. But that, of itself, will cause a conflict between the view's inherent autoresizing constraints and the existing constraints that were positioning it under autolayout; those existing constraints must therefore be removed as well, which may require considerable preparation in advance.

CHAPTER 5

Touches

[*Winifred the Woebegone illustrates hit-testing:*]
Hey nonny nonny, is it you? — Hey nonny nonny
nonny no! — Hey nonny nonny, is it you? — *Hey*
nonny nonny nonny no!

—Marshall Barer, *Once Upon a Mattress*

A *touch* is an instance of the user putting a finger on the screen. The system and the hardware, working together, know *when* a finger contacts the screen and *where* it is. A finger is fat, but its location is cleverly reduced to a single appropriate point.

A UIView, by virtue of being a UIResponder, is the visible locus of touches. There are other UIResponder subclasses, but none of them is visible on the screen. What the user sees are views; what the user is touching are views. (The user actually sees layers, but a layer is not a UIResponder and is not involved with touches.)

It would make sense, therefore, if every touch were reported directly to the view in which it occurred. However, what the system "sees" is not particular views but an app as a whole. So a touch is represented as an object (a UITouch instance) which is bundled up in an envelope (a UIEvent) which the system delivers to your app. It is then up to your app to deliver the envelope to an appropriate UIView. In the vast majority of cases, this will happen automatically the way you expect, and you will respond to a touch by way of the view in which the touch occurred.

In fact, usually you won't concern yourself with UIEvents and UITouches at all. Most built-in interface views deal with these low-level touch reports themselves, and notify your code at a higher level — you hear about functionality and intention rather than raw touches. When a UIButton emits an action message to report a control event such as Touch Up Inside, it has already performed a reduction of a complex sequence of touches ("the user put a finger down inside me and then, possibly with some dragging hither and yon, raised it when it was still reasonably close to me"). A UITextField reports touches on the keyboard as changes in its own text. A UITableView reports that the user selected a cell. A UIScrollView, when dragged, reports that it scrolled; when pinched outward, it reports that it zoomed.

Nevertheless, it is useful to know how to respond to touches directly, so that you can implement your own touchable views, and so that you understand what Cocoa's built-in views are actually doing. In this chapter, I'll start by discussing touch detection and response by views (and other UIResponders) at their lowest level, along with a higher-level, more practical mechanism, gesture recognizers, that categorizes touches into gesture types for you. Then I'll deconstruct the touch-delivery architecture by which touches are reported to your views in the first place.

Touch Events and Views

Imagine a screen that the user is not touching at all: the screen is "finger-free." Now the user touches the screen with one or more fingers. From that moment until the time the screen is once again finger-free, all touches and finger movements together constitute what Apple calls a single *multitouch sequence.*

The system reports to your app, during a given multitouch sequence, every change in finger configuration, so that your app can figure out what the user is doing. Every such report is a UIEvent. In fact, every report having to do with the same multitouch sequence is *the same UIEvent instance*, arriving repeatedly, each time there's a change in finger configuration.

Every UIEvent reporting a change in the user's finger configuration contains one or more UITouch objects. Each UITouch object corresponds to a single finger; conversely, every finger touching the screen is represented in the UIEvent by a UITouch object. Once a UITouch instance has been created to represent a finger that has touched the screen, *the same UITouch instance* is used to represent that finger throughout this multitouch sequence until the finger leaves the screen.

Now, it might sound as if the system, during a multitouch sequence, constantly has to bombard the app with huge numbers of reports. But that's not really true. The system needs to report only *changes* in the finger configuration. For a given UITouch object (representing, remember, a specific finger), only four things can happen. These are called *touch phases*, and are described by a UITouch instance's `phase` property (UITouchPhase):

`.Began`
> The finger touched the screen for the first time; this UITouch instance has just been created. This is always the first phase, and arrives only once.

`.Moved`
> The finger moved upon the screen.

`.Stationary`

The finger remained on the screen without moving. Why is it necessary to report this? Well, remember, once a UITouch instance has been created, it must be present every time the UIEvent for this multitouch sequence arrives. So if the UIEvent arrives because something *else* happened (e.g., a new finger touched the screen), we must report what *this* finger has been doing, even if it has been doing nothing.

`.Ended`

The finger left the screen. Like `.Began`, this phase arrives only once. The UITouch instance will now be destroyed and will no longer appear in UIEvents for this multitouch sequence.

Those four phases are sufficient to describe everything that a finger can do. Actually, there is one more possible phase:

`.Cancelled`

The system has aborted this multitouch sequence because something interrupted it. What might interrupt a multitouch sequence? There are many possibilities. Perhaps the user clicked the Home button or the screen lock button in the middle of the sequence. A local notification alert may have appeared (Chapter 13); on an iPhone, a call may have come in. And as we shall see, a gesture recognizer recognizing its gesture may also trigger touch cancellation. The point is, if you're dealing with touches yourself, you cannot afford to ignore touch cancellation; they are your opportunity to get things into a coherent state when the sequence is interrupted.

When a UITouch first appears (`.Began`), your app works out which UIView it is associated with. (I'll give full details, later in this chapter, as to how it does that.) This view is then set as the touch's `view` property, and *remains* so; from then on, this UITouch is *always* associated with this view (until that finger leaves the screen).

The same UIEvent containing the same UITouches can be sent to multiple views. Accordingly, a UIEvent is distributed to *all the views of all the UITouches it contains.* Conversely, if a view is sent a UIEvent, it's because that UIEvent contains at least one UITouch whose `view` is this view.

If every UITouch in a UIEvent associated with a certain UIView has the phase `.Stationary`, that UIEvent is *not* sent to that UIView. There's no point, because as far as that view is concerned, nothing happened.

 Although you can distinguish a particular UITouch or UIEvent object over time by keeping a reference to it, you mustn't retain that reference; it doesn't belong to you.

Receiving Touches

A UIResponder, and therefore a UIView, has four methods corresponding to the four UITouch phases that require UIEvent delivery. A UIEvent is delivered to a view by calling one of these four methods (the *touches methods*):

touchesBegan:withEvent:
> A finger touched the screen, creating a UITouch.

touchesMoved:withEvent:
> A finger previously reported to this view with touchesBegan:withEvent: has moved.

touchesEnded:withEvent:
> A finger previously reported to this view with touchesBegan:withEvent: has left the screen.

touchesCancelled:withEvent:
> We are bailing out on a finger previously reported to this view with touches-Began:withEvent:.

The parameters of these methods are:

The relevant touches
> These are the event's touches whose phase corresponds to the name of the method and (normally) whose view is this view. They arrive as a Set. If there is only one touch in the set, or if any touch in the set will do, you can retrieve it with first (a set is unordered, so *which* element is first is arbitrary).

The event
> This is the UIEvent instance. It contains its touches as a Set, which you can retrieve with the allTouches message. This means *all* the event's touches, including but not necessarily limited to those in the first parameter; there might be touches in a different phase or intended for some other view. You can call touchesForView: or touchesForWindow: to ask for the set of touches associated with a particular view or window.

A UITouch has some useful methods and properties:

locationInView:, previousLocationInView:
> The current and previous location of this touch with respect to the coordinate system of a given view. The view you'll be interested in will often be self or self.superview; supply nil to get the location with respect to the window. The previous location will be of interest only if the phase is .Moved.

timestamp
> When the touch last changed. A touch is timestamped when it is created (.Began) and each time it moves (.Moved). There can be a delay between the occurrence of a physical touch and the delivery of the corresponding UITouch, so to learn about the timing of touches, consult the timestamp, not the clock.

tapCount
> If two touches are in roughly the same place in quick succession, and the first one is brief, the second one may be characterized as a repeat of the first. They are different touch objects, but the second will be assigned a tapCount one larger than the previous one. The default is 1, so if (for example) a touch's tapCount is 3, then this is the third tap in quick succession in roughly the same spot.

view
> The view with which this touch is associated.

majorRadius, majorRadiusTolerance
> Respectively, the radius of the touch (approximately half its size) and the uncertainty of that measurement, in points.

Here are some additional UIEvent properties:

type
> This will be UIEventType.Touches. There are other event types, but you're not going to receive any of them this way.

timestamp
> When the event occurred.

So, when we say that a certain view *is receiving a touch*, that is a shorthand expression meaning that it is being sent a UIEvent containing this UITouch, over and over, by calling one of its touches methods, corresponding to the phase this touch is in, from the time the touch is created until the time it is destroyed.

Restricting Touches

Touch events can be turned off entirely at the application level with UIApplication's beginIgnoringInteractionEvents. It is quite common to do this during animations and other lengthy operations during which responding to a touch could cause undesirable results. This call should be balanced by endIgnoringInteractionEvents. Pairs can be nested, in which case interactivity won't be restored until the outermost endIgnoringInteractionEvents has been reached.

A number of UIView properties also restrict the delivery of touches to particular views:

`userInteractionEnabled`

> If set to `false`, this view (along with its subviews) is excluded from receiving touches. Touches on this view or one of its subviews "fall through" to a view behind it.

`alpha`

> If set to `0.0` (or extremely close to it), this view (along with its subviews) is excluded from receiving touches. Touches on this view or one of its subviews "fall through" to a view behind it.

`hidden`

> If set to `true`, this view (along with its subviews) is excluded from receiving touches. This makes sense, since from the user's standpoint, the view and its subviews are not even present.

`multipleTouchEnabled`

> If set to `false`, this view never receives more than one touch simultaneously; once it receives a touch, it doesn't receive any other touches until that first touch has ended.

`exclusiveTouch`

> An `exclusiveTouch` view receives a touch only if no other views in the same window have touches associated with them; once an `exclusiveTouch` view has received a touch, then while that touch exists no other view in the same window receives any touches. (This is the only one of these properties that can't be set in the nib editor.)

Interpreting Touches

Thanks to gesture recognizers (discussed later in this chapter), in most cases you won't have to interpret touches at all; you'll let a gesture recognizer do most of that work. Even so, it is beneficial to be conversant with the nature of touch interpretation; this will help you interact with a gesture recognizer, write your own gesture recognizer, or subclass an existing one. Furthermore, not every touch sequence can be codified through a gesture recognizer; sometimes, directly interpreting touches is the best approach.

To figure out what's going on as touches are received by a view, your code must essentially function as a kind of state machine. You'll receive various `touches` method calls, and your response will partly depend upon what happened previously, so you'll have to record somehow, such as in instance properties, the information that you'll need in order to decide what to do when the next `touches` method is called. Such an architecture can make writing and maintaining touch-analysis code quite tricky.

To illustrate the business of interpreting touches, we'll start with a view that can be dragged with the user's finger. For simplicity, I'll assume that this view receives only a single touch at a time. (This assumption is easy to enforce by setting the view's multiple-TouchEnabled to false, which is the default.)

The trick to making a view follow the user's finger is to realize that a view is positioned by its center, which is in superview coordinates, but the user's finger might not be at the center of the view. So at every stage of the drag we must change the view's center by the change in the user's finger position in superview coordinates:

```
override func touchesMoved(touches: Set<UITouch>, withEvent e: UIEvent?) {
    let t = touches.first!
    let loc = t.locationInView(self.superview)
    let oldP = t.previousLocationInView(self.superview)
    let deltaX = loc.x - oldP.x
    let deltaY = loc.y - oldP.y
    var c = self.center
    c.x += deltaX
    c.y += deltaY
    self.center = c
}
```

Next, let's add a restriction that the view can be dragged only vertically or horizontally. All we have to do is hold one coordinate steady; but which coordinate? Everything seems to depend on what the user does initially. So we'll do a one-time test the first time we receive touchesMoved:withEvent:. Now we're maintaining two Bool state properties, self.decided and self.horiz:

```
override func touchesBegan(touches: Set<UITouch>, withEvent e: UIEvent?) {
    self.decided = false
}
override func touchesMoved(touches: Set<UITouch>, withEvent e: UIEvent?) {
    let t = touches.first!
    if !self.decided {
        self.decided = true
        let then = t.previousLocationInView(self)
        let now = t.locationInView(self)
        let deltaX = fabs(then.x - now.x)
        let deltaY = fabs(then.y - now.y)
        self.horiz = deltaX >= deltaY
    }
    let loc = t.locationInView(self.superview)
    let oldP = t.previousLocationInView(self.superview)
    let deltaX = loc.x - oldP.x
    let deltaY = loc.y - oldP.y
    var c = self.center
    if self.horiz {
        c.x += deltaX
    } else {
        c.y += deltaY
    }
    self.center = c
}
```

Look at how things are trending. We are maintaining multiple state properties, which we are managing across multiple methods, and we are subdividing a `touches` method implementation into tests depending on the state of our state machine. Our state machine is very simple, but already our code is becoming difficult to read and to maintain — and things will only become more messy as we try to make our view's behavior more sophisticated.

Another area in which manual touch handling can rapidly prove overwhelming is when it comes to distinguishing between different gestures that the user is to be permitted to perform on a view. Imagine, for example, a view that distinguishes between a finger tapping briefly and a finger remaining down for a longer time. We can't know how long a tap is until it's over, so we must wait until then before deciding; once again, this requires maintaining state in a property (`self.time`):

```
override func touchesBegan(touches: Set<UITouch>, withEvent e: UIEvent?) {
    self.time = touches.first!.timestamp
}
override func touchesEnded(touches: Set<UITouch>, withEvent e: UIEvent?) {
    let diff = event.timestamp - self.time
    if (diff < 0.4) {
        print("short")
    } else {
        print("long")
    }
}
```

A similar challenge is distinguishing between a single tap and a double tap. The UITouch `tapCount` property already makes this distinction, but that, by itself, is not enough to help us react differently to the two. What we must do, having received a tap whose `tapCount` is 1, is to use delayed performance in responding to it, so that we wait long enough to give a second tap a chance to arrive. This is unfortunate, because it means that if the user intends a single tap, some time will elapse before anything happens in response to it; however, there's nothing we can readily do about that.

Distributing our various tasks correctly is tricky. We *know* when we have a double tap as early as `touchesBegan:withEvent:`, but we *respond* to the double tap in `touchesEnded:withEvent:`. Therefore we use a property (`self.single`) to communicate between the two. We don't start our delayed response to a single tap until `touchesEnded:withEvent:`, because what matters is the time between the taps as a whole, not between the starts of the taps:

```
override func touchesBegan(touches: Set<UITouch>, withEvent e: UIEvent?) {
    let ct = touches.first!.tapCount
    switch ct {
    case 2:
        self.single = false
    default: break
    }
```

```
}
override func touchesEnded(touches: Set<UITouch>, withEvent e: UIEvent?) {
    let ct = touches.first!.tapCount
    switch ct {
    case 1:
        self.single = true
        delay(0.3) {
            if self.single { // no second tap intervened
                print("single tap")
            }
        }
    case 2:
        print("double tap")
    default: break
    }
}
```

As that code weren't confusing enough, let's now consider combining our detection for
a single or double tap with our earlier code for dragging a view horizontally or vertically.
This is to be a view that can detect four kinds of gesture: a single tap, a double tap, a
horizontal drag, and a vertical drag. We must include the code for all possibilities and
make sure they don't interfere with each other. The result is horrifying — a forced join
between two already complicated sets of code, along with an additional pair of state
properties (self.drag, self.decidedTapOrDrag) to track the decision between the tap
gestures on the one hand and the drag gestures on the other:

```
override func touchesBegan(touches: Set<UITouch>, withEvent e: UIEvent?) {
    // be undecided
    self.decidedTapOrDrag = false
    // prepare for a tap
    let ct = touches.first!.tapCount
    switch ct {
    case 2:
        self.single = false
        self.decidedTapOrDrag = true
        self.drag = false
        return
    default: break
    }
    // prepare for a drag
    self.decidedDirection = false
}
override func touchesMoved(touches: Set<UITouch>, withEvent e: UIEvent?) {
    if self.decidedTapOrDrag && !self.drag {return}
    let t = touches.first!
    self.decidedTapOrDrag = true
    self.drag = true
    if !self.decidedDirection {
        self.decidedDirection = true
        let then = t.previousLocationInView(self)
        let now = t.locationInView(self)
```

```
            let deltaX = fabs(then.x - now.x)
            let deltaY = fabs(then.y - now.y)
            self.horiz = deltaX >= deltaY
        }
        let loc = t.locationInView(self.superview)
        let oldP = t.previousLocationInView(self.superview)
        let deltaX = loc.x - oldP.x
        let deltaY = loc.y - oldP.y
        var c = self.center
        if self.horiz {
            c.x += deltaX
        } else {
            c.y += deltaY
        }
        self.center = c
    }
    override func touchesEnded(touches: Set<UITouch>, withEvent e: UIEvent?) {
        if !self.decidedTapOrDrag || !self.drag {
            // end for a tap
            let ct = touches.first!.tapCount
            switch ct {
            case 1:
                self.single = true
                delay(0.3) {
                    if self.single {
                        print("single tap")
                    }
                }
            case 2:
                print("double tap")
            default: break
            }
        }
    }
}
```

That code seems to work, but it's hard to say whether it covers all possibilities coherently; it's barely legible and the logic borders on the mysterious. This is the kind of situation for which gesture recognizers were devised.

 New in iOS 9, if you're collecting raw touches, you can obtain more touches than in previous systems, thus allowing you to reduce the latency between the user's touches and your app's rendering to the screen. On certain devices, the touch detection rate is doubled, and you can obtain the extra touches by calling coalesced-TouchesForTouch: on the current UIEvent. On all devices, a few future touches may be predicted, and you can obtain these by calling predictedTouchesForTouch: on the current UIEvent. Watch WWDC 2015 video 233 for more information. — This edition does *not* document touch, responder, gesture recognizer, and application features related to screen presses, force touch, and 3D touch, as they are too new and still evolving.

Gesture Recognizers

Writing and maintaining a state machine that interprets touches across a combination of three or four touches methods is hard enough when a view confines itself to expecting only one kind of gesture, such as dragging. It becomes even more involved when a view wants to accept and respond differently to different kinds of gesture. Furthermore, many types of gesture are conventional and standard; it seems insane to require developers to implement independently the elements that constitute what is, in effect, a universal vocabulary.

The solution is gesture recognizers, which standardize common gestures and allow the code for different gestures to be separated and encapsulated into different objects. Thanks to gesture recognizers, it is unnecessary to subclass UIView merely in order to implement touch analysis.

Gesture Recognizer Classes

A *gesture recognizer* (a subclass of UIGestureRecognizer) is an object whose job is to detect that a multitouch sequence equates to *one particular type of gesture*. It is attached to a UIView, which has for this purpose methods addGestureRecognizer: and remove-GestureRecognizer:, and a gestureRecognizers property.

A UIGestureRecognizer implements the four touches handlers, but it is not a responder (a UIResponder), so it does not participate in the responder chain. If, however, a new touch is going to be delivered to a view, it is also associated with and delivered to that view's gesture recognizers if it has any, *and* to that view's *superview's* gesture recognizers if *it* has any, and so on up the view hierarchy. Thus, the place of a gesture recognizer in the view hierarchy matters, even though it isn't part of the responder chain.

UITouch and UIEvent provide complementary ways of learning how touches and gesture recognizers are associated. UITouch's gestureRecognizers lists the gesture recognizers that are currently handling this touch. UIEvent's touchesForGesture-Recognizer: lists the touches that are currently being handled by a particular gesture recognizer.

Each gesture recognizer maintains its own state as touch events arrive, building up evidence as to what kind of gesture this is. When one of them decides that it has recognized *its own particular type of gesture*, it emits either a single message (to indicate, for example, that a finger has tapped) or a series of messages (to indicate, for example, that a finger is moving); the distinction here is between a *discrete* and a *continuous* gesture.

What message a gesture recognizer emits, and to what object it sends it, is set through a target–action dispatch table attached to the gesture recognizer; a gesture recognizer is rather like a UIControl in this regard. Indeed, one might say that a gesture recognizer simplifies the touch handling of *any* view to be like that of a control. The difference is that one control may report several different control events, whereas each gesture recognizer reports only one gesture type, with different gestures being reported by different gesture recognizers.

UIGestureRecognizer itself is abstract, providing methods and properties to its subclasses. Among these are:

init(target:action:)
> The designated initializer. Each message emitted by a UIGestureRecognizer is a matter of sending the action message to the target. Further target–action pairs may be added with addTarget:action: and removed with removeTarget:action:.
>
> Two forms of action: selector are possible: either there is no parameter, or there is a single parameter which will be the gesture recognizer. Most commonly, you'll use the second form, so that the target can identify and query the gesture recognizer through one of its various methods and properties.

locationOfTouch:inView:
> The touch is specified by an index number. The numberOfTouches property provides a count of current touches; the touches themselves are inaccessible by way of the gesture recognizer.

enabled
> A convenient way to turn a gesture recognizer off without having to remove it from its view.

state, view
> I'll discuss state later on. The view is the view to which this gesture recognizer is attached.

Built-in UIGestureRecognizer subclasses are provided for six common gesture types: tap, pinch (inward or outward), pan (drag), swipe, rotate, and long press. Each embodies properties and methods likely to be needed for each type of gesture, either in order to configure the gesture recognizer beforehand or in order to query it as to the state of an ongoing gesture:

UITapGestureRecognizer (discrete)
> Configuration: numberOfTapsRequired, numberOfTouchesRequired ("touches" means simultaneous fingers).

UIPinchGestureRecognizer (continuous)
> Two fingers moving toward or away from each other. State: scale, velocity.

UIRotationGestureRecognizer (continuous)
> Two fingers moving round a common center. State: rotation, velocity.

UISwipeGestureRecognizer (discrete)

A straight-line movement in one of the four cardinal directions. Configuration: `direction` (meaning permitted directions, a bitmask), `numberOfTouchesRequired`.

UIPanGestureRecognizer (continuous)

Dragging. Configuration: `minimumNumberOfTouches`, `maximumNumberOfTouches`. State: `translationInView:`, `setTranslation:inView:`, and `velocityInView:`; the coordinate system of the specified view is used.

UIScreenEdgePanGestureRecognizer

A UIPanGestureRecognizer subclass. It recognizes a pan gesture that starts at an edge of the screen. It adds a configuration property, `edges`, a UIRectEdge; despite the name (and the documentation), this must be set to a single edge.

UILongPressGestureRecognizer (continuous)

Configuration: `numberOfTapsRequired`, `numberOfTouchesRequired`, `minimumPressDuration`, `allowableMovement`. The `numberOfTapsRequired` is the count of taps *before* the tap that stays down, so it can be 0 (the default). The `allowableMovement` setting lets you compensate for the fact that the user's finger is unlikely to remain steady during an extended press; thus we need to provide some limit before deciding that this gesture is, say, a drag, and not a long press after all. On the other hand, once the long press is recognized, the finger is permitted to drag as part of the long press gesture.

UIGestureRecognizer also provides a `locationInView:` method. This is a single point, even if there are multiple touches. The subclasses implement this variously. For example, for UIPanGestureRecognizer, the location is where the touch is if there's a single touch, but it's a sort of midpoint ("centroid") if there are multiple touches.

We already know enough to implement, using a gesture recognizer, a view that responds to a single tap, or a view that responds to a double tap. Here's code that implements a view (`self.v`) that responds to a single tap by calling our `singleTap` method:

```
let t1 = UITapGestureRecognizer(target:self, action:"singleTap")
self.v.addGestureRecognizer(t1)
```

And here's code that implements a view (`self.v`) that responds to a double tap by calling our `doubleTap` method:

```
let t2 = UITapGestureRecognizer(target:self, action:"doubleTap")
t2.numberOfTapsRequired = 2
self.v.addGestureRecognizer(t2)
```

For a continuous gesture like dragging, we need to know both when the gesture is in progress and when the gesture ends. This brings us to the subject of a gesture recognizer's state.

A gesture recognizer implements a notion of *states* (the `state` property, UIGesture-RecognizerState); it passes through these states in a definite progression. The gesture recognizer remains in the `.Possible` state until it can make a decision one way or the other as to whether this is in fact the correct gesture. The documentation neatly lays out the possible progressions:

Wrong gesture
> `.Possible` → `.Failed`. No action message is sent.

Discrete gesture (like a tap), recognized
> `.Possible` → `.Ended`. One action message is sent, when the state changes to `.Ended`.

Continuous gesture (like a drag), recognized
> `.Possible` → `.Began` → `.Changed` (repeatedly) → `.Ended`. Action messages are sent once for `.Began`, as many times as necessary for `.Changed`, and once for `.Ended`.

Continuous gesture, recognized but later cancelled
> `.Possible` → `.Began` → `.Changed` (repeatedly) → `.Cancelled`. Action messages are sent once for `.Began`, as many times as necessary for `.Changed`, and once for `.Cancelled`.

The same action message arrives at the same target every time, so the handler must differentiate by asking about the gesture recognizer's `state`. To illustrate, we will implement, using a gesture recognizer, a view that lets itself be dragged around in any direction by a single finger. Our maintenance of state is greatly simplified, because a UIPan-GestureRecognizer maintains a delta (translation) for us. This delta, available using `translationInView:`, is reckoned from the touch's initial position. We don't even need to record the view's original `center`, because we are allowed to reset the UIPanGesture-Recognizer's delta, using `setTranslation:inView:`. So:

```
func dragging(p : UIPanGestureRecognizer) {
    let v = p.view!
    switch p.state {
    case .Began, .Changed:
        let delta = p.translationInView(v.superview)
        var c = v.center
        c.x += delta.x; c.y += delta.y
        v.center = c
        p.setTranslation(CGPointZero, inView: v.superview)
    default: break
    }
}
```

A pan gesture recognizer can be used also to make a view draggable under the influence of a UIDynamicAnimator (Chapter 4). The strategy here is that the view is attached to one or more anchor points through a UIAttachmentBehavior; as the user drags, we move the anchor point(s), and the view follows. In this example, I set up the whole UIKit dynamics "stack" of objects as the gesture begins, anchoring the view at the point where the touch is; then I move the anchor point to stay with the touch. Instance properties `self.anim` and `self.att` store the UIDynamicAnimator and the UIAttachmentBehavior, respectively; `self.view` is our view's superview, and is the animator's reference view:

```
@IBAction func dragging(g: UIPanGestureRecognizer) {
    switch g.state {
    case .Began:
        self.anim = UIDynamicAnimator(referenceView:self.view)
        let loc = g.locationOfTouch(0, inView:g.view)
        let cen = CGPointMake(g.view!.bounds.midX, g.view!.bounds.midY)
        let off = UIOffsetMake(loc.x-cen.x, loc.y-cen.y)
        let anchor = g.locationOfTouch(0, inView:self.view)
        let att = UIAttachmentBehavior(item:g.view!,
            offsetFromCenter:off, attachedToAnchor:anchor)
        self.anim.addBehavior(att)
        self.att = att
    case .Changed:
        self.att.anchorPoint = g.locationOfTouch(0, inView: self.view)
    default:
        self.anim = nil
    }
}
```

The outcome is that the view both moves and rotates in response to dragging, like a plate being pulled about on a table by a single finger.

By adding behaviors to the dynamic animator, we can limit further what the view is permitted to do as it is being dragged by its anchor. For example, imagine a view that can be lifted vertically and dropped, but cannot be moved horizontally. As I demonstrated earlier, you can prevent horizontal dragging through the implementation of your response to touch events (and later in this chapter, I'll show how to do this by subclassing UIPanGestureRecognizer). But the same sort of limitation can imposed by way of the underlying physics of the world in which the view exists — with a sliding attachment, for example.

Gesture Recognizer Conflicts

The question naturally arises of what happens when multiple gesture recognizers are in play. This isn't a matter merely of multiple recognizers attached to a single view; as I have said, if a view is touched, not only its own gesture recognizers but also any gesture recognizers attached to views further up the view hierarchy are in play simultaneously. I like to think of a view as surrounded by a *swarm* of gesture recognizers — its own, and those of its superview, and so on. (In reality, it is a touch that has a swarm of gesture recognizers; that's why a UITouch has a `gestureRecognizers` property, in the plural.)

The superview gesture recognizer swarm comes as a surprise to beginners, but it makes sense, because without it, certain gestures would be impossible. Imagine, for example, a pair of views, each of which the user can tap individually, but which the user can also touch simultaneously (one finger on each view) to rotate them together around their mutual centroid. Neither view can detect the rotation *qua* rotation, because neither view receives both touches; only the superview can detect it, so the fact that the views themselves respond to touches must not prevent the superview's gesture recognizer from operating.

In general, once a gesture recognizer succeeds in recognizing its gesture, any *other* gesture recognizers associated with its touches are *forced into the* `.Failed` *state*, and whatever touches were associated with those gesture recognizers are no longer sent to them; in effect, the first gesture recognizer in a swarm that recognizes its gesture owns the gesture (and its touches) from then on.

In many cases, this "first past the post" behavior, on its own, will correctly eliminate conflicts. If it doesn't, you can modify it.

For example, we can add *both* our UITapGestureRecognizer for a single tap *and* our UIPanGestureRecognizer to a view and everything will just work; "first past the post" is exactly the desired behavior. What happens, though, if we also add the UITapGesture-Recognizer for a double tap? Dragging works, and single tap works; double tap works too, but without preventing the single tap from working. So, on a double tap, both the single tap action handler and the double tap action handler are called.

If that isn't what we want, we don't have to use delayed performance, as we did earlier. Instead, we can create a *dependency* between one gesture recognizer and another, telling the first to suspend judgement until the second has decided whether this is its gesture. We can do this by sending the first gesture recognizer the `requireGestureRecognizer-ToFail:` message. (This message is rather badly named; it doesn't mean "force this other recognizer to fail," but rather, "you can't succeed unless this other recognizer has failed.")

So our view `self.v` is now configured as follows:

```
let t2 = UITapGestureRecognizer(target:self, action:"doubleTap")
t2.numberOfTapsRequired = 2
self.v.addGestureRecognizer(t2)
let t1 = UITapGestureRecognizer(target:self, action:"singleTap")
t1.requireGestureRecognizerToFail(t2) // *
self.v.addGestureRecognizer(t1)
let p = UIPanGestureRecognizer(target: self, action: "dragging:")
self.v.addGestureRecognizer(p)
```

Another conflict that can arise is between a gesture recognizer and a view that already knows how to respond to the same gesture, such as a UIControl. This problem pops up particularly when the gesture recognizer belongs to the UIControl's superview. The UIControl's mere presence does not "block" the superview's gesture recognizer from recognizing a gesture on the UIControl, even if it is a UIControl that responds autonomously to touches. For example, your window's root view might have a UITapGesture-

Recognizer attached to it (perhaps because you want to be able to recognize taps on the background), but there is also a UIButton within it. How is that gesture recognizer to ignore a tap on the button?

The UIView instance method `gestureRecognizerShouldBegin:` solves the problem. It is called automatically; to modify its behavior, use a custom UIView subclass and override it. Its parameter is a gesture recognizer belonging to this view or to a view further up the view hierarchy. That gesture recognizer has recognized its gesture as taking place in this view; but by returning `false`, the view can tell the gesture recognizer to bow out and do nothing, not sending any action messages, and permitting this view to respond to the touch as if the gesture recognizer weren't there.

Thus, for example, a UIButton could return `false` for a single tap UITapGesture-Recognizer; a single tap on the button would then trigger the button's action message, not the gesture recognizer's action message. And in fact a UIButton, by default, *does* return `false` for a single tap UITapGestureRecognizer whose view is not the UIButton itself. (If the gesture recognizer is for some gesture other than a tap, then the problem never arises, because a tap on the button won't cause the gesture recognizer to recognize in the first place.) Other built-in controls may also implement `gestureRecognizer-ShouldBegin:` in such a way as to prevent accidental interaction with a gesture recognizer; the documentation says that a UISlider implements it in such a way that a UISwipeGestureRecognizer won't prevent the user from sliding the "thumb," and there may be other cases that aren't documented explicitly. Naturally, you can take advantage of this feature in your own UIView subclasses as well.

Another way of resolving possible gesture recognizer conflicts is through the gesture recognizer's delegate, or with a gesture recognizer subclass. I'll discuss those in a moment.

Subclassing Gesture Recognizers

To subclass UIGestureRecognizer or a built-in gesture recognizer subclass, you must do the following things:

- Import `UIKit.UIGestureRecognizerSubclass`. This file contains a category on UIGestureRecognizer that allows you to set the gesture recognizer's state (which is otherwise read-only), along with declarations for the methods you may need to override.

- Override any `touches` methods you need to (as if the gesture recognizer were a UIResponder); if you're subclassing a built-in gesture recognizer subclass, you will almost certainly call `super` so as to take advantage of the built-in behavior. In overriding a `touches` method, you need to think like a gesture recognizer. As these methods are called, a gesture recognizer is setting its state; you must interact with that process.

To illustrate, we will subclass UIPanGestureRecognizer so as to implement a view that can be moved only horizontally or vertically. Our strategy will be to make *two* UIPan-GestureRecognizer subclasses — one that allows only horizontal movement, and another that allows only vertical movement. They will make their recognition decisions in a mutually exclusive manner, so we can attach an instance of each to our view. This separates the decision-making logic in a gorgeously encapsulated object-oriented manner — a far cry from the spaghetti code we wrote earlier to do this same task.

I will show only the code for the horizontal drag gesture recognizer, because the vertical recognizer is symmetrically identical. We maintain just one property, `self.origLoc`, which we will use once to determine whether the user's initial movement is horizontal. We override `touchesBegan:withEvent:` to set our property with the first touch's location:

```
override func touchesBegan(touches: Set<UITouch>, withEvent e: UIEvent) {
    self.origLoc = touches.first!.locationInView(self.view!.superview)
    super.touchesBegan(touches, withEvent:e)
}
```

We then override `touchesMoved:withEvent:`; all the recognition logic is here. This method will be called for the first time with the state still at `.Possible`. At that moment, we look to see if the user's movement is more horizontal than vertical. If it isn't, we set the state to `.Failed`. But if it is, we just step back and let the superclass do its thing:

```
override func touchesMoved(touches: Set<UITouch>, withEvent e: UIEvent) {
    if self.state == .Possible {
        let loc = touches.first!.locationInView(self.view!.superview)
        let deltaX = fabs(loc.x - self.origLoc.x)
        let deltaY = fabs(loc.y - self.origLoc.y)
        if deltaY >= deltaX {
            self.state = .Failed
        }
    }
    super.touchesMoved(touches, withEvent:e)
}
```

We now have a view that moves only if the user's initial gesture is horizontal. But that isn't the entirety of what we want; we want a view that, itself, moves horizontally only. To implement this, we'll simply lie to our client about where the user's finger is, by overriding `translationInView::`

```
override func translationInView(view: UIView?) -> CGPoint {
    var proposedTranslation = super.translationInView(view)
    proposedTranslation.y = 0
    return proposedTranslation
}
```

That example was simple, because we subclassed a fully functional built-in UIGesture-Recognizer subclass. If you were to write your own UIGestureRecognizer subclass entirely from scratch, there would be more work to do:

- You should definitely implement all four `touches` handlers. Their job, at a minimum, is to advance the gesture recognizer through the canonical progression of its states. When the first touch arrives at a gesture recognizer, its state will be `.Possible`; you never explicitly set the recognizer's state to `.Possible` yourself. As soon as you know this can't be our gesture, you set the state to `.Failed` (Apple says that a gesture recognizer should "fail early, fail often"). If the gesture gets past all the failure tests, you set the state instead either to `.Ended` (for a discrete gesture) or to `.Began` (for a continuous gesture); if `.Began`, then you might set it to `.Changed`, and ultimately you must set it to `.Ended`. Action messages will be sent automatically at the appropriate moments.

- You should probably implement `reset`. This is called after you reach the end of the progression of states to notify you that the gesture recognizer's state is about to be set back to `.Possible`; it is your chance to return your state machine to its starting configuration (resetting properties, for example).

Keep in mind that your gesture recognizer might stop receiving touches without notice. Just because it gets a `touchesBegan:withEvent:` call for a particular touch doesn't mean it will ever get `touchesEnded:withEvent:` for that touch. If your gesture recognizer fails to recognize its gesture, either because it declares failure or because it is still in the `.Possible` state when another gesture recognizer recognizes, it won't get any more `touches` calls for any of the touches that were being sent to it. This is why `reset` is so important; it's the one reliable signal that it's time to clean up and get ready to receive the beginning of another possible gesture.

Gesture Recognizer Delegate

A gesture recognizer can have a delegate (UIGestureRecognizerDelegate), which can perform two types of task.

These delegate methods can *block a gesture recognizer's operation*:

`gestureRecognizerShouldBegin:`
Sent to the delegate before the gesture recognizer passes out of the `.Possible` state; return `false` to force the gesture recognizer to proceed to the `.Failed` state. (This happens *after* `gestureRecognizerShouldBegin:` has been sent to the view in which the touch took place. That view must not have returned `false`, or we wouldn't have reached this stage.)

`gestureRecognizer:shouldReceiveTouch:`

> Sent to the delegate before a touch is sent to the gesture recognizer's `touches-Began:withEvent:` method; return `false` to prevent that touch from ever being sent to the gesture recognizer.

These delegate methods can *mediate gesture recognition conflict*:

`gestureRecognizer:shouldRecognizeSimultaneouslyWithGestureRecognizer:`

> Sent when a gesture recognizer recognizes its gesture, if this will force the failure of another gesture recognizer, to the delegates of *both* gesture recognizers. Return `true` to prevent that failure, thus allowing both gesture recognizers to operate simultaneously. For example, a view could respond to both a two-fingered pinch and a two-fingered pan, the one applying a scale transform, the other changing the view's center.

`gestureRecognizer:shouldRequireFailureOfGestureRecognizer:`
`gestureRecognizer:shouldBeRequiredToFailByGestureRecognizer:`

> Sent very early in the life of a gesture, when all gesture recognizers in a view's swarm are still in the `.Possible` state, to the delegates of *all* of them, pairing the gesture recognizer whose delegate this is with every other gesture recognizer in the swarm. Return `true` to prioritize between a pair, saying that one gesture recognizer cannot succeed until another has first failed. In essence, these delegate methods turn the decision made once and permanently in `requireGestureRecognizerToFail:` into a live decision that can be made freshly every time a gesture occurs.

As an example, we will use delegate messages to combine a UILongPressGesture-Recognizer and a UIPanGestureRecognizer, as follows: the user must perform a tap-and-a-half (tap, then tap and hold) to "get the view's attention," which we will indicate by a pulsing animation on the view; then (and only then) the user can drag the view.

The UIPanGestureRecognizer's handler will take care of the drag, as shown earlier in this chapter. The UILongPressGestureRecognizer's handler will take care of starting and stopping the animation:

```
func longPress(lp:UILongPressGestureRecognizer) {
    switch lp.state {
    case .Began:
        let anim = CABasicAnimation(keyPath: "transform")
        anim.toValue = NSValue(
            CATransform3D:CATransform3DMakeScale(1.1, 1.1, 1))
        anim.fromValue = NSValue(CATransform3D:CATransform3DIdentity)
        anim.repeatCount = Float.infinity
        anim.autoreverses = true
        lp.view!.layer.addAnimation(anim, forKey:nil)
    case .Ended, .Cancelled:
```

```
            lp.view!.layer.removeAllAnimations()
        default: break
        }
    }
```

As we created our gesture recognizers, we kept a reference to the UILongPressGesture-Recognizer (`self.longPresser`), and we made ourself the UIPanGestureRecognizer's delegate. So we will receive delegate messages. If the UIPanGestureRecognizer tries to declare success while the UILongPressGestureRecognizer's state is `.Failed` or still at `.Possible`, we prevent it. If the UILongPressGestureRecognizer succeeds, we permit the UIPanGestureRecognizer to operate as well:

```
func gestureRecognizerShouldBegin(g: UIGestureRecognizer) -> Bool {
    // g is the pan gesture recognizer
    switch self.longPresser.state {
    case .Possible, .Failed:
        return false
    default:
        return true
    }
}
func gestureRecognizer(g: UIGestureRecognizer,
    shouldRecognizeSimultaneouslyWithGestureRecognizer
    g2: UIGestureRecognizer) -> Bool {
        return true
}
```

The result is that the view can be dragged only while it is pulsing; in effect, what we've done is to compensate, using delegate methods, for the fact that UIGestureRecognizer has no `requireGestureRecognizerToSucceed:` method.

If you are subclassing a gesture recognizer class, you can incorporate delegate-like behavior into the subclass, by overriding the following methods:

- `canPreventGestureRecognizer:`
- `canBePreventedByGestureRecognizer:`
- `shouldRequireFailureOfGestureRecognizer:`
- `shouldBeRequiredToFailByGestureRecognizer:`

The `Prevent` methods are similar to the delegate `shouldBegin:` method, and the `Fail` methods are similar to the delegate `Fail` methods. In this way, you can mediate gesture recognizer conflict at the class level. The built-in gesture recognizer subclasses already do this; that is why, for example, a single tap UITapGestureRecognizer does not, by recognizing its gesture, cause the failure of a double tap UITapGestureRecognizer.

You can also, in a gesture recognizer subclass, send `ignoreTouch:forEvent:` directly to a gesture recognizer (typically, to `self`). This has the same effect as the delegate method `gestureRecognizer:shouldReceiveTouch:` returning `false`, blocking all future delivery of that touch to the gesture recognizer. For example, if you're in the middle of an already recognized gesture and a new touch arrives, you might well elect to ignore it.

Gesture Recognizers in the Nib

Instead of instantiating a gesture recognizer in code, you can create and configure it in a *.xib* or *.storyboard* file. In the nib editor, drag a gesture recognizer from the Object library onto a view; the gesture recognizer becomes a top-level nib object, and the view's `gestureRecognizers` outlet is connected to the gesture recognizer. (You can add more than one gesture recognizer to a view in the nib: the view's `gestureRecognizers` property is an array, and its `gestureRecognizers` outlet is an outlet collection.) The gesture recognizer's properties are configurable in the Attributes inspector, and the gesture recognizer has a `delegate` outlet. The gesture recognizer is a full-fledged nib object, so you can make an outlet to it.

To configure a gesture recognizer's target–action pair in the nib, treat it like a UIControl's control event. The action method's signature should be marked `@IBAction`, and it should take a single parameter, which will be a reference to the gesture recognizer. You will then be able to form the Sent Action connection in the usual way. (A gesture recognizer can have multiple target–action pairs, but only one target–action pair can be configured for a gesture recognizer using the nib editor.) A view retains its gesture recognizers, so there will usually be no need for additional memory management on a gesture recognizer instantiated from a nib.

Touch Delivery

Here's the full standard procedure by which a touch is delivered to views and gesture recognizers:

- Whenever a new touch appears, the application performs hit-testing to determine the view that was touched. This view will be permanently associated with this touch, and is called, appropriately, the *hit-test view*. The logic of ignoring a view (denying it the ability to become the hit-test view) in response to its `userInteractionEnabled`, `hidden`, and `alpha` properties is implemented at this stage.

- Each time the touch situation changes, the application calls its own `sendEvent:`, which in turn calls the window's `sendEvent:`. The window delivers each of an event's touches by calling the appropriate `touches` method(s), as follows:

    - As a touch first appears, the logic of obedience to `multipleTouchEnabled` and `exclusiveTouch` is considered. If permitted by that logic:

        ◦ The touch is delivered to the hit-test view's swarm of gesture recognizers.

○ The touch is delivered to the hit-test view itself.

- If a gesture is recognized by a gesture recognizer, then for any touch associated with this gesture recognizer:

  ○ `touchesCancelled:forEvent:` is sent to the touch's view, and the touch is no longer delivered to its view.

  ○ If that touch was associated with any other gesture recognizer, that gesture recognizer is forced to fail.

- If a gesture recognizer fails, either because it declares failure or because it is forced to fail, its touches are no longer delivered to it, but (except as already specified) they continue to be delivered to their view.

- If a touch would be delivered to a view, but that view does not respond to the appropriate `touches` method, a responder further up the responder chain is sought that does respond to it, and the touch is delivered there.

The rest of this chapter discusses the details. As you'll see, nearly every bit of the standard procedure can be customized to some extent.

Hit-Testing

Hit-testing is the determination of what view the user touched. View hit-testing uses the UIView instance method `hitTest:withEvent:`, which returns either a view (the hit-test view) or `nil`. The idea is to find the frontmost view containing the touch point. This method uses an elegant recursive algorithm, as follows:

1. A view's `hitTest:withEvent:` first calls the same method on its own subviews, if it has any, because a subview is considered to be in front of its superview. The subviews are queried in front-to-back order (Chapter 1): thus, if two sibling views overlap, the one in front reports the hit first.

2. If, as a view hit-tests its subviews, any of those subviews responds by returning a view, it stops querying its subviews and immediately returns the view that was returned to it. Thus, the very first view to declare itself the hit-test view immediately percolates all the way to the top of the call chain and *is* the hit-test view.

3. If, on the other hand, a view has no subviews, or if all of its subviews return `nil` (indicating that neither they nor their subviews was hit), then the view calls `pointInside:withEvent:` on itself. If this call reveals that the touch was inside this view, the view returns itself, declaring itself the hit-test view; otherwise it returns `nil`.

No problem arises if a view has a transform, because `pointInside:withEvent:` takes the transform into account. That's why a rotated button continues to work correctly.

It is also up to `hitTest:withEvent:` to implement the logic of touch restrictions exclusive to a view. If a view's `userInteractionEnabled` is `false`, or its `hidden` is `true`, or its `alpha` is close to `0.0`, it returns `nil` without hit-testing any of its subviews and without calling `pointInside:withEvent:`. Thus these restrictions do not, of themselves, exclude a view from being hit-tested; on the contrary, they operate precisely by modifying a view's hit-test result.

However, hit-testing knows nothing about `multipleTouchEnabled` (which involves multiple touches) or `exclusiveTouch` (which involves multiple views). The logic of obedience to these properties is implemented at a later stage of the story.

You can use hit-testing yourself at any moment where it might prove useful. In calling `hitTest:withEvent:`, supply a point *in the coordinates of the view to which the message is sent*. The second parameter can be `nil` if you have no event.

For example, suppose we have a UIView with two UIImageView subviews. We want to detect a tap in either UIImageView, but we want to handle this at the level of the UIView. We can attach a UITapGestureRecognizer to the UIView, but then the gesture recognizer's `view` is the UIView, so how will we know which subview, if any, the tap was in?

First, verify that `userInteractionEnabled` is `true` for both UIImageViews. UIImageView is one of the few built-in view classes where this property is `false` by default, and a view whose `userInteractionEnabled` is `false` won't normally be the result of a call to `hitTest:withEvent:`. Then, when our gesture recognizer's action handler is called, we can use hit-testing to determine where the tap was:

```
// g is the gesture recognizer
let p = g.locationOfTouch(0, inView: g.view)
let v = g.view!.hitTest(p, withEvent: nil)
if let v = v as? UIImageView { // ...
```

You can also override `hitTest:withEvent:` in a view subclass, to alter its results during touch delivery, thus customizing the touch delivery mechanism. I call this *hit-test munging*. Hit-test munging can be used selectively as a way of turning user interaction on or off in an area of the interface. In this way, some unusual effects can be produced.

An important use of hit-test munging is to permit the touching of parts of subviews outside the bounds of their superview. If a view's `clipsToBounds` is `false`, a paradox arises: the user can *see* the regions of its subviews that are outside its bounds, but can't *touch* them. This can be confusing and seems wrong. The solution is for the view to override `hitTest:withEvent:` as follows:

```
override func hitTest(point: CGPoint, withEvent e: UIEvent?) -> UIView? {
    if let result = super.hitTest(point, withEvent:e) {
        return result
    }
    for sub in self.subviews.reverse() {
        let pt = self.convertPoint(point, toView:sub)
```

```
            if let result = sub.hitTest(pt, withEvent:e) {
                return result
            }
        }
    }
    return nil
}
```

Hit-testing for layers

Layers do *not* receive touches. A touch is reported to a view, not a layer. A layer, except insofar as it is a view's underlying layer and gets touch reporting because of its view, is completely untouchable; from the point of view of touches and touch reporting, it's as if the layer weren't on the screen at all. No matter where a layer may appear to be, a touch falls through the layer, to whatever view is behind it.

Nevertheless, hit-testing for layers is possible. It doesn't happen automatically, as part of sendEvent: or anything else; it's up to you. It's just a convenient way of finding out which layer *would* receive a touch at a point, if layers *did* receive touches. To hit-test layers, call hitTest: on a layer, with a point *in superlayer coordinates.*

In the case of a layer that is a view's underlying layer, you don't need hit-testing. It is the view's drawing; where it appears is where the view is. So a touch in that layer is equivalent to a touch in its view. Indeed, one might say (and it is often said) that this is what views are actually for: to provide layers with touchability.

The only layers on which you'd need special hit-testing, then, would presumably be layers that are not themselves any view's underlying layer, because those are the only ones you don't find out about by normal view hit-testing. However, all layers, including a layer that is its view's underlying layer, are part of the layer hierarchy, and can participate in layer hit-testing. So the most comprehensive way to hit-test layers is to start with the topmost layer, the window's layer. In this example, we subclass UIWindow (see Chapter 1) and override its hitTest:withEvent: so as to get layer hit-testing every time there is view hit-testing:

```
override func hitTest(point: CGPoint, withEvent e: UIEvent?) -> UIView? {
    let lay = self.layer.hitTest(point)
    // ... possibly do something with that information
    return super.hitTest(point, withEvent:e)
}
```

In that example, self is the window, which is a special case. In general, you'll have to convert to superlayer coordinates. In this next example, we return to the CompassView developed in Chapter 3, in which all the parts of the compass are layers; we want to know whether the user tapped on the arrow layer, and if so, we'll rotate the arrow. For simplicity, we've given the CompassView a UITapGestureRecognizer, and this is its action handler, in the CompassView itself. We convert to our superview's coordinates, because these are also our layer's superlayer coordinates:

```
@IBAction func tapped(t:UITapGestureRecognizer) {
    let p = t.locationOfTouch(0, inView: self.superview)
    let hitLayer = self.layer.hitTest(p)
    let arrow = (self.layer as! CompassLayer).arrow
    if hitLayer == arrow { // respond to touch
        arrow.transform = CATransform3DRotate(
            arrow.transform, CGFloat(M_PI)/4.0, 0, 0, 1)
    }
}
```

Layer hit-testing knows nothing of the restrictions on touch delivery; it just reports on every sublayer, even one whose view (for example) has userInteractionEnabled set to false.

 The documentation warns that hitTest: must not be called on a CATransform-Layer.

Hit-testing for drawings

The preceding example (letting the user tap on the compass arrow) worked, but we might complain that it is reporting a hit on the arrow even if the hit misses the *drawing* of the arrow. That's true for view hit-testing as well. A hit is reported if we are within the view or layer as a whole; hit-testing knows nothing of drawing, transparent areas, and so forth.

If you know how the region is drawn and can reproduce the edge of that drawing as a CGPath, you can test whether a point is inside it with CGPathContainsPoint. So, in our compass layer, we could override hitTest along these lines:

```
override func hitTest(p: CGPoint) -> CALayer? {
    var lay = super.hitTest(p)
    if lay == self.arrow {
        // artificially restrict touchability to roughly the arrow area
        let pt = self.arrow.convertPoint(p, fromLayer:self.superlayer)
        let path = CGPathCreateMutable()
        CGPathAddRect(path, nil, CGRectMake(10,20,20,80))
        CGPathMoveToPoint(path, nil, 0, 25)
        CGPathAddLineToPoint(path, nil, 20, 0)
        CGPathAddLineToPoint(path, nil, 40, 25)
        CGPathCloseSubpath(path)
        if !CGPathContainsPoint(path, nil, pt, false) {
            lay = nil;
        }
    }
    return lay
}
```

(Layer hit-testing works by calling `containsPoint:`. However, `containsPoint:` takes a point in the layer's coordinates, so to hand it a point that arrives through `hitTest:` we must first convert from superlayer coordinates.)

Alternatively, it might be the case that if a pixel of the drawing is transparent, it's outside the drawn region, so that it suffices to detect whether the pixel tapped is transparent. Unfortunately, there's no way to ask a drawing (or a view, or a layer) for the color of a pixel; you have to make a bitmap and copy the drawing into it, and then ask the bitmap for the color of a pixel. If you can reproduce the content as an image, and all you care about is transparency, you can make a one-pixel alpha-only bitmap, draw the image in such a way that the pixel you want to test is the pixel drawn into the bitmap, and examine the transparency of the resulting pixel:

```
// assume im is a UIImage, point is the CGPoint to test
let info = CGImageAlphaInfo.Only.rawValue
let pixel = UnsafeMutablePointer<CUnsignedChar>.alloc(1)
pixel[0] = 0
let context = CGBitmapContextCreate(pixel,
    1, 1, 8, 1, nil, info)!
UIGraphicsPushContext(context)
im.drawAtPoint(CGPointMake(-point.x, -point.y))
UIGraphicsPopContext()
let p = pixel[0]
let alpha = Double(p)/255.0
let transparent = alpha < 0.01
```

However, there may not be a one-to-one relationship between the pixels of the underlying drawing and the points of the drawing as portrayed on the screen — because the drawing is stretched, for example. In many cases, the CALayer method `renderIn-Context:` can be helpful here. This method allows you to copy a layer's actual drawing into a graphics context of your choice. If that context is an image context created with `UIGraphicsBeginImageContextWithOptions`, you can use the resulting image as `im` in the code above.

Hit-testing during animation

The simplest solution to the problem of touch during animation is to disallow it entirely. By default, view animation turns off touchability of a view while it's being animated (though you can prevent that with `.AllowUserInteraction` in the `options:` argument), and you can temporarily turn off touchability altogether with UIApplication's `begin-IgnoringInteractionEvents`, as I mentioned earlier in this chapter.

If user interaction is allowed during an animation that moves a view from one place to another, then if the user taps on the animated view, the tap might mysteriously fail because the view (the model layer) is elsewhere; conversely, the user might accidentally tap where the view actually is, and the tap will hit the animated view even though it appears to be elsewhere. If the position of a view or layer is being animated and you want the user to be able to tap on it, therefore, you'll need to *hit-test the presentation layer.*

In this simple example, we have a superview containing a subview. To allow the user to tap on the subview even when it is being animated, we implement hit-test munging in the subview:

```
override func hitTest(point: CGPoint, withEvent e: UIEvent?) -> UIView? {
    let pres = self.layer.presentationLayer() as! CALayer
    let suppt = self.convertPoint(point, toView: self.superview!)
    let prespt = self.superview!.layer.convertPoint(suppt, toLayer: pres)
    return super.hitTest(prespt, withEvent: e)
}
```

However, as Apple puts it in the WWDC 2011 videos, the animated view "swallows the touch." For example, suppose the view in motion is a button. Although our hit-test munging makes it possible for the user to tap the button as it is being animated, and although the user sees the button highlight in response, the button's action message is not sent in response to this highlighting if the animation is in-flight when the tap takes place. This behavior seems unfortunate, but it's generally possible to work around it (for instance, with a gesture recognizer).

Initial Touch Event Delivery

When the touch situation changes, an event containing all touches is handed to the UIApplication instance by calling its `sendEvent:`, and the UIApplication in turn hands it to the relevant UIWindow by calling *its* `sendEvent:`. The UIWindow then performs the complicated logic of examining, for every touch, the hit-test view and its superviews and their gesture recognizers and deciding which of them should be sent a `touches` message, and does so.

You can override `sendEvent:` in a subclass of UIWindow or UIApplication (this is, indeed, just about the *only* reason you might have for subclassing UIApplication). These are delicate and crucial maneuvers, however, and you wouldn't want to lame your application by interfering with them. Moreover, it is unlikely, nowadays, that you would need to resort to such measures. A typical case before the advent of gesture recognizers was that you needed to detect touches directed to an object of some built-in interface class in a way that subclassing it wouldn't permit. For example, you want to know when the user swipes a UIWebView; you're not allowed to subclass UIWebView, and in any case it eats the touch. The solution used to be to subclass UIWindow and override `sendEvent:`; you would then work out whether this was a swipe on the UIWebView and respond accordingly, or else call `super`. Now, however, you can attach a UISwipeGestureRecognizer to the UIWebView.

Gesture Recognizer and View

When a touch first appears and is delivered to a gesture recognizer, it is also delivered to its hit-test view, the same `touches` method being called on both. Later, if a gesture recognizer in a view's swarm recognizes its gesture, that view is sent `touches-Cancelled:withEvent:` for any touches that went to that gesture recognizer and were hit-tested to that view, and subsequently the view no longer receives those touches.

This comes as a surprise to beginners, but it is the most reasonable approach, as it means that touch interpretation by a view isn't jettisoned just because gesture recognizers are in the picture. Later on in the multitouch sequence, if all the gesture recognizers in a view's swarm declare failure to recognize their gesture, that view's internal touch interpretation just proceeds as if gesture recognizers had never been invented.

Moreover, touches and gestures are two different things; sometimes you want to respond to both. In one of my apps, where the user can tap cards, each card has a single tap gesture recognizer and a double tap gesture recognizer, but it also responds directly to `touchesBegan:withEvent:` by reducing its own opacity, and to `touchesEnded:with-Event:` and `touchesCancelled:withEvent:` by restoring its opacity. The result is that the user always sees feedback when touching a card, *instantly*, regardless of what the gesture turns out to be.

This behavior can be changed by setting a gesture recognizer's `cancelsTouchesIn-View` property to `false`. If this is the case for every gesture recognizer in a view's swarm, the view will receive touch events more or less as if no gesture recognizers were in the picture.

If a gesture recognizer happens to be ignoring a touch (because, for example, it was told to do so by `ignoreTouch:forEvent:`), then `touchesCancelled:withEvent:` *won't* be sent to the view for that touch when that gesture recognizer recognizes its gesture. Thus, a gesture recognizer's ignoring a touch is the same as simply letting it fall through to the view, as if the gesture recognizer weren't there.

Gesture recognizers can also *delay* the delivery of touches to a view, and by default they do. The UIGestureRecognizer property `delaysTouchesEnded` is `true` by default, meaning that when a touch reaches `.Ended` and the gesture recognizer's `touchesEnded:with-Event:` is called, if the gesture recognizer is still allowing touches to be delivered to the view because its state is still `.Possible`, it doesn't deliver this touch until it has resolved the gesture. When it does, either it will recognize the gesture, in which case the view will have `touchesCancelled:withEvent:` called instead (as already explained), or it will declare failure and *now* the view will have `touchesEnded:withEvent:` called.

The reason for this behavior is most obvious with a gesture where multiple taps are required. The first tap ends, but this is insufficient for the gesture recognizer to declare success or failure, so it withholds that touch from the view. In this way, the gesture recognizer gets the proper priority. In particular, if there is a second tap, the gesture recognizer should succeed and send touchesCancelled:withEvent: to the view — but it can't do that if the view has already been sent touchesEnded:withEvent:.

It is also possible to delay the entire suite of touches methods from being called on a view, by setting a gesture recognizer's delaysTouchesBegan property to true. Again, this delay would be until the gesture recognizer can resolve the gesture: either it will recognize it, in which case the view will have touchesCancelled:withEvent: called, or it will declare failure, in which case the view will receive touchesBegan:withEvent: plus any further touches calls that were withheld — except that it will receive *at most* one touchesMoved:withEvent: call, the last one, because if a lot of these were withheld, to queue them all up and send them all at once now would be simply insane.

It is unlikely that you'll change a gesture recognizer's delaysTouchesBegan property to true, however. You might do so, for example, if you have an elaborate touch analysis within a view that simply cannot operate simultaneously with a gesture recognizer, but this is improbable, and the latency involved may look strange to your user.

When touches are delayed and then delivered, what's delivered is the original touch with the original event, which still have their original timestamps. Because of the delay, these timestamps may differ significantly from now. For this reason (and many others), Apple warns that touch analysis that is concerned with timing should always look at the time-stamp, not the clock.

Touch Exclusion Logic

It is up to the UIWindow's sendEvent: to implement the logic of multipleTouch-Enabled and exclusiveTouch.

If a new touch is hit-tested to a view whose multipleTouchEnabled is false and which already has an existing touch hit-tested to it, then sendEvent: never delivers the new touch to that view. However, that touch *is* delivered to the view's swarm of gesture recognizers.

Similarly, if there's an exclusiveTouch view in the window, then sendEvent: must decide whether a particular touch should be delivered, in accordance with the meaning of exclusiveTouch, which I described earlier. If a touch is not delivered to a view because of exclusiveTouch restrictions, it is *not* delivered to its swarm of gesture recognizers either.

For example, suppose you have two views with touch handling, and their common superview has a pinch gesture recognizer. Normally, if you touch both views simulta-nously and pinch, the pinch gesture recognizer recognizes. But if both views are marked exclusiveTouch, the pinch gesture recognizer does *not* recognize.

A comment in Apple's Simple Gesture Recognizers sample code gets this wrong. It says: "Recognizers ignore the exclusive touch setting for views. This is so that they can consistently recognize gestures even if they cross other views. For example, suppose you had two buttons, each marked exclusive touch, and you added a pinch gesture recognizer to their superview. That a finger came down in one of the buttons shouldn't prevent you from pinching in the general case." That is *false*; the exclusiveTouch setting *does* prevent you from pinching.

Gesture Recognition Logic

When a gesture recognizer recognizes its gesture, everything changes. As we've already seen, the touches for this gesture recognizer are sent to their hit-test views as a touches-Cancelled:forEvent: message, and then no longer arrive at those views (unless the gesture recognizer's cancelsTouchesInView is false). Moreover, all other gesture recognizers pending with regard to these touches are made to fail, and then are no longer sent the touches they were receiving either.

If the very same event would cause more than one gesture recognizer to recognize, there's an algorithm for picking the one that will succeed and make the others fail: a gesture recognizer lower down the view hierarchy (closer to the hit-test view) prevails over one higher up the hierarchy, and a gesture recognizer more recently added to its view prevails over one less recently added.

There are various means for modifying this "first past the post" behavior:

Dependency order
    Certain methods institute a dependency order, causing a gesture recognizer to be put on hold when it tries to transition from the .Possible state to the .Began (continuous) or .Ended (discrete) state; only if a certain other gesture recognizer fails is this one permitted to perform that transition. Apple says that in a dependency like this, the gesture recognizer that fails first is not sent reset (and won't receive any touches) until the second finishes its state sequence and is sent reset, so that they resume recognizing together. The methods are:

- requireGestureRecognizerToFail: (sent to a gesture recognizer)

- shouldRequireFailureOfGestureRecognizer: (overridden in a subclass)

- shouldBeRequiredToFailByGestureRecognizer: (overridden in a subclass)

- gestureRecognizer:shouldRequireFailureOfGestureRecognizer: (implemented by the delegate)

- gestureRecognizer:shouldBeRequiredToFailByGestureRecognizer: (implemented by the delegate)

The first of those methods sets up a permanent relationship between two gesture recognizers, and cannot be undone; but the others are sent every time a gesture starts in a view whose swarm includes both gesture recognizers, and each applies only on this occasion.

The delegate methods work together as follows. For each pair of gesture recognizers in the hit-test view's swarm, the members of that pair are arranged in a fixed order (as I've already described). The first of the pair is sent `shouldRequire` and then `shouldBeRequired`, and then the second of the pair is sent `shouldRequire` and then `shouldBeRequired`. But if any of those four methods returns `true`, the relationship between that pair is settled and we proceed to the next pair.

Success into failure

Certain methods, by returning `false`, turn success into failure; at the moment when the gesture recognizer is about to declare that it recognizes its gesture, transitioning from the `.Possible` state to the `.Began` (continuous) or `.Ended` (discrete) state, it is forced to fail instead:

- UIView's `gestureRecognizerShouldBegin:`
- The delegate's `gestureRecognizerShouldBegin:`

Simultaneous recognition

A gesture recognizer succeeds, but some other gesture recognizer is *not* forced to fail, in accordance with these methods:

- `gestureRecognizer:shouldRecognizeSimultaneouslyWithGesture-Recognizer:` (implemented by the delegate)
- `canPreventGestureRecognizer:` (overridden in a subclass)
- `canBePreventedByGestureRecognizer:` (overridden in a subclass)

In the subclass methods, `Prevent` means "by succeeding, you force failure upon this other," and `BePrevented` means "by succeeding, this other forces failure on you." They work together as follows. `canPreventGestureRecognizer:` is called first; if it returns `false`, that's the end of the story for that gesture recognizer, and `canPreventGestureRecognizer:` is called on the other gesture recognizer. But if `canPreventGestureRecognizer:` returns `true` when it is first called, the other gesture recognizer is sent `canBePreventedByGestureRecognizer:`. If it returns `true`, that's the end of the story; if it returns `false`, the process starts over the other way around, sending `canPreventGestureRecognizer:` to the second gesture recognizer, and so forth. In this way, conflicting answers are resolved without the device exploding: prevention is regarded as exceptional (even though it is in fact the norm) and will happen only if it is acquiesced to by everyone involved.

Touches and the Responder Chain

A UIView is a responder, and participates in the responder chain. In particular, if a touch is to be delivered to a UIView (because, for example, it's the hit-test view) and that view doesn't implement the relevant `touches` method, a walk up the responder chain is performed, looking for a responder that *does* implement it; if such a responder is found, the touch is delivered to that responder. Moreover, the default implementation of the `touches` methods — the behavior that you get if you call `super` — is to perform the same walk up the responder chain, starting with the next responder in the chain.

The relationship between touch delivery and the responder chain can be useful, but you must be careful not to allow it to develop into an incoherency. For example, if `touches-Began:withEvent:` is implemented in a superview but not in a subview, then a touch to the subview will result in the superview's `touchesBegan:withEvent:` being called, with the first parameter (the touches) containing a touch whose `view` is the subview. But most UIView implementations of the `touches` methods rely upon the assumption that the first parameter consists of all and only touches whose `view` is `self`; built-in UIView subclasses certainly assume this.

Again, if `touchesBegan:withEvent:` is implemented in both a superview and a subview, and you call `super` in the subview's implementation, passing along the same arguments that came in, then the same touch delivered to the subview will trigger both the subview's `touchesBegan:withEvent:` and the superview's `touchesBegan:withEvent:` (and once again the first parameter to the superview's `touchesBegan:withEvent:` will contain a touch whose `view` is the subview).

The solution is to behave rationally, as follows:

- If all the responders in the affected part of the responder chain are instances of your own subclass of UIView itself or of your own subclass of UIViewController, you will generally want to follow the simplest possible rule: implement *all* the `touches` events together in one class, so that touches arrive at an instance either because it was the hit-test view or because it is up the responder chain from the hit-test view, and do *not* call `super` in any of them. In this way, "the buck stops here" — the touch handling for this object or for objects below it in the responder chain is bottlenecked into one well-defined place.

- If you subclass a built-in UIView subclass and you override its touch handling, you don't have to override every single `touches` event, but you *do* need to call `super` so that the built-in touch handling can occur.

- Don't allow touches to arrive from lower down the responder chain at an instance of a built-in UIView subclass that implements built-in touch handling, because such a class is completely unprepared for the first parameter of a `touches` method containing a touch not intended for itself. Judicious use of userInteractionEnabled or hit-test munging can be a big help here.

I'm not saying, however, that you have to block all touches from percolating up the responder chain; it's normal for unhandled touches to arrive at the UIWindow or UIApplication, for example, because these classes do not (by default) do any touch handling — so those touches will remain unhandled and will percolate right off the end of the responder chain, which is perfectly fine.

- Never call a touches method directly (except to call super).

Apple's documentation has some discussion of a technique called *event forwarding* where you *do* call touches methods directly. But you are far less likely to need this now that gesture recognizers exist, and it can be extremely tricky and even downright dangerous to implement, so I won't give an example, and I suggest that you not use it.

PART II

Interface

This part of the book is about view controllers, and about all the various kinds of view provided by the Cocoa framework — the built-in building blocks with which you'll construct an app's interface.

- Chapter 6 is about view controllers, the fundamental iOS mechanism for allowing an entire interface to be replaced by another. Every app you write will have its interface managed by at least one view controller.

- Chapter 7 is about scroll views, the iOS mechanism for letting the user scroll and zoom the interface.

- Chapter 8 explains table views, a type of scroll view that lets the user navigate through any amount of data, along with collection views, a generalization of table views.

- Chapter 9 is about two forms of interface especially characteristic of the iPad — popovers and split views — along with iPad multitasking.

- Chapter 10 describes several ways of presenting text (including styled text) in an app's interface — labels, text fields, text views, and text drawn directly.

- Chapter 11 discusses web views. A web view is an easy-to-use interface object backed by the power of a full-fledged web browser.

- Chapter 12 describes all the remaining built-in iOS (UIKit) interface objects.

- Chapter 13 is about the forms of modal dialog that can appear in front of an app's interface.

CHAPTER 6

View Controllers

An iOS app's interface is dynamic, and with good reason. On the desktop, an application's windows can be big, and there can be more than one of them, so there's room for lots of interface. With iOS, everything needs to fit on a single display consisting of a single window, which in the case of the iPhone can be almost forbiddingly tiny. The iOS solution is to introduce, at will, completely new interface — a new view, possibly with an elaborate hierarchy of subviews — replacing or covering the previous interface.

For this to work, regions of interface material — often the entire contents of the screen — must come and go in an agile fashion that is understandable to the user. There will typically be a logical, structural, and functional relationship between the view that was present and the view that replaces or covers it, and this relationship will need to be maintained behind the scenes, in your code, as well as being indicated to the user: multiple views may be pure alternatives or siblings of one another, or one view may be a temporary replacement for another, or views may be like successive pages of a book. Animation is often used to emphasize and clarify these relationships as one view is superseded by another. Navigational interface and a vivid, suggestive gestural vocabulary give the user an ability to control what's seen and an understanding of the possible options: a tab bar whose buttons summon alternate views, a back button or a swipe gesture for returning to a previously visited view, a tap on an interface element to dive deeper into a conceptual world, a Done or Cancel button to escape from a settings screen, and so forth.

In iOS, the management of this dynamic interface is performed through view controllers. A *view controller* is an instance of UIViewController. Actually, a view controller is most likely to be an instance of a UIViewController subclass; the UIViewController class is designed to be subclassed, and you are very unlikely to use a plain vanilla UIViewController object without subclassing it. You might write your own UIViewController subclass; you might use a built-in UIViewController subclass such as

UINavigationController or UITabBarController; or you might subclass a built-in UIViewController subclass such as UITableViewController (Chapter 8).

A view controller manages a single view (which can, of course, have subviews); its `view` property points to the view it manages. This is the view controller's *main view*, or simply its view. A view controller's main view has no explicit pointer to the view controller that manages it, but a view controller is a UIResponder and is in the responder chain just above its view, so it is the view's `nextResponder`.

View Controller Responsibilities

A view controller's most important responsibility is its view. A view controller must have a view (it is useless without one). If that view is to be useful, it must somehow *get into the interface*, and hence onto the screen; a view controller is usually responsible for seeing to that, too, but typically *not* the view controller whose view this is; rather, this will be taken care of by some view controller whose view is *already* in the interface. In many cases, this will happen automatically (I'll talk more about that in the next section), but you can participate in the process, and for some view controllers you may have to do the work yourself. The reverse is also true: a view that comes may also eventually go, and the view controller responsible for putting a view into the interface will also be responsible for removing it.

A view controller will typically provide *animation* of the interface as a view comes or goes. Built-in view controller subclasses and built-in ways of summoning or removing a view controller and its view come with built-in animations. We are all familiar, for example, with tapping something to make new interface slide in from the side of the screen, and then later tapping a back button to make that interface slide back out again. In cases where you are responsible for getting a view controller's view onto the screen, you are also responsible for providing the animation. And you can take complete charge of the animation even for built-in view controllers.

View controllers, working together, can *save and restore state* automatically. This feature helps you ensure that if your app is terminated in the background and subsequently relaunched, it will quickly resume displaying the same interface that was showing when the user last saw it.

The most powerful view controller is the *root view controller*. This is the view controller managing the *root view*, the view that sits at the top of the view hierarchy, as the one and only direct subview of the main window, acting as the superview for all other interface. I described in Chapter 1 how this view controller attains its lofty position: it is assigned to the window's `rootViewController` property. The window then takes that view controller's main view, gives it the correct frame (resizing it if necessary), and makes it its own subview. The root view controller bears ultimate responsibility for two important decisions about the behavior of your app:

Rotation of the interface

> The user can rotate the device, and you might like the interface to rotate in response, to compensate. This decision is made, in large part, by the root view controller.

Manipulation of the status bar

> The status bar is actually a secondary window belonging to the runtime, but the runtime consults the root view controller as to whether the status bar should be present and, if so, whether its text should be light or dark.

Above and beyond all this, view controllers are typically the heart of any app, by virtue of their role in the model–view–controller architecture: view controllers are *controllers* (hence the name). Views give the user something to tap, and display data for the user to see; they are *view*. The data itself is *model*. But the logic of determining, at any given moment, *what* views are shown, *what* data those views display, and *what* the response to the user's gestures should be, is *controller* logic. Typically, that means view controller logic. In any app, view controllers will be the most important controllers — frequently, in fact, the only controllers. View controllers are where you'll put the bulk of the code that actually makes your app do what your app does.

View Controller Hierarchy

As I said in the previous section, there is always one root view controller, along with its view, the root view. There may also be other view controllers, each of which has its own main view. Such view controllers are *subordinate* to the root view controller. In iOS, there are two subordination relationships between view controllers:

Parentage (containment)

> A view controller can *contain* another view controller. The containing view controller is the *parent* of the contained view controller; the contained view controller is a *child* of the containing view controller. A containment relationship between two view controllers is reflected in their views: the child view controller's view, if it is in the interface at all, is a *subview* (at some depth) of the parent view controller's view.
>
> The parent view controller is responsible for getting a child view controller's view into the interface, by making it a subview of its own view, and (if necessary) for removing it later. Introduction of a view, removal of a view, and replacement of one view with another often involve a parent view controller managing its children and their views.
>
> A familiar example is the navigation interface: the user taps something and new interface slides in from the side, replacing the current interface. Figure 6-1 shows the TidBITS News app displaying a typical iPhone interface, consisting of a list of story headlines and summaries. This interface is managed by a parent view controller (a UINavigationController) with a child view controller whose view is the

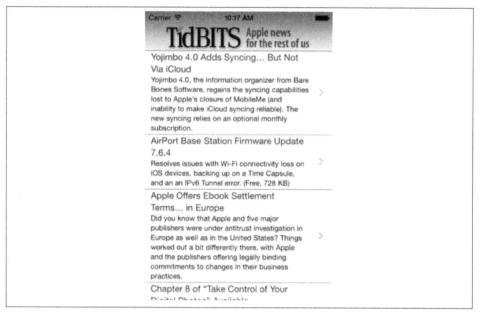

Figure 6-1. The TidBITS News app

list of headlines and summaries. If the user taps an entry in the list, the whole list will slide away to one side and the text of that story will slide in from the other side; the parent view controller has added a new child view controller, and has manipulated the views of its children to bring about this animated change of the interface. The parent view controller itself, meanwhile, stays put — and so does its own view. (In this example, the UINavigationController is the root view controller, and its view is the root view.)

Presentation (modal views)

A view controller can *present* another view controller. The first view controller is the *presenting* view controller (not the parent) of the second; the second view controller is the *presented* view controller (not a child) of the first. The second view controller's view replaces or covers, completely or partially, the first view controller's view.

The name of this mechanism, and of the relationship between the view controllers involved, has changed over time. In iOS 4 and before, the presented view controller was called a *modal view controller*, and its view was a *modal view*; there is an analogy here to the desktop, where a window is modal if it sits in front of, and denies the user access to, the rest of the interface until it is explicitly dismissed. The terms *presented view controller* and *presented view* are more recent and more general, but the historical term "modal" still appears in the documentation and in the API.

A presented view controller's view does indeed sometimes look rather like a desktop modal view; for example, it might have a button such as Done or Save for dismissing the view, the implication being that this is a place where the user must make a decision and can do nothing else until the decision is made. However, as I'll explain later, that isn't the only use of a presented view controller.

There is thus a *hierarchy of view controllers*. In a properly constructed iOS app, there should be exactly one root view controller, and it is the *only* nonsubordinate view controller — it has neither a parent view controller nor a presenting view controller. Any other view controller, if its view appears in the interface, *must* be a child view controller of some parent view controller or a presented view controller of some presenting view controller.

Moreover, there is a clear relationship between the view hierarchy and the view controller hierarchy. Recall that, for a parent view controller and child view controller, the child's view, if present in the interface, must be a subview of the parent's view. Similarly, for a presenting view controller and presented view controller, the presented view controller's view is either a subview of, or completely replaces, the presenting view controller's view. In this way, the actual views of the interface form a hierarchy dictated by *and parallel to* some portion of the view controller hierarchy: *every* view visible in the interface owes its presence to a view controller's view, either because it *is* a view controller's view, or because it's a subview of a view controller's view.

The place of a view controller's view in the view hierarchy will often be automatic. You might never need to put a UIViewController's view into the view hierarchy manually. You'll manipulate view controllers; their hierarchy and their built-in functionality will construct and manage the view hierarchy for you.

For example, in Figure 6-1, we see two interface elements:

- The navigation bar, containing the TidBITS logo.
- The list of stories, which is actually a UITableView.

I will describe how all of this comes to appear on the screen through the view controller hierarchy and the view hierarchy (Figure 6-2):

- The app's root view controller is a UINavigationController; the UINavigationController's view is the window's sole immediate subview (the root view). The navigation bar is a subview of that view.
- The UINavigationController contains a second UIViewController — a parent–child relationship. The child is a custom UIViewController subclass; *its* view is what occupies the rest of the window, as another subview of the UINavigationController's view. That view is the UITableView. This architecture means that when the user

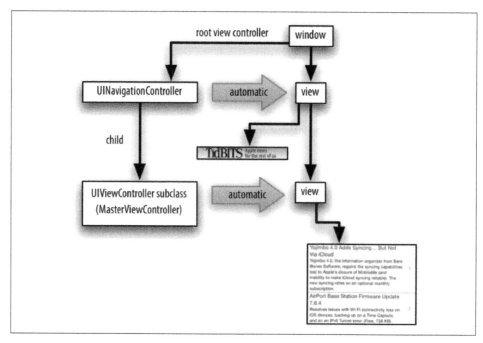

Figure 6-2. The TidBITS News app's initial view controller and view hierarchy

taps a story listing in the UITableView, the whole table will slide out, to be replaced by the view of a different UIViewController, while the navigation bar stays.

In Figure 6-2, notice the word "automatic" in the two large right-pointing arrows associating a view controller with its view. This is intended to tell you how the view controller's view became part of the view hierarchy. The UINavigationController's view became the window's subview automatically, by virtue of the UINavigationController being the window's `rootViewController`. The custom UIViewController's view became the UINavigationController's view's subview automatically, by virtue of the UIViewController being the UINavigationController's child.

Sometimes, you'll write your own parent view controller class. In that case, *you* will be doing the kind of work that the UINavigationController was doing in that example, so you will need to put a child view controller's view into the interface *manually*, as a subview (at some depth) of the parent view controller's view.

I'll illustrate with another app of mine (Figure 6-3). The interface displays a flashcard containing information about a Latin word, along with a toolbar (the dark area at the bottom) where the user can tap an icon to choose additional functionality.

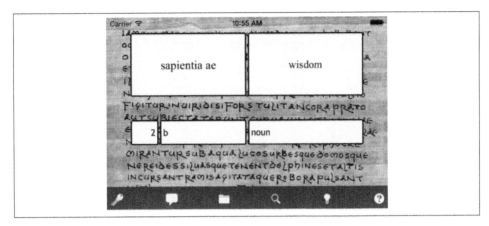

Figure 6-3. A Latin flashcard app

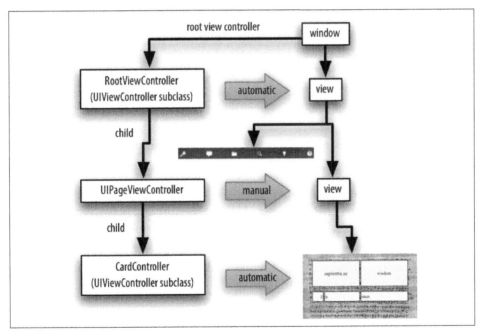

Figure 6-4. The Latin flashcard app's initial view controller and view hierarchy

Again, I will describe how the interface shown in Figure 6-3 comes to appear on the screen through the view controller hierarchy and the view hierarchy (Figure 6-4). The app actually contains over a thousand of these Latin words, and I want the user to be able to navigate between flashcards to see the next or previous word; there is an excellent built-in view controller for this purpose, the UIPageViewController. However, that's just

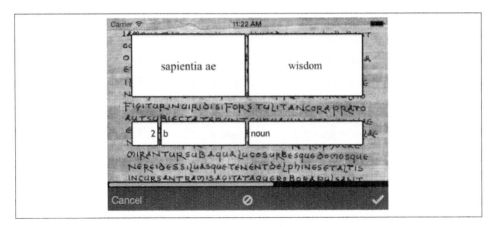

Figure 6-5. The Latin flashcard app, in drill mode

for the card; the toolbar at the bottom stays there, so the toolbar can't be inside the UIPageViewController's view. Therefore:

- The app's root view controller is my own UIViewController subclass, which I call RootViewController; its view contains the toolbar, and is also to contain the UIPageViewController's view. My RootViewController's view becomes the window's subview (the root view) automatically, by virtue of the RootViewController's being the window's `rootViewController`.

- In order for the UIPageViewController's view to appear in the interface, since it is not the root view controller, it *must* be some view controller's child. There is only one possible parent — my RootViewController. My RootViewController must function as a custom parent view controller, with the UIPageViewController as its child. So I have made that happen, and I have therefore also had to put the UIPage-ViewController's view *manually* into my RootViewController's view.

- I hand the UIPageViewController an instance of my CardController class (another UIViewController subclass) as its child, and the UIPageViewController displays the CardController's view automatically.

Finally, here's an example of a presented view controller. My Latin flashcard app has a second mode, where the user is drilled on a subset of the cards in random order; the interface looks very much like the first mode's interface (Figure 6-5), but it behaves completely differently.

To implement this, I have another UIViewController subclass, DrillViewController; it is structured very much like RootViewController. When the user is in drill mode, a DrillViewController is being *presented* by the RootViewController, meaning that the DrillViewController's interface takes over the screen automatically: the DrillView-

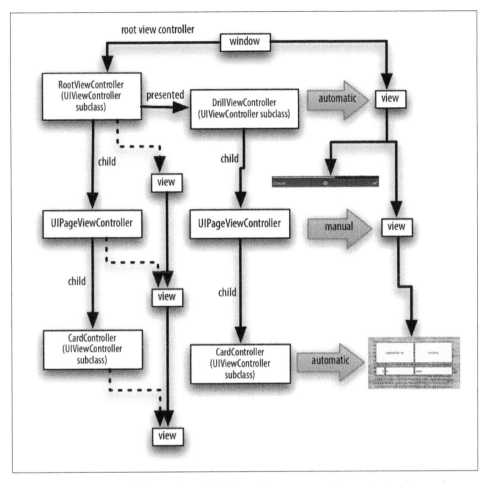

Figure 6-6. The Latin flashcard app's drill mode view controller and view hierarchy

Controller's view, with its whole subview hierarchy, including the views of the Drill-ViewController's children in the view controller hierarchy, replaces the RootView-Controller's view and *its* whole subview hierarchy (Figure 6-6). The RootViewController and its hierarchy of child view controllers remains in place, but the corresponding view hierarchy is not in the interface; it will be returned to the interface automatically when we leave drill mode (because the presented DrillViewController is dismissed), and the situation will look like Figure 6-4 once again.

For any app that you write, you should be able to construct a diagram showing the hierarchy of view controllers and charting how each view controller's view fits into the view hierarchy. The diagram should be similar to mine! The view hierarchy should run neatly parallel with the view controller hierarchy; there should be no crossed wires or orphan views. And every view controller's view should be placed automatically into the view hierarchy, unless you have written your own parent view controller.

 Do *not* put a view controller's view into the interface manually, unless one of the following is the case:

- The view controller is the child of your custom parent view controller. There is a complicated parent–child dance you have to do. See "Container View Controllers" on page 339.
- You're doing a custom transition animation. See "Custom Transition" on page 315.

View Controller Creation

A view controller is an instance like any other instance, and it is created like any other instance — by instantiating its class. You might perform this instantiation in code; in that case, you will of course have to initialize the instance properly as you create it. Here's an example from one of my own apps:

```
let llc = LessonListController(terms: self.data)
let nav = UINavigationController(rootViewController:llc)
```

In that example, LessonListController is my own UIViewController subclass, so I have called its designated initializer, which I myself have defined; UINavigationController is a built-in UIViewController subclass, and I have used one of its convenience initializers.

Alternatively, a view controller instance might come into existence through the loading of a nib. To make it possible to get a view controller into the nib in the first place, view controllers are included among the object types available through the Object library in the nib editor.

It is legal, though in practice not common, for a *.xib* file to contain a view controller. A *.storyboard* file, on the other hand, is chock full of view controllers; view controllers are the basis of a storyboard's structure, with each scene consisting of and corresponding to one view controller object. A view controller in a storyboard will go into a nib file in the built app, and that nib file will be loaded when the view controller instance is needed. Usually, that happens automatically. Nevertheless, a view controller in a storyboard is an ordinary nib object and, if it is to be used in the running app, will be instantiated through the loading of the nib just like any other nib object. I'll give full details on how and why a view controller is instantiated from a storyboard later in this chapter.

Once a view controller comes into existence, it must be retained so that it will persist. This will happen automatically when the view controller is assigned a place in the view controller hierarchy that I described in the previous section. A view controller assigned as a window's `rootViewController` is retained by the window. A view controller assigned as another view controller's child is retained by the parent view controller. A presented view controller is retained by the presenting view controller. The parent view controller or presenting view controller then takes ownership, and will release the other view controller in good order when it is no longer needed.

Here's an example, from one of my apps, of view controllers being instantiated and then being retained by being placed into the view controller hierarchy:

```
let llc = LessonListController(terms: self.data) ❶
let nav = UINavigationController(rootViewController:llc) ❷
self.presentViewController(nav, animated:true, completion:nil) ❸
```

That's the same code I showed a moment ago, extended by one line. It comes from a view controller class called RootViewController. Here's how view controller creation and memory management works in those three lines:

❶ I instantiate LessonListController.

❷ I instantiate UINavigationController, and I assign the LessonListController instance to the UINavigationController instance as its child; the navigation controller retains the LessonListController instance and takes ownership of it.

❸ I present the UINavigationController instance on `self`, a RootViewController instance; the RootViewController instance is the presenting view controller, and it retains and takes ownership of the UINavigationController instance as its presented view controller. The RootViewController instance itself is already the window's `rootViewController`, and is retained by the window — and so the view controller hierarchy is safely established.

All of this sounds straightforward, but it is worth dwelling on, because things can go wrong. It is quite possible, if things are mismanaged, for a view controller's view to get into the interface while the view controller itself is allowed to go out of existence. *This must not be permitted.* If such a thing happens, at the very least the view will apparently misbehave, failing to perform its intended functionality, because that functionality is embodied by the view controller, which no longer exists. (I've made this mistake, so I speak from experience here.) If you instantiate a view controller in code, you should immediately ask yourself who will be retaining this view controller.

If a view controller is instantiated automatically from a storyboard, it will be retained automatically. That isn't magic, however; it's done in exactly the same ways I just listed — by assigning it as the window's `rootViewController`, or by making it another view controller's child view controller or presented view controller.

How a View Controller Gets Its View

Initially, when it first comes into existence, a view controller has no view. A view controller is a small, lightweight object; a view is a relatively heavyweight object, involving interface elements that occupy memory. Therefore, a view controller postpones obtaining its view until it has to do so, namely, when it is asked for the value of its `view` property. At that moment, if its `view` property is `nil`, the view controller sets about obtaining its view. (We say that a view controller loads its view *lazily*.) Typically, this happens because it is time to put the view controller's view into the interface.

In working with a newly instantiated view controller, be careful not to refer to its `view` property if you don't need to, since this will trigger the view controller's obtaining its view prematurely. (As usual, I speak from experience here.) To learn whether a view controller has a view without causing it to load its view, call `isViewLoaded`. New in iOS 9, you can refer to a view controller's view safely, without loading it, as its `viewIfLoaded` (an Optional); you can also cause the view controller to load its view explicitly, rather than as a side effect of mentioning its `view`, by calling `loadViewIfNeeded`.

As soon as a view controller has its view, its `viewDidLoad` method is called. If this view controller is an instance of your own UIViewController subclass, `viewDidLoad` is your opportunity to modify the contents of this view — to populate it with subviews, to tweak the subviews it already has, and so forth — as well as to perform other initializations of the view controller consonant with its acquisition of a view. The `view` property is now pointing to the view, so it is safe to refer to `self.view`. Bear in mind, however, that the view may not yet be part of the interface! In fact, it almost certainly is not. (To confirm this, check whether `self.view.window` is nil.) Thus, for example, you cannot necessarily rely on the *dimensions* of the view at this point to be the dimensions that the view will assume when it becomes visible in the interface. Performing certain customizations prematurely in `viewDidLoad` is a common beginner mistake. I'll have more to say about that later in the chapter.

Before `viewDidLoad` will be called, however, the view controller must obtain its view. The question of where and how the view controller will get its view is often crucial. In some cases, to be sure, you won't care about this; in particular, when a view controller is an instance of a built-in UIViewController subclass such as UINavigationController or UITabBarController, its view is out of your hands — you might never even have cause to refer to it over the entire course of your app's lifetime — and you simply trust that the view controller will somehow generate its view. But when the view controller is an instance of your own subclass of UIViewController, and when you yourself will design or modify its view, it becomes essential to understand the process whereby a view controller gets its view.

This process is not difficult to understand, but it is rather elaborate, because there are multiple possibilities. Most important, this process is *not magic*. Yet it quite possibly causes more confusion to beginners than any other matter connected with iOS programming. Therefore, I will explain it in detail. The more you know about the details of how a view controller gets its view, the deeper and clearer will be your understanding of the entire workings of your app, its view controllers, its *.storyboard* and *.xib* files, and so on.

The alternatives are as follows:

- The view may be created in the view controller's own code, manually.
- The view may be created as an empty generic view, automatically.
- The view may be created in its own separate nib.
- The view may be created in a nib, which is the same nib from which the view controller itself is instantiated.

Manual View

To supply a UIViewController's view manually, in code, implement its `loadView` method. Your job here is to obtain an instance of UIView (or a subclass of UIView) and *assign it to `self.view`*. You must *not* call `super` (for reasons that I'll make clear later on).

 Do not confuse `loadView` with `viewDidLoad`. Yes, I've made this mistake myself. I confess! `loadView` creates the view; `viewDidLoad` is called afterward.

Let's try it. We are going to do everything manually, so we don't need or want a storyboard; therefore, start with an app without a main storyboard (I explained how to make such an app at the start of Chapter 1), and modify it as follows:

1. We need a UIViewController subclass, so choose File → New → File; specify iOS → Source → Cocoa Touch Class. Click Next.

2. Name the class RootViewController, and specify that it is to be a UIViewController subclass. Uncheck "Also create XIB file" (if it happens to be checked). Click Next.

3. Confirm that we're saving into the appropriate folder and group, and that these files will be part of the app target. Click Create.

We now have a RootViewController class, and we proceed to edit its code. In *RootViewController.swift*, we'll implement `loadView`. To convince ourselves that the example is working correctly, we'll give the view an identifiable color, and we'll put some interface inside it, namely a "Hello, World" label:

```
override func loadView() {
    let v = UIView()
    v.backgroundColor = UIColor.greenColor()
    self.view = v
    let label = UILabel()
    v.addSubview(label)
    label.text = "Hello, World!"
    label.autoresizingMask = [
        .FlexibleTopMargin,
        .FlexibleLeftMargin,
        .FlexibleBottomMargin,
        .FlexibleRightMargin]
    label.sizeToFit()
    label.center = CGPointMake(v.bounds.midX, v.bounds.midY)
    label.frame.makeIntegralInPlace()
}
```

We have not yet given a RootViewController instance a place in our view controller hierarchy — in fact, we have no view controller hierarchy. Let's make one. To do so, we turn to *AppDelegate.swift*. (It's a little frustrating having to set things up in two different places before our labors can bear any visible fruit, but such is life.)

In *AppDelegate.swift*, modify the implementation of `application:didFinish-LaunchingWithOptions:` to create a RootViewController instance and make it the window's `rootViewController` (see Example 1-1):

```
import UIKit
@UIApplicationMain
class AppDelegate : UIResponder, UIApplicationDelegate {
    var window : UIWindow?
    func application(application: UIApplication,
        didFinishLaunchingWithOptions launchOptions: [NSObject: AnyObject]?)
        -> Bool {
            self.window = UIWindow()
            let theRVC = RootViewController() // *
            self.window!.rootViewController = theRVC // *
            self.window!.backgroundColor = UIColor.whiteColor()
            self.window!.makeKeyAndVisible()
            return true
    }
}
```

Build and run the app. Sure enough, there's our green background and our "Hello, world" label!

When we created our view controller's view (`self.view`), we never gave it a reasonable frame. This is because we are relying on someone else to frame the view appropriately. In this case, the "someone else" is the window, which responds to having its `rootView-Controller` property set to a view controller by framing the view controller's view appropriately as the root view before putting it into the window as a subview. In general, it is the responsibility of whoever puts a view controller's view into the interface to give the view the correct frame — and this will never be the view controller itself (although under some circumstances the view controller can express a preference in this regard). Indeed, the size of a view controller's view may be changed as it is placed into the interface, and you must keep in mind, as you design your view controller's view and its subviews, that this can happen. (That's why, in the preceding code, I used autoresizing to keep the label centered in the view, no matter how the view may be resized.)

Generic Automatic View

We should distinguish between creating a view and populating it. The preceding example fails to draw this distinction. The lines that create our RootViewController's view are merely these:

```
let v = UIView()
self.view = v
```

Everything else configures and populates the view, turning it green and putting a label into it. A more appropriate place to populate a view controller's view is its viewDid-Load implementation, which, as I've already mentioned, is called after the view exists and can be referred to as self.view. We could therefore rewrite the preceding example like this (just for fun, I'll use autolayout this time):

```
override func loadView() {
    let v = UIView()
    self.view = v
}
override func viewDidLoad() {
    super.viewDidLoad()
    let v = self.view
    v.backgroundColor = UIColor.greenColor()
    let label = UILabel()
    v.addSubview(label)
    label.text = "Hello, World!"
    label.translatesAutoresizingMaskIntoConstraints = false
    NSLayoutConstraint.activateConstraints([
        label.centerXAnchor.constraintEqualToAnchor(v.centerXAnchor),
        label.centerYAnchor.constraintEqualToAnchor(v.centerYAnchor),
    ])
}
```

But if we're going to do that, we can go even further and remove our implementation of loadView altogether! It turns out that if you don't implement loadView, and if no view is supplied in any other way, then UIViewController's default implementation of loadView will do exactly what we are already doing in code: it creates a generic UIView object and assigns it to self.view. If we needed our view controller's view to be a particular UIView subclass, that wouldn't be acceptable; but in this case, our view controller's view *is* a generic UIView object, so it *is* acceptable. Comment out or delete the entire `loadView` implementation from the preceding code, and build and run the app; our example still works!

View in a Separate Nib

A view controller's view can be supplied from a nib file. This approach gives you the convenience of configuring and populating the view by designing it graphically in the nib editor interface.

When the nib loads, the view controller instance will already have been created, and it will serve as the nib's owner. The view controller's proxy in the nib has the same class as the view controller, and its `view` outlet points to the view object in the nib. Thus, when the nib loads, the view controller obtains its view through the nib-loading mechanism!

I'll illustrate by modifying the preceding example to use a *.xib* file. (I'll deal later with the use of a *.storyboard* file; knowing first how the process works for a *.xib* file will greatly enhance your understanding of how it works for a *.storyboard* file.)

In a *.xib* file, the nib owner is represented by the File's Owner proxy object. Therefore, in a *.xib* file that is to serve as the source of a view controller's view, the following two things must be true:

- The File's Owner class must be set to a UIViewController subclass (depending on the class of the view controller whose view this will be).

- The File's Owner proxy now has a `view` outlet, corresponding to a UIView-Controller's `view` property. This outlet must be connected to the view.

Let's try it. We begin with the example we've already developed, with our RootView-Controller class. Delete the implementation of `loadView` and `viewDidLoad` from *Root-ViewController.swift*, because we want the view to come from a nib and we're going to populate it in the nib. Then:

1. Choose File → New → File and specify iOS → User Interface → View. This will be a *.xib* file containing a UIView object. Click Next.

2. Name the file *MyNib* (meaning *MyNib.xib*). Confirm the appropriate folder and group, and make sure that the file will be part of the app target. Click Create.

3. Edit *MyNib.xib*. Prepare it in the way I described a moment ago:

   a. Set the File's Owner class to RootViewController (in the Identity inspector).

   b. Connect the File's Owner `view` outlet to the View object.

4. Design the view. To make it clear that this is not the same view we were creating previously, perhaps you should give the view a red background color (in the

Attributes inspector). Drag a UILabel into the middle of the view and give it some text, such as "Hello, World!"

We have designed the nib, but we have done nothing as yet to associate this nib with our RootViewController instance. To do so, let's once again return to *App-Delegate.swift*, where we create our RootViewController instance:

```
let theRVC = RootViewController()
self.window!.rootViewController = theRVC
```

We're going to modify this code so that our RootViewController instance, theRVC, is aware of this nib file, *MyNib.xib*, as its own nib file. That way, when theRVC needs to acquire its view, it will load that nib file with itself as owner, thus ending up with the correct view as its own view property. A UIViewController has a nibName property for this purpose. However, we are not allowed to set its nibName property (it is read-only). Instead, as we instantiate the view controller, we use the designated initializer, init(nibName:bundle:), like this:

```
let theRVC = RootViewController(nibName:"MyNib", bundle:nil)
self.window!.rootViewController = theRVC
```

(The nil argument to the bundle: parameter specifies the main bundle, which is almost always what you want.)

To prove that this works, build and run. The red background appears! Our view is loading from the nib.

Now I'm going to describe a shortcut based on the name of the nib. It turns out that if the nib name passed to init(nibName:bundle:) is nil, a nib will be sought automatically *with the same name as the view controller's class*. Moreover, UIViewController's init() calls init(nibName:bundle:), passing nil for both arguments. This means, in effect, that we can return to using init() to initialize the view controller, provided that the nib file has a name that matches the name of the view controller class.

Let's try it. Rename *MyNib.xib* to *RootViewController.xib*, and change the code that instantiates and initializes our RootViewController back to what it was before, like this:

```
let theRVC = RootViewController()
self.window!.rootViewController = theRVC
```

Build and run. It works!

There's an additional aspect to this shortcut based on the name of the nib. It seems ridiculous that we should end up with a nib that has "Controller" in its name merely because our view controller, as is so often the case, has "Controller" in *its* name. A nib, after all, is not a controller. It turns out that the runtime, in looking for a view controller's corresponding nib, will in fact try stripping "Controller" off the end of the view controller class's name. Thus, we can name our nib file *RootView.xib* instead of *RootView-*

Controller.xib, and it will *still* be properly associated with our RootViewController instance.

When you create a UIViewController subclass, the Xcode dialog has a checkbox (which we unchecked earlier) offering to create an eponymous *.xib* file at the same time. If you accept that option, the nib is created with the File's Owner's class already set to the view controller's class and with its `view` outlet already hooked up to the view. This automatically created *.xib* file does *not* have "Controller" stripped off the end of its name; you can rename it manually later (I generally do) if the default name bothers you.

Another convention involving the nib name has to do with the rules for loading resources by name generally. The same naming rule that I mentioned in Chapter 2 for an image file extended by the suffix ~`ipad` applies to nib files. A nib file named *RootViewController~ipad.xib* will be loaded on an iPad when a nib named "`RootView-Controller`" is sought. This principle can greatly simplify your life when you're writing a universal app (though conditional constraints, described in Chapter 1, may permit you to design an interface differing on iPad and iPhone in a single nib).

We are now in a position to summarize the sequence whereby a view controller's view is obtained:

1. When the view controller first decides that it needs its view, `loadView` is *always* called.

2. If we override `loadView`, we supply and set the `view` in code, and we do *not* call `super`. Therefore the process of seeking a view comes to an end.

3. If we *don't* override `loadView`, UIViewController's built-in default implementation of `loadView` is used. It is this default implementation of `loadView` that loads the view controller's associated nib. That is why, if we *do* override `loadView`, we must *not* call `super` — that would cause us to get *both* behaviors!

4. If the previous steps all fail — we don't override `loadView`, and there is no associated nib — UIViewController's default implementation of `loadView` creates a generic UIView.

 It follows from what I've just said that if a view controller's view is to come from a nib, you should *not* implement `loadView`. I've made this mistake. The results were not pretty.

Nib-Instantiated View Controller

As I mentioned earlier, a view controller can be a nib object, to be instantiated through the loading of the nib. In the nib editor, the Object library contains a View Controller

Nib Name Matching in iOS 8

Swift has some funny ideas about class names. You may think a class is called Root-ViewController, but Swift's name for it prepends the name of the module; for example, if this project is called TestApp, then Swift thinks that this class is called `TestApp.Root-ViewController`. This means that the eponymous *.xib* file would actually have to be named *TestApp.RootViewController.xib*. Fortunately, in iOS 9, when that file isn't found, the module name is stripped off the class name and we try again — thus finding *Root-ViewController.xib* or *RootView.xib* if it exists.

But this stripping of the module name doesn't happen in iOS 8. Therefore, the view controller fails to find the eponymous *.xib* file — because it isn't seen as eponymous. There are four ways to work around this problem:

- Change the name of the *.xib* file to match Swift's idea of the class name. For example, if this project is called TestApp, call the *.xib* file *TestApp.RootViewController.xib*.

- Strip the module name from the class name yourself. To do so, use the `@objc()` notation when the view controller is declared, like this:

  ```
  @objc(RootViewController) class RootViewController : UIViewController {
  ```

- Call `init(nibName:bundle:)` with an explicit nib name. An elegant approach is to implement `init()` in your view controller subclass, so that other classes can call `init()`:

  ```
  required init?(coder: NSCoder) {
      fatalError("NSCoding not supported")
  }
  init() {
      super.init(nibName:"RootViewController", bundle:nil)
  }
  ```

- Override the getter for the UIViewController read-only `nibName` property:

  ```
  override var nibName : String { return "RootView" }
  ```

  Note, however, that this approach does *not* participate in the automatic stripping of "Controller" from the name; if the nib is named *RootView.xib* and you supply `"RootViewController"` as the value of the `nibName` property in its getter, your app will crash. (The documentation is misleading on this point.)

(UIViewController) as well as several built-in UIViewController subclasses. Any of these can be dragged into the canvas. This is the standard way of creating a scene in a *.storyboard* file; doing the same with a *.xib* file is rare but perfectly possible.

When a view controller has been instantiated from a nib, and when it comes eventually to obtain its view, all the ways I've already described whereby a view controller can obtain its view still apply. (There's also an additional way, which I'll discuss in a moment.)

To try this with a *.xib* file, start over with an empty project without a storyboard:

1. Choose File → New → File and specify iOS → User Interface → Empty. Click Next.
2. Name the new file *Main.xib*, make sure it's being saved into the right place and that it is part of the app target, and click Create.
3. Edit *Main.xib*. Drag a plain vanilla View Controller object into the canvas.
4. In the view controller you just dragged into the canvas, there's a View object serving as the main view. Select it and delete it! Don't worry, we'll discuss in a moment what it's for.

In *AppDelegate.swift*, we must now arrange to load *Main.xib* and extract the view controller instance created from the nib object we just put into the nib, making that view controller our app's root view controller. Here's one very simple way to do that:

```
let arr = UINib(nibName: "Main", bundle: nil)
    .instantiateWithOwner(nil, options: nil)
self.window!.rootViewController = arr[0] as? UIViewController
```

You can now proceed, if you like, to experiment with various ways of helping this view controller get its view. At the moment it is a plain UIViewController instance. Let's make it a class of our own:

1. Give the project a RootViewController class (a UIViewController subclass).
2. In *Main.xib*, select the view controller object and use its Identity inspector to set its class to RootViewController.

Now you can help RootViewController get its view, in any of the ways we've already explored:

- Implement loadView in RootViewController.
- Or, implement viewDidLoad but not loadView in RootViewController.
- Or, add another nib called *RootViewController.xib* (or *RootView.xib*).

If this nib-instantiated view controller is to get its view from another nib, there's a way to specify the name of that nib in the nib editor: select the view controller in its nib, and enter the name of the view's nib in the NIB Name field in its Attributes inspector. This is the equivalent of specifying a nib name when you call init(nibName:bundle:).

When a nib contains a view controller, there is, as I hinted a moment ago, *an additional way* for it to obtain its view — and you've probably already guessed what it is. When you first drag a View Controller object into the canvas in the nib editor, it *already* contains a view, hooked up and ready to act as its main view! The view controller, in fact, is portrayed in the canvas more or less as if it *were* this view. Thus, using the nib editor we can design the view controller's main view's interface *in the view controller itself.* Let's try it:

1. If you've been experimenting with the code in *RootViewController.swift*, remove any implementation of loadView or viewDidLoad.

2. In *Main.xib*, find the plain vanilla View object in the Object library and drag it *into the view controller object* in the canvas. (This restores the view that we deleted earlier.) This view object automatically becomes the view controller's view, and is drawn inside it in the canvas. Thus, you can now add further interface objects to this view.

Build and run. The interface you designed inside the view object inside the view controller object in *Main.xib* appears in the running app.

 When a view controller is instantiated from a nib, your implementation of its init(nibName:bundle:) initializer is *not* called. If your nib-instantiated UIView-Controller subclass needs access to the view controller instance very early in its lifetime, override init(coder:) or awakeFromNib.

Storyboard-Instantiated View Controller

If you've ever used a storyboard, it will not have escaped your attention that the *.xib* file we constructed in the previous section, consisting of a view controller directly containing its view, looks a lot like a scene in a storyboard. That's because, by default, this *is* the structure of a scene in a storyboard. Indeed, we are now ready to appreciate and understand how a storyboard works.

Each scene in a *.storyboard* file is rather like a *.xib* file containing a view controller nib object. A scene's view controller is instantiated only when needed; the underlying mechanism is that the scene's view controller is stored in a nib file in the built app, inside the *.storyboardc* bundle, and this nib file is loaded on demand and the view controller is instantiated from it, as we did in the previous section.

Moreover, by default, the view controller in a scene in a *.storyboard* file comes equipped with a view, which appears inside it in the canvas. You design the view and its subviews in the nib editor. When the app is built, each view controller's view goes into *a separate nib file*, inside the *.storyboardc* bundle, and the view controller, once instantiated, loads its view from that nib file lazily, exactly as we did earlier.

In this way, a storyboard embodies the very same mechanisms we've already explored through *.xib* files. Even though a storyboard may appear, in the nib editor, to contain many view controllers and their main views, each view controller and each main view constitutes an individual nib, which is loaded on demand, when needed by the running app, just as if we had configured the project with multiple *.xib* files. Thus a storyboard combines the memory management advantages of *.xib* files, which are not loaded until they're needed, and can be loaded multiple times to give additional instances of the same nib objects, with the convenience to you of being able to see and edit a lot of your app's interface simultaneously in one place.

You don't *have* to use the default scene structure in a storyboard. The default is that a view controller in a storyboard contains its view — *but you can delete the view*. If you do, then that view controller will obtain its view in any of the *other* ways we've already discussed: by an implementation of `loadView` in the code of that view controller class, or by loading an eponymous nib file, or even (if all of that fails) by creating a generic UIView.

 There's no way in a *.storyboard* file to specify as the source of a view controller's view a *.xib* file with a different name from the view controller's class; the nib editor lacks the NIB Name field in a view controller's Attributes inspector when you're working in a storyboard.

The Xcode app templates start with a single main storyboard called *Main.storyboard*, which is designated the app's main storyboard by the *Info.plist* key "Main storyboard file base name" (`UIMainStoryboardFile`). Therefore, as the app launches, `UIApplicationMain` gets a reference to this storyboard by calling the UIStoryboard initializer `init(name:bundle:)`, instantiates its initial view controller by calling `instantiateInitialViewController`, and makes that instance the window's `rootViewController`.

If you add segues to your storyboard, then when one of those segues is performed — which can be configured to happen automatically in response to the user tapping an interface object — the destination view controller is automatically instantiated. In this way it is perfectly possible for a single storyboard to be the source of every view controller that your app will ever instantiate, and for all of that instantiation to take place automatically.

That doesn't mean, however, that an app's interface must be configured as a single monolithic main storyboard. It is perfectly possible to use a main storyboard for some view controllers and to instantiate other view controllers in code (perhaps getting their views from corresponding *.xib* files). You can also have different storyboards containing different view controllers. In Xcode 7, using multiple storyboards is easier than ever — you no longer have to load your ancillary storyboards manually, because a segue in one storyboard can lead through a storyboard reference to a view controller in another storyboard, which will be loaded automatically. (I'll discuss storyboard references later in this chapter.)

You can get a reference to a storyboard either by calling the UIStoryboard initializer `init(name:bundle:)` or through the `storyboard` property of a view controller that has already been instantiated from that storyboard. With a storyboard instance in hand, a view controller can be instantiated from that storyboard in one of four ways:

- At most one view controller in the storyboard is designated the storyboard's *initial view controller*. To instantiate that view controller, call `instantiateInitialViewController`. The instance is returned.

- A view controller in a storyboard can be assigned an arbitrary string identifier; this is its Storyboard ID in the Identity inspector. To instantiate that view controller, call `instantiateViewControllerWithIdentifier:`. The instance is returned.

- A parent view controller in a storyboard may have immediate children, such as a UINavigationController and its initial child view controller. The nib editor will show a *relationship* connection between them. When the parent is instantiated (the source of the relationship), the initial children (the destination of the relationship) are instantiated automatically.

- A view controller in a storyboard may be (or contain) the source of a *segue* whose destination is a *future* child view controller or a *future* presented view controller. When the segue is triggered and performed, it instantiates the new view controller.

I'll go into much greater detail about storyboards and segues later in this chapter.

View Resizing

A view controller's view is likely to be resized. Other views can be resized as well, of course, but quite often this is a direct consequence of the resizing of a view controller's view, of which they are subviews. A view controller's view is resized when it is put into the interface. It is resized when the app rotates. It may be resized in response to interface changes, such as when a navigation bar gets taller or shorter, appears or disappears. On the iPhone 6, it may even be resized because a change in the Display Zoom setting changes the effective size of the screen. Apple describes views and view controllers as *adaptive* to size changes.

Because a view controller is a controller, it is typically the locus of logic for helping the interface to cope with all this resizing. A view controller has properties and receives events connected to the resizing of its view, so that it can correctly dictate the arrangement of the interface.

View Size in the Nib Editor

When you design your interface in the nib editor, every view controller's view has to be displayed at some definite size. But that size may not be the size at which the view will appear at runtime. If you design the interface only for the size you see in the nib editor, you can get a rude surprise when you actually run the app and the view appears at some other size. Failing to take account of this possibility is a common beginner mistake. On the contrary, you should assume that the size at which a view controller's main view is portrayed in the nib editor canvas is probably *not* the size it will assume at runtime.

In the nib editor, you can display the view at the size of any actual device: for a storyboard, select the view controller (for a *.xib* file, select the top-level view) and choose a specific device from the Size pop-up menu under Simulated Metrics at the top of the Attributes inspector. You can also specify an orientation, as well as the presence or absence of interface elements that can affect layout (status bar, top bar, bottom bar).

But don't forget that the specific size you see in the nib still may not reflect runtime reality. Suppose you design the interface for a view controller's view sized like an iPhone 4s; then when the app loads on an iPhone 5, or one of the two iPhone 6 models, the view is a different size, and the interface as designed isn't the interface you actually see. The Interface Builder Preview feature can be a big help here, allowing you to view your interface laid out for multiple devices simultaneously.

From this point of view, Xcode's "Use Size Classes" option is a boon (see Chapter 1). By default, it shows a view controller's main view as a square — a neutral shape that will never be encountered in real life. This serves as a reminder that the interface you are designing must adapt to a variety of real sizes when the app runs.

Bars and Underlapping

A view controller's view will often have to adapt to the presence of bars at the top and bottom of the screen:

The status bar is underlapped
> The status bar is transparent, so that the region of a view behind it is visible through it. The root view, and any other fullscreen view, must occupy the *entire window*, including the status bar area, the top of the view being visible behind the transparent status bar. You'll want to design your view so that its top doesn't contain any interface objects that will be overlapped by the status bar.

Top and bottom bars may be underlapped
> The top and bottom bars displayed by a navigation controller (navigation bar, toolbar) or tab bar controller (tab bar) can be translucent. When they are, your view controller's view is, by default, extended *behind* the translucent bar, underlapping it. Again, you'll want to design your view so that this underlapping doesn't conceal any of your view's important interface.

The status bar may be present or absent. Top and bottom bars may be present or absent, and, if present, their height can change. How will your interface cope with such changes? The primary coping mechanism is the view controller's *layout guides*.

Recall (from Chapter 1) that a view controller supplies two properties, its topLayout-Guide and its bottomLayoutGuide. The position of these guide objects moves automatically at runtime to reflect the view's environment:

topLayoutGuide
> The topLayoutGuide is positioned as follows:
>
> - If there is a status bar and no top bar, the topLayoutGuide is positioned at the bottom of the status bar.
> - If there is a top bar, the topLayoutGuide is positioned at the bottom of the top bar.
> - If there is no top bar and no status bar, the topLayoutGuide is positioned at the top of the view.

bottomLayoutGuide
> The bottomLayoutGuide is positioned as follows:
>
> - If there is a bottom bar, the bottomLayoutGuide is positioned at the top of the bottom bar.
> - If there is no bottom bar, the bottomLayoutGuide is positioned at the bottom of the view.

The easiest way to involve the layout guides in your view layout is through autolayout and constraints. By constraining a view by its top to the bottom of the topLayout-Guide, or by its bottom to the top of the bottomLayoutGuide, you guarantee that the view will move when the layout guide moves. Such constraints are easy to form in the nib editor — they are the default. When you're using the new iOS 9 anchor notation for creating a constraint in code, you'll use the topLayoutGuide's bottomAnchor and the bottomLayoutGuide's topAnchor.

If you need actual numbers in order to perform layout-related calculations, a layout guide's spacing from the corresponding edge of the view controller's main view is reported by its length property. Note that viewDidLoad is too early to obtain a meaningful value; the earliest coherent opportunity is probably viewWillLayoutSubviews (I'll discuss this event later). New in iOS 9, if you are constructing a constraint relative to the height of a layout guide, you can use its heightAnchor property.

Status bar visibility

The default behavior of the status bar is that it is present, except in landscape orientation on an iPhone, where it is absent. The root view controller, as I mentioned at the start of this chapter, gets a say in this behavior; it also determines the look of the status bar when present. Your UIViewController subclass can override these methods:

preferredStatusBarStyle

> Your choices (UIStatusBarStyle) are `.Default` and `.LightContent`, meaning dark text and light text, respectively. Use light text for legibility if the view content underlapping the status bar is dark.

prefersStatusBarHidden

> Return `true` to make the status bar invisible; return `false` to make the status bar visible, even in landscape orientation on an iPhone. (Return the result of a call to `super` to get the default behavior.)

childViewControllerForStatusBarStyle
childViewControllerForStatusBarHidden

> Used to delegate the decision on the status bar style or visibility to a child view controller's `preferredStatusBarStyle` or `prefersStatusBarHidden`. For example, a tab bar controller implements these methods to allow your view controller to decide the status bar style and visibility when your view controller's view occupies the tab bar controller's view. Thus, your view controller gets to make the decisions even though the tab bar controller is the root view controller.

You never call any of those methods yourself; they are called automatically when the view controller situation changes (including when the interface rotates). If you want them to be called immediately, because they are not being called when you need them to be, or because the situation has changed and a call to one of them would now give a different answer, call `setNeedsStatusBarAppearanceUpdate` on your view controller. If this call is inside an animation block, the animation of the change in the look of the status bar will have the specified duration. The character of the animation from visible to invisible (and *vice versa*) is set by your view controller's implementation of `preferredStatusBarUpdateAnimation`; the value you return (UIStatusBarAnimation) can be `.Fade`, `.Slide`, or `.None`.

When you toggle the visibility of the status bar, the top layout guide will move up or down by 20 points. If your main view has subviews with constraints to the top layout guide, those subviews will move. If this happens when the main view is visible, the user will see this movement as a jump. That is probably not what you want. To prevent it, call `layoutIfNeeded` on your view in the same animation block in which you call `setNeedsStatusBarAppearanceUpdate`; your layout update will then be animated together with the change in status bar visibility. In this example, a button's action method toggles the visibility of the status bar with smooth animation:

```
var hide = false
override func prefersStatusBarHidden() -> Bool {
    return self.hide
}
@IBAction func doButton(sender: AnyObject) {
    self.hide = !self.hide
    UIView.animateWithDuration(0.4, animations: {
        self.setNeedsStatusBarAppearanceUpdate()
        self.view.layoutIfNeeded()
    })
}
```

Extended layout

If your UIViewController's parent is a navigation controller or tab bar controller, you can govern whether its view underlaps a top bar (navigation bar) or bottom bar (toolbar, tab bar) with these UIViewController properties:

edgesForExtendedLayout

> A UIRectEdge. The default is .All, meaning that this view controller's view will underlap a translucent top bar or a translucent bottom bar. The other extreme is .None, meaning that this view controller's view won't underlap top and bottom bars. Other possibilities are .Top (underlap translucent top bars only) and .Bottom (underlap translucent bottom bars only).

extendedLayoutIncludesOpaqueBars

> If true, then if edgesForExtendedLayout permits underlapping of bars, those bars will be underlapped *even if they are opaque*. The default is false, meaning that only translucent bars are underlapped.

Resizing Events

A UIViewController receives events that notify it of pending view size changes. (Trait collections, size classes, and view layout events were discussed in Chapter 1.)

The following events are associated primarily with rotation of the interface; new in iOS 9, they are associated also with iPad multitasking (Chapter 9):

willTransitionToTraitCollection:withTransitionCoordinator:

> Sent when the app is about to undergo a change in the trait collection (because the size classes will change). Common examples are rotation of 90 degrees on an iPhone, or a change between fullscreen and splitscreen on an iPad. This event is *not* sent on launch or when your view controller's view is first embedded into the interface. If you override this method, call super.
>
> UIViewController receives this event by virtue of adopting the UIContentContainer protocol.

`viewWillTransitionToSize:withTransitionCoordinator:`
> Sent when the app is about to undergo rotation (even if the rotation turns out to be 180 degrees and the size won't actually change) or an iPad multitasking size change. The new size is the first parameter; the old size is still available as `self.view.bounds.size`. This event is *not* sent on launch or when your view controller's view is first embedded into the interface. If you override this method, call `super`.
>
> UIViewController receives this event by virtue of adopting the UIContent-Container protocol.

`traitCollectionDidChange:`
> Sent after the trait collection changes. The parameter is the old trait collection; the new trait collection is available as `self.traitCollection`. Sent after the trait collection changes, *including* on launch or when the trait collection is set for the first time (in which case the parameter will be `nil`).
>
> UIViewController receives this event by virtue of adopting the UITraitEnvironment protocol.

(I'll describe the use of the `transitionCoordinator:` parameter later in this chapter.)

In addition, a UIViewController receives these events related to the layout of its view:

`updateViewConstraints`
> The view is about to be told to update its constraints (`updateConstraints`), *including* at application launch. If you override this method, call `super`.

`viewWillLayoutSubviews`
`viewDidLayoutSubviews`
> These events surround the moment when the view is sent `layoutSubviews`, *including* at application launch.

In a situation where all these events are sent, the order is:

- `willTransitionToTraitCollection:withTransitionCoordinator:`
- `viewWillTransitionToSize:withTransitionCoordinator:`
- `updateViewConstraints`
- `traitCollectionDidChange:`
- `viewWillLayoutSubviews`
- `viewDidLayoutSubviews`

There is no guarantee that any of these events, if sent, will be sent exactly once.

Your view can be resized under many circumstances, such as the showing and hiding of a navigation bar that isn't underlapped, *without* the viewWillTransition-ToSize:... event being sent. Thus, to detect these changes, you'll have to fall back on layout events such as viewWillLayoutSubviews. I regard this as a flaw in the iOS view controller event architecture.

Rotation

Your app can rotate, moving its top to correspond to a different edge of the device's screen. In iOS 7 and before, this rotation was something of an illusion: the window remained pinned to the screen, and rotation was a matter of applying a transform to the root view and changing the bounds size to match the new orientation. In iOS 8 and later, however, the app really does rotate. Rotation expresses itself in two ways:

The status bar orientation changes
You can hear about this (though this will rarely be necessary) by way of these app delegate events and notifications:

- application:willChangeStatusBarOrientation:duration: (and the corresponding UIApplicationWillChangeStatusBarOrientationNotification)

- application:didChangeStatusBarOrientation: (and the corresponding UIApplicationDidChangeStatusBarOrientationNotification)

The current orientation (which is also the app's current orientation) is available from the UIApplication as its statusBarOrientation; the app delegate methods also provide the other orientation (the one we are changing to or from, respectively) as the second parameter. Possible values (UIInterfaceOrientation) are:

- .Portrait
- .PortraitUpsideDown
- .LandscapeLeft
- .LandscapeRight

Two global convenience functions, UIInterfaceOrientationIsLandscape and UIInterfaceOrientationIsPortrait, take a UIInterfaceOrientation and return a Bool.

The view controller's view is resized
The view controller receives events related to resizing, as I described in the preceding section. These may or may not include a change in the trait collection. Thus, the most general way to learn that rotation is taking place is through viewWillTransitionToSize:withTransitionCoordinator:. On the other hand, you are more likely to care about a 90 degree rotation on an iPhone than any other kind of

rotation, and in that case `willTransitionToTraitCollection:withTransition-Coordinator:` applies.

There are two complementary uses for rotation:

Compensatory rotation

> The app rotates to compensate for the orientation of the device, so that the app appears right way up with respect to how the user is holding the device. The challenge of compensatory rotation stems, quite simply, from the fact that the screen is not square. This means that if the app rotates 90 degrees, the interface no longer fits the screen, and must be changed to compensate.

Forced rotation

> The app rotates when a particular view appears in the interface, or when the app launches, to indicate that the user needs to rotate the device in order to view the app the right way up. This is typically because the interface has been specifically designed, in the face of the fact that the screen is not square, to appear in one orientation (portrait or landscape).

In the case of the iPhone, no law says that your app has to perform compensatory rotation. Most of my iPhone apps do not do so; indeed, I have no compunction about doing just the opposite. My view controller views often look best in just one orientation (or one pair of opposed orientations, either just portrait or just landscape), and they stubbornly stay there regardless of how the user holds the device. A single app may contain view controller views that work best in different orientations; thus, my app forces the user to rotate the device differently depending on what view is being displayed. This is reasonable, because the iPhone is small and easily reoriented with a twist of the user's wrist, and it has a natural right way up, especially because it's a phone. (The iPod touch isn't a phone, but the same argument works by analogy.)

On the other hand, Apple would prefer iPad apps to rotate to at least two opposed orientations (such as landscape with the button on the right and landscape with the button on the left), and preferably to all four possible orientations, so that the user isn't restricted in how the device is held.

It's fairly trivial to let your app rotate to two opposed orientations, because once the app is set up to work in one of them, it can work with no change in the other. But allowing a single interface to rotate between two orientations that are 90 degrees apart is trickier, because its dimensions must change — roughly speaking, its height and width are transposed — and this may require a change of layout and might even call for more substantial alterations, such as removal or addition of part of the interface. A good example is the behavior of Apple's Mail app on the iPad: in landscape, the master pane and the detail pane appear side by side, but in portrait, the master pane is removed and must be summoned as a temporary overlay on top of the detail pane.

Permitting compensatory rotation

By default, when you create an Xcode project, the resulting app will perform compensatory rotation in response to the user's rotation of the device. For an iPhone app, this means that the app can appear with its top at the top of the device or either of the two sides of the device. For an iPad app, this means that the app can assume any orientation.

If the default behavior isn't what you want, it is up to you to change it. There are three levels at which you can make changes:

- The app itself, in its *Info.plist*, may declare once and for all every orientation the interface will ever be permitted to assume. It does this under the "Supported interface orientations" key, `UISupportedInterfaceOrientations` (supplemented, for a universal app, by "Supported interface orientations (iPad)," `UISupportedInterfaceOrientations~ipad`). These keys can also be set through checkboxes when you edit the app target, in the General tab.

- The app delegate may implement the `application:supportedInterfaceOrientationsForWindow:` method, returning a bitmask listing every orientation the interface is permitted to assume. This list *overrides* the *Info.plist* settings. Thus, the app delegate can do dynamically what the *Info.plist* can do only statically. `application:supportedInterfaceOrientationsForWindow:` is called at least once every time the device rotates.

- The top-level view controller — that is, the root view controller, or a view controller presented fullscreen — may implement `supportedInterfaceOrientations`, returning a bitmask listing a set of orientations that *intersects* the set of orientations permitted by the app or the app delegate. The resulting intersection will then be the set of orientations permitted at that moment. This intersection must not be empty; if it is, your app will crash (with a useful message: "Supported orientations has no common orientation with the application"). `supportedInterfaceOrientations` is called at least once every time the device rotates.

  The top-level view controller can also implement `shouldAutorotate`. This method returns a Bool, and the default is `true`. `shouldAutorotate` is called at least once every time the device rotates; if it returns `false`, the interface will not rotate to compensate at this moment, and `supportedInterfaceOrientations` is not called.

 Built-in parent view controllers, when they are top-level view controller, do *not* automatically consult their children about rotation. If your view controller is a child view controller of a UITabBarController or a UINavigationController, it has no direct say in how the app rotates. Those parent view controllers, however, do consult their *delegates* about rotation, as I'll explain later.

A UIViewController class method `attemptRotationToDeviceOrientation` prompts the runtime to do immediately what it would do if the user were to rotate the device, namely to walk the three levels I've just described and, if the results permit rotation of the interface to match the current device orientation, to rotate the interface. This would be useful if, say, your view controller had previously returned `false` from `should-Autorotate`, but is now for some reason prepared to return `true` and wants to be asked again, immediately.

The bitmask you return from `application:supportedInterfaceOrientationsFor-Window:` or `supportedInterfaceOrientations` is a UIInterfaceOrientationMask. It may be one of these values, or multiple values combined:

- `.Portrait`
- `.LandscapeLeft`
- `.LandscapeRight`
- `.PortraitUpsideDown`
- `.Landscape` (a combination of `.Left` and `.Right`)
- `.All` (a combination of `.Portrait`, `.UpsideDown`, `.Left`, and `.Right`)
- `.AllButUpsideDown` (a combination of `.Portrait`, `.Left`, and `.Right`)

For example:

```
override func supportedInterfaceOrientations()
    -> UIInterfaceOrientationMask {
        return .Portrait
}
```

If your code needs to know the current physical orientation of the device (as opposed to the current orientation of the app), it can ask the device:

```
let orientation = UIDevice.currentDevice().orientation
```

Possible results (UIDeviceOrientation) are `.Unknown`, `.Portrait`, and so on. Global convenience functions `UIDeviceOrientationIsPortrait` and `UIDeviceOrientation-IsLandscape` take a UIDeviceOrientation and return a Bool. By the time you get a rotation-related event, the device's orientation has already changed.

 In iOS 9, because of the new iPad multitasking architecture (Chapter 9), an iPad app that doesn't permit all four orientations must include in its *Info.plist* the `UIRequiresFullScreen` key with a value of YES. Moreover, if the app's *Info.plist* does *not* include `UIRequiresFullScreen` and *does* permit all four orientations, then `supportedInterfaceOrientations` and `shouldAutorotate` are never called, presumably because the answer is known in advance.

Initial orientation

I've talked about how to determine what orientations your app can support in the course of its lifetime; but what about its initial orientation, the very first orientation your app will assume when it launches?

On the iPad, an app has no fixed initial orientation. iPad apps are supposed to be more or less orientation-agnostic, so the app will launch into whatever permitted orientation is closest to the device's current orientation at launch time.

On the iPhone, in iOS 9, the app's initial orientation is always portrait orientation if your *Info.plist* includes portrait orientation (`UIInterfaceOrientationPortrait`). If your initial root view controller also permits portrait orientation, but the user is holding the device in a landscape orientation that is also permitted, then the app will launch normally, correctly, and fully into portrait orientation, appearing to the user in portrait, and will then almost immediately afterward visibly rotate to landscape. This is essentially no different than if the user had been holding the device in portrait orientation while launching your app and then rotated it to landscape later.

If your *Info.plist* does not include portrait orientation, then the app launches directly into landscape. Which landscape orientation the app will prefer is dictated by the *order* in which the landscape orientations are listed in the *Info.plist*. If, say, the first listing is "Landscape (left home button)" (`UIInterfaceOrientationLandscapeLeft`), but the user is holding the device in landscape with the Home button at the right, then the app will launch directly into landscape upside down (from the user's point of view), and will then visibly rotate 180 degrees.

If your *Info.plist does* include portrait orientation but your initial root view controller does *not* permit portrait orientation, then in iOS 9 the app will start out in portrait orientation but will rotate to landscape (with a trait collection transition, but no size transition) before performing layout and appearing to the user. In this situation, the order of orientations listed in the *Info.plist* makes no difference: the app will initially appear to the user as if the home button were on the right, and if in fact it is on the left, the app will then visibly rotate 180 degrees. This behavior is a change from how things worked in iOS 8, where the order of orientations in the *Info.plist* mattered; I regard it as somewhat incoherent. A possible workaround is to exclude portrait orientation from the *Info.plist* but include it in your implementation of `application:supported-InterfaceOrientationsForWindow:`.

Initial layout

If you have code that performs or contributes to the initial construction and layout of your app's interface, where should that code go? What events your root view controller will receive at launch differs depending on various rotation-related factors mentioned in the previous section, but at a minimum, you can certainly count on the following:

- `viewDidLoad`

- `traitCollectionDidChange:`

- `viewWillLayoutSubviews`

There is a natural temptation to perform initial layout-related tasks in `viewDidLoad`, just because it's so convenient. It is called *exactly once* as early as possible in the life of the view controller's view; that's why it is a conventional locus for preparation of the interface (as well as other view controller initializations). However, keep in mind that at the time `viewDidLoad` is called, the view has been loaded, but it has not yet been inserted into the interface! Thus it has not yet been fully resized for the first time. A layout-related task that depends upon the absolute dimensions of the view is therefore destined to generate erroneous results. As long as you *don't* rely on a knowledge of the final absolute dimensions of your view — in particular, if your initial layout configuration involves autolayout — `viewDidLoad` is a reasonable place to do it.

In this (completely artifical) example, our goal is to insert a small black square at the top center of the interface. This code could be a mistake:

```
override func viewDidLoad() {
    super.viewDidLoad()
    let square = UIView(frame:CGRectMake(0,0,10,10))
    square.backgroundColor = UIColor.blackColor()
    square.center = CGPointMake(self.view.bounds.midX,5) // top center?
    self.view.addSubview(square)
}
```

That might work, but then again it might not. On an iPhone, under certain circumstances, at the time `viewDidLoad` is called, the width (and hence the `midX`) of `self.view` might not yet have the value it will have when the interface settles down, and our square will be misplaced. This still might not matter, however, if our square also has the ability to compensate for subsequent rotation and resizing. It might be enough to add autoresizing:

```
override func viewDidLoad() {
    super.viewDidLoad()
    let square = UIView(frame:CGRectMake(0,0,10,10))
    square.backgroundColor = UIColor.blackColor()
    square.center = CGPointMake(self.view.bounds.midX,5)
    square.autoresizingMask =
        [.FlexibleLeftMargin, .FlexibleRightMargin, .FlexibleBottomMargin]
    self.view.addSubview(square)
}
```

The best approach is to use autolayout:

```
override func viewDidLoad() {
    super.viewDidLoad()
    let square = UIView()
    square.backgroundColor = UIColor.blackColor()
    self.view.addSubview(square)
    square.translatesAutoresizingMaskIntoConstraints = false
    let side : CGFloat = 10
    var con = [NSLayoutConstraint]()
    con.appendContentsOf([
        square.widthAnchor.constraintEqualToConstant(side),
        square.centerXAnchor.constraintEqualToAnchor(self.view.centerXAnchor)
    ])
    con.appendContentsOf(
        NSLayoutConstraint.constraintsWithVisualFormat("V:|[square(side)]",
            options:[], metrics:["side":side],
            views:["square":square]))
    NSLayoutConstraint.activateConstraints(con)
}
```

Our view (`self.view`) may proceed to be resized further as the interface settles down, but the small black square will still be positioned correctly, because the constraints determine that position relative to *whatever* the size of our view may be.

If we decide to perform layout initializations in `traitCollectionDidChange:` or `viewWillLayoutSubviews`, we face the quandary that these methods can be called multiple times over the lifetime of a view controller. To ensure that we perform initializations just once, we can make use of a Bool property flag:

```
var viewInitializationDone = false
override func viewWillLayoutSubviews() {
    if !self.viewInitializationDone {
        self.viewInitializationDone = true // ensure we do this just once
        // perform initializations here
    }
}
```

Responding to rotation

When your app rotates 90 degrees, your view controller's main view may have its height and width bounds dimensions effectively transposed. This is an extraordinarily dramatic and extreme resizing, especially on an iPhone. Your interface may need to be rearranged, perhaps quite heavily, to cope with this change in your view's size. You may need not only to move and resize views but even to insert or remove views.

In many cases, autoresizing or (more likely) autolayout will handle the situation — and you can get a serious boost from conditional constraints and the ability to configure things in the nib editor so that views and constraints are removed and inserted *automatically* in response to a trait collection change (see Chapter 1).

Sometimes, however, code is needed to perform or supplement the rearrangement of your interface at rotation time. Such code is not at all easy to implement. In iOS 7 and before, rotation events (with `rotate` in their names) arrived on both iPad and iPhone to let you know what's happening. But in iOS 8, those rotation events were deprecated, and were replaced with `willTransitionToTraitCollection:...` and `viewWill-TransitionToSize:....` Unfortunately those new events do not arrive in a consistently helpful way; in particular, the former event is *not* sent when an iPad rotates, because iPad rotation does not cause any change in the trait collection.

Rotation is animated, and you'll probably want your layout changes to harmonize with and participate in that animation. This is where the `transitionCoordinator:` parameter comes in. It is (not surprisingly) a transition coordinator; in particular, it's an object adopting the UIViewControllerTransitionCoordinator protocol, which means that it is reponsible for governing a runtime animation (in this case, the rotation animation), and that it implements this method:

`animateAlongsideTransition:completion:`
> Takes an animation block and a completion block. The animation you supply is incorporated into the transition coordinator's animation. Returns a Bool, informing you in case your commands couldn't be animated.

> Both blocks receive as parameter a context object implementing the UIViewControllerTransitionCoordinatorContext protocol. This object, among other things, has a `targetTransform` method that you can call to learn how far and in what direction the interface is rotating. (The transition coordinator, too, is such a context object.) In particular, if `rot` is the result of calling `targetTransform`, the rotation is 180 degrees — the thing you're most likely to want to know — if and only if both `rot.b` and `rot.c` are 0.

(Other methods implemented by the transition coordinator and context object are irrelevant to rotation; I'll discuss them later in this chapter, in connection with custom view controller transitions.)

In this (completely artificial) example, I'll specify that our interface should display a large green rectangle occupying the left side of the screen if the device is in landscape orientation, but not if the device is in portrait orientation. Let's stipulate that this will be an iPhone app; thus, I can be notified of rotation by implementing `willTransition-ToTraitCollection:withTransitionCoordinator:`, and I can test which way we're about to rotate by examining the new trait collection's vertical size class. I'll animate the green rectangle on and off the screen in coordination with the rotation animation:

```
lazy var greenRect : UIView = self.makeGreenRect()
func makeGreenRect() -> UIView {
    var f = self.view.bounds
    if self.traitCollection.verticalSizeClass != .Compact {
        (f.size.width, f.size.height) = (f.size.height, f.size.width)
```

```
        }
        f.size.width /= 3.0
        f.origin.x = -f.size.width
        let gr = UIView(frame:f)
        gr.backgroundColor = UIColor.greenColor()
        return gr
    }
    override func willTransitionToTraitCollection(
        newCollection: UITraitCollection,
        withTransitionCoordinator coordinator:
        UIViewControllerTransitionCoordinator) {
            super.willTransitionToTraitCollection(newCollection,
                withTransitionCoordinator: coordinator)
            let v = self.greenRect
            var newFrameOriginX = v.frame.origin.x
            if newCollection.verticalSizeClass == .Compact { // landscape
                if v.superview == nil {
                    self.view.addSubview(v)
                    newFrameOriginX = 0
                }
            } else { // portrait
                if v.superview != nil {
                    newFrameOriginX = -v.frame.size.width
                }
            }
            coordinator.animateAlongsideTransition({
                _ in
                v.frame.origin.x = newFrameOriginX // animate!
                }, completion: {
                    _ in
                    if newCollection.verticalSizeClass != .Compact {
                        self.greenRect.removeFromSuperview()
                    }
            })
    }
```

As usual, a constraint-based solution would be more robust. This is a good use of the
technique I described in Chapter 1, where we prepare two sets of constraints and swap
them in and out. I won't even bother to remove the green rectangle from the interface;
I'll add it once and for all as I configure the view initially, and just slide it onscreen and
offscreen as needed:

```
var greenRectConstraintsOnscreen : [NSLayoutConstraint]!
var greenRectConstraintsOffscreen : [NSLayoutConstraint]!
override func viewDidLoad() {
    super.viewDidLoad()
    let gr = UIView()
    gr.translatesAutoresizingMaskIntoConstraints = false
    gr.backgroundColor = UIColor.greenColor()
    self.view.addSubview(gr)
    var c = [NSLayoutConstraint]()
    // "g.r. is pinned to top and bottom of superview"
```

```
            c.appendContentsOf(
                NSLayoutConstraint.constraintsWithVisualFormat("V:|[gr]|",
                    options:[], metrics:nil, views:["gr":gr]))
            // "g.r. is 1/3 the width of superview"
            c.append(
                gr.widthAnchor.constraintEqualToAnchor(self.view.widthAnchor,
                    multiplier: 1.0/3.0))
            // "onscreen, g.r.'s left is pinned to superview's left"
            let marrOn =
                NSLayoutConstraint.constraintsWithVisualFormat("H:|[gr]",
                    options:[], metrics:nil, views:["gr":gr])
            // "offscreen, g.r.'s right is pinned to superview's left"
            let marrOff = [
                gr.trailingAnchor.constraintEqualToAnchor(self.view.leadingAnchor)!
            ]
            self.greenRectConstraintsOnscreen = marrOn
            self.greenRectConstraintsOffscreen = marrOff
            // start out offscreen!
            c.appendContentsOf(marrOff)
            NSLayoutConstraint.activateConstraints(c)
    }
    override func willTransitionToTraitCollection(
        newCollection: UITraitCollection,
        withTransitionCoordinator coordinator:
        UIViewControllerTransitionCoordinator) {
            super.willTransitionToTraitCollection(newCollection,
                withTransitionCoordinator: coordinator)
            NSLayoutConstraint.deactivateConstraints(
                self.greenRectConstraintsOnscreen)
            NSLayoutConstraint.deactivateConstraints(
                self.greenRectConstraintsOffscreen)
            if newCollection.verticalSizeClass == .Compact {
                NSLayoutConstraint.activateConstraints(
                    self.greenRectConstraintsOnscreen)
            } else {
                NSLayoutConstraint.activateConstraints(
                    self.greenRectConstraintsOffscreen)
            }
    }
```

The movement of the green rectangle is animated as the interface rotates, because *any* constraint-based layout performed as the interface rotates is animated!

For this particular example, an even more elegant solution is possible: the entire change of interface can be configured in the nib, using conditional constraints. The details are left as an exercise for the reader.

But none of those approaches will work if this app runs natively on an iPad! When an iPad rotates, there is no change of trait collection. Thus, willTransitionToTrait-Collection:withTransitionCoordinator: will never be sent; we can't learn how we are oriented by looking at the trait collection; and conditional constraints configured in the nib won't operate. Instead, we have to concentrate on our main view's *size*. We can implement viewWillTransitionToSize:withTransitionCoordinator: to detect rotation, and we can learn our new orientation by comparing the new size's height to its width. But this event won't be sent if we launch into landscape on the iPad, so we'll have to factor out our constraint-swapping code and call it from viewDidLoad as well:

```
override func viewDidLoad() {
    super.viewDidLoad()
    let gr = UIView()
    // ... create constraints as before ...
    self.adjustInterfaceForSize(self.view.bounds.size)
}
override func viewWillTransitionToSize(size: CGSize,
    withTransitionCoordinator coordinator:
    UIViewControllerTransitionCoordinator) {
        super.viewWillTransitionToSize(size,
            withTransitionCoordinator: coordinator)
        if size != self.view.bounds.size {
            self.adjustInterfaceForSize(size)
        }
}
func adjustInterfaceForSize(size: CGSize) {
    NSLayoutConstraint.deactivateConstraints(
        self.greenRectConstraintsOnscreen)
    NSLayoutConstraint.deactivateConstraints(
        self.greenRectConstraintsOffscreen)
    if size.width > size.height {
        NSLayoutConstraint.activateConstraints(
            self.greenRectConstraintsOnscreen)
    } else {
        NSLayoutConstraint.activateConstraints(
            self.greenRectConstraintsOffscreen)
    }
}
```

Presented View Controller

Back when the only iOS device was an iPhone, a presented view controller was called a *modal view controller*. When a modal view controller was summoned (presented), the root view controller remained in place, but its view was taken out of the interface and the modal view controller's view was used instead. Thus, this was the simplest way to replace the entire interface with a different interface.

You can see why this configuration was characterized as "modal." The presented view controller's view has, in a sense, blocked access to the "real" view, the root view controller's view. The user is forced to work in the presented view controller's view, until that view is "dismissed" and the "real" view is visible again — similar to a modal dialog

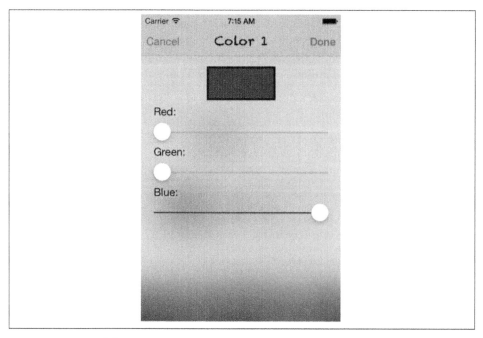

Figure 6-7. A modal view

in a desktop application, where the user can't do anything else but work in the dialog as long as it is present. A presented view controller's view often reinforces this analogy with obvious dismissal buttons with titles like Save, Done, or Cancel.

The color picker view in my own Zotz! app is a good example (Figure 6-7); this is an interface that says, "You are now configuring a color, and that's all you can do; change the color or cancel, or you'll be stuck here forever." The user can't get out of this view without tapping Cancel or Done, and the view that the user was previously using is visible as a blur behind this view, waiting for the user to return to it.

Figure 6-5, from my Latin flashcard app, is another example of a presented view. It has a Cancel button, and the user is in a special "mode," performing a drill exercise rather than scrolling through flashcards.

Nevertheless, the "modal" characterization is not always apt. A presented view controller might be no more than a technique that you, the programmer, have used to alter the interface; the user needn't be conscious of this. A presented view controller's view may have a complex interface; it may have child view controllers; it may present yet *another* view controller; it may take over the interface *permanently*, with the user *never* returning to the interface that it replaced.

Furthermore, the range of ways in which a presented view controller's view can be displayed now goes far beyond merely replacing the root view controller's view. For example:

- Instead of replacing the entire interface, a presented view controller's view can replace a *subview* within the existing interface. (This ability was originally confined to the iPad alone; starting in iOS 8, it became available on the iPhone as well.)
- A presented view controller's view may cover the existing interface only *partially*; the existing interface is never removed. (This, too, was originally an iPad-only feature; it became possible on the iPhone starting in iOS 7.)

Presenting a View

The two key methods for presenting and dismissing a view are:

`presentViewController:animated:completion:`
> To make a view controller present another view controller, you send the first view controller this message, handing it the second view controller, which you will probably instantiate for this very purpose. (The first view controller is very typically `self`.)
>
> We now have two view controllers that stand in the relationship of being one another's `presentingViewController` and `presentedViewController` respectively. The presented view controller is retained, and its view effectively replaces or covers the presenting view controller's view in the interface (I'll talk later about ways to refine that arrangement).

`dismissViewControllerAnimated:completion:`
> The "presented" state of affairs described in the previous paragraph persists until the presenting view controller is sent this message. The presented view controller's view is then removed from the interface, the original interface is restored, and the presented view controller is released; it will thereupon typically go out of existence, together with its view, its child view controllers and *their* views, and so on.

As the view of the presented view controller appears, and again when it is dismissed, there's an option for animation to be performed as the transition takes place (the `animated:` argument, a Bool). The `completion:` parameter, which can be `nil`, lets you supply a block of code to be run after the transition (including the animation) has occurred. I'll talk later about how to govern the nature of the animation.

The presenting view controller (the presented view controller's `presentingViewController`) is not necessarily the view controller to which you sent `presentViewController:animated:completion:`. It will help if we distinguish *three* roles that view controllers can play in presenting a view controller:

Presented view controller

The view controller specified as the first argument to `presentView-Controller:animated:completion:`.

Original presenter

The view controller to which `presentViewController:animated:completion:` was sent. Apple sometimes refers to this view controller as the *source*; "original presenter" is my own term.

The presented view controller is set as the original presenter's `presentedView-Controller`.

Presenting view controller

The presented view controller's `presentingViewController`. This is the view controller whose view is replaced or covered by the presented view controller's view. By default, it is *the view controller whose view is the entire interface* — namely, either the root view controller or an already existing presented view controller. It might not be the same as the original presenter.

The presented view controller is set as the presenting view controller's `presented-ViewController`. Thus, the presented view controller might be the `presentedView-Controller` of two different view controllers.

The receiver of `dismissViewControllerAnimated:completion:` may be *any* of those three objects; the runtime will use the linkages between them to transmit the necessary messages up the chain on your behalf to the `presentingViewController`.

You can test whether a view controller's `presentedViewController` or `presentingView-Controller` is `nil` to learn whether view presentation is occurring. For example, a view controller whose `presentingViewController` is `nil` is not a presented view controller at this moment.

A view controller can have at most one `presentedViewController`. If you send `present-ViewController:animated:completion:` to a view controller whose `presentedView-Controller` isn't `nil`, nothing will happen and the completion handler is not called (and you'll get a warning from the runtime).

However, a presented view controller can itself present a view controller, so there can be a chain of presented view controllers. If you send `dismissViewController-Animated:completion:` to a view controller in the middle of a presentation chain — a view controller that has both a `presentingViewController` and a `presentedView-Controller` — then its `presentedViewController` is dismissed.

If you send `dismissViewControllerAnimated:completion:` to a view controller whose `presentedViewController` is `nil` and that has no `presentingViewController`, nothing will happen (not even a warning in the console), and the `completion:` handler is not called.

Let's make one view controller present another. We could do this simply by connecting one view controller to another in a storyboard with a modal segue, but I don't want you to do that: a modal segue calls `presentViewController:animated:completion:` for you, whereas I want you to call it yourself.

So start with an iPhone project made from the Single View Application template. This contains one view controller class, called ViewController. Our first move must be to add a second view controller class, an instance of which will function as the presented view controller:

1. Choose File → New → File and specify iOS → Source → Cocoa Touch Class. Click Next.

2. Name the class SecondViewController, make sure it is a subclass of UIView-Controller, and check the XIB checkbox so that we can design this view controller's view quickly and easily in a nib. (We could use the storyboard instead, but that would not be as educational.) Click Next.

3. Confirm the folder, group, and app target membership, and click Create.

4. Edit *SecondViewController.xib*, and do something there to make the view distinctive, so that you'll recognize it when it appears; for example, give it a red background color.

5. We need a way to trigger the presentation of SecondViewController. Edit *Main.storyboard* and add a button to the ViewController's view's interface. Connect that button to an action method in *ViewController.swift*; let's call it `doPresent:`.

6. In *ViewController.swift*, write the code for `doPresent:`, as follows:

```
@IBAction func doPresent(sender:AnyObject?) {
    let svc = SecondViewController(
        nibName: "SecondViewController", bundle: nil)
    self.presentViewController(svc, animated:true, completion:nil)
}
```

Run the project. In ViewController's view, tap the button. SecondViewController's view slides into place over ViewController's view.

In our lust for instant gratification, we have neglected to provide a way to dismiss the presented view controller. If you'd like to do that, edit *SecondViewController.xib*, put a button into SecondViewController's view, and connect it to an action method in *SecondViewController.swift*:

```
@IBAction func doDismiss(sender:AnyObject?) {
    self.presentingViewController!.dismissViewControllerAnimated(
        true, completion: nil)
}
```

Run the project. You can now alternate between ViewController's view and Second-ViewController's view, presenting and dismissing in turn. Go ahead and play for a while with your exciting new app; I'll wait.

Communication With a Presented View Controller

In real life, it is highly probable that the original presenter will have additional information to impart to the presented view controller as the latter is created and presented, and that the presented view controller will want to pass information back to the original presenter as it is dismissed. Knowing how to arrange this exchange of information is very important.

Passing information from the original presenter to the presented view controller is usually easy, because the original presenter typically has a reference to the presented view controller before the latter's view appears in the interface. For example, suppose the presented view controller has a public data property. Then the original presenter can easily set this property:

```
@IBAction func doPresent(sender:AnyObject?) {
    let svc = SecondViewController(
        nibName: "SecondViewController", bundle: nil)
    svc.data = "This is very important data!" // *
    self.presentViewController(svc, animated:true, completion:nil)
}
```

Indeed, if you're calling presentViewController:animated:completion: explicitly like this, you might even give your SecondViewController a designated initializer that accepts — and thus requires — this data. In my Latin vocabulary app, for example, I've given DrillViewController a designated initializer init(data:) precisely so that whoever creates it *must* pass it the data it will need to do its job while it exists.

Passing information back from the presented view controller to the original presenter is a more interesting problem. The presented view controller will need to know who the original presenter is, but it doesn't automatically have a reference to it (the original presenter, remember, is not necessarily the same as the presentingViewController). Moreover, the presented view controller will need to know the signature of some method, implemented by the original presenter, which it can call in order to hand over the information — and this needs to work regardless of the original presenter's class.

The standard solution is to use delegation, as follows:

1. The presented view controller defines a *protocol* declaring a method that the presented view controller wants to call before it is dismissed.

2. The original presenter conforms to this protocol: it declares adoption of the protocol, and it implements the required method.

3. The presented view controller provides a means whereby it can be handed a reference to an object conforming to this protocol. Think of that reference as the presented view controller's *delegate*. Very often, this will be a property — perhaps called delegate! — typed as the protocol. (Such a property should be weak, since an object usually has no business retaining its delegate.)

4. As the original presenter creates and configures the presented view controller, it hands the presented view controller a reference to itself, in its role as adopter of the protocol, by assigning itself as the presented view controller's delegate.

This sounds elaborate, but with practice you'll find yourself able to implement it very quickly. And you can see why it works: because its delegate is typed as the protocol, the presented view controller is guaranteed that this delegate, if it has one, implements the method declared in the protocol. Thus, the desired communication from the presented view controller to whoever configured and created it is assured.

Let's modify our example to embody this architecture. First, edit *SecondView-Controller.swift* to look like this:

```
protocol SecondViewControllerDelegate : class {
    func acceptData(data:AnyObject!)
}
class SecondViewController : UIViewController {
    var data : AnyObject?
    weak var delegate : SecondViewControllerDelegate?
    @IBAction func doDismiss(sender:AnyObject?) {
        self.delegate?.acceptData("Even more important data!")
    }
}
```

It is now ViewController's job to adopt the SecondViewControllerDelegate protocol, and to set itself as the SecondViewController's delegate. When the delegate method is called, ViewController will be handed the data, and it should then dismiss the Second-ViewController:

```
class ViewController : UIViewController, SecondViewControllerDelegate {
    @IBAction func doPresent(sender:AnyObject?) {
        let svc = SecondViewController(
            nibName: "SecondViewController", bundle: nil)
        svc.data = "This is very important data!"
        svc.delegate = self // *
        self.presentViewController(svc, animated:true, completion:nil)
    }
    func acceptData(data:AnyObject!) {
```

```
        // do something with data here
        self.dismissViewControllerAnimated(true, completion: nil)
    }
}
```

That is a perfectly satisfactory implementation, and we could stop at this point. For completeness, I'll just show a possible variation. You might object that too much responsibility rests upon the original presenter (the delegate): it is sent the data and then it must also dismiss the presented view controller. Surely the presented view controller should hand back any data and should then dismiss itself (as in the preceding section). Even better, the presented view controller should hand back any data *automatically*, regardless of how it is dismissed.

We can arrange that by putting all the responsibility on the presented view controller. First, edit ViewController's acceptData: so that it accepts the data and no more (it no longer performs the dismissal). Second, back in SecondViewController, we will implement *both* the task of dismissal *and* the task of handing back the data, *separately*. To make the latter task automatic, SecondViewController will arrange to hear about its own dismissal by implementing viewWillDisappear: (discussed later in this chapter), which will then call acceptData: to ensure that the data is handed across. There is more than one reason why viewWillDisappear: might be called; we can ensure that this really is the moment of our own dismissal by calling isBeingDismissed. Here is what Second-ViewController looks like now:

```
protocol SecondViewControllerDelegate : class {
    func acceptData(data:AnyObject!)
}
class SecondViewController : UIViewController {
    var data : AnyObject?
    weak var delegate : SecondViewControllerDelegate?
    @IBAction func doDismiss(sender:AnyObject?) {
        self.presentingViewController!.dismissViewControllerAnimated(
            true, completion: nil)
    }
    override func viewWillDisappear(animated: Bool) {
        super.viewWillDisappear(animated)
        if self.isBeingDismissed() {
            self.delegate?.acceptData("Even more important data!")
        }
    }
}
```

If you're using a storyboard, things are a bit different. You don't have access to the presented view controller at the moment of creation; instead, in the original presenter (the source of the segue) you implement prepareForSegue:sender: as a moment when the original presenter and the presented view controller will meet, and the former can hand across any needed data, set itself as delegate, and so forth. If you dismiss the presented view controller automatically by way of an unwind segue, the same is true in reverse: the presented view controller calls the delegate method in its own `prepareFor-Segue:sender:`. I'll give more details later in this chapter.

Presented View Animation

When a view is presented and later when it is dismissed, a simple animation can be performed, according to whether the `animated:` parameter of the corresponding method is `true`. There are a few different built-in animation styles (*modal transition styles*) to choose from.

 Instead of choosing a simple built-in modal transition style, you can supply your own animation, as I'll explain later in the chapter.

Your choice of built-in animation style is not passed as a parameter when presenting or dismissing a view controller; rather, it is attached beforehand to a presented view controller as its `modalTransitionStyle` property. This value can be set in code or in the nib editor. Your choices (UIModalTransitionStyle) are:

`.CoverVertical` *(the default)*
> The presented view slides up from the bottom to cover the presenting view on presentation and down to reveal the presenting view on dismissal. "Bottom" is defined differently depending on the orientation of the device and the orientations the view controllers support.

`.FlipHorizontal`
> The view flips on the vertical axis as if the two views were the front and back of a piece of paper. The "vertical axis" is the device's long axis, regardless of the app's orientation.

> This animation style provides one of those rare occasions where the user may directly glimpse the window behind the transitioning views. You may want to set the window's background color appropriately.

`.CrossDissolve`
> The views remain stationary, and one fades into the other.

`.PartialCurl`
> The first view curls up like a page in a notepad to expose most of the second view, but remains covering the top-left region of the second view. Thus there must not be any important interface in that region, as the user will not be able to see it.

> If the user clicks on the curl, `dismissViewControllerAnimated:completion:` is called on the original presenter. That's convenient, but make sure it doesn't disrupt communication between your view controllers; this is another reason for factoring

out any final handing back of information from the presented view controller into its `viewWillDisappear:`, as I did in the previous section.

 In iOS 8 and iOS 9, after the Partial Curl animation, the curled page is not present, but tapping where it would be dismisses the presented view controller. That's confusing, not to say incoherent, and is presumably a bug; this style should be avoided until it is fixed.

Presentation Styles

By default, the presented view controller's view occupies the entire screen, completely replacing that of the presenting view controller. But you can choose from a few other built-in options expressing how the presented view controller's view should cover the screen (*modal presentation styles*).

 Instead of choosing a simple built-in modal presentation style, you can customize the presentation to place the presented view controller's view anywhere you like, as I'll explain later in this chapter.

To choose a presentation style, set the presented view controller's `modalPresentation-Style` property. This value can be set in code or in the nib editor. Your choices (UIModal-PresentationStyle) are:

`.FullScreen`
> The default. The presenting view controller is the root view controller or a fullscreen presented view controller, and its view — meaning the entire interface — is replaced.

`.OverFullScreen`
> Similar to `.FullScreen`, but the presenting view controller's view is *not* replaced; instead, it stays where it is, possibly being visible during the transition, and remaining visible behind the presented view controller's view if the latter has some transparency.

`.PageSheet`
> Similar to `.FullScreen`, but in portrait orientation on the iPad it's a little shorter (leaving a gap behind the status bar), and in landscape orientation on the iPad and the iPhone 6 Plus it's also narrower, with the presenting view controller's view remaining partially visible (and dimmed) behind it. Treated as `.FullScreen` on the iPhone (including the iPhone 6 Plus in portrait).

`.FormSheet`
> Similar to `.PageSheet`, but on the iPad it's even smaller, allowing the user to see more of the presenting view controller's view behind it. As the name implies, this

is intended to allow the user to fill out a form (Apple describes this as "gathering structured information from the user"). On the iPhone 6 Plus in landscape, indistinguishable from `.PageSheet`. Treated as `.FullScreen` on the iPhone (including the iPhone 6 Plus in portrait).

`.CurrentContext`

> The presenting view controller can be *any* view controller, such as a child view controller. The presented view controller's view replaces the presenting view controller's view, which may have been occupying only a portion of the screen. I'll explain in a moment how to specify the presenting view controller.

`.OverCurrentContext`

> Like `.CurrentContext`, but the presented view controller's view covers the presenting view controller's view rather than replacing it. Again, this may mean that the presented view controller's view now covers only a portion of the screen. `.OverCurrentContext` will often be a better choice than `.CurrentContext`, because some subviews don't behave well when automatically removed from their superview and restored later.

When the presented view controller's `modalPresentationStyle` is `.CurrentContext` or `.OverCurrentContext`, a decision has to be made by the runtime as to what view controller should be the presenting view controller. This will determine what view will be replaced or covered by the presented view controller's view. The decision involves another UIViewController property, `definesPresentationContext` (a Bool), and possibly still *another* UIViewController property, `providesPresentationContextTransitionStyle`. Here's how the decision operates:

1. Starting with the original presenter (the view controller to which `presentViewController:animated:completion:` was sent), we walk up the chain of parent view controllers, looking for one whose `definesPresentationContext` property is `true`. If we find one, that's the one; it will be the `presentingViewController`, and its view will be replaced or covered by the presented view controller's view.

   (If we *don't* find one, things work as if the presented view controller's `modalPresentationStyle` had been `.FullScreen`.)

2. If, during the search just described, we find a view controller whose `definesPresentationContext` property is `true`, we look to see if that view controller's `providesPresentationContextTransitionStyle` property is *also* `true`. If so, *that* view controller's `modalTransitionStyle` is used for this transition animation, instead of using the presented view controller's `modalTransitionStyle`.

To illustrate, I need a parent–child view controller arrangement to work with. This chapter hasn't yet discussed any parent view controllers in detail, but the simplest is

UITabBarController, which I discuss in the next section, and it's easy to create a working app with a UITabBarController-based interface, so that's the example I'll use.

Start with the Tabbed Application project template. As in the previous example, I want us to create and present the presented view controller manually, rather than letting the storyboard do it automatically; so make a new view controller class with an accompanying *.xib* file, to use as a presented view controller — call it ExtraViewController. In *ExtraViewController.xib*, give the view a distinctive background color, so you'll recognize it when it appears.

In the storyboard, put a button in the First View Controller view, and connect it to an action method in *FirstViewController.swift* that summons the new view controller as a presented view controller:

```
@IBAction func doPresent(sender:AnyObject?) {
    let vc = ExtraViewController(nibName: "ExtraViewController", bundle: nil)
    self.presentViewController(vc, animated: true, completion: nil)
}
```

Run the project and tap the button. Observe that the presented view controller's view occupies the *entire* interface, covering even the tab bar; it replaces the root view, because the presentation style is .FullScreen. The presenting view controller is the root view controller, which is the UITabBarController.

Now change the code to look like this:

```
@IBAction func doPresent(sender:AnyObject?) {
    let vc = ExtraViewController(nibName: "ExtraViewController", bundle: nil)
    self.definesPresentationContext = true // *
    vc.modalPresentationStyle = .CurrentContext // *
    self.presentViewController(vc, animated: true, completion: nil)
}
```

Run the project and tap the button. The presented view controller's view replaces only the first view controller's view; the tab bar remains, and you can switch back and forth between the tab bar's first and second views even while the first view remains covered by the presented view. That's because the presented view controller's modal-PresentationStyle is .CurrentContext, and definesPresentationContext is true in FirstViewController, which is the original presenter. Thus the search for a context stops in FirstViewController, which thus becomes the presenting view controller — meaning that the presented view replaces FirstViewController's view instead of the root view.

We can also override the presented view controller's transition animation through the modalTransitionStyle property of the presenting view controller:

```
@IBAction func doPresent(sender:AnyObject?) {
    let vc = ExtraViewController(nibName: "ExtraViewController", bundle: nil)
    self.definesPresentationContext = true
    self.providesPresentationContextTransitionStyle = true // *
    self.modalTransitionStyle = .CoverVertical // *
    vc.modalPresentationStyle = .CurrentContext
    vc.modalTransitionStyle = .FlipHorizontal // this will be overridden
    self.presentViewController(vc, animated: true, completion: nil)
}
```

Because the presenting view controller's `providesPresentationContextTransition-Style` is `true`, the transition uses the `.CoverVertical` animation belonging to the presenting view controller, rather than the `.FlipHorizontal` animation of the presented view controller.

When a view controller is presented, if its presentation style is *not* `.FullScreen`, a question arises of whether its status bar methods (`prefersStatusBarHidden` and `preferredStatusBarStyle`) should be consulted. By default, the answer is no, because this view controller is not the top-level view controller. To make the answer be yes, set this view controller's `modalPresentationCapturesStatusBarAppearance` to `true`.

Adaptive Presentation

When a view controller with a `modalPresentationStyle` of `.PageSheet` or `.FormSheet` is about to appear, you get a second opportunity to change its effective `modalPresentationStyle`, and even to substitute a different view controller, based on the current trait collection environment. This is called *adaptive presentation*. The idea is that your presented view controller might appear one way for certain trait collections and another way for others — for example, on an iPad as opposed to an iPhone.

To implement adaptive presentation, you use a view controller's *presentation controller* (`presentationController`, a UIPresentationController). Before presenting a view controller, you set its presentation controller's `delegate` (adopting the UIAdaptivePresentationControllerDelegate protocol). Before the presented view controller's view appears, the delegate is sent these messages:

`adaptivePresentationStyleForPresentationController:traitCollection:`
 Asks for a modal presentation style. The first parameter is the presentation controller; you can consult its `presentationStyle` to learn what the `modalPresentationStyle` *would* be. Return `.None` if you don't want to change the presentation style.

 (This method, introduced in iOS 8.3, supersedes the simpler `adaptivePresentationStyleForPresentationController:`, which doesn't include the `traitCollection:` information, and which isn't called under all circumstances.)

`presentationController:willPresentWithAdaptiveStyle:transition-`
`Coordinator:`

> Called just before the presentation takes place. If the `adaptiveStyle:` is `.None`, adaptive presention is *not* going to take place.

`presentationController:viewControllerForAdaptivePresentationStyle:`

> Called only if adaptive presention *is* going to take place. Return a view controller to be presented, substituting it for the current presented view controller.

What adaptations are you permitted to perform? First, as I've already said, the original `modalPresentationStyle` should be `.PageSheet` or `.FormSheet`. It isn't illegal to try to adapt from other presentation styles, but it isn't going to work either. Then the possibilities are as follows:

Adapt sheet to full screen

> You can adapt `.PageSheet` or `.FormSheet` to `.FullScreen` or `.OverFullScreen`.
>
> If the trait collection's horizontal size class is `.Compact` (an iPhone, including an iPhone 6 Plus in portrait), then if you adapt `.PageSheet` or `.FormSheet` to `.Page-Sheet`, `.CurrentContext`, `.OverCurrentContext`, or even `.Popover`, the runtime behaves as if you had adapted to `.FullScreen`.)

Adapt page sheet to form sheet

> You can adapt `.PageSheet` to `.FormSheet`.
>
> On an iPad, the difference is clearly visible; on an iPhone 6 Plus in landscape, the two sheet types are indistinguishable.
>
> On an iPhone (including an iPhone 6 Plus in portrait), the result is something a little unusual and unexpected. It's similar to `.PageSheet` on the iPad in portrait orientation: it is full width, but a little shorter than full height, leaving a gap behind the status bar. (You can also obtain this configuration by adapting `.PageSheet` or `.FormSheet` to `.None`.)

For example, here's how to present a view controller as a `.PageSheet` on iPad but as `.OverFullScreen` on iPhone:

```
extension ViewController : UIAdaptivePresentationControllerDelegate {
    @IBAction func doPresent(sender:AnyObject?) {
        let svc = SecondViewController(
            nibName: "SecondViewController", bundle: nil)
        svc.modalPresentationStyle = .FormSheet
        svc.presentationController!.delegate = self // *
        self.presentViewController(svc, animated:true, completion:nil)
    }
    func adaptivePresentationStyleForPresentationController(
        controller: UIPresentationController,
        traitCollection: UITraitCollection) -> UIModalPresentationStyle {
            if traitCollection.horizontalSizeClass == .Compact {
```

```
                return .OverFullScreen
        }
        return .None // don't adapt
    }
}
```

Now let's extend that example by also replacing the view controller presented on iPad with a different view controller to be presented on iPhone:

```
extension ViewController : UIAdaptivePresentationControllerDelegate {
    // ... same as before ...
    func presentationController(controller: UIPresentationController,
        viewControllerForAdaptivePresentationStyle
        style: UIModalPresentationStyle) -> UIViewController? {
            let newvc = ThirdViewController(
                nibName: "ThirdViewController", bundle: nil)
            return newvc
    }
}
```

In real life, of course, when substituting a different view controller, you might need to prepare it before returning it (for example, giving it data and setting its delegate). A common scenario is to return the *same* view controller wrapped in a navigation controller; I'll illustrate in Chapter 9.

Rotation of a Presented View

When the presenting view controller is the top-level view controller — the root view controller, or a fullscreen presented view controller — the presented view controller becomes the new top-level view controller. This means that its supportedInterfaceOrientations is consulted and honored. If these supportedInterfaceOrientations do not intersect with the app's current orientation, the app's orientation will rotate, as the presented view appears, to an orientation that the presented view controller supports — and the same thing will be true in reverse when the presented view controller is dismissed.

Thus, a presented view controller allows you to *force* the interface to rotate. In fact, a presented view controller is the *only* officially sanctioned way to force the interface to rotate.

Forced rotation is a perfectly reasonable thing to do, especially on the iPhone, where the user can easily rotate the device to compensate for the new orientation of the interface. Some views work better in portrait than landscape, or better in landscape than portrait (especially on the small screen). Forced rotation lets you ensure that each view appears only in the orientation in which it works best.

The presented view controller's supportedInterfaceOrientations bitmask might permit multiple possible orientations. The view controller may then also wish to specify which of those multiple orientations it should have *initially* when it is presented. To do so, override `preferredInterfaceOrientationForPresentation`; this method is called before `supportedInterfaceOrientations`, and should return a single UIInterface-Orientation (*not* a bitmask). For example:

```
override func preferredInterfaceOrientationForPresentation()
    -> UIInterfaceOrientation {
        return .LandscapeLeft
}
```

Tab Bar Controller

A *tab bar* (UITabBar, see also Chapter 12) is a horizontal bar containing items. Each item is a UITabBarItem; it displays, by default, an image and a title. At all times, exactly one of these items is selected (highlighted); when the user taps an item, it becomes the selected item.

If there are too many items to fit on a tab bar, the excess items are automatically subsumed into a final More item. When the user taps the More item, a list of the excess items appears, and the user can select one; the user can also be permitted to edit the tab bar, determining which items appear in the tab bar itself and which ones spill over into the More list.

A tab bar is an independent interface object, but it is most commonly used in conjunction with a *tab bar controller* (UITabBarController, a subclass of UIViewController) to form a *tab bar interface.* The tab bar controller displays the tab bar at the bottom of its own view. From the user's standpoint, the tab bar items correspond to views; when the user selects a tab bar item, the corresponding view appears. The user is thus employing the tab bar to choose an entire area of your app's functionality. In reality, the UITab-BarController is a parent view controller; you give it child view controllers, which the tab bar controller then contains, and the views summoned by tapping the tab bar items are the views of those child view controllers.

Familiar examples of a tab bar interface on the iPhone are Apple's Clock app and Music app.

You can get a reference to the tab bar controller's tab bar through its `tabBar` property. In general, you won't need this. When using a tab bar interface by way of a UITabBar-Controller, you do not interact (as a programmer) with the tab bar itself; you don't create it or set its delegate. You provide the UITabBarController with children, and it does the rest; when the UITabBarController's view is displayed, there's the tab bar along with the view of the selected item. You can, however, customize the *look* of the tab bar (see Chapter 12 for details).

If a tab bar controller is the top-level view controller, it determines your app's compensatory rotation behavior. To take a hand in that determination without having to subclass

UITabBarController, make one of your objects the tab bar controller's delegate (UITab-BarControllerDelegate) and implement these methods, as needed:

- `tabBarControllerSupportedInterfaceOrientations:`
- `tabBarControllerPreferredInterfaceOrientationForPresentation:`

A top-level tab bar controller also determines your app's status bar appearance. However, a tab bar controller implements `childViewControllerForStatusBarStyle` and `childViewControllerForStatusBarHidden` so that the actual decision is relegated to the child view controller whose view is currently being displayed. Thus, your `preferredStatusBarStyle` and `prefersStatusBarHidden` are consulted and obeyed.

Tab Bar Items

For each view controller you assign as a tab bar controller's child, you're going to need a *tab bar item*, which will appear as its representative in the tab bar. This tab bar item will be your child view controller's `tabBarItem`. A tab bar item is a UITabBarItem; this is a subclass of UIBarItem, an abstract class that provides some of its most important properties, such as `title`, `image`, and `enabled`.

There are two ways to make a tab bar item:

By borrowing it from the system
    Instantiate UITabBarItem using `init(tabBarSystemItem:tag:)`, and assign the instance to your child view controller's `tabBarItem`. Consult the documentation for the list of available system items. Unfortunately, you can't customize a system tab bar item's title; you must accept the title the system hands you. (You can't work around this restriction by somehow copying a system tab bar item's image.)

By making your own
    Instantiate UITabBarItem using `init(title:image:tag:)` and assign the instance to your child view controller's `tabBarItem`. Alternatively, use the view controller's existing `tabBarItem` and set its `image` and `title`. Instead of setting the `title` of the `tabBarItem`, you can set the `title` property of the view controller itself; doing this automatically sets the `title` of its current `tabBarItem` (unless the tab bar item is a system tab bar item), though the converse is not true.

    You can add a separate `selectedImage` later, or possibly by initializing with `init(title:image:selectedImage:)`. The `selectedImage` will be displayed in place of the normal `image` when this tab bar item is selected in the tab bar.

The `image` (and `selectedImage`) for a tab bar item should be a 30×30 PNG; if it is larger, it will be scaled down as needed. By default, it will be treated as a transparency mask (a template): the hue of its pixels will be ignored, and the transparency of its pixels will be combined with the tab bar's `tintColor`, which may be inherited from higher up the view hierarchy. However, you can instead display the image as is, and not as a transparency mask, by deriving an image whose rendering mode is `.AlwaysOriginal` (see Chapter 2).

You can also give a tab bar item a badge (see the documentation on the `badgeValue` property). Other ways in which you can customize the look of a tab bar item are discussed in Chapter 12. For example, you can control the font and style of the title, or you can give it an empty title and offset the image.

Configuring a Tab Bar Controller

Basic configuration of a tab bar controller is very simple: just hand it the view controllers that will be its children. To do so, collect those view controllers into an array and set the UITabBarController's `viewControllers` property to that array. The view controllers in the array are now the tab bar controller's child view controllers; the tab bar controller is the `parentViewController` of the view controllers in the array. The tab bar controller is also the `tabBarController` of the view controllers in the array and of all their children; thus a child view controller at any depth can learn that it is contained by a tab bar controller and can get a reference to that tab bar controller. The tab bar controller retains the array, and the array retains the child view controllers.

Here's a simple example from one of my apps, in which I construct and display a tab bar interface in code:

```
var tabBarController = UITabBarController()
func application(application: UIApplication,
    didFinishLaunchingWithOptions launchOptions: [NSObject:AnyObject]?)
    -> Bool {
        self.window = UIWindow()
        let viewController1 = GameBoardController()
        let viewController2 = UINavigationController(
            rootViewController:SettingsController())
        self.tabBarController.viewControllers =
            [viewController1, viewController2]
        self.tabBarController.selectedIndex = 0
        self.tabBarController.delegate = self
        self.window!.rootViewController = self.tabBarController
        self.window!.makeKeyAndVisible()
        return true
}
```

The tab bar controller's tab bar will automatically display the `tabBarItem` of each child view controller. The order of the tab bar items is the order of the view controllers in the tab bar controller's `viewControllers` array. Thus, a child view controller will probably want to configure its `tabBarItem` property early in its lifetime, so that the `tabBarItem` is ready by the time the view controller is handed as a child to the tab bar controller.

Observe that `viewDidLoad` is *not* early enough! That's because the view controllers (other than the initially selected view controller) have no view when the tab bar controller initially appears. Thus it is common to implement an initializer for this purpose.

Here's an example from the same app as the previous code (in the GameBoardController class):

```
init() {
    super.init(nibName:nil, bundle:nil)
    // tab bar configuration
    self.tabBarItem.image = UIImage(named: "game.png")
    self.title = "Game"
}
```

In the tab bar, the image `"game.png"` is displayed as is, not as a template. I don't have to call `imageWithRenderingMode:` because the rendering mode is set directly in the asset catalog that holds the image.

If you change the tab bar controller's view controllers array later in its lifetime and you want the corresponding change in the tab bar's display of its items to be animated, call `setViewControllers:animated:`.

Initially, by default, the first child view controller's tab bar item is selected and its view is displayed. To ask the tab bar controller which tab bar item the user has selected, you can couch your query in terms of the child view controller (`selectedView-Controller`) or by index number in the array (`selectedIndex`). You can also *set* these properties to switch between displayed child view controllers programmatically. (In fact, it is legal to set a tab bar controller's tab bar's `hidden` to `true` and take charge of switching between children yourself — though if that's your desired architecture, a UIPageView-Controller without animation or gesture response might be more appropriate.)

 You can supply an animation when a tab bar controller's selected tab item changes and one child view controller's view is replaced by another. I'll discuss that topic later in the chapter.

You can also set the UITabBarController's delegate (adopting UITabBarController-Delegate). The delegate gets messages allowing it to prevent a given tab bar item from being selected, and notifying it when a tab bar item is selected and when the user is customizing the tab bar from the More item.

If the tab bar contains few enough items that it doesn't need a More item, there won't be one, and the tab bar won't be user-customizable. If there *is* a More item, you can exclude some tab bar items from being customizable by setting the `customizableView-Controllers` property to an array that lacks them; setting this property to `nil` means that the user can see the More list but can't rearrange the items. Setting the `view-`

Controllers property sets the `customizableViewControllers` property to the same value, so if you're going to set the `customizableViewControllers` property, do it *after* setting the `viewControllers` property. The `moreNavigationController` property can be compared with the `selectedViewController` property to learn whether the user is currently viewing the More list; apart from this, the More interface is mostly out of your control, but I'll discuss some sneaky ways of customizing it in Chapter 12.

(If you allow the user to rearrange items, you would presumably want to save the new arrangement and restore it the next time the app runs. You might use NSUserDefaults for this; you could also take advantage of the built-in automatic state saving and restoration facilities, discussed later in this chapter.)

You can configure a UITabBarController in a *.storyboard* or *.xib* file. The UITabBar-Controller's contained view controllers can be set directly — in a storyboard, there will be a "view controllers" relationship between the tab bar controller and each of its children — and the contained view controllers will be instantiated together with the tab bar controller. Moreover, each contained view controller has a Tab Bar Item; you can select this and set many aspects of the `tabBarItem`, such as its system item or its title, image, selected image, and tag, directly in the nib. (If a view controller in a nib doesn't have a Tab Bar Item and you want to configure this view controller for use in a tab bar interface, drag a Tab Bar Item from the Object library onto the view controller.)

To start a project with a main storyboard that has a UITabBarController as its root view controller, begin with the Tabbed Application template.

Navigation Controller

A *navigation bar* (UINavigationBar, see also Chapter 12) is a horizontal bar displaying a center title and a right button. When the user taps the right button, the navigation bar animates, sliding its interface out to the left and replacing it with a new interface that enters from the right. The new interface displays a back button at the left side, and a new center title — and possibly a new right button. The user can tap the back button to go back to the first interface, which slides in from the left; or, if there's a right button in the second interface, the user can tap it to go further forward to a third interface, which slides in from the right.

The successive interfaces of a navigation bar thus behave like a stack. In fact, a navigation bar does represent an actual stack — an internal stack of *navigation items* (UINavigationItem). It starts out with one navigation item: the *root* or *bottom item* of the stack. Since there is just one navigation item, this is also the *top item* of the stack (the navigation bar's `topItem`). It is the top item whose interface is always reflected in the navigation bar. When the user taps a right button, a new navigation item is pushed onto the stack; it becomes the top item, and its interface is seen. When the user taps a back button, the top item is popped off the stack, and what was previously the next item beneath it in the stack — the *back item* (the navigation bar's backItem) — becomes the top item, and its interface is seen.

The state of the stack is thus reflected in the navigation bar's interface. The navigation bar's center title comes automatically from the top item, and its back button comes from the back item. (See Chapter 12 for a complete description.) Thus, the title tells the user what item is current, and the left side is a button telling the user what item we would return to if the user were to tap that button. The animations reinforce this notion of directionality, giving the user a sense of position within a chain of items.

A navigation bar is an independent interface object, but it is most commonly used in conjunction with a *navigation controller* (UINavigationController, a subclass of UIViewController) to form a *navigation interface*. Just as there is a stack of navigation items in the navigation bar, there is a stack of view controllers in the navigation controller. These view controllers are the navigation controller's children, and each navigation item belongs to a view controller — it is a view controller's navigationItem.

The navigation controller performs automatic coordination of the navigation bar and the overall interface. Whenever a view controller comes to the top of the navigation controller's stack, its view is displayed in the interface. At the same time, its navigation-Item is automatically pushed onto the top of the navigation bar's stack — and is thus displayed in the navigation bar. Moreover, the animation in the navigation bar is reinforced by animation of the interface as a whole: by default, a view controller's view slides into the main interface from the left or right just as its navigation item slides into the navigation bar from the left or right.

 You can supply a different animation when a view controller is pushed onto or popped off of a navigation controller's stack. I'll discuss this topic later in the chapter.

Your code can control the overall navigation, so in real life, the user may well navigate to the right, not by tapping the right button in the navigation bar, but by tapping something inside the main interface, such as a listing in a table view. (Figure 6-1 is a navigation interface that works this way.) In this situation, your code is deciding in real time what the next view should be; typically, you won't even create the next view controller until the user asks to navigate to it. The navigation interface thus becomes a *master–detail interface*.

Conversely, you might put a view controller inside a navigation controller just to get the convenience of the navigation bar, with its title and buttons, even when no actual push-and-pop navigation is going to take place.

You can get a reference to the navigation controller's navigation bar through its navigationBar property. In general, you won't need this. When using a navigation interface by way of a UINavigationController, you do not interact (as a programmer) with the navigation bar itself; you don't create it or set its delegate. You provide the UINavigationController with children, and it does the rest, handing each child view controller's `navigationItem` to the navigation bar for display and showing the child view controller's view each time navigation occurs. You can, however, customize the *look* of the navigation bar (see Chapter 12 for details).

A navigation interface may also optionally display a toolbar at the bottom. A toolbar (UIToolbar) is a horizontal view displaying a row of items, any of which the user can tap. Typically, the tapped item may highlight momentarily, but it is not selected; it represents the initiation of an action, like a button. You can get a reference to a UINavigationController's toolbar through its `toolbar` property. The look of the toolbar can be customized (Chapter 12). In a navigation interface, however, the *contents* of the toolbar are determined automatically by the view controller that is currently the top item in the stack: they are its `toolbarItems`.

 A UIToolbar can also be used independently, and often is. It then typically appears at the bottom on an iPhone — Figure 6-3 has a toolbar at the bottom — but often appears at the top on an iPad, where it plays something of the role that the menu bar plays on the desktop. When a toolbar is displayed by a navigation controller, though, it always appears at the bottom.

A familiar example of a navigation interface is Apple's Settings app on the iPhone. The Mail app on the iPhone is a navigation interface that includes a toolbar.

If a navigation controller is the top-level view controller, it determines your app's compensatory rotation behavior. To take a hand in that determination without having to subclass UINavigationController, make one of your objects the navigation controller's delegate (UINavigationControllerDelegate) and implement these methods, as needed:

- `navigationControllerSupportedInterfaceOrientations:`
- `navigationControllerPreferredInterfaceOrientationForPresentation:`

A top-level navigation controller also determines your app's status bar appearance. However, a navigation controller implements `childViewControllerForStatusBar-Hidden` so that the actual decision is relegated to the child view controller whose view is currently being displayed.

Your child view controllers can implement `preferredStatusBarStyle`, and the navigation controller's `childViewControllerForStatusBarStyle` defers to its top child view controller — but only if the navigation bar is hidden. If the navigation bar is showing, the navigation controller sets the status bar style based on the navigation bar's `barStyle` — to `.Default` if the bar style is `.Default`, and to `.LightContent` if the bar style is `.Black`. So, the way to change the status bar style is to change the navigation bar style. Alternatively, you can subclass UINavigationController and compel the navigation controller to respect the top child view controller's `preferredStatusBarStyle`, like this:

```
override func childViewControllerForStatusBarStyle() -> UIViewController? {
    let vc = super.childViewControllerForStatusBarStyle()
    return self.topViewController
}
```

Bar Button Items

The buttons in a UIToolbar or a UINavigationBar are bar button items — UIBarButtonItem, a subclass of UIBarItem. A bar button item comes in one of two broadly different flavors:

Basic bar button item
> The bar button item behaves like a simple button.

Custom view
> The bar button item has no inherent behavior, but has (and displays) a `customView`.

UIBarItem is not a UIView subclass. A basic bar button item is button-like, but it has no frame, no UIView touch handling, and so forth. A UIBarButtonItem's `customView`, however, *is* a UIView — indeed, it can be *any* kind of UIView. Thus, a bar button item with a `customView` can display any sort of view in a toolbar or navigation bar, and that view can implement touch handling however it likes.

Let's start with the basic bar button item (no custom view). A bar button item, like a tab bar item, inherits from UIBarItem the `title`, `image`, and `enabled` properties. The title text color, by default, comes from the bar button item's `tintColor`, which may be inherited from the bar itself or from higher up the view hierarchy. Assigning an image removes the title. The image should usually be quite small; Apple recommends 22×22. By default, it will be treated as a transparency mask (a template): the hue of its pixels will be ignored, and the transparency of its pixels will be combined with the bar button item's `tintColor`. However, you can instead display the image as is, and not as a transparency mask, by deriving an image whose rendering mode is `.AlwaysOriginal` (see Chapter 2).

A basic bar button item has a `style` property (UIBarButtonItemStyle); this will usually be `.Plain`. The alternative, `.Done`, causes the title to be bold. You can further refine the title font and style. In addition, a bar button item can have a background image; this will typically be a small, resizable image, and can be used to provide a border. Full details appear in Chapter 12.

A bar button item also has `target` and `action` properties. These contribute to its button-like behavior: tapping a bar button item can trigger an action method elsewhere.

There are three ways to make a bar button item:

By borrowing it from the system

Make a UIBarButtonItem with `init(barButtonSystemItem:target: action:)`. Consult the documentation for the list of available system items; they are not the same as for a tab bar item. You can't assign a title or change the image. (But you can change the tint color or assign a background image.)

By making your own basic bar button item

Make a UIBarButtonItem with `init(title:style:target:action:)` or with `init(image:style:target:action:)`.

An additional initializer, `init(image:landscapeImagePhone:style:target: action:)`, lets you supply two images, one for portrait orientation, the other for landscape orientation; this is because by default, the bar's height might change when the interface is rotated. Alternatively, you can use size class–aware images to handle this situation (see Chapter 2).

By making a custom view bar button item

Make a UIBarButtonItem with `init(customView:)`, supplying a UIView that the bar button item is to display. The bar button item has no action and target; the UIView itself must somehow implement button behavior if that's what you want. For example, the `customView` might be a UISegmentedButton, but then it is the UISegmentedButton's target and action that give it button behavior.

Bar button items in a toolbar are horizontally positioned automatically by the system. You can provide hints to help with this positioning. If you know that you'll be changing an item's title dynamically, you'll probably want its width to accommodate the longest possible title right from the start; to arrange that, set the `possibleTitles` property to a Set of strings that includes the longest title. Alternatively, you can supply an absolute `width`. Also, you can incorporate spacers into the toolbar; these are created with `init(barButtonSystemItem:target:action:)`, but they have no visible appearance, and cannot be tapped. Place `.FlexibleSpace` system items between the visible items to distribute the visible items equally across the width of the toolbar. There is also a `.Fixed-Space` system item whose `width` lets you insert a space of defined size.

Navigation Items and Toolbar Items

What appears in a navigation bar (UINavigationBar) depends upon the navigation items (UINavigationItem) in its stack. In a navigation interface, the navigation controller will manage the navigation bar's stack for you, but you must still configure each navigation item by setting properties of the `navigationItem` of each child view controller. The UINavigationItem properties are as follows (see also Chapter 12):

Figure 6-8. A segmented control in the center of a navigation bar

title *or* titleView

Determines what is to appear in the center of the navigation bar when this navigation item is at the top of the stack.

The title is a string. Setting the view controller's title property sets the title of the navigationItem automatically, and is usually the best approach.

The titleView can be any kind of UIView; if set, it will be displayed instead of the title. The titleView can implement further UIView functionality; for example, it can be tappable. Even if you are using a titleView, you should still give your view controller a title, as it will be needed for the back button when a view controller is pushed onto the stack on top of this one.

Figure 6-1 shows the TidBITS News master view, with the navigation bar displaying a titleView which is a (tappable) image view; the master view controller's title, which is "TidBITS", is therefore not displayed. In the TidBITS News detail view controller's navigation item, the titleView is a segmented control providing a Previous and Next button; when it is pushed onto the stack, the back button displays the master view controller's title (Figure 6-8).

prompt

An optional string to appear centered above everything else in the navigation bar. The navigation bar's height will be increased to accommodate it.

rightBarButtonItem *or* rightBarButtonItems

A bar button item or, respectively, an array of bar button items to appear at the right side of the navigation bar; the first item in the array will be rightmost.

In Figure 6-8, the text size button is a right bar button item; it has nothing to do with navigation, but is placed here merely because space is at a premium on the small iPhone screen.

backBarButtonItem

When a view controller is pushed on top of this view controller, the navigation bar will display at its left a button pointing to the left, whose title is this view controller's title. That button is *this* view controller's navigation item's backBarButtonItem. That's right: the back button displayed in the navigation bar belongs, not to the top item (the navigationItem of the current view controller), but to the back item (the navigationItem of the view controller that is one level down in the stack). In

Figure 6-8, the back button in the detail view is the master view controller's default back button, displaying its `title`.

The vast majority of the time, the default behavior is the behavior you'll want, and you'll leave the back button alone. If you wish, though, you can customize the back button by setting a view controller's `navigationItem.backBarButtonItem` so that it contains an image, or a title differing from the view controller's `title`. The best technique is to provide a new UIBarButtonItem whose target and action are `nil`; the runtime will add a correct target and action, so as to create a working back button. Here's how to create a back button with a custom image instead of a title:

```
let b = UIBarButtonItem(
    image:UIImage(named:"files.png"), style:.Plain, target:nil, action:nil)
self.navigationItem.backBarButtonItem = b
```

A Bool property, `hidesBackButton`, allows the top navigation item to suppress display of the back item's back bar button item. If you set this to `true`, you'll probably want to provide some other means of letting the user navigate back.

The visible indication that the back button *is* a back button is a left-pointing chevron (the *back indicator*) that's separate from the button itself. This chevron can also be customized, but it's a feature of the navigation bar, not the bar button item: set the navigation bar's `backIndicatorImage` and `backIndicatorTransitionMask`. (I'll give an example in Chapter 12.) Alternatively, if the back button is assigned a background image, the back indicator is removed; it is up to the background image to point left, if desired.

`leftBarButtonItem` *or* `leftBarButtonItems`
A bar button item or, respectively, an array of bar button items to appear at the left side of the navigation bar; the first item in the array will be leftmost. The `leftItems-SupplementBackButton` property, if set to `true`, allows both the back button and one or more left bar button items to appear.

A view controller's navigation item can have its properties set at any time while being displayed in the navigation bar. This (and not direct manipulation of the navigation bar) is the way to change the navigation bar's contents dynamically. For example, in one of my apps, the `titleView` is a progress view (UIProgressView, Chapter 12) that needs updating every second, and the right bar button should be either the system Play button or the system Pause button, depending on whether music from the library is playing, paused, or stopped. So I have a timer that periodically checks the state of the music player; observe how we access the progress view and the right bar button by way of `self.navigationItem`:

```
// change the progress view
let prog = self.navigationItem.titleView as! UIProgressView
if let item = self.nowPlayingItem {
    let current = self.mp.currentPlaybackTime
```

```
    let total = item.valueForProperty(
        MPMediaItemPropertyPlaybackDuration) as! Double
    prog.progress = Float(current / total)
} else {
    prog.progress = 0
}
// change the bar button
let whichButton : UIBarButtonSystemItem?
switch self.mp.currentPlaybackRate {
case 0..<0.1:
    whichButton = .Play
case 0.1...1.0:
    whichButton = .Pause
default:
    whichButton = nil
}
if let which = whichButton {
    let bb = UIBarButtonItem(barButtonSystemItem: which,
        target: self, action: "doPlayPause:")
    self.navigationItem.rightBarButtonItem = bb
}
```

Each view controller to be pushed onto the navigation controller's stack is responsible also for supplying the items to appear in the navigation interface's toolbar, if there is one. To configure this, set the view controller's `toolbarItems` property to an array of UIBarButtonItem instances. You can change the toolbar items even while the view controller's view and current `toolbarItems` are showing, optionally with animation, by sending `setToolbarItems:animated:` to the view controller.

Configuring a Navigation Controller

You configure a navigation controller by manipulating its stack of view controllers. This stack is the navigation controller's `viewControllers` array property, though you will rarely need to manipulate that property directly.

The view controllers in a navigation controller's `viewControllers` array are the navigation controller's child view controllers; the navigation controller is the `parentViewController` of the view controllers in the array. The navigation controller is also the `navigationController` of the view controllers in the array and of all their children; thus a child view controller at any depth can learn that it is contained by a navigation controller and can get a reference to that navigation controller. The navigation controller retains the array, and the array retains the child view controllers.

The normal way to manipulate a navigation controller's stack is by pushing or popping one view controller at a time. When the navigation controller is instantiated, it is usually initialized with `init(rootViewController:)`; this is a convenience method that assigns the navigation controller a single initial child view controller, the root view controller that goes at the bottom of the stack:

```
let fvc = FirstViewController()
let nav = UINavigationController(rootViewController:fvc)
```

Instead of init(rootViewController:), you might choose to create the navigation controller with init(navigationBarClass:toolbarClass:), in order to set a custom subclass of UINavigationBar or UIToolbar. Typically, this will be in order to customize the appearance of the navigation bar and toolbar; sometimes you'll create, say, a UIToolbar subclass for no other reason than to mark this kind of toolbar as needing a certain appearance. I'll explain about that in Chapter 12. If you use this initializer, you'll have to set the navigation controller's root view controller separately.

You can also set the UINavigationController's delegate (adopting UINavigation-ControllerDelegate). The delegate receives messages before and after a child view controller's view is shown.

A navigation controller will typically appear on the screen initially containing just its root view controller, and displaying its root view controller's view. There will be no back button, because there is no back item; there is nowhere to go back to. Subsequently, when the user asks to navigate to a new view, you (typically meaning code in the current view controller) obtain the next view controller (typically by creating it) and push it onto the stack by calling pushViewController:animated: on the navigation controller. The navigation controller performs the animation, and displays the new view controller's view:

```
let svc = SecondViewController()
self.navigationController!.pushViewController(svc, animated: true)
```

There is usually no need to worry about going back; when the user taps the back button to navigate back, the runtime will call popViewControllerAnimated: for you. When a view controller is popped from the stack, the viewControllers array removes and releases the view controller, which is usually permitted to go out of existence at that point.

Alternatively, there's a second way to push a view controller onto the navigation controller's stack, without referring to the navigation controller: showView-Controller:sender:. This method lets the caller be agnostic about the current interface situation; for example, it pushes onto a navigation controller if the view controller to which it is sent is in a navigation interface, but generates a presented view controller if not. I'll talk more about this method in Chapter 9; meanwhile, I'll continue using push-ViewController:animated: in my examples.

Instead of tapping the back button, the user can go back by dragging a pushed view controller's view from the left edge of the screen. This is actually a way of calling pop-ViewControllerAnimated:, with the difference that the animation is interactive. (Interactive view controller transition animation is the subject of the next section.) The UINavigationController uses a UIScreenEdgePanGestureRecognizer to detect and track the user's gesture. You can obtain a reference to this gesture recognizer as the navigation controller's `interactivePopGestureRecognizer`; thus you can disable the gesture recognizer and prevent this way of going back, or you can mediate between your own gesture recognizers and this one (see Chapter 5).

You can manipulate the stack more directly if you wish. You can call `popViewController-Animated:` explicitly; to pop multiple items so as to leave a particular view controller at the top of the stack, call `popToViewController:animated:`, or to pop all the items down to the root view controller, call `popToRootViewControllerAnimated:`. All of these methods return the popped view controller (or view controllers, as an array), in case you want to do something with them.

To set the entire stack at once, call `setViewControllers:animated:`. You can access the stack through the `viewControllers` property. Manipulating the stack directly is the only way, for instance, to delete or insert a view controller in the middle of the stack.

The view controller at the top of the stack is the `topViewController`; the view controller whose view is displayed is the `visibleViewController`. Those will normally be the same, but they needn't be, as the `topViewController` might present a view controller, in which case the presented view controller will be the `visibleViewController`. Other view controllers can be accessed through the `viewControllers` array by index number. The root view controller is at index 0; if the array's `count` is c, the back view controller (the one whose `navigationItem.backBarButtonItem` is currently displayed in the navigation bar) is at index c-2.

The `topViewController` may need to communicate with the next view controller as the latter is pushed onto the stack, or with the back view controller as it itself is popped off the stack. The problem is parallel to that of communication between an original presenter and a presented view controller, which I discussed earlier in this chapter ("Communication With a Presented View Controller" on page 290), so I won't say more about it here.

A child view controller will probably want to configure its `navigationItem` early in its lifetime, so as to be ready for display in the navigation bar by the time the view controller is handed as a child to the navigation controller. Apple warns (in the UIViewController class reference, under `navigationItem`) that `loadView` and `viewDidLoad` are not appropriate places to do this, because the circumstances under which the view is needed are not related to the circumstances under which the navigation item is needed. Apple's own code examples routinely violate this warning, but it is probably best to override `init(nibName:bundle:)` — or `init(coder:)` or `awakeFromNib`, if appropriate — for this purpose.

A navigation controller's navigation bar is accessible as its `navigationBar`, and can be hidden and shown with `setNavigationBarHidden:animated:`. (It is possible, though not common, to maintain and manipulate a navigation stack through a navigation controller whose navigation bar never appears.) Its toolbar is accessible as its `toolbar`, and can be hidden and shown with `setToolbarHidden:animated:`.

A view controller also has the power to specify that its ancestor's bottom bar (a navigation controller's toolbar, or a tab bar controller's tab bar) should be hidden as this view controller is pushed onto a navigation controller's stack. To do so, set the view controller's `hidesBottomBarWhenPushed` property to `true`. The trick is that you must do this very early, before the view loads; the view controller's initializer is a good place. The bottom bar remains hidden from the time this view controller is pushed to the time it is popped, even if other view controllers are pushed and popped on top of it in the meantime.

A navigation controller can perform automatic hiding and showing of its navigation bar (and, if normally shown, its toolbar) in response to various situations, as configured by properties:

When tapped
> If the navigation controller's `hidesBarsOnTap` is `true`, a tap that falls through the top view controller's view is taken as a signal to toggle bar visibility. The relevant gesture recognizer is the navigation controller's `barHideOnTapGestureRecognizer`.

When swiped
> If the navigation controller's `hidesBarsOnSwipe` is `true`, an upward or downward swipe respectively hides or shows the bars. The relevant gesture recognizer is the navigation controller's `barHideOnSwipeGestureRecognizer`.

In landscape
> If the navigation controller's `hidesBarsWhenVerticallyCompact` is `true`, bars are automatically hidden when the app rotates to landscape on the iPhone (and `hidesBarsOnTap` is treated as `true`, so the bars can be shown again by tapping).

When the user is typing
> If the navigation controller's `hidesBarsWhenKeyboardAppears` is `true`, bars are automatically hidden when the onscreen keyboard appears (see Chapter 10).

You can configure a UINavigationController, or any view controller that is to serve in a navigation interface, in a *.storyboard* or *.xib* file. In the Attributes inspector, use a navigation controller's Bar Visibility and Hide Bars checkboxes to determine the presence of the navigation bar and toolbar. The navigation bar and toolbar are themselves subviews of the navigation controller, and you can configure them with the Attributes inspector as well. A navigation controller's root view controller can be specified; in a storyboard, there will be a "root view controller" relationship between the navigation controller and its root view controller.

A view controller in a *.storyboard* or *.xib* file has a Navigation Item where you can specify its title, its prompt, and the text of its back button. (If a view controller in a nib doesn't have a Navigation Item and you want to configure this view controller for use in a navigation interface, drag a Navigation Item from the Object library onto the view controller.) You can drag Bar Button Items into a view controller's navigation bar in the canvas to set the left buttons and right buttons of its navigationItem. Moreover, the Navigation Item has outlets, one of which permits you to set its titleView. Similarly, you can give a view controller Bar Button Items that will appear in the toolbar.

To start an iPhone project with a main storyboard that has a UINavigationController as its root view controller, begin with the Master–Detail Application template. Alternatively, start with the Single View Application template, remove the existing view controller from the storyboard, and add a Navigation Controller in its place. Unfortunately, the nib editor assumes that the navigation controller's root view controller should be a UITableViewController. If that's not the case, here's a better way: start with the Single View Application template, select the existing view controller, and choose Editor → Embed In → Navigation Controller. A view controller to be subsequently pushed onto the navigation stack can be configured in the storyboard as the destination of a push segue; I'll talk more about that later in the chapter.

Custom Transition

You can customize the transition that occurs between view controller views, as follows:

- When a tab bar controller changes which of its child view controllers is selected, you can *animate* the change of views.

- When a navigation controller pushes or pops a child view controller, you can *customize* the animation of views.

- When a view controller is presented or dismissed, you can customize the animation of views *and the placement* of the presented view.

Given the extensive animation resources of iOS (see Chapter 4), this is an excellent chance for you to provide your app with variety, interest, and distinctiveness. The view of a child view controller pushed onto a navigation controller's stack, for example, needn't arrive sliding from the side; it can expand by zooming from the middle of the screen, drop from above and fall into place with a bounce, snap into place like a spring, or whatever else you can dream up. A familiar example is Apple's Calendar app, which transitions from a year to a month, in a navigation controller, by zooming in.

A custom transition animation can optionally be *interactive* — meaning that it is driven in real time by the user's gesture. The user does not merely tap and cause an animation to take place; the user performs an extended gesture and gradually summons the new view to supersede the old one. The user can thus participate in the progress of the transition. An example is the way a navigation controller's view can be popped by dragging from the left edge of the screen. Another example is the Photos app, which lets the user pinch a photo, in a navigation controller, to pop to the album containing it.

In the case of a presented view controller, you also get to dictate the ultimate size and position of the presented view, and how the presenting view is seen behind it; you can also provide intermediate views that remain during the presentation. The presentation controller (introduced earlier in this chapter) participates in, and is crucial to, the transition.

I'll start by talking about how to add a custom animation to a tab bar controller transition, and work up to the more involved business of customizing a view controller presentation.

Noninteractive Custom Transition Animation

Let's start with the base case, where the custom animation is *not* interactive. Configuring your custom animation requires three steps:

1. The view controller in charge of the transition must have a delegate.

2. As the transition begins, the delegate will be asked for an *animation controller*, meaning any object adopting the UIViewControllerAnimatedTransitioning protocol. Return `nil` to specify that the default animation (if any) should be used.

3. The animation controller will be sent two messages:

    `transitionDuration:`
       The animation controller must return the duration of the custom animation.

    `animateTransition:`
       The animation controller should perform the animation.

The implementation of `animateTransition:` works, in general, as follows:

1. The parameter is an object called the *transition context* (adopting the UIViewControllerContextTransitioning protocol). By querying the transition context, you can obtain:

   - The *container view*, an already existing view within which all the action is to take place.

   - The outgoing and incoming view controllers.

   - The outgoing and incoming views. These are probably the main views of the outgoing and incoming view controllers, but you should obtain the views directly from the transition context, just in case they aren't. The outgoing view is already inside the container view.

- The initial frame of the outgoing view, and the ultimate frame of the incoming view.

2. Having gathered this information, your mission is to *put the incoming view into the container view* and *animate* it in such a way as to *end up at its correct ultimate position*. You may also animate the outgoing view if you wish.

3. When the animation ends, you *must* call the transition context's `complete-Transition:` to tell it that the animation is over. The outgoing view is then *removed automatically*.

To illustrate, consider the transition between two child view controllers of a tab bar controller. By default, this transition isn't animated; one view just replaces the other. Let's animate the transition.

One obvious custom animation is that the new view controller's view should slide in from one side while the old view controller's view should slide out the other side. The direction of the slide should depend on whether the index of the new view controller is greater or less than that of the old view controller.

Take the steps in order. First, configure a delegate for the tab bar controller. Assume that the tab bar controller is our app's root view controller. For simplicity, I'll set its delegate in code, in the app delegate's `application:didFinishLaunchingWith-Options:`, and I'll make that delegate be the app delegate itself:

```
(self.window!.rootViewController as! UITabBarController).delegate = self
```

On to the second step. The app delegate, in its role as UITabBarControllerDelegate, will now be sent a message whenever the tab bar controller is about to change view controllers. That message is:

- `tabBarController:animationControllerForTransitionFromView-Controller:toViewController:`

We must implement this method to return an animation controller, namely, some object implementing UIViewControllerAnimatedTransitioning. In this case, to keep things simple, I'll return `self`. Here we go:

```
func tabBarController(tabBarController: UITabBarController,
    animationControllerForTransitionFromViewController
    fromVC: UIViewController,
    toViewController toVC: UIViewController)
    -> UIViewControllerAnimatedTransitioning? {
        return self
}
```

(There is no particular reason why the animation controller should be `self`; it can be any object — even a dedicated lightweight object instantiated just to govern this transition. There is also no particular reason why the animation controller should be the same object every time this method is called. We know, in real time, what's about to happen, because we receive the tab bar controller and both child view controllers as parameters. Thus we could readily provide a different animation controller under different circumstances, or we could return nil to use the default transition — meaning, in this case, no animation.)

On to the third step! Here we are in the animation controller (UIViewController-AnimatedTransitioning). Our first job is to reveal in advance the duration of our animation:

```
func transitionDuration(
    transitionContext: UIViewControllerContextTransitioning?)
    -> NSTimeInterval {
        return 0.4
}
```

(Again, the value returned needn't be the same every time this method is called. The transition context has arrived as parameter, and we could query it to identify the two view controllers involved and make a decision based on that. But make sure that the value you return here is indeed the duration of the animation you'll perform in animate-Transition:.)

Finally, we come to animateTransition: itself:

```
func animateTransition(
    transitionContext: UIViewControllerContextTransitioning) {
        // ...
}
```

Once more, simply perform the steps in order. First, query the transition context. This code is practically boilerplate for any custom view controller transition animation:

```
let vc1 = transitionContext.viewControllerForKey(
    UITransitionContextFromViewControllerKey)!
let vc2 = transitionContext.viewControllerForKey(
    UITransitionContextToViewControllerKey)!
let con = transitionContext.containerView()!
let r1start = transitionContext.initialFrameForViewController(vc1)
let r2end = transitionContext.finalFrameForViewController(vc2)
let v1 = transitionContext.viewForKey(UITransitionContextFromViewKey)!
let v2 = transitionContext.viewForKey(UITransitionContextToViewKey)!
```

We have the view controllers and their views, and the initial frame of the outgoing view and the destination frame of the incoming view. Now, to prepare for our intended animation, we want to calculate the converse, namely the final frame of the outgoing view and the initial frame of the incoming view. We are sliding the views sideways, so those frames should be positioned sideways from the initial frame of the outgoing view and the final frame of the incoming view. *Which* side they go on depends upon the relative place of these view controllers among the children of the tab bar controller — is this to be a leftward slide or a rightward slide? Since the animation controller is the app delegate, we can get a reference to the tab bar controller the same way we did before:

```
let tbc = self.window!.rootViewController as! UITabBarController
let ix1 = tbc.viewControllers!.indexOf(vc1)!
let ix2 = tbc.viewControllers!.indexOf(vc2)!
let dir : CGFloat = ix1 < ix2 ? 1 : -1
var r1end = r1start
r1end.origin.x -= r1end.size.width * dir
var r2start = r2end
r2start.origin.x += r2start.size.width * dir
```

We are now ready for the second step: put the second view controller's view into the container view at its initial frame, and perform the animation. The end of the animation is also the moment to perform the all-important third step, namely to call `complete-Transition:` to signal that our part has been played and our hands are off the views:

```
v2.frame = r2start
con.addSubview(v2)
UIView.animateWithDuration(0.4, animations: {
    v1.frame = r1end
    v2.frame = r2end
    }, completion: {
        _ in
        transitionContext.completeTransition(true)
    })
```

That's all there is to it. Of course, that wasn't a very complex animation; but an animation needn't be complex to be interesting, significant, and helpful to the user. And even a more complex animation would be implemented along the same basic lines. One possibility that I didn't illustrate in my example is that you are free to introduce additional views temporarily into the container view during the course of the animation; you'll probably want to remove them in the completion handler.

A custom transition for a navigation controller is similar to a custom transition for a tab bar controller, so I don't need to give a separate example. The only slight difference lies in the name of the navigation controller delegate method that will be called to discover whether there's an animation controller:

- `navigationController:animationControllerForOperation:fromView-Controller:toViewController:`

The `operation:` parameter allows you to distinguish a push from a pop.

 Implementing a navigation controller custom push animation while returning `nil` for the pop animation controller will cause the built-in swipe-to-pop interactive transition to stop working. I regard this as a bug.

Interactive Custom Transition Animation

With an interactive custom transition animation, the idea is that we track something the user is doing, typically by means of a gesture recognizer (see Chapter 5), and perform the "frames" of the transition in response. There are two ways to write an interactive custom transition animation. In both cases, we're going to need an *interaction controller*, namely an object that conforms to the UIViewControllerInteractiveTransitioning protocol. The two ways of writing the code correspond to the two ways of supplying this object:

Create a UIPercentDrivenInteractiveTransition instance

We supply an instance of the built-in UIPercentDrivenInteractiveTransition class (let's call this the *percent driver*). This percent driver object performs the frames of the animation for us by calling our `animateTransition:` and "freezing" the animation. All we have to do is track the gesture and repeatedly call the percent driver's `updateInteractiveTransition:`, telling it how far the gesture has proceeded; the percent driver updates the interface, changing our animation's "frame" to match the extent of the gesture. At the end of the gesture, we decide whether to finish or cancel the transition; accordingly, we call the percent driver's `finishInteractive-Transition` or `cancelInteractiveTransition`. Finally, we call the transition context's `completeTransition:`.

Adopt UIViewControllerInteractiveTransitioning

We supply our own object with our own code. This object, conforming to the UIViewControllerInteractiveTransitioning protocol, will need to respond to `start-InteractiveTransition:`, whose parameter will be the transition context. Once we are told that the transition has started, we will set up the initial conditions for the animation and then constantly track the gesture, changing the interface and calling the transition context's `updateInteractiveTransition:`. When the interaction ends, we decide whether to finish or cancel the transition; accordingly, we animate into the final or initial conditions, and call the transition context's `finish-InteractiveTransition` or `cancelInteractiveTransition`. Finally, we call the transition context's `completeTransition:`.

Using a percent driver

If we have already written a noninteractive version of our transition animation, using the percent driver is going to be simplest, because we get to keep our existing `animate-Transition:` code. The steps build upon those of a noninteractive transition animation:

1. The view controller in charge of the transition must have a delegate.

2. We observe that the user is gesturing in a way that should trigger a change of view controller. We respond by triggering that change.

3. The delegate will be asked for an animation controller, as before. We return an object adopting the UIViewControllerAnimatedTransitioning protocol, as before.

4. The delegate is also asked for an *interaction controller*. (This happened before, but we didn't supply one, which is why our transition animation wasn't interactive.) We have elected to use a UIPercentDrivenInteractiveTransition object. So we return that object.

5. The animation controller is sent the same two messages as before:

   transitionDuration:
   > The duration of the custom animation.

   animateTransition:
   > The animation controller should perform the animation. But the animation will not in fact proceed at this moment; it will be "frozen" and its "frames" will be produced as the interaction proceeds.
   >
   > (To perform this magic, the percent driver takes advantage of the fact that a CALayer conforms to the CAMediaTiming protocol, as I explained in Chapter 4. It asks the transition context for the container view, obtains that view's layer, and sets the layer's speed to 0. Subsequently, as we call the percent driver's updateInteractiveTransition:, it adjusts that layer's timeOffset accordingly, thus displaying a different "frame" of the animation.)

6. We continue tracking the interaction, calling our percent driver's updateInteractiveTransition: to tell it how far the gesture has proceeded. The percent driver displays that frame of our animation for us.

7. Sooner or later the gesture will end. At this point, we must decide whether to declare the transition completed or cancelled. The usual approach is to say that if the user performed more than half the full gesture, that constitutes completion; otherwise, it constitutes cancellation. We call the percent driver's finishInteractiveTransition or cancelInteractiveTransition accordingly. The percent driver either completes the animation or (if we cancelled) reverses the animation.

8. The animation is now completed, and its completion block is called. We call completeTransition:, with the argument stating whether the transition was finished or cancelled.

As an example, I'll describe how to make an interactive version of the tab bar controller transition animation that we developed in the previous section, such that the user can drag the tab bar controller's adjacent view controller in from the right or from the left. All the code we've already written can be left more or less as is! To track the user's gesture, I'll put a pair of UIScreenEdgePanGestureRecognizers into the interface, and keep references to them so they can be identified later. The gesture recognizers are attached to the tab bar controller's view (`tbc.view`), as this will remain constant while the views of its view controllers are sliding across the screen:

```
let sep = UIScreenEdgePanGestureRecognizer(target:self, action:"pan:")
sep.edges = UIRectEdge.Right
tbc.view.addGestureRecognizer(sep)
sep.delegate = self
self.rightEdger = sep
let sep2 = UIScreenEdgePanGestureRecognizer(target:self, action:"pan:")
sep2.edges = UIRectEdge.Left
tbc.view.addGestureRecognizer(sep2)
sep2.delegate = self
self.leftEdger = sep2
```

Acting as the delegate of the two gesture recognizers, we prevent either pan gesture recognizer from operating unless there is another child of the tab bar controller available on that side of the current child:

```
func gestureRecognizerShouldBegin(g: UIGestureRecognizer) -> Bool {
    let tbc = self.window!.rootViewController as! UITabBarController
    var result = false
    if g == self.rightEdger {
        result = (tbc.selectedIndex < tbc.viewControllers!.count - 1)
    }
    else {
        result = (tbc.selectedIndex > 0)
    }
    return result
}
```

If the gesture recognizer action handler `pan:` is called, we now know that this means our interactive transition animation is to take place. I'll break down the discussion according to the gesture recognizer's stages. First, I collect some information that will be needed later:

```
func pan(g:UIScreenEdgePanGestureRecognizer) {
    let v = g.view!
    let tbc = self.window!.rootViewController as! UITabBarController
    let delta = g.translationInView(v)
    let percent = fabs(delta.x/v.bounds.size.width)
    switch g.state {
        // ... to be continued ...
    }
}
```

As the gesture begins, we create the UIPercentDrivenInteractiveTransition object and store it in a property (`self.inter`). We then set the tab bar controller's `selectedIndex`:

```
case .Began:
    self.inter = UIPercentDrivenInteractiveTransition()
    self.interacting = true
    if g == self.rightEdger {
```

```
        tbc.selectedIndex = tbc.selectedIndex + 1
    } else {
        tbc.selectedIndex = tbc.selectedIndex - 1
    }
```

Changing the tab bar controller's `selectedIndex` causes the runtime to turn to the tab bar controller's delegate to see whether there is an animation controller, and hence a custom animation; as before, we make ourselves the animation controller:

```
func tabBarController(tabBarController: UITabBarController,
    animationControllerForTransitionFromViewController
    fromVC: UIViewController,
    toViewController toVC: UIViewController)
    -> UIViewControllerAnimatedTransitioning? {
        return self
}
```

The runtime now asks if there is also an interaction controller. There wasn't one in our previous example, but now there is — the percent driver:

```
func tabBarController(tabBarController: UITabBarController,
    interactionControllerForAnimationController
    animationController: UIViewControllerAnimatedTransitioning)
    -> UIViewControllerInteractiveTransitioning? {
        let result : UIViewControllerInteractiveTransitioning? =
            self.interacting ? self.inter : nil
        return result
}
```

The runtime now calls our percent driver's `startInteractiveTransition:`, handing it a reference to the transition context. The percent driver immediately turns around and calls our `animateTransition:` method, *without performing the animation*. The percent driver "freezes" the animation instead. Our job now is to keep calling the percent driver, telling it what "frame" of the animation to display at every moment; the percent driver will also call the transition context on our behalf.

We are now back in the gesture recognizer's action handler. As the gesture proceeds, we keep sending `updateInteractiveTransition:` to the percent driver:

```
case .Changed:
    self.inter.updateInteractiveTransition(percent)
```

When the gesture ends, we decide whether this counts as finishing or canceling, and we report to the percent driver accordingly:

```
case .Ended:
    if percent > 0.5 {
        self.inter.finishInteractiveTransition()
    } else {
        self.inter.cancelInteractiveTransition()
    }
    self.interacting = false
```

If we call `finishInteractiveTransition`, the percent driver quickly plays the rest of the animation forward to completion. If we call `cancelInteractiveTransition`, the percent driver plays the animation backward to its beginning.

Finally, we find ourselves back inside `animateTransition:`, in the animation `completion:` handler. This is the only place where a change is needed in our previously existing code. As I've just said, the transition can complete in one of two ways. We must still call `completeTransition:` ourselves, but we must tell the transition context which way things turned out, so that the transition context can restore the previous state of things if the transition was cancelled. Luckily, the transition context already knows whether the transition was cancelled! So we simply ask it:

```
UIView.animateWithDuration(0.4, delay:0, options:opts, animations: {
    v1.frame = r1end
    v2.frame = r2end
    }, completion: {
        _ in
        let cancelled = transitionContext.transitionWasCancelled()
        transitionContext.completeTransition(!cancelled)
    })
```

That's all there is to it, and in fact, as a bonus, I have sneakily added a bit of extra functionality to our code: not only does this work as an interactive transition, but I've also kept the noninteractive transition that we developed earlier. In other words, the user can tap a tab bar item to get the original sliding animation left or right, or the user can manually slide a view to get the interactive animation.

Without a percent driver

If we *don't* use a percent driver, then the entire interactive transition is up to us. We ourselves must repeatedly reposition the views at every stage of the gesture, and when the gesture ends, we ourselves must animate them either into their final position or back into their initial position. We will no longer need an `animateTransition:` method (it must be present, to satisfy the protocol requirements, but it can be empty); all the logic of initializing, positioning, and finalizing the moving views must be effectively deconstructed and folded into the various stages of our gesture recognizer action handler. At every stage, we must keep talking to the transition context itself.

The resulting code is verbose, and can be difficult to express in a compact or object-oriented way. However, it is more powerful, more flexible, and possibly more reliable than using a percent driver. We don't need to rely on the percent driver's trick of using a frozen animation; we can reposition the actual views (or their snapshots) as the gesture proceeds.

I'll just sketch out how to rewrite our tab bar controller interactive transition without a percent driver. We have our gesture recognizer(s) as before. When the gesture begins, the `.Began` section of the action handler triggers the transition as before. The delegate is asked for an animation controller and an interaction controller; the interaction controller is now not a percent driver, but some object that we will supply — let's say it's `self`.

The result is that, in our role as adopter of the UIViewControllerInteractiveTransitioning protocol, our `startInteractiveTransition:` is called. Here, we set up the initial conditions of the transition, putting the views into place, and storing a reference to the `transitionContext` in a property where our gesture recognizer action handler can access it:

```
func startInteractiveTransition(
    transitionContext: UIViewControllerContextTransitioning){
    // store transition context so the gesture recognizer can get at it
    self.context = transitionContext
    // ... set up initial conditions ...
    // ... store any additional instance variables ...
    self.r1end = r1end
    self.r2start = r2start
}
```

Our gesture recognizer action handler is called again, repeatedly, at the `.Changed` stage. We keep repositioning our views in accordance with the progress of the interactive gesture. At the same time, we keep informing the transition context of that progress:

```
case .Changed:
    // ... calculate progress (percent)
    // ... put views into position corresponding to current "frame" ...
    // ... and finally, notify the transition context
    v1.frame = // whatever
    v2.frame = // whatever
    tc.updateInteractiveTransition(percent)
```

(Why must we call `updateInteractiveTransition:` throughout the progress of the gesture? For a tab bar controller's transition, this call has little or no significance. But in the case, say, of a navigation controller, the animation has a component separate from what you're doing — the change in the appearance of the navigation bar, as the old title departs and the new title arrives and so forth. The transition context needs to coordinate that animation with the interactive gesture and with your animation. So you need to keep telling it where things are in the course of the interaction.)

Finally, our gesture recognizer action handler is called one last time, at the `.Ended` stage. We now animate our views the rest of the way, or else back to the start, and call either `finishInteractiveTransition` or `cancelInteractiveTransition` followed by `completeTransition:` with the appropriate argument:

```
case .Ended:
    if percent > 0.5 {
        UIView.animateWithDuration(0.2, animations:{
            v1.frame = self.r1end
            v2.frame = r2end
            }, completion: { _ in
```

```
                    tc.finishInteractiveTransition()
                    tc.completeTransition(true)
            })
        }
        else {
            UIView.animateWithDuration(0.2, animations:{
                v1.frame = r1start
                v2.frame = self.r2start
                }, completion: { _ in
                    tc.cancelInteractiveTransition()
                    tc.completeTransition(false)
            })
        }
```

Custom Presented View Controller Transition

Customizing what happens when a view controller is presented is more complex, and more powerful, than customizing a tab bar controller or navigation controller transition. With a presented view controller, you can customize not only the *animation* but also the final *position* of the presented view. Moreover, you can introduce extra views which *remain in the scene* until dismissal; for example, if the presented view is smaller than the presenting view and covers it only partially, you might add a dimming view between them, to darken the presenting view (just as a .FormSheet presentation does).

What the runtime must do while a view is being presented in order to make the presentation customizable is also more complex. There is no existing view to serve as the container view; therefore, when the presentation starts, the runtime must construct the container view and insert it into the interface and leave it there for only as long as the view remains presented. In the case of a .FullScreen presentation, the runtime must also rip the presenting view out of the interface and insert it into the container view, because you might want the presenting view to participate in the animation. For other styles of presentation, the container view is *in front of* the presenting view, which can't be animated and is left in place as the presentation proceeds.

The work of customizing a presentation is distributed between *two* objects: the animation controller (or interaction controller) on the one hand, and the presentation controller on the other. The idea is that the animation controller should be responsible for *only* the animation, the movement of the presented view into its final position. The *determination* of that final position is the job of the presentation controller. The presentation controller is also responsible for inserting any extra views, such as a dimming view, into the container view; Apple says that the animation controller animates the content, while the presentation controller animates the "chrome." This distribution of responsibilities may require some extra effort on your part, but in fact it also simplifies considerably the task of customizing the animation itself.

Customizing the animation

I'll start with a situation where we *don't* need to use the presentation controller: all we want to do is customize the animation part of a built-in presentation style. The steps are almost completely parallel to how we customized a tab bar controller animation:

1. Give the presented view controller a delegate. Here, we assign to the presented view controller's `transitioningDelegate` property an object adopting the UIView-ControllerTransitioningDelegate protocol.

2. The delegate will be asked for an animation controller, and will return an object adopting the UIViewControllerAnimatedTransitioning protocol. Unlike a tab bar controller or navigation controller, a presented view controller's view undergoes *two* animations — the presentation and the dismissal — and therefore the delegate is asked *separately* for controllers:

   - `animationControllerForPresentedController:presentingController: sourceController:`

   - `interactionControllerForPresentation:`

   - `animationControllerForDismissedController:`

   - `interactionControllerForDismissal:`

   You are free to customize just one animation, leaving the other at the default by not providing a controller for it.

3. The animation controller will implement `transitionDuration` and `animate-Transition:`.

To illustrate, let's say we're running on an iPad, and we want to present a view using the `.FormSheet` presentation style. But instead of using any of the built-in animation styles, we'll have the presented view appear to grow from the middle of the screen. The only mildly tricky step is the first one. The problem is that the delegate must be assigned very early in the presented view controller's life — before the presentation begins. But the presented view controller doesn't *exist* before the presentation begins. The most reliable approach, therefore, is for the presented view controller to assign its own delegate in its own initializer:

```
required init?(coder aDecoder: NSCoder) {
    super.init(coder:aDecoder)
    self.transitioningDelegate = self
}
```

On to step two. The transitioning delegate is asked for an animation controller; here, I'll have it supply `self` once again, and I'll do this only for the presentation, leaving the dismissal to use the default animation:

```
func animationControllerForPresentedController(
    presented: UIViewController,
    presentingController presenting: UIViewController,
    sourceController source: UIViewController)
    -> UIViewControllerAnimatedTransitioning? {
        return self
}
```

Finally, step three — the actual animation. This is extremely simple, especially because we don't care or inquire about the From view controller, which remains in place during the presentation (indeed, its view isn't even in the container view):

```
func transitionDuration(
    transitionContext: UIViewControllerContextTransitioning?)
    -> NSTimeInterval {
        return 0.4
}
func animateTransition(
    transitionContext: UIViewControllerContextTransitioning) {
        let vc2 = transitionContext.viewControllerForKey(
            UITransitionContextToViewControllerKey)
        let con = transitionContext.containerView()!
        let r2end = transitionContext.finalFrameForViewController(vc2!)
        let v2 = transitionContext.viewForKey(UITransitionContextToViewKey)!
        v2.frame = r2end
        v2.transform = CGAffineTransformMakeScale(0.1, 0.1)
        v2.alpha = 0
        con.addSubview(v2)
        UIView.animateWithDuration(0.4, animations: {
            v2.alpha = 1
            v2.transform = CGAffineTransformIdentity
        }, completion: {
            _ in
            transitionContext.completeTransition(true)
        })
}
```

There is just one complication when you animate a presented view controller's view. If you also animate the dismissal of that view, and if the animation controller is the same object so that the same animateTransition: implementation is called, the roles are reversed: on presentation, the presented view controller is the To view controller (UITransitionContextToViewControllerKey and UITransitionContextToViewKey), but on dismissal, it is the From view controller (UITransitionContextFromView-ControllerKey and UITransitionContextFromViewKey). For a presentation that isn't .FullScreen, the unused view is nil, so you can distinguish the cases by structuring your code like this:

```
let v1 = transitionContext.viewForKey(UITransitionContextFromViewKey)
let v2 = transitionContext.viewForKey(UITransitionContextToViewKey)
if let v2 = v2 { // presenting
    // ...
} else if let v1 = v1 {
    // ...
}
```

Customizing the presentation

Now let's involve the presentation controller. This will require some additional steps:

1. In addition to setting a `transitioningDelegate`, we set the presented view controller's `modalPresentationStyle` to `.Custom`.

2. The result of the preceding step is that the delegate is sent an additional message:

   • `presentationControllerForPresentedViewController:presentingViewController:sourceViewController:`

   (The `sourceViewController:` parameter is what I have termed the "original presenter.") Your mission is to return an instance of a *custom UIPresentationController subclass* which you have previously declared and implemented. This will then be the presented view controller's presentation controller during the course of this presentation, from the time presentation begins to the time dismissal ends. You must create this instance by calling (directly or indirectly) the designated initializer:

   • `init(presentedViewController:presentingViewController:)`

3. By overriding appropriate UIPresentationController methods in your UIPresentationController subclass, you participate in the presentation, setting the presented view controller's position and adding "chrome" to the presentation as desired.

 It is perfectly legal for the transitioning delegate to supply a custom presentation controller and *no* animation controller! In that case, a default animation will be performed, but the presented view will end up at the position your custom presentation controller dictates. This is a good example of the delightful "separation of powers" of the presentation controller and the animation controller.

The UIPresentationController has properties pointing to the `presentingViewController` as well the `presentedViewController` and the `presentedView`, plus the `presentationStyle` set by the presented view controller. It also obtains the `containerView`, which it subsequently communicates to the animation controller's transition context. It has some methods that you can override in your subclass, but you only need to override the ones that require customization for your particular implementation:

`frameOfPresentedViewInContainerView`

> Returns the final position of the presented view. The animation coordinator, if there is one, will obtain this frame through the transition context's `finalFrameForView-Controller:` method and must cause the presented view to end up there (as you already know).

`presentationTransitionWillBegin`
`presentationTransitionDidEnd`
`dismissalTransitionWillBegin`
`dismissalTransitionDidEnd`

> Use these events as signals to add or remove "chrome" (extra views) to the container view.

`containerViewWillLayoutSubviews`
`containerViewDidLayoutSubviews`

> Use these layout events as signals to update the "chrome" views if needed.

`shouldPresentInFullscreen`

> The default is to return `true`; returning `false` turns this presentation into a `.CurrentContext` presentation.

`shouldRemovePresentersView`

> The default is to return `false`, except that of course it is `true` for a standard `.Full-Screen` presentation, meaning that the presenting view is ripped out of the interface at the end of the presentation transition. You can return `true` for a custom presentation, but it would be rare to do this; even if the presented view completely covers the presenting view, there is no harm in leaving the presenting view in place.

A UIPresentationController is not a UIViewController, but it adopts some protocols that UIViewController adopts, and thus gets the same resizing-related messages that a UIViewController gets, as I described earlier in this chapter. It adopts UITrait-Environment, meaning that it has a `traitCollection` and participates in the trait collection inheritance hierarchy, and receives the `traitCollectionDidChange:` message. It also adopts UIContentContainer, meaning that it receives `willTransitionToTrait-Collection:withTransitionCoordinator:` and `viewWillTransitionToSize:with-TransitionCoordinator:`.

In addition, a presentation controller functions as the *parent* of the presented view controller, and can override its inherited trait collection and respond to changes in its `preferredContentSize`, as I'll explain later.

To illustrate the use of a custom presentation controller, I'll expand the preceding example to implement a custom presentation style that looks like a .FormSheet *even on an iPhone*. The first step is to set the presentation style to .Custom at the same time that we set the transitioning delegate:

```
required init?(coder aDecoder: NSCoder) {
    super.init(coder:aDecoder)
    self.transitioningDelegate = self
    self.modalPresentationStyle = .Custom // *
}
```

The result (step two) is that the extra delegate method is called so that we can provide a custom presentation controller, and we do so:

```
func presentationControllerForPresentedViewController(
    presented: UIViewController,
    presentingViewController presenting: UIViewController,
    sourceViewController source: UIViewController)
    -> UIPresentationController? {
        let pc = MyPresentationController(
            presentedViewController: presented,
            presentingViewController: presenting)
        return pc
}
```

Everything else happens in our implementation of MyPresentationController. To make the presentation look like a .FormSheet, we inset the presented view's frame:

```
override func frameOfPresentedViewInContainerView() -> CGRect {
    return super.frameOfPresentedViewInContainerView()
        .insetBy(dx: 40, dy: 40)
}
```

We could actually stop at this point! The presented view now appears in the correct position. However, the presenting view is appearing undimmed behind it. Let's add dimming, by inserting a translucent dimming view into the container view. Note that we are careful to deal with the possibility of subsequent rotation:

```
override func presentationTransitionWillBegin() {
    let con = self.containerView!
    let shadow = UIView(frame:con.bounds)
    shadow.backgroundColor = UIColor(white:0, alpha:0.4)
    con.insertSubview(shadow, atIndex: 0)
    shadow.autoresizingMask = [.FlexibleWidth, .FlexibleHeight]
}
```

Again, this works perfectly, but now I don't like what happens when the presented view is dismissed: the dimming view vanishes suddenly at the end of the dismissal. I'd rather have the dimming view fade out, and I'd like it to fade out *in coordination with the dismissal animation*. The way to arrange that is through the object vended by the presented view controller's transitionCoordinator method. This object is just like the transition coordinator I've already discussed earlier in this chapter in connection with resizing events and rotation: in particular, we can call its `animateAlongside-Transition:` method to add our own animation:

```
override func dismissalTransitionWillBegin() {
    let con = self.containerView!
    let shadow = con.subviews[0]
    let tc = self.presentedViewController.transitionCoordinator()!
    tc.animateAlongsideTransition({
        _ in
        shadow.alpha = 0
        }, completion: nil)
}
```

Once again, we could stop at this point. But I'd like to add a further refinement. A `.Form-Sheet` view has rounded corners. I'd like to make our presented view look the same way:

```
override func presentedView() -> UIView? {
    let v = super.presentedView()!
    v.layer.cornerRadius = 6
    v.layer.masksToBounds = true
    return v
}
```

Finally, for completeness, it would be nice, during presentation, to dim the appearance of any button titles and other tinted interface elements visible through the dimming view, to emphasize that they are disabled:

```
override func presentationTransitionDidEnd(completed: Bool) {
    let vc = self.presentingViewController
    let v = vc.view
    v.tintAdjustmentMode = .Dimmed
}
override func dismissalTransitionDidEnd(completed: Bool) {
    let vc = self.presentingViewController
    let v = vc.view
    v.tintAdjustmentMode = .Automatic
}
```

Transition Coordinator

A UIViewController, as I mentioned in the previous section, has a `transition-Coordinator` method, which yields an object adopting the UIViewControllerTransition-Coordinator protocol. This object, the *transition coordinator*, is a kind of wrapper around the current transition context, and also adopts the UIViewControllerTransition-CoordinatorContext protocol, just like the transition context. Thus, in effect, view controllers can find out about the transition they are involved in.

In addition to the methods that it implements by virtue of adopting the UIView-ControllerTransitionCoordinatorContext protocol, a transition coordinator implements the following methods:

animateAlongsideTransition:completion:

Takes an animation block and a completion block. The animation you supply is incorporated into the transition coordinator's animation. Returns a Bool, informing you in case your commands couldn't be animated. Both blocks receive the transition context as a parameter. (See also "Responding to rotation" on page 281, where I discussed this method in connection with rotation.)

A view controller's use of this method will typically be to add animation of its view's internal interface as part of a transition animation. Observe that this works equally for a custom animation or a built-in animation; in fact, the point is that the view controller can behave agnostically with regard to how its own view is being animated. In this example, a presented view controller animates part of its interface into place as the animation proceeds (whatever that animation may be):

```
override func viewWillAppear(animated: Bool) {
    super.viewWillAppear(animated)
    if let tc = self.transitionCoordinator() {
        tc.animateAlongsideTransition({
            _ in
            self.buttonTopConstraint.constant += 200
            self.view.layoutIfNeeded()
        }, completion: nil)
    }
}
```

animateAlongsideTransitionInView:animation:completion:

Just like the previous method, except that the animated view can be outside the container view.

notifyWhenInteractionEndsUsingBlock:

Called at the moment the user abandons an interactive gesture and the transition is about to be either completed or cancelled. This is useful particularly if the interactive transition is being cancelled, as it may well be that what your view controller wants to do will differ in this situation. The parameter to the block is the transition context.

In this example, a navigation controller has pushed a view controller, and now the user is popping it interactively (using the default drag-from-the-left-edge gesture). If the user cancels, the back view controller can hear about it, like this:

```
override func viewWillAppear(animated: Bool) {
    super.viewWillAppear(animated)
    guard let tc = self.transitionCoordinator() else {return}
    guard tc.initiallyInteractive() else {return}
    tc.notifyWhenInteractionEndsUsingBlock {
```

```
        context in
        if context.isCancelled() {
            // ...
        }
    }
}
```

 I have not found any occasion when the child of a tab bar controller has a non-nil transition coordinator. This feels like a bug.

Page View Controller

A page view controller (UIPageViewController) displays its child view controller's view. The user, by a gesture, can navigate in one direction or the other to see the next or the previous child view controller's view, successively — like turning the pages of a book. In reality, the page view controller has only one child view controller at a time (or, if so configured, two at a time); it navigates by releasing its existing child view controller and replacing it with another.

Think of a page view controller as being like a book that *pretends* to have multiple pages, but in fact has just *one* page at a time, and replaces that page with another when the reader "turns the page." This is a very efficient architecture: it makes no difference whether the page view controller lets the user page through three pages or ten thousand pages, because the pages are created in real time, on demand, and each page exists only as long as the user is looking at it.

Preparing a Page View Controller

To create a UIPageViewController, use its designated initializer:

- `init(transitionStyle:navigationOrientation:options:)`

Here's what the parameters mean:

`transitionStyle:`
    The animation style during navigation (UIPageViewControllerTransitionStyle). Your choices are:

    - `.PageCurl`
    - `.Scroll` (sliding)

`navigationOrientation:`
    The direction of navigation (UIPageViewControllerNavigationOrientation). Your choices are:

- `.Horizontal`
- `.Vertical`

`options:`

A dictionary. Possible keys are:

`UIPageViewControllerOptionSpineLocationKey`

If you're using the page curl transition, this is the position of the pivot line around which those page curl transitions rotate. The value (UIPageView-ControllerSpineLocation) is one of the following:

- `.Min` (left or top)
- `.Mid` (middle; two pages are shown at once)
- `.Max` (right or bottom)

`UIPageViewControllerOptionInterPageSpacingKey`

If you're using the scroll transition, this is the spacing between successive pages, visible as a gap during the transition (the default is 0).

You configure the page view controller's initial content by handing it its initial child view controller(s). You do that by calling this method:

- `setViewControllers:direction:animated:completion:`

Here's what the parameters mean:

`viewControllers:`

An array of one view controller — unless you're using the page curl transition and the `.Mid` spine location, in which case it's an array of two view controllers.

`direction:`

The animation direction (UIPageViewControllerNavigationDirection). This probably won't matter when you're assigning the page view controller its initial content, as you are not likely to want any animation. Possible values are:

- `.Forward`
- `.Backward`

`animated:, completion:`

A Bool and a completion handler.

To allow the user to page through the page view controller, and to supply the page view controller with a new page at that time, you also assign the page view controller a `data-Source`, which should conform to the UIPageViewControllerDataSource protocol. The `dataSource` is told whenever the user starts to change pages, and should respond by immediately providing another view controller whose view will constitute the new page. Typically, the data source will create this view controller on the spot.

Here's a minimal example. Each page in the page view controller is to portray an image of a named Pep Boy. The first question is where the pages will come from. My data model consists of an array (self.pep) of the string names of the three Pep Boys, along with three eponymous image files in my app bundle portraying each Pep Boy. I've also got a UIViewController subclass called Pep, capable of displaying a Pep Boy. I initialize a Pep object with the designated initializer init(pepBoy:), supplying the name of a Pep Boy from the array; the Pep object sets its own boy property:

```
init(pepBoy boy:String) {
    self.boy = boy
    super.init(nibName: "Pep", bundle: nil)
}
```

Pep's viewDidLoad then fetches the corresponding image and assigns it as the image of a UIImageView within its own view:

```
override func viewDidLoad() {
    super.viewDidLoad()
    self.pic.image = UIImage(named:"\(self.boy.lowercaseString).jpg")
}
```

Here's how I create the page view controller itself (in my app delegate):

```
// make a page view controller
let pvc = UIPageViewController(
    transitionStyle: .Scroll,
    navigationOrientation: .Horizontal, options: nil)
// give it an initial page
let page = Pep(pepBoy: self.pep[0])
pvc.setViewControllers(
    [page], direction: .Forward, animated: false, completion: nil)
// give it a data source
pvc.dataSource = self
// puts its view into the interface
self.window!.rootViewController = pvc
```

The page view controller is a UIViewController, and its view must get into the interface by standard means. You can make the page view controller the window's rootView-Controller, as I do here; you can make it a presented view controller; you can make it a child view controller of a tab bar controller or a navigation controller. If you want the page view controller's view to be a subview of a custom view controller's view, that view controller must be a custom container view controller, as I'll describe later.

Page View Controller Navigation

We now have a page view controller's view in our interface, itself containing and displaying the view of a Pep view controller that is its child. In theory, we also have three pages, because we have three Pep Boys and their images — but the page view controller knows about only one of them. Just as with a navigation controller, you don't supply (or even create) a page *until the moment comes to navigate to it*. When that happens, one of these data source methods will be called:

- pageViewController:viewControllerAfterViewController:
- pageViewController:viewControllerBeforeViewController:

The job of those methods is to return the requested successive view controller. You'll need a strategy for doing that; the strategy you devise will depend on how your model maintains the data.

My data is an array of unique strings, so all I have to do is find the previous name or the next name in the array. Here's one of my data source methods:

```
func pageViewController(pageViewController: UIPageViewController,
    viewControllerAfterViewController viewController: UIViewController)
    -> UIViewController? {
        let boy = (viewController as! Pep).boy
        let ix = self.pep.indexOf(boy)! + 1
        if ix >= self.pep.count {
            return nil
        }
        return Pep(pepBoy: self.pep[ix])
}
```

You can also, at any time, call setViewControllers:... to change programmatically what page is being displayed, possibly with animation.

Page indicator

If you're using the scroll style, the page view controller will optionally display a page indicator (a UIPageControl, see Chapter 12). The user can look at this to get a sense of what page we're on, and can tap to the left or right of it to navigate. To get the page indicator, you must implement two more data source methods; they are consulted in response to setViewControllers:.... We called that method initially to configure the page view controller; if we never call it again (because the user simply keeps navigating to the next or previous page), these data source methods won't be called again either, but they don't need to be: the page view controller will thenceforth keep track of the current index on its own. Here's my implementation for the Pep Boy example:

```
func presentationCountForPageViewController(
    pageViewController: UIPageViewController) -> Int {
        return self.pep.count
}
func presentationIndexForPageViewController(
    pvc: UIPageViewController) -> Int {
```

```
        let page = pvc.viewControllers![0] as! Pep
        let boy = page.boy
        return self.pep.indexOf(boy)!
}
```

Unfortunately, the page view controller's page indicator by default has white dots and a clear background, so it is invisible in front of a white background. You'll want to customize it to change that. Unfortunately, there is no direct access to it, so it's simplest to use the appearance proxy (Chapter 12). For example:

```
let proxy = UIPageControl.appearance()
proxy.pageIndicatorTintColor = UIColor.redColor().colorWithAlphaComponent(0.6)
proxy.currentPageIndicatorTintColor = UIColor.redColor()
proxy.backgroundColor = UIColor.yellowColor()
```

Navigation gestures

If you've assigned the page view controller the `.PageCurl` transition style, the user can ask for navigation by tapping at either edge of the view or by dragging across the view. These gestures are detected through two gesture recognizers, which you can access through the page view controller's `gestureRecognizers` property. The documentation suggests that you might change where the user can tap or drag by attaching them to a different view, and other customizations are possible as well. In this code, I change a `.PageCurl` page view controller's behavior so that the user must double tap to request navigation:

```
for g in pvc.gestureRecognizers {
    if let g = g as? UITapGestureRecognizer {
        g.numberOfTapsRequired = 2
    }
}
```

Of course you are also free to add to the user's stock of gestures for requesting navigation. You can supply any controls or gesture recognizers that make sense for your app, and respond by calling `setViewControllers:...`. For example, if you're using the `.Scroll` transition style, there's no tap gesture recognizer, so the user can't tap at either edge of the page view controller's view to request navigation. Let's change that. I've added invisible views at either edge of my Pep view controller's view, with tap gesture recognizers attached. When the user taps, the tap gesture recognizer fires, and the action handler posts a notification whose `object` is the tap gesture recognizer:

```
@IBAction func tap (sender: UIGestureRecognizer?) {
    NSNotificationCenter.defaultCenter().postNotificationName(
        "tap", object: sender)
}
```

I receive this notification and use the tap gesture recognizer's view's `tag` to learn which view it is; I then navigate accordingly (`n` is the notification, `pvc` is the page view controller):

```
let g = n.object as! UIGestureRecognizer
let which = g.view!.tag
let vc0 = pvc.viewControllers![0]
let vc = (which == 0 ?
    self.pageViewController(pvc, viewControllerBeforeViewController: vc0) :
    self.pageViewController(pvc, viewControllerAfterViewController: vc0))
if vc == nil {
    return
}
let dir : UIPageViewControllerNavigationDirection =
    which == 0 ? .Reverse : .Forward
UIApplication.sharedApplication().beginIgnoringInteractionEvents()
pvc.setViewControllers([vc!], direction: dir, animated: true, completion: {
    _ in
    UIApplication.sharedApplication().endIgnoringInteractionEvents()
})
```

Other Page View Controller Configurations

It is possible to assign a page view controller a delegate (UIPageViewController-Delegate), which gets an event when the user starts turning the page and when the user finishes turning the page, and can change the spine location dynamically in response to a change in device orientation. As with a tab bar controller's delegate or a navigation controller's delegate, a page view controller's delegate also gets messages allowing it to specify the page view controller's rotation policy, so there's no need to subclass UIPage-ViewController solely for that purpose.

One further bit of configuration applicable to a .PageCurl page view controller is the doubleSided property. If it is true, the next page occupies the back of the previous page. The default is false, unless the spine is in the middle, in which case it's true and can't be changed. Your only option here, therefore, is to set it to true when the spine isn't in the middle, and in that case the back of each page would be a sort of throwaway page, glimpsed by the user during the page curl animation.

A page view controller in a storyboard lets you configure its transition style, navigation orientation, page spacing, spine location, and doubleSided property. (It also has delegate and data source outlets, but you're not allowed to connect them to other view controllers, because you can't draw an outlet from one scene to another in a storyboard.) It has no child view controller relationship, so you can't set the page view controller's initial child view controller in the storyboard; you'll have to complete the page view controller's initial configuration in code.

Container View Controllers

UITabBarController, UINavigationController, and UIPageViewController are built-in *parent view controllers*: you hand them a child view controller and they put that child view controller's view into the interface for you, inside their own view. What if you want your own view controller to do the same thing?

Back in iOS 3 and 4, that was illegal; the only way a view controller's view could get into the interface was if a built-in parent view controller put it there. You could put a view into the interface, of course — but not a view controller's view. (Naturally, developers ignored this restriction, and got themselves into all kinds of difficulties.) In iOS 5, Apple introduced a coherent way for you to create your own parent view controllers, which can legally manage child view controllers and put their views into the interface. A custom parent view controller of this sort is called a *container view controller*.

Container view controllers give you the flexibility and power to construct the kind of hierarchy shown in Figure 6-4 from your own view controllers and their views, nesting them in what whatever manner and degree you like. Your own view controller becomes like one of the built-in parent view controllers, except that *you* get to define what it does — what it means for a view controller to be a child of this kind of parent view controller, how many children it has, which of its children's views appear in the interface and where they appear, and so on. A container view controller can also participate actively in the business of trait collection inheritance and view resizing.

Adding and Removing Children

A view controller has a childViewControllers array. This is what gives it the power to be a parent! You must not, however, just wantonly populate this array. A child view controller needs to receive certain definite events at particular moments:

- As it becomes a child view controller
- As its view is added to and removed from the interface
- As it ceases to be a child view controller

Therefore, to act as a parent view controller, your UIViewController subclass must fulfill certain responsibilities:

Adding a child
When a view controller is to *become your view controller's child*, your view controller must do these things, in this order:

1. Send addChildViewController: to itself, with the child as argument. The child is automatically added to your childViewControllers array and is retained.

2. Get the child view controller's view into the interface (as a subview of your view controller's view), if that's what adding a child view controller means.

3. Send didMoveToParentViewController: to the child with your view controller as its argument.

Removing a child

When a view controller is to *cease being your view controller's child*, your view controller must do these things, in this order:

1. Send `willMoveToParentViewController:` to the child with a `nil` argument.

2. Remove the child view controller's view from your interface.

3. Send `removeFromParentViewController` to the child. The child is automatically removed from your `childViewControllers` array and is released.

This is a clumsy and rather confusing dance. The underlying reason for it is that a child view controller must always receive `willMoveToParentViewController:` followed by `didMoveToParentViewController:` (and your own child view controllers can take advantage of these events however you like). But it turns out that you don't always send both these messages explicitly, because:

- `addChildViewController:` sends `willMoveToParentViewController:` for you *automatically*.

- `removeFromParentViewController` sends `didMoveToParentViewController:` for you *automatically*.

Thus, in each case you must send manually the *other* message, the one that adding or removing a child view controller *doesn't* send for you — and of course you must send it so that everything happens in the correct order, as dictated by the rules I just listed.

Example 6-1 provides a schematic approach for how to obtain an initial child view controller and put its view into the interface, where no child view controller's view was previously. (Alternatively, a storyboard can do this work for you, with no code, as I'll explain later in this chapter.)

Example 6-1. Adding an initial child view controller

```
let vc = // whatever; this is the initial child view controller
self.addChildViewController(vc) // "will" called for us
vc.view.frame = // whatever, or use constraints
// insert view into interface between "will" and "did"
self.view.addSubview(vc.view)
// when we call add, we must call "did" afterwards
vc.didMoveToParentViewController(self)
```

The next question is how to *replace* one child view controller's view in the interface with another (comparable to how UITabBarController behaves when a different tab bar item is selected). The simplest, most convenient way is for the parent view controller to send itself this message:

- transitionFromViewController:toViewController:duration:options:
  animations:completion:

That method manages the stages in good order, adding one child view controller's view to the interface before the transition and removing the other child view controller's view from the interface after the transition, and seeing to it that the child view controllers receive lifetime events (such as viewWillAppear:) at the right moment. Here's what the last three arguments are for:

options:

A bitmask (UIViewAnimationOptions) comprising the same possible options that apply to any block-based view transition (see "Transitions" on page 155).

animations:

A block that may be used for additional view animations, besides the transition animation specified in the options: argument. Alternatively, if none of the built-in transition animations is suitable, you can animate the views yourself here; they are both in the interface during this block.

completion:

This block will be important if the transition involves the removal or addition of a child view controller. At the time when transitionFromViewController:toView-Controller:... is called, both view controllers must be children of the parent view controller; so if you're going to remove one of the view controllers as a child, you'll do it in the completion: block. Similarly, if you owe a new child view controller a didMoveToParentViewController: call, you'll use the completion: block to fulfill that debt.

Here's an example. To keep things simple, suppose that our view controller has just one child view controller at a time, and displays the view of that child view controller within its own view. So let's say that when our view controller is handed a new child view controller, it substitutes that new child view controller for the old child view controller and replaces the old child view controller's view with the new child view controller's view. Here's code that does that correctly; the view controllers are fromvc and tovc:

```
// we have already been handed the new view controller
// set up the new view controller's view's frame
tovc.view.frame = // ... whatever
// must have both as children before we can transition between them
self.addChildViewController(tovc) // "will" called for us
// note: when we call remove, we must call "will" (with nil) beforehand
fromvc.willMoveToParentViewController(nil)
// then perform the transition
self.transitionFromViewController(fromvc,
    toViewController:tovc,
    duration:0.4,
    options:.TransitionFlipFromLeft,
```

```
        animations:nil,
        completion:{
            _ in
            // finally, finish up
            // note: when we call add, we must call "did" afterwards
            tovc.didMoveToParentViewController(self)
            fromvc.removeFromParentViewController() // "did" called for us
        })
```

If we're using constraints to position the new child view controller's view, where will we set up those constraints? Before `transitionFromViewController:...` is too soon, as the new child view controller's view is not yet in the interface. The `completion:` block is too late: if the view is added with no constraints, it will have no initial size or position, so the animation will be performed and then the view will suddenly seem to pop into existence as we provide its constraints. The `animations:` block turns out to be a very good place:

```
// must have both as children before we can transition between them
self.addChildViewController(tovc) // "will" called for us
// note: when we call remove, we must call "will" (with nil) beforehand
fromvc.willMoveToParentViewController(nil)
// then perform the transition
self.transitionFromViewController(fromvc,
    toViewController:tovc,
    duration:0.4,
    options:.TransitionFlipFromLeft,
    animations: {
        tovc.view.translatesAutoresizingMaskIntoConstraints = false
        // ... configure tovc.view constraints here ...
    },
    completion:{
        _ in
        // finally, finish up
        // note: when we call add, we must call "did" afterwards
        tovc.didMoveToParentViewController(self)
        fromvc.removeFromParentViewController() // "did" called for us
    })
```

Alternatively, you can use a layout-related event, such as `viewWillLayoutSubviews`; still, I prefer the `animations:` block, as it is called just once at exactly the right moment.

If the built-in transition animations are unsuitable, you can set the `options:` argument to `.None` and provide your own animation in the `animations:` block, at which time both views are in the interface. In this example, I animate a substitute view (an image view showing a snapshot of `tovc.view`) to grow from the top left corner; then I configure the real view's constraints and remove the substitute:

```
// tovc.view.frame is already set
UIGraphicsBeginImageContextWithOptions(tovc.view.bounds.size, true, 0)
tovc.view.layer.renderInContext(UIGraphicsGetCurrentContext()!)
let im = UIGraphicsGetImageFromCurrentImageContext()
```

```
UIGraphicsEndImageContext()
let iv = UIImageView(image:im)
iv.frame = CGRectZero
self.view.addSubview(iv)
tovc.view.alpha = 0
// must have both as children before we can transition between them
self.addChildViewController(tovc) // "will" called for us
// note: when we call remove, we must call "will" (with nil) beforehand
fromvc.willMoveToParentViewController(nil)
// then perform the transition
self.transitionFromViewController(fromvc,
    toViewController:tovc,
    duration:0.4,
    options:.TransitionNone,
    animations: {
        iv.frame = tovc.view.frame // animate bounds change
        // ... configure tovc.view constraints here ...
    },
    completion:{
        _ in
        tovc.view.alpha = 1
        iv.removeFromSuperview()
        // finally, finish up
        // note: when we call add, we must call "did" afterwards
        tovc.didMoveToParentViewController(self)
        fromvc.removeFromParentViewController() // "did" called for us
    })
```

If your parent view controller is going to be consulted about the status bar (whether it should be shown or hidden, and if shown, whether its text should be light or dark), it can elect to defer the decision to one of its children, by implementing these methods (just as a UITabBarController does):

- childViewControllerForStatusBarStyle
- childViewControllerForStatusBarHidden

Container View Controllers, Traits, and Resizing

A container view controller participates in trait collection inheritance and view resizing. In fact, you may well insert a container view controller into your view controller hierarchy for no other purpose than to engage in such participation.

Thus far, I have treated trait collection inheritance as immutable; and for the most part, it is. A UITraitEnvironment (an object with a traitCollection property: UIScreen, UIView, UIViewController, or UIPresentationController) ultimately gets its trait collection from the environment, and the environment is simply a fact. Nevertheless, a parent view controller has the amazing ability to lie to a child view controller about the environment, thanks to this method:

- `setOverrideTraitCollection:forChildViewController:`

The first parameter is a UITraitCollection that will be combined with the inherited trait collection and communicated to the specified child.

This is a UIViewController instance method, so only view controllers have this mighty power. Moreover, you have to specify a child view controller, so only *parent* view controllers have this mighty power. However, UIPresentationController has a similar power, through its `overrideTraitCollection` property; setting this property combines the override trait collection with the inherited collection and communicates it to the presented view controller.

Why would you want to do such a thing as lie to a child view controller about its environment? Well, imagine that we're writing an iPad app, and we have a view controller whose view can appear either fullscreen or as a small subview of a parent view controller's main view. The view's interface might need to be different when it appears in the smaller size. You could configure that using size classes (conditional constraints) in the nib editor, with one interface for a `.Regular` horizontal size class (iPad) and another interface for a `.Compact` horizontal size class (iPhone). Then, when the view is to appear in its smaller size, we lie to its view controller and tell it that this *is* an iPhone:

```
let vc = // the view controller we're going to use as a child
self.addChildViewController(vc)
let tc = UITraitCollection(horizontalSizeClass: .Compact)
self.setOverrideTraitCollection(tc, forChildViewController: vc) // heh heh
vc.view.frame = // whatever
self.view.addSubview(vc.view)
vc.didMoveToParentViewController(self)
```

Apple's own motivating example involves UISplitViewController, a class that behaves differently depending on its trait environment. For example, by lying to a split view controller and making it believe we're on an iPad, you can cause the split view controller to *look* like a split view controller (displaying two subviews, such as a master table view and a detail view) even on an iPhone. I'll talk more about that in Chapter 9.

A parent view controller sets the size of a child view controller's view. A child view controller, however, can express a preference as to what size it would like its view to be, by setting its own `preferredContentSize` property. The chief purpose of this property is to be consulted by a parent view controller when this view controller is its child. This property is a preference and no more; no law says that the parent must consult the child, or that the parent must obey the child's preference.

If a view controller's `preferredContentSize` is set while it is a child view controller, the runtime automatically communicates this fact to the parent view controller, by calling this UIContentContainer method:

- `preferredContentSizeDidChangeForChildContentContainer:`

The parent view controller may implement this method to consult the child's `preferred-ContentSize` and change the child's view's size in response. Again, no law requires the parent to do this. This method, and the `preferredContentSize` property, are ways of allowing a child view controller a voice in its view's size; it is the parent who dictates what that size will actually be.

A parent view controller, as an adopter of the UIContentContainer protocol (along with UIPresentationController), is also responsible for communicating to its children that their sizes are changing and what their new sizes will be. It is the parent view controller's duty to implement this method:

`sizeForChildContentContainer:withParentContainerSize:`
> Should be implemented to return each child view controller's correct size at any moment. Failure to implement this method will cause the child view controller to be handed the wrong size in its implementation of `viewWillTransitionTo-Size:withTransitionCoordinator:` — it will be given the *parent's* new size rather than its own new size!

If your parent view controller implements `viewWillTransitionToSize:with-TransitionCoordinator:`, calling `super` is sufficient to get the same message passed on to the children. This works even if your implementation explicitly changed the size of a child view controller at this time, provided that you implemented `sizeForChild-ContentContainer:withParentContainerSize:` to return the new size.

Storyboards

Throughout this chapter, I've been describing how to create a view controller and present it or make it another view controller's child *manually*, entirely in code. But if you're using a storyboard, you will often (or always) allow the storyboard to do those things for you *automatically*. A storyboard can be helpful and convenient in this regard, though not, perhaps, for the reasons one might expect. It doesn't necessarily reduce the amount of code you'll have to write; indeed, in some cases using a storyboard may compel you to write *more* code, and in a less readable and maintainable way, than if you were creating your view controllers manually. But a storyboard does clarify the relationships between your view controllers over the course of your app's lifetime. Instead of having to hunt around in each of your classes to see which class creates which view controller and when, you can view and manage the chain of view controller creation graphically in the nib editor. Figure 6-9 shows the storyboard of a small test app.

A storyboard, as I've already explained, is basically a collection of view controller nibs (scenes) and view nibs. Each view controller is instantiated from its own nib, as needed, and will then obtain its view, as needed — typically from a view nib that you've config-

---

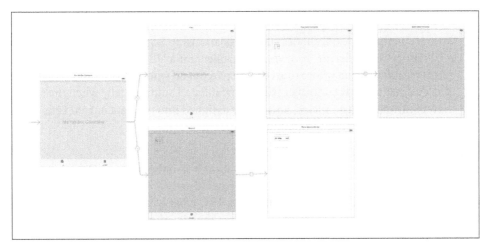

Figure 6-9. The storyboard of an app

ured in the same storyboard by editing the view controller's view. I described this process in detail, and listed the ways in which a view controller in a storyboard can be instantiated, in "Storyboard-Instantiated View Controller" on page 267.

One of those ways is that your code could instantiate a view controller *directly* from a storyboard, by calling `instantiateInitialViewController` or `instantiateView-ControllerWithIdentifier:`. The other three ways are automatic:

Initial view controller
> If your app has a main storyboard, as specified by its *Info.plist*, that storyboard's initial view controller will be instantiated and assigned as the window's `rootView-Controller` automatically as the app launches. To specify that a view controller is a storyboard's initial view controller, check the "Is Initial View Controller" checkbox in its Attributes inspector. This will cause any existing initial view controller to lose its initial view controller status. The initial view controller is distinguished graphically in the canvas by an arrow pointing to it from the left, and in the document outline by the presence of the Storyboard Entry Point.

Relationship
> Two built-in parent view controllers can specify their children directly in the storyboard, setting their `viewControllers` array:

> - UITabBarController can specify multiple children.
> - UINavigationController can specify its single initial child (its root view controller).

To add a view controller as a `viewControllers` child to a parent view controller, Control-drag from the parent view controller to the child view controller; in the little HUD that appears, choose (under Relationship Segue) "view controllers" for a UITabBarController, or "root view controller" for a UINavigationController. The result is a *relationship* whose source is the parent and whose destination is the child. The destination view controller will be instantiated automatically when the source view controller is instantiated, and will be assigned into its `viewControllers` array, thus making it a child and retaining it.

Triggered segue

A triggered segue configures a *future* situation, when the segue will be *triggered*. At that time, one view controller that already exists will cause the instantiation of another, bringing the latter into existence. Two types of triggered segue are particularly common; they have special names in the nib editor if your storyboard uses size classes:

Show (without size classes: "push")

The future view controller will be pushed onto the stack of the navigation controller of which the existing view controller is already a child.

The name "show" comes from the `showViewController:sender:` method, which pushes a view controller onto the parent navigation controller if there is one, but behaves adaptively if there is not (I'll talk more about that in Chapter 9).

Present modally (without size classes: "modal")

The future view controller will be a presented view controller (and the existing view controller will be its original presenter).

Unlike a relationship, a triggered segue does not have to emanate from a view controller; it can emanate from certain kinds of gesture recognizer, or from an appropriate view (such as a button or a table view cell) in the first view controller's view. This is a graphical shorthand signifying that the segue should be triggered, bringing the second view controller into existence, when a tap or other gesture occurs.

To create a triggered segue, Control-drag from the view in the first view controller, or from the first view controller itself, to the second view controller. In the little HUD that appears, choose the type of segue you want (listed under Action Segue if you dragged from a button, or Manual Segue if you dragged from the view controller).

Apple's segue nomenclature is confusing and inconsistent, and Apple itself seems unsettled by its own choice of names. Is a relationship a kind of segue, as in the HUD ("relationship segue") or a different kind of connection altogether, as in the document outline ("relationship")? Is a triggered segue a triggered segue, as in the WWDC 2015 videos, a manual segue or action segue, as in the HUD, or simply a segue, as in the document outline? Even the individual segue names are in doubt: in the Segue pop-up menu in the Attributes inspector, a push segue is called "Show (e.g. Push)" — a clear case of namer's remorse.

Triggered Segues

A triggered segue (or simply segue), such as a push segue (show) or a modal segue (present modally), is a full-fledged object, an instance of UIStoryboardSegue (or your custom subclass thereof), and it can be configured in the nib editor through its Attributes inspector. In a storyboard, however, it is not a nib object, in the sense that it is not instantiated by the loading of a nib, and it cannot be pointed to by an outlet. Rather, it will be instantiated when the segue is triggered, at which time its designated initializer will be called, namely `init(identifier:source:destination:)`.

A segue's `source` and `destination` are the two view controllers between which it runs. The segue is directional, so the source and destination are clearly distinguished. The source view controller is the one that will exist already, before the segue is triggered; the destination view controller will be instantiated together with the segue itself, when the segue is triggered.

A segue's `identifier` is a string. You can set this string for a segue in a storyboard through its Attributes inspector; this can be useful when you want to trigger the segue manually in code (you'll specify it by means of its identifier), or when you have code that can receive a segue as parameter and you need to distinguish which segue this is.

Triggered segue behavior

The default behavior of a segue, when it is triggered, is exactly the behavior of the corresponding manual transition described earlier in this chapter:

Push segue

> The segue is going to call `pushViewController:animated:` for you (if we are in a navigation interface).

Modal segue

> The segue is going to call `presentViewController:animated:completion:` for you. Therefore, the Attributes inspector for this kind of segue also lets you specify the Presentation (equivalent to the view controller's `modalPresentationStyle`) and the Transition (equivalent to the view controller's `modalTransitionStyle`); if you change these settings from Default, the segue will set that property of the destination

view controller, overriding whatever setting the destination view controller already has. The Animates checkbox is effectively the same as the second argument in `presentViewController:animated:completion:`.

You can further customize a triggered segue's behavior by providing your own UIStoryboardSegue subclass. The key thing is that you must implement your custom segue's `perform` method, which will be called after the segue is triggered and instantiated, in order to do the actual transition from one view controller to another. New in Xcode 7 and iOS 9, you can do this even for a push segue or a modal segue: in the Attributes inspector for the segue, you specify your UIStoryboardSegue subclass, and in that subclass, you call `super` in your `perform` implementation. Let's say, for example, that you want to add a custom transition animation to a modal segue. You can do this by writing a segue class that makes itself the destination controller's transitioning delegate in its `perform` implementation before calling `super`:

```
class MyCoolSegue: UIStoryboardSegue {
    override func perform() {
        let dest = self.destinationViewController
        dest.modalPresentationStyle = .Custom
        dest.transitioningDelegate = self
        super.perform()
    }
}
```

The rest is then exactly as in "Custom Presented View Controller Transition" on page 326. For example, the segue might proceed to make itself the animation controller as well:

```
extension MyCoolSegue: UIViewControllerTransitioningDelegate {
    func animationControllerForPresentedController(
        presented: UIViewController,
        presentingController presenting: UIViewController,
        sourceController source: UIViewController)
        -> UIViewControllerAnimatedTransitioning? {
            return self
    }
    func animationControllerForDismissedController(
        dismissed: UIViewController)
        -> UIViewControllerAnimatedTransitioning? {
            return self
    }
}
```

It would then provide the custom animations:

```
extension MyCoolSegue: UIViewControllerAnimatedTransitioning {
    func transitionDuration(
        transitionContext: UIViewControllerContextTransitioning?)
        -> NSTimeInterval {
            return 0.8
    }
```

```
func animateTransition(transitionContext: UIViewControllerContextTransitioning) {
    let vc1 = transitionContext.viewControllerForKey(
        UITransitionContextFromViewControllerKey)!
    let vc2 = transitionContext.viewControllerForKey(
        UITransitionContextToViewControllerKey)!
    let con = transitionContext.containerView()!
    let r1start = transitionContext.initialFrameForViewController(vc1)
    let r2end = transitionContext.finalFrameForViewController(vc2)
    if let v2 = transitionContext.viewForKey(
        UITransitionContextToViewKey) {
            // ... provide presenting animation ...
    } else if let v1 = transitionContext.viewForKey(
        UITransitionContextFromViewKey) {
            // ... provide dismissing animation ...
    }
  }
}
```

You can also create a *completely* custom segue. To do so, in the HUD when you Control-drag to create the segue, ask for a Custom segue, and then, in the Attributes inspector, specify your UIStoryboardSegue subclass. Again, you must override perform, but now you *don't* call super — the whole transition is completely up to you. Your perform implementation can access the segue's identifier, sourceViewController, and destinationViewController properties. The destinationViewController has already been instantiated, but that's all; doing something with this view controller so as to make it a child view controller or presented view controller, retaining it and causing its view to appear in the interface, is entirely up to your code.

How a segue is triggered

A triggered segue will be triggered in one of two ways:

Through a user gesture
> If a segue emanates from a gesture recognizer or from a tappable view, it will be triggered automatically when the tap or other gesture occurs. Your source view controller class can prevent this, if you have overridden shouldPerformSegueWith-Identifier:sender:. It returns a Bool (and the default is true), so if you don't want this segue triggered on this occasion, return false.

In code
> If a segue emanates from a view controller as a whole, then triggering it is up to your code. Send performSegueWithIdentifier:sender: to the source view controller. (In this case, shouldPerformSegueWithIdentifier:sender: will not be called.)

View controller communication

When a segue is triggered, the destination view controller is instantiated automatically; your code does not instantiate it. This raises a crucial question: how on earth are you going to communicate between the source view controller and the destination view controller? This, you'll remember, was the subject of an earlier section of this chapter ("Communication With a Presented View Controller" on page 290), where I used this code as an example:

```
let svc = SecondViewController(
    nibName: "SecondViewController", bundle: nil)
svc.data = "This is very important data!"
svc.delegate = self
self.presentViewController(svc, animated:true, completion:nil)
```

In that code, the first view controller creates the second view controller, and therefore has a reference to it at that moment. Thus, it has an opportunity of passing along some data to it before presenting it. With a modal segue, however, the second view controller is instantiated for you, and the segue itself is going to call `presentView-Controller:animated:completion:`. So when and how will the first view controller be able to set `svc.data` and set itself as `svc`'s delegate?

The answer is that, after the segue has instantiated the second view controller but before it is performed, the source view controller is sent `prepareForSegue:sender:`. This is the moment when the source view controller and the destination view controller meet! The source view controller can thus perform configurations on the destination view controller, hand it data, and so forth. The source view controller can work out which segue is being triggered by examining the segue's `identifier` and `destinationView-Controller` properties, and the `sender` is the interface object that was tapped to trigger the segue (or, if `performSegueWithIdentifier:sender:` was called in code, whatever object was supplied as the `sender:` argument).

This solves the communication problem, though in a clumsy way; `prepareFor-Segue:sender:` feels like a blunt instrument. The `destinationViewController` arrives typed as a generic UIViewController, and it is up to your code to know its actual type, cast it, and configure it. Moreover, if more than one segue emanates from a view controller, they are all bottlenecked through the same `prepareForSegue:sender:` implementation, which thus devolves into an ugly collection of conditions to distinguish them.

Container Views and Embed Segues

As I mentioned earlier, the only parent view controllers for which you can create relationship segues specifying their children in a storyboard are the built-in UITabBar-Controller and UINavigationController. That's because the nib editor understands how they work. If you write your own custom container view controller, the nib editor doesn't even know that your view controller *is* a container view controller, so it can't be the source of a relationship segue.

Nevertheless, you can perform some initial parent–child configuration of your custom container view controller in a storyboard, if your situation conforms to these assumptions:

- Your parent view controller will have one initial child view controller.
- You want the child view controller's view placed somewhere in the parent view controller's view when the child view controller is instantiated.

Those are reasonable assumptions, and you can work around them if they don't quite give the desired effect. For example, if your parent view controller is to have additional children, you can always add them later, in code; and if the child view controller's view is not to be initially visible in the parent view controller's view, you can always hide it.

To configure your parent view controller in a storyboard, drag a Container View object from the Object library into the parent view controller's view in the canvas. The result is a view, together with an *embed* segue from it to an additional child view controller. You can then assign the child view controller its correct class in its Identity inspector. Alternatively, delete the child view controller, replace it with a different view controller, and Control-drag from the container view to this view controller and, in the HUD, specify an embed segue.

When an embed segue is triggered, the destination view controller is instantiated and made the source view controller's child, and its view is placed exactly inside the container view as its subview. Thus, the container view is not only a way of generating the embed segue, but also a way of specifying where you want the child view controller's view to go. The entire child-addition dance is performed correctly and automatically for you: addChildViewController: is called, the child's view is put into the interface, and didMoveToParentViewController: is called.

Despite its superficial resemblance to a relationship segue, an embed segue is a triggered segue. It can have an identifier, and the standard messages are sent to the source view controller when the segue is triggered. Nevertheless, it has this similarity to a relationship: when the source (parent) view controller is instantiated, the runtime wants to trigger the segue automatically, instantiating the child view controller and embedding its view in the container view *now*. If that isn't what you want, override shouldPerformSegueWithIdentifier:sender: in the parent view controller to return false for this segue, and call performSegueWithIdentifier:sender: later when you do want the child view controller instantiated.

The parent view controller is sent prepareForSegue:sender: before the child's view loads. At this time, the child has not yet been added to the parent's childViewControllers array. If you allow the segue to be triggered when the parent view controller is instantiated, then by the time the parent's `viewDidLoad` is called, the child's `viewDid-Load` has been called, the child has been added to the parent's `childViewControllers`, and the child's view is inside the parent's view.

Subsequently replacing one child view controller's view with another in the interface will require that you call `transitionFromViewController:...` just as you would have done if a storyboard weren't involved (as I described earlier in this chapter). Still, you can configure this through a storyboard as well, by using a custom segue and a UIStoryboardSegue subclass.

Storyboard References

New in Xcode 7 and iOS 9, when you create a triggered segue in the storyboard, you don't have to Control-drag to a view controller as the destination; instead, you can Control-drag to a *storyboard reference* which you have previously placed in the canvas of this storyboard. A storyboard reference is a *placeholder* for a specific view controller. Thus, instead of a large and complicated network of segues running all over your storyboard, possibly crisscrossing in confusing ways, you can effectively *jump* through the storyboard reference to the actual view controller.

To specify what view controller a storyboard reference stands for, you need to perform two steps:

1. Select the view controller and, in the Identity inspector, give it a Storyboard ID.
2. Select the storyboard reference and, in the Attributes inspector, enter that same Storyboard ID value as its Referenced ID.

But wait — there's more! The referenced view controller doesn't even have to be in the same storyboard as the storyboard reference. You can use a storyboard reference to jump to *a different storyboard*. This allows you to organize your app's interface into multiple storyboards. This was always possible, but loading any storyboards apart from the automatically loaded main storyboard was up to you (in code). With a storyboard reference that leads into a different storyboard, that storyboard is loaded *automatically*.

To configure a storyboard reference to refer to a view controller in a different storyboard, use the Storyboard pop-up menu in its Attributes inspector. The rule is that if you specify the Storyboard but not the Referenced ID, the storyboard reference stands for the target storyboard's initial view controller (the one marked as the Storyboard Entry Point in that storyboard's document outline). If you do specify the Referenced ID, then of course the storyboard reference stands for the view controller with that Storyboard ID in the target storyboard.

This is a welcome and long-anticipated feature, which should make storyboards much more convenient to use.

Unwind Segues

Storyboards and segues would appear to be useful only half the time, because segues are asymmetrical. There is a push segue but no pop segue. There is a present modally segue but no dismiss segue.

In a nutshell, you can't use a normal segue to mean "go back." Triggering a triggered segue *instantiates* the destination view controller; it *creates a new view controller instance*. But when dismissing a presented view controller or popping a pushed view controller, we don't need any *new* view controller instances. We want to return, somehow, to an *existing instance* of a view controller.

 A common mistake among beginners is to make a triggered segue from view controller A to view controller B, and then try to express the notion "go back" by making *another* triggered segue from view controller B to view controller A. The result, of course, is not presentation and subsequent dismissal, but presentation piled on presentation, or push piled on push, one view controller instantiated on top of another on top of another. *Do not construct a cycle of segues.* (Unfortunately, the nib editor doesn't alert you to this mistake.)

The solution is an *unwind segue*. An unwind segue *does* let you express the notion "go back" in a storyboard. Basically, it lets you jump to *any* view controller that is already instantiated further up your view controller hierarchy, destroying the source view controller and any intervening view controllers in good order.

Creating an unwind segue

Before you can create an unwind segue, you must implement an *unwind method* in the class of any view controller represented in the storyboard. This should be a method marked @IBAction as a hint to the storyboard editor, and taking a single parameter, a UIStoryboardSegue. You can call it unwind: if you like, but the name doesn't really matter:

```
@IBAction func unwind(seg:UIStoryboardSegue!) {
    // ...
}
```

Think of this method as a marker, specifying that the view controller in which it appears can be the destination for an unwind segue. It is, in fact, a little more than a marker: it will also be called when the unwind segue is triggered. But its marker functionality is much more important — so much so that, in many cases, you won't give this method any code at all. Its *presence*, and its name, are what matters.

Now you can create an unwind segue. Doing so involves the use of the Exit proxy object that appears in every scene of a storyboard. Control-drag from the view controller you

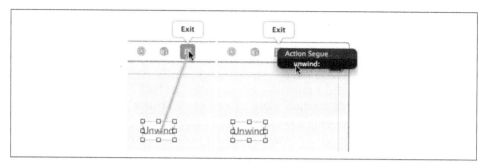

Figure 6-10. Creating an unwind segue

want to go back *from*, or from something like a button in that view controller's view, connecting it to the Exit proxy object *in the same scene* (Figure 6-10). A little HUD appears, listing all the unwind methods known to this storyboard (similar to how action methods are listed in the HUD when you connect a button to its target). Click the name of the unwind method you want. You have now made an unwind segue, bound to that unwind method.

How an unwind segue works

When the unwind segue is triggered, the following steps are performed:

1. The source view controller's `shouldPerformSegueWithIdentifier:sender:` is called — just as for a normal segue. This is your chance to stop the whole process dead at this point by returning `false`.

2. The name of the unwind method to which the unwind segue is bound is *only a name*. The unwind segue's source view controller is the view controller that contains it. But *its destination view controller is unknown*. Therefore, the runtime now starts walking *up the view controller hierarchy* looking for a destination view controller. Put simply, the first view controller it finds that *implements the unwind method* will, by default, be the destination view controller.

3. The source view controller's `prepareForSegue:sender:` is called — just as for a normal segue. The two view controllers are now in contact (because the other view controller is the segue's `destinationViewController`). This is an opportunity for the source view controller to hand information to the destination view controller before being destroyed! (Thus, an unwind segue is an alternative to a `delegate` property as a way of putting one view controller into communication with another: see "Communication With a Presented View Controller" on page 290.)

4. The destination view controller's unwind method is called. Its parameter is the segue; this segue can be identified through its `identifier` property. The two view controllers are now in contact *again* (because the other view controller is the segue's

`sourceViewController`). It is perfectly reasonable, as I've already said, for the unwind method body to be empty; the unwind method's real purpose is to mark this view controller as the destination view controller.

5. The segue is performed, *destroying* the source controller and any intervening view controllers up to (but not including) the destination view controller, in good order.

Now I'll go back and explain in detail the second step and the last step: how the destination view controller is found, and how the segue is actually performed. This is partly out of sheer interest (they are both devilishly clever), and partly in case you need to customize the process.

 These procedures are both new in iOS 9. Apple has revised unwind segues, sometimes quite dramatically, with each major iOS update since they were introduced in iOS 6; this newest revision is a brilliant simplification and rationalization.

How the destination view controller is found

We begin with how the destination view controller is located. The process is initially one of walking *up* the view controller hierarchy. What do I mean by "up" the hierarchy? Well, every view controller has either a `parentViewController` or a `presentingView-Controller`, so the next view controller up the hierarchy is that view controller. However, it might also be necessary to walk back *down* the hierarchy, to a child (at some depth) of one of the parents we encounter. In iOS 8 and before, it was necessary for every parent view controller to know how to find the unwind segue's destination view controller amongst its children. But in iOS 9, the runtime discovers the view controller hierarchy and, if needed, walks both up and then down the hierarchy for you.

Here's how it does that:

1. At each step up the view controller hierarchy, the runtime sends this view controller the following event:

   • `allowedChildViewControllersForUnwindingFromSource:`

   This view controller's job is to supply an *array of its own direct children*. The array can be empty, but it must be an array. To do so, the view controller calls this method:

   • `childViewControllerContainingSegueSource:`

   This tells the view controller which of its own children is, or is the ultimate parent of, the source view controller. We don't want to go down *that* branch of the view hierarchy; that's the branch we just came *up*. So this view controller *subtracts* that view controller from the array of its own child view controllers, and returns the resulting array.

2. There are two possible kinds of result from the previous step (the value returned from `allowedChildViewControllers...`):

There are children

> If the previous step yielded an array with one or more child view controllers in it, the runtime performs step 1 on all of them (until it finds the destination), thus going *down* the view hierarchy.

There are no children

> If, on the other hand, the previous step yielded an *empty* array, the runtime asks *this same* view controller the following question:
>
> • `canPerformUnwindSegueAction(fromViewController:withSender:)`
>
> The default implementation of this method is simply to call `respondsTo-Selector:` on `self`, asking whether this view controller contains an implementation of the unwind method we're looking for. The result is a Bool. If it is `true`, we *stop. This is the destination view controller.* If it is `false`, we continue with the search *up* the view controller hierarchy, finding the next view controller and performing step 1 again.

A moment's thought will reveal that the recursive application of this algorithm will eventually arrive at an existing view controller instance with an implementation of the unwind method if there is one. Okay, maybe a moment's thought didn't reveal that to you, so here's an actual example. I'll use the app whose storyboard is pictured in Figure 6-9. Its root view controller is a UITabBarController with two children:

• The first child is a UINavigationController with a root view controller called First-ViewController, which has a push segue to another view controller called Extra-ViewController.

• The second child is called SecondViewController, which has a modal segue to another view controller called ExtraViewController2.

The unwind method is in FirstViewController, and is called `iAmFirst:`. The corresponding unwind segue, whose action is `"iAmFirst:"`, is triggered from a button in ExtraViewController2. Assume that the user starts in the tab bar controller's first view controller, where she triggers the push segue, thus showing ExtraViewController. She then switches to the tab bar controller's second view controller, where she triggers the modal segue, thus showing ExtraViewController2. All the view controllers pictured in Figure 6-9 now exist simultaneously.

The user now taps the button in ExtraViewController2 and thus triggers the `"iAm-First:"` unwind segue. *What will happen?* First, ExtraViewController2 is sent `should-PerformSegueWithIdentifier:` and returns `true`, permitting the segue to go forward.

The runtime now needs to walk the view controller hierarchy and locate the iAmFirst: method. Here's how it does that:

1. We start by walking *up* the view hierarchy. We thus arrive at the original presenter from which ExtraViewController2 was presented, namely SecondViewController. The runtime sends SecondViewController allowedChildViewControllersFor- UnwindingFromSource:; the childless SecondViewController returns an empty array. So the runtime also asks SecondViewController canPerformUnwindSegue- Action:... to find out whether this is the destination; SecondViewController returns false, so we know this is *not* the destination.

2. We therefore proceed *up* the view hierarchy to SecondViewController's parent, the UITabBarController. The runtime sends the UITabBarController allowedChild- ViewControllersForUnwindingFromSource:. The UITabBarController has two child view controllers, namely the UINavigationController and SecondView- Controller — but one of them, SecondViewController, contains the source (as it discovers by calling childViewControllerContainingSegueSource:). Therefore the UITabBarController returns an array containing just one child view controller, namely the UINavigationController.

3. The runtime has received an array with a child in it; it therefore proceeds *down* the view hierarchy to that child, the UINavigationController, and asks it the same question: allowedChildViewControllersForUnwindingFromSource:. The navigation controller has two children, namely FirstViewController and ExtraView- Controller, and neither of them is or contains the source, so it returns an array containing both of them.

4. The runtime therefore notes down that it has two hierarchy branches to explore, and proceeds to explore them:

   a. The runtime starts with ExtraViewController, asking it allowedChildView- ControllersForUnwindingFromSource:. The reply is an empty array, so the runtime asks canPerformUnwindSegueAction:... to find out whether this is the destination — but ExtraViewController replies false.

   b. So much for that branch of the UINavigationController's children; we've reached a dead end. So the runtime proceeds to the other branch, namely FirstView- Controller. The runtime asks FirstViewController allowedChildView- ControllersForUnwindingFromSource:. The reply is an empty array, so the runtime asks canPerformUnwindSegueAction:... to find out whether this is the destination — and FirstViewController replies true. We've found the des- tination view controller!

The destination having been found, the runtime now sends prepareForSegue:sender: to the source, and then calls the destination's unwind method, iAmFirst:. We are now ready to *perform* the segue.

How an unwind segue is performed

The way an unwind segue is performed is just as ingenious as how the destination is found. During the walk, the runtime *remembers* the walk. Thus, it knows where all the presented view controllers are, and it knows where all the parent view controllers are — the view controllers that returned an array containing view controllers from allowed-ChildViewControllersForUnwindingFromSource:. Thus we have a *path* of presenting view controllers and parent view controllers between the source and the destination. The runtime then proceeds as follows:

- For any presented view controllers, the runtime itself calls dismissViewController-Animated:completion: on the presenting view controller.

- For any parent view controllers, the runtime tells each of them, in turn, to unwind-ForSegue:towardsViewController:.

The second parameter of unwindForSegue:towardsViewController: is the *direct child* of this parent view controller leading down the branch where the destination lives. This child might or might not *be* the destination, but that's no concern of this parent view controller. Its job is merely to *get us onto that branch*, whatever that may mean for this kind of parent view controller. A moment's thought will reveal (don't you wish I'd stop saying that?) that if each parent view controller along the path of parent view controllers does this correctly, we will in fact end up at the destination, releasing in good order all intervening view controllers that need to be released. This procedure, new to iOS 9, is called *incremental unwind*.

Thus, the unwind procedure for our example runs as follows:

1. The runtime sends dismissViewControllerAnimated:completion: to the root view controller, namely the UITabBarController. Thus, ExtraViewController2 is destroyed in good order.

2. The runtime sends unwindForSegue:towardsViewController: to the UITabBar-Controller. The second parameter is the tab bar controller's first child, the UINavigationController. The UITabBarController therefore changes its selected-ViewController to be the UINavigationController.

3. The runtime sends unwindForSegue:towardsViewController: to the UINavigationController. The second parameter is the FirstViewController. The navigation controller therefore pops its stack down to the FirstViewController.

Thus, ExtraViewController is destroyed in good order, and we are back at the First-ViewController — which is exactly what was supposed to happen.

Unwind segue customization

Knowing how an unwind segue works, you can see how to intervene in and customize the process:

- In a custom view controller that contains an implementation of the unwind method, you might implement `canPerformUnwindSegueAction:fromViewController:withSender:` to return `false` instead of `true` so that it doesn't become the destination on this occasion.

- In a custom parent view controller, you might implement `allowedChildViewControllersForUnwindingFromSource:`. In all probability, your implementation will consist simply of listing your `childViewControllers`, calling `childViewControllerContainingSegueSource:` to find out which of your children is or contains the source, subtracting that child from the array, and returning the array.

- In a custom parent view controller, you might implement `unwindForSegue:towardsViewController:`. The second parameter is one of your current children; you will do whatever it means for this parent view controller to make this the currently displayed child.

 Do *not* override `childViewControllerContainingSegueSource:`. It knows more than you do; you wouldn't want to interfere with its operation.

View Controller Lifetime Events

As views come and go, driven by view controllers and the actions of the user, events arrive that give your view controller the opportunity to respond to the various stages of its own existence and the management of its view. By overriding these methods, your UIViewController subclass can perform appropriate tasks at appropriate moments. Here's a list:

viewDidLoad
> The view controller has obtained its view. See the discussion earlier in this chapter of how a view controller gets its view. Recall that this does *not* mean that the view is in the interface or even that it has been given its correct size.

`willTransitionToTraitCollection:withTransitionCoordinator:`
`viewWillTransitionToSize:withTransitionCoordinator:`
`traitCollectionDidChange:`

> The view controller's view is being resized or the trait environment is changing (or both). See the discussion of resizing events earlier in this chapter. Your implementation of the first two methods should call `super`.

`updateViewConstraints`
`viewWillLayoutSubviews`
`viewDidLayoutSubviews`

> The view is receiving `updateConstraints` and `layoutSubviews` events. See Chapter 1, and the discussion of resizing events earlier in this chapter. Your implementation of `updateViewConstraints` should call `super`.

`willMoveToParentViewController:`
`didMoveToParentViewController:`

> The view controller is being added or removed as a child of another view controller. See the discussion of container view controllers earlier in this chapter.

`viewWillAppear:`
`viewDidAppear:`
`viewWillDisappear:`
`viewDidDisappear:`

> The view is being added to or removed from the interface. This includes being supplanted by another view controller's view or being restored through the removal of another view controller's view. A view that has appeared (or has not yet disappeared) is in the window; it is part of your app's active view hierarchy. A view that has disappeared (or has not yet appeared) is not in the window; its `window` is `nil`. You should call `super` in your override of any of these four methods; if you forget to do so, things may go wrong in subtle ways.

> To distinguish more precisely *why* your view is appearing or disappearing, call any of these methods on `self`:

> - `isBeingPresented`
> - `isBeingDismissed`
> - `isMovingToParentViewController`
> - `isMovingFromParentViewController`

A good way to get a sense for when these events are useful is to track the sequence in which they normally occur. Take, for example, a UIViewController being pushed onto the stack of a navigation controller. It receives, in this order, the following messages:

- `willMoveToParentViewController:`
- `viewWillAppear:`
- `updateViewConstraints`
- `traitCollectionDidChange:`
- `viewWillLayoutSubviews`
- `viewDidLayoutSubviews`
- `viewDidAppear:`
- `didMoveToParentViewController:`

(There is then a second round of layout messages.)

When this same UIViewController is popped off the stack of the navigation controller, it receives, in this order, the following messages:

- `willMoveToParentViewController:` (with parameter `nil`)
- `viewWillDisappear:`
- `updateViewConstraints`
- `viewWillLayoutSubviews`
- `viewDidLayoutSubviews`
- `viewDidDisappear:`
- `didMoveToParentViewController:` (with parameter `nil`)

Disappearance, as I mentioned a moment ago, can happen because another view controller's view supplants this view controller's view. For example, consider a UIView-Controller functioning as the top (and visible) view controller of a navigation controller. When another view controller is pushed on top of it, the first view controller gets these messages:

- `viewWillDisappear:`
- `updateViewConstraints`
- `viewWillLayoutSubviews`
- `viewDidLayoutSubviews`
- `viewDidDisappear:`
- `didMoveToParentViewController:`

The converse is also true. For example, when a view controller is popped from a navigation controller, the view controller that was below it in the stack (the back view controller) receives these events:

- `viewWillAppear:`
- `updateViewConstraints`
- `viewWillLayoutSubviews`
- `viewDidLayoutSubviews`
- `viewDidAppear`
- `didMoveToParentViewController:`

(There is then a second round of layout messages.)

Incoherencies in View Controller Events

Unfortunately, the exact sequence of events and the number of times they will be called for any given view controller transition situation sometimes seems nondeterministic or incoherent. The previous section contains a number of cases in point, and there are others. For example:

- Sometimes `didMoveToParentViewController:` arrives without a corresponding `willMoveToParentViewController:`.
- Sometimes `didMoveToParentViewController:` arrives even though this view controller was previously the child of this parent and remains the child of this parent.
- Sometimes the layout events (`updateViewConstraints`, `viewWillLayoutSubviews`, `viewDidLayoutSubviews`) arrive more than once for the same view controller for the same transition.
- Sometimes the layout events arrive needlessly, as when the view controller's view is about to leave the interface and the view controller is about to be destroyed.
- Sometimes `viewWillAppear:` or `viewWillDisappear:` arrives without the corresponding `viewDidAppear:` or `viewDidDisappear:`. For example, if an interactive transition animation begins and is cancelled, the cancelled view controller receives `viewWillAppear:` at the start, *without* `viewDidAppear:`, and receives `viewWillDisappear:` and `viewDidDisappear:` at the end.

The best advice I can offer is that you should try to structure your code in such a way that incoherencies of this sort don't matter. For example, if you do something in `viewWillAppear:` that needs to be cancelled or reversed in `viewDidAppear:`, you should also cancel or reverse it in `viewWillDisappear:`.

Appear and Disappear Events

The Appear and Disappear events are particularly appropriate for making sure that a view reflects the model or some form of saved state whenever it appears. Changes to the interface performed in viewDidAppear: or viewWillDisappear: may be visible to the user as they occur! If that's not what you want, use the other member of the pair. For example, in a certain view containing a long scrollable text, I want the scroll position to be the same when the user returns to this view as it was when the user left it, so I save the scroll position in viewWillDisappear: and restore it in viewWillAppear: (not view-DidAppear:, where the user might see the scroll position jump).

These methods are useful also when something must be true exactly so long as a view is in the interface. For example, a repeating NSTimer that must be running while a view is present can be started in the view controller's viewDidAppear: and stopped in its view-WillDisappear:. (This architecture also allows you to avoid the retain cycle that could result if you waited to invalidate the timer in a deinit that might otherwise never arrive.)

A view does not disappear if a presented view controller's view merely covers it rather than supplanting it. For example, a view controller that presents another view controller using the .FormSheet presentation style gets no lifetime events during presentation and dismissal.

A view does not disappear merely because the app is backgrounded and suspended. Once suspended, your app might be killed. So you cannot rely on viewWillDisappear: and viewDidDisappear: alone for saving data that the app will need the next time it launches. If you are to cover every case, you may need to ensure that your data-saving code also runs in response to an application lifetime event such as applicationWill-ResignActive: or applicationDidEnterBackground: (and see Appendix A for a discussion of the application lifetime events).

Event Forwarding to a Child View Controller

A custom container (parent) view controller, as I explained earlier, must effectively send willMoveToParentViewController: and didMoveToParentViewController: to its children manually.

It must also forward resizing events to its children. This will happen automatically if you call super in your implementation of willTransitionToTraitCollection:... and viewWillTransitionToSize:.... By the same token, if you implement these methods, failure to call super may prevent them from being forwarded correctly to the child view controller.

The Appear and Disappear events are normally passed along automatically. However, you can take charge by implementing this method:

shouldAutomaticallyForwardAppearanceMethods

> If you override this method to return `false`, you are responsible for seeing that these methods on your view controller's children are called:
>
> - viewWillAppear:
> - viewDidAppear:
> - viewWillDisappear:
> - viewDidDisappear:
>
> You do *not* do this by calling these methods directly. The reason is that you have no access to the correct moment for sending them. Instead, you call these two methods on your child view controller:
>
> - beginAppearanceTransition:animated:; the first parameter is a Bool saying whether this view controller's view is about to appear (true) or disappear (false)
> - endAppearanceTransition

Here's what to do if you've implemented shouldAutomaticallyForwardAppearance-Methods to return false. There are two main occasions on which your custom container view controller must forward Appear and Disappear events to a child.

First, what happens when your custom container view controller's own view itself appears or disappears? If it has a child view controller's view within its own view, it must implement and forward all four Appear and Disappear events to that child. You'll need an implementation along these lines, for each of the four events:

```
override func viewWillAppear(animated: Bool) {
    super.viewWillAppear(animated)
    let child = // whatever
    if child.isViewLoaded() && child.view.superview != nil {
        child.beginAppearanceTransition(true, animated: true)
    }
}
override func viewDidAppear(animated: Bool) {
    super.viewDidAppear(animated)
    let child = // whatever
    if child.isViewLoaded() && child.view.superview != nil {
        child.endAppearanceTransition()
    }
}
```

(The implementations for viewDidAppear: and viewDidDisappear: are similar, except that the first argument for beginAppearanceTransition: is false.)

Second, what happens when you swap one view controller's child for another in your interface? You must *not* call the UIViewController method transitionFromView-Controller:toViewController:...! It takes charge of sending the four events to the children itself, and it isn't going to do so correctly in this situation. Instead, you must perform the transition animation directly. A minimal correct implementation might involve the UIView class method transitionFromView:toView:... (see Chapter 4). Here, you can and should call beginAppearanceTransition: and endAppearanceTransition yourself.

Here's an example of a parent view controller swapping one child view controller and its view for another, while taking charge of notifying the child view controllers of the appearance and disappearance of their views. I've put asterisks to call attention to the additional method calls that forward the Appear and Disappear events to the children (fromvc and tovc):

```
self.addChildViewController(tovc)
fromvc.willMoveToParentViewController(nil)
fromvc.beginAppearanceTransition(false, animated:true) // *
tovc.beginAppearanceTransition(true, animated:true) // *
UIView.transitionFromView(fromvc.view,
    toView:tovc.view,
    duration:0.4,
    options:.TransitionFlipFromLeft,
    completion:{
        _ in
        tovc.endAppearanceTransition() // *
        fromvc.endAppearanceTransition() // *
        tovc.didMoveToParentViewController(self)
        fromvc.removeFromParentViewController()
})
```

View Controller Memory Management

Memory is at a premium on a mobile device. Thus you want to minimize your app's use of memory. Your motivations are partly altruistic and partly selfish. While your app is running, other apps are suspended in the background; you want to keep your memory usage as low as possible so that those other apps have room to remain suspended and the user can readily switch to them from your app. You also want to prevent your own app from being terminated! If your app is backgrounded and suspended while using a lot of memory, it may be terminated in the background when memory runs short. If your app uses an inordinate amount of memory while in the foreground, it may be summarily killed before the user's very eyes.

One strategy for avoiding using too much memory is to release any memory-hogging objects you're retaining if they are not needed at this moment. Because a view controller is the basis of so much of your application's architecture, it is likely to be a place where you'll concern yourself with releasing unneeded memory.

One of your view controller's most memory-intensive objects is its view. Fortunately, the iOS runtime manages a view controller's view's memory for you. If a view controller's view is not in the interface, it can be temporarily dispensed with. In such a situation, if memory is getting tight, then even though the view controller itself persists, and even though it retains its actual view, the runtime may release its view's backing store (the cached bitmap representing the view's drawn contents). The view will then be redrawn when and if it is to be shown again later.

In addition, if memory runs low, your view controller may be sent this message:

didReceiveMemoryWarning

Sent to a view controller to advise it of a low-memory situation. It is preceded by a call to the app delegate's applicationDidReceiveMemoryWarning:, together with a UIApplicationDidReceiveMemoryWarningNotification posted to any registered objects. You are invited to respond by releasing any data that you can do without. Do not release data that you can't readily and quickly recreate! The documentation advises that you should call super.

If you're going to release data in didReceiveMemoryWarning, you must concern yourself with how you're going to get it back. A simple and reliable mechanism is *lazy loading* — a getter that reconstructs or fetches the data if it is nil.

For example, suppose we have a property myBigData which might be a big piece of data. We make this a calculated property, storing the real data in a private property (I'll call it myBigDataReal). Our calculated property's setter simply writes through to the private property. In didReceiveMemoryWarning we write myBigData out as a file to disk (Chapter 23) and set myBigData to nil — thus setting myBigDataReal to nil as well, and releasing the big data from memory. The getter for myBigData implements lazy loading: if we try to get myBigData when myBigDataReal is nil, we attempt to fetch the data from disk — and if we succeed, we delete it from disk (to prevent stale data):

```
private var myBigDataReal : NSData!
var myBigData : NSData! {
    set (newdata) {
        self.myBigDataReal = newdata
    }
    get {
        if myBigDataReal == nil {
            let fm = NSFileManager()
            let f = (NSTemporaryDirectory() as NSString)
                .stringByAppendingPathComponent("myBigData")
            if fm.fileExistsAtPath(f) {
                self.myBigDataReal = NSData(contentsOfFile: f)
                do {
                    try fm.removeItemAtPath(f)
```

```
                } catch {
                    print("Couldn't remove temp file")
                }
            }
        }
        return self.myBigDataReal
    }
}
func saveAndReleaseMyBigData() {
    if let myBigData = self.myBigData {
        let f = (NSTemporaryDirectory() as NSString)
            .stringByAppendingPathComponent("myBigData")
        myBigData.writeToFile(f, atomically:false)
        self.myBigData = nil
    }
}
override func didReceiveMemoryWarning() {
    super.didReceiveMemoryWarning()
    self.saveAndReleaseMyBigData()
}
```

When your big data can be reconstructed from scratch on demand, you can take advantage of the built-in NSCache class, which is like a dictionary with the ability to clear out its own entries automatically under memory pressure. As in the previous example, a calculated property can be used as a façade:

```
let cache = NSCache()
var cachedData : NSData {
    let key = // ...
    var data = self.cache.objectForKey(key) as? NSData
    if data != nil {
        return data!
    }
    // ... recreate data here ...
    data = // recreated data
    self.cache.setObject(data!, forKey: key)
    return data!
}
```

Another built-in class that knows how to clear itself out is NSPurgeableData. It is a subclass of NSMutableData that adopts the NSDiscardableContent protocol (which your own classes can also adopt). NSCache knows how to work with classes that adopt NSDiscardableContent, or you can use such classes independently. To signal that the data should be discarded, send your object discardContentIfPossible. Wrap any access to data in calls to beginContentAccess and endContentAccess; the former returns a Bool to indicate whether the data was accessible. The tricky part is getting those access calls right; when you create an NSPurgeableData, you must send it an unbalanced endContentAccess to make its content discardable:

```
var purgeable = NSPurgeableData()
var purgeabledata : NSData {
    if self.purgeable.beginContentAccess() && self.purgeable.length > 0 {
        let result = self.purgeable.copy() as! NSData
        self.purgeable.endContentAccess()
        return result
    } else {
        // ... recreate data here ...
        let data = // recreated data
        self.purgeable = NSPurgeableData(data:data)
        self.purgeable.endContentAccess()
        return data
    }
}
```

(For more about NSCache and NSPurgeableData, see the "Caching and Purgeable Memory" chapter of Apple's *Memory Usage Performance Guidelines*.)

At an even lower level, you can store your data on disk (in some reasonable location such the Caches directory) and read it using NSData(contentsOfURL:options:) with an options: argument .DataReadingMappedAlways. This creates a memory-mapped data object, which has the remarkable feature that it isn't considered to belong to your memory at all; the system has no hesitation in clearing it from RAM, because it is backed through the virtual memory system by the file on disk, and will be read back into memory automatically when you next access it. This is suitable only for large immutable data, because small data runs the risk of fragmenting a virtual memory page.

To test low-memory circumstances artificially, run your app in the Simulator and choose Hardware → Simulate Memory Warning. I don't believe this has any actual effect on memory, but a memory warning of sufficient severity is sent to your app, so you can see the results of triggering your low-memory response code, including the app delegate's applicationDidReceiveMemoryWarning: and your view controller's didReceive-MemoryWarning.

On the device, the equivalent is to call an undocumented method:

```
UIApplication.sharedApplication().performSelector("_performMemoryWarning")
```

(Be sure to remove that code when it is no longer needed for testing, as the App Store won't accept it.)

You will also wish to concern yourself with releasing memory when your app is about to be suspended. If your app has been backgrounded and suspended and the system later discovers it is running short of memory, it will go hunting through the suspended apps, looking for memory hogs that it can kill in order to free up that memory. If the system decides that your suspended app is a memory hog, it isn't politely going to wake your app and send it a memory warning; it's just going to terminate your app in its sleep. The time to be concerned about releasing memory, therefore, is *before* the app is suspended. You'll probably want your view controller to be registered with the shared

application to receive `UIApplicationDidEnterBackgroundNotification`. The arrival
of this notification is an opportunity to release any easily restored memory-hogging
objects, such as `myBigData` in the previous example:

```
override func viewDidLoad() {
    super.viewDidLoad()
    NSNotificationCenter.defaultCenter().addObserver(
        self, selector: "backgrounding:",
        name: UIApplicationDidEnterBackgroundNotification,
        object: nil)
}
func backgrounding(n:NSNotification) {
    self.saveAndReleaseMyBigData()
}
```

 A very nice feature of NSCache is that it evicts its objects automatically when your
app goes into the background.

Testing how your app's memory behaves in the background isn't easy. In a WWDC 2011
video, an interesting technique is demonstrated. The app is run under Instruments on
the device, using the virtual memory instrument, and is then backgrounded by pressing
the Home button, thus revealing how much memory it voluntarily relinquishes at that
time. Then a special memory-hogging app is launched on the device: its interface loads
and displays a very large image in a UIImageView. Even though your app is backgrounded and suspended, the virtual memory instrument continues to track its memory
usage, and you can see whether further memory is reclaimed under pressure from the
demands of the memory-hogging app in the foreground.

State Restoration

When the user leaves your app and then later returns to it, one of two things might have
happened in the meantime (see Appendix A):

Your app was suspended

Your app was suspended in the background, and remained suspended while the
user did something else. When the user returns to your app, the system simply
unfreezes your app, and there it is, looking just as it did when the user left it.

Your app was terminated

Your app was suspended in the background, and then, as the user worked with other
apps, a moment came where the system decided it needed the resources (such as
memory) being held by your suspended app. Therefore it terminated your app.
When the user returns to your app, the app launches from scratch.

The user, however, doesn't know the difference between those two things, so why should the app behave differently some of the time? Ideally, it should *always* feel to the user as if the app is being resumed from where it left off the last time it was in the foreground, even if in fact the app was terminated while suspended in the background. Otherwise, as the WWDC 2013 video on this topic puts it, the user will feel that the app has "lost my place."

That's where *state restoration* comes in. Your app has a state at every moment: some view controller's view is occupying the screen, and views within it are displaying certain values (for example, a certain switch is set to On, or a certain table view is scrolled to a certain position). The idea of state restoration is to save that information when the app goes into the background, and use it to make all those things true again if the app is subsequently launched from scratch.

iOS provides a general solution to the problem of state restoration. This solution is centered around view controllers, which makes sense, since view controllers are the heart of the problem. What is the user's "place" in the app, which we don't want to "lose"? It's the chain of view controllers that got us to where we were when the app was back-grounded, along with the configuration of each one. The goal of state restoration must therefore be to *reconstruct all existing view controllers*, initializing each one into the state it previously had.

Note that *state*, in this sense, is neither user defaults nor data. If something is a preference, store it in NSUserDefaults. If something is data, keep it in a file (Chapter 23). Don't misuse the state saving and restoration mechanism for such things. The reason for this is not only conceptual; it's also because *saved state can be lost*. You don't want to commit anything to the state restoration mechanism if it would be a disaster to have lost it the next time the app launches.

For example, suppose the user kills your app outright by double-clicking the Home button to show the app switcher interface and flicking your app's snapshot upward; the system will throw away its state. Similarly, if your app crashes, the system will throw away its state. In both cases, the system assumes that something went wrong, and doesn't want to launch your app into what might be a troublesome saved state. Instead, your app will launch cleanly, from the beginning. There's no problem for the user, barring a mild inconvenience — as long as the only thing that gets thrown away is state.

How to Test State Restoration

To test whether your app is saving and restoring state as you expect:

1. Run the app as usual, in the Simulator or on a device.
2. At some point, in the Simulator or on the device, click the Home button (Hardware → Home in the Simulator). This causes the app to be suspended in good order, and state is saved.

3. Now, back in Xcode, stop the running project (Product → Stop).

4. Run the project again. If there is saved state, it is restored.

(To test the app's behavior from a truly cold start, delete it from the Simulator or device. You might need to do this after changing something about the underlying save-and-restore model.)

Apple also provides (at *http://developer.apple.com/downloads*) some debugging tools:

restorationArchiveTool *plutil* *data.data files*

> A command-line tool letting you examine a saved state archive in textual format. The archive is in a folder called Saved Application State in your app's sandboxed Library. See Chapter 23 for more about the app's sandbox, and how to copy it to your computer from a device.

StateRestorationDebugLogging.mobileconfig

> A configuration profile. When installed on a device, it causes the console to dump information as state saving and restoration proceeds.

StateRestorationDeveloperMode.mobileconfig

> A configuration profile. When installed on a device, it prevents the state archive from being jettisoned after unexpected termination of the app (a crash, or manual termination through the app switcher interface). This can allow you to test state restoration a bit more conveniently.

To install a *.mobileconfig* file on a device, the simplest approach is to email it to yourself on the device and tap the file in the Mail message. You can subsequently delete the file, if desired, through the Settings app.

Participating in State Restoration

Built-in state restoration is an opt-in technology: it operates only if you explicitly tell the system that you want to participate in it. To do so, you take three basic steps:

Implement app delegate methods

> The app delegate must implement these methods to return `true`:
>
> * `application:shouldSaveApplicationState:`
> * `application:shouldRestoreApplicationState:`
>
> (Naturally, your code can instead return `false` to prevent state from being saved or restored on some particular occasion.)

Implement `application:willFinishLaunchingWithOptions:`

> Although it is very early, `application:didFinishLaunchingWithOptions:` is too late for state restoration. Your app needs its basic interface *before* state restoration

begins. The solution is to use a different app delegate method, `application:will-`
`FinishLaunchingWithOptions:`.

Typically, you can just change "did" to "will" in the name of this method, keeping your existing code unchanged. However, your implementation *must* call `makeKey-` `AndVisible` explicitly on the window if the existing code doesn't already call it! Otherwise, the interface doesn't come into existence soon enough for restoration to happen during launch.

Provide restoration IDs

Both UIViewController and UIView have a `restorationIdentifier` property, which is a string. Setting this string to a non-`nil` value is your signal to the system that you want this view controller (or view) to participate in state restoration. If a view controller's `restorationIdentifier` is `nil`, neither it nor any subsequent view controllers down the chain will be saved or restored. (A nice feature of this architecture is that it lets you participate *partially* in state restoration, omitting some view controllers by not assigning them a restoration identifier.)

You can set the `restorationIdentifier` manually, in code; typically you'll do that early in a view controller's lifetime. If a view controller or view is instantiated from a nib, you'll want to set the restoration identifier in the nib editor; the Identity inspector has a Restoration ID field for this purpose. (If you're using a storyboard, it's a good idea, in general, to make a view controller's restoration ID in the storyboard the same as its storyboard ID, the string used to identify the view controller in a call to `instantiateViewControllerWithIdentifier:`; in fact, it's such a good idea that the storyboard editor provides a checkbox, "Use Storyboard ID," that makes the one value automatically the same as the other.)

In the case of a simple storyboard-based app, where each needed view controller instance can be reconstructed directly from the storyboard, those steps alone can be sufficient to bring state restoration to life, operating correctly at the view controller level. Let's test it. Start with a storyboard-based app with the following architecture (Figure 6-11):

- A navigation controller.
- Its root view controller, connected by a relationship from the navigation controller. Call its class RootViewController.
  - A presented view controller, connected by a modal segue from a Present button in the root view controller's view. Call its class PresentedViewController. Its view contains a Dismiss button.
- A second view controller, connected by a push segue from a Push bar button item in the root view controller's navigation item. Call its class SecondViewController.

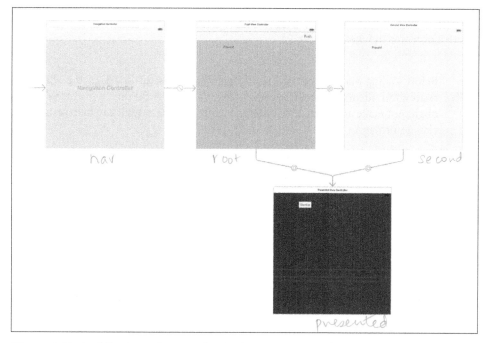

Figure 6-11. Architecture of an app for testing state restoration

- The very same presented view controller (PresentedViewController), also connected by a modal segue from a Present button in the second view controller's view.

This storyboard-based app runs perfectly with just about no code at all; all we need is an empty implementation of an unwind method in RootViewController and Second-ViewController so that we can create an unwind segue from the PresentedView-Controller Dismiss button.

We will now make this app implement state restoration:

1. Change the name of `application:didFinishLaunchingWithOptions:` in the app delegate to `application:willFinishLaunchingWithOptions:`, and insert this line of code if it isn't already present:

   ```
   self.window?.makeKeyAndVisible()
   ```

2. Implement `application:shouldSaveApplicationState:` and `application:shouldRestoreApplicationState:` in the app delegate to return `true`.

3. Give all four view controller instances in the storyboard restoration IDs: let's call them `"nav"`, `"root"`, `"second"`, and `"presented"`.

That's all! The app now saves and restores state. When we run the app, navigate to another view controller, quit, and later relaunch, the app appears in the same view controller it was in when we quit.

 Before calling makeKeyAndVisible, it may also be useful to assign the window a restoration identifier: self.window?.restorationIdentifier = "window". This might not make any detectable difference, but in some cases it can help restore size class information.

Restoration ID, Identifier Path, and Restoration Class

Having everything done for us by the storyboard reveals nothing about what's really happening. To learn more, let's rewrite the example without a storyboard. Throw away the storyboard (and delete the Main Storyboard entry from the *Info.plist*) and implement the same architecture using code alone:

```
// AppDelegate.swift:
func application(application: UIApplication,
    didFinishLaunchingWithOptions launchOptions: [NSObject: AnyObject]?)
    -> Bool {
        self.window = UIWindow()
        let rvc = RootViewController()
        let nav = UINavigationController(rootViewController:rvc)
        self.window!.rootViewController = nav
        self.window!.backgroundColor = UIColor.whiteColor()
        self.window!.makeKeyAndVisible()
        return true
}

// RootViewController.swift:
override func viewDidLoad() {
    super.viewDidLoad()
    // ... color view background, create buttons ...
}
func doPresent(sender:AnyObject?) {
    let pvc = PresentedViewController()
    self.presentViewController(pvc, animated:true, completion:nil)
}
func doPush(sender:AnyObject?) {
    let svc = SecondViewController()
    self.navigationController!.pushViewController(svc, animated:true)
}

// SecondViewController.swift:
override func viewDidLoad() {
    super.viewDidLoad()
    // ... color view background, create button ...
}
func doPresent(sender:AnyObject?) {
```

```
    let pvc = PresentedViewController()
    self.presentViewController(pvc, animated:true, completion:nil)
}

// PresentedViewController.m:
override func viewDidLoad() {
    super.viewDidLoad()
    // ... color view background, create button ...
}
func doDismiss(sender:AnyObject?) {
    self.dismissViewControllerAnimated(true, completion: nil)
}
```

That's a working app. Now let's start adding state restoration, just as before:

1. Change the name of `application:didFinishLaunchingWithOptions:` in the app delegate to `application:willFinishLaunchingWithOptions:`.

2. Implement `application:shouldSaveApplicationState:` and `application:shouldRestoreApplicationState:` in the app delegate to return `true`.

3. Give all four view controller instances restoration IDs: let's call them `"nav"`, `"root"`, `"second"`, and `"presented"`. We'll have to do this in code. We're creating each view controller instance manually, so we may as well assign its `restorationIdentifier` in the next line, like this:

   ```
   let rvc = RootViewController()
   rvc.restorationIdentifier = "root"
   let nav = UINavigationController(rootViewController:rvc)
   nav.restorationIdentifier = "nav"
   ```

   And so on.

Run the app. We are *not* getting state restoration. Why not?

The reason is that the `restorationIdentifier` alone is not sufficient to tell the state restoration mechanism what to do as the app launches. The restoration mechanism knows the chain of view controller *classes* that needs to be generated, but it is up to us to generate the *instances* of those classes. (Our storyboard-based example didn't exhibit this problem, because the storyboard itself was the source of the instances.) To do that, we need to know about the *identifier path* and the *restoration class*.

The `restorationIdentifier` serves as a guide during restoration as to what view controller is needed at each point in the view controller hierarchy. Any particular view controller instance, given its position in the view controller hierarchy, is uniquely identified by the sequence of `restorationIdentifier` values of *all* the view controllers (including itself) in the chain that leads to it. Those `restorationIdentifier` values, taken together and in sequence, constitute the *identifier path* for any given view controller instance.

Each identifier path is, in fact, merely an array of strings. In effect, the identifier paths are like a trail of breadcrumbs that you left behind as you created each view controller while the app was running, and that will now be used to identify each view controller again as the app launches.

For example, if we launch the app and press the Push button and then the Present button, then all four view controllers have been instantiated; those instances are identified as:

- `["nav"]`
- `["nav", "root"]`
- `["nav", "second"]`
- `["nav", "presented"]` (because the navigation controller is the actual presenting view controller)

Observe that a view controller's identifier path is not a record of the full story of how we got here. It's just an identifier! The state-saving mechanism also saves a relational tree of identifiers. For example, if the app is suspended in the current situation, then the state-saving mechanism will record the true state of affairs, namely that the root view controller has two children and a presented view controller, along with their identifiers.

Now consider what the state restoration mechanism needs to do when the app has been suspended and killed, and comes back to life, from the situation I just described. We need to restore four view controllers; we know their identifiers and mutual relationships. State restoration doesn't start until *after* `application:willFinishLaunchingWith-Options:`. So when the state restoration mechanism starts examining the situation, it discovers that the `["nav"]` and `["nav", "root"]` view controller instances have already been created! However, the view controller instances for `["nav", "second"]` and `["nav", "presented"]` must also be created now. The state restoration mechanism doesn't know how to do that — so it's going to ask your code for the instances.

But *what* code should it ask? One way of specifying this is for you to provide a *restoration class* for each view controller instance that is *not* restored by the time `application:will-FinishLaunchingWithOptions:` returns. Here's how you do that:

1. Give the view controller a `restorationClass`. Typically, this will be the view controller's own class, or the class of the view controller responsible for creating this view controller instance.

2. Implement the class method `viewControllerWithRestorationIdentifier-Path:coder:` on the class named by each view controller's `restorationClass` property, returning a view controller instance as specified by the identifier path. Very often, the implementation will be to instantiate the view controller directly and return that instance.

3. Specify formally that each class named as a restorationClass implements the UIViewControllerRestoration protocol. (If you omit this step, you'll get a helpful warning message at runtime: "Restoration class for view controller does not conform to UIViewControllerRestoration protocol.")

Let's make our PresentedViewController and SecondViewController instances restorable. I'll start with PresentedViewController. Our app can have *two* PresentedViewController instances (though not simultaneously) — the one created by RootViewController, and the one created by SecondViewController. Let's start with the one created by RootViewController.

Since RootViewController creates and configures a PresentedViewController instance, it can reasonably act also as the restoration class for that instance. In its implementation of viewControllerWithRestorationIdentifierPath:coder:, RootViewController should then create and configure a PresentedViewController instance *exactly* as it was doing before we added state restoration to our app — except for putting it into the view controller hierarchy! The state restoration mechanism itself, remember, is responsible for assembling the view controller hierarchy; our job is merely to supply any needed view controller instances.

So RootViewController now must adopt UIViewControllerRestoration, and will contain this code:

```
func doPresent(sender:AnyObject?) {
    let pvc = PresentedViewController()
    pvc.restorationIdentifier = "presented"
    pvc.restorationClass = self.dynamicType // *
    self.presentViewController(pvc, animated:true, completion:nil)
}
class func viewControllerWithRestorationIdentifierPath(ip: [AnyObject],
    coder: NSCoder) -> UIViewController? {
        var vc : UIViewController? = nil
        let last = ip.last as! String
        switch last {
        case "presented":
            let pvc = PresentedViewController()
            pvc.restorationIdentifier = "presented"
            pvc.restorationClass = self
            vc = pvc
        default: break
        }
        return vc
}
```

You can see what I mean when I say that the restoration class must do exactly what it was doing before state restoration was added. Clearly this situation has led to some annoying code duplication, so let's factor out the common code. In doing so, we must bear in mind that doPresent: is an instance method, whereas viewControllerWith-

RestorationIdentifierPath:coder: is a class method; our factored-out code must therefore be a class method, so that they can both call it:

```
class func makePresentedViewController () -> UIViewController {
    let pvc = PresentedViewController()
    pvc.restorationIdentifier = "presented"
    pvc.restorationClass = self
    return pvc
}
func doPresent(sender:AnyObject?) {
    let pvc = self.dynamicType.makePresentedViewController()
    self.presentViewController(pvc, animated:true, completion:nil)
}
class func viewControllerWithRestorationIdentifierPath(ip: [AnyObject],
    coder: NSCoder) -> UIViewController? {
        var vc : UIViewController? = nil
        let last = ip.last as! String
        switch last {
        case "presented":
            vc = self.makePresentedViewController()
        default: break
        }
        return vc
}
```

The structure of our viewControllerWithRestorationIdentifierPath:coder: is typical. We test the identifier path — usually, it's sufficient to examine its last element — and return the corresponding view controller; ultimately, we are also prepared to return nil, in case we are called with an identifier path we can't interpret. We can also return nil deliberately, to tell the restoration mechanism, "Go no further; don't restore the view controller you're asking for here, or any view controller further down the same path."

Continuing in the same vein, we expand RootViewController still further to make it also the restoration class for SecondViewController, and SecondViewController can make itself the restoration class for the PresentedViewController instance that it creates. There's no conflict in the notion that both RootViewController and SecondView-Controller can fulfill the role of PresentedViewController restoration class, as we're talking about two different PresentedViewController instances. The app now performs state saving and restoration correctly! (The details are left as an exercise for the reader.)

I said earlier that the state restoration mechanism can ask your code for needed instances in two ways. The second way is that you implement this method in your app delegate:

- application:viewControllerWithRestorationIdentifierPath:coder:

If you implement this method, it will be called for *every* view controller that doesn't have a restoration class. This works in a storyboard-based app, and thus is a chance for you to intervene and prevent the restoration of a particular view controller on a particular occasion (by returning `nil`). Be prepared to receive identifier paths for an existing view controller! If that happens, return the existing view controller — don't make a new one.

For example, if we were to implement `application:viewControllerWithRestoration-IdentifierPath:coder:` in the example app I've been describing, it would be called for `["nav"]` and for `["nav", "root"]`, because those view controllers have no restoration class. But we needn't, and we mustn't, create a new view controller; those view controller instances have already been created, and we must return those existing instances.

Restoring View Controller State

I have explained how the state restoration mechanism creates a view controller and places it into the view controller hierarchy. But at that point, the work of restoration is only half done. What about the *state* of that view controller?

A newly restored view controller probably won't yet have the data and property values it was holding at the time the app was terminated. The history of the creation and configuration of this view controller is *not* magically recapitulated during restoration. If the view controller comes from a storyboard, then any settings in its Attributes inspector are obeyed, but the segue that generated the view controller in the first place is never run, so the previous view controller's `prepareForSegue:sender:` is never called, and the previous view controller never gets to hand this view controller any data. If the view controller is created by a restoration class, it may have been given some initial configuration, but this very likely falls short of the full state that the view controller was holding when the app was terminated. Any additional communication between one view controller and another to hand it data will be missing from the process. Indeed, since the history of the app during its previous run is not recapitulated, there will be no data to hand over in the first place.

It is up to each view controller, therefore, to *restore its own state* when it itself is restored. And in order to do that, it must previously *save its own state* when the app is backgrounded. The state saving and restoration mechanism provides a way of helping your view controllers do this, through the use of a *coder* (an NSCoder object). Think of this coder as a box in which the view controller is invited to place its valuables for safekeeping, and from which it can retrieve them later. Each of these valuables needs to be identified, so it is tagged with a key (an arbitrary string) when it is placed into the box, and is then later retrieved by using the same key, much as in a dictionary.

Anyone who has anything to save at the time it is handed a coder can do so by sending the coder an appropriate encode message with a key, such as `encodeFloat:forKey:` or `encodeObject:forKey:`. If an object's class doesn't adopt the NSCoding protocol, you may have to archive it to an NSData object before you can encode it. However, views and view controllers can be handled by the coder directly, because they are treated as references. Whatever was saved in the coder can later be extracted by sending the coder the reverse operation using the same key, such as decodeFloatForKey: or decodeObject-ForKey:.

The keys do not have to be unique across the entire app; they only need to be unique for a particular view controller. Each object that is handed a coder is handed *its own personal coder*. It is handed this coder at state saving time, and it is handed the same coder (that is, a coder with the same archived objects and keys) at state restoration time.

Here's the sequence of events involving coders:

When state is saved

When it's time to save state (as the app is about to be backgrounded), the state saving mechanism provides coders as follows:

1. The app delegate is sent `application:shouldSaveApplicationState:`. The coder is the second parameter.

2. The app delegate is sent `application:willEncodeRestorableStateWith-Coder:`. This is the same coder as in the previous step, because this is the same object (the app delegate).

3. Each view controller down the chain, starting at the root view controller, is sent `encodeRestorableStateWithCoder:` if it implements it. The implementation should call `super`. Each view controller gets its own coder.

When state is restored

When the app is launched, if state is to be restored, the state restoration mechanism provides coders as follows:

1. The app delegate is sent `application:shouldRestoreApplicationState:`. The coder (the one belonging to the app delegate) is the second parameter.

2. As each view controller down the chain is to be created, one of these methods is called (as I've already explained):

   • The restoration class's `viewControllerWithRestorationIdentifier-Path:coder:`, if the view controller has a restoration class.

   • The app delegate's `application:viewControllerWithRestorationIden-tifierPath:coder:`, if implemented.

   The coder is the one appropriate to the view controller that's to be created.

3. Each view controller down the chain, starting at the root view controller, is sent `decodeRestorableStateWithCoder:` if it implements it. The implementation should call `super`. The coder is the one appropriate to this view controller.

4. The app delegate is sent `application:didDecodeRestorableStateWith-Coder:`. The coder is the same one sent to `application:shouldRestore-ApplicationState:` (the one belonging to the app delegate).

The *UIStateRestoration.h* header file describes five built-in keys that are available from every coder during restoration:

`UIStateRestorationViewControllerStoryboardKey`
A reference to the storyboard from which this view controller came, if any.

`UIApplicationStateRestorationBundleVersionKey`
Your *Info.plist* `CFBundleVersion` string at the time of state saving.

`UIApplicationStateRestorationUserInterfaceIdiomKey`
An NSNumber wrapping a UIUserInterfaceIdiom value, either `.Phone` or `.Pad`, telling what kind of device we were running on when state saving happened. You can extract this information as follows:

```
if let idiomraw = coder.decodeObjectForKey(
    UIApplicationStateRestorationUserInterfaceIdiomKey) as? Int {
        if let idiom = UIUserInterfaceIdiom(rawValue:idiomraw) {
            if idiom == .Phone {
                // ...
            }
        }
}
```

`UIApplicationStateRestorationTimestampKey`
An NSDate telling when state saving happened.

`UIApplicationStateRestorationSystemVersionKey`
A NSString telling the system version under which state saving happened.

One purpose of these keys is to allow your app to opt out of state restoration, wholly or in part, because the archive is too old, was saved on the wrong kind of device (and presumably migrated to this one by backup and restore), and so forth.

A typical implementation of `encodeRestorableStateWithCoder:` and `decode-RestorableStateWithCoder:` will concern itself with properties and interface views. `decodeRestorableStateWithCoder:` is guaranteed to be called *after* `viewDidLoad`, so you know that `viewDidLoad` won't overwrite any direct changes to the interface performed in `decodeRestorableStateWithCoder:`.

To illustrate, I'll add state saving and restoration to my earlier UIPageViewController example, the one that displays a Pep Boy on each page. Recall how that example is architected. The project has no storyboard. The code defines just two classes, the app delegate and the Pep view controller. The app delegate creates a UIPageViewController and makes it the window's root view controller, and makes itself the page view controller's data source. The page view controller's data source methods create and supply an appropriate Pep instance whenever a page is needed for the page view controller, along these lines:

```
// ... work out index of new name ...
return Pep(pepBoy: self.pep[ix])
```

The challenge is to restore the Pep object displayed in the page view controller as the app launches. One solution involves recognizing that a Pep object is completely configured once created, and it is created just by handing it the name of a Pep Boy in its designated initializer, which becomes its boy property. Thus we can mediate between a Pep object and a mere string, and all we really need to save and restore is that string.

All the additional work, therefore, can be performed in the app delegate. As usual, we change "did" to "will" so that we are now implementing `application:willFinish-LaunchingWithOptions:`, and we implement `application:shouldSaveApplication-State:` and `application:shouldRestoreApplicationState:` to return true. Now we save and restore the current Pep Boy name in the app delegate's Encode and Decode methods:

```
func application(application: UIApplication,
    willEncodeRestorableStateWithCoder coder: NSCoder) {
        let pvc = self.window!.rootViewController as! UIPageViewController
        let boy = (pvc.viewControllers![0] as! Pep).boy
        coder.encodeObject(boy, forKey:"boy")
}
func application(application: UIApplication,
    didDecodeRestorableStateWithCoder coder: NSCoder) {
        let boy: AnyObject? = coder.decodeObjectForKey("boy")
        if let boy = boy as? String {
            let pvc = self.window!.rootViewController as! UIPageViewController
            let pep = Pep(pepBoy: boy)
            pvc.setViewControllers(
                [pep], direction: .Forward, animated: false, completion: nil)
        }
}
```

A second, more general solution is to make our Pep view controller class itself capable of saving and restoration. This means that every view controller down the chain from the root view controller to our Pep view controller must have a restoration identifier. In our simple app, there's just one such view controller, the UIPageViewController; the app delegate can assign it a restoration ID when it creates it:

```
let pvc = UIPageViewController(transitionStyle: .Scroll,
    navigationOrientation: .Horizontal, options: nil)
pvc.restorationIdentifier = "pvc" // *
```

We'll have a Pep object assign itself a restoration ID in its own designated initializer. The Pep object will also need a restoration class; as I mentioned earlier, this can perfectly well be the Pep class itself, and that seems most appropriate here:

```
required init(pepBoy boy:String) {
    self.boy = boy
    super.init(nibName: "Pep", bundle: nil)
    self.restorationIdentifier = "pep" // *
    self.restorationClass = self.dynamicType // *
}
```

The only state that a Pep object needs to save is its boy string. The coder in which that boy value is saved will come back to us in Pep's `viewControllerWithRestoration-IdentifierPath:coder:`, so we can use it to create the new Pep object by calling the designated initializer, thus avoiding code duplication:

```
override func encodeRestorableStateWithCoder(coder: NSCoder) {
    super.encodeRestorableStateWithCoder(coder)
    coder.encodeObject(self.boy, forKey:"boy")
}
class func viewControllerWithRestorationIdentifierPath(
    ip: [AnyObject], coder: NSCoder) -> UIViewController? {
        let boy = coder.decodeObjectForKey("boy") as! String
        return self.init(pepBoy: boy)
}
```

(Swift won't permit a class to instantiate itself through an initializer on `self` unless we guarantee that any subclass implements that initializer; our marking of `init(pepBoy:)` as `required` constitutes just such a guarantee.)

Now comes a surprise. We run the app and test it, and we find that we're *not* getting saving and restoration of our Pep object. It isn't being archived; its `encodeRestorable-StateWithCoder:` isn't even being called! The reason is that the state saving mechanism doesn't work automatically for a UIPageViewController and its children (or for a custom container view controller and *its* children, for that matter). It is up to us to see to it that the current Pep object is archived.

To do so, we can archive and unarchive the current Pep object in an implementation of `encodeRestorableStateWithCoder:` and `decodeRestorableStateWithCoder:` that *is* being called. For our app, that would have to be in the app delegate. The code we've written so far has all been necessary to make the current Pep object archivable and restorable; now the app delegate will make sure that it *is* archived and restored:

```
func application(application: UIApplication,
    willEncodeRestorableStateWithCoder coder: NSCoder) {
        let pvc = self.window!.rootViewController as! UIPageViewController
        let pep = pvc.viewControllers![0] as! Pep
        coder.encodeObject(pep, forKey:"pep")
}
func application(application: UIApplication,
    didDecodeRestorableStateWithCoder coder: NSCoder) {
        let pep : AnyObject? = coder.decodeObjectForKey("pep")
        if let pep = pep as? Pep {
            let pvc = self.window!.rootViewController as! UIPageViewController
```

```
                pvc.setViewControllers(
                    [pep], direction: .Forward, animated: false, completion: nil)
            }
        }
```

This solution may seem rather heavyweight, but it isn't. We're not really archiving an entire Pep instance; it's just a reference. The actual Pep instance is the one created by `viewControllerWithRestorationIdentifierPath:coder:`.

Restoration Order of Operations

When you implement state saving and restoration for a view controller, the view controller ends up with two different ways of being configured. One way involves the view controller lifetime events I discussed earlier ("View Controller Lifetime Events" on page 361). The other involves the state restoration events I've been discussing here. You want your view controller to be correctly configured no matter whether this view controller is undergoing state restoration or not.

Before state saving and restoration, you were probably configuring your view controller, at least in part, in `viewWillAppear:` and `viewDidAppear:`. With state saving and restoration added to the picture, you may also be receiving `decodeRestorableStateWith-Coder:`. If you configure your view controller here, will you be overriding what happens in `viewWillAppear:` and `viewDidAppear:`, or will they come along later and override what you do in `decodeRestorableStateWithCoder:`?

The unfortunate fact is that you don't know. For `viewWillAppear:` and `viewDid-Appear:`, in particular, the only thing you *do* know during state restoration is that you'll get both of them for the top view controller (the one whose view actually appears). You don't know *when* they will arrive; it might be before or after `decodeRestorableState-WithCoder:`. For other view controllers, you don't even know *whether* `viewDidAppear:` will arrive: it might well *never* arrive, even if `viewWillAppear:` arrives. This is another of those view controller lifetime event incoherencies I complained about earlier in this chapter.

However, there's another view controller event I haven't mentioned yet: `application-FinishedRestoringState`. If you implement this method in a view controller subclass, it will be called if and only if we're doing state restoration, at a time when *all* view controllers have already been sent `decodeRestorableStateWithCoder:`.

Thus, the known order of events during state restoration is like this:

1. `application:shouldRestoreApplicationState:`

2. `application:viewControllerWithRestorationIdentifierPath:coder:`

3. `viewControllerWithRestorationIdentifierPath:coder:`, in order down the chain

4. `viewDidLoad`, in order down the chain; possibly interleaved with the foregoing

5. `decodeRestorableStateWithCoder:`, in order down the chain

6. `application:didDecodeRestorableStateWithCoder:`

7. `applicationFinishedRestoringState`, in order down the chain

You still don't know when `viewWillAppear:` and `viewDidAppear:` will arrive, or whether `viewDidAppear:` will arrive at all. But in `applicationFinishedRestoring-State` you can reliably finish configuring your view controller and your interface.

A typical situation is that you will want to update your interface after all properties have been set. So you'll factor out your interface-updating code into a single method. Now there are two possibilities, and they are both handled coherently:

We're not restoring state
    Properties will be set through initialization and configuration, and then `viewWill-Appear:` calls your interface-updating method.

We are restoring state
    Properties will be set by `decodeRestorableStateWithCoder:`, and then `applicationFinishedRestoringState` calls your interface-updating method.

There is still some indeterminacy as to what's going to happen, but the interface-updating method can mediate that indeterminacy by checking for two things that can go wrong:

It is called too soon
    The interface-updating method should check to see that the properties have in fact been set; if not, it should just return. It will be called again when the properties *have* been set.

It is called unnecessarily
    The interface-updating method might run twice in quick succession with the same set of properties. This is not a disaster, but if you don't like it, you can prevent it by comparing the properties to the interface and return if the interface has already been configured with these properties.

 If your app has additional state restoration work to do on a background thread (Chapter 25), the documentation says you should call UIApplication's `extendState-Restoration` as you begin and `completeStateRestoration` when you've finished. The idea is that if you *don't* call `completeStateRestoration`, the system can assume that something has gone very wrong and will throw away the saved state information in case it is faulty.

Restoration of Other Objects

A view will participate in automatic saving and restoration of state if its view controller does, and if it itself has a restoration identifier. Some built-in UIView subclasses also have built-in restoration abilities. For example, a scroll view that participates in state saving and restoration will automatically return to the point to which it was scrolled previously. You should consult the documentation on each UIView subclass to see whether it participates usefully in state saving and restoration, and I'll mention a few significant cases when we come to discuss those views in later chapters.

In addition, an arbitrary object can be made to participate in automatic saving and restoration of state. There are three requirements for such an object:

- The object's class must adopt the UIStateRestoring protocol. This declares three optional methods:
    - encodeRestorableStateWithCoder:
    - decodeRestorableStateWithCoder:
    - applicationFinishedRestoringState
- When the object is created, someone must register it with the runtime by calling this UIApplication class method:
    - registerObjectForStateRestoration:restorationIdentifier:
- Someone who participates in state saving and restoration, such as a view controller, must make the archive aware of this object by storing a reference to it in the archive (typically in encodeRestorableStateWithCoder:) — much as we did with the Pep object earlier.

So, for example, here's an NSObject subclass Thing with a word property, that participates in state saving and restoration:

```
class Thing : NSObject, UIStateRestoring {
    var word = ""
    func encodeRestorableStateWithCoder(coder: NSCoder) {
        coder.encodeObject(self.word, forKey:"word")
    }
    func decodeRestorableStateWithCoder(coder: NSCoder) {
        self.word = coder.decodeObjectForKey("word") as! String
    }
    func applicationFinishedRestoringState() {
        // not used
    }
}
```

And here's a view controller with a Thing property (self.thing):

```
class func makeThing () -> Thing {
    let thing = Thing()
    UIApplication.registerObjectForStateRestoration(
        thing, restorationIdentifier: "thing")
    return thing
}
override func awakeFromNib() {
    super.awakeFromNib()
    self.thing = self.dynamicType.makeThing()
}
override func encodeRestorableStateWithCoder(coder: NSCoder) {
    super.encodeRestorableStateWithCoder(coder)
    coder.encodeObject(self.thing, forKey: "mything") // important!
}
```

That last line is crucial; it introduces our Thing object to the archive and brings its UIStateRestoring methods to life.

There is an optional `objectRestorationClass` property of the restorable object, and an `objectWithRestorationIdentifierPath:coder:` method that the designated class must implement. But our object is restorable even without an `objectRestoration-Class`! Presumably, just calling `registerObjectForStateRestoration:restoration-Identifier:` sufficiently identifies this object to the runtime. If you do want to assign an `objectRestorationClass`, you'll have to declare it:

```
var objectRestorationClass: UIObjectRestoration.Type?
```

The class in question should adopt the UIObjectRestoration protocol; its `objectWith-RestorationIdentifierPath:coder:` will then be called, and can return the restorable object, by creating it or pointing to it. Alternatively, it can return `nil` to prevent restoration.

Another optional property of the restorable object is `restorationParent`. Again, if you want to assign to it, you'll have to declare it:

```
var restorationParent: UIStateRestoring?
```

The parent should adopt the UIStateRestoring protocol. The purpose of the parent is to give the restorable object an identifier path. For example, if we have a chain of view controllers with a path `["nav", "second"]`, then if that last view controller is the `restorationParent` of our Thing object, the Thing object's identifier path in `object-WithRestorationIdentifierPath:coder:` will be `["nav", "second", "thing"]`, rather than simply `["thing"]`. This is useful if we are worried that `["thing"]` alone will not uniquely identify this object.

Snapshot Suppression

When your app is backgrounded, the system takes a snapshot of your interface. It is used in the app switcher interface, and as a launch image when your app is resumed. But what happens if your app is killed in the background and relaunched?

If your app isn't participating in state restoration, then its default launch image is used. This makes sense, because your app is starting from scratch. But if your app *is* participating in state restoration, then the snapshot is used as a launch image. This makes sense, too, because the interface that was showing when the app was backgrounded is presumably the very interface your state restoration process is about to restore.

However, you might decide, while saving state, that there is reason not to use the system's snapshot when relaunching. (Perhaps there is something in your interface that would be inappropriate to display when the app is subsequently launched.) In that case, you can call the UIApplication instance method `ignoreSnapshotOnNextApplication-Launch`. When the app launches with state restoration, the user will see your app's default launch image, followed by a change to the restored interface. They may not match, but at least there is a nice cross-dissolve between them.

By the same token, if the view controller whose view was showing at state saving time is not restorable (it has no restoration ID), then if the app is killed in the background and subsequently launches with state restoration, the restoration mechanism knows that the snapshot taken at background time doesn't match the interface we're about to restore to, so the user will initially see your app's default launch image.

CHAPTER 7

Scroll Views

A scroll view (UIScrollView) is a view whose content is larger than its bounds. To reveal a desired area, the user can scroll the content by dragging, or you can reposition the content in code.

A scroll view isn't magic; it takes advantage of ordinary UIView features (Chapter 1). The content is simply the scroll view's subviews. When the scroll view scrolls, what's really changing is the scroll view's own bounds origin; the subviews are positioned with respect to the bounds origin, so they move with it. The scroll view's `clipsToBounds` is usually `true`, so any content positioned within the scroll view is visible and any content positioned outside it is not.

In addition, a scroll view brings to the table some nontrivial abilities:

- It knows how to shift its bounds origin in response to the user's gestures.
- It provides scroll indicators whose size and position give the user a clue as to the content's size and position.
- It can enforce paging, whereby the user can scroll only by a fixed amount.
- It supports zooming, so that the user can resize the content with a pinch gesture.
- It provides a plethora of delegate methods, so that your code knows exactly how the user is scrolling and zooming.

As I've just said, a scroll view's subviews, like those of any view, are positioned with respect to its bounds origin; to scroll is to change the bounds origin. The scroll view thus already knows how far it should be allowed to slide its subviews downward and rightward — the limit is reached when the scroll view's bounds origin is (0.0,0.0). What the scroll view *needs* to know is how far it should be allowed to slide its subviews upward and leftward. That is the scroll view's *content size* — its `contentSize` property. The scroll view uses its `contentSize`, in combination with its own bounds size, to set the limits on how large its bounds origin can become. It may also be helpful to think of the scroll view's scrollable *content* as the rectangle defined by `CGRect(origin:CGPoint-Zero, size:contentSize)`; this is the rectangle that the user can inspect by scrolling.

If a dimension of the `contentSize` isn't larger than the same dimension of the scroll view's own bounds, the content won't be scrollable in that dimension: there is nothing to scroll, as the entire scrollable content is already showing. The default is that the `contentSize` is `(0.0,0.0)` — meaning that the scroll view *isn't scrollable*.

To get a working scroll view, therefore, it will be crucial to set its `contentSize` correctly. You can do this directly, in code; or, if you're using autolayout (Chapter 1), the `contentSize` is calculated for you based on the constraints of the scroll view's subviews. I'll demonstrate both approaches.

Creating a Scroll View in Code

I'll start by creating a scroll view, providing it with subviews, and making those subviews viewable by scrolling, entirely in code.

Manual Content Size

In the first instance, let's not use autolayout. Our project is based on the Single View Application template, with a single view controller class, ViewController. In the ViewController's `viewDidLoad`, I'll create the scroll view to fill the main view, and populate it with 30 UILabels whose text contains a sequential number so that we can see where we are when we scroll:

```
let sv = UIScrollView(frame: self.view.bounds)
sv.autoresizingMask = [.FlexibleWidth, .FlexibleHeight]
self.view.addSubview(sv)
sv.backgroundColor = UIColor.whiteColor()
var y : CGFloat = 10
for i in 0 ..< 30 {
    let lab = UILabel()
    lab.text = "This is label \(i+1)"
    lab.sizeToFit()
    lab.frame.origin = CGPointMake(10,y)
    sv.addSubview(lab)
    y += lab.bounds.size.height + 10
}
var sz = sv.bounds.size
sz.height = y
sv.contentSize = sz // *
```

The crucial move is the last line, where we tell the scroll view how large its content is to be. If we omit this step, the scroll view won't be scrollable; the window will appear to consist of a static column of labels.

There is no rule about the order in which you perform the two operations of setting the contentSize and populating the scroll view with subviews. In that example, we set the contentSize afterward because it is more convenient to track the heights of the subviews as we add them than to calculate their total height in advance. Similarly, you can alter a scroll view's content (subviews) or contentSize, or both, dynamically as the app runs.

Any direct subviews of the scroll view may need to have their autoresizing set appropriately in case the scroll view is resized, as would happen, for instance, if our app performs compensatory rotation. To see this, add these lines to the preceding example, inside the for loop:

```
lab.frame.width = self.view.bounds.width - 20
lab.backgroundColor = UIColor.redColor()
lab.autoresizingMask = .FlexibleWidth
```

Run the app, and rotate the device or the Simulator. The labels are wider in portrait orientation because the scroll view itself is wider.

This, however, has nothing to do with the contentSize! The contentSize does not change just because the scroll view's bounds change; if you want the contentSize to change in response to rotation, you will need to change it manually, in code. Conversely, resizing the contentSize has no effect on the size of the scroll view's subviews; it merely determines the scrolling limit.

Automatic Content Size With Autolayout

With autolayout, things are different. The difficult thing to understand — and it is certainly counterintuitive — is that a constraint between a scroll view and its direct subview is *not* a way of positioning the subview relative to the scroll view (as it would be if the superview were an ordinary UIView). Instead, it's a way of describing the scroll view's contentSize.

To see this, let's rewrite the preceding example to use autolayout. The scroll view and its subviews have their translatesAutoresizingMaskIntoConstraints set to false, and we're giving them explicit constraints:

```
let sv = UIScrollView()
sv.backgroundColor = UIColor.whiteColor()
sv.translatesAutoresizingMaskIntoConstraints = false
self.view.addSubview(sv)
var con = [NSLayoutConstraint]()
con.appendContentsOf(
    NSLayoutConstraint.constraintsWithVisualFormat(
        "H:|[sv]|",
        options:[], metrics:nil,
        views:["sv":sv]))
con.appendContentsOf(
```

```
    NSLayoutConstraint.constraintsWithVisualFormat(
        "V:|[sv]|",
        options:[], metrics:nil,
        views:["sv":sv]))
var previousLab : UILabel? = nil
for i in 0 ..< 30 {
    let lab = UILabel()
    // lab.backgroundColor = UIColor.redColor()
    lab.translatesAutoresizingMaskIntoConstraints = false
    lab.text = "This is label \(i+1)"
    sv.addSubview(lab)
    con.appendContentsOf(
        NSLayoutConstraint.constraintsWithVisualFormat(
            "H:|-(10)-[lab]",
            options:[], metrics:nil,
            views:["lab":lab]))
    if previousLab == nil { // first one, pin to top
        con.appendContentsOf(
            NSLayoutConstraint.constraintsWithVisualFormat(
                "V:|-(10)-[lab]",
                options:[], metrics:nil,
                views:["lab":lab]))
    } else { // all others, pin to previous
        con.appendContentsOf(
            NSLayoutConstraint.constraintsWithVisualFormat(
                "V:[prev]-(10)-[lab]",
                options:[], metrics:nil,
                views:["lab":lab, "prev":previousLab!]))
    }
    previousLab = lab
}
NSLayoutConstraint.activateConstraints(con)
```

The labels are correctly positioned relative to one another, but the scroll view isn't scrollable. Moreover, setting the contentSize manually doesn't help. The reason is that we are *missing a constraint.* We have to add one more constraint, showing the scroll view what the height of its contentSize should be. Replace the last line of that code with this:

```
// ... everything else as before ...
// last one, pin to bottom, this dictates content size height!
con.appendContentsOf(
    NSLayoutConstraint.constraintsWithVisualFormat(
        "V:[lab]-(10)-|",
        options:[], metrics:nil,
        views:["lab":previousLab!]))
NSLayoutConstraint.activateConstraints(con)
```

The constraints of the scroll view's subviews now describe the contentSize height: the top label is pinned to the top of the scroll view, the next one is pinned to the one above it, and so on — *and the bottom one is pinned to the bottom of the scroll view.*

Consequently, the runtime calculates the `contentSize` height from the inside out, as it were, as the sum of all the vertical constraints (including the intrinsic heights of the labels), and the scroll view is vertically scrollable to show all the labels.

Using a Content View

Instead of putting all of our scroll view's content directly inside the scroll view as its immediate subviews, we can provide a generic UIView as the sole immediate subview of the scroll view; everything else inside the scroll view is to be a subview of this generic UIView, which we may term the *content view*. This is a commonly used arrangement.

Under autolayout, we then have two choices for setting the scroll view's `contentSize`:

- Set the content view's `translatesAutoresizingMaskIntoConstraints` to `true`, and set the scroll view's `contentSize` manually to the size of the content view.

- Set the content view's `translatesAutoresizingMaskIntoConstraints` to `false`, set its size with constraints, and pin its edges to its superview (the scroll view) with a `constant` of `0`.

A convenient consequence of this arrangement is that it works independently of whether the content view's own subviews are positioned explicitly by their frames or using constraints. There are thus four possible combinations:

No constraints
The content view is sized by its frame, its contents are positioned by its frame, and the scroll view's `contentSize` is set explicitly.

Content view constraints
The content view is sized by *its own height and width constraints* and is pinned to the scroll view to set its content size.

Content view and content constraints
The content view is sized from the inside out *by the constraints of its subviews* and is pinned to the scroll view to set its content size.

Content constraints only
The content view is sized by its frame and the scroll view's `contentSize` is set explicitly, but the content view's subviews are positioned using constraints.

I'll illustrate by rewriting the previous example to use a content view. All four possible combinations start the same way:

```
let sv = UIScrollView()
sv.backgroundColor = UIColor.whiteColor()
sv.translatesAutoresizingMaskIntoConstraints = false
self.view.addSubview(sv)
var con = [NSLayoutConstraint]()
```

```
con.appendContentsOf(
    NSLayoutConstraint.constraintsWithVisualFormat(
        "H:|[sv]|",
        options:[], metrics:nil,
        views:["sv":sv]))
con.appendContentsOf(
    NSLayoutConstraint.constraintsWithVisualFormat(
        "V:|[sv]|",
        options:[], metrics:nil,
        views:["sv":sv]))
let v = UIView() // content view
sv.addSubview(v)
```

The differences lie in what happens next. The first combination is that *no* constraints are used (apart from the constraints that frame the scroll view), and the scroll view's content size is set explicitly. It's just like the first example in the chapter, except that the labels are added to the content view, not to the scroll view:

```
var y : CGFloat = 10
for i in 0 ..< 30 {
    let lab = UILabel()
    lab.text = "This is label \(i+1)"
    lab.sizeToFit()
    lab.frame.origin = CGPointMake(10,y)
    v.addSubview(lab) // *
    y += lab.bounds.size.height + 10
}
// set content view frame and content size explicitly
v.frame = CGRectMake(0,0,0,y)
sv.contentSize = v.frame.size
NSLayoutConstraint.activateConstraints(con)
```

The second combination is that the content view uses explicit constraints, but its subviews don't. It's just like the preceding code, except that we set the content view's constraints rather than the scroll view's content size:

```
var y : CGFloat = 10
for i in 0 ..< 30 {
    let lab = UILabel()
    lab.text = "This is label \(i+1)"
    lab.sizeToFit()
    lab.frame.origin = CGPointMake(10,y)
    v.addSubview(lab)
    y += lab.bounds.size.height + 10
}
// set content view width, height, and frame-to-superview constraints
// content size is calculated for us
v.translatesAutoresizingMaskIntoConstraints = false
con.appendContentsOf(
    NSLayoutConstraint.constraintsWithVisualFormat("V:|[v(y)]|",
        options:[], metrics:["y":y], views:["v":v]))
```

```
con.appendContentsOf(
    NSLayoutConstraint.constraintsWithVisualFormat("H:|[v(0)]|",
        options:[], metrics:nil, views:["v":v]))
NSLayoutConstraint.activateConstraints(con)
```

The third combination is that explicit constraints are used throughout. This is just like
the second example in the chapter, except that the labels are added to the content view:

```
var previousLab : UILabel? = nil
for i in 0 ..< 30 {
    let lab = UILabel()
    // lab.backgroundColor = UIColor.redColor()
    lab.translatesAutoresizingMaskIntoConstraints = false
    lab.text = "This is label \(i+1)"
    v.addSubview(lab) // *
    con.appendContentsOf( // *
        NSLayoutConstraint.constraintsWithVisualFormat(
            "H:|-(10)-[lab]",
            options:[], metrics:nil,
            views:["lab":lab]))
    if previousLab == nil { // first one, pin to top
        con.appendContentsOf( // *
            NSLayoutConstraint.constraintsWithVisualFormat(
                "V:|-(10)-[lab]",
                options:[], metrics:nil,
                views:["lab":lab]))
    } else { // all others, pin to previous
        con.appendContentsOf( // *
            NSLayoutConstraint.constraintsWithVisualFormat(
                "V:[prev]-(10)-[lab]",
                options:[], metrics:nil,
                views:["lab":lab, "prev":previousLab!]))
    }
    previousLab = lab
}
// last one, pin to bottom, this dictates content size height!
con.appendContentsOf( // *
    NSLayoutConstraint.constraintsWithVisualFormat(
        "V:[lab]-(10)-|",
        options:[], metrics:nil,
        views:["lab":previousLab!]))
// pin content view to scroll view, sized by its subview constraints
// content size is calculated for us
v.translatesAutoresizingMaskIntoConstraints = false
con.appendContentsOf(
    NSLayoutConstraint.constraintsWithVisualFormat("V:|[v]|",
        options:[], metrics:nil, views:["v":v])) // *
con.appendContentsOf(
    NSLayoutConstraint.constraintsWithVisualFormat("H:|[v]|",
        options:[], metrics:nil, views:["v":v])) // *
NSLayoutConstraint.activateConstraints(con)
```

The fourth combination is that the content view's subviews are positioned using constraints, but we set the content view's frame and the scroll view's content size explicitly. There is no y to track as we position the subviews, so how can we find out the final content size height? Fortunately, `systemLayoutSizeFittingSize:` tells us:

```
// ... same as previous ...
// last one, pin to bottom, this dictates content size height!
con.appendContentsOf( // *
    NSLayoutConstraint.constraintsWithVisualFormat(
        "V:[lab]-(10)-|",
        options:[], metrics:nil,
        views:["lab":previousLab!]))
NSLayoutConstraint.activateConstraints(con)
// autolayout helps us learn the consequences of those constraints
let minsz = v.systemLayoutSizeFittingSize(UILayoutFittingCompressedSize)
// set content view frame and content size explicitly
v.frame = CGRectMake(0,0,0,minsz.height)
sv.contentSize = v.frame.size
```

Scroll View in a Nib

A UIScrollView is available in the nib editor in the Object library, so you can drag it into a view in the canvas and give it subviews. Alternatively, you can wrap existing views in the canvas in a UIScrollView as an afterthought: to do so, select the views and choose Editor → Embed In → Scroll View. The scroll view can't be scrolled in the nib editor, so to design its subviews, you make the scroll view large enough to accommodate them; if this makes the scroll view too large, you can resize the actual scroll view instance when the nib loads. If the scroll view is inside the view controller's main view, you may have to make *that* view too large as well, in order to see and work with the full scroll view and its contents (Figure 7-1). Set the view controller's Size pop-up menu in the Simulated Metrics section of its Attributes inspector to Freeform; now you can change the main view's size.

If you're not using autolayout, judicious use of autoresizing settings in the nib editor can be a big help here. In Figure 7-1, the scroll view is the main view's subview; the scroll view's edges are pinned (struts) to its superview, and its width and height are flexible (springs). Thus, when the app runs and the main view is resized (as I discussed in Chapter 6), the scroll view will be resized too, to fit the main view. The content view, on the other hand, must not be resized, so its width and height are not flexible (they are struts, not springs), and only its top and left edges are pinned to its superview (struts).

But although everything is correctly sized at runtime, the scroll view doesn't scroll. That's because we have failed to set the scroll view's `contentSize`. Unfortunately, the nib editor provides no way to do that! Thus, we'll have to do it in code. This, in fact, is why I'm using a content view. The content view is the correct size in the nib, and it won't be resized through autoresizing, so at runtime, when the nib loads, its size will be the desired

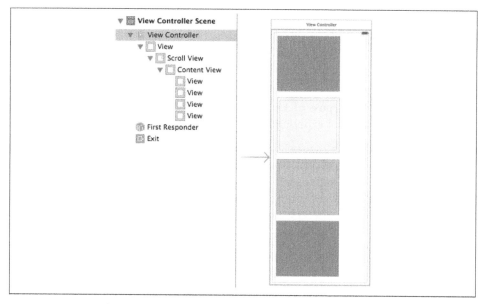

Figure 7-1. A scroll view in the nib editor

contentSize. I have an outlet to the scroll view (self.sv) and an outlet to the content view (self.cv), and I set the scroll view's contentSize to the content view's size in view-DidLayoutSubviews:

```
var didSetup = false
override func viewDidLayoutSubviews() {
    if !self.didSetup {
        self.didSetup = true
        self.sv.contentSize = self.cv.bounds.size
    }
}
```

If you *are* using autolayout, constraints take care of everything; there is no need for any code to set the scroll view's contentSize. The scroll view's own size is determined by constraints; typically, its edges are pinned to those of its superview. The content view's edges are also pinned to those of *its* superview, the scroll view. Be sure to set the constant of each constraint between the content view and the scroll view to 0! That tells the scroll view: "The contentSize is the size of the content view."

The only question now is how you'd like to dictate the content view's size. You have two choices, corresponding to the second and third combinations in the preceding section: you can set the content view's width and height constraints explicitly, or you can let the content view's width and height be completely determined by the constraints of its subviews. Do whichever feels suitable. The nib editor understands this aspect of scroll view configuration, and will alert you with a warning (about the "scrollable content size") until you've provided enough constraints to determine unambiguously the scroll view's contentSize.

Scrolling

For the most part, the purpose of a scroll view will be to let the user scroll. A number of properties affect the user experience with regard to scrolling:

scrollEnabled

> If false, the user can't scroll, but you can still scroll in code (as explained later in this section). You could put a UIScrollView to various creative purposes other than letting the user scroll; for example, scrolling in code to a different region of the content might be a way of replacing one piece of interface by another, possibly with animation.

scrollsToTop

> If true (the default), and assuming scrolling is enabled, the user can tap on the status bar as a way of making the scroll view scroll its content to the top (that is, the content moves all the way down). You can also override this setting dynamically through the scroll view's delegate, discussed later in this chapter.

bounces

> If true (the default), then when the user scrolls to a limit of the content, it is possible to scroll somewhat further (possibly revealing the scroll view's backgroundColor behind the content, if a subview was covering it); the content then snaps back into place when the user releases it. Otherwise, the user experiences the limit as a sudden inability to scroll further in that direction.

alwaysBounceVertical
alwaysBounceHorizontal

> If true, and assuming that bounces is true, then even if the contentSize in the given dimension isn't larger than the scroll view (so that no scrolling is actually possible in that dimension), the user can nevertheless scroll somewhat and the content then snaps back into place when the user releases it; otherwise, the user experiences a simple inability to scroll in that dimension.

directionalLockEnabled

> If true, and if scrolling is possible in both dimensions (even if only because the appropriate alwaysBounce... is true), then the user, having begun to scroll in one dimension, can't scroll in the other dimension without ending the gesture and starting over. In other words, the user is constrained to scroll vertically or horizontally but not both at once.

`decelerationRate`

> The rate at which scrolling is damped out, and the content comes to a stop, after the user's gesture ends. As convenient examples, standard constants are provided:
>
> - `UIScrollViewDecelerationRateNormal` (0.998)
> - `UIScrollViewDecelerationRateFast` (0.99)
>
> Lower values mean faster damping; experimentation suggests that values lower than 0.5 are viable but barely distinguishable from one another. You can also effectively override this value dynamically through the scroll view's delegate, discussed later in this chapter.

`showsHorizontalScrollIndicator`
`showsVerticalScrollIndicator`

> The scroll indicators are bars that appear only while the user is scrolling in a scrollable dimension (where the content is larger than the scroll view), and serve to indicate both the size of the content in that dimension relative to the scroll view and where the user is within it. The default is `true` for both.
>
> Because the user cannot see the scroll indicators except when actively scrolling, there is normally no indication that the view is scrollable. I regard this as somewhat unfortunate, because it makes the possibility of scrolling less discoverable; I'd prefer an option to make the scroll indicators constantly visible. Apple suggests that you call `flashScrollIndicators` when the scroll view appears, to make the scroll indicators visible momentarily.

 The scroll indicators are subviews of the scroll view (they are actually UIImage-Views). Do not assume that the subviews you add to a UIScrollView are its only subviews!

`indicatorStyle`

> The way the scroll indicators are drawn. Your choices (UIScrollViewIndicatorStyle) are `.Black`, `.White`, and `.Default` (black with a white border).

You can scroll in code even if the user can't scroll. The content simply moves to the position you specify, with no bouncing and no exposure of the scroll indicators. You can specify the new position in two ways:

`contentOffset`

> The point (CGPoint) of the content that is located at the scroll view's top left (effectively the same thing as the scroll view's bounds origin). You can get this property to learn the current scroll position, and set it to change the current scroll position. The values normally go up from (`0.0,0.0`) until the limit dictated by the `content-Size` and the scroll view's own bounds size is reached.

To set the `contentOffset` with animation, call `setContentOffset:animated:`. The animation does not cause the scroll indicators to appear; it just slides the content to the desired position.

If a scroll view participates in state restoration (Chapter 6), its `contentOffset` is saved and restored, so when the app is relaunched, the scroll view will reappear scrolled to the same position as before.

`scrollRectToVisible:animated:`
Adjusts the content so that the specified CGRect of the content is within the scroll view's bounds. This is less precise than setting the `contentOffset`, because you're not saying exactly what the resulting scroll position will be, but sometimes guaranteeing the visibility of a certain portion of the content is exactly what you're after.

If you call a method to scroll with animation and you need to know when the animation ends, implement `scrollViewDidEndScrollingAnimation:` in the scroll view's delegate.

Finally, these properties affect the scroll view's structural dimensions:

`contentInset`
A UIEdgeInsets struct (four CGFloats: `top`, `left`, `bottom`, `right`) specifying margin space around the content.

If a scroll view participates in state restoration (Chapter 6), its `contentInset` is saved and restored.

`scrollIndicatorInsets`
A UIEdgeInsets struct specifying a shift in the position of the scroll indicators.

A typical use for the `contentInset` would be that your scroll view underlaps an interface element, such as a status bar, navigation bar, or toolbar, and you want your content to be visible even when scrolled to its limit.

A good example is the app with 30 labels that we created at the start of this chapter. The scroll view occupies the entirety of the view controller's main view. But that means that the scroll view underlaps the status bar. And *that* means that at launch time, and whenever the scroll view's content is scrolled all the way down, the first label, which is as far down as it can go, is partly hidden by the text of the status bar. We can prevent this by setting the scroll view's `contentInset`:

```
sv.contentInset = UIEdgeInsetsMake(20, 0, 0, 0)
```

The scroll view still underlaps the status bar, and its scrolled content is still visible behind the status bar; what's changed is only that at the extreme scrolled-down position, where the content offset is (`0.0,0.0`), the scroll view's content is *not* behind the status bar.

When changing the `contentInset`, you will probably want to change the `scroll-IndicatorInsets` to match. Consider again the scroll view whose `contentInset` we have just set. When scrolled all the way down, it now has a nice gap between the bottom of the status bar and the top of the first label; but the top of the scroll indicator is still up behind the status bar. We can prevent this by setting the `scrollIndicatorInsets` to the same value as the `contentInset`:

```
sv.contentInset = UIEdgeInsetsMake(20, 0, 0, 0)
sv.scrollIndicatorInsets = sv.contentInset
```

As I mentioned in Chapter 6, top bars and bottom bars are likely to be translucent, and the runtime would like to make your view underlap them. With a scroll view, this looks cool, because the scroll view's contents are visible in a blurry way through the translucent bar; but the `contentInset` and `scrollIndicatorInsets` need to be adjusted so that the scrolling limits stay between the top bar and the bottom bar. Moreover, the height of the bars can change, depending on such factors as how the interface is rotated.

Therefore, if a scroll view is going to underlap top and bottom bars, it would be nice, instead of hard-coding the top inset as in the preceding code, to make the scroll view's inset respond to its environment. A layout event seems the best place for such a response, and we can use the view controller's `topLayoutGuide` and `bottomLayoutGuide` to help us:

```
override func viewWillLayoutSubviews() {
    if let sv = self.sv {
        let top = self.topLayoutGuide.length
        let bot = self.bottomLayoutGuide.length
        sv.contentInset = UIEdgeInsetsMake(top, 0, bot, 0)
        sv.scrollIndicatorInsets = self.sv.contentInset
    }
}
```

Even better, if our view controller's main view contains one primary scroll view, and if it contains it sufficiently early — in the nib, for example — then if our view controller's `automaticallyAdjustsScrollViewInsets` property is `true`, the runtime will adjust our scroll view's `contentInset` and `scrollIndicatorInsets` with no code on our part. This property won't help us in the examples earlier in this chapter where we create the scroll view in code. But if the scroll view is created from the nib, as in Figure 7-1, this property applies and works. Moreover, a value of `true` is the default! In the nib editor, you can change it with the Adjust Scroll View Insets checkbox in the Attributes inspector. Be sure to set this property to `false` if you want to take charge of adjusting a scroll view's `contentInset` and `scrollIndicatorInsets` yourself.

Paging

If its `pagingEnabled` property is `true`, the scroll view doesn't let the user scroll freely; instead, the content is considered to consist of equal-sized sections. The user can scroll only in such a way as to move to a different section. The size of a section is set automatically to the size of the scroll view's bounds. The sections are the scroll view's *pages*.

When the user stops dragging, a paging scroll view gently snaps automatically to the nearest whole page. For example, let's say that the scroll view scrolls only horizontally, and that its subviews are image views showing photos, sized to match the scroll view's bounds. If the user drags horizontally to the left to a point where *less* than half of the next photo to the right is visible, and raises the dragging finger, the paging scroll view snaps its content back to the right until the entire first photo is visible again. If the user drags horizontally to the left to a point where *more* than half of the next photo to the right is visible, and raises the dragging finger, the paging scroll view snaps its content further to the left until the entire second photo is visible.

The usual arrangement is that a paging scroll view is at least as large, or nearly as large, in its scrollable dimension, as the screen. A moment's thought will reveal that, under this arrangement, it is impossible for the user to move the content more than a single page in any direction with a single gesture. The reason is that the size of the page is the size of the scroll view's bounds. Thus the user will run out of surface area to drag on before being able to move the content the distance of a page and a half, which is what would be needed to make the scroll view snap to a page not adjacent to the page we started on.

Sometimes, indeed, the paging scroll view will be slightly *larger* than the window in its scrollable dimension. This allows each page's content to fill the scroll view while also providing gaps between the pages, visible when the user starts to scroll. The user is still able to move from page to page, because it is still readily possible to drag more than half a new page into view (and the scroll view will then snap the rest of the way when the user raises the dragging finger).

When the user raises the dragging finger, the scroll view's action in adjusting its content is considered to be *decelerating*, and the scroll view's delegate (discussed in more detail later in this chapter) will receive scrollViewWillBeginDecelerating:, followed by scrollViewDidEndDecelerating: when the scroll view's content has stopped moving and a full page is showing. Thus, these messages can be used to detect efficiently that the page may have changed.

You can take advantage of this, for example, to coordinate a paging scroll view with a UIPageControl (Chapter 12). In this example, a page control (self.pager) is updated whenever the user causes a horizontally scrollable scroll view (self.sv) to display a different page:

```
func scrollViewDidEndDecelerating(scrollView: UIScrollView) {
    let x = self.sv.contentOffset.x
    let w = self.sv.bounds.size.width
    self.pager.currentPage = Int(x/w)
}
```

Conversely, we can scroll the scroll view to a new page manually when the user taps the page control; in this case we have to calculate the page boundaries ourselves:

```
@IBAction func userDidPage(sender:AnyObject?) {
    let p = self.pager.currentPage
    let w = self.sv.bounds.size.width
    self.sv.setContentOffset(CGPointMake(CGFloat(p)*w,0), animated:true)
}
```

A useful interface is a paging scroll view where you supply pages dynamically as the user scrolls. In this way, you can display a huge number of pages without having to put them all into the scroll view at once. A scrolling UIPageViewController (Chapter 6) provides exactly that interface. Its `UIPageViewControllerOptionInterPageSpacing-Key` even provides the gap between pages that I mentioned earlier.

A compromise between a UIPageViewController and a completely preconfigured paging scroll view is a scroll view whose `contentSize` can accommodate all pages, but whose actual page content is supplied lazily. The only pages that have to be present at all times are the page visible to the user and the two pages adjacent to it on either side (so that there is no delay in displaying a new page's content when the user starts to scroll). This approach is exemplified by Apple's PageControl sample code. Unfortunately, that example does not also remove page content that is no longer needed, so there is ultimately no conservation of memory.

There are times when a scroll view, even one requiring a good deal of dynamic configuration, is better than a scrolling UIPageViewController, because the scroll view provides full information to its delegate about the user's scrolling activity (as described later in this chapter). For example, if you wanted to respond to the user's dragging one area of the interface by programmatically scrolling another area of the interface in a coordinated fashion, you might want what the user is dragging to be a scroll view, because it tells you what the user is up to at every moment.

Tiling

Suppose we have some finite but really big content that we want to display in a scroll view, such as a very large image that the user can inspect, piecemeal, by scrolling. To hold the entire image in memory may be onerous or impossible.

Tiling is one solution to this kind of problem. It takes advantage of the insight that there's really no need to hold the entire image in memory; all we need at any given moment is the part of the image visible to the user right now. Mentally, divide the content rectangle into a matrix of rectangles; these rectangles are the tiles. In reality, divide the huge image into corresponding rectangles. Then whenever the user scrolls, we look to see whether part of any empty tile has become visible, and if so, we supply its content. At the same time, we can release the content of all tiles that are completely offscreen. Thus, at any given moment, only the tiles that are showing have content. There is some latency associated with this approach (the user scrolls, then any empty newly visible tiles are filled in), but we will have to live with that.

There is actually a built-in CALayer subclass for helping us implement tiling — CATiledLayer. Its `tileSize` property sets the dimensions of a tile. Its `drawLayer:inContext:` is called when content for an empty tile is needed; calling `CGContextGetClipBoundingBox` on the context reveals the location of the desired tile, and now we can supply that tile's content.

The usual approach is to implement `drawRect:` in a UIView that hosts the CATiledLayer. Here, the CATiledLayer is the view's underlying layer; therefore the view is the CATiledLayer's delegate (see Chapter 3). This means that when the CATiledLayer's `drawLayer:inContext:` is called, the host view's `drawRect:` is called, and the `drawRect:` parameter is the same as the result of calling `CGContextGetClipBoundingBox` — namely, it's the rect of the tile we are to draw.

The `tileSize` may need to be adjusted for the screen resolution. On a double-resolution device, for example, the CATiledLayer's `contentsScale` will be doubled, and the tiles will be half the size that we ask for. If that isn't acceptable, we can double the `tileSize` dimensions.

To illustrate, we'll use some tiles already created for us as part of Apple's own Photo-Scroller sample code. In particular, I'll use a few of the "CuriousFrog_500" images. These all have names of the form *CuriousFrog_500_x_y.png*, where *x* and *y* are integers corresponding to the picture's position within the matrix. The images are 256×256 pixels, except for the ones on the extreme right and bottom edges of the matrix, which are shorter in one dimension, but I won't be using those in this example; I've selected a square matrix of 9 square images.

We will give our scroll view (`self.sv`) one subview, a TiledView, a UIView subclass that exists purely to give our CATiledLayer a place to live. `TILESIZE` is defined as 256, to match the image dimensions:

```
override func viewDidLoad() {
    let f = CGRectMake(0,0,3*TILESIZE,3*TILESIZE)
    let content = TiledView(frame:f)
    let tsz = TILESIZE * content.layer.contentsScale
    (content.layer as! CATiledLayer).tileSize = CGSizeMake(tsz, tsz)
    self.sv.addSubview(content)
    self.sv.contentSize = f.size
    self.content = content
}
```

Here's the code for TiledView. As Apple's sample code points out, we must fetch images with `init(contentsOfFile:)` in order to avoid the automatic caching behavior of `init(named:)` — after all, we're going to all this trouble exactly to avoid using more memory than we have to:

```
override class func layerClass() -> AnyClass {
    return CATiledLayer.self
}
override func drawRect(r: CGRect) {
    let tile = r
    let x = Int(tile.origin.x/TILESIZE)
    let y = Int(tile.origin.y/TILESIZE)
    let tileName = String(format:"CuriousFrog_500_\(x+3)_\(y)")
    let path = NSBundle.mainBundle().pathForResource(tileName, ofType:"png")!
    let image = UIImage(contentsOfFile:path)!
    image.drawAtPoint(CGPointMake(CGFloat(x)*TILESIZE,CGFloat(y)*TILESIZE))
}
```

In this configuration, our TiledView's `drawRect` is called *on a background thread*. This is unusual, but it shouldn't cause any trouble as long as you confine yourself to standard thread-safe activities. Fortunately, fetching the image and drawing it *are* thread-safe.

 You may encounter a nasty issue where a CATiledLayer's `drawRect:` is called simultaneously on *multiple* background threads. It isn't clear to me whether this problem is confined to the Simulator or whether it can also occur on a device. The workaround is to wrap the whole interior of `drawRect:` in a call to `dispatch_sync` on a serial queue (see Chapter 25).

There is no special call for invalidating an offscreen tile. You can call `setNeedsDisplay` or `setNeedsDisplayInRect:` on the TiledView, but this doesn't erase offscreen tiles. You're just supposed to trust that the CATiledLayer will eventually clear offscreen tiles if needed to conserve memory.

CATiledLayer has a class method `fadeDuration` that dictates the duration of the animation that fades a new tile into view. You can create a CATiledLayer subclass and override this method to return a value different from the default (`0.25`), but this is probably not worth doing, as the default value is a good one. Returning a smaller value won't make tiles appear faster; it just replaces the nice fade-in with an annoying flash.

Zooming

To implement zooming of a scroll view's content, you set the scroll view's `minimumZoomScale` and `maximumZoomScale` so that at least one of them isn't 1 (the default). You also implement `viewForZoomingInScrollView:` in the scroll view's delegate to tell the scroll view which of its subviews is to be the scalable view. The scroll view then zooms by applying a scale transform (Chapter 1) to this subview. The amount of that transform is the scroll view's `zoomScale` property. Typically, you'll want the scroll view's entire content to be scalable, so you'll have one direct subview of the scroll view that acts as the scalable view, and anything else inside the scroll view will be a subview of the scalable view, so as to be scaled together with it. This is another reason for arranging your scroll view's subviews inside a single content view, as I suggested earlier.

To illustrate, we can start with any of the four content view–based versions of our scroll view containing 30 labels. I called the content view v. Now we add these lines:

```
v.tag = 999
sv.minimumZoomScale = 1.0
sv.maximumZoomScale = 2.0
sv.delegate = self
```

We have assigned a tag to the view that is to be scaled, so that we can refer to it later. We have set the scale limits for the scroll view. And we have made ourselves the scroll view's delegate. Now all we have to do is implement viewForZoomingInScrollView: to return the scalable view:

```
func viewForZoomingInScrollView(scrollView: UIScrollView) -> UIView? {
    return scrollView.viewWithTag(999)
}
```

This works: the scroll view now responds to pinch gestures by scaling appropriately! But it doesn't look quite as good as I'd like when we zoom, and in particular I don't like the way the labels snap into place when we stop zooming. The reason is that, in my earlier examples, I gave the content view and the contentSize a zero width; that was sufficient to prevent the scroll view from scrolling horizontally, which was all that mattered. Now, however, these widths also affect how the content behaves as the user zooms it. This particular example, I think, looks best while zooming if the content view width is a bit wider than the widest label. (Implementing that is left as an exercise for the reader.)

The user can actually scale considerably beyond the limits we set in both directions; in that case, when the gesture ends, the scale snaps back to the limit value. If we wish to confine scaling strictly to our defined limits, we can set the scroll view's bouncesZoom to false; when the user reaches a limit, scaling will simply stop.

The actual amount of zoom is reflected as the scroll view's current zoomScale. If a scroll view participates in state restoration, its zoomScale is saved and restored, so when the app is relaunched, the scroll view will reappear zoomed by the same amount as before.

If the minimumZoomScale is less than 1, then when the scalable view becomes smaller than the scroll view, it is pinned to the scroll view's top left. If you don't like this, you can change it by subclassing UIScrollView and overriding layoutSubviews, or by implementing the scroll view delegate method scrollViewDidZoom:. Here's a simple example (drawn from a WWDC 2010 video) demonstrating an override of layout-Subviews that keeps the scalable view centered in either dimension whenever it is smaller than the scroll view in that dimension:

```
override func layoutSubviews() {
    super.layoutSubviews()
    if let v = self.delegate?.viewForZoomingInScrollView?(self) {
        let svw = self.bounds.width
        let svh = self.bounds.height
        let vw = v.frame.width
        let vh = v.frame.height
        var f = v.frame
        if vw < svw {
            f.origin.x = (svw - vw) / 2.0
        } else {
            f.origin.x = 0
        }
        if vh < svh {
            f.origin.y = (svh - vh) / 2.0
        } else {
            f.origin.y = 0
        }
        v.frame = f
    }
}
```

Earlier, I said that the scroll view zooms by applying a scale transform to the scalable view. This has two important secondary consequences that can surprise you if you're unprepared:

- *The frame of the scalable view* is scaled to match the current zoomScale. This follows as a natural consequence of applying a scale transform to the scalable view.

- The scroll view is concerned to make scrolling continue to work correctly: the limits as the user scrolls should continue to match the limits of the content, and commands like scrollRectToVisible:animated: should continue to work the same way for the same values. Therefore, the scroll view automatically scales *its own content-Size* to match the current zoomScale.

Zooming Programmatically

To zoom programmatically, you have two choices:

setZoomScale:animated:
> Zooms in terms of scale value. The contentOffset is automatically adjusted to keep the current center centered and the content occupying the entire scroll view.

zoomToRect:animated:
> Zooms so that the given rectangle of the content occupies as much as possible of the scroll view's bounds. The contentOffset is automatically adjusted to keep the content occupying the entire scroll view.

In this example, I implement double tapping as a zoom gesture. In my action handler for the double-tap UITapGestureRecognizer attached to the scalable view, a double tap means to zoom to maximum scale, minimum scale, or actual size, depending on the current scale value:

```
@IBAction func tapped(tap : UIGestureRecognizer) {
    let v = tap.view!
    let sv = v.superview as! UIScrollView
    if sv.zoomScale < 1 {
        sv.setZoomScale(1, animated:true)
    }
    else if sv.zoomScale < sv.maximumZoomScale {
        sv.setZoomScale(sv.maximumZoomScale, animated:true)
    }
    else {
        sv.setZoomScale(sv.minimumZoomScale, animated:true)
    }
}
```

Zooming with Detail

By default, when a scroll view zooms, it merely applies a scale transform to the scaled view. The scaled view's drawing is cached beforehand into its layer, so when we zoom in, the bits of the resulting bitmap are drawn larger. This means that a zoomed-in scroll view's content may be fuzzy (pixellated). In some cases this might be acceptable, but in others you might like the content to be redrawn more sharply at its new size.

(On a high-resolution device, this might not be such an issue. For example, if the user is allowed to zoom only up to double scale, you can draw at double scale right from the start; the results will look good at single scale, because the screen has high resolution, as well as at double scale, because that's the scale you drew at.)

One solution is to take advantage of a CATiledLayer feature that I didn't mention earlier. It turns out that CATiledLayer is aware not only of scrolling but also of scaling: you can configure it to ask for tiles to be drawn when the layer is scaled to a new order of magnitude. When your drawing routine is called, the graphics context itself has already been scaled appropriately by a transform.

In the case of an image into which the user is to be permitted to zoom deeply, you would be forearmed with multiple tile sets constituting the image, each set having double the tile size of the previous set (as in Apple's PhotoScroller example). In other cases, you may not need tiles at all; you'll just draw again, at the new resolution.

Besides its `tileSize`, you'll need to set two additional CATiledLayer properties:

levelsOfDetail

The number of different resolutions at which you want to redraw, where each level has twice the resolution of the previous level. So, for example, with two levels of detail we can ask to redraw when zooming to double size (2x) and when zooming back to single size (1x).

levelsOfDetailBias

> The number of levels of detail that are *larger* than single size (1x). For example, if levelsOfDetail is 2, then if we want to redraw when zooming to 2x and when zooming back to 1x, the levelsOfDetailBias needs to be 1, because one of those levels is larger than 1x. (If we were to leave levelsOfDetailBias at 0, the default, we would be saying we want to redraw when zooming to 0.5x and back to 1x — we have two levels of detail but neither is larger than 1x, so one must be smaller than 1x.)

The CATiledLayer will ask for a redraw at a higher resolution as soon as the view's size becomes larger than the previous resolution. In other words, if there are two levels of detail with a bias of 1, the layer will be redrawn at 2x as soon as it is zoomed even a little bit larger than 1x. This is an excellent approach, because although a level of detail would look blurry if scaled up, it looks pretty good scaled down.

For example, let's say I have a TiledView that hosts a CATiledLayer, in which I intend to draw an image. I haven't broken the image into tiles, because the maximum size at which the user can view it isn't prohibitively large; the original image is 838×958, and can be held in memory easily. Rather, I'm using a CATiledLayer in order to take advantage of its ability to change resolutions automatically. The image will be displayed initially at 208×238, and if the user never zooms in to view it larger, we can save memory by drawing a quarter-size version of the image.

The CATiledLayer is configured as follows:

```
let scale = lay.contentsScale
lay.tileSize = CGSizeMake(208*scale,238*scale)
lay.levelsOfDetail = 3
lay.levelsOfDetailBias = 2
```

The tileSize has been adjusted for screen resolution, so the result is as follows:

- As originally displayed at 208×238, there is one tile and we can draw our image at quarter size.

- If the user zooms in, to show the image larger than its originally displayed size, there will be 4 tiles and we can draw our image at half size.

- If the user zooms in still further, to show the image larger than double its originally displayed size (416×476), there will be 16 tiles and we can draw our image at full size, which will continue to look good as the user zooms all the way in to the full size of the original image.

We do not, however, need to draw each tile individually. Each time we're called upon to draw a tile, we'll draw the entire image into the TiledView's bounds; whatever falls outside the requested tile will be clipped out and won't be drawn.

Here's my TiledView's drawRect: implementation. I have a UIImage property current-Image, initialized to nil, and a CGRect property currentSize initialized to CGSize-Zero. Each time drawRect: is called, I compare the tile size (the incoming rect parameter's size) to currentSize. If it's different, I know that we've changed by one level of detail and we need a new version of currentImage, so I create the new version of current-Image at a scale appropriate to this level of detail. Finally, I draw currentImage into the TiledView's bounds:

```
override func drawRect(rect: CGRect) {
    let oldSize = self.currentSize
    if !CGSizeEqualToSize(oldSize, rect.size) {
        // make a new size
        self.currentSize = rect.size
        // make a new image
        let lay = self.layer as! CATiledLayer
        let tr = CGContextGetCTM(UIGraphicsGetCurrentContext()!)
        let sc = tr.a/lay.contentsScale
        let scale = sc/4.0
        let path = NSBundle.mainBundle().pathForResource(
            "earthFromSaturn", ofType:"png")!
        let im = UIImage(contentsOfFile:path)!
        let sz = CGSizeMake(im.size.width * scale, im.size.height * scale)
        UIGraphicsBeginImageContextWithOptions(sz, true, 1)
        im.drawInRect(CGRectMake(0,0,sz.width,sz.height))
        self.currentImage = UIGraphicsGetImageFromCurrentImageContext()
        UIGraphicsEndImageContext()
    }
    self.currentImage.drawInRect(self.bounds)
}
```

An alternative and much simpler approach (from a WWDC 2011 video) is to make yourself the scroll view's delegate so that you get an event when the zoom ends, and then change the scalable view's contentScaleFactor to match the current zoom scale, compensating for the high-resolution screen at the same time:

```
func scrollViewDidEndZooming(scrollView: UIScrollView,
    withView view: UIView?,
    atScale scale: CGFloat) {
        if let view = view {
            view.contentScaleFactor = scale * UIScreen.mainScreen().scale
        }
}
```

In response, the scalable view's drawRect: will be called, and its rect parameter will be the CGRect to draw into. Thus, the view may appear fuzzy for a while as the user zooms in, but when the user stops zooming, the view is redrawn sharply. That approach comes with a caveat, however: you mustn't overdo it. If the zoom scale, screen resolution, and scalable view size are high, you will be asking for a very large graphics context to be maintained in memory, which could cause your app to run low on memory or even to be abruptly terminated by the system.

For more about displaying a large image in a zoomable scroll view, see Apple's Large Image Downsizing example.

Scroll View Delegate

The scroll view's delegate (adopting the UIScrollViewDelegate protocol) receives lots of messages that can help you track, in great detail, exactly what the scroll view is up to:

`scrollViewDidScroll:`
> If you scroll in code without animation, you will receive this message *once* afterward. If the user scrolls, either by dragging or with the scroll-to-top feature, or if you scroll in code with animation, you will receive this message *repeatedly* throughout the scroll, including during the time the scroll view is decelerating after the user's finger has lifted; there are other delegate messages that tell you, in those cases, when the scroll has finally ended.

`scrollViewDidEndScrollingAnimation:`
> If you scroll in code with animation, you will receive this message afterward, when the animation ends.

`scrollViewWillBeginDragging:`
`scrollViewWillEndDragging:withVelocity:targetContentOffset:`
`scrollViewDidEndDragging:willDecelerate:`
> If the user scrolls by dragging, you will receive these messages at the start and end of the user's finger movement. If the user brings the scroll view to a stop before lifting the finger, `willDecelerate` is `false` and the scroll is over. If the user lets go of the scroll view while the finger is moving, or when paging is turned on, `willDecelerate` is `true` and we proceed to the delegate messages reporting deceleration.
>
> The purpose of `scrollViewWillEndDragging:...` is to let you customize the outcome of the content's deceleration. The third argument is a pointer to a CGPoint; you can use it to set a different CGPoint, specifying the `contentOffset` value the scroll view should have when the deceleration is over.

`scrollViewWillBeginDecelerating:`
`scrollViewDidEndDecelerating:`
> Sent once each after `scrollViewDidEndDragging:willDecelerate:` arrives with a value of `true`. When `scrollViewDidEndDecelerating:` arrives, the scroll is over.

`scrollViewShouldScrollToTop:`
`scrollViewDidScrollToTop:`
> These have to do with the feature where the user can tap the status bar to scroll the scroll view's content to its top. You won't get either of them if `scrollsToTop` is `false`, because the scroll-to-top feature is turned off in that case. The first lets you prevent the user from scrolling to the top on this occasion even if `scrollsToTop` is `true`. The second tells you that the user has employed this feature and the scroll is over.

So, if you wanted to do something after a scroll ends completely regardless of how the scroll was performed, you'd need to implement multiple delegate methods:

- `scrollViewDidEndDragging:willDecelerate:` in case the user drags and stops (`willDecelerate` is `false`).
- `scrollViewDidEndDecelerating:` in case the user drags and the scroll continues afterward.
- `scrollViewDidScrollToTop:` in case the user uses the scroll-to-top feature.
- `scrollViewDidEndScrollingAnimation:` in case you scroll with animation.

(You don't need a delegate method to tell you when the scroll is over after you scroll in code *without* animation: it's over immediately, so if you have work to do after the scroll ends, you can do it in the next line of code.)

In addition, the scroll view has read-only properties reporting its state:

`tracking`
> The user has touched the scroll view, but the scroll view hasn't decided whether this is a scroll or some kind of tap.

`dragging`
> The user is dragging to scroll.

`decelerating`
> The user has scrolled and has lifted the finger, and the scroll is continuing.

There are also three delegate messages that report zooming:

`scrollViewWillBeginZooming:withView:`
> If the user zooms or you zoom in code, you will receive this message as the zoom begins.

`scrollViewDidZoom:`
> If you zoom in code, even with animation, you will receive this message *once*. If the user zooms, you will receive this message *repeatedly* as the zoom proceeds. (You

will probably also receive `scrollViewDidScroll:`, possibly many times, as the zoom proceeds.)

`scrollViewDidEndZooming:withView:atScale:`

If the user zooms or you zoom in code, you will receive this message after the last `scrollViewDidZoom:`.

In addition, the scroll view has read-only properties reporting its state during a zoom:

`zooming`

The scroll view is zooming. It is possible for `dragging` to be true at the same time.

`zoomBouncing`

The scroll view is returning automatically from having been zoomed outside its minimum or maximum limit. As far as I can tell, you'll get only one `scrollView-DidZoom:` while the scroll view is in this state.

Scroll View Touches

Improvements in UIScrollView's internal implementation have eliminated most of the worry once associated with scroll view touches. A scroll view will interpret a drag or a pinch as a command to scroll or zoom, and any other gesture will fall through to the subviews; thus buttons and similar interface objects inside a scroll view work just fine.

You can even put a scroll view inside a scroll view, and this can be quite a useful thing to do, in contexts where you might not think of it at first. Apple's PhotoScroller example, based on principles discussed in a delightful WWDC 2010 video, is an app where a single photo fills the screen: you can page-scroll from one photo to the next, and you can zoom into the current photo with a pinch gesture. This is implemented as a scroll view inside a scroll view: the outer scroll view is for paging between images, and the inner scroll view contains the current image and is for zooming (and for scrolling to different parts of the zoomed-in image). Similarly, a WWDC 2013 video deconstructs the iOS 7 lock screen in terms of scroll views embedded in scroll views.

Gesture recognizers (Chapter 5) have also greatly simplified the task of adding custom gestures to a scroll view. For instance, some older code in Apple's documentation, showing how to implement a double tap to zoom in and a two-finger tap to zoom out, uses old-fashioned touch handling, but this is no longer necessary. Simply attach to your scroll view's scalable subview any gesture recognizers for these sorts of gesture, and they will mediate automatically among the possibilities.

In the past, making something inside a scroll view draggable required setting the scroll view's `canCancelContentTouches` property to `false`. (The reason for the name is that the scroll view, when it realizes that a gesture is a drag or pinch gesture, normally sends `touchesCancelled:forEvent:` to a subview tracking touches, so that the scroll view and not the subview will be affected.) However, unless you're implementing old-fashioned direct touch handling, you probably won't have to concern yourself with this. Regardless of how `canCancelContentTouches` is set, a draggable control, such as a UISlider, remains draggable inside a scroll view.

Here's an example of a draggable object inside a scroll view implemented through a gesture recognizer. Suppose we have an image of a map, larger than the screen, and we want the user to be able to scroll it in the normal way to see any part of the map, but we also want the user to be able to drag a flag into a new location on the map. We'll put the map image in an image view and wrap the image view in a scroll view, with the scroll view's `contentSize` the same as the map image view's size. The flag is a small image view; it's another subview of the scroll view, and it has a UIPanGestureRecognizer. The gesture recognizer's action handler allows the flag to be dragged, exactly as described in Chapter 5:

```
@IBAction func dragging (p : UIPanGestureRecognizer) {
    let v = p.view!
    switch p.state {
    case .Began, .Changed:
        let delta = p.translationInView(v.superview!)
        v.center.x += delta.x
        v.center.y += delta.y
        p.setTranslation(CGPointZero, inView: v.superview)
    default: break
    }
}
```

The user can now drag the map or the flag (Figure 7-2). Dragging the map brings the flag along with it, but dragging the flag doesn't move the map. The state of the scroll view's `canCancelContentTouches` is irrelevant, because the flag view isn't tracking the touches manually.

An interesting addition to that example would be to implement *autoscrolling*, meaning that the scroll view scrolls itself when the user drags the flag close to its edge. This, too, is greatly simplified by gesture recognizers; in fact, we can add autoscrolling code directly to the `dragging:` action handler:

```
@IBAction func dragging (p : UIPanGestureRecognizer) {
    let v = p.view!
    switch p.state {
    case .Began, .Changed:
        let delta = p.translationInView(v.superview!)
        v.center.x += delta.x
        v.center.y += delta.y
        p.setTranslation(CGPointZero, inView: v.superview)
        if p.state == .Changed {fallthrough}
    case .Changed:
        // autoscroll
        let sv = self.sv
        let loc = p.locationInView(sv)
```

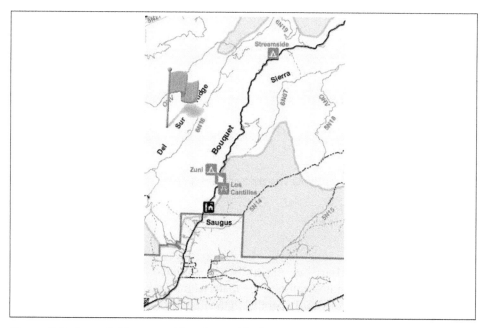

Figure 7-2. A scrollable map with a draggable flag

```
let f = sv.bounds
var off = sv.contentOffset
let sz = sv.contentSize
var c = v.center
// to the right
if loc.x > CGRectGetMaxX(f) - 30 {
    let margin = sz.width - CGRectGetMaxX(sv.bounds)
    if margin > 6 {
        off.x += 5
        sv.contentOffset = off
        c.x += 5
        v.center = c
        self.keepDragging(p)
    }
}
// to the left
if loc.x < f.origin.x + 30 {
    let margin = off.x
    if margin > 6 {
        // ...
    }
}
// to the bottom
if loc.y > CGRectGetMaxY(f) - 30 {
    let margin = sz.height - CGRectGetMaxY(sv.bounds)
    if margin > 6 {
```

```
                    // ...
                }
            }
            // to the top
            if loc.y < f.origin.y + 30 {
                let margin = off.y
                if margin > 6 {
                    // ...
                }
            }
        default: break
        }
    }
    func keepDragging (p : UIPanGestureRecognizer) {
        let del = 0.1
        delay(del) {
            self.dragging(p)
        }
    }
}
```

The `delay` in `keepDragging:` (see Appendix B), combined with the change in offset, determines the speed of autoscrolling. The material marked as omitted in the second, third, and fourth cases is obviously parallel to the first case, and is left as an exercise for the reader.

A scroll view's touch handling is itself based on gesture recognizers attached to the scroll view, and these are available to your code through the scroll view's `panGesture-Recognizer` and `pinchGestureRecognizer` properties. This means that if you want to customize a scroll view's touch handling, it's easy to add more gesture recognizers and have them interact with those already attached to the scroll view.

To illustrate, I'll build on the previous example. Suppose we want the flag to start out offscreen, and we'd like the user to be able to summon it with a rightward swipe. We can attach a UISwipeGestureRecognizer to our scroll view, but it will never recognize its gesture because the scroll view's own pan gesture recognizer will recognize first. But we have access to the scroll view's pan gesture recognizer, so we can compel it to yield to our swipe gesture recognizer by sending it `requireGestureRecognizerToFail::`:

```
self.sv.panGestureRecognizer.requireGestureRecognizerToFail(self.swipe)
```

The UISwipeGestureRecognizer will recognize a rightward swipe. In my implementation of its action handler, we position the flag, which has been waiting invisibly offscreen, just off to the top left of the scroll view's visible content, and animate it onto the screen:

```
@IBAction func swiped (g: UISwipeGestureRecognizer) {
    let sv = self.sv
    let p = sv.contentOffset
    self.flag.frame.origin = p
    self.flag.frame.origin.x -= self.flag.bounds.size.width
    self.flag.hidden = false
```

```
    UIView.animateWithDuration(0.25, animations:{
        self.flag.frame.origin.x = p.x
        // thanks for the flag, now stop operating altogether
        g.enabled = false
    })
}
```

Floating Scroll View Subviews

A scroll view's subview will appear to "float" over the scroll view if it remains stationary while the rest of the scroll view's content is being scrolled. Before autolayout, this sort of thing was rather tricky to arrange; you had to use a delegate event to respond to every change in the scroll view's bounds origin by shifting the "floating" view's position to compensate, so as to appear to remain fixed. With autolayout, however, all you have to do is set up constraints pinning the subview to something *outside* the scroll view. Here's an example:

```
let iv = UIImageView(image:UIImage(named:"smiley.png"))
iv.translatesAutoresizingMaskIntoConstraints = false
self.sv.addSubview(iv)
let sup = self.sv.superview!
NSLayoutConstraint.activateConstraints([
    iv.rightAnchor.constraintEqualToAnchor(sup.rightAnchor, constant: -5),
    iv.topAnchor.constraintEqualToAnchor(sup.topAnchor, constant: 25)
])
```

Scroll View Performance

At several points in earlier chapters I've mentioned performance problems and ways to increase drawing efficiency. Nowhere are you so likely to need these as in connection with a scroll view. As a scroll view scrolls, views must be drawn very rapidly as they appear on the screen. If the drawing system can't keep up with the speed of the scroll, the scrolling will visibly stutter.

Performance testing and optimization is a big subject, so I can't tell you exactly what to do if you encounter stuttering while scrolling. But certain general suggestions (mostly extracted from a really great WWDC 2010 video) should come in handy:

- Everything that can be opaque should be opaque: don't force the drawing system to composite transparency, and remember to tell it that an opaque view or layer *is* opaque by setting its opaque property to true. If you really must composite transparency, keep the size of the nonopaque regions to a minimum; for example, if a large layer is transparent at its edges, break it into five layers — the large central layer, which is opaque, and the four edges, which are not.

- If you're drawing shadows, don't make the drawing system calculate the shadow shape for a layer: supply a shadowPath, or use Core Graphics to create the shadow with a drawing. Similarly, avoid making the drawing system composite the shadow as a transparency against another layer; for example, if the background layer is white, your opaque drawing can itself include a shadow already drawn on a white background.

- Don't make the drawing system scale images for you; supply the images at the target size for the correct resolution.

- In a pinch, you can just eliminate massive swatches of the rendering operation by setting a layer's `shouldRasterize` to `true`. You could, for example, do this when scrolling starts and then set it back to `false` when scrolling ends.

Apple's documentation also says that setting a view's `clearsContextBeforeDrawing` to `false` may make a difference. I can't confirm or deny this; it may be true, but I haven't encountered a case that positively proves it.

Xcode provides tools that will help you detect inefficiencies in the drawing system. In the Simulator, the Debug menu shows you blended layers (where transparency is being composited) and images that are being copied, misaligned, or rendered offscreen. On the device, the Core Animation module of Instruments provides the same functionality, plus it tracks the frame rate for you, allowing you to scroll and measure performance objectively where it really counts.

CHAPTER 8

Table Views and Collection Views

*I'm gonna ask you the three big questions. — Go
ahead. — Who made you? — You did. — Who
owns the biggest piece of you? — You do. — What
would happen if I dropped you? — I'd go right
down the drain.*

—Dialogue by Garson Kanin and Ruth Gordon,
Pat and Mike

A table view (UITableView) is a vertically scrolling UIScrollView (Chapter 7) containing
a single column of rectangular cells (UITableViewCell, a UIView subclass). It is a key-
stone of Apple's strategy for making the small iPhone screen useful and powerful, and
has three main purposes:

Presentation of information

> The cells typically contain text, which the user can read. The cells are usually quite
> small, in order to maximize the quantity appearing on the screen at once, so this
> text is often condensed, truncated, or simplified.

Selection

> A table view can provide the user with a column of choices. The user chooses by
> tapping a cell, which selects the cell; the app responds appropriately to that choice.

Navigation

> The appropriate response to the user's choosing a cell is often navigation to another
> interface. This might be done, for example, through a presented view controller or
> a navigation interface (Chapter 6). An extremely common configuration is a *mas-
> ter–detail interface*, where the master view is a table view within a navigation inter-
> face: the user taps a table view cell to navigate to the details about that cell. This is
> one reason why truncation of text in a table view cell is acceptable: the detail view
> contains the full information.

In addition to its column of cells, a table view can be extended by a number of other features that make it even more useful and flexible:

- A table can display a header view at the top and a footer view at the bottom.
- The cells can be clumped into sections. Each section can have a header and footer, and these remain visible as long as the section itself occupies the screen, giving the user a clue as to where we are within the table. Moreover, a section index can be provided, in the form of an overlay column of abbreviated section titles, which the user can tap or drag to jump to the start of a section, thus making a long table tractable.
- Tables can be editable: the user can be permitted to insert, delete, and reorder cells.
- A table can have a grouped format, with large section headers and footers that travel with their neighbor cells. This is often used for presenting small numbers of related cells; the headers and footers can provide ancillary information.

Table view cells, too, can be extremely flexible. Some basic cell formats are provided, such as a text label along with a small image view, but you are free to design your own cell as you would any other view. There are also some standard interface items that are commonly used in a cell, such as a checkmark to indicate selection or a right-pointing chevron to indicate that tapping the cell navigates to a detail view.

Figure 8-1 shows a familiar table view: Apple's Music app. Each table cell displays a song's name, artist, and album, in truncated form; the user can tap to play the song or to see further options. The table is divided into sections; as the user scrolls, the current section header stays pinned to the top of the table view. The table can also be navigated using the section index at the right.

Figure 8-2 shows a familiar grouped table: Apple's Settings app. It's a master–detail interface. The master view has sections, but they aren't labeled: they merely clump related topics. The detail view often has a single cell per section, using section headers and footers to explain what that cell does.

It would be difficult to overstate the importance of table views. An iOS app without a table view somewhere in its interface would be a rare thing, especially on the small iPhone screen. I've written apps consisting almost entirely of table views. Indeed, it is not uncommon to use a table view even in situations that have nothing particularly table-like about them, simply because it is so convenient.

For example, in one of my apps I want the user to be able to choose between three levels of difficulty and two sets of images. In a desktop application I'd probably use radio buttons; but there are no radio buttons among the standard iOS interface objects. Instead, I use a grouped table view so small that it doesn't even scroll. This gives me section headers, tappable cells, and a checkmark indicating the current choice (Figure 8-3).

Figure 8-1. A familiar table view

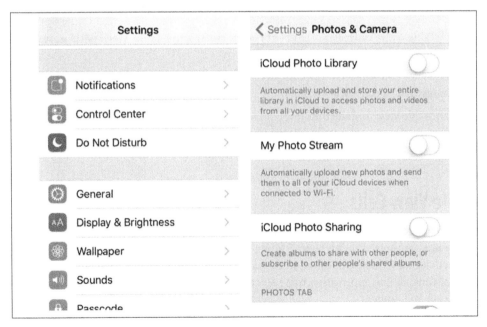

Figure 8-2. A familiar grouped table

Figure 8-3. A grouped table view as an interface for choosing options

There is a UIViewController subclass, UITableViewController, whose main view is a table view. You never really *need* to use a UITableViewController; it's a convenience, but it doesn't do anything that you couldn't do yourself by other means. Here's some of what using a UITableViewController gives you:

- UITableViewController's `init(style:)` creates the table view with a plain or grouped format.
- The view controller is automatically made the table view's delegate and data source, unless you specify otherwise.
- The table view is made the view controller's `tableView`. It is also, of course, the view controller's `view`, but the `tableView` property is typed as a UITableView, so you can send table view messages to it without casting.

Table View Cells

Beginners may be surprised to learn that a table view's structure and contents are generally not configured in advance. Rather, you supply the table view with a data source and a delegate (which will often be the same object), and the table view turns to these in real time, as the app runs, whenever it needs a piece of information about its own structure and contents.

This architecture may sound odd, but in fact it is part of a brilliant strategy to conserve resources. Imagine a long table consisting of thousands of rows. It must appear, therefore, to consist of thousands of cells as the user scrolls. But a cell is a UIView and is memory-intensive; to maintain thousands of cells internally would put a terrible strain on memory. Therefore, the table typically maintains only as many cells as are showing simultaneously at any one moment (about twelve, let's say). As the user scrolls to reveal new cells, those cells are created on the spot; meanwhile, the cells that have been scrolled out of view are permitted to die.

That's ingenious, but wouldn't it be even cleverer if, instead of letting a cell die as it is scrolled *out* of view, it were whisked around to the other side and used again as one of the cells being scrolled *into* view? Yes, and in fact that's exactly what you're supposed to do. You do it by assigning each cell a *reuse identifier*.

As cells with a given reuse identifier are scrolled out of view, the table view maintains a bunch of them in a pile. As cells are scrolled into view, you ask the table view for a cell from that pile, specifying it by means of the reuse identifier. The table view hands an old used cell back to you, and now you can configure it as the cell that is about to be scrolled into view. Cells are thus *reused* to minimize not only the number of actual cells in existence at any one moment, but the number of actual cells *ever created*. A table of 1000 rows might very well never need to create more than about a dozen cells over the entire lifetime of the app.

To facilitate this architecture, your code must be prepared, on demand, to supply the table with pieces of requested data. Of these, the most important is the cell to be slotted into a given position. A position in the table is specified by means of an index path (NSIndexPath), a class used here to combine a section number with a row number, and is often referred to simply as a *row* of the table. Your data source object may at any moment be sent the message `tableView:cellForRowAtIndexPath:`, and must respond by returning the UITableViewCell to be displayed at that row of the table. And you must return it *fast*: the user is scrolling *now*, so the table needs the next cell *now*.

In this section, I'll discuss *what* you're going to be supplying — the table view cell. After that, I'll talk about *how* you supply it.

Built-In Cell Styles

The simplest way to obtain a table view cell is to start with one of the four built-in table view cell styles. To create a cell using a built-in style, call `init(style:reuseIdentifier:)`. The `reuseIdentifier:` is what allows cells previously assigned to rows that are no longer showing to be reused for cells that are; it will usually be the same for all cells in a table. Your choices of cell style (UITableViewCellStyle) are:

.Default
> The cell has a UILabel (its `textLabel`), with an optional UIImageView (its `imageView`) at the left. If there is no image, the label occupies the entire width of the cell.

.Value1

The cell has two UILabels (its `textLabel` and its `detailTextLabel`) side by side, with an optional UIImageView (its `imageView`) at the left. The first label is left-aligned; the second label is right-aligned. If the first label's text is too long, the second label won't appear.

.Value2

The cell has two UILabels (its `textLabel` and its `detailTextLabel`) side by side. No UIImageView will appear. The first label is right-aligned; the second label is left-aligned. The label sizes are fixed, and the text of either will be truncated if it's too long.

.Subtitle

The cell has two UILabels (its `textLabel` and its `detailTextLabel`), one above the other, with an optional UIImageView (its `imageView`) at the left.

To experiment with the built-in cell styles, do this:

1. Start with an empty application without a storyboard (I explained how to do that at the start of Chapter 1).

2. Choose File → New → File and specify iOS → Source → Cocoa Touch Class. Click Next.

3. Make this class a UITableViewController subclass called RootViewController. The XIB checkbox should be checked; Xcode will create an eponymous *.xib* file containing a table view, correctly configured with its File's Owner as our RootViewController class. Click Next.

4. Make sure you're saving into the correct folder and group, and that the app target is checked. Click Create.

To get our table view into the interface, insert this line into AppDelegate's `application:didFinishLaunchingWithOptions:` at the appropriate spot:

```
self.window!.rootViewController = RootViewController()
```

Now modify the RootViewController class (which comes with a lot of templated code), as in Example 8-1. Run the app to see the world's simplest table (Figure 8-4).

Example 8-1. The world's simplest table

```
let cellIdentifier = "Cell"
override func numberOfSectionsInTableView(tableView: UITableView)
    -> Int {
        return 1 ❶
}
override func tableView(tableView: UITableView,
    numberOfRowsInSection section: Int) -> Int {
        return 20 ❷
```

Figure 8-4. The world's simplest table

```
}
override func tableView(tableView: UITableView,
    cellForRowAtIndexPath indexPath: NSIndexPath) -> UITableViewCell {
        var cell : UITableViewCell! =
            tableView.dequeueReusableCellWithIdentifier(cellIdentifier) ❸
        if cell == nil {
            cell = UITableViewCell(
                style:.Default, reuseIdentifier:cellIdentifier) ❹
            cell.textLabel!.textColor = UIColor.redColor() ❺
        }
        cell.textLabel!.text = "Hello there! \(indexPath.row)" ❻
        return cell
}
```

The key parts of the code are:

❶ Our table will have one section.

❷ Our table will consist of 20 rows. Having multiple rows will give us a sense of how our cell looks when placed next to other cells.

❸ In cellForRowAtIndexPath:, you always start by asking the table view for a reusable cell. Here, we will receive either an already existing reused cell or nil; in the latter case, we must create the cell from scratch, ourselves.

❹ If we did receive nil, we do create the cell. This is where you specify the built-in table view cell style you want to experiment with.

❺ At this point in the code you can modify characteristics of the cell (cell) that are to be the same for *every* cell of the table. For the moment, I've symbolized this by assuming that every cell's text is to be the same color.

❻ We now have the cell to be used for *this* row of the table, so at this point in the code you can modify characteristics of the cell (cell) that are unique to this row. I've symbolized this by appending successive numbers to the text of each row. Of course, in real life the different cells would reflect meaningful data. I'll talk about that later in this chapter.

Now you can experiment with your cell's appearance by tweaking the code and running the app. Feel free to try different built-in cell styles in the place where we are now specifying `.Default`.

The flexibility of each built-in style is based mostly on the flexibility of UILabels. Not everything can be customized, because after you return the cell some further configuration takes place, which may override your settings. For example, the size and position of the cell's subviews are not up to you. (I'll explain, a little later, how to get around that.) But you get a remarkable degree of freedom. Here are a few basic UILabel properties for you to play with now (by customizing `cell.textLabel`), and I'll talk much more about UILabels in Chapter 10:

text
> The string shown in the label.

textColor, highlightedTextColor
> The color of the text. The `highlightedTextColor` applies when the cell is highlighted or selected (tap on a cell to select it).

textAlignment
> How the text is aligned; some possible choices (NSTextAlignment) are `.Left`, `.Center`, and `.Right`.

numberOfLines
> The maximum number of lines of text to appear in the label. Text that is long but permitted to wrap, or that contains explicit linefeed characters, can appear completely in the label if the label is tall enough and the number of permitted lines is sufficient. 0 means there's no maximum; the default is 1.

font
> The label's font. You could reduce the font size as a way of fitting more text into the label. A font name includes its style. For example:
>
>   cell.textLabel!.font = UIFont(name:"Helvetica-Bold", size:12.0)

shadowColor, shadowOffset
> The text shadow. Adding a little shadow can increase clarity and emphasis for large text.

You can also assign the image view (`cell.imageView`) an image. The frame of the image view can't be changed, but you can inset its apparent size by supplying a smaller image and setting the image view's `contentMode` to `.Center`. It's probably a good idea in any case, for performance reasons, to supply images at their drawn size and resolution rather than making the drawing system scale them for you (see the last section of Chapter 7). For example:

```
let im = UIImage(named:"moi.png")!
UIGraphicsBeginImageContextWithOptions(CGSizeMake(36,36), true, 0.0)
im.drawInRect(CGRectMake(0,0,36,36))
let im2 = UIGraphicsGetImageFromCurrentImageContext()
UIGraphicsEndImageContext()
cell.imageView!.image = im2
cell.imageView!.contentMode = .Center
```

The cell itself also has some properties you can play with:

accessoryType

A built-in type (UITableViewCellAccessoryType) of accessory view, which appears at the cell's right end. For example:

```
cell.accessoryType = .DisclosureIndicator
```

accessoryView

Your own UIView, which appears at the cell's right end (overriding the accessory-Type). For example:

```
let b = UIButton(type:.System)
b.setTitle("Tap Me", forState:.Normal)
b.sizeToFit()
// ... also assign button a target and action ...
cell.accessoryView = b
```

indentationLevel, indentationWidth

These properties give the cell a left margin, useful for suggesting a hierarchy among cells. You can also set a cell's indentation level in real time, with respect to the table row into which it is slotted, by implementing the delegate's table-View:indentationLevelForRowAtIndexPath: method.

separatorInset

A UIEdgeInsets. Only the left and right insets matter. The default is a left inset of 15, but the built-in table view cell styles may shift it; for example, it's 16 for the .Basic cell style. This property affects both the drawing of the separator between cells and the indentation of content of the built-in cell styles.

If you try to set the separatorInset, you may run up against the cell's layout margins. For example, setting a cell's separatorInset to UIEdgeInsetsZero results in a left inset of 8. A workaround is to set the cell's layoutMargins to UIEdgeInsets-Zero as well.

selectionStyle

How the background looks when the cell is selected (UITableViewCellSelection-Style). The default is solid gray (.Default), or you can choose .None.

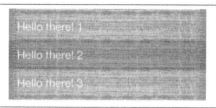

Figure 8-5. A cell with an image background

backgroundColor
backgroundView
selectedBackgroundView

What's behind everything else drawn in the cell. The selectedBackgroundView is drawn in front of the backgroundView (if any) when the cell is selected, and will appear instead of whatever the selectionStyle dictates. The backgroundColor is behind the backgroundView. There is no need to set the frame of the background-View and selectedBackgroundView; they will be resized automatically to fit the cell.

multipleSelectionBackgroundView

If defined (not nil), and if the table's allowsMultipleSelection (or, if editing, allowsMultipleSelectionDuringEditing) is true, used instead of the selected-BackgroundView when the cell is selected.

In this example, we set the cell's backgroundView to display an image with some transparency at the outside edges, so that the backgroundColor shows behind it, and we set the selectedBackgroundView to an almost transparent blue rectangle, to darken that image when the cell is selected (Figure 8-5):

```
cell.textLabel!.textColor = UIColor.whiteColor()
let v = UIImageView() // no need to set frame
v.contentMode = .ScaleToFill
v.image = UIImage(named:"linen.png")
cell.backgroundView = v
let v2 = UIView() // no need to set frame
v2.backgroundColor = UIColor.blueColor().colorWithAlphaComponent(0.2)
cell.selectedBackgroundView = v2;
cell.backgroundColor = UIColor.redColor()
```

If those features are to be true of every cell ever displayed in the table, then that code should go in the spot numbered 4 in Example 8-1; there's no need to waste time doing the same thing all over again when an existing cell is reused.

Finally, here are a few properties of the table view itself worth playing with:

`rowHeight`

> The height of a cell. A taller cell may accommodate more information. You can also change this value in the nib editor; the table view's row height appears in the Size inspector. The cell's subviews have their autoresizing set so as to compensate correctly. You can also set a cell's height in real time by implementing the delegate's `tableView:heightForRowAtIndexPath:` method; thus a table's cells may differ from one another in height (more about that later in this chapter).

`separatorStyle`, `separatorColor`, `separatorInset`

> These can also be set in the nib. The table's `separatorInset` is adopted by individual cells that don't have their own explicit `separatorInset`. Separator styles (UITable-ViewCellSeparatorStyle) are `.None` and `.SingleLine`.

`backgroundColor`, `backgroundView`

> What's behind all the cells of the table; this may be seen if the cells have transparency, or if the user scrolls the cells beyond their limit. The `backgroundView` is drawn on top of the `backgroundColor`.

`tableHeaderView`, `tableFooterView`

> Views to be shown before the first row and after the last row, respectively (as part of the table's scrolling content). Their background color is, by default, the background color of the table, but you can change that. You dictate their heights; their widths will be dynamically resized to fit the table. The user can, if you like, interact with these views (and their subviews); for example, a view can be (or can contain) a UIButton.
>
> You can alter a table header or footer view dynamically during the lifetime of the app; if you change its height, you must set the corresponding table view property afresh to notify the table view of what has happened.

Registering a Cell Class

In Example 8-1, I used this method to obtain the reusable cell:

- `dequeueReusableCellWithIdentifier:`

However, there's another way:

- `dequeueReusableCellWithIdentifier:forIndexPath:`

(The second parameter should always be the index path you received to begin with as the last parameter of `tableView:cellForRowAtIndexPath:`.)

Even though these two methods look nearly identical, they behave quite differently. The second method has three advantages:

The result is never `nil`

Unlike `dequeueReusableCellWithIdentifier:`, the value returned by `dequeue-ReusableCellWithIdentifier:forIndexPath:` is never `nil` (in Swift, it isn't an Optional). If there is a free reusable cell with the given identifier, it is returned. If there isn't, a new one is created for you. Step 4 of Example 8-1 can thus be eliminated!

The cell size is known earlier

Unlike `dequeueReusableCellWithIdentifier:`, the cell returned by `dequeue-ReusableCellWithIdentifier:forIndexPath:` has its final bounds. That's possible because you've passed the index path as an argument, so the runtime knows this cell's ultimate destination within the table, and has already consulted the table's `rowHeight` or the delegate's `tableView:heightForRowAtIndexPath:`. This makes laying out the cell's contents much easier.

The identifier is consistent

A danger with `dequeueReusableCellWithIdentifier:` is that you may accidentally pass an incorrect reuse identifier, and end up not reusing cells. With `dequeue-ReusableCellWithIdentifier:forIndexPath:`, that can't happen.

Before you call `dequeueReusableCellWithIdentifier:forIndexPath:` for the first time, you must *register* with the table itself (unless the cell is coming from a storyboard, as I'll explain in a moment). You can do this by calling `registerClass:forCellReuse-Identifier:`. This associates a class (which must be UITableViewCell or a subclass thereof) with a string identifier. That's how `dequeueReusableCellWithIdentifier:for-IndexPath:` knows what class to instantiate when it creates a new cell for you: you pass an identifier, and you've already told the table what class it signifies. The only cell types you can obtain are those for which you've registered in this way; if you pass a bad identifier, the app will crash (with a helpful log message).

This is a very elegant mechanism. It also raises some new questions:

When should I register with the table view?

Do it early, before the table view starts generating cells; `viewDidLoad` is a good place:

```
override func viewDidLoad() {
    super.viewDidLoad()
    self.tableView.registerClass(
        UITableViewCell.self, forCellReuseIdentifier: "Cell")
}
```

How do I specify a built-in table view cell style?

We are no longer calling `init(style:reuseIdentifier:)`, so where do we make our choice of built-in cell style? The default cell style is `.Default`, so if that's what you wanted, the problem is solved. Otherwise, subclass UITableViewCell and override `init(style:reuseIdentifier:)` to substitute the cell style you're after (passing along the reuse identifier you were handed).

For example, suppose we want the `.Subtitle` style. Let's call our UITableViewCell subclass MyCell. So we now specify `MyCell.self` in our call to `registerClass:for-CellReuseIdentifier:`. MyCell's initializer looks like this:

```
override init(style: UITableViewCellStyle, reuseIdentifier: String?) {
    super.init(style:.Subtitle, reuseIdentifier: reuseIdentifier)
}
```

How do I know whether the returned cell is new or reused?

Good question! It's important to know this, because our call never returns `nil`, so we need some *other* way to distinguish between configurations that are to apply once and for all to a *new cell* (step 5 of Example 8-1) and configurations that differ for *each row* (step 6). The answer is: It's up to you, when performing one-time configuration on a cell, to give that cell some distinguishing mark that you can look for later to determine whether a cell requires one-time configuration.

For example, if every cell is to have a two-line text label, there is no point configuring the text label of *every* cell returned by `dequeueReusableCellWithIdentifier:for-IndexPath:`; the reused cells have already been configured. But how will we know which cells need their text label to be configured? It's easy: they are the ones whose text label *hasn't* been configured:

```
override func tableView(tableView: UITableView,
    cellForRowAtIndexPath indexPath: NSIndexPath) -> UITableViewCell {
        let cell = tableView.dequeueReusableCellWithIdentifier(
            "Cell", forIndexPath:indexPath) as! MyCell
        if cell.textLabel!.numberOfLines != 2 { // never configured
            cell.textLabel!.numberOfLines = 2
            // other one-time configurations here ...
        }
        cell.textLabel!.text = // ...
        // other individual configurations here ...
        return cell
}
```

Custom Cells

The built-in cell styles give the beginner a leg up in getting started with table views, but there is nothing sacred about them, and soon you'll probably want to transcend them, putting yourself in charge of how a table's cells look and what subviews they contain. You are perfectly free to do this. The thing to remember is that the cell has a `content-View` property, which is one of its subviews; things like the `accessoryView` are outside the `contentView`. All *your* customizations must be confined to subviews of the `content-View`; this allows the cell to continue working correctly.

I'll illustrate four possible approaches to customizing the contents of a cell:

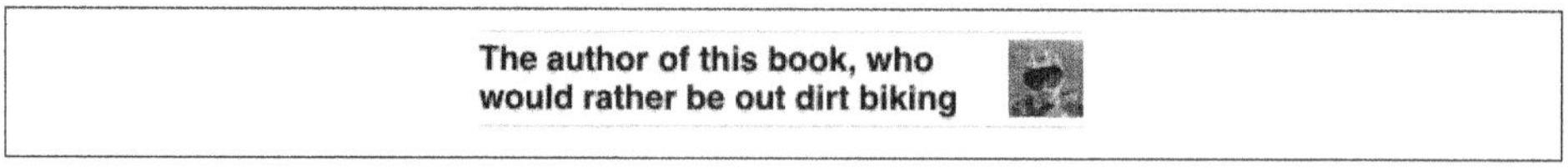

The author of this book, who
would rather be out dirt biking

Figure 8-6. A cell with its label and image view swapped

- Start with a built-in cell style, but supply a UITableViewCell subclass and override `layoutSubviews` to alter the frames of the built-in subviews.

- In `tableView:cellForRowAtIndexPath:`, add subviews to each cell's `contentView` as the cell is created. This approach can be combined with the previous one, or you can ignore the built-in subviews and use your own exclusively.

- Design the cell in a nib, and load that nib in `tableView:cellForRowAtIndexPath:` each time a cell needs to be created.

- Design the cell in a storyboard.

What causes the built-in subviews to be present is not the cell style but the fact that you refer to them. As long as you never speak of the cell's `textLabel`, `detailTextLabel`, or `imageView`, they are never created or inserted into the cell. Thus, you don't need to remove them if you don't want to use them.

Overriding a cell's subview layout

You can't directly change the frame of a built-in cell style subview in `tableView:cellForRowAtIndexPath:`, because the cell's `layoutSubviews` comes along later and overrides your changes. The workaround is to override the cell's `layoutSubviews`! This is a straightforward solution if your main objection to a built-in style is the frame of an existing subview.

To illustrate, let's modify a `.Default` cell so that the image is at the right end instead of the left end (Figure 8-6). We'll make a UITableViewCell subclass, MyCell, remembering to register MyCell with the table view, so that `dequeueReusableCellWithIdentifier:forIndexPath:` produces a MyCell instance; here is MyCell's `layoutSubviews`:

```
override func layoutSubviews() {
    super.layoutSubviews()
    let cvb = self.contentView.bounds
    let imf = self.imageView!.frame
    self.imageView!.frame.origin.x = cvb.size.width - imf.size.width - 15
    self.textLabel!.frame.origin.x = 15
}
```

Adding subviews in code

Instead of modifying the existing default subviews, you can add completely new views to each UITableViewCell's content view. The best place to do this in code is `table-View:cellForRowAtIndexPath:`. Here are some things to keep in mind:

- The new views must be added when we instantiate a new cell, but not when we reuse a cell (because a reused cell already has them).
- We must never send `addSubview:` to the cell itself — only to its `contentView` (or some subview thereof).
- We should assign the new views an appropriate `autoresizingMask` or constraints, because the cell's content view might be resized.
- Each new view should be assigned a tag so that it can be identified and referred to elsewhere.

I'll rewrite the previous example (Figure 8-6) to use this technique. We are no longer using a UITableViewCell subclass; the registered cell class is UITableViewCell itself. If this is a new cell, we add the subviews and assign them tags. If this is a reused cell, we don't add the subviews (the cell already has them), and we use the tags to refer to the subviews:

```
override func tableView(tableView: UITableView,
    cellForRowAtIndexPath indexPath: NSIndexPath) -> UITableViewCell {
        let cell = tableView.dequeueReusableCellWithIdentifier(
            "Cell", forIndexPath:indexPath)
        if cell.viewWithTag(1) == nil { // no subviews! add them
            let iv = UIImageView()
            iv.tag = 1
            cell.contentView.addSubview(iv)
            let lab = UILabel()
            lab.tag = 2
            cell.contentView.addSubview(lab)
            // since we are now adding the views ourselves,
            // we can use autolayout to lay them out
            let d = ["iv":iv, "lab":lab]
            iv.translatesAutoresizingMaskIntoConstraints = false
            lab.translatesAutoresizingMaskIntoConstraints = false
            var con = [NSLayoutConstraint]()
            // image view is vertically centered
            con.append(iv.centerYAnchor.constraintEqualToAnchor(
                cell.contentView.centerYAnchor))
            // it's a square
            con.append(iv.widthAnchor.constraintEqualToAnchor(
                iv.heightAnchor))
            // label has height pinned to superview
            con.appendContentsOf(
                NSLayoutConstraint.constraintsWithVisualFormat(
                    "V:|[lab]|",
```

```
                options:[], metrics:nil, views:d))
        // horizontal margins
        con.appendContentsOf(
            NSLayoutConstraint.constraintsWithVisualFormat(
                "H:|-15-[lab]-15-[iv]-15-|",
                options:[], metrics:nil, views:d))
        NSLayoutConstraint.activateConstraints(con)
    }
    // can refer to subviews by their tags
    let lab = cell.viewWithTag(2) as! UILabel
    let iv = cell.viewWithTag(1) as! UIImageView
    // ...
    return cell
}
```

Designing a cell in a nib

We can avoid the verbosity of the previous code by designing the cell in a nib. To do so, we start by creating a *.xib* file that will consist, in effect, solely of this one cell. In Xcode, create the *.xib* file by specifying iOS → User Interface → View. Let's call it *MyCell.xib*. In the nib editor, delete the existing View and replace it with a Table View Cell from the Object library.

The cell's design window shows a standard-sized cell; you can resize it as desired, but the actual size of the cell in the interface will be dictated by the table view's width and its rowHeight (or the delegate's response to tableView:heightForRowAtIndexPath:). The cell already has a contentView, and any subviews you add will be inside that; do not subvert that arrangement.

You can choose a built-in table view cell style in the Style pop-up menu of the Attributes inspector, and this gives you the default subviews, locked in their standard positions; for example, if you choose Basic, the textLabel appears, and if you specify an image, the imageView appears. If you set the Style pop-up menu to Custom, you start with a blank slate. Let's do that.

We'll implement, from scratch, the same subviews we've already implemented in the preceding two examples: a UILabel on the left side of the cell, and a UIImageView on the right side. Just as when adding subviews in code, we should set each subview's autoresizing behavior or constraints, and *give each subview a tag*, so that later, in table-View:cellForRowAtIndexPath:, we'll be able to refer to the label and the image view using viewWithTag:, exactly as in the previous example:

```
let lab = cell.viewWithTag(2) as! UILabel
let iv = cell.viewWithTag(1) as! UIImageView
// ...
return cell
```

The only remaining question is how to load the cell from the nib. It's simple! When we register with the table view, which we're currently doing in viewDidLoad, instead of calling `registerClass:forCellReuseIdentifier:`, we call a different method: `registerNib:forCellReuseIdentifier:`. To specify the nib, call UINib's class method `nibWithNibName:bundle:`, like this:

```
self.tableView.registerNib(
    UINib(nibName:"MyCell", bundle:nil), forCellReuseIdentifier: "Cell")
```

That's all there is to it. In `tableView:cellForRowAtIndexPath:`, when we call `dequeue-ReusableCellWithIdentifier:forIndexPath:`, if the table has no free reusable cell already in existence, the nib will automatically be loaded and the cell will be instantiated from it and returned to us.

You may wonder how that's possible, when we haven't specified a File's Owner class or added an outlet from the File's Owner to the cell in the nib. The answer is that the nib conforms to a specific format. The UINib instance method `instantiateWith-Owner:options:` can load a nib with a `nil` owner; regardless, it returns an array of the nib's instantiated top-level objects. A nib registered with the table view is expected to have exactly one top-level object, and that top-level object is expected to be a UITable-ViewCell; that being so, the cell can easily be extracted from the resulting array, as it is the array's only element. Our nib meets those expectations!

The advantages of this approach should be immediately obvious. The subviews can now be designed in the nib, and code that was creating *and configuring* each subview can be deleted. For example, suppose we previously had this code:

```
if cell.viewWithTag(1) == nil {
    let iv = UIImageView()
    iv.tag = 1
    cell.contentView.addSubview(iv)
    let lab = UILabel()
    lab.tag = 2
    cell.contentView.addSubview(lab)
    // ... position views ...
    lab.font = UIFont(name:"Helvetica-Bold", size:16)
    lab.lineBreakMode = .ByWordWrapping
    lab.numberOfLines = 2
}
```

All of that can now be eliminated, including setting the label's `font`, `lineBreakMode`, and `numberOfLines`; those configurations are to be applied to the label in *every* cell, so they can be performed in the nib instead.

 The nib *must* conform to the format I've described: it must have exactly one top-level object, a UITableViewCell. This means that some configurations are difficult or impossible in the nib. For example, a cell's `backgroundView` cannot be configured in the nib, because this would require the presence of a second top-level nib object. The simplest workaround is to add the `backgroundView` in code.

In `tableView:cellForRowAtIndexPath:`, we are still referring to the cell's subviews by way of `viewWithTag:`. There's nothing wrong with that, but perhaps you'd prefer to use names. Now that we're designing the cell in a nib, that's easy. Provide a UITableViewCell subclass with outlet properties, and configure the nib file accordingly:

1. Create a UITableViewCell subclass — let's call it MyCell — and declare two outlet properties:

    ```
    class MyCell : UITableViewCell {
        @IBOutlet var theLabel : UILabel!
        @IBOutlet var theImageView : UIImageView!
    }
    ```

    That is the *entirety* of MyCell's code; it exists solely so that we can create these outlets.

2. Edit the table view cell nib *MyCell.xib*. Change the class of the cell (in the Identity inspector) to MyCell, and connect the outlets from the cell to the respective subviews.

The result is that in our implementation of `tableView:cellForRowAtIndexPath:`, once we've typed the cell as a MyCell, the compiler will let us use the property names to access the subviews:

```
let cell = tableView.dequeueReusableCellWithIdentifier(
    "Cell", forIndexPath:indexPath) as! MyCell
let lab = cell.theLabel
let iv = cell.theImageView
```

Designing a cell in a storyboard

When your table view comes from a storyboard, it is open to you to employ any of the ways of obtaining and designing its cells that I've already described. There is also an additional option, available only in a UITableViewController scene in the storyboard: you can have the table view obtain the cells from the storyboard itself, and you can also *design* the cell directly in the table view in the storyboard.

To experiment with this way of obtaining and designing a cell, start with a project based on the Single View Application template:

1. In the storyboard, delete the View Controller scene. In the project, delete the View Controller class file.

2. In the project, create a file for a UITableViewController subclass called RootView-Controller, *without* a corresponding *.xib* file.

3. In the storyboard, drag a Table View Controller into the empty canvas, and set its class to RootViewController (and make sure it's the initial view controller).

4. The table view controller in the storyboard comes with a table view. In the storyboard, select that table view, and, in the Attributes inspector, set the Content pop-

up menu to Dynamic Prototypes, and set the number of Prototype Cells to 1 (these are the defaults).

The table view now contains a single table view cell with a content view. You can do in this cell exactly what we were doing before when designing a table view cell in a *.xib* file.

So, let's do that. I like being able to refer to my custom cell subviews with property names. Our procedure is just like what we did in the previous example:

1. In the project, add a UITableViewCell subclass — let's call it MyCell — and declare two outlet properties:

   ```
   class MyCell : UITableViewCell {
       @IBOutlet var theLabel : UILabel!
       @IBOutlet var theImageView : UIImageView!
   }
   ```

2. In the storyboard, select the prototype cell and change its class to MyCell.

3. Drag a label and an image view into the prototype cell, position and configure them as desired, and connect the cell's outlets to them appropriately.

So far, so good; but there is one crucial question I have not yet answered: How will your code tell the table view to get its cells from the storyboard? Clearly, *not* by calling `registerClass:forCellReuseIdentifier:`, and *not* by calling `registerNib:forCell-ReuseIdentifier:`; each of those would do something perfectly valid, but not the thing we want done in this case. The answer is that you *don't register anything at all* with the table view!_ Instead, when you call `dequeueReusableCellWithIdentifier:forIndex-Path:`, you supply an identifier that matches the *prototype cell's identifier* in the storyboard.

So, return once more to the storyboard:

1. Select the prototype cell.

2. In the Attributes inspector, enter `Cell` in the Identifier field (capitalization counts).

Now RootViewController's `tableView:cellForRowAtIndexPath:` works exactly as it did in the previous example:

```
let cell = tableView.dequeueReusableCellWithIdentifier(
    "Cell", forIndexPath:indexPath) as! MyCell
let lab = cell.theLabel
let iv = cell.theImageView
```

If you call `dequeueReusableCellWithIdentifier:forIndexPath:` with an identifier that you have *not* registered with the table view and that *doesn't* match the identifier of a prototype cell in the storyboard, your app will crash (with a helpful message in the console).

Even though I've said it before, I'll say it again: You must *not* call `registerClass:for-CellReuseIdentifier:` or `registerNib:forCellReuseIdentifier:` in this situation. If you do, you will be telling the runtime *not* to get the cell from the storyboard. This is a common beginner mistake.

Table View Data

The structure and content of the actual data portrayed in a table view comes from the data source, an object pointed to by the table view's `dataSource` property and adopting the UITableViewDataSource protocol. The data source is thus the heart and soul of the table. What surprises beginners is that the data source operates not by *setting* the table view's structure and content, but by *responding on demand*. The data source, *qua* data source, consists of a set of methods that the table view will call when it needs information; in effect, it will ask your data source some questions. This architecture has important consequences for how you write your code, which can be summarized by these simple guidelines:

Be ready

Your data source cannot know *when* or *how often* any of these methods will be called, so it must be prepared to answer *any question at any time*.

Be fast

The table view is asking for data in real time; the user is probably scrolling through the table *right now*. So you mustn't gum up the works; you must be ready to supply responses just as fast as you possibly can. (If you can't supply a piece of data fast enough, you may have to skip it, supply a placeholder, and insert the data into the table later. This may involve you in threading issues that I don't want to get into here. I'll give an example in Chapter 24.)

Be consistent

There are multiple data source methods, and you cannot know *which* one will be called at a given moment. So you must make sure your responses are mutually consistent at *any* moment. For example, a common beginner error is forgetting to take into account, in your data source methods, the possibility that the data might not yet be ready.

This may sound daunting, but you'll be fine as long as you maintain an unswerving adherence to the principles of model–view–controller. How and when you accumulate the actual data, and how that data is structured, is a *model* concern. Acting as a data source is a *controller* concern. So you can acquire and arrange your data whenever and however you like, just so long as when the table view actually turns to you and asks what to do, you can lay your hands on the relevant data rapidly and consistently. You'll want to design the model in such a way that the controller can access any desired piece of data more or less instantly.

Another source of confusion for beginners is that methods are rather oddly distributed between the data source and the delegate, an object pointed to by the table view's delegate property and adopting the UITableViewDelegate protocol; in some cases, one may seem to be doing the job of the other. This is not usually a cause of any real difficulty, because the object serving as data source will probably also be the object serving as delegate. Nevertheless, it is rather inconvenient when you're consulting the documentation; you'll probably want to keep the data source and delegate documentation pages open simultaneously as you work.

 If a table view's contents are known beforehand, you can alternatively design the entire table, *including the contents of individual cells*, in a storyboard. I'll give an example later in this chapter.

The Three Big Questions

Like Katherine Hepburn in *Pat and Mike*, the basis of your success (as a data source) is your ability, at any time, to answer the Three Big Questions. The questions the table view will ask you are a little different from the questions Mike asks Pat, but the principle is the same: know the answers, and be able to recite them at any moment. Here they are:

How many sections does this table have?
The table will call numberOfSectionsInTableView:; respond with an integer. In theory you can sometimes omit this method, as the default response is 1, which is often correct. However, I never omit it; for one thing, returning 0 is a good way to say that the table has no data, and will prevent the table view from asking any other questions.

How many rows does this section have?
The table will call tableView:numberOfRowsInSection:. The table supplies a section number — the first section is numbered 0 — and you respond with an integer. In a table with only one section, of course, there is probably no need to examine the incoming section number.

What cell goes in this row of this section?
The table will call tableView:cellForRowAtIndexPath:. The index path is expressed as an NSIndexPath; this is a sophisticated and powerful class, but you don't actually have to know anything about it, because UITableView provides a category on it that adds two read-only properties — section and row. Using these, you extract the requested section number and row number, and return a fully configured UITableViewCell, ready for display in the table view. The first row of a section is numbered 0. I have already explained how to obtain the cell in the first place, by calling dequeueReusableCellWithIdentifier:forIndexPath:.

I have nothing particular to say about precisely how you're going to fulfill these obligations. It all depends on your data model and what your table is trying to portray. The important thing is to remember that you're going to be receiving an NSIndexPath specifying a section and a row, and you need to be able to lay your hands on the data corresponding to that slot *now* and configure the cell *now*. So construct your model, and your algorithm for consulting it in the Three Big Questions, and your way of configuring the cell, in accordance with that necessity.

For example, suppose our table is to list the names of the Pep Boys. Our data model might be an array of string names (`self.pep`). Our table has only one section. So our code might look like this:

```
override func numberOfSectionsInTableView(tableView: UITableView) -> Int {
    if self.pep == nil {
        return 0
    }
    return 1
}
override func tableView(tableView: UITableView,
    numberOfRowsInSection section: Int) -> Int {
        return self.pep.count
}
override func tableView(tableView: UITableView,
    cellForRowAtIndexPath indexPath: NSIndexPath) -> UITableViewCell {
        let cell = tableView.dequeueReusableCellWithIdentifier(
            "Cell", forIndexPath: indexPath)
        cell.textLabel!.text = pep[indexPath.row]
        return cell
}
```

At this point you may be feeling some exasperation. You want to object: "But that's trivial!" Exactly so! Your access to the data model *should* be trivial. That's the sign of a data model that's well designed for access by your table view's data source. Your implementation of `tableView:cellForRowAtIndexPath:` might have some interesting work to do in order to configure the *form* of the cell, but accessing the actual *data* should be simple and boring.

Reusing Cells

Another important goal of `tableView:cellForRowAtIndexPath:` should be to conserve resources by reusing cells. As I've already explained, once a cell's row is no longer visible on the screen, that cell can be slotted into a row that *is* visible — with its portrayed data appropriately modified, of course! — so that only a few more than the number of simultaneously visible cells will ever need to be instantiated.

A table view is ready to implement this strategy for you; all you have to do is call `dequeue-ReusableCellWithIdentifier:forIndexPath:`. For any given identifier, you'll be handed either a newly minted cell or a reused cell that previously appeared in the table view but is now no longer needed because it has scrolled out of view.

The table view can maintain more than one cache of reusable cells; this could be useful if your table view contains more than one type of cell (where the meaning of the concept "type of cell" is pretty much up to you). This is why you must *name* each cache, by attaching an identifier string to any cell that can be reused. All the examples in this chapter (and in this book, and in fact in every UITableView I've ever created) use just one cache and just one identifier, but there can be more than one. If you're using a storyboard as a source of cells, there would then need to be more than one prototype cell.

To prove to yourself the efficiency of the cell-caching architecture, do something to differentiate newly instantiated cells from reused cells, and count the newly instantiated cells, like this:

```
override func numberOfSectionsInTableView(tableView: UITableView) -> Int {
    return 1
}
override func tableView(
    tableView: UITableView, numberOfRowsInSection section: Int) -> Int {
        return 1000 // make a lot of rows this time!
}
override func tableView(tableView: UITableView,
    cellForRowAtIndexPath indexPath: NSIndexPath) -> UITableViewCell {
        let cell = tableView.dequeueReusableCellWithIdentifier(
            "Cell", forIndexPath:indexPath) as! MyCell
        let lab = cell.theLabel
        // prove that many rows does not mean many cell objects
        lab.text = "Row \(indexPath.row) of section \(indexPath.section)"
        if lab.tag != 999 {
            lab.tag = 999
            print("New cell \(++self.cells)")
        }
    }
```

When we run this code and scroll through the table, every cell is numbered correctly, so there appear to be 1000 cells. But the console messages show that only about a dozen distinct cells are ever actually created.

Be certain that *your* table view code passes that test, and that you are truly reusing cells! Fortunately, one of the benefits of calling dequeueReusableCellWithIdentifier:for-IndexPath: is that it forces you to use a valid reuse identifier.

 A common beginner error is to obtain a cell in some other way, such as instantiating it directly every time tableView:cellForRowAtIndexPath: is called. I have even seen beginners call dequeueReusableCellWithIdentifier:forIndexPath:, only to instantiate a fresh cell manually in the *next* line. Don't do that.

When your `tableView:cellForRowAtIndexPath:` implementation configures *individual* cells (step 6 in Example 8-1), the cell might be new or reused; at this point in your code, you don't know or care which. Therefore, you should always configure *everything* about the cell that might need configuring. If you fail to do this, and if the cell is reused, you might be surprised when some aspect of the cell is left over from its previous use; similarly, if you fail to do this, and if the cell is new, you might be surprised when some aspect of the cell isn't configured at all.

As usual, I learned that lesson the hard way. In the TidBITS News app, there is a little loudspeaker icon that should appear in a given cell in the master view's table view only if there is a recording associated with this article. So I initially wrote this code:

```
if (item.enclosures != nil) && (item.enclosures.count > 0) {
    cell.speaker.hidden = false
}
```

That turned out to be a mistake, because the cell might be reused. Every reused call *always* had a visible loudspeaker icon if, in a previous usage, that cell had *ever* had a visible loudspeaker icon! The solution was to rewrite the logic to cover all possibilities completely, like this:

```
cell.speaker.hidden =
    !((item.enclosures != nil) && (item.enclosures.count > 0))
```

You do get a sort of second bite of the cherry: there's a delegate method, `tableView:will-DisplayCell:forRowAtIndexPath:`, that is called for every cell just before it appears in the table. This is absolutely the last minute to configure a cell. But don't misuse this method. You're functioning as the delegate here, not the data source; you may set the final details of the cell's appearance, but you shouldn't be consulting the data model at this point.

An additional delegate method is `tableView:didEndDisplayingCell:forRowAtIndex-Path:`. This tells you that the cell no longer appears in the interface and has become free for reuse. You could take advantage of this to tear down any resource-heavy customization of the cell — I'll give an example in Chapter 24 — or simply to prepare it somehow for subsequent future reuse.

Table View Sections

Your table data may be expressed as divided into sections. You might clump your data into sections for various reasons (and doubtless there are other reasons beyond these):

- You want to supply section headers (or footers, or both).
- You want to make navigation of the table easier by supplying an index down the right side. You can't have an index without sections.

- You want to facilitate programmatic rearrangement of the table. For example, it's very easy to hide or move an entire section at once, possibly with animation.

Section headers and footers

A section header or footer appears between the cells, before the first row of a section or after the last row of a section, respectively. In a nongrouped table, a section header or footer detaches itself while the user scrolls the table, pinning itself to the top or bottom of the table view and floating over the scrolled rows, giving the user a sense, at every moment, of where we are within the table. Also, a section header or footer can contain custom views, so it's a place where you might put additional information, or even functional interface, such as a button the user can tap.

 Don't confuse the section headers and footers with the header and footer of the table as a whole. The latter are view properties of the table view itself, its `tableHeaderView` and `tableFooterView`, discussed earlier in this chapter. The table header appears only when the table is scrolled all the way down; the table footer appears only when the table is scrolled all the way up.

The number of sections is determined by your reply to `numberOfSectionsInTableView:`. For each section, the table view will consult your data source and delegate to learn whether this section has a header or a footer, or both, or neither (the default).

The UITableViewHeaderFooterView class is a UIView subclass intended specifically for use as the view of a header or footer; much like a table view cell, it is reusable. It has the following properties:

`textLabel`
Label (UILabel) for displaying the text of the header or footer.

`detailTextLabel`
This label, if you set its text, appears only in a grouped style table.

`contentView`
A subview of the header or footer, to which you can add custom subviews. If you do, you probably should not use the built-in `textLabel`; the `textLabel` is not inside the `contentView` and in a sense doesn't belong to you.

`backgroundView`
Any view you want to assign. The `contentView` is in front of the `backgroundView`. The `contentView` has a clear background by default, so the `backgroundView` shows through. An opaque `contentView.backgroundColor`, on the other hand, would completely obscure the `backgroundView`.

If the backgroundView is nil (the default), the header or footer view will supply its own background view whose backgroundColor is derived (in some annoyingly unspecified way) from the table's backgroundColor.

 Don't set a UITableViewHeaderFooterView's backgroundColor; instead, set the backgroundColor of its contentView, or assign a backgroundView and configure it as you like. Also, setting its tintColor has no effect. (This feels like a bug; the tintColor should affect the color of subviews, such as a UIButton's title, but it doesn't.)

There are two ways in which you can supply a header or footer. You can use both, but it is better to pick just one:

Header or footer title string

You implement the data source method tableView:titleForHeaderInSection: or tableView:titleForFooterInSection: (or both). Return nil to indicate that the given section has no header (or footer). The header or footer view itself is a UITableViewHeaderFooterView, and is reused automatically: there will be only as many as needed for simultaneous display on the screen. The string you supply becomes the view's textLabel.text.

(In a grouped style table, the string's capitalization may be changed. To avoid that, use the second way of supplying the header or footer.)

Header or footer view

You implement the delegate method tableView:viewForHeaderInSection: or tableView:viewForFooterInSection: (or both). The view you supply is used as the entire header or footer and is automatically resized to the table's width and the section header or footer height (I'll discuss how the height is determined in a moment).

You are not required to return a UITableViewHeaderFooterView, but you will probably want to, in order to take advantage of reusability. To do so, the procedure is much like making a cell reusable. You register beforehand with the table view by calling registerClass:forHeaderFooterViewReuseIdentifier:. To supply the reusable view, send the table view dequeueReusableHeaderFooterViewWithIdentifier:; the result will be either a newly instantiated view or a reused view.

You can then configure this view as desired. For example, you can set its textLabel.text, or you can give its contentView custom subviews. In the latter case, be sure to set proper autoresizing or constraints, so that the subviews will be positioned and sized appropriately when the view itself is resized.

The documentation lists a second way of registering a header or footer view for reuse — `registerNib:forHeaderFooterViewReuseIdentifier:`. But the nib editor's Object library doesn't include a UITableViewHeaderFooterView, so this method is useless.

In addition, two pairs of delegate methods permit you to perform final configurations on your header or footer views:

`tableView:willDisplayHeaderView:forSection:`
`tableView:willDisplayFooterView:forSection:`

> You can perform further configuration here, if desired. A useful possibility is to generate the default UITableViewHeaderFooterView by implementing `title-For...` and then tweak its form slightly here. These delegate methods are matched by `tableView:didEndDisplayingHeaderView:forSection:` and `tableView:did-EndDisplayingFooterView:forSection:`.

`tableView:heightForHeaderInSection:`
`tableView:heightForFooterInSection:`

> The runtime resizes your header or footer before displaying it. Its width will be the table view's width; its height will be the table view's `sectionHeaderHeight` or `sectionFooterHeight` unless you implement one of these methods to say otherwise. Returning `UITableViewAutomaticDimension` means 0 if `titleFor...` returns `nil` or the empty string (or isn't implemented); otherwise, it means the table view's `sectionHeaderHeight` or `sectionFooterHeight`. Be sure to dictate the height *somehow* or you might not see any headers (or footers).

Some lovely effects can be created by making use of the fact that a header or footer view in a nongrouped table will be further forward than the table's cells. For example, a header with transparency shows the cells as they scroll behind it; a header with a shadow casts that shadow on the adjacent cell.

When a header or footer view appears in the middle of the table view (between two table cells), there is a transparent gap behind it. If the header or footer view has some transparency, the table view's background is visible through this gap. You'll want to take this into account when planning your color scheme.

Section data

Clearly, a table that is to have sections may require some advance planning in the formation of its data model. The row data must somehow be clumped into sections, because you're going to be asked for a row *with respect to its section*. And, just as with a cell, a section title must be readily available so that it can be supplied quickly in real time. A structure that I commonly use is a pair of parallel arrays: an array of strings containing the section names, and an array of subarrays containing the data for each section.

For example, suppose we intend to display the names of all 50 U.S. states in alphabetical order as the rows of a table view, and that we wish to divide the table into sections according to the first letter of each state's name. Let's say I have the alphabetized list as a text file, which starts like this:

```
Alabama
Alaska
Arizona
Arkansas
California
Colorado
Connecticut
Delaware
...
```

I have properties already initialized as empty arrays, waiting to hold the data model:

```
var sectionNames = [String]()
var sectionData = [[String]]()
```

I'll prepare the data model by loading the text file and walking through it, line by line, creating a new section name and a new subarray when I encounter a new first letter:

```
let s = try! String(contentsOfFile: NSBundle.mainBundle()
    .pathForResource("states", ofType: "txt")!,
    encoding: NSUTF8StringEncoding)
let states = s.componentsSeparatedByString("\n")
var previous = ""
for aState in states {
    // get the first letter
    let c = String(aState.characters.prefix(1))
    // only add a letter to sectionNames when it's a different letter
    if c != previous {
        previous = c
        self.sectionNames.append(c.uppercaseString)
        // and in that case also add new subarray to our array of subarrays
        self.sectionData.append([String]())
    }
    sectionData[sectionData.count-1].append(aState)
}
```

The value of this preparatory dance is evident when we are bombarded with questions from the table view about cells and headers; supplying the answers is trivial, just as it should be:

```
override func numberOfSectionsInTableView(tableView: UITableView) -> Int {
    return self.sectionNames.count
}
override func tableView(tableView: UITableView,
    numberOfRowsInSection section: Int) -> Int {
        return self.sectionData[section].count
}
override func tableView(tableView: UITableView,
```

```
cellForRowAtIndexPath indexPath: NSIndexPath) -> UITableViewCell {
    let cell = tableView.dequeueReusableCellWithIdentifier(
        "Cell", forIndexPath: indexPath)
    let s = self.sectionData[indexPath.section][indexPath.row]
    cell.textLabel!.text = s
    return cell
}
override func tableView(tableView: UITableView,
    titleForHeaderInSection section: Int) -> String? {
        return self.sectionNames[section]
}
```

Let's modify that example to illustrate customization of a header view. I've already registered my header identifier in `viewDidLoad`:

```
self.tableView.registerClass(UITableViewHeaderFooterView.self,
    forHeaderFooterViewReuseIdentifier: "Header")
```

Now, instead of `tableView:titleForHeaderInSection:`, I'll implement `tableView:viewForHeaderInSection:`. For completely new views, I'll place my own label and an image view inside the `contentView` and give them their basic configuration; then I'll perform individual configuration on all views, new or reused (very much like `tableView:cellForRowAtIndexPath:`). Note my deliberate misuse of the otherwise useless `tintColor` property to mark whether a view needs basic configuration:

```
override func tableView(tableView: UITableView,
    viewForHeaderInSection section: Int) -> UIView? {
        let h = tableView
            .dequeueReusableHeaderFooterViewWithIdentifier("Header")!
        if h.tintColor != UIColor.redColor() {
            h.tintColor = UIColor.redColor() // invisible marker, tee-hee
            h.backgroundView = UIView()
            h.backgroundView?.backgroundColor = UIColor.blackColor()
            let lab = UILabel()
            lab.tag = 1
            lab.font = UIFont(name:"Georgia-Bold", size:22)
            lab.textColor = UIColor.greenColor()
            lab.backgroundColor = UIColor.clearColor()
            h.contentView.addSubview(lab)
            let v = UIImageView()
            v.tag = 2
            v.backgroundColor = UIColor.blackColor()
            v.image = UIImage(named:"us_flag_small.gif")
            h.contentView.addSubview(v)
            lab.translatesAutoresizingMaskIntoConstraints = false
            v.translatesAutoresizingMaskIntoConstraints = false
            NSLayoutConstraint.activateConstraints([
                NSLayoutConstraint.constraintsWithVisualFormat(
                    "H:|-5-[lab(25)]-10-[v(40)]",
                    options:[], metrics:nil, views:["v":v, "lab":lab]),
                NSLayoutConstraint.constraintsWithVisualFormat(
                    "V:|[v]|",
```

```
                options:[], metrics:nil, views:["v":v]),
            NSLayoutConstraint.constraintsWithVisualFormat(
                "V:|[lab]|",
                options:[], metrics:nil, views:["lab":lab])
        ].flatten().map{$0})
    }
    let lab = h.contentView.viewWithTag(1) as! UILabel
    lab.text = self.sectionNames[section]
    return h
}
```

Section index

If your table view has the plain style, you can add an index down the right side of the table, where the user can tap or drag to jump to the start of a section — helpful for navigating long tables. To generate the index, implement the data source method `sectionIndexTitlesForTableView:`, returning an array of string titles to appear as entries in the index. For our list of state names, that's trivial once again, just as it should be:

```
override func sectionIndexTitlesForTableView(tableView: UITableView)
    -> [String]? {
        return self.sectionNames
}
```

The index can appear even if there are no section headers. It will appear only if the number of rows exceeds the table view's `sectionIndexMinimumDisplayRowCount` property value; the default is 0, so the index is always displayed by default. You will want the index entries to be short — preferably just one character — because they will be partially obscuring the right edge of the table; plus, each cell's content view will shrink to compensate, so you're sacrificing some cell real estate.

You can modify three properties that affect the index's appearance:

sectionIndexColor
    The index text color.

sectionIndexBackgroundColor
    The index background color. I advise giving the index some background color, even if it is clearColor, because otherwise the index distorts the colors of what's behind it in a distracting way.

sectionIndexTrackingBackgroundColor
    The index background color while the user's finger is sliding over it. By default, it's the same as the sectionIndexBackgroundColor.

Normally, there will be a one-to-one correspondence between the index entries and the sections; when the user taps an index entry, the table jumps to the start of the corresponding section. However, under certain circumstances you may want to customize this correspondence.

For example, suppose there are 100 sections, but there isn't room to display 100 index entries comfortably on the iPhone. The index will automatically curtail itself, omitting some index entries and inserting bullets to suggest the omission, but you might prefer to take charge of the situation.

To do so, supply a shorter index, and implement the data source method `table-View:sectionForSectionIndexTitle:atIndex:`, returning the number of the section to jump to. You are told both the title and the index number of the section index listing that the user chose, so you can use whichever is convenient.

Refreshing Table View Data

The table view has no direct connection to the underlying data. If you want the table view display to change because the underlying data have changed, you have to cause the table view to refresh itself; basically, you're requesting that the Big Questions be asked all over again. At first blush, this seems inefficient ("regenerate *all* the data??"); but it isn't. Remember, in a table that caches reusable cells, there are no cells of interest other than those actually showing in the table at this moment. Thus, having worked out the layout of the table through the section header and footer heights and row heights, the table has to regenerate only those cells that are actually visible.

You can cause the table data to be refreshed using any of several methods:

`reloadData`
> The table view will ask the Three Big Questions all over again, including heights of rows and section headers and footers, and the index, exactly as it does automatically when the table view first appears.

`reloadRowsAtIndexPaths:withRowAnimation:`
> The table view will ask the Three Big Questions all over again, including heights, but not index entries. Cells are requested only for visible cells among those you specify. The first parameter is an array of index paths; to form an index path, use the initializer `init(forRow:inSection:)`.

`reloadSections:withRowAnimation:`
> The table view will ask the Three Big Questions all over again, including heights of rows and section headers and footers, and the index. Cells, headers, and footers are requested only for visible elements of the sections you specify. The first parameter is an NSIndexSet.

The latter two methods can perform animations that cue the user as to what's changing. For the `rowAnimation:` argument, you'll pass one of the following (UITableViewRow-Animation):

`.Fade`

The old fades into the new.

`.Right, .Left, .Top, .Bottom`

The old slides out in the stated direction, and is replaced from the opposite direction.

`.None`

No animation.

`.Middle`

Hard to describe; it's a sort of venetian blind effect on each cell individually.

`.Automatic`

The table view just "does the right thing." This is especially useful for grouped style tables, because if you pick the wrong animation, the display can look very funny as it proceeds.

If all you need to do is to refresh the index, call `reloadSectionIndexTitles`; this calls the data source's `sectionIndexTitlesForTableView:`.

If you want the table view to be laid out freshly without reloading *any* cells, send it `beginUpdates` immediately followed by `endUpdates`. The section and row structure of the table will be asked for, along with calculation of all heights, but no cells and no headers or footers are requested. This is useful as a way of alerting the table that its measurements have changed. It might be considered a misuse of an updates block (the real use of such a block is discussed later in this chapter); but Apple takes advantage of this trick in the Table View Animations and Gestures example, in which a pinch gesture is used to change a table's row height in real time, so it must be legal.

It is also possible to access and alter a table's individual cells directly. This can be a lightweight approach to refreshing the table, plus you can supply your own animation within the cell as it alters its appearance. It is important to bear in mind, however, that the cells are not the data (view is not model). If you change the content of a cell manually, make sure that you have also changed the model corresponding to it, so that the row will appear correctly if its data is reloaded later.

To do this, you need direct access to the cell you want to change. You'll probably want to make sure the cell is visible within the table view's bounds; nonvisible cells don't really exist (except as potential cells waiting in the reuse cache), and there's no point changing them manually, as they'll be changed when they are scrolled into view, through the usual call to `tableView:cellForRowAtIndexPath:`.

Here are some UITableView properties and methods that mediate between cells, rows, and visibility:

`visibleCells`

An array of the cells actually showing within the table's bounds.

`indexPathsForVisibleRows`

An array of the rows actually showing within the table's bounds.

`cellForRowAtIndexPath:`

Returns a UITableViewCell if the table is maintaining a cell for the given row (typically because this is a visible row); otherwise, returns `nil`.

`indexPathForCell:`

Given a cell obtained from the table view, returns the row into which it is slotted.

By the same token, you can get access to the views constituting headers and footers, by calling `headerViewForSection:` or `footerViewForSection:`. Thus you could modify a view directly. You should assume that if a section is returned by `indexPathsForVisibleRows`, its header or footer might be visible.

If you want to grant the user some interface for requesting that a table view be refreshed, you might like to use a UIRefreshControl. You aren't required to use this; it's just Apple's attempt to provide a standard interface. It is located behind the top of the scrolling part of the table view. To request a refresh, the user scrolls the table view downward to reveal the refresh control and holds long enough to indicate that this scrolling is deliberate. The refresh control then acknowledges visually that it is refreshing, and remains visible until refreshing is complete.

 The refresh control is located *behind the table view's backgroundView*. If the table view has an opaque background view, the refresh control will be impossible to see.

To give a table view a refresh control, assign a UIRefreshControl to the table view controller's `refreshControl` property; to do this in the nib editor, set the table view controller's Refreshing pop-up menu to Enabled. A refresh control is a control (UIControl, Chapter 12), and you will want to hook its Value Changed event to an action method; you can do that in the nib editor by making an action connection, or you can do it in code. Here's an example of creating and configuring a refresh control entirely in code:

```
self.refreshControl = UIRefreshControl()
self.refreshControl!.addTarget(
    self, action: "doRefresh", forControlEvents: .ValueChanged)
```

Once a refresh control's action message has fired, the control remains visible and indicates by animation (similar to an activity indicator) that it is refreshing, until you send it the `endRefreshing` message:

```
@IBAction func doRefresh(sender: AnyObject) {
    // ... refresh ...
    (sender as! UIRefreshControl).endRefreshing()
}
```

You can initiate a refresh animation in code with `beginRefreshing`, but this does not fire the action message or display the refresh control; to display it, scroll the table view:

```
self.tableView.setContentOffset(
    CGPointMake(0, -self.refreshControl!.bounds.height), animated:true)
self.refreshControl!.beginRefreshing()
self.doRefresh(self.refreshControl!) // fire action message manually
```

A refresh control also has these properties:

`refreshing` *(read-only)*
> Whether the refresh control is refreshing.

`tintColor`
> The refresh control's color. It is *not* inherited from the view hierarchy (I regard this as a bug).

`attributedTitle`
> Styled text displayed below the refresh control's activity indicator. On attributed strings, see Chapter 10.

`backgroundColor` *(inherited from UIView)*
> If you give a table view controller's `refreshControl` a background color, that color completely covers the table view's own background color when the refresh control is revealed. For some reason, I find the drawing of the `attributedTitle` more reliable if the refresh control has a background color.

Variable Row Heights

Most tables have rows that are all the same height, as set by the table view's `rowHeight`. However, the delegate's `tableView:heightForRowAtIndexPath:` can be used to make different rows different heights. You can see an example in the TidBITS News app (Figure 6-1).

Back when I first wrote TidBITS News, variable row heights were possible but virtually unheard-of; I knew of no other app that was using them, and Apple provided no guidance, so I had to invent my own technique by sheer trial-and-error. There were three main challenges:

Measurement
> *What* should the height of a given row be?

Timing
> *When* should the determination of each row's height be made?

Layout

How should the *subviews* of each cell be configured for its individual height?

Over the years since then, implementing variable row heights has become considerably easier. In iOS 6, with the advent of constraints, both measurement and layout became much simpler. In iOS 7, new table view properties made it possible to improve the timing. And iOS 8 permitted variable row heights to be implemented *automatically*, without your having to worry about any of these problems.

I will briefly describe four different approaches that I have used, in historical order. Perhaps you won't use any of the first three, because the automatic variable row heights feature makes them unnecessary; nevertheless, a basic understanding of them will give you an appreciation of what the fourth approach is doing for you. Besides, in my experience, the automatic variable row heights feature can be slow; for efficiency and speed, you might want to revert to one of the earlier techniques.

Manual row height measurement

The TidBITS News app, in its earliest implementation, works as follows. Each cell contains two labels. The *measurement* question is, then, given the content that each label will have in a particular cell in a particular row of the table, how tall should the cell be in order to accomodate both labels and their contents?

The cells don't use autolayout, so we have to measure them manually. The procedure is simple but somewhat laborious. The NSAttributedString method `boundingRectWith-Size:options:context:` (Chapter 10) answers the question, "How tall would this text be if laid out at a fixed width?" Thus, for each cell, we must answer that question for each label, allow for any vertical spacing above the first label, below the second label, and between the labels, and sum the results.

Then, however, the question of *timing* intrudes. The problem is that the moment when `tableView:heightForRowAtIndexPath:` is called is very different from the moment when `tableView:cellForRowAtIndexPath:` is called. The runtime needs to know the heights of *everything* in the table immediately, before it starts asking for *any* cells. Thus, before we are asked `tableView:cellForRowAtIndexPath:` for even *one* row, we are asked `tableView:heightForRowAtIndexPath:` for *every* row.

In effect, this means we have to gather *all* the data and lay out *all* the cells before we can start showing the data in any *single* row. You can see why this can be problematic. We are being asked up front to measure the entire table, row by row. If that measurement takes a long time, the table view will remain blank during the calculation.

In addition, there is now a danger of duplicating our own work later on, during *layout* (in `tableView:cellForRowAtIndexPath:`, or perhaps in `tableView:willDisplay-Cell:forRowAtIndexPath:`); it appears we will ultimately be laying out every cell *twice*, once when we're asked for all the heights initially, and again later when we're asked for an actual cell.

My solution is to start with an empty array of CGFloat stored in a property, `self.row-Heights`. (A single array is all that's needed, because the table has just one section; the row number can thus serve directly as an index into the array.) Once that array is constructed, it can be used to supply a requested height *instantly*.

Calculating a cell height requires me to lay out that cell in at least a theoretical way. Thus, I have a utility method that lays out a cell for a given row, using the actual data for that row; let's say its name is `setUpCell:forIndexPath:`. It takes a cell and an index path, lays out the cell, and returns the cell's required height as a CGFloat.

When the delegate's `tableView:heightForRowAtIndexPath:` is called, either this is the very first time it's been called or it isn't. Thus, either we've already constructed `self.row-Heights` or we haven't. If we haven't, we construct it, by immediately calling the `setUpCell:forIndexPath:` utility method for *every* row and storing each resulting height in `self.rowHeights`. I have no real cells at this point in the story, but I'm using a UITableViewCell subclass designed in a nib, so I simply load the nib directly and pull out the cell to use a model.

Now I'm ready to answer `tableView:heightForRowAtIndexPath:` for *any* row, *immediately* — all I have to do is return the appropriate value from the `self.rowHeights` array.

Finally, we come to `tableView:cellForRowAtIndexPath:`. Every time it is called, I call my `setUpCell:forIndexPath:` utility method *again* — but this time, I'm laying out the *real* cell (and ignoring the returned height value).

Measurement and layout with constraints

Constraints assist the process in two ways. Early in the process, in `tableView:heightForRowAtIndexPath:`, they perform the *measurement* for us. How do they do that? Well, if the cell is designed with constraints that ultimately pin every subview to the `contentView` in such a way as to size the `contentView` height unambiguously *from the inside out* — because every subview either is given explicit size constraints or else is the kind of view that has an implicit size based on its contents, like a label or an image view — then we can simply call `systemLayoutSizeFittingSize:` to tell us the resulting height of the cell.

Later in the process, when we come to `tableView:cellForRowAtIndexPath:`, constraints obviously help with *layout* of each cell, because that's what constraints do. Thanks to `dequeueReusableCellWithIdentifier:forIndexPath:`, the cell has the correct height, so the constraints are now determining the size of the subviews *from the outside in*.

The one danger to watch out for here is that a .SingleLine separator eats into the cell height. This can cause the height of the cell in real life to differ very slightly from its height as calculated by systemLayoutSizeFittingSize:. If you've overdetermined the subview constraints, this can result in a conflict among constraints. Careful use of lowered constraint priorities can solve this problem nicely if it arises (though it is simpler, in practice, to set the cell separator to .None).

I'll show the actual code from another app of mine that uses this technique. My setUp-Cell:forIndexPath: no longer needs to return a value; I hand it a reference to a cell, it sets up the cell, and now I can do whatever I like with that cell. If this is the model cell being used for measurement in tableView:heightForRowAtIndexPath:, I call system-LayoutSizeFittingSize: to get the height; if it's the real cell generated by dequeuing in tableView:cellForRowAtIndexPath:, I return it. Thus, setUpCell:forIndexPath: is extremely simple: it just configures the cell with actual data from the model:

```
func setUpCell(cell:UITableViewCell, forIndexPath indexPath:NSIndexPath) {
    let row = indexPath.row
    (cell.viewWithTag(1) as! UILabel).text = self.titles[row]
    (cell.viewWithTag(2) as! UILabel).text = self.artists[row]
    (cell.viewWithTag(3) as! UILabel).text = self.composers[row]
}
```

My self.rowHeights property is typed as [CGFloat?], and has been initialized to an array the same size as my data model (self.titles and so on) with every element set to nil. My implemention of tableView:heightForRowAtIndexPath:: is called repeatedly (self.titles.count times, in fact) before the table is displayed; the *first* time it is called, I calculate *all* the row height values *once* and store them all in self.rowHeights:

```
override func tableView(tableView: UITableView,
    heightForRowAtIndexPath indexPath: NSIndexPath) -> CGFloat {
        let ix = indexPath.row
        if self.rowHeights[ix] == nil {
            let objects = UINib(nibName: "TrackCell2", bundle: nil)
                .instantiateWithOwner(nil, options: nil)
            let cell = objects.first as! UITableViewCell
            for ix in 0..<self.rowHeights.count {
                let indexPath = NSIndexPath(forRow: ix, inSection: 0)
                self.setUpCell(cell, forIndexPath: indexPath)
                let v = cell.contentView
                let sz = v.systemLayoutSizeFittingSize(
                    UILayoutFittingCompressedSize)
                self.rowHeights[ix] = sz.height
            }
        }
        return self.rowHeights[ix]!
}
```

My `tableView:cellForRowAtIndexPath:` implementation is trivial, because `setUp-Cell:forIndexPath:` does all the real work:

```
override func tableView(tableView: UITableView,
    cellForRowAtIndexPath indexPath: NSIndexPath) -> UITableViewCell {
        let cell = tableView.dequeueReusableCellWithIdentifier(
            "TrackCell", forIndexPath: indexPath)
        self.setUpCell(cell, forIndexPath:indexPath)
        return cell
}
```

Estimated height

In iOS 7, three new table view properties were introduced:

- `estimatedRowHeight`
- `estimatedSectionHeaderHeight`
- `estimatedSectionFooterHeight`

To accompany those, there are also three table view delegate methods:

- `tableView:estimatedHeightForRowAtIndexPath:`
- `tableView:estimatedHeightForHeaderInSection:`
- `tableView:estimatedHeightForFooterInSection:`

The purpose of these properties and methods is to reduce the amount of time spent calculating row heights at the outset. If you supply an estimated row height, for example, then when `tableView:heightForRowAtIndexPath:` is called repeatedly before the table is displayed, it is called *only for the visible cells* of the table; for the remaining cells, the *estimated* height is used. The runtime thus has enough information to lay out the entire table very quickly: in a table with 300 rows, you don't have to provide the real heights for all 300 rows up front — you only have to provide real heights for, say, the half dozen visible rows. The downside is that this layout is incorrect, and will have to be corrected later: as new rows are scrolled into view, `tableView:heightForRowAtIndexPath:` will be called *again* for those new rows, and the layout of the whole table will be revised accordingly.

Thus, using an estimated height changes the *timing* of when `tableView:heightForRow-AtIndexPath:` is called. To illustrate, I'll revise the previous example to use estimated heights. The estimated height is set in `viewDidLoad`:

```
self.tableView.estimatedRowHeight = 75
```

Now in my `tableView:heightForRowAtIndexPath:` implementation, when I find that a requested height value in `self.rowHeights` is `nil`, I don't fill in *all* the values of `self.rowHeights` — I fill in *just that one height*. It's simply a matter of removing the for loop:

```
override func tableView(tableView: UITableView,
    heightForRowAtIndexPath indexPath: NSIndexPath) -> CGFloat {
        let ix = indexPath.row
        if self.rowHeights[ix] == nil {
            let objects = UINib(nibName: "TrackCell2", bundle: nil)
                .instantiateWithOwner(nil, options: nil)
            let cell = objects.first as! UITableViewCell
            let indexPath = NSIndexPath(forRow: ix, inSection: 0)
            self.setUpCell(cell, forIndexPath: indexPath)
            let v = cell.contentView
            let sz = v.systemLayoutSizeFittingSize(
                UILayoutFittingCompressedSize)
            self.rowHeights[ix] = sz.height
        }
        return self.rowHeights[ix]!
}
```

Automatic row height

In iOS 8, a completely automatic calculation of variable row heights was introduced. This, in effect, simply does automatically what I'm already doing in `tableView:height-ForRowAtIndexPath:` in the preceding code: it relies upon autolayout for the calculation of each row's height, and it calculates and caches a row's height the first time it is needed, as it is about to appear on the screen.

To use this mechanism, first configure your cell using autolayout to determine the size of the `contentView` from the inside out. Now all you have to do is to set the table view's `estimatedRowHeight` and *don't* implement `tableView:heightForRowAtIndexPath:` at all!

Thus, to adopt this approach in my app, all I have to do at this point is delete my `table-View:heightForRowAtIndexPath:` implementation entirely.

Obviously, that's very easy: but easy does not necessarily mean best. There is also a question of performance. The four techniques I've outlined here run not only from oldest to newest but also from fastest to slowest. Manual layout is faster than calling `systemLayoutSizeFittingSize:`, and calculating the heights of all rows up front, though it may cause a longer pause initially, makes *scrolling* faster for the user because no row heights have to be calculated while scrolling. You will have to measure and decide which approach is most suitable.

And there's one more thing to watch out for. I said earlier that the cell returned to you from `dequeueReusableCellWithIdentifier:forIndexPath:` in your implementation of `tableView:cellForRowAtIndexPath:` already has its final size. But if you use automatic variable row heights, that's not true, because automatic calculation of a cell's height can't take place until after the cell exists! Any code that relies on the cell having its final size in `tableView:cellForRowAtIndexPath:` will break when you switch to automatic variable row heights, and may need to be moved to `tableView:willDisplayCell:for-RowAtIndexPath:`, where the final cell size has definitely been achieved.

Table View Cell Selection

A table view cell has a normal state, a highlighted state (according to its `highlighted` property), and a selected state (according to its `selected` property). It is possible to change these states directly, possibly with animation, by calling `set-Highlighted:animated:` or `setSelected:animated:` on the cell. But you don't want to act behind the table's back, so you are more likely to manage selection through the table view, letting the table view manage and track the state of its cells.

Selection implies highlighting. When a cell is selected, it propagates the highlighted state down through its subviews by setting each subview's `highlighted` property if it has one. That is why a UILabel's `highlightedTextColor` applies when the cell is selected. Similarly, a UIImageView (such as the cell's `imageView`) can have a `highlightedImage` that is shown when the cell is selected, and a UIControl (such as a UIButton) takes on its `highlighted` state when the cell is selected.

One of the chief purposes of your table view is likely to be to let the user select a cell. This will be possible, provided you have not set the value of the table view's `allows-Selection` property to `false`. The user taps a cell, and the cell switches to its selected state. Table views can also permit the user to select multiple cells simultaneously. Set the table view's `allowsMultipleSelection` property to `true`. If the user taps an already selected cell, by default it stays selected if the table doesn't allow multiple selection, but is deselected if the table does allow multiple selection.

By default, being selected will mean that the cell is redrawn with a gray background view, but you can change this at the individual cell level, as I've already explained: you can set a cell's `selectedBackgroundView` (or `multipleSelectionBackgroundView`), or change its `selectionStyle`.

Managing Cell Selection

Your code can learn and manage the selection through these UITableView properties and instance methods:

`indexPathForSelectedRow`
`indexPathsForSelectedRows`

These read-only properties report the currently selected row(s), or `nil` if there is no selection. Don't accidentally call the wrong one. For example, asking for `index-PathForSelectedRow` when the table view allows multiple selection gives a result that will have you scratching your head in confusion. (As usual, I speak from experience.)

`selectRowAtIndexPath:animated:scrollPosition:`
The animation involves fading in the selection, but the user may not see this unless the selected row is already visible. The last parameter dictates whether and how the table view should scroll to reveal the newly selected row; your choices (UITableViewScrollPosition) are `.Top`, `.Middle`, `.Bottom`, and `.None`. For the first three options, the table view scrolls (with animation, if the second parameter is `true`) so that the selected row is at the specified position among the visible cells. For `.None`, the table view does not scroll; if the selected row is not already visible, it does not become visible.

`deselectRowAtIndexPath:animated:`
Deselects the given row (if it is selected); the optional animation involves fading out the selection. No automatic scrolling takes place.

To deselect *all* currently selected rows, call `selectRowAtIndexPath:animated:scrollPosition:` with a `nil` index path. Reloading a cell's data also deselects that cell, and calling `reloadData` deselects all selected rows.

Responding to Cell Selection

Response to user selection is through the table view's delegate:

- `tableView:shouldHighlightRowAtIndexPath:`
- `tableView:didHighlightRowAtIndexPath:`
- `tableView:didUnhighlightRowAtIndexPath:`
- `tableView:willSelectRowAtIndexPath:`
- `tableView:didSelectRowAtIndexPath:`
- `tableView:willDeselectRowAtIndexPath:`
- `tableView:didDeselectRowAtIndexPath:`

Despite their names, the two `will` methods are actually `should` methods and expect a return value:

- Return `nil` to prevent the selection (or deselection) from taking place.
- Return the index path handed in as argument to permit the selection (or deselection), or a different index path to cause a different cell to be selected (or deselected).

The Highlight methods are more sensibly named, and they arrive first, so you can return false from tableView:shouldHighlightRowAtIndexPath: to prevent a cell from being selected.

Let's focus in more detail on the relationship between a cell's highlighted state and its selected state. They are, in fact, two different states. When the user touches a cell, the cell passes through a complete highlight cycle. Then, if the touch turns out to be the beginning of a scroll motion, the cell is unhighlighted immediately, and the cell is not selected. Otherwise, the cell is unhighlighted and selected.

But the user doesn't know the difference between these two states: whether the cell is highlighted or selected, the cell's subviews are highlighted, and the selectedBackgroundView appears. Thus, if the user touches and scrolls, what the user sees is the flash of the selectedBackgroundView and the highlighted subviews, until the table begins to scroll and the cell returns to normal. If the user touches and lifts the finger, the selectedBackgroundView and highlighted subviews appear and remain; there is actually a moment in the sequence where the cell has been highlighted and then unhighlighted and not yet selected, but the user doesn't see any momentary unhighlighting of the cell, because no redraw moment occurs (see Chapter 4).

Here's a summary of the sequence:

1. The user's finger goes down. If shouldHighlight permits, the cell highlights, which propagates to its subviews. Then didHighlight arrives.

2. There is a redraw moment. Thus, the user will *see* the cell as highlighted (including the appearance of the selectedBackgroundView), regardless of what happens next.

3. The user either starts scrolling or lifts the finger. The cell unhighlights, which also propagates to its subviews, and didUnhighlight arrives.

    a. If the user starts scrolling, there is a redraw moment, so the user now sees the cell unhighlighted. The sequence ends.

    b. If the user merely lifts the finger, there is no redraw moment, so the cell keeps its highlighted appearance. The sequence continues.

4. If willSelect permits, the cell is selected, and didSelect arrives. The cell is *not* highlighted, but highlighting is propagated to its subviews.

5. There's another redraw moment. The user still sees the cell as highlighted (including the appearance of the selectedBackgroundView).

When tableView:willSelectRowAtIndexPath: is called because the user taps a cell, and if this table view permits only single cell selection, tableView:willDeselectRowAtIndexPath: will be called subsequently for any previously selected cells.

Here's an example of implementing `tableView:willSelectRowAtIndexPath:`. The default behavior for `allowsSelection` (not multiple selection) is that the user can select by tapping, and the cell remains selected; if the user taps a selected row, the selection does not change. We can alter this so that tapping a selected row deselects it:

```
override func tableView(tableView: UITableView,
    willSelectRowAtIndexPath indexPath: NSIndexPath) -> NSIndexPath? {
        if tableView.indexPathForSelectedRow == indexPath {
            tableView.deselectRowAtIndexPath(indexPath, animated:false)
            return nil
        }
        return indexPath
}
```

Navigation From a Table View

An extremely common response to user selection is navigation. A master–detail architecture is typical: the table view lists things the user can see in more detail, and a tap displays the detailed view of the selected thing. On the iPhone, very often the table view will be in a navigation interface, and you will respond to user selection by creating the detail view and pushing it onto the navigation controller's stack.

For example, here's the code from my Albumen app that navigates from the list of albums to the list of songs in the album that the user has tapped:

```
override func tableView(tableView: UITableView,
    didSelectRowAtIndexPath indexPath: NSIndexPath) {
        let t = TracksViewController(
            mediaItemCollection: self.albums[indexPath.row])
        self.navigationController!.pushViewController(t, animated: true)
}
```

In a storyboard, when you draw a segue from a UITableViewCell, you are given a choice of two segue triggers: Selection Segue and Accessory Action. If you create a Selection Segue, the segue will be triggered when the user selects a cell. Thus you can readily push or present another view controller in response to cell selection.

If you're using a UITableViewController, then by default, whenever the table view appears, the selection is cleared automatically in `viewWillAppear:`, and the scroll indicators are flashed in `viewDidAppear:`. You can prevent this automatic clearing of the selection by setting the table view controller's `clearsSelectionOnViewWillAppear` to `false`. I sometimes do that, preferring to implement deselection in `viewDidAppear:`; the effect is that when the user returns to the table, the row is still momentarily selected before it deselects itself.

By convention, if selecting a table view cell causes navigation, the cell should be given an `accessoryType` (UITableViewCellAccessory) of `.DisclosureIndicator`. This is a plain gray right-pointing chevron at the right end of the cell. The chevron itself doesn't respond to user interaction; it is not a button, but just a visual cue that the user can tap the cell to learn more.

Two additional `accessoryType` settings *are* buttons:

`.DetailButton`
> Drawn as a letter "i" in a circle.

`.DetailDisclosureButton`
> Drawn like `.DetailButton`, along with a disclosure indicator chevron to its right.

To respond to the tapping of an accessory button, implement the table view delegate's `tableView:accessoryButtonTappedForRowWithIndexPath:`. Or, in a storyboard, you can Control-drag a connection from a cell and choose an Accessory Action segue.

A common convention is that selecting the cell as a whole does one thing and tapping the detail button does something else. For example, in Apple's Phone app, tapping a contact's listing in the Recents table places a call to that contact, but tapping the detail button navigates to that contact's detail view.

Cell Choice and Static Tables

Another use of cell selection is to implement a choice among cells, where a section of a table effectively functions as an iOS alternative to OS X radio buttons. The table view usually has the grouped format. An `accessoryType` of `.Checkmark` is typically used to indicate the current choice. Implementing radio button behavior is up to you.

As an example, I'll implement the interface shown in Figure 8-3. The table view has the grouped style, with two sections. The first section, with a "Size" header, has three mutually exclusive choices: "Easy," "Normal," or "Hard." The second section, with a "Style" header, has two choices: "Animals" or "Snacks."

This is a *static table*; its contents are known beforehand and won't change. In a case like this, if we're using a UITableViewController subclass instantiated from a storyboard, the nib editor lets us design the entire table, including the headers and the cells *and their content*, directly in the storyboard. Select the table and set its Content pop-up menu in the Attributes inspector to Static Cells to make the table editable in this way (Figure 8-7).

Even though each cell is designed initially in the storyboard, I can still implement `tableView:cellForRowAtIndexPath:` to call `super` and then add further functionality. That's how I'll add the checkmarks. The user defaults are storing the current choice in each of the two categories; there's a `"Size"` preference and a `"Style"` preference, each consisting of a string denoting the title of the chosen cell:

```
override func tableView(tv: UITableView,
    cellForRowAtIndexPath indexPath: NSIndexPath) -> UITableViewCell {
        let cell = super.tableView(
            tv, cellForRowAtIndexPath:indexPath)
```

Figure 8-7. Designing a static table in the storyboard editor

```
let ud = NSUserDefaults.standardUserDefaults()
cell.accessoryType = .None
if ud.valueForKey("Style") as? String == cell.textLabel!.text! ||
    ud.valueForKey("Size") as? String == cell.textLabel!.text! {
        cell.accessoryType = .Checkmark
}
return cell
}
```

When the user taps a cell, the cell is selected. I want the user to see that selection momentarily, as feedback, but then I want to deselect, adjusting the checkmarks so that that cell is the only one checked in its section. In `tableView:didSelectRowAtIndexPath:`, I set the user defaults, and then I reload the table view's data. This removes the selection and causes `tableView:cellForRowAtIndexPath:` to be called to adjust the checkmarks:

```
override func tableView(tv: UITableView,
    didSelectRowAtIndexPath indexPath: NSIndexPath) {
        let ud = NSUserDefaults.standardUserDefaults()
        let setting = tv.cellForRowAtIndexPath(indexPath)!.textLabel!.text
        let header = self.tableView(
            tv, titleForHeaderInSection:indexPath.section)!
        ud.setValue(setting, forKey:header)
        tv.reloadData()
}
```

Table View Scrolling and Layout

A UITableView is a UIScrollView, so everything you already know about scroll views is applicable (Chapter 7). In addition, a table view supplies two convenience scrolling methods:

- scrollToRowAtIndexPath:atScrollPosition:animated:
- scrollToNearestSelectedRowAtScrollPosition:animated:

The scrollPosition parameter is as for selectRowAtIndexPath:..., discussed earlier in this chapter.

The following UITableView methods mediate between the table's bounds coordinates on the one hand and table structure on the other:

- indexPathForRowAtPoint:
- indexPathsForRowsInRect:
- rectForSection:
- rectForRowAtIndexPath:
- rectForFooterInSection:
- rectForHeaderInSection:

The table's own header and footer are direct subviews of the table view, so their positions within the table's bounds are given by their frames.

Table View State Restoration

If a UITableView participates in state saving and restoration (Chapter 6), the restoration mechanism would like to restore the selection and the scroll position. This behavior is automatic; the restoration mechanism knows both what cells should be visible and what cells should be selected, in terms of their index paths. If that's satisfactory, you've no further work to do.

In some apps, however, there is a possibility that when the app is relaunched, the underlying data may have been rearranged somehow. Perhaps what's meaningful in dictating what the user should see in such a case is not the previous *rows* but the previous *data*. The state saving and restoration mechanism doesn't know anything about the relationship between the cells and the underlying data. If you'd like to tell it, adopt the UIDataSourceModelAssociation protocol and implement two methods:

modelIdentifierForElementAtIndexPath:inView:
    Based on the index path, you return some string that you will *later* be able to use to identify uniquely this bit of model data.

indexPathForElementWithModelIdentifier:inView:
    Based on the unique identifier you provided earlier, you return the index path at which this bit of model data is displayed in the table *now*.

Devising a system of unique identification and incorporating it into your data model is up to you.

Table View Searching

A common need is to make a table view searchable, typically through a search field (a UISearchBar; see Chapter 12). A commonly used interface for presenting the results of such a search is a table view! Thus, in effect, entering characters in the search field appears to filter the original table.

This interface is managed through a UIViewController subclass, UISearchController. It is extremely important to understand, before I tell you about UISearchController, that it has nothing to do, *per se*, with table views! A table view is not the only thing you might want to search, and a table view is not the only way you might want to present the results of a search. UISearchController itself is completely agnostic about the form of those results. However, I'm introducing this class in a chapter about table views, so what I'm going to describe is the particular (and common) case of how to use a table view to present the results of searching a table view.

Configuring a Search Controller

Here are the steps for configuring a UISearchController:

1. Create *and retain* a UISearchController instance. To do so, you'll call the designated initializer, `init(searchResultsController:)`. The parameter is a view controller — a UIViewController subclass instance that you will have created for this purpose. The search controller will retain this view controller as a child view controller. When the time comes to display search results, the search controller will *present* itself as a presented view controller, with this view controller's view inside its own view; that is where the search results are to be displayed.

2. Assign to the search controller's `searchResultsUpdater` an object to be notified when the search results change. This must be an object adopting the UISearchResultsUpdating protocol, which means that it implements one method: `updateSearchResultsForSearchController:`. Very typically, this will be the same view controller that you passed as the `searchResultsController:` parameter when you initialized the search controller, but no law says that it has to be the same object or even that it has to be a view controller.

3. Acquire the search controller's `searchBar` and put it into the interface.

Thinking about these steps, you can see what the search controller is proposing to do for you — and what it *isn't* going to do for you. It isn't going to display the search results. It isn't going to manage the search results. It isn't even going to do any searching! It owns a search bar, which you have placed into the interface; and it's going to keep an eye on that search bar. When the user taps in that search bar to begin searching, the search controller will respond by presenting itself and managing the view controller you specified. Then, as the user enters characters in the search bar, the search controller will keep calling the search results updater's `updateSearchResultsForSearchController:`. Finally, when the user taps the search bar's Cancel button, the search controller will dismiss itself.

A UISearchController has just a few other properties you might want to configure:

`dimsBackgroundDuringPresentation`
> Whether a "dimming view" should appear behind the search controller's own view. Defaults to `true`, but I'll give an example later where it needs to be set to `false`.

`hidesNavigationBarDuringPresentation`
> Whether a navigation bar, if present, should be hidden. The default is `true`.

A UISearchController can also be assigned a delegate (UISearchControllerDelegate), which is notified before and after presentation and dismissal (and has one more important ability that I'll mention a bit later).

The minimalistic nature of the search controller's behavior is exactly the source of its power and flexibility, because it leaves you the freedom to take care of the details: what searching means, and what displaying search results means, is up to you.

Using a Search Controller

I'll demonstrate several variations on the theme of using a search controller to make a table view searchable. In this example, searching will mean finding the search bar text within the text displayed in the table view's cells.

Minimal search results table

Let's start with the simplest possible case. We will have two table view controllers — one managing the original table view, the other managing the search results table view. The original table view can be elaborate; we'll use the table of U.S. states, with sections and an index, developed earlier in this chapter. The search results table view will be as minimal as possible: I propose to use a rock-bottom table view with `.Default` style cells, where each search result will be the `text` of a cell's `textLabel` (Figure 8-8).

Here's the configuration of the original table's UITableViewController. I have a property, `self.searcher`, waiting to retain the search controller. I also have a second UITable-ViewController subclass, which I have rather boringly called SearchResultsController, whose job will be to obtain and present the search results. In `viewDidLoad`, I instantiate SearchResultsController, create the UISearchController, and put its search bar into the interface as the table view's header view (and scroll to hide that search bar initially, a common convention):

Figure 8-8. Searching a table

```
let src = SearchResultsController(data: self.sectionData)
let searcher = UISearchController(searchResultsController: src)
self.searcher = searcher
searcher.searchResultsUpdater = src
let b = searcher.searchBar
b.sizeToFit() // crucial, trust me on this one
b.autocapitalizationType = .None
self.tableView.tableHeaderView = b
self.tableView.reloadData()
self.tableView.scrollToRowAtIndexPath(
    NSIndexPath(forRow: 0, inSection: 0),
    atScrollPosition:.Top, animated:false)
```

 Adding the search bar as the table view's header view has an odd side effect: it causes the table view's background color to be covered by an ugly gray color, visible above the search bar when the user scrolls down. The official workaround is to assign the table view a backgroundView with the desired color.

Now we turn to SearchResultsController. It is a completely vanilla table view controller, *qua* table view controller. But I've given it two special features:

- It is capable of *receiving the searchable data.* You can see this happening, in fact, in the first line of the preceding code.
- It is capable of *filtering* that data and displaying the filtered data in its table view.

I'm not using sections in the SearchResultsController's table, so it will simplify things if, as I receive the searchable data in the SearchResultsController, I flatten it from an array of arrays to a simple array:

```
init(data:[[String]]) {
    self.originalData = data.flatten().map{$0}
    super.init(nibName: nil, bundle: nil)
}
```

I have stored the flattened data in the `self.originalData` array, but what I display in the table view is a *different* array, `self.filteredData`. This is initially empty, because there are no search results until the user starts typing in the search field:

```
override func numberOfSectionsInTableView(tableView: UITableView) -> Int {
    return 1
}
override func tableView(tableView: UITableView,
    numberOfRowsInSection section: Int) -> Int {
        return self.filteredData.count
}
override func tableView(tableView: UITableView,
    cellForRowAtIndexPath indexPath: NSIndexPath) -> UITableViewCell {
        let cell = tableView.dequeueReusableCellWithIdentifier(
            "Cell", forIndexPath: indexPath)
        cell.textLabel!.text = self.filteredData[indexPath.row]
        return cell
}
```

All of that is sheer boilerplate and is perfectly obvious; but how does our search results table go from being empty to displaying any search results? That's the second special feature of SearchResultsController. It adopts UISearchResultsUpdating, so it implements updateSearchResultsForSearchController:. In that implementation, it uses the current text of the search controller's searchBar to filter `self.originalData` into `self.filteredData` and reloads the table view:

```
func updateSearchResultsForSearchController(
    searchController: UISearchController) {
        let sb = searchController.searchBar
        let target = sb.text!
        self.filteredData = self.originalData.filter {
            s in
            let options = NSStringCompareOptions.CaseInsensitiveSearch
            let found = s.rangeOfString(target, options: options)
            return (found != nil)
        }
        self.tableView.reloadData()
}
```

That's all! Of course, it's an artificially simple example; I'm describing the interface and the use of a UISearchController, not a real app. In real life you would presumably want to allow the user to *do* something with the search results, perhaps by tapping on a cell in the search results table.

Search bar scope buttons

If we wanted our search bar to have scope buttons, we would set its `scopeButton-Titles` immediately after calling `sizeToFit` in the preceding code:

```
let b = searcher.searchBar
b.sizeToFit() // crucial, trust me on this one
b.scopeButtonTitles = ["Starts", "Contains"]
```

The scope buttons don't appear in the table header view, but they do appear when the search controller presents itself. However, the search controller does not automatically call us back in `updateSearchResultsForSearchController:` when the user taps on a scope button. I regard that as a bug, but it's easy to work around it: we must simply make ourselves the search bar's `delegate`, so as to be notified through the delegate method `searchBar:selectedScopeButtonIndexDidChange:` — which can then turn right around and call `updateSearchResultsForSearchController:` (provided it has a reference to the search controller, which is easy to arrange beforehand). Here, I'll make our SearchResultsController respond to the distinction that a state name either starts with or contains the search text:

```
func updateSearchResultsForSearchController(
    searchController: UISearchController) {
        self.searchController = searchController // weak reference
        let sb = searchController.searchBar
        let target = sb.text!
        self.filteredData = self.originalData.filter {
            s in
            var options = NSStringCompareOptions.CaseInsensitiveSearch
            // we now have scope buttons; 0 means "starts with"
            if searchController.searchBar.selectedScopeButtonIndex == 0 {
                options.insert(.AnchoredSearch)
            }
            let found = s.rangeOfString(target, options: options)
            return (found != nil)
        }
        self.tableView.reloadData()
}
func searchBar(searchBar: UISearchBar,
    selectedScopeButtonIndexDidChange selectedScope: Int) {
        self.updateSearchResultsForSearchController(self.searchController!)
}
```

Customizing the presentation

The search controller is a presented view controller. This means that the presentation is customizable, as I explained in "Custom Presented View Controller Transition" on page 326. In particular:

• You can customize the presentation *animation* by setting the search controller's `transitioningDelegate`. As part of customizing the animation, you can (in fact you must) take charge of *placing the search bar* into the search controller's view; of course you can animate this however you like.

- The search controller's presentation controller is a normal presentation controller, and thus can be adaptive.

- If the search controller's delegate implements `presentSearchController:`, the very act of *presenting the search controller* is left up to you. If you don't call `presentViewController:animated:completion:` here, it will be called for you, but this is your chance to perform preparatory customizations, to add a completion handler, to present without animation, and so on.

In this excerpt from the animation controller's `animateTransition:`, I cause the search bar to appear during the presentation by sliding it down from above:

```
if let v2 = v2 { // presenting, vc2 is the search controller
    con.addSubview(v2) // con is the container view
    v2.frame = r2end
    let sc = vc2 as! UISearchController
    let sb = sc.searchBar
    sb.removeFromSuperview() // take it out of the original table view
    sb.showsScopeBar = true
    sb.sizeToFit()
    v2.addSubview(sb)
    sb.frame.origin.y = -sb.frame.height
    UIView.animateWithDuration(0.3, animations: {
        sb.frame.origin.y = 0
    }, completion: {
        _ in
        sb.setShowsCancelButton(true, animated: true)
        transitionContext.completeTransition(true)
    })
}
```

Search bar in navigation bar

No law says that you have to put the UISearchController's search bar into a table view's header view. Another common interface is for the search bar to appear in a navigation bar at the top of the screen. For example, assuming we are already in a navigation interface, you might make the search bar your view controller's `navigationItem.titleView`. You won't want the navigation bar to vanish when the user searches, so you'll set the search controller's `hidesNavigationBarDuringPresentation` to `false`. To prevent the presented search controller's view from covering the navigation bar, set your view controller's `definesPresentationContext` to `true`; the presented search controller's view will cover your view controller's view, but not the navigation bar, which belongs to the navigation controller's view:

```
let src = SearchResultsController(data: self.sectionData)
let searcher = UISearchController(searchResultsController: src)
self.searcher = searcher
searcher.searchResultsUpdater = src
let b = searcher.searchBar
```

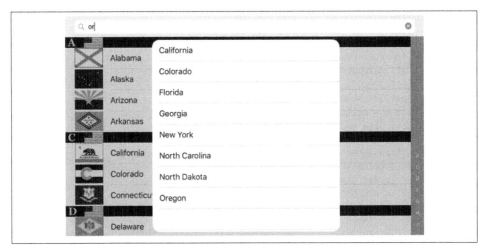

Figure 8-9. Searching from a navigation bar

```
b.sizeToFit()
b.autocapitalizationType = .None
self.navigationItem.titleView = b // *
searcher.hidesNavigationBarDuringPresentation = false // *
self.definesPresentationContext = true // *
```

An interesting question is how the search results should be displayed on an iPad. The usual thing is that they should pop down from the search bar as the user types. In iOS 7 and before, this was typically done by means of a popover (Chapter 9), but starting in iOS 8, Apple seems to prefer a small view that floats in front of everything. Apple's Safari app on the iPad is a familiar case in point. I'll imitate that interface (Figure 8-9).

It's a surprisingly tricky interface to achieve. The UISearchController is a presented view controller, so I would have expected to be able to customize its view position and chrome by setting its `modalPresentationStyle` to `.Custom` and injecting my own custom UIPresentationController; but I can't find a place to do that, because for some reason the transitioning delegate's `presentationControllerForPresentedViewController:...` is never called.

So I've resorted to a different strategy: the UISearchController's `searchResultsController` is a custom parent view controller with a transparent view, and its child view controller is the UITableViewController whose table view will display the search results:

```
class SearchResultsController : UIViewController {
    let child : ChildViewController // a UITableViewController
    init(data:[[String]]) {
        self.child = ChildViewController(data:data)
        super.init(nibName:nil, bundle:nil)
```

```
    }
    required init?(coder aDecoder: NSCoder) {
        fatalError("init(coder:) has not been implemented")
    }
    override func viewDidLoad() {
        self.automaticallyAdjustsScrollViewInsets = false
        self.view.backgroundColor = UIColor.clearColor()
        self.addChildViewController(self.child)
        let v = self.child.view
        self.view.addSubview(self.child.view)
        v.layer.cornerRadius = 15
        v.translatesAutoresizingMaskIntoConstraints = false
        NSLayoutConstraint.activateConstraints([
            v.heightAnchor.constraintEqualToConstant(400),
            v.widthAnchor.constraintEqualToConstant(400),
            v.topAnchor.constraintEqualToAnchor(
                self.view.topAnchor, constant: 50),
            v.centerXAnchor.constraintEqualToAnchor(self.view.centerXAnchor)
        ])
        self.child.didMoveToParentViewController(self)
        let t = UITapGestureRecognizer(target: self, action: "tap:")
        t.delegate = self
        self.view.addGestureRecognizer(t)
    }
}
```

The purpose of the tap gesture recognizer is so that a tap on the background can dismiss the search controller's view. We respond to the tap by walking up the responder chain until we come to our parent, the UISearchController; setting its `active` to `false` dismisses it. We don't want this to happen if the tap is on the results table itself, so we act as the tap gesture recognizer's delegate to prevent it:

```
extension SearchResultsController : UIGestureRecognizerDelegate {
    func tap(g:UITapGestureRecognizer) {
        var r : UIResponder = g.view!
        while !(r is UISearchController) {r = r.nextResponder()!}
        (r as! UISearchController).active = false
    }
    func gestureRecognizerShouldBegin(g: UIGestureRecognizer) -> Bool {
        let pt = g.locationOfTouch(0, inView: self.child.view)
        if self.child.tableView.pointInside(pt, withEvent: nil) {
            return false
        }
        return true
    }
}
```

Finally, the child table view controller adopts the UISearchResultsUpdating protocol, and we pass any `updateSearchResultsForSearchController:` calls along to it:

```
extension SearchResultsController : UISearchResultsUpdating {
    func updateSearchResultsForSearchController(sc: UISearchController) {
        self.child.updateSearchResultsForSearchController(sc)
    }
}
```

No secondary search results view controller

As a final variation, I'll demonstrate how to use a search controller *without* a distinct search results view controller. There will be no SearchResultsController; instead, we'll present the search results *in the original table view*.

To configure our search controller, we pass `nil` as its `searchResultsController` and set ourselves as the `searchResultsUpdater`. We also set the search controller's `dims-BackgroundDuringPresentation` to `false`; this allows the original table view to remain *visible and touchable* behind the search controller's view:

```
let searcher = UISearchController(searchResultsController:nil)
self.searcher = searcher
searcher.dimsBackgroundDuringPresentation = false
searcher.searchResultsUpdater = self
searcher.delegate = self
```

The implementation is a simple problem in table data source management. We keep an immutable copy of our data model arrays, `self.sectionData` and `self.section-Names` — let's call the copies `self.originalSectionData` and `self.originalSection-Names`. These copies are unused if we're not searching. If we *are* searching, we hear about it through the search controller's delegate methods, and we raise a Bool flag in a property:

```
func willPresentSearchController(searchController: UISearchController) {
    self.searching = true
}
func willDismissSearchController(searchController: UISearchController) {
    self.searching = false
}
```

Any of our table view delegate or data source methods can consult this flag. For example, it might be nice to remove the index while searching is going on:

```
override func sectionIndexTitlesForTableView(tableView: UITableView)
    -> [String]? {
        return self.searching ? nil : self.sectionNames
}
```

All that remains is to implement `updateSearchResultsForSearchController`: to filter `self.originalSectionData` and `self.originalSectionNames` into the data model arrays `self.sectionData` and `self.sectionNames` — or to copy them unfiltered if the search bar's text is empty, which is also the signal that the search controller presentation is over:

```
func updateSearchResultsForSearchController(
    searchController: UISearchController) {
        let sb = searchController.searchBar
        let target = sb.text
        if target == "" {
            self.sectionNames = self.originalSectionNames
            self.sectionData = self.originalSectionData
            self.tableView.reloadData()
            return
        }
        // we have a target string
        self.sectionData = self.originalSectionData.map {
            $0.filter {
                let options = NSStringCompareOptions.CaseInsensitiveSearch
                let found = $0.rangeOfString(target, options: options)
                return (found != nil)
            }
        }.filter {$0.count > 0}
        self.sectionNames =
            self.sectionData.map {String($0[0].characters.prefix(1))}
        self.tableView.reloadData()
}
```

Table View Editing

A table view cell has a normal state and an editing state, according to its `editing` property. The editing state (or *edit mode*) is typically indicated visually by one or more of the following:

Editing controls

At least one editing control will usually appear, such as a Minus button (for deletion) at the left side.

Shrinkage

The content of the cell will usually shrink to allow room for an editing control. If there is no editing control, you can prevent a cell shifting its left end rightward in edit mode with the table delegate's `tableView:shouldIndentWhileEditingRowAt-IndexPath:`. (There is also a cell property `shouldIndentWhileEditing`, but I find it unreliable.)

Changing accessory view

The cell's accessory view will change automatically in accordance with its `editing-AccessoryType` or `editingAccessoryView`. If you assign neither, so that they are `nil`, the cell's existing accessory view will vanish when in edit mode.

As with selection, you could set a cell's `editing` property directly (or use `set-Editing:animated:` to get animation), but you are more likely to let the table view manage editability. Table view editability is controlled through the table view's `editing` property, usually by sending the table the `setEditing:animated:` message. The table is then responsible for putting its cells into edit mode.

A cell in edit mode can also be selected by the user if the table view's `allowsSelection-DuringEditing` or `allowsMultipleSelectionDuringEditing` is `true`. But this would be unusual.

Putting the table into edit mode is usually left up to the user. A typical interface would be an Edit button that the user can tap. In a navigation interface, we might have our view controller supply the button as a bar button item in the navigation bar:

```
let b = UIBarButtonItem(
    barButtonSystemItem: .Edit, target: self, action: "doEdit:")
self.navigationItem.rightBarButtonItem = b
```

Our action handler will be responsible for putting the table into edit mode, so in its simplest form it might look like this:

```
func doEdit(sender:AnyObject?) {
    self.tableView.setEditing(true, animated:true)
}
```

But that does not solve the problem of getting *out* of edit mode. The standard solution is to have the Edit button replace itself by a Done button:

```
func doEdit(sender:AnyObject?) {
    var which : UIBarButtonSystemItem
    if !self.tableView.editing {
        self.tableView.setEditing(true, animated:true)
        which = .Done
    } else {
        self.tableView.setEditing(false, animated:true)
        which = .Edit
    }
    let b = UIBarButtonItem(
        barButtonSystemItem: which, target: self, action: "doEdit:")
    self.navigationItem.rightBarButtonItem = b
}
```

However, it turns out that all of that is completely unnecessary! If we want standard behavior, it's already implemented for us. A UIViewController's `editButtonItem` method vends a bar button item that calls the UIViewController's `set-Editing:animated:` when tapped, tracks whether we're in edit mode with the UIViewController's `editing` property, and changes its own title accordingly (Edit or Done). Moreover, a UITableViewController's implementation of `setEditing:animated:` is to call `setEditing:animated:` on its table view. Thus, if we're using a UITableViewController, we get all of that behavior for free, just by calling `editButtonItem` and inserting the resulting button into our interface:

```
self.navigationItem.rightBarButtonItem = self.editButtonItem()
```

When the table view enters edit mode, it consults its data source and delegate about the editability of individual rows:

`tableView:canEditRowAtIndexPath:` *to the data source*
> The default is `true`. The data source can return `false` to prevent the given row from entering edit mode.

`tableView:editingStyleForRowAtIndexPath:` *to the delegate*
> Each standard editing style corresponds to a control that will appear in the cell. The choices (UITableViewCellEditingStyle) are:
>
> `.Delete`
>> The cell shows a Minus button at its left end. The user can tap this to summon a Delete button, which the user can then tap to confirm the deletion. This is the default.
>
> `.Insert`
>> The cell shows a Plus button at its left end; this is usually taken to be an insert button.
>
> `.None`
>> No editing control appears.

If the user taps an insert button (the Plus button) or a delete button (the Delete button that appears after the user taps the Minus button), the data source is sent the `table-View:commitEditingStyle:forRowAtIndexPath:` message and is responsible for obeying it. In your response, you will probably want to alter the structure of the table, and UITableView methods for doing this are provided:

- `insertRowsAtIndexPaths:withRowAnimation:`
- `deleteRowsAtIndexPaths:withRowAnimation:`
- `insertSections:withRowAnimation:`
- `deleteSections:withRowAnimation:`
- `moveSection:toSection:`
- `moveRowAtIndexPath:toIndexPath:`

The row animations here are effectively the same ones discussed earlier in connection with refreshing table data; `.Left` for an insertion means to slide in from the left, and for a deletion it means to slide out to the left, and so on. The two "move" methods provide animation with no provision for customizing it.

If you're issuing more than one of these commands, you can combine them by surrounding them with `beginUpdates` and `endUpdates`, forming an *updates block*. An updates block combines not just the animations but the requested changes themselves.

This relieves you from having to worry about how a command is affected by earlier commands in the same updates block; indeed, the order of commands within an updates block doesn't really matter.

For example, if you delete row 1 of a certain section and then (in a separate command in the same updates block) delete row 2 of the same section, you delete two successive rows, just as you would expect; the notion "2" does not change its meaning because you deleted an earlier row first, because you *didn't* delete an earlier row first — the updates block combines the commands for you, interpreting both index paths with respect to the state of the table before any changes are made. If you perform insertions and deletions together in one updates block, the deletions are performed first, regardless of the order of your commands, and the insertion row and section numbers refer to the state of the table after the deletions.

An updates block can also include `reloadRows...` and `reloadSections...` commands (but not `reloadData`).

I need hardly emphasize once again (but I will anyway) that view is not model. It is one thing to rearrange the appearance of the table, another to alter the underlying data. It is up to you to make certain you do both together. Do not, even for a moment, permit the data and the view to get out of synch with each other! If you delete a row, you must first remove from the model the datum that it represents. The runtime will try to help you with error messages if you forget to do this, but in the end the responsibility is yours. I'll give examples as we proceed.

Deleting Cells

Deletion of cells is the default, so there's not much for us to do in order to implement it. If our view controller is a UITableViewController and we've displayed the Edit button in a navigation bar, everything happens automatically: when the user taps the Edit button, the view controller's `setEditing:animated:` is called, the table view's `setEditing:animated:` is called, and the cells all show the Minus button at the left end. The user can then tap a Minus button; a Delete button is shown at the cell's right end. You can customize the Delete button's title with the table view delegate method `tableView:titleForDeleteConfirmationButtonForRowAtIndexPath:`.

What is *not* automatic is the actual response to the Delete button. For that, we need to implement `tableView:commitEditingStyle:forRowAtIndexPath:`. Typically, you'll remove the corresponding entry from the underlying model data, and you'll call `deleteRowsAtIndexPaths:withRowAnimation:` or `deleteSections:withRowAnimation:` to update the appearance of the table.

To illustrate, let's suppose once again that the underlying model is a pair of parallel arrays of strings (`self.sectionNames`) and arrays (`self.sectionData`). Our approach will be in two stages:

1. Deal with the model data. We'll delete the datum for the requested row; if this empties the section array, we'll also delete that section array and the corresponding section name.

2. Deal with the table's appearance. If we deleted the section array, we'll call `delete-Sections:withRowAnimation:` (and reload the section index if there is one); otherwise, we'll call `deleteRowsAtIndexPaths:withRowAnimation:`.

That's the strategy; here's the implementation:

```
override func tableView(tableView: UITableView,
    commitEditingStyle editingStyle: UITableViewCellEditingStyle,
    forRowAtIndexPath ip: NSIndexPath) {
        switch editingStyle {
        case .Delete:
            if self.sectionData[ip.section].count == 0 {
                self.sectionData.removeAtIndex(ip.section)
                self.sectionNames.removeAtIndex(ip.section)
                tableView.deleteSections(NSIndexSet(index: ip.section),
                    withRowAnimation:.Automatic)
                tableView.reloadSectionIndexTitles()
            } else {
                tableView.deleteRowsAtIndexPaths([ip],
                    withRowAnimation:.Automatic)
            }
        default: break
        }
}
```

The user can also delete a row by sliding it to the left to show its Delete button *without* having explicitly entered edit mode; no other row is editable, and no other editing controls are shown. This feature is implemented "for free" by virtue of our having supplied an implementation of `tableView:commitEditingStyle:forRowAtIndexPath:`.

If you're like me, your first response will be: "Thanks for the free functionality, Apple, and now how do I turn this off?" Because the Edit button is already using the UIView-Controller's `editing` property to track edit mode, we can take advantage of this and refuse to let any cells be edited unless the view controller *is* in edit mode:

```
override func tableView(tableView: UITableView,
    editingStyleForRowAtIndexPath indexPath: NSIndexPath)
    -> UITableViewCellEditingStyle {
        return self.editing ? .Delete : .None
}
```

Custom Action Buttons

The table cell is itself inside a little horizontal scroll view; the user who slides a cell to the left is actually scrolling the cell to the left, revealing the Delete button behind it. You can customize what buttons will appear when the user slides a cell leftward to enter edit mode, or enters edit mode and taps the Minus button.

To configure the buttons for a row of the table, implement the table view delegate method `tableView:editActionsForRowAtIndexPath:` and return an array of UITableView-RowAction objects in right-to-left order (or `nil` to get the default Delete button). Create a row action button with its initializer, `init(style:title:handler:)`. The parameters are:

style:
>   A UITableViewRowActionStyle, either `.Default` or `.Normal`. By default, `.Default` is a red button signalling a destructive action, like the Delete button, while `.Normal` is a gray button. You can subsequently change the color by setting the button's `backgroundColor`.

title:
>   The text of the button.

handler:
>   A function to be called when the button is tapped; it takes two parameters, a reference to the row action and the index path for this cell.

If you want the user to be able to slide the cell to reveal the buttons, you must implement `tableView:commitEditingStyle:forRowAtIndexPath:`, even if your implementation is empty. But even if you *don't* implement this method, the buttons can be revealed by putting the table view into edit mode and tapping the Minus button. Your `handler:` can call `tableView:commitEditingStyle:forRowAtIndexPath:` if appropriate; a custom Delete button, for example, might do so.

In this example, we give our cells a blue Mark button in addition to the default Delete button:

```
override func tableView(tableView: UITableView,
    editActionsForRowAtIndexPath indexPath: NSIndexPath)
    -> [UITableViewRowAction]? {
        let act = UITableViewRowAction(style: .Normal, title: "Mark") {
            action, ip in
            print("Mark") // in real life, do something here
        }
        act.backgroundColor = UIColor.blueColor()
        let act2 = UITableViewRowAction(style: .Default, title: "Delete") {
            action, ip in
            self.tableView(self.tableView, commitEditingStyle:.Delete,
                forRowAtIndexPath:ip)
        }
        return [act2, act]
}
```

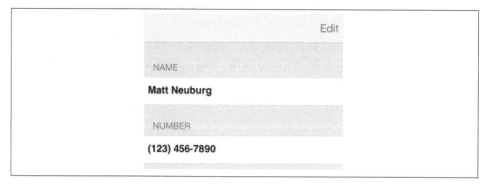

Figure 8-10. A simple phone directory app

Configuration of these buttons is disappointingly inflexible — for example, you can't achieve anything like the Mail app's interface — and many developers will prefer to continue rolling their own sliding table cells, as in the past.

Editable Content in Cells

A cell might have content that the user can edit directly, such as a UITextField (Chapter 10). Because the user is working in the view, you need a way to reflect the user's changes into the model. This will probably involve putting yourself in contact with the interface objects where the user does the editing.

To illustrate, I'll implement a table view cell with a text field that is editable when the cell is in edit mode. Imagine an app that maintains a list of names and phone numbers. A name and phone number are displayed as a grouped style table, and they become editable when the user taps the Edit button (Figure 8-10).

We don't need a button at the left end of the cell when it's being edited:

```
override func tableView(tableView: UITableView,
    editingStyleForRowAtIndexPath indexPath: NSIndexPath)
    -> UITableViewCellEditingStyle {
        return .None
}
```

A UITextField is editable if its `enabled` is `true`. To tie this to the cell's `editing` state, it is probably simplest to implement a custom UITableViewCell class. I'll call it MyCell, and I'll design it in the nib, giving it a single UITextField that's pointed to through an outlet property called `textField`. In the code for MyCell, we override `didTransition-ToState:`, as follows:

```
class MyCell : UITableViewCell {
    @IBOutlet weak var textField : UITextField!
    override func didTransitionToState(state: UITableViewCellStateMask) {
        self.textField.enabled = state.contains(.ShowingEditControlMask)
        super.didTransitionToState(state)
    }
}
```

In the table view's data source, we make ourselves the text field's delegate when we create and configure the cell:

```
override func tableView(tableView: UITableView,
    cellForRowAtIndexPath indexPath: NSIndexPath) -> UITableViewCell {
        let cell = tableView.dequeueReusableCellWithIdentifier(
            "Cell", forIndexPath:indexPath) as! MyCell
            switch indexPath.section {
        case 0:
            cell.textField.text = self.name
        case 1:
            cell.textField.text = self.numbers[indexPath.row]
            cell.textField.keyboardType = .NumbersAndPunctuation
        default: break
        }
        cell.textField.delegate = self
        return cell
}
```

We are the UITextField's delegate, so we are responsible for implementing the Return button in the keyboard to dismiss the keyboard (I'll talk more about this in Chapter 10):

```
func textFieldShouldReturn(textField: UITextField) -> Bool {
    textField.endEditing(true)
    return false
}
```

When a text field stops editing, we are its delegate, so we can hear about it in `textFieldDidEndEditing:`. We work out which cell this text field belongs to — I like to do this by simply walking up the view hierarchy until I come to a table view cell — and update the model accordingly:

```
func textFieldDidEndEditing(textField: UITextField) {
    // some cell's text field has finished editing; which cell?
    var v : UIView = textField
    repeat { v = v.superview! } while !(v is UITableViewCell)
    let cell = v as! MyCell
    // update data model to match
    let ip = self.tableView.indexPathForCell(cell)!
    if ip.section == 1 {
        self.numbers[ip.row] = cell.textField.text!
    } else if ip.section == 0 {
        self.name = cell.textField.text!
    }
}
```

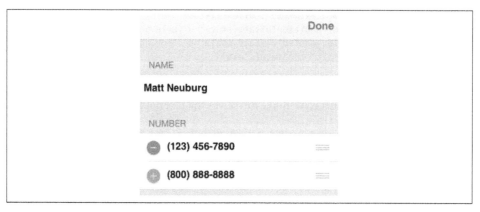

Figure 8-11. Phone directory app in edit mode

Inserting Cells

You are unlikely to attach a Plus (insert) button to every row. A more likely interface is that when a table is edited, every row has a Minus button except the last row, which has a Plus button; this shows the user that a new row can be appended at the end of the list.

Let's implement this for phone numbers in our name-and-phone-number app, allowing the user to give a person any quantity of phone numbers (Figure 8-11):

```
override func tableView(tableView: UITableView,
    editingStyleForRowAtIndexPath indexPath: NSIndexPath)
    -> UITableViewCellEditingStyle {
        if indexPath.section == 1 {
            let ct = self.tableView(
                tableView, numberOfRowsInSection:indexPath.section)
            if ct-1 == indexPath.row {
                return .Insert
            }
            return .Delete;
        }
        return .None
}
```

The person's name has no editing control (a person must have exactly one name), so we prevent it from indenting in edit mode:

```
override func tableView(tableView: UITableView,
    shouldIndentWhileEditingRowAtIndexPath indexPath: NSIndexPath)
    -> Bool {
        if indexPath.section == 1 {
            return true
        }
        return false
}
```

When the user taps an editing control, we must respond. We immediately force our text fields to cease editing: the user have may tapped the editing control while editing, and we want our model to contain the very latest changes, so this is effectively a way of causing our `textFieldDidEndEditing:` to be called. The model for our phone numbers is an array of strings (`self.numbers`). We already know what to do when the tapped control is a delete button; things are similar when it's an insert button, but we've a little more work to do. The new row will be empty, and it will be at the end of the table; so we append an empty string to the `self.numbers` model array, and then we insert a corresponding row at the end of the table view. But now two successive rows have a Plus button; the way to fix that is to reload the first of those rows. Finally, we also show the keyboard for the new, empty phone number, so that the user can start editing it immediately; we do that outside the updates block:

```
override func tableView(tableView: UITableView,
    commitEditingStyle editingStyle: UITableViewCellEditingStyle,
    forRowAtIndexPath indexPath: NSIndexPath) {
        tableView.endEditing(true)
        if editingStyle == .Insert {
            self.numbers += [""]
            let ct = self.numbers.count
            tableView.beginUpdates()
            tableView.insertRowsAtIndexPaths(
                [NSIndexPath(forRow:ct-1, inSection:1)],
                withRowAnimation:.Automatic)
            tableView.reloadRowsAtIndexPaths(
                [NSIndexPath(forRow:ct-2, inSection:1)],
                withRowAnimation:.Automatic)
            tableView.endUpdates()
            // crucial that this next bit be *outside* the update block
            let cell = self.tableView.cellForRowAtIndexPath(
                NSIndexPath(forRow:ct-1, inSection:1))
            (cell as! MyCell).textField.becomeFirstResponder()
        }
        if editingStyle == .Delete {
            self.numbers.removeAtIndex(indexPath.row)
            tableView.beginUpdates()
            tableView.deleteRowsAtIndexPaths(
                [indexPath], withRowAnimation:.Automatic)
            tableView.reloadSections(
                NSIndexSet(index:1), withRowAnimation:.Automatic)
            tableView.endUpdates()
        }
}
```

Rearranging Cells

If the data source implements `tableView:moveRowAtIndexPath:toIndexPath:`, the table displays a reordering control at the right end of each row in edit mode (Figure 8-11), and the user can drag it to rearrange cells. The reordering control can be suppressed for individual cells by implementing `tableView:canMoveRowAtIndex-Path:`. The user is free to move rows that display a reordering control, but the delegate can limit where a row can be moved to by implementing `tableView:targetIndexPath-ForMoveFromRowAtIndexPath:toProposedIndexPath:`.

To illustrate, we'll add to our name-and-phone-number app the ability to rearrange phone numbers. There must be multiple phone numbers to rearrange:

```
override func tableView(tableView: UITableView,
    canMoveRowAtIndexPath indexPath: NSIndexPath) -> Bool {
        if indexPath.section == 1 && self.numbers.count > 1 {
            return true
        }
        return false
}
```

A phone number must not be moved out of its section, so we implement the delegate method to prevent this. We also take this opportunity to dismiss the keyboard if it is showing:

```
override func tableView(tableView: UITableView,
    targetIndexPathForMoveFromRowAtIndexPath sourceIndexPath: NSIndexPath,
    toProposedIndexPath proposedDestinationIndexPath: NSIndexPath)
    -> NSIndexPath {
        tableView.endEditing(true)
        if proposedDestinationIndexPath.section == 0 {
            return NSIndexPath(forRow:0, inSection:1)
        }
        return proposedDestinationIndexPath
}
```

After the user moves an item, `tableView:moveRowAtIndexPath:toIndexPath:` is called, and we trivially update the model to match. We also reload the table, to fix the editing controls:

```
override func tableView(tableView: UITableView,
    moveRowAtIndexPath fromIndexPath: NSIndexPath,
    toIndexPath: NSIndexPath) {
        let s = self.numbers[fromIndexPath.row]
        self.numbers.removeAtIndex(fromIndexPath.row)
        self.numbers.insert(s, atIndex: toIndexPath.row)
        tableView.reloadData()
}
```

Dynamic Cells

A table may be rearranged not just in response to the user working in edit mode, but for some other reason entirely. In this way, many interesting and original interfaces are possible.

In this example, we permit the user to double tap on a section header as a way of collapsing or expanding the section — that is, we'll suppress or permit the display of the rows of the section, with a nice animation as the change takes place. (This idea is shamelessly stolen from a WWDC 2010 video.)

One more time, our data model consists of the two arrays, self.sectionNames and self.sectionData. I've also got a Set (of Int), self.hiddenSections, in which I'll list the sections that aren't displaying their rows. That list is all I'll need, since either a section is showing all its rows or it's showing none of them:

```
override func tableView(tableView: UITableView,
    numberOfRowsInSection section: Int) -> Int {
        if self.hiddenSections.contains(section) {
            return 0
        }
        return self.sectionData[section].count
}
```

We need a correspondence between a section header and the number of its section. It's odd that UITableView doesn't give us such a correspondence; it provides indexPathFor-Cell:, but there is no sectionForHeaderFooterView:. My solution is to subclass UITableViewHeaderFooterView and give my subclass a public property section:

```
class MyHeaderView : UITableViewHeaderFooterView {
    var section = 0
}
```

Whenever tableView:viewForHeaderInSection: is called, I set the header view's section property:

```
override func tableView(tableView: UITableView,
    viewForHeaderInSection section: Int) -> UIView? {
        let h = tableView.dequeueReusableHeaderFooterViewWithIdentifier(
            "Header") as! MyHeaderView
        // ...
        h.section = section // *
        return h
}
```

The section headers are a UITableViewHeaderFooterView subclass with user-InteractionEnabled set to true and a UITapGestureRecognizer attached, so we can detect a double tap. When the user double taps a section header, we learn from the header what section this is, we find out from the model how many rows this section has, and we derive the index paths of the rows we're about to insert or remove. Now we look for the section number in our hiddenSections set. If it's there, we're about to display the rows, so we *remove* that section number from hiddenSections, and we *insert* the rows. If it's *not* there, we're about to hide the rows, so we *insert* that section number into hiddenSections, and we *delete* the rows:

```
func tap (g : UIGestureRecognizer) {
    let v = g.view as! MyHeaderView
    let sec = v.section
    let ct = self.sectionData[sec].count
    let arr = Array(0..<ct).map {NSIndexPath(forRow:$0, inSection:sec)}
    if self.hiddenSections.contains(sec) {
        self.hiddenSections.remove(sec)
        self.tableView.beginUpdates()
        self.tableView.insertRowsAtIndexPaths(arr,
            withRowAnimation:.Automatic)
        self.tableView.endUpdates()
        self.tableView.scrollToRowAtIndexPath(arr[ct-1],
            atScrollPosition:.None,
            animated:true)
    } else {
        self.hiddenSections.insert(sec)
        self.tableView.beginUpdates()
        self.tableView.deleteRowsAtIndexPaths(arr,
            withRowAnimation:.Automatic)
        self.tableView.endUpdates()
    }
}
```

Table View Menus

A menu, in iOS, is a sort of balloon containing tappable words such as Copy, Cut, and
Paste. You can permit the user to display a menu from a table view cell by performing
a long press on the cell. The long press followed by display of the menu gives the cell a
selected appearance, which goes away when the menu is dismissed.

To allow the user to display a menu from a table view's cells, you implement three
delegate methods:

tableView:shouldShowMenuForRowAtIndexPath:
> Return true if the user is to be permitted to summon a menu by performing a long
> press on this cell.

tableView:canPerformAction:forRowAtIndexPath:withSender:
> You'll be called repeatedly with selectors for various actions that the system knows
> about. Returning true, regardless, causes the Copy, Cut, and Paste menu items to
> appear in the menu, corresponding to the copy:, cut:, and paste: actions; return
> false to prevent the menu item for an action from appearing. The menu itself will
> then appear unless you return false to all three actions. The sender is the shared
> UIMenuController.

tableView:performAction:forRowAtIndexPath:withSender:
> The user has tapped one of the menu items; your job is to respond to it somehow.

Here's an example where the user can summon a Copy menu from any cell (Figure 8-12):

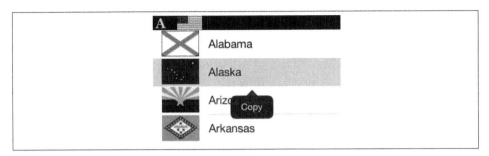

Figure 8-12. A table view cell with a menu

```
override func tableView(tableView: UITableView,
    shouldShowMenuForRowAtIndexPath indexPath: NSIndexPath) -> Bool {
        return true
}
override func tableView(tableView: UITableView,
    canPerformAction action: Selector,
    forRowAtIndexPath indexPath: NSIndexPath,
    withSender sender: AnyObject?) -> Bool {
        return action == "copy:"
}
override func tableView(tableView: UITableView,
    performAction action: Selector,
    forRowAtIndexPath indexPath: NSIndexPath,
    withSender sender: AnyObject?) {
        if action == "copy:" {
            // ... do whatever copying consists of ...
        }
}
```

To add a custom menu item to the menu (other than `copy:`, `cut:`, and `paste:`) is a little more work. First, you must tell the shared UIMenuController to append the menu item to the global menu; the `tableView:shouldShowMenuForRowAtIndexPath:` delegate method is a good place to do this:

```
override func tableView(tableView: UITableView,
    shouldShowMenuForRowAtIndexPath indexPath: NSIndexPath) -> Bool {
        let mi = UIMenuItem(title: "Abbrev", action: "abbrev:")
        UIMenuController.sharedMenuController().menuItems = [mi]
        return true
}
```

We have now given the menu an additional menu item whose title is Abbrev, and whose action when the menu item is tapped is `abbrev:`. (I am imagining here a table of the names of U.S. states, where one can copy a state's two-letter abbreviation to the clipboard.) If we want this menu item to appear in the menu, and if we want to respond to it when the user taps it, we must add that selector to the two `performAction:` delegate methods:

```
override func tableView(tableView: UITableView,
    canPerformAction action: Selector,
    forRowAtIndexPath indexPath: NSIndexPath,
    withSender sender: AnyObject) -> Bool {
        return action == "copy:" || action == "abbrev:"
}
override func tableView(tableView: UITableView,
    performAction action: Selector,
    forRowAtIndexPath indexPath: NSIndexPath,
    withSender sender: AnyObject) {
        if action == "copy:" {
            // ... do whatever copying consists of ...
        }
        if action == "abbrev:" {
            // ... do whatever abbreviating consists of ...
        }
}
```

Now comes the tricky part: we must implement our custom selector, abbrev:, *in the cell*. We will therefore need our table to use a custom UITableViewCell subclass. Let's call it MyCell:

```
class MyCell : UITableViewCell {
    func abbrev(sender:AnyObject!) {
        // ...
    }
}
```

The Abbrev menu item now appears when the user long-presses a cell of our table, and the cell's abbrev: method is called when the user taps that menu item. We could respond directly to the tap in the cell, but it seems more consistent that our table view delegate should respond. So we work out what table view this cell belongs to and send its delegate the very message it is already expecting:

```
func abbrev(sender:AnyObject!) {
    // find my table view
    var v : UIView = self
    repeat {v = v.superview!} while !(v is UITableView)
    let tv = v as! UITableView
    // ask it what index path we are
    let ip = tv.indexPathForCell(self)!
    // talk to its delegate
    let action = Selector(__FUNCTION__ + ":") // *
    tv.delegate?.tableView?(
        tv, performAction:action, forRowAtIndexPath:ip, withSender:sender)
}
```

 The starred line calls attention to the fact that Swift's __FUNCTION__ literal does not evaluate to a valid Objective-C selector string; I regard this as a bug.

Collection Views

A collection view (UICollectionView) is a UIScrollView subclass that generalizes the notion of a UITableView. Indeed, knowing about table views, you know a great deal about collection views already; they are extremely similar:

- You can manage your UICollectionView through a UIViewController subclass — a subclass of UICollectionViewController.
- A collection view has reusable cells. These are UICollectionViewCell instances.
- Where a table view has *rows*, a collection view has *items.*
- A collection view can clump its items into sections, identified by section number.
- You'll make the cells reusable by registering a class or nib with the collection view:
  - `registerClass:forCellWithReuseIdentifier:`
  - `registerNib:forCellWithReuseIdentifier:`.

  Alternatively, if you've started with a UICollectionViewController in a storyboard, just assign the reuse identifier to the cell prototype in the storyboard.
- A collection view has a data source (UICollectionViewDataSource) and a delegate (UICollectionViewDelegate), and it's going to ask the data source Three Big Questions:
  - `numberOfSectionsInCollectionView:`
  - `collectionView:numberOfItemsInSection:`
  - `collectionView:cellForItemAtIndexPath:`
- To answer the third Big Question, your data source will supply a cell by calling `dequeueReusableCellWithReuseIdentifier:forIndexPath:`.
- A collection view allows the user to select a cell, or multiple cells. The delegate is notified of highlighting and selection. Your code can rearrange the cells, inserting, moving, and deleting cells or entire sections. If the delegate permits, the user can long-press a cell to produce a menu.

With a collection view, a section can have a header and footer, but the collection view itself does not call them that; instead, it generalizes its subview types into cells, on the one hand, and *supplementary views*, on the other. A supplementary view is just a UICollectionReusableView, which happens to be UICollectionViewCell's superclass. A supplementary view is associated with a *kind*, which is just a string identifying its type; thus you can have a header as one kind, a footer as another kind, and anything else you can imagine. A supplementary view in a collection view is then similar to a header or footer view in a table view:

- You can make supplementary views reusable by registering a class with the collection view.
- The data source method where you are asked for a supplementary view will be:
  - `collectionView:viewForSupplementaryElementOfKind:atIndexPath:`
- In that method, your data source will supply a supplementary view by calling `dequeueReusableSupplementaryViewOfKind:....`

The big *difference* between a table view and a collection view is *how the collection view lays out its elements* (cells and supplementary views). A table view lays out its cells in just one way: a vertically scrolling column, where the cells' widths are the width of the table view, their heights are dictated by the table view or the delegate, and touching one another. A collection view doesn't do that. In fact, a collection view doesn't lay out its elements at all! That job is left to another class, a subclass of UICollectionViewLayout.

A UICollectionViewLayout subclass instance is responsible for the overall layout of the collection view that owns it. It does this by answering some Big Questions of its own, posed by the collection view; the most important are these:

`collectionViewContentSize`
How big is the entire layout? The collection view needs to know this, because the collection view is a scroll view (Chapter 7), and this will be the content size of the scrollable material that it will display.

`layoutAttributesForElementsInRect:`
Where do all the elements go? The layout attributes, as I'll explain in more detail in a moment, are bundles of positional information.

To answer these questions, the collection view layout needs to ask the collection view some questions of its own, such as `numberOfSections` and `numberOfItemsIn-Section:`. (The collection view, in turn, gets the answers to those questions from its data source.)

The collection view layout can thus assign the elements any positions it likes, and the collection view will faithfully draw them in those positions within its content rectangle. That seems very open-ended, and indeed it is. To get you started, there's a built-in UICollectionViewLayout subclass — UICollectionViewFlowLayout.

UICollectionViewFlowLayout arranges its cells in something like a grid. The grid can be scrolled either horizontally or vertically, but not both; so this grid is a series of rows or columns. Through properties and a delegate protocol of its own (UICollectionView-DelegateFlowLayout), the UICollectionViewFlowLayout instance lets you provide hints about how big the cells are and how they should be spaced out. It defines two supplementary view types, using them to let you give each section a header and a footer.

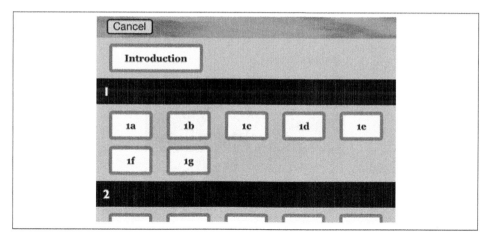

Figure 8-13. A collection view in my Latin flashcard app

Figure 8-13 shows a collection view, laid out with a flow layout, from my Latin flashcard app. This interface simply lists the chapters and lessons into which the flashcards themselves are divided, and allows the user to jump to a desired lesson by tapping it. Previously, I was using a table view to present this list; when collection views were introduced (in iOS 6), I adopted one for this interface, and you can see why. Instead of a lesson item like "1a" occupying an entire row that stretches the whole width of a table, it's just a little rectangle; in landscape orientation, the flow layout fits five of these rectangles onto a line for me. So a collection view is a much more compact and appropriate way to present this interface than a table view.

If UICollectionViewFlowLayout doesn't quite meet your needs, you can subclass it, or you can subclass UICollectionViewLayout itself. (I'll talk more about that later on.)

Figure 8-14 shows a familiar collection view: the Moments view of Apple's Photos app. It lays out square photo thumbnails as a grid that can be scrolled vertically. The thumbnail cells are clumped into sections, and each section has a header with a label displaying the date. My guess is that this collection view probably uses a UICollectionViewFlowLayout subclass.

(In addition to cells and supplementary views, a collection view supports *decoration views*. These are not directly analogous to anything in a table view; they are closest, perhaps, to the section index. They don't represent data; the collection view won't ask the data source about them, and the collection view has no methods about them. They are purely up to the collection view layout; it defines any decoration view types, gives its decoration views actual view content, and states the positions its decoration views are to have. I've never written or used a collection view layout that implemented decoration views, and I'm not going to say any more about them.)

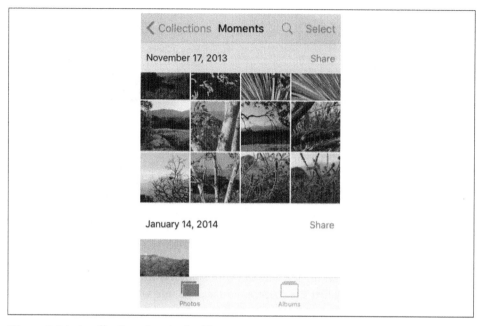

Figure 8-14. A collection view in the Photos app

Collection View Classes

Here are the main classes associated with UICollectionView. This is just a conceptual overview; I don't recite all the properties and methods of each class, which you can learn from the documentation:

UICollectionViewController

A UIViewController subclass. Like a table view controller, UICollectionView-Controller is convenient if a UICollectionView is to be a view controller's view, but is not required. It is the delegate and data source of its `collectionView` by default. In the nib editor, there is a Collection View Controller nib object. The designated initializer requires you to supply a layout instance:

```
let rvc =
    RootViewController(collectionViewLayout:UICollectionViewFlowLayout())
```

UICollectionView

A UIScrollView subclass. It has a `backgroundColor` (because it's a view) and optionally a `backgroundView` in front of that. Its designated initializer requires you to supply a layout instance, which will be its `collectionViewLayout`. In the nib editor, there is a Collection View nib object, which comes with a Collection View Flow Layout by default; you can change the collection view layout class with the Layout pop-up menu in the Collection View's Attributes inspector.

A collection view's methods are very much parallel to those of a UITableView, but fewer and simpler:

- Where a table view speaks of rows, a collection view speaks of *items*. UICollectionView extends NSIndexPath so that you can refer to its item property instead of its row property.

- Where a table view speaks of a header or footer, a collection view speaks of a *supplementary view*.

- A UICollectionView doesn't do layout, so it is not where things like header and cell size are configured.

- A UICollectionView has no notion of editing.

- A UICollectionView has no section index.

- Where a table view batches updates with beginUpdates and endUpdates, a collection view uses performBatchUpdates:completion:, which takes functions.

- A collection view performs animation when you insert, delete, or move sections or items, but you don't specify an animation type. (The layout can modify the animation.)

UICollectionViewLayoutAttributes

UICollectionViewLayoutAttributes is a value class (a bunch of properties), tying together an element's indexPath with the specifications for how and where it should be drawn — specifications that are remarkably reminiscent of view or layer properties, with names like frame, center, size, transform, and so forth. Layout attributes objects function as the mediators between the layout and the collection view; they are what the layout passes to the collection view to tell it where all the elements of the view should go.

UICollectionViewCell

An extremely minimal view class. It has a highlighted property and a selected property. It has a contentView, a selectedBackgroundView, a backgroundView, and of course (since it's a view) a backgroundColor, layered in that order, just like a table view cell; everything else is up to you.

If you start with a collection view controller in a storyboard, you get prototype cells, which you obtain by dequeuing. Otherwise, you obtain cells through registration and dequeuing.

UICollectionReusableView

The superclass of UICollectionViewCell — so it is even more minimal! This is the class of supplementary views such as headers and footers. You obtain reusable views through registration and dequeuing; if you're using a flow layout in a storyboard, you are given a header and footer prototype view.

UICollectionViewLayout

The layout workhorse class for a collection view. A collection view cannot exist without a layout instance! As I've already said, the layout knows how much room all the subviews occupy, and supplies the `collectionViewContentSize` that sets the `contentSize` of the collection view, *qua* scroll view. In addition, the layout must answer questions from the collection view, by supplying a UICollectionView-LayoutAttributes object, or an array of such objects, saying where and how elements should be drawn. These questions come in two categories:

Static attributes

The collection view wants to know the layout attributes of an item, supplementary view, or decoration view, specified by index path, or of all elements within a given rect.

Dynamic attributes

The collection view is inserting or removing elements. It asks for the layout attributes that an element, specified by index path, should have before insertion or after removal. The collection view can thus animate between the element's static attributes and these dynamic attributes. For example, if an element's layout attributes `alpha` is `0` after removal, the element will appear to fade away as it is removed.

The collection view also notifies the layout of pending changes through some methods whose names start with `prepare` and `finalize`. This is another way for the layout to participate in animations, or to perform other kinds of preparation and cleanup.

UICollectionViewLayout is an abstract class; to use it, you must subclass it, or start with the built-in subclass, UICollectionViewFlowLayout.

UICollectionViewFlowLayout

A concrete subclass of UICollectionViewLayout; you can use it as is, or you can subclass it. It lays out items in a grid that can be scrolled either horizontally or vertically, and it defines two supplementary element types to serve as the header and footer of a section. A collection view in the nib editor has a Layout pop-up menu that lets you choose a Flow layout, and you can configure the flow layout in the Size inspector; in a storyboard, you can even add and design a header and a footer.

A flow layout has the following configurations:

- A scroll direction
- A `sectionInset` (the margins for a section)

- An itemSize, along with a minimumInteritemSpacing and minimumLine-Spacing

- A headerReferenceSize and footerReferenceSize

- New in iOS 9, sectionHeadersPinToVisibleBounds and sectionFootersPin-ToVisibleBounds (causing the headers and footers to behave like table view headers and footers when the user scrolls)

At a minimum, if you want to see any section headers, you must assign the flow layout a headerReferenceSize, because the default is (0.0,0.0). Otherwise, you get initial defaults that will at least allow you to see something immediately, such as an itemSize of (50.0,50.0) and reasonable default spacing between items and lines.

UICollectionViewFlowLayout also defines a delegate protocol of its own, UICollectionViewDelegateFlowLayout. The flow layout automatically treats the collection view's delegate as its own delegate. The section margins, item size, item spacing, line spacing, and header and footer size can be set for individual sections, cells, and supplementary views through this delegate.

Using a Collection View

Basic use of a collection view is easy. Here's how the view shown in Figure 8-13 is created. I have a UICollectionViewController subclass, LessonListController. Every collection view must have a layout, so LessonListController's designated initializer initializes itself with a UICollectionViewFlowLayout:

```
init?(terms data:NSArray) {
    self.terms = data
    // ... other self-initializations here ...
    let layout = UICollectionViewFlowLayout()
    super.init(collectionViewLayout:layout)
}
```

In viewDidLoad, we give the flow layout its hints about the sizes of the margins, cells, and headers, as well as registering for cell and header reusability:

```
let HEADERID = "LessonHeader"
let CELLID = "LessonCell"
override func viewDidLoad() {
    super.viewDidLoad()
    let layout = self.collectionView!
        .collectionViewLayout as! UICollectionViewFlowLayout
    layout.sectionInset = UIEdgeInsetsMake(10, 20, 10, 20)
    layout.headerReferenceSize = CGSizeMake(0,40)
    layout.itemSize = CGSizeMake(70,45)
    self.collectionView!.registerNib(
        UINib(nibName:CELLID, bundle:nil),
```

```
        forCellWithReuseIdentifier:CELLID)
    self.collectionView!.registerClass(
        UICollectionReusableView.self,
        forSupplementaryViewOfKind:UICollectionElementKindSectionHeader,
        withReuseIdentifier:HEADERID)
    self.collectionView!.backgroundColor = UIColor.myGolden()
    // ...
}
```

The first two of the Three Big Questions to the data source are boring and familiar:

```
override func numberOfSectionsInCollectionView(
    collectionView: UICollectionView) -> Int {
        return self.sectionNames.count
}
override func collectionView(collectionView: UICollectionView,
    numberOfItemsInSection section: Int) -> Int {
        return self.sectionData[section].count
}
```

The third of the Three Big Questions to the data source creates and configures the cells. In a *.xib* file, I've designed the cell with a single subview, a UILabel with tag 1; if the text of that label is still "Label", this is a sign that the cell has come freshly minted from the nib and needs further initial configuration. Among other things, I assign each new cell a selectedBackgroundView and give the label a highlightedTextColor, to get an automatic indication of selection:

```
override func collectionView(collectionView: UICollectionView,
    cellForItemAtIndexPath indexPath: NSIndexPath)
    -> UICollectionViewCell {
        let cell = collectionView.dequeueReusableCellWithReuseIdentifier(
            CELLID, forIndexPath: indexPath)
        let lab = cell.viewWithTag(1) as! UILabel
        if lab.text == "Label" {
            lab.highlightedTextColor = UIColor.whiteColor()
            cell.backgroundColor = UIColor.myPaler()
            cell.layer.borderColor = UIColor.brownColor().CGColor
            cell.layer.borderWidth = 5
            cell.layer.cornerRadius = 5
            let v = UIView()
            v.backgroundColor =
                UIColor.blueColor().colorWithAlphaComponent(0.8)
            cell.selectedBackgroundView = v
        }
        let term = self.sectionData[indexPath.section][indexPath.item]
        lab.text = term.lesson + term.sectionFirstWord
        return cell
}
```

The fourth data source method asks for the supplementary element views; in my case, these are the section headers. I configure the header entirely in code. Again I distinguish between newly minted views and reused views; the latter will already have a single sub-view, a UILabel:

```
override func collectionView(collectionView: UICollectionView,
    viewForSupplementaryElementOfKind kind: String,
    atIndexPath indexPath: NSIndexPath)
    -> UICollectionReusableView {
        let v = collectionView.dequeueReusableSupplementaryViewOfKind(
            UICollectionElementKindSectionHeader,
            withReuseIdentifier: HEADERID,
            forIndexPath: indexPath)
        if v.subviews.count == 0 {
            let lab = UILabel(frame:CGRectMake(10,0,100,40))
            lab.font = UIFont(name:"GillSans-Bold", size:20)
            lab.backgroundColor = UIColor.clearColor()
            v.addSubview(lab)
            v.backgroundColor = UIColor.blackColor()
            lab.textColor = UIColor.myPaler()
        }
        let lab = v.subviews[0] as! UILabel
        lab.text = self.sectionNames[indexPath.section]
        return v
}
```

As you can see from Figure 8-13, the first section is treated specially — it has no header, and its cell is wider. I take care of that with two UICollectionViewDelegateFlowLayout methods:

```
func collectionView(collectionView: UICollectionView,
    layout collectionViewLayout: UICollectionViewLayout,
    sizeForItemAtIndexPath indexPath: NSIndexPath) -> CGSize {
        var sz =
            (collectionViewLayout as! UICollectionViewFlowLayout)
                .itemSize
        if indexPath.section == 0 {
            sz.width = 150
        }
        return sz
}
func collectionView(collectionView: UICollectionView,
    layout collectionViewLayout: UICollectionViewLayout,
    referenceSizeForHeaderInSection section: Int) -> CGSize {
        var sz =
            (collectionViewLayout as! UICollectionViewFlowLayout)
                .headerReferenceSize
        if section == 0 {
            sz.height = 0
        }
        return sz
}
```

When the user taps a cell, I hear about it through the delegate method `collection-`
`View:didSelectItemAtIndexPath:` and respond accordingly. That is the entire code
for managing this collection view!

Here's an example of deleting cells in a collection view. Let's assume that the cells to be
deleted have been selected, with multiple selection being possible. If there are selected
cells, they are provided as an array of NSIndexPaths. My data model is once again the
usual pair of parallel arrays of strings (`sectionNames`) and arrays (`sectionData`); each
NSIndexPath gets me directly to the corresponding piece of data in `sectionData`, so I
delete each piece of data in reverse order, keeping track of any arrays (sections) that end
up empty. Finally, I delete the items from the collection view, and then do the same for
the sections:

```
func doDelete(sender:AnyObject) { // button, delete selected cells
    let arr = self.collectionView!.indexPathsForSelectedItems()!
    if arr.count == 0 {
        return
    }
    // sort
    let arr2 = ((arr as NSArray).sortedArrayUsingSelector(
        Selector("compare:")) as! [NSIndexPath])
    // delete data
    var empties = [Int]() // keep track of what sections get emptied
    for ip in arr2.reverse() {
        self.sectionData[ip.section].removeAtIndex(ip.item)
        if self.sectionData[ip.section].count == 0 {
            empties += [ip.section]
        }
    }
    // will need an NSIndexSet version of that empties list
    let emptyset = NSMutableIndexSet()
    for i in empties {
        emptyset.addIndex(i)
    }
    // delete from view, deal with empty sections
    self.collectionView!.performBatchUpdates({
        self.collectionView!.deleteItemsAtIndexPaths(arr2)
        if empties.count > 0 { // delete empty sections
            self.sectionNames.removeAtIndexes(empties)
            self.sectionData.removeAtIndexes(empties)
            self.collectionView!.deleteSections(emptyset)
        }
    }, completion: nil)
}
```

(For the `removeAtIndexes:` utility, see Appendix B.)

Menu handling is also completely parallel to a table view; if you want additional menu
items beyond the standard Copy, Cut, and Paste, the corresponding custom selectors
must be implemented in a UICollectionViewCell subclass.

Custom Collection View Layouts

To explore what might be involved in writing your own layout class, let's introduce a simple modification of UICollectionViewFlowLayout.

By default, the flow layout wants to full-justify every row of cells horizontally, spacing the cells evenly between the left and right margins, except for the last row, which is left-aligned. Let's say that this isn't what you want — you'd rather that *every* row be left-aligned, with every cell as far to the left as possible given the size of the preceding cell and the minimum spacing between cells.

To achieve this, you'll need to subclass UICollectionViewFlowLayout and override two methods, `layoutAttributesForElementsInRect:` and `layoutAttributesForItemAt-IndexPath:`. Fortunately, we're starting with a layout, UICollectionViewFlowLayout, whose answers to these questions are almost right. So we call `super` and make modifications as necessary.

The really important method here is `layoutAttributesForItemAtIndexPath:`, which returns a single UICollectionViewLayoutAttributes object.

If the index path's `item` is `0`, we have a degenerate case: the answer we got from `super` is right. Alternatively, if this cell is at the start of a row — we can find this out by asking whether the left edge of its frame is close to the margin — we have another degenerate case: the answer we got from `super` is right.

Otherwise, where this cell goes depends on where the previous cell goes, so we obtain the frame of the previous cell recursively; we propose to position our left edge a minimal spacing amount from the right edge of the previous cell. We do that by copying the layout attributes object that we got from `super` and changing the frame of that copy. Then we return that object:

```
override func layoutAttributesForItemAtIndexPath(indexPath: NSIndexPath)
    -> UICollectionViewLayoutAttributes? {
        var atts = super.layoutAttributesForItemAtIndexPath(indexPath)!
        if indexPath.item == 0 {
            return atts // degenerate case 1
        }
        if atts.frame.origin.x - 1 <= self.sectionInset.left {
            return atts // degenerate case 2
        }
        let ipPv = NSIndexPath(
            forItem:indexPath.item-1, inSection:indexPath.section)
        let fPv = self.layoutAttributesForItemAtIndexPath(ipPv)!.frame
        let rightPv =
            fPv.origin.x + fPv.size.width + self.minimumInteritemSpacing
        atts = atts.copy() as! UICollectionViewLayoutAttributes
        atts.frame.origin.x = rightPv
        return atts
    }
```

The other method, `layoutAttributesForElementsInRect:`, returns an array of UICollectionViewLayoutAttributes objects for all the cells and supplementary views in a rect. Again we call `super` and modify the resulting array so that if an element is a cell, its UICollectionViewLayoutAttributes is the result of our `layoutAttributesForItemAtIndexPath::`

```
override func layoutAttributesForElementsInRect(rect: CGRect)
    -> [UICollectionViewLayoutAttributes]? {
        let arr = super.layoutAttributesForElementsInRect(rect)!
        return arr.map {
            (var atts) in
            if atts.representedElementKind == nil {
                let ip = atts.indexPath
                atts = self.layoutAttributesForItemAtIndexPath(ip)!
            }
            return atts
        }
}
```

Apple supplies some further interesting examples of subclassing UICollectionViewFlowLayout. For instance, the LineLayout example (accompanying the WWDC 2012 videos) implements a single row of horizontally scrolling cells, where a cell grows as it approaches the center of the screen and shrinks as it moves away. To do this, it first of all overrides a UICollectionViewLayout method I didn't mention earlier, `shouldInvalidateLayoutForBoundsChange:`; this causes layout to happen repeatedly while the collection view is scrolled. It then overrides `layoutAttributesForElementsInRect:` to do the same sort of thing I did a moment ago: it calls `super` and then modifies, as needed, the `transform3D` property of the UICollectionViewLayoutAttributes for the onscreen cells.

You can also subclass UICollectionViewLayout itself. The WWDC 2012 videos demonstrate a UICollectionViewLayout subclass that arranges its cells in a circle; the WWDC 2013 videos demonstrate a UICollectionViewLayout subclass that piles its cells into a single stack in the center of the collection view, like a deck of cards seen from above.

A collection view layout can be powerful and complex, but getting started writing one from scratch is not difficult. To illustrate, I'll write a collection view layout that ignores sections and presents all cells as a simple grid of squares.

In my UICollectionViewLayout subclass, called MyLayout, the really big questions I need to answer are `collectionViewContentSize` and `layoutAttributesForElementsInRect:`. To answer them, I'll calculate the entire layout of my grid beforehand. The `prepareLayout` method is the perfect place to do this; it is called every time something about the collection view or its data changes. I'll calculate the grid of cells and express their positions as an array of UICollectionViewLayoutAttributes objects; I'll store that information in a property `self.atts`, which is a dictionary keyed by index path so that

I can retrieve a given layout attributes object by its index path quickly. I'll also store the size of the grid in a property `self.sz`:

```
override func prepareLayout() {
    let sections = self.collectionView!.numberOfSections()
    // work out cell size based on bounds size
    let sz = self.collectionView!.bounds.size
    let width = sz.width
    let shortside = floor(width/50.0)
    let cellside = width/shortside
    // generate attributes for all cells
    var x = 0
    var y = 0
    var atts = [UICollectionViewLayoutAttributes]()
    for i in 0 ..< sections {
        let jj = self.collectionView!.numberOfItemsInSection(i)
        for j in 0 ..< jj {
            let att = UICollectionViewLayoutAttributes(
                forCellWithIndexPath:
                NSIndexPath(forItem:j, inSection:i))
            att.frame = CGRectMake(
                CGFloat(x)*cellside,CGFloat(y)*cellside,cellside,cellside)
            atts += [att]
            x++
            if CGFloat(x) >= shortside {
                x = 0
                y++
            }
        }
    }
    for att in atts {
        self.atts[att.indexPath] = att
    }
    let fluff = (x == 0) ? 0 : 1
    self.sz = CGSizeMake(width, CGFloat(y+fluff) * cellside)
}
```

`collectionViewContentSize` and `layoutAttributesForElementsInRect:` are easy: I'll just fetch the requested information from the `sz` or `atts` property, respectively:

```
override func collectionViewContentSize() -> CGSize {
    return self.sz
}
override func layoutAttributesForElementsInRect(rect: CGRect)
    -> [UICollectionViewLayoutAttributes]? {
        return Array(self.atts.values)
}
```

`layoutAttributesForItemAtIndexPath:` is implemented by looking up the corresponding value in my `self.atts` dictionary:

```
    override func layoutAttributesForItemAtIndexPath(indexPath: NSIndexPath)
        -> UICollectionViewLayoutAttributes? {
            return self.atts[indexPath]
    }
```

Finally, I want to implement shouldInvalidateLayoutForBoundsChange: to return true, so that if the interface is rotated, my prepareLayout will be called again to recalculate the grid. There's a potential source of inefficiency here, though: the user scrolling the collection view counts as a bounds change as well. Therefore I return false unless the bounds width has changed:

```
    override func shouldInvalidateLayoutForBoundsChange(newBounds: CGRect)
        -> Bool {
            let ok = newBounds.size.width != self.sz.width
            return ok
    }
```

Switching Layouts

An astonishing feature of a collection view is that its layout object can be swapped out on the fly. You can substitute one layout for another, by calling setCollectionView-Layout:animated:completion:. The data hasn't changed, and the collection view can identify each element uniquely and persistently, so it responds by moving every element from its position according to the old layout to its position according to the new layout — and, if the animated: argument is true, it does this with animation! Thus the elements are seen to rearrange themselves, as if by magic.

This animated change of layout can even be driven interactively (in response, for example, to a user gesture; compare Chapter 6 on interactive transitions). You call start-InteractiveTransitionToCollectionViewLayout:completion: on the collection view, and a special layout object is returned — a UICollectionViewTransitionLayout instance (or a subclass thereof; to make it a subclass, you need to have implemented collectionView:transitionLayoutForOldLayout:newLayout: in your collection view delegate). This transition layout is temporarily made the collection view's layout, and your job is then to keep it apprised of the transition's progress (through its transitionProgress property) and ultimately to call finishInteractive-Transition or cancelInteractiveTransition on the collection view.

Furthermore, when one collection view controller is pushed on top of another in a navigation interface, the runtime will do exactly the same thing for you, as a custom view controller transition (again, compare Chapter 6). To arrange this, the first collection view controller's useLayoutToLayoutNavigationTransitions property must be false and the second collection view controller's useLayoutToLayoutNavigation-Transitions property must be true. The result is that when the second collection view controller is pushed onto the navigation controller, *the collection view remains in place*, and the layout specified by the second collection view controller is substituted for the collection view's existing layout, with animation.

As the second collection view controller is pushed onto the navigation stack, although there are two collection view controllers, and although the second view controller has a view (the collection view), and its `viewDidLoad` and `viewWillAppear:` (as well as the first view controller's `viewWillDisappear:`) are called as you would expect, the same collection view is also still the *first* view controller's view, and the collection view's data source and delegate are still the *first* view controller. Later, after the transition is complete, the collection view's delegate becomes the *second* view controller, but its data source is *still* the *first* view controller. I find this profoundly weird.

Collection Views and UIKit Dynamics

The UICollectionViewLayoutAttributes class adopts the UIDynamicItem protocol (see Chapter 4). Thus, collection view elements can be animated under UIKit dynamics. The world of the animator here is not a superview but the layout itself; instead of `init(referenceView:)`, you'll create the UIDynamicAnimator with `init(collectionViewLayout:)`. The layout's `collectionViewContentSize` determines the bounds of this world. Convenience methods are provided so that your code can access an animated collection view item's layout attributes directly from the animator.

You'll need a custom collection view layout subclass, because otherwise you won't be able to see any animation. On every frame of its animation, the UIDynamicAnimator is going to change the layout attributes of some items, but the collection view is still going to draw those items in accordance with the layout's `layoutAttributesFor-ElementsInRect:`. The simplest solution is to override `layoutAttributesForElements-InRect:` so as to obtain those layout attributes from the UIDynamicAnimator. This cooperation will be easiest if the layout itself owns and configures the animator.

In this example, we're in the layout subclass, setting up the animation. The layout subclass has a property to hold the animator, as well as a Bool property to signal when an animation is in progress:

```
let visworld = self.collectionView!.bounds
let anim = UIDynamicAnimator(collectionViewLayout:self)
self.animator = anim
self.animating = true
// ... configure rest of animation
```

Our implementation of `layoutAttributesForElementsInRect:`, if we are animating, substitutes the layout attributes that come from the animator for those we would normally return; the technique I use here relies on the fact that the animator convenience methods `layoutAttributesForCellAtIndexPath:` and so forth return `nil` if the specified item is not being animated. In this particular example, both cells and supplementary items (headers and footers) can be animated, so the two cases have to be distinguished:

```
override func layoutAttributesForElementsInRect(rect: CGRect)
    -> [UICollectionViewLayoutAttributes]? {
        var arr = super.layoutAttributesForElementsInRect(rect)!
        if self.animating {
            return arr.map {
                atts in
                let path = atts.indexPath
                switch atts.representedElementCategory {
                case .Cell:
                    if let atts2 = self.animator?
                        .layoutAttributesForCellAtIndexPath(path) {
                            return atts2
                    }
                case .SupplementaryView:
                    if let kind = atts.representedElementKind {
                        if let atts2 = self.animator?
                            .layoutAttributesForSupplementaryViewOfKind(
                                kind, atIndexPath:path) {
                                    return atts2
                        }
                    }
                default: break
                }
                return atts
            }
        }
        return arr
}
```

iPad Interface

This chapter discusses some iOS interface features that differ between the iPad and the iPhone.

Popovers and split views are forms of interface designed originally for the iPad. In iOS 7 and before, they existed *only* on the iPad. Starting in iOS 8, both became available also on the iPhone, where they can either adapt — appearing in an altered form, more appropriate to the smaller screen — or appear just as they do on the iPad.

iPad multitasking, new in iOS 9, is an interface confined to a subset of iPad models, where two apps can occupy the screen simultaneously.

Popovers

A *popover* is a sort of secondary window or dialog: it displays a view layered on top of the main interface. It is usually associated, through a sort of arrow, with a view in the main interface — usually the button that the user tapped to summon the popover. It might be effectively modal, preventing the user from working in the rest of the interface; alternatively, it might vanish if the user taps outside it.

A popover can bring to the larger iPad the smaller, more lightweight flavor of the iPhone. For example, in my LinkSame app, both the settings view (where the user configures the game) and the help view (which describes how to play the game) are popovers (Figure 9-1). On the iPhone, both these views would occupy the entire screen; for each, we'd need a way to navigate to it, and then the user would have to return to the main interface afterward. But with the larger iPad screen, neither view is large enough, or important enough, to occupy the entire screen exclusively. As popovers, they are characterized as smaller, secondary views which the user summons temporarily and then dismisses.

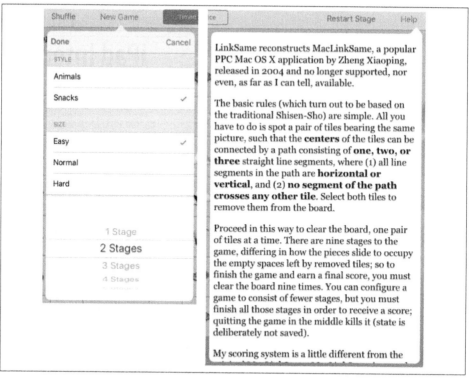

Figure 9-1. *Two popovers*

A popover, in iOS 8 and later, is actually a form of presented view controller — a presented view controller with a modalPresentationStyle of .Popover (which I didn't tell you about in Chapter 6). Among the advantages of this architecture are:

Memory management

In iOS 7 and before, it was necessary to create a UIPopoverController and retain it explicitly. A presented view controller, on the other hand, is retained *automatically* by its presenting view controller.

Singularity

In iOS 7 and before, nothing enforced Apple's guideline that a maximum of one popover at a time should be shown. A presented view controller, on the other hand, enforces it *automatically* (a view controller can't have more than one presented view controller at a time).

Adaptibility

In iOS 7 and before, a popover was illegal on the iPhone. Your universal app therefore had to be filled with conditional code: "If we're running on an iPad, show this view controller as a popover; otherwise, make it a presented view controller." Dismissal and cleanup were conditional too, and could be even harder to manage. A presented view controller, on the other hand, can adapt. A `.Popover` presented view controller, like a `.FormSheet` presented view controller, is *automatically* treated by default as `.FullScreen` on the iPhone. Moreover, if you don't want the default, you don't have to accept it; it is legal for a popover to appear on the iPhone as a popover.

Preparing a Popover

To show a popover, you're going to present a view controller. Before that presentation takes place, you'll turn this into a popover presentation by setting the view controller's `modalPresentationStyle` to `.Popover`:

```
let vc = MyViewController()
vc.modalPresentationStyle = .Popover
self.presentViewController(vc, animated: true, completion: nil)
```

This, however, is insufficient; without a little further configuration, that code will crash at runtime when the popover is presented. The additional configuration is performed through the UIPopoverPresentationController (a UIPresentationController subclass) that is responsible for showing this popover. Setting the view controller's `modalPresentationStyle` to `.Popover` causes its `presentationController` to become a UIPopoverPresentationController, and its `popoverPresentationController` points to that same UIPopoverPresentationController.

Arrow source and direction

At a minimum, the UIPopoverPresentationController needs you to set one of the following:

barButtonItem
> A bar button item in the interface, with which the popover should be associated. The popover's arrow will point to this bar button item. Typically, this will be the bar button item that was tapped in order to summon the popover (as in Figure 9-1).

sourceView, sourceRect
> A UIView in the interface, along with the CGRect *in that view's coordinate system*, with which the popover should be associated. The popover's arrow will point to this rect. Typically, the `sourceView` will be the view that was tapped in order to summon the popover, and the `sourceRect` will be its bounds.

Thus, here's a minimal popover presentation that actually works; the popover is summoned by tapping a UIButton in the interface, and this is that button's action method:

```
@IBAction func doButton(sender: AnyObject) {
    let vc = MyViewController()
    vc.modalPresentationStyle = .Popover
    self.presentViewController(vc, animated: true, completion: nil)
    if let pop = vc.popoverPresentationController {
```

```
        let v = sender as! UIView
        pop.sourceView = v
        pop.sourceRect = v.bounds
    }
}
```

(Observe that it is legal and effective to finish configuring the popover *after* presenting it. That's because the presentation hasn't actually started yet, as your code has not yet come to an end.)

In addition to the arrow source, you can set the desired arrow direction, as the popover presentation controller's `permittedArrowDirections`. This is a bitmask with possible values `.Up`, `.Down`, `.Left`, and `.Right`. The default is `.Any`, comprising all four bitmask values; this will usually be what you want.

Popover size and position

The presentation of the popover won't fail if you don't supply a size for the popover, but you probably will want to supply one, as the default is unlikely to be desirable. This information is provided through the presented view controller's `preferredContentSize`.

Recall (from Chapter 6) that a view controller can use its `preferredContentSize` to communicate to a parent view controller the size that it would like to be. The popover presentation controller is a presentation controller (UIPresentationController), and is therefore also a UIContentContainer; the presentation controller acts as the parent of the presented view controller, and in this situation will consult the presented view controller's wishes and will try to respect them.

I'm deliberately leaving open the question of who will set the presented view controller's `preferredContentSize` and when. The presented view controller might set its own value here; its `viewDidLoad` is a reasonable place, or, if the view controller is instantiated from a nib, the nib editor provides Content Size fields in the Attributes inspector. Alternatively, you can set the presented view controller's `preferredContentSize` as you present it:

```
if let pop = vc.popoverPresentationController {
    let v = sender as! UIView
    pop.sourceView = v
    pop.sourceRect = v.bounds
    vc.preferredContentSize = CGSizeMake(200,500)
}
```

It is possible to change the presented view controller's `preferredContentSize` while the popover is showing. The popover presentation controller will hear about this (through the mechanism discussed in Chapter 6) and will respond by changing the popover's size, with animation.

If the popover is a navigation controller, the navigation controller will look at its current view controller's `preferredContentSize`, adjust for the presence of the navigation bar, and set its own `preferredContentSize` appropriately. This is delightful, but it is probably unwise to press it too far; subsequently pushing or popping a view controller with a *different* `preferredContentSize` may not work as you expect — to be precise, the popover's *width* will change to match the new preferred width, but the popover's *height* will change only if the new preferred height is *taller*. (It is possible to work around this by resetting the navigation controller's `preferredContentSize` in a navigation controller delegate method.)

 In theory, it should also be possible to set the popover presentation controller's `popoverLayoutMargins` as a way of encouraging the popover to keep a certain distance from the edges of the presenting view controller's view. In fact, however, my experience is that this setting is ignored; I regard this as a bug.

Popover appearance

By default, a popover presentation controller takes charge of the background color of the presented view controller's view, including the arrow, as well the navigation bar in a navigation interface. If the resulting color isn't to your taste, you can set the popover presentation controller's `backgroundColor`. In a navigation interface, you can change the navigation bar's color separately, and customize the position and appearance of the navigation bar's bar button items (see Chapter 12).

You can also customize the outside of the popover — that is, the "frame" surrounding the content, including the arrow. To do so, you set the UIPopoverPresentationController's `popoverBackgroundViewClass` to your own subclass of UIPopoverBackgroundView (a UIView subclass) — at which point you can achieve just about anything you want, including the very silly popover shown in Figure 9-2.

Configuring your UIPopoverBackgroundView subclass is a bit tricky, because this single view is responsible for drawing both the arrow and the frame. Thus, in a complete and correct implementation, you'll have to draw differently depending on the arrow direction, which you can learn from the UIPopoverBackgroundView's `arrowDirection` property.

I'll give a simplified example in which I cheat by assuming that the arrow direction will be `.Up`. I start by defining some class-level constants that I'll need later:

```
class MyPopoverBackgroundView : UIPopoverBackgroundView {
    static let ARBASE : CGFloat = 20
    static let ARHEIGHT : CGFloat = 20
    // ...
}
```

Figure 9-2. A very silly popover

Drawing the frame (drawRect:) is easy: here, I divide the view's overall rect into two areas, the arrow area on top and the frame area on the bottom, and I draw the frame into the bottom area as a resizable image (Chapter 2):

```
let linOrig = UIImage(named: "linen.png")!
let capw = linOrig.size.width / 2.0 - 1
let caph = linOrig.size.height / 2.0 - 1
let lin = linOrig.resizableImageWithCapInsets(
    UIEdgeInsetsMake(caph, capw, caph, capw), resizingMode:.Tile)
// ... draw arrow here ...
var arrow = CGRectZero
var body = CGRectZero
CGRectDivide(rect, &arrow, &body, Arrow.ARHEIGHT, .MinYEdge)
lin.drawInRect(body)
```

I omitted the drawing of the arrow; now let's insert it. The UIPopoverBackgroundView has arrowHeight and arrowBase class methods that we've overridden to describe the arrow dimensions to the runtime; here, their values are the two constant static variables, ARHEIGHT and ARBASE:

```
override class func arrowBase() -> CGFloat {
    return self.ARBASE
}
override class func arrowHeight() -> CGFloat {
    return self.ARHEIGHT
}
```

My arrow will consist simply of a texture-filled isosceles triangle, with an excess base consisting of a rectangle joining it to the frame. The UIPopoverBackgroundView has an `arrowOffset` property that the runtime has set to tell you where to draw the arrow: this offset measures the positive distance between the center of the view's edge and the center of the arrow. However, the runtime will have no hesitation in setting the `arrow-Offset` all the way at the edge of the view, or even beyond its bounds (in which case it won't be drawn); to prevent this, I provide a maximum offset limit:

```
let con = UIGraphicsGetCurrentContext()!
CGContextSaveGState(con)
var propX = self.arrowOffset
let limit : CGFloat = 22.0
let maxX = rect.size.width/2.0 - limit
if propX > maxX {
    propX = maxX
}
if propX < limit {
    propX = limit
}
let klass = self.dynamicType
CGContextTranslateCTM(con, rect.size.width/2.0 + propX - klass.ARBASE/2.0, 0)
CGContextMoveToPoint(con, 0, klass.ARHEIGHT)
CGContextAddLineToPoint(con, klass.ARBASE / 2.0, 0)
CGContextAddLineToPoint(con, klass.ARBASE, klass.ARHEIGHT)
CGContextClosePath(con)
CGContextAddRect(con, CGRectMake(0,klass.ARHEIGHT,klass.ARBASE,15))
CGContextClip(con)
lin.drawAtPoint(CGPointMake(-40,-40))
CGContextRestoreGState(con)
```

Finally, the thickness of the four sides of the frame is dictated by implementing the `contentViewInsets` class method:

```
override class func contentViewInsets() -> UIEdgeInsets {
    return UIEdgeInsetsMake(20,20,20,20)
}
```

Passthrough views

When you're configuring your popover, you'll want to plan ahead for how the popover is to be dismissed. The default is that the user can tap anywhere outside the popover to dismiss it, and this will often be what you want. You can, however, modify this behavior in two ways:

UIPopoverPresentationController's `passthroughViews` *property*

An array of views in the interface behind the popover; the user can interact normally with these views while the popover is showing, and the popover will *not* be dismissed.

What happens if the user taps a view that is *not* listed in the `passthroughViews` array depends on the `modalInPopover` property.

UIViewController's `modalInPopover` *property*

If this is `true` for the presented view controller (or for its current child view controller, as in a tab bar interface or navigation interface), then if the user taps outside the popover on a view *not* listed in the popover presentation controller's `passthroughViews`, *nothing* happens (the popover is *not* dismissed). The default is `false`.

Clearly, if you've set this property to `true`, you've removed the user's ability to dismiss the popover by tapping outside it. You would then presumably provide some other way of letting the user dismiss the popover — typically, a button *inside* the popover which the user can then tap to call `dismissViewController-Animated:completion:`.

 The claim made by the documentation that `modalInPopover` prevents *all* user interaction outside a popover is wrong. The user can still interact with a view listed in the `passthroughViews`, even if `modalInPopover` is `true`.

Unfortunately — and I can't believe I'm still having to warn about this after all these years — if a popover is summoned by the user tapping a UIBarButton item in a toolbar, other UIBarButtonItems in that toolbar are automatically turned into passthrough views! This means that the user can tap any other button in the toolbar — including a button that summons another popover.

Working around this annoying problem is not easy. Setting the popover presentation controller's `passthroughViews` to `nil` or an empty array just after presenting it doesn't help; your setting is overridden by the runtime. My rather hacky solution is to provide some extra delay, so as to assert my will *after* the runtime:

```
if let pop = vc.popoverPresentationController {
    // ... other configurations go here ...
    delay(0.1) {
        pop.passthroughViews = nil
    }
}
```

Popover Presentation, Dismissal, and Delegate

Because a popover is just a form of presented view controller, it is shown with `present-ViewController:animated:completion:`. Similarly, if you want to dismiss a popover in code, rather than letting the user dismiss it by tapping outside it, you'll dismiss it with `dismissViewControllerAnimated:completion:`.

Messages to the popover presentation controller's delegate (UIPopoverPresentation-ControllerDelegate) provide further information and control. Typically, you'll set the delegate in the same place you're performing the other configurations:

```
if let pop = vc.popoverPresentationController {
    // ... other configurations go here ...
    pop.delegate = self
}
```

The three most commonly used delegate methods are:

prepareForPopoverPresentation:
: The popover is being presented. There is time to perform further initial configurations here (but this method is still called too early for you to work around the passthroughViews issue I discussed a moment ago).

popoverPresentationControllerShouldDismissPopover:
: The user is dismissing the popover by tapping outside it. Return false to prevent dismissal. *Not* called when you dismiss the popover in code.

popoverPresentationControllerDidDismissPopover:
: The user has dismissed the popover by tapping outside it. The popover is gone from the screen and dismissal is complete, even though the popover presentation controller still exists. *Not* called when you dismissed the popover in code.

The delegate methods provide the popover presentation controller as parameter, and if necessary you can probably identify the popover more precisely by querying it further. For example, you can learn what view controller is being presented by examining its presentedViewController, or what interface object its arrow is connected to by examining its sourceView or barButtonItem.

The delegate methods make up for the fact that, when the user dismisses the popover, you don't have the sort of direct information and control that you get from calling dismissViewControllerAnimated:completion: and setting a completion handler. If the user can dismiss the popover *either* by tapping outside the popover *or* by tapping an interface item that calls dismissViewControllerAnimated:completion:, you may have to duplicate some code in order to cover all cases.

For example, consider the first popover shown in Figure 9-1. It has a Done button and a Cancel button; the idea here is that the user sets up a desired game configuration and then, while dismissing the popover, either saves it (Done) or doesn't (Cancel). My approach is to save the user's configuration into NSUserDefaults in real time as the user works within the popover; for example, if the user changes the Style by tapping Animals, I write this change into NSUserDefaults then and there (in my implementation of table-View:didSelectRowAtIndexPath:). So far, so good; but what if the user then cancels? To prepare for that possibility, I copy the relevant user defaults into a property (self.old-Defs) *before* the popover appears:

```
func prepareForPopoverPresentation(pop: UIPopoverPresentationController) {
    self.oldDefs = ud.dictionaryWithValuesForKeys(
        [Default.Style, Default.Size, Default.LastStage])
}
```

If the user taps Done, I dismiss the popover, clear out that property, and proceed to start a new game:

```
func startNewGame() { // user tapped Done
    self.dismissViewControllerAnimated(true, completion: {
        self.oldDefs = nil
        self.prepareNewStage(nil)
    })
}
```

If the user taps Cancel, I dismiss the popover, restore the defaults from the property, and clear out the property:

```
func cancelNewGame() { // user tapped Cancel
    self.dismissViewControllerAnimated(true, completion: nil)
    if (self.oldDefs != nil) {
        ud.setValuesForKeysWithDictionary(self.oldDefs)
        self.oldDefs = nil
    }
}
```

But what if the user taps outside the popover? I interpret that as cancellation. So I've implemented the didDismiss delegate method to duplicate what I would have done if the user had tapped Cancel:

```
func popoverPresentationControllerDidDismissPopover(
    pop: UIPopoverPresentationController) {
        if (self.oldDefs != nil) {
            ud.setValuesForKeysWithDictionary(self.oldDefs)
            self.oldDefs = nil
        }
}
```

There is one further delegate method:

popoverPresentationController:willRepositionPopoverToRect:inView:
> Called because the popover's sourceView is involved in new layout activity. Typically, this is because the interface is rotating. The rect: and view: parameters are mutable pointers, so you can set their memory properties to change the source-Rect or sourceView, thus changing the attachment of the arrow.

In this (unlikely) example, when the interface rotates, I move the popover's arrow from one button to another:

```
func popoverPresentationController(
    popoverPresentationController: UIPopoverPresentationController,
    willRepositionPopoverToRect rect: UnsafeMutablePointer<CGRect>,
    inView view: AutoreleasingUnsafeMutablePointer<UIView?>) {
```

```
        if view.memory == self.button {
            rect.memory = self.button2.bounds
            view.memory = self.button2
        }
    }
```

Adaptive Popovers

Back in iOS 7 and before, popovers were confined to the iPad. If you tried to summon a popover on an iPhone, you'd crash. This meant that you had to summon your view controller in two different ways, conditioned on the environment — for example, as a popover on iPad, but as a presented view controller on iPhone. Thus, you had to write two interleaved sets of code. And it wasn't just a matter of summoning the view controller; you had the same problem on dismissal, because a popover and a presented view controller were dismissed in two different ways.

In iOS 8 and later, however, a popover *is* a presented view controller. So much for that problem! Moreover, this presented view controller is *adaptive*. By default, in a horizontally compact environment (such as an iPhone), the .Popover modal presentation style will be treated as .FullScreen; what appears as a popover on the iPad will appear as a fullscreen presented view on the iPhone, completely replacing the interface. Thus, by default, with no extra code, you'll get something eminently sensible on both types of device.

Sometimes, however, the default is not quite what you want. A case in point appears in Figure 9-1. The popover on the right, containing our help info, has no internal button for dismissal. It doesn't need one on the iPad, because the user can dismiss the popover by tapping outside it. But suppose this is a universal app. The same help info will appear on the iPhone as a fullscreen presented view — *and the user will have no way to dismiss it.*

Clearly, we need a Done button that appears inside the presented view controller's view — but only on the iPhone. How might we achieve this? One approach would be to design the interface in the nib editor with conditional constraints: this view controller's view could then have one interface for a .Regular horizontal size class (iPad) and another interface for a .Compact horizontal size class (iPhone) — and the difference might involve the presence or absence of a Done button.

Another approach is to take advantage of UIPresentationController delegate methods. A UIPopoverPresentationController is also a UIPresentationController — and you can set its delegate (UIAdaptivePresentationControllerDelegate). The adaptive presentation delegate methods (see "Adaptive Presentation" on page 297) thus spring to life, allowing you to tweak how the popover adapts, and how it behaves when it adapts. The trick is that you must set the presentation controller's delegate *before* calling presentView-

Controller:animated:completion:; otherwise, the adaptive presentation delegate methods won't be called.

For example, we can implement the delegate method `presentationController:view-ControllerForAdaptivePresentationStyle:` to substitute a different view controller. This might be nothing but the old view controller wrapped in a UINavigationController! If our view controller has a `navigationItem` with a working Done button, the problem is now solved: on the iPhone, there's a navigation bar at the top of the interface, and the Done button appears in it:

```
@IBAction func doButton(sender: AnyObject) {
    let vc = MyViewController()
    vc.preferredContentSize = CGSizeMake(400,500)
    vc.modalPresentationStyle = .Popover
    if let pres = vc.presentationController {
        pres.delegate = self
    }
    self.presentViewController(vc, animated: true, completion: nil)
    if let pop = vc.popoverPresentationController {
        pop.sourceView = (sender as! UIView)
        pop.sourceRect = (sender as! UIView).bounds
    }
}
func presentationController(controller: UIPresentationController,
    viewControllerForAdaptivePresentationStyle style:
    UIModalPresentationStyle)
    -> UIViewController? {
        if style != .Popover {
            let vc = controller.presentedViewController
            let nav = UINavigationController(rootViewController: vc)
            let b = UIBarButtonItem(barButtonSystemItem: .Done,
                target: self, action: "dismissHelp:")
            vc.navigationItem.rightBarButtonItem = b
            return nav
        }
        return nil
    }
}
```

The outcome is that in a `.Regular` horizontal size class we get a popover that can be dismissed by tapping outside it; otherwise, we get a fullscreen presented view controller that can be dismissed with a Done button.

You can also implement the `adaptivePresentationStyleForPresentationController:traitCollection:` delegate method to customize how the popover adapts. In a `.Compact` horizontal size class, you don't have to return `.FullScreen`; you can return some other adaptive presentation style. In iOS 9 you can return `.FormSheet` to get a slightly smaller view on iPhone. Another possibility is to return `.None` — in which case the presented view controller will be a popover *even on iPhone* (Figure 9-3):

This game reconstructs MacLinkSame, a popular PPC Mac OS X application by Zheng Xiaoping, released in 2004 and no longer supported, nor even, as far as I can tell, available.

The basic rules (which turn out to be based on the traditional Shisen-Sho) are simple. All you have to do is spot a pair of tiles bearing the same picture, such that the **centers** of the tiles can be connected by a path consisting of **one, two, or three** straight line segments, where (1) all line segments in the path are **horizontal or vertical**, and (2) **no segment**

Help

Figure 9-3. A popover appears on an iPhone

```
func adaptivePresentationStyleForPresentationController(
    controller: UIPresentationController,
    traitCollection: UITraitCollection)
    -> UIModalPresentationStyle {
        return .None
}
```

Popover Segues

If you're using a storyboard, you can draw (Control-drag) a segue from the button (or view controller) that is to *summon* the popover to the view controller that is to *be* the popover, and specify "popover presentation" as the segue type. The result is a *popover segue*.

The segue, as it is triggered, configures the presentation just as you would configure it in code. It instantiates and initializes the presented view controller, sets its modal presentation style to `.Popover`, and presents it. You can implement `prepareForSegue:sender:` to perform additional configurations: obtain the segue's `destinationViewController`, get a reference to its `popoverPresentationController`, and configure it. At the time `prepareForSegue:sender:` is called, the presentation has not yet begun, so you can successfully set the popover presentation controller's delegate here as well. You can set its `passthroughViews` too, but you'll still have to provide a delay if your goal is to overcome the default behavior of bar button items:

```
override func prepareForSegue(segue: UIStoryboardSegue, sender: AnyObject?) {
    if segue.identifier == "MyPopover" {
        let dest = segue.destinationViewController
        if let pop = dest.popoverPresentationController {
            pop.delegate = self
            delay(0.1) {
                pop.passthroughViews = nil
            }
        }
    }
}
```

You'll notice that I didn't set the `sourceView` or `barButtonItem` in that code; that's because those properties can be set in the nib editor (Anchor, in the segue's Attributes inspector). You can set the `permittedArrowDirections` in the nib editor as well; they appear as the Directions checkboxes. You can also set the passthrough views in the nib editor, but not in such a way as to override the unwanted default bar button item behavior; thus, I've had to do that in code.

The popover version of an unwind segue is dismissal of the popover. Thus, both presentation and dismissal can be managed through the storyboard.

In iOS 9, you can specify a custom segue class. As I discussed in Chapter 6, your `perform` method can call `super`, so it can concentrate on things that are specific to this segue. Thus, for example, I can create a popover segue that encapsulates our workaround for the `passthroughViews` issue:

```
class MyPopoverSegue: UIStoryboardSegue {
    override func perform() {
        let dest = self.destinationViewController
        if let pop = dest.popoverPresentationController {
            delay(0.1) {
                pop.passthroughViews = nil
            }
        }
        super.perform()
    }
}
```

 In Xcode 7, you *must* be using size classes in your storyboard in order to create a popover segue.

Popover Presenting a View Controller

A popover can present a view controller internally; you'll specify a `modalPresentation-Style` of `.CurrentContext` or `.OverCurrentContext`, because otherwise the presented view will be fullscreen by default (see Chapter 6). In iOS 7 and before, it was necessary to restrict the modal transition style to `.CoverVertical`; in iOS 8, that restriction was lifted.

This raises the question of what happens when the user taps *outside* a popover that is currently *presenting* a view controller and displaying its view internally. Different systems behave differently. Here's a sample:

iOS 7 and before
> Nothing happens; `modalInPopover` is `true`.

iOS 8.1
> The entire popover, including the internal presented view controller, is dismissed.

iOS 8.3
> The internal presented view controller is dismissed, while the popover remains.

iOS 9
> Like iOS 8.1.

This variety of responses is extremely unfortunate (and confusing). In my opinion, the iOS 7 behavior was correct. Presented view controllers are supposed to be modal. They don't spontaneously dismiss themselves because the user taps elsewhere; there has to be some internal interface, such as a Done button or a Cancel button, that the user must tap in order to dismiss the view controller and proceed.

You can restore the iOS 7 behavior by implementing the delegate method `popover-PresentationControllerShouldDismissPopover:` to prevent dismissal if the popover is itself presenting a view controller:

```
func popoverPresentationControllerShouldDismissPopover(
    pop: UIPopoverPresentationController) -> Bool {
        let ok = pop.presentedViewController.presentedViewController == nil
        return ok
}
```

In iOS 9 only, there's another way to achieve the same effect. When the presented view controller appears, you set the `modalInPopover` of *both* the presented view controller *and* the popover's view controller to `true`, restoring things when you dismiss the presented view controller. Here, we implement that workaround in the presented view controller itself:

```
    var oldModal = false
    override func viewWillAppear(animated: Bool) {
        if let pres = self.presentingViewController {
            self.modalInPopover = true
            self.oldModal = pres.modalInPopover
            pres.modalInPopover = true
        }
    }
    @IBAction func doDone(sender: AnyObject) {
        if let pres = self.presentingViewController {
            self.modalInPopover = false
            pres.modalInPopover = self.oldModal
        }
        self.dismissViewControllerAnimated(true, completion: nil)
    }
```

Split Views

A *split view* appears in its typical configuration on the iPad as a combination of two views, the first having (by default) the width of an iPhone screen in portrait orientation. Under the hood, there is a *split view controller* (UISplitViewController); the two views are the main views of its two child view controllers. The child view controllers are the split view controller's viewControllers. A UIViewController that is a child, at any depth, of a UISplitViewController has a reference to the UISplitViewController through its splitViewController property.

The split view controller manages its children's views differently depending on the orientation of the device:

The iPad is in landscape orientation
    The two views appear side by side.

The iPad is in portrait orientation
    There are two possibilities:

> • Both views continue to appear side by side; the second view is narrower than in landscape orientation, because the screen is narrower. Apple's Settings app is an example.

> • Only the second view appears, with an option to summon the first view from the left as an overlay, either by tapping a bar button item or by swiping from left to right. Apple's Mail app is an example (Figure 9-4).

A split view typically expresses a *master–detail architecture*. The smaller, first view is a UITableView where the user is presented with a list (the *master*). The user taps an item of that list to specify what should appear in the larger, second view (the *detail*). We may

---

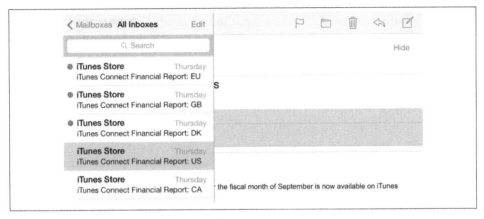

Figure 9-4. A familiar split view interface

thus speak of the two children of the split view controller as the *master view controller* and the *detail view controller*. Apple also sometimes calls them the *primary* and *secondary* view controllers.

On the smaller iPhone screen, a master–detail interface would usually be expressed as a navigation interface: the user sees the master list, which occupies the entire interface, and taps an item of the list to navigate to the corresponding detail view, which again occupies the entire interface — because the detail view controller has been pushed onto the navigation stack. On the larger iPad screen, that interface seems overblown and unnecessary: there is room, especially in landscape orientation, for the master view and the detail view to appear *simultaneously*. In the split view interface, that's exactly what happens.

In iOS 7 and before, writing a universal app that uses a split view in its iPad incarnation was challenging. You had to implement two completely different interfaces using two completely different types of view controller:

Split view controller on the iPad
    When the user taps an item of the master table view, the iPad version alters the split view controller's detail view controller.

Navigation controller on the iPhone
    When the user taps an item of the master table view, the iPhone version pushes a new view controller onto the navigation stack.

In iOS 8 and later, a split view interface is *adaptive*. This means that a single UISplit-ViewController can create and manage *both* of those architectures on *both* types of device. And the split view controller's interface is structurally more flexible than in earlier systems; for example, in the side by side arrangement, the width of the views is up to you.

If a split view controller is the top-level view controller, it determines your app's compensatory rotation behavior. To take a hand in that determination without having to subclass UISplitViewController, make one of your objects the split view controller's delegate (UISplitViewControllerDelegate) and implement these methods, as needed:

- `splitViewControllerSupportedInterfaceOrientations:`
- `splitViewControllerPreferredInterfaceOrientationForPresentation:`

 A split view controller does not relegate decisions about the status bar appearance to its children. Thus, for example, to hide the status bar when a split view controller is the root view controller, you will have to subclass UISplitViewController. Alternatively, you might wrap the split view controller in a custom container view controller, as I describe later in this chapter.

Expanded Split View Controller (iPad)

Xcode's Master–Detail Application template will give you an adaptive UISplitView-Controller with no work on your part, but for pedagogical purposes I'll start by constructing a split view architecture entirely in code, starting from a completely empty app project with no storyboard (see Chapter 1). We'll get it working on the iPad before proceeding to the iPhone version. For reasons that will be clear later, a split view controller on the iPad, by default, is called an *expanded* split view controller. An expanded split view controller has two child view controllers, as I've already described.

Our master view (owned by MasterViewController) will be a table view listing the names of the three Pep Boys. Our detail view (owned by DetailViewController) will contain a single label displaying the name of the Pep Boy selected in the master view.

Our first cut at writing MasterViewController merely displays the table view:

```
class MasterViewController: UITableViewController {
    let model = ["Manny", "Moe", "Jack"]
    override func viewDidLoad() {
        super.viewDidLoad()
        self.tableView.registerClass(
            UITableViewCell.self, forCellReuseIdentifier: "Cell")
    }
    override func numberOfSectionsInTableView(
        tableView: UITableView) -> Int {
            return 1
    }
    override func tableView(tableView: UITableView,
        numberOfRowsInSection section: Int) -> Int {
            return model.count
    }
    override func tableView(tableView: UITableView,
```

```
        cellForRowAtIndexPath indexPath: NSIndexPath) -> UITableViewCell {
            let cell = tableView.dequeueReusableCellWithIdentifier(
                "Cell", forIndexPath: indexPath)
            cell.textLabel!.text = model[indexPath.row]
            return cell
        }
    }
```

DetailViewController, in its `viewDidLoad` implementation, puts the label (`self.lab`) into the interface; it also has a public boy string property whose value appears in the label. We are deliberately agnostic about the order of events; our interface works correctly regardless of whether boy is set before or after `viewDidLoad` is called:

```
class DetailViewController: UIViewController {
    var lab : UILabel!
    var boy : String = "" {
        didSet {
            if self.lab != nil {
                self.lab.text = self.boy
            }
        }
    }
    override func viewDidLoad() {
        super.viewDidLoad()
        self.view.backgroundColor = UIColor.whiteColor()
        let lab = UILabel(frame:CGRectMake(100,100,100,30))
        self.view.addSubview(lab)
        self.lab = lab
        self.lab.text = self.boy
    }
}
```

Our app delegate constructs the interface by making a UISplitViewController, giving it its two initial children, and putting its view into the window:

```
func application(application: UIApplication,
    didFinishLaunchingWithOptions launchOptions: [NSObject: AnyObject]?)
    -> Bool {
        self.window = UIWindow()
        let svc = UISplitViewController()
        svc.viewControllers = [MasterViewController(), DetailViewController()]
        self.window!.rootViewController = svc
        self.window!.backgroundColor = UIColor.whiteColor()
        self.window!.makeKeyAndVisible()
        return true
}
```

This is already a working split view interface. In landscape orientation, the two views appear side by side. In portrait orientation, only the detail view appears; but the master view can be summoned by swiping from left to right, and can be dismissed by tapping outside it. However, the app itself doesn't yet *do* anything. In particular, when we tap on a Pep Boy's name in the master view, the detail view doesn't change. Let's add that code (to MasterViewController):

```
override func tableView(tableView: UITableView,
    didSelectRowAtIndexPath indexPath: NSIndexPath) {
        let detail = DetailViewController()
        detail.boy = model[indexPath.row]
        self.showDetailViewController(detail, sender: self)
}
```

The last line is a major surprise. We have not implemented any `showDetailView‐Controller:sender:` method; yet we are able to send this message to ourselves, and it works: the new, correctly configured detail view seamlessly replaces the existing detail view, causing the selected Pep Boy's name to appear in the interface. How can this be? This method effectively walks up the view controller hierarchy, looking for someone to handle it. (I'll discuss the details later.) Our DetailViewController can't handle it, but its parent view controller, the UISplitViewController, can! It responds by making the specified view controller its second child.

Our app still doesn't quite look like a standard master–detail view interface. The usual thing is for both the master view and the detail view to contain a navigation bar. The detail view in portrait orientation can then display in its navigation bar a left button that summons the master view, so that the user doesn't have to know about the swipe gesture. This button is vended by the UISplitViewController, through the `displayModeButton‐Item` method. Thus, we need to change our app delegate code as follows:

```
let svc = UISplitViewController()
let master = MasterViewController()
master.title = "Pep" // *
let nav1 = UINavigationController(rootViewController:master) // *
let detail = DetailViewController()
let nav2 = UINavigationController(rootViewController:detail) // *
svc.viewControllers = [nav1, nav2]
self.window!.rootViewController = svc
let b = svc.displayModeButtonItem() // *
detail.navigationItem.leftBarButtonItem = b // *
```

But we are still not quite done. Consider what will happen when the user taps a Pep Boy name in the master view. At the moment, we are making a new DetailViewController and making it the split view controller's second child. That is now wrong; we must make a new UINavigationController instead, with a new DetailViewController as its child. Moreover, this new DetailViewController doesn't automatically have the `displayMode‐ButtonItem` as its `leftBarButtonItem` — we have to set it:

```
override func tableView(tableView: UITableView,
    didSelectRowAtIndexPath indexPath: NSIndexPath) {
        let detail = DetailViewController()
        detail.boy = model[indexPath.row]
        let b = self.splitViewController!.displayModeButtonItem()
```

```
            detail.navigationItem.leftBarButtonItem = b
            detail.navigationItem.leftItemsSupplementBackButton = true
            let nav = UINavigationController(rootViewController: detail)
            self.showDetailViewController(nav, sender: self)
    }
```

When the app is in landscape orientation with the two views displayed side by side, the displayModeButtonItem automatically hides itself. Our iPad split view implementation is therefore finished.

Collapsed Split View Controller (iPhone)

Astoundingly, if we now launch our existing app on iPhone, it works almost perfectly! There's a navigation interface. Tapping a Pep Boy's name in the master view pushes the new detail view controller onto the navigation stack, with its view displaying that name. The detail view's navigation bar has a back button that pops the detail view controller and returns us to the master view.

The only thing that isn't quite right is that the app launches with the detail view showing, rather than the master view. To fix that, we first modify our app delegate to function as the UISplitViewController's delegate:

```
    let svc = UISplitViewController()
    svc.delegate = self
    // ... the rest as before ...
```

We then implement splitViewController:collapseSecondaryViewController: ontoPrimaryViewController: to return true:

```
    func splitViewController(svc: UISplitViewController,
        collapseSecondaryViewController vc2: UIViewController,
        ontoPrimaryViewController vc1: UIViewController) -> Bool {
            return true
    }
```

That's all! On the iPhone, the app now behaves correctly.

How can this be? To understand what the split view controller is up to, you need to know that it adopts one of two states: it is or it isn't collapsed. This distinction corresponds to whether or not the environment's trait collection has a .Compact horizontal size class: if so, the split view controller collapses. Thus, the split view controller collapses as it launches on an iPhone.

A collapsed split view controller has only *one* child view controller. This raises the question of how to get from the expanded state to the collapsed state. As the split view controller collapses, it *asks its delegate* how to proceed. In particular, it calls these delegate methods:

`primaryViewControllerForCollapsingSplitViewController:`

> The collapsed split view controller will have only one child view controller. *What* view controller should this be? By default, it will be the current *first* view controller, but you can implement this method to return a different answer.

`splitViewController:collapseSecondaryViewController:ontoPrimaryView-Controller:`

> The collapsing split view controller is going to remove its *second* view controller, leaving its *first* view controller as its only child view controller. Return `true` to permit this to happen.
>
> If this method returns `false` (the default), the split view controller sends `collapse-SecondaryViewController:forSplitViewController:` to the *first* view controller. What happens to the second view controller is now up to the first view controller.

Our first view controller is a UINavigationController, which responds to `collapse-SecondaryViewController:forSplitViewController:` by pushing the specified secondary view controller onto its own stack. That explains what we've just seen. If we *don't* implement the `splitViewController:collapse...` delegate method to return `true`, we end up launching with the detail view showing on the iPhone. Therefore, we *do* implement `splitViewController:collapse...` to return `true`, thus permitting the split view controller to remove its second view controller, so that we end up launching with the master view showing on the iPhone.

Our app has now launched. Its root view controller is the split view controller. The split view controller has one child — a UINavigationController which, in turn, has one child, namely our MasterViewController. Thus, the table view is visible in a navigation interface. The user taps a row of the table, and our code sends `showDetailView-Controller:sender:` to the MasterViewController. As I mentioned before, the result is a walk up the view controller hierarchy, looking for someone to handle this method. Here's what happens:

1. MasterViewController doesn't handle it, so we proceed to its parent, the UINavigationController.

2. UINavigationController doesn't handle it either! So we proceed to *its* parent, the UISplitViewController.

3. UISplitViewController *does* handle this message, in one of two ways:

   • If the split view controller is *not* collapsed, it accepts the specified view controller and substitutes it as its own second view controller. The second view controller's view is displayed, so the user now sees it as the detail view. That is what happened when our app ran on the iPad.

- If the split view controller *is* collapsed, it sends `showViewController:sender:` to its first view controller. The first view controller happens to be a UINavigation-Controller, and we already know (from Chapter 6) how it responds: it pushes the specified view controller onto its stack.

 In our example, the second view controller is a UINavigationController. We are therefore pushing a UINavigationController onto a UINavigationController's stack. This is an odd thing to do, but thanks to some internal voodoo, the parent UINavigationController will do the right thing: in displaying this child's view, it turns to the child UINavigationController's `topViewController` and displays *its* view (and its `navigationItem`), and the child UINavigationController's navigation bar never gets into the interface.

Expanding Split View Controller (iPhone 6 Plus)

The iPhone 6 Plus is an interesting hybrid case: it's horizontally compact in portrait orientation, but *not* in landscape orientation. Thus, in effect, the split view controller thinks it's on an iPhone when the iPhone 6 Plus is in portrait, but it thinks it has been magically moved over to an iPad when the iPhone 6 Plus interface rotates to landscape. Thus, the split view controller *alternates* between `collapsed` being `true` and `false` on a single device. In portrait, the split view displays a single navigation interface, with the master view controller at its root, like an iPhone. In landscape, the master and detail views are displayed side by side, like an iPad.

When the app, running on the iPhone 6 Plus, rotates to portrait, or if it launches into portrait, the split view controller goes through the very same procedure I just described for an iPhone. When it rotates to landscape, it performs the opposite of collapsing — which Apple, not surprisingly, describes as *expanding*. As the split view controller expands, it *asks its delegate* how to proceed:

`primaryViewControllerForExpandingSplitViewController:`
> The collapsed split view controller has just one child. The expanded split view controller will have two children. What view controller should be its *first* child view controller? By default, it will be the *current* child view controller, but you can implement this method to return a different answer.

`splitViewController:separateSecondaryViewControllerFromPrimaryViewController:`
> What view controller should be the expanded split view controller's *second* child view controller? Implement this method to provide an answer.
>
> If you don't implement this method, or if you return `nil`, the split view controller sends `separateSecondaryViewControllerForSplitViewController:` to the *first* view controller. This method returns a view controller, or `nil`. If it returns a view

controller, the split view controller makes that view controller its second view controller.

The default response of a plain vanilla UIViewController to separateSecondaryViewControllerForSplitViewController: is to return nil. A UINavigationController, however, pops its own topViewController and returns that view controller. Thus, when our app is rotated from portrait to landscape, exactly the right thing happens: if the navigation controller has pushed a DetailViewController onto its stack, it now pops it and hands it to the split view controller, which displays its view as the detail view.

One other new feature of our app's behavior on the iPhone 6 Plus is that the displayModeButtonItem is present in landscape (whereas it disappears automatically on an iPad in landscape). It takes on a new form: instead of appearing as a "back" chevron, it's an "expand" symbol (two arrows pointing away from each other). When the user taps it, the master view is hidden and the detail view occupies the entire screen — and the displayModeButtonItem changes to a chevron. Tapping the chevron toggles back the other way: the master view is shown again.

An interesting problem arises when we rotate from landscape to portrait on the iPhone 6 Plus. Suppose we're in landscape (.Regular horizontal size class) and the user is looking at the *detail* view controller. Now the user rotates to portrait (.Compact horizontal size class). The split view controller collapses. Without extra precautions, we'll end up displaying the *master* view controller — because we went to the trouble of arranging that, back when we thought the only way to collapse was to *launch* into a .Compact horizontal size class:

```
func splitViewController(svc: UISplitViewController,
    collapseSecondaryViewController vc2: UIViewController,
    ontoPrimaryViewController vc1: UIViewController) -> Bool {
        return true
}
```

The result is that the user's place in the application has been lost. I think we can solve this satisfactorily simply by having the split view controller's delegate keep track of whether the user has ever chosen a detail view. I'll use an instance property, self.didChooseDetail:

```
override func tableView(tableView: UITableView,
    didSelectRowAtIndexPath indexPath: NSIndexPath) {
        // ...
        let del = UIApplication.sharedApplication().delegate as! AppDelegate
        del.didChooseDetail = true
}
```

Now the split view controller's delegate uses that instance property to decide what to do — that is, whether to display the master view controller or the detail view controller — when the split view controller collapses:

```
func splitViewController(svc: UISplitViewController,
    collapseSecondaryViewController vc2: UIViewController,
    ontoPrimaryViewController vc1: UIViewController) -> Bool {
        return !self.didChooseDetail
}
```

Customizing a Split View Controller

Properties and delegate methods of a UISplitViewController allow it to be customized:

presentsWithGesture

A Bool. If `false`, the left-to-right swipe gesture that shows the master view in portrait orientation on an iPad is disabled. The default is `true`.

preferredDisplayMode

Set this to change the current display mode of an expanded split view controller programmatically, or set it to `.Automatic` to allow the display mode to adopt its default value. To learn the actual display mode being used, ask for the current `displayMode`.

An expanded split view controller has three possible display modes (UISplitViewControllerDisplayMode):

- `.PrimaryHidden`
- `.AllVisible`
- `.PrimaryOverlay`

The default automatic behaviors are:

iPad in landscape

The `displayModeButtonItem` is hidden, and the display mode is `.AllVisible`.

iPad in portrait

The `displayModeButtonItem` is shown, and the display mode toggles between `.PrimaryHidden` and `.PrimaryOverlay`.

iPhone 6 Plus in landscape

The `displayModeButtonItem` is shown, and the display mode toggles between `.PrimaryHidden` and `.AllVisible`.

preferredPrimaryColumnWidthFraction

Sets the master view width in `.AllVisible` and `.PrimaryOverlay` display modes, as a percentage of the whole split view (between 0 and 1). Your setting may have no effect unless you also constrain the width limits absolutely through the `minimumPrimaryColumnWidth` and `maximumPrimaryColumnWidth` properties. To specify the default width, use `UISplitViewControllerAutomaticDimension`. To learn the actual width being used, ask for the current `primaryColumnWidth`.

You can also track and govern the display mode with these delegate methods:

`splitViewController:willChangeToDisplayMode:`
The `displayMode` of an expanded split view controller is about to change, meaning that its first view controller's view will be shown or hidden. You might want to alter the interface somehow in response.

`targetDisplayModeForActionInSplitViewController:`
Called whenever something happens that might affect the display mode, such as:

- The split view controller is showing for the first time.
- The interface is rotating.
- The user summons or dismisses the primary view.

Return a display mode to specify what the user's tapping the `displayModeButtonItem` should subsequently do (and, by extension, how the button is portrayed), or `.Automatic` to accept what the split view would normally do.

Customizations on a more structural level are performed through the other delegate methods. For example, there might be additional view controllers present, or you might use a split view controller in some completely different way, so that the default collapsed version of a split view controller might not be appropriate. Thus you would implement the delegate methods I described in the preceding sections to determine how the view controller structure should be rearranged when the split view controller collapses and expands:

- `primaryViewControllerForCollapsingSplitViewController:`
- `splitViewController:collapseSecondaryViewController:ontoPrimaryViewController:`
- `primaryViewControllerForExpandingSplitViewController:`
- `splitViewController:separateSecondaryViewControllerFromPrimaryViewController:`

Also, your custom view controller can implement `collapseSecondaryViewController:forSplitViewController:` and `separateSecondaryViewControllerForSplitViewController:`, so that it can take a hand in what happens during collapsing and expanding when it is the primary view controller.

After collapsing or expanding, a UISplitViewController emits the `UIViewControllerShowDetailTargetDidChangeNotification`.

Setting the Collapsed State

The split view controller can be in a collapsed or an expanded state — its `collapsed` property can be `true` or `false`. But this property is read-only. How, then, would you *set* the collapsed state? For example, perhaps you want side-by-side display of the two child view controllers' views in landscape *even on an iPhone*. How would you arrange that?

The split view controller decides which state to adopt depending on the environment — in particular, whether the current trait collection's horizontal size class is `.Compact`. The solution, therefore, is to *lie to the split view controller* about its trait collection environment, effectively making it believe, for example, that it's on an iPad even though it's really on an iPhone.

You can do that by interposing your own custom container view controller above the split view controller in the view controller hierarchy — typically, as the split view controller's direct parent. You can then send your container view controller the `setOverride-TraitCollection:forChildViewController:` message, thus causing it to pass the trait collection of your choosing down the view controller hierarchy to the split view controller.

In this example, our container view controller is the app's root view controller; its child is a split view controller. The split view controller's view completely occupies the container view controller's view (in other words, the container's own view is never seen independently; the container view controller exists *solely* in order to manage the split view controller). Early in the life of the app, the container view controller configures the split view controller and lies to it about the environment:

```
override func viewWillLayoutSubviews() {
    if !self.didInitialSetup {
        self.didInitialSetup = true
        let svc = self.childViewControllers[0] as! UISplitViewController
        svc.preferredDisplayMode = .AllVisible
        svc.preferredPrimaryColumnWidthFraction = 0.5
        svc.maximumPrimaryColumnWidth = 500
        let traits = UITraitCollection(traitsFromCollections: [
            UITraitCollection(horizontalSizeClass: .Regular)])
        self.setOverrideTraitCollection(
            traits, forChildViewController: svc)
    }
}
```

The result is that the split view controller displays both its children's views side by side, both in portrait and landscape, like the Settings app on the iPad, *even on the iPhone.*

Another possibility, based on Apple's AdaptivePhotos sample code, might be to make the iPhone behave like an iPhone 6 Plus, with a `.Regular` horizontal size class in landscape (the split view controller expands) but a `.Compact` horizontal size class in portrait (the split view controller collapses):

```
override func viewWillTransitionToSize(size: CGSize,
    withTransitionCoordinator
    coordinator: UIViewControllerTransitionCoordinator) {
        let svc = self.childViewControllers[0] as! UISplitViewController
        if size.width > size.height {
            let traits = UITraitCollection(traitsFromCollections: [
                UITraitCollection(horizontalSizeClass: .Regular)])
            self.setOverrideTraitCollection(
                traits, forChildViewController: svc)
        } else {
            self.setOverrideTraitCollection(
                nil, forChildViewController: svc)
        }
        super.viewWillTransitionToSize(
            size, withTransitionCoordinator: coordinator)
}
```

Replacing the Child View Controllers

The master–detail architecture that I've been using as an example throughout this discussion uses showDetailViewController:sender: as the standard response to the user tapping an entry in the master list. However, I have not been sending this message directly to the split view controller; instead, I've sent it to self (the master view controller), with an assurance that the message will percolate up to the split view controller. It's now time to talk in more detail about this percolation process.

iOS provides a generalized architecture for percolating a message up the view controller hierarchy. The heart of this architecture is the method targetViewControllerForAction:sender:, where the action: parameter is the selector for the method we're inquiring about. This method, using some deep introspective voodoo, looks to see whether the view controller to which the message was sent *overrides the UIViewController implementation* of the method in question. If so, it returns self; if not, it effectively recurses *up* the view controller hierarchy, returning the result of calling the same method with the same parameters on its parent view controller or presenting view controller — or nil if no view controller is ultimately returned to it.

 A view controller subclass that *does* override the method in question but does *not* want to be the target view controller can implement the UIResponder method canPerformAction:withSender: to return false.

The idea is that any UIViewController method can be implemented so as to percolate up the view controller hierarchy in this way, analogously to how the responder chain operates. In particular, two UIViewController methods *are* implemented in this way — showViewController:sender: and showDetailViewController:sender:.

These methods are implemented to call `targetViewControllerForAction:sender:`. If this returns a target, they send themselves to that target. If it *doesn't* return a target, they call `presentViewController:animated:completion:`.

Thus, what actually happens when the master view controller sends `showDetailViewController:sender:` to `self` is as follows:

1. The master view controller doesn't implement any override of `showDetailViewController:sender:`; it inherits the UIViewController implementation, which is called.

2. The UIViewController implementation of `showDetailViewController:sender:` calls `targetViewControllerForAction:sender:` on `self` (the master view controller) with "`showDetailViewController:sender:`" as its `action:` parameter.

3. `targetViewControllerForAction:sender:` sees that the method in question, namely `showDetailViewController:sender:`, is *not* overridden by this view controller (the master view controller); so it calls `targetViewControllerForAction:sender:` on the parent view controller, which is a UINavigationController.

4. Here we are, looking at the UINavigationController. `targetViewControllerForAction:sender:` sees that the method in question, namely `showDetailViewController:sender:`, is not overridden by *this* view controller either! So it calls `targetViewControllerForAction:sender:` on *its* parent view controller, which is a UISplitViewController.

5. Now we're looking at the UISplitViewController. It turns out that UISplitViewController *does* override the UIViewController implementation of `showDetailViewController:sender:`. Thus, `targetViewControllerForAction:sender:` in the split view controller returns the split view controller instance, and all the nested calls to `targetViewControllerForAction:sender:` return with the split view controller as the result.

6. We are now back in `showDetailViewController:sender:`, originally sent to the master view controller. From its call to `targetViewControllerForAction:sender:`, it has acquired a target — the split view controller. So it finishes by sending `showDetailViewController:sender:` to the split view controller.

The flexibility illustrated here is what allows the two methods, `showViewController:sender:` and `showDetailViewController:sender:`, to work *differently* depending on how the view controller to which they are originally sent is situated *in the view controller hierarchy*. Two built-in UIViewController subclasses override one or both of these methods, and thus, if they are further up the view controller hierarchy than the view controller on which these methods are called, they will take charge of what happens:

UINavigationController showViewController:sender:

UINavigationController implements showViewController:sender: to call push-ViewController:animated:.

Thus, if you send showViewController:sender: to a view controller whose parent is a UINavigationController, it is the navigation controller's implementation that will be called, meaning that the parameter view controller is *pushed* onto the stack. But if you send showViewController:sender: to a view controller *without* a parent that overrides this method, the default implementation is used, meaning that the parameter view is *presented.*

UISplitViewController showDetailViewController:sender:

UISplitViewController implements showDetailViewController:sender: as follows. First, it calls the delegate method splitViewController:showDetailViewController:sender:; if the delegate returns true, UISplitViewController does nothing. (In that case, *you* would be responsible for getting the parameter view controller's view into the interface.) Otherwise:

If the split view controller is expanded
It replaces its second child view controller with the parameter view controller.

If the split view controller is collapsed
If its first (and only) child view controller is a UINavigationController, it sends showViewController:sender: to it. Otherwise, it calls presentViewController:animated:completion:.

UISplitViewController showViewController:sender:

UISplitViewController implements showViewController:sender: as follows. First, it calls the delegate method splitViewController:showViewController:sender:; if the delegate returns true, UISplitViewController does nothing. (In that case, *you* would be responsible for getting the parameter view controller's view into the interface.) Otherwise:

If the split view controller is expanded
If the sender: is its first view controller, the split view controller replaces the *first* view controller with the parameter view controller. Otherwise, it replaces its *second* view controller with the parameter view controller.

If the split view controller is collapsed
It calls presentViewController:animated:completion:.

Now that you understand the percolation mechanism, perhaps you'd like to know whether your own custom methods can participate in it. They can! Extend UIView-Controller to implement your method such that it calls targetViewControllerFor-Action:sender: on self and sends the action method to the target if there is one. For example:

```
extension UIViewController {
    func showHide(sender:AnyObject?) {
        let target =
            self.targetViewControllerForAction("showHide:", sender:sender)
        if target != nil {
            target!.showHide(self)
        }
    }
}
```

In that example, I don't know what any particular UIViewController subclass's override of showHide: may do, and I don't care! What matters is that if showHide: is sent to a view controller that *doesn't* override it, it will percolate up the view controller hierarchy until we find a view controller that *does* override it, and it is *that override* that will be called.

Split View Controller in a Storyboard

To see how to configure a split view controller in a storyboard, make a new project from the Universal version of the Master–Detail Application template and study the storyboard that it provides. This storyboard contains essentially the same configuration I created in code at the start of this section. The split view controller has two relationships, "master view controller" and "detail view controller," specifying its two children. Those two children are both navigation controllers. The first navigation controller has a "root view controller" relationship to a MasterViewController, which is a UITableViewController; the second has a "root view controller" relationship to a DetailViewController (Figure 9-5).

There's one more object in the storyboard, and it's the interesting object: from the prototype table view cell in the master table view comes a segue triggered by the user selecting the cell — a "show detail" segue whose destination is the detail navigation controller. It should now be clear what a "show detail" segue does: it calls showDetailViewController:sender:. As you know, this means that when the split view controller is expanded, the newly instantiated detail navigation controller will replace the split view controller's second child view controller; when the split view controller is collapsed, the newly instantiated detail navigation controller will be pushed onto the master navigation controller's stack.

Unfortunately, that's not the end of the initial configuration required to get this split view controller to work. The app delegate template code also configures and adds the displayModeButtonItem; to do this, it must verbosely obtain a reference to the split view controller and to the detail view controller:

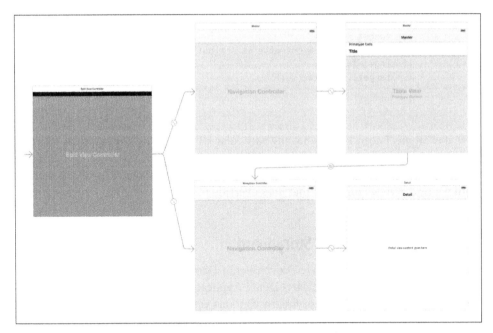

Figure 9-5. How the storyboard configures a split view interface

```
let splitViewController =
    self.window!.rootViewController as! UISplitViewController
let navigationController = splitViewController.viewControllers[
    splitViewController.viewControllers.count-1] as! UINavigationController
navigationController.topViewController!.navigationItem.leftBarButtonItem =
    splitViewController.displayModeButtonItem()
```

Similarly, the master view controller, when the "show detail" segue is triggered, must verbosely get a reference to the detail view controller:

```
let controller =
    (segue.destinationViewController as! UINavigationController)
        .topViewController as! DetailViewController
```

That sort of thing is error-prone and opaque. The problem is that the architecture has been constructed automatically, behind the code's back, and so the code must scramble to get references to the pieces of that architecture. For this reason, I prefer to create and assemble my split view controllers in code. Code that creates a view controller manually has a direct reference to that view controller, and is clearer and cleaner.

iPad Multitasking

New in iOS 9, certain models of iPad can perform a kind of multitasking where the windows of two different apps can appear simultaneously. There are two multitasking modes:

Slideover

> One app appears in a narrow format in front of the other. The rear app is deactivated but not backgrounded. The front app has a `.Compact` horizontal size class (and is 320 points wide).

Splitscreen

> The two apps appear side by side, both being active simultaneously. The one on the right might have the same physical characteristics as the front app in slideover mode, or the two apps might share the screen equally, in which case they *both* have a `.Compact` horizontal size class. This multitasking mode is available on an even narrower range of iPad models.

Your iPad or Universal app, by default, will participate in iPad multitasking if it is built against iOS 9, permits all four orientations, and uses a launch screen storyboard or *.xib*.

If you would like your app to opt out of participation in iPad multitasking, you can set the *Info.plist* key `UIRequiresFullScreen` to YES. An app that doesn't participate in iPad multitasking can still be deactivated while another app appears in front of it in slideover mode, but it cannot itself appear as the front app in slideover mode, and it cannot be involved in splitscreen mode at all.

From what I've said, it follows that if your app participates in iPad multitasking:

- It can be launched or summoned into a `.Compact` horizontal size class situation even on an iPad.
- It can be toggled between a `.Compact` horizontal size class and a `.Regular` horizontal size class even on an iPad (and without an accompanying rotation).

When your app's window changes size because of multitasking, your view controller will receive `viewWillTransitionToSize:withTransitionCoordinator:`. It may receive this event more than once, and it will receive it *while the app is inactive*. If the size change also involves a transition from one horizontal size class to another, then of course your view controller will also receive `willTransitionToTraitCollection:withTransitionCoordinator:` and `traitCollectionDidChange:`, also while the app is inactive.

Thus, on the whole, if your app is prepared to respond coherently to these events — as it would be already, if it is a universal app — it can probably participate in iPad multitasking with no significant change. You can't assume that a `.Compact` horizontal size class means you're on an iPhone, but you probably weren't thinking in those terms anyway — and if even if you were, you can still detect what kind of device you are *really* on simply by looking at the trait collection's userInterfaceIdiom.

You also can't assume that screen bounds and window bounds are identical (something that all previous editions of this book *have* assumed). Your app's width, under iPad multitasking, is its window width, which could be as little as 320 points; the screen, meanwhile, is unchanged. A button's position in window coordinates could be very different from its position in screen coordinates. However, once again, it's unlikely that you were thinking in those terms to begin with.

If a view controller has been presented, then if the size transition involves a trait collection transition, the view controller will adapt. Thus, for example, a .FormSheet or .Popover presented view controller will, by default, turn into a .FullScreen presented view controller as the app transitions from a .Regular horizontal size class to .Compact — and will then change back again as the app transitions back to .Regular. And of course you can take a hand in how it adapts by functioning as the presentation controller's delegate.

Similarly, if a split view controller is operative, it will collapse and expand as the app transitions from a .Regular horizontal size class to .Compact and back again. This is no different from the ability of a split view controller to collapse and expand when an iPhone 6 Plus is rotated, and the same precautions will take care of it satisfactorily. In landscape in splitscreen mode .Regular horizontal size class, the split view controller's display mode toggles between .PrimaryHidden and .PrimaryOverlay, as if we were in portrait; but that's automatic and shouldn't affect your code.

From a purely dimensional point of view, iPad multitasking certainly introduces your app to some new size possibilities. Here are some of the sizes your app can assume:

.Regular *horizontal size class*
> We're on an iPad, or an iPhone 6 Plus in landscape:
>
> - 1024×768 (iPad in landscape)
> - 768×1024 (iPad in portrait)
> - 736×414 (iPhone 6 Plus in landscape)
> - 694×768 (iPad splitscreen in landscape)

.Compact *horizontal size class*
> We're on an iPad under multitasking, or an iPhone:
>
> - 507×768 (iPad splitscreen in landscape)
> - 438×1024 (iPad splitscreen in portrait)
> - 320×768 (iPad slideover or splitscreen in landscape)

- 320×1024 (iPad slideover or splitscreen in portrait)
- 414×736 (iPhone 6 Plus in portrait)
- 320×480 (iPhone 4s in portrait)

The new iPad Pro will introduce additional sizes; and of course there are a range of sizes between the iPhone 6 Plus and the iPhone 4s, along with their landscape sizes (which have a .Compact vertical size class). Clearly, however, it would be foolish to concern yourself with these sizes *explicitly*. If this is a universal app, then you are *already* taking care of a wide range of possible sizes through size classes and autolayout, and you probably won't have to do anything new to cover these new sizes.

What iPad multitasking *does* introduce that's completely new is the possibility that your app will effectively be frontmost at the same time as some other app. This means that another app can be using both the processor (especially the main thread) and memory at a time when your app is not suspended. All apps participating in iPad multitasking need to be on their best behavior, adhering to best practices with regard to threading (see Chapter 25) and memory usage (see "View Controller Memory Management" on page 367).

CHAPTER 10

Text

Drawing text into your app's interface is one of the most complex and powerful things that iOS does for you. Fortunately, iOS also shields you from much of that complexity. All you need is some text to draw, and possibly an interface object to draw it for you.

Text to appear in your app's interface will be an NSString or an NSAttributedString. NSAttributedString adds text styling to an NSString, including runs of different character styles, along with paragraph-level features such as alignment, line spacing, and margins.

To make your NSString or NSAttributedString appear in the interface, you can draw it into a graphics context, or hand it to an interface object that knows how to draw it:

Self-drawing text

> Both NSString and NSAttributedString have methods (supplied by the NSString-Drawing category) for drawing themselves into any graphics context.

Text-drawing interface objects

> Interface objects that know how to draw an NSString or NSAttributedString are:

> *UILabel*

>> Displays text, possibly consisting of multiple lines; neither scrollable nor editable.

> *UITextField*

>> Displays a single line of user-editable text; may have a border, a background image, and overlay views at its right and left end.

> *UITextView*

>> Displays scrollable multiline text, possibly user-editable.

Deep under the hood, all text drawing is performed through a low-level technology with a C API called Core Text. Before iOS 7, certain powerful and useful text-drawing features were available *only* by working with Core Text. Now, however, iOS provides Text Kit, a middle-level technology lying on top of Core Text. UITextView is largely just a lightweight drawing wrapper around Text Kit, and Text Kit can also draw directly into a graphics context. By working with Text Kit, you can readily do all sorts of useful text-drawing tricks that previously would have required you to sweat your way through Core Text.

(Another way of drawing text is to use a web view, a scrollable view displaying rendered HTML. A web view can also display various additional document types, such as PDF, RTF, and *.doc*. Web views draw their text using a somewhat different technology, and are discussed in Chapter 11.)

Fonts and Font Descriptors

There are two ways of describing a font: as a UIFont (suitable for use with an NSString or a UIKit interface object) or as a CTFont (suitable for Core Text). Before iOS 7, CTFont and UIFont were unfortunately *not* toll-free bridged to one another, and what you usually started with and wanted to end with was a UIFont; thus, in order to perform font transformations, it was necessary to convert a UIFont to a CTFont manually, work with the CTFont, and then convert back to a UIFont manually — which was by no means trivial. Now, however, UIFont and CTFont *are* toll-free bridged to one another. Moreover, another important Core Text type, CTFontDescriptor, is toll-free bridged to UIFontDescriptor, which can be helpful for performing font transformations.

Fonts

A font (UIFont, toll-free bridged to Core Text's CTFont) is an extremely simple object. You specify a font by its name and size by calling the UIFont initializer `init(name:size:)`, and you can also transform a font of one size to the same font in a different size. UIFont also provides some methods for learning a font's various measurements, such as its `lineHeight` and `capHeight`.

To ask for a font by name, you have to *know* the font's name. Every font variant (bold, italic, and so on) counts as a different font, and font variants are clumped into families. UIFont has class methods that tell you the names of the families and the names of the fonts within them. To learn, in the console, the name of every installed font, you would say:

```
UIFont.familyNames().map {UIFont.fontNamesForFamilyName($0)}
    .forEach {(n:[String]) in n.forEach {print($0)}}
```

When calling `init(name:size:)`, you can specify a font by its family name or by its font name (technically, its PostScript name). For example, `"Avenir"` is a family name; the plain font within that family is `"Avenir-Book"`. Either is legal as the `name:` argument.

The initializer is failable, so you'll know if you've specified the font incorrectly — you'll get `nil`.

The system font (used, for example, by default in a UIButton) can be obtained by calling `systemFontOfSize:weight:`. The `weight:` parameter is new in iOS 9 (actually, I believe it was introduced quietly in iOS 8.2); possible weights, expressed as constant names of CGFloats, in order from lightest to heaviest, are:

- `UIFontWeightUltraLight`
- `UIFontWeightThin`
- `UIFontWeightLight`
- `UIFontWeightRegular`
- `UIFontWeightMedium`
- `UIFontWeightSemibold`
- `UIFontWeightBold`
- `UIFontWeightHeavy`
- `UIFontWeightBlack`

In iOS 9, the system font comes in all of these weights, except at sizes smaller than 20 points, where the extreme ultralight, thin, and black are missing.

 New in iOS 9, the system font is San Francisco, and system font names begin with `.SF`, but that name, like any font name that starts with a dot, should never be used directly; you should regard it as private and subject to change.

Dynamic Type fonts

The Dynamic Type fonts (originally introduced in iOS 7) have two salient features:

Their size is up to the user
> The Dynamic Type fonts are linked to the slider that the user can adjust in the Settings app, under Display & Brightness → Text Size.

They are specified by role
> You specify a Dynamic Type font, not by its size (which, as I've just said, is up to the user), but in terms of the *role* it is to play in your layout. Call the UIFont class method `preferredFontForTextStyle:`. Possible roles that you can supply as the argument are:
>
> - `UIFontTextStyleTitle1` (new in iOS 9)
> - `UIFontTextStyleTitle2` (new in iOS 9)

- UIFontTextStyleTitle3 (new in iOS 9)

- UIFontTextStyleHeadline

- UIFontTextStyleSubheadline

- UIFontTextStyleBody

- UIFontTextStyleCallout (new in iOS 9)

- UIFontTextStyleFootnote

- UIFontTextStyleCaption1

- UIFontTextStyleCaption2

The idea is that if you have text for the user to read or edit, you can use a Dynamic Type font; it will be sized and styled for you in accordance with the user's Text Size preference and the role that you have specified.

You'll probably want to experiment with specifying various roles for your individual pieces of text, to see which looks appropriate in context. For example, in Figure 6-1, the headlines are UIFontTextStyleSubheadline and the blurbs are UIFontTextStyle-Caption1.

Disappointingly, Dynamic Type fonts are *not* actually dynamic; preferredFontForText-Style: will return a font whose size is proportional to the user's Text Size preference only at the moment when it is called. If the user changes that preference, you are expected to call preferredFontForTextStyle: again. To hear about such changes, register for UIContentSizeCategoryDidChangeNotification. When the notification arrives, you are supposed to set the fonts for your Dynamic Type–savvy text all over again. This, in turn, may have consequences for the physical features of your interface as a whole; autolayout can be a big help here (Chapter 1).

In the nib editor, wherever the Attributes inspector lets you supply a font for an interface object, the Dynamic Type roles are available in a pop-up menu. But you will *still* have to set the font of every such interface object again, in code, when UIContentSize-CategoryDidChangeNotification arrives.

In this example, we have a label (self.lab) whose font uses Dynamic Type; we have set its font to UIFontTextStyleHeadline in the nib editor. We must therefore also update its font manually whenever UIContentSizeCategoryDidChangeNotification subsequently arrives:

```
override func viewDidLoad() {
    super.viewDidLoad()
    NSNotificationCenter.defaultCenter().addObserver(
        self, selector: "doDynamicType:",
        name: UIContentSizeCategoryDidChangeNotification, object: nil)
}
```

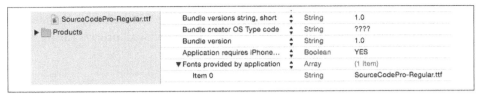

SourceCodePro-Regular.ttf	Bundle versions string, short	⬍	String	1.0
▶ Products	Bundle creator OS Type code	⬍	String	????
	Bundle version	⬍	String	1.0
	Application requires iPhone...	⬍	Boolean	YES
	▼ Fonts provided by application	⬍	Array	(1 Item)
	Item 0		String	SourceCodePro-Regular.ttf

Figure 10-1. Embedding a font in an app bundle

```
func doDynamicType(n:NSNotification) {
    let style = self.lab.font.fontDescriptor()
        .objectForKey(UIFontDescriptorTextStyleAttribute) as! String
    self.lab.font = UIFont.preferredFontForTextStyle(style)
}
```

Needless to say, that kind of thing gets very old very fast — it's enough to put one off using Dynamic Type at all. Fortunately, starting in iOS 8, a UITableView whose cells contain labels will watch for UIContentSizeCategoryDidChangeNotification for you and will update the label fonts automatically. So Dynamic Type in a table view, at least, *is* dynamic.

In iOS 9, the Dynamic Type fonts are the system fonts — that is, they are forms of the new San Francisco font. But this should probably be regarded as an opaque implementation detail.

Adding fonts

You are not limited to the fonts installed by default as part of the system. There are two ways to obtain additional fonts:

Include a font in your app bundle
> A font included at the top level of your app bundle will be loaded at launch time if your *Info.plist* lists it under the "Fonts provided by application" key (UIAppFonts).

Download a font in real time
> All OS X fonts are available for download from Apple's servers; you can obtain and install one while your app is running.

Figure 10-1 shows a font included in the app bundle, along with the *Info.plist* entry that lists it. Observe that what you're listing here is the name of the font *file*.

To download a font in real time, you'll have specify the font as a font descriptor (discussed in the next section) and drop down to the level of Core Text (import Core-Text) to call CTFontDescriptorMatchFontDescriptorsWithProgressHandler. It takes a function which is called repeatedly at every stage of the download process; it will be called on a background thread, so if you want to use the downloaded font immediately in the interface, you must step out to the main thread (see Chapter 25).

In this example, I'll attempt to use Nanum Brush Script as my UILabel's font; if it isn't installed, I'll attempt to download it and *then* use it as my UILabel's font. I've inserted a lot of unnecessary logging to mark the stages of the download process (using `NSLog` because `print` isn't thread-safe):

```
let name = "NanumBrush"
let size : CGFloat = 24
let f : UIFont! = UIFont(name:name, size:size)
if f != nil {
    self.lab.font = f
    print("already installed")
    return
}
print("attempting to download font")
let desc = UIFontDescriptor(name:name, size:size)
CTFontDescriptorMatchFontDescriptorsWithProgressHandler(
    [desc], nil, {
        (state:CTFontDescriptorMatchingState, prog:CFDictionary!)
            -> Bool in
        switch state {
        case .DidBegin:
            NSLog("%@", "matching did begin")
        case .WillBeginDownloading:
            NSLog("%@", "downloading will begin")
        case .Downloading:
            let d = prog as NSDictionary
            let key = kCTFontDescriptorMatchingPercentage
            let cur : AnyObject? = d[key as NSString]
            if let cur = cur as? NSNumber {
                NSLog("progress: %@%%", cur)
            }
        case .DidFinishDownloading:
            NSLog("%@", "downloading did finish")
        case .DidFailWithError:
            NSLog("%@", "downloading failed")
        case .DidFinish:
            NSLog("%@", "matching did finish")
            dispatch_async(dispatch_get_main_queue(), {
                let f : UIFont! = UIFont(name:name, size:size)
                if f != nil {
                    NSLog("%@", "got the font!")
                    self.lab.font = f
                }
            })
        default:break
        }
        return true
    })
```

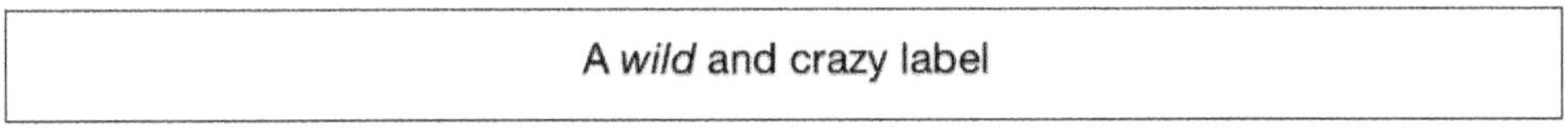

A *wild* and crazy label

Figure 10-2. A Dynamic Type font with an italic variant

Font Descriptors

A font descriptor (UIFontDescriptor, toll-free bridged to Core Text's CTFont-Descriptor) is a way of specifying a font, or converting between one font description and another, in terms of its features. For example, given a font descriptor desc, you can ask for a corresponding italic font descriptor like this:

```
let desc2 = desc.fontDescriptorWithSymbolicTraits(.TraitItalic)
```

If desc was originally a descriptor for Avenir-Book 15, desc2 is now a descriptor for Avenir-BookOblique 15. However, it is not the *font* Avenir-BookOblique 15; a font descriptor is not a font.

You can obtain a font descriptor just as you would obtain a font, by calling its initializer init(name:size:). Alternatively, to convert from a font to a font descriptor, call its fontDescriptor method; to convert from a font descriptor to a font, call the UIFont initializer init(descriptor:size:), typically supplying a size of 0 to signify that the size should not change. Thus, this will be a typical pattern in your code, as you convert from font to font descriptor to perform some transformation, and then back to font:

```
let f = UIFont(name: "Avenir", size: 15)!
let desc = f.fontDescriptor()
let desc2 = desc.fontDescriptorWithSymbolicTraits(.TraitItalic)
let f2 = UIFont(descriptor: desc2, size: 0) // Avenir-BookOblique 15
```

This same technique is useful for obtaining styled variants of the Dynamic Type fonts. A UIFontDescriptor class method, preferredFontDescriptorWithTextStyle:, saves you from having to start with a UIFont. In this example, I prepare to form an NSAttributedString whose font is mostly UIFontTextStyleBody, but with one italicized word (Figure 10-2):

```
let body = UIFontDescriptor
    .preferredFontDescriptorWithTextStyle(UIFontTextStyleBody)
let emphasis = body.fontDescriptorWithSymbolicTraits(.TraitItalic)
fbody = UIFont(descriptor: body, size: 0)
femphasis = UIFont(descriptor: emphasis, size: 0)
```

You can explore a font's features by way of UIFontDescriptor's fontAttributes method, which returns a dictionary of attributes and their values. If you know the name of the attribute whose value you want, you can send objectForKey: directly to a UIFont-Descriptor, as I did in an earlier example.

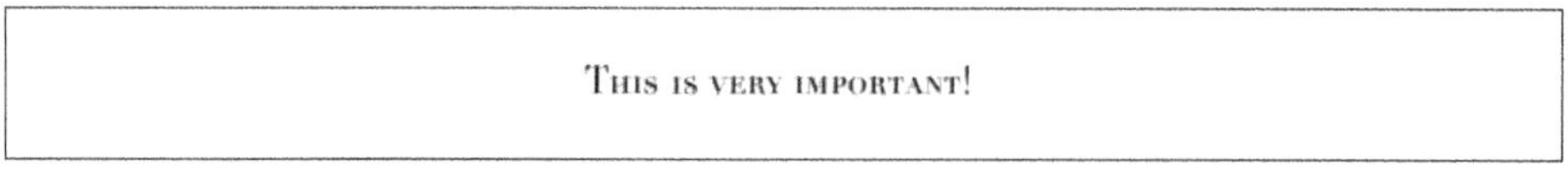

Figure 10-3. A small caps font variant

Another use of font descriptors is to access hidden built-in typographical features of individual fonts. In this example, I'll obtain a variant of the Didot font that draws its minuscules as small caps (Figure 10-3):

```
let desc = UIFontDescriptor(name:"Didot", size:18)
let d = [
    UIFontFeatureTypeIdentifierKey:kLetterCaseType,
    UIFontFeatureSelectorIdentifierKey:kSmallCapsSelector
]
let desc2 = desc.fontDescriptorByAddingAttributes([
    UIFontDescriptorFeatureSettingsAttribute:[d]
])
let f = UIFont(descriptor: desc2, size: 0)
```

Typographical feature identifier constants such as kSmallCapsSelector are listed in the Core Text header *SFNTLayoutTypes.h*. There is also useful information at *https://devel oper.apple.com/fonts/TrueType-Reference-Manual/RM09/AppendixF.html*.

What isn't so clear is how you're supposed to *discover* what features a font contains, and what name accesses a given feature. For example, the system (and Dynamic Type) font in iOS 9 provides an alternative form of the digits "6" and "9" through the identifer/ selector pair kStylisticAlternativesType and kStylisticAltOneOnSelector. But how can you discover that fact? The easiest way to explore a font's features is obtain a copy of the font on the desktop, install it, open TextEdit, choose Format → Font → Show Fonts, select the font, and open the Typography panel (Figure 10-4). Now you can experiment on selected text within TextEdit.

Attributed Strings

Styled text — that is, text consisting of multiple style runs, with different font, size, color, and other text features in different parts of the text — is expressed as an *attributed string*. Attributed strings (NSAttributedString and its mutable subclass, NSMutableAttributedString) have been around in iOS for a long time, but before iOS 6 they were difficult to use — you had to drop down to the level of Core Text — and they couldn't be used at all in connection with UIKit interface classes such as UILabel and UITextView. Thus, such interface classes couldn't display styled text. In iOS 6, NSAttributedString became a first-class citizen; it can now be used to draw styled text directly, and can be drawn by built-in interface classes.

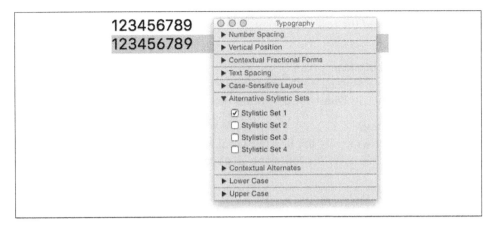

Figure 10-4. Exploring font variants with TextEdit

 In general, interface object methods and properties that accept attributed strings stand side by side with their pre-iOS 6 equivalents; the new ones tend to have "attributed" in their name. Thus, you don't *have* to use attributed strings. If a UILabel, for example, is to display text in a single font, size, color, and alignment, it might be easiest to use the pre-iOS 6 plain-old-NSString features of UILabel. If you do use an attributed string with an interface object, it is best not to mix in any of the pre-iOS 6 settings: let the attributed string do *all* the work of dictating text style features.

An NSAttributedString consists of an NSString (its `string`) plus the attributes, applied in ranges. For example, if the string "one red word" is blue except for the word "red" which is red, and if these are the only changes over the course of the string, then there are three distinct style runs — everything before the word "red," the word "red" itself, and everything after the word "red." However, we can apply the attributes in two steps, first making the whole string blue, and then making the word "red" red, just as you would expect.

Attributed String Attributes

The attributes applied to a range of an attributed string are described in dictionaries. Each possible attribute has a predefined name, used as a key in these dictionaries; here are some of the most important attributes (for the full list, see Apple's *NSAttributedString UIKit Additions Reference*):

NSFontAttributeName
   A UIFont. The default is Helvetica 12 (not San Francisco, the new system font).

NSForegroundColorAttributeName
   The text color, a UIColor.

`NSBackgroundColorAttributeName`

The color *behind* the text, a UIColor. You could use this to highlight a word, for example.

`NSLigatureAttributeName`

An NSNumber wrapping 0 or 1, expressing whether or not you want ligatures used. Some fonts, such as Didot, have ligatures that are on by default.

`NSKernAttributeName`

An NSNumber wrapping the floating-point amount of kerning. A negative value brings a glyph closer to the following glyph; a positive value adds space between them.

`NSStrikethroughStyleAttributeName`
`NSUnderlineStyleAttributeName`

An NSNumber wrapping one of these values (NSUnderlineStyle) describing the line weight:

- `.StyleNone`
- `.StyleSingle`
- `.StyleDouble`
- `.StyleThick`

Optionally, you may append a specification of the line pattern, with names like `.PatternDot`, `.PatternDash`, and so on.

Optionally, you may append `.ByWord`; if you do not, then if the underline or strikethrough range involves multiple words, the whitespace between the words will be underlined or struck through.

 The value corresponding to the `NSStrikethroughStyleAttributeName` key needs to be an NSNumber, but Swift sees NSUnderlineStyle as an enum. Therefore, you will have to take its `rawValue`, and if you want to append another piece of information such as the line pattern, you'll have to use bitwise-or to form the bitmask from two raw values. I regard this as a bug.

`NSStrikethroughColorAttributeName`
`NSUnderlineColorAttributeName`

A UIColor. If not defined, the foreground color is used.

`NSStrokeWidthAttributeName`

An NSNumber wrapping a Float. The stroke width is peculiarly coded. If it's positive, then the text glyphs are stroked but not filled, giving an outline effect, and the foreground color is used unless a separate stroke color is defined. If it's negative, then its absolute value is the width of the stroke, and the glyphs are both filled (with the foreground color) and stroked (with the stroke color).

NSStrokeColorAttributeName
: The stroke color, a UIColor.

NSShadowAttributeName
: An NSShadow object. An NSShadow is just a value class, combining a shadow-Offset, shadowColor, and shadowBlurRadius.

NSTextEffectAttributeName
: If defined, the only possible value is NSTextEffectLetterpressStyle.

NSAttachmentAttributeName
: An NSTextAttachment object. A text attachment is basically an inline image. I'll discuss text attachments later on.

NSLinkAttributeName
: An NSURL. In a noneditable, selectable UITextView, the link is tappable to go to the URL (depending on your implementation of the UITextViewDelegate method textView:shouldInteractWithURL:inRange:). By default, appears as blue without an underline in a UITextView. Appears as blue with an underline in a UILabel, but is not a tappable link there.

NSBaselineOffsetAttributeName
NSObliquenessAttributeName
NSExpansionAttributeName
: An NSNumber wrapping a Float.

NSParagraphStyleAttributeName
: An NSParagraphStyle object. This is basically just a value class, assembling text features that apply properly to paragraphs as a whole, not merely to characters, even if your string consists only of a single paragraph. Here are its most important properties:

- alignment (NSTextAlignment)
    - .Left
    - .Center
    - .Right
    - .Justified
    - .Natural (left-aligned or right-aligned depending on the writing direction)
- lineBreakMode (NSLineBreakMode)
    - .ByWordWrapping

- .ByCharWrapping

- .ByClipping

- .ByTruncatingHead

- .ByTruncatingTail

- .ByTruncatingMiddle

- firstLineHeadIndent, headIndent (left margin), tailIndent (right margin)

- lineHeightMultiple, maximumLineHeight, minimumLineHeight

- lineSpacing

- paragraphSpacing, paragraphSpacingBefore

- hyphenationFactor (0 or 1)

- defaultTabInterval, tabStops (the tab stops are an array of NSTextTab objects; I'll give an example in a moment)

- allowsDefaultTighteningForTruncation (new in iOS 9; if true, permits some negative kerning to be applied automatically to a Truncating paragraph if this would prevent truncation)

To construct an NSAttributedString, you can call init(string:attributes:) if the entire string has the same attributes; otherwise, you'll use its mutable subclass NSMutableAttributedString, which lets you set attributes over a range.

To construct an NSParagraphStyle, you'll use its mutable subclass NSMutableParagraphStyle. (The properties of NSParagraphStyle itself are all read-only, for historical reasons.) It is sufficient to apply a paragraph style to the first character of a paragraph; to put it another way, the paragraph style of the first character of a paragraph dictates how the whole paragraph is rendered.

Both NSAttributedString and NSParagraphStyle come with default values for all attributes, so you only have to set the attributes you care about.

Making an Attributed String

We now know enough for an example! I'll draw my attributed strings in a disabled (noninteractive) UITextView; its background is white, but its superview's background is gray, so you can see the text view's bounds relative to the text. (Ignore the text's vertical positioning, which is configured independently as a feature of the text view itself.)

First, two words of my attributed string are made extra-bold by stroking in a different color. I start by dictating the entire string and the overall style of the text; then I apply the special style to the two stroked words (Figure 10-5):

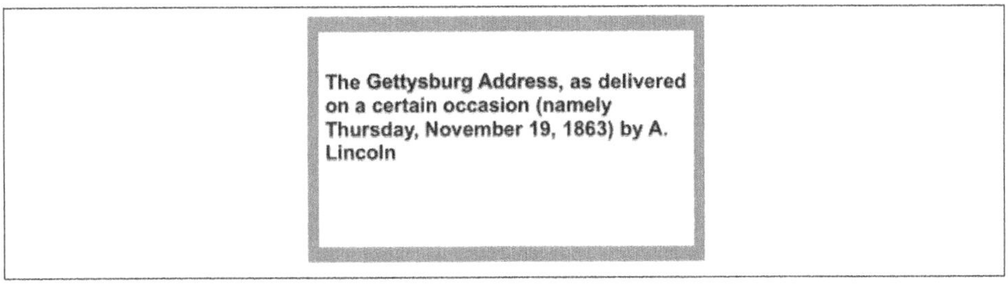

The Gettysburg Address, as delivered
on a certain occasion (namely
Thursday, November 19, 1863) by A.
Lincoln

Figure 10-5. An attributed string

```
let s1 = "The Gettysburg Address, as delivered on a certain occasion " +
    "(namely Thursday, November 19, 1863) by A. Lincoln"
let content = NSMutableAttributedString(string:s1, attributes:[
    NSFontAttributeName: UIFont(name:"Arial-BoldMT", size:15)!,
    NSForegroundColorAttributeName: UIColor(
        red:0.251, green:0.000, blue:0.502, alpha:1)
    ])
let r = (s1 as NSString).rangeOfString("Gettysburg Address")
content.addAttributes([
    NSStrokeColorAttributeName: UIColor.redColor(),
    NSStrokeWidthAttributeName: -2.0
    ], range: r)
self.tv.attributedText = content
```

Carrying on from the previous example, I'll also make the whole paragraph centered and indented from the edges of the text view. To do so, I create a paragraph style and apply it to the first character. Note how the margins are dictated: the tailIndent is negative, to bring the right margin leftward, and the firstLineHeadIndent must be set separately, as the headIndent does not automatically apply to the first line (Figure 10-6):

```
let para = NSMutableParagraphStyle()
para.headIndent = 10
para.firstLineHeadIndent = 10
para.tailIndent = -10
para.lineBreakMode = .ByWordWrapping
para.alignment = .Center
para.paragraphSpacing = 15
content.addAttribute(
    NSParagraphStyleAttributeName,
    value:para, range:NSMakeRange(0,1))
self.tv.attributedText = content
```

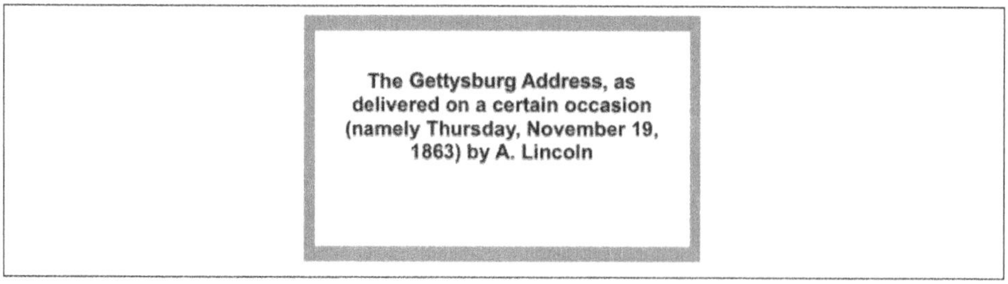

Figure 10-6. An attributed string with a paragraph style

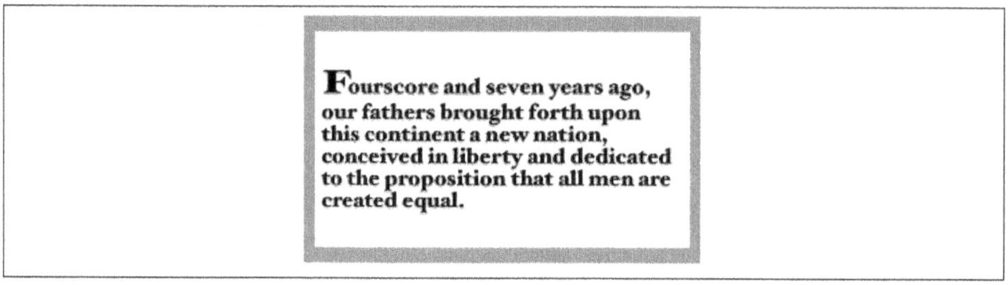

Figure 10-7. An attributed string with an expanded first character

When working with a value class such as NSMutableParagraphStyle, it feels clunky to be forced to instantiate the class and configure the instance *before* using it for the one and only time. So I've written a little Swift generic function, lend (see Appendix B), that lets me do all that in an anonymous function at the point where the value class is used.

In this next example, I'll enlarge the first character of a paragraph. I assign the first character a larger font size, I expand its width slightly, and I reduce its kerning (Figure 10-7):

```
let s2 = "Fourscore and seven years ago, our fathers brought forth " +
    "upon this continent a new nation, conceived in liberty and " +
    "dedicated to the proposition that all men are created equal."
let content2 = NSMutableAttributedString(string:s2, attributes: [
    NSFontAttributeName: UIFont(name:"HoeflerText-Black", size:16)!
])
content2.addAttributes([
    NSFontAttributeName: UIFont(name:"HoeflerText-Black", size:24)!,
    NSExpansionAttributeName: 0.3,
    NSKernAttributeName: -4
], range:NSMakeRange(0,1))
self.tv.attributedText = content2
```

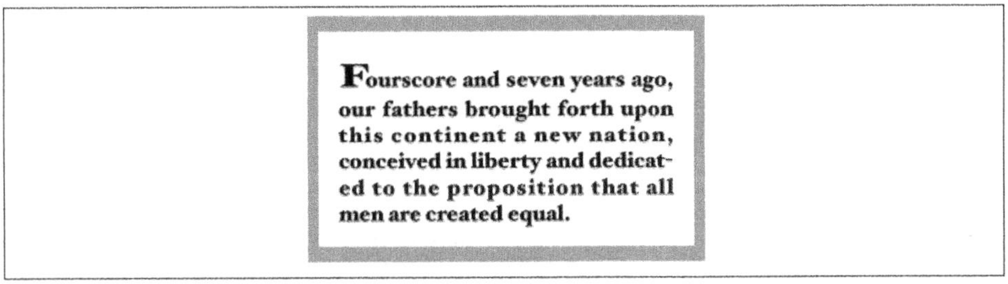

Figure 10-8. An attributed string with justification and autohyphenation

Carrying on from the previous example, I'll once again construct a paragraph style and add it to the first character. My paragraph style illustrates full justification and automatic hyphenation (Figure 10-8):

```
content2.addAttribute(NSParagraphStyleAttributeName,
    value:lend {
        (para:NSMutableParagraphStyle) in
        para.headIndent = 10
        para.firstLineHeadIndent = 10
        para.tailIndent = -10
        para.lineBreakMode = .ByWordWrapping
        para.alignment = .Justified
        para.lineHeightMultiple = 1.2
        para.hyphenationFactor = 1.0
    }, range:NSMakeRange(0,1))
self.tv.attributedText = content2
```

Now we come to the Really Amazing Part. I can make a *single* attributed string consisting of *both* paragraphs, and a single text view can portray it (Figure 10-9):

```
let end = content.length
content.replaceCharactersInRange(NSMakeRange(end, 0), withString:"\n")
content.appendAttributedString(content2)
self.tv.attributedText = content
```

Tab stops

A tab stop is an NSTextTab, a value class whose initializer lets you set its location (points from the left edge) and alignment. An options dictionary lets you set the tab stop's column terminator characters; a common use is to create a decimal tab stop, for aligning currency values at their decimal point. The key, in that case, is NSTabColumnTerminators-AttributeName; you can obtain a value appropriate to a given NSLocale by calling NSTextTab's class method columnTerminatorsForLocale:.

Here's an example (Figure 10-10); I have deliberately omitted the last digit from the second currency value, to prove that the tab stop really is aligning the numbers at their decimal points:

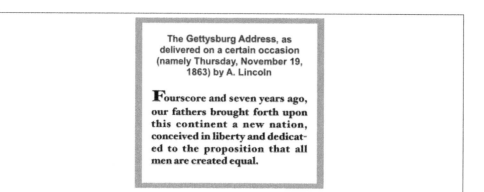

Figure 10-9. A single attributed string comprising differently styled paragraphs

Figure 10-10. Tab stops in an attributed string

```
let s = "Onions\t$2.34\nPeppers\t$15.2\n"
let mas = NSMutableAttributedString(string:s, attributes:[
    NSFontAttributeName:UIFont(name:"GillSans", size:15)!,
    NSParagraphStyleAttributeName:lend {
        (p:NSMutableParagraphStyle) in
        let terms = NSTextTab.columnTerminatorsForLocale(
            NSLocale.currentLocale())
        let tab = NSTextTab(
            textAlignment:.Right, location:170, options:[
                NSTabColumnTerminatorsAttributeName:terms])
        p.tabStops = [tab]
        p.firstLineHeadIndent = 20
    }
])
self.tv.attributedText = mas
```

In that code, I set the paragraph style's entire `tabStops` array at once. New in iOS 9, the `tabStops` array can also be modified by calling `addTabStop:` or `removeTabStop:` on the paragraph style. However, a paragraph style comes with default tab stops, so you might want to remove them, or replace the `tabStops` array with an empty array, before you start adding tab stops.

Text attachments

A text attachment is basically an inline image. To make one, you need an instance of NSTextAttachment initialized with image data; the easiest way is to start with a UIImage

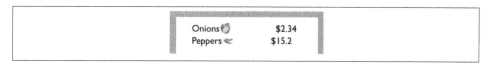

Figure 10-11. Text attachments in an attributed string

and assign directly to the NSTextAttachment's `image` property. You must also give the NSTextAttachment a nonzero bounds; the image will be scaled to the size of the bounds you provide, and a zero origin places the image on the text baseline.

A text attachment is attached to an NSAttributedString using the `NSAttachment-AttributeName` key; the text attachment itself is the value. The range of the string that has this attribute must be a special nonprinting character whose codepoint is `NSAttachmentCharacter` (0xFFFC). The simplest way to arrange that is to call the NSAttributedString initializer `init(attachment:)`; you hand it an NSTextAttachment and it hands you an attributed string consisting of the `NSAttachmentCharacter` with the `NSAttachmentAttributeName` attribute set to that text attachment. You can then insert this attributed string into your own attributed string at the point where you want the image to appear.

To illustrate, I'll add an image of onions and an image of peppers just after the words "Onions" and "Peppers" in the attributed string (`mas`) that I created in the previous example (Figure 10-11):

```
let onions = // ... get image ...
let peppers = // ... get image ...
let onionatt = NSTextAttachment()
onionatt.image = onions
onionatt.bounds = CGRectMake(0,-5,onions.size.width,onions.size.height)
let onionattchar = NSAttributedString(attachment:onionatt)
let pepperatt = NSTextAttachment()
pepperatt.image = peppers
pepperatt.bounds = CGRectMake(0,-1,peppers.size.width,peppers.size.height)
let pepperattchar = NSAttributedString(attachment:pepperatt)
let r = (mas.string as NSString).rangeOfString("Onions")
mas.insertAttributedString(onionattchar, atIndex:(r.location + r.length))
let r2 = (mas.string as NSString).rangeOfString("Peppers")
mas.insertAttributedString(pepperattchar, atIndex:(r2.location + r2.length))
self.tv.attributedText = mas
```

Other ways to create an attributed string

The nib editor provides an ingenious interface for letting you construct attributed strings wherever built-in interface objects (such as UILabel or UITextView) accept them as a property; it's not perfect, however, and isn't suitable for lengthy or complex text.

It is also possible to import an attributed string from text in some other standard format, such as HTML or RTF. To do so, get the target text into an NSData and call `init(data:options:documentAttributes:)`; alternatively, start with a file and call `init(URL:options:documentAttributes:)`. The `options:` allow you to specify the target text's format. For example, here we read an RTF file from the app bundle as an attributed string and show it in a UITextView:

```
let url = NSBundle.mainBundle().URLForResource("test",withExtension:"rtf")!
let opts = [NSDocumentTypeDocumentAttribute: NSRTFTextDocumentType]
var d : NSDictionary? = nil
let s = try! NSAttributedString(
    URL: url, options: opts, documentAttributes: &d)
self.tv.attributedText = s
```

I have not experimented to see how much can get lost in the translation or whether longer strings can cause a delay, but this is certainly an excellent way to generate attributed strings painlessly. There are also corresponding export methods.

Modifying and Querying an Attributed String

Although attributes are *applied* to ranges, they actually *belong* to each individual character. Thus we can coherently modify just the string part of a mutable attributed string. The key method here is `replaceCharactersInRange:withString:`, which can be used to replace characters with a plain string or, using a zero range length, to insert a plain string at the start, middle, or end of an attributed string. The question is then what attributes will be applied to the inserted string. The rule is:

- If we *replace* characters, the inserted string takes on the attributes of the *first replaced* character.

- If we *insert* characters, the inserted string takes on the attributes of the character *preceding* the insertion — except that, if we insert at the *start*, there is no preceding character, so the inserted string takes on the attributes of the character *following* the insertion.

You can query an attributed string about its attributes one character at a time — asking either about all attributes at once (`attributesAtIndex:effectiveRange:`) or about a particular attribute by name (`attribute:atIndex:effectiveRange:`). In those methods, the `effectiveRange` parameter is a pointer to an NSRange variable, which will be set by indirection to the range over which this same attribute value, or set of attribute values, applies:

```
var range : NSRange = NSMakeRange(0,0)
let d = content.attributesAtIndex(content.length-1, effectiveRange:&range)
```

Because style runs are something of an artifice, the `effectiveRange` might not be what you would think of as the *entire* style run. The methods with `longestEffectiveRange:`

in their names do (at the cost of some efficiency) work out the entire style run for you. In practice, however, you typically don't need the entire style run range, because you're cycling through ranges, and speed, even at the cost of *more* iterations, matters more than getting the longest effective range on *every* iteration.

In this example, I start with the combined two-paragraph Gettysburg Address attributed string constructed earlier, and change all the size 15 material to Arial Bold 20. I don't care whether I'm handed longest effective ranges (and my code explicitly says so); I just want to cycle efficiently:

```
let opts : NSAttributedStringEnumerationOptions =
    .LongestEffectiveRangeNotRequired
content.enumerateAttribute(NSFontAttributeName,
    inRange:NSMakeRange(0,content.length),
    options:opts, usingBlock: {
        value, range, stop in
        let font = value as! UIFont
        if font.pointSize == 15 {
            content.addAttribute(NSFontAttributeName,
                value:UIFont(name: "Arial-BoldMT", size:20)!,
                range:range)
        }
    })
```

Custom Attributes

You are permitted to apply your own custom attributes to a stretch of text in an attributed string. Your attributes won't directly affect how the string is drawn, because the text engine doesn't know what to make of them; but it doesn't object to them either. In this way, you can mark a stretch of text invisibly for your own future use.

In this example, I have a UILabel containing some text and a date. Every so often, I want to replace the date by the current date. The problem is that when the moment comes to replace the date, I don't know where it is: I know neither its length nor the length of the text that precedes it. The solution is to use an attributed string, and to mark the date with a secret custom attribute when I first insert it. (My attribute is called "HERE", and I've assigned it a value of 1.) Now I can readily find the date again later, because the text engine will tell me where it is:

```
let mas =
    self.lab.attributedText.mutableCopy() as! NSMutableAttributedString
mas.enumerateAttribute(
    "HERE", inRange: NSMakeRange(0, mas.length), options: []) {
        value, r, stop in
        if let value = value as? Int where value == 1 {
            mas.replaceCharactersInRange(
                r, withString: NSDate().description)
```

```
            stop.memory = true
        }
    }
    self.lab.attributedText = mas
```

Drawing and Measuring an Attributed String

You can draw an attributed string directly, without hosting it in a built-in interface object, and sometimes this will prove to be the most reliable approach. An NSString can be drawn into a rect with drawInRect:withAttributes: and related methods; an NSAttributedString can be drawn with drawAtPoint:, drawInRect:, and drawWith-Rect:options:context:.

Here, I draw an attributed string, content, into an image graphics context and extract the image (which might then be displayed by an image view):

```
UIGraphicsBeginImageContextWithOptions(rect.size, true, 0)
UIColor.whiteColor().setFill()
CGContextFillRect(UIGraphicsGetCurrentContext()!, rect)
content.drawInRect(rect) // draw attributed string
let im = UIGraphicsGetImageFromCurrentImageContext()
UIGraphicsEndImageContext()
```

Similarly, you can draw an attributed string directly in a UIView's drawRect:. For example, imagine that we have a UIView subclass called StringDrawer that has an attributedText property. The idea is that we just assign an attributed string to that property and the StringDrawer redraws itself:

```
self.drawer.attributedText = content
```

And here's StringDrawer:

```
class StringDrawer : UIView {
    @NSCopying var attributedText : NSAttributedString! {
        didSet {
            self.setNeedsDisplay()
        }
    }
    override func drawRect(rect: CGRect) {
        let r = rect.offsetBy(dx: 0, dy: 2)
        let opts : NSStringDrawingOptions = .UsesLineFragmentOrigin
        self.attributedText.drawWithRect(r, options: opts, context: nil)
    }
}
```

The use of .UsesLineFragmentOrigin is crucial here. Without it, the string is drawn with its *baseline* at the rect origin (so that it appears *above* that rect) and it doesn't wrap. The rule is that .UsesLineFragmentOrigin is the implicit default for simple drawIn-Rect:, but with drawWithRect:options:context: you must specify it explicitly.

NSAttributedString also provides methods to *measure* an attributed string, such as `boundingRectWithSize:options:context:`. Again, the option `.UsesLineFragment-Origin` is crucial; without it, the measured text doesn't wrap and the returned height will be very small. The documentation warns that the returned height can be fractional and that you should round up with the `ceil` function if the height of a view is going to depend on this result.

The `context:` parameter of methods such as `drawWithRect:options:context:` lets you attach an instance of NSStringDrawingContext, a simple value class whose `total-Bounds` property tells you where you just drew.

 Other features of NSStringDrawingContext, such as its `minimumScaleFactor`, appear to be nonfunctional.

Labels

A label (UILabel) is a simple built-in interface object for displaying text. I listed some of its chief properties in Chapter 8 (in "Built-In Cell Styles" on page 425).

If you're displaying a plain NSString in a label, by way of the label's `text` property, then you are likely also to set its `font`, `textColor`, and `textAlignment` properties, and possibly its `shadowColor` and `shadowOffset` properties. The label's text can have an alternate `highlightedTextColor`, to be used when its `highlighted` property is `true` — as happens, for example, when the label is in a selected cell of a table view.

On the other hand, if you're using an NSAttributedString, then you'll set just the label's `attributedText` property and let the attributes dictate things like color, alignment, and shadow. Those other UILabel properties do mostly still work, but they're going to change the attributes of your *entire* attributed string, in ways that you might not intend. Setting the `text` of a UILabel that has `attributedText` will basically eliminate the attributes. The `highlightedTextColor` property affects the `attributedText` only if the latter is black.

Number of Lines

A UILabel's `numberOfLines` property is extremely important. Together with the label's line breaking behavior and resizing behavior, it determines how much of the text will appear. The default is `1` — a single line — which can come as a surprise. To make a label display more than one line of text, you must explicitly set its `numberOfLines` to a value greater than 1, or to `0` to indicate that there is to be no maximum.

Line break characters in a label's text are honored. Thus, for example, in a single-line label, you won't see whatever follows the first line break character.

Wrapping and Truncation

UILabel line breaking (wrapping) and truncation behavior, which applies to both single-line and multiline labels, is determined by the `lineBreakMode` (of the label or the attributed string). The options (NSLineBreakMode) are those that I listed earlier in discussing NSParagraphStyle, but their *behavior* within a label needs to be described:

`.ByWordWrapping`
> Lines break at word-end, but if this is a single-line label, indistinguishable from `.By-Clipping`.

`.ByClipping`
> Lines break at word-end, but the *last* line can continue past its boundary, even if this leaves a character showing only partially.

`.ByCharWrapping`
> Lines break in midword in order to maximize the number of characters in each line.

`.ByTruncatingHead`
`.ByTruncatingMiddle`
`.ByTruncatingTail`
> Lines break at word-end; if the text is too long for the label, then the *last* line displays an ellipsis at the start, middle, or end of the line respectively, and text is omitted at the point of the ellipsis.

The default line break mode for a new label is `.ByTruncatingTail`. But the default line break mode for an attributed string's NSParagraphStyle is `.ByWordWrapping`.

New in iOS 9, `allowsDefaultTighteningForTruncation`, if `true`, permits some negative kerning to be applied automatically to a `Truncating` label if this would prevent truncation.

 UILabel line break behavior is *not the same* as what happens when an NSAttributedString draws itself in an image context or a plain UIView, as I described earlier. An NSAttributedString whose NSParagraphStyle's `lineBreakMode` doesn't have `Wrapping` in its name *doesn't wrap* when it draws itself — it consists of a single line.

Resizing a Label to Fit Its Text

If a label is too small for its text, the entire text won't show. If a label is too big for its text, the text is vertically centered in the label, with space above and below. Either of those might be undesirable. You might like to shrink or grow a label to fit its text exactly.

If you're not using autolayout, in most simple cases `sizeToFit` will do exactly the right thing; I believe that behind the scenes it is calling `boundingRectWithSize:options:context:`.

 There are cases where UILabel's `sizeToFit` will misbehave. The problem arises particularly with paragraph styles involving margins (`headIndent` and `tailIndent`) — presumably because `boundingRectWithSize:options:context:` ignores the margins.

If you're using autolayout, a label will correctly configure its own `intrinsicContentSize` automatically, based on its contents — and therefore, all other things being equal, will size itself to fit its contents *with no code at all*. Every time you reconfigure the label in a way that affects its contents (setting its text, changing its font, setting its attributed text, and so forth), the label automatically invalidates and recalculates its intrinsic content size. There are two general cases to consider:

Short single-line label
> You might give the label no width or height constraints; you'll constrain its position, but you'll let the label's `intrinsicContentSize` provide both the label's width and its height.

Multiline label
> In this case, it is more likely that you'll want to dictate the label's width, while letting the label's height change automatically to accommodate its contents. There are two ways to do this:

Set the label's width constraint
> This is appropriate particularly when the label's width is to remain fixed ever after.

Set the label's `preferredMaxLayoutWidth`
> This property is a hint to help the label's calculation of its `intrinsicContentSize`. It is the width at which the label, as its contents increase, will stop growing horizontally to accommodate those contents, and start growing vertically instead.

If a label's width is to be permitted to vary because of constraints, you can tell it recalculate its height to fit its contents by setting its `preferredMaxLayoutWidth` to its actual width. For example, consider a label whose left and right edges are both pinned to the superview. And imagine that the superview's width can change, thus changing the width of the label. For example, perhaps the superview is a view controller's main view, and is resized as the nib loads; and perhaps the app's interface is permitted to rotate, thus changing the main view's width to match the new orientation of the screen. Nevertheless, if the `preferredMaxLayoutWidth` is adjusted after every such change, the label's height will always perfectly fit its contents.

So how will you ensure that the `preferredMaxLayoutWidth` is adjusted when the label's width changes? Before giving the label constraints and text, set its `preferredMaxLayoutWidth` to 0! This happens to be the default, so there is nothing to do. Now the label will change its `preferredMaxLayoutWidth` *automatically* as its width changes, and will therefore *always* fit its contents, with no further effort on your part. Here's an example of creating such a label in code:

```
let lab = UILabel() // preferredMaxLayoutWidth is 0
lab.numberOfLines = 0
lab.backgroundColor = UIColor.yellowColor() // show bounds
lab.translatesAutoresizingMaskIntoConstraints = false
self.view.addSubview(lab)
NSLayoutConstraint.activateConstraints([
    NSLayoutConstraint.constraintsWithVisualFormat(
        "H:|-(30)-[v]-(30)-|",
        options: [], metrics: nil, views: ["v":lab]),
    NSLayoutConstraint.constraintsWithVisualFormat(
        "V:|-(30)-[v]",
        options: [], metrics: nil, views: ["v":lab])
    ].flatten().map{$0})
lab.attributedText = // whatever
```

You can also perform this configuration in the nib editor: at the top of the Size Inspector, uncheck the Explicit checkbox. The Preferred Width field says "Automatic," meaning that the `preferredMaxLayoutWidth` will change automatically to match the label's actual width as dictated by its constraints.

Instead of letting a label grow, you can permit its text font size to shrink if this would allow more of the text to fit. How the text is repositioned when the font size shrinks is determined by the label's `baselineAdjustment` property. For this feature to operate, *all* of the following conditions must be the case:

- The label's `adjustsFontSizeToFitWidth` property must be `true`.
- The label's `minimumScaleFactor` must be less than `1.0`.
- The label's size must be limited.
- *Either* this must be a single-line label (`numberOfLines` is 1) *or* the line break mode (of the label or the attributed string) must *not* have `Wrapping` in its name.

Customized Label Drawing

Methods that you can override in a subclass to modify a label's drawing are `drawTextInRect:` and `textRectForBounds:limitedToNumberOfLines:`.

For example, this is the code for a UILabel subclass that outlines the label with a black rectangle and puts a five-point margin around the label's contents:

```
class BoundedLabel: UILabel {
    override func awakeFromNib() {
        super.awakeFromNib()
        self.layer.borderWidth = 2.0
        self.layer.cornerRadius = 3.0
    }
    override func drawTextInRect(rect: CGRect) {
        super.drawTextInRect(
            rect.insetBy(dx: 5, dy: 5).integral)
    }
}
```

 A CATextLayer (Chapter 3) is like a lightweight, layer-level version of a UILabel. If the width of the layer is insufficient to display the entire string, we can get truncation behavior with the truncationMode property. If the wrapped property is set to true, the string will wrap. We can also set the alignment with the alignmentMode property. And its string property can be an NSAttributedString.

Text Fields

A text field (UITextField) portrays just a single line of text; any line break characters in its text are treated as spaces. It has many of the same properties as a label. You can provide it with a plain NSString, setting its text, font, textColor, and textAlignment, or provide it with an attributed string, setting its attributedText. You can learn a text field's overall text attributes as an attributes dictionary through its defaultTextAttributes property.

Under autolayout, a text field's intrinsicContentSize will attempt to set its width to fit its contents; if its width is fixed, you can set its adjustsFontSizeToFitWidth and minimumFontSize properties to allow the text size to shrink somewhat.

Text that is too long for the text field is displayed with an ellipsis at the end. A text field has no lineBreakMode, but you can change the position of the ellipsis by assigning the text field an attributed string with different truncation behavior, such as .ByTruncating-Head. When long text is being edited, the ellipsis (if any) is removed, and the text shifts horizontally to show the insertion point.

Regardless of whether you originally supplied a plain string or an attributed string, if the text field's allowsEditingTextAttributes property is true, the user, when editing in the text field, can summon a menu toggling the selected text's bold, italics, or underline features. (Oddly, there's no way to set this property in a nib.)

A text field has a `placeholder` property, which is the text that appears faded within the text field when it has no text (its `text` or `attributedText` has been set to `nil`, or the user has removed all the text); the idea is that you can use this to suggest to the user what the text field is for. It has a styled text alternative, `attributedPlaceholder`.

If a text field's `clearsOnBeginEditing` property is `true`, it automatically deletes its existing text (and displays the placeholder) when editing begins within it. If a text field's `clearsOnInsertion` property is `true`, then when editing begins within it, the text remains, but is invisibly selected, and will be replaced by the user's typing.

A text field's border drawing is determined by its `borderStyle` property. Your options (UITextFieldBorderStyle) are:

`.None`
    No border.

`.Line`
    A plain black rectangle.

`.Bezel`
    A gray rectangle, where the top and left sides have a very slight, thin shadow.

`.RoundedRect`
    A larger rectangle with slightly rounded corners and a flat, faded gray color.

You can supply a background image (`background`); if you combine this with a `borderStyle` of `.None`, or if the image has no transparency, you thus get to supply your own border — unless the `borderStyle` is `.RoundedRect`, in which case the `background` is ignored. The image is automatically resized as needed (and you will probably supply a resizable image). A second image (`disabledBackground`) can be displayed when the text field's `enabled` property, inherited from UIControl, is `false`. The user can't interact with a disabled text field, but without a `disabledBackground` image, the user may lack any visual clue to this fact (though a `.Line` or `.RoundedRect` disabled text field is subtly different from an enabled one). You can't set the `disabledBackground` unless you have also set the `background`.

A text field may contain one or two ancillary overlay views, its `leftView` and `rightView`, and possibly a Clear button (a gray circle with a white X). The automatic visibility of each of these is determined by the `leftViewMode`, `rightViewMode`, and `clearButtonMode`, respectively. The view mode values (UITextFieldViewMode) are:

`.Never`
    The view never appears.

`.WhileEditing`
    A Clear button appears if there is text in the field and the user is editing. A left or right view appears if there is *no* text in the field and the user is editing.

`.UnlessEditing`
> A Clear button appears if there is text in the field and the user is not editing. A left or right view appears if the user is not editing, or if the user is editing but there is no text in the field.

`.Always`
> A Clear button appears if there is text in the field. A left or right view always appears.

Depending on what sort of view you use, your `leftView` and `rightView` may have to be sized manually so as not to overwhelm the text view contents. If a right view and a Clear button appear at the same time, the right view may cover the Clear button unless you reposition it.

The positions and sizes of *any* of the components of the text field can be set in relation to the text field's bounds by overriding the appropriate method in a subclass:

- `clearButtonRectForBounds:`
- `leftViewRectForBounds:`
- `rightViewRectForBounds:`
- `borderRectForBounds:`
- `textRectForBounds:`
- `placeholderRectForBounds:`
- `editingRectForBounds:`

 You should make no assumptions about when or how frequently these methods will be called; the same method might be called several times in quick succession. Also, these methods should all be called with a parameter that is the bounds of the text field, but some are sometimes called with a 100×100 bounds; this feels like a bug.

You can also override in a subclass the methods `drawTextInRect:` and `drawPlaceholderInRect:`. You should either draw the specified text or call `super` to draw it; if you do neither, the text won't appear. Both these methods are called with a parameter whose size is the dimensions of the text field's text area, but whose origin is (0.0,0.0). In effect what you've got is a graphics context for just the text area; any drawing you do outside the given rectangle will be clipped.

Summoning and Dismissing the Keyboard

Making the onscreen simulated keyboard appear when the user taps in a text field is no work at all — it's automatic. Making the keyboard vanish again, on the other hand, can be a bit tricky. (Another problem is that the keyboard can cover the text field that the user just tapped in; I'll talk about that in a moment.)

The presence or absence of the keyboard, and a text field's editing state, are intimately tied to one another, and to the text field's status as the *first responder*:

- When a text field is first responder, it is being edited and the keyboard is present.
- When a text field is no longer first responder, it is no longer being edited, and if no other text field (or text view) becomes first responder, the keyboard is not present. The keyboard is not dismissed if one text field takes over first responder status from another.

Thus, you can programmatically control the presence or absence of the keyboard, together with a text field's editing state, by way of the text field's first responder status:

Becoming first responder
> To make the insertion point appear within a text field and to cause the keyboard to appear, you send becomeFirstResponder to that text field.
>
> You won't typically have to do that; usually, the user will tap in a text field and it will become first responder automatically. Still, sometimes it's useful to make a text field the first responder programmatically; an example appeared in Chapter 8 ("Inserting Cells" on page 484).

Resigning first responder
> To make a text field stop being edited and to cause the keyboard to disappear, you send resignFirstResponder to that text field. (Actually, resignFirstResponder returns a Bool, because a responder might return false to indicate that for some reason it refuses to obey this command.)
>
> Alternatively, send the UIView endEditing: method to the first responder *or any superview* (including the window) to ask or compel the first responder to resign first responder status.

 In a view presented in the .FormSheet modal presentation style on the iPad (Chapter 6), the keyboard, by default, does *not* disappear when a text field resigns first responder status. This is presumably because a form sheet is intended primarily for text input, so the keyboard is felt as accompanying the form as a whole, not individual text fields. Optionally, you can prevent this exceptional behavior: in your UIViewController subclass, override disablesAutomaticKeyboardDismissal to return false.

There is no simple way to learn what view is first responder! This is very odd, because a window surely *knows* what its first responder is — but it won't tell you. There's a method `isFirstResponder`, but you'd have to send it to every view in a window until you find the first responder. One workaround is to store a reference to the first responder yourself, typically in your implementation of the text field delegate's `textFieldDidBegin-Editing:`.

Once the user has tapped in a text field and the keyboard has automatically appeared, how is the user supposed to get rid of it? On the iPad, and on the iPhone 6 and iPhone 6 Plus in landscape, the keyboard contains a button that dismisses the keyboard. Otherwise, this is an oddly tricky issue. You would think that the "return" button in the keyboard would dismiss the keyboard; but, of itself, it doesn't.

One solution is to be the text field's delegate and to implement a text field delegate method, `textFieldShouldReturn:`. When the user taps the Return key in the keyboard, we hear about it through this method, and we tell the text field to resign its first responder status, which dismisses the keyboard:

```
func textFieldShouldReturn(tf: UITextField) -> Bool {
    tf.resignFirstResponder()
    return true
}
```

Keyboard Covers Text Field

The keyboard has a position "docked" at the bottom of the screen. This may cover the text field in which the user wants to type, even if it is first responder. On the iPad, this may not be an issue, because the user can "undock" the keyboard (possibly also splitting and shrinking it) and slide it up and down the screen freely. On the iPhone, you'll typically want to do something to reveal the text field.

To help with this, you can register for keyboard-related notifications:

- `UIKeyboardWillShowNotification`
- `UIKeyboardDidShowNotification`
- `UIKeyboardWillHideNotification`
- `UIKeyboardDidHideNotification`

Those notifications all have to do with the *docked* position of the keyboard. On the iPhone, keyboard docking and keyboard visibility are equivalent: the keyboard is visible if and only if it is docked. On the iPad, the keyboard is said to Show if it is being docked, whether that's because it is appearing from offscreen or because the user is docking it; and it is said to Hide if it is undocked, whether that's because it is moving offscreen or because the user is undocking it.

Two additional notifications are sent *both* when the keyboard enters and leaves the screen *and* (on the iPad) when the user drags it, splits or unsplits it, and docks or undocks it:

- `UIKeyboardWillChangeFrameNotification`
- `UIKeyboardDidChangeFrameNotification`

The notification's `userInfo` dictionary contains information about the keyboard describing what it will do or has done, under these keys:

- `UIKeyboardFrameBeginUserInfoKey`
- `UIKeyboardFrameEndUserInfoKey`
- `UIKeyboardAnimationDurationUserInfoKey`
- `UIKeyboardAnimationCurveUserInfoKey`

Thus, to a large extent, you can coordinate your actions with those of the keyboard. In particular, by looking at the `UIKeyboardFrameEndUserInfoKey`, you know what position the keyboard is moving to; you can compare this with the screen bounds to learn whether the keyboard will now be on or off the screen and, if it will now be on the screen, you can see whether it will cover a text field.

Finding a strategy for dealing with the keyboard's presence depends on the needs of your particular app. I'll concentrate on the most universal case, where the keyboard moves into and out of docked position and we detect this with `UIKeyboardWillShow-Notification` and `UIKeyboardWillHideNotification`. What should we do if, when the keyboard is shown, it covers the text field being edited?

Sliding the interface

One natural-looking approach is to slide the entire interface upward as the keyboard appears. To make this easy, you might start with a view hierarchy like this: the root view contains a transparent view that's the same size as the root view; everything else is contained in that transparent view. The transparent view's purpose is to host the rest of the interface; if we slide it upward, the whole interface will slide upward.

Here's an implementation involving constraints. The transparent view, which I'll called the *sliding view*, is pinned by constraints at the top and bottom to its superview with a `constant` of 0, and we have outlets to those constraints. We also have an outlet to the sliding view itself, and we've got a property prepared to hold the first responder:

```
@IBOutlet var topConstraint : NSLayoutConstraint!
@IBOutlet var bottomConstraint : NSLayoutConstraint!
@IBOutlet var slidingView : UIView!
var fr : UIView? // first responder
```

In our view controller's `viewDidLoad`, we register for the keyboard notifications:

```
super.viewDidLoad()
NSNotificationCenter.defaultCenter().addObserver(
    self, selector: "keyboardShow:",
    name: UIKeyboardWillShowNotification, object: nil)
NSNotificationCenter.defaultCenter().addObserver(
    self, selector: "keyboardHide:",
    name: UIKeyboardWillHideNotification, object: nil)
```

We are the delegate of the various text fields in our interface. When one of them starts editing, we keep a reference to it as first responder:

```
func textFieldDidBeginEditing(tf: UITextField) {
    self.fr = tf // keep track of first responder
}
```

As I suggested in the previous section, we also dismiss the keyboard by resigning first responder when the user taps the Return button in the keyboard:

```
func textFieldShouldReturn(tf: UITextField) -> Bool {
    tf.resignFirstResponder()
    self.fr = nil
    return true
}
```

As the keyboard threatens to appear, we examine where its top will be. If the keyboard will cover the text field that's about to be edited, we animate the sliding view upward to compensate, by changing the `constant` value of the constraints that pin its top and bottom:

```
func keyboardShow(n:NSNotification) {
    let d = n.userInfo!
    var r = (d[UIKeyboardFrameEndUserInfoKey] as! NSValue).CGRectValue()
    r = self.slidingView.convertRect(r, fromView:nil)
    if let f = self.fr?.frame {
        let y : CGFloat =
            f.maxY + r.size.height - self.slidingView.bounds.height + 5
        if r.origin.y < f.maxY {
            self.topConstraint.constant = -y
            self.bottomConstraint.constant = y
            self.view.layoutIfNeeded()
        }
    }
}
```

When the keyboard disappears, we put the sliding view back again:

```
func keyboardHide(n:NSNotification) {
    self.topConstraint.constant = 0
    self.bottomConstraint.constant = 0
    self.view.layoutIfNeeded()
}
```

In iOS 8 and later, our code is executed inside the keyboard's animation block; our changes to animatable view properties and layout are thus *automatically* animated together with the keyboard!

Text field in a scroll view

Changing the sliding view's constraints is a way of changing its *frame origin*. Since all we really want is to move the sliding view's subviews, it would be more suitable to change its *bounds origin*. If we're going to do that, we might as well make the sliding view a view that already knows all about shifting its bounds origin — a scroll view! This approach has two notable advantages over the preceding approach:

- We can permit the user to scroll the view within the area not covered by the keyboard. This is a job for contentInset, whose purpose, you will recall (Chapter 7), is precisely to make it possible for the user to view all of the scroll view's content even though part of the scroll view is being covered by something.

  (This behavior is in fact implemented automatically by a UITableViewController. When a text field inside a table cell is first responder, the table view controller adjusts the table view's contentInset and scrollIndicatorInsets to compensate for the keyboard. The result is that the entire table view content is available within the space between the top of the table view and the top of the keyboard.)

- A scroll view has some built-in behavior that will help us: it scrolls automatically to reveal the first responder. Furthermore, a UIScrollView has a keyboardDismiss-Mode, governing what will happen to the keyboard when the user scrolls.

Let's imitate UITableViewController's behavior with a scroll view containing text fields. In viewDidLoad, we register for keyboard notifications, and we are the delegate of any text fields, exactly as in the previous example. When the keyboard appears, we store the current content offset, content inset, and scroll indicator insets; then we alter the insets and allow the scroll view to scroll the first responder into view for us:

```
func keyboardShow(n:NSNotification) {
    self.oldContentInset = self.scrollView.contentInset
    self.oldIndicatorInset = self.scrollView.scrollIndicatorInsets
    self.oldOffset = self.scrollView.contentOffset
    let d = n.userInfo!
    var r = (d[UIKeyboardFrameEndUserInfoKey] as! NSValue).CGRectValue()
    r = self.scrollView.convertRect(r, fromView:nil)
    self.scrollView.contentInset.bottom = r.size.height
    self.scrollView.scrollIndicatorInsets.bottom = r.size.height
}
```

When the keyboard disappears, we restore the saved values:

```
func keyboardHide(n:NSNotification) {
    self.scrollView.bounds.origin = self.oldOffset
    self.scrollView.scrollIndicatorInsets = self.oldIndicatorInset
    self.scrollView.contentInset = self.oldContentInset
}
```

UIScrollView's `keyboardDismissMode` provides ways of letting the user dismiss the keyboard. The options (UIScrollViewKeyboardDismissMode) are:

`.None`
> The default; we must use code to dismiss the keyboard.

`.Interactive`
> The user can dismiss the keyboard by dragging it down.

`.OnDrag`
> The keyboard dismisses itself if the user scrolls the scroll view.

A scroll view with a `keyboardDismissMode` that isn't `.None`, in addition to hiding the keyboard, also calls `resignFirstResponder` on the text field. Such a scroll view is thus a great alternative solution to our misuse of `textFieldShouldReturn:` as a way of removing the keyboard. If you're going to embed your interface in a scroll view as a way of preventing text fields from being covered by the keyboard, you might use a strategy like this:

1. Set the scroll view's `keyboardDismissMode:` to `.Interactive`.

2. Respond to the keyboard being shown or hidden as I've already demonstrated.

3. Implement `textFieldShouldReturn:`, or not, depending on what you think the user will expect.

4. Don't bother keeping track of the first responder! You don't need that information any longer.

I also like to keep track of whether the keyboard is showing and prevent rotation of the interface if it is; otherwise, it becomes necessary to compensate for the change in dimensions, which can get tricky:

```
var keyboardShowing = false
func keyboardShow(n:NSNotification) {
    // ...
    self.keyboardShowing = true
}
func keyboardHide(n:NSNotification) {
    // ...
    self.keyboardShowing = false
}
override func shouldAutorotate() -> Bool {
    return !self.keyboardShowing
}
```

Configuring the Keyboard

A UITextField adopts the UITextInputTraits protocol, which defines properties on the
UITextField that you can set to determine how the keyboard will look and how typing
in the text field will behave. (These properties can also be set in the nib.) For example,
you can set the `keyboardType` to `.PhonePad` to make the keyboard for this text field
consist of digits. You can set the `returnKeyType` to determine the text of the Return key
(if the keyboard is of a type that has one). You can give the keyboard a dark or light
shade (`keyboardAppearance`). You can turn off autocapitalization or autocorrection
(`autocapitalizationType`, `autocorrectionType`), make the Return key disable itself
if the text field has no content (`enablesReturnKeyAutomatically`), and make the text
field a password field (`secureTextEntry`). You can even supply your own keyboard or
other input mechanism by setting the text field's `inputView`.

 Starting in iOS 8, your app can supply *other* apps with a keyboard. See the "Custom
Keyboard" chapter of Apple's *App Extension Programming Guide*.

You can attach an accessory view to the top of the keyboard by setting the text field's
`inputAccessoryView`. In this example, the accessory view contains a button that lets
the user navigate to the next text field. The accessory view is loaded from a nib and is
available through a property, `self.accessoryView`. When editing starts, we configure
the keyboard and store a reference to the text field:

```
func textFieldDidBeginEditing(tf: UITextField!) {
    self.fr = tf // keep track of first responder
    tf.inputAccessoryView = self.accessoryView
}
```

We have an array property populated with references to all our text fields (this might be an appropriate use of an outlet collection). The accessory view contains a Next button. The button's action method moves editing to the next text field:

```
var ix = self.textFields.indexOf(self.fr as! UITextField)!
ix = ++ix % self.textFields.count
let v = self.textFields[ix]
v.becomeFirstResponder()
```

The user can control the localization of the keyboard character set in the Settings app, either through a choice of the system's base language or with General → Keyboard → Keyboards (and possibly Add New Keyboard). In the latter case, the user can switch among keyboard character sets while the keyboard is showing. But, as far as I can tell, your code can't make this choice; you cannot, for example, *force* a certain text field to display the Cyrillic keyboard. You can ask the user to switch keyboards manually, but if you really want a particular keyboard to appear regardless of the user's settings and behavior, you'll have to create it yourself and provide it as the `inputView`.

 Some keyboard types, such as `.NumberPad`, `.PhonePad`, and `.DecimalPad`, may have no Return key. You'll need to supply some other interface for dismissing the keyboard!

New in iOS 9, bar button items can appear on the iPad in the spelling suggestion bar at the top of the keyboard. You can modify those bar button items. The spelling suggestion bar is the text field's `inputAssistantItem` (inherited from UIResponder), and it has `leadingBarButtonGroups` and `trailingBarButtonGroups`. A button group is a UIBarButtonItemGroup (also new in iOS 9), an array of UIBarButtonItems along with an optional `representativeItem` to be shown if there isn't room for the whole array; if the representative item has no target–action pair, tapping it will summon a popover containing the actual group.

In this example, we add a Camera bar button item to the right (trailing) side of the spelling suggestion bar for our text field (`self.tf`):

```
let bbi = UIBarButtonItem(
    barButtonSystemItem: .Camera, target: self, action: "doCamera:")
let group = UIBarButtonItemGroup(
    barButtonItems: [bbi], representativeItem: nil)
let shortcuts = self.tf.inputAssistantItem
shortcuts.trailingBarButtonGroups.append(group)
```

Text Field Delegate and Control Event Messages

As editing begins and proceeds in a text field, various messages are sent to the text field's delegate, adopting the UITextFieldDelegate protocol. Some of these messages are also available as notifications. Using them, you can customize the text field's behavior during editing:

`textFieldShouldBeginEditing:`
　　Return `false` to prevent the text field from becoming first responder.

`textFieldDidBeginEditing:`
`UITextFieldTextDidBeginEditingNotification`
　　The text field has become first responder.

`textFieldShouldClear:`
　　Return `false` to prevent the operation of the Clear button or of automatic clearing on entry (`clearsOnBeginEditing`). This event is *not* sent when the text is cleared because `clearsOnInsertion` is `true`, because the user is not clearing the text but rather changing it.

`textFieldShouldReturn:`
　　The user has tapped the Return button in the keyboard. We have already seen that this can be used as a signal to dismiss the keyboard.

`textField:shouldChangeCharactersInRange:replacementString:`
`UITextFieldTextDidChangeNotification`
　　In the delegate method, you can distinguish whether the user is typing or pasting, on the one hand, or backspacing or cutting, on the other; in the latter case, the replacement string will have zero length. Return `false` to prevent the proposed change; you can substitute text by changing the text field's `text` directly (there is no circularity, as this delegate method is not called when you do that).

　　In this example, the user can enter only lowercase characters:

```
func textField(textField: UITextField,
    shouldChangeCharactersInRange range: NSRange,
    replacementString string: String) -> Bool {
        if string == "\n" {
            return true
        }
        let lc = string.lowercaseString
        textField.text =
            (textField.text! as NSString)
                .stringByReplacingCharactersInRange(
                    range, withString:lc)
        return false
}
```

It is common practice to implement `textField:shouldChangeCharactersIn-Range:replacementString:` as a way of learning that the text has been changed, even if you then always return `true`. You are *not* notified when the user changes text styling through the Bold, Italics, or Underline menu items.

`textFieldShouldEndEditing:`

Return `false` to prevent the text field from resigning first responder (even if you just sent `resignFirstResponder` to it). You might do this, for example, because the text is invalid or unacceptable in some way. The user will not know why the text field is refusing to end editing, so the usual thing is to put up an alert (Chapter 13) explaining the problem.

`textFieldDidEndEditing:`
`UITextFieldTextDidEndEditingNotification`

The text field has resigned first responder. See Chapter 8 ("Editable Content in Cells" on page 482) for an example of using `textFieldDidEndEditing:` to fetch the text field's current text and store it in the model.

A text field is also a control (UIControl; see also Chapter 12). This means you can attach a target–action pair to any of the events that it reports in order to receive a message when that event occurs:

- The user can touch and drag, triggering Touch Down and the various Touch Drag events.

- If the user touches in such a way that the text field enters edit mode (and the keyboard appears), Editing Did Begin and Touch Cancel are triggered; if the user causes the text field to enter edit mode in some other way (such as by tabbing into it), Editing Did Begin is triggered without any Touch events.

- As the user edits (including changing attributes), Editing Changed is triggered.

- If the user taps while in edit mode, Touch Down (and possibly Touch Down Repeat) and Touch Cancel are triggered.

- When editing ends, Editing Did End is triggered; if the user stops editing by tapping Return in the keyboard, Did End on Exit is triggered first.

In general, you're more likely to treat a text field as a text field (through its delegate messages) than as a control (through its control events). However, the Did End on Exit event message has an interesting property: it provides an alternative way to dismiss the keyboard when the user taps a text field keyboard's Return button. If there is a Did End on Exit target–action pair for this text field, then if the text field's delegate does not return `false` from `textFieldShouldReturn:`, the keyboard will be dismissed *automatically* when the user taps the Return key. The action handler for Did End on Exit doesn't actually have to *do* anything.

Thus we have a splendid trick for getting automatic keyboard dismissal *with no code at all*. In the nib, edit the First Responder proxy object in the Attributes inspector, adding a new First Responder Action; let's call it dummy:. Now hook the Did End on Exit event of the text field to the dummy: action of the First Responder proxy object. That's it! Because the text field's Did End on Exit event now has a target–action pair, the text field automatically dismisses its keyboard when the user taps Return; there is no penalty for not finding a handler for a message sent up the responder chain, so the app doesn't crash even though there is no implementation of dummy: anywhere.

Alternatively, you can implement the same trick in code:

```
textField.addTarget(
    nil, action:"dummy:", forControlEvents:.EditingDidEndOnExit)
```

 A disabled text field emits no delegate messages or control events.

Text Field Menu

When the user double-taps or long-presses in a text field, the menu appears. It contains menu items such as Select, Select All, Paste, Copy, Cut, and Replace; which menu items appear depends on the circumstances. Many of the selectors for these standard menu items are listed in the UIResponderStandardEditActions informal protocol. Commonly used standard actions are:

- cut:
- copy:
- select:
- selectAll:
- paste:
- delete:
- _promptForReplace:
- _define:
- _showTextStyleOptions:
- toggleBoldface:
- toggleItalics:
- toggleUnderline:

The menu can also be customized; just as with a table view cell's menus (Chapter 8), this involves setting the shared UIMenuController object's `menuItems` property to an array of UIMenuItem instances representing the menu items that *may* appear *in addition* to those that the system puts there.

Actions for menu items are `nil`-targeted, so they percolate up the responder chain. You can thus implement a menu item's action anywhere up the responder chain; if you do this for a standard menu item at a point in the responder chain *before* the system receives it, you can interfere with and customize what it does. You govern the presence or absence of a menu item by implementing the UIResponder method `canPerformAction:with-Sender:` in the responder chain.

As an example, we'll devise a text field whose menu includes our own menu item, Expand. I'm imagining here, for instance, a text field where the user can select a U.S. state two-letter abbreviation (such as "CA") and can then summon the menu and tap Expand to replace it with the state's full name (such as "California").

I'll implement this in a UITextField subclass, in order to guarantee that the Expand menu item will be available when an instance of this subclass is first responder, but at no other time. My subclass has a property, `self.list`, which has been set to an array of state name abbreviations, each followed by its expanded state name. A utility function looks to see whether a string appears in the list:

```
func stateForAbbrev(abbrev:String) -> String? {
    let ix = self.list.indexOf(abbrev.uppercaseString)
    return ix != nil ? list[ix!+1] : nil
}
```

At some moment before the user taps in an instance of our UITextField subclass (such as `viewDidLoad`), we modify the global menu:

```
let mi = UIMenuItem(title:"Expand", action:"expand:")
let mc = UIMenuController.sharedMenuController()
mc.menuItems = [mi]
```

We implement `canPerformAction:withSender:` to govern the contents of the menu. Let's presume that we want our Expand menu item to be present only if the selection consists of a two-letter state abbreviation. UITextField itself provides no way to learn the selected text, but it conforms to the UITextInput protocol, which does:

```
override func canPerformAction(action: Selector,
    withSender sender: AnyObject?) -> Bool {
        if action == "expand:",
            let r = self.selectedTextRange,
            let s = self.textInRange(r) {
                return s.characters.count == 2 &&
```

```
                    self.stateForAbbrev(s) != nil
        }
        return super.canPerformAction(action, withSender:sender)
}
```

When the user chooses the Expand menu item, the `expand:` message is sent up the responder chain. We catch it in our UITextField subclass and obey it by replacing the selected text with the corresponding state name:

```
func expand(sender:AnyObject?) {
    if let r = self.selectedTextRange,
        let s = self.textInRange(r),
        let ss = self.stateForAbbrev(s) {
            self.replaceRange(r, withText:ss)
    }
}
```

We can also implement the selector for, and thus modify the behavior of, any of the standard menu items. For example, I'll implement `copy:` and modify its behavior. First we call `super` to get standard copying behavior; then we modify what's now on the pasteboard:

```
override func copy(sender:AnyObject?) {
    super.copy(sender)
    let pb = UIPasteboard.generalPasteboard()
    if let s = pb.string {
        let ss = // ... alter s here ...
        pb.string = ss
    }
}
```

 Implementing the selectors for `toggleBoldface:`, `toggleItalics:`, and `toggle-Underline:` is probably the best way to get an event when the user changes these attributes.

Text Views

A text view (UITextView) is a scroll view subclass (UIScrollView); it is *not* a control. Many of its properties are similar to those of a text field:

- A text view has `text`, `font`, `textColor`, and `textAlignment` properties; it can be user-editable or not, according to its `editable` property.

- A text view has `attributedText`, `allowsEditingTextAttributes`, and `typing-Attributes` properties, as well as `clearsOnInsertion`.

- An editable text view governs its keyboard just as a text field does: when it is first responder, it is being edited and shows the keyboard, and it adopts the UITextInput protocol and has `inputView` and `inputAccessoryView` properties.
- A text view's menu works the same way as a text field's.

A text view provides information about, and control of, its selection: it has a `selected-Range` property which you can get and set, along with a `scrollRangeToVisible:` method so that you can scroll in terms of a range of its text.

A text view's delegate messages (UITextViewDelegate protocol) and notifications, too, are similar to those of a text field. The following delegate methods (and notifications) should have a familiar ring:

- `textViewShouldBeginEditing:`
- `textViewDidBeginEditing:`
- `UITextViewTextDidBeginEditingNotification`
- `textViewShouldEndEditing:`
- `textViewDidEndEditing:`
- `UITextViewTextDidEndEditingNotification`
- `textView:shouldChangeTextInRange:replacementText:`

Some differences are:

`textViewDidChange:`
`UITextViewTextDidChangeNotification`
> Sent when the user changes text or attributes. A text field has no corresponding delegate method, though the Editing Changed control event and notification are similar.

`textViewDidChangeSelection:`
> In contrast, a text field is officially uninformative about the selection (though you can learn about and manipulate a UITextField's selection by way of the UITextInput protocol).

A text view's delegate can also decide how to respond when the user taps on a text attachment or a link. The text view must have its `selectable` property set to `true`, and its `editable` property set to `false`:

`textView:shouldInteractWithTextAttachment:inRange:`
> The default is `false`. If you return `true`, the user sees (in response to a long press) an action sheet offering to copy the image to the clipboard or the photo library.

`textView:shouldInteractWithURL:inRange:`
> The default is `true`: the URL is opened in Safari, or if the user long-presses, an action sheet appears with options Open, Add to Reading List, and Copy.

By returning `false` from either of those methods, you can substitute your own response, effectively treating the image or link as a button.

A text view also has a `dataDetectorTypes` property; this, too, if the text view is selectable but not editable, allows text of certain types, specified as a bitmask (and presumably located using NSDataDetector), to be treated as tappable links; the types (UIDataDetectorTypes) are:

`.Link`
> The default response is the same as for a link created using `NSLinkAttributeName`.

`.PhoneNumber`
> The default response to a tap is an alert with an option to call the number; the default response to a long press is an action sheet with options Call, Send Message, Add to Contacts, and Copy.

`.Address`
> The default response to a tap is to search for the address in the Maps app; the default response to a long press is an action sheet with options Open in Maps, Add to Contacts, and Copy.

`.CalendarEvent`
> The default response is an action sheet with options Create Event, Show in Calendar, and Copy.

The delegate's implementation of `textView:shouldInteractWithURL:inRange:` will catch data detector taps as well, so you can prevent the default behavior and substitute your own. You can distinguish a phone number through the URL's `scheme` (it will be `"tel"`), but an address or calendar event will be more or less opaque (the scheme is `"x-apple-data-detectors"`); however, you have the range so you can obtain the tapped text. The delegate method doesn't distinguish a tap from a long press for you.

Text View as Scroll View

A text view is a scroll view, so everything you know about scroll views applies (see Chapter 7). It has, by default, no border, because a scroll view has no border. It can be user-scrollable or not.

A text view's `contentSize` is maintained for you automatically as the text changes, so as to contain the text exactly; thus, if the text view is scrollable, the user can see any of its text. You can track changes to the content size by tracking changes to the text. A common reason for doing so is to implement a *self-sizing* text view, that is, a text view that adjusts its height automatically to embrace the amount of text it contains. In this example, we have an outlet to the text view's internal height constraint; the rather hacky quality of the code prevents some unfortunate misbehaviors of the text view:

```
func adjustHeight(tv:UITextView) {
    self.heightConstraint.constant = ceil(tv.contentSize.height)
}
func textView(textView: UITextView, shouldChangeTextInRange range: NSRange,
    replacementText text: String) -> Bool {
        let sel = textView.selectedRange
        textView.text = (textView.text as NSString)
            .stringByReplacingCharactersInRange(range, withString:text)
        self.adjustHeight(textView)
        textView.selectedRange =
            text.isEmpty && sel.length == 0 ?
                NSMakeRange(sel.location - 1,0) :
                NSMakeRange(sel.location + text.utf16.count, 0)
        return false
}
```

Text View and Keyboard

The fact that a text view is a scroll view comes in handy also when the keyboard partially covers a text view. The text view quite often dominates the screen, or a large portion of the screen, and you can respond to the keyboard partially covering it by adjusting the text view's contentInset, just as we did earlier in this chapter with a scroll view ("Text field in a scroll view" on page 574). As with a scroll view, once we play our part by setting the contentInset, the text view will scroll as needed to reveal the insertion point.

Now let's talk about what happens when the keyboard is dismissed. First of all, *how* is the keyboard to be dismissed? On the iPad, the virtual keyboard usually contains a button that dismisses the keyboard. But what about the iPhone? The Return key is meaningful for character entry; you aren't likely to want to misuse it as a way of dismissing the keyboard.

On the iPhone, the interface might well consist of a text view and the keyboard, which is *always* showing: instead of dismissing the keyboard, the user dismisses the entire interface. For example, in Apple's Mail app on the iPhone, when the user is composing a message, in what is presumably a presented view controller, the keyboard is present the whole time; the keyboard is dismissed because the user sends or cancels the message and the presented view controller is dismissed.

Alternatively, you can provide interface for dismissing the keyboard explicitly. For example, in Apple's Notes app, a note alternates between being read fullscreen and being edited with the keyboard present; in the latter case, a Done button appears, and the user taps it to dismiss the keyboard. If there's no good place to put a Done button in the interface, you could attach an accessory view to the keyboard itself.

Here's a possible implementation of a Done button's action method, with resulting dismissal of the keyboard:

```
func doDone(sender:AnyObject?) {
    self.view.endEditing(false)
}
func keyboardHide(n:NSNotification) {
    self.tv.contentInset = UIEdgeInsetsZero
    self.tv.scrollIndicatorInsets = UIEdgeInsetsZero
}
```

Finally, a text view is a scroll view, so it can have a `keyboardDismissMode`. Thus, by making the keyboard dismiss mode `.Interactive`, you can permit the user to hide the keyboard by dragging it. Again, the Mail message compose view is a case in point.

Text Kit

Text Kit comes originally from OS X, where you may already be more familiar with its use than you realize. For example, much of the text-editing "magic" of Xcode is due to Text Kit. It comprises a small group of classes that are responsible for drawing text; simply put, they turn an NSAttributedString into graphics. You can take advantage of Text Kit to modify text drawing in ways that were once possible (if at all) only by dipping down to the low-level C-based world of Core Text.

A UITextView provides direct access to the underlying Text Kit engine. It has the following Text Kit–related properties:

textContainer
> The text view's text container (an NSTextContainer instance). UITextView's designated initializer is `init(frame:textContainer:)`; the `textContainer:` can be `nil` to get a default text container, or you can supply your own custom text container.

textContainerInset
> The margins of the text container, designating the area within the `contentSize` rectangle in which the text as a whole is drawn. Changing this value changes the margins immediately, causing the text to be freshly laid out.

layoutManager
> The text view's layout manager (an NSLayoutManager instance).

textStorage
> The text view's text storage (an NSTextStorage instance).

When you initialize a text view with a custom text container, you hand it the entire "stack" of Text Kit instances: a text container, a layout manager, and a text storage. In the simplest and most common case, a text storage has a layout manager, and a layout manager has a text container, thus forming the "stack." If the text container is a UIText-

View's text container, the stack is retained, and the text view is operative. Thus, the simplest case might look like this:

```
let r = // frame for the new text view
let lm = NSLayoutManager()
let ts = NSTextStorage()
ts.addLayoutManager(lm)
let tc = NSTextContainer(size:CGSizeMake(r.width, CGFloat.max))
lm.addTextContainer(tc)
let tv = UITextView(frame:r, textContainer:tc)
```

Here's what the three chief Text Kit classes do:

NSTextStorage

A subclass of NSMutableAttributedString. It is, or holds, the underlying text. It has one or more layout managers, and notifies them when the text changes. By subclassing and delegation (NSTextStorageDelegate), its behavior can be modified so that it applies attributes in a custom fashion.

NSTextContainer

It is owned by a layout manager, and helps that layout manager by defining the region in which the text is to be laid out. It does this in three primary ways:

Size

The text container's top left is the origin for the text layout coordinate system, and the text will be laid out within the text container's rectangle.

Exclusion paths

The exclusionPaths property consists of UIBezierPath objects within which no text is to be drawn.

Subclassing

By overriding lineFragmentRectForProposedRect:atIndex:writing-Direction:remainingRect:, you can place each chunk of text drawing anywhere at all (except inside an exclusion path).

NSLayoutManager

This is the master text drawing class! It has one or more text containers, and is owned by a text storage — thus forming the Text Kit stack. It draws the text storage's text into the boundaries defined by the text container(s).

A layout manager can have a delegate (NSLayoutManagerDelegate), and can be subclassed. This, as you may well imagine, is a powerful and sophisticated class.

Text Container

An NSTextContainer has a size, within which the text will be drawn. By default, as in the preceding code, a text view's text container's width is the width of the text view, while its height is effectively infinite, allowing the drawing of the text to grow vertically but not horizontally beyond the bounds of the text view, and making it possible to scroll the text vertically.

It also has `heightTracksTextView` and `widthTracksTextView` properties, causing the text container to be resized to match changes in the size of the text view — for example, if the text view is resized because of interface rotation. By default, as you might expect, `widthTracksTextView` is `true` (the documentation is wrong about this), while `heightTracksTextView` is `false`: the text fills the width of the text view, and is laid out freshly if the text view's width changes, but its height remains effectively infinite. The text view itself, of course, configures its own `contentSize` so that the user can scroll just to the bottom of the existing text.

When you change a text view's `textContainerInset`, it modifies its text container's size to match, as necessary. In the default configuration, this means that it modifies the text container's width; the top and bottom insets are implemented through the text container's position within the content rect. Within the text container, additional side margins correspond to the text container's `lineFragmentPadding`; the default is 5, but you can change it.

If the text view's `scrollEnabled` is `false`, then by default its text container's `heightTracksTextView` and `widthTracksTextView` are both `true`, and the text container size is adjusted so that the text fills the text view. In that case, you can also set the text container's `lineBreakMode`. This works like the line break mode of a UILabel. For example, if the line break mode is `.ByTruncatingTail`, then the last line has an ellipsis at the end (if the text is too long for the text view). You can also set the text container's `maximumNumberOfLines`, which is like a UILabel's `numberOfLines`. In effect, you've turned the text view into a label!

But, of course, a nonscrolling text view isn't *just* a label, because you've got access to the Text Kit stack that backs it. For example, you can apply exclusion paths to the text container. Figure 10-12 shows a case in point. The text wraps in longer and longer lines, and then in shorter and shorter lines, because there's an exclusion path on the right side of the text container that's a rectangle with a large V-shaped indentation.

In Figure 10-12, the text view (`self.tv`) is initially configured in the view controller's `viewDidLoad`:

```
self.tv.attributedText = // ...
self.tv.textContainerInset = UIEdgeInsetsMake(20, 20, 20, 0)
self.tv.scrollEnabled = false
```

The exclusion path is then drawn and applied in `viewDidLayoutSubviews`:

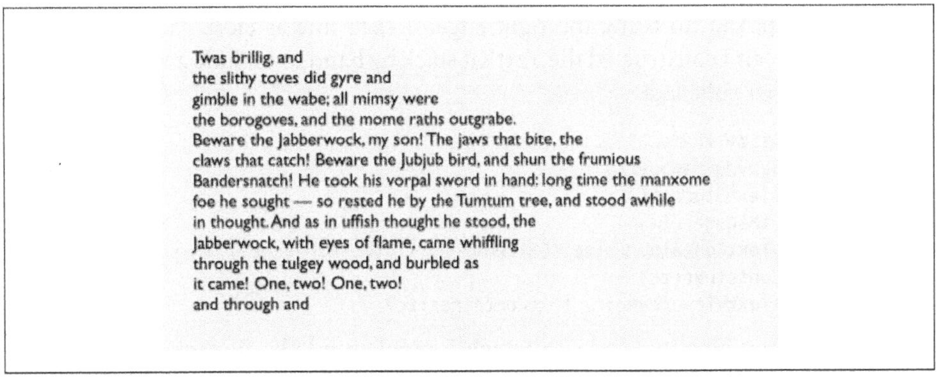

Figure 10-12. A text view with an exclusion path

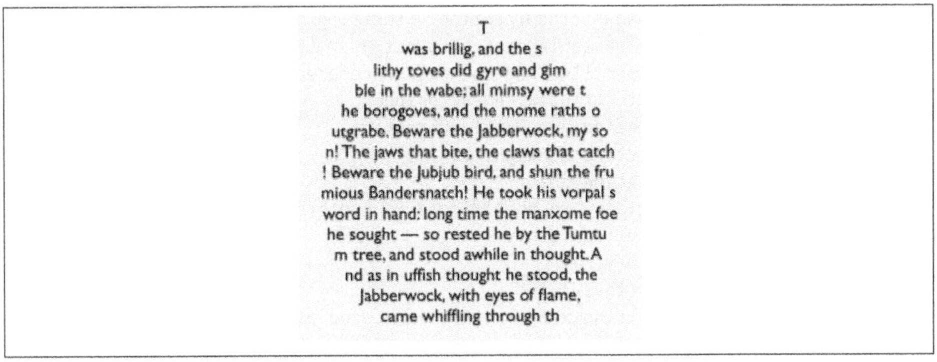

Figure 10-13. A text view with a subclassed text container

```
override func viewDidLayoutSubviews() {
    let sz = self.tv.textContainer.size
    let p = UIBezierPath()
    p.moveToPoint(CGPointMake(sz.width/4.0,0))
    p.addLineToPoint(CGPointMake(sz.width,0))
    p.addLineToPoint(CGPointMake(sz.width,sz.height))
    p.addLineToPoint(CGPointMake(sz.width/4.0,sz.height))
    p.addLineToPoint(CGPointMake(sz.width,sz.height/2.0))
    p.closePath()
    self.tv.textContainer.exclusionPaths = [p]
}
```

Instead of (or in addition to) an exclusion path, you can subclass NSTextContainer to modify the rectangle in which the layout manager wants to position a piece of text. (Each piece of text is actually a line fragment; I'll explain in the next section what a line fragment is.) In Figure 10-13, the text is inside a circle.

To achieve the layout shown in Figure 10-13, I set the attributed string's line break mode to .ByCharWrapping (to bring the right edge of each line as close as possible to the circular shape), and constructed the TextKit stack by hand to include an instance of my NSTextContainer subclass:

```
let r = self.tv.frame
let lm = NSLayoutManager()
let ts = NSTextStorage()
ts.addLayoutManager(lm)
let tc = MyTextContainer(size:CGSizeMake(r.width, r.height))
lm.addTextContainer(tc)
let tv = UITextView(frame:r, textContainer:tc)
```

That subclass contains this code, in which I simplemindedly fit each line fragment's horizontal origin and width entirely within a circle:

```
override func lineFragmentRectForProposedRect(
    proposedRect: CGRect, atIndex characterIndex: Int,
    writingDirection baseWritingDirection: NSWritingDirection,
    remainingRect: UnsafeMutablePointer<CGRect>) -> CGRect {
        var result = super.lineFragmentRectForProposedRect(
            proposedRect, atIndex:characterIndex,
            writingDirection:baseWritingDirection,
            remainingRect:remainingRect)
        let r = self.size.height / 2.0
        // convert initial y so that circle is centered at origin
        let y = r - result.origin.y
        let theta = asin(y/r)
        let x = r * cos(theta)
        // convert resulting x from circle centered at origin
        result.origin.x = r-x
        result.size.width = 2*x
        return result
}
```

Alternative Text Kit Stack Architectures

The default Text Kit stack is one text storage, which has one layout manager, which has one text container. But a text storage can have multiple layout managers, and a layout manager can have multiple text containers. What's that all about?

If one layout manager has multiple text containers, the overflow from each text container is drawn in the next one. For example, in Figure 10-14, there are two text views; the text has filled the first text view, and has then continued by flowing into and filling the second text view. As far as I can tell, the text views can't be made editable in this configuration. But clearly this is a way to achieve a multicolumn or multipage layout, or you could use text views of different sizes for a magazine-style layout.

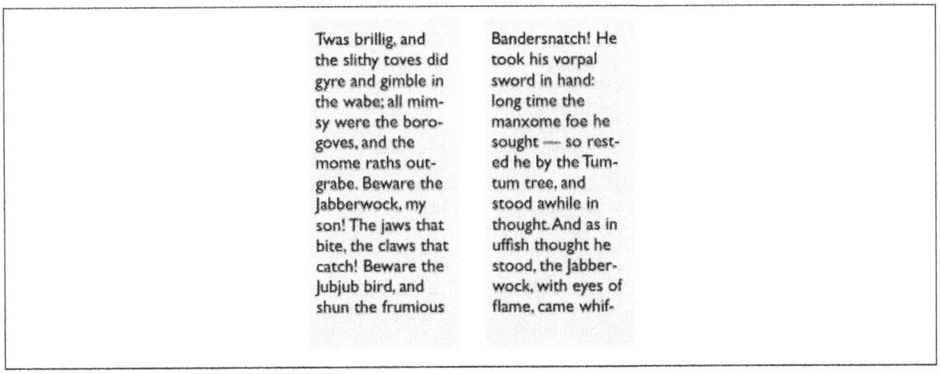

Figure 10-14. A layout manager with two text containers

It is possible to achieve that arrangement by disconnecting the layout managers of existing text views from their text containers and rebuilding the stack from below. In this example, though, I'll build the entire stack by hand:

```
let r = // frame
let r2 = // frame
let mas = // content
let ts1 = NSTextStorage(attributedString:mas)
let lm1 = NSLayoutManager()
ts1.addLayoutManager(lm1)
let tc1 = NSTextContainer(size:r.size)
lm1.addTextContainer(tc1)
let tv = UITextView(frame:r, textContainer:tc1)
let tc2 = NSTextContainer(size:r2.size)
lm1.addTextContainer(tc2)
let tv2 = UITextView(frame:r2, textContainer:tc2)
```

If one text storage has multiple layout managers, then each layout manager is laying out the same text. For example, in Figure 10-15, there are two text views displaying the same text. The remarkable thing is that if you edit one text view, the other changes to match. (That's how Xcode lets you edit the same code file in different windows, tabs, or panes.)

Again, this arrangement is probably best achieved by building the entire text stack by hand:

```
let r = // frame
let r2 = // frame
let mas = // content
let ts1 = NSTextStorage(attributedString:mas)
let lm1 = NSLayoutManager()
ts1.addLayoutManager(lm1)
let lm2 = NSLayoutManager()
ts1.addLayoutManager(lm2)
let tc1 = NSTextContainer(size:r.size)
```

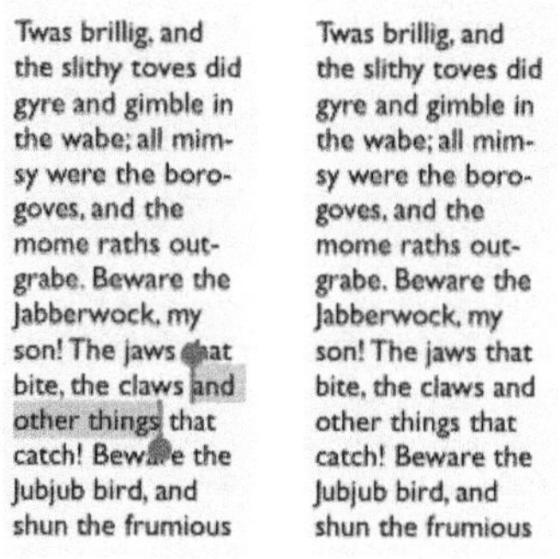

Figure 10-15. A text storage with two layout managers

```
let tc2 = NSTextContainer(size:r2.size)
lm1.addTextContainer(tc1)
lm2.addTextContainer(tc2)
let tv = UITextView(frame:r, textContainer:tc1)
let tv2 = UITextView(frame:r2, textContainer:tc2)
```

Layout Manager

The first thing to know about a layout manager is the geometry in which it thinks. To envision a layout manager's geometrical world, think in terms of glyphs and line fragments:

Glyph
> The drawn analog of a character. The layout manager's primary job is to get glyphs from a font and draw them.

Line fragment
> A rectangle in which glyphs are drawn, one after another. (The reason it's a line *fragment*, and not just a line, is that a line might be interrupted by the text container's exclusion paths.)

A glyph has a location in terms of the line fragment into which it is drawn. A line fragment's coordinates are in terms of the text container. The layout manager can convert between these coordinate systems, and between text and glyphs. Given a range of text in the text storage, it knows where the corresponding glyphs are drawn in the text container. Conversely, given a location in the text container, it knows what glyph is drawn there and what range of text in the text storage that glyph represents.

What's missing from that geometry is what, if anything, the text container corresponds to in the real world. A text container is not, itself, a real rectangle in the real world; it's just a class that tells the layout manager a size to draw into. Making that rectangle meaningful for drawing purposes is up to some other class outside the Text Kit stack.

A UITextView, for example, has a text container, which it shares with a layout manager. The text view knows how its own content is scrolled and how the rectangle represented by its text container is inset within that scrolling content. The layout manager, however, doesn't know anything about that; it sees the text container as a purely theoretical rectangular boundary. Only when the layout manager actually draws does it make contact with the real world of some graphics context — and it must be told, on those occasions, how the text container's rectangle is offset within that graphics context.

To illustrate, I'll use a TextKit method to learn the index of the first character visible at the top left of a text view (self.tv); I'll then use NSLinguisticTagger to derive the first *word* visible at the top left of the text view. I can ask the layout manager what character or glyph corresponds to a certain point in the text container, but what point should I ask about? Translating from the real world to text container coordinates is up to me; I must take into account both the scroll position of the text view's content and the inset of the text container within that content:

```
let off = self.tv.contentOffset
let top = self.tv.textContainerInset.top
var tctopleft = CGPointMake(0, off.y - top)
```

Now I'm speaking in terms of text container coordinates, which are layout manager coordinates. One possibility is then to ask directly for the index (in the text storage's string) of the corresponding character:

```
var ix = self.tv.layoutManager.characterIndexForPoint(tctopleft,
    inTextContainer:self.tv.textContainer,
    fractionOfDistanceBetweenInsertionPoints:nil)
```

That, however, does not give quite the results one might intuitively expect. If *any* of a word is poking down from above into the visible area of the text view, that is the word whose first character is returned. I think we intuitively expect, if a word isn't fully visible, that the answer should be the word that starts the *next* line, which *is* fully visible. So I'll modify that code in a simpleminded way. I'll obtain the index of the *glyph* at my initial point; from this, I can derive the rect of the line fragment containing it. If that line fragment is not at least three-quarters visible, I'll add one line fragment height to the starting point and derive the glyph index again. Then I'll convert the glyph index to a character index:

```
var ix = self.tv.layoutManager.glyphIndexForPoint(tctopleft,
    inTextContainer:self.tv.textContainer,
    fractionOfDistanceThroughGlyph:nil)
let frag = self.tv.layoutManager.lineFragmentRectForGlyphAtIndex(
    ix, effectiveRange:nil)
if tctopleft.y > frag.origin.y + 0.5*frag.size.height {
    tctopleft.y += frag.size.height
    ix = self.tv.layoutManager.glyphIndexForPoint(tctopleft,
        inTextContainer:self.tv.textContainer,
        fractionOfDistanceThroughGlyph:nil)
```

```
    }
let charRange = self.tv.layoutManager.characterRangeForGlyphRange(
    NSMakeRange(ix,0), actualGlyphRange:nil)
ix = charRange.location
```

Finally, I'll use NSLinguisticTagger to get the range of the entire word to which this character belongs:

```
let sch = NSLinguisticTagSchemeTokenType
let t = NSLinguisticTagger(tagSchemes:[sch], options:0)
t.string = self.tv.text
var r : NSRange = NSMakeRange(0,0)
let tag = t.tagAtIndex(ix, scheme:sch, tokenRange:&r, sentenceRange:nil)
if tag == NSLinguisticTagWord {
    print((self.tv.text as NSString).substringWithRange(r))
}
```

Clearly, the same sort of technique could be used to formulate a custom response to a tap ("what word did the user just tap on?").

By subclassing NSLayoutManager (and by implementing its delegate), many powerful effects can be achieved. As a simple example, I'll carry on from the preceding code by drawing a rectangular outline around the word we just located. To make this possible, I have an NSLayoutManager subclass, MyLayoutManager, an instance of which is built into the Text Kit stack for this text view. MyLayoutManager has a public NSRange property, wordRange. Having worked out what word I want to outline, I set the layout manager's wordRange and invalidate its drawing of that word, to force a redraw:

```
let lm = self.tv.layoutManager as! MyLayoutManager
lm.wordRange = r
lm.invalidateDisplayForCharacterRange(r)
```

In MyLayoutManager, I've overridden the method that draws the background behind glyphs. At the moment this method is called, there is already a graphics context.

First, I call super. Then, if the range of glyphs to be drawn includes the glyphs for the range of characters in self.wordRange, I ask for the rect of the bounding box of those glyphs, and stroke it to form the rectangle. As I mentioned earlier, the bounding box is in text container coordinates, but now we're drawing in the real world, so I have to compensate by offsetting the drawn rectangle by the same amount that the text container is supposed to be offset in the real world; fortunately, the text view tells us (through the origin: parameter) what that offset is:

```
override func drawBackgroundForGlyphRange(
    glyphsToShow: NSRange, atPoint origin: CGPoint) {
        super.drawBackgroundForGlyphRange(
            glyphsToShow, atPoint:origin)
        if self.wordRange.length == 0 {
            return
        }
        var range = self.glyphRangeForCharacterRange(
```

```
        self.wordRange, actualCharacterRange:nil)
    range = NSIntersectionRange(glyphsToShow, range)
    if range.length == 0 {
        return
    }
    if let tc = self.textContainerForGlyphAtIndex(
        range.location, effectiveRange:nil,
        withoutAdditionalLayout:true) {
            var r = self.boundingRectForGlyphRange(
                range, inTextContainer:tc)
            r.origin.x += origin.x
            r.origin.y += origin.y
            let c = UIGraphicsGetCurrentContext()!
            CGContextSaveGState(c)
            CGContextSetStrokeColorWithColor(
                c, UIColor.blackColor().CGColor)
            CGContextSetLineWidth(c, 1.0)
            CGContextStrokeRect(c, r)
            CGContextRestoreGState(c)
    }
}
```

Text Kit Without a Text View

UITextView is the only built-in iOS class that has a Text Kit stack to which you are given programmatic access. But that doesn't mean it's the only place where you can draw with Text Kit! You can draw with Text Kit *anywhere you can draw* — that is, in any graphics context (Chapter 2). When you do so, you should always call both drawBackgroundFor-GlyphRange:atPoint: (the method I overrode in the previous example) and draw-GlyphsForGlyphRange:atPoint:, in that order. The point: argument is where you consider the text container's origin to be within the current graphics context.

To illustrate, I'll change the implementation of the StringDrawer class that I described earlier in this chapter. Previously, StringDrawer's drawRect: implementation told the attributed string (self.attributedText) to draw itself:

```
override func drawRect(rect: CGRect) {
    let r = rect.offsetBy(dx: 0, dy: 2)
    let opts : NSStringDrawingOptions = .UsesLineFragmentOrigin
    self.attributedText.drawWithRect(r, options: opts, context: nil)
}
```

Instead, I'll construct the Text Kit stack and tell its layout manager to draw the text:

```
override func drawRect(rect: CGRect) {
    let lm = NSLayoutManager()
    let ts = NSTextStorage(attributedString:self.attributedText)
    ts.addLayoutManager(lm)
    let tc = NSTextContainer(size:rect.size)
    lm.addTextContainer(tc)
    tc.lineFragmentPadding = 0
```

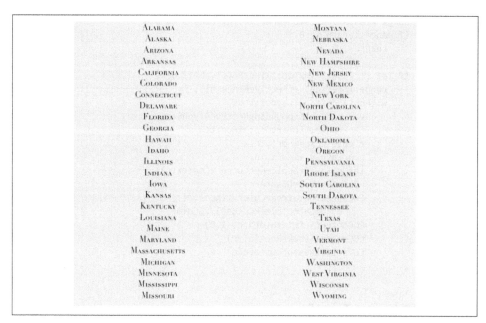

Alabama	Montana
Alaska	Nebraska
Arizona	Nevada
Arkansas	New Hampshire
California	New Jersey
Colorado	New Mexico
Connecticut	New York
Delaware	North Carolina
Florida	North Dakota
Georgia	Ohio
Hawaii	Oklahoma
Idaho	Oregon
Illinois	Pennsylvania
Indiana	Rhode Island
Iowa	South Carolina
Kansas	South Dakota
Kentucky	Tennessee
Louisiana	Texas
Maine	Utah
Maryland	Vermont
Massachusetts	Virginia
Michigan	Washington
Minnesota	West Virginia
Mississippi	Wisconsin
Missouri	Wyoming

Figure 10-16. Two-column text in small caps

```
    let r = lm.glyphRangeForTextContainer(tc)
    lm.drawBackgroundForGlyphRange(r, atPoint:CGPointMake(0,2))
    lm.drawGlyphsForGlyphRange(r, atPoint:CGPointMake(0,2))
}
```

Building the entire Text Kit stack by hand may seem like overkill for that simple example, but imagine what *else* I could do now that I have access to the entire Text Kit stack! I can use properties, subclassing and delegation, and alternative stack architectures to achieve customizations and effects that, before TextKit was migrated to iOS, were difficult or impossible to achieve without dipping down to the level of Core Text.

For example, the two-column display of U.S. state names on the iPad shown in Figure 10-16 was a Core Text example in early editions of this book, requiring 50 or 60 lines of elaborate C code, complicated by the necessity of flipping the context to prevent the text from being drawn upside-down. Nowadays, it can be achieved easily through Text Kit — effectively just by reusing code from earlier examples in this chapter.

Furthermore, the example from previous editions went on to describe how to make the display of state names interactive, with the name of the tapped state briefly outlined with a rectangle (Figure 10-17). With Core Text, this was almost insanely difficult, not least because we had to keep track of all the line fragment rectangles ourselves. But it's easy with Text Kit, because the layout manager knows all the answers.

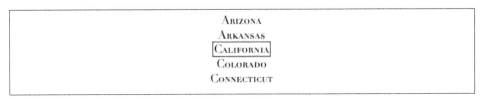

ARIZONA
ARKANSAS
CALIFORNIA
COLORADO
CONNECTICUT

Figure 10-17. The user has tapped on California

We have a UIView subclass, StyledText. In its `layoutSubviews`, it creates the Text Kit stack — a layout manager with two text containers, to achieve the two-column layout — and stores the whole stack, along with the rects at which the two text containers are to be drawn, in properties:

```
override func layoutSubviews() {
    super.layoutSubviews()
    var r1 = self.bounds
    r1.origin.y += 2 // a little top space
    r1.size.width /= 2.0 // column 1
    var r2 = r1
    r2.origin.x += r2.size.width // column 2
    let lm = MyLayoutManager()
    let ts = NSTextStorage(attributedString:self.text)
    ts.addLayoutManager(lm)
    let tc = NSTextContainer(size:r1.size)
    lm.addTextContainer(tc)
    let tc2 = NSTextContainer(size:r2.size)
    lm.addTextContainer(tc2)
    self.lm = lm; self.ts = ts; self.tc = tc; self.tc2 = tc2
    self.r1 = r1; self.r2 = r2
}
```

Our `drawRect:` is just like the previous example, except that we have two text containers to draw:

```
override func drawRect(rect: CGRect) {
    let range1 = self.lm.glyphRangeForTextContainer(self.tc)
    self.lm.drawBackgroundForGlyphRange(range1, atPoint: self.r1.origin)
    self.lm.drawGlyphsForGlyphRange(range1, atPoint: self.r1.origin)
    let range2 = self.lm.glyphRangeForTextContainer(self.tc2)
    self.lm.drawBackgroundForGlyphRange(range2, atPoint: self.r2.origin)
    self.lm.drawGlyphsForGlyphRange(range2, atPoint: self.r2.origin)
}
```

So much for drawing the text!

When the user taps on our view, a tap gesture recognizer's action handler is called. We are using the same layout manager subclass developed in the preceding section of this chapter: it draws a rectangle around the glyphs corresponding to the characters of its `wordRange` property. Thus, all we have to do in order to make the flashing rectangle around the tapped word is work out what that range is, set our layout manager's word-Range property and redraw ourselves, and then (after a short delay) set the wordRange property back to a zero range and redraw ourselves again to remove the rectangle.

We start by working out which column the user tapped in; this tells us which text container it is, and what the tapped point is in text container coordinates:

```
var p = g.locationInView(self) // g is the tap gesture recognizer
var tc = self.tc
if !CGRectContainsPoint(self.r1, p) {
    tc = self.tc2
    p.x -= self.r1.size.width
}
```

Now we can ask the layout manager what glyph the user tapped on, and hence the whole range of glyphs within the line fragment the user tapped in. If the user tapped to the left of the first glyph or to the right of the last glyph, no word was tapped, and we return:

```
var f : CGFloat = 0
let ix = self.lm.glyphIndexForPoint(
    p, inTextContainer:tc, fractionOfDistanceThroughGlyph:&f)
var glyphRange : NSRange = NSMakeRange(0,0)
self.lm.lineFragmentRectForGlyphAtIndex(ix, effectiveRange:&glyphRange)
if ix == glyphRange.location && f == 0.0 {
    return
}
if ix == glyphRange.location + glyphRange.length - 1 && f == 1.0 {
    return
}
```

If the last glyph of the line fragment is a whitespace glyph, we don't want to include it in our rectangle, so we subtract it from the end of our range. Then we're ready to convert to a character range, and thus we can learn the name of the state that the user tapped on:

```
func lastCharIsControl () -> Bool {
    let lastCharRange = glyphRange.location + glyphRange.length - 1
    let property = self.lm.propertyForGlyphAtIndex(lastCharRange)
    let mask1 = property.rawValue
    let mask2 = NSGlyphProperty.ControlCharacter.rawValue
    return mask1 & mask2 != 0
}
while lastCharIsControl() {
    glyphRange.length -= 1
}
let characterRange =
    self.lm.characterRangeForGlyphRange(glyphRange, actualGlyphRange:nil)
let s = (self.text.string as NSString).substringWithRange(characterRange)
```

Finally, we flash the rectangle around the state name by setting and resetting the word-Range property of the subclassed layout manager:

```
let lm = self.lm as! MyLayoutManager
lm.wordRange = characterRange
self.setNeedsDisplay()
delay(0.3) {
    lm.wordRange = NSMakeRange(0, 0)
    self.setNeedsDisplay()
}
```

CHAPTER 11

Web Views

A web view is a web browser: it knows how to fetch resources from the Internet, and it understands and can render text coded in HTML, along with associated instructions coded as CSS and JavaScript. Thus it is an asynchronous network communication device on the one hand, and a powerful engine for layout, animation, and media display on the other.

All of that power comes "for free" with a web view. It gives your app a browser interface, comparable to Mobile Safari; you can just stand back and let it do its work. You don't have to know anything about networking. Links and other ancillary resources work automatically. If your web view's HTML refers to an image, the web view will fetch it and display it. If the user taps on a link, the web view will fetch that content and display it; if the link is to some sort of media (a sound or video file), the web view will allow the user to play it.

A web view also knows how to display various other types of content commonly encountered as Internet resources. For example, a web view is an excellent way to display PDF files. It can also display documents in such formats as *.rtf*, Microsoft Word (*.doc* and *.docx*), and Pages. (A Pages file that is actually a bundle must be compressed to form a single *.pages.zip* resource.)

 A web view should also be able to display *.rtfd* files, but in iOS 8 and 9, it can't. Apple suggests that you convert to an attributed string (as I described in Chapter 10; specify a document type of NSRTFDTextDocumentType), or use a QLPreview-Controller (Chapter 23).

Web view content is loaded *asynchronously* (gradually, in a thread of its own), and it might not be loaded at all (because the user might not be connected to the Internet, the server might not respond properly, and so on). If you're loading a resource directly from disk, loading is quick and nothing is going to go wrong; nevertheless, rendering the content can take time, and even a resource loaded from disk, or content formed directly as an HTML string, might refer to material out on the Internet that takes time to fetch.

Your app's interface, however, is not blocked or frozen while the content is loading. On the contrary, it remains accessible and operative; that's what "asynchronous" means. The web view, in fetching a web page and its linked components, is doing something quite complex, involving both threading and network interaction — I'll have a lot more to say about this in Chapters 24 and 25 — but it shields you from this complexity. Your own interaction with the web view stays on the main thread and is straightforward. You ask the web view to load some content; then you sit back and let it worry about the details.

 iOS 9 introduces App Transport Security. Your app, by default, cannot load external URLs that are not secure (https:). You can turn off this restriction completely or in part in your *Info.plist*. See Chapter 24 for details.

In iOS 9, there are actually *three* web view objects:

UIWebView

UIWebView, a UIView subclass, has been around since the earliest days of iOS. Apple would like you to move away from use of UIWebView, though as far as I can tell it has not yet been formally deprecated as of this writing.

WKWebView

WKWebView, a UIView subclass, appeared in iOS 8. The "WK" stands for WebKit; confusingly, both WKWebView and UIWebView use WebKit as their rendering engine, but WebKit is also the name of a framework that was introduced in iOS 8 as well. The arrival of the WebKit framework allows WKWebKit to perform some cool tricks that UIWebKit can't do.

SFSafariViewController

SFSafariViewController, a UIViewController subclass, is new in iOS 9, as part of the Safari Services framework, which is also new. It is a full-fledged browser, in effect identical to introducing Mobile Safari into your app, except that the initially loaded page is up to you, and the user cannot navigate to an arbitrary URL. It is, in effect, a form of Safari itself, running as a separate process within your app; in addition to built-in interface such as Forward and Back buttons and the Share button, it provides Safari features such as autofill and Reader, and shares its cookies with the real Safari app.

In this edition, I'll describe WKWebView and SFSafariViewController. For a discussion of UIWebView, consult an earlier edition of this book.

It is possible to design an entire app that is effectively nothing but a web view — especially if you have control of the server with which the user is interacting. Indeed, before the advent of iOS, an iPhone app *was* a web application. There are still iOS apps that work this way, including some Apple apps; but such an approach to app design is outside the scope of this book.

WKWebView

WKWebView is part of the WebKit framework; to use it, you'll need to `import Web‐ Kit` and create the web view in code. The designated initializer for WKWebView is `init(frame:configuration:)`, where the `configuration:` is a WKWebView‐Configuration. You can create a configuration beforehand:

```
let config = WKWebViewConfiguration()
// ... configure config here ...
let wv = WKWebView(frame: CGRectZero, configuration:config)
```

Alternatively, you can initialize your web view with `init(frame:)` to get a default configuration and modify it through the web view's `configuration` property later:

```
let wv = WKWebView(frame: CGRectZero)
// ... configure wv.configuration here ...
```

Either way, you'll probably want to perform configurations before the web view has a chance to load any content, because some settings will affect *how* it loads or renders that content.

Here are some of the more important WKWebViewConfiguration properties:

`suppressesIncrementalRendering`
> If `true`, the web view's visible content doesn't change until all linked renderable resources (such as images) have finished loading. The default is `false`.

`allowsInlineMediaPlayback`
> If `true`, linked media are played inside the web page. The default is `false` (the fullscreen player is used).

`requiresUserActionForMediaPlayback`
> If `false`, linked media are played automatically. The default is `true`.

`websiteDataStore`
> A WKWebsiteDataStore (new in iOS 9). By supplying a data store, you get control over stored resources. You can thus implement private browsing, examine and delete cookies, and so forth. For the types of data stored here, see the documentation on WKWebsiteDataRecord.

preferences

A WKPreferences object. This is a value class embodying three properties:

- `minimumFontSize`
- `javaScriptEnabled`
- `javaScriptCanOpenWindowsAutomatically`

`userContentController`

A WKUserContentController object. This is how you can inject JavaScript into a web page and communicate between your code and the web page's content. I'll give an example later.

Having created your web view, you'll place it in your interface and, if necessary, size and position it:

```
self.view.addSubview(wv)
wv.translatesAutoresizingMaskIntoConstraints = false
NSLayoutConstraint.activateConstraints([
    NSLayoutConstraint.constraintsWithVisualFormat(
        "H:|[wv]|", options: [], metrics: nil, views: ["wv":wv]),
    NSLayoutConstraint.constraintsWithVisualFormat(
        "V:|[wv]|", options: [], metrics: nil, views: ["wv":wv])
].flatten().map{$0})
```

A WKWebView is not a scroll view, but it *has* a scroll view (`scrollView`). You can use this to scroll the web view's content programatically; you can also get references to its gesture recognizers, and add gesture recognizers of your own (see Chapter 7).

WKWebView Content

You can supply a web view with content in one of four forms:

An NSURLRequest

Formed with an NSURL, using `init(URL:)`. Optionally, you can add a cache policy and a timeout interval, using `init(URL:cachePolicy:timeoutInterval:)`. For additional configuration, start with an NSMutableURLRequest; now you can set such properties as `allowsCellularAccess`. When ready, call `loadRequest:`. For example:

```
let url = NSURL(string: "http://www.apple.com")!
self.wv.loadRequest(NSURLRequest(URL:url))
```

A local file

Obtain a local file URL and call `loadFileURL:allowingReadAccessToURL:` (new in iOS 9). The second parameter effectively sandboxes the web view into a single file or directory. For example:

```
let path = NSBundle.mainBundle().pathForResource(
    "zotzhelp", ofType: "html")!
let url = NSURL.fileURLWithPath(path)
self.wv.loadFileURL(url, allowingReadAccessToURL: url)
```

An HTML string

> Prepare a string consisting of valid HTML, and call `loadHTMLString:baseURL:`.
> The `baseURL:` specifies how partial URLs in your HTML are to be resolved; for
> example, the HTML might refer to resources within your app bundle.

A NSData object

> Call `loadData:MIMEType:characterEncodingName:baseURL:` (new in iOS 9).

Starting with an HTML string is useful particularly when you want to construct your
HTML programmatically or make changes to it before handing it to the web view. In
this example, I have a template file in my app bundle containing placeholders to be filled
in depending on the circumstances at runtime:

```
let templatepath = NSBundle.mainBundle().pathForResource(
    "htmlTemplate", ofType:"txt")!
let base = NSURL.fileURLWithPath(templatepath)
var s = try! String(
    contentsOfFile:templatepath, encoding:NSUTF8StringEncoding)
let ss = // actual body content for this page
s = s.stringByReplacingOccurrencesOfString("<content>", withString:ss)
// ... additional modifications go here ...
self.wv.loadHTMLString(s, baseURL:base)
```

All four methods return a WKNavigation object, though I'm not capturing it in any of
these examples; it's an opaque object that can be used to identify a single page-loading
operation.

Tracking Changes in a WKWebView

A WKWebView has properties that can be tracked with key–value observing, such as:

- `loading`
- `estimatedProgress`
- `URL`
- `title`

You can observe these properties to be notified as a web page loads or changes. For
example, as preparation to give the user feedback while a page is loading, I'll put an
activity indicator (Chapter 12) in the center of my web view, keep a reference to it, and
observe the web view's `loading` property:

```
let act = UIActivityIndicatorView(activityIndicatorStyle:.WhiteLarge)
act.backgroundColor = UIColor(white:0.1, alpha:0.5)
self.activity = act
wv.addSubview(act)
act.translatesAutoresizingMaskIntoConstraints = false
NSLayoutConstraint.activateConstraints([
    act.centerXAnchor.constraintEqualToAnchor(wv.centerXAnchor),
    act.centerYAnchor.constraintEqualToAnchor(wv.centerYAnchor)
])
wv.addObserver(self, forKeyPath: "loading", options: .New, context: nil)
```

When the web view starts loading or stops loading, I'm notified, so I can show or hide the activity view:

```
override func observeValueForKeyPath(keyPath: String?,
    ofObject object: AnyObject?, change: [String : AnyObject]?,
    context: UnsafeMutablePointer<()>) {
        guard let wv = object as? WKWebView else {return}
        guard let keyPath = keyPath else {return}
        guard let change = change else {return}
        switch keyPath {
        case "loading":
            if let val = change[NSKeyValueChangeNewKey] as? Bool {
                if val {
                    self.activity.startAnimating()
                } else {
                    self.activity.stopAnimating()
                }
            }
        default:break
        }
}
```

Do not forget to remove yourself as an observer as you go out of existence. If, as is usually the case, this means also that the web view itself is going out of existence, I like to stop any loading that it may be doing at that moment as well:

```
deinit {
    self.wv.removeObserver(self, forKeyPath: "loading")
    self.wv.stopLoading()
}
```

WKWebView Navigation

A WKWebView maintains a back and forward list of the URLs to which the user has navigated. The list is its backForwardList, a WKBackForwardList, which is a collection of read-only properties (and one method) such as:

- currentItem
- backItem

- `forwardItem`

- `itemAtIndex:`

Each item in the list is a WKBackForwardItem, a simple value class basically consisting of a URL and a `title`.

The WKWebView itself responds to `goBack`, `goForward` and `goToBackForwardList-Item:`, so you can tell it in code to navigate the list. Its properties `canGoBack` and `canGoForward` are key–value observable; typically you would use that fact to enable or disable a Back and Forward button in your interface in response to the list changing.

A WKWebView also has one settable property, `allowsBackForwardNavigation-Gestures`. The default is `false`; if `true`, the user can swipe sideways to go back and forward in the list.

To prevent or reroute navigation that the user tries to perform by tapping links, set yourself as the WKWebView's `navigationDelegate` (WKNavigationDelegate) and implement `webView:decidePolicyForNavigationAction:decisionHandler:`. You are handed a `decisionHandler` function which you must call, handing it a WKNavigationActionPolicy — either `.Cancel` or `.Allow`. You can examine the incoming `navigationAction` (a WKNavigationAction) to help make your decision. It has a `request` which is the NSURLRequest we are proposing to perform — and you can look at its URL to see where we are proposing to go — along with a `navigationType` which will be one of the following (WKNavigationType):

- `.LinkActivated`

- `.BackForward`

- `.Reload`

- `.FormSubmitted`

- `.FormResubmitted`

- `.Other`

In this example, I permit navigation in the most general case — otherwise nothing would ever appear in my web view! — but if the user taps a link, I forbid it and show that URL in Mobile Safari instead:

```
func webView(webView: WKWebView,
    decidePolicyForNavigationAction navigationAction: WKNavigationAction,
    decisionHandler: ((WKNavigationActionPolicy) -> Void)) {
        if navigationAction.navigationType == .LinkActivated {
            if let url = navigationAction.request.URL {
                UIApplication.sharedApplication().openURL(url)
                decisionHandler(.Cancel)
                return
```

```
            }
        }
        decisionHandler(.Allow)
    }
```

In iOS 9, you needn't be as reluctant as you might have been previously to navigate the user away from your app to display web content in Safari, because the status bar displays a Back button making it easy for the user to return to your app. Moreover, iOS 9 offers a further alternative: you can present an SFSafariViewController within your own app, as I'll explain later in this chapter.

Several other WKNavigationDelegate methods can notify you as a page loads (or fails to load). Under normal circumstances, you'll receive them in this order:

- `webView:didStartProvisionalNavigation:`

- `webView:didCommitNavigation:`

- `webView:didFinishNavigation:`

Those delegate methods, and all navigation commands, like the four ways of loading your web view with initial content, supply a WKNavigation object. This object is completely opaque and has no properties, but you can use it in an equality comparison to determine whether the navigations referred to in different methods are the same navigation (roughly speaking, the same page-loading operation).

Communicating With a WKWebView Web Page

Your code can pass messages into and out of a WKWebView's web page, thus allowing you to change the page's contents or respond to changes within it, even while it is being displayed.

To send a message into an already loaded WKWebView web page, call `evaluateJava-Script:completionHandler:`. Your JavaScript runs within the context of the web page.

In this example, the user is able to decrease the size of the text in the web page. We have prepared some JavaScript that generates a `<style>` element containing CSS that sets the `font-size` for the page's `<body>` in accordance with a property, `self.fontsize`:

```
var fontsize = 18
var cssrule : String {
    var s = "var s = document.createElement('style');\n"
    s += "s.textContent = '"
    s += "body { font-size: \(self.fontsize)px; }"
    s += "';\n"
    s += "document.documentElement.appendChild(s);\n"
    return s
}
```

When the user taps a button, we decrement `self.fontsize`, construct that JavaScript, and send it to the web page:

```
func doDecreaseSize (sender:AnyObject) {
    self.fontsize -= 1
    if self.fontsize < 10 {
        self.fontsize = 20
    }
    let s = self.cssrule
    self.wv.evaluateJavaScript(s, completionHandler: nil)
}
```

That's clever, but we have not done anything about setting the web page's *initial* `font-size`. A WKWebView allows us to inject JavaScript into the web page at the time it is loaded. To do so, we use the `userContentController` of the WKWebView's `configuration`. We create a WKUserScript, specifying the JavaScript it contains, along with an `injectionTime` which can be either before (`.DocumentStart`) or after (`.DocumentEnd`) a page's content has loaded. In this case, we want it to be before; otherwise, the user will see the font size change suddenly:

```
let s = self.cssrule
let script = WKUserScript(
    source: s, injectionTime: .AtDocumentStart, forMainFrameOnly: true)
self.wv.configuration.userContentController.addUserScript(script)
```

To communicate out of a web page, you need first to install a message handler to receive the communication. Again, this involves the `userContentController`. You call `add-ScriptMessageHandler:name:`, where the first argument is an object that must implement the WKScriptMessageHandler protocol, so that its `userContentController:did-ReceiveScriptMessage:` method can be called later:

```
self.wv.configuration.userContentController.addScriptMessageHandler(
    self, name: "playbutton")
```

We have now installed a `playbutton` message handler. This means that the DOM for our web page now contains an element, among its `window.webkit.messageHandlers`, called `playbutton`. A message handler sends its message when it receives a `post-Message()` function call. Thus, to sum up, the WKScriptMessageHandler (`self` in this example) will get a call to its `userContentController:didReceiveScriptMessage:` method if JavaScript inside the web page sends `postMessage()` to the `window.webkit.messageHandlers.playbutton` object.

To make that actually happen, I've put an `<img>` tag into my web page's HTML, specifying an image that will act as a tappable button:

```
<img src=\"listen.png\"
onclick=\"window.webkit.messageHandlers.playbutton.postMessage('play')\">
```

When the user taps that image, the message is posted, and so my code runs and I can respond:

```
func userContentController(
    userContentController: WKUserContentController,
    didReceiveScriptMessage message: WKScriptMessage) {
        if message.name == "playbutton" {
            if let body = message.body as? String {
                if body == "play" {
                    // ... do stuff here! ...
                }
            }
        }
}
```

There's just one little problem: that code causes a retain cycle. The reason is that a WKUserContentController leaks, and it retains the WKScriptMessageHandler, which in this case is self — and so self will never be deallocated. My solution is to create an intermediate trampoline object that can be harmlessly retained, and that has a weak reference to self:

```
class MyMessageHandler : NSObject, WKScriptMessageHandler {
    weak var delegate : WKScriptMessageHandler?
    init(delegate:WKScriptMessageHandler) {
        self.delegate = delegate
        super.init()
    }
    func userContentController(
        userContentController: WKUserContentController,
        didReceiveScriptMessage message: WKScriptMessage) {
            delegate?.userContentController(
                userContentController, didReceiveScriptMessage: message)
    }
}
```

Now when I add myself as a script message handler, I do it by way of the trampoline object:

```
self.wv.configuration.userContentController.addScriptMessageHandler(
    MyMessageHandler(delegate:self), name: "playbutton")
```

The trampoline object leaks, but it's an extremely lightweight object so it doesn't matter much. However, I can do even better; now that I've broken the retain cycle, my own deinit is called, and I can release the offending objects:

```
deinit {
    self.wv.removeObserver(self, forKeyPath: "loading")
    self.wv.stopLoading()
    // break all retains
    self.wv.configuration.userContentController
```

```
        .removeAllUserScripts()
    self.wv.configuration.userContentController
        .removeScriptMessageHandlerForName("playbutton")
}
```

WKWebView Shortcomings

A WKWebView can't be instantiated from a nib. The Web View object in the nib editor's Object library is a UIWebView, not a WKWebView.

In iOS 8, a URL pointing to a resource on disk — including inside your app's bundle — will fail to load with a WKWebView. This makes WKWebView unsuitable, say, for presentation of internal help documentation in iOS 8. The problem is fixed in iOS 9, but the fix isn't backward-compatible, so if your app runs on iOS 8 you might have to continue using UIWebView.

WKWebView, as far as I can tell, does not automatically participate in any way in the iOS view controller state saving and restoration mechanism. This is a *major* flaw in WKWebView. With UIWebView, if it has an actual URL request as the source of its content at the time the user leaves the app, then that URL request is archived by the state saving mechanism, along with the UIWebView's Back and Forward lists and the content offset of its scroll view. If state restoration takes place, the UIWebView's request property, and its Back and Forward lists, and its scroll view's content offset, including the offsets of all previously viewed pages, are restored automatically; all you have to do is load the restored request, which you can easily do in applicationFinishedRestoring-State, like this:

```
override func applicationFinishedRestoringState() {
    if self.wv.request != nil { // self.wv is a UIWebView
        self.wv.reload()
    }
}
```

But you can't do anything like that with a WKWebView. It has no request property. It has a URL property, but that property is not saved and restored. Moreover, a WKWebView's backForwardList is not writable. Thus, there is no way to save and restore a WKWebView's state as a web browser. This could be a reason for staying with UIWebView for now.

If you are using a WKWebView purely for display of internally provided material, such as an HTML string, then you can manually save and restore how it is scrolled. In encode-RestorableStateWithCoder:, we save the current scroll state; we can't archive a CGPoint, so we wrap it in an NSValue:

```
override func encodeRestorableStateWithCoder(coder: NSCoder) {
    super.encodeRestorableStateWithCoder(coder)
    let off = self.wv.scrollView.contentOffset
    coder.encodeObject(NSValue(CGPoint:off), forKey:"oldOffset")
}
```

In decodeRestorableStateWithCoder:, we unarchive the saved NSValue and store it in a property, self.oldOffset, which is an Optional wrapping an NSValue:

```
override func decodeRestorableStateWithCoder(coder: NSCoder) {
    super.decodeRestorableStateWithCoder(coder)
    if let oldOffset = coder.decodeObjectForKey("oldOffset") as? NSValue {
        self.oldOffset = oldOffset
    }
}
```

Observe that I have not yet set the contentOffset of the web view's scrollView. That's because we don't yet have any content! Subsequently, we load the content manually; when the content has loaded, we hear about it through key–value observing in our observeValueForKeyPath:..., and now (with a delay) we can set the web view's scroll offset:

```
if self.oldOffset != nil {
    if wv.estimatedProgress == 1 {
        delay(0.1) {
            wv.scrollView.contentOffset = self.oldOffset!.CGPointValue()
            self.oldOffset = nil
        }
    }
}
```

Safari View Controller

A Safari view controller (SFSafariViewController, new in iOS 9) puts the Mobile Safari interface in a separate process inside your app. It provides the user with a browser interface familiar from Mobile Safari itself. In a toolbar, which can be shown or hidden by scrolling, there are Back and Forward buttons, a Share button including standard Safari features such as Add Bookmark and Add to Reading List, and a Safari button that lets the user load the same page in the *real* Safari app. In a navigation bar, which can be shrunk or grown by scrolling, are a read-only URL field with a Reader button (if this page has a Reader mode available) and a Refresh button, and a Done button. The user has access to autofill and to Safari cookies with no intervention by your app.

The idea, according to Apple, is that when you want to present internal HTML content, such as an HTML string, you'll use a WKWebView, but when you really want to allow the user to access the web, you'll use a Safari view controller. In this way, you are saved from the trouble of trying to build a full-fledged web browser yourself.

To use a Safari view controller, you'll need to `import SafariServices`. Create the SFSafariViewController, initialize it with a URL, and present it:

```
let svc = SFSafariViewController(URL: url)
self.presentViewController(svc, animated: true, completion: nil)
```

If you use the initializer `init(URL:entersReaderIfAvailable:)`, then if the initially loaded URL page has a Reader mode available, the Safari view controller will switch to Reader mode automatically.

When the user taps the Done button, the Safari view controller is dismissed.

If you like, you can make yourself the Safari view controller's delegate (SFSafariViewControllerDelegate) and implement any of these methods:

`safariViewController:didCompleteInitialLoad:`
`safariViewControllerDidFinish:`
> Called on presentation and dismissal of the Safari view controller, respectively.

`safariViewController:activityItemsForURL:title:`
> Allows you to supply your own Share button items; I'll explain what activity items are in Chapter 13.

 I have not found any way in which a Safari view controller participates in view controller state saving and restoration. Needless to say, I regard this as a bug.

Developing Web View Content

Before designing the HTML to be displayed in a web view, you might want to read up on the brand of HTML native to the mobile WebKit rendering engine. There are certain limitations; for example, mobile WebKit notoriously doesn't use plug-ins, such as Flash, and it imposes limits on the size of resources (such as images) that it can display. On the plus side, WebKit is in the forefront of the march toward HTML 5 and CSS 3, and has many special capabilities suited for display on a mobile device. For documentation and other resources, see Apple's Safari Dev Center.

A good place to start is the *Safari Web Content Guide*. It contains links to other relevant documentation, such as the *Safari CSS Visual Effects Guide*, which describes some things you can do with WebKit's implementation of CSS3 (like animations), and the *Safari HTML5 Audio and Video Guide*, which describes WebKit's audio and video player support.

If nothing else, you'll want to be aware of one important aspect of web page content — the *viewport*. This is typically set through a `<meta>` tag in the `<head>` area. For example:

```
<meta name="viewport" content="initial-scale=1.0, user-scalable=no">
```

Figure 11-1. The Web Inspector inspects an app running in the Simulator

Without that line, or something similar, a web page may be laid out incorrectly when it is rendered. Without a viewport, your content may appear tiny (because it is being rendered as if the screen were large), or it may be too wide for the view, forcing the user to scroll horizontally to read it. See the *Safari Web Content Guide* for details.

Another important section of the *Safari Web Content Guide* describes how you can use a `media` attribute in the `<link>` tag that loads your CSS to load *different* CSS depending on what kind of device your app is running on. For example, you might have one CSS file that lays out your web view's content on an iPhone, and another that lays it out on an iPad.

Inspecting, debugging, and experimenting with web view content is greatly eased by the Web Inspector, built into Safari on the desktop. It can see a web view in your app running in the Simulator, and lets you analyze every aspect of how it works. For example, in Figure 11-1, I'm examining an image to understand how it is sized and scaled.

You can hover the mouse over a web page element in the Web Inspector to highlight the rendering of that element in the running app. Moreover, the Web Inspector lets you change your web view's content in real time, with many helpful features such as CSS autocompletion.

JavaScript and the document object model (*DOM*) are also extremely powerful. Event listeners allow JavaScript code to respond directly to touch and gesture events, so that the user can interact with elements of a web page much as if they were iOS-native touchable views; it can also take advantage of Core Location and Core Motion facilities to respond to where the user is on earth and how the device is positioned (Chapter 22). Additional helpful documentation includes Apple's *WebKit DOM Programming Topics* and *Safari DOM Additions Reference*.

 Be sure also to peruse Apple's Safari release notes, *What's New in Safari*; these release notes often inform you of CSS and JavaScript details that are documented nowhere else. For example, this is the only place you would learn about the `-apple-system` font family, which lets your CSS specify a font that matches the iOS system font.

CHAPTER 12

Controls and Other Views

This chapter discusses all UIView subclasses provided by UIKit that haven't been discussed already. It's remarkable how few of them there are; UIKit exhibits a notable economy of means in this regard.

Additional UIView subclasses, as well as UIViewController subclasses that create interface, are provided by other frameworks. There will be examples in Part III. For example, the Map Kit framework provides the MKMapView (Chapter 21), which displays an interactive map; and the MessageUI framework provides MFMailComposeViewController, which supplies an interface for composing and sending a mail message (Chapter 20).

UIActivityIndicatorView

An activity indicator (UIActivityIndicatorView) appears as the spokes of a small wheel. You set the spokes spinning with `startAnimating`, giving the user a sense that some time-consuming process is taking place. You stop the spinning with `stopAnimating`. If the activity indicator's `hidesWhenStopped` is `true` (the default), it is visible only while spinning.

An activity indicator comes in a style, its `activityIndicatorViewStyle`; if it is created in code, you'll set its style with `init(activityIndicatorStyle:)`. Your choices (UIActivityIndicatorViewStyle) are:

- `.WhiteLarge`
- `.White`
- `.Gray`

Figure 12-1. A large activity indicator

An activity indicator has a standard size, which depends on its style. Changing its size in code changes the size of the view, but not the size of the spokes. For bigger spokes, you can resort to a scale transform.

You can assign an activity indicator a `color`; this overrides the color assigned through the style. An activity indicator is a UIView, so you can set its `backgroundColor`; a nice effect is to give an activity indicator a contrasting background color and to round its corners by way of the view's layer (Figure 12-1).

Here's some code from a UITableViewCell subclass in one of my apps. In this app, it takes some time, after the user taps a cell to select it, for me to construct the next view and navigate to it; to cover the delay, I show a spinning activity indicator in the center of the cell while it's selected:

```
override func setSelected(selected: Bool, animated: Bool) {
    if selected {
        let v = UIActivityIndicatorView(activityIndicatorStyle: .WhiteLarge)
        v.color = UIColor.yellowColor()
        dispatch_async(dispatch_get_main_queue()) {
            v.backgroundColor = UIColor(white:0.2, alpha:0.6)
        }
        v.layer.cornerRadius = 10
        v.frame = v.frame.insetBy(dx: -10, dy: -10)
        let cf = self.contentView.convertRect(self.bounds, fromView:self)
        v.center = CGPointMake(cf.midX, cf.midY)
        v.tag = 1001
        self.contentView.addSubview(v)
        v.startAnimating()
    } else {
        if let v = self.viewWithTag(1001) {
            v.removeFromSuperview()
        }
    }
    super.setSelected(selected, animated: animated)
}
```

If activity involves the network, you might want to set UIApplication's `networkActivity-IndicatorVisible` to `true`. This displays a small spinning activity indicator in the status bar. The indicator is not reflecting actual network activity; if it's visible, it's spinning. Be sure to set it back to `false` when the activity is over.

Figure 12-2. A custom activity indicator

An activity indicator is simple and standard, but you can't change the way it's drawn. One obvious alternative would be a UIImageView with an animated image, as described in Chapter 4. Another solution is a CAReplicatorLayer, a layer that makes multiple copies of its sublayer; by animating the sublayer, you animate the copies. This is a very common approach (in fact, it wouldn't surprise me to hear that UIActivityIndicatorView is implemented using CAReplicatorLayer). For example:

```
let lay = CAReplicatorLayer()
lay.frame = CGRectMake(0,0,100,20)
let bar = CALayer()
bar.frame = CGRectMake(0,0,10,20)
bar.backgroundColor = UIColor.redColor().CGColor
lay.addSublayer(bar)
lay.instanceCount = 5
lay.instanceTransform = CATransform3DMakeTranslation(20, 0, 0)
let anim = CABasicAnimation(keyPath: "opacity")
anim.fromValue = 1.0
anim.toValue = 0.2
anim.duration = 1
anim.repeatCount = Float.infinity
bar.addAnimation(anim, forKey: nil)
lay.instanceDelay = anim.duration / Double(lay.instanceCount)
self.view.layer.addSublayer(lay)
lay.position = CGPointMake(
    self.view.layer.bounds.midX, self.view.layer.bounds.midY)
```

Our single red vertical bar (bar) is replicated to make five red vertical bars. We repeatedly fade the opacity of the bar to 0, but because we've set the replicator layer's instance-Delay, the replicated bars fade in sequence, so that the darkest bar appears to be marching repeatedly to the right (Figure 12-2).

UIProgressView

A progress view (UIProgressView) is a "thermometer," graphically displaying a percentage. It is often used to represent a time-consuming process whose percentage of completion is known (if the percentage of completion is unknown, you're more likely to use an activity indicator). But it's good for static percentages too. In one of my apps, I use a progress view to show the current position within the song being played by the built-in music player; in another app, which is a card game, I use a progress view to show how many cards are left in the deck.

Figure 12-3. A progress view

A progress view comes in a style, its `progressViewStyle`; if the progress view is created in code, you'll set its style with `init(progressViewStyle:)`. Your choices (UIProgress-ViewStyle) are:

- `.Default`
- `.Bar`

A `.Bar` progress view is intended for use in a UIBarButtonItem, as the title view of a navigation item, and so on. Both styles by default draw the thermometer extremely thin — just 2 pixels and 3 pixels, respectively. (Figure 12-3 shows a `.Default` progress view.) Changing a progress view's frame height directly has no visible effect on how the thermometer is drawn. Under autolayout, to make a thicker thermometer, supply a height constraint with a larger value (thus overriding the intrinsic content height). Alternatively, subclass UIProgressView and override `sizeThatFits:`.

The fullness of the thermometer is the progress view's `progress` property. This is a value between 0 and 1, inclusive; you'll usually need to do some elementary arithmetic in order to convert from the actual value you're reflecting to a value within that range. (It is also a Float; in Swift, you may have to coerce explicitly.) For example, to reflect the number of cards remaining in a deck of 52 cards:

```
let r = self.deck.cards().count
self.prog.progress = Float(r) / 52
```

A change in `progress` value can be animated by calling `setProgress:animated:`.

The default color of the filled portion of a progress view is the `tintColor` (which may be inherited from higher up the view hierarchy). The default color for the unfilled portion is gray for a `.Default` progress view and transparent for a `.Bar` progress view. You can customize the colors; set the progress view's `progressTintColor` and `trackTint-Color`, respectively. This can also be done in the nib.

Alternatively, you can customize the image used to draw the filled portion of the progress view, its `progressImage`, along with the image used to draw the unfilled portion, the `trackImage`. This can also be done in the nib. Each image must be stretched to the length of the filled or unfilled area, so you'll want to use a resizable image.

Here's a simple example from one of my apps (Figure 12-4):

Figure 12-4. A thicker progress view using a custom progress image

```
self.prog.backgroundColor = UIColor.blackColor()
self.prog.trackTintColor = UIColor.blackColor()
UIGraphicsBeginImageContextWithOptions(CGSizeMake(10,10), true, 0)
let con = UIGraphicsGetCurrentContext()!
CGContextSetFillColorWithColor(con, UIColor.yellowColor().CGColor)
CGContextFillRect(con, CGRectMake(0, 0, 10, 10))
let r = CGRectInset(CGContextGetClipBoundingBox(con),1,1)
CGContextSetLineWidth(con, 2)
CGContextSetStrokeColorWithColor(con, UIColor.blackColor().CGColor)
CGContextStrokeRect(con, r)
CGContextStrokeEllipseInRect(con, r)
let im =
    UIGraphicsGetImageFromCurrentImageContext()
        .resizableImageWithCapInsets(
            UIEdgeInsetsMake(4, 4, 4, 4), resizingMode:.Stretch)
UIGraphicsEndImageContext()
self.prog.progressImage = im
```

> That code works in iOS 9, and in iOS 7.0 and before. But in between, from iOS 7.1 through all versions of iOS 8, it breaks; setting the progressImage has no effect. A possible workaround, which is extremely fragile and hacky, is to try to find the UIImageView that is intended to hold the UIProgressView's progressImage and set its image directly.

For maximum flexibility, you can design your own UIView subclass that draws something similar to a thermometer. Figure 12-5 shows a simple custom thermometer view; it has a value property, and you set this to something between 0 and 1 and call setNeeds-Display to make the view redraw itself. Here's its drawRect: code:

```
override func drawRect(rect: CGRect) {
    let c = UIGraphicsGetCurrentContext()!
    UIColor.whiteColor().set()
    let ins : CGFloat = 2.0
    let r = self.bounds.insetBy(dx: ins, dy: ins)
    let radius : CGFloat = r.size.height / 2.0
    let mpi = CGFloat(M_PI)
    let path = CGPathCreateMutable()
    CGPathMoveToPoint(path, nil, r.maxX - radius, ins)
    CGPathAddArc(path, nil,
        radius+ins, radius+ins, radius, -mpi/2.0, mpi/2.0, true)
    CGPathAddArc(path, nil,
        r.maxX - radius, radius+ins, radius, mpi/2.0, -mpi/2.0, true)
```

Figure 12-5. A custom progress view

Figure 12-6. A circular custom progress view

```
    CGPathCloseSubpath(path)
    CGContextAddPath(c, path)
    CGContextSetLineWidth(c, 2)
    CGContextStrokePath(c)
    CGContextAddPath(c, path)
    CGContextClip(c)
    CGContextFillRect(c, CGRectMake(
        r.origin.x, r.origin.y, r.size.width * self.value, r.size.height))
}
```

Your custom view doesn't have to look like a thermometer. Apple has introduced many other variants on the notion of graphically indicating progress, and you can readily adopt these. For instance, the Music app shows the current playing position within an album's song by drawing the arc of a circle (Figure 12-6). This effect is easily achieved by setting the strokeEnd of a CAShapeLayer with a circular path (and possibly a rotation transform, to start the circle at the top).

New in iOS 9, a progress view has an observedProgress property. This is an instance of NSProgress, a class that abstracts the notion of task progress: it has a totalUnit-Count property and a completedUnitCount property, and their ratio generates its fractionCompleted, which can be tracked with KVO and can thus be used to update a UIProgressView. The UIProgressView observedProgress property, however, saves you the trouble of using KVO; its fractionCompleted is *automatically* used to update this progress view.

The power of NSProgress comes from two features:

Unification

> Often, an operation's progress is distributed over multiple methods. A network download is an obvious case in point: the expected size, the accumulated data, and the fact of completion are reported in three different delegate methods. A single

NSProgress object, visible to all these methods, provides a unified locus where each method can play its part in updating the progress information.

Composability

An NSProgress object can have child NSProgress objects. The progress of an operation reported to a child NSProgress automatically forms an appropriate fraction of the progress reported by the parent. Thus, a single NSProgress, acting as the ultimate parent, can conglomerate the progress of numerous individual operations.

In general, there are three ways in which you might configure a UIProgressView's `observedProgress`:

- Set the UIProgressView's `observedProgress` *directly* to an NSProgress object created, vended, and updated by some other object that performs the operation. This has the advantage of simplicity, but we now have two objects with strong references to the same NSProgress object.

- Set the UIProgressView's `observedProgress` to a new NSProgress object. Also, configure some other object that performs the operation and also has an NSProgress object. Now set up an *explicit* parent–child relationship between the two NSProgress objects. You can do this from the point of view of the parent by calling `add-Child:withPendingUnitCount:`, or from the point of view of the child by creating it with `init(totalUnitCount:parent:pendingUnitCount:)`.

- Set the UIProgressView's `observedProgress` to a new NSProgress object. Now create and configure some other object that performs the operation and also has an NSProgress object, which it initializes in such a way that it becomes the child *implicitly*. To do so:

  1. Tell the prospective parent NSProgress to `becomeCurrentWithPendingUnit-Count:`. The notion "current" means that this NSProgress is waiting to accept another NSProgress as its child.

  2. Create the operation object, which initializes its NSProgress with `init(total-UnitCount:)`. As if by magic, this NSProgress becomes the other NSProgress's child (because the other NSProgress is "current").

  3. Tell the parent to `resignCurrent`. This balances the earlier `becomeCurrentWith-PendingUnitCount:` and brings the configuration to an end.

Here's a simple illustration of the third approach. I have a ProgressingOperation class that performs an operation that can be divided into stages:

```
class ProgressingOperation {
    let progress : NSProgress
    init(units:Int) {
        self.progress = NSProgress(totalUnitCount: Int64(units))
```

```
    }
    func start() {
        // ... whatever ...
    }
}
```

In the view controller that manages the UIProgressView (self.prog), I also have a property (self.op) that is an Optional wrapping a ProgressingOperation. I begin the operation by configuring the progress view and the operation object, like this:

```
self.prog.progress = 0
self.prog.observedProgress =
    NSProgress.discreteProgressWithTotalUnitCount(10)
self.prog.observedProgress?.becomeCurrentWithPendingUnitCount(10)
self.op = ProgressingOperation(units:10)
self.prog.observedProgress?.resignCurrent()
self.op!.start()
```

The ProgressingOperation's `progress` is now the child of the UIProgressView's `observedProgress`, and the view controller that configured everything takes its hands off: the rest will happen *automatically*. The ProgressingOperation object begins its operation. At each stage, it increments its own `self.progress.completedUnitCount`. This change percolates up to the parent NSProgress belonging to our UIProgressView, which increases its own `progress` to match, moving the visible thermometer.

UIPickerView

A picker view (UIPickerView) displays selectable choices using a rotating drum metaphor. New in iOS 9, its default height is adaptive: the default height is 162 in an environment with a `.Compact` vertical size class (an iPhone in landscape orientation) and 216 otherwise. Also new in iOS 9, you are free to set the height; in earlier systems, there were restrictions that would thwart your attempts to set a picker view's height outside an undocumented range, but these have now been removed. A picker view's width is generally up to you.

Each drum, or column, is called a *component*. Your code configures the UIPickerView's content through its data source (UIPickerViewDataSource) and delegate (UIPicker-ViewDelegate), which are usually the same object. Your data source and delegate must answer questions similar to those posed by a UITableView (Chapter 8):

numberOfComponentsInPickerView: *(data source)*
> How many components (drums) does this picker view have?

pickerView:numberOfRowsInComponent: *(data source)*
> How many rows does this component have? The first component is numbered 0.

```
pickerView:titleForRow:forComponent:
pickerView:attributedTitleForRow:forComponent:
pickerView:viewForRow:forComponent:reusingView: (delegate)
```
What should this row of this component display? The first row is numbered 0. You can supply a simple string, an attributed string (Chapter 10), or an entire view such as a UILabel; but you should supply every row of every component the same way.

 The reusingView: parameter, if not nil, is supposed to be a view that you supplied for a row now no longer visible, giving you a chance to reuse it, much as cells are reused in a table view. In actual fact, the reusingView: parameter is *always* nil; views are not reused. They don't leak — they go out of existence in good order when they are no longer visible — but they aren't reused. I regard this as a bug.

Here's the code for a UIPickerView (Figure 12-7) that displays the names of the 50 U.S. states, stored in an array. We implement pickerView:viewForRow:for-Component:reusingView: just because it's the most interesting case; as our views, we supply UILabel instances. The state names appear centered because the labels are centered within the picker view:

```
func numberOfComponentsInPickerView(pickerView: UIPickerView) -> Int {
    return 1
}
func pickerView(pickerView: UIPickerView,
    numberOfRowsInComponent component: Int) -> Int {
        return 50
}
func pickerView(pickerView: UIPickerView, viewForRow row: Int,
    forComponent component: Int, reusingView view: UIView?) -> UIView {
        let lab : UILabel
        if let label = view as? UILabel { // never happens
            lab = label
        } else {
            lab = UILabel()
        }
        lab.text = self.states[row]
        lab.backgroundColor = UIColor.clearColor()
        lab.sizeToFit()
        return lab
}
```

The delegate may further configure the UIPickerView's physical appearance by means of these methods:

- pickerView:rowHeightForComponent:

- pickerView:widthForComponent:

Figure 12-7. A picker view

The delegate may implement `pickerView:didSelectRow:inComponent:` to be notified each time the user spins a drum to a new position. You can also query the picker view directly by sending it `selectedRowInComponent:`.

You can set the value to which any drum is turned using `selectRow:in-Component:animated:`. Other handy picker view methods allow you to request that the data be reloaded, and there are properties and methods to query the picker view's structure:

- `reloadComponent:`
- `reloadAllComponents`
- `numberOfComponents`
- `numberOfRowsInComponent:`
- `viewForRow:forComponent:`

By implementing `pickerView:didSelectRow:inComponent:` and calling `reload-Component:`, you can make a picker view where the values displayed by one drum depend dynamically on what is selected in another. For example, one can imagine expanding our U.S. states example to include a second drum listing major cities in each state; when the user switches to a different state in the first drum, a different set of major cities appears in the second drum.

UISearchBar

A search bar (UISearchBar) is essentially a wrapper for a text field; it has a text field as one of its subviews, though there is no official access to it. It is displayed by default as a rounded rectangle containing a magnifying glass icon, where the user can enter text (Figure 12-8). It does not, of itself, do any searching or display the results of a search; a common interface involves displaying the results of a search as a table, and the UISearchController class makes this easy to do (see Chapter 8).

Figure 12-8. A search bar with a search results button

A search bar's current text is its `text` property. It can have a `placeholder`, which appears when there is no text. A `prompt` can be displayed above the search bar to explain its purpose. Delegate methods (UISearchBarDelegate) notify you of editing events; for their use, compare the text field and text view delegate methods discussed in Chapter 10:

- `searchBarShouldBeginEditing:`
- `searchBarTextDidBeginEditing:`
- `searchBar:textDidChange:`
- `searchBar:shouldChangeTextInRange:replacementText:`
- `searchBarShouldEndEditing:`
- `searchBarTextDidEndEditing:`

A search bar has a `barStyle`, for which your choices and their default appearances are (UIBarStyle):

- `.Default`, a flat light gray background and a white search field
- `.Black`, a black background and a black search field

In addition, there's a `searchBarStyle` property (UISearchBarStyle):

- `.Default`, as already described
- `.Prominent`, identical to `.Default`
- `.Minimal`, transparent background and dark transparent search field

Alternatively, you can set a search bar's `barTintColor` to change its background color; if the bar style is `.Black`, the `barTintColor` will also tint the search field itself. An opaque `barTintColor` is a way to make a search bar opaque. The `tintColor` property, meanwhile, whose value may be inherited from higher up the view hierarchy, governs the color of search bar components such as the Cancel button title and the flashing insertion cursor.

A search bar can also have a custom `backgroundImage`; this will be treated as a resizable image. The full setter method is `setBackgroundImage:forBarPosition:bar-Metrics:`; I'll talk later about what bar position and bar metrics are. The background-

Image overrides all other ways of determining the background, and the search bar's backgroundColor, if any, appears behind it — though under some circumstances, if the search bar's translucent is false, the barTintColor may appear behind it instead.

The search field area where the user enters text can be offset with respect to its background, using the searchFieldBackgroundPositionAdjustment property; you might do this, for example, if you had enlarged the search bar's height and wanted to position the search field within that height. The text can be offset within the search field with the searchTextPositionAdjustment property.

You can also replace the image of the search field itself; this is the image that is normally a rounded rectangle. To do so, call setSearchFieldBackgroundImage:forState:. According to the documentation, the possible state: values are .Normal and .Disabled; but the API provides no way to disable a search field, so what does Apple have in mind here? The only way I've found is to cycle through the search bar's subviews, find the text field, and disable that:

```
for v in self.sb.subviews[0].subviews {
    if let tf = v as? UITextField {
        tf.enabled = false
        break
    }
}
```

The search field image will be drawn vertically centered in front of the background and behind the contents of the search field (such as the text); its width will be adjusted for you, but it is up to you choose an appropriate height, and to ensure an appropriate background color so the user can read the text.

A search bar displays an internal cancel button automatically (normally an X in a circle) if there is text in the search field. Internally, at its right end, a search bar may display a search results button (showsSearchResultsButton), which may be selected or not (searchResultsButtonSelected), or a bookmark button (showsBookmarkButton); if you ask to display both, you'll get the search results button. These buttons vanish if text is entered in the search bar so that the cancel button can be displayed. There is also an option to display a Cancel button externally (showsCancelButton, or call setShows-CancelButton:animated:). The internal cancel button works automatically to remove whatever text is in the field; the other buttons do nothing, but delegate methods notify you when they are tapped:

- searchBarResultsListButtonClicked:
- searchBarBookmarkButtonClicked:
- searchBarCancelButtonClicked:

You can customize the images used for the search icon (a magnifying glass, by default) and any of the internal right icons (the internal cancel button, the search results button, and the bookmark button) with setImage:forSearchBarIcon:state:. The images will be resized for you, except for the internal cancel button, for which about 20×20 seems to be a good size. The icons are specified with constants (UISearchBarIcon):

- .Search
- .Clear (the internal cancel button)
- .Bookmark
- .ResultsList

The documentation says that the possible state: values are .Normal and .Disabled, but this is wrong; the choices are .Normal and .Highlighted. The highlighted image appears while the user taps on the icon (except for the search icon, which isn't a button). If you don't supply a normal image, the default image is used; if you supply a normal image but no highlighted image, the normal image is used for both. Setting search-ResultsButtonSelected to true reverses the search results button's behavior: it displays the highlighted image, but when the user taps it, it displays the normal image. The position of an icon can be adjusted with setPositionAdjustment:forSearchBarIcon:.

A search bar may also display scope buttons (see the example in Chapter 8). These are intended to let the user alter the meaning of the search; precisely how you use them is up to you. To make the scope buttons appear, use the showsScopeBar property; the button titles are the scopeButtonTitles property, and the currently selected scope button is the selectedScopeButtonIndex property. The delegate is notified when the user taps a different scope button:

- searchBar:selectedScopeButtonIndexDidChange:

The overall look of the scope bar can be heavily customized. Its background is the scope-BarBackgroundImage, which will be stretched or tiled as needed. To set the background of the smaller area constituting the actual buttons, call setScopeBarButtonBackground-Image:forState:; the states are .Normal and .Selected. If you don't supply a separate selected image, a darkened version of the normal image is used. If you don't supply a resizable image, the image will be made resizable for you; the runtime decides what region of the image will be stretched behind each button.

The dividers between the buttons are normally vertical lines, but you can customize them as well: call setScopeBarButtonDividerImage:forLeftSegmentState:right-SegmentState:. A full complement of dividers consists of three images, one when the buttons on both sides of the divider are normal (unselected) and one each when a button on one side or the other is selected; if you supply an image for just one state combination,

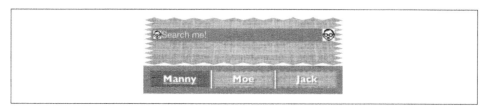

Figure 12-9. A horrible search bar

it is used for the other two state combinations. The height of the divider image is adjusted for you, but the width is not; you'll normally use an image just a few pixels wide.

The font attributes of the titles of the scope buttons can customized by calling `setScope-BarButtonTitleTextAttributes:forState:`. The `attributes:` argument is the attributes dictionary of an NSAttributedString (Chapter 10).

 It may appear that there is no way to customize the external Cancel button, but in fact, although you've no official direct access to it through the search bar, the Cancel button is a UIBarButtonItem and you can customize it using the UIBarButtonItem appearance proxy, discussed later in this chapter.

By combining the various customization possibilities, a completely unrecognizable search bar of inconceivable ugliness can easily be achieved (Figure 12-9). Let's be careful out there.

The problem of allowing the keyboard to appear without hiding the search bar is exactly as for a text field (Chapter 10). Text input properties of the search bar configure its keyboard and typing behavior like a text field as well.

When the user taps the Search key in the keyboard, the delegate is notified, and it is then up to you to dismiss the keyboard (`resignFirstResponder`) and perform the search:

- `searchBarSearchButtonClicked:`

A common interface is a search bar at the top of the screen. On the iPad, a search bar can be embedded as a bar button item's view in a toolbar at the top of the screen. On the iPhone, a search bar can be a navigation item's `titleView`. In Chapter 9, I gave an example of a search bar in a navigation bar. A search bar used in this way, however, has some limitations: for example, there may be no room for a prompt, scope buttons, or an external Cancel button, and you might not be able to assign it a background image or change its `barTintColor`.

Alternatively, a UISearchBar can itself function as a top bar, *like* a navigation bar without being *in* a navigation bar. If you use a search bar in this way, you'll want its height to be extended automatically under the status bar; I'll explain later in this chapter how to arrange that.

UIControl

UIControl is a subclass of UIView whose chief purpose is to be the superclass of several further built-in classes (controls) and to endow them with common behavior.

The most important thing that controls have in common is that they automatically track and analyze touch events (Chapter 5) and report them to your code as significant control events by way of action messages. Each control implements some subset of the possible control events. The full set of control events is listed under UIControlEvents in the Constants section of the UIControl class documentation:

- `.TouchDown`
- `.TouchDownRepeat`
- `.TouchDragInside`
- `.TouchDragOutside`
- `.TouchDragEnter`
- `.TouchDragExit`
- `.TouchUpInside`
- `.TouchUpOutside`
- `.TouchCancel`
- `.ValueChanged`
- `.EditingDidBegin`
- `.EditingChanged`
- `.EditingDidEnd`
- `.EditingDidEndOnExit`
- `.AllTouchEvents`
- `.AllEditingEvents`
- `.AllEvents`

The control events also have informal names that are visible in the Connections inspector when you're editing a nib. I'll mostly use the informal names in the next couple of paragraphs.

Control events fall roughly into three groups: the user has touched the screen (Touch Down, Touch Drag Inside, Touch Up Inside, etc.), edited text (Editing Did Begin, Editing Changed, etc.), or changed the control's value (Value Changed).

Apple's documentation is rather coy about which controls normally emit actions for which control events, so here's a list obtained through experimentation (but keep in mind that Apple's silence on this matter may mean that the details are subject to change):

UIButton
All Touch events.

UIDatePicker
Value Changed.

UIPageControl
All Touch events, Value Changed.

UIRefreshControl
Value Changed.

UISegmentedControl
Value Changed.

UISlider
All Touch events, Value Changed.

UISwitch
All Touch events, Value Changed.

UIStepper
All Touch events, Value Changed.

UITextField
All Touch events except the Up events, and all Editing events (see Chapter 10 for details).

UIControl (generic)
All Touch events.

New in iOS 9 is the notion of a control's *primary* control event, a UIControlEvent called .PrimaryActionTriggered. The primary control event is Value Changed for all controls except for UIButton, where it is Touch Up Inside, and UITextField, where it is Did End On Exit.

 A UIDatePicker has no primary control event. Its primary control event should presumably be Value Changed, but it isn't. This feels like a bug.

For each control event that you want to hear about, you attach to the control one or more target–action pairs. You can do this in the nib or in code.

For any given control, each control event and its target–action pairs form a dispatch table. The following methods permit you to manipulate and query the dispatch table:

- `addTarget:action:forControlEvents:`
- `removeTarget:action:forControlEvents:`
- `actionsForTarget:forControlEvent:`
- `allTargets`
- `allControlEvents` (a bitmask of control events to which a target–action pair is attached)

An action method (the method that will be called on the target when the control event occurs) may adopt any of three signatures, whose parameters are:

- The control and the UIEvent
- The control only
- No parameters

The second signature is by far the most common. It's unlikely that you'd want to dispense altogether with the parameter telling you which control sent the control event. On the other hand, it's equally unlikely that you'd want to examine the original UIEvent that triggered this control event, since control events deliberately shield you from dealing with the nitty-gritty of touches. (I suppose you might, on rare occasions, have some reason to examine the UIEvent's timestamp.)

When a control event occurs, the control consults its dispatch table, finds all the target–action pairs associated with that control event, and reports the control event by sending each action message to the corresponding target.

 The action messaging mechanism is actually more complex than I've just stated. The UIControl does not really send the action message directly; rather, it tells the shared application to send it. When a control wants to send an action message reporting a control event, it calls its own sendAction:to:forEvent: method. This in turn calls the shared application instance's sendAction:to:from:forEvent:, which actually sends the specified action message to the specified target. In theory, you could call or override either of these methods to customize this aspect of the message-sending architecture, but it is extremely unlikely that you would do so.

To make a control emit its action message(s) corresponding to a particular control event right now, in code, call its sendActionsForControlEvents: method (which is never called automatically by the runtime). For example, suppose you tell a UISwitch programmatically to change its setting from Off to On. This doesn't cause the switch to report a control event, as it would if the *user* had slid the switch from Off to On; if you wanted it to do so, you could use sendActionsForControlEvents:, like this:

```
self.sw.setOn(true, animated: true)
self.sw.sendActionsForControlEvents(.ValueChanged)
```

You might also use sendActionsForControlEvents: in a subclass to customize the circumstances under which a control reports control events. I'll give an example later in this chapter.

A control has enabled, selected, and highlighted properties; any of these can be true or false independently of the others. Together, they correspond to the control's state, which is reported as a bitmask of three possible values (UIControlState):

- .Highlighted
- .Disabled
- .Selected

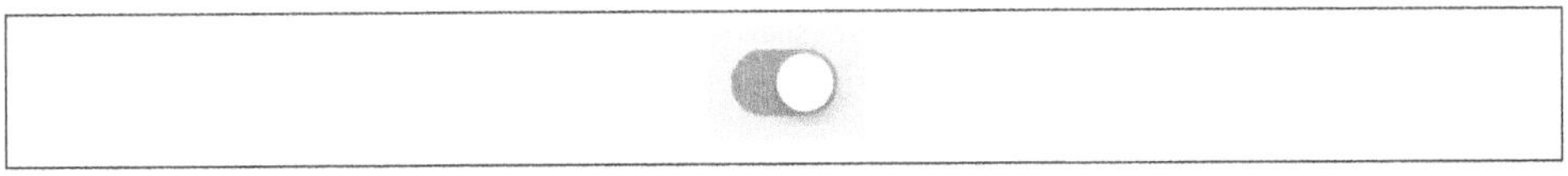

Figure 12-10. A switch

A fourth state, .Normal, corresponds to a zero state bitmask, and means that enabled is true, and selected and highlighted are both false.

A control that is not enabled does not respond to user interaction. Whether the control also portrays itself differently, to cue the user to this fact, depends upon the control. For example, a disabled UISwitch is faded; but a rounded rect text field gives the user no cue that it is disabled. The visual nature of control selection and highlighting, too, depends on the control. Neither highlighting nor selection make any difference to the appearance of a UISwitch, but a highlighted UIButton usually looks quite different from a nonhighlighted UIButton.

A control has contentHorizontalAlignment and contentVerticalAlignment properties. These matter only if the control has content that can be aligned. You are most likely to use them in connection with a UIButton to position its title and internal image.

A text field (UITextField) is a control; see Chapter 10. A refresh control (UIRefresh-Control) is a control; see Chapter 8. The remaining controls are covered here, and then I'll give a simple example of writing your own custom control.

UISwitch

A switch (UISwitch, Figure 12-10) portrays a Bool value: it looks like a sliding switch, and its on property is either true or false. The user can slide or tap to toggle the switch's setting. When the user changes the switch's setting, the switch reports a Value Changed control event. To change the on property's value with accompanying animation, call set-On:animated:.

A switch has only one size (51×31); any attempt to set its size will be ignored.

You can customize a switch's appearance by setting these properties:

onTintColor
    The color of the track when the switch is at the On setting.

thumbTintColor
    The color of the slidable button.

tintColor
    The color of the outline when the switch is at the Off setting.

Figure 12-11. A stepper

A switch's track when the switch is at the Off setting is transparent, and can't be customized. I regard this as a bug. (Changing the switch's `backgroundColor` is not a successful workaround, because the background color shows outside the switch's outline.)

 The UISwitch properties `onImage` and `offImage`, added in iOS 6 after much clamoring (and hacking) by developers, were unfortunately withdrawn in iOS 7, making a UISwitch once again almost impossible to customize to any appreciable degree. I regard this as a bug.

UIStepper

A stepper (UIStepper, Figure 12-11) lets the user increase or decrease a numeric value: it looks like two buttons side by side, one labeled (by default) with a minus sign, the other with a plus sign. The user can tap or hold a button, and can slide a finger from one button to the other as part of the same interaction with the stepper. It has only one size (apparently 94×29). It maintains a numeric value, which is its `value`. Each time the user increments or decrements the value, it changes by the stepper's `stepValue`. If the `minimumValue` or `maximumValue` is reached, the user can go no further in that direction, and to show this, the corresponding button is disabled — unless the stepper's `wraps` property is `true`, in which case the value goes beyond the maximum by starting again at the minimum, and *vice versa*.

As the user changes the stepper's `value`, a Value Changed control event is reported. Portraying the numeric value itself is up to you; you might, for example, use a label or (as here) a progress view:

```
@IBAction func doStep(sender:AnyObject!) {
    let step = sender as! UIStepper
    self.prog.setProgress(
        Float(step.value / (step.maximumValue - step.minimumValue)),
        animated:true)
}
```

If a stepper's `continuous` is `true` (the default), a long touch on one of the buttons will update the value repeatedly; the updates start slowly and get faster. If the stepper's `autorepeat` is `false`, the updated value is not reported as a Value Changed control event until the entire interaction with the stepper ends; the default is `true`.

Figure 12-12. A customized stepper

The appearance of a stepper can be customized. The color of the outline and the button captions is the stepper's `tintColor`, which may be inherited from further up the view hierarchy. You can also dictate the images that constitute the stepper's structure with these methods:

- `setDecrementImageForState:`
- `setIncrementImageForState:`
- `setDividerImage:forLeftSegmentState:rightSegmentState:`
- `setBackgroundImage:forState:`

The images work similarly to a search bar's scope bar (described earlier in this chapter). The background images should probably be resizable. They are stretched behind both buttons, half the image being seen as the background of each button. If the button is disabled (because we've reached the value's limit in that direction), it displays the `.Disabled` background image; otherwise, it displays the `.Normal` background image, except that it displays the `.Highlighted` background image while the user is tapping it. You'll probably want to provide all three background images if you're going to provide any; the default is used if a state's background image is `nil`. You'll probably want to provide three divider images as well, to cover the three combinations of one or neither segment being highlighted. The increment and decrement images, replacing the default minus and plus signs, are composited on top of the background image; they are treated as template images, colored by the `tintColor`, unless you explicitly provide an `.Always-Original` image. If you provide only a `.Normal` image, it will be adjusted automatically for the other two states. Figure 12-11 shows a customized stepper.

UIPageControl

A page control (UIPageControl) is a row of dots; each dot is called a *page*, because it is intended to be used in conjunction with some other interface that portrays something analogous to pages, such as a UIScrollView with its `pagingEnabled` set to `true`. Coordinating the page control with this other interface is usually up to you; see Chapter 7 for an example. A UIPageViewController in scroll style can optionally display a page control that's automatically coordinated with its content (Chapter 6).

The number of dots is the page control's `numberOfPages`. To learn the minimum size required for a given number of pages, call `sizeForNumberOfPages:`. You can make the page control wider than the dots to increase the target region on which the user can tap. The user can tap to one side or the other of the current page's dot to increment or decrement the current page; the page control then reports a Value Changed control event.

The dot colors differentiate the current page, the page control's currentPage, from the others; by default, the current page is portrayed as a solid dot, while the others are slightly transparent. You can customize a page control's pageIndicatorTintColor (the color of the dots in general) and currentPageIndicatorTintColor (the color of the current page's dot); you will almost certainly want to do this, as the default dot color is white, which under normal circumstances may be impossible to see.

It is possible to set a page control's backgroundColor; you might do this to show the user the tappable area, or to make the dots more clearly visible by contrast.

If a page control's hidesForSinglePage is true, the page control becomes invisible when its numberOfPages changes to 1.

If a page control's defersCurrentPageDisplay is true, then when the user taps to increment or decrement the page control's value, the display of the current page is not changed. A Value Changed control event is reported, but it is up to your code to handle this action and call updateCurrentPageDisplay. A case in point might be if the user's changing the current page triggers an animation, and you don't want the current page dot to change until the animation ends.

UIDatePicker

A date picker (UIDatePicker) looks like a UIPickerView (discussed earlier in this chapter), but it is not a UIPickerView subclass; it uses a UIPickerView to draw itself, but it provides no official access to that picker view. Its purpose is to express the notion of a date and time, taking care of the calendrical and numerical complexities so that you don't have to. When the user changes its setting, the date picker reports a Value Changed control event.

A UIDatePicker has one of four modes (datePickerMode), determining how it is drawn (UIDatePickerMode):

.Time
> The date picker displays a time; for example, it has an hour component and a minutes component.

.Date
> The date picker displays a date; for example, it has a month component, a day component, and a year component.

`.DateAndTime`

> The date picker displays a date and time; for example, it has a component showing day of the week, month, and day, plus an hour component and a minutes component.

`.CountDownTimer`

> The date picker displays a number of hours and minutes; for example, it has an hours component and a minutes component.

Exactly what components a date picker displays, and what values they contain, depends by default upon the user's preferences in the Settings app (General → Language & Region → Region). For example, a U.S. time displays an hour numbered 1 through 12 plus minutes and AM or PM, but a British time displays an hour numbered 1 through 24 plus minutes. If the user changes the region format in the Settings app, the date picker's display will change immediately.

A date picker has `calendar` and `timeZone` properties, respectively an NSCalendar and an NSTimeZone; these are `nil` by default, meaning that the date picker responds to the user's system-level settings. You can also change these values manually; for example, if you live in California and you set a date picker's `timeZone` to GMT, the displayed time is shifted forward by 8 hours, so that 11 AM is displayed as 7 PM (if it is winter).

 Don't change the `timeZone` of a `.CountDownTimer` date picker; if you do, the displayed value will be shifted, and you will confuse the heck out of yourself (and your users).

The minutes component, if there is one, defaults to showing every minute, but you can change this with the `minuteInterval` property. The maximum value is 30, in which case the minutes component values are 0 and 30. An attempt to set the `minuteInterval` to a value that doesn't divide evenly into 60 will be silently ignored.

The date represented by a date picker (unless its mode is `.CountDownTimer`) is its `date` property, an NSDate. The default date is now, at the time the date picker is instantiated. For a `.Date` date picker, the time by default is 12 AM (midnight), local time; for a `.Time` date picker, the date by default is today. The internal value is reckoned in the local time zone, so it may be different from the displayed value, if you have changed the date picker's `timeZone`.

The maximum and minimum values enabled in the date picker are determined by its `maximumDate` and `minimumDate` properties. Values outside this range may appear disabled. There isn't really any practical limit on the range that a date picker can display, because the "drums" representing its components are not physical, and values are added dynamically as the user spins them. In this example, we set the initial minimum and maximum dates of a date picker (dp) to the beginning and end of 1954. We also set the actual date, so that the date picker will be set initially to a value within the minimum–maximum range:

```
dp.datePickerMode = .Date
let dc = NSDateComponents()
dc.year = 1954
dc.month = 1
dc.day = 1
let c = NSCalendar(calendarIdentifier:NSCalendarIdentifierGregorian)!
let d1 = c.dateFromComponents(dc)!
dp.minimumDate = d1
dp.date = d1
dc.year = 1955
let d2 = c.dateFromComponents(dc)!
dp.maximumDate = d2
```

 Don't set the maximumDate and minimumDate properties values for a .CountDown-Timer date picker; if you do, you might cause a crash with an out-of-range exception.

To convert between an NSDate and a string, you'll need an NSDateFormatter (see Apple's *Date and Time Programming Guide*):

```
func dateChanged(sender:AnyObject) {
    let dp = sender as! UIDatePicker
    let d = dp.date
    let df = NSDateFormatter()
    df.timeStyle = .FullStyle
    df.dateStyle = .FullStyle
    print(df.stringFromDate(d))
    // Tuesday, August 10, 1954 at 3:16:00 AM GMT-07:00
}
```

The value displayed in a .CountDownTimer date picker is its countDownDuration; this is an NSTimeInterval, which is a Double representing a number of seconds, even though the minimum interval displayed is a minute. A .CountDownTimer date picker does not actually do any counting down! You are expected to use some other interface to display the countdown. The Timer tab of Apple's Clock app shows a typical interface; the user configures the date picker to set the countDownDuration initially, but once the counting starts, the date picker is hidden and a label displays the remaining time.

Converting the countDownDuration from an NSTimeInterval to hours and minutes is up to you; if your purpose is to display a string, you could use NSDateComponents-Formatter (introduced in iOS 8):

```
let t = dp.countDownDuration
let f = NSDateComponentsFormatter()
f.allowedUnits = [.Hour, .Minute]
f.unitsStyle = .Abbreviated
if let s = f.stringFromTimeInterval(t) {
    print(s) // "1h 12m"
}
```

 A nasty bug makes the Value Changed event from a `.CountDownTimer` date picker unreliable (especially just after the app launches, and whenever the user has tried to set the timer to zero). The workaround is not to rely on the Value Changed event; for example, provide a button in the interface that the user can tap to make your code read the date picker's `countDownDuration`.

UISlider

A slider (UISlider) is an expression of a continuously settable value (its `value`, a Float) between some minimum and maximum (its `minimumValue` and `maximumValue`; they are 0 and 1 by default). It is portrayed as an object, the *thumb*, positioned along a *track*. As the user changes the thumb's position, the slider reports a Value Changed control event; it may do this continuously as the user presses and drags the thumb (if the slider's `continuous` is `true`, the default) or only when the user releases the thumb (if its `continuous` is `false`). While the user is pressing on the thumb, the slider is in the `highlighted` state.

 According to the documentation, you should be able to change a slider's value with animation by calling `setValue:animated:`. But this broke in iOS 7 — there is no animation — and has not been fixed in iOS 8 or iOS 9.

A commonly expressed desire is to modify a slider's behavior so that if the user taps on its track, the slider moves to the spot where the user tapped. Unfortunately, a slider does not, of itself, respond to taps on its track; such a tap doesn't even cause it to report a Touch Up Inside control event. However, with a gesture recognizer, most things are possible; here's the action handler for a UITapGestureRecognizer attached to a UISlider:

```
func tapped(g:UIGestureRecognizer) {
    let s = g.view as! UISlider
    if s.highlighted {
        return // tap on thumb, let slider deal with it
    }
    let pt = g.locationInView(s)
    let track = s.trackRectForBounds(s.bounds)
    if !CGRectContainsPoint(CGRectInset(track, 0, -10), pt) {
        return // not on track, forget it
    }
```

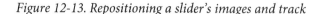

Figure 12-13. Repositioning a slider's images and track

```
        let percentage = Float(pt.x / s.bounds.size.width)
        let delta = percentage * (s.maximumValue - s.minimumValue)
        let value = s.minimumValue + delta
        s.setValue(value, animated:true) // but animation is broken
    }
```

A slider's `tintColor` (which may be inherited from further up the view hierarchy) determines the color of the track to the left of the thumb. You can change the color of the thumb with the `thumbTintColor` property. You can change the color of the two parts of the track with the `minimumTrackTintColor` and `maximumTrackTintColor` properties.

To go further, you can provide your own thumb image and your own track image, along with images to appear at each end of the track, and you can override in a subclass the methods that position these.

The images at the ends of the track are the slider's `minimumValueImage` and `maximum-ValueImage`, and they are `nil` by default. If you set them to actual images (which can also be done in the nib), the slider will attempt to position them within its own bounds, shrinking the drawing of the track to compensate.

You can change that behavior by overriding `minimumValueImageRectForBounds:`, `maximumValueImageRectForBounds:`, and `trackRectForBounds:` in a subclass. The bounds passed in are the slider's bounds. In this example (Figure 12-13), we expand the track width to the full width of the slider, and draw the images outside the slider's bounds. The images are still visible, because the slider does not clip its subviews to its bounds. In the figure, I've given the slider a background color so you can see how the track and images are related to its bounds:

```
override func maximumValueImageRectForBounds(bounds: CGRect) -> CGRect {
    return super.maximumValueImageRectForBounds(bounds)
        .offsetBy(dx: 31, dy: 0)
}
override func minimumValueImageRectForBounds(bounds: CGRect) -> CGRect {
    return super.minimumValueImageRectForBounds(bounds)
        .offsetBy(dx: -31, dy: 0)
}
override func trackRectForBounds(bounds: CGRect) -> CGRect {
    var result = super.trackRectForBounds(bounds)
    result.origin.x = 0
    result.size.width = bounds.size.width
    return result
}
```

Figure 12-14. Replacing a slider's thumb

The thumb is also an image, and you set it with `setThumbImage:forState:`. There are two chiefly relevant states, `.Normal` and `.Highlighted`. If you supply images for both, the thumb will change automatically while the user is dragging it. By default, the image will be centered in the track at the point represented by the slider's current value; you can shift this position by overriding `thumbRectForBounds:trackRect:value:` in a subclass. In this example, the image is repositioned upward slightly (Figure 12-14):

```
override func thumbRectForBounds(
    bounds: CGRect, trackRect rect: CGRect, value: Float) -> CGRect {
        return super.thumbRectForBounds(
            bounds, trackRect: rect, value: value)
                .offsetBy(dx: 0, dy: -7)
}
```

Enlarging or offsetting a slider's thumb can mislead the user as to the area on which it can be touched to drag it. The slider, not the thumb, is the touchable UIControl; only the part of the thumb that intersects the slider's bounds will be draggable. The user may try to drag the part of the thumb that is drawn outside the slider's bounds, and will fail (and be confused). A solution is to increase the slider's height; if you're using autolayout, you can add an explicit height constraint in the nib, or override `intrinsicContent-Size` in code (Chapter 1).

The track is two images, one appearing to the left of the thumb, the other to its right. They are set with `setMinimumTrackImage:forState:` and `setMaximumTrackImage:for-State:`. If you supply images both for `.Normal` state and for `.Highlighted` state, the images will change while the user is dragging the thumb.

The images should be resizable, because that's how the slider cleverly makes it look like the user is dragging the thumb along a single static track. In reality, there are two images; as the user drags the thumb, one image grows horizontally and the other shrinks horizontally. For the left track image, the right end cap inset will be partially or entirely hidden under the thumb; for the right track image, the left end cap inset will be partially or entirely hidden under the thumb. Figure 12-15 shows a track derived from a single 15×15 image of a circular object (a coin):

```
let coinEnd = UIImage(named:"coin.png")!.resizableImageWithCapInsets(
    UIEdgeInsetsMake(0,7,0,7), resizingMode: .Stretch)
self.setMinimumTrackImage(coinEnd, forState: .Normal)
self.setMaximumTrackImage(coinEnd, forState: .Normal)
```

Figure 12-15. Replacing a slider's track

Figure 12-16. A segmented control

UISegmentedControl

A segmented control (UISegmentedControl, Figure 12-16) is a row of tappable segments; a segment is rather like a button. The user is thus choosing among options. By default (`momentary` is `false`), the most recently tapped segment remains selected. Alternatively (`momentary` is `true`), the tapped segment is shown as highlighted momentarily (by default, highlighted is indistinguishable from selected, but you can change that); afterward, no segment selection is displayed, though internally the tapped segment remains the selected segment.

The selected segment can be set and retrieved with the `selectedSegmentIndex` property; when you set it in code, the selected segment remains visibly selected, even for a `momentary` segmented control. A `selectedSegmentIndex` value of `UISegmentedControlNoSegment` means no segment is selected. When the user taps a segment that isn't already visibly selected, the segmented control reports a Value Changed event.

A segmented control's change of selection is animatable. To animate the change in code, wrap it in a UIView animation:

```
UIView.animateWithDuration(0.4, animations: {
    self.seg.selectedSegmentIndex = 1
})
```

To animate the change more slowly when the user taps on a segment, set the segmented control's layer's `speed` to a fractional value.

A segment can be separately enabled or disabled with `setEnabled:forSegmentAtIndex:`, and its enabled state can be retrieved with `isEnabledForSegmentAtIndex:`. A disabled segment, by default, is drawn faded; the user can't tap it, but it can still be selected in code.

A segment has either a title or an image; when one is set, the other becomes `nil`. An image is treated as a template image, colored by the `tintColor`, unless you explicitly provide an `.AlwaysOriginal` image. The methods for setting and fetching the title and image for existing segments are:

- `setTitle:forSegmentAtIndex:`, `titleForSegmentAtIndex:`
- `setImage:forSegmentAtIndex:`, `imageForSegmentAtIndex:`

You will also want to set the title or image when creating the segment. You can do this in code if you're creating the segmented control from scratch, with `init(items:)`, which takes an array each item of which is either a string or an image:

```
let seg = UISegmentedControl(
    items: [
        UIImage(named:"smiley")!.imageWithRenderingMode(.AlwaysOriginal),
        "Two"
    ])
seg.frame.origin = CGPointMake(30,30)
self.view.addSubview(seg)
```

Methods for managing segments dynamically are:

- `insertSegmentWithTitle:atIndex:animated:`
- `insertSegmentWithImage:atIndex:animated:`
- `removeSegmentAtIndex:animated:`
- `removeAllSegments`

The number of segments can be retrieved with the read-only `numberOfSegments` property.

A segmented control has a standard height; if you're using autolayout, you can change the height through constraints or by overriding `intrinsicContentSize` — or by setting its background image, as I'll describe in a moment.

If you're using autolayout, the widths of all segments and the `intrinsicContentSize` width of the entire segmented control are adjusted automatically whenever you set a segment's title or image. If the segmented control's `apportionsSegmentWidthsBy-Content` property is `false`, segment sizes will be made equal to one another; if it is `true`, each segment will be sized individually to fit its content. Alternatively, you can set a segment's width explicitly with `setWidth:forSegmentAtIndex:` (and retrieve it with `widthForSegmentAtIndex:`); setting a width of `0` means that this segment is to be sized automatically.

To change the position of the content (title or image) within a segment, call `setContent-Offset:forSegmentAtIndex:` (and retrieve it with `contentOffsetForSegmentAt-Index:`).

Figure 12-17. A segmented control, customized

The color of a segmented control's outline, title text, and selection are dictated by its tintColor, which may be inherited from further up the view hierarchy.

Further methods for customizing a segmented control's appearance are parallel to those for setting the look of a stepper or the scope bar portion of a search bar, both described earlier in this chapter. You can set the overall background, the divider image, the text attributes for the segment titles, and the position of segment contents:

- setBackgroundImage:forState:barMetrics:
- setDividerImage:forLeftSegmentState:rightSegmentState:barMetrics:
- setTitleTextAttributes:forState:
- setContentPositionAdjustment:forSegmentType:barMetrics:

You don't have to customize for every state, as the segmented control will use the .Normal state setting for the states you don't specify. As I mentioned a moment ago, setting a background image changes the segmented control's height.

Here's the code that achieved Figure 12-17. Selecting a segment automatically darkens the background image for us (similar to a button's adjustsImageWhenHighlighted, described in the next section), so there's no need to specify a separate selected image; for imageOfSize:, see Appendix B:

```
// background, set desired height but make width resizable
// sufficient to set for Normal only
let sz = CGSizeMake(100,60)
let im = imageOfSize(sz) {
    UIImage(named:"linen.png")!
        .drawInRect(CGRect(origin: CGPoint(), size: sz))
    }.resizableImageWithCapInsets(
        UIEdgeInsetsMake(0,10,0,10), resizingMode: .Stretch)
self.seg.setBackgroundImage(im, forState: .Normal, barMetrics: .Default)
// segment images, redraw at final size
let pep = ["manny", "moe", "jack"].map {$0 + ".jpg"}
for (i, boy) in pep.enumerate() {
    let sz = CGSizeMake(30,30)
    let im = imageOfSize(sz) {
        UIImage(named:boy)!
            .drawInRect(CGRect(origin: CGPoint(), size: sz))
        }.imageWithRenderingMode(.AlwaysOriginal)
    self.seg.setImage(im, forSegmentAtIndex: i)
```

```
        self.seg.setWidth(80, forSegmentAtIndex: i)
    }
    // divider, set at desired width, sufficient to set for Normal only
    let sz2 = CGSizeMake(2,10)
    let div = imageOfSize(sz2) {
        UIColor.whiteColor().set()
        CGContextFillRect(UIGraphicsGetCurrentContext()!,
            CGRect(origin: CGPoint(), size: sz2))
    }
    self.seg.setDividerImage(div,
        forLeftSegmentState: .Normal, rightSegmentState: .Normal,
        barMetrics: .Default)
```

The segmentType: parameter in setContentPositionAdjustment:forSegmentType:
barMetrics: is needed because, by default, the segments at the two extremes have
rounded ends (and, if a segment is the lone segment, both its ends are rounded). The
argument (UISegmentedControlSegment) allows you distinguish between the various
possibilities:

- .Any
- .Left
- .Center
- .Right
- .Alone

The barMetrics: parameter will be ignored unless its value is .Default.

UIButton

A button (UIButton) is a fundamental tappable control, which may contain a title, an
image, and a background image (and may have a backgroundColor). A button has a
type, and the initializer is init(type:). The types (UIButtonType) are:

.System
> The title text appears in the button's tintColor, which may be inherited from fur-
> ther up the view hierarchy; when the button is tapped, the title text color momen-
> tarily changes to a color derived from what's behind it (which might be the button's
> backgroundColor). The image is treated as a template image, colored by the tint-
> Color, unless you explicitly provide an .AlwaysOriginal image; when the button
> is tapped, the image (even if it isn't a template image) is momentarily tinted to a
> color derived from what's behind it.

.DetailDisclosure, .InfoLight, .InfoDark, .ContactAdd
> Basically, these are all .System buttons whose image is set automatically to standard
> button images. The first three are an "i" in a circle, and the last is a Plus in a circle;

the two `Info` types are identical, and they differ from the `DetailDisclosure` type only in that their `showsTouchWhenHighlighted` is `true` by default.

`.Custom`

Similar to `.System`, except that there's no automatic coloring of the title or image by the `tintColor` or the color of what's behind the button, and the image is a normal image by default.

There is no built-in button type with an outline (border), comparable to the Rounded Rect style of iOS 6 and before. You can add an outline — by adding a background image, for example, or by manipulating the button's layer — but the default look of a button is the text or image alone. In one of my apps, I make a button appear as a rounded rectangle, entirely through settings made in the nib:

1. In the Attributes inspector, I give the button a background color.

2. In the Identity inspector, I use the User Defined Runtime Attributes to set the button's `layer.borderWidth` to 2 and its `layer.cornerRadius` to 5.

I'll give a more sophisticated example later in this chapter (see Figure 12-20).

A button has a title, a title color, and a title shadow color — or you can supply an attributed title, thus dictating these features and more in a single value through an NSAttributedString (Chapter 10).

Distinguish a button's image, which is an internal image, from its background image. The background image, if any, is stretched, if necessary, to fill the button's bounds (technically, its `backgroundRectForBounds:`). The internal image, on the other hand, if smaller than the button, is not resized. The button can have both a title and an image, if the image is small enough; in that case, the image is shown to the left of the title by default.

These six features — title, title color, title shadow color, attributed title, image, and background image — can all be made to vary depending on the button's current state: `.Highlighted`, `.Selected`, `.Disabled`, and `.Normal`. The button can be in more than one state at once, except for `.Normal` which means "none of the other states." A state change, whether automatic (the button is highlighted while the user is tapping it) or programmatically imposed, will thus in and of itself alter a button's appearance. The methods for setting these button features, therefore, all involve specifying a corresponding state — or multiple states, using a bitmask:

- `setTitle:forState:`
- `setTitleColor:forState:`
- `setTitleShadowColor:forState:`
- `setAttributedTitle:forState:`

- setImage:forState:
- setBackgroundImage:forState:

Similarly, when getting these button features, you must either specify a single state you're interested in or ask about the feature as currently displayed:

- titleForState:, currentTitle
- titleColorForState:, currentTitleColor
- titleShadowColorForState:, currentTitleShadowColor
- attributedTitleForState:, currentAttributedTitle
- imageForState:, currentImage
- backgroundImageForState:, currentBackgroundImage

If you don't specify a feature for a particular state, or if the button adopts more than one state at once, an internal heuristic is used to determine what to display. I can't describe all possible combinations, but here are some general observations:

- If you specify a feature for a particular state (highlighted, selected, or disabled), and the button is in *only* that state, that feature will be used.
- If you *don't* specify a feature for a particular state (highlighted, selected, or disabled), and the button is in *only* that state, the normal version of that feature will be used as fallback. (That's why many examples earlier in this book have assigned a title for .Normal only; this is sufficient to give the button a title in every state.)
- Combinations of states often cause the button to fall back on the feature for normal state. For example, if a button is both highlighted and selected, the button will display its normal title, even if it has a highlighted title, a selected title, or both.

A .System button with an attributed normal title will tint the title to the tintColor if you don't give the attributed string a color, and will tint the title while highlighted to the color derived from what's behind the button if you haven't supplied a highlighted title with its own color. But a .Custom button will not do any of that; it leaves control of the title color for each state completely up to you.

In addition, a UIButton has some properties determining how it draws itself in various states, which can save you the trouble of specifying different images for different states:

showsTouchWhenHighlighted
 If true, then the button projects a circular white glow when highlighted. If the button has an internal image, the glow is centered behind it. Thus, this feature is suitable particularly if the button image is small and circular; for example, it's the default behavior for an .InfoLight or .InfoDark button. If the button has no

internal image, the glow is centered at the button's center. The glow is drawn on top of the background image or color, if any.

adjustsImageWhenHighlighted

In a .Custom button, if this property is true (the default), then if there is no separate highlighted image (and if showsTouchWhenHighlighted is false), the normal image is darkened when the button is highlighted. This applies equally to the internal image and the background image. (A .System button is already tinting its highlighted image, so this property doesn't apply.)

adjustsImageWhenDisabled

If true, then if there is no separate disabled image, the normal image is shaded when the button is disabled. This applies equally to the internal image and the background image. The default is true for a .Custom button and false for a .System button.

A button has a natural size in relation to its contents. If you're using autolayout, the button can adopt that size automatically as its intrinsicContentSize, and you can modify the way it does this by overriding intrinsicContentSize in a subclass or by applying explicit constraints. If you're not using autolayout and you create a button in code, send it sizeToFit or give it an explicit size; otherwise, the button may have a zero size, and you'll be left wondering why your button hasn't appeared in the interface.

The title is a UILabel (Chapter 10), and the label features of the title can be accessed through the button's titleLabel. For example, beginners often wonder how to make a button's title consist of more than one line; the answer is obvious, once you remember that the title is displayed in a label: increase the button's titleLabel.numberOfLines. In general, the label's properties may be set, provided they do not conflict with existing UIButton features. For example, you can set the title's font and shadowOffset by way of the label, but the title's text, color, and shadow color should be set using the appropriate button methods specifying a button state. If the title is given a shadow in this way, then the button's reversesTitleShadowWhenHighlighted property also applies: if true, the shadowOffset values are replaced with their additive inverses when the button is highlighted. The modern way, however, is to do that sort of thing through the button's attributed title.

The internal image is drawn by a UIImageView (Chapter 2), whose features can be accessed through the button's imageView. Thus, for example, you can change the internal image view's alpha to make the image more transparent.

The internal position of the image and title as a whole are governed by the button's contentVerticalAlignment and contentHorizontalAlignment (inherited from UIControl). You can also tweak the position of the image and title, together or separately, by setting the button's contentEdgeInsets, titleEdgeInsets, or imageEdgeInsets.

Increasing an inset component increases that margin; thus, for example, a positive top component makes the distance between that object and the top of the button larger than normal (where "normal" is where the object would be according to the alignment settings). The titleEdgeInsets or imageEdgeInsets values are added to the overall contentEdgeInsets values. So, for example, if you really wanted to, you could make the internal image appear to the right of the title by decreasing the left titleEdge-Insets and increasing the left imageEdgeInsets.

Four methods also provide access to the button's positioning of its elements:

- titleRectForContentRect:
- imageRectForContentRect:
- contentRectForBounds:
- backgroundRectForBounds:

These methods are called whenever the button is redrawn, including every time it changes state. The content rect is the area in which the title and image are placed. By default, contentRectForBounds: and backgroundRectForBounds: yield the same result. You can override these methods in a subclass to change the way the button's elements are positioned.

Here's an example of a customized button. In a UIButton subclass, we increase the button's intrinsicContentSize to give it larger margins around its content, and we override backgroundRectForBounds to shrink the button slightly when highlighted as a way of providing feedback (for sizeByDelta, see Appendix B):

```
override func backgroundRectForBounds(bounds: CGRect) -> CGRect {
    var result = super.backgroundRectForBounds(bounds)
    if self.highlighted {
        result.insetInPlace(dx: 3, dy: 3)
    }
    return result
}
override func intrinsicContentSize() -> CGSize {
    return super.intrinsicContentSize().sizeByDelta(dw:25, dh: 20)
}
```

The button, which is a .Custom button, is assigned an internal image and a background image from the same resizable image, along with attributed titles for the .Normal and .Highlighted states. The internal image glows when highlighted, thanks to adjusts-ImageWhenHighlighted (Figure 12-18).

Figure 12-18. A custom button

Custom Controls

If you create your own UIControl subclass, you automatically get the built-in Touch events; in addition, there are several methods that you can override in order to customize touch tracking, along with properties that tell you whether touch tracking is going on:

- `beginTrackingWithTouch:withEvent:`
- `continueTrackingWithTouch:withEvent:`
- `endTrackingWithTouch:withEvent:`
- `cancelTrackingWithEvent:`
- `tracking` (property)
- `touchInside` (property)

With the advent of gesture recognizers (Chapter 5), such direct involvement with touch tracking is probably less needed than it used to be, especially if your purpose is to modify the behavior of a built-in UIControl subclass. So, to illustrate their use, I'll give a simple example of creating a custom control. The main reason for doing this (rather than using, say, a UIView and gesture recognizers) would probably be to obtain the convenience of control events. Also, the touch-tracking methods, though not as high-level as gesture recognizers, are at least a level up from the UIResponder `touches` methods (Chapter 5): they track a single touch, and both `beginTracking...` and `continueTracking...` return a Bool, giving you a chance to stop tracking the current touch.

We'll build a simplified knob control (Figure 12-19). The control starts life at its minimum position, with an internal angle value of 0; it can be rotated clockwise with a single finger as far as its maximum position, with an internal angle value of 5 (radians). To keep things simple, the words "Min" and "Max" appearing in the interface are actually labels; the control just draws the knob, and to rotate it we'll apply a rotation transform.

Our control is a UIControl subclass, MyKnob. It has a public CGFloat `angle` property, and a private CGFloat property `self.initialAngle` that we'll use internally during rotation. Because a UIControl is a UIView, it can draw itself, which it does with an image file included in our app bundle:

Figure 12-19. A custom control

```
override func drawRect(rect: CGRect) {
    UIImage(named:"knob.png")!.drawInRect(rect)
}
```

We'll need a utility function for transforming a touch's Cartesian coordinates into polar coordinates, giving us the angle to be applied as a rotation to the view:

```
func pToA (touch:UITouch) -> CGFloat {
    let loc = touch.locationInView(self)
    let c = CGPointMake(self.bounds.midX, self.bounds.midY)
    return atan2(loc.y - c.y, loc.x - c.x)
}
```

Now we're ready to override the tracking methods. beginTrackingWithTouch:with-Event: simply notes down the angle of the initial touch location. continueTracking-WithTouch:withEvent: uses the difference between the current touch location's angle and the initial touch location's angle to apply a transform to the view, and updates the angle property. endTrackingWithTouch:withEvent: triggers the Value Changed control event. So our first draft looks like this:

```
override func beginTrackingWithTouch(
    touch: UITouch, withEvent event: UIEvent?) -> Bool {
        self.initialAngle = pToA(touch)
        return true
}
override func continueTrackingWithTouch(
    touch: UITouch, withEvent event: UIEvent?) -> Bool {
        let ang = pToA(touch) - self.initialAngle
        let absoluteAngle = self.angle + ang
        self.transform = CGAffineTransformRotate(self.transform, ang)
        self.angle = absoluteAngle
        return true
}
override func endTrackingWithTouch(
    touch: UITouch, withEvent event: UIEvent) {
        self.sendActionsForControlEvents(.ValueChanged)
}
```

This works: we can put a MyKnob into the interface and hook up its Value Changed control event (this can be done in the nib editor), and sure enough, when we run the app, we can rotate the knob and, when our finger lifts from the knob, the Value Changed action handler is called.

However, our class needs modification. When the angle is set programmatically, we should respond by rotating the knob; at the same time, we need to peg the incoming value at the allowable minimum or maximum:

```
var angle : CGFloat = 0 {
    didSet {
        if self.angle < 0 {
            self.angle = 0
        }
        if self.angle > 5 {
            self.angle = 5
        }
        self.transform = CGAffineTransformMakeRotation(self.angle)
    }
}
```

Now we should revise continueTrackingWithTouch:withEvent:. We no longer need to perform the rotation, since setting the angle will do that for us. On the other hand, we do need to peg the gesture when the minimum or maximum rotation is exceeded. My solution is simply to stop tracking; in that case, endTracking... will never be called, so we also need to trigger the Value Changed control event. Also, it might be nice to give the programmer the option to have the Value Changed control event reported continuously as continueTracking... is called repeatedly; so we'll add a public continuous Bool property and obey it:

```
override func continueTrackingWithTouch(
    touch: UITouch, withEvent event: UIEvent) -> Bool {
        let absoluteAngle = self.angle + pToA(touch) - self.initialAngle
        switch absoluteAngle {
        case -CGFloat.max...0:
            self.angle = 0
            self.sendActionsForControlEvents(.ValueChanged)
            return false
        case 5...CGFloat.max:
            self.angle = 5
            self.sendActionsForControlEvents(.ValueChanged)
            return false
        default:
            self.angle = absoluteAngle
            if self.continuous {
                self.sendActionsForControlEvents(.ValueChanged)
            }
            return true
        }
}
```

Bars

There are three bar types: navigation bar (UINavigationBar), toolbar (UIToolbar), and tab bar (UITabBar). They are often used in conjunction with a built-in view controller (Chapter 6):

- A UINavigationController has a UINavigationBar.
- A UINavigationController has a UIToolbar.
- A UITabBarController has a UITabBar.

You can also use these bar types independently. You are most likely to do that with a UIToolbar, which is often used as an independent bottom bar. On the iPad, it can also be used as a top bar, adopting a role analogous to a menu bar on the desktop.

This section summarizes the facts about the three bar types — along with UISearchBar, which can act as a top bar — and about the items that populate them.

Bar Position and Bar Metrics

If a bar is to occupy the top of the screen, its apparent height should be increased to underlap the transparent status bar. To make this possible, iOS provides the notion of a *bar position*. The UIBarPositioning protocol, adopted by UINavigationBar, UIToolbar, and UISearchbar (the bars that can go at the top of the screen), defines one property, `barPosition`, whose possible values (UIBarPosition) are:

- `.Any`
- `.Bottom`
- `.Top`
- `.TopAttached`

But `barPosition` is read-only, so how are you supposed to set it? Use the bar's delegate! The delegate protocols UINavigationBarDelegate, UIToolbarDelegate, and UISearch-BarDelegate all conform to UIBarPositioningDelegate. The UIBarPositioningDelegate protocol defines one method, `positionForBar:`. This provides a way for a bar's delegate to dictate the bar's `barPosition`.

The rule is that the bar's apparent height will be extended upward, so that its top can go behind the status bar, if the bar's delegate returns `.TopAttached` from its implementation of `positionForBar:`. To get the final position right, the bar's top should also have a zero-length constraint to the view controller's top layout guide. If you're not using autolayout, then the bar's top should have a y value of `20`.

I say that a bar's *apparent* height is extended upward, because in fact its height remains untouched. It is *drawn* extended upward, and this drawing is visible because the bar's clipsToBounds is false. For this reason (and others), you should not set a top bar's clipsToBounds to true.

A bar's height is reflected also by its *bar metrics*. This refers to a change in the standard height of the bar in reponse to a change in the orientation of the app. This change is *not* an automatic feature of the bar itself; rather, it is performed automatically by a UINavigationController on its own navigation bar or toolbar in a .Compact horizontal size class environment. The standard heights are 44 (.Regular vertical size class) and 32 (.Compact vertical size class). Possible bar metrics values are (UIBarMetrics):

- .Default
- .Compact
- .DefaultPrompt
- .CompactPrompt

The Compact metrics apply in a .Compact vertical size class environment. The Prompt metrics apply to a bar whose height is extended downward to accommodate prompt text (and to a search bar whose scope buttons are showing).

When you're customizing a feature of a bar, you may find yourself calling a method that takes a bar metrics parameter, and possibly a bar position parameter as well. The idea is that you can customize that feature differently depending on the bar position and the bar metrics. But you don't have to set that value for *every* possible combination of bar position and bar metrics; in general (though, unfortunately, the details are a little inconsistent from class to class), UIBarPosition.Any and UIBarMetrics.Default are treated as defaults that encompass any positions and metrics you don't specify.

The interface object classes and their features that participate in this system are:

UISearchBar
> A search bar can function as a top bar and can have a prompt. You can set its background image.

UINavigationBar
> A navigation bar can function as a top bar, it can have a prompt, and its height in a navigation interface is changed automatically in a .Compact horizontal size class environment depending on the vertical size class. You can set its background image. In addition, the vertical offset of its title can depend on the bar metrics.

UIToolbar

A toolbar can function as a top bar or a bottom bar, and its height in a navigation interface is changed automatically in a `.Compact` horizontal size class environment depending on the vertical size class. You can set its background image. In addition, its shadow can depend on its bar position.

UIBarButtonItem

You can set a bar button item's image, image inset, background image, title offset, and background offset, so as to depend upon the bar metrics of the containing bar, either a UINavigationBar or a UIToolbar (and the bar position is irrelevant).

Bar Appearance

A bar can be styled at three levels:

`barStyle, translucent`

The `barStyle` options are (UIBarStyle):

- `.Default`
- `.Black`

The bar styles are flat white and flat black respectively. The `translucent` property turns on or off the characteristic blurry translucency. The degree of translucency can vary from one device type to another; don't expect complete control of a translucent bar's appearance.

`barTintColor`

This property tints the bar with a solid color. Like the transparency color, you should not expect complete control of the resulting color. It is best to set the bar's `translucent` to `true`; otherwise, odd things can happen. (For example, a toolbar whose `translucent` is `false` may ignore the bar tint color and appear transparent instead.)

`backgroundImage`

The background image is set, as I explained earlier, with `setBackgroundImage:forBarPosition:barMetrics:`. If the image is too large, it is sized down to fit; if it is too small, it is tiled by default, but you can change that behavior by supplying a resizable image.

If a bar's `translucent` is `false`, then the `barTintColor` may appear behind the background image, but a `translucent` bar with a background image is transparent behind the image; thus, a background image provides maximum control over the appearance of the bar.

In a UINavigationController, there is a reason why you might set the navigation bar's barStyle even if you are configuring the bar's appearance in some other way — namely, because the navigation controller will pass this setting along in its implementation of preferredStatusBarStyle. In other words, you set the navigation controller's navigation bar's bar style as a way of setting the *status bar's* bar style.

If you assign a bar a background image, you can also customize its shadow, which is cast from the bottom of the bar (if the bar is at the top) or the top of the bar (if the bar is at the bottom) on whatever is behind it. To do so, set the shadowImage property — except that a toolbar can be either at the top or the bottom, so its setter is setShadow-Image:forToolbarPosition:, and the barPosition is used to decide whether the shadow should appear at the top or the bottom of the toolbar.

You'll want a shadow image to be very small and very transparent; the image will be tiled horizontally. If you're going to set the bar's translucent, you should do so *after* setting both the background image and the shadow image. You won't see the shadow if the bar's clipsToBounds is true. Here's an example for a navigation bar:

```
let sz = CGSizeMake(4,4)
self.navbar.shadowImage = imageOfSize(sz) {
    UIColor.grayColor().colorWithAlphaComponent(0.3).setFill()
    CGContextFillRect(UIGraphicsGetCurrentContext()!, CGRectMake(0,0,4,2))
    UIColor.grayColor().colorWithAlphaComponent(0.15).setFill()
    CGContextFillRect(UIGraphicsGetCurrentContext()!, CGRectMake(0,2,4,2))
}
```

UIBarButtonItem

The only things that can appear inside a navigation bar or a toolbar — aside from a navigation bar's title and prompt — are bar button items (UIBarButtonItem, a subclass of UIBarItem). This is not much of a limitation, however, because a bar button item can contain a custom view, which can be any type of UIView at all. A bar button item itself, however, is not a UIView subclass.

A bar button item may be instantiated with any of five methods:

- init(barButtonSystemItem:target:action:)
- init(title:style:target:action:)
- init(image:style:target:action:)
- init(image:landscapeImagePhone:style:target:action:)
- init(customView:)

A bar button item's image is treated by default as a template image, unless you explicitly provide an `.AlwaysOriginal` image.

The `style:` options are (UIBarButtonItemStyle):

- `.Plain`
- `.Done` (the title text is bold)

As I mentioned a moment ago, many aspects of a bar button item can be made dependent upon the bar metrics of the containing bar. Thus, you can initialize a bar button item with both an `image` and a `landscapeImagePhone`, the latter to be used when the bar metrics has `Compact` in its name. A bar button item inherits from UIBarItem the ability to adjust the image position with `imageInsets` (and `landscapeImagePhoneInsets`), plus the `enabled` and `tag` properties. Recall from Chapter 6 that you can also set a bar button item's `possibleTitles` and `width` properties, to determine its width.

A bar button item's `tintColor` property tints the title text or template image of the button; it is inherited from the `tintColor` of the bar, or you can override it for an individual bar button item.

You can apply an attributes dictionary to a bar button item's title, and you can give a bar button item a background image:

- `setTitleTextAttributes:forState:` (inherited from UIBarItem)
- `setTitlePositionAdjustment:forBarMetrics:`
- `setBackgroundImage:forState:barMetrics:`
- `setBackgroundImage:forState:style:barMetrics:`
- `setBackgroundVerticalPositionAdjustment:forBarMetrics:`

In addition, these methods apply only if the bar button item is being used as a back button item in a navigation bar (as I'll describe in the next section):

- `setBackButtonTitlePositionAdjustment:forBarMetrics:`
- `setBackButtonBackgroundImage:forState:barMetrics:`
- `setBackButtonBackgroundVerticalPositionAdjustment:forBarMetrics:`

No bar button item style supplies an outline (border); the default look of a button is just the text or image. (The pre–iOS 7 bar button item style `.Bordered` is now deprecated, and its appearance is identical to `.Plain`.) If you want an outline, you have to supply it yourself. For the left bar button item in the settings view of my Zotz! app (Figure 12-20), I use a custom view that's a UIButton with a background image:

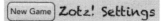

Figure 12-20. A bar button item with a border

```
let b = UIButton(type:.Custom)
// ...
let im = imageOfSize(CGSizeMake(15,15)) {
    let grad = CAGradientLayer()
    grad.frame = CGRectMake(0,0,15,15)
    grad.colors = [
        UIColor(red: 1, green: 1, blue: 0, alpha: 0.8).CGColor,
        UIColor(red: 0.7, green: 0.7, blue: 0.3, alpha: 0.8).CGColor
    ]
    let p = UIBezierPath(roundedRect: CGRectMake(0,0,15,15), cornerRadius: 8)
    p.addClip()
    grad.renderInContext(UIGraphicsGetCurrentContext()!)
    UIColor.blackColor().setStroke()
    p.lineWidth = 2
    p.stroke()
    }.resizableImageWithCapInsets(
        UIEdgeInsetsMake(7,7,7,7), resizingMode: .Stretch)
b.setBackgroundImage(im, forState: .Normal)
let bb = UIBarButtonItem(customView: b)
self.navigationItem.leftBarButtonItem = bb
```

UINavigationBar

A navigation bar (UINavigationBar) is populated by navigation items (UINavigation-Item). The UINavigationBar maintains a stack; UINavigationItems are pushed onto and popped off of this stack. Whatever UINavigationItem is currently topmost in the stack (the UINavigationBar's topItem), in combination with the UINavigationItem just beneath it in the stack (the UINavigationBar's backItem), determines what appears in the navigation bar:

title, titleView

> The title (string) or titleView (UIView) of the topItem appears in the center of the navigation bar.

prompt

> The prompt (string) of the topItem appears at the top of the navigation bar, whose height increases to accommodate it.

rightBarButtonItem, leftBarButtonItem

> The rightBarButtonItem and leftBarButtonItem appear at the right and left ends of the navigation bar. A UINavigationItem can have multiple right bar button items and multiple left bar button items; its rightBarButtonItems and leftBarButton-

Figure 12-21. A back button animating to the left

Items properties are arrays (of bar button items). The bar button items are displayed from the outside in: that is, the first item in the leftBarButtonItems is leftmost, while the first item in the rightBarButtonItems is rightmost. If there are multiple buttons on a side, the rightBarButtonItem is the first item of the rightBarButton-Items array, and the leftBarButtonItem is the first item of the leftBarButton-Items array.

backBarButtonItem

The backBarButtonItem *of the backItem* appears at the left end of the navigation bar. It is automatically configured so that, when tapped, the topItem is popped off the stack. If the backItem has *no* backBarButtonItem, then there is *still* a back button at the left end of the navigation bar, taking its title from the title of the backItem. However, if the topItem has its hidesBackButton set to true, the back button is suppressed. Also, unless the topItem has its leftItemsSupplementBack-Button set to true, the back button is suppressed if the topItem has a leftBar-ButtonItem.

The indication that the back button *is* a back button is supplied by the navigation bar's backIndicatorImage, which by default is a left-pointing chevron appearing to the left of the back button. You can customize this image; the image that you supply is treated as a template image by default. If you set the backIndicatorImage, you must also supply a backIndicatorTransitionMaskImage. The purpose of the mask image is to indicate the region where the back button should disappear as it slides out to the left when a new navigation item is pushed onto the stack. For example, in Figure 12-21, the back button title, which is sliding out to the left, is visible to the right of the chevron but not to the left of the chevron; that's because on the left side of the chevron it is masked out.

In this example, I replace the chevron with a vertical bar. The vertical bar is not the entire image; the image is actually a wider rectangle, with the vertical bar at its right side. The mask is the entire wider rectangle, and is completely transparent; thus, the back button disappears as it passes behind the bar and stays invisible as it continues on to the left:

```
self.navbar.backIndicatorImage =
    imageOfSize(CGSizeMake(10,20)) {
        CGContextFillRect(
            UIGraphicsGetCurrentContext()!, CGRectMake(6,0,4,20))
self.navbar.backIndicatorTransitionMaskImage =
    imageOfSize(CGSizeMake(10,20)) {}
```

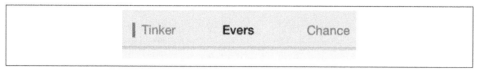

Figure 12-22. A navigation bar

Changes to the navigation bar's buttons can be animated by sending its `topItem` any of these messages:

- `setRightBarButtonItem:animated:`
- `setLeftBarButtonItem:animated:`
- `setRightBarButtonItems:animated:`
- `setLeftBarButtonItems:animated:`
- `setHidesBackButton:animated:`

UINavigationItems are pushed and popped with `pushNavigationItem:animated:` and `popNavigationItemAnimated:`, or you can set all items on the stack at once with `set-Items:animated:`.

You can set the title's attributes dictionary (`titleTextAttributes`), and you can shift the title's vertical position by calling `setTitleVerticalPositionAdjustment:forBar-Metrics:`.

When you use a UINavigationBar implicitly as part of a UINavigationController interface, the navigation controller is the navigation bar's delegate. If you were to use a UINavigationBar on its own, you might want to supply your own delegate. The delegate methods are:

- `navigationBar:shouldPushItem:`
- `navigationBar:didPushItem:`
- `navigationBar:shouldPopItem:`
- `navigationBar:didPopItem:`

This simple (and silly) example of a standalone UINavigationBar implements the legendary baseball combination trio of Tinker to Evers to Chance; see the relevant Wikipedia article if you don't know about them (Figure 12-22, which also shows the custom back indicator and shadow I described earlier):

Figure 12-23. A toolbar

```
override func viewDidLoad() {
    super.viewDidLoad()
    let ni = UINavigationItem(title: "Tinker")
    let b = UIBarButtonItem(
        title: "Evers", style: .Plain, target: self, action: "pushNext:")
    ni.rightBarButtonItem = b
    self.navbar.items = [ni]
}
func pushNext(sender:AnyObject) {
    let oldb = sender as! UIBarButtonItem
    let s = oldb.title!
    let ni = UINavigationItem(title:s)
    if s == "Evers" {
        let b = UIBarButtonItem(title:"Chance",
            style: .Plain, target:self, action:"pushNext:")
        ni.rightBarButtonItem = b
    }
    self.navbar.pushNavigationItem(ni, animated:true)
}
```

UIToolbar

A toolbar (UIToolbar, Figure 12-23) is intended to appear at the bottom of the screen; on the iPad, it may appear at the top. It displays a row of UIBarButtonItems, which are its items. The items are displayed from left to right in the order in which they appear in the items array. You can set the items with animation by calling set-Items:animated:. The items within the toolbar are positioned automatically; you can intervene in this positioning by using the system bar button items .FlexibleSpace and .FixedSpace, along with the UIBarButtonItem width property.

UITabBar

A tab bar (UITabBar) displays tab bar items (UITabBarItem), its items, each consisting of an image and a name. To change the items in an animated fashion, call set-Items:animated:.

The tab bar maintains a current selection among its items, its selectedItem, which is a UITabBarItem, not an index number; you can set it in code, or the user can set it by tapping on a tab bar item. To hear about the user changing the selection, implement tabBar:didSelectItem: in the delegate (UITabBarDelegate).

You get some control over how the tab bar items are laid out:

`itemPositioning`

There are three possible values (UITabBarItemPositioning):

`.Centered`

The items are crowded together at the center.

`.Fill`

The items are spaced out evenly.

`.Automatic`

On the iPad, the same as `.Centered`; on the iPhone, the same as `.Fill`.

`itemSpacing`

The space between items, if the positioning is `.Centered`. For the default space, specify 0.

`itemWidth`

The width of items, if the positioning is `.Centered`. For the default width, specify 0.

You can set the image drawn behind the selected tab bar item to indicate that it's selected, the `selectionIndicatorImage`.

A UITabBarItem is created with one of these methods:

- `init(tabBarSystemItem:tag:)`
- `init(title:image:tag:)`
- `init(title:image:selectedImage:)`

UITabBarItem is a subclass of UIBarItem, so in addition to its `title` and `image` it inherits the ability to adjust the image position with `imageInsets`, plus the `enabled` and `tag` properties. The UITabBarItem itself adds the `selectedImage` property.

A tab bar item's title text and template image are tinted, by default, with the tab bar's `tintColor` *when selected*; there's no way to set the deselected tint color (this was possible before iOS 7, so I regard the change as a bug). You can customize the title (including its color) with an attributes dictionary (`setTitleTextAttributes:forState:`, inherited from UIBarItem), and you can adjust the title's position with the `titlePosition-Adjustment` property. The image is treated as a template image, but you can override that by supplying an `.AlwaysOriginal` image; in this way, you can control the color of both the `image` and `selectedImage`.

Figure 12-24 is an example of a customized tab bar; I've set the selection indicator image (the checkmark), the tint color, and the text attributes (including the color, when selected) of the tab bar items.

Figure 12-24. A tab bar

The user can be permitted to alter the contents of the tab bar, setting its tab bar items from among a larger repertory of tab bar items. To summon the interface that lets the user do this, call beginCustomizingItems:, passing an array of UITabBarItems that may or may not appear in the tab bar. (To prevent the user from removing an item from the tab bar, include it in the tab bar's items and *don't* include it in the argument passed to beginCustomizingItems:.) A presented view with a Done button appears, behind the tab bar but in front of everything else, displaying the customizable items. The user can then drag an item into the tab bar, replacing an item that's already there. To hear about the customizing view appearing and disappearing, implement delegate methods:

- tabBar:willBeginCustomizingItems:

- tabBar:didBeginCustomizingItems:

- tabBar:willEndCustomizingItems:changed:

- tabBar:didEndCustomizingItems:changed:

A UITabBar on its own (outside a UITabBarController) does not provide any automatic access to the user customization interface; it's up to you. In this (silly) example, we populate a UITabBar with four system tab bar items and a More item; we also populate an instance variable array with those same four system tab bar items, plus three more. When the user taps the More item, we show the user customization interface with all seven tab bar items:

```
var items : [UITabBarItem] = {
    Array(1..<8).map {
        UITabBarItem(
            tabBarSystemItem:UITabBarSystemItem(rawValue:$0)!, tag:$0)
    }
}()
override func viewDidLoad() {
    super.viewDidLoad()
    self.tabbar.items = Array(self.items[0..<4]) +
        [UITabBarItem(tabBarSystemItem: .More, tag: 0)]
    self.tabbar.selectedItem = self.tabbar.items![0]
}
func tabBar(tabBar: UITabBar, didSelectItem item: UITabBarItem) {
    if item.tag == 0 {
        // More button
        tabBar.selectedItem = nil
        tabBar.beginCustomizingItems(self.items)
```

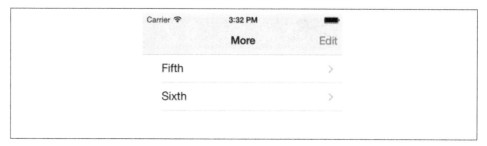

Figure 12-25. Automatically generated More list

```
        }
    }
    func tabBar(tabBar: UITabBar, didEndCustomizingItems items: [UITabBarItem],
        changed: Bool) {
            self.tabbar.selectedItem = self.tabbar.items![0]
    }
```

When used in conjunction with a UITabBarController, the customization interface is provided automatically, in an elaborate way. If there are a lot of items, a More item is automatically present, and can be used to access the remaining items in a table view. In this table view, the user can select any of the excess items, navigating to the corresponding view; or the user can switch to the customization interface by tapping the Edit button. Figure 12-25 shows how a More list looks by default.

The way this works is that the automatically provided More item corresponds to a UINavigationController with a root view controller (UIViewController) whose view is a UITableView. Thus, a navigation interface containing this UITableView appears through the tabbed interface when the user taps the More button. When the user selects an item in the table, the corresponding UIViewController is pushed onto the UINavigationController's stack.

You can access this UINavigationController: it is the UITabBarController's more-NavigationController. Through it, you can access the root view controller: it is the first item in the UINavigationController's viewControllers array. And through that, you can access the table view: it is the root view controller's view. This means you can customize what appears when the user taps the More button! For example, let's make the navigation bar red with white button titles, and let's remove the word More from its title:

```
    let more = self.tabBarController.moreNavigationController
    let list = more.viewControllers[0]
    list.title = ""
    let b = UIBarButtonItem()
```

```
b.title = "Back"
list.navigationItem.backBarButtonItem = b
more.navigationBar.barTintColor = UIColor.redColor()
more.navigationBar.tintColor = UIColor.whiteColor()
```

We can go even further by supplementing the table view's data source with a data source of our own, thus proceeding to customize the table itself. This is tricky because we have no internal access to the actual data source, and we mustn't accidentally disable it from populating the table. Still, it can be done. I'll start by replacing the table view's data source with an instance of my own MyDataSource, initializing it with a reference to the *original* data source object:

```
let tv = list.view as! UITableView
let mds = MyDataSource(originalDataSource: tv.dataSource!)
self.myDataSource = mds
tv.dataSource = mds
```

In MyDataSource, I'll use message forwarding (see Apple's *Objective-C Runtime Programming Guide*) so that MyDataSource acts as a front end for originalDataSource. MyDataSource will magically appear to respond to any message that originalDataSource responds to, and any message that arrives that MyDataSource can't handle will be magically forwarded to originalDataSource. This way, the insertion of the MyDataSource instance as data source doesn't break whatever the original data source does:

```
override func forwardingTargetForSelector(aSelector: Selector)
    -> AnyObject? {
        if self.originalDataSource.respondsToSelector(aSelector) {
            return self.originalDataSource
        }
        return super.forwardingTargetForSelector(aSelector)
}
```

Finally, we'll implement the two Big Questions required by the UITableViewDataSource protocol, to quiet the compiler. In both cases, we first pass the message along to originalDataSource (somewhat analogous to calling super); then we add our own customizations as desired. Here, just as a proof of concept, I'll change each cell's text font (Figure 12-26):

```
func tableView(tv: UITableView, numberOfRowsInSection sec: Int) -> Int {
    return self.originalDataSource.tableView(
        tv, numberOfRowsInSection: sec)
}
func tableView(tv: UITableView, cellForRowAtIndexPath ip: NSIndexPath)
    -> UITableViewCell {
        let cell = self.originalDataSource.tableView(
            tv, cellForRowAtIndexPath: ip)
        cell.textLabel!.font = UIFont(name: "GillSans-Bold", size: 14)!
        return cell
}
```

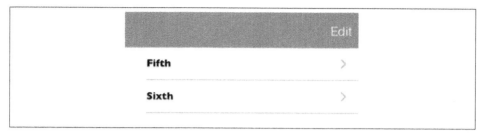

Figure 12-26. Customized More list

Tint Color

The UIView and UIBarButtonItem `tintColor` property has a remarkable built-in feature: its value, if not set explicitly (or if set to `nil`), is inherited from its superview. The idea is to simplify the task of giving your app a consistent overall appearance. Many built-in interface objects use the `tintColor` for some aspect of their appearance, as I've already described. For example, if a `.System` button's `tintColor` is red, either because you've set it directly or because it has inherited that color from higher up the view hierarchy, it will have red title text by default.

This works exactly the way you would expect:

Inheritance

When you set the `tintColor` of a view, that value is inherited by all subviews of that view. The ultimate superview is the window; thus, you can set the `tintColor` of your UIWindow instance, and its value will be inherited by *every* view that ever appears in your interface.

Overriding

The inherited `tintColor` can be overridden by setting a view's `tintColor` explicitly. Thus, you can set the `tintColor` of a view partway down the view hierarchy so that it and all its subviews have a different `tintColor` from the rest of the interface. In this way, you might subtly suggest that the user has entered a different world.

Propagation

If you change the `tintColor` of a view, the change immediately propagates down the hierarchy of its subviews — except, of course, that a view whose `tintColor` has been explicitly set to a color of its own is unaffected, along with its subviews.

Whenever a view's `tintColor` changes, including when its `tintColor` is initially set at launch time, and including when *you* set it in code, *this view and all its affected subviews* are sent the `tintColorDidChange` message. A subview whose `tintColor` has previously been explicitly set to a color of its own isn't affected, so it is *not* sent the `tintColorDidChange` message merely because its superview's `tintColor` changes — the subview's own `tintColor` *didn't* change.

When you ask a view for its `tintColor`, what you get is the `tintColor` of the view itself, if its own `tintColor` has been explicitly set to a color, or else the `tintColor` inherited from up the view hierarchy. In this way, you can always learn what the *effective* tint color of a view is.

A UIView also has a `tintAdjustmentMode`. Under certain circumstances, such as the summoning of an alert (Chapter 13) or a popover (Chapter 9), the system will set the `tintAdjustmentMode` of the view at the top of the view hierarchy to `.Dimmed`. This causes the `tintColor` to change to a variety of gray. The idea is that the tinting of the background should become monochrome, thus emphasizing the primacy of the view that occupies the foreground (the alert or popover). See "Custom Presented View Controller Transition" on page 326 for an example of my own code making this change.

By default, this change in the `tintAdjustmentMode` propagates all the way down the view hierarchy, changing *all* `tintAdjustmentMode` values and *all* `tintColor` values — and sending *all* subviews the `tintColorDidChange` message. When the foreground view goes away, the system will set the topmost view's `tintAdjustmentMode` to `.Normal`, and that change, too, will propagate down the hierarchy.

This propagation behavior is governed by the `tintAdjustmentMode` of the subviews. The default `tintAdjustmentMode` value is `.Automatic`, meaning that you want this view's `tintAdjustmentMode` to adopt its superview's `tintAdjustmentMode` automatically. When you ask for such a view's `tintAdjustmentMode`, what you get is just like what you get for `tintColor` — you're told the *effective* tint adjustment mode (`.Normal` or `.Dimmed`) inherited from up the view hierarchy.

If, on the other hand, you set a view's `tintAdjustmentMode` *explicitly* to `.Normal` or `.Dimmed`, this tells the system that you want to be left in charge of the `tintAdjustment-Mode` for this part of the hierarchy; the automatic propagation of the `tintAdjustment-Mode` down the view hierarchy is prevented. To turn automatic propagation back on, set the `tintAdjustmentMode` back to `.Automatic`.

You can take advantage of `tintColorDidChange` to make your custom UIView subclass behave like a built-in UIView subclass. For example, a `.Custom` UIButton might not automatically dim the title text color. But the button's `tintColor` is still being dimmed, even though that color isn't being applied to the visible interface; thus, to imitate a `.System` UIButton, you can apply the `tintColor` yourself.

In this example, my UIButton has an attributed title, configured in the nib editor, so its title doesn't automatically change color when the superview's `tintColor` changes. But I want my button to participate in dimming. So I subclass UIButton and change the attributed title to a gray version of itself when the inherited `tintAdjustmentMode` changes to `.Dimmed`:

```
class MySpecialButton : UIButton {
    var originalTitle : NSAttributedString?
    var dimmedTitle : NSAttributedString?
    override func awakeFromNib() {
        super.awakeFromNib()
        self.originalTitle = self.attributedTitleForState(.Normal)!
        let t = NSMutableAttributedString(
            attributedString: self.attributedTitleForState(.Normal)!)
        t.addAttribute(
            NSForegroundColorAttributeName, value: UIColor.grayColor(),
            range: NSMakeRange(0,t.length))
        self.dimmedTitle = t
    }
    override func tintColorDidChange() {
        self.setAttributedTitle(
            self.tintAdjustmentMode == .Dimmed ?
                self.dimmedTitle : self.originalTitle,
            forState: .Normal)
    }
}
```

Appearance Proxy

When you want to customize the look of an interface object, instead of sending a message to the object itself, you can send that message to an *appearance proxy* for that object's class. The appearance proxy then passes that same message along to the actual *future* instances of that class. You'll usually configure your appearance proxies once very early in the lifetime of the app, and never again. The app delegate's `application:didFinish-LaunchingWithOptions:`, before the app's window has been displayed, is the most obvious and common location.

Like the `tintColor` that I discussed in the previous section, this architecture helps you give your app a consistent appearance, as well as saving you from having to write a lot of code. For example, instead of having to send `setTitleTextAttributes:forState:` to *every* UIBarButtonItem your app *ever* instantiates, you send it *once* to the appearance proxy, and it is sent to all future UIBarButtonItems for you:

```
UIBarButtonItem.appearance()
    .setTitleTextAttributes(
        [NSFontAttributeName: UIFont(name:"GillSans-Bold", size:16)!],
        forState: .Normal)
```

Also, the appearance proxy sometimes provides access to interface objects that might otherwise be difficult to refer to. For example, you don't get direct access to a search bar's external Cancel button, but it is a UIBarButtonItem and you can customize it through the UIBarButtonItem appearance proxy.

There are four class methods for obtaining an appearance proxy:

appearance
Returns a general appearance proxy for the receiver class.

appearanceForTraitCollection:
Returns an appearance proxy applicable to situations where the environment matches the specified trait collection.

appearanceWhenContainedInInstancesOfClasses:
The argument is an array of classes, arranged in order of containment from inner to outer. The method you send to the appearance proxy returned from this call will be passed on only to instances of the receiver class that are actually contained in the way you describe. The notion of what "contained" means is deliberately left vague; basically, it works the way you intuitively expect it to work.

appearanceForTraitCollection:whenContainedInInstancesOfClasses:
A combination of the preceding two: returns an appearance proxy applicable when both the specified trait collection and the specified containment hierarchy are matched.

 The two whenContainedIn... methods are new in iOS 9, superseding two existing methods that unfortunately could not be called in Swift.

When configuring appearance proxy objects, *specificity trumps generality*. Thus, you could call appearance to say what should happen for *most* instances of some class, and call appearanceForTraitCollection: or appearanceWhenContainedIn...: to say what should happen *instead* for *certain* instances of that class. Similarly, longer appearanceWhenContainedIn...: chains are more specific than shorter ones.

For example, here's some code from my Latin flashcard app (myGolden and myPaler are class methods defined by an extension on UIColor):

```
UIBarButtonItem.appearance().tintColor = UIColor.myGolden() ❶
UIBarButtonItem.appearanceWhenContainedInInstancesOfClasses(
    [UIToolbar.self]).tintColor = UIColor.myPaler() ❷
UIBarButtonItem.appearanceWhenContainedInInstancesOfClasses(
    [UIToolbar.self, DrillViewController.self])
        .tintColor = UIColor.myGolden() ❸
```

That means:

❶ In general, bar button items should be tinted golden.

❷ But bar button items in a toolbar are an exception: they should be tinted paler.

❸ But bar button items in a toolbar in DrillViewController's view are an exception to the exception: they should be tinted golden.

Sometimes, in order to express sufficient specificity, I find myself defining subclasses for no other purpose than to refer to them when obtaining an appearance proxy. For example, here's some more code from my Latin flashcard app:

```
UINavigationBar.appearance()
    .setBackgroundImage(marble2, forBarMetrics:.Default)
// counteract the above for the black navigation bar
BlackNavigationBar.appearance()
    .setBackgroundImage(nil, forBarMetrics:.Default)
```

In that code, BlackNavigationBar is a UINavigationBar subclass that does nothing whatever. Its sole purpose is to tag one navigation bar in my interface so that I can refer to it in that code! Thus, I'm able to say, in effect, "All navigation bars in this app should have marble2 as their background image, unless they are instances of BlackNavigation-Bar."

The ultimate in specificity is, of course, to customize the look of an instance directly. Thus, for example, if you set one particular UIBarButtonItem's tintColor property, then setting the tint color by way of a UIBarButtonItem appearance proxy will have no effect on that particular bar button item.

Be warned, however, that not every message that can be sent to an instance of a class can be sent to that class's appearance proxy. Unfortunately, the compiler can't help you here; illegal code like this will compile, but will crash at runtime:

```
UIBarButtonItem.appearance().action = "crashme" // thanks, I will
```

When in doubt, look at the class documentation; there should be a section that lists the properties and methods applicable to the appearance proxy for this class. For example, the UINavigationBar class documentation has a section called "Customizing the Bar Appearance," the UIBarButtonItem class documentation has a section called "Customizing Appearance," and so forth.

 The headers and other documentation may appear to warn that tintColor is not a legal appearance proxy message. Don't worry; it *is* legal. However, it is also true that the *normal* tintColor property can conflict with appearance proxy settings. For example, setting an object's tintColor directly can undo a UIBarButtonItem's title font set previously through the appearance proxy's title text attributes.

CHAPTER 13

Modal Dialogs

A modal dialog demands attention; while it is present, the user can do nothing other than work within it or dismiss it. You might need to put up a simple modal dialog in order to give the user some information or to ask the user how to proceed. iOS provides two types of rudimentary modal dialog — alerts and action sheets.

A local notification is an alert that the system presents at a predetermined time on your app's behalf when your app isn't frontmost. I discuss local notifications in this chapter as well. I'll also talk about today extensions, a mechanism whereby your app can present interface on the Today side of the device's notification center.

An activity view is a modal dialog displaying icons representing possible courses of action, and intended in certain circumstances to replace the action sheet. For example, Mobile Safari's Share button presents an activity view whose icons represent possible operations on a URL, such as handing it off to Mail, Message, or Twitter, or saving it internally as a bookmark or reading list item. I'll describe how to present an activity view and how to provide your own activities, either privately within your app or publicly as an action extension or share extension.

Alerts and Action Sheets

Alerts and action sheets are both forms of presented view controller. They are managed through the UIAlertController class, a UIViewController subclass. To show an alert or an action sheet is a three-step process:

1. Instantiate UIAlertController with `init(title:message:preferredStyle:)`. The `title:` and `message:` are large and small descriptive text to appear at the top of the dialog. The `preferredStyle:` (UIAlertControllerStyle) will be either `.Alert` or `.ActionSheet`.

2. Configure the dialog by calling `addAction:` on the UIAlertController as many times as needed. An action is a UIAlertAction, which basically means it's a button to appear in the dialog, along with a function to be executed when the button is tapped; to create one, call `init(title:style:handler:)`. Possible `style:` values are (UIAlertActionStyle):

- `.Default`
- `.Cancel`
- `.Destructive`

An alert may also have text fields (I'll talk about that in a moment).

3. Call `presentViewController:animated:completion:` to present the UIAlertController.

The dialog is automatically dismissed when the user taps any button.

Alerts

An alert (UIAlertController style `.Alert`) pops up unexpectedly in the middle of the screen, with an elaborate animation, and may be thought of as an attention-getting interruption. It contains a title, a message, and some number of buttons, one of which may be the cancel button, meaning that it does nothing but dismiss the alert. In addition, an alert may contain one or two text fields.

Alerts are minimal, but intentionally so; they are intended for simple, quick interaction or display of information. Often there is only a cancel button, the primary purpose of the alert being to show the user the message ("You won the game"); additional buttons may be used to give the user a choice of how to proceed ("You won the game; would you like to play another?" "Yes," "No," "Replay"). Text fields might allow the user to supply login credentials.

Figure 13-1 shows a basic alert, illustrating the title, the message, and the three button styles: `.Destructive`, `.Default`, and `.Cancel` respectively. Here's the code that generated it:

```
let alert = UIAlertController(title: "Not So Fast!",
    message: "Do you really want to do this " +
        "tremendously destructive thing?",
    preferredStyle: .Alert)
func handler(act:UIAlertAction) {
    print("User tapped \(act.title)")
}
alert.addAction(UIAlertAction(
    title: "No", style: .Cancel, handler: handler))
alert.addAction(UIAlertAction(
```

Figure 13-1. An alert

```
    title: "Yes", style: .Destructive, handler: handler))
alert.addAction(UIAlertAction(
    title: "Maybe", style: .Default, handler: handler))
self.presentViewController(alert, animated: true, completion: nil)
```

In Figure 13-1, observe that the `.Destructive` button appears first and the `.Cancel` button appears last, without regard to the order in which they are defined. The `.Default` button order of definition, on the other hand, will be the order of the buttons themselves. If no `.Cancel` button is defined, the last `.Default` button will be displayed as a `.Cancel` button.

New in iOS 9, you can designate an action as the alert's `preferredAction`. This appears to boldify the title of that button. For example, suppose I append this to the preceding code:

```
alert.preferredAction = alert.actions[2]
```

The order of the `actions` array is the order in which we added actions; thus, the preferred action is now the Maybe button. The order isn't changed — the Maybe button is still second — but the bold styling is removed from the No button and placed on the Maybe button instead.

As I've already mentioned, the dialog is dismissed automatically when the user taps a button. If you don't want to respond to the tap of a particular button, you can supply `nil` as the `handler:` argument. In the preceding code, I've provided a minimal `handler:` function for each button, just to show what one looks like. As the example demonstrates, the function receives the original UIAlertAction as a parameter, and can examine it as desired. The function can also access the alert controller itself, provided the alert controller is in scope at the point where the handler function is defined (which will usually be the case). My example code assigns the same function to all three buttons, but more often you'll give each button its own individual handler.

Now let's talk about adding text fields to an alert. Because space is limited on the smaller iPhone screen, especially when the keyboard is present, an alert that is to contain a text field should probably should have at most two buttons, with short titles such as "OK" and "Cancel," and at most two text fields. To add a text field to an alert, call `addText-FieldWithConfigurationHandler:`. The handler will receive the text field as a parameter; it is called before the alert appears, and can be used to configure the text field. Other handlers, such as the handler of a button, can access the text field through the alert's `textFields` property, which is an array. In this example, the user is invited to enter a number in the text field; if the alert is dismissed with the OK button, its handler reads the text from the text field:

```
let alert = UIAlertController(
    title: "Enter a number:", message: nil, preferredStyle: .Alert)
alert.addTextFieldWithConfigurationHandler {
    (tf:UITextField) in
    tf.keyboardType = .NumberPad
}
func handler(act:UIAlertAction) {
    let tf = alert.textFields![0]
    let s = tf.text // ... and now do something with the text ...
}
alert.addAction(UIAlertAction(
    title: "Cancel", style: .Cancel, handler: nil))
alert.addAction(UIAlertAction(
    title: "OK", style: .Default, handler: handler))
self.presentViewController(alert, animated: true, completion: nil)
```

A puzzle arises as to how to prevent the user from dismissing the alert if the text fields are not acceptably filled in. The alert will be dismissed if the user taps a button, and no button handler can prevent this. The solution is to disable the relevant buttons until the text fields are satisfactory. A UIAlertAction has an `enabled` property for this very purpose. I'll modify the preceding example so that the OK button can't initially be tapped:

```
alert.addAction(
    UIAlertAction(title: "Cancel", style: .Cancel, handler: nil))
alert.addAction(
    UIAlertAction(title: "OK", style: .Default, handler: handler))
alert.actions[1].enabled = false
self.presentViewController(alert, animated: true, completion: nil)
```

But this raises a new puzzle: how will the OK button be enabled? The text field can have a delegate or a control event target–action pair (Chapter 10), and so we can hear about the user typing in it. I'll modify the example again so that I'm notified as the user edits in the text field:

```
alert.addTextFieldWithConfigurationHandler {
    (tf:UITextField) in
    tf.keyboardType = .NumberPad
    tf.addTarget(self,
        action: "textChanged:", forControlEvents: .EditingChanged)
}
```

Our `textChanged:` method will now be called when the user edits, but this raises one final puzzle: how will this method, which receives a reference to the text field, get a reference to the OK button in the alert in order to enable it? My approach is to work my way up the responder chain from the text field to the alert controller. Here, I enable the OK button if and only if the text field contains some text:

```
func textChanged(sender:AnyObject) {
    let tf = sender as! UITextField
    var resp : UIResponder! = tf
    while !(resp is UIAlertController) { resp = resp.nextResponder() }
    let alert = resp as! UIAlertController
    alert.actions[1].enabled = (tf.text != "")
}
```

Action Sheets

An action sheet (UIAlertController style `.ActionSheet`) may be considered the iOS equivalent of a menu; it consists primarily of buttons. On the iPhone, it slides up from the bottom of the screen; on the iPad, it appears as a popover.

Where an alert is an interruption, an action sheet is a logical branching of what the user is already doing: it typically divides a single piece of interface into multiple possible courses of action. For example, in Apple's Mail app, a single Action button summons an action sheet that lets the user reply to the current message, forward it, or print it (or cancel and do nothing).

Figure 13-2 shows a basic action sheet on the iPhone. Here's the code that constructed it:

```
let action = UIAlertController(
    title: "Choose New Layout", message: nil, preferredStyle: .ActionSheet)
action.addAction(UIAlertAction(
    title: "Cancel", style: .Cancel, handler: nil))
func handler(act:UIAlertAction) {
    let s = act.title // ... and do something with that info here ...
}
for s in ["3 by 3", "4 by 3", "4 by 4", "5 by 4", "5 by 5"] {
    action.addAction(
        UIAlertAction(title: s, style: .Default, handler: handler))
}
self.presentViewController(action, animated: true, completion: nil)
```

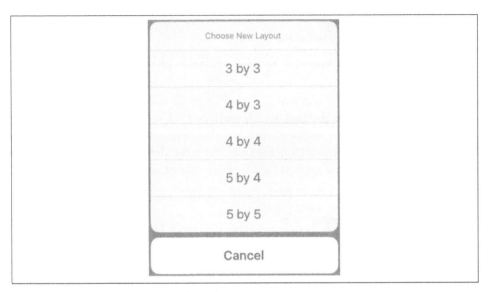

Figure 13-2. An action sheet on the iPhone

On the iPad, the action sheet wants to be a popover. This means that a UIPopover-PresentationController will take charge of it. It will thus be incumbent upon you to provide something for the popover's arrow to point to; otherwise, you'll crash at runtime (with an unbelievably helpful error message). You already know from Chapter 9 how to do that:

```
self.presentViewController(action, animated: true, completion: nil)
if let pop = action.popoverPresentationController {
    let v = sender as! UIView
    pop.sourceView = v
    pop.sourceRect = v.bounds
}
```

In that code, we're assuming that the sender (whatever was tapped in order to summon the action sheet) is a UIView. If it's a UIBarButtonItem, then obviously you'll set the popover presentation controller's barButtonItem, and you may want to do the little dance I demonstrated in Chapter 9 to set its passthroughViews to nil.

The Cancel button for a popover action sheet on the iPad is suppressed, because the user can dismiss the popover by tapping outside it. On the iPhone, too, where the Cancel button is displayed, the user can *still* dismiss the action sheet by tapping outside it. When the user does that, the Cancel button's handler function will be called, just as if the user had tapped the Cancel button — even if the Cancel button is not displayed.

An action sheet can also be presented *inside* a popover. In that case, the containing popover is treated as an iPhone: the action sheet slides up from the bottom of the

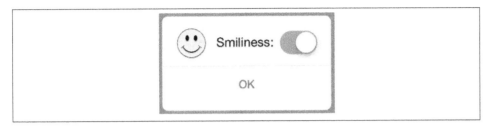

Figure 13-3. A presented view behaving like an alert

popover, and the Cancel button is *not* suppressed. The action sheet's modal presentation style defaults to `.OverCurrentContext`, which is exactly what we want, so there is no need to set it. You are then presenting a view controller inside a popover; see "Popover Presenting a View Controller" on page 521 for the considerations that apply. In iOS 9, the user can dismiss the popover and the action sheet by tapping outside the popover, unless you take precautions to prevent this. The user can dismiss the action sheet by tapping outside the action sheet but inside the popover; that's the same behavior I described in the preceding paragraph.

Dialog Alternatives

Alerts and action sheets are limited, inflexible, and inappropriate to any but the simplest cases. Their interface can contain title text, buttons, and (for an alert) one or two text fields, and that's all. What if you wanted more interface than that?

Some developers have hacked into their alerts or action sheets in an attempt to force them to be more customizable. *This is wrong*, and in any case there is no need for such extremes. These are just presented view controllers, and if you don't like what they contain, you can make your own presented view controller with its own customized view. If you also want that view to look and behave like an alert or an action sheet, then simply make it so! As I have already shown ("Custom Presented View Controller Transition" on page 326), it is easy to create a small presented view that looks and behaves quite like an alert or action sheet, floating in front of the main interface and darkening everything behind it — the difference being that this is an ordinary view controller's view, belonging entirely to you, and capable of being populated with any interface you like (Figure 13-3). You can even add a UIMotionEffect to your presented view, giving it the same parallax as a real alert.

Often, however, there will no need for such elaborate measures. A popover, after all, is virtually a secondary window, and can be truly modal. The popovers in Figure 9-1, for example, are effectively modal dialogs. A popover can internally display a secondary presented view or even an action sheet, as we've already seen. Also, a presented view can use the `.FormSheet` presentation style, which is effectively a dialog window smaller than the screen. On the iPhone, furthermore, *any* presented view is essentially a modal

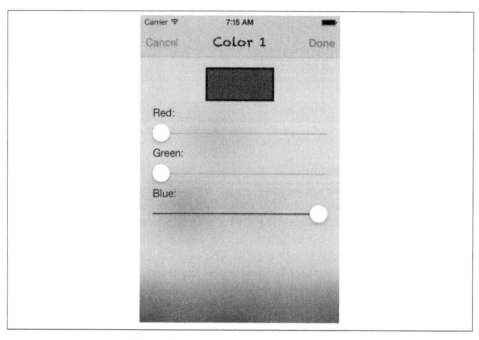

Figure 13-4. A presented view functioning as a modal dialog

dialog. The color picker in my Zotz! app (Figure 13-4) has the same lightweight, temporary quality that an alert offers, and on the desktop would probably be presented as part of a secondary Preferences window; it happens that, on the iPhone, it occupies the entire screen, but it is still effectively a modal dialog.

Local Notifications

A *local notification* is an alert to the user that can appear even if your app is not running. Where it may appear depends upon the user's preferences in the Settings app, either under Notification Center or under your app's own listing. In addition to optionally producing a sound, a local notification's interface possibilities are (Figure 13-5, clockwise from the top left):

- A modal alert, similar to a UIAlertController's alert
- A momentary banner at the top of the screen, which vanishes automatically if the user does nothing; this interface is mutually exclusive with the modal alert interface
- A row on the lock screen
- A row in the notification center

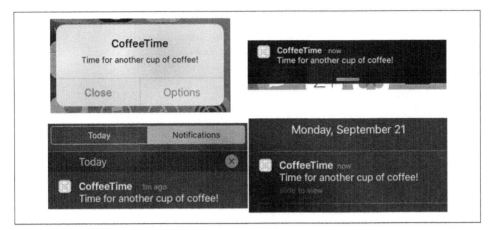

Figure 13-5. Local notification interface possibilities

 This use of the term *notification* has nothing to do with NSNotification; the ambiguity is unfortunate.

Your app does not present a local notification; the system does. You hand the system instructions for when the local notification is to *fire*, and then you just stand back and let the system deal with it. That's why the local notification can appear even if your app isn't frontmost or isn't even running. Indeed, if your app *is* frontmost, the local notification's alert or banner does *not* automatically appear when it fires; instead, your app is notified, and you can notify the user if you like. The only local notification alert that can appear when your app is frontmost is some *other* app's local notification (and in that case, your app will become inactive; see Appendix A).

The user, in the Settings app, can veto any of your local notification's interface options, or turn off your app's local notifications entirely. Thus, your local notification can be effectively suppressed; you can still create a local notification, but when it fires, only your app will hear about it, and only if it is frontmost. Moreover, the system will suppress your local notifications entirely unless the user approves first; thus, the user must deliberately opt in if your notification is ever to appear in any form. Figure 13-6 shows the alert that the system will show your user, once, offering the initial opportunity to opt in to your local notifications.

The interface whereby a notification is presented by the system to the user also provides a way for the user to summon your app in response, bringing it to the front if it is backgrounded, and launching it if it isn't running, by way of action buttons. An action button can appear in any of a notification's forms, you can customize it, you can have more than one, and an action button can communicate with your app without bringing

Figure 13-6. The user will see this only once

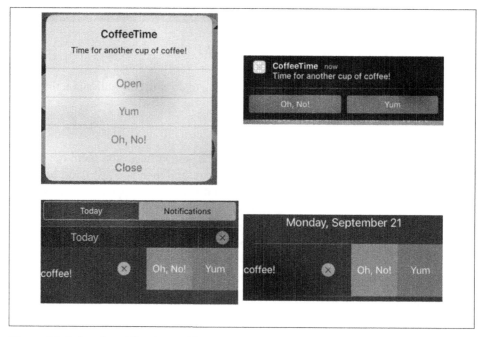

Figure 13-7. Local notifications with custom actions

it to the front. Thus, from a presented notification, the user can elect to open your app or to tap an action button; either way, your app will know what happened, as I'll explain in a moment. Figure 13-7 shows the various forms of interface through which the user might expose your notification's action buttons.

Creation of a local notification involves three steps, which I'll discuss in order:

1. Your app must *register* for notifications. Registration states what sorts of interface your notifications will want to use, and ensures that the user has seen the opt-in

dialog (Figure 13-6). This is also the moment when you provide action buttons. You may register as many times as you like (the opt-in dialog won't be repeated); each registration cancels the previous registration settings and replaces them with new ones.

2. Your app creates and schedules a local notification.

3. Your app is prepared to hear about the user responding to the notification.

Registering a Notification

When should registration be performed? Apple has not provided clear guidance; they say only "during your launch cycle." This would seem to suggest `application:did-FinishLaunchingWithOptions:` as a possible location. But there seems to be no clear reason why you shouldn't register just before creating a local notification for the first time, and this might make more sense if your app might never create a local notification, or if you think the user will be more eager to approve your notifications after using your app for a while. So that's the architecture I'll describe.

To register, you must supply two things:

Interface types

> Interface types (UIUserNotificationType) are `.Alert` (meaning alerts and banners), `.Sound`, and `.Badge`, forming a bitmask. Omit any that your app will never use, and that type will be omitted from Settings for your app; regardless of your registered interface types, the user will always see the options to show your notifications in the notification center and the lock screen.

Categories

> A category (UIUserNotificationCategory, along with its mutable subclass) is a value class comprising a string identifier along with any custom action buttons. When you create and schedule a local notification, you will associate it with a category by using the string identifier, thus determining what custom action buttons will be present.

An action button (UIUserNotificationAction, along with its mutable subclass) has the following properties:

`identifier`

> A private string identifier; this is how your app will know what button was tapped.

`title`

> The visible title of the button. Keep it short!

`destructive`

> If `true`, the button will be shown in red.

activationMode

A UIUserNotificationActivationMode, either `.Foreground` or `.Background`. In the latter case, your app will not be brought to the front when the user taps this button; instead, your app will be permitted to run briefly in the background.

authenticationRequired

If `true`, and if this is a `.Background` button, then if the user's device requires a passcode to go beyond the lock screen, tapping this button in the lock screen will also require a passcode. The idea is to prevent performance of a dangerous action without authentication directly from the lock screen.

behavior

New in iOS 9: a UIUserNotificationActionBehavior, either `.Default` or `.Text-Input`. I'll explain more about it in a moment.

We now know enough for an example! Here's some code that registers the notification shown in Figure 13-7:

```
let categoryIdentifier = "coffee"
func registerMyNotification() {
    let types : UIUserNotificationType = [.Alert, .Sound]
    let category = UIMutableUserNotificationCategory()
    category.identifier = self.categoryIdentifier
    let action1 = UIMutableUserNotificationAction()
    action1.identifier = "yum"
    action1.title = "Yum" // user will see this
    action1.destructive = false
    action1.activationMode = .Foreground
    let action2 = UIMutableUserNotificationAction()
    action2.identifier = "ohno"
    action2.title = "Oh, No!" // user will see this
    action2.destructive = false
    action2.activationMode = .Background
    category.setActions([action1, action2], forContext: .Default)
    let settings = UIUserNotificationSettings(
        forTypes: types, categories: [category])
    UIApplication.sharedApplication()
        .registerUserNotificationSettings(settings)
}
```

In `setActions:forContext:`, the possible contexts are `.Default` and `.Minimal`. A `.Default` context, a full-fledged alert, can have a maximum of four buttons; the other forms of interface can have a maximum of two. Thus, if you had more than two buttons for the `.Default` context, you would use an additional call to `setActions:forContext:` to say which buttons should appear in the `.Minimal` context.

New in iOS 9, an action button can secondarily summon a text field. To arrange this, set the UIUserNotificationAction's `behavior` property to `.TextInput`. The result is that when the user taps this button, regardless of how this notification is being presented, a banner appears at the top of the screen with a text field and a Send button. That Send button constitutes the actual action; your app won't be notified if the user doesn't tap it.

By calling the shared application's `currentUserNotificationSettings` method, you can check to see what UIUserNotificationCategory objects are already registered. In this way, we can avoid registering the same category twice (not that there is any harm in doing so, as the previous registration is simply replaced with the new one). I'll add such a check to the previous example:

```
func registerMyNotification() {
    if let settings =
        UIApplication.sharedApplication().currentUserNotificationSettings() {
            if let cats = settings.categories {
                for cat in cats {
                    if cat.identifier == self.categoryIdentifier {
                        return
                    }
                }
            }
    }
    // ... and the rest is as before ...
}
```

You can also learn whether the user has granted permissions for the notification types you requested when you registered. For example:

```
if let settings =
    UIApplication.sharedApplication().currentUserNotificationSettings() {
        if settings.types.contains(.Alert) {
            // alerts are enabled
        }
}
```

It is difficult, however, to see how that information is useful, as it is insufficiently fine-grained. Even if `settings.types` doesn't contain `.Alert` — even if, in fact, it is `.None` — that doesn't prove the user has completely turned off notifications for your app. There is always a chance that your notification might appear in the notification center or the lock screen; and you have no way to learn that this is not the case. Thus, although Apple claims you might call `currentUserNotificationSettings` in order to save yourself the trouble of preparing a certain notification, I don't follow that logic.

After you call `registerUserNotificationSettings:`, your app delegate will receive `application:didRegisterUserNotificationSettings:`. This is useful if you want to carry on after registering the notification. Registration might take time, because the permission dialog might appear (Figure 13-6). If it does, `application:didRegister-UserNotificationSettings:` won't be called until after the user has dismissed it.

We can thus see how to architect a single operation that registers, creates, and schedules a local notification. First, register the notification, and stop. Eventually, the app delegate's application:didRegisterUserNotificationSettings: is called; here, tell the appropriate instance to proceed to create and schedule the local notification. An NSNotification is a good medium of communication:

```
// in the app delegate:
func application(application: UIApplication,
    didRegisterUserNotificationSettings s: UIUserNotificationSettings) {
    NSNotificationCenter.defaultCenter().postNotificationName(
        "didRegisterUserNotificationSettings", object: self)
}

// in the place where the real action is:
func registerMyNotification() {
    // ... as before ...
    var ob : NSObjectProtocol! = nil
    ob = NSNotificationCenter.defaultCenter().addObserverForName(
        "didRegisterUserNotificationSettings", object: nil, queue: nil) {
            _ in
            NSNotificationCenter.defaultCenter().removeObserver(ob)
            self.createLocalNotification()
    }
    UIApplication.sharedApplication()
        .registerUserNotificationSettings(settings)
}
```

It remains to write `self.createLocalNotification()`. That's the subject of the next section.

Scheduling a Notification

We are now ready for the second step — creating and scheduling a notification. To create a local notification, you configure a UILocalNotification object and hand it to the shared UIApplication instance by calling `scheduleLocalNotification:`. The UILocal-Notification object has properties as follows:

category
> The identifier of a category you provided when you registered. If your category has actions, this also tells the runtime to provide them.

alertBody
> The message to be displayed in the notification.

soundName
> The name of a sound file at the top level of your app bundle, to be played when the alert appears. This should be an uncompressed sound (AIFF or WAV). Alternatively, you can specify the default sound, `UILocalNotificationDefaultSound-Name`. If you don't set this property, there won't be a sound (and of course the user can prevent your app's notifications from emitting any sound).

userInfo
> An optional dictionary whose contents are up to you. Your app can retrieve this dictionary later on, if it receives the notification after the notification fires.

fireDate, timeZone
> When you want the local notification to fire. The fireDate is an NSDate. If you don't include a timeZone, the date is measured against universal time; if you do include a timeZone, the date is measured against the user's local time zone, and thus it keeps working correctly if that time zone changes (because the user travels, for instance).

repeatInterval, repeatCalendar
> If set, the local notification will recur. The repeatInterval (an NSCalendarUnit) must be a minute or longer; setting it to .Second will result in a value of .Minute. Recurrence survives a restart of the device.

Additional UIApplication methods let you manipulate the list of local notifications you've already scheduled. You can cancel one or all scheduled local notifications (cancelLocalNotification:, cancelAllLocalNotifications:); you can also manipulate the list directly by setting the application's scheduledLocalNotifications array.

 Canceling a recurring local notification is up to your code; if you don't provide a way of doing that, and if the user wants to prevent the notification from recurring, the user's only recourse will be to delete your app.

Here's the code for creating and scheduling the local notification that results in Figure 13-5:

```
func createLocalNotification() {
    let ln = UILocalNotification()
    ln.alertBody = "Time for another cup of coffee!"
    ln.category = self.categoryIdentifier // adds action buttons
    ln.fireDate = NSDate(timeIntervalSinceNow:15)
    ln.soundName = UILocalNotificationDefaultSoundName
    UIApplication.sharedApplication().scheduleLocalNotification(ln)
}
```

Hearing About a Local Notification

Now let's talk about what happens when one of your scheduled local notifications fires. There are three possibilities, depending on the state of your app at that moment:

Your app is frontmost

The user won't be informed by the system that the notification has fired; there won't be any sound, alert, or banner. Your notification *will* be listed in the notification center if the user has granted permission.

Your app delegate will receive `application:didReceiveLocalNotification:`, where the second parameter is the UILocalNotification, and your application's `applicationState` will be `.Active`.

Your app is suspended or not running

What happens depends on what the user does in response to the firing of the alert:

The user summons your app

If the user taps the top of the banner or the Open button in the alert, or taps your notification in the notification center, or slides your notification in the lock screen to the right, your app is brought to the front, and:

If your app was suspended

Your app delegate will receive `application:didReceiveLocal-Notification:`, where the second parameter is the UILocalNotification, and your application's `applicationState` will be `.Inactive`.

If your app was not running

Your app delegate will receive `application:didFinishLaunchingWith-Options:`, with a dictionary parameter that includes the `UIApplication-LaunchOptionsLocalNotificationKey`, whose value is the UILocal-Notification.

The user taps an action button

Your app delegate will receive `application:handleActionWithIdentifier:forLocalNotification:withResponseInfo:completionHandler:`. You *must* call the completion handler at the end of your implementation! If this is a `.Background` button, your app is now running in the background. You have very little time before being suspended, so respond quickly.

The `responseInfo:` parameter, which is new in iOS 9, is a dictionary. If we got here because this action button has a `.TextInput` behavior and the user tapped the Send button in the text field, this dictionary will contain the text field's text, by way of its `UIUserNotificationActionResponseTypedTextKey`.

(If your app wasn't running and your app delegate thus also receives `application:didFinishLaunchingWithOptions:`, the options dictionary will be `nil`.)

Nothing (or close)

If the user does nothing, or closes the banner, or taps Close in the alert, that's the end of the matter; your app will never be informed that the notification fired.

Thus, to cover all possible cases, you should implement all three app delegate methods:

`application:didFinishLaunchingWithOptions:`

Check its second parameter to see whether we are launching in response to a local notification.

`application:didReceiveLocalNotification:`

Check the UIApplication's `applicationState` and the notification as desired.

`application:handleActionWithIdentifier:forLocalNotification:withResponse-Info:completionHandler:`

Check the identifier and notification as desired, look for the text field string if appropriate, and remember to call the completion handler. Here's a minimal implementation:

```
func application(application: UIApplication,
    handleActionWithIdentifier id: String?,
    forLocalNotification n: UILocalNotification,
    withResponseInfo d: [NSObject : AnyObject],
    completionHandler: () -> Void) {
        // ... examine id and n as desired ...
        if let s =
            d[UIUserNotificationActionResponseTypedTextKey] as? String {
                // ... do something with typed string ....
        }
        completionHandler() // crucial!
}
```

It comes as a surprise to beginners that your app can't always learn that a notification fired. For example, if a notification fired while your app wasn't in the foreground, and if the user didn't respond by summoning your app or tapping an action button, your app will never hear about the notification. The simple fact is that notifications are *between the system and the user.* They don't absolve your app from doing its homework, and they cannot be used to guarantee that your app will be running at a certain time. If your app's logic is about things happening at certain times, you'll need to implement your own internal model to keep track of those times and look to see, when you come the front, whether those times have passed.

If your app wasn't frontmost and the user summons it from a notification, you may want to show the user, immediately, some interface appropriate to this local notification. However, as your app appears, the user will first see either your default launch image (if the app is launched from scratch) or the screenshot image taken by the system when your app was suspended (if the app is activated from the background). To prevent a

Figure 13-8. A today extension

mismatch between that image and what the user will see when your app's interface actually appears, you can include in the original UILocalNotification an alertLaunchImage that more closely matches your app's interface.

Under some special circumstances (addressed, for example, in Chapters 14 and 22), your app might be running, *not* suspended, in the background, when your notification fires. In this case, the situation is similar to what happens when your app *is* suspended: the user may be notified, and can summon your app to the front. Your running-in-the-background app can even schedule a notification to fire immediately with the convenience method presentLocalNotificationNow:.

 A local notification can also fire in response to the user's location, rather than in reponse to the arrival of a certain time. I'll talk about that in Chapter 21.

Today Extensions

Your app can obtain a bit of real estate on the other side of the notification center — the Today side, as opposed to the Notifications side. To do so, you add to your app a *today extension*. Your app vends the extension, and the user has the option of adding it to the Today side of the notification center (Figure 13-8).

To add a today extension to your app, create a new target and specify iOS → Application Extension → Today Extension. The template gives you a good start on your extension. You have a storyboard with a single scene, and the code for a corresponding view controller that adopts the NCWidgetProviding protocol. You might need to edit the extension's *Info.plist* and set the "Bundle display name" entry — this is the title that will appear above your extension in the notification center.

 The today extension target will be explicitly linked to the NotificationCenter framework. This framework is crucial; without it, your today extension target will compile, but the today extension itself will crash.

Design your extension's interface in the storyboard provided. Use autolayout to position your views, and provide sufficient constraints to determine the full height of your extension's interface from the inside out. (Apple says that you can alternatively determine your extension's height by setting your view controller's preferredContentSize, but in my experimentation, autolayout proved more reliable.) If you want to add a UIVisualEffectView with vibrancy, do so in code, initializing the view's effect by calling UIVibrancyView's class method notificationCenterVibrancyEffect:

```
let v = UIVisualEffectView(
    effect: UIVibrancyEffect.notificationCenterVibrancyEffect())
```

Your interface will appear aligned to the notification center's margins, which by default involve a large left margin. To counteract that, implement the NCWidgetProviding protocol method widgetMarginInsetsForProposedMarginInsets:. For example:

```
func widgetMarginInsetsForProposedMarginInsets(
    defaultMarginInsets: UIEdgeInsets) -> UIEdgeInsets {
        return UIEdgeInsetsMake(0,16,0,16)
}
```

Each time your today extension's interface is about to appear, your code is given an opportunity to update its interface, through its implementation of widgetPerform-UpdateWithCompletionHandler:. Be sure to finish up by calling the completion-Handler, handing it an NCUpdateResult, which will be .NewData, .NoData, or .Failed. Time-consuming work should be performed off the main thread (see Chapter 25):

```
func widgetPerformUpdateWithCompletionHandler(
    completionHandler: ((NCUpdateResult) -> Void)) {
        // ... do stuff off the main thread here ...
        // ... then get back on the main thread and call:
        completionHandler(NCUpdateResult.NewData)
}
```

That's basically all there is to a today extension, but be sure to read the NCWidget-Providing protocol header and the "Today" chapter of Apple's *App Extension Programming Guide*. Also, look at the "Handling Common Scenarios" section to understand how to communicate data and messages between your app and the extension. The extension is not running within your app, but is being hosted by some other app; thus, there are some calls you can't make — for example, there is no shared application object — and communication can be a bit tricky.

In Figure 13-8, two buttons invite the user to set up a reminder; I've implemented these to open our CoffeeTime app by calling openURL:completionHandler: — a method of the automatically provided extensionContext, not the shared application:

▼ URL types		Array	(1 item)
▼ Item 0 (Viewer)		Dictionary	(3 items)
Document Role		String	Viewer
URL identifier		String	com.neuburg.matt.coffeetime
▼ URL Schemes		Array	(1 item)
Item 0		String	coffeetime

Figure 13-9. A custom URL declaration

```swift
@IBAction func doButton(sender: AnyObject) {
    let v = sender as! UIView
    let t = v.tag // tag is number of minutes
    if let url = NSURL(string:"coffeetime://\(t)") {
        self.extensionContext?.openURL(url, completionHandler: nil)
    }
}
```

The CoffeeTime app receives this message because I've given it two things:

A custom URL scheme

The `coffeetime` scheme is declared in the app's *Info.plist* (Figure 13-9).

An implementation of `application:openURL:options:`

In the app delegate, I've implemented `application:openURL:options:` to analyze the URL when it arrives. I've coded the original URL so that the "host" is actually the number of minutes announced in the tapped button; thus, I can respond appropriately (presumably by scheduling a local notification for that number of minutes from now):

```swift
func application(app: UIApplication,
    openURL url: NSURL, options: [String : AnyObject]) -> Bool {
        let scheme = url.scheme
        let host = url.host
        if scheme == "coffeetime" {
            if let host = host, min = Int(host) {
                // ... do something here ...
                return true
            }
        }
        return false
}
```

Activity Views

An activity view is the view belonging to a UIActivityViewController, typically appearing when the user taps a Share button. To display it, you start with one or more pieces of data, such as a string, that you want the user to have the option of sharing or working with. The activity view, when it appears, will then contain an icon for every activity (UIActivity) that can work with this type of data. The user may tap an icon in the activity

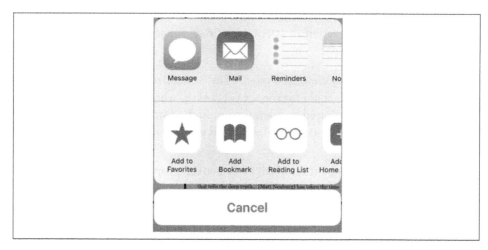

Figure 13-10. An activity view

view, and is then perhaps shown additional interface, belonging to the provider of the chosen activity. Figure 13-10 shows an example, from Mobile Safari.

In Figure 13-10, the top row of the activity view lists some applicable built-in system-wide activities; the bottom row shows some activities provided internally by Safari itself. When you present an activity view within your app, your app can add to the lower row additional activities that are available only within your app. Moreover, your app can provide system-wide activities that are available when *any* app presents an activity view; such system-wide activities come in two forms:

Share extensions

A *share extension* is shown in the *upper* row of an activity view. Share extensions are for apps that can accept information into themselves, either for storage, such as Notes and Reminders, or for sending out to a server, such as Twitter and Facebook.

Action extensions

An *action extension* is shown in the *lower* row of an activity view. Action extensions offer to perform some kind of manipulation on the data provided by the host app, and can hand back the resulting data in reply.

I'll describe how to present an activity view and how to construct an activity that's private to your app. Then I'll give an example of writing an action extension, and finally an example of writing a share extension.

 Don't confuse UIActivityViewController, UIActivity, UIActivityItemProvider, and UIActivityItemSource, on the one hand, with UIActivityIndicatorView (Chapter 12) on the other. The similarity of the names is unfortunate.

Presenting an Activity View

You will typically want to present an activity view in response to the user tapping a Share button in your app. To do so:

1. Instantiate UIActivityViewController. The initializer you'll be calling is init(activityItems:applicationActivities:), where the first argument is an array of objects to be shared or operated on, such as string or image objects. Presumably these are objects associated somehow with the interface the user is looking at right now.

2. Set the controller's completionWithItemsHandler property to a function that will be called when the user's interaction with the activity interface ends.

3. Present the controller, as a presented view controller; on the iPad, it will be a popover, so you'll also configure the popover presentation controller. The presented view or popover will be dismissed automatically when the user cancels or chooses an activity.

So, for example:

```
let url = NSBundle.mainBundle().URLForResource(
    "sunglasses", withExtension:"png")!
let things = ["This is a cool picture", url] // a string and an image URL
let avc = UIActivityViewController(
    activityItems:things, applicationActivities:nil)
avc.completionWithItemsHandler = {
    (s: String?, ok: Bool, items: [AnyObject]?, err:NSError?) -> Void in
    // ... optionally do something here; only the ok parameter matters ...
}
self.presentViewController(avc, animated:true, completion:nil)
if let pop = avc.popoverPresentationController {
    let v = sender as! UIView
    pop.sourceView = v
    pop.sourceRect = v.bounds
}
```

There is no Cancel button in the popover presentation of the activity view; the user cancels by tapping outside the popover. Actually, the user can cancel by tapping outside the activity view even on the iPhone.

The activity view is populated automatically with known system-wide activities that can handle any of the types of data you provided as the activityItems: argument. These activities represent UIActivity types, and are designated by string constants:

- UIActivityTypePostToFacebook
- UIActivityTypePostToTwitter
- UIActivityTypePostToWeibo

- UIActivityTypeMessage

- UIActivityTypeMail

- UIActivityTypePrint

- UIActivityTypeCopyToPasteboard

- UIActivityTypeAssignToContact

- UIActivityTypeSaveToCameraRoll

- UIActivityTypeAddToReadingList

- UIActivityTypePostToFlickr

- UIActivityTypePostToVimeo

- UIActivityTypePostToTencentWeibo

- UIActivityTypeAirDrop

- UIActivityTypeOpenInIBooks

Consult the UIActivity class documentation to learn what types of activity item each of these activities can handle. For example, the UIActivityTypeMail activity will accept a string, an image, or a file on disk (such as an image file) designated by an NSURL; it will present a mail composition interface with the activity item(s) in the body.

Since the default is to include all the system-wide activities that can handle the provided data, if you *don't* want a certain system-wide activity included in the activity view, you must exclude it explicitly. You do this by setting the UIActivityViewController's excludedActivityTypes property to an array of activity type constants.

 The Notes and Reminders activities have no corresponding UIActivity, because they are implemented as share extensions; it is up to the *user* to turn them off if desired.

In the UIActivityViewController initializer init(activityItems:application-Activities:), if you would prefer that an element of the activityItems: array be an object that will supply the data, instead of the data itself, make that object adopt the UIActivityItemSource protocol. Typically, this object will be self (the view controller in charge of all this code). Here's a minimal example:

```
extension ViewController : UIActivityItemSource {
    func activityViewControllerPlaceholderItem(
        activityViewController: UIActivityViewController)
        -> AnyObject {
            return ""
    }
    func activityViewController(
```

```
        activityViewController: UIActivityViewController,
        itemForActivityType activityType: String)
        -> AnyObject? {
            return "Coolness"
    }
}
```

The first method provides a placeholder that exemplifies the type of data that will be returned; the second method returns the actual data. Observe that the second method can return different data depending on the activity type that the user chose; for example, you could provide one string to Notes and another string to Mail.

The UIActivitySource protocol also answers a commonly asked question about how to get the Mail activity to populate the mail composition form with a default subject:

```
extension ViewController : UIActivityItemSource {
    // ...
    func activityViewController(
        activityViewController: UIActivityViewController,
        subjectForActivityType activityType: String?) -> String {
            return "This is cool"
    }
}
```

(There is no official way to provide a default recipient, presumably because sharing is up to the user. For a mail composition interface where you *can* provide a default recipient, see Chapter 20.)

If your `activityItems:` data is time-consuming to provide, substitute an instance of a `UIActivityItemProvider` subclass:

```
let avc = UIActivityViewController(
    activityItems:[MyProvider(placeholderItem: "")],
    applicationActivities:nil)
```

The `placeholderItem:` in the initializer signals the type of data that this UIActivityItem-Provider object will actually provide. Your UIActivityItemProvider subclass should implement the `item` method to return the actual object; this method runs on a background thread, and UIActivityItemProvider is itself an NSOperation subclass (see Chapter 25).

Custom Activities

The purpose of the `applicationActivities:` parameter of `init(activity-Items:applicationActivities:)` is for you to list any additional activities implemented internally by your own app, so that their icons will appear as choices in the lower row when your app presents an activity view. Each activity will be an instance of one of your own UIActivity subclasses.

To illustrate, I'll create a minimal (and nonsensical) activity called Be Cool that accepts string activity items. It is a UIActivity subclass called MyCoolActivity. So, to include Be Cool among the choices presented to the user by a UIActivityViewController, I'd say:

```
let things = ["This is a cool picture", url] // a string and an image URL
let avc = UIActivityViewController(
    activityItems:things, applicationActivities:[MyCoolActivity()])
```

Now let's implement MyCoolActivity. It has an array property called items, for reasons that will be apparent in a moment. We need to arm ourselves with an image to represent this activity in the activity view; this will be treated as a template image. It should be no larger than 60×60 (76×76 on iPad); it can be smaller, and looks better if it is, because the system will draw a rounded rectangle around it, and the image should be somewhat inset from this. It needn't be square, as it will be centered in the rounded rectangle automatically.

Here's the preparatory part of the implementation of MyCoolActivity:

```
override class func activityCategory() -> UIActivityCategory {
    return .Action // the default
}
override func activityType() -> String? {
    return "com.neuburg.matt.coolActivity"
}
override func activityTitle() -> String? {
    return "Be Cool"
}
override func activityImage() -> UIImage? {
    return self.image // prepared beforehand
}
override func canPerformWithActivityItems(
    activityItems: [AnyObject]) -> Bool {
        for obj in activityItems {
            if obj is String {
                return true
            }
        }
        return false
}
override func prepareWithActivityItems(activityItems: [AnyObject]) {
    self.items = activityItems
}
```

If we return true from canPerformWithActivityItems:, then an icon for this activity, labeled Be Cool and displaying our activityImage, will appear in the activity view. If the user taps our icon, prepareWithActivityItems: will be called. We retain the activityItems into a property, because they won't be arriving again when we are actually told to perform the activity.

The next step, if the user has tapped our icon in the activity view, is that we will be called upon to perform the activity. To do so, we implement one of two methods:

`performActivity`

   We simply perform the activity directly, using the activity items we've already retained. If the activity is time-consuming, the activity should be performed on a background thread (Chapter 25) so that we can return immediately; the activity view interface will be taken down and the user will be able to go on interacting with the app.

`activityViewController`

   We have further interface that we'd like to show the user as part of the activity, so we return an instance of a UIViewController subclass. The activity view mechanism will present this view controller for us; it is not our job to present or dismiss it. (We may, however, present or dismiss dependent interface. For example, if our view controller is a navigation controller with a custom root view controller, we might push another view controller onto its stack while the user is interacting with the activity.)

No matter which of these two methods we implement, we *must* eventually call this activity instance's `activityDidFinish:`. This is the signal to the activity view mechanism that the activity is over. If the activity view mechanism is still presenting any interface, it will be taken down, and the argument we supply here, a Bool signifying whether the activity completed successfully, will be passed into the block we supplied earlier as the activity view controller's `completionWithItemsHandler`. So, for example:

```
override func performActivity() {
    // ... do something with self.items here ...
    self.activityDidFinish(true)
}
```

If your UIActivity is returning a view controller from `activityViewController`, it will want to hand that view controller a reference to `self` beforehand, so that the view controller can call its `activityDidFinish:` when the time comes.

For example, suppose our activity involves letting the user draw a mustache on a photo of someone. Our view controller will provide interface for doing that, including some way of letting the user signal completion, such as a Cancel button and a Done button. When the user taps either of those, we'll do whatever else is necessary (such as saving the altered photo somewhere if the user tapped Done) and then call `activityDid-Finish:`. Thus, we could implement `activityViewController` like this:

```
override func activityViewController() -> UIViewController? {
    let mvc = MustacheViewController(activity: self, items: self.items!)
    return mvc
}
```

And then MustacheViewController would have code like this:

```
weak var activity : UIActivity?
var items: [AnyObject]
init(activity:UIActivity, items:[AnyObject]) {
    self.activity = activity
    self.items = items
    super.init(nibName: "MustacheViewController", bundle: nil)
}
// ... other stuff ...
@IBAction func doCancel(sender:AnyObject) {
    self.activity?.activityDidFinish(false)
}
@IBAction func doDone(sender:AnyObject) {
    self.activity?.activityDidFinish(true)
}
```

Note that MustacheViewController's reference to the UIActivity (`self.activity`) is weak; otherwise, a retain cycle ensues.

> The purpose of the SFSafariViewController delegate method `safariView-Controller:activityItemsForURL:title:` (Chapter 11) is now clear. This view controller's view appears inside your app, but it isn't your view controller, its Share button is not your button, and the activity view that it presents is not your activity view. Therefore you need some other way to add custom UIActivity items to that activity view; to do so, implement this method.

Action Extensions

To provide a system-wide activity — one that appears when some *other* app puts up an activity view — you can write a share extension (to appear in the upper row) or an action extension (to appear in the lower row). Your app can provide just one share extension, but can provide multiple action extensions. I'll describe first the basics of writing an action extension. (For full information, study the relevant documentation and WWDC 2014 videos.)

As with today extensions, start with the appropriate target template, iOS → Application Extension → Action Extension. There are two kinds of action extension, with or without an interface; you'll make your choice in the second pane as you create the target.

Preparation of the *Info.plist* is a bit more elaborate than for a today extension. In addition to setting the bundle name, which will appear below the activity's icon in the activity view, you'll use the *Info.plist* to specify what types of data this activity accepts as its operands. In the `NSExtensionActivationRule` dictionary, you'll provide one or more keys, such as:

- `NSExtensionActivationSupportsFileWithMaxCount`
- `NSExtensionActivationSupportsImageWithMaxCount`

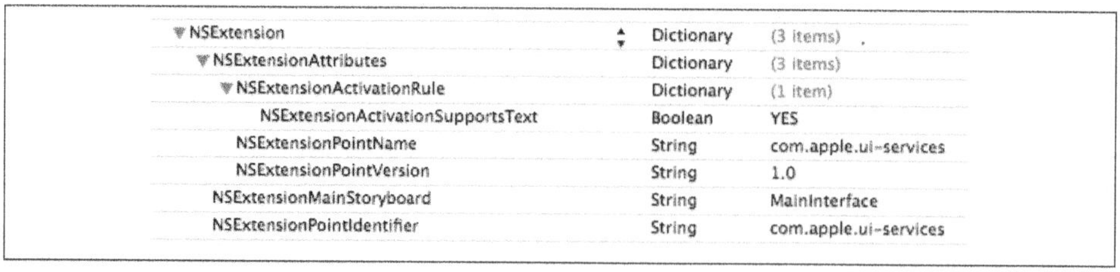

▼ NSExtension		Dictionary	(3 items)
▼ NSExtensionAttributes		Dictionary	(3 items)
▼ NSExtensionActivationRule		Dictionary	(1 item)
NSExtensionActivationSupportsText		Boolean	YES
NSExtensionPointName		String	com.apple.ui-services
NSExtensionPointVersion		String	1.0
NSExtensionMainStoryboard		String	MainInterface
NSExtensionPointIdentifier		String	com.apple.ui-services

Figure 13-11. An action extension Info.plist

- `NSExtensionActivationSupportsMovieWithMaxCount`

- `NSExtensionActivationSupportsText`

- `NSExtensionActivationSupportsWebURLWithMaxCount`

For the full list, see the "Action Extension Keys" section of Apple's *Information Property List Key Reference*. It is also possible to declare in a more sophisticated way what types of data your activity accepts, by writing an NSPredicate string as the value of the `NSExtensionActivationRule` key. Figure 13-11 shows the relevant part of the *Info.plist* for an action extension that accepts one text object.

When your action extension appears in an activity view within some other app that provides the appropriate type(s) of data, it will be represented by an icon which you need to specify by editing your action extension target; this icon is the same size as an app icon, and can conveniently come from an asset catalog, but it will be treated as a template image.

There is one big difference between an action extension and a custom UIActivity: an action extension can return data to the calling app. The transport mechanism for this data is rather elaborate, as I shall now explain.

Action extension without an interface

I'll start by giving an example of an action extension that has no interface. Our code goes into the class provided by the template, ActionRequestHandler, an NSObject subclass.

Our example extension takes a string object and returns a string. In particular, it accepts a string that might be the two-letter abbreviation of one of the U.S. states, and if it is, it returns the name of the actual state. To prepare, we provide some properties:

```
let list : [String] = {
    let path = NSBundle.mainBundle().URLForResource(
        "abbreviations", withExtension:"txt")!
    let s = try! String(contentsOfURL:path, encoding:NSUTF8StringEncoding)
```

```
        return s.componentsSeparatedByString("\n")
    }()
    var extensionContext: NSExtensionContext?
    let desiredType = kUTTypePlainText as String // import MobileCoreServices
```

`self.list` is a string alternating abbreviations with state names; observe that we are permitted to read a text file out of our extension's bundle. `self.extensionContext` is a place to store the NSExtensionContext that will be provided to us. `self.desired-Type` is just a convenient constant expressing the acceptable data type.

There is just one entry point into our extension's code — `beginRequestWithExtension-Context:`. Here we must store a reference to the incoming NSExtensionContext, retrieve the data, process the data, and return the result. You will probably want to factor the processing of the data out into a separate function; I've called mine `processItem:`. Here's a sketch of my `beginRequestWithExtensionContext:` implementation; as it shows, my plan is to make one of two possible calls to `self.processItem:`, either passing the string retrieved from `items`, or else passing `nil` to signify that there was no data:

```
    func beginRequestWithExtensionContext(context: NSExtensionContext) {
        self.extensionContext = context
        let items = self.extensionContext!.inputItems
        // ... if there is no data, call self.processItem with nil ...
        // ... if there is data, call self.processItem with the data ...
    }
```

Now let's implement the retrieval of the data from `items`. Think of this as a series of envelopes (or nested matryoshka dolls) that we must examine and open:

- Our local `items` variable is an array of NSExtensionItem objects.

- An NSExtensionItem as an `attachments` array of NSItemProvider objects.

- An NSItemProvider vends items, each of which represents the data in a particular format. In particular:

    - We can *ask* whether an NSItemProvider has an item of a particular type, by calling `hasItemConformingToTypeIdentifier:`.

    - We can *retrieve* the item of a particular type, by calling `loadItemForType-Identifier:options:completionHandler:`. The item may be vended lazily, and can thus take time to prepare and provide; so we proceed in the `completion-Handler:` to receive the item and do something with it.

We are expecting only one item, so it will be provided by the first NSItemProvider inside the first NSExtensionItem. Here, then, is the code that I omitted from `beginRequest-WithExtensionContext:`

```
guard let extensionItem = items[0] as? NSExtensionItem,
    let provider = extensionItem.attachments?[0] as? NSItemProvider
    where provider.hasItemConformingToTypeIdentifier(self.desiredType)
    else {
        return self.processItem(nil)
}
provider.loadItemForTypeIdentifier(self.desiredType, options: nil) {
    (item:NSSecureCoding?, err:NSError!) -> () in
    dispatch_async(dispatch_get_main_queue()) {
        self.processItem(item as? String)
    }
}
}
```

Now we have the data, and we're ready to do something with it. In my code, that happens in the method that I've named processItem:. This method must do two things:

1. Call the NSExtensionContext's completeRequestReturningItems:completion-Handler: to hand back the data.

2. Release the NSExtensionContext by setting our retaining property to nil.

I'll start with the simplest case: we didn't get any data. In that case, the returned value is nil:

```
func processItem(item:String?) {
    var result : [NSExtensionItem]? = nil
    // ... hmmm ...
    self.extensionContext?.completeRequestReturningItems(
        result, completionHandler: nil)
    self.extensionContext = nil
}
```

That was easy, because we cleverly omitted the only case where we have any work to do. Now let's implement that case. We have received a string in the item parameter. The first question is: is it the abbreviation of a state? To answer that question, I've implemented a utility function:

```
func stateForAbbrev(abbrev:String) -> String? {
    let ix = list.indexOf(abbrev.uppercaseString)
    return ix != nil ? list[ix!+1] : nil
}
```

If we call that method with our item string and the answer comes back nil, we simply proceed just as before — we return nil:

```
func processItem(item:String?) {
    var result : [NSExtensionItem]? = nil
    if let item = item,
        let abbrev = self.stateForAbbrev(item) {
            // ... hmmm ...
    }
```

```
    self.extensionContext?.completeRequestReturningItems(
        result, completionHandler: nil)
    self.extensionContext = nil
}
```

We come at last to the dreaded moment that I have been postponing all this time: what if we get an abbreviation? In that case, we must reverse the earlier process of opening envelopes: we must put envelopes within envelopes and hand back an array of NSExtensionItems. We have only one result, so this will be an array of one NSExtension-Item, whose `attachments` is an array of one NSItemProvider, whose `item` is the string and whose `typeIdentifier` is the type of that string. Confused? Here, I've written a little utility function that should clarify:

```
func stuffThatEnvelope(item:String) -> [NSExtensionItem] {
    let extensionItem = NSExtensionItem()
    let itemProvider = NSItemProvider(
        item: item, typeIdentifier: self.desiredType)
    extensionItem.attachments = [itemProvider]
    return [extensionItem]
}
```

We can now write the full implementation of `processItem:`, and our action extension is finished:

```
func processItem(item:String?) {
    var result : [NSExtensionItem]? = nil
    if let item = item,
        let abbrev = self.stateForAbbrev(item) {
            result = self.stuffThatEnvelope(abbrev)
    }
    self.extensionContext?.completeRequestReturningItems(
        result, completionHandler: nil)
    self.extensionContext = nil
}
```

Action extension with an interface

If an action extension has an interface, then the template provides a storyboard with one scene, along with the code for a corresponding UIViewController class. The code is actually simpler, because:

- A view controller already has an `extensionContext` property, and it is automatically set for us.

- There are no special entry points to our code. This is a UIViewController, and everything happens just as you would expect.

So, in my implementation, I use `viewDidLoad` to open the data envelope from `self.extensionContext`, get the abbreviation if there is one, get the expansion if there is one (storing it in a property, `self.expansion`), *and stop*. I've equipped my interface with a Done button and a Cancel button. The action handlers for those buttons are where I hand the result back to the extensionContext:

```
@IBAction func cancel(sender: AnyObject) {
    self.extensionContext?.completeRequestReturningItems(
        nil, completionHandler: nil)
}
@IBAction func done(sender: AnyObject) {
    self.extensionContext?.completeRequestReturningItems(
        self.stuffThatEnvelope(self.expansion!), completionHandler: nil)
}
```

The runtime responds by dismissing the interface in good order.

Receiving data from an action extension

Now switch roles and pretend that your app is presenting a UIActivityViewController. We now know that this activity view might contain action extension icons. If the user taps one, how will your code retrieve the result? In my earlier implementation, I avoided this issue by pretending that action extensions didn't exist. Here's a more complete sketch:

```
let avc = UIActivityViewController(
    activityItems:things, applicationActivities:nil)
avc.completionWithItemsHandler = {
    (s: String?, ok: Bool, items: [AnyObject]?, err:NSError?) -> Void in
    if ok {
        guard let items = items where items.count > 0 else {
            return // nothing returned, nothing to do
        }
        // ... open the envelopes! ...
    }
}
self.presentViewController(avc, animated:true, completion:nil)
```

If what the user interacted with in the activity view is one of the built-in UIActivity types, or is one of our own internal custom UIActivity subclasses, then only the ok parameter matters. It will be either true or false, but even if it is true, the other parameters will be empty. No data value has been returned.

But if the user interacted with an action extension, then it is up to us to open the items envelopes. The structure here is exactly the same as the items of an NSExtension-Context: items is an array, each element of which is presumably an NSExtensionItem, whose attachments is presumably an array of NSItemProvider objects, each of which can be queried for its data. In the case where we know in advance that we are expecting a single string, therefore, the code is effectively just the same as the envelope-opening code we've already written:

```
        if ok {
            guard let items = items where items.count > 0 else {
                return
            }
            guard let extensionItem = items[0] as? NSExtensionItem,
                let provider = extensionItem.attachments?[0] as? NSItemProvider
                where provider.hasItemConformingToTypeIdentifier(self.desiredType)
                else {
                    return
            }
            provider.loadItemForTypeIdentifier(self.desiredType, options: nil) {
                (item:NSSecureCoding?, err:NSError!) -> () in
                dispatch_async(dispatch_get_main_queue()) {
                    if let s = item as? String {
                        self.tf.text = s
                    }
                }
            }
        }
    }
```

In the more general case, however, you would presumably need to be more exploratory. Unfortunately, Apple has not demonstrated how you're supposed to do this, and there seems to be insufficient API for your UIActivityViewController to determine what action extensions the user may have loaded into it, how their returned data is structured, and whether that data is something your app wants to receive and do something with.

Share Extensions

Your app can appear in the top row of an activity view if it provides a share extension. A share extension is similar to an action extension, but simpler: it accepts some data and returns nothing. As I've already said, the idea is that it will then do something with that data, such as storing it or posting it to a server.

The user, after tapping an app's icon in the activity view, is given an opportunity to interact further with the data, possibly modifying it or canceling the share operation. To make this possible, the Share Extension template, when you create the target (iOS → Application Extension → Share Extension), will give you a storyboard and a view controller. This view controller can be one of two types:

An SLComposeServiceViewController
> The SLComposeServiceViewController provides a standard interface for displaying editable text in a UITextView along with a possible preview view, plus user-configurable option buttons, along with a Cancel button and a Post button.

A plain view controller subclass
> If you opt for a plain view controller subclass, then designing its interface, including providing a way to dismiss it, will be up to you.

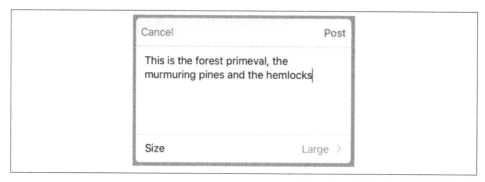

Figure 13-12. A share extension

Whichever form of interface you elect to use, your way of dismissing it will be this familiar-looking incantation:

```
self.extensionContext?.completeRequestReturningItems(
    [], completionHandler: nil)
```

As you are most likely to use an SLComposeServiceViewController, I'll briefly describe some of the basics of working with one. An SLComposeServiceViewController's view is displayed with its text view already populated with the text passed along from the host app, so there's very little more for you to do; you can add a preview view and option buttons, and that's just about all. I'll concentrate on option buttons.

An option button displays a title string and a value string. When tapped, it will typically summon interface where the user can change the value string. In Figure 13-12, I've created a single option button — a Size button, whose value can be Large, Medium, or Small. (I have no idea what this choice is supposed to signify for my app; it's only an example!)

To create the configuration option, I override the SLComposeServiceViewController `configurationItems` method to return an array of one SLComposeSheetConfigurationItem. Its `title` and `value` are displayed in the button. Its `tapHandler` will be called when the button is tapped. Typically, you'll create a view controller and push it into the interface with `pushConfigurationViewController`:

```
weak var config : SLComposeSheetConfigurationItem?
var selectedText = "Large" {
    didSet {
        self.config?.value = self.selectedText
    }
}
override func configurationItems() -> [AnyObject]! {
    let c = SLComposeSheetConfigurationItem()
    c.title = "Size"
    c.value = self.selectedText
```

```
        c.tapHandler = {
            [unowned self] in
            let tvc = TableViewController(style: .Grouped)
            tvc.selectedSize = self.selectedText
            tvc.delegate = self
            self.pushConfigurationViewController(tvc)
        }
        self.config = c
        return [c]
    }
```

My view controller is a table view controller that I've prepared in advance. Its table view displays three rows whose cells are labeled Large, Medium, and Small, along with a checkmark (compare the table view described in "Cell Choice and Static Tables" on page 464). The tricky part is that I need a way to communicate with this table view controller: I need to tell it what the configuration item's value is now, and I need to hear from it what the user chooses in the table view. So I've given the table view controller a property (selectedSize) where I can deposit the configuration item's value, and I've declared a delegate protocol so that the table view controller can set a property of mine (selected-Text). This is the relevant portion of my TableViewController class:

```
protocol SizeDelegate : class {
    var selectedText : String {get set}
}
class TableViewController: UITableViewController {
    var selectedSize : String?
    weak var delegate : SizeDelegate?
    override func tableView(tableView: UITableView,
        didSelectRowAtIndexPath indexPath: NSIndexPath) {
            let cell = tableView.cellForRowAtIndexPath(indexPath)!
            let s = cell.textLabel!.text!
            self.selectedSize = s
            self.delegate?.selectedText = s
            tableView.reloadData()
    }
}
```

The navigation interface is provided for me, so I don't have to do anything about popping the table view controller: the user will do that by tapping the Back button after choosing a size. In my configurationItems implementation, I cleverly kept a reference to my configuration item as self.config. When the user chooses from the table view, its did-SelectRowAtIndexPath sets my selectedText, and my selectedText setter observer promptly changes the value of the configuration item to whatever the user chose.

The user, when finished interacting with the share extension interface, will tap one of the provided buttons, either Cancel or Post. The Cancel button is handled automatically: the interface is dismissed. The Post button is hooked automatically to my didSelect-Post implementation, where I fetch the text from my own contentText property, do something with it, and dismiss the interface:

```
override func didSelectPost() {
    let s = self.contentText
    // and do something with it
    self.extensionContext?.completeRequestReturningItems(
        [], completionHandler: nil)
}
```

If the material provided from the host app were more elaborate, I would pull it out of
self.extensionContext in the same way as for an action extension. If there were networking to do at this point, I would initiate a background NSURLSession (Chapter 24).

 There is no supported way, as far as I can tell, to change the title or appearance of
the Cancel and Post buttons. Apps that show different buttons, such as Reminders
and Notes, are either not using SLComposeServiceViewController or are using a
technique available only to Apple.

PART III

Some Frameworks

Cocoa supplies numerous specialized optional frameworks. This part of the book explains the basics of some of these frameworks, showing you how to get started, and training you to understand and explore these and related frameworks independently if your app requires a further level of depth and detail.

- Chapter 14 introduces the various iOS means for playing sound files, including audio sessions and playing sounds in the background.
- Chapter 15 describes some basic ways of playing video (movies), along with an introduction to the powerful AV Foundation framework.
- Chapter 16 is about how an app can access the user's music library.
- Chapter 17 is about how an app can access the user's photo library, along with the ability to take photos and capture movies.
- Chapter 18 discusses how an app can access the user's contacts.
- Chapter 19 talks about how an app can access the user's calendar data.
- Chapter 20 describes how an app can allow the user to compose and send email and SMS messages and social media posts.
- Chapter 21 explains how an app can display a map, along with custom annotations and overlays. It also talks about how a map can display the user's current location and how to convert between a location and an address.
- Chapter 22 is about how an app can learn where the device is located, how it is moving, and how it is oriented.

CHAPTER 14

Audio

iOS provides various means and technologies for allowing your app to produce, record, and process sound. The topic is a large one, so this chapter can only introduce it; I'll concentrate on basic sound production. You'll want to read Apple's *Multimedia Programming Guide* and *Core Audio Overview*.

None of the classes discussed in this chapter provides any interface within your app for allowing the user to stop and start playback of sound (transport control). If you want transport interface, here are some options:

- You can create your own interface.
- You can associate the built-in "remote control" buttons with your application, as I'll explain in this chapter.
- A web view (Chapter 11) supports the HTML 5 `<audio>` tag; this can be a simple, lightweight way to play audio and to allow the user to control playback (including use of AirPlay).
- You could treat the sound as a movie and use the interface-providing classes that I'll discuss in Chapter 15; this can also be a good way to play a sound file located remotely over the Internet.

System Sounds

The simplest form of sound is *system sound*, which is the iOS equivalent of the basic computer "beep." This is implemented through System Sound Services, part of the Audio Toolbox framework; you'll need to `import AudioToolbox`.

The API for playing a system sound has changed in iOS 9. I'll show you the old code first (it still works in iOS 9); then I'll demonstrate the new code. The old code involves calling one of two C functions, which behave very similarly to one another:

AudioServicesPlayAlertSound

On an iPhone, may also vibrate the device, depending on the user's settings.

AudioServicesPlaySystemSound

On an iPhone, there won't be an accompanying vibration, but you can specifically elect to have this "sound" *be* a device vibration (by passing kSystemSound-ID_Vibrate as the name of the "sound").

The sound file to be played needs to be an uncompressed AIFF or WAV file (or an Apple CAF file wrapping one of these). To hand the sound to these functions, you'll need a SystemSoundID, which you obtain by calling AudioServicesCreateSystemSoundID with an NSURL that points to a sound file. In this example, the sound file is in our app bundle:

```
let sndurl = NSBundle.mainBundle().URLForResource(
    "test", withExtension: "aif")!
var snd : SystemSoundID = 0
AudioServicesCreateSystemSoundID(sndurl, &snd)
AudioServicesPlaySystemSound(snd)
```

That code works — we hear the sound — but there's a problem: we have failed to exercise proper memory management. We need to call AudioServicesDisposeSystemSoundID to release our SystemSoundID. But when shall we do this? AudioServicesPlaySystem-Sound executes asynchronously. So the solution can't be to call AudioServicesDispose-SystemSoundID in the next line of the same snippet, because this would release our sound just as it is about to start playing, resulting in silence.

The solution is to implement a *sound completion handler*, a function that is called when the sound has finished playing. The sound completion handler is specified by calling AudioServicesAddSystemSoundCompletion. The sound completion handler must be supplied as a C pointer-to-function. In Swift 1.2 and before, this was impossible, so you couldn't call this function without dropping momentarily into Objective-C. But Swift 2.0 allows you to pass a global or local Swift function (including an anonymous function) where a C pointer-to-function is expected. So our code now looks like this:

```
let sndurl = NSBundle.mainBundle().URLForResource(
    "test", withExtension: "aif")!
var snd : SystemSoundID = 0
AudioServicesCreateSystemSoundID(sndurl, &snd)
AudioServicesAddSystemSoundCompletion(snd, nil, nil, {
    sound, context in
    AudioServicesRemoveSystemSoundCompletion(sound)
    AudioServicesDisposeSystemSoundID(sound)
}, nil)
AudioServicesPlaySystemSound(snd)
```

Note that when we are about to release the sound, we first release the sound completion handler information applied to it.

Now for the new iOS 9 way. Instead of calling `AudioServicesAddSystemSound-Completion` beforehand, we can provide the completion handler as part of the call that plays the sound, using new functions whose names end `WithCompletion`. Thus, instead of `AudioServicesPlaySystemSound`, we'll call `AudioServicesPlaySystemSoundWith-Completion`.

The new calls take *two* parameters: a SystemSoundID and a completion function. The completion function takes no parameters; we can still refer to the SystemSoundID in order to dispose of its memory, because it is in scope. We no longer need to call `Audio-ServicesRemoveSystemSoundCompletion` because we never called `AudioServicesAdd-SystemSoundCompletion`. So here's the new version of the same code:

```
let sndurl = NSBundle.mainBundle().URLForResource(
    "test", withExtension: "aif")!
var snd : SystemSoundID = 0
AudioServicesCreateSystemSoundID(sndurl, &snd)
AudioServicesPlaySystemSoundWithCompletion(snd) {
    AudioServicesDisposeSystemSoundID(snd)
}
```

Audio Session

If your app is going to use a more sophisticated way of producing sound, such as an audio player (discussed in the next section), it must specify a *policy* regarding that sound. This policy will answer such questions as:

- Should your app's sound stop when the screen is locked?
- Should your app stop other sound (being played, for example, by the Music app) or should your app's sound be layered on top of other sound?

Your policy is declared in an *audio session*, which is a singleton AVAudioSession instance created automatically as your app launches. This is part of the AV Foundation framework; you'll need to `import AVFoundation`. You'll refer to your app's AVAudioSession by way of the class method `sharedInstance`. This shared audio session instance is actually your pipeline to the part of the system that mediates *all* audio belonging to *all* apps and processes, the *media services daemon*; this daemon must juggle many demands, which is why your app's audio can be affected and even overruled by other apps and external factors.

To declare your audio session's policy, you'll set its *category*, by calling `set-Category:withOptions:`. The basic policies for audio playback are:

Ambient (`AVAudioSessionCategoryAmbient`)
    Your app's audio plays even while another app is playing audio, and is silenced by the phone's Silent switch and screen locking.

Solo Ambient (`AVAudioSessionCategorySoloAmbient,` *the default)*
> Your app stops any audio being played by other apps, and is silenced by the phone's Silent switch and screen locking.

Playback (`AVAudioSessionCategoryPlayback`*)*
> Your app stops any audio being played by other apps, and is *not* silenced by the Silent switch. It is silenced by screen locking, unless it is also configured to play in the background (as explained later in this chapter).

New in iOS 9, the audio session's `availableCategories` property can tell you in advance whether this device is capable of the policy you're thinking of using.

Audio session category options, supplied as the `withOptions:` parameter of `set-Category:withOptions:`, allow you to modify the playback policies (AVAudioSession-CategoryOptions):

Mixable audio (`.MixWithOthers`*)*
> You can override the Playback policy so as to allow other apps to continue playing audio. Your sound is then said to be *mixable*. Note that mixability can also affect you in the other direction: another app's mixable audio can continue to play even when your app's Playback policy is *not* mixable.

Ducking audio (`.DuckOthers`*)*
> You can override a policy that allows other audio to play, so as to *duck* (diminish the volume of) that audio. Ducking is thus a form of mixing.

Mixable except for speech (`.InterruptSpokenAudioAndMixWithOthers`*)*
> New in iOS 9, you can be mixable with other audio *except* for speech audio. Audio is marked as speech by setting the *mode* of its audio session (`setMode:`) with a value of `AVAudioSessionModeSpokenAudio`. Your app will stop audio marked in this way, but otherwise will be mixable (and can perform ducking).

It is common practice to declare your app's initial audio session policy very early in the life of the app, possibly as early as `application:didFinishLaunchingWithOptions:`. You can later, if necessary, change your audio session policy as your app runs.

Activation

Your audio session policy is not in effect unless your audio session is also *active*. By default, it isn't. Thus, asserting your audio session policy is done by a combination of configuring the audio session and activating the audio session. To activate (or deactivate) your audio session, you call `setActive:withOptions:`.

The question then is *when* to call `setActive:withOptions:`. This is a little tricky because your audio session can be deactivated automatically if your app is no longer active. So if you want your policy to be obeyed under all circumstances, you must explicitly activate your audio session each time your app becomes active. The best place to do this is in `applicationDidBecomeActive:`, as this is the only method guaranteed to be called every time your app is reactivated under circumstances where your audio session might have been deactivated in the background (see Appendix A).

The first parameter to `setActive:withOptions:` is a Bool saying whether we want to activate or deactivate our audio session. There are various reasons why you might deactivate (and perhaps reactivate) your audio session over the lifetime of your app.

One possible reason is that you want to *change* something about your audio session policy. Certain changes in your audio session category and options don't take effect unless you deactivate the existing policy and activate the new policy. Ducking is a good example. Ducking does *not* depend automatically on whether your app is actively producing any sound; rather, it starts as soon as the `.DuckOthers` option is added to your audio session's policy, and remains in place until your audio session is deactivated. Thus, to play audio that ducks background audio, you won't add ducking to your audio session policy until just before playing; after playing, you'll deactivate your audio session and activate it without ducking. I'll demonstrate in the next section.

Another reason for deactivating your audio session is that you no longer need to hog the device's audio, and you want to yield to other apps so that they can resume playing. You can even send a message to other apps as you do this. The second parameter to `setActive:withOptions:` lets you supply the AVAudioSessionSetActiveOptions value `.NotifyOthersOnDeactivation` (only when you are in fact deactivating your audio session). I'll demonstrate later in this chapter.

 Apple suggests that you might want to register for `AVAudioSessionMediaServices-WereResetNotification`. If this notification arrives, the media services daemon was somehow hosed, and your whole audio session has probably been blown away as well. Thus you should activate your audio session in response, as well as resetting and recreating any audio-related objects. See Apple's *Technical Q&A QA1749*.

Ducking

As an example of deactivating and activating your audio session, I'll describe how to implement ducking. Let's say that, in general, we don't play any sounds, and we want sound from other apps, such as the Music app, to continue playing while our app runs. So we configure our audio session to use the Ambient policy in `application:didFinish-LaunchingWithOptions:`, as follows:

```
func application(application: UIApplication,
    didFinishLaunchingWithOptions launchOptions: [NSObject: AnyObject]?)
    -> Bool {
        _ = try? AVAudioSession.sharedInstance().setCategory(
            AVAudioSessionCategoryAmbient, withOptions: [])
        return true
}
```

 Methods that set features of your AVAudioSession, such as those I've already mentioned — setCategory:withOptions:, setActive:withOptions:, and setMode: — can throw an error. It isn't clear how best to deal with this in Swift 2.0. Little is to be learned by catching the error; in fact, I've never actually experienced an error, and I'm not even sure why an error might be thrown. But calling these methods with try! is risky, because if an error *is* thrown, the app will crash. What I generally do, therefore, is call them with try? and assign the result (an Optional wrapping Void) to a dummy variable to silence the compiler.

We aren't stopping other audio with our Ambient policy, so it does no harm to activate our audio session every time our app becomes active, no matter how, in application-DidBecomeActive:, like this:

```
func applicationDidBecomeActive(application: UIApplication) {
    _ = try? AVAudioSession.sharedInstance().setActive(
        true, withOptions: [])
}
```

That's all it takes to set and enforce your app's overall audio session policy. Now let's say we do *sometimes* play a sound, but it's brief and doesn't require other sound to stop entirely; it suffices for other audio to be quieter momentarily while we're playing our sound. That's ducking! So, just before we play our sound, we duck any other sound by changing the options on our Ambient category:

```
_ = try? AVAudioSession.sharedInstance().setCategory(
    AVAudioSessionCategoryAmbient, withOptions: .DuckOthers)
```

In that code, we didn't have to activate or deactivate our audio session. Not so, however, when we finish playing our sound and we want to turn *off* ducking. To do so, we must *deactivate our audio session* to make the change take effect immediately and bring the other sound back to its original level; there is then no harm in reactivating our audio session without ducking:

```
let sess = AVAudioSession.sharedInstance()
_ = try? sess.setActive(false, withOptions: [])
_ = try? sess.setCategory(AVAudioSessionCategoryAmbient, withOptions: [])
_ = try? sess.setActive(true, withOptions: [])
```

Interruptions

Your audio session can be *interrupted*. This could mean that some other app deactivates it: for example, on an iPhone a phone call can arrive or an alarm can go off. It could mean that another app asserts its audio session over yours.

To learn of interruptions, register for AVAudioSessionInterruptionNotification. The notification can arrive either because an interruption begins or because it ends. To learn whether the interruption began or ended, examine the AVAudioSession-InterruptionTypeKey entry in the notification's userInfo dictionary; this will be a UInt equating to an AVAudioSessionInterruptionType, either .Began or .Ended. So, for example:

```
NSNotificationCenter.defaultCenter().addObserverForName(
    AVAudioSessionInterruptionNotification, object: nil, queue: nil) {
        (n:NSNotification) in
        guard let why =
            n.userInfo?[AVAudioSessionInterruptionTypeKey] as? UInt
                else {return}
        guard let type = AVAudioSessionInterruptionType(rawValue: why)
            else {return}
        if type == .Began {
            // began
        } else {
            // ended
        }
}
```

When an interruption ends, the notification's userInfo dictionary may also contain an AVAudioSessionInterruptionOptionKey entry. If so, it will be a UInt whose value, as an AVAudioSessionInterruptionOptions, may be .ShouldResume:

```
guard let opt =
    n.userInfo![AVAudioSessionInterruptionOptionKey] as? UInt
        else {return}
let opts = AVAudioSessionInterruptionOptions(rawValue: opt)
if opts.contains(.ShouldResume) {
    // ...
}
```

.ShouldResume is the flip side of .NotifyOthersOnDeactivation, which I mentioned earlier: some other app that interrupted you has now deactivated its audio session, and is telling you to feel free to resume your audio.

Interruptions are not as intrusive as you might suppose. When your audio session is interrupted, your audio has already stopped and your audio session has been deactivated; you might respond by altering something about your app's user interface to reflect the fact that your audio isn't playing, but apart from this there's no particular work for you to do. When the interruption ends, on the other hand, activating your audio session and possibly resuming playback of your audio might be up to you.

When your app switches to the background, your audio is paused (unless your app plays audio in the background, as discussed later in this chapter). What messages you get depends on whether you were playing audio with an audio player (AVAudioPlayer, discussed in the next section):

You were playing audio with an audio player
> The audio player will probably handle the entire situation. When your app comes back to the front, it will automatically reactivate your audio session and resume playing, and *you won't get any interruption notifications.*

You were not playing audio with an audio player
> It is likely that being moved into the background will count as an interruption of your audio session. You'll get an interruption notification just after your app delegate's `applicationDidEnterBackground:` is called. When your app comes back to the front, you'll be notified that the interruption ended, and then your app delegate's `applicationDidBecomeActive:` will be called.

Secondary Audio

When your app is frontmost and the user brings up the control center and uses the Play button to resume, say, the current Music app song, there may be no interruption of your audio session, because your app never went into the background. Instead, what you'll get, if you've registered for it, is a notification of a different kind, namely `AVAudioSessionSilenceSecondaryAudioHintNotification`. You'll receive this notification only while your app is in the foreground.

This notification, corresponding to the AVAudioSession Bool property `secondaryAudioShouldBeSilencedHint`, expresses a fine-grained distinction between primary and secondary audio. Apple's example is a game app, where intermittent sound effects are the primary audio, while an ongoing underlying soundtrack is the secondary audio. The idea is that the user might start playing a song from the Music app, and that your app would therefore pause its secondary audio while continuing to produce its primary audio — because the user's chosen Music track will do just as well as a background soundtrack behind your game's sound effects.

To respond to this notification, examine the `AVAudioSessionSilenceSecondaryAudioHintTypeKey` entry in the notification's `userInfo` dictionary; this will be a UInt equating to an AVAudioSessionSilenceSecondaryAudioHintType, either `.Begin` or `.End`. So, for example:

```
NSNotificationCenter.defaultCenter().addObserverForName(
    AVAudioSessionSilenceSecondaryAudioHintNotification,
    object: nil, queue: nil) {
        (n:NSNotification) in
        guard let why =
            n.userInfo?[AVAudioSessionSilenceSecondaryAudioHintTypeKey]
                as? UInt else {return}
        guard let type =
            AVAudioSessionSilenceSecondaryAudioHintType(rawValue:why)
                else {return}
        if type == .Begin {
            // silence secondary audio
        } else {
            // resume secondary audio
        }
}
```

Routing Changes

Your audio is routed through a particular output (and input). The user can make changes in this routing — for example, by plugging headphones into the device, which causes sound to stop coming out of the speaker and to come out of the headphones instead. By default, your playing audio continues uninterrupted when routing is changed, but you can register for AVAudioSessionRouteChangeNotification to hear about routing changes and respond to them.

The notification's userInfo dictionary is chock full of useful information about what just happened. Here's the console display of the dictionary that results when I detach headphones from the device:

```
AVAudioSessionRouteChangeReasonKey: 2,
AVAudioSessionRouteChangePreviousRouteKey:
    <AVAudioSessionRouteDescription: 0x17d8e910,
        inputs = (null);
        outputs = (
            "<AVAudioSessionPortDescription: 0x17d76e20,
                type = Headphones;
                name = Headphones;
                UID = Wired Headphones;
                selectedDataSource = (null)>"
        )>
```

Upon receipt of this notification, I can find out what the audio route is now, by calling AVAudioSession's currentRoute method:

```
<AVAudioSessionRouteDescription: 0x17d74ea0,
    inputs = (null);
    outputs = (
        "<AVAudioSessionPortDescription: 0x17d828b0,
            type = Speaker;
```

```
                    name = Speaker;
                    UID = Built-In Speaker;
                    selectedDataSource = (null)>"
        )>
```

The classes mentioned here — AVAudioSessionRouteDescription and AVAudioSession-
PortDescription — are value classes. The `AVAudioSessionRouteChangeReasonKey`
refers to an AVAudioSessionRouteChangeReason; the value here, 2, is `.OldDevice-
Unavailable` — we stopped using the headphones because there are no headphones
any longer.

A routing change may not of itself interrupt your sound, but Apple suggests that in this
particular situation you might like to respond by stopping your audio deliberately,
because otherwise sound may now suddenly be coming out of the speaker in a public
place.

Audio Player

An *audio player* (AVAudioPlayer) is the easiest way to play sounds with any degree of
sophistication. AVAudioPlayer is part of the AV Foundation framework; you'll need to
`import AVFoundation`. An audio player should always be used in conjunction with an
audio session. A wide range of sound types is acceptable, including MP3, AAC, and
ALAC, as well as AIFF and WAV. You can set a sound's volume and stereo pan features,
loop a sound, change the playing rate, and set playback to begin somewhere in the middle
of a sound. A single audio player can possess and play only one sound; but you can have
multiple audio players, they can play separately or simultaneously, and you can even
synchronize them.

An audio player is initialized with its sound, using a local file URL or NSData; optionally,
the initializer can also state the expected sound file format. Having created and initialized an audio player, *retain it*, typically by assigning it to an instance property; assigning
an audio player to a *local* variable and telling it to play, and hearing nothing — because
the player has gone out of existence at the end of the method, before it has a chance
even to start playing — is a common beginner mistake.

To play the sound, first tell the audio player to `prepareToPlay`, causing it to load buffers
and initialize hardware; then tell it to `play`. The audio player's delegate (AVAudio-
PlayerDelegate) is notified when the sound finishes playing (`audioPlayerDidFinish-
Playing:successfully:`); do *not* repeatedly check the audio player's `playing` property
to learn its state. Other useful methods include `pause` and `stop`; the chief difference
between them is that `pause` doesn't release the buffers and hardware set up by `prepare-
ToPlay`, but `stop` does, so you'd want to call `prepareToPlay` again before resuming play.
Neither `pause` nor `stop` changes the playhead position, the point in the sound where
playback will start if `play` is sent again; for that, use the `currentTime` property.

Devising a strategy for instantiating, retaining, and releasing your audio players is up to you. In one of my apps, I define a class called Player, which implements a `playFile-AtPath:` method expecting a string path to a sound file. This method creates a new AVAudioPlayer, stores it as a property, and tells it to play the sound file; it also sets itself as that audio player's delegate, and notifies its own delegate when the sound finishes playing (by way of a PlayerDelegate protocol that I also define). In this way, by maintaining a single Player instance, I can play different sounds in succession:

```
protocol PlayerDelegate : class {
    func soundFinished(sender : AnyObject)
}
class Player : NSObject, AVAudioPlayerDelegate {
    var player : AVAudioPlayer!
    weak var delegate : PlayerDelegate?
    func playFileAtPath(path:String) {
        self.player?.delegate = nil
        self.player?.stop()
        let fileURL = NSURL(fileURLWithPath: path)
        guard let p = try? AVAudioPlayer(contentsOfURL: fileURL)
            else {return}
        self.player = p
        self.player.prepareToPlay()
        self.player.delegate = self
        self.player.play()
    }
    func audioPlayerDidFinishPlaying(AVAudioPlayer!, successfully: Bool) {
        self.delegate?.soundFinished(self)
    }
}
```

Here are some useful audio player properties:

pan, volume

  Stereo positioning and loudness, respectively.

numberOfLoops

  How many times the sound should repeat after it finishes playing; 0 (the default) means it doesn't repeat. A negative value causes the sound to repeat indefinitely (until told to stop).

duration

  The length of the sound (read-only).

currentTime

  The playhead position within the sound. If the sound is paused or stopped, play will start at the currentTime. You can set this in order to "seek" to a playback position within the sound.

Figure 14-1. The software remote controls in the control center

`enableRate, rate`

> These properties allow the sound to be played at anywhere from half speed (`0.5`) to double speed (`2.0`). Set `enableRate` to `true` *before* calling `prepareToPlay`; you are then free to set the `rate`.

`meteringEnabled`

> If `true` (the default is `false`), you can call `updateMeters` followed by `averagePowerForChannel:` and/or `peakPowerForChannel:` periodically to track how loud the sound is. Presumably this would be so you could provide some sort of graphical representation of this value in your interface.

`settings`

> A read-only dictionary describing features of the sound, such as its bit rate (`AVEncoderBitRateKey`), its sample rate (`AVSampleRateKey`), and its data format (`AVFormatIDKey`).

The `playAtTime:` method allows playing to be scheduled to start at a certain time. The time should be described in terms of the audio player's `deviceCurrentTime` property.

As I mentioned earlier, an audio player handles interruptions seamlessly; in particular, it resumes playing when your app comes to the front if it was playing and was forced to stop playing when your app was moved to the background.

Remote Control of Your Sound

Various sorts of signal constitute *remote control*. There is hardware remote control: for example, the user might be using earbuds with buttons. There is also software remote control — the playback controls that you see in the control center (Figure 14-1) and in the lock screen (Figure 14-2).

Figure 14-2. The software remote controls on the lock screen

Your app can arrange to be targeted by *remote control events* reporting that the user has tapped a remote control. Your sound-playing app can respond to the remote play/pause button, for example, by playing or pausing its sound.

Remote control events are a form of UIEvent, and they are sent initially to the first responder. To arrange to be a recipient of remote control events:

- Your app must contain a UIResponder in its responder chain that returns true from canBecomeFirstResponder, and that responder must actually be first responder.
- Some UIResponder in the responder chain, at or above the first responder, must implement remoteControlReceivedWithEvent:.
- Your app must call the UIApplication instance method beginReceivingRemote-ControlEvents.
- Your app's audio session policy must be Playback.
- Your app must emit some sound. The rule is that the running app that is capable of receiving remote control events and that last actually produced sound is the target of remote control events. The remote control event target defaults to the Music app if no other app takes precedence by this rule.

A typical place to put all of this is in your view controller, which is, after all, a UIResponder:

```
override func canBecomeFirstResponder() -> Bool {
    return true
}
override func viewDidAppear(animated: Bool) {
    super.viewDidAppear(animated)
    self.becomeFirstResponder()
    UIApplication.sharedApplication().beginReceivingRemoteControlEvents()
}
override func remoteControlReceivedWithEvent(event: UIEvent?) {
    // ...
}
```

The question is then how to implement remoteControlReceivedWithEvent:. Your implementation will examine the subtype of the incoming UIEvent to decide what to do. There are various possible subtype values (UIEventSubtype). Earbuds with a central button will probably send `.RemoteControlTogglePlayPause`. In iOS 6 and before, the software remote control play/pause button *used* to send `.RemoteControlTogglePlay-Pause` as well; starting with iOS 7, however, it now sends `.RemoteControlPlay` or `.RemoteControlPause`. So your code needs to cover all three possibilities at a minimum. Here's an example in an app where sound is produced by an AVAudioPlayer:

```
override func remoteControlReceivedWithEvent(event: UIEvent?) {
    let rc = event!.subtype
    let p = // our AVAudioPlayer
    switch rc {
    case .RemoteControlTogglePlayPause:
        if p.playing { p.pause() } else { p.play() }
    case .RemoteControlPlay:
        p.play()
    case .RemoteControlPause:
        p.pause()
    default:break
    }
}
```

You can also influence what information the user will see, in the remote control interface, about what's being played. For that, you'll use MPNowPlayingInfoCenter, from the Media Player framework; you'll need to `import MediaPlayer`. Call the class method `defaultCenter` and set the resulting instance's `nowPlayingInfo` property to a dictionary. The relevant keys are listed in the class documentation; they will make more sense after you've read Chapter 16, which discusses the Media Player framework. Here's some example code from my TidBITS News app:

```
let mpic = MPNowPlayingInfoCenter.defaultCenter()
mpic.nowPlayingInfo = [
    MPMediaItemPropertyTitle:self.titleLabel!.text!,
    MPMediaItemPropertyArtist:self.authorLabel!.text!
]
```

Playing Sound in the Background

When the user switches away from your app to another app, by default, your app is suspended and stops producing sound. But if the business of your app is to play sound, you might like your app to continue playing sound in the background. To play sound in the background, your app must do these things:

- In your *Info.plist*, you must include the "Required background modes" key (`UIBackgroundModes`) with a value that includes "App plays audio or streams audio/video using AirPlay" (`audio`). The simplest way to arrange this is through the a Background Modes checkbox in the Capabilities tab of the target editor (Figure 14-3).

Figure 14-3. Using Capabilities to enable background audio

- Your audio session's policy must be active and must be Playback.

If those things are true, then the sound that your app is playing will go right on playing when the user clicks the Home button and dismisses your app, or when the user switches to another app, or when the screen is locked. Your app is now running in the background for the purpose of playing sound.

Moreover, your app may be able to start playing in the background even if it was *not* playing previously — namely, if it is mixable (`.MixWithOthers`, see earlier in this chapter), or if it is capable of being the remote control target.

Indeed, an extremely cool feature of playing sound in the background is that remote control events continue to work. Even if your app was *not* actively playing at the time it was put into the background, it may nevertheless be the remote control target (because it *was* playing sound earlier, as explained in the preceding section). In that case, if the user causes a remote control event to be sent, your app, if suspended in the background, will be woken up (still in the background) in order to receive the remote control event and can begin playing sound.

Your app, playing in the background, if interrupted by the foreground app's audio session policy, may be able subsequently to resume playing. To illustrate with an AVAudioPlayer, let's have two apps called BackgroundPlayer and Interrupter. Suppose Interrupter has an audio session policy of Ambient. This means that when Interrupter comes to the front, background audio doesn't stop. But now Interrupter wants to play a brief sound of its own, temporarily stopping background audio. To pause the background audio, it sets its own audio session policy to Playback before telling its AVAudioPlayer to play:

```
_ = try? AVAudioSession.sharedInstance().setCategory(
    AVAudioSessionCategoryPlayback, withOptions: [])
_ = try? AVAudioSession.sharedInstance().setActive(
    true, withOptions: [])
self.player.prepareToPlay()
self.player.delegate = self
self.player.play()
```

When Interrupter's sound finishes playing, its AVAudioPlayer's delegate is notified. In response, Interrupter deactivates its audio session with the `.NotifyOthersOn-`

Deactivation option; then it's fine for it to switch its audio session policy back to Ambient and activate it once again:

```
func audioPlayerDidFinishPlaying(
    player: AVAudioPlayer, successfully flag: Bool) {
        let sess = AVAudioSession.sharedInstance()
        // this is the key move
        _ = try? sess.setActive(
            false, withOptions: .NotifyOthersOnDeactivation)
        // now go back to ambient
        _ = try? sess.setCategory(
            AVAudioSessionCategoryAmbient, withOptions: [])
        _ = try? sess.setActive(true, withOptions: [])
}
```

So much for Interrupter. Now let's turn to BackgroundPlayer, which was playing in the background when Interrupter came along:

When Interrupter changes its audio session policy to Playback

BackgroundPlayer receives AVAudioSessionInterruptionNotification (if registered for it) with AVAudioSessionInterruptionTypeKey set to .Began — and BackgroundPlayer's AVAudioPlayer *automatically* stops playing.

When Interrupter deactivates its audio session

BackgroundPlayer receives AVAudioSessionInterruptionNotification (if registered for it) with AVAudioSessionInterruptionTypeKey set to .Ended — but its AVAudioPlayer does *not* automatically resume.

Thus, it is up to BackgroundPlayer to notice that the interruption has ended, and to resume its AVAudioPlayer manually. For example:

```
self.observer = NSNotificationCenter.defaultCenter().addObserverForName(
    AVAudioSessionInterruptionNotification, object: nil, queue: nil) {
        [weak self](n:NSNotification) in
        guard let why =
            n.userInfo?[AVAudioSessionInterruptionTypeKey] as? UInt
                else {return}
        guard let type = AVAudioSessionInterruptionType(rawValue: why)
            else {return}
        if type == .Ended {
            guard let opt =
                n.userInfo![AVAudioSessionInterruptionOptionKey] as? UInt
                    else {return}
            let opts = AVAudioSessionInterruptionOptions(rawValue: opt)
            if opts.contains(.ShouldResume) {
                self?.player.prepareToPlay()
                self?.player.play()
            }
        }
}
```

In that code, when the interruption ends, I examine the secondary `AVAudioSession-InterruptionOptionKey` to see whether the `.ShouldResume` option is present. In this case, it is — because Interrupter deactivated its audio session with the `.NotifyOthers-OnDeactivation` option. Thus, everyone in this story is a good citizen.

When your app is capable of playing sound in the background, there's an interesting byproduct: while it *is* playing sound, an NSTimer can fire in the background. The timer must have been created and scheduled in the foreground, but after that, it will fire even while your app is in the background, unless your app is currently not playing any sound. This is remarkable, because many other sorts of activity are forbidden when your app is running in the background.

Another byproduct of your app playing sound in the background has to do with app delegate events (see Appendix A). Typically, your app delegate will probably never receive the `applicationWillTerminate:` message, because by the time the app terminates, it will already have been suspended and incapable of receiving any events. However, an app that is playing sound in the background is obviously *not* suspended, even though it is in the background. If it is terminated while playing sound in the background, it will receive `applicationDidEnterBackground:`, even though it has *already* received this event previously when it was moved into the background, and then it *will* receive `applicationWillTerminate:`.

AVAudioEngine

AVAudioEngine, introduced in iOS 8, is modeled after a mixer board. You can construct and manipulate a graph of sound-producing objects in real time, varying their relative volumes and other attributes, mixing them down to a single sound (which can optionally be recorded into a file as it plays). This is a deep topic; I'll just provide an introductory overview.

The key classes are:

AVAudioEngine
> The overall engine object, representing the world in which everything else happens. You'll probably make and retain just one. Its chief jobs are:
>
> * To connect and disconnect *nodes* (AVAudioNode), analogous to patch cords on a mixer board. The engine has three built-in nodes: its `inputNode`, its `outputNode`, and its `mixerNode`.
> * To start and stop the production of sound.

AVAudioNode
> An abstract class embracing the various types of object for producing, processing, mixing, and receiving sound. An audio node has inputs and outputs, and may

optionally be given a *tap*, a buffer through which the node's sound can be analyzed and recorded. Some subclasses are:

AVAudioMixerNode

A node with an output volume; it mixes its inputs down to a single output. The AVAudioEngine's built-in `mixerNode` is an AVAudioMixerNode.

AVAudioIONode

A node that patches through to the system's (device's) own input (AVAudio-InputNode) or output (AVAudioOutputNode). The AVAudioEngine's built-in `inputNode` and `outputNode` are AVAudioIONodes.

AVAudioPlayerNode

A node that produces sound, analogous to an AVAudioPlayer. It can play from a file or from a buffer.

AVAudioUnit

A node that processes its input with special effects before passing it to the output. Built-in subclasses include:

AVAudioUnitTimePitch

Independently changes the pitch and rate of the input.

AVAudioUnitVarispeed

Changes the pitch and rate of the input together.

AVAudioUnitDelay

Adds to the input a delayed version of itself.

AVAudioUnitDistortion

Adds distortion to the input.

AVAudioUnitEQ

Constructs an equalizer, for processing different frequency bands separately.

AVAudioUnitReverb

Adds a reverb effect to the input.

Just to give an idea of what working with AVAudioEngine looks like, I'll start by simply playing a file. We need an AVAudioPlayerNode and an AVAudioFile. We hand the AVAudioPlayerNode to the engine and patch it to the engine's built-in mixer node. (In this simple case, we could have patched the player node to the engine's output node; but the engine's mixer node is already patched to the output node, so it makes no difference.) We associate the file with the player node and start the engine running. Finally, we tell the player node to play:

```
let player = AVAudioPlayerNode()
let url = NSBundle.mainBundle().URLForResource(
    "aboutTiagol", withExtension: "m4a")!
let f = try! AVAudioFile(forReading: url)
let mixer = engine.mainMixerNode
engine.attachNode(player)
engine.connect(player, to: mixer, format: f.processingFormat)
player.scheduleFile(f, atTime: nil, completionHandler:nil)
engine.prepare()
do {
    try engine.start()
    player.play()
} catch {}
```

You can also play sound from a buffer. This is a little more involved, but not much. Here, I'll start with an AVAudioFile again, but this time I'll feed it into a buffer; this allows me to do a little trickery, such as cutting out everything but the first third of the file:

```
let url2 = NSBundle.mainBundle().URLForResource(
    "Hooded", withExtension: "mp3")!
let f2 = try! AVAudioFile(forReading: url2)
let buffer = AVAudioPCMBuffer(
    PCMFormat: f2.processingFormat, frameCapacity: UInt32(f2.length/3))
try! f2.readIntoBuffer(buffer)
let player2 = AVAudioPlayerNode()
engine.attachNode(player2)
let mixer = engine.mainMixerNode
engine.connect(player2, to: mixer, format: f2.processingFormat)
player2.scheduleBuffer(
    buffer, atTime: nil, options: [], completionHandler: nil)
engine.prepare()
do {
    try engine.start()
    player2.play()
} catch {}
```

So far, we've done virtually nothing that we couldn't have done with an AVAudioPlayer. But now let's start patching some more nodes into the graph. I'll play both files simultaneously; I'll pass the first sound through a time-pitch effect node and then through a reverb effect node; I'll loop the second sound; and I'll set the volumes and pan positions of the sounds:

```
// first sound
let player = AVAudioPlayerNode()
let url = NSBundle.mainBundle().URLForResource(
    "aboutTiagol", withExtension: "m4a")!
let f = try! AVAudioFile(forReading: url)
engine.attachNode(player)
// add some effect nodes to the chain
let effect = AVAudioUnitTimePitch()
effect.rate = 0.9
effect.pitch = -300
```

```
engine.attachNode(effect)
engine.connect(player, to: effect, format: f.processingFormat)
let effect2 = AVAudioUnitReverb()
effect2.loadFactoryPreset(.Cathedral)
effect2.wetDryMix = 40
engine.attachNode(effect2)
engine.connect(effect, to: effect2, format: f.processingFormat)
// patch last node into engine mixer and start playing first sound
let mixer = engine.mainMixerNode
engine.connect(effect2, to: mixer, format: f.processingFormat)
player.scheduleFile(f, atTime: nil, completionHandler:nil)
engine.prepare()
do {
    try engine.start()
    player.play()
} catch { return }
// second sound; loop it this time
let url2 = NSBundle.mainBundle().URLForResource(
    "Hooded", withExtension: "mp3")!
let f2 = try! AVAudioFile(forReading: url2)
let buffer = AVAudioPCMBuffer(
    PCMFormat: f2.processingFormat, frameCapacity: UInt32(f2.length/3))
try! f2.readIntoBuffer(buffer)
let player2 = AVAudioPlayerNode()
engine.attachNode(player2)
engine.connect(player2, to: mixer, format: f2.processingFormat)
player2.scheduleBuffer(
    buffer, atTime: nil, options: .Loops, completionHandler: nil)
// mix down a little, start playing second sound
player.pan = -0.5
player2.volume = 0.5
player2.pan = 0.5
player2.play()
```

New in iOS 9, you can *split* a node's output between multiple nodes. Instead of calling connect:to:format:, you call connect:toConnectionPoints:fromBus:format:. The connectionPoints: argument is an array of AVAudioConnectionPoint objects, each of which is simply a node and a bus. In this example, I'll split my player's output three ways: I'll connect it simultaneously to a delay effect and a reverb effect, both of which are connected to the output mixer, and I'll connect the player itself directly to the output mixer as well:

```
let effect = AVAudioUnitDelay()
effect.delayTime = 0.4
effect.feedback = 0
engine.attachNode(effect)
let effect2 = AVAudioUnitReverb()
effect2.loadFactoryPreset(.Cathedral)
effect2.wetDryMix = 40
engine.attachNode(effect2)
let mixer = engine.mainMixerNode
```

```
// patch player node to _both_ effect nodes _and_ the mixer
let cons = [
    AVAudioConnectionPoint(node: effect, bus: 0),
    AVAudioConnectionPoint(node: effect2, bus: 0),
    AVAudioConnectionPoint(node: mixer, bus: 1),
]
engine.connect(player, toConnectionPoints: cons,
    fromBus: 0, format: f.processingFormat)
// patch both effect nodes into the mixer
engine.connect(effect, to: mixer, format: f.processingFormat)
engine.connect(effect2, to: mixer, format: f.processingFormat)
```

Finally, I'll demonstrate how to patch the sound produced from one file into a new file. This is done by installing a tap on a node to collect its sound into a buffer and writing the buffer into a file. When I started writing this example, I was hoping that the processing would be done rapidly in the background, but that's not how AVAudioEngine works: you have to play the sound in real time.

So, I'll pass a sound file through a reverb effect and patch the output into a new file. The most interesting challenge in this example turned out to be knowing when to stop! You can't just stop when the original input file buffer empties, because the reverb effect has yet to finish fading away. To know when that happens, I watch for the last output buffer value to become very small:

```
let url2 = NSBundle.mainBundle().URLForResource(
    "Hooded", withExtension: "mp3")!
let f2 = try! AVAudioFile(forReading: url2)
let buffer = AVAudioPCMBuffer(
    PCMFormat: f2.processingFormat, frameCapacity: UInt32(f2.length/3))
try! f2.readIntoBuffer(buffer)
let player2 = AVAudioPlayerNode()
engine.attachNode(player2)
let effect = AVAudioUnitReverb()
effect.loadFactoryPreset(.Cathedral)
effect.wetDryMix = 40
engine.attachNode(effect)
engine.connect(player2, to: effect, format: f2.processingFormat)
let mixer = engine.mainMixerNode
engine.connect(effect, to: mixer, format: f2.processingFormat)
// create the output file
let fm = NSFileManager.defaultManager()
let doc = try! fm.URLForDirectory(.DocumentDirectory,
    inDomain: .UserDomainMask, appropriateForURL: nil, create: true)
let outurl = doc.URLByAppendingPathComponent("myfile.aac")
let outfile = try! AVAudioFile(forWriting: outurl, settings: [
    AVFormatIDKey : NSNumber(unsignedInt:kAudioFormatMPEG4AAC),
    AVNumberOfChannelsKey : 1,
    AVSampleRateKey : 22050,
    AVEncoderBitRatePerChannelKey : 16
])
// install a tap on the reverb effect node
```

```
var done = false // flag: don't stop until input buffer is empty!
effect.installTapOnBus(0, bufferSize: 4096,
    format: outfile.processingFormat) {
        (buffer : AVAudioPCMBuffer!, time : AVAudioTime!) in
        let dataptrptr = buffer.floatChannelData
        let dataptr = dataptrptr.memory
        let datum = dataptr[Int(buffer.frameLength) - 1]
        // stop when input is empty and sound is very quiet
        if done && fabs(datum) < 0.000001 {
            print("stopping")
            self.engine.stop()
            return
        }
        do {
            try outfile.writeFromBuffer(buffer)
        } catch {
            print(error)
        }
}
player2.scheduleBuffer(buffer, atTime: nil, options: []) {
    done = true
}
engine.prepare()
do {
    try engine.start()
    player2.play()
} catch {}
```

An AVAudioNode subclass that I haven't talked about is AVAudioEnvironmentNode, which gives three-dimensional spatial control over sound sources (suitable for games). With it, a bunch of interesting AVAudioNode properties spring to life.

MIDI Playback

iOS allows interaction with MIDI devices through the CoreMIDI framework, which I'm not going to discuss here. But playing a MIDI file is another matter. Before iOS 8, this required use of the rather tricky Audio Toolbox framework. But starting in iOS 8, playing a MIDI file became just as simple as playing an audio file. In this example, I'm already armed with a MIDI file, which provides the music, and a SoundFont file, which provides the instrument that will play it; self.player will be an AVMIDIPlayer:

```
let midurl = NSBundle.mainBundle().URLForResource(
    "presto", withExtension: "mid")!
let sndurl = NSBundle.mainBundle().URLForResource(
    "PianoBell", withExtension: "sf2")!
self.player = try! AVMIDIPlayer(
    contentsOfURL: midurl, soundBankURL: sndurl)
self.player.prepareToPlay()
self.player.play(nil)
```

New in iOS 9, a MIDI player can also act as a source in an AVAudioEngine. In this case, you'll want an AVAudioUnitSampler as your starting AVAudioUnit. The MIDI file will be parsed by an AVAudioSequencer; this is not part of the audio engine node structure, but rather it *has* the audio engine as a property, so you'll need to retain it in a property (`self.seq` in this example):

```
let midurl = NSBundle.mainBundle().URLForResource(
    "presto", withExtension: "mid")!
let sndurl = NSBundle.mainBundle().URLForResource(
    "PianoBell", withExtension: "sf2")!
let unit = AVAudioUnitSampler()
engine.attachNode(unit)
let mixer = engine.outputNode
engine.connect(unit, to: mixer, format: mixer.outputFormatForBus(0))
try! unit.loadInstrumentAtURL(sndurl) // note the order here!
self.seq = AVAudioSequencer(audioEngine: engine)
try! self.seq.loadFromURL(midurl, options: [])
engine.prepare()
try! engine.start()
try! self.seq.start()
```

That code is rather mysterious: where's the connection between the AVAudioSequencer and the AVAudioUnitSampler? The answer is that the sequencer just finds the first AVAudioUnitSampler in the audio engine graph and proceeds to drive it. If that isn't what you want, get the AVAudioSequencer's `tracks` property, which is an array of AVMusicTrack; now you can set each track's `destinationAudioUnit` explicitly.

Speech Synthesis

Text can be transformed into synthesized speech. This can be extremely easy to do, using the AVSpeechUtterance and AVSpeechSynthesizer classes. As with an AVAudioPlayer, you'll need to retain the AVSpeechSynthesizer (`self.talker` in my example); here, I also use the AVSpeechSynthesisVoice class to make sure the device speaks the text in English, regardless of the user's language settings:

```
let utter = AVSpeechUtterance(string:"Polly, want a cracker?")
let v = AVSpeechSynthesisVoice(language: "en-US")
utter.voice = v
self.talker.delegate = self
self.talker.speakUtterance(utter)
```

You can also set the speech rate. The delegate (AVSpeechSynthesizerDelegate) is told when the speech starts, when it comes to a new range of text (usually a word), and when it finishes.

Further Topics in Sound

iOS is a powerful milieu for production and processing of sound; its sound-related technologies are extensive. This is a big topic, and an entire book could be written about it (in fact, such books do exist). I'll talk in Chapter 16 about accessing sound files in the user's music library. But here are some further topics that there is no room to discuss here:

Other audio session policies

If your app accepts sound input or does audio processing, you'll want to look into additional audio session policies I didn't talk about earlier — Record, Play and Record, and Audio Processing. In addition, if you're using Record or Play and Record, there are modes — voice chat, video recording, and measurement (of the sound being input) — that optimize how sound is routed (for example, what microphone is used) and how it is modified.

 Your app must obtain the user's permission to use the microphone. This permission will be requested on your behalf when you adopt a Record audio session policy. You can modify the body of the system alert by setting the "Privacy — Microphone Usage Description" key (NSMicrophoneUsageDescription) in your app's *Info.plist*. You can learn whether permission has been granted by calling the audio session's recordPermission method.

Recording sound

To record sound simply, use AVAudioRecorder. Your audio session will need to adopt a Record policy before recording begins.

Audio queues

Audio queues — Audio Queue Services, part of the Audio Toolbox framework — implement sound playing and recording through a C API with more granularity than the Objective-C AVAudioPlayer and AVAudioRecorder (though it is still regarded as a high-level API), giving you access to the buffers used to move chunks of sound data between a storage format (a sound file) and sound hardware.

Extended Audio File Services

A C API for reading and writing sound files in chunks. It is useful in connection with technologies such as audio queues.

Audio Converter Services

A C API for converting sound files between formats. New in iOS 9, the AVAudioConverter class (along with AVAudioCompressedBuffer) gives this API an object-oriented structure.

Streaming audio

Audio streamed in real time over the network, such as an Internet radio station, can be played with Audio File Stream Services, in connection with audio queues.

OpenAL

An advanced technology for playing sound with fine control over its stereo stage and directionality. AVAudioEngine is an easier front end.

Audio units

Plug-ins that generate sound or modify sound as it passes through them. New in iOS 9, the API has been migrated from C into Objective-C and given a modern object-oriented structure; audio units can vend interface (AUViewController); and an audio unit from one app can be hosted inside another (audio unit extensions).

CHAPTER 15

Video

Video playback is performed using classes such as AVPlayer provided by the AV Foundation framework (`import AVFoundation`). An AVPlayer is not a view; rather, an AVPlayer's content is made visible through a CALayer subclass, AVPlayerLayer, which can be added to your app's interface.

An AV Foundation video playback interface can be wrapped in a simple view controller, AVPlayerViewController (introduced in iOS 8): you provide an AVPlayer, and the AVPlayerViewController *automatically* hosts an associated AVPlayerLayer in its own main view, providing standard playback transport controls so that the user can start and stop play, seek to a different frame, and so forth. AVPlayerViewController is provided by the AVKit framework; you'll need to `import AVKit`.

 AVPlayerViewController effectively supersedes the Media Player framework's MPMoviePlayerController and MPMoviePlayerViewController, which are deprecated in iOS 9 and are not discussed in this edition.

A simple interface for letting the user trim video (UIVideoEditorController) is also supplied. Sophisticated video editing can be performed through the AV Foundation framework, as I'll demonstrate later in this chapter.

If an AVPlayer produces sound, you may need to concern yourself with your application's audio session; see Chapter 14. AVPlayer deals gracefully with the app being sent into the background: it will pause when your app is backgrounded and resume when your app returns to the foreground.

A movie file can be in a standard movie format, such as *.mov* or *.mp4*, but it can also be a sound file. An AVPlayerViewController is thus an easy way to play a sound file, including a sound file obtained in real time over the Internet, along with standard controls for pausing the sound and moving the playhead — unlike AVAudioPlayer, which, as I pointed out in Chapter 14, lacks a user interface.

A mobile device does not have unlimited power for decoding and presenting video in real time. A video that plays on your computer might not play at all on an iOS device. See the "Media Layer" chapter of Apple's *iOS Technology Overview* for a list of specifications and limits within which video is eligible for playing.

A web view (Chapter 11) supports the HTML 5 <video> tag. This can be a simple lightweight way to present video and to allow the user to control playback. Both web view video and AVPlayer support AirPlay.

AVPlayerViewController

An AVPlayerViewController is a view controller; thus, you already know (from Chapter 6) how to work with it. The only other thing you need to know, in order to get started, is that an AVPlayerViewController must be assigned a player, which is an AVPlayer, and that an AVPlayer can be initialized directly from the URL of the video it is to play, with init(URL:). Thus, you'll instantiate AVPlayerViewController, create and set its AVPlayer, and get the AVPlayerViewController into the view controller hierarchy; AVPlayerViewController adapts intelligently to its place in the hierarchy.

 You can instantiate an AVPlayerViewController from a storyboard; look for the AVKit Player View Controller object in the Object library. However, you will then need to link your target manually to the AVKit framework: edit the target and add *AVKit.framework* under Linked Frameworks and Libraries in the General tab.

The absolute rock-bottom simplest approach is to use an AVPlayerViewController as a presented view controller. In this example, I present a video from the app bundle:

```
let av = AVPlayerViewController()
let url = NSBundle.mainBundle().URLForResource(
    "ElMirage", withExtension: "mp4")!
let player = AVPlayer(URL: url)
av.player = player
self.presentViewController(av, animated: true, completion: nil)
```

The AVPlayerViewController knows that it's being shown as a fullscreen presented view controller, so it provides fullscreen video controls, including a Done button which *automatically* dismisses the presented view controller! Thus, there is literally no further work for you to do.

Figure 15-1 shows a fullscreen presented AVPlayerViewController. Exactly what controls you'll see depends on the circumstances; in my case, at the top there's the Done button, the current playhead position slider, and the expand/contract button, and at the

Figure 15-1. A presented AVPlayerViewController

Figure 15-2. A presented AVPlayerViewController with a sound file

bottom there are the three standard transport buttons and a volume slider. (If my net-work were more interesting, we would also see an AirPlay button.) The user can hide or show the controls by tapping the video, and can expand or contract the video by double-tapping it.

The black color of the background is the `backgroundColor` of the AVPlayerView-Controller's view, which you are free to change.

If the movie file is in fact a sound file, the central region is replaced by a QuickTime symbol, and the controls can't be hidden (Figure 15-2).

Figure 15-3. An embedded AVPlayerViewController's view

Instead of presenting an AVPlayerViewController, you might push it onto a navigation controller's stack. Again, the AVPlayerViewController behaves intelligently. There is now no Done button. Instead, the lower controls include a fullscreen button. Tapping the fullscreen button results in almost exactly the same interface shown in Figure 15-1: the view is displayed fullscreen, and its controls then include a Done button which exits fullscreen mode.

If you want the convenience and the control interface that come from using an AVPlayerViewController, while displaying its view as a *subview* of your own view controller's view, make your view controller a parent view controller and add the AVPlayerViewController's view in good order (see "Container View Controllers" on page 339):

```
let url = NSBundle.mainBundle().URLForResource(
    "ElMirage", withExtension:"mp4")!
let player = AVPlayer(URL:url)
let av = AVPlayerViewController()
av.player = player
av.view.frame = CGRectMake(10,10,300,200)
self.addChildViewController(av)
self.view.addSubview(av.view)
av.didMoveToParentViewController(self)
```

Once again, the AVPlayerViewController behaves intelligently, reducing its controls to a minimum to adapt to the reduced size of its view. On my device, at the given view size, there is room for a play button, a playhead position slider, a full-screen button, and nothing else (Figure 15-3). However, the user can enter full-screen mode, either by tapping the full-screen button or by pinching outwards on the video view, and now the full complement of controls is present.

Other AVPlayerViewController Properties

An AVPlayerViewController has very few properties:

player

> The view controller's AVPlayer, whose AVPlayerLayer will be hosted in the view
> controller's view. You can set the player while the view is visible, to change what
> video it displays (though you are more likely to keep the player and tell *it* to change
> the video). It is legal to assign an AVQueuePlayer, an AVPlayer subclass; an
> AVQueuePlayer has multiple items, and the AVPlayerViewController will treat
> these as chapters of the video. (I'll give an example of using an AVQueuePlayer in
> Chapter 16.)

showsPlaybackControls

> If false, the controls are hidden. This could be useful, for example, if you want to
> display a video for decorative purposes, or if you are substituting your own controls.

contentOverlayView

> A UIView to which you are free to add subviews. These subviews will appear over-
> laid in front of the video but behind the playback controls. This is a great way to
> cover that dreadful QuickTime symbol (Figure 15-2).

videoGravity

> How the video should be positioned within the view. Possible values are:
>
> - AVLayerVideoGravityResizeAspect (the default)
> - AVLayerVideoGravityResizeAspectFill
> - AVLayerVideoGravityResize (fills the view, possibly distorting the video)

videoBounds
readyForDisplay

> The video position within the view, and the ability of the video to display its first
> frame and start playing, respectively. If the video is not ready for display, we prob-
> ably don't yet know its bounds either. In any case, readyForDisplay will initially
> be false and the videoBounds will initially be reported as CGRectZero. This is
> because, with video, things take time to prepare. I'll explain further later in this
> chapter.

Everything else there is to know about an AVPlayerViewController comes from its
player, an AVPlayer. I'll discuss AVPlayer in more detail in a moment.

Picture-in-Picture

New in iOS 9, an iPad that supports iPad multitasking also supports picture-in-picture
video playback. This means that the user can move your playing video into a small
system window that floats in front of everything else on the screen. This floating window
persists even if your app is put into the background. Your iPad app will support picture-
in-picture if it supports background audio, as I described in Chapter 14: you check the

Figure 15-4. The picture-in-picture button appears

checkbox in the Capabilities tab of the target editor (Figure 14-3), and your audio session's policy must be active and must be Playback.

 If you want to do those things *without* supporting picture-in-picture, set the AVPlayerViewController's allowsPictureInPicturePlayback to false. Note that even if you *do* support picture-in-picture, the user can turn it off in the Settings app.

The result is that, on an iPad that supports picture-in-picture, an extra button appears among the lower set of playback controls (Figure 15-4). When the user taps this button, the video is moved into the system window (and the AVPlayerViewController's view displays a placeholder). The user is now free to leave your app while continuing to see and hear the video. Moreover, if you are using a fullscreen AVPlayerViewController and the user leaves your app while the video is playing, the video is moved into the picture-in-picture system window *automatically*.

The user can move the system window to any corner. Buttons in the system window, which can be shown or hidden by tapping, allow the user to play and pause the video, to dismiss the system window, or to dismiss the system window plus return to your app.

If you're using a pushed or embedded AVPlayerViewController, then when the user dismisses the system window, the right thing happens automatically: back in your app, the video is restored to the AVPlayerViewController's view. But if you're using a presented AVPlayerViewController, the presented view controller, by default, has been dismissed — there is no AVPlayerViewController any longer. If that isn't what you want, declare yourself the AVPlayerViewController's delegate (AVPlayerViewController-Delegate) and deal with it in a delegate method. You have two choices:

Don't dismiss the presented view controller

Implement playerViewControllerShouldAutomaticallyDismissAtPictureIn-PictureStart: to return false. Now the presented view controller remains, and the video has a place in your app to which it can be restored.

Recreate the presented view controller

Implement playerViewController:restoreUserInterfaceForPictureInPic-tureStopWithCompletionHandler:. Do what the name tells you: restore the user interface! The first parameter is your original AVPlayerViewController; all you have to do is get it back into the view controller hierarchy. At the end of the process, *call the completion handler.*

I'll demonstrate the second approach:

```
func playerViewController(pvc: AVPlayerViewController,
    restoreUserInterfaceForPictureInPictureStopWithCompletionHandler
    ch: (Bool) -> Void) {
        self.presentViewController(pvc, animated:true) {
            _ in
            ch(true)
        }
}
```

Other delegate methods inform you of various stages as picture-in-picture mode begins and ends. Thus you could respond by rearranging the interface. For example, if you're using a pushed AVPlayerViewController, you might want to pop it when picture-in-picture mode starts. And there's another reason for being conscious that you've entered picture-in-picture mode: once that happens, you are effectively a background app, and you should reduce resources and activity so that playing the video is *all* you're doing until picture-in-picture mode ends.

Introducing AV Foundation

The video display performed by AVPlayerViewController is supplied by classes from the AV Foundation framework. This is a big framework with a lot of classes; the *AV Foundation Framework Reference* lists about 150 classes and 20 protocols. This may seem daunting, but there's a good reason for it: video has a lot of structure and can be manipulated in many ways, and AV Foundation very carefully and correctly draws all the distinctions needed for good object-oriented encapsulation.

Because AV Foundation is so big, all I can do here is introduce it. I'll point out some of the principal classes, features, and techniques associated with video. Further AV Foundation examples will appear in Chapters 16 and 17. Eventually you'll want to read Apple's *AV Foundation Programming Guide* for a full overview.

Some AV Foundation Classes

The heart of AV Foundation video playback is AVPlayer. It is not a UIView; rather, it is the locus of video transport (and the actual video, if shown, appears in an AVPlayerLayer associated with the AVPlayer). For example, AVPlayerViewController provides a play button, but what if you wanted to start video playback in code? You'd tell the AVPlayerViewController's `player` (an AVPlayer) to `play`.

An AVPlayer's video is its `currentItem`, an AVPlayerItem. This may come as a surprise, because in the examples earlier in this chapter we initialized an AVPlayer directly from a URL, with no reference to any AVPlayerItem. That, however, was just a shortcut.

AVPlayer's *real* initializer is `init(playerItem:)`; when we called `init(URL:)`, the AVPlayerItem was created for us.

An AVPlayerItem, too, can be initialized from a URL with `init(URL:)`, but again, this is just a shortcut. AVPlayerItem's *real* initalizer is `init(asset:)`, which takes an AVAsset. An AVAsset is an actual video resource, and comes in one of two subclasses:

`AVURLAsset`
> An asset specified through an NSURL.

`AVComposition`
> An asset constructed by editing video in code. I'll give an example later in this chapter.

Thus, to configure an AVPlayer using the complete "stack" of objects that constitute it, you could say something like this:

```
let url = NSBundle.mainBundle().URLForResource(
    "ElMirage", withExtension:"mp4")!
let asset = AVURLAsset(URL:url, options:nil)
let item = AVPlayerItem(asset:asset)
let player = AVPlayer(playerItem:item)
```

Once an AVPlayer exists and has an AVPlayerItem, that player item's tracks, as seen from the player's perspective, are AVPlayerItemTrack objects, which can be individually enabled or disabled. That's different from an AVAssetTrack, which is a fact about an AVAsset. This distinction is a good example of what I said earlier about how AV Foundation encapsulates its objects correctly: an AVAssetTrack is a hard and fast reality, but an AVPlayerItemTrack lets a track be manipulated for purposes of playback on a particular occasion.

Another important use of an AVPlayerItem is as the locus of information about the arrival and playback of an AVAsset from across the network. Properties such as `playbackLikelyToKeepUp` and `accessLog`, along with notifications such as `AVPlayer-ItemPlaybackStalledNotification`, can be helpful in keeping you abreast of any issues.

Things Take Time

Working with video is time-consuming. Just because you give an AVPlayer a command or set a property doesn't mean that reaction time is immediate. All sorts of operations, from reading a video file and learning its metadata to transcoding and saving a video file, take a significant amount of time. The user interface must not freeze while a video task is in progress, so AV Foundation relies heavily on threading (Chapter 25). In this way, AV Foundation covers the complex and time-consuming nature of its operations; but your code must cooperate. You'll frequently use key–value observing and callbacks to run your code at the right moment.

Here's a simple example. There's an elementary interface flaw in the code presented earlier for displaying an embedded video:

```
let url = NSBundle.mainBundle().URLForResource(
    "ElMirage", withExtension:"mp4")!
let player = AVPlayer(URL:url)
let av = AVPlayerViewController()
av.player = player
av.view.frame = CGRectMake(10,10,300,200)
self.addChildViewController(av)
self.view.addSubview(av.view)
av.didMoveToParentViewController(self)
```

The problem is that the AVPlayerViewController's view is appearing in the interface when the video is not yet ready for display — resulting in a visible flash when the video *is* ready for display. To prevent this flash, let's start with the AVPlayerViewController's view hidden, and not show it until readyForDisplay is true.

But how will we know when that is? *Not* by repeatedly polling the readyForDisplay property! That sort of behavior is absolutely wrong. Rather, we will use KVO to register as an observer of this property:

```
av.view.frame = CGRectMake(10,10,300,200)
av.view.hidden = true // *
self.addChildViewController(av)
self.view.addSubview(av.view)
av.didMoveToParentViewController(self)
av.addObserver(self,
    forKeyPath: "readyForDisplay", options: .New, context: nil) // *
```

Sooner or later, readyForDisplay will become true, and we'll be notified. Now we can unregister from KVO and show the AVPlayerViewController's view:

```
override func observeValueForKeyPath(keyPath: String?,
    ofObject object: AnyObject?, change: [String : AnyObject]?,
    context: UnsafeMutablePointer<()>) {
        guard keyPath == "readyForDisplay" else {return}
        guard let obj = object as? AVPlayerViewController else {return}
        guard let ok = change?[NSKeyValueChangeNewKey] as? Bool else {return}
        guard ok else {return}
        vc.removeObserver(self, forKeyPath:"readyForDisplay")
        dispatch_async(dispatch_get_main_queue(), {
            self.finishConstructingInterface(obj)
        })
}
func finishConstructingInterface (vc:AVPlayerViewController) {
    vc.view.hidden = false
}
```

Note that, in that code, I make no assumptions about what thread KVO calls me back on: I intend to operate on the interface, so I step out to the main thread.

In the same way, you can observe an embedded AVPlayerViewController's `video-Bounds` property as a way of learning when the user toggles it into fullscreen mode.

For the sake of efficiency, many AV Foundation object properties are *never* evaluated unless you specifically ask for them. AV Foundation objects that behave this way conform to the AVAsynchronousKeyValueLoading protocol. You call `loadValues-AsynchronouslyForKeys:completionHandler:` for any properties you're going to be interested in. When your completion handler function is called, you check the status of a key and, if its status is `.Loaded`, you are now free to access it.

Here's a rather overblown example (deliberately so, because I want to illustrate asynchronous key loading). In the preceding code, I've been assigning the AVPlayerView-Controller's view an arbitrary size, thus causing some letterboxing above and below the actual video when it appears (visible in Figure 15-3). Let's say that I'd like to learn the video's actual size and give the AVPlayerViewController's view the same aspect ratio. An AVAsset has `tracks` (AVAssetTrack); in particular, an AVAsset representing a video has a video track. A video track has a `naturalSize`. Both AVAsset's `tracks` and AVAsset-Track's `naturalSize` are properties that we can load asynchronously. I'll start by creating the AVAsset and then stop, waiting to hear that its `tracks` property is ready:

```
let url = NSBundle.mainBundle().URLForResource(
    "ElMirage", withExtension:"mp4")!
let asset = AVURLAsset(URL:url, options:nil)
asset.loadValuesAsynchronouslyForKeys(["tracks"]) {
    let status = asset.statusOfValueForKey("tracks", error: nil)
    if status == .Loaded {
        dispatch_async(dispatch_get_main_queue(), {
            self.getVideoTrack(asset)
        })
    }
}
```

When the `tracks` property is ready, my `getVideoTrack` method is called. I obtain the video track and stop once again, waiting to hear when the video track's `naturalSize` property is ready:

```
func getVideoTrack(asset:AVAsset) {
    let visual = AVMediaCharacteristicVisual
    let vtrack = asset.tracksWithMediaCharacteristic(visual)[0]
    vtrack.loadValuesAsynchronouslyForKeys(["naturalSize"]) {
        let status =
            vtrack.statusOfValueForKey("naturalSize", error: nil)
        if status == .Loaded {
            dispatch_async(dispatch_get_main_queue(), {
                self.getNaturalSize(vtrack, asset)
            })
        }
    }
}
```

When the `naturalSize` property is ready, my `getNaturalSize` method is called. I get the natural size and use it to finish constructing the AVPlayer and to set AVPlayer-Controller's frame — and the rest is as before:

```
func getNaturalSize(vtrack:AVAssetTrack, _ asset:AVAsset) {
    let sz = vtrack.naturalSize
    let item = AVPlayerItem(asset:asset)
    let player = AVPlayer(playerItem:item)
    let av = AVPlayerViewController()
    av.view.frame = AVMakeRectWithAspectRatioInsideRect(
        sz, CGRectMake(10,10,300,200))
    av.player = player
    // ...
}
```

AVPlayerItem provides another way of loading an asset's properties: initialize it with `init(asset:automaticallyLoadedAssetKeys:)` and observe its `status` using KVO. When that `status` is `.ReadyToPlay`, you are guaranteed that the player item's `asset` has attempted to load those keys, and you can query them just as you would in `loadValuesAsynchronouslyForKeys:`.

Time is Measured Oddly

Another peculiarity of AV Foundation is that time is measured in an unfamiliar way. This is necessary because calculations using an ordinary built-in numeric class such as CGFloat will always have slight rounding errors that quickly begin to matter when you're trying to specify a time within a large piece of media.

Therefore, the Core Media framework (`import CoreMedia`) provides the CMTime class, which under the hood is a pair of integers; they are called the `value` and the `timescale`, but they are simply the numerator and denominator of a rational number. The denominator represents the degree of granularity; a typical value is 600, sufficient to specify individual frames in common video formats.

In the convenience function `CMTimeMakeWithSeconds`, however, the two arguments are *not* the numerator and denominator; they are the time's equivalent in seconds and the denominator. For example, `CMTimeMakeWithSeconds(2.5,600)` yields the CMTime (`1500,600`).

 Swift extends CMTime and some related types to make them easier to use. For example, instead of calling `CMTimeMakeWithSeconds`, you can call an initializer `init(seconds:preferredTimescale:)`.

Constructing Media

AV Foundation allows you to construct your own media asset in code as an AVCom-position, an AVAsset subclass, using *its* subclass, AVMutableComposition. An AVMutableComposition is an AVAsset, so given an AVMutableComposition comp we could make an AVPlayerItem from it and hand it over to an AVPlayerViewController's player; we will thus be creating and displaying our own movie:

```
let item = AVPlayerItem(asset:comp)
let vc = self.childViewControllers[0] as! AVPlayerViewController
let p = vc.player!
p.replaceCurrentItemWithPlayerItem(item)
```

Let's try it! In this example, I start with an AVAsset (a video file) and assemble its first 5 seconds of video and its last 5 seconds of video into a new AVAsset:

```
let oldAsset = p.currentItem!.asset
let type = AVMediaTypeVideo
let arr = oldAsset.tracksWithMediaType(type)
let track = arr.last!
let duration : CMTime = track.timeRange.duration
let comp = AVMutableComposition()
let comptrack = comp.addMutableTrackWithMediaType(type,
    preferredTrackID: Int32(kCMPersistentTrackID_Invalid))
try! comptrack.insertTimeRange(
    CMTimeRangeMake(
        CMTimeMakeWithSeconds(0,600), CMTimeMakeWithSeconds(5,600)
    ), ofTrack:track, atTime:CMTimeMakeWithSeconds(0,600))
try! comptrack.insertTimeRange(CMTimeRangeMake(CMTimeSubtract(
    duration, CMTimeMakeWithSeconds(5,600)), CMTimeMakeWithSeconds(5,600)),
    ofTrack:track, atTime:CMTimeMakeWithSeconds(5,600))
```

This works perfectly. We are not very good video editors, however, as we have forgotten the corresponding soundtrack. Let's go back and get it and add it to our AVMutable-Composition (comp):

```
let type2 = AVMediaTypeAudio
let arr2 = oldAsset.tracksWithMediaType(type2)
let track2 = arr2.last!
let comptrack2 = comp.addMutableTrackWithMediaType(type2,
    preferredTrackID:Int32(kCMPersistentTrackID_Invalid))
try! comptrack2.insertTimeRange(
    CMTimeRangeMake(
        CMTimeMakeWithSeconds(0,600), CMTimeMakeWithSeconds(5,600)
    ), ofTrack:track2, atTime:CMTimeMakeWithSeconds(0,600))
try! comptrack2.insertTimeRange(CMTimeRangeMake(CMTimeSubtract(
    duration, CMTimeMakeWithSeconds(5,600)), CMTimeMakeWithSeconds(5,600)),
    ofTrack:track2, atTime:CMTimeMakeWithSeconds(5,600))
```

But wait! Now let's overlay *another* audio track; this might be, for example, some additional narration:

```
let type3 = AVMediaTypeAudio
let s = NSBundle.mainBundle().URLForResource(
    "aboutTiagol", withExtension:"m4a")!
let asset = AVURLAsset(URL:s, options:nil)
let arr3 = asset.tracksWithMediaType(type3)
let track3 = arr3.last!
let comptrack3 = comp.addMutableTrackWithMediaType(type3,
    preferredTrackID:Int32(kCMPersistentTrackID_Invalid))
try! comptrack3.insertTimeRange(
    CMTimeRangeMake(
        CMTimeMakeWithSeconds(0,600), CMTimeMakeWithSeconds(10,600)
    ), ofTrack:track3, atTime:CMTimeMakeWithSeconds(0,600))
```

You can also apply audio volume changes and video opacity and transform changes to the playback of individual tracks. I'll continue from the previous example, applying a fadeout to the last three seconds of the narration track (comptrack3) by creating an AVAudioMix:

```
let params = AVMutableAudioMixInputParameters(track:comptrack3)
params.setVolume(1, atTime:CMTimeMakeWithSeconds(0,600))
params.setVolumeRampFromStartVolume(1, toEndVolume:0,
    timeRange:CMTimeRangeMake(
        CMTimeMakeWithSeconds(7,600), CMTimeMakeWithSeconds(3,600)))
let mix = AVMutableAudioMix()
mix.inputParameters = [params]
```

The audio mix must be applied to a playback milieu, such as an AVPlayerItem. So when we make an AVPlayerItem out of our AVComposition (comp), as I showed at the start of this section, we can set its audioMix property to mix.

Similar to AVAudioMix, you can use AVVideoComposition to dictate how video tracks are to be composited. New in iOS 9, you can easily add a CIFilter (Chapter 2) to be applied to your video.

Synchronizing Animation With Video

An intriguing feature of AV Foundation is AVSynchronizedLayer, a CALayer subclass that effectively crosses the bridge between video time (the CMTime within the progress of a movie) and Core Animation time (the time within the progress of an animation). This means that you can coordinate animation in your interface (Chapter 4) with the playback of a movie. You attach an animation to a layer in more or less the usual way, but the animation takes place in movie playback time: if the movie is stopped, the animation is stopped; if the movie is run at double rate, the animation runs at double rate; and the current "frame" of the animation always corresponds to the current frame, within its entire duration, of the video.

The synchronization is performed with respect to an AVPlayer's AVPlayerItem. To demonstrate, I'll draw a long thin gray rectangle containing a little black square; the

Figure 15-5. The black square's position is synchronized to the movie

horizontal position of the black square within the gray rectangle will be synchronized to the movie playhead position:

```
let vc = self.childViewControllers[0] as! AVPlayerViewController
let p = vc.player!
let item = p.currentItem!
let syncLayer = AVSynchronizedLayer(playerItem:item)
// put synch layer into the interface
syncLayer.frame = CGRectMake(10,220,300,10)
syncLayer.backgroundColor = UIColor.lightGrayColor().CGColor
self.view.layer.addSublayer(syncLayer)
// give synch layer a sublayer
let subLayer = CALayer()
subLayer.backgroundColor = UIColor.blackColor().CGColor
subLayer.frame = CGRectMake(0,0,10,10)
syncLayer.addSublayer(subLayer)
// animate the sublayer
let anim = CABasicAnimation(keyPath:"position")
anim.fromValue = NSValue(CGPoint: subLayer.position)
anim.toValue = NSValue(CGPoint: CGPointMake(295,5))
anim.removedOnCompletion = false
anim.beginTime = AVCoreAnimationBeginTimeAtZero // important trick
anim.duration = CMTimeGetSeconds(item.asset.duration)
subLayer.addAnimation(anim, forKey:nil)
```

The result is shown in Figure 15-5. The gray rectangle is the AVSynchronizedLayer, tied to our movie. The little black square inside it is its sublayer; when we animate the black square, that animation will be synchronized to the movie, changing its position from the left end of the gray rectangle to the right end, starting at the beginning of the movie and with the same duration as the movie. Thus, although we attach this animation to the black square layer in the usual way, that animation is frozen: the black square *doesn't move* until we start the movie playing. Moreover, if we pause the movie, the black square stops. The black square is thus *automatically* representing the current play position within the movie. This may seem a silly example, but if you were to suppress the video controls it could prove downright useful.

AVPlayerLayer

An AVPlayer is not an interface object. The corresponding interface object — an AVPlayer made visible, as it were — is an AVPlayerLayer (a CALayer subclass). It has no controls for letting the user play and pause a movie and visualize its progress; it just shows the movie, acting as a bridge between the AV Foundation world of media and the CALayer world of things the user can see.

An AVPlayerViewController's view hosts an AVPlayerLayer for you automatically; otherwise you would not see any video in the AVPlayerViewController's view. But there may certainly be situations where you find AVPlayerViewController too heavyweight, where you don't need the standard transport controls, where you don't want the video to be expandable or to have a fullscreen mode — you just want the simple direct power that can be obtained only by putting an AVPlayerLayer into the interface yourself. And you are free to do so!

Here, I'll display the same movie as before, but without an AVPlayerViewController:

```
let m = NSBundle.mainBundle().URLForResource(
    "ElMirage", withExtension:"mp4")!
let asset = AVURLAsset(URL:m, options:nil)
let item = AVPlayerItem(asset:asset)
let p = AVPlayer(playerItem:item)
self.player = p // might need a reference later
let lay = AVPlayerLayer(player:p) // *
lay.frame = CGRectMake(10,10,300,200)
self.view.layer.addSublayer(lay) // *
```

As before, if we want to prevent a flash when the video becomes ready for display, we can postpone adding the AVPlayerLayer to our interface until its readyForDisplay property becomes true — which we can learn through KVO.

The movie is now visible in the interface, but it isn't doing anything. We haven't told our AVPlayer to play, and there are no transport controls, so the user can't tell the video to play either. This is why I kept a reference to the AVPlayer in a property! We can start play either by calling play or by setting the AVPlayer's rate. Here, I imagine that we've provided a simple play/pause button that toggles the playing status of the movie by changing its rate:

```
@IBAction func doButton (sender:AnyObject!) {
    let rate = self.player.rate
    if rate < 0.01 {
        self.player.rate = 1
```

```
    } else {
        self.player.rate = 0
    }
}
```

Without trying to replicate the transport controls, we might also like to give the user a way to jump the playhead back to the start of the movie. The playhead position is a feature, not of an AVPlayer, but of an AVPlayerItem:

```
@IBAction func restart (sender:AnyObject!) {
    let item = self.player.currentItem!
    item.seekToTime(CMTimeMake(0, 1))
}
```

If we want our AVPlayerLayer to support picture-in-picture, then (in addition to making the app itself support picture-in-picture, as I've already described) we need to call upon AVKit to supply us with an AVPictureInPictureController. This is *not* a view controller; it merely endows our AVPlayerLayer with picture-in-picture behavior. You create the AVPictureInPictureController (checking first to see whether the environment supports picture-in-picture in the first place), initialize it with the AVPlayerLayer, *and retain it*:

```
if AVPictureInPictureController.isPictureInPictureSupported() {
    let pic = AVPictureInPictureController(playerLayer: lay)
    self.pic = pic
}
```

There are no transport controls, so there is no picture-in-picture button. Supplying one is up to you. Don't forget to hide the button if picture-in-picture isn't supported! When the button is tapped, tell the AVPictureInPictureController to startPictureInPicture:

```
if self.pic.pictureInPicturePossible {
    self.pic.startPictureInPicture()
}
```

You might also want to set yourself as the AVPictureInPictureController's delegate (AVPictureInPictureControllerDelegate). This is very similar to the AVPlayerView-Controller delegate, and serves the same purpose: you are informed of stages in the life of the picture-in-picture window so that you can adjust your interface accordingly. If the AVPlayerLayer is still sitting in your interface, there may be no work to do. If not, then if you implement pictureInPictureController:restoreUserInterfaceFor-PictureInPictureStopWithCompletionHandler: because you removed the AVPlayer-Layer from your interface, just be sure that the AVPlayerLayer that you now put into your interface is *the same one* that was removed earlier; in other words, your player layer must continue to be the same as the AVPictureInPictureController's playerLayer.

Further Exploration of AV Foundation

Here are some other things you can do with AV Foundation:

- Extract single images ("thumbnails") from a movie (AVAssetImageGenerator).

- Export a movie in a different format (AVAssetExportSession), or read/write raw uncompressed data through a buffer to or from a track (AVAssetReader, AVAsset-ReaderOutput, AVAssetWriter, AVAssetWriterInput, and so on).

- Capture audio, video, and stills through the device's hardware (AVCaptureSession and so on). I'll say more about this in Chapter 17.

- Tap into video and audio being captured or played, including capturing video frames as still images (AVPlayerItemVideoOutput, AVCaptureVideoDataOutput, and so on; and see Apple's *Technical Q&A QA1702*).

UIVideoEditorController

UIVideoEditorController is a view controller that presents an interface where the user can trim video. Its view and internal behavior are outside your control, and you're not supposed to subclass it. You are expected to treat the view controller as a presented view controller on the iPhone or as a popover on the iPad, and respond by way of its delegate.

 UIVideoEditorController is one of the creakiest pieces of interface in iOS. It dates back to iOS 3.1, and hasn't been revised since its inception — and it looks and feels like it. It has *never* worked properly on the iPad, and still doesn't. I'm going to show how to use it, but I'm not going to explore its bugginess in any depth or we'd be here all day.

Before summoning a UIVideoEditorController, be sure to call its class method `canEdit-VideoAtPath:`. (This call can take some noticeable time to return.) If this call returns `false`, don't instantiate UIVideoEditorController to edit the given file. Not every video format is editable, and not every device supports video editing. You must also set the UIVideoEditorController instance's `delegate` and `videoPath` before presenting it; the delegate should adopt both UINavigationControllerDelegate and UIVideoEditor-ControllerDelegate. Setting the UIVideoEditorController's `modalPresentationStyle` to `.Popover` on the iPad is up to you (a good instance of the creakiness I was just referring to):

```
let path = NSBundle.mainBundle().pathForResource(
    "ElMirage", ofType: "mp4")!
let can = UIVideoEditorController.canEditVideoAtPath(path)
if !can {
    print("can't edit this video")
    return
}
```

```
let vc = UIVideoEditorController()
vc.delegate = self
vc.videoPath = path
if UIDevice.currentDevice().userInterfaceIdiom == .Pad {
    vc.modalPresentationStyle = .Popover
}
self.presentViewController(vc, animated: true, completion: nil)
if let pop = vc.popoverPresentationController {
    let v = sender as! UIView
    pop.sourceView = v
    pop.sourceRect = v.bounds
    pop.delegate = self
}
```

The view's interface (on the iPhone) contains Cancel and Save buttons, a trimming box displaying thumbnails from the movie, a play/pause button, and the movie itself. The user slides the ends of the trimming box to set the beginning and end of the saved movie. The Cancel and Save buttons do *not* dismiss the presented view; you must do that in your implementation of the delegate methods. There are three of them, and you should implement all three and dismiss the presented view in all of them:

- videoEditorController:didSaveEditedVideoToPath:

- videoEditorControllerDidCancel:

- videoEditorController:didFailWithError:

Implementing the second two delegate methods is straightforward:

```
func videoEditorControllerDidCancel(editor: UIVideoEditorController) {
    self.dismissViewControllerAnimated(true, completion: nil)
}
func videoEditorController(editor: UIVideoEditorController,
    didFailWithError error: NSError) {
        print("error: \(error.localizedDescription)")
        self.dismissViewControllerAnimated(true, completion: nil)
}
```

Saving the trimmed video is more involved. Like everything else about a movie, it takes time. When the user taps Save, there's a progress view while the video is trimmed and compressed. By the time the delegate method videoEditorController:didSaveEdited-VideoToPath: is called, the trimmed video has *already* been saved to a file in your app's temporary directory (the same directory returned from a call to NSTemporary-Directory).

Doing something useful with the saved file at this point is up to you; if you merely leave it in the temporary directory, you can't rely on it to persist. In this example, I copy the edited movie into the user's photo library. That takes time too, so when I call UISave-VideoAtPathToSavedPhotosAlbum, I configure a callback to a method that dismisses the editor *after* the saving is over:

```
func videoEditorController(editor: UIVideoEditorController,
    didSaveEditedVideoToPath editedVideoPath: String) {
        if UIVideoAtPathIsCompatibleWithSavedPhotosAlbum(
            editedVideoPath) {
                UISaveVideoAtPathToSavedPhotosAlbum(
                    editedVideoPath, self,
                    "video:savedWithError:ci:", nil)
            } else {
                // need to think of something else to do with it
            }
}
```

In our callback method (here, `video:savedWithError:ci:`), it's important to check for errors, because things can still go wrong. In particular, the user could deny us access to the photo library (see Chapter 17 for more about that). If that's the case, we'll get an NSError whose `domain` is `ALAssetsLibraryErrorDomain`:

```
func video(video:NSString!, savedWithError error:NSError!,
    ci:UnsafeMutablePointer<()>) {
        if error != nil {
            print("error:\(error)")
        }
        self.dismissViewControllerAnimated(true, completion: nil)
}
```

Music Library

An iOS device can be used for the same purpose as the original iPod — to hold and play music, podcasts, and audiobooks. These items constitute the device's *music library*. (The relevant guide in Apple's documentation, *iPod Library Access Programming Guide*, preserves a more archaic name.) iOS provides the programmer with various forms of access to the device's music library; you can:

- Explore the music library.
- Play an item from the music library.
- Learn and control what the Music app's music player is doing.
- Present a standard interface for allowing the user to select a music library item.

These abilities are provided by the Media Player framework; you'll need to `import MediaPlayer`.

Exploring the Music Library

Everything in the music library, as seen by your code, is an MPMediaEntity. This is an abstract class. It has two concrete subclasses:

MPMediaItem
> An MPMediaItem is a single item (a "song").

MPMediaCollection
> An MPMediaCollection is an ordered list of MPMediaItems, rather like an array; it has a `count`, and its `items` property *is* an array.

MPMediaEntity endows its subclasses with the ability to describe themselves through key–value pairs called *properties*. The property keys have names like `MPMediaItem-PropertyTitle`. To fetch a property's value, call `valueForProperty:` with its key. You can fetch multiple properties with `enumerateValuesForProperties:usingBlock:`. Thus, the use of the word "properties" here has nothing to do with object properties; these properties are more like entries in a dictionary. On the other hand, MPMediaEntity and its subclasses have instance properties whose names correspond to the property names. Thus, for example, with an MPMediaItem you can say either `myItem.valueForProperty(MPMediaItemPropertyTitle)` or `myItem.title`, and in most cases you will surely prefer the latter. (You will, however, still need the full property key name if you're going to form an MPMediaPropertyPredicate, as I'll demonstrate later.)

An MPMediaItem has a type, according to the value of its `MPMediaItemPropertyMediaType`: it might, for example, be music, a podcast, or an audiobook. A media item's properties will be intuitively familiar from your use of iTunes: it has a title, an album title, a track number, an artist, a composer, and so on. Different types of item have slightly different properties; for example, a podcast, in addition to its normal title, has a podcast title.

A playlist is an MPMediaPlaylist, a subclass of MPMediaCollection. Its properties include a title, a flag indicating whether it is a "smart" playlist, and so on.

An item's artwork image is an instance of the MPMediaItemArtwork class, from which you are supposed to be able to get the image itself scaled to a specified size by calling `imageWithSize:`. My experience, however, is that in reality you'll receive an image of any old size the system cares to give you, so you may have to scale it further yourself. This, for example, is what my Albumen app does (see Appendix B for my `imageOfSize:` utility):

```
let art : MPMediaItemArtwork = // ...
guard let im = art.imageWithSize(CGSizeMake(36,36)) else {
    return // no image
}
let r = AVMakeRectWithAspectRatioInsideRect(im.size, CGRectMake(0,0,36,36))
let im2 = imageOfSize(CGSizeMake(36,36)) { im.drawInRect(r) }
```

Querying the Music Library

Obtaining actual information from the music library requires a *query*, an MPMediaQuery. First, you *form* the query. There are three main ways to do this:

Without limits

Create a simple MPMediaQuery by calling `init` (that is, `MPMediaQuery()`). The result is an unlimited query; it asks for everything in the music library.

With a convenience constructor

MPMediaQuery provides several class methods that form a query ready to ask the music library for a limited subset of its contents — all of its songs, or all of its podcasts, and so on. Here's the complete list:

- songsQuery

- podcastsQuery

- audiobooksQuery

- playlistsQuery

- albumsQuery

- artistsQuery

- composersQuery

- genresQuery

- compilationsQuery

With filter predicates

You can limit a query more precisely by attaching to the query one or more MPMediaPropertyPredicate instances. These predicates filter the music library according to criteria you specify; to be included in the result, a media item must successfully pass through all the filters (in other words, the predicates are combined using logical-and). A predicate is a simple comparison. It has three aspects:

A property

The key name of the property you want to compare against. Not every property can be used in a filter predicate; the documentation makes the distinction clear (and you can get additional help from an MPMediaEntity class method, can-FilterByProperty:).

A value

The value that the property must have in order to pass through the filter.

A comparison type (optional)

An MPMediaPredicateComparison. In order to pass through the filter, a media item's property value can either *match* the value you provide (.EqualTo, the default) or *contain* the value you provide (.Contains).

The two ways of forming a limited query are actually the same; a convenience constructor is just a quick way of obtaining a query already endowed with a filter predicate.

A query also *groups* its results, according to its groupingType (MPMediaGrouping). Your choices are:

- .Title
- .Album
- .Artist
- .AlbumArtist

- `.Composer`

- `.Genre`

- `.Playlist`

- `.PodcastTitle`

The query convenience constructors all supply a `groupingType` in addition to a filter predicate. Indeed, the grouping is often the salient aspect of the query. For example, an `albumsQuery` is in fact merely a `songsQuery` with the added feature that its results are grouped by album.

The groups resulting from a query are *collections*; that is, each is an MPMediaItem-Collection. This class, you will recall, is an MPMediaEntity subclass, so a collection has properties. In addition, it has `items` and a `count`. It also has a `representativeItem` property, which gives you just one item from the collection. The reason you need this is that properties of a collection are often embodied in its items rather than in the collection itself. For example, an album has no title; rather, its items have album titles that are all the same. So to learn the title of an album, you ask for the album title of a representative item.

After you form the query, you *perform* the query. You do this simply by asking for the query's results. You can ask either for its `collections`, if you care about the groups returned from the query, or for its `items`. Here, I'll discover the titles of all the albums:

```
let query = MPMediaQuery.albumsQuery()
guard let result = query.collections else {return}
// prove we've performed the query, by logging the album titles
for album in result {
    print(album.representativeItem!.albumTitle!)
}
/*
Bach, CPE, Symphonies
Beethoven Canons
Beethoven Dances
Scarlatti Continuo
*/
```

Now let's make our query more elaborate; we'll get the titles of all the albums whose name contains "Beethoven." We simply add a filter predicate to the previous query:

```
let query = MPMediaQuery.albumsQuery()
let hasBeethoven = MPMediaPropertyPredicate(value:"Beethoven",
    forProperty:MPMediaItemPropertyAlbumTitle,
    comparisonType:.Contains)
query.addFilterPredicate(hasBeethoven)
guard let result = query.collections else {return}
for album in result {
    print(album.representativeItem!.albumTitle!)
}
```

```
/*
Beethoven Canons
Beethoven Dances
*/
```

Similarly, we can get the titles of all the albums containing any songs whose name contains "Sonata." This is like the previous example, but here we are concerned with the song's own title rather than its album title:

```
let query = MPMediaQuery.albumsQuery()
let hasSonata = MPMediaPropertyPredicate(value:"Sonata",
    forProperty:MPMediaItemPropertyTitle,
    comparisonType:.Contains)
query.addFilterPredicate(hasSonata)
guard let result = query.collections else {return}
for album in result {
    print(album.representativeItem!.albumTitle!)
}
/*
Scarlatti Continuo
*/
```

The results of an `albumsQuery` are actually songs (MPMediaItems). That means we can immediately access any song in any of those albums. Let's modify the output from our previous query to print the titles of all the matching songs in the first album returned, which happens to be the only album returned. We don't have to change our query, so I'll start at the point where we perform it; `result` is the array of collections returned from our query, so `result[0]` is an MPMediaItemCollection holding the filtered songs of one album:

```
// ... same as before ...
let album = result[0]
for song in album.items {
    print(song.title!)
}
/*
Sonata in E minor Kk 81 - I Grave
Sonata in E minor Kk 81 - II Allegro
Sonata in E minor Kk 81 - III Grave
Sonata in E minor Kk 81 - IV Allegro
Sonata in G minor Kk 88 - I Grave
... and so on ...
*/
```

Here are some more examples of query filter predicates that arise in my own apps. The user's music library can include songs that are actually off in "the cloud." For example, suppose the user subscribes to iTunes Match (now termed iCloud Music Library in the Music settings). Some songs may have been downloaded for offline listening; others may still be in the cloud. But they are all listed in the library. In my Albumen app, I don't want to include cloud-based songs in my results:

```
let notCloud = MPMediaPropertyPredicate(value: false,
    forProperty: MPMediaItemPropertyIsCloudItem,
    comparisonType: .EqualTo)
query.addFilterPredicate(notCloud)
```

When gathering playlists, I don't want to include smart playlists, genius playlists, or on-the-go playlists created on the user's device. Here's how I eliminate those:

```
let notSmart = MPMediaPropertyPredicate(value: 0,
    forProperty: MPMediaPlaylistPropertyPlaylistAttributes,
    comparisonType: .EqualTo)
query.addFilterPredicate(notSmart)
```

Persistence and Change in the Music Library

One of the properties of an MPMediaEntity is its *persistent ID*, which uniquely identifies this song (`MPMediaItemPropertyPersistentID`, or an MPMediaItem's `persistentID`) or playlist (`MPMediaPlaylistPropertyPersistentID`, or an MPMediaPlaylist's `persistentID`). No other means of identification is guaranteed unique; two songs or two playlists can have the same title, for example. Using the persistent ID, you can retrieve again at a later time the same song or playlist you retrieved earlier, even across launches of your app. All sorts of things have persistent IDs — entities in general (`MPMediaEntityPropertyPersistentID`), albums, artists, composers, and more.

While you are maintaining the results of a search, the contents of the music library may themselves change. For example, the user might connect the device to a computer and add or delete music with iTunes; or the user might switch away from your app and turn iTunes Match (iCloud Music Library) on or off. This can put your results out of date. For this reason, the library's own modified date is available through the MPMedia-Library class. Call the class method `defaultMediaLibrary` to get the actual library instance; now you can ask it for its `lastModifiedDate`. You can also register to receive a notification, `MPMediaLibraryDidChangeNotification`, when the music library is modified. This notification is not emitted unless you first send the library `begin-GeneratingLibraryChangeNotifications`; you should eventually balance this with `endGeneratingLibraryChangeNotifications`.

 The library's notion of what constitutes a change can be somewhat surprising with regard to cloud-based items. For example, the user playing or downloading a cloud song can cause `MPMediaLibraryDidChangeNotification` to be triggered numerous times in quick succession.

Music Player

The Media Player framework class for playing an MPMediaItem is MPMusicPlayer-Controller. It comes in two flavors, depending on which class method you use to get an instance:

systemMusicPlayer
> The global music player — the very same player used by the Music app. This might already be playing an item, or it might be paused with a current item, at any time while your app runs; you can learn or change what item this is. The global music player continues playing independently of the state of your app, and the user, by way of the Music app, can at any time alter what it is doing. (The name systemMusic-Player supersedes the name iPodMusicPlayer from iOS 7 and before, which is deprecated.)

applicationMusicPlayer
> The song being played by the applicationMusicPlayer can be different from the Music app's current song; what you do with this music player doesn't affect, and is not affected by, what the Music app does. Nevertheless, the applicationMusic-Player is actually the global music player behaving differently; it isn't really inside your app. It has its own audio session. You cannot play its audio when your app is in the background. You cannot make it the target of remote control events. If these limitations prove troublesome, use the systemMusicPlayer (or some other means of playing the song, as discussed later in this chapter).

A music player doesn't merely play an item; it plays from a *queue* of items. This behavior is familiar from iTunes and the Music app. For example, in the Music app, when you tap the first song of a playlist to start playing it, when the end of that song is reached, we proceed by default to the next song in the playlist. That's because tapping the first song of a playlist causes the queue to be the totality of songs in the playlist. The music player behaves the same way: when it reaches the end of a song, it proceeds to the next song in its queue.

Your methods for controlling playback also reflect this queue-based orientation. In addition to the expected play, pause, and stop commands, there's a skipToNextItem and skipToPreviousItem command. Anyone who has ever used iTunes or the Music app (or, for that matter, an old-fashioned iPod) will have an intuitive grasp of this and everything else a music player does. For example, you can also set a music player's repeat-Mode and shuffleMode, just as in iTunes.

You provide a music player with its queue in one of two ways:

With a query
> You hand the music player an MPMediaQuery. The query's items are the items of the queue.

With a collection

You hand the music player an MPMediaItemCollection. This might be obtained from a query you performed, but you can also assemble your own collection of MPMediaItems in any way you like, putting them into an array and calling MPMediaItemCollection's init(items:).

In this example, we collect all songs actually present in the library shorter than 30 seconds and set them playing in random order using the application music player. Observe that I explicitly stop the player before setting its queue; I have found (in iOS 8.4 and later) that this is the most reliable approach:

```
let query = MPMediaQuery.songsQuery()
let isPresent = MPMediaPropertyPredicate(value:false,
    forProperty:MPMediaItemPropertyIsCloudItem,
    comparisonType:.EqualTo)
query.addFilterPredicate(isPresent)
guard let items = query.items else {return}
let shorties = items.filter {
    let dur = $0.playbackDuration
    return dur < 30
}
guard shorties.count > 0 else {
    print("no songs that short!")
    return
}
let queue = MPMediaItemCollection(items:shorties)
let player = MPMusicPlayerController.applicationMusicPlayer()
player.stop()
player.setQueueWithItemCollection(queue)
player.shuffleMode = .Songs
player.play()
```

You can ask a music player for its nowPlayingItem, and since this is an MPMediaItem, you can learn all about it through its properties. Unfortunately, you can't query a music player as to its queue, but you can keep your own pointer to the MPMediaItemCollection constituting the queue when you hand it to the music player, and you can ask the music player which song within the queue is currently playing (indexOfNowPlayingItem). The user can completely change the queue of the systemMusicPlayer, however, so if control over the queue is important to you, use the applicationMusicPlayer.

A music player has a playbackState that you can query to learn what it's doing (whether it is playing, paused, stopped, or seeking). It also emits notifications informing you of changes in its state:

- MPMusicPlayerControllerPlaybackStateDidChangeNotification
- MPMusicPlayerControllerNowPlayingItemDidChangeNotification

- `MPMusicPlayerControllerVolumeDidChangeNotification`

These notifications are not emitted until you tell the music player to `beginGenerating-`
`PlaybackNotifications`. (You should eventually balance this call with `endGenerating-`
`PlaybackNotifications`.) This is an instance method, so you can arrange to receive
notifications from just one of the two possible music players. If you do receive notifications from both, you can distinguish them by examining the NSNotification's `object`
and comparing it to each player.

To illustrate, I'll extend the previous example to set the text of a UILabel in our interface
(`self.label`) every time a different song starts playing. Before we start the player playing, we insert these lines to generate the notifications:

```
player.beginGeneratingPlaybackNotifications()
NSNotificationCenter.defaultCenter().addObserver(
    self, selector: "changed:",
    name: MPMusicPlayerControllerNowPlayingItemDidChangeNotification,
    object: player)
self.q = queue // retain a pointer to the queue
```

And here's how we respond to those notifications:

```
func changed(n:NSNotification) {
    self.label.text = ""
    let player = MPMusicPlayerController.applicationMusicPlayer()
    guard n.object === player else { return } // just playing safe
    guard let title = player.nowPlayingItem?.title else {return}
    let ix = player.indexOfNowPlayingItem
    guard ix != NSNotFound else {return}
    self.label.text = "\(ix+1) of \(self.q.count): \(title)"
}
```

There's no periodic notification as a song plays and the current playhead position
advances. To get this information, you'll have to resort to polling. This is not objectionable as long as your polling interval is reasonably sparse; your display may occasionally fall a little behind reality, but this won't usually matter. To illustrate, let's add to
our existing example a UIProgressView (`self.prog`) showing the current percentage
of the current song being played by the music player. I'll use an NSTimer to poll the
state of the player every second:

```
self.timer = NSTimer.scheduledTimerWithTimeInterval(
    1, target: self, selector: "timerFired:",
    userInfo: nil, repeats: true)
self.timer.tolerance = 0.1
```

When the timer fires, the progress view displays the state of the currently playing item:

```
func timerFired(_:AnyObject) {
    let player = MPMusicPlayerController.applicationMusicPlayer()
    guard let item = player.nowPlayingItem
        where player.playbackState != .Stopped else {
```

```
            self.prog.hidden = true
            return
    }
    self.prog.hidden = false
    let current = player.currentPlaybackTime
    let total = item.playbackDuration
    self.prog.progress = Float(current / total)
}
```

The `applicationMusicPlayer` has no user interface. It displays its currently playing song in the MPNowPlayingInfoCenter, but the remote playback controls do not automatically work on it (Figure 14-1); if you want the user to have controls for playing and stopping a song, you'll have to create them yourself. The `systemMusicPlayer`, on the other hand, has a complete user interface — the Music app, to which it is effectively a back door.

MPVolumeView

The Media Player framework offers a slider for letting the user set the system output volume, along with an AirPlay route button if appropriate; this is an MPVolumeView. An MPVolumeView works only on a device — not in the Simulator. It is customizable similarly to a UISlider (Chapter 12); you can set the images for the two halves of the track, the thumb, and even the AirPlay route button, for both the normal and the highlighted state (while the user is touching the thumb).

For further customization, you can subclass MPVolumeView and override `volume-SliderRectForBounds:`. (An additional overridable method is documented, `volume-ThumbRectForBounds:volumeSliderRect:value:`, but in my testing it is never called; I regard this as a bug.)

You can register for notifications when a wireless route (Bluetooth or AirPlay) appears or disappears and when a wireless route becomes active or inactive.

- `MPVolumeViewWirelessRoutesAvailableDidChangeNotification`
- `MPVolumeViewWirelessRouteActiveDidChangeNotification`

Playing Songs With AV Foundation

MPMusicPlayerController is convenient and simple, but it's also simpleminded. Its audio session isn't your audio session; the music player doesn't really belong to you. An MPMediaItem, however, has an `MPMediaItemPropertyAssetURL` key (or `assetURL` property) whose value is a URL. That gives you a reference to the music file on disk, and everything from Chapters 14 and 15 comes into play.

So, for example, having obtained an MPMediaItem's asset URL, you could use that URL to initialize an AVAudioPlayer, an AVPlayer, or an AVAsset. Each of these ways of playing an MPMediaItem has its advantages. For example, an AVAudioPlayer is easy to use, and lets you loop a sound, poll the power value of its channels, and so forth. An AVPlayer assigned to an AVPlayerViewController gives you a built-in play/pause button and playhead slider. An AVAsset gives you the full power of the AV Foundation framework, letting you edit the sound, assemble multiple sounds, perform a fadeout effect, and even attach the sound to a video (and then play it with an AVPlayer).

In this example, I'll use an AVQueuePlayer (an AVPlayer subclass) to play a sequence of MPMediaItems, just as MPMusicPlayerController does:

```
let arr = // array of MPMediaItem
let items = arr.map {
    let url = $0.assetURL!
    let asset = AVAsset(URL:url)
    return AVPlayerItem(asset: asset)
}
self.qp = AVQueuePlayer(items:items)
self.qp.play()
```

That works, but I have the impression, based on something said in one of the WWDC 2011 videos, that instead of adding a whole batch of AVPlayerItems to an AVQueue-Player all at once, you're supposed to add just a few AVPlayerItems to start with and then append each additional AVPlayerItem when an item finishes playing. So I'll start out by adding just three AVPlayerItems, and use key–value observing to watch for changes in the AVQueuePlayer's currentItem:

```
let arr = // array of MPMediaItem
self.items = arr.map {
    let url = $0.assetURL!
    let asset = AVAsset(URL:url)
    return AVPlayerItem(asset: asset)
}
self.total = self.items.count
let seed = min(3,self.items.count)
self.qp = AVQueuePlayer(items:Array(self.items.prefixUpTo(seed)))
self.items = Array(self.items.suffixFrom(seed))
// use .Initial option so that we get an observation for the first item
self.qp.addObserver(
    self, forKeyPath:"currentItem", options:.Initial, context:nil)
self.qp.play()
```

In observeValueForKeyPath:..., we pull an AVPlayerItem off the front of our items array and add it to the end of the AVQueuePlayer's queue. The AVQueuePlayer itself deletes an item from the start of its queue after playing it, so in this way the queue never exceeds three items in length:

```
let item = self.qp.currentItem
guard self.items.count > 0 else {return}
let newItem = self.items.removeFirst()
self.qp.insertItem(newItem, afterItem:nil) // means "at end"
```

As long as `observeValueForKeyPath:...` is notifying us each time a new song starts playing, let's insert some code to update a label's text with the title of each successive song. This will demonstrate how to extract metadata from an AVAsset by way of an AVMetadataItem; here, we fetch the `AVMetadataCommonKeyTitle` and get its `value` property:

```
self.curnum++
var arr = item.asset.commonMetadata
arr = AVMetadataItem.metadataItemsFromArray(arr,
    withKey:AVMetadataCommonKeyTitle,
    keySpace:AVMetadataKeySpaceCommon)
let met = arr[0]
met.loadValuesAsynchronouslyForKeys(["value"]) {
    if met.statusOfValueForKey("value", error: nil) == .Loaded {
        guard let title = met.value as? String else {return}
        dispatch_async(dispatch_get_main_queue()) {
            self.label.text = "\(self.curnum) of \(self.total): \(title)"
        }
    }
}
```

We can also update a progress view to reflect the current item's current time and duration. Unlike MPMusicPlayerController, we don't need to poll with an NSTimer; we can install a time observer on our AVQueuePlayer:

```
self.ob = self.qp.addPeriodicTimeObserverForInterval(
    CMTimeMakeWithSeconds(0.5, 600), queue: nil,
    usingBlock: self.timerFired)
```

To get our AVPlayerItems to load their `duration` property, we'll need to go back and modify the code we used to initialize them:

```
let url = $0.assetURL!
let asset = AVAsset(URL:url)
return AVPlayerItem(
    asset: asset, automaticallyLoadedAssetKeys: ["duration"])
```

Our time observer calls us periodically, reporting the current time of the current player item; we obtain the current item's `duration` and configure our progress view (`self.prog`):

```
func timerFired(time:CMTime) {
    if let item = self.qp.currentItem {
        let asset = item.asset
        if asset.statusOfValueForKey("duration", error: nil) == .Loaded {
            let dur = asset.duration
            self.prog.setProgress(
```

```
                Float(time.seconds/dur.seconds), animated: false)
            self.prog.hidden = false
        }
    }
}
```

Media Picker

The media picker (MPMediaPickerController), supplied by the Media Player frame-work, is a view controller whose view is a self-contained navigation interface in which the user can select a media item from the music library, similar to the Music app. You are expected to treat the picker as a presented view controller.

You can use the initializer, init(mediaTypes:), to limit the type of media items dis-played. You can make a prompt appear at the top of the navigation bar (prompt). You can govern whether the user can choose multiple media items or just one, with the allowsPickingMultipleItems property. You can filter out items stored in the cloud by setting showsCloudItems to false.

 In iOS 9, the mediaTypes: values .Podcast and .AudioBook don't work. I believe that this is because podcasts are considered to be the purview of the Podcasts app, and audiobooks are considered to be the purview of iBooks — not the Music app. You can see podcasts and audiobooks as MPMediaEntity objects in the user's music library, but *not* by way of an MPMediaPickerController.

While the view is showing, you learn what the user is doing through two delegate meth-ods (MPMediaPickerControllerDelegate); the presented view controller is not auto-matically dismissed, so it is up to you dismiss it in these delegate methods:

- mediaPicker:didPickMediaItems:
- mediaPickerDidCancel:

The behavior of the delegate methods depends on the value of the controller's allows-PickingMultipleItems:

The controller's allowsPickingMultipleItems *is* false *(the default)*
> There's a Cancel button. When the user taps a media item, your mediaPicker:did-PickMediaItems: is called, handing you an MPMediaItemCollection consisting of that item; you are likely to dismiss the presented view controller at this point. When the user taps Cancel, your mediaPickerDidCancel: is called.

The controller's allowsPickingMultipleItems *is* true
> There's a Done button. Every time the user taps a media item, it is checked to indicate that it has been selected. When the user taps Done, your mediaPicker:didPick-

MediaItems: is called, handing you an MPMediaItemCollection consisting of all items the user tapped — unless the user tapped no items, in which case your media-PickerDidCancel: is called.

In this example, we put up the media picker; we then play the user's chosen media item(s) with the application's music player. The example works equally well whether allows-PickingMultipleItems is true or false:

```
func presentPicker (sender:AnyObject) {
    let picker = MPMediaPickerController(mediaTypes: .Music)
    picker.delegate = self
    // picker.allowsPickingMultipleItems = true
    self.presentViewController(picker, animated: true, completion: nil)
}
func mediaPicker(mediaPicker: MPMediaPickerController,
    didPickMediaItems mediaItemCollection: MPMediaItemCollection) {
        let player = MPMusicPlayerController.applicationMusicPlayer()
        player.setQueueWithItemCollection(mediaItemCollection)
        player.play()
        self.dismissViewControllerAnimated(true, completion: nil)
}
func mediaPickerDidCancel(mediaPicker: MPMediaPickerController) {
    self.dismissViewControllerAnimated(true, completion: nil)
}
```

On the iPad, the media picker can be displayed as a fullscreen presented view, but it also works reasonably well in a popover, especially if we increase its preferredContent-Size. This code presents as fullscreen on an iPhone and as a reasonably-sized popover on an iPad:

```
func presentPicker (sender:AnyObject) {
    let picker = MPMediaPickerController(mediaTypes: .Music)
    picker.delegate = self
    picker.allowsPickingMultipleItems = true
    picker.modalPresentationStyle = .Popover
    picker.preferredContentSize = CGSizeMake(500,600)
    self.presentViewController(picker, animated: true, completion: nil)
    if let pop = picker.popoverPresentationController {
        if let b = sender as? UIBarButtonItem {
            pop.barButtonItem = b
        }
    }
}
```

CHAPTER 17

Photo Library and Image Capture

The photos and videos accessed by the user through the Photos app constitute the device's photo library. Your app can give the user an interface for exploring this library through the UIImagePickerController class.

In addition, the Photos framework lets you access the photo library and its contents programmatically — including the ability to modify a photo's image. You'll need to `import Photos`.

The UIImagePickerController class can also be used to give the user an interface similar to the Camera app, letting the user take photos and videos on devices with the necessary hardware. At a deeper level, the AV Foundation framework (Chapter 15) provides direct control over the camera hardware. You'll need to `import AVFoundation` (and probably `CoreMedia`).

Constants such as kUTTypeImage, referred to in this chapter, are provided by the Mobile Core Services framework; you'll need to `import MobileCoreServices`.

Photo Library Authorization

Access to the photo library requires user authorization. You can use UIImagePicker-Controller without prior authorization, as authorization will automatically be requested for you and the interface works coherently if authorization has been refused. Still, it is probably good policy for any app that's going to need photo library access to ascertain authorization status beforehand, and to try to obtain authorization if needed. My strategy is to check the authorization status every time the root view controller appears and whenever the app is brought to the foreground:

```
override func viewDidAppear(animated: Bool) {
    super.viewDidAppear(animated)
    self.determineStatus()
    NSNotificationCenter.defaultCenter().addObserver(self,
```

```
        selector: "determineStatus",
        name: UIApplicationWillEnterForegroundNotification,
        object: nil)
    }
```

My determineStatus method returns a Bool, even though I'm disregarding the returned value in the preceding code; that way, I can also learn authorization status at *any* time while the app runs. In determineStatus, I first ask what our authorization status is. That's done by way of the Photos framework, by calling PHPhoto-Library.authorizationStatus(). There are four PHAuthorizationStatus responses:

.NotDetermined

> Authorization has never been requested. In that case, I explicitly request it by calling PHPhotoLibrary.requestAuthorization(), which causes the runtime to present an authorization request alert on our behalf. It is possible to supply a completion handler here, which will be called when the user dismisses the alert; but there is nothing of any particular importance to be learned at this point, since I can always check the status again later, so I use an effectively empty completion handler.

.Authorized

> There is nothing to do; we're already authorized.

.Restricted

> This means that we have been denied authorization and that the user may not have the power to authorize us. There's no point harassing the user about this, so I do nothing.

.Denied

> This means that we have been denied authorization. I could do nothing, but it is also reasonable to put up an alert begging for authorization. You can take the user directly to the spot in the Settings app where the user can provide authorization, so I offer to do that.

Here's my determineStatus method for the photo library:

```
func determineStatus() -> Bool {
    let status = PHPhotoLibrary.authorizationStatus()
    switch status {
    case .Authorized:
        return true
    case .NotDetermined:
        PHPhotoLibrary.requestAuthorization() {_ in}
        return false
    case .Restricted:
        return false
    case .Denied:
        let alert = UIAlertController(
            title: "Need Authorization",
            message: "Wouldn't you like to authorize this app " +
```

Figure 17-1. The system prompts for photo library access

```
        "to use your Photo library?",
    preferredStyle: .Alert)
alert.addAction(UIAlertAction(
    title: "No", style: .Cancel, handler: nil))
alert.addAction(UIAlertAction(
    title: "OK", style: .Default, handler: {
    _ in
    let url = NSURL(string:UIApplicationOpenSettingsURLString)!
    UIApplication.sharedApplication().openURL(url)
}))
    self.presentViewController(alert, animated:true, completion:nil)
    return false
    }
}
```

One final bit of preparation is needed: The *Info.plist* should contain some text that the system authorization request alert can use to explain why your app wants access. For the photo library, the relevant key is "Privacy — Photo Library Usage Description" (`NSPhotoLibraryUsageDescription`). Figure 17-1 shows the authorization request alert containing my (rather bland) usage description:

 To retest the system authorization request alert and other access-related behaviors, go to the Settings app and choose General → Reset → Reset Location & Privacy. This, unfortunately, causes the system to revert to its default settings for *everything* in the Privacy section of Settings: all permissions lists will be empty, but Location Services and all System Services will be On.

Choosing From the Photo Library

UIImagePickerController is a view controller providing an interface in which the user can choose an item from the photo library, similar to the Photos app. You are expected treat the UIImagePickerController as a presented view controller. You can use a popover on the iPad, but it looks good as a fullscreen presented view.

The documentation claims that a fullscreen presented view is forbidden on the iPad; this is not true (though it was true in early versions of iOS).

To let the user choose an item from the photo library, instantiate UIImagePicker-Controller and assign its `sourceType` one of these values (UIImagePickerController-SourceType):

`.PhotoLibrary`
> The user is shown a table of all albums, and can navigate into any of them.

`.SavedPhotosAlbum`
> In theory, the user is confined to the contents of the Camera Roll album. Instead, in iOS 8 and 9, the user sees the Moments interface and all photos are shown (I regard this as an atrocious bug).

You should call the class method `isSourceTypeAvailable:` beforehand; if it doesn't return `true`, don't present the controller with that source type.

You'll probably want to specify an array of `mediaTypes` you're interested in. This array will usually contain `kUTTypeImage`, `kUTTypeMovie`, or both; or you can specify all available types by calling the class method `availableMediaTypesForSourceType:`.

After doing all of that, and having supplied a delegate (adopting UIImagePicker-ControllerDelegate and UINavigationControllerDelegate), present the picker:

```
let src = UIImagePickerControllerSourceType.SavedPhotosAlbum
let ok = UIImagePickerController.isSourceTypeAvailable(src)
if !ok {
    print("alas")
    return
}
let arr = UIImagePickerController.availableMediaTypesForSourceType(src)
if arr == nil {
    print("no available types")
    return
}
let picker = UIImagePickerController()
picker.sourceType = src
picker.mediaTypes = arr!
picker.delegate = self
self.presentViewController(picker, animated: true, completion: nil)
```

If authorization has not been granted, the UIImagePickerController is presented, but it will be empty (with a reminder that the user has denied your app access to the photo library) and the user won't be able to do anything but cancel (Figure 17-2). Thus, your code is unaffected.

The delegate will receive one of these messages:

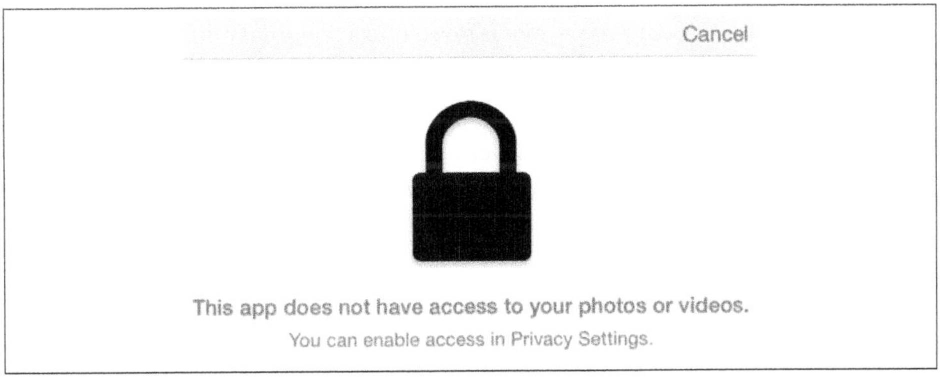

Cancel

This app does not have access to your photos or videos.
You can enable access in Privacy Settings.

Figure 17-2. The image picker, when the user has denied access

- `imagePickerController:didFinishPickingMediaWithInfo:`
- `imagePickerControllerDidCancel:`

If a UIImagePickerControllerDelegate method is not implemented, the view controller is dismissed automatically at the point where that method would be called; but rather than relying on this, you should probably implement both delegate methods and dismiss the view controller yourself in each.

The `didFinish...` method is handed a dictionary of information about the chosen item. The keys in this dictionary depend on the media type:

An image
The keys are:

`UIImagePickerControllerMediaType`
A UTI; probably `"public.image"`, which is the same as `kUTTypeImage`.

`UIImagePickerControllerReferenceURL`
An asset URL pointing to the image file in the library.

`UIImagePickerControllerOriginalImage`
A UIImage. This is the output you are expected to use. For example, you might display it in a UIImageView.

A movie
The keys are:

`UIImagePickerControllerMediaType`
A UTI; probably `"public.movie"`, which is the same as `kUTTypeMovie`.

`UIImagePickerControllerReferenceURL`
An asset URL pointing to the movie file in the library.

`UIImagePickerControllerMediaURL`
> A file URL to a copy of the movie saved into a temporary directory. This is the output you are expected to use. For example, you might display it in an AVPlayerViewController's view or an AVPlayerLayer (Chapter 15).

Optionally, you can set the view controller's `allowsEditing` to `true`. In the case of an image, the interface then allows the user to scale the image up and to move it so as to be cropped by a preset rectangle; the dictionary will include two additional keys:

`UIImagePickerControllerCropRect`
> An NSValue wrapping a CGRect.

`UIImagePickerControllerEditedImage`
> A UIImage. This becomes the image you are expected to use.

In the case of a movie, if the view controller's `allowsEditing` is `true`, the user can trim the movie just as with a UIVideoEditorController (Chapter 15). The dictionary keys are the same as before.

Here's an example implementation of `imagePickerController:didFinishPicking-MediaWithInfo:` that covers the fundamental cases:

```
func imagePickerController(picker: UIImagePickerController,
    didFinishPickingMediaWithInfo info: [String : AnyObject]) {
        let url = info[UIImagePickerControllerMediaURL] as? NSURL
        var im = info[UIImagePickerControllerOriginalImage] as? UIImage
        let edim = info[UIImagePickerControllerEditedImage] as? UIImage
        if edim != nil {
            im = edim
        }
        self.dismissViewControllerAnimated(true) {
            let type = info[UIImagePickerControllerMediaType] as? String
            if type != nil {
                switch type! {
                case kUTTypeImage as NSString as String:
                    if im != nil {
                        self.showImage(im!)
                    }
                case kUTTypeMovie as NSString as String:
                    if url != nil {
                        self.showMovie(url!)
                    }
                default:break
                }
            }
        }
}
```

UIImagePickerController provides no way to govern its supported interface orientations (rotation). The delegate method `navigationControllerSupportedInterfaceOrientations:` is ineffective. My solution is to subclass.

Photos Framework

The Photos framework, also known as *Photo Kit*, does for the photo library roughly what the Media Player framework does for the music library (Chapter 16), letting your code explore the library's contents — and then some. You can manipulate albums, and can even perform edits on the user's photos.

 The Assets Library framework from iOS 7 and before is now deprecated, and is not discussed in this edition.

The photo library itself is represented by the PHPhotoLibrary class — which I used earlier in this chapter to authorize access — and by its shared instance, which you can obtain through the `sharedPhotoLibrary` method. You will not often need to use this class, however, and you do not need to retain the shared photo library instance. More important are the classes representing the kinds of things that inhabit the library (the *photo entities*):

PHAsset
A single photo or video file.

PHCollection
An abstract class representing collections of all kinds. Its concrete subclasses are:

PHAssetCollection
A collection of photos; albums and moments are PHAssetCollections.

PHCollectionList
A collection of asset collections. For example, a year of moments is a collection list; a folder of albums is a collection list.

Finer typological distinctions are drawn, not through subclasses, but through a system of types and subtypes. For example, a PHAsset might have a type of `.Image` and a subtype of `.PhotoPanorama`; a PHAssetCollection might have a type of `.Album` and a subtype of `.AlbumRegular`; and so on.

The photo entity classes are actually all subclasses of PHObject, an abstract class that endows them all with a `localIdentifier` property that functions as a persistent unique identifier.

Querying the Photo Library

When you want to know what's in the photo library, start with one of the photo entity classes — the one that represents the type of entity you want to know about. The photo entity class will supply class methods whose names begin with fetch; you'll pick the class method that expresses the kind of criteria you're starting with. For example, to fetch one or more PHAssets, you'll call a PHAsset fetch method; you can fetch by containing asset collection, by local identifier, by media type, or by asset URL (such as you might get from a UIImagePickerController). Similarly, you can fetch PHAssetCollections by identifier, by URL, by whether they contain a given PHAsset; you can fetch PHCollectionLists by identifier, by whether they contain given a PHAssetCollection; and so on.

Many of these fetch methods have options that help to limit and define the search. In addition, you can supply a PHFetchOptions object letting you refine the results even further: you can set its predicate to limit your request results, and its sort-Descriptors to determine the results order. New in iOS 9, a PHFetchOptions object's fetchLimit can limit the number of results returned, and its includeAssetSource-Types can limit where the results should come from, such as eliminating cloud items (as we did with MPMediaItems in Chapter 16). You may even be able to fetch based *entirely* on a PHFetchOptions object (for instance, there's PHAsset's fetchAssetsWith-Options:).

What you get back from a fetch method query is not images or videos but *information*. A fetch method returns a collection of PHObjects of the type to which you sent the fetch method originally; these *refer* to entities in the photo library, rather than handing you an entire file (which would be huge). The collection itself is expressed as a PHFetchResult, which behaves very like an array: you can ask for its count, obtain the object at a given index (including the use of subscripting), look for an object within the collection, and enumerate the collection with an enumerate method.

You cannot enumerate a PHFetchResult with for...in in Swift, even though you can do so in Objective-C. I regard this as a bug. The workaround is to extend PHFetchResult to adopt the SequenceType protocol; you then *can* enumerate it with for...in (and I do so in my examples):

```
extension PHFetchResult: SequenceType {
    public func generate() -> NSFastGenerator {
        return NSFastGenerator(self)
    }
}
```

For example, let's say we want to know how moments are divided into years. A clump of moments grouped by year is a PHCollectionList, so the relevant class is PHCollectionList. This code is a fairly standard template for any sort of information fetching:

```
let opts = PHFetchOptions()
let desc = NSSortDescriptor(key: "startDate", ascending: true)
opts.sortDescriptors = [desc]
let result = PHCollectionList.fetchCollectionListsWithType(
    .MomentList, subtype: .MomentListYear, options: opts)
for obj in result {
    let list = obj as! PHCollectionList
    let f = NSDateFormatter()
    f.dateFormat = "yyyy"
    print(f.stringFromDate(list.startDate!))
}
/*
1987
1988
1989
1990
...
*/
```

Each resulting `list` object in the preceding code is a PHCollectionList comprising a list of moments. Let's dive into that object to see how those moments are clumped into clusters. A cluster of moments is a PHAssetCollection, so the relevant class is PHAssetCollection:

```
let result = PHAssetCollection.fetchMomentsInMomentList(
    list, options: nil)
for (ix,obj) in result.enumerate() {
    let coll = obj as! PHAssetCollection
    if ix == 0 {
        print("======= \(result.count) clusters")
    }
    f.dateFormat = ("yyyy-MM-dd")
    print("starting \(f.stringFromDate(coll.startDate!)): " +
        "\(coll.estimatedAssetCount)")
}
/*
======= 12 clusters
starting 1987-05-15: 2
starting 1987-05-16: 6
starting 1987-05-17: 2
starting 1987-05-20: 4
....
*/
```

Observe that in that code we can learn how many moments are in each cluster only as its `estimatedAssetCount`. This is probably the right answer, but to obtain the real count, we'd have to dive one level deeper and fetch the cluster's actual moments.

Next, let's list all albums that have been synced onto the device from iPhoto. An album is a PHAssetCollection, so the relevant class is PHAssetCollection:

```
let result = PHAssetCollection.fetchAssetCollectionsWithType(
    .Album, subtype: .AlbumSyncedAlbum, options: nil)
for obj in result {
    let album = obj as! PHAssetCollection
    print("\(album.localizedTitle): " +
        "approximately \(album.estimatedAssetCount) photos")
}
```

Again, let's dive further: given an album, let's fetch its contents. An album's contents are its assets (photos and videos), so the relevant class is PHAsset:

```
let result = PHAsset.fetchAssetsInAssetCollection(album, options: nil)
for obj in result {
    let asset = obj as! PHAsset
    print(asset)
}
```

 There is no PHAsset fetch method for fetching from a collection all assets of a certain type! Thus, for example, you cannot simply get all photos (and no videos) from the user's Camera Roll. You can perform such a fetch, but to do so, you need to form an NSPredicate and use a PHFetchOptions object; I'll give an example later. This is a case of Apple making something easy into something hard.

Modifying the Library

Structural modifications to the photo library are performed through a change request class corresponding to the class of photo entity we wish to modify. The name of the change request class is the name of a photo entity class followed by "ChangeRequest." Thus, for PHAsset, there's the PHAssetChangeRequest class — and so on.

A change request is usable only by calling a performChanges method on the shared photo library. Typically, the method you'll call will be performChanges:completion-Handler:, which takes two functions. The first function is where you describe the changes you want performed; the second function is called back after the changes have been performed. The reason for this peculiar structure is that the photo library is a live database. While we are working, the photo library can change. Therefore, a perform-Changes: block is used to batch our desired changes and send them off as a single transaction to the photo library, which responds when the outcome of the entire batch is known.

Each change request class comes with methods that ask for a change of some particular type. For example, PHAssetChangeRequest has class methods deleteAssets:, creationRequestForAssetFromImage:, and so on. PHAssetCollectionChangeRequest, in addition to the class methods deleteAssetCollections: and creationRequestFor-AssetCollectionWithTitle:, has initializers init?(forAssetCollection:) and init?(forAssetCollection:assets:), along with instance methods addAssets:, removeAssets:, and so on. The creationRequest class methods also return change request instances, but you won't need them unless you plan to perform further changes as part of the same batch.

For example, let's create an album called "Test Album." An album is a PHAsset-Collection, so we start with the PHAssetCollectionChangeRequest class and call its creation class method in the performChanges: block. This method returns a PHAsset-CollectionChangeRequest instance, but we don't need that instance for anything, so we simply throw it away:

```
PHPhotoLibrary.sharedPhotoLibrary().performChanges({
    let t = "TestAlbum"
    _ = PHAssetCollectionChangeRequest
        .creationRequestForAssetCollectionWithTitle(t)
    }, completionHandler: {
        (ok:Bool, err:NSError?) in
        print("created TestAlbum: \(ok)")
})
```

It may appear, in that code, that we didn't actually do anything — we asked for a creation request, but we didn't tell it to do any creating. Nevertheless, that code is sufficient; generating the creation request for a new asset collection in the performChanges: block constitutes an instruction to create an asset collection.

That code, however, is rather silly, in that we created an album but are left with no reference to it. To fix that, we need a PHObjectPlaceholder. This minimal PHObject subclass has just one property — localIdentifier, which it inherits from PHObject. But this is enough to permit a reference to the created object to survive into the completion handler, where we can do something useful with it. So our code now looks like this:

```
var ph : PHObjectPlaceholder?
PHPhotoLibrary.sharedPhotoLibrary().performChanges({
    let t = "TestAlbum"
    let cr = PHAssetCollectionChangeRequest
        .creationRequestForAssetCollectionWithTitle(t)
    ph = cr.placeholderForCreatedAssetCollection
    }, completionHandler: {
        (ok:Bool, err:NSError?) in
        print("created TestAlbum: \(ok)")
        if let ph = ph {
            print("and its id is \(ph.localIdentifier)")
        }
})
```

Now suppose we subsequently want to populate our newly created album. For example, let's say we want to make the first asset in the user's Recently Added smart album a member of our new album as well. No problem! First, we need a reference to the Recently Added album; then we need a reference to its first asset; and finally, we need a reference to our newly created album (which is easy if we have captured its localIdentifier from the preceding code). Those are all basic fetch requests:

```
// find Recently Added smart album
let result = PHAssetCollection.fetchAssetCollectionsWithType(
    .SmartAlbum, subtype: .SmartAlbumRecentlyAdded, options: nil)
guard let rec = result.firstObject as? PHAssetCollection else {
    print("no recently added album")
    return
}
// find its first asset
let result2 = PHAsset.fetchAssetsInAssetCollection(rec, options: nil)
guard let asset1 = result2.firstObject as? PHAsset else {
    print("no first item in recently added album")
    return
}
// find our newly created album by its local id
let result3 = PHAssetCollection
    .fetchAssetCollectionsWithLocalIdentifiers(
        [self.newAlbumId!], options: nil)
guard let alb2 = result3.firstObject as? PHAssetCollection else {
    print("no target album")
    return
}
```

Carrying on from there, it's easy to make the change request; we are asking to add asset1 to alb2:

```
PHPhotoLibrary.sharedPhotoLibrary().performChanges({
    let cr = PHAssetCollectionChangeRequest(forAssetCollection: alb2)
    cr?.addAssets([asset1])
    }, completionHandler: {
        (ok:Bool, err:NSError?) in
        print("added it: \(ok)")
})
```

What if we created an asset collection and wanted to add *it* to something (presumably to a PHCollectionList), all in one batch request? Requesting the creation of an asset collection gives us a PHAssetCollectionChangeRequest; you can't add *that* to a collection. And the requested PHAssetCollection itself hasn't been created yet! Once again, the solution would be to use placeholderForCreatedAssetCollection to obtain a PHObjectPlaceholder object. The placeholder object has the remarkable feature that, because it is a PHObject, it can be used instead of a "real" object in the argument of calls such as addChildCollections:.

A PHAssetChangeRequest is a little different from a collection change request: you can create an asset or delete an asset, but you obviously are not going to add or remove anything from an asset. You can, however, change the asset's features, such as its creation date or its associated geographical location. By default, creating a PHAsset puts it into the user's Camera Roll album immediately. I'll give an example later in this chapter.

Being Notified of Changes

When the library is modified, either by your code or by some other means while your app is running, any information you've collected about the library — information which you may even be displaying in your interface at that very moment — may become out-of-date. To cope with this possibility, you should, early in the life of your app, register a change observer (adopting the PHPhotoLibraryChangeObserver protocol) with the photo library:

```
PHPhotoLibrary.sharedPhotoLibrary().registerChangeObserver(self)
```

The outcome is that, whenever the library changes, the observer's `photoLibraryDid-Change:` method is called, with a PHChange object encapsulating a description of the change. The observer can then probe the PHChange object, using one (or both) of these methods:

`changeDetailsForObject:`

> The parameter is a single PHAsset, PHAssetCollection, or PHCollectionList you're interested in. The result is a PHObjectChangeDetails object, with properties like `objectBeforeChanges`, `objectAfterChanges`, and `objectWasDeleted`.

`changeDetailsForFetchResult:`

> The parameter is a previously obtained PHFetchResult. The result is a PHFetch-ResultChangeDetails object, with properties like `fetchResultBeforeChanges`, `fetchResultAfterChanges`, `removedObjects`, `insertedObjects`, and so on.

For example, suppose my interface is displaying a list of album names, which I obtained originally through a PHAssetCollection fetch request. At the time that I performed the fetch request, I also *retained*, as an instance property (`self.albums`), the fetch result that it returned. Thus, if my `photoLibraryDidChange:` method is called, I can find out whether any albums in that fetch result were added or removed; from there, I can update the fetch result and change my interface accordingly:

```
func photoLibraryDidChange(changeInfo: PHChange) {
    if self.albums !== nil {
        if let details =
            changeInfo.changeDetailsForFetchResult(self.albums) {
                dispatch_async(dispatch_get_main_queue()) {
                    if details.insertedObjects != nil {
                        self.albums = details.fetchResultAfterChanges
                        // adjust interface here ...
                    }
                }
            }
    }
}
```

Merely performing a fetch request can generate a PHChange report. If you don't want that, supply to the fetch request a PHFetchOptions object whose wants-IncrementalChangeDetails is false.

Displaying Images

Sooner or later, you'll probably want to go beyond information about the structure of the photo library and fetch an actual photo or video for display in your app. PHAsset image data is retrieved, in the first instance, through the PHImageManager default-Manager object. For an image, you can ask for a UIImage or its NSData; for a video, you can ask for an AVPlayerItem, an AVAsset, or an AVAssetExportSession suitable for exporting the video file to a new location (see Chapter 15).

All of the methods for obtaining an image or video take a completion handler called resultHandler:. The thing you requested is not returned as the method call's result; rather, it is supplied as the first parameter of the completion handler. The reason is that the process of obtaining an image can be time-consuming, so there has to be a way in which you can be called back asynchronously. This is true not only because the data may be large but also because it may be stored in the cloud.

In fact, if you're asking for a UIImage, information about the image may increase in accuracy and detail in the course of this process — with the curious consequence that your resultHandler: is not only called asynchronously but may be called multiple times. The idea is to give you *some* image to display as fast as possible, with better versions of the image arriving later. If you would rather receive just *one* version of the image, you can, by passing into your call an appropriate PHImageRequestOptions object (as I'll explain in a moment).

You can specify details of the data-retrieval process by using the parameters of the method that you call. For example, when asking for a UIImage, you supply these parameters:

targetSize:
    The size of the desired image. It is a waste of memory to ask for an image larger than you need for actual display, and a larger image may take longer to supply. The image retrieval process performs the desired downsizing so that you don't have to. For the largest possible size, pass PHImageManagerMaximumSize.

contentMode:
    A PHImageContentMode, either .AspectFit or .AspectFill, with respect to your targetSize. Again, with .AspectFill, the image retrieval process does any needed cropping so that you don't have to.

options:

A PHImageRequestOptions object. This is a value class representing a grab-bag of additional tweaks, such as:

- Do you want the original image or the edited image?

- Do you want one `resultHandler:` call or many, and if one, do you want a degraded thumbnail or the best possible quality?

- Do you want custom cropping?

- Do you want the image fetched over the network if necessary, and if so, do you want to install a progress handler?

- Do you want the image fetched synchronously? If you do, you will get only one `resultHandler` call. Keep in mind that in this case you *must* make your call on a background thread, and the image will arrive on that same background thread (see Chapter 25).

It sounds involved, but it needn't be. In this simple example, I have a view controller called DataViewController, good for viewing one photo. It has an image view outlet (`self.iv`). It also has a PHAsset property, `self.asset`, which is assumed to have been set when this DataViewController instance was created. In `viewDidLoad`, I call my `setUpInterface` utility method to populate the interface:

```
func setUpInterface() {
    guard let asset = self.asset else { return }
    PHImageManager.defaultManager().requestImageForAsset(asset,
        targetSize: CGSizeMake(300,300), contentMode: .AspectFit,
        options: nil) {
            (im:UIImage?, info:[NSObject : AnyObject]?) in
            if let im = im {
                self.iv.image = im
            }
    }
}
```

This may result in the image view's `image` being set multiple times as the requested image's quality improves, but there is nothing wrong with that.

Now imagine an app whose interface is a UIPageViewController permitting the user to view each individual image in an album. I can use my DataViewController as the pages of the UIPageViewController. Let's say that the album is the user's Camera Roll. I'll start by obtaining a fetch result collecting all the image assets in the Camera Roll:

```
self.recentAlbums = PHAssetCollection.fetchAssetCollectionsWithType(
    .SmartAlbum, subtype: .SmartAlbumUserLibrary, options: nil)
guard let rec = self.recentAlbums.firstObject as? PHAssetCollection
    else {return}
let options = PHFetchOptions() // photos only, please
```

```
let pred = NSPredicate(format: "mediaType = %@", NSNumber(
    integer:PHAssetMediaType.Image.rawValue))
options.predicate = pred
self.photos = PHAsset.fetchAssetsInAssetCollection(rec, options: options)
```

The fetch result, `self.photos`, is now our model object. Given an index number, I can provide a DataViewController displaying the corresponding photo:

```
func viewControllerAtIndex(index: Int, storyboard: UIStoryboard)
    -> DataViewController? {
        if self.photos == nil ||
        self.photos.count == 0 ||
        index >= self.photos.count {
            return nil
        }
        let dvc = storyboard.instantiateViewControllerWithIdentifier(
            "DataViewController") as! DataViewController
        dvc.asset = self.photos[index] as! PHAsset
        return dvc
}
```

I can also find the index of any DataViewController's corresponding `asset` in `self.photos`:

```
func indexOfViewController(dvc: DataViewController) -> Int {
    let asset = dvc.asset
    let ix = self.photos.indexOfObject(asset)
    return ix
}
```

Writing the UIPageViewControllerDataSource methods is now trivial — and presto, you've written a photo album browser! For a more elaborate example, displaying photos in a UICollectionView, look at Apple's SamplePhotosApp sample code.

The `info` parameter in an image request's result handler is a dictionary whose elements may be useful in a variety of circumstances; for example:

PHImageResultRequestIDKey

Uniquely identifies a single image request for which this result handler is being called multiple times. This value is also *returned* by the original request method call (I didn't bother to capture it in the previous example). You can also use this identifier to call `cancelImageRequest:` if it turns out that you don't need this image after all.

PHImageResultIsInCloudKey

Warns that the image is in the cloud and that your request must be resubmitted with explicit permission to use the network.

PHImageCancelledKey

Reports that an attempt to cancel an image request with `cancelImageRequest:` succeeded.

If you imagine that your interface is a table view or collection view, you can see why the asynchronous, time-consuming nature of image fetching can be of importance. As the user scrolls, a cell comes into view and you request the corresponding image. But as the user keeps scrolling, that cell goes out of view, and now the requested image, if it hasn't arrived, is no longer needed, so you cancel the request. (I'll tackle the same sort of problem with regard to Internet-based images in a table view in Chapter 24.) There is also a PHImageManager subclass, PHCachingImageManager, that can help do the opposite: you can prefetch some images *before* the user scrolls to view them, thus improving response time.

 New in iOS 9, you can access an asset's various kinds of data directly through the PHAssetResource and PHAssetResourceManager classes. Conversely, PHAsset-ChangeRequest has a subclass PHAssetCreationRequest, which allows you to supply the asset's NSData directly. For a list of the data types we're talking about here, see the documentation on the PHAssetResourceType enum.

Editing Images

Astonishingly, Photo Kit allows you to *change* an image in the user's photo library. Why is this even legal? There are two reasons:

- The user will have to give permission every time your app proposes to modify a photo in the library.
- Changes to library photos are undoable, because the original image remains in the database along with the changed image that the user sees (and the user can revert to that original at any time).

To change a photo is a three-step process:

1. You send a PHAsset the requestContentEditingInputWithOptions:completion-Handler: message. Your completionHandler: is called, and is handed a PHContentEditingInput object. This object wraps some image data which you can display to the user (displaySizeImage), along with a pointer to the real image data on disk (fullSizeImageURL).

2. You create a PHContentEditingOutput object by calling init(contentEditing-Input:), handing it the PHContentEditingInput object. This PHContentEditing-Output object has a renderedContentURL property, which is an NSURL represent-ing a URL on disk. Your mission is to *write the edited photo image data to that URL*. Thus, what you'll typically do is:

   a. Fetch the image data from the PHContentEditingInput object's fullSizeImage-URL.

b. Process the image.

c. Write the resulting image data to the PHContentEditingOutput object's renderedContentURL.

3. You notify the photo library that it should pick up the edited version of the photo. To do so, you call performChanges:completionHandler: and, inside the perform-Changes: block, create a PHAssetChangeRequest and set its contentEditing-Output property to the PHContentEditingOutput object. This is when the user will be shown the alert requesting permission to modify this photo; your completion-Handler: is then called, with a first parameter of false if the user refuses (or if anything else goes wrong).

However, if you do *only* what I have just described, your attempt to modify the photo will fail. The reason is that I have omitted something: before the third step, you *must* set the PHContentEditingOutput object's adjustmentData property to a newly instantiated PHAdjustmentData object. The initializer is init(formatIdentifier:format-Version:data:). What goes into these parameters is completely up to you; the idea, however, is to send a message to your future self in case you are called upon to edit the same photo again later.

The adjustmentData, too, works in three steps, interwoven with the three steps I already outlined:

1. When you call the requestContentEditingInputWithOptions:completion-Handler: method, the options: argument should be a PHContentEditingInput-RequestOptions object. You are to create this object and set its canHandle-AdjustmentData property to a function that takes a PHAdjustmentData and returns a Bool. This Bool should be based simply on whether you recognize this PHAdjustmentData as yours — typically because you recognize its format-Identifier. That determines what image you'll get when you receive your PHContentEditingInput object:

    Your canHandleAdjustmentData *function returns* false
        The image you'll be editing is the edited image displayed in the Photos app.

    Your canHandleAdjustmentData *function returns* true
        The image you'll be editing is the *original* image, stripped of your edits. This is because, by returning true, you are asserting that you can recreate the content of your edits based on what's in the PHAdjustmentData's data.

2. When your completionHandler: is called and you receive your PHContentEditing-Input object, it has (you guessed it) an adjustmentData property! Naturally, it is a PHAdjustmentData object. Its data is the data you put in the last time you edited

this image, and you are expected to extract it and use it to recreate the edited state of the image.

3. When you prepare the PHContentEditingOutput, you give it a new PHAdjustmentData object, as I already explained. If you are performing edits, the `data` of this new PHAdjustmentData object can be a summary of the edited state of the photo from your point of view — and so the whole cycle can start again if the same photo is to be edited again later.

 If this image has no PHAdjustmentData, or if your `canHandleAdjustmentData` returns `false`, the PHContentEditingInput's `adjustmentData` property *will be nil*. Unfortunately, in iOS 9, this property is typed as a PHAdjustmentData, *not an Optional*. This is a serious mistake on Apple's part. To work around it, you must assign the `adjustmentData` immediately to an Optional variable.

This may sound confusing or complicated, but in fact an actual implementation is quite straightforward and almost pure boilerplate. The details will vary only in regard to the actual editing of the photo and the actual `data` by which you'll summarize that editing — so, in constructing an example, I'll keep that part very simple. Recall, from Chapter 2 ("CIFilter and CIImage" on page 85), my example of a custom "vignette" CIFilter called MyVignetteFilter. I'll provide an interface whereby the user can apply that filter to a photo. My interface will include a slider that allows the user to set the *degree* of vignetting that should be applied (MyVignetteFilter's `inputPercentage`). Moreover, my interface will include a button that lets the user remove *all* vignetting from the photo, even if that vignetting was applied in a previous editing session.

First, I'll plan the structure of the PHAdjustmentData. The `formatIdentifier` can be any unique string; I'll use `"com.neuburg.matt.PhotoKitImages.vignette"`, a constant that I'll store in a property (`self.myidentifier`). The `formatVersion` is likewise arbitrary; I'll use `"1.0"`. Finally, the `data` will express the only thing about my editing that is adjustable — the `inputPercentage`. The `data` will wrap an NSNumber which itself wraps a Double whose value is the `inputPercentage`.

As editing begins, I construct the PHContentEditingInputRequestOptions object that expresses whether a photo's most recent editing belongs to me. I then obtain the photo that is to be edited (a PHAsset) and ask for the PHContentEditingInput object:

```
let options = PHContentEditingInputRequestOptions()
options.canHandleAdjustmentData = {
    (adjustmentData : PHAdjustmentData!) in
    return adjustmentData.formatIdentifier == self.myidentifier
}
```

```
let asset = self.asset
asset.requestContentEditingInputWithOptions(options, completionHandler: {
    // ...
})
```

Inside the completionHandler:, I receive my PHContentEditingInput object. I'm going to need this object later when editing ends, so I immediately store it in a property. I then unwrap its adjustmentData and construct the editing interface; in this case, that happens to be a presented view controller, but the details are irrelevant and are omitted here:

```
(input:PHContentEditingInput?, info:[NSObject : AnyObject]) in
guard let input = input else { return }
self.input = input
let im = input.displaySizeImage! // show this to the user during editing
let adj : PHAdjustmentData? = input.adjustmentData
if let adj = adj where adj.formatIdentifier == self.myidentifier {
    if let vigAmount =
        NSKeyedUnarchiver.unarchiveObjectWithData(adj.data) as? Double {
            // ... store vigAmount ...
    }
}
// ... present editing interface ...
```

The idea is that if we were able to extract a vigAmount from the adjustmentData, then the displaySizeImage is the *original, unvignetted image*. Meanwhile, our editing interface itself initially applies the vigAmount of vignetting to this image — thus *reconstructing the vignetted state of the photo* as shown in the Photos app, while allowing the user to *change* the amount of vignetting, or even to remove all vignetting entirely. On the other hand, if we *weren't* able to extract a vigAmount from the adjustmentData, then there is nothing to reconstruct; the displaySizeImage is just the photo image from the Photos app, and we will apply vignetting to it directly.

Let's skip ahead now to the point where the user's interaction with our editing interface comes to an end. If the user cancelled, that's all; the user doesn't want to modify the photo after all. Otherwise, the user either asked to apply a certain amount of vignetting (vignette) or asked to remove *all* vignetting from the *original* image. In the latter case, I use an arbitrary vignette value of -1 as a signal. Recall that we have been working all this time, in the editing interface, with the PHContentEditingInput's displaySizeImage. Now, however, we must apply this amount of vignetting to the *real* photo image, which has been sitting waiting for us all this time, untouched, at the PHContentEditingInput's fullSizeImageURL. This is a *much* bigger image, which will take significant time to load, to alter, and to save — which is why we haven't been working with it live in the editing interface. Now, however, is the moment! So, depending on the value of vignette requested by the user, I either run the input image from the fullSizeImageURL through my vignette filter or I don't; either way, I write a JPEG to the PHContentEditing-Output's renderedContentURL:

```
let input = self.input
let inurl = input.fullSizeImageURL!
let inorient = input.fullSizeImageOrientation
let output = PHContentEditingOutput(contentEditingInput: input)
let outurl = output.renderedContentURL
let outcgimage = {
    () -> CGImage in
    var ci = CIImage(contentsOfURL: inurl)!
        .imageByApplyingOrientation(inorient)
    if vignette >= 0.0 {
        let vig = MyVignetteFilter()
        vig.setValue(ci, forKey: "inputImage")
        vig.setValue(vignette, forKey: "inputPercentage")
        ci = vig.outputImage!
    }
    return CIContext(options: nil).createCGImage(ci, fromRect: ci.extent)
}()
let dest = CGImageDestinationCreateWithURL(outurl, kUTTypeJPEG, 1, nil)!
CGImageDestinationAddImage(dest, outcgimage, [
    kCGImageDestinationLossyCompressionQuality as String:1
])
CGImageDestinationFinalize(dest)
```

(The image that we save at the renderedContentURL must be a maximum-quality JPEG. I achieve that by using the ImageIO framework, discussed in Chapter 23.)

But we are not quite done. As I've already mentioned, it is *crucial* that we set the PHContentEditingOutput's adjustmentData, and the goal here is to send a message to myself, in case I am asked later to edit this same image again, as to what amount of vignetting is already applied to the image. That amount is represented by vignette — so that's the value I store in the adjustmentData:

```
let data = NSKeyedArchiver.archivedDataWithRootObject(vignette)
output.adjustmentData = PHAdjustmentData(
    formatIdentifier: self.myidentifier, formatVersion: "1.0", data: data)
```

The finished image is now sitting at the renderedContentURL, and we conclude by telling the photo library to retrieve it:

```
PHPhotoLibrary.sharedPhotoLibrary().performChanges({
    let asset = self.asset
    let req = PHAssetChangeRequest(forAsset: asset)
    req.contentEditingOutput = output
    }, completionHandler: {
        (ok:Bool, err:NSError?) in
        if ok {
            // image changed! adjust interface
        } else {
            print(err)
        }
})
```

Photo Editing Extension

A photo editing extension is photo-modifying code supplied by your app that is effectively injected into the Photos app. When the user edits a photo from within the Photos app, your extension appears as an option and can modify the photo being edited.

To make a photo editing extension, create a new target in your app, specifying iOS → Application Extension → Photo Editing Extension. The template supplies a storyboard containing one scene, along with the code file for a corresponding UIViewController subclass. This file imports not only the Photos framework but also the PhotosUI framework, which supplies the PHContentEditingController protocol, to which the view controller conforms. This protocol specifies the methods through which the runtime will communicate with your extension's code.

A photo editing extension works almost exactly the same way as modifying photo library assets in general, as I described in the preceding section. The chief differences are:

- You don't put a Done or a Cancel button into your editing interface. The Photos app will wrap your editing interface in its own interface, which supplies them when it presents your view.
- You must situate the pieces of your code in such a way that those pieces respond to the calls that will come through the PHContentEditingController methods.

The PHContentEditingController methods are as follows:

canHandleAdjustmentData:
> You will not be instantiating PHContentEditingInput; the runtime will do it for you. Therefore, instead of configuring a PHContentEditingInputRequestOptions object and setting its canHandleAdjustmentData, you implement this method to return a Bool.

startContentEditingWithInput:placeholderImage:
> The runtime has obtained the PHContentEditingInput object for you. Now it supplies that object to you, along with a very temporary initial version of the image to be displayed in your interface; you are expected to replace this with the PHContentEditingInput object's displaySizeImage. Just as in the previous section's code, you should retain the PHContentEditingInput object in a property, as you will need it again later.

cancelContentEditing
> The user tapped Cancel. You may well have nothing to do here.

finishContentEditingWithCompletionHandler:
> The user tapped Done. In your implementation, you get onto a background thread (the template configures this for you) and do *exactly* the same thing you would do if this were not a photo editing extension — get the PHContentEditingOutput

object and set its `adjustmentData`; get the photo from the PHContentEditingInput object's `fullSizeImageURL`, modify it, and save the modified image as a full-quality JPEG at the PHContentEditingOutput object's `renderedContentURL`. When you're done, *don't* notify the PHPhotoLibrary; instead, call the `completionHandler` that arrived as a parameter, handing it the PHContentEditingOutput object.

Using the Camera

The simplest way to prompt the user to take a photo or video is to use our old friend UIImagePickerController, which provides an interface similar to the Camera app. I'll describe this approach first, and then proceed to talk about controlling the camera directly through the AV Foundation framework.

 Use of the camera is greatly curtailed, and is interruptible, under iOS 9's new iPad multitasking. Watch 2015 WWDC video 211 for details.

Camera Authorization

Starting in iOS 8, use of the camera requires explicit authorization from the user. The system will present the access request dialog; you should modify the body of this dialog by setting the "Privacy — Camera Usage Description" key (`NSCameraUsage-Description`) in your app's *Info.plist*.

Using the UIImagePickerController to control the camera for the first time will cause the system to present the authorization dialog on your behalf, but if you'd like to ascertain the authorization status beforehand and summon the authorization dialog, you can. The relevant calls are completely parallel to the photo library authorization code I presented at the start of this chapter; the difference is that you'll be talking to the AVCaptureDevice class (you'll need to `import AVFoundation`). Here's how to learn the current authorization status for use of the camera:

```
let status =
    AVCaptureDevice.authorizationStatusForMediaType(AVMediaTypeVideo)
```

The term `AVMediaTypeVideo` here embraces both stills and video. If the status is `.Not-Determined` and you'd like to summon the authorization dialog explicitly, here's how:

```
AVCaptureDevice.requestAccessForMediaType(
    AVMediaTypeVideo, completionHandler: nil)
```

If your app will let the user record actual video (as opposed to stills), you will also need to obtain permission from the user to access the microphone. The same methods apply, but with argument `AVMediaTypeAudio`. You should modify the body of the authorization alert by setting the "Privacy — Microphone Usage Description" key (NSMicrophone-UsageDescription) in your app's *Info.plist*.

Using the Camera with UIImagePickerController

To use UIImagePickerController to control the camera, first check isSourceType-Available: for .Camera; it will be false if the user's device has no camera or the camera is unavailable. If it is true, call availableMediaTypesForSourceType: to learn whether the user can take a still photo (kUTTypeImage), a video (kUTTypeMovie), or both. Now instantiate UIImagePickerController, set its source type to .Camera, and set its media-Types in accordance with which types you just learned are available; if your setting is an array of both kUTTypeImage and kUTTypeMovie, the user will see a Camera-like interface allowing a choice of either one. Finally, set a delegate (adopting UINavigation-ControllerDelegate and UIImagePickerControllerDelegate), and present the picker.

So, for example:

```
let cam = UIImagePickerControllerSourceType.Camera
let ok = UIImagePickerController.isSourceTypeAvailable(cam)
if (!ok) {
    print("no camera")
    return
}
let desiredType = kUTTypeImage as NSString as String
let arr = UIImagePickerController.availableMediaTypesForSourceType(cam)
if arr?.indexOf(desiredType) == nil {
    print("no capture")
    return
}
let picker = UIImagePickerController()
picker.sourceType = .Camera
picker.mediaTypes = [desiredType]
picker.delegate = self
self.presentViewController(picker, animated: true, completion: nil)
```

For video, you can also specify the videoQuality and videoMaximumDuration. More-over, these additional properties and class methods allow you to discover the camera capabilities:

isCameraDeviceAvailable:
 Checks to see whether the front or rear camera is available, using one of these values as argument (UIImagePickerControllerCameraDevice):

  - .Front
  - .Rear

cameraDevice
 Lets you learn and set which camera is being used.

---

availableCaptureModesForCameraDevice:

Checks whether the given camera can capture still images, video, or both. You specify the front or rear camera; returns an array of integers. Possible modes are (UIImagePickerControllerCameraCaptureMode):

- .Photo
- .Video

cameraCaptureMode

Lets you learn and set the capture mode (still or video).

isFlashAvailableForCameraDevice:

Checks whether flash is available.

cameraFlashMode

Lets you learn and set the flash mode (or, for a movie, toggles the LED "torch"). Your choices are (UIImagePickerControllerCameraFlashMode):

- .Off
- .Auto
- .On

When the view controller's view appears, the user will see the interface for taking a picture, familiar from the Camera app, possibly including flash options, camera selection button, digital zoom (if the hardware supports it), photo/video option (if your mediaTypes setting allows both), and Cancel and shutter buttons. If the user takes a picture, the presented view offers an opportunity to use the picture or to retake it.

Allowing the user to edit the captured image or movie (allowsEditing), and handling the outcome with the delegate messages, is the same as I described earlier for dealing with an image or movie selected from the photo library. There won't be any UIImage-PickerControllerReferenceURL key in the dictionary delivered to the delegate, because the image isn't in the photo library. A still image might report a UIImagePicker-ControllerMediaMetadata key containing the metadata for the photo. The photo library was not involved in the process of media capture, so no user permission to access the photo library is needed; of course, if you *now* propose to save the media into the photo library, you *will* need permission. The minimal case is that you want to save into the user's Camera Roll, just as the Camera app would do; this is as simple as can be — creating the PHAsset is sufficient:

```
func imagePickerController(picker: UIImagePickerController,
    didFinishPickingMediaWithInfo info: [String : AnyObject]) {
        var im = info[UIImagePickerControllerOriginalImage] as? UIImage
        let edim = info[UIImagePickerControllerEditedImage] as? UIImage
        if edim != nil {
```

```
            im = edim
        }
        self.dismissViewControllerAnimated(true) {
            let type = info[UIImagePickerControllerMediaType] as? String
            if type != nil {
                switch type! {
                case kUTTypeImage as NSString as String:
                    if im != nil {
                        let lib = PHPhotoLibrary.sharedPhotoLibrary()
                        lib.performChanges({
                            PHAssetChangeRequest
                                .creationRequestForAssetFromImage(im!)
                        }, completionHandler: nil)
                    }
                default:break
                }
            }
        }
    }
```

Customizing the Image Capture Interface

You can customize the UIImagePickerController interface. If you need to do that, you should probably consider dispensing with UIImagePickerController altogether and designing your own image capture interface from scratch, based around AV Foundation and AVCaptureSession, which I'll introduce in the next section. Still, it may be that a modified UIImagePickerController is all you need.

In the image capture interface, you can hide the standard controls by setting shows-CameraControls to false, replacing them with your own overlay view, which you supply as the value of the cameraOverlayView. In this case, you're probably going to want some means in your overlay view to allow the user to take a picture! You can do that through these methods:

- takePicture

- startVideoCapture

- stopVideoCapture

In this example, I'll remove all the default controls and use a gesture recognizer on the cameraOverlayView to permit the user to double-tap the image in order to take a picture:

```
picker.showsCameraControls = false
let f = self.view.window!.bounds
let v = UIView(frame:f)
let t = UITapGestureRecognizer(target:self, action:"tap:")
```

```
t.numberOfTapsRequired = 2
v.addGestureRecognizer(t)
picker.cameraOverlayView = v
self.picker = picker // we'll need this later
```

Our `tap:` gesture recognizer action handler simply calls `takePicture:`

```
func tap (g:UIGestureRecognizer) {
    self.picker?.takePicture()
}
```

It would be nice, however, to *tell* the user to double-tap to take a picture; we also need to give the user a way to dismiss the image capture interface. We could put a button and a label into the `cameraOverlayView`, but here, I'll take advantage of the fact that the UIImagePickerController is a UINavigationController. Thus, it has a toolbar that we can bend to our own purposes. Moreover, we are the UIImagePickerController's delegate, meaning that we are not only its UIImagePickerControllerDelegate but also its UINavigationControllerDelegate; I'll use a delegate method to populate the toolbar:

```
func navigationController(nc: UINavigationController,
    didShowViewController vc: UIViewController, animated: Bool) {
        nc.toolbarHidden = false
        let sz = CGSizeMake(10,10)
        let im = imageOfSize(sz) {
            UIColor.blackColor().colorWithAlphaComponent(0.1).setFill()
            CGContextFillRect(
                UIGraphicsGetCurrentContext()!,
                CGRect(origin: CGPoint(), size: sz))
        }
        nc.toolbar.setBackgroundImage(
            im, forToolbarPosition: .Any, barMetrics: .Default)
        nc.toolbar.translucent = true
        let b = UIBarButtonItem(
            title: "Cancel", style: .Plain,
            target: self, action: "doCancel:")
        let lab = UILabel()
        lab.text = "Double tap to take a picture"
        lab.textColor = UIColor.whiteColor()
        lab.backgroundColor = UIColor.clearColor()
        lab.sizeToFit()
        let b2 = UIBarButtonItem(customView: lab)
        nc.topViewController.toolbarItems = [b,b2]
}
```

When the user double-taps to take a picture, our `imagePickerController:didFinish-PickingMediaWithInfo:` delegate method is called, just as before. We don't automatically get the secondary interface where the user is shown the resulting image and offered an opportunity to use it or retake the image. But we can provide such an interface ourselves, by pushing another view controller onto the navigation controller:

```
func imagePickerController(picker: UIImagePickerController,
    didFinishPickingMediaWithInfo info: [NSObject : AnyObject]) {
        var im = info[UIImagePickerControllerOriginalImage] as? UIImage
        if im == nil {
            return
        }
        let svc = SecondViewController(image:im)
        picker.pushViewController(svc, animated: true)
}
```

(Designing the SecondViewController class is left as an exercise for the reader.)

Image Capture With AV Foundation

Instead of using UIImagePickerController, you can control the camera and capture images directly using the AV Foundation framework (Chapter 15). You get no help with interface (except for displaying in your interface what the camera "sees"), but you get vastly more detailed control than UIImagePickerController can give you; for example, for stills, you can control focus and exposure directly and independently, and for video, you can determine the quality, size, and frame rate of the resulting movie.

The heart of all AV Foundation capture operations is an AVCaptureSession object. You configure this and provide it as desired with inputs (such as a camera) and outputs (such as a file); then you call startRunning to begin the actual capture. You can reconfigure an AVCaptureSession, possibly adding or removing an input or output, while it is running — indeed, doing so is far more efficient than stopping the session and starting it again — but you should wrap your configuration changes in beginConfiguration and commitConfiguration.

As a rock-bottom example, let's start by displaying in our interface, in real time, what the camera sees. This requires an AVCaptureVideoPreviewLayer, a CALayer subclass. This layer is not an AVCaptureSession output; rather, the layer receives its imagery by *owning* the AVCaptureSession. Our AVCaptureSession's input is the default video camera. We have no intention, as yet, of doing anything with the captured video other than displaying it in the interface, so our AVCaptureSession doesn't need an output:

```
self.sess = AVCaptureSession()
let cam = AVCaptureDevice.defaultDeviceWithMediaType(AVMediaTypeVideo)
guard let input = try? AVCaptureDeviceInput(device:cam) else {return}
self.sess.addInput(input)
let lay = AVCaptureVideoPreviewLayer(session:self.sess)
lay.frame = self.previewRect
self.view.layer.addSublayer(lay)
self.previewLayer = lay // keep a ref
self.sess.startRunning()
```

Presto! Our interface now contains a window on the world, so to speak.

Expanding on that example, let's permit the user to snap a still photo, which our interface will then display. Now we *do* need an output for our AVCaptureSession; since all we want is a still image, this will be an AVCaptureStillImageOutput, and we'll set its output-Settings to specify the quality of the JPEG image we're after. We also need to configure the quality of image that the camera is to capture; the simplest and most common way is to apply a sessionPreset to the AVCaptureSession. In this case, since this image is to go directly into our interface, we won't need the vast multimegapixel image size of which the camera is capable; so we'll configure our AVCaptureSession's session-Preset to ask for a much smaller image:

```
self.sess = AVCaptureSession()
self.sess.sessionPreset = AVCaptureSessionPreset640x480
self.snapper = AVCaptureStillImageOutput()
self.snapper.outputSettings = [
    AVVideoCodecKey: AVVideoCodecJPEG,
    AVVideoQualityKey: 0.6
]
self.sess.addOutput(self.snapper)
// ... and the rest is as before ...
```

When the user asks to snap a picture, we send captureStillImageAsynchronouslyFrom-Connection:completionHandler: to our AVCaptureStillImageOutput object. The first argument is an AVCaptureConnection; to obtain it, we ask the output for its connection that is currently inputting video. The second argument is the function that will be called, possibly on a background thread, when the image data is ready; in that function, we capture the data into a UIImage and, stepping out to the main thread (Chapter 25), we remove the AVCaptureVideoPreviewLayer and stop the AVCaptureSession (and at that point we can do something with the UIImage, such as displaying it in the interface):

```
if self.sess == nil || !self.sess.running { return }
let vc = self.snapper.connectionWithMediaType(AVMediaTypeVideo)
self.snapper.captureStillImageAsynchronouslyFromConnection(vc) {
    (buf:CMSampleBuffer!, err:NSError!) in
    let data = AVCaptureStillImageOutput
        .jpegStillImageNSDataRepresentation(buf)
    let im = UIImage(data:data)
    dispatch_async(dispatch_get_main_queue()) {
        self.previewLayer.removeFromSuperlayer()
        self.sess.stopRunning()
        self.sess = nil
        // ... do something with im here ...
    }
}
```

My favorite part of that example is that capturing the image produces, automatically, the built-in "shutter" sound!

Our code has not illustrated setting the focus, changing the flash settings, and so forth; doing so is not difficult (see the class documentation on AVCaptureDevice), but note that you should wrap such changes in calls to `lockForConfiguration:` and `unlockFor-Configuration`. Also, always call the corresponding `is...Supported:` method before setting any feature of an AVCaptureDevice; for example, before setting the `flashMode`, call `isFlashModeSupported:` for that mode. Starting in iOS 8, you get direct hardware-level control over the camera focus, manual exposure, and white balance; for a good introduction, watch the WWDC 2014 video on camera capture, and look at the AVCam-Manual sample code. Also, the BracketStripes example shows how to capture multiple bracketed images.

You can stop the flow of video data by setting the AVCaptureConnection's `enabled` to `false`, and there are some other interesting AVCaptureConnection features, mostly involving stabilization of the video image (not relevant to the example, because a preview layer's video isn't stabilized). Plus, AVCaptureVideoPreviewLayer provides methods for converting between layer coordinates and capture device coordinates; without such methods, this can be a very difficult problem to solve. You can also scan bar codes, shoot video at 60 frames per second (on some devices), and more. You can turn on the LED "torch" by setting the back camera's `torchMode` to `AVCaptureTorchModeOn`, even if no AVCaptureSession is running.

AV Foundation's control over the camera, and its ability to process incoming data — especially video data — goes far deeper than there is room to discuss here, so consult the documentation; in particular, see the "Media Capture" chapter of the *AV Foundation Programming Guide*. There are also excellent WWDC videos on AV Foundation, and some fine sample code; I found Apple's AVCam example very helpful while preparing this discussion.

CHAPTER 18

Contacts

The user's contacts, which the user sees through the Contacts app, constitute a database that your code can access programmatically through the Contacts framework. You'll need to `import Contacts`.

A user interface for interacting with the contacts database is provided by the Contacts UI framework. You'll need to `import ContactsUI`.

 The Contacts framework, which is new in iOS 9, replaces the Address Book framework and the Address Book UI framework. The Address Book framework was an archaic C API without memory management information, so it was almost impossible to use in Swift, and it wasn't all that usable in Objective-C either. The Address Book framework is not discussed in this edition.

Contacts Authorization

Access to the contacts database requires authorization from the user. To learn whether you have authorization, call the CNContactStore class method `authorizationStatus-ForEntityType:`; there is only one possible entity type (CNEntityType), namely `.Contacts`. To request authorization if your status is `.NotDetermined`, call the CNContactStore instance method `requestAccessForEntityType:completion-Handler:`. The first time you do this with a `.NotDetermined` status, the user will see the system alert requesting access on your behalf. Your *Info.plist* should contain some text that the system authorization request alert can use to explain why your app wants access; the relevant key is "Privacy — Contacts Usage Description" (`NSContactsUsage-Description`).

A possible authorization strategy would thus be completely parallel to the strategy I described at the start of Chapter 17. However, you will probably end up calling request-

`AccessForEntityType:completionHandler:` even when you believe that you already have access. The reason is that talking to the contacts database, to fetch or save contacts, is time-consuming and should therefore always be done on a background thread. The `completionHandler:` function *is* called on a background thread. Thus you can assure access and do your fetching and saving on a background thread all in one move.

 To retest the system authorization request alert and other access-related behaviors, go to the Settings app and choose General → Reset → Reset Location & Privacy. This, unfortunately, causes the system to revert to its default settings for *everything* in the Privacy section of Settings: all permissions lists will be empty, but Location Services and all System Services will be On.

Fetching Contact Information

Here are the chief object types you'll be concerned with when you work with the user's contacts:

CNContactStore
> The user's database of contacts is accessed through an instance of the CNContact-Store class. You do not need to keep a reference to an instance of this class. When you want to fetch a contact from the database, or when you want to save a created or modified contact into the database, instantiate CNContactStore, do your fetching or saving, and let the CNContactStore instance vanish.

CNContact
> An individual contact is an instance of the CNContact class. Its properties correspond to the fields displayed in the Contacts app. In addition, it has an `identifier` which is unique and persistent. A CNContact that comes from the CNContactStore is immutable (its properties are read-only) and has no connection with the database; it is safe to preserve it and to pass it around between objects and between threads. To create your own CNContact, start with its mutable subclass, CNMutableContact; to modify an existing CNContact, call `mutableCopy` to make it a CNMutable-Contact.

> The properties of a CNContact are matched by constant key names designating those properties. For example, a CNContact has a `familyName` property, and there is also a `CNContactFamilyNameKey`. This should remind you of MPMediaItem (Chapter 16), and indeed the purpose is similar: the key names allow you, when you fetch a CNContact from the CNContactStore, to state which properties of the CNContact you want populated. By limiting the properties to be fetched, you fetch more efficiently and quickly.

CNContactFormatter, CNPostalAddressFormatter

A formatter is an engine for displaying aspects of a CNContact as a string. For example, a CNContactFormatter whose `style` is `.FullName` assembles the name-related properties of a CNContact into a name string. Moreover, a formatter will hand you the key names of the properties that it needs in order to form its string, so that you can easily include them in the list of contact properties you fetch from the store.

Now let's put it all together and fetch some contacts. When we perform a fetch, there are two parameters to provide in order to limit the information to be returned to us:

`predicate:`

An NSPredicate. CNContact provides class methods that will generate some common predicates; you are most likely to use `predicateForContactsMatchingName:` and `predicateForContactsWithIdentifiers:`.

`keysToFetch:`

An array of objects adopting the CNKeyDescriptor protocol; such an object will be either a string key name such as `CNContactFamilyNameKey` or a descriptor (actually an instance of a hidden class called CNAggregateKeyDescriptor) provided by a formatter such as CNContactFormatter.

I'll start by finding myself as a contact in my contacts database. To do so, I'll first fetch all contacts whose name is Matt. I'll call the CNContactStore instance method `unified-ContactsMatchingPredicate:keysToFetch:`. To determine which resulting Matt is me, I don't need more than the first name and the last name of those contacts. I'll cycle through the resulting array of contacts in an attempt to find one whose last name is Neuburg. The structure of this code is very typical; we start with `requestAccessFor-EntityType:` so that our actual fetch takes place on a background thread, and the fetch is wrapped in a `do...catch` construct because it can throw:

```
CNContactStore().requestAccessForEntityType(.Contacts) {
    ok, err in
    guard ok else {
        print("not authorized")
        return
    }
    do {
        let pred = CNContact.predicateForContactsMatchingName("Matt")
        var matts = try CNContactStore().unifiedContactsMatchingPredicate(
            pred, keysToFetch:
                [CNContactFamilyNameKey, CNContactGivenNameKey])
        matts = matts.filter{$0.familyName == "Neuburg"}
        guard var moi = matts.first else {
            print("couldn't find myself")
            return
        }
        // do something with moi here
```

```
        } catch {
            print(error)
        }
    }
```

Alternatively, since I intend to cycle through the fetched contacts, I could call enumerate-ContactsWithFetchRequest:, which hands me contacts one at a time. The parameter is a CNContactFetchRequest, a simple value class; in addition to keysToFetch and predicate, it has some convenient properties allowing me to retrieve CNMutableContacts instead of CNContacts, to dictate the sort order, and to suppress the unification of linked contacts. I don't need those extra features here, but I'll demonstrate the syntax anyway:

```
CNContactStore().requestAccessForEntityType(.Contacts) {
    ok, err in
    guard ok else {
        print("not authorized")
        return
    }
    do {
        let pred = CNContact.predicateForContactsMatchingName("Matt")
        let req = CNContactFetchRequest(keysToFetch: [
            CNContactFamilyNameKey, CNContactGivenNameKey])
        req.predicate = pred
        var matt : CNContact? = nil
        try CNContactStore().enumerateContactsWithFetchRequest(req) {
            con, stop in
            if con.familyName == "Neuburg" {
                matt = con
                stop.memory = true
            }
        }
        guard var moi = matt else {
            print("couldn't find myself")
            return
        }
        // do something with moi here
    } catch {
        print(error)
    }
}
```

In those examples, I boldly read the familyName from each fetched contact, because I know that I included the CNContactFamilyNameKey in my list of properties to be fetched. Nevertheless, this contact is only partially populated. To illustrate, let's say that I now want to access my email addresses. If I were to carry on directly from the preceding code by reading the emailAddresses property of moi, I'd crash because that property isn't populated:

```
let emails = moi.emailAddresses // crash
```

If I'm unsure what properties of a particular contact are populated, I can test for safety beforehand with the `isKeyAvailable:` method:

```
if moi.isKeyAvailable(CNContactEmailAddressesKey) {
    let emails = moi.emailAddresses
}
```

But even though I'm not crashing any more, I still want those email addresses. One solution, obviously, would have been to plan ahead and include `CNContactEmail-AddressesKey` in the list of properties to be fetched. Unfortunately, I failed to do that. Luckily, there's another way; I can go back to the store and repopulate this contact, based on its identifier:

```
moi = try CNContactStore().unifiedContactWithIdentifier(
    moi.identifier, keysToFetch: [
        CNContactFamilyNameKey, CNContactGivenNameKey,
        CNContactEmailAddressesKey
    ]
)
let emails = moi.emailAddresses
```

Now let's talk about the structure of the thing I've just obtained — the value of the `email-Addresses` property. It's an array of CNLabeledValue objects. A CNLabeledValue has a `label` and a `value` (and an `identifier`). This class handles the fact that some contact attributes can have more than one value, each intended for a specific purpose (the label). For example, I might have a home email address and a work email address. These addresses are not keyed by their labels — we cannot, for example, use a dictionary here — because I can have, say, *two* work email addresses. Rather, the label is simply another piece of information accompanying the value. You can make up your own labels, or you can use the built-in labels. Under the hood, the built-in labels are very strange-looking strings like `"_$!<Work>!$_"`, but there are also some constants that you can use instead, such as `CNLabelWork`. Carrying on from the previous example, I'll look for all my work email addresses:

```
let workemails = emails.filter{$0.label == CNLabelWork}.map{$0.value}
```

Postal addresses are similar, except that their `value` is a CNPostalAddress. (Recall that there's a CNPostalAddressFormatter, to be used when presenting an address as a string.) Phone number values are CNPhoneNumber objects. And so on.

To illustrate the point about formatters and keys, let's say that now I want to present the full name and work email of this contact to the user, as a string. I should not assume either that the full name is to be constructed as `givenName` followed by `familyName` nor that those are the only two pieces that constitute it. Rather, I should rely on the intelligence of a CNContactFormatter:

```
let full = CNContactFormatterStyle.FullName
let keys = CNContactFormatter.descriptorForRequiredKeysForStyle(full)
moi = try CNContactStore().unifiedContactWithIdentifier(
    moi.identifier, keysToFetch: [keys, CNContactEmailAddressesKey])
if let name = CNContactFormatter.stringFromContact(moi, style: full) {
    print("\(name): \(workemails[0])") // Matt Neuburg: matt@tidbits.com
}
```

One more thing to watch out for regarding contact properties: dates, such as a birthday, are not NSDates. Rather, they are NSDateComponents. This is because they do not require full date information; for example, I know when someone's birthday is without knowing the year they were born.

The user's contacts database can change while your app is running. To detect this, register for the `CNContactStoreDidChangeNotification`. The arrival of this notification means that any contacts-related objects that you are retaining, such as CNContacts, may be outdated.

Saving Contact Information

All saving of information into the user's contacts database involves a CNContactSave object. This object batches the proposed changes that you give it by using instance methods such as `addContact:toContainerWithIdentifier:`, `updateContact:`, and `deleteContact:`. You then hand the CNContactSave object over to the CNContactStore with `executeSaveRequest:`.

In this example, I'll create a contact for Snidely Whiplash with a Home email `snidely@villains.com` and add him to the contacts database:

```
let snidely = CNMutableContact()
snidely.givenName = "Snidely"
snidely.familyName = "Whiplash"
let email = CNLabeledValue(
    label: CNLabelHome, value: "snidely@villains.com")
snidely.emailAddresses.append(email)
snidely.imageData =
    UIImagePNGRepresentation(UIImage(named:"snidely.jpg")!)
let save = CNSaveRequest()
save.addContact(snidely, toContainerWithIdentifier: nil)
CNContactStore().requestAccessForEntityType(.Contacts) {
    ok, error in
    guard ok else {
        print("not authorized")
        return
    }
    do {
        try CNContactStore().executeSaveRequest(save)
        print("created snidely!")
```

Figure 18-1. A contact created programmatically

```
    } catch {
        print(error)
    }
}
```

Sure enough, if we then check the state of the database through the Contacts app, our Snidely contact exists (Figure 18-1).

Contact Sorting, Groups, and Containers

Contacts are naturally sorted either by family name or by given name, and the user can choose between them (in the Settings app) in arranging the list of contacts to be displayed by the Contacts app and other apps that display the same list. The CNContact class provides a comparator, through the `comparatorForNameSortOrder:` class method, suitable for handing to NSArray methods such as `sortedArrayUsingComparator:`. To make sure your CNContact is populated with the properties needed for sorting, call the class method `descriptorForAllComparatorKeys()`. Your choices (CNContactSort-Order) are:

- `.GivenName`
- `.FamilyName`
- `.UserDefault`

Contacts can belong to groups, and the Contacts application in OS X provides an interface for manipulating contact groups — though the Contacts app on an iOS device does not. (The Contacts app on an iOS device allows contacts to be filtered by group, but does not permit editing of groups — creation of groups, addition of contacts to groups, and so on. I am not clear on the reason for this curious omission.) A group in the Contacts framework is a CNGroup; its mutable subclass, CNMutableGroup, allows you to create a group and set its name. All manipulation of contacts and groups — creating, renaming, or deleting a group, adding a contact to a group or removing a contact from a group — is performed through CNSaveRequest instance methods.

Contacts come from sources. A contact or group might be on the device or might come from an Exchange server or a CardDAV server. The source really does, in a sense, own the group or contact; a contact can't belong to two sources. A complicating factor, however, is that the same real person might be listed in two different sources as two different contacts; to deal with this, it is possible for multiple contacts to be linked, indicating that they are the same person. This is why the methods that fetch contacts from the database describe the resulting contacts as "unified" — the linkage between linked contacts from different sources has already been used to assemble the information before you receive them as a single contact. In the Contacts framework, a source is a CNContainer. When I called the CNSaveRequest instance method `addContact:toContainer-WithIdentifier:` earlier, I supplied a container identifier of `nil`, signifying the user's default container.

Contacts Interface

The Contacts UI framework puts a user interface, similar to the Contacts app, in front of common tasks involving the listing, display, and editing of contacts in the database. This is a great help, because designing your own interface to do the same thing would be tedious and involved. The framework provides two UIViewController subclasses:

CNContactPickerViewController
> Presents a navigation interface, effectively the same as the Contacts app but without an Edit button: it lists the contacts in the database and allows the user to pick one and view the details.

CNContactViewController
> Presents an interface showing the properties of a specific contact. It comes in three variants:

> *Existing contact*
>> Displays the details, possibly editable, of an existing contact fetched from the database.

> *Unknown contact*
>> Displays a proposed contact with a partial set of properties, for editing and saving or merging into an existing contact in the database.

> *New contact*
>> Displays editable properties of a new contact, allowing the user to save the edited contact into the database.

CNContactPickerViewController

A CNContactPickerViewController is a UINavigationController. With it, the user can see a list of all contacts in the database, and can filter that list by group. In effect, the user appears to be inside the Contacts app — and in a sense, that is indeed the case, as is shown by the fact that the picker operates *without* the user having to grant your app permission to access the database.

 How does this view controller operate without the user granting Contact database access? It may be because, as Apple puts it, the view controller is "out of process" with respect to your application — meaning that the user, though still inside your app, is effectively using the Contacts app, something that, of itself, requires no access permission. It's true that your app can receive information about contacts through the CNContactPickerViewController, despite the lack of permission; but perhaps Apple's rationale is that you receive only the information that the user explicitly grants you by tapping on a contact — if the user cancels, you get nothing — and so the user tapping *is* a form of permission.

To use CNContactPickerViewController, instantiate it, assign it a delegate (CNContactPickerDelegate), and present it as a presented view controller:

```
let picker = CNContactPickerViewController()
picker.delegate = self
self.presentViewController(picker, animated:true, completion:nil)
```

That code works — the picker appears, and there's a Cancel button so the user can dismiss it — but it's completely impractical, because we have provided no way for any *information* to travel from the picker to our app. For that, we need to configure the picker a bit further, and we need to implement at least one delegate method.

To understand configuration of the picker, we need to consider what the picker does *without* configuration. At present, when the user taps a contact, that contact's details are pushed onto the navigation controller. And when the user taps a piece of information among the details, some default action is performed: for a postal address, it is displayed in the Maps app; for an email address, it becomes the addressee of a new message in the Mail app; for a phone number, the number is dialed; and so on. Our goal is thus that, under some circumstances at least, a tap should instead convey the corresponding information to our app. This is called *selecting* a contact or a property.

There are two stages to the accomplishing of this goal:

1. We must permit selection to occur. This is done by providing an NSPredicate, setting the picker's `predicateForSelectionOfContact` or its `predicateForSelectionOfProperty`, or both. When the user taps a contact or property, our predicate is evaluated; if it evalutes to `true`, selection is permitted.

2. We must implement a delegate method. If the user taps and the predicate evaluates to `true`, then the interface doesn't change; instead, the corresponding delegate method is called, either `contactPicker:didSelectContact:` or `contactPicker:didSelectContactProperty:` — along with information about that contact or property. We will then presumably dismiss the picker, which has done its work.

For example, suppose our goal is that the user should hand us a contact's email address. Then we would enable selection of email addresses. For purposes of working with arbitrary properties in these view controllers, there's a CNContactProperty class, consisting of a `key`, a `value`, a `label`, a `contact`, and an `identifier`. In the case of `predicateForSelectionOfProperty`, the predicate will be evaluated against a CNContactProperty. So our predicate looks like this:

```
picker.predicateForSelectionOfProperty =
    NSPredicate(format: "key == 'emailAddresses'")
```

The result is that when the user taps an email address, our delegate method is called, and we do something with the result and dismiss the picker:

```
func contactPicker(picker: CNContactPickerViewController,
    didSelectContactProperty prop: CNContactProperty) {
        // ... do something with CNContactProperty here ...
        self.dismissViewControllerAnimated(true, completion: nil)
}
```

The CNContactProperty that we receive in our delegate method contains not only an email address (its `value`) but the contact to which it belongs (its `contact`), which is fully populated.

Now, our interface is not very sensible if our goal was to let the user choose only an email address. The user is seeing all the other properties of every contact, and tapping one of them will perform its action; for example, tapping a phone number will place a phone call. That's likely to be surprising. To prevent it, we can limit what properties are displayed in the first place, by way of the picker's `displayedPropertyKeys` property:

```
picker.displayedPropertyKeys = [CNContactEmailAddressesKey]
picker.predicateForSelectionOfProperty =
    NSPredicate(format: "key == 'emailAddresses'")
```

Interestingly, the CNContactProperty that we receive in our delegate method is *still* fully populated. We may thus end up with information, such as the contact's postal addresses, that the user never saw.

There are two further bits of configuration we can perform on a CNContactPickerViewController. First, we can disable contacts selectively, so that they cannot be tapped. To do so, set the picker's `predicateForEnablingContact`. This would make sense in our example; we are after an email address, so it is pointless to enable a contact who has *no* email address:

```
picker.displayedPropertyKeys = [CNContactEmailAddressesKey]
picker.predicateForSelectionOfProperty =
    NSPredicate(format: "key == 'emailAddresses'")
picker.predicateForEnablingContact =
    NSPredicate(format: "emailAddresses.@count > 0")
```

Second, we can enable multiple selection. To do so, there is no picker property to set; rather, we simply implement a different delegate method, either `contactPicker:did-SelectContacts:` or `contactPicker:didSelectContactProperties:` (or both). This causes a Done button to appear in the interface, and our delegate method is called when the user taps it.

 The interface for letting the user select multiple properties is clumsy and confusing at best, and downright broken at worst; an injudicious combination of `predicate-ForSelectionOfProperty` and `contactPicker:didSelectContactProperties:` can send your app into limbo. Experiment with this interface before deciding to use it.

CNContactViewController

A CNContactViewController is a UIViewController. It comes, as I've already said, in three flavors, depending on how you instantiate it.

Existing contact

To display an existing contact in a CNContactViewController, call `init(for-Contact:)`. However, there's a catch. This call will crash your app unless the contact has already been populated with all the information needed to display it in this view controller. Therefore, CNContactViewController supplies a class method `descriptorFor-RequiredKeys`, and you will want to call it to set the keys when you fetch your contact from the store.

Having instantiated CNContactViewController, you set its delegate (CNContactView-ControllerDelegate) and *push* the view controller onto an existing UINavigation-Controller's stack. The user's only way out of the resulting interface will be through the back button.

An Edit button appears at the top right, and the user can tap it to edit this contact in a presented view controller — unless you have set the view controller's `allowsEditing` property to `false`, in which case the Edit button is suppressed.

The `allowsActions` property refers to extra buttons that can appear in the interface if it is `true` — things like Send Message, FaceTime, Share Contact, and Add to Favorites. Exactly what buttons appear depends on what categories of information are displayed.

As with CNContactPickerViewController, displayedPropertyKeys limits the properties shown for this contact. The message is a string displayed beneath the contact's name.

Here's a minimal working example; I'll display the Snidely Whiplash contact that I created earlier. Observe that, having successfully *fetched* Snidely on a background thread, we need to step out to the main thread before we can *display* Snidely in the interface:

```
CNContactStore().requestAccessForEntityType(.Contacts) {
    ok, err in
    guard ok else {
        print("not authorized")
        return
    }
    do {
        let pred = CNContact.predicateForContactsMatchingName("Snidely")
        let keys = CNContactViewController.descriptorForRequiredKeys()
        let snides = try CNContactStore()
            .unifiedContactsMatchingPredicate(pred, keysToFetch: [keys])
        guard let snide = snides.first else {
            print("no snidely")
            return
        }
        let vc = CNContactViewController(forContact:snide)
        dispatch_async(dispatch_get_main_queue()) {
            self.navigationController?
                .pushViewController(vc, animated: true)
        }
    } catch {
        print(error)
    }
}
```

The situation is like our first attempt with CNContactPickerViewController: it works in the sense that Snidely's contact is displayed, but the interface is silly in that the user can't do anything related to our app. We need to tweak our code depending on the purpose of showing this view controller.

For example, suppose our goal is to let the user *edit* Snidely. By default, the user can do that. So we need to do two things. First, we should turn off "actions" in our view controller, so that the user doesn't get rocketed off to the Mail app by accidentally tapping an email address. Second, we should capture the Snidely contact when the user is finished editing. We can do both of those things by setting ourself as delegate and implementing the two delegate methods:

contactViewController:shouldPerformDefaultActionForContactProperty:
    This is like a live version of the picker predicateForSelectionOfProperty, except that the meaning is reversed: returning true means that the tapped property should proceed to trigger the Mail app or the Maps app or whatever is appropriate.

`contactViewController:didCompleteWithContact:`

> Sent when the user dismisses *the editing interface*. If you have set the view controller's `contactStore` property to a contact store instance, then the edited contact is also saved into the database. If not, then you have the edited contact and what happens to it is up to you. (If the user cancels from the editing interface, the contact returned to you will be `nil`.)

Unknown contact

To use a CNContactViewController to allow the user to edit an unknown contact, instantiate it with `init(forUnknownContact:)`. You must provide a CNContact parameter, which you may have made up from scratch using a CNMutableContact. You must have database access, and you must set the view controller's `contactStore` to a CNContactStore instance; it's not an error otherwise, but the view controller is useless. You then set a delegate and push the view controller onto an existing navigation controller:

```
let con = CNMutableContact()
con.givenName = "Johnny"
con.familyName = "Appleseed"
con.phoneNumbers.append(CNLabeledValue(
    label: "woods", value: CNPhoneNumber(stringValue: "555-123-4567")))
let unkvc = CNContactViewController(forUnknownContact: con)
unkvc.message = "He knows his trees"
unkvc.contactStore = CNContactStore()
unkvc.delegate = self
unkvc.allowsActions = false
self.navigationController?.pushViewController(unkvc, animated: true)
```

Aside from the actions such as Share Contact (which you can suppress), and the ability to tap a phone number to call that number and so forth (which you can prevent), the only thing the user can do besides pop the view controller is tap one of two buttons, Create New Contact or Add to Existing Contact. Let's take them in turn:

Create New Contact
> The editing interface is presented, with a Cancel button and a Done button. If the user taps Cancel, you'll never hear about it. If the user taps Done, your `contactViewController:didCompleteWithContact:` is called with the edited contact, which has already been saved into the database.

Add to Existing Contact
> The picker is presented. The user can tap Cancel or tap an existing contact. If the user taps an existing contact, that contact is presented for editing, with fields from the partial contact merged in, along with a Cancel button and an Update button. If the taps Cancel, you'll never hear about it. If the user taps Update, your `contactViewController:didCompleteWithContact:` is called with the edited contact, which has already been saved into the database.

If the framework thinks that this partial contact is the same as an existing contact, there will be a third button offering explicitly to update that particular contact. The result is as if the user had tapped Add to Existing Contact and picked this existing contact: the editing interface for that contact appears, with the fields from the partial contact merged in, along with Cancel and Update buttons.

 Unfortunately, as of this writing, after tapping Add to Existing Contact or Update, the surrounding navigation interface is destroyed and the user can never leave this view controller to return to your app. This is a major bug; ascertain whether it is fixed before using this form of CNContactViewController.

New contact

To use a CNContactViewController to allow the user to create a new contact, instantiate it with init(forNewContact:). The parameter can be nil, or it can be a CNMutable-Contact that you've created and partially populated; but your properties will be only suggestions, because the user is going to be launched directly into the contact editing interface and can change anything you've put.

 You should check for authorization before using this flavor of CNContactView-Controller, because if you don't have it or can't get it, the interface the user sees will lack a Done button and this view controller will be pointless.

Having set the view controller's delegate, you then do a little dance: you instantiate a UINavigationController with the CNContactViewController as its root view controller, and present the navigation controller. Thus, this is a minimal implementation:

```
let con = CNMutableContact()
con.givenName = "Dudley"
con.familyName = "Doright"
let npvc = CNContactViewController(forNewContact: con) // or nil
npvc.delegate = self
self.presentViewController(
    UINavigationController(rootViewController: npvc),
    animated: true, completion:nil)
```

Your implementation of the delegate method contactViewController:didComplete-WithContact: *must* call dismissViewControllerAnimated:completion:. If the user tapped Cancel, the contact returned to you will be nil. If the contact returned to you is *not* nil, then that contact has already been saved into the database. You can't prevent this, but you have the new contact's identifier, so you are perfectly free at this point to delete that contact from the database once again (which you can certainly do, because the user would not have been able to save into the database if your app didn't have authorization in the first place).

CHAPTER 19

Calendar

The user's calendar information, which the user sees through the Calendar app, is effectively a database of calendar events. The calendar database also includes reminders, which the user sees through the Reminders app. This database can be accessed directly through the Event Kit framework. You'll need to `import EventKit`.

A user interface for interacting with the calendar is also provided, through the Event Kit UI framework. You'll need to `import EventKitUI`.

Calendar Database

The calendar database is accessed as an instance of the EKEventStore class. This instance is expensive to obtain but lightweight to maintain, so your usual strategy will be to instantiate and retain one EKEventStore instance. There is no harm in initializing a property as an EKEventStore instance and keeping that reference for the rest of the app's lifetime:

```
let database = EKEventStore()
```

In the examples in this chapter, my EKEventStore instance is called `self.database` throughout.

Calendar Database Authorization

Although there is one database, access to calendar events and access to reminders are considered two separate forms of access and require separate authorizations. To learn authorization status, call the EKEventStore class method `authorizationStatusFor-EntityType:` with an EKEntityType, either `.Event` (for access to calendar events) or `.Reminder` (for access to reminders). To request authorization if the status is `.Not-Determined`, call the EKEventStore instance method `requestAccessToEntity-Type:completion:`. You should supply the body of the authorization request alert by setting the "Privacy — Calendars Usage Description" key (NSCalendarsUsage-Description) or the "Privacy — Reminders Usage Description" key (NSReminders-UsageDescription) in your app's *Info.plist*. A possible strategy is thus completely parallel to the code at the start of Chapter 17 for access to the photo library.

 To retest the system authorization request alert and other access-related behaviors, go to the Settings app and choose General → Reset → Reset Location & Privacy. This, unfortunately, causes the system to revert to its default settings for *everything* in the Privacy section of Settings: all permissions lists will be empty, but Location Services and all System Services will be On.

Calendar Database Contents

Starting with an EKEventStore instance, you can obtain two kinds of object — a calendar or a calendar item.

Calendars

A calendar represents a named (title) collection of calendar items, meaning events or reminders. It is an instance of EKCalendar. Curiously, however, an EKCalendar instance doesn't contain or link to its calendar items; to obtain and create calendar items, you work directly with the EKEventStore itself. A calendar's allowedEntityTypes, despite the plural, will probably return just one entity type; you can't create a single calendar that allows both.

Calendars have various types (type, an EKCalendarType), reflecting the nature of their origin: a calendar can be created and maintained by the user locally (.Local), but it might also live remotely on the network (.CalDAV, .Exchange); the Birthday calendar (.Birthday) is generated automatically from information in the address book; and so on.

The type is supplemented and embraced by the calendar's source, an EKSource whose sourceType (EKSourceType) can be .Local, .Exchange, .CalDAV (which includes iCloud), and so forth; a source can also have a title, and it has a unique identifier (sourceIdentifier). You can get an array of all sources known to the EKEventStore, or specify a source by its identifier. You'll probably use the source exclusively and ignore the calendar's type property.

There are three ways of requesting a calendar:

All calendars
> Fetch all calendars permitting a particular calendar item type (.Event or .Reminder) by calling calendarsForEntityType:. You can send this message either to the EKEventStore or to an EKSource.

Particular calendar

Fetch an individual calendar by means of a previously obtained `calendar-Identifier` by calling `calendarWithIdentifier:`.

Default calendar

Fetch the default calendar for a particular calendar item type through the `default-CalendarForNewEvents` property or the `defaultCalendarForNewReminders` property; this is appropriate particularly if your intention is to create a new calendar item.

You can also create a calendar with the initializer `init(forEntityType:event-Store:)`. At that point, you can specify the source to which the calendar belongs.

Depending on the source, a calendar will be modifiable in various ways. The calendar might be `subscribed`. If the calendar is `immutable`, you can't delete the calendar or change its attributes; but its `allowsContentModifications` might still be `true`, in which case you can add, remove, and alter its events. You can update your copy of the calendar from any remote sources by calling `refreshSourcesIfNecessary`.

Calendar items

A calendar item (EKCalendarItem) is either a calendar event (EKEvent) or a reminder (EKReminder). Think of it as a memorandum describing when something happens. As I mentioned a moment ago, you don't get calendar items from a calendar; rather, a calendar item *has* a `calendar`, but you get it from the EKEventStore as a whole. There are two chief ways of doing so:

By predicate

Fetch all events or reminders according to a predicate:

- `eventsMatchingPredicate:`
- `enumerateEventsMatchingPredicate:`
- `fetchRemindersMatchingPredicate:completion:`

Methods starting with `predicate...` help you to form the predicate.

By identifier

Fetch an individual calendar item by means of a previously obtained `calendarItem-Identifier` by calling `calendarItemWithIdentifier:`.

Calendar Database Changes

Changes to the database can be atomic. There are two prongs to the implementation of this feature:

- The methods for saving and removing calendar items and calendars have a `commit:` parameter. If you pass `false` as the argument, the changes that you're ordering are batched; later, you can call `commit:` (or `reset` if you change your mind). If you pass `false` and fail to call `commit:` later, your changes will never happen.

- An abstract class, EKObject, functions as the superclass for all the other persistent object types, such as EKCalendar, EKCalendarItem, EKSource, and so on. It endows those classes with methods `new` and `hasChanges`, along with `refresh`, `rollback`, and `reset`.

A calendar can change while your app is running (the user might sync, or the user might edit with the Calendar app), which can put your information out of date. You can register for a single EKEventStore notification, `EKEventStoreChangedNotification`; if you receive it, you should assume that any calendar-related instances you're holding are invalid. This situation is made relatively painless by the fact that every calendar-related instance can be refreshed with `refresh`. Keep in mind that `refresh` returns a Boolean; if it returns `false`, this object is *really* invalid and you should stop working with it entirely (it may have been deleted from the database).

Creating Calendars and Events

Let's start by creating an events calendar. We need to assign a source type (EKSource-Type); we'll choose `.Local`, meaning that the calendar will be created on the device itself. We can't ask the database for the local source directly, so we have to cycle through all sources looking for it. When we find it, we make a new calendar called "CoolCal":

```
if !self.determineStatus() { // not authorized
    return
}
let locals = self.database.sources.filter {$0.sourceType == .Local}
guard let src = locals.first else {
    print("failed to find local source")
    return
}
let cal = EKCalendar(forEntityType:.Event, eventStore:self.database)
cal.source = src
cal.title = "CoolCal"
do {
    try self.database.saveCalendar(cal, commit:true)
} catch {
    print("save calendar error: \(error)")
    return
}
```

If a device's calendar is subscribed to a remote source (such as iCloud), .Local calendars are inaccessible. The examples in this chapter use a local calendar (because I don't want to risk damaging your online calendars); to test them, you'll have to turn off iCloud for your Calendar app.

Now let's create an event. EKEvent is a subclass of EKCalendarItem, from which it inherits some of its important properties. If you've ever used the Calendar app in iOS or OS X, you already have a sense for how an EKEvent can be configured. It has a title and optional notes. It is associated with a calendar, as I've already said. It can have one or more alarms and one or more recurrence rules; I'll talk about both of those in a moment. All of that is inherited from EKCalendarItem. EKEvent itself adds the all-important startDate and endDate properties; these are NSDates and involve both date and time. If the event's allDay property is true, the time aspect of its dates is ignored; the event is associated with a day or a stretch of days as a whole. If the event's allDay property is false, the time aspect of its dates matters; an event will then typically be bounded by two times on the same day.

Making an event is simple, if tedious. You *must* provide a startDate and an endDate! The simplest way to construct dates, and to do the date math that you'll often need in order to derive one date from another, is with NSDateComponents. I'll create an event and add it to our new calendar. First, I need a way to locate the new calendar. I'll locate it by its title. I really should be using the calendarIdentifier; the title isn't reliable, since the user might change it, and since multiple calendars can have the same title. However, it's only an example:

```
func calendarWithName( name:String ) -> EKCalendar? {
    let cals = self.database.calendarsForEntityType(.Event)
    return cals.filter {$0.title == name}.first
}
```

Now I'll create an event, configure it, and add it to our CoolCal calendar:

```
if !self.determineStatus() { // not authorized
    return
}
guard let cal = self.calendarWithName("CoolCal") else { // no calendar
    return
}
let greg = NSCalendar(calendarIdentifier:NSCalendarIdentifierGregorian)!
let comp = NSDateComponents()
(comp.year, comp.month, comp.day, comp.hour) = (2016,8,10,15)
let d1 = greg.dateFromComponents(comp)!
comp.hour = comp.hour + 1
let d2 = greg.dateFromComponents(comp)!
let ev = EKEvent(eventStore:self.database)
ev.title = "Take a nap"
ev.notes = "You deserve it!"
```

```
ev.calendar = cal
(ev.startDate, ev.endDate) = (d1,d2)
do {
    try self.database.saveEvent(ev, span:.ThisEvent, commit:true)
} catch {
    print("save simple event \(error)")
    return
}
```

An alarm is an EKAlarm, a very simple class; it can be set to fire either at an absolute
date or at a relative offset from the event time. On an iOS device, an alarm fires through
a local notification (Chapter 13). We could easily have added an alarm to our event as
we were configuring it:

```
let alarm = EKAlarm(relativeOffset:-3600) // one hour before
ev.addAlarm(alarm)
```

Recurrence

Recurrence is embodied in a recurrence rule (EKRecurrenceRule); a calendar item can
have multiple recurrence rules, which you manipulate through its recurrenceRules
property, along with methods addRecurrenceRule: and removeRecurrenceRule:. A
simple EKRecurrenceRule is described by three properties:

Frequency
> By day, by week, by month, or by year.

Interval
> Fine-tunes the notion "by" in the frequency. A value of 1 means "every." A value of
> 2 means "every other." And so on.

End
> Optional, because the event might recur forever. It is an EKRecurrenceEnd instance,
> describing the limit of the event's recurrence either as an end date or as a maximum
> number of occurrences.

The options for describing a more complex EKRecurrenceRule are best summarized by
its initializer:

```
init(recurrenceWithFrequency type: EKRecurrenceFrequency,
                     interval: Int,
            daysOfTheWeek days: [EKRecurrenceDayOfWeek]?,
       daysOfTheMonth monthDays: [NSNumber]?,
        monthsOfTheYear months: [NSNumber]?,
                weeksOfTheYear: [NSNumber]?,
                 daysOfTheYear: [NSNumber]?,
                  setPositions: [NSNumber]?,
                          end: EKRecurrenceEnd?)
```

The meanings of all these parameters are mostly obvious from their names and types. The EKRecurrenceDayOfWeek class allows specification of a week number as well as a day number so that you can say things like "the fourth Thursday of the month." Many of the numeric values can be negative to indicate counting backward from the last one. Numbers are all 1-based, not 0-based. The `setPositions` parameter is an array of numbers filtering the occurrences defined by the rest of the specification against the interval; for example, if `daysOfTheWeek` is Sunday, `-1` means the final Sunday.

An EKRecurrenceRule is intended to embody the `RRULE` event component in the iCalendar standard specification (*http://datatracker.ietf.org/doc/rfc5545*); in fact, the documentation tells you how each EKRecurrenceRule property corresponds to an `RRULE` attribute, and if you log an EKRecurrenceRule, what you're shown *is* the underlying `RRULE`. `RRULE` can describe some amazingly sophisticated recurrence rules, such as this one:

```
RRULE:FREQ=YEARLY;INTERVAL=2;BYMONTH=1;BYDAY=SU
```

That means "every Sunday in January, every other year." Let's form this rule. Observe that we should attach it to an event whose `startDate` and `endDate` make sense as an example of the rule — that is, on a Sunday in January. Fortunately, NSDateComponents makes that easy:

```
// ... make sure we have authorization ...
// ... obtain our calendar (cal) ...
// form the rule
let everySunday = EKRecurrenceDayOfWeek(.Sunday)
let january = 1
let recur = EKRecurrenceRule(
    recurrenceWithFrequency:.Yearly, // every year
    interval:2, // no, every *two* years
    daysOfTheWeek:[everySunday],
    daysOfTheMonth:nil,
    monthsOfTheYear:[january],
    weeksOfTheYear:nil,
    daysOfTheYear:nil,
    setPositions: nil,
    end:nil)
let ev = EKEvent(eventStore:self.database)
ev.title = "Mysterious biennial Sunday-in-January morning ritual"
ev.addRecurrenceRule(recur)
ev.calendar = cal
// need a start date and end date
let greg = NSCalendar(calendarIdentifier:NSCalendarIdentifierGregorian)!
let comp = NSDateComponents()
comp.year = 2016
comp.month = 1
comp.weekday = 1 // Sunday
comp.weekdayOrdinal = 1 // *first* Sunday
comp.hour = 10
ev.startDate = greg.dateFromComponents(comp)!
```

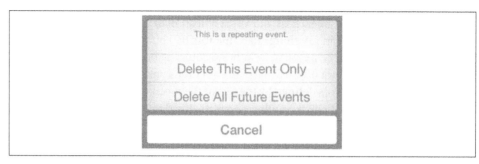

Figure 19-1. The user specifies a span

```
comp.hour = 11
ev.endDate = greg.dateFromComponents(comp)!
do {
    try self.database.saveEvent(ev, span:.FutureEvents, commit:true)
} catch {
    print("save recurring event \(error)")
    return
}
```

In that code, the event we save into the database is a recurring event. When we save or delete a recurring event, we must specify a `span:` argument (EKSpan). This is either `.ThisEvent` or `.FutureEvents`, and corresponds to the two buttons the user sees in the Calendar interface when saving or deleting a recurring event (Figure 19-1). The buttons and the span types reflect their meaning exactly: the change affects either this event alone, or this event plus all *future* (not past) recurrences. This choice determines not only how this and future recurrences of the event are affected now, but also how they relate to one another from now on.

Fetching Events

Now let's talk about how to extract an event from the database. One way, as I mentioned earlier, is by its identifier (`calendarItemIdentifier`). Not only is this identifier a fast and unique way to obtain an event, but also it's just a string, which means that it persists even if the EKEventStore subsequently goes out of existence. Remember to obtain it, though, while the EKEventStore *is* still in existence; an EKEvent drawn from the database loses its meaning and its usability if the EKEventStore instance is destroyed. (Even this unique identifier *might* not survive changes in a calendar between launches of your app.)

You can also extract events from the database by matching a predicate (NSPredicate). To form this predicate, you specify a start and end date and an array of eligible calendars, and call the EKEventStore method `predicateForEventsWithStartDate:end-Date:calendars:`. That's the only kind of predicate you can use, so any further filtering of events is then up to you. In this example, I'll look through the events of our CoolCal calendar to find the nap event I created earlier; because I have to specify a date range, I ask for events occurring over the next two years (see Appendix B for my `lend` function). Because `enumerateEventsMatchingPredicate:` can be time-consuming, it's best to run it on a background thread (Chapter 25):

```
// ... make sure we have authorization ...
// ... obtain our calendar (cal) ...
let d1 = NSDate() // today
let greg = NSCalendar(calendarIdentifier:NSCalendarIdentifierGregorian)!
let d2 = greg.dateByAddingComponents(lend {
        (comp:NSDateComponents) in comp.year = 2
    }, toDate:d1, options:[])!
let pred = self.database.predicateForEventsWithStartDate(
    d1, endDate:d2, calendars:[cal])
dispatch_async(dispatch_get_global_queue(0, 0)) {
    self.database.enumerateEventsMatchingPredicate(pred) {
        (event:EKEvent, stop:UnsafeMutablePointer<ObjCBool>) in
        if event.title.rangeOfString("nap") != nil {
            self.napid = event.calendarItemIdentifier
            stop.memory = true
        }
    }
}
```

When you fetch events from the database, they are provided in no particular order; the convenience method `compareStartDateWithEvent:` is provided as a sort selector to put them in order by start date.

When you extract events from the database, event recurrences are treated as separate events. Recurrences of the same event will have different start and end dates but the same `calendarItemIdentifier`. When you fetch an event by identifier, you get the *earliest* event with that identifier. This makes sense, because if you're going to make a change affecting this and future recurrences of the event, you need the option to start with the earliest possible recurrence (so that "future" means "all").

Reminders

A reminder (EKReminder) is very parallel to an event (EKEvent); the chief difference is that EKReminder was invented some years after EKEvent and so its API is a little more modern. They both inherit from EKCalendarItem, so a reminder has a calendar (which the Reminders app refers to as a "list"), a title, notes, alarms, and recurrence rules. Instead of a start date and an end date, it has a start date, a due date, a completion date, and a `completed` property. The start date and due date are expressed directly as NSDateComponents, so you can supply as much detail as you wish: if you don't include any time components, it's an all-day reminder.

To illustrate, I'll make an all-day reminder for today:

```
if !self.determineStatus() { // no authorization
    return
}
let cal = self.database.defaultCalendarForNewReminders()
let rem = EKReminder(eventStore:self.database)
rem.title = "Get bread"
rem.calendar = cal
let today = NSDate()
let greg = NSCalendar(calendarIdentifier:NSCalendarIdentifierGregorian)!
let comps : NSCalendarUnit = [.Year, .Month, .Day]
rem.dueDateComponents = greg.components(comps, fromDate:today)
do {
    try self.database.saveReminder(rem, commit:true)
} catch {
    print("save calendar \(error)")
    return
}
```

When you call fetchRemindersMatchingPredicate:completion:, the possible predicates let you fetch all reminders in given calendars, incomplete reminders, or completed
reminders. You don't have to call it on a background thread, because it calls your
completion function asynchronously.

Proximity Alarms

A proximity alarm is triggered by the user's approaching or leaving a certain location
(also known as *geofencing*). This is appropriate particularly for reminders: one might
wish to be reminded of some task when approaching the place where that task can be
accomplished. To form the location, you'll need to use the CLLocation class (see Chapter 22). Here, I'll attach a proximity alarm to a reminder (rem); the alarm will fire when
I'm near my local Trader Joe's:

```
let alarm = EKAlarm()
let loc = EKStructuredLocation(title:"Trader Joe's")
loc.geoLocation = CLLocation(latitude:34.271848, longitude:-119.247714)
loc.radius = 10*1000 // metres
alarm.structuredLocation = loc
alarm.proximity = .Enter // alarm when *arriving*
rem.addAlarm(alarm)
```

Use of a proximity alarm requires Location Services authorization, but that's of no concern here, because the app that needs this authorization is not our app but the Reminders
app! Now that we've placed a reminder with a proximity alarm into the database, the
Reminders app will request authorization, if needed, the next time the user brings it
frontmost. If you add a proximity alarm to the event database and the Reminders app
can't perform background geofencing, the alarm will not fire (unless the Reminders app
is frontmost).

You can also construct a local notification based on geofencing without involving reminders or the Reminders app. See Chapter 22.

Calendar Interface

The Event Kit UI framework provides three view controller classes that manage views for letting the user work with events and calendars:

EKEventViewController
Shows the description of a single event, possibly editable.

EKEventEditViewController
Allows the user to create or edit an event.

EKCalendarChooser
Allows the user to pick a calendar.

These view controllers automatically listen for changes in the database and, if needed, will automatically call refresh on the information being edited, updating their display to match. If a view controller is displaying an event in the database and the event is deleted while the user is viewing it, the delegate will get the same notification as if the user had deleted it.

EKEventViewController

EKEventViewController shows the event display listing the event's title, date and time, calendar, alert, and notes, familiar from the Calendar app (Figure 19-2). To use EKEventViewController, instantiate it, give it an event from the database, assign it a delegate (EKEventViewDelegate), and push it onto an existing navigation controller:

```
let evc = EKEventViewController()
evc.event = ev
evc.allowsEditing = true
evc.delegate = self
self.navigationController?.pushViewController(evc, animated: true)
```

Do *not* use EKEventViewController for an event that isn't in the database, or at a time when the database isn't open! It won't function correctly if you do.

If allowsEditing is true, an Edit button appears in the navigation bar, and by tapping this, the user can edit the various aspects of an event in the same interface as the Calendar app, including the Delete button at the bottom. If the user ultimately deletes the event, or edits it and taps Done, the change is saved into the database.

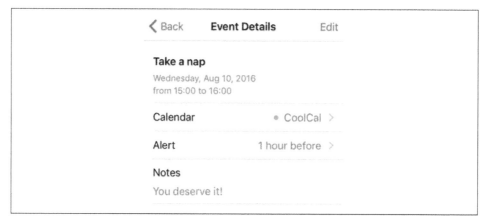

Figure 19-2. The event interface

If the user deletes the event, you will be notified in the delegate method, eventView-
Controller:didCompleteWithAction:; it is then up to you to pop the navigation controller:

```
func eventViewController(controller: EKEventViewController,
    didCompleteWithAction action: EKEventViewAction) {
        if action == .Deleted {
            self.navigationController?.popViewControllerAnimated(true)
        }
}
```

 Even if allowsEditing is false (the default), the user can change what calendar
this event belongs to, can change an alert's firing time if there is one, and can delete
the event. I regard this as a bug.

EKEventEditViewController

EKEventEditViewController (a UINavigationController) presents the interface for editing an event. To use it, set its eventStore and editViewDelegate (EKEventEditView-
Delegate, *not* delegate), and optionally its event, and present it as a presented view
controller (which looks best on the iPad as a popover). The event can be nil for a
completely empty new event; it can be an event you've just created (and possibly partially
configured) and not stored in the database; or it can be an existing event from the
database. If access to the database has been denied, the interface will be empty and the
user will simply cancel.

The delegate method eventEditViewControllerDefaultCalendarForNewEvents:
may be implemented to specify what calendar a completely new event should be assigned

to. If you're partially constructing a new event, you can assign it a calendar then, and of course an event from the database already has a calendar.

You must implement the delegate method `eventEditViewController:didComplete-WithAction:` so that you can dismiss the presented view controller. Possible actions are that the user cancelled, saved the edited event into the database, or deleted an already existing event from the database. You can get a reference to the edited event as the EKEventEditViewController's `event`.

EKCalendarChooser

EKCalendarChooser displays a list of calendars, choosable by tapping; a chosen calendar displays a checkmark. To use it, instantiate it with `init(selectionStyle:display-Style:entityType:eventStore:)`, set a `delegate` (EKCalendarChooserDelegate), make it the root view controller of a UINavigationController, and show the navigation controller as a presented view controller (which looks best as a popover on the iPad). The `selectionStyle` dictates whether the user can pick one or multiple calendars; the `displayStyle` states whether all calendars or only writable calendars will be displayed. If access to the database has been denied, the interface will be empty and the user will simply cancel.

Two properties, `showsCancelButton` and `showsDoneButton`, determine whether these buttons will appear in the navigation bar. In a fullscreen presented view controller, you'll certainly show at least one and probably both, because otherwise the user has no way to dismiss the presented view controller!

There are three delegate methods, the first two being required:

- `calendarChooserDidFinish:` (the user tapped Done)
- `calendarChooserDidCancel:`
- `calendarChooserSelectionDidChange:`

In the `Finish` and `Cancel` methods, you should dismiss the presented view controller.

In this example, we implement a potentially destructive action: we offer to delete the selected calendar. Because this is potentially destructive, we pass through an action sheet for confirmation:

```
@IBAction func deleteCalendar (sender:AnyObject!) {
    let choo = EKCalendarChooser(
        selectionStyle:.Single,
        displayStyle:.AllCalendars,
        entityType:.Event,
        eventStore:self.database)
    choo.showsDoneButton = true
    choo.showsCancelButton = true
```

```
        choo.delegate = self
        let nav = UINavigationController(rootViewController: choo)
        nav.modalPresentationStyle = .Popover
        self.presentViewController(nav, animated: true, completion: nil)
        if let pop = nav.popoverPresentationController {
            if let v = sender as? UIView {
                pop.sourceView = v
                pop.sourceRect = v.bounds
            }
        }
    }
}
func calendarChooserDidCancel(calendarChooser: EKCalendarChooser) {
    self.dismissViewControllerAnimated(true, completion: nil)
}
func calendarChooserDidFinish(chooser: EKCalendarChooser) {
    let cals = chooser.selectedCalendars
    guard cals.count > 0 else {
        self.dismissViewControllerAnimated(true, completion:nil)
        return
    }
    let calsToDelete = cals.map {$0.calendarIdentifier}
    let alert = UIAlertController(
        title: "Delete selected calendar?", message: nil,
        preferredStyle: .ActionSheet)
    alert.addAction(UIAlertAction(
        title: "Cancel", style: .Cancel, handler: nil))
    alert.addAction(UIAlertAction(
        title: "Delete", style: .Destructive, handler: {
            _ in
            for id in calsToDelete {
                if let cal = self.database.calendarWithIdentifier(id) {
                    _ = try? self.database.removeCalendar(cal, commit:true)
                }
            }
            // dismiss *everything*
            self.dismissViewControllerAnimated(true, completion: nil)
    }))
    // alert sheet inside presented-or-popover
    chooser.presentViewController(alert, animated: true, completion: nil)
}
```

CHAPTER 20

Mail and Messages

Your app can present an interface allowing the user to edit and send a mail message or an SMS message. Two view controller classes are provided by the Message UI framework; you'll need to import MessageUI. In addition, the Social framework lets you post to Twitter or Facebook on the user's behalf. You'll need to import Social. The classes are:

MFMailComposeViewController
   Allows composition and sending of a mail message.

MFMessageComposeViewController
   Allows composition and sending of an SMS message.

SLComposeViewController
   Allows composition and sending of a Twitter or Facebook post. Alternatively, you can prepare and post a message directly using SLRequest.

UIActivityViewController (Chapter 13) also provides a unified interface for permitting the user to choose any of the built-in messaging milieus and to send a message through it. However, the Message UI framework and the Social framework remain important, because the user can be presented with a message form without having to pass through an activity view, and because you can fill in fields, such as the recipient field in a mail composition form, that UIActivityViewController doesn't let you fill in.

Another option is to form a URL of the appropriate scheme and hand it to UIApplication's openURL: method. For example, given a mailto: URL, openURL: can generate a proposed mail message with an initial recipient field and subject field. (See the *Apple URL Scheme Reference* for a list of built-in URL schemes.) That takes the user to the Mail app — and out of *your* app — but in iOS 9 that might not be so terrible, because a Back button appears in the status bar.

Mail Message

The MFMailComposeViewController class, a UINavigationController, allows the user to edit a mail message. The user can attempt to send the message there and then, or can cancel but save a draft, or can cancel completely. Before using this class to present a view, call `canSendMail`; if the result is `false`, go no further, as a negative result means that the device is not configured for sending mail. A positive result does not mean that the device is connected to the network and can send mail right now, only that sending mail is generally possible with this device; actually sending the mail message (or storing it as a draft) will be up to the device's internal processes.

To use MFMailComposeViewController, instantiate it, provide a `mailCompose-Delegate` (*not* `delegate`) adopting MFMailComposeViewControllerDelegate, and configure the message to any desired extent. Configuration methods are:

- `setSubject:`
- `setToRecipients:`
- `setCcRecipients:`
- `setBccRecipients:`
- `setMessageBody:isHTML:`
- `addAttachmentData:mimeType:fileName:`

Typically, you'll show the MFMailComposeViewController as a presented view controller. (On the iPad, a `.FormSheet` presentation feels less overwhelming.) The user can later alter your preset configurations, at which time the message details will be out of your hands.

The delegate method `mailComposeController:didFinishWithResult:error:` will be called, describing the user's final action, which might be any of these:

- `MFMailComposeResultCancelled`
- `MFMailComposeResultSaved`
- `MFMailComposeResultSent`
- `MFMailComposeResultFailed`

Dismissing the presented view controller is up to you, in the delegate method. Here's a minimal example:

```
@IBAction func doMail (sender:AnyObject!) {
    guard MFMailComposeViewController.canSendMail() else { return }
    let vc = MFMailComposeViewController()
    vc.mailComposeDelegate = self
```

```
        self.presentViewController(vc, animated:true, completion:nil)
    }
    func mailComposeController(
        controller: MFMailComposeViewController,
        didFinishWithResult result: MFMailComposeResult,
        error: NSError?) {
            // can do something with result here
            self.dismissViewControllerAnimated(true, completion: nil)
    }
```

Text Message

The MFMessageComposeViewController class is a UINavigationController subclass. Before using this class to present a view, call `canSendText`; if the result is `false`, go no further. The user has no option to save an SMS message as a draft, so even if this device sometimes *can* send text, there's no point proceeding if the device can't send text *now*. However, you can register for the `MFMessageComposeViewControllerTextMessage-AvailabilityDidChangeNotification` in the hope that the device might later be able to send text; if the notification arrives, examine its `MFMessageComposeViewController-TextMessageAvailabilityKey`.

To use MFMessageComposeViewController, instantiate the class, give it a `message-ComposeDelegate` (*not* `delegate`) adopting MFMessageComposeViewController-Delegate, and configure it as desired through the `recipients` (phone number strings) and body properties. You can also configure the message subject and provide attachments. For the subject, call the class method `canSendSubject`, and if it returns `true`, you can set the `subject`. For attachments, call the class method `canSendAttachments`, and if it returns `true`, you may want to call `isSupportedAttachmentUTI:` to see if a particular file type can be sent as an attachment; finally, call `addAttachmentURL:with-AlternateFilename:` (if you have a file URL) or `addAttachmentData:type-Identifier:filename:`. Conversely, you can prevent the user from adding attachments by calling `disableUserAttachments`.

When you've finished configuring the MFMessageComposeViewController, show it as a presented view controller. The user can later alter your preset configurations, at which time the message details will be out of your hands.

The delegate method `messageComposeViewController:didFinishWithResult:` will be called with a description of the user's final action, which might be any of these:

- `MessageComposeResultCancelled`
- `MessageComposeResultSent`
- `MessageComposeResultFailed`

Dismissing the presented view controller is up to you, in the delegate method. Here's a minimal example:

```
@IBAction func doMessage (sender:AnyObject!) {
    guard MFMessageComposeViewController.canSendText() else { return }
    let vc = MFMessageComposeViewController()
    vc.messageComposeDelegate = self
    self.presentViewController(vc, animated:true, completion:nil)
}
func messageComposeViewController(
    controller: MFMessageComposeViewController,
    didFinishWithResult result: MessageComposeResult) {
        // can do something with result here
        self.dismissViewControllerAnimated(true, completion: nil)
}
```

Twitter Post

The interface for letting the user construct a Twitter post is SLComposeViewController, part of the Social framework. Twitter, together with Facebook (and Weibo), are represented by constant strings starting with SLServiceType. You'll use the class method isAvailableForServiceType: to learn whether the desired service is available; if it is, you can instantiate SLComposeViewController for that service and present it as a presented view controller.

SLComposeViewController has a more modern API than the mail and message view controllers. Instead of a delegate, SLComposeViewController has a completion-Handler. Set it to a function taking one parameter, an SLComposeViewControllerResult. In the function, dismiss the view controller. The SLComposeViewControllerResult parameter will be .Cancelled or .Done. Here's a minimal example:

```
@IBAction func doTwitter (sender:AnyObject!) {
    guard SLComposeViewController
        .isAvailableForServiceType(SLServiceTypeTwitter) else { return }
    guard let vc = SLComposeViewController(
        forServiceType:SLServiceTypeTwitter) else { return }
    vc.completionHandler = {
        (result:SLComposeViewControllerResult) in
        // can do something with result here
        self.dismissViewControllerAnimated(true, completion:nil)
    };
    self.presentViewController(vc, animated:true, completion:nil)
}
```

You can also, with the user's permission, gain secure access to the user's account information through the ACAccountStore class (part of the Accounts framework). Using this, along with the SLRequest class, your app can construct and post a message *directly*, without passing through the message composition interface. The ACAccount-

Store class can manipulate accounts in other ways as well, without violating the user's privacy.

CHAPTER 21

Maps

Your app can imitate the Maps app, displaying a map interface and placing annotations and overlays on the map. The relevant classes are provided by the Map Kit framework. You'll need to `import MapKit`. The classes used to describe locations in terms of latitude and longitude, whose names start with "CL," come from the Core Location framework, but you won't need to import it explicitly.

Displaying a Map

A map is displayed through a UIView subclass, an MKMapView.

 You can instantiate an MKMapView from a nib. However, you will then need to link your target manually to the MapKit framework: edit the target and add *MapKit.framework* under Linked Frameworks and Libraries in the General tab.

A map has a `type`, which is one of the following (MKMapType):

- `.Standard`
- `.Satellite`
- `.Hybrid`

The area displayed on the map is its `region`, an MKCoordinateRegion. This is a struct comprising a location (its `center`, a CLLocationCoordinate2D), describing the latitude and longitude of the point at the center of the region, along with a `span` (an MKCoordinateSpan), describing the quantity of latitude and longitude embraced by the region and hence the scale of the map. Convenience functions help you construct an MKCoordinateRegion.

Figure 21-1. A map view showing a happy place

In this example, I'll initialize the display of an MKMapView (`self.map`) to show a place where I like to go dirt biking (Figure 21-1):

```
let loc = CLLocationCoordinate2DMake(34.927752,-120.217608)
let span = MKCoordinateSpanMake(0.015, 0.015)
let reg = MKCoordinateRegionMake(loc, span)
self.map.region = reg
```

An MKCoordinateSpan is described in degrees of latitude and longitude. It may be, however, that what you know is the region's proposed dimensions in meters. To convert, call `MKCoordinateRegionMakeWithDistance`. The ability to perform this conversion is important, because an MKMapView shows the world through a Mercator projection, where longitude lines are parallel and equidistant, and scale increases at higher latitudes.

I happen to know that the area I want to display is about 1200 meters on a side. Hence, this is another way of displaying roughly the same region:

```
let loc = CLLocationCoordinate2DMake(34.927752,-120.217608)
let reg = MKCoordinateRegionMakeWithDistance(loc, 1200, 1200)
self.map.region = reg
```

Yet another way of describing a map region is with an MKMapRect, a struct built up from MKMapPoint and MKMapSize. The earth has already been projected onto the map for us, and now we are describing a rectangle of that map, in terms of the units in which the map is drawn. The exact relationship between an MKMapPoint and the corresponding latitude/longitude coordinates is arbitrary and of no interest; what matters is that you can ask for the conversion, along with the ratio of points to meters (which will vary with latitude):

- `MKMapPointForCoordinate`

- MKCoordinateForMapPoint

- MKMetersPerMapPointAtLatitude

- MKMapPointsPerMeterAtLatitude

- MKMetersBetweenMapPoints

To determine what the map view is showing in MKMapRect terms, use its visibleMap-Rect property. Thus, this is another way of displaying approximately the same region:

```
let loc = CLLocationCoordinate2DMake(34.927752,-120.217608)
let pt = MKMapPointForCoordinate(loc)
let w = MKMapPointsPerMeterAtLatitude(loc.latitude) * 1200
self.map.visibleMapRect = MKMapRectMake(pt.x - w/2.0, pt.y - w/2.0, w, w)
```

In none of those examples did I bother with the question of the actual dimensions of the map view itself. I simply threw a proposed region at the map view, and it decided how best to portray the corresponding area. Values you assign to the map's region and visibleMapRect are unlikely to be the exact values the map adopts in any case; that's because the map view will optimize for display without distorting the map's scale. You can perform this same optimization in code by calling these methods:

- regionThatFits:

- mapRectThatFits:

- mapRectThatFits:edgePadding:

By default, the user can zoom and scroll the map with the usual gestures; you can turn this off by setting the map view's zoomEnabled and scrollEnabled to false. Usually you will set them both to true or both to false. For further customization of an MKMapView's response to touches, use a UIGestureRecognizer (Chapter 5).

You can change programmatically the region displayed, optionally with animation, by calling these methods:

- setRegion:animated:

- setCenterCoordinate:animated:

- setVisibleMapRect:animated:

- setVisibleMapRect:edgePadding:animated:

The map view's delegate (MKMapViewDelegate) is notified as the map loads and as the region changes (including changes triggered programmatically):

- mapViewWillStartLoadingMap:

- mapViewDidFinishLoadingMap:

- `mapViewDidFailLoadingMap:withError:`

- `mapView:regionWillChangeAnimated:`

- `mapView:regionDidChangeAnimated:`

You can also enable 3D viewing of the map (`pitchEnabled`), and there's a large and powerful API putting control of 3D viewing in your hands. Discussion of 3D map viewing is beyond the scope of this chapter; an excellent WWDC 2013 video surveys the topic. New in iOS 9 are 3D flyover map types `.SatelliteFlyover` and `.Hybrid-Flyover`; a WWDC 2015 video explains about these.

Also new in iOS 9, an MKMapView has Bool properties `showsCompass`, `showsScale`, and `showsTraffic`.

 Data types such as MKCoordinateSpan are documented in the *Map Kit Data Types Reference*, but convenience functions such as `MKCoordinateSpanMake` are documented in the *Map Kit Functions Reference* — and there are some useful constants in the *Map Kit Constants Reference*. For a better overview, refer to the *MKGeometry.h* header.

Annotations

An annotation is a marker associated with a location on a map. To make an annotation appear on a map, two objects are needed:

The object attached to the MKMapView
> The annotation itself is attached to the MKMapView. It consists of any instance whose class adopts the MKAnnotation protocol, which specifies a `coordinate`, a `title`, and a `subtitle` for the annotation. You might have reason to define your own class to handle this task, or you can use the simple built-in MKPointAnnotation class. The annotation's coordinate is crucial; it says where on earth the annotation should be drawn. The title and subtitle are optional, to be displayed in a callout.

The object that draws the annotation
> An annotation is drawn by an MKAnnotationView, a UIView subclass. This can be extremely simple. In fact, even a `nil` MKAnnotationView might be perfectly satisfactory: it draws a red pin. If red is not your favorite color, a built-in MKAnnotation-View subclass, MKPinAnnotationView, displays a pin in red, green, or purple (conventionally designating destination points, starting points, and user-specified points, respectively) — or, new in iOS 9, you are free to set an MKPinAnnotation-View's pin color (its `pinTintColor` property) to *any* UIColor.

Figure 21-2. A simple annotation

If a pin is not your thing, you can provide your own UIImage as the MKAnnotation-View's `image` property. And for even more flexibility, you can take over the drawing of an MKAnnotationView by overriding `drawRect:` in a subclass.

Not only does an annotation require two separate objects, but in fact those objects do not initially exist together. An annotation object has no pointer to the annotation view object that will draw it. Rather, it is up to you to supply the annotation view object in real time, on demand, in the MKMapView's delegate. This architecture may sound confusing, but in fact it's a very clever way of reducing the amount of resources needed at any given moment. An annotation itself is merely a lightweight object that a map can always possess; the corresponding annotation view is a heavyweight object that is needed only so long as that annotation's coordinates are within the visible portion of the map.

Let's add the simplest possible annotation to our map. The point where the annotation is to go has been stored in an instance variable:

```
self.annloc = CLLocationCoordinate2DMake(34.923964,-120.219558)
```

We create the annotation, configure its properties, and add it to the MKMapView:

```
let ann = MKPointAnnotation()
ann.coordinate = self.annloc
ann.title = "Park here"
ann.subtitle = "Fun awaits down the road!"
self.map.addAnnotation(ann)
```

That code is sufficient to produce Figure 21-2. I didn't implement any MKMapView delegate methods, so the MKAnnotationView is `nil`. But a `nil` MKAnnotationView, as I've already said, produces a red pin. I've also tapped the annotation, to display its callout, containing the annotation's title and subtitle.

Custom Annotation View

The location marked by our annotation is the starting point of a suggested dirt bike ride, so by convention the pin should be green. We can easily create a green pin using MKPinAnnotationView, which has a `pinTintColor` property. To supply the annotation view, we must give the map view a delegate (MKMapViewDelegate) and implement `map-View:viewForAnnotation:`.

The structure of `mapView:viewForAnnotation:` is rather similar to the structure of `tableView:cellForRowAtIndexPath:` (Chapter 8), which is not surprising, considering that they both do the same sort of thing. Recall that the goal of `tableView:cellForRow-AtIndexPath:` is to allow the table view to reuse cells, so that at any given moment only as many cells are needed as are *visible* in the table view, regardless of how many rows the table as a whole may consist of. The same thing holds for a map and its annotation views. The map may have a huge number of annotations, but it needs to display annotation views for only those annotations that are within its current `region`. Any extra annotation views that have been scrolled out of view can thus be reused and are held for us by the map view in a cache for exactly this purpose.

So, in `mapView:viewForAnnotation:`, we start by calling `dequeueReusableAnnotation-ViewWithIdentifier:` to see whether there's an already existing annotation view that's not currently being displayed and that we might be able to reuse. If there isn't, we create one, attaching to it an appropriate reuse identifier.

Here's our implementation of `mapView:viewForAnnotation:`. Observe that in creating our green pin, we explicitly set its `canShowCallout` to `true`, as this is not the default:

```
func mapView(mapView: MKMapView,
    viewForAnnotation annotation: MKAnnotation) -> MKAnnotationView? {
        var v : MKAnnotationView! = nil
        if let t = annotation.title where t == "Park here" { ❶
            let ident = "greenPin" ❷
            v = mapView.dequeueReusableAnnotationViewWithIdentifier(ident)
            if v == nil {
                v = MKPinAnnotationView(
                    annotation:annotation, reuseIdentifier:ident)
                (v as! MKPinAnnotationView).pinTintColor =
                    MKPinAnnotationView.greenPinColor()
                v.canShowCallout = true
            }
            v.annotation = annotation ❸
        }
        return v
}
```

The structure of this implementation of `mapView:viewForAnnotation:` is typical (though it seems pointlessly elaborate when we have only one annotation in our map):

❶   We might have more than one reusable type of annotation view, so we must somehow distinguish the possible cases, based on *something about the incoming annotation*. Here, I use the annotation's title as a distinguishing mark; later in this chapter, I'll suggest a much better approach.

❷ For each reusable type, we proceed much as with table view cells. We have an identifier that categorizes this sort of reusable view. We try to dequeue an unused annotation view of the appropriate type. If we can't, we'll get `nil`; in that case, we create an MKAnnotationView and configure it (compare Example 8-1).

❸ Even if we *can* dequeue an unused annotation view, and even if we have no other configuration to perform, we *must* associate the annotation view with the incoming annotation by assigning the annotation to this annotation view's `annotation` property. Forgetting to do this is a common beginner mistake.

MKPinAnnotationView has one more option of which we might avail ourselves: when it draws the annotation view (the pin), it can animate it into place, dropping it in the manner familiar from the Maps app. All we have to do is add one line of code:

```
(v as! MKPinAnnotationView).animatesDrop = true
```

Now let's go further. Instead of a pin, we'll substitute our own artwork. I'll revise the code at the heart of my `mapView:viewForAnnotation:` implementation, such that instead of creating an MKPinAnnotationView, I create an instance of its superclass, MKAnnotationView, and give it a custom image showing a dirt bike. The image is too large, so I shrink the view's bounds before returning it; I also move the view up a bit, so that the bottom of the image is at the coordinates on the map (Figure 21-3):

```
func mapView(mapView: MKMapView,
    viewForAnnotation annotation: MKAnnotation) -> MKAnnotationView? {
        var v : MKAnnotationView! = nil
        if let t = annotation.title where t == "Park here" {
            let ident = "bike"
            v = mapView.dequeueReusableAnnotationViewWithIdentifier(ident)
            if v == nil {
                v = MKAnnotationView(
                    annotation:annotation, reuseIdentifier:ident)
                v.image = UIImage(named:"clipartdirtbike.gif")
                v.bounds.size.height /= 3.0
                v.bounds.size.width /= 3.0
                v.centerOffset = CGPointMake(0,-20)
                v.canShowCallout = true
            }
            v.annotation = annotation
        }
        return v
}
```

For more flexibility, we can create our own MKAnnotationView subclass and endow it with the ability to draw itself. At a minimum, such a subclass should override the initializer and assign itself a frame, and should implement `drawRect:`. Here's the implementation for a class MyAnnotationView that draws a dirt bike:

Figure 21-3. A custom annotation image

```
class MyAnnotationView : MKAnnotationView {
    override init(annotation:MKAnnotation?, reuseIdentifier:String?) {
        super.init(
            annotation: annotation, reuseIdentifier: reuseIdentifier)
        let im = UIImage(named:"clipartdirtbike.gif")!
        self.frame = CGRectMake(
            0, 0, im.size.width / 3.0 + 5, im.size.height / 3.0 + 5)
        self.centerOffset = CGPointMake(0,-20)
        self.opaque = false
    }
    override init(frame: CGRect) {
        super.init(frame:frame)
    }
    required init(coder: NSCoder) {
        fatalError("NSCoding not supported")
    }
    override func drawRect(rect: CGRect) {
        let im = UIImage(named:"clipartdirtbike.gif")!
        im.drawInRect(self.bounds.insetBy(dx: 5, dy: 5))
    }
}
```

The corresponding implementation of `mapView:viewForAnnotation:` now has much less work to do:

```
func mapView(mapView: MKMapView,
    viewForAnnotation annotation: MKAnnotation) -> MKAnnotationView? {
        var v : MKAnnotationView! = nil
        if let t = annotation.title where t == "Park here" {
            let ident = "bike"
            v = mapView.dequeueReusableAnnotationViewWithIdentifier(ident)
            if v == nil {
                v = MyAnnotationView(
                    annotation:annotation, reuseIdentifier:ident)
                v.canShowCallout = true
            }
            v.annotation = annotation
        }
        return v
}
```

Custom Annotation Class

For ultimate flexibility, we can provide our own annotation class as well. A minimal annotation class will look like this:

```
class MyAnnotation : NSObject, MKAnnotation {
    dynamic var coordinate: CLLocationCoordinate2D
    var title: String?
    var subtitle: String?
    init(location coord:CLLocationCoordinate2D) {
        self.coordinate = coord
        super.init()
    }
}
```

Now when we create our annotation and add it to our map, our code looks like this:

```
let ann = MyAnnotation(location:self.annloc)
ann.title = "Park here"
ann.subtitle = "Fun awaits down the road!"
self.map.addAnnotation(ann)
```

A major advantage of this change appears in our implementation of `mapView:viewForAnnotation:`, where we test for the annotation type. Formerly, it wasn't easy to distinguish those annotations that needed to be drawn as a dirt bike; we were rather artificially examining the title:

```
if let t = annotation.title where t == "Park here" {
```

Now, however, we can just look at the class:

```
if annotation is MyAnnotation {
```

A further advantage of supplying our own annotation class is that this approach gives our implementation room to grow. For example, at the moment, every MyAnnotation is drawn as a bike, but we could now add another property to MyAnnotation that tells us what drawing to use. We could also give MyAnnotation further properties saying such things as which way the bike should face, what angle it should be drawn at, and so on. Each instance of MyAnnotationView will end up with a reference to the corresponding MyAnnotation instance (as its `annotation` property), so it would be able to read those MyAnnotation properties and draw itself appropriately.

Other Annotation Features

To add our own animation to an annotation view as it appears on the map, analogous to the built-in MKPinAnnotationView pin-drop animation, we implement the map view delegate method `mapView:didAddAnnotationViews:`. The key fact here is that at the moment this method is called, the annotation view has been added but the redraw moment has not yet arrived (Chapter 4). So if we animate the view, that animation will be performed at the moment the view appears onscreen. Here, I'll animate the opacity of the view so that it fades in, while growing the view from a point to its full size; I identify the view type through its `reuseIdentifier`:

```
func mapView(mapView: MKMapView,
    didAddAnnotationViews views: [MKAnnotationView]) {
        for aView in views {
            if aView.reuseIdentifier == "bike" {
                aView.transform = CGAffineTransformMakeScale(0, 0)
                aView.alpha = 0
                UIView.animateWithDuration(0.8) {
                    aView.alpha = 1
                    aView.transform = CGAffineTransformIdentity
                }
            }
        }
    }
}
```

The callout is visible in Figures 21-2 and 21-3 because before taking the screenshot, I tapped on the annotation, thus *selecting* it. MKMapView has methods allowing annotations to be selected or deselected programmatically, thus (by default) causing their callouts to appear or disappear. The delegate has methods notifying you when the user selects or deselects an annotation, and you are free to override your custom MKAnnotationView's `setSelected:animated:` if you want to change what happens when the user taps an annotation. For example, you could show and hide a custom view instead of, or in addition to, the built-in callout.

A callout can contain left and right accessory views; these are the MKAnnotationView's `leftCalloutAccessoryView` and `rightCalloutAccessoryView`. They are UIViews, and should be small (less than 32 pixels in height). New in iOS 9, there is also a `detail-CalloutAccessoryView` which replaces the subtitle; for example, you could supply a multiline label with smaller text, something that was quite difficult in earlier system versions. The map view's `tintColor` (see Chapter 12) affects such accessory view elements as template images and button titles. You can respond to taps on these views as you would any view or control; as a convenience, a delegate method `mapView:annotationView:calloutAccessoryControlTapped:` is called when the user taps an accessory view, provided it is a UIControl.

An MKAnnotationView can optionally be draggable by the user; set its `draggable` property to `true` and implement the map view delegate's `mapView:annotationView:didChangeDragState:fromOldState:`. A minimal implementation must update the MKAnnotationView's `dragState`, like this:

```
func mapView(mapView: MKMapView, annotationView view: MKAnnotationView,
    didChangeDragState newState: MKAnnotationViewDragState,
    fromOldState oldState: MKAnnotationViewDragState) {
        switch (newState) {
        case .Starting:
            view.dragState = .Dragging
```

```
        case .Ending, .Canceling:
            view.dragState = .None
        default: break
        }
    }
```

(You can also customize changes to the appearance of the view as it is dragged, by implementing your annotation view class's `setDragState:animated:` method.) If you're using a custom annotation class, its `coordinate` property must also be settable; in our custom annotation class, MyAnnotation, the `coordinate` property is explicitly declared as a read-write property (`var`), as opposed to the `coordinate` property in the MKAnnotation protocol which is read-only.

Certain annotation properties and annotation view properties are automatically animatable through view animation, provided you've implemented them in a KVO compliant way. For example, in MyAnnotation, the `coordinate` property is KVO compliant (because we declared it `dynamic`); therefore, we are able to animate shifting the annotation's position:

```
UIView.animateWithDuration(0.25) {
    var loc = ann.coordinate
    loc.latitude = loc.latitude + 0.0005
    loc.longitude = loc.longitude + 0.001
    ann.coordinate = loc
}
```

MKMapView has extensive support for adding and removing annotations. Also, given a bunch of annotations, you can ask your MKMapView to zoom in such a way that all of them are showing (`showAnnotations:animated:`).

Annotation views don't change size as the map is zoomed in and out, so if there are several annotations and they are brought close together by the user zooming out, the display can become crowded. Moreover, if too many annotations are being drawn simultaneously in a map view, scroll and zoom performance can degrade. The only way to prevent this is to respond to changes in the map's visible region (for example, in the delegate method `mapView:regionDidChangeAnimated:`) by removing and adding annotations dynamically. This is a tricky problem; MKMapView's `annotationsInMapRect:` efficiently lists the annotations within a given MKMapRect, but deciding which ones to eliminate or restore, and when, is still up to you.

Overlays

An overlay differs from an annotation in being drawn entirely with respect to points on the surface of the earth. Thus, whereas an annotation's size is always the same, an overlay's size is tied to the zoom of the map view.

Figure 21-4. An overlay

Overlays are implemented much like annotations. You provide an object that adopts the MKOverlay protocol (which itself conforms to the MKAnnotation protocol) and add it to the map view. When the map view delegate method `mapView:viewForOverlay:` is called, you provide an MKOverlayRenderer and hand it the overlay object; the overlay renderer then draws the overlay on demand. As with annotations, this architecture means that the overlay itself is a lightweight object, and the overlay is drawn only if the part of the earth that the overlay covers is actually being displayed in the map view. An MKOverlayRenderer has no reuse identifier.

Some built-in MKShape subclasses adopt the MKOverlay protocol: MKCircle, MKPolygon, and MKPolyline. In parallel to those, MKOverlayRenderer has built-in subclasses MKCircleRenderer, MKPolygonRenderer, and MKPolylineRenderer, ready to draw the corresponding shapes. Thus, as with annotations, you can base your overlay entirely on the power of existing classes.

In this example, I'll use MKPolygonRenderer to draw an overlay triangle pointing up the road from the parking place annotated in our earlier examples (Figure 21-4). We add the MKPolygon as an overlay to our map view, and derive the MKPolygonRenderer from it in our implementation of `mapView:viewForOverlay:`. First, the MKPolygon overlay:

```
let lat = self.annloc.latitude
let metersPerPoint = MKMetersPerMapPointAtLatitude(lat)
var c = MKMapPointForCoordinate(self.annloc)
c.x += 150/metersPerPoint
c.y -= 50/metersPerPoint
var p1 = MKMapPointMake(c.x, c.y)
p1.y -= 100/metersPerPoint
var p2 = MKMapPointMake(c.x, c.y)
p2.x += 100/metersPerPoint
var p3 = MKMapPointMake(c.x, c.y)
p3.x += 300/metersPerPoint
p3.y -= 400/metersPerPoint
var pts = [
```

```
        p1, p2, p3
    ]
    let tri = MKPolygon(points:&pts, count:3)
    self.map.addOverlay(tri)
```

Second, the delegate method, where we provide the MKPolygonRenderer:

```
func mapView(mapView: MKMapView,
    rendererForOverlay overlay: MKOverlay) -> MKOverlayRenderer {
        if let overlay = overlay as? MKPolygon {
            let v = MKPolygonRenderer(polygon:overlay)
            v.fillColor = UIColor.redColor().colorWithAlphaComponent(0.1)
            v.strokeColor = UIColor.redColor().colorWithAlphaComponent(0.8)
            v.lineWidth = 2
            return v
        }
        return MKOverlayRenderer()
}
```

Custom Overlay Class

The triangle in Figure 21-4 is rather crude; I could draw a better arrow shape using a CGPath (Chapter 2). The built-in MKOverlayRenderer subclass that lets me do that is MKOverlayPathRenderer. To structure things similarly to the preceding example, I'd like to supply the CGPath when I add the overlay instance to the map view. No built-in class lets me do that, so I'll use a custom class, MyOverlay, that adopts the MKOverlay protocol.

A minimal overlay class looks like this:

```
class MyOverlay : NSObject, MKOverlay {
    var coordinate : CLLocationCoordinate2D {
        get {
            let pt = MKMapPointMake(
                MKMapRectGetMidX(self.boundingMapRect),
                MKMapRectGetMidY(self.boundingMapRect))
            return MKCoordinateForMapPoint(pt)
        }
    }
    var boundingMapRect : MKMapRect
    init(rect:MKMapRect) {
        self.boundingMapRect = rect
        super.init()
    }
}
```

Our actual MyOverlay class will also have a path property; this will be a UIBezierPath that holds our CGPath and supplies it to the MKOverlayPathRenderer.

Just as the coordinate property of an annotation tells the map view where on earth the annotation is to be drawn, the boundingMapRect property of an overlay tells the map view where on earth the overlay is to be drawn. Whenever any part of the boundingMap-Rect is displayed within the map view's bounds, the map view will have to concern itself with drawing the overlay. With MKPolygon, we supplied the points of the polygon in earth coordinates and the boundingMapRect was calculated for us. With our custom overlay class, we must supply or calculate it ourselves.

At first it may appear that there is a typological impedance mismatch: the boundingMap-Rect is an MKMapRect, whereas a CGPath is defined by CGPoints. However, it turns out that these units are interchangeable: the CGPoints of our CGPath will be translated for us directly into MKMapPoints on the same scale — that is, the *distance* between any two CGPoints will be the distance between the two corresponding MKMapPoints. However, the *origins* are different: the CGPath must be described relative to the top-left corner of the boundingMapRect — to put it another way, the boundingMapRect is described in earth coordinates, but the top-left corner of the boundingMapRect is (0.0,0.0) as far as the CGPath is concerned. (You might think of this difference as analogous to the difference between a UIView's frame and its bounds.)

To make life simple, I'll think in meters; actually, I'll think in chunks of 75 meters, because this turns out to be a good unit for positioning and laying out the arrow. Thus, a line one unit long would in fact be 75 meters long if I were to arrive at this actual spot on the earth and discover the overlay literally drawn on the ground. Having derived this chunk (unit), I use it to lay out the boundingMapRect, four units on a side and positioned slightly east and north of the annotation point (because that's where the road is). Then I simply construct the arrow shape within the 4×4-unit square, rotating it so that it points in roughly the same direction as the road:

```
// start with our position and derive a nice unit for drawing
let lat = self.annloc.latitude
let metersPerPoint = MKMetersPerMapPointAtLatitude(lat)
let c = MKMapPointForCoordinate(self.annloc)
let unit = CGFloat(75.0/metersPerPoint)
// size and position the overlay bounds on the earth
let sz = CGSizeMake(4*unit, 4*unit)
let mr = MKMapRectMake(
    c.x + 2*Double(unit), c.y - 4.5*Double(unit),
    Double(sz.width), Double(sz.height))
// describe the arrow as a CGPath
let p = CGPathCreateMutable()
let start = CGPointMake(0, unit*1.5)
let p1 = CGPointMake(start.x+2*unit, start.y)
let p2 = CGPointMake(p1.x, p1.y-unit)
let p3 = CGPointMake(p2.x+unit*2, p2.y+unit*1.5)
let p4 = CGPointMake(p2.x, p2.y+unit*3)
let p5 = CGPointMake(p4.x, p4.y-unit)
let p6 = CGPointMake(p5.x-2*unit, p5.y)
var points = [
    start, p1, p2, p3, p4, p5, p6
]
```

Figure 21-5. A nicer overlay

```
// rotate the arrow around its center
let t1 = CGAffineTransformMakeTranslation(unit*2, unit*2)
let t2 = CGAffineTransformRotate(t1, CGFloat(-M_PI)/3.5)
var t3 = CGAffineTransformTranslate(t2, -unit*2, -unit*2)
CGPathAddLines(p, &t3, &points, 7)
CGPathCloseSubpath(p)
// create the overlay and give it the path
let over = MyOverlay(rect:mr)
over.path = UIBezierPath(CGPath:p)
// add the overlay to the map
self.map.addOverlay(over)
```

The delegate method, where we provide the MKOverlayPathRenderer, is simple. We pull the CGPath out of the MyOverlay instance and hand it to the MKOverlayPathRenderer, also telling the MKOverlayPathRenderer how to stroke and fill that path:

```
func mapView(mapView: MKMapView,
    rendererForOverlay overlay: MKOverlay) -> MKOverlayRenderer {
        if let overlay = overlay as? MyOverlay {
            let v = MKOverlayPathRenderer(overlay:overlay)
            v.path = overlay.path.CGPath
            v.fillColor = UIColor.redColor().colorWithAlphaComponent(0.2)
            v.strokeColor = UIColor.blackColor()
            v.lineWidth = 2
            return v
        }
        return MKOverlayRenderer()
}
```

The result is a much nicer arrow (Figure 21-5), and of course this technique can be generalized to draw an overlay from any CGPath we like.

Custom Overlay Renderer

For full generality, you could define your own MKOverlayRenderer subclass; your subclass must override and implement drawMapRect:zoomScale:inContext:. The incoming mapRect: parameter describes a tile of the visible map (not the size and position of the overlay). The overlay itself is available through the inherited overlay property, and conversion methods such as `rectForMapRect:` are provided for converting between the map's `mapRect:` coordinates and the overlay renderer's graphics context coordinates.

In our example, we can move the entire functionality for drawing the arrow into an MKOverlayRenderer subclass, which I'll call MyOverlayRenderer. Its initializer takes an `angle:` parameter, with which I'll set its `angle` property; now our arrow can point in any direction. Another nice benefit of this architectural change is that we can use the `zoomScale:` parameter to determine the stroke width. For simplicity, our implementation of `drawMapRect:zoomScale:inContext:` ignores the incoming `mapRect` value and just draws the entire arrow every time it is called:

```
var angle : CGFloat
init(overlay:MKOverlay, angle:CGFloat) {
    self.angle = angle
    super.init(overlay:overlay)
}
override func drawMapRect(
    mapRect: MKMapRect, zoomScale: MKZoomScale,
    inContext context: CGContext) {
        CGContextSetStrokeColorWithColor(
            context, UIColor.blackColor().CGColor)
        CGContextSetFillColorWithColor(context,
            UIColor.redColor().colorWithAlphaComponent(0.2).CGColor)
        CGContextSetLineWidth(context, 1.2/zoomScale)
        let unit =
            CGFloat(MKMapRectGetWidth(self.overlay.boundingMapRect)/4.0)
        let p = CGPathCreateMutable()
        let start = CGPointMake(0, unit*1.5)
        let p1 = CGPointMake(start.x+2*unit, start.y)
        let p2 = CGPointMake(p1.x, p1.y-unit)
        let p3 = CGPointMake(p2.x+unit*2, p2.y+unit*1.5)
        let p4 = CGPointMake(p3.x, p2.y+unit*3)
        let p5 = CGPointMake(p4.x, p4.y-unit)
        let p6 = CGPointMake(p5.x-2*unit, p5.y)
        let points = [
            start, p1, p2, p3, p4, p5, p6
        ]
        // rotate the arrow around its center
        let t1 = CGAffineTransformMakeTranslation(unit*2, unit*2)
        let t2 = CGAffineTransformRotate(t1, self.angle)
        var t3 = CGAffineTransformTranslate(t2, -unit*2, -unit*2)
        CGPathAddLines(p, &t3, points, 7)
        CGPathCloseSubpath(p)
        CGContextAddPath(context, p)
        CGContextDrawPath(context, .FillStroke)
}
```

To add the overlay to our map, we still must determine its MKMapRect:

```
    let lat = self.annloc.latitude
    let metersPerPoint = MKMetersPerMapPointAtLatitude(lat)
    let c = MKMapPointForCoordinate(self.annloc)
    let unit = 75.0/metersPerPoint
    // size and position the overlay bounds on the earth
    let sz = CGSizeMake(4*CGFloat(unit), 4*CGFloat(unit))
    let mr = MKMapRectMake(
        c.x + 2*unit, c.y - 4.5*unit,
        Double(sz.width), Double(sz.height))
    let over = MyOverlay(rect:mr)
    self.map.addOverlay(over)
```

The delegate, providing the overlay renderer, now has very little work to do; in our implementation, it merely supplies an angle for the arrow:

```
func mapView(mapView: MKMapView,
    rendererForOverlay overlay: MKOverlay) -> MKOverlayRenderer {
        if overlay is MyOverlay {
            let v = MyOverlayRenderer(
                overlay:overlay, angle: -CGFloat(M_PI)/3.5)
            return v
        }
        return MKOverlayRenderer()
}
```

Other Overlay Features

Our MyOverlay class, adopting the MKOverlay protocol, also implements the coordinate getter method to return the center of the boundingMapRect. This is crude, but it's a good minimal implementation. The purpose of the MKOverlay coordinate property is to specify the position where you would add an annotation describing the overlay. For example:

```
// ... create overlay and assign it a path as before ...
self.map.addOverlay(over)
let annot = MKPointAnnotation()
annot.coordinate = over.coordinate
annot.title = "This way!"
self.map.addAnnotation(annot)
```

The MKOverlay protocol also lets you provide an implementation of intersectsMap-Rect: to refine your overlay's definition of what constitutes an intersection with itself; the default is to use the boundingMapRect, but if your overlay is drawn in some non-rectangular shape, you might want to use its actual shape as the basis for determining intersection.

Overlays are maintained by the map view as an array and are drawn from back to front starting at the beginning of the array. MKMapView has extensive support for adding and removing overlays, and for managing their layering order. When you add the overlay to the map, you can say where you want it drawn among the map view's sublayers;

methods for adding and inserting overlays have a `level:` parameter (for example, `add-Overlay:level:`). The levels are (MKOverlayLevel):

- `.AboveRoads` (and below labels)
- `.AboveLabels`

The MKTileOverlay class, adopting the MKOverlay protocol, lets you superimpose, or even substitute (`canReplaceMapContent`), a map view's drawing of the map itself. It works much like CATiledLayer (Chapter 7): you provide a set of tiles at multiple sizes to match multiple zoom levels, and the map view fetches and draws the tiles needed for the current `region` and degree of zoom. In this way, for example, you could integrate your own topo map into an MKMapView's display. It takes a lot of tiles to draw an area of any size, so MKTileOverlay starts with a URL, which can be a remote URL for tiles to be fetched across the Internet.

Map Kit and Current Location

A device may have sensors that can report its current location (Chapter 22). Map Kit provides simple integration with these facilities. Keep in mind that the user can turn off these sensors or can refuse your app access to them (in the Settings app, under Privacy → Location Services), so trying to use these features may fail. Also, determining the device's location can take time.

You can ask an MKMapView in your app to display the device's location just by setting its `showsUserLocation` property to `true`; the map will then automatically put an annotation at that location. However, you must obtain authorization first. You'll need a CLLocationManager instance — the usual thing is to retain it in a property — and you'll request authorization through the instance method `requestWhenInUse-Authorization`. Also, you must have an `NSLocationWhenInUseUsageDescription` entry in your app's *Info.plist*. (I'll talk more about location authorization in Chapter 22.)

The `userLocation` property of the map view is an MKUserLocation, adopting the MKAnnotation protocol. It has a `location` property, a CLLocation, whose `coordinate` is a CLLocationCoordinate2D; if the map view's `showsUserLocation` is `true` and the map view has actually worked out the user's location, the `coordinate` describes that location. It also has `title` and `subtitle` properties, plus you can check whether it is currently `updating`. The default annotation appearance comes from the map view's `tintColor`. You are free to supply your own annotation view to be displayed for this annotation, just as for any annotation.

Displaying the appropriate region of the map — that is, actually *showing* the part of the world where the user is located — is a separate task. The simplest way is to take advantage of the MKMapView's `userTrackingMode` property, which determines how the user's real-world location should be tracked *automatically* by the map display; your options are (MKUserTrackingMode):

.None

> If showsUserLocation is true, the map gets an annotation at the user's location, but that's all; the map's region is unchanged. You could set it manually by responding to the delegate method mapView:didUpdateUserLocation:.

.Follow

> Setting this mode sets showsUserLocation to true. The map automatically centers the user's location and scales appropriately. When the map is in this mode, you should *not* set the map's region manually, as you'll be struggling against the tracking mode's attempts to do the same thing.

.FollowWithHeading

> Like .Follow, but the map is also rotated so that the direction the user is facing is up. In this case, the userLocation annotation also has a heading property, a CLHeading; I'll talk more about headings in Chapter 22.

So, presume we have a CLLocationManager property:

```
let locman = CLLocationManager()
```

Then this code is sufficient to start displaying the user's location:

```
self.locman.requestWhenInUseAuthorization()
self.map.userTrackingMode = .Follow // sets showsUserLocation to true
```

When the userTrackingMode is one of the Follow modes, if the user is left free to zoom and scroll the map, and if the user scrolls in such a way that the user location annotation is no longer visible, the userTrackingMode may be automatically changed back to .None (and the user location annotation may be removed). You'll probably want to provide a way to let the user turn tracking back on again, or to toggle among the three tracking modes.

One way to do that is with an MKUserTrackingBarButtonItem, a UIBarButtonItem subclass. You initialize MKUserTrackingBarButtonItem with a map view, and its behavior is automatic from then on: when the user taps it, it switches the map view to the next tracking mode, and its icon reflects the current tracking mode. This is the same bar button item that appears at the far left in the toolbar of the Maps app.

You can ask the map view whether the user's location, if known, is in the visible region of the map (isUserLocationVisible).

It is also possible to ask the Maps app to display the device's current location, as I'll describe in the next section.

Figure 21-6. The Maps app displays our point of interest

Communicating With the Maps App

Your app can communicate with the Maps app. For example, instead of displaying a point of interest in a map view in our own app, we can ask the Maps app to display it. The user could then bookmark or share the location. The channel of communication between your app and the Maps app is the MKMapItem class.

Here, I'll ask the Maps app to display the same point marked by the annotation in our earlier examples, on a hybrid map portraying the same region of the earth (Figure 21-6):

```
let p = MKPlacemark(coordinate:self.annloc, addressDictionary:nil)
let mi = MKMapItem(placemark: p)
mi.name = "A Great Place to Dirt Bike" // label to appear in Maps app
let opts = [
    MKLaunchOptionsMapTypeKey: MKMapType.Hybrid.rawValue
]
mi.openInMapsWithLaunchOptions(opts)
```

 In theory it should be possible to set the zoom level of the Maps app display with the MKLaunchOptionsMapSpanKey key, but in my experimentation this has no effect. I regard that as a bug.

If you start with an MKMapItem returned by the class method `mapItemForCurrentLocation`, you're asking the Maps app to display the device's current location. This call doesn't attempt to determine the device's location, nor does it contain any location information; it merely generates an MKMapItem which, when sent to the Maps app, will cause *it* to attempt to determine (and display) the device's location:

```
let mi = MKMapItem.mapItemForCurrentLocation()
mi.openInMapsWithLaunchOptions(
    [MKLaunchOptionsMapTypeKey: MKMapType.Standard.rawValue])
```

Geocoding, Searching, and Directions

Map Kit provides your app with three services that involve performing queries over the network. These services take time and might not succeed at all, as they depend upon network and server availability; moreover, results may be more or less uncertain. Therefore, they involve a completion handler that is called back asynchronously on the main thread. The three services are:

Geocoding
Translation of a street address to a coordinate and *vice versa*. For example, what address am I at right now? Or conversely, what are the coordinates of my home address?

Searching
Lookup of possible matches for a natural language search. For example, what are some Thai restaurants near me?

Directions
Lookup of turn-by-turn instructions and route mapping from a source location to a destination location.

The completion handler is called, in every case, with a single response object plus an NSError. If the response object is `nil`, the NSError tells you what the problem was.

Geocoding

Geocoding functionality is encapsulated in the CLGeocoder class. The response, if things went well, is an array of CLPlacemark objects, a series of guesses from best to worst; if things went *really* well, the array will contain exactly one CLPlacemark.

A CLPlacemark can be used to initialize an MKPlacemark, a CLPlacemark subclass that adopts the MKAnnotation protocol, and is therefore suitable to be handed directly over to an MKMapView for display.

Here is an (unbelievably simpleminded) example that allows the user to enter an address in a UISearchBar (Chapter 12) to be displayed in an MKMapView:

```
let s = searchBar.text
let geo = CLGeocoder()
geo.geocodeAddressString(s) {
    (placemarks : [CLPlacemark]?, error : NSError?) in
```

```
        guard let placemarks = placemarks else { return }
        self.map.showsUserLocation = false
        let p = placemarks[0]
        let mp = MKPlacemark(placemark:p)
        self.map.removeAnnotations(self.map.annotations)
        self.map.addAnnotation(mp)
        self.map.setRegion(
            MKCoordinateRegionMakeWithDistance(mp.coordinate, 1000, 1000),
            animated: true)
    }
```

By default, the resulting annotation's callout `title` contains a nicely formatted string describing the address.

The converse operation is *reverse geocoding*: you start with a coordinate — actually a CLLocation, which you'll obtain from elsewhere, or construct from a coordinate using `init(latitude:longitude:)` — and call `reverseGeocodeLocation:completion-Handler:` in order to obtain an address. The address is expressed through the CLPlacemark `addressDictionary` property, whose rather curious key names are left over from the now-deprecated Address Book framework (they have not been updated to match the structure of a CNPostalAddress; see Chapter 18). You can consult directly various CLPlacemark properties, such as `subthoroughfare` (a house number), `thoroughfare` (a street name), `locality` (a town), and `administrativeArea` (a state); the `"FormattedAddressLines"` key yields an array of strings, one per line of the printed address.

In this example of reverse geocoding, we have an MKMapView that is already tracking the user, and so we have the user's location as the map's `userLocation`; we ask for the corresponding address:

```
    guard let loc = self.map.userLocation.location else { return }
    let geo = CLGeocoder()
    geo.reverseGeocodeLocation(loc) {
        (placemarks : [CLPlacemark]?, error : NSError?) in
        guard let ps = placemarks where ps.count > 0 else {return}
        let p = ps[0]
        if let d = p.addressDictionary {
            if let add = d["FormattedAddressLines"] as? [String] {
                for line in add {
                    print(line)
                }
            }
        }
    }
```

Searching

The MKLocalSearch class, along with MKLocalSearchRequest and MKLocalSearch-Response, lets you ask the server to perform a natural language search for you. This is less formal than forward geocoding, described in the previous section; instead of searching for an address, you can search for a point of interest by name or description. It can be useful, for some types of search, to constrain the area of interest by setting the MKLocalSearchRequest's `region`. In this example, I'll do a natural language search for a Thai restaurant near the user location currently displayed in the map, and I'll display it with an annotation in our map view:

```
guard let loc = self.map.userLocation.location else { return }
let req = MKLocalSearchRequest()
req.naturalLanguageQuery = "Thai restaurant"
req.region = MKCoordinateRegionMake(
    loc.coordinate, MKCoordinateSpanMake(1,1))
let search = MKLocalSearch(request:req)
search.startWithCompletionHandler() {
    (response : MKLocalSearchResponse?, error : NSError?) in
    guard let response = response else { print(error); return }
    self.map.showsUserLocation = false
    let mi = response.mapItems[0] // I'm feeling lucky
    let place = mi.placemark
    let loc = place.location!.coordinate
    let reg = MKCoordinateRegionMakeWithDistance(loc, 1200, 1200)
    self.map.setRegion(reg, animated:true)
    let ann = MKPointAnnotation()
    ann.title = mi.name
    ann.subtitle = mi.phoneNumber
    ann.coordinate = loc
    self.map.addAnnotation(ann)
}
```

Directions

The MKDirections class, along with MKDirectionsRequest and MKDirections-Response, looks up walking or driving directions between two locations expressed as MKMapItem objects. The resulting MKDirectionsResponse includes an array of MKRoute objects; each MKRoute includes an MKPolyline suitable for display as an overlay in your map, as well as an array of MKRouteStep objects, each of which provides its own MKPolyline plus instructions and distances. The MKDirectionsResponse also has its own `source` and `destination` MKMapItems, which may be different from what we started with.

To illustrate, I'll continue from the Thai food example in the previous section, starting at the point where we obtained the Thai restaurant's MKMapItem:

```
// ... same as before up to this point ...
let mi = response.mapItems[0] // I'm still feeling lucky
let req = MKDirectionsRequest()
req.source = MKMapItem.mapItemForCurrentLocation()
req.destination = mi
let dir = MKDirections(request:req)
```

```
dir.calculateDirectionsWithCompletionHandler() {
    (response:MKDirectionsResponse?, error:NSError?) in
    guard let response = response else { print(error); return }
    let route = response.routes[0] // I'm feeling really lucky
    let poly = route.polyline
    self.map.addOverlay(poly)
    for step in route.steps {
        print("After \(step.distance) metres: \(step.instructions)")
    }
}
```

The step-by-step instructions appear in the console; in real life, of course, we would presumably display these in our app's interface. The route is drawn in our map view, provided we have an appropriate implementation of mapView:rendererForOverlay:, such as this:

```
func mapView(mapView: MKMapView,
    rendererForOverlay overlay: MKOverlay) -> MKOverlayRenderer {
        if let overlay = overlay as? MKPolyline {
            let v = MKPolylineRenderer(polyline:overlay)
            v.strokeColor = UIColor.blueColor().colorWithAlphaComponent(0.8)
            v.lineWidth = 2
            return v
        }
        return MKOverlayRenderer()
}
```

You can also ask MKDirections to estimate the time of arrival, by calling calculate-ETAWithCompletionHandler:, and iOS 9 introduces arrival time estimation for some public transit systems (and you can tell the Maps app to display a transit directions map).

CHAPTER 22

Sensors

A device may contain hardware for sensing the world around itself — where it is located, how it is oriented, how it is moving.

Information about the device's current location and how that location is changing over time, using its Wi-Fi, cellular networking, and GPS capabilities, along with information about the device's orientation relative to north, using its magnetometer, is provided through the Core Location framework. You'll need to `import CoreLocation`.

Information about the device's change in speed and attitude using its accelerometer is provided through the UIEvent class (for device shake) and the Core Motion framework, which provides increased accuracy by incorporating the device's gyroscope, if it has one, as well as the magnetometer; you'll need to `import CoreMotion`. In addition, the device may have an extra chip that analyzes and records the user's activity, such as walking or running; the Core Motion framework provides access to this information.

One of the major challenges associated with writing code that takes advantage of the sensors is that different devices have different hardware. If you don't want to impose stringent restrictions on what devices your app will run on in the first place (`UIRequired-DeviceCapabilities` in the *Info.plist*), your code must be prepared to fail gracefully and possibly provide a subset of its full capabilities when it discovers that the current device lacks certain features.

Moreover, certain sensors may experience momentary inadequacy; for example, Core Location might not be able to get a fix on the device's position because it can't see cell towers, GPS satellites, or both. And some sensors take time to "warm up," so that the values you'll get from them initially will be invalid. You'll want to respond to such changes in the external circumstances, in order to give the user a decent experience of your application regardless.

In addition, all sensor usage means battery usage, to a lesser or greater degree — sometimes to a *considerably* greater degree. There's a compromise to be made here: you want to please the user with your app's convenience and usefulness without disagreeably surprising and annoying the user through the device's rapid depletion of its battery charge.

Core Location

The Core Location framework provides facilities for the device to determine and report its location (*location services*). It takes advantage of three sensors:

Wi-Fi
> The device, if Wi-Fi is turned on, may scan for nearby Wi-Fi devices and compare these against an online database.

Cell
> The device, if it has cell capabilities and they are not turned off, may compare nearby telephone cell towers against an online database.

GPS
> The device's GPS, if it has one, may be able to obtain a position fix from GPS satellites. The GPS is obviously the most accurate location sensor, but it takes the longest to get a fix, and in some situations it will fail — indoors, for example, or in a city of tall buildings, where the device can't "see" enough of the sky.

Core Location will automatically use whatever facilities the device has available; all *you* have to do is ask for the device's location. Core Location allows you to specify how accurate a position fix you want; more accurate fixes may require more time.

The notion of a location is encapsulated by the CLLocation class and its properties, which include:

`coordinate`
> A CLLocationCoordinate2D, a struct consisting of two Doubles representing latitude and longitude.

`altitude`
> A CLLocationDistance, which is a Double representing a number of meters.

`speed`
> A CLLocationSpeed, which is a Double representing meters per second.

`course`
> A CLLocationDirection, which is a Double representing degrees (*not* radians) clockwise from north.

`horizontalAccuracy`
> A CLLocationAccuracy, which is a Double representing meters.

```
timestamp
```
   An NSDate.

Behavior of your app may depend on the device's physical location. To help you test, Xcode lets you pretend that the device is at a particular location on earth. The Simulator's Debug → Location menu lets you enter a location; the Scheme editor lets you set a default location (under Options); and the Debug → Simulate Location menu lets you switch among locations. You can set a built-in location or supply a standard GPX file containing a waypoint. You can also set the location to None; it's important to test for what happens when no location information is available.

Location Manager and Delegate

Use of Core Location requires a *location manager* object, an instance of CLLocation-Manager. There is no reason not to create this object early and maintain it as a property. Moreover, your location manager will generally be useless without a delegate (CLLocationManagerDelegate), so you will probably want to set its delegate as early as possible. Thus, a good strategy is to initialize the location manager property lazily and set its delegate at the same time:

```
lazy var locman : CLLocationManager = {
    let locman = CLLocationManager()
    locman.delegate = self
    return locman
}()
```

Core Location Authorization

Use of Core Location requires that you explicitly request authorization from the user; moreover, there are two types of authorization (starting in iOS 8):

When In Use
   When In Use authorization allows your app to perform basic location determination and no more. Modes where the system tracks the device's location on your behalf, and notifies your app even if your app isn't running, are unavailable. Your app, tracking location in the foreground, can continue tracking location if the user backgrounds it, but the device will make the user aware that this is happening through a blue double-height status bar (similar to the in-call status bar).

Always
   Always authorization gives your app use of all Core Location modes and features. When you track location in the background, the blue double-height status bar doesn't appear. However, even after you are granted authorization, if your app does in fact track location in the background, the system may present the authorization dialog again, every few days, to remind the user of the situation.

In contrast to other types of authorization, you are unlikely to request authorization in advance (merely because your app launches, or because a certain view controller appears). Rather, you'll probably request authorization on demand, in connection with some specific action on the user's part, such as tapping a button that initiates functionality requiring authorization.

At the broadest level, the CLLocationManager class method locationServices-Enabled reports whether location services as a whole are switched off; if they are, and if you proceed to try to use Core Location anyway, the system may put up an alert on your behalf offering to switch to the Settings app so that the user can turn location services on. Thus, a good strategy is to call locationServicesEnabled and, if it is false, immediately send your location manager the startUpdatingLocation message. Your attempt to learn the device's location will fail in good order (and you can hear about this in the delegate method locationManager:didFailWithError:), and this failure was worthwhile because it may have caused the user to see the system alert.

Once location services *are* enabled, call the CLLocationManager class method authorizationStatus to learn your app's actual authorization status; two possible results correspond to the two types of authorization, .AuthorizedWhenInUse and .AuthorizedAlways. To request authorization if the status is .NotDetermined, call one of two instance methods, either requestWhenInUseAuthorization or request-AlwaysAuthorization; you must also have a corresponding entry in your app's *Info.plist*, either NSLocationWhenInUseUsageDescription or NSLocationAlwaysUsage-Description, providing the body of the authorization request alert.

Here's a utility method expressing a good general strategy for checking authorization:

```
func determineStatus() -> Bool {
    guard CLLocationManager.locationServicesEnabled() else {
        self.locman.startUpdatingLocation() // might get "enable" dialog
        return false
    }
    let status = CLLocationManager.authorizationStatus()
    switch status {
    case .AuthorizedAlways, .AuthorizedWhenInUse:
        return true
    case .NotDetermined:
        self.locman.requestWhenInUseAuthorization()
        // locman.requestAlwaysAuthorization()
        return false
    case .Restricted:
        return false
    case .Denied:
        let message = "Wouldn't you like to authorize" +
            "this app to use Location Services?"
        let alert = UIAlertController(title: "Need Authorization",
            message: message, preferredStyle: .Alert)
        alert.addAction(UIAlertAction(title: "No",
```

```
                style: .Cancel, handler: nil))
            alert.addAction(UIAlertAction(title: "OK",
                style: .Default, handler: {
                    _ in
                    let url = NSURL(string:UIApplicationOpenSettingsURLString)!
                    UIApplication.sharedApplication().openURL(url)
            }))
            self.presentViewController(alert, animated:true, completion:nil)
            return false
        }
    }
```

The two request methods have no completion handler. Instead, if you want to be notified as soon as the user authorizes you, implement the delegate method location-
Manager:didChangeAuthorizationStatus:. A good strategy here might be to raise a
flag of some kind before requesting authorization, telling yourself that you are in the
middle of trying to start whatever procedure requires authorization. If the user authorizes you in response to the authorization request alert, you can then start that procedure
immediately.

So, for example, here I've prepared an instance property which might or might not
contain a method call representing what I was trying to do when I requested authorization:

```
var doThisWhenAuthorized : (() -> ())?
```

Now imagine that the user taps a button asking for the device's location. At the start of
the button's action handler, I raise my flag and check my authorization status:

```
@IBAction func doFindMe (sender:AnyObject!) {
    self.doThisWhenAuthorized = {
        [unowned self] in self.doFindMe(sender)
    }
    guard self.determineStatus() else { return }
    // if we get here, we have authorization
    self.doThisWhenAuthorized = nil
    // ... and now proceed to use the location manager ...
}
```

If my implementation of locationManager:didChangeAuthorizationStatus: hears
that we have changed to being authorized and we have a function waiting in self.do-
ThisWhenAuthorized, it calls that function:

```
func locationManager(manager: CLLocationManager,
    didChangeAuthorizationStatus status: CLAuthorizationStatus) {
        switch status {
        case .AuthorizedAlways, .AuthorizedWhenInUse:
            self.doThisWhenAuthorized?()
        default: break
        }
}
```

To retest the system authorization request alert and other access-related behaviors, go to the Settings app and choose General → Reset → Reset Location & Privacy. This, unfortunately, causes the system to revert to its default settings for *everything* in the Privacy section of Settings: all permissions lists will be empty, but Location Services and all System Services will be On.

Location Tracking

To use the location manager to track the user's location:

1. Set yourself as the location manager's delegate (CLLocationManagerDelegate). I've already suggested a strategy for making sure you've done that in advance.

2. Configure the location manager (I'll go into more detail in a moment).

3. Tell the location manager to `startUpdatingLocation`. The location manager, in turn, will begin calling your `locationManager:didUpdateLocations:` delegate method repeatedly. You'll deal with each such call as it arrives. In this way, you will be kept more or less continuously informed of where the device is — until you call `stopUpdatingLocation`. Don't forget to call it when you no longer need location services.

   Your delegate will also always implement `locationManager:didFailWithError:` to receive error messages.

The pattern here is common to virtually *all* use of the location manager. It can do various kinds of tracking, but they all work the same way: you'll tell it to start, a corresponding delegate method will be called repeatedly, and ultimately you'll tell it to stop.

Here are some location manager configuration properties that are useful to set *before* you start location tracking:

`desiredAccuracy`
 Your choices are:

- `kCLLocationAccuracyBestForNavigation`
- `kCLLocationAccuracyBest`
- `kCLLocationAccuracyNearestTenMeters`
- `kCLLocationAccuracyHundredMeters`
- `kCLLocationAccuracyKilometer`
- `kCLLocationAccuracyThreeKilometers`

 It might be sufficient for your purposes to know very quickly but very roughly the device's location. Highest accuracy may also cause the highest battery drain; indeed, `kCLLocationAccuracyBestForNavigation` is supposed to be used only when the device is connected to external power. The accuracy setting is not a filter: the location manager will send you whatever location information it has, even if it isn't as accurate as you asked for, and checking a location's `horizontalAccuracy` is then up to you.

`distanceFilter`
Perhaps you don't need a location report unless the device has moved a certain distance since the previous report. This property can help keep you from being bombarded with events you don't need.

`activityType`
Your choices are (CLActivityType):

- `.Fitness`
- `.AutomotiveNavigation`
- `.OtherNavigation`
- `.Other`

This affects how persistently and frequently updates will be sent, based on the movement of the device. With `.AutomotiveNavigation`, updates can cease temporarily if the device is not moving significantly. With `.Fitness`, on the other hand, the user is assumed to be on foot, so updates may arrive even if the device is stationary.

Where Am I?

Curiously, the previous section does not answer in any simple way the most basic question you are likely to ask — namely, where is the device *now*? In this scenario, you don't want to *track* the location; you just want to *learn* the location, without being subjected to ongoing calls to `locationManager:didUpdateLocations:`. Before iOS 9, this was remarkably difficult to do. The location manager wasn't configured to answer this question, so your only option was to turn on location tracking for just long enough to answer it yourself, and then turn location tracking off again.

This isn't as simple as it might sound. You might think that it would be enough to receive `locationManager:didUpdateLocations:` once and stop; but that is not at all the case. On the contrary, many calls to `locationManager:didUpdateLocations:` may be needed before the sensors warm up sufficiently to give a reading of the desired accuracy. What's more, a reading of the desired accuracy might never arrive, so we must be prepared also to time out and accept whatever we've got.

I'll demonstrate, even though in iOS 9 this approach is no longer necessary. A Bool property, `self.trying`, acts as a flag stating whether we are in the middle of this attempt, and an Optional NSDate property, self.startTime, tracks how long this attempt has been going on:

```
if self.trying { return }
self.trying = true
self.locman.desiredAccuracy = kCLLocationAccuracyBest
self.locman.activityType = .Fitness
self.startTime = nil
self.locman.startUpdatingLocation()
```

We have a utility method for turning off updates and resetting our properties:

```
func stopTrying () {
    self.locman.stopUpdatingLocation()
    self.startTime = nil
    self.trying = false
}
```

If something goes wrong, we'll turn updates back off:

```
func locationManager(manager: CLLocationManager,
    didFailWithError error: NSError) {
        print("failed: \(error)")
        self.stopTrying()
}
```

If things go well, we'll be handed our location as soon as it is determined, in location-Manager:didUpdateLocations:. For purposes of this example, I'm going to insist on a fairly high level of accuracy; if I don't get it, I wait for the next update. But I don't want to wait too long, either, so on the very first pass I record the current time, so that I can compare the location's timestamp on subsequent calls. (Observe that I also return immediately from the first update, as I find that it contains spurious information.) If I get the desired accuracy within the desired time, I turn off updates and am ready to use the location information:

```
let REQ_ACC : CLLocationAccuracy = 10
let REQ_TIME : NSTimeInterval = 10
func locationManager(manager: CLLocationManager,
    didUpdateLocations locations: [CLLocation]) {
        print("did update location ")
        let loc = locations.last!
        let acc = loc.horizontalAccuracy
        let time = loc.timestamp
        let coord = loc.coordinate
        if self.startTime == nil {
            self.startTime = NSDate()
            return // ignore first attempt
        }
        print(acc)
        let elapsed = time.timeIntervalSinceDate(self.startTime)
        if elapsed > REQ_TIME {
            print("This is taking too long")
```

```
            self.stopTrying()
            return
        }
        if acc < 0 || acc > REQ_ACC {
            return // wait for the next one
        }
        // got it
        print("You are at \(coord.latitude) \(coord.longitude)")
        self.stopTrying()
    }
```

Feel free to experiment with different values for the required accuracy and the required time. On my device, it was clearly worth waiting a few cycles to get better accuracy; you can see the accuracy improving as the sensors warm up:

```
did update location 1285.19869645162
did update location 1285.19869645172
did update location 1285.19869645173
did update location 65.0
did update location 65.0
did update location 30.0
did update location 30.0
did update location 30.0
did update location 10.0
You are at ...
```

Starting in iOS 9, however, none of that is necessary; it is all done for us. Instead of calling startUpdatingLocation, call requestLocation:

```
self.locman.desiredAccuracy = kCLLocationAccuracyBest
self.locman.requestLocation()
```

Your locationManager:didUpdateLocations: will be called *once* with a good location, based on the desiredAccuracy you've already set and some internal sense of when to time out (based on the fact that accuracy is failing to improve fast enough):

```
func locationManager(manager: CLLocationManager,
    didUpdateLocations locations: [CLLocation]) {
        let loc = locations.last!
        let coord = loc.coordinate
        print("You are at \(coord.latitude) \(coord.longitude)")
}
```

You do not have to call stopUpdatingLocation, though you can do so if you change your mind and decide before the location arrives that it is no longer needed.

Heading

For appropriately equipped devices, Core Location supports use of the magnetometer to determine which way the device is facing (its *heading*). Although this information is accessed through a location manager, you do *not* need location services to be turned on merely to use the magnetometer to report the device's orientation with respect to *magnetic* north; but you do need location services to be turned on in order to report *true* north, as this depends on the device's location.

As with location, you'll first check that the desired feature is available (`heading-Available`); then you'll instantiate and configure the location manager, and call `start-UpdatingHeading`. The delegate will be sent `locationManager:didUpdateHeading:` repeatedly until you call `stopUpdatingHeading` (or else `locationManager:didFail-WithError:` will be called).

A heading object is a CLHeading instance; its `magneticHeading` and `trueHeading` properties are CLLocationDirection values, which report degrees (*not* radians) clockwise from the reference direction (magnetic or true north, respectively). If the `true-Heading` is not available, it will be reported as `-1`. The `trueHeading` will *not* be available unless both of the following are true in the Settings app:

- Location services are turned on (Privacy → Location Services).
- Compass calibration is turned on (Privacy → Location Services → System Services).

Beyond that, explicit user authorization is *not* needed in order to get the device's heading with respect to true north.

In this example, I'll use the device as a compass. The `headingFilter` setting is to prevent us from being bombarded constantly with readings. For best results, the device should probably be held level (like a tabletop, or a compass); we are setting the `heading-Orientation` so that the reported heading will be the direction in which the top of the device (the end away from the Home button) is pointing:

```
guard CLLocationManager.headingAvailable() else {return} // no hardware
if self.updating {return}
self.locman.headingFilter = 5
self.locman.headingOrientation = .Portrait
self.updating = true
self.locman.startUpdatingHeading()
```

In the delegate, I'll display our heading as a rough cardinal direction in a label in the interface (`self.lab`). If we have a `trueHeading`, I'll use it; otherwise I'll use the `magnetic-Heading`:

```
func locationManager(manager: CLLocationManager,
    didUpdateHeading newHeading: CLHeading) {
        var h = newHeading.magneticHeading
        let h2 = newHeading.trueHeading
        if h2 >= 0 {
            h = h2
        }
        let cards = ["N", "NE", "E", "SE", "S", "SW", "W", "NW"]
        var dir = "N"
```

```
        for (ix, card) in cards.enumerate() {
            if h < 45.0/2.0 + 45.0*Double(ix) {
                dir = card
                break
            }
        }
        if self.lab.text != dir {
            self.lab.text = dir
        }
    }
```

Background Location

You can use Core Location when your app is not in the foreground. There are two quite different ways to do this:

Continuous background location
> This is an extension of basic location tracking. You tell the location manager to startUpdatingLocation, and updates are permitted to continue even if the app goes into the background. Your app runs in the background in order to receive these updates (except during periods when you elect to receive deferred updates, if the hardware supports it).

Location monitoring
> Your app does *not* run in the background! Rather, the system monitors location for you. If a significant location event occurs, your app may be awakened in the background (or launched in the background, if it is not running) and notified.

Continuous background location

Use of Core Location to perform continuous background updates is parallel to production of sound in the background (Chapter 14). In your app's *Info.plist*, the "Required background modes" key (UIBackgroundModes) should include location; you can set this up easily by checking "Location updates" under Background Modes in the Capabilities tab when editing the target.

 New in iOS 9, you *must* also set your location manager's allowsBackgroundLocation-Updates to true. If you are retaining multiple location managers, you must do this for *all* of them.

The result is that if you have a location manager to which you have sent startUpdating-Location and the user sends your app into the background, your app is not suspended: the use of location services continues, and your delegate keeps receiving location updates. If your app has When In Use authorization, the blue double-height status bar will be present as long as your app is in the background and is actively updating the device's location (and the user can tap it to summon your app to the front).

Background use of location services can cause a power drain, but if you want your app to function as a positional data logger, for instance, it may be the only way; you can also help conserve power by making judicious choices, such as setting a coarse `distance-Filter` value, by not requiring overly high accuracy, and by being correct about the `activityType`.

Core Location may be able to operate in deferred mode (`allowDeferredLocation-UpdatesUntilTraveled:timeout:`) so that your background app doesn't receive updates until the user has moved a specified amount or until a fixed time interval has elapsed; this, too, can help conserve power, especially if the user locks the screen, as the device may be able to power down some of its sensors temporarily, and your app can be allowed to stop running in the background. This feature is dependent on hardware capabilities; use it only if the class method `deferredLocationUpdatesAvailable` returns `true`. For this feature to work, the location manager's `desiredAccuracy` must be `kCLLocationAccuracyBest` or `kCLLocationAccuracyBestForNavigation`, and its `distanceFilter` must be `kCLDistanceFilterNone` (the default).

Deferred mode doesn't mean that location updates are fewer or filtered; it affects only the *delivery* of those updates. Updates are accumulated and then delivered all at once after the specified distance or time: the delegate is sent these messages:

- `locationManager:didFinishDeferredUpdatesWithError:`
- `locationManager:didUpdateLocations:`

The `locations:` parameter of `locationManager:didUpdateLocations:` in this situation is an array of *all the accumulated updates*. At this point, deferred updating has ceased; asking for the next set of updates to be deferred is up to you, by calling `allow-Deferred...` again. If the user brings your app to the foreground, any undelivered accumulated updates are delivered then and there, so that your interface can present the most recent information.

Location monitoring

Using Core Location to perform location monitoring without being in the foreground *doesn't* require your app to run continuously in the background, and you do *not* have to set the `UIBackgroundModes` of your *Info.plist*. That's because the system is going to do all the work on your behalf. Your app still needs appropriate authorization, however.

Some forms of location monitoring involve use of a CLRegion, which basically expresses a *geofence*, an area that triggers a notification when the user enters or leaves it (or both). This class is divided into two subclasses, CLBeaconRegion and CLCircularRegion.

CLBeaconRegion is used in connection with iBeacon monitoring; I'm not going to discuss iBeacon in this book, so that leaves us with CLCircularRegion. Its initializer is init(center:radius:identifier:); the center: parameter is a CLLocation-Coordinate2D, and the identifier: serves as a unique key. You should also set the region's notifyOnEntry or notifyOnExit to false if you're interested in just one type of event.

There are four distinct forms of location monitoring:

Geofenced local notifications

This is a local notification (UILocalNotification, Chapter 13) that is triggered, not by the arrival of a certain time, but by the user's crossing a geofence. You will need a location manager and When In Use authorization. Create the local notification and set its region to a CLRegion. The notification's regionTriggersOnce is true by default; if false, the notification will be triggered *every* time the region is entered or exited (in accordance with the notifyOnEntry and notifyOnExit settings). Apart from this, the local notification is a standard local notification, and you'll hear about it only if the user uses the notification to summon your app (or if your app is in the foreground when the notification fires).

Significant location monitoring

If the class method significantLocationChangeMonitoringAvailable returns true, you can call startMonitoringSignificantLocationChanges. You will need a location manager and Always authorization. The delegate's locationManager:did-UpdateLocations: will be called whenever the device's location has changed significantly.

Visit monitoring

By tracking significant changes in your location along with the *pauses* between those changes, the system decides that the user is visiting a spot. Visit monitoring is basically a form of significant location monitoring, but requires even less power and notifies you less often, because locations that don't involve pauses are filtered out. You will need a location manager and Always authorization. If the class method significantLocationChangeMonitoringAvailable returns true, you can call startMonitoringVisits. The delegate's locationManager:didVisit: will be called whenever the user's location pauses in a way that suggests a visit is beginning, and again whenever a visit ends. The second parameter is a CLVisit, a simple value class wrapping visit data; in addition to coordinate and horizontalAccuracy, you get an arrivalDate and departureDate. If this is an arrival, the departureDate will be NSDate.distantFuture(). If this is a departure and we were not monitoring visits when the user arrived, the arrivalDate will be NSDate.distantPast().

Region monitoring

If the class method `isMonitoringAvailableForClass:` with an argument of `CLCircularRegion.self` returns `true`, then you can call `startMonitoringFor-Region:` for each region in which you are interested. You will need a location manager and Always authorization. Regions being monitored are maintained as a set, which is the location manager's `monitoredRegions`. A region's `identifier` serves as a unique key, so that if you start monitoring for a region whose identifier matches that of a region already in the `monitoredRegions` set, the latter will be ejected from the set. The following delegate methods may be called:

- `locationManager:didEnterRegion:`
- `locationManager:didExitRegion:`
- `locationManager:monitoringDidFailForRegion:withError:`

Location monitoring is much less battery-intensive than full-fledged location tracking. That's because it relies on cell tower positions to estimate the device's location. Since the cell is probably working anyway — for example, the device is a phone, so the cell is always on and is always concerned with what cell towers are available — little or no additional power is required. Apple says that the system will also take advantage of other clues (requiring no extra battery drain) to decide that there may have been a change in location: for example, the device may observe a change in the available Wi-Fi networks, strongly suggesting that the device has moved.

Every `startMonitoring` method has a corresponding `stopMonitoring` method. Don't forget to call that method when location monitoring is no longer needed! The system is performing this work on your behalf, and it will continue to do so until you tell it not to.

If your app isn't in the foreground at the time the system wants to send your location manager delegate a location monitoring event, there are two possible states in which your app might find itself:

Your app is suspended in the background

Your app is woken up (remaining in the background) long enough to receive the delegate event and do something with it.

Your app is not running at all

Your app is relaunched (remaining in the background), and your app delegate will be sent `application:didFinishLaunchingWithOptions:` with a dictionary containing `UIApplicationLaunchOptionsLocationKey`, thus allowing it to discern the special nature of the situation. At this point you probably have no location manager — your app has just launched from scratch. So you should get yourself a location manager and assign it a delegate so that you have a way to receive the delegate event.

Acceleration, Attitude, and Activity

Acceleration results from the application of a force to the device, and is detected through the device's accelerometer, supplemented by the gyroscope if it has one. Gravity is a force, so the accelerometer always has something to measure, even if the user isn't consciously applying a force to the device; thus the device can report its attitude relative to the vertical.

Acceleration information can arrive in two ways:

As a prepackaged UIEvent
> You can receive a UIEvent notifying you of a predefined gesture performed by accelerating the device. At present, the only such gesture is the user shaking the device.

With the Core Motion framework
> You instantiate CMMotionManager and then obtain information of a desired type. You can ask for accelerometer information, gyroscope information, or device motion information (and you can also use Core Motion to get magnetometer information); device motion combines the gyroscope data with data from the other sensors to give you the best possible description of the device's attitude in space.

Shake Events

A shake event is a UIEvent (Chapter 5). Receiving shake events is rather like receiving remote control events (Chapter 14), involving the notion of the first responder. To receive shake events, your app must contain a UIResponder which:

- Returns `true` from `canBecomeFirstResponder`
- Is in fact first responder

This responder, or a UIResponder further up the responder chain, should implement some or all of these methods:

`motionBegan:withEvent:`
> Something has started to happen that might or might not turn out to be a shake.

`motionEnded:withEvent:`
> The motion reported in `motionBegan:withEvent:` is over and has turned out to be a shake.

`motionCancelled:withEvent:`
> The motion reported in `motionBegan:withEvent:` wasn't a shake after all.

It might be sufficient to implement `motionEnded:withEvent:`, because this arrives if and only if the user performs a shake gesture. The first parameter will be the event subtype, but at present this is guaranteed to be `.MotionShake`, so testing it is pointless.

The view controller in charge of the current view is a good candidate to receive shake events. Thus, a minimal implementation might look like this:

```
override func canBecomeFirstResponder() -> Bool {
    return true
}
override func viewDidAppear(animated: Bool) {
    super.viewDidAppear(animated)
    self.becomeFirstResponder()
}
override func motionEnded(
    motion: UIEventSubtype, withEvent event: UIEvent?) {
        print("hey, you shook me!")
}
```

By default, if some other object is first responder, and is of a type that supports undo (such as a UITextField), and if `motionBegan:withEvent:` is sent up the responder chain, and if you have not set the shared UIApplication's `applicationSupportsShakeToEdit` property to `false`, a shake will be handled through an Undo or Redo alert. Your view controller might not want to rob any responders in its view of this capability. A simple way to prevent this is to test whether the view controller is itself the first responder; if it isn't, we call `super` to pass the event on up the responder chain:

```
override func motionEnded(
    motion: UIEventSubtype, withEvent event: UIEvent?) {
        if self.isFirstResponder() {
            print("hey, you shook me!")
        } else {
            super.motionEnded(motion, withEvent: event)
        }
}
```

Raw Acceleration

If the device has an accelerometer but no gyroscope, you can learn about the forces being applied to it, but some compromises will be necessary. The chief problem is that, even if the device is completely motionless, its acceleration values will constitute a normalized vector pointing toward the center of the earth, popularly known as *gravity*. The accelerometer is thus constantly reporting a combination of gravity and user-induced acceleration. This is good and bad. It's good because it means that, with certain restrictions, you can use the accelerometer to detect the device's attitude in space. It's bad because gravity values and user-induced acceleration values are mixed together. Fortunately, there are ways to separate these values mathematically:

With a low-pass filter

A low-pass filter will damp out user acceleration so as to report gravity only.

With a high-pass filter

A high-pass filter will damp out the effect of gravity so as to detect user acceleration only, reporting a motionless device as having zero acceleration.

In some situations, it is desirable to apply both a low-pass filter and a high-pass filter, so as to learn both the gravity values and the user acceleration values. A common additional technique is to run the output of the high-pass filter itself through a low-pass filter to reduce noise and small twitches. Apple provides some nice sample code for implementing a low-pass or a high-pass filter; see especially the AccelerometerGraph example, which is also very helpful for exploring how the accelerometer behaves.

The technique of applying filters to the accelerometer output has some serious downsides, which are inevitable in a device that lacks a gyroscope:

- It's up to you to apply the filters; you have to implement boilerplate code and hope that you don't make a mistake.
- Filters mean *latency*. Your response to the accelerometer values will lag behind what the device is actually doing; this lag may be noticeable.

Reading raw accelerometer values with Core Motion is really a subset of how you read *any* values with Core Motion; in some ways it is similar to how you use Core Location:

1. You start by instantiating CMMotionManager; retain the instance somewhere, typically as a property. There is no reason not to initialize the property directly:

   ```
   let motman = CMMotionManager()
   ```

2. Confirm that the desired hardware is available.

3. Set the interval at which you wish the motion manager to update itself with new sensor readings.

4. Call the appropriate `start` method.

5. You probably expect me to say that the motion manager will call into a delegate. Surprise! A motion manager has no delegate. You have two choices:

   - Poll the motion manager whenever you want data, asking for the appropriate `data` property. The polling interval doesn't have to be the same as the motion manager's update interval; when you poll, you'll obtain the motion manager's *current* data — that is, the data generated by its most recent update, whenever that was.

   - If your app's purpose is to collect *all* the data, then instead of calling a `start` method, you can call a `start...UpdatesToQueue:withHandler:` method and receive callbacks to your `handler:` function, possibly on a background thread, managed by an NSOperationQueue (Chapter 25).

6. Don't forget to call the corresponding `stop` method when you no longer need data.

In this example, I will simply report whether the device is lying flat on its back. I start by configuring my motion manager; then I launch a repeating timer to trigger polling:

```
guard self.motman.accelerometerAvailable else { return }
self.motman.accelerometerUpdateInterval = 1.0 / 30.0
self.motman.startAccelerometerUpdates()
self.timer = NSTimer.scheduledTimerWithTimeInterval(
    self.motman.accelerometerUpdateInterval,
    target: self, selector: "pollAccel:",
    userInfo: nil, repeats: true)
```

My `pollAccel:` method is now being called repeatedly. In `pollAccel:`, I ask the motion manager for its accelerometer data. This arrives as a CMAccelerometerData object, which is a timestamp plus a CMAcceleration; a CMAcceleration is simply a struct of three values, one for each axis of the device, measured in Gs. The positive x-axis points to the right of the device. The positive y-axis points toward the top of the device, away from the Home button. The positive z-axis points out the front of the screen.

The two axes orthogonal to gravity, which are the x- and y-axes when the device is lying more or less on its back, are much more accurate and sensitive to small variation than the axis pointing toward or away from gravity. So our approach is to ask first whether the x and y values are close to zero; only then do we use the z value to learn whether the device is on its back or on its face. To keep from updating our interface constantly, we implement a crude state machine; the state property (`self.state`) starts out at `.Unknown`, and then switches between `.LyingDown` (device on its back) and `.NotLying-Down` (device not on its back), and we update the interface only when there is a state change:

```
guard let dat = self.motman.accelerometerData else {return}
let acc = dat.acceleration
let x = acc.x
let y = acc.y
let z = acc.z
let accu = 0.08
if abs(x) < accu && abs(y) < accu && z < -0.5 {
    if self.state == .Unknown || self.state == .NotLyingDown {
        self.state = .LyingDown
        self.label.text = "I'm lying on my back... ahhh..."
    }
} else {
    if self.state == .Unknown || self.state == .LyingDown {
```

```
            self.state = .NotLyingDown
            self.label.text = "Hey, put me back down on the table!"
        }
    }
```

This works, but it's sensitive to small motions of the device on the table. To damp this sensitivity, we can run our input through a low-pass filter. The low-pass filter code comes straight from Apple's own examples, and involves maintaining the previously filtered reading as a set of properties:

```
func addAcceleration(accel:CMAcceleration) {
    let alpha = 0.1
    self.oldX = accel.x * alpha + self.oldX * (1.0 - alpha)
    self.oldY = accel.y * alpha + self.oldY * (1.0 - alpha)
    self.oldZ = accel.z * alpha + self.oldZ * (1.0 - alpha)
}
```

Our polling code now starts out by passing the data through the filter:

```
guard let dat = self.motman.accelerometerData else {return}
self.addAcceleration(dat.acceleration)
let x = self.oldX
let y = self.oldY
let z = self.oldZ
// ... and the rest is as before ...
```

As I mentioned earlier, instead of polling, you can receive callbacks to a function. This approach is useful particularly if your goal is to receive every update or to receive updates on a background thread (or both). To illustrate, I'll rewrite the previous example to use this technique; to keep things simple, I'll ask for my callbacks on the main thread (the documentation advises against this, but Apple's own sample code does it). We now start our accelerometer updates like this:

```
self.motman.startAccelerometerUpdatesToQueue(
    NSOperationQueue.mainQueue(), withHandler: {
        (accelerometerData:CMAccelerometerData?, error:NSError?) in
        guard let dat = accelerometerData else {
            print(error)
            self.stopAccelerometer()
            return
        }
        self.receiveAccel(dat)
})
```

receiveAccel: is just like our earlier pollAccel:, except that we already have the accelerometer data:

```
func receiveAccel (dat:CMAccelerometerData) {
    self.addAcceleration(dat.acceleration)
    // ... and the rest is as before ...
}
```

In this next example, the user is allowed to slap the side of the device into an open hand — perhaps as a way of telling it to go to the next or previous image or whatever it is we're displaying. We pass the acceleration input through a high-pass filter to eliminate gravity (again, the filter code comes straight from Apple's examples):

```
func addAcceleration(accel:CMAcceleration) {
    let alpha = 0.1
    self.oldX = accel.x - ((accel.x * alpha) + (self.oldX * (1.0 - alpha)))
    self.oldY = accel.y - ((accel.y * alpha) + (self.oldY * (1.0 - alpha)))
    self.oldZ = accel.z - ((accel.z * alpha) + (self.oldZ * (1.0 - alpha)))
}
```

What we're looking for, in our polling routine, is a high positive or negative x value. A single slap is likely to consist of several consecutive readings above our threshold, but we want to report each slap only once, so we take advantage of the timestamp attached to a CMAccelerometerData, maintaining the timestamp of our previous high reading as a property and ignoring readings that are too close to one another in time. Another problem is that a sudden jerk involves both an acceleration (as the user starts the device moving) and a deceleration (as the device stops moving); thus a left slap might be preceded by a high value in the opposite direction, which we might interpret wrongly as a right slap. We can compensate crudely, at the expense of some latency, with delayed performance; for the CancelableTimer object stored at self.canceltimer, see Appendix B:

```
func pollAccel(_:AnyObject!) {
    guard let dat = self.motman.accelerometerData else {return}
    self.addAcceleration(dat.acceleration)
    let x = self.oldX
    let thresh = 1.0
    if x < -thresh {
        if dat.timestamp - self.oldTime > 0.5 || self.lastSlap == .Right {
            self.oldTime = dat.timestamp
            self.lastSlap = .Left
            self.canceltimer?.cancel()
            self.canceltimer = CancelableTimer(once: true) {
                print("left")
            }
            self.canceltimer.startWithInterval(0.5)
        }
    } else if x > thresh {
        if dat.timestamp - self.oldTime > 0.5 || self.lastSlap == .Left {
            self.oldTime = dat.timestamp
            self.lastSlap = .Right
            self.canceltimer?.cancel()
            self.canceltimer = CancelableTimer(once: true) {
                print("right")
            }
```

```
            self.canceltimer.startWithInterval(0.5)
        }
    }
}
```

The gesture we're detecting is a little tricky to make: the user must slap the device into an open hand *and hold it there*; if the device jumps out of the open hand, that movement may be detected as the last in the series, resulting in the wrong report (left instead of right, or *vice versa*). And the latency of our gesture detection is very high.

Of course we might try tweaking some of the magic numbers in this code to improve accuracy and performance, but a more sophisticated analysis would probably involve storing a stream of all the most recent CMAccelerometerData objects and studying the entire stream to work out the overall trend.

 New in iOS 9, some devices may be capable of recording accelerometer data for later analysis. You'll want to look into the CMSensorRecorder class (along with CMSensorDataList and CMRecordedAccelerometerData).

Gyroscope

The inclusion of an electronic gyroscope in the panoply of onboard hardware in some devices has made a huge difference in the accuracy and speed of gravity and attitude reporting. A gyroscope has the property that its attitude in space remains constant; thus it can detect any change in the attitude of the containing device. This has two important consequences for accelerometer measurements:

- The accelerometer can be supplemented by the gyroscope to detect quickly the difference between gravity and user-induced acceleration.

- The gyroscope can observe pure rotation, where little or no acceleration is involved and so the accelerometer would not have been helpful. The extreme case is constant attitudinal rotation around the gravity axis, which the accelerometer alone would be completely unable to detect (because there is no user-induced force, and gravity remains constant).

It is possible to track the raw gyroscope data: make sure the device has a gyroscope (gyroAvailable), and then call startGyroUpdates. What we get from the motion manager is a CMGyroData object, which combines a timestamp with a CMRotationRate that reports the *rate of rotation* around each axis, measured in radians per second, where a positive value is *counterclockwise* as seen by someone whose eye is pointed to by the positive axis. (This is the opposite of the direction graphed in Figure 3-9.) The problem, however, is that the gyroscope values are *scaled* and *biased*. This means that the values are based on an arbitrary scale and are gradually increasing (or decreasing) over time at a roughly constant rate. Thus there is very little merit in the exercise of dealing with the raw gyroscope data.

What you are likely to be interested in is a combination of at least the gyroscope and the accelerometer. The mathematics required to combine the data from these sensors can be daunting. Fortunately, there's no need to know anything about that. Core Motion will happily package up the calculated combination of data as a CMDeviceMotion instance, with the effects of the sensors' internal bias and scaling already factored out. CMDeviceMotion consists of the following properties, all of which provide a triple of values corresponding to the device's natural 3D frame (x increasing to the right, y increasing to the top, z increasing out the front):

gravity
> A CMAcceleration expressing a vector with value 1 pointing to the center of the earth, measured in Gs.

userAcceleration
> A CMAcceleration describing user-induced acceleration, with no gravity component, measured in Gs.

rotationRate
> A CMRotationRate describing how the device is rotating around its own center. This is essentially the CMGyroData rotationRate with scale and bias accounted for.

magneticField
> A CMCalibratedMagneticField describing (in its field, a CMMagneticField) the magnetic forces acting on the device, measured in microteslas. The sensor's internal bias has already been factored out. The accuracy is one of the following:
>
> - CMMagneticFieldCalibrationAccuracyUncalibrated
> - CMMagneticFieldCalibrationAccuracyLow
> - CMMagneticFieldCalibrationAccuracyMedium
> - CMMagneticFieldCalibrationAccuracyHigh

attitude
> A CMAttitude, descriptive of the device's instantaneous attitude in space. When you ask the motion manager to start generating updates, you can specify a reference frame for the attitude (having first called the class method availableAttitude-ReferenceFrames to ascertain that the desired reference frame is available on this device). In every case, the negative z-axis points at the center of the earth:
>
> CMAttitudeReferenceFrameXArbitraryZVertical
>> The x-axis and y-axis, though orthogonal to the other axes, could be pointing anywhere.

`CMAttitudeReferenceFrameXArbitraryCorrectedZVertical`
> The same as in the previous option, but the magnetometer is used to maintain accuracy (preventing drift of the reference frame over time).

`CMAttitudeReferenceFrameXMagneticNorthZVertical`
> The x-axis points toward magnetic north.

`CMAttitudeReferenceFrameXTrueNorthZVertical`
> The x-axis points toward true north. This value will be inaccurate unless you are also using Core Location to obtain the device's location.

The `attitude` value's numbers can be accessed through various CMAttitude properties corresponding to three different systems, each being convenient for a different purpose:

`pitch, roll, yaw`
> The device's angle of offset from the reference frame, in radians, around the device's natural x-axis, y-axis, and z-axis respectively.

`rotationMatrix`
> A CMRotationMatrix struct embodying a 3×3 matrix expressing a rotation in the reference frame.

`quaternion`
> A CMQuaternion describing an attitude. (Quaternions are commonly used in OpenGL.)

In this example, we turn the device into a simple compass/clinometer, merely by asking for its `attitude` with reference to magnetic north and taking its `pitch`, `roll`, and `yaw`. We begin by making the usual preparations; notice the use of the `showsDeviceMovementDisplay` property, intended to allow the runtime to prompt the user if the magnetometer needs calibration:

```
guard self.motman.deviceMotionAvailable else { return }
let ref = CMAttitudeReferenceFrame.XMagneticNorthZVertical
let avail = CMMotionManager.availableAttitudeReferenceFrames()
guard avail.contains(ref) else { return }
self.motman.showsDeviceMovementDisplay = true
self.motman.deviceMotionUpdateInterval = 1.0 / 30.0
self.motman.startDeviceMotionUpdatesUsingReferenceFrame(ref)
let t = self.motman.deviceMotionUpdateInterval * 10
self.timer = NSTimer.scheduledTimerWithTimeInterval(t, target:self,
    selector:"pollAttitude:",userInfo:nil, repeats:true)
```

In `pollAttitude:`, we wait until the magnetometer is ready, and then we start taking attitude readings (converted to degrees):

```
guard let mot = self.motman.deviceMotion else {return}
let acc = mot.magneticField.accuracy.rawValue
if acc <= CMMagneticFieldCalibrationAccuracyLow.rawValue {
    return // not ready yet
}
let att = mot.attitude
let to_deg = 180.0 / M_PI
print("\(att.pitch * to_deg), \(att.roll * to_deg), \(att.yaw * to_deg)")
```

The values are all close to zero when the device is level with its x-axis pointing to magnetic north, and each value increases as the device is rotated *counterclockwise* with respect to an eye that has the corresponding positive axis pointing at it. So, for example, a device held upright (top pointing at the sky) has a `pitch` approaching 90; a device lying on its right edge has a `roll` approaching 90; and a device lying on its back with its top pointing north has a `yaw` approaching -90.

There are some quirks in the way Euler angles operate mathematically:

- `roll` and `yaw` increase with counterclockwise rotation from 0 to π (180 degrees) and then jump to $-\pi$ (-180 degrees) and continue to increase to 0 as the rotation completes a circle; but `pitch` increases to $\pi/2$ (90 degrees) and then decreases to 0, then decreases to $-\pi/2$ (-90 degrees) and increases to 0. This means that `attitude` alone, if we are exploring it through `pitch`, `roll`, and `yaw`, is insufficient to describe the device's attitude, since a `pitch` value of, say, $\pi/4$ (45 degrees) could mean two different things. To distinguish those two things, we can supplement `attitude` with the z-component of `gravity`:

  ```
  let g = mot.gravity
  let whichway = g.z > 0 ? "forward" : "back"
  print("pitch is tilted \(whichway)")
  ```

- Values become inaccurate in certain orientations. In particular, when `pitch` is ±90 degrees (the device is upright or inverted), `roll` and `yaw` become erratic. (You may see this effect referred to as "the singularity" or as "gimbal lock.") I believe that, depending on what you are trying to accomplish, you can solve this by using a different expression of the attitude, such as the `rotationMatrix`, which does not suffer from this limitation.

This next (simple and very silly) example illustrates a use of CMAttitude's `rotationMatrix` property. Our goal is to make a CALayer rotate in response to the current attitude of the device. We start as before, except that our reference frame is `CMAttitudeReferenceFrameXArbitraryZVertical`; we are interested in how the device moves from its initial attitude, without reference to any particular fixed external direction such as magnetic north. In `pollAttitude`, our first step is to store the device's current attitude in a CMAttitude property, `self.ref`:

```
guard let mot = self.motman.deviceMotion else {return}
let att = mot.attitude
if self.ref == nil {
    self.ref = att
    return
}
```

That code works correctly because on the first few polls, as the attitude-detection hardware warms up, att is nil, so we don't get past the return call until we have a valid initial attitude. Our next step is highly characteristic of how CMAttitude is used: we call the CMAttitude instance method multiplyByInverseOfAttitude:, which transforms our attitude so that it is relative *to the stored initial attitude*:

```
att.multiplyByInverseOfAttitude(self.ref)
```

Finally, we apply the attitude's rotation matrix directly to a layer in our interface as a transform. Well, not quite directly: a rotation matrix is a 3×3 matrix, whereas a CATransform3D, which is what we need in order to set a layer's transform, is a 4×4 matrix. However, it happens that the top left nine entries in a CATransform3D's 4×4 matrix constitute its rotation component, so we start with an identity matrix and set those entries directly:

```
let r = att.rotationMatrix
var t = CATransform3DIdentity
t.m11 = CGFloat(r.m11)
t.m12 = CGFloat(r.m12)
t.m13 = CGFloat(r.m13)
t.m21 = CGFloat(r.m21)
t.m22 = CGFloat(r.m22)
t.m23 = CGFloat(r.m23)
t.m31 = CGFloat(r.m31)
t.m32 = CGFloat(r.m32)
t.m33 = CGFloat(r.m33)
let lay = // whatever
CATransaction.setAnimationDuration(1.0/10.0)
lay.transform = t
```

The result is that the layer apparently tries to hold itself still as the device rotates. The example is rather crude because we aren't using OpenGL to draw a three-dimensional object, but it illustrates the principle well enough.

There is a quirk to be aware of in this case as well: over time, the transform has a tendency to drift. Thus, even if we leave the device stationary, the layer will gradually rotate. That is the sort of effect that CMAttitudeReferenceFrameXArbitraryCorrectedZVertical is designed to help mitigate, by bringing the magnetometer into play.

Here are some additional considerations to be aware of when using Core Motion:

- The documentation warns that your app should create only one CMMotion-Manager instance. This is not a terribly onerous restriction, but it's rather odd that, if this is important, the API doesn't provide a shared singleton instance accessed through a class method.

- Use of Core Motion is legal while your app is running in the background. To take advantage of this, your app would need to be running in the background for some *other* reason; there is no Core Motion UIBackgroundModes setting in an *Info.plist*. For example, you might run in the background because you're using Core Location, and take advantage of this to employ Core Motion as well.

- Core Motion requires that various sensors be turned on, such as the magnetometer and the gyroscope. This can result in some increased battery drain, so try not to use any sensors you don't have to, and remember to stop generating updates as soon as you no longer need them.

 Newer devices tend to have more hardware. For example, the iPhone 6 and iPhone 6 Plus have a barometer! You can get altitude information using the CMAltimeter and CMAltitudeData classes.

Motion Activity

Some devices have a motion coprocessor chip with the ability to detect, analyze, and keep a record of device motion even while the device is asleep and with very little drain on power. This is *not* a form of location determination; it is an analysis of the device's physical motion and attitude in order to draw conclusions about what the user has been doing while carrying or wearing the device. You can learn that the user is walking, or walked for an hour, but not where the user was walking.

Interaction with the motion coprocessor is through a CMMotionActivityManager instance. There is no reason not to initialize a property with this instance:

```
let actman = CMMotionActivityManager()
```

The device must actually *have* a motion coprocessor; call the class method isActivity-Available. The user must also grant authorization, and, having granted it, can later deny it (in the Settings app, under Privacy → Motion Activity). There are no authorization methods; the technique is to "tickle" the activity manager by trying to query it and seeing if you get an error. In this example, I have a Bool property, self.authorized, which I set based on the outcome of trying to query the activity manager:

```
let now = NSDate()
self.actman.queryActivityStartingFromDate(now,
    toDate:now, toQueue:NSOperationQueue.mainQueue()) {
        (arr:[CMMotionActivity]?, err:NSError?) in
        let notauth = Int(CMErrorMotionActivityNotAuthorized.rawValue)
        if err != nil && err!.code == notauth {
```

```
            self.authorized = false
        } else {
            self.authorized = true
        }
    }
```

On the first run of that code, the system puts up the authorization request alert. The completion handler is not called until the user deals with the alert, so the outcome tells you what the user decided. On subsequent runs, that code reports the current authorization status.

There are two approaches to querying the activity manager:

Real-time updates

This is similar to getting motion manager updates with a handler. You call `start-ActivityUpdatesToQueue:withHandler:`, and the handler is called periodically. When you no longer need updates, call `stopActivityUpdates`.

Historical data

The motion coprocessor records about a week's-worth of data. You ask for a chunk of that recorded data by calling `queryActivityStartingFromDate:toDate:toQueue:withHandler:`.

I'll illustrate querying for historical data. In this example, I fetch the data for the past 24 hours. I have prepared an NSOperationQueue property, `self.queue`:

```
let now = NSDate()
let yester = now.dateByAddingTimeInterval(-60*60*24)
self.actman.queryActivityStartingFromDate(yester,
    toDate: now, toQueue: self.queue) {
        (arr:[CMMotionActivity]?, err:NSError?) -> Void in
        guard var acts = arr else {return}
        // ...
}
```

We now have an array of CMMotionActivity objects representing every *change* in the device's activity status. This is a value class. It has a `startDate`, a `confidence` (a CMMotionActivityConfidence, `.Low`, `.Medium`, or `.High`) ranking the activity manager's faith in its own categorization of what the user was doing, and a bunch of Bool properties actually categorizing the activity:

- `stationary`
- `walking`
- `running`
- `automotive`

- cycling

- unknown

A common first response to the flood of data is to pare it down (sometimes referred to as *smoothing*). To help with this, I've extended CMMotionActivity with a utility method that summarizes its Bool properties as a string:

```
extension CMMotionActivity {
    private func tf(b:Bool) -> String {
        return b ? "t" : "f"
    }
    func overallAct() -> String {
        let s = tf(self.stationary)
        let w = tf(self.walking)
        let r = tf(self.running)
        let a = tf(self.automotive)
        let c = tf(self.cycling)
        let u = tf(self.unknown)
        return "\(s) \(w) \(r) \(a) \(c) \(u)"
    }
}
```

So, as a straightforward way of paring down the data, I walk backwards through the data, removing every CMMotionActivity with no definite activity, with a low degree of confidence, or whose activity is the same as its predecessor. Then I set a property, and my data are ready for use:

```
let blank = "f f f f f f"
acts = acts.filter {act in act.overallAct() != blank}
acts = acts.filter {act in act.confidence == .High}
for i in (1..<acts.count).reverse() {
    if acts[i].overallAct() == acts[i-1].overallAct() {
        acts.removeAtIndex(i)
    }
}
dispatch_async(dispatch_get_main_queue()) {
    self.data = acts
}
```

There is also a CMPedometer class; before using it, check the isStepCounting-Available class method. Some devices can deduce the size of the user's stride and compute distance (isDistanceAvailable); some devices can use barometric data to estimate whether the user mounted a flight of stairs (isFloorCountingAvailable). New in iOS 9, you can also ask for instantaneous cadence (isCadenceAvailable) and pace (isPaceAvailable). Pedometer data is queried just like motion activity data; you can either ask for constant updates or you can ask for the stored history. Each bit of data arrives as a CMPedometerData object. The pedometer may work reliably under circumstances where Core Location doesn't.

PART IV

Final Topics

This part of the book is a miscellany of topics.

- Chapter 23 is about files. It explains how your app can store data on disk to be retrieved the next time the app runs (including both standalone files and user defaults). It also discusses sharing files with the user through iTunes and with other apps, plus the document architecture and iCloud, and concludes with a survey of how iOS can work with some common file formats (XML, SQLite, Core Data, and image files).

- Chapter 24 introduces networking, with an emphasis on HTTP downloading of data. It also introduces some specialized forms of networking such as on-demand resources and in-app purchasing.

- Chapter 25 is about threads. Making your code multithreaded can introduce great complexity and is not a beginner topic, but you still might need to understand the basic concepts of multithreading, either in order to prevent a lengthy task from blocking user interaction with your app, or because some framework explicitly relies on it. Particular attention is paid to the advantages of NSOperation and Grand Central Dispatch.

- Chapter 26 describes how iOS supports undo in your app.

CHAPTER 23

Persistent Storage

The device on which your app runs contains flash memory that functions as the equivalent of a hard disk, holding files that survive between runs of your app, even if the device is powered down. This chapter is about how and where files are saved and retrieved, and about some of the additional ways in which files can be manipulated: for example, apps can define document types in which they specialize and can hand such documents to one another, and can share documents into the cloud (iCloud), so that multiple copies of the same app can retrieve them on different devices. The chapter also explains how user preferences are maintained in NSUserDefaults, and describes some specialized file formats and ways of working with their data, such as XML, SQLite, Core Data, and images.

The Sandbox

The hard disk as a whole is not open to your app's view. A limited portion of the hard disk is dedicated to your app alone: this is your app's *sandbox*. The idea is that every app, seeing only its own sandbox, is hindered from spying or impinging on the files belonging to other apps, and in turn is protected from having its own files spied or impinged on by other apps. Your app's sandbox is thus a safe place for you to store your data. Your sandbox, and hence your data, will be deleted if the user deletes your app; otherwise, it should reliably persist.

Standard Directories

The sandbox contains some standard directories, and there are built-in methods for referring to them. For example, suppose you want a reference to the Documents directory. Here's one way to access it:

```
let docs = NSSearchPathForDirectoriesInDomains(
    .DocumentDirectory, .UserDomainMask, true).last!
```

That code returns a path string for the Documents directory. The preferred way to refer to a file or directory, however, is with a URL. You can obtain this from an NSFileManager instance:

```
do {
    let fm = NSFileManager()
    let docsurl = try fm.URLForDirectory(
        .DocumentDirectory, inDomain: .UserDomainMask,
        appropriateForURL: nil, create: false)
    // use docsurl here
} catch {
    // examine error here
}
```

A question that will immediately occur to you is: *where* should I put files and folders that I want to save now and read later? The Documents directory can be a good place. But if your app supports file sharing (discussed later in this chapter), the user can see and modify your app's Documents directory through iTunes, so you might not want to put things there that the user isn't supposed to see and change.

Personally, I favor the Application Support directory for most purposes. In OS X, this directory is shared by multiple applications, each of which must confine itself to an individual subfolder, but on iOS each app has its own private Application Support directory in its own sandbox, so you can safely put files anywhere within it. This directory may not exist initially, but you can obtain it and create it at the same time:

```
do {
    let fm = NSFileManager()
    let docsurl = try fm.URLForDirectory(
        .ApplicationSupportDirectory, inDomain: .UserDomainMask,
        appropriateForURL: nil, create: true)
    // use docsurl here
} catch {
    // examine error here
}
```

Temporary files, whose loss you are willing to accept (because their contents can be recreated), can be written into the Caches directory (NSCachesDirectory) or the Temporary directory (NSTemporaryDirectory). You can write temporary files into the Application Support folder, but by default this means they can be backed up by the user through iTunes or iCloud; to prevent that, exclude such a file from backup by way of its file URL:

```
try myDocumentURL.setResourceValue(
    true, forKey: NSURLIsExcludedFromBackupKey)
```

Although URLs are the favored way of referring to files and folders, they are a more recent innovation than path strings, and you may encounter file operations that still require a string. To derive a path string from an NSURL, send it the path message.

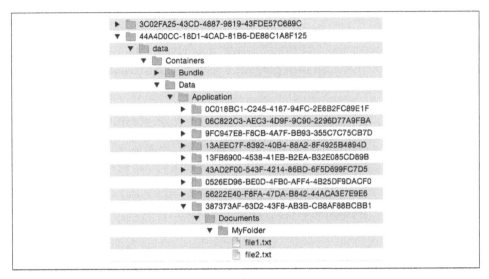

Figure 23-1. An app's sandbox in the Simulator

Visually Inspecting the Sandbox

The Simulator's sandbox is a folder on your Mac that you can, with some difficulty, inspect visually. In your user *~/Library/Developer/CoreSimulator/Devices* folder, you'll find mysteriously named folders representing the different simulators. The *device.plist* file inside each folder can help you identify which simulator a folder represents; so can `xcrun simctl list` at the command line. Inside a simulator's *data/Containers/Data/Application* folder are more mysteriously named folders representing apps on that simulator. I don't know how to identify the different apps, but one of them is the app you're interested in, and inside it is that app's sandox.

In Figure 23-1, I've drilled down from my user *Library* to an app that I've run in the Simulator. My app's Documents folder is visible, and I've opened it to show a folder and a couple of files that I've created programmatically (the code that created them will appear later in this chapter).

You can also view the file structure of your app's sandbox on the device. When the device is connected and no app is being run from Xcode, choose Window → Devices. Select your device on the left; on the right, under Installed Apps, select your app. Click the Gear icon and choose Show Container to view your app's sandbox hierarchy in a modal sheet. Alternatively, choose Download Container to copy your app's sandbox to your computer; the sandbox arrives on your computer as an *.xcappdata* package, and you can open it in the Finder with Show Package Contents.

Basic File Operations

Let's say we intend to create a folder *MyFolder* inside the Documents directory. Assume that we have an NSFileManager instance `fm` and an NSURL `docsurl` pointing at the Documents directory. We can then generate a reference to *MyFolder*, from which we can ask our NSFileManager instance to create the folder if it doesn't exist already:

```
let myfolder = docsurl.URLByAppendingPathComponent("MyFolder")
try fm.createDirectoryAtURL(
    myfolder, withIntermediateDirectories: true, attributes: nil)
```

To learn what files and folders exist within a directory, you can ask for an array of the directory's contents:

```
let arr = try fm.contentsOfDirectoryAtURL(
    docsurl, includingPropertiesForKeys: nil, options: [])
arr.forEach{ print($0.lastPathComponent!) } // MyFolder
```

The array resulting from `contentsOfDirectoryAtURL:...` lists full URLs of the directory's *immediate* contents; it is shallow. For a deep traversal of a directory's contents, you can enumerate it; you are handed only one file reference at a time:

```
let dir = fm.enumeratorAtURL(docsurl, includingPropertiesForKeys: nil,
    options: [], errorHandler: nil)!
for case let f as NSURL in dir where f.pathExtension == "txt" {
    print(f.lastPathComponent!) // file1.txt, file2.txt
}
```

A directory enumerator also permits you to decline to dive into a particular subdirectory (`skipDescendants`), so you can make your traversal even more efficient.

Consult the NSFileManager class documentation for more about what you can do with files, and see also Apple's *File System Programming Guide*.

Saving and Reading Files

To save or read a simple file, you are likely to use one of the convenience methods for the class appropriate to the file's contents. NSString, NSData, NSArray, and NSDictionary provide methods `writeToURL:...` (for writing) and `init(contentsOfURL:...)` (for reading).

NSString and NSData objects map directly between their own contents and the contents of the file. Here, I'll generate a text file directly from a string:

```
try "howdy".writeToURL(myfolder.URLByAppendingPathComponent("file1.txt"),
    atomically: true, encoding: NSUTF8StringEncoding)
```

You can also read and write an attributed string using a file in a standard format, as I mentioned in Chapter 10.

NSArray and NSDictionary files are actually property lists, and will work only if all the contents of the array or dictionary are property list types (NSString, NSData, NSDate, NSNumber, NSArray, and NSDictionary).

So how do you save to a file an object of some other class? Well, if an object's class adopts the NSCoding protocol, you can convert it to an NSData and back again using NSKeyed-Archiver and NSKeyedUnarchiver; the problem is then solved, because an NSData can be saved as a file or in a property list.

You can make your own class adopt the NSCoding protocol. This can become somewhat complicated because an object can refer (through a property) to another object, which may also adopt the NSCoding protocol, and thus you can end up saving an entire graph of interconnected objects if you wish. However, I'll confine myself to illustrating a simple case (and you can read Apple's *Archives and Serializations Programming Guide* for more information).

Let's say, then, that we have a simple Person class with a firstName property and a last-Name property. We'll declare that it adopts the NSCoding protocol:

```
class Person: NSObject, NSCoding {
    var firstName : String
    var lastName : String
    override var description : String {
        return self.firstName + " " + self.lastName
    }
    init(firstName:String, lastName:String) {
        self.firstName = firstName
        self.lastName = lastName
        super.init()
    }
}
```

To make this class actually conform to NSCoding, we must implement encodeWith-Coder: to archive the object, and init(coder:) to unarchive the object. In encodeWith-Coder:, we must first call super if the superclass adopts NSCoding — in this case, it doesn't — and then call the appropriate encode method for each property we want preserved:

```
func encodeWithCoder(coder: NSCoder) {
    // do not call super in this case
    coder.encodeObject(self.lastName, forKey: "last")
    coder.encodeObject(self.firstName, forKey: "first")
}
```

In init(coder:), we call the appropriate decode method for each property stored earlier, thus restoring the state of our object. We must also call super, using either init(coder:) if the superclass adopts the NSCoding protocol or the designated initializer if not:

```
    required init(coder: NSCoder) {
        self.lastName = coder.decodeObjectForKey("last") as! String
        self.firstName = coder.decodeObjectForKey("first") as! String
        // do not call super init(coder:) in this case
        super.init()
    }
```

We can test our code by creating, configuring, and saving a Person instance as a file:

```
let moi = Person(firstName: "Matt", lastName: "Neuburg")
let moidata = NSKeyedArchiver.archivedDataWithRootObject(moi)
let moifile = docsurl.URLByAppendingPathComponent("moi.txt")
moidata.writeToURL(moifile, atomically: true)
```

We can retrieve the saved Person at a later time:

```
let persondata = NSData(contentsOfURL: moifile)!
let person =
    NSKeyedUnarchiver.unarchiveObjectWithData(persondata) as! Person
print(person) // Matt Neuburg
```

If the NSData object is itself the entire content of the file, as here, then instead of using `archivedDataWithRootObject:` and `unarchiveObjectWithData:`, you can skip the intermediate NSData object and use `archiveRootObject:toFile:` and `unarchive-ObjectWithFile:`.

Saving a single Person as an archive may seem like overkill; why didn't we just make a text file consisting of the first and last names? But imagine that a Person has a lot more properties, or that we have an array of hundreds of Persons, or an array of hundreds of dictionaries where one value in each dictionary is a Person; now the power of an archivable Person is evident. Even though Person now adopts the NSCoding protocol, an NSArray containing a Person object still cannot be written to disk using NSArray's `writeToURL...`, because Person is still not a property list type. But the array can be archived and written to disk with NSKeyedArchiver.

User Defaults

User defaults (NSUserDefaults) are intended as the persistent storage of the user's preferences. They are little more, really, than a special case of an NSDictionary property list file. You talk to the NSUserDefaults `standardUserDefaults` object much as if it were a dictionary; it has keys and values. And the only legal values are property list values; thus, for example, to store a Person in user defaults, you'd have to archive it first to an NSData object.

Somewhere on disk, this dictionary is being saved for you automatically as a property list file — though you don't concern yourself with that. You simply set or retrieve values from the dictionary by way of their keys, secure in the knowledge that the file is being read into memory or written to disk as needed. Your chief concern is to make sure that you've written everything needful into user defaults before your app terminates; this will usually mean when the app delegate receives `applicationDidEnterBackground:` at the latest. If you're worried that your app might crash, you can tell the `standardUser-Defaults` object to `synchronize` as a way of forcing it to save right now, but this is rarely necessary.

To provide the value for a key before the user has had a chance to do so — the default default, as it were — use `registerDefaults:`. What you're supplying here is a dictionary whose key–value pairs will each be written into the user defaults, but only if there is no such key already. For example:

```
NSUserDefaults.standardUserDefaults().registerDefaults([
    Default.HazyStripy : HazyStripy.Hazy.rawValue,
    Default.Color1 :
        NSKeyedArchiver.archivedDataWithRootObject(UIColor.blueColor()),
    Default.Color2 :
        NSKeyedArchiver.archivedDataWithRootObject(UIColor.redColor()),
    Default.Color3 :
        NSKeyedArchiver.archivedDataWithRootObject(UIColor.greenColor()),
    Default.CardMatrixRows : 4,
    Default.CardMatrixColumns : 3
])
```

The idea is that we call `registerDefaults:` extremely early as the app launches. Either the app has run at some time previously and the user has set these preferences, in which case this call has no effect and does no harm, or not, in which case we now have initial values for these preferences with which to get started. So, for example, in the game app from which that code comes, we start out with a 4×3 game layout, but the user can change this at any time.

This leaves only the question of how the user is to interact with the defaults. One way is that your app provides some kind of interface. For example, the game app from which the previous code comes has a tab bar interface; the second tab is where the user sets preferences (Figure 23-2).

Alternatively, you can provide a *settings bundle*, consisting mostly of one or more property list files describing an interface and the corresponding user default keys and their initial values; the Settings app is then responsible for translating your instructions into an actual interface, and for presenting it to the user.

Using a settings bundle has some obvious disadvantages: the user has to leave your app to access preferences, and you don't get the kind of control over the interface that you have within your own app. Also, the user can set your preferences while your app is backgrounded or not running; you'll need to register for `NSUserDefaultsDidChange-Notification` in order to hear about this.

In some situations, though, a settings bundle has some clear advantages. Keeping the preferences interface out of your app can make your app's own interface cleaner and

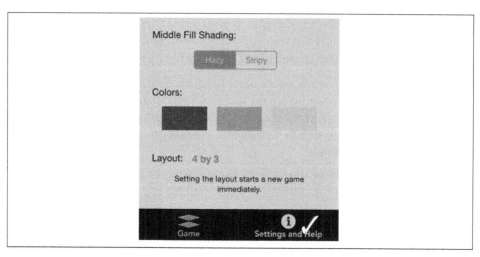

Figure 23-2. An app's preferences interface

simpler. You don't have to write any of the "glue" code that coordinates the preferences interface with the user default values. And it may be appropriate for the user to be able to set at least certain preferences for your app when your app isn't running.

In iOS 7 and before, another objection to a settings bundle was that the user might not think to look in the Settings app for your preferences. Nowadays, however, this is less of an issue, because you can transport your user directly from your app to your app's preferences in the Settings app (and in iOS 9, a Back button appears in the status bar, making it easy for the user to return from Settings to your app):

```
let url = NSURL(string:UIApplicationOpenSettingsURLString)!
UIApplication.sharedApplication().openURL(url)
```

Writing a settings bundle is described in Apple's *Preferences and Settings Programming Guide.*

It is common practice to misuse NSUserDefaults ever so slightly for various purposes. For example, every method in your app can access the `standardUserDefaults` object, so it often serves as a global "drop" where one instance can deposit a piece of information for another instance to pick up later, when those two instances might not have ready communication with one another or might not even exist simultaneously.

NSUserDefaults is also a lightweight alternative to the built-in view controller–based state saving and restoration mechanism discussed in Chapter 6. My Zotz! app (Figure 23-2) is a case in point. In addition to using the user defaults to store the user's actual preferences, it also misuses them to store state information: it records the state of the game board and the card deck into user defaults every time these change, so that if the app is terminated and then launched again later, we can restore the game as it was when the user left off. One might argue that the contents of the card deck are not a user preference, so I am misusing the user defaults to store data. However, while purists may grumble, it's a very small amount of data and I don't think the distinction is terribly significant in this case.

Yet another use of NSUserDefaults is as a way to communicate data between your app and an extension provided by your app. For example, let's say you've written a today extension (Chapter 13) whose interface details depend upon some data belonging to your app. After configuring your extension and your app to constitute an app group, both the extension and the app can access the NSUserDefaults associated with the app group (call `init(suiteName:)` instead of `standardUserDefaults`). For more information, see the "Handling Common Scenarios" chapter of Apple's *App Extension Programming Guide*.

Simple Sharing and Previewing of Files

iOS provides some simple and safe passageways by which a file can pass in and out of your sandbox. File sharing lets the user manipulate the contents of your app's Documents directory. UIDocumentInteractionController allows the user to tell another app to hand your app a copy of a document, or to tell your app to hand a copy of a document to another app. UIDocumentInteractionController also permits previewing a document, provided it is compatible with Quick Look.

 Starting in iOS 8, iOS provides an elaborate mechanism for allowing one app to share an area of its sandbox directly with other apps — document provider extensions, along with related classes such as UIDocumentMenuViewController and UIDocumentPickerViewController. This edition does *not* discuss this topic; see the "Document Provider" chapter of Apple's *App Extension Programming Guide*.

File Sharing

File sharing means simply that an app's Documents directory becomes available to the user through iTunes (Figure 23-3). The user can add files to your app's Documents directory, and can save files and folders from your app's Documents directory to the computer, as well as renaming and deleting files and folders. This could be appropriate, for example, if your app works with common types of file that the user might obtain elsewhere, such as PDFs or JPEGs.

To support file sharing, set the *Info.plist* key "Application supports iTunes file sharing" (`UIFileSharingEnabled`).

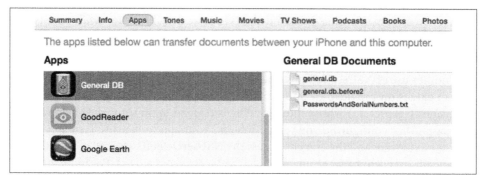

Figure 23-3. The iTunes file sharing interface

Once your entire Documents directory is exposed to the user this way, you are unlikely to use the Documents directory to store private files. As I mentioned earlier, I like to use the Application Support directory instead.

Your app doesn't get any automatic notification when the user has altered the contents of the Documents directory. Noticing that the situation has changed and responding appropriately is entirely up to you; Apple's DocInteraction sample code demonstrates one approaching using the kernel-level kqueue mechanism.

Document Types and Receiving a Document

Your app can declare itself willing to open documents of a certain type. In this way, if another app obtains a document of this type, it can propose to hand a copy of the document over to your app. For example, the user might download the document with Mobile Safari, or receive it in a mail message with the Mail app; now we need a way to get it from Safari or Mail to you.

To let the system know that your app is a candidate for receiving a certain kind of document, you will configure the "Document types" (CFBundleDocumentTypes) key in your *Info.plist*. This is an array, where each entry will be a dictionary specifying a document type by using keys such as "Document Content Type UTIs" (LSItemContentTypes), "Document Type Name" (CFBundleTypeName), CFBundleTypeIconFiles, and LSHandlerRank. Far and away the simplest method for configuring the *Info.plist* is through the interface available in the Info tab when you edit the target.

For example, suppose I want to declare that my app opens PDFs and text files. In my target's Info tab in Xcode, I would edit the Document Types section to look like Figure 23-4.

Now suppose the user receives a PDF in an email message. The Mail app can display this PDF, but the user can also bring up an activity view offering, among other things,

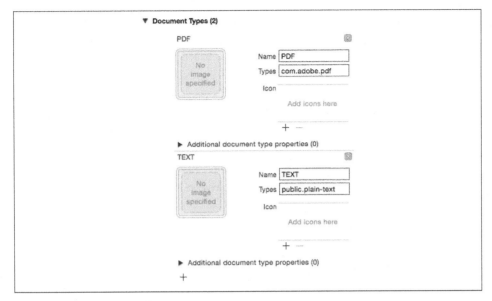

Figure 23-4. Creating a document type

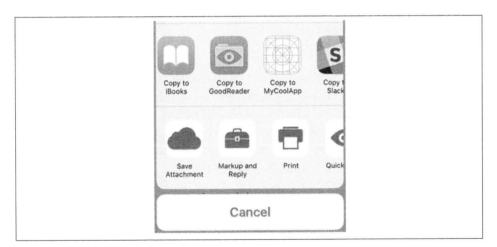

Figure 23-5. The Mail app offers to hand off a PDF

to copy the file to some other app. The interface will resemble Figure 23-5; various apps that can deal with a PDF are listed here, and my app is among them.

So far, so good. But what if the user actually *taps* the button that sends the PDF over to my app? For this to work, my app delegate must implement `application:open-URL:options:`. When that method is called, my app has been brought to the front, either by launching it from scratch or by reviving it from background suspension; its job is now to handle the opening of the document whose URL has arrived as the second parameter. The system has already copied the document into my app's Inbox directory, which it has created in my Documents folder for exactly this purpose.

 The Inbox directory is created in your Documents folder. Thus, if your app implements file sharing, the user can see the Inbox folder; you may wish to delete the Inbox folder, therefore, as soon as you're done retrieving files from it.

In this simple example, my app has just one view controller, which has an outlet to a web view where we will display any PDFs that arrive in this fashion. So my app delegate contains this code:

```
func application(app: UIApplication, openURL url: NSURL,
    options: [String : AnyObject]) -> Bool {
        let vc = self.window!.rootViewController as! ViewController
        vc.displayDoc(url)
        return true
}
```

And my view controller contains this code:

```
func displayDoc (url:NSURL) {
    let req = NSURLRequest(URL: url)
    self.wv.loadRequest(req)
}
```

In real life, things might be more complicated. Our implementation of `application:openURL:options:` might check to see whether this really *is* a PDF, and return `false` if it isn't. Also, our app might be in the middle of something else, possibly displaying a completely different view controller's view; because `application:openURL:options:` can arrive at any time, we may have to be prepared to drop whatever we were doing and display the incoming document instead.

If our app is launched from scratch by the arrival of this URL, `application:didFinishLaunchingWithOptions:` will be sent to our app delegate as usual. The options dictionary (the second parameter) will contain the `UIApplicationLaunchOptionsURLKey`, and we can take into account, if we like, the fact that we are being launched specifically to open a document. We can also return `false` to refuse to open the document. If we return `true` as usual, `application:openURL:options:` will arrive in good order after our interface has been set up.

The example I've been discussing assumes that the UTI for the document type is standard and well-known. It is also possible that your app will operate on a new document type, that is, a type of document that the app itself defines. In that case, you'll also want to add this UTI to your app's list of Exported UTIs in the *Info.plist*. I'll give an example later in this chapter.

Handing Over a Document

The converse of the situation discussed in the previous section is this: your app has somehow acquired a document and wants to let the user hand over a copy of it to some other app to deal with it. This is done through the UIDocumentInteractionController class. This class operates asynchronously, so retaining an instance of it is up to you; typically, you'll store it in a property, and there is no reason not to initialize this property directly:

```
let dic = UIDocumentInteractionController()
```

For example, assuming we have a file URL `url` pointing to a document on disk, presenting the interface for handing the document over to some other application could be as simple as this (`sender` is a button that the user has just tapped):

```
self.dic.URL = url
let v = sender as! UIView
let ok = self.dic.presentOpenInMenuFromRect(
    v.bounds, inView: v, animated: true)
```

The interface is an activity view (Chapter 13). There are actually two activity views available:

`presentOpenInMenuFromRect:inView:animated:`
`presentOpenInMenuFromBarButtonItem:animated:`
Presents an activity view listing apps to which the document can be copied.

`presentOptionsMenuFromRect:inView:animated:`
`presentOptionsMenuFromBarButtonItem:animated:`
Presents an activity view listing apps to which the document can be copied, along with other possible actions, such as Copy and Print.

Previewing a Document

A UIDocumentInteractionController can be used for an entirely different purpose: it can present a preview of the document, if the document is of a type for which preview is enabled, by calling `presentPreviewAnimated:`. You must give the UIDocument-InteractionController a delegate (UIDocumentInteractionControllerDelegate), and the delegate must implement `documentInteractionControllerViewControllerFor-Preview:`, returning an existing view controller that will contain the preview's view controller. So, here we ask for the preview:

```
self.dic.URL = url
self.dic.delegate = self
self.dic.presentPreviewAnimated(true)
```

In the delegate, we supply the view controller; it happens that, in my code, this delegate *is* a view controller, so it simply returns `self`:

```
func documentInteractionControllerViewControllerForPreview(
    controller: UIDocumentInteractionController) -> UIViewController {
        return self
}
```

If the view controller returned were a UINavigationController, the preview's view controller would be pushed onto it. In this case it isn't, so the preview's view controller is a presented view controller with a Done button. The preview interface also contains an Action button that lets the user summon the Options activity view.

There is another way for the user to reach this interface. If you call `presentOptions-Menu...` on your UIDocumentInteractionController, and if the UIDocument-InteractionController has a delegate that implements `documentInteraction-ControllerViewControllerForPreview:`, then the activity view will contain a Quick Look icon that the user can tap to summon the preview interface.

Additional delegate methods allow you to track what's happening in the interface presented by the UIDocumentInteractionController. Probably most important are those that inform you that key stages of the interaction are ending:

- `documentInteractionControllerDidDismissOptionsMenu:`
- `documentInteractionControllerDidDismissOpenInMenu:`
- `documentInteractionControllerDidEndPreview:`
- `documentInteractionController:didEndSendingToApplication:`

Previews are actually provided through the Quick Look framework, and you can skip the UIDocumentInteractionController and present the preview yourself through a QLPreviewController; you'll need to `import QuickLook`. It's a view controller, so to display the preview you show it as a presented view controller or push it onto a navigation controller's stack, just as UIDocumentInteractionController would have done. A nice feature of QLPreviewController is that you can give it more than one document to preview; the user can move between these, within the preview, by paging sideways or using a table of contents summoned by a button at the bottom of the interface. Apart from this, the interface looks like the interface presented by the UIDocument-InteractionController.

In this example, I may have in my Documents directory one or more PDF or text documents. I acquire a list of their URLs and present a preview for them (`self.exts` has been initialized to a set consisting of [`"pdf"`, `"txt"`]):

```
self.docs = [NSURL]()
do {
    let fm = NSFileManager()
    let docsurl = try fm.URLForDirectory(.DocumentDirectory,
        inDomain: .UserDomainMask, appropriateForURL: nil, create: false)
    let dir = fm.enumeratorAtURL(docsurl, includingPropertiesForKeys: nil,
        options: [], errorHandler: nil)!
    for case let f as NSURL in dir {
        if self.exts.contains(f.pathExtension!) {
            if QLPreviewController.canPreviewItem(f) {
                self.docs.append(f)
            }
        }
    }
    guard self.docs.count > 0 else { return }
    let preview = QLPreviewController()
    preview.dataSource = self
    preview.currentPreviewItemIndex = 0
    self.presentViewController(preview, animated: true, completion: nil)
} catch {
    print(error)
}
```

You'll notice that I haven't told the QLPreviewController what documents to preview.
That is the job of QLPreviewController's data source. In my code, I (self) am also the
data source. I simply fetch the requested information from the list of URLs, which I
previously saved into self.docs:

```
func numberOfPreviewItemsInPreviewController(
    controller: QLPreviewController!) -> Int {
        return self.docs.count
}
func previewController(controller: QLPreviewController!,
    previewItemAtIndex index: Int) -> QLPreviewItem! {
        return self.docs[index]
}
```

The second data source method requires us to return an object that adopts the
QLPreviewItem protocol. By a wildly improbable coincidence, NSURL *does* adopt this
protocol, so the example works.

Document Architecture

If your app opens and saves documents of a type peculiar to itself, you may want to take
advantage of the *document architecture*. This architecture revolves around a class,
UIDocument, that takes care of a number of pesky issues:

- Reading or writing your data might take some time, so UIDocument does those
  things on a background thread.

- A document owned by your app may be exposed to reading and writing by other apps. Thus, there needs to be a coherent way for your app to read and write to that document without interference from other apps. The solution is to use an NSFile-Coordinator. UIDocument does this.

- Your document data needs to be synchronized to the document on disk. UIDocument provides autosaving behavior, so that your data is written out automatically whenever it changes.

- Conversely, information about an open document can become stale. To prevent this, the NSFilePresenter protocol notifies editors that a document has changed. UIDocument participates in this system.

- With iCloud, your app's documents on one of the user's devices can automatically be mirrored onto another of the user's devices. UIDocument is the simplest gateway for allowing your documents to participate in iCloud.

Getting started with UIDocument is not difficult. You'll declare a UIDocument subclass, and you'll override two methods:

`loadFromContents:ofType:`
Called when it's time to open a document from disk. You are expected to convert the `contents` value into a model object that your app can use, and to store that model object.

`contentsForType:`
Called when it's time to save a document to disk. You are expected to convert the app's model object into an NSData instance (or, if your document is a package, an NSFileWrapper) and return it.

Your UIDocument subclass will need a place to store and retrieve the data model object. Obviously, this can be a property of the UIDocument subclass itself. At the same time, keep in mind that your UIDocument instance will probably be partnered in some way with a view controller instance, which will also need access to the same data.

To instantiate a UIDocument, call its designated initializer, `init(fileURL:)`. This sets the UIDocument's `fileURL` property, and associates the UIDocument with this file on disk, typically for the remainder of its lifetime.

In my description of the two key UIDocument methods that your subclass will override, I used the phrase, "when it's time" (to open or save the document). This raises the question of how your UIDocument instance will know when to open and save a document. There are three circumstances to distinguish:

Make a new document
The `fileURL:` points to a nonexistent file. Immediately after instantiating the UIDocument, you send it `saveToURL:forSaveOperation:completionHandler:`, where the second argument (a UIDocumentSaveOperation) is `.ForCreating`. (The

first argument will be the UIDocument's own `fileURL`.) This in turn causes `contentsForType:` to be called, and the contents of an empty document are saved out to disk. This implies that your UIDocument subclass should know of some default value that represents the model data when there is no data.

Open an existing document

Send the UIDocument instance `openWithCompletionHandler:`. This in turn causes `loadFromContents:ofType:` to be called.

Save an existing document

There are two approaches to saving an existing document:

Autosave

Usually, you'll mark the document as "dirty" by calling `updateChangeCount:`. From time to time, the UIDocument will notice this situation and will save the document to disk, calling `contentsForType:` in the process.

Manual save

On certain occasions, waiting for autosave won't be appropriate. We've already seen an example of such an occasion — when the file itself needs to be created on the spot. Another is when the app is going into the background; we will want to preserve our document there and then, in case the app is terminated. You'll call `saveToURL:forSaveOperation:completionHandler:`; if the file is not being created for the first time, the second argument will be `.For-Overwriting`. Alternatively, if you know you're finished with the document (perhaps the interface displaying the document is about to be torn down) you can call `closeWithCompletionHandler:`.

The `open...`, `close...`, and `saveTo...` methods have a `completionHandler:` argument. This is UIDocument's solution to the fact that reading and saving may take time. The file operations themselves take place on a background thread; the `completionHandler:` function is then called on the main thread.

We now know enough for an example! I'll reuse my Person class from earlier in this chapter. Imagine a document effectively consisting of multiple Person instances; I'll call each such document a *people group*. Our app, People Groups, will list all people groups in the user's Documents folder; it will also open any people group from disk and display its contents, allowing the user to edit any Person's `firstName` or `lastName` (Figure 23-6).

My first step is to define a custom UTI in my app's *Info.plist*, associating a file type `com.neuburg.pplgrp` with a file extension `"pplgrp"`. I then also define a document type that uses this UTI, as shown earlier in this chapter (Figure 23-7).

A document consists of multiple Persons, so a natural model implementation is an array of Persons. Moreover, as I mentioned earlier, since Person implements NSCoding, an array of Persons can be archived directly into an NSData. Thus, our UIDocument sub-

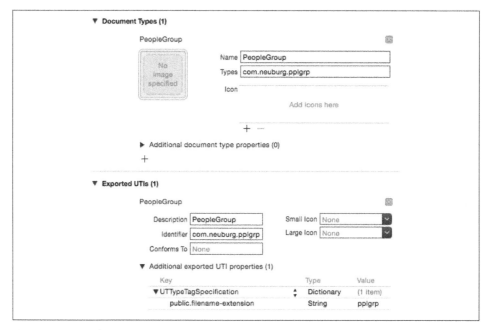

Figure 23-6. The People Groups interface

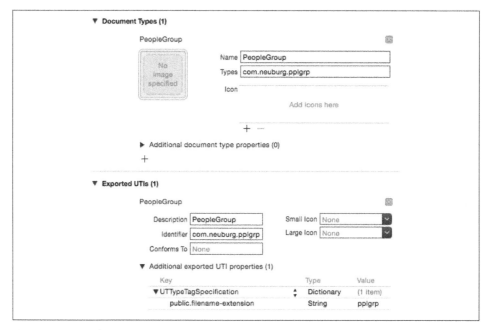

Figure 23-7. Defining a custom UTI

class (which I'll call PeopleDocument) has a public array `people` property, and can be implemented very simply: we initialize our `people` property to an empty Person array, so that we have something to save into a new empty document, and to mediate between

our model and the data on disk, we use NSKeyedUnarchiver and NSKeyedArchiver
exactly as in our earlier examples:

```
class PeopleDocument: UIDocument {
    var people = [Person]()
    override func loadFromContents(contents: AnyObject,
        ofType typeName: String?) throws {
            if let contents = contents as? NSData {
                if let arr = NSKeyedUnarchiver
                    .unarchiveObjectWithData(contents) as? [Person] {
                        self.people = arr
                        return // all's well that ends well
                }
            }
            throw NSError(domain: "NoDataDomain", code: -1, userInfo: nil)
    }
    override func contentsForType(typeName: String) throws -> AnyObject {
        let data = NSKeyedArchiver.archivedDataWithRootObject(self.people)
        return data
    }
}
```

The remaining questions are architectural: when should a PeopleDocument be initialized, where should it be stored, and what should be the nature of communications with
it?

The first view controller, DocumentLister, merely lists documents by name, and provides an interface for letting the user create a new group; only the second view controller,
PeopleLister, the one that displays the first and last names of the people in the group,
actually needs to work with PeopleDocument.

PeopleLister's designated initializer therefore requires that it be given a fileURL: argument, with which it sets its own fileURL property. In its viewDidLoad implementation,
PeopleLister instantiates a PeopleDocument with that same fileURL, and retains it
through a PeopleDocument property (self.doc); PeopleLister's own people property
will be nothing but a front for this PeopleDocument's people property. If fileURL points
to a nonexistent file, PeopleLister requests that it be created by calling saveToURL:for-
SaveOperation:completionHandler:; otherwise, it requests that the document be
read, by calling openWithCompletionHandler:. Either way, the completion handler
refreshes the interface:

```
let fileURL : NSURL
var doc : PeopleDocument!
var people : [Person] { // front end for the document's model object
    get {
        return self.doc.people
    }
    set (val) {
        self.doc.people = val
    }
```

```
    }
    init(fileURL:NSURL) {
        self.fileURL = fileURL
        super.init(nibName: "PeopleLister", bundle: nil)
    }
    required init(coder: NSCoder) {
        fatalError("NSCoding not supported")
    }
    override func viewDidLoad() {
        super.viewDidLoad()
        self.title = (self.fileURL.lastPathComponent! as NSString)
            .stringByDeletingPathExtension
        // ...
        let fm = NSFileManager()
        self.doc = PeopleDocument(fileURL:self.fileURL)
        func listPeople(success:Bool) {
            if success {
                self.tableView.reloadData()
            }
        }
        if !fm.fileExistsAtPath(self.fileURL.path!) {
            self.doc.saveToURL(self.doc.fileURL,
                forSaveOperation: .ForCreating,
                completionHandler: listPeople)
        } else {
            self.doc.openWithCompletionHandler(listPeople)
        }
    }
}
```

When the user performs a significant editing maneuver, such as creating or deleting a
person or editing a person's first or last name, PeopleLister tells its PeopleDocument
that the document is dirty, and allows autosaving to take it from there:

```
self.doc.updateChangeCount(.Done)
```

When the app is about to go into the background, or when PeopleLister's own view is
disappearing, PeopleLister forces PeopleDocument to save immediately:

```
func forceSave(_:AnyObject?) {
    self.tableView.endEditing(true)
    self.doc.saveToURL(self.doc.fileURL,
        forSaveOperation:.ForOverwriting, completionHandler:nil)
}
```

That's all it takes; adding UIDocument support to your app is easy, because UIDocument
is merely acting as a supplier and preserver of your app's data model object. UIDocument
presents itself in the documentation as a large and complex class, but that's chiefly
because it is so heavily customizable both at high and low levels; for the most part, you
won't need any of that heavy customization, and use of UIDocument really will be as
simple as what I've shown here. You might go further in order to give your UIDocument
a more sophisticated understanding of what constitutes a significant change in your

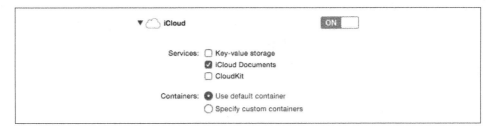

Figure 23-8. Turning on iCloud support

data by working with its undo manager; I'll talk about undo managers in Chapter 26. For further details, see Apple's *Document-based App Programming Guide for iOS.*

iCloud

Once your app is operating through UIDocument, basic iCloud compatibility effectively falls right into your lap. You have just two steps to perform:

Obtain iCloud entitlements
  Edit the target and, in the Capabilities tab, set the iCloud switch to On. This causes a transaction to take place between Xcode and the Member Center; automatically, your app gets a ubiquity container, and an appropriately configured entitlements file is added to the project (Figure 23-8).

Obtain an iCloud-compatible directory
  Early in your app's lifetime, call NSFileManager's URLForUbiquityContainer-Identifier: (typically passing nil as the argument), on a background thread, to obtain the URL of the cloud-shared directory. Any documents your app puts here by way of a UIDocument subclass will be automatically shared into the cloud.

Thus, having thrown the switch in the Capabilities tab (Figure 23-8), I can make my People Groups example app iCloud-compatible with just two code changes. In the app delegate, as my app launches, I step out to a background thread (Chapter 25), obtain the cloud-shared directory's URL, and then step back to the main thread and retain the URL through a property, self.ubiq:

```
dispatch_async(dispatch_get_global_queue(0, 0)) {
    let fm = NSFileManager()
    let ubiq = fm.URLForUbiquityContainerIdentifier(nil)
    dispatch_async(dispatch_get_main_queue()) {
        self.ubiq = ubiq
    }
}
```

When I specify where to seek and save people groups, I continue using the user's Documents folder if ubiq is nil, but otherwise I use ubiq itself:

```
var docsurl : NSURL {
    var url = NSURL()
    let del = UIApplication.sharedApplication().delegate
    if let ubiq = (del as! AppDelegate).ubiq {
        url = ubiq
    } else {
        do {
            let fm = NSFileManager()
            url = try fm.URLForDirectory(.DocumentDirectory,
                inDomain: .UserDomainMask, appropriateForURL: nil,
                create: false)
        } catch {
            print(error)
        }
    }
    return url
}
```

To test, iCloud Drive must be turned on under iCloud in my Settings. I run the app and create a people group with some people in it. I then switch to a different device and run the app there, and tap the Refresh button. This is a very crude implementation, purely for testing purposes; it looks through the `docsurl` directory, first for cloud items to download, and then for `pplgrp` files:

```
do {
    let fm = NSFileManager()
    self.files = try fm.contentsOfDirectoryAtURL(
        self.docsurl, includingPropertiesForKeys: nil, options: [])
        .filter {
            if fm.isUbiquitousItemAtURL($0) {
                try fm.startDownloadingUbiquitousItemAtURL($0)
            }
            return $0.pathExtension! == "pplgrp"
        }
    self.tableView.reloadData()
} catch {
    print(error)
}
```

Presto, the app on this device now displays my people group containing my people, created on a different device! It's quite thrilling.

Although it works — possibly after a couple of tries — my Refresh button approach is crude. My UIDocument works with iCloud, but my app is not yet a good iCloud citizen. The truth is that I should not be using NSFileManager like this. Instead, I should be running an NSMetadataQuery. The usual strategy is:

1. Instantiate NSMetadataQuery and retain the instance.

2. Configure the search. This means giving the metadata query a search scope of `NSMetadataQueryUbiquitousDocumentsScope`, and supplying a serial queue (NSOperationQueue, see Chapter 25) for it to run on.

3. Register for notifications such as `NSMetadataQueryDidFinishGathering-Notification` and `NSMetadataQueryDidUpdateNotification`.

4. Start the search (`startQuery`). The NSMetadataQuery instance then remains in place, with the search continuing to run more or less constantly, for the entire lifetime of the app.

5. When a notification arrives, check the NSMetadataQuery's `results`. These will be NSMetadataItem objects, whose `valueForAttribute(NSMetadataItemURLKey)` is the document URL.

Similarly, in my earlier code I called `fileExistsAtPath:`, but for a cloud item I should be calling NSURL's `checkPromisedItemIsReachableAndReturnError:` instead.

Further iCloud details are outside the scope of this discussion; see Apple's *iCloud Design Guide*. Getting started is easy; making your app a good iCloud citizen, capable of dealing with the complexities that iCloud may entail, is not. There are many complications to deal with: What if the currently open document changes because someone edited it on another device? What if that change is in conflict with changes I've made on *this* device? What if the availability of iCloud changes while the app is open — for example, the user switches it on, or switches it off? Apple's sample code has a bad habit of skirting the knottier issues; for instance, the ShapeEdit example fails to demonstrate how to accommodate the possibility that iCloud may be turned off.

XML

XML is a highly flexible and widely used general-purpose text file format for storage and retrieval of structured data. You might use it yourself to store data that you'll need to retrieve later, or you could encounter it when obtaining information from elsewhere, such as the Internet.

OS X Cocoa provides a set of classes (NSXMLDocument and so forth) for reading, parsing, maintaining, searching, and modifying XML data in a completely general way, but iOS does *not* include these. I think the reason must be that their tree-based approach is too memory-intensive. Instead, iOS provides NSXMLParser, a much simpler class that walks through an XML document, sending delegate messages as it encounters elements. With this, you can parse an XML document once, but what you do with the pieces as you encounter them is up to you. The general assumption here is that you know in advance the structure of the particular XML data you intend to read and that you have provided classes for storage of the same data in object form and for transforming the XML pieces into that storage.

To illustrate, let's return once more to our Person class with a `firstName` and a `last-Name` property. Imagine that as our app starts up, we would like to populate it with Person objects, and that we've stored the data describing these objects as an XML file in our app bundle, like this:

```
<?xml version="1.0" encoding="utf-8"?>
<people>
    <person>
        <firstName>Matt</firstName>
        <lastName>Neuburg</lastName>
    </person>
    <person>
        <firstName>Snidely</firstName>
        <lastName>Whiplash</lastName>
    </person>
    <person>
        <firstName>Dudley</firstName>
        <lastName>Doright</lastName>
    </person>
</people>
```

This data could be mapped to an array of Person objects, each with its `firstName` and `lastName` properties appropriately set. (This is a deliberately easy example, of course; not all XML is so readily expressed as objects.) Let's consider how we might do that.

Using NSXMLParser is not difficult in theory. You create the NSXMLParser, handing it the URL of a local XML file (or an NSData, perhaps downloaded from the Internet), set its delegate, and tell it to `parse`. The delegate starts receiving delegate messages. For simple XML like ours, there are only three delegate messages of interest:

`parser:didStartElement:namespaceURI:qualifiedName:attributes:`
The parser has encountered an opening element tag. In our document, this would be <people>, <person>, <firstName>, or <lastName>.

`parser:didEndElement:namespaceURI:qualifiedName:`
The parser has encountered the corresponding closing element tag. In our document this would be </people>, </person>, </firstName>, or </lastName>.

`parser:foundCharacters:`
The parser has encountered some text between the starting and closing tags for the current element. In our document this would be, for example, Matt or Neuburg and so on.

In practice, responding to these delegate messages poses challenges of maintaining state. If there is just one delegate, it will have to bear in mind at every moment what element it is currently encountering; this could make for a lot of properties and a lot of if-statements in the implementation of the delegate methods. To aggravate the issue, `parser:foundCharacters:` can arrive multiple times for a single stretch of text; that is, the text may arrive in pieces, so we have to accumulate it into a property.

An elegant way to meet these challenges is by resetting the NSXMLParser's delegate to different objects at different stages of the parsing process. We make each delegate responsible for parsing one element; when a child of that element is encountered, we make a new object and make *it* the delegate. The child element delegate is then responsible for making the parent the delegate once again when it finishes parsing its own element. This is slightly counterintuitive because it means `parser:didStart-Element...` and `parser:didEndElement...` for the same element are arriving at *two different objects*. Imagine, for example, what the job of our <people> parser will be:

1. When `parser:didStartElement...` arrives, the <people> parser looks to see if this is a <person>. If so, it creates an object that knows how to deal with a <person> (a <person> parser), handing that object a reference to itself (the <people> parser), and makes it the delegate.

2. Delegate messages now arrive at this newly created <person> parser. If any text is encountered, `parser:foundCharacters:` will be called, and the text must be accumulated into a property.

3. Eventually, `parser:didEndElement...` arrives. The <person> parser now uses its reference to make the <people> parser the delegate once again. The <people> parser, having received from the <person> parser any data it may have collected, is now ready in case another <person> element is encountered (and the old <person> parser might now go quietly out of existence).

With this in mind, we can design a simple all-purpose base class for parsing an element (simple especially because we are taking no account of namespaces, attributes, and other complications). I'll show you the design and explain its architecture before I fill in the blanks with actual code:

```
class MyXMLParserDelegate : NSObject {
    var name : String!
    var text = ""
    weak var parent : MyXMLParserDelegate?
    var child : MyXMLParserDelegate!
    required init(name:String, parent:MyXMLParserDelegate?) {/*...*/}
    func makeChild(klass:MyXMLParserDelegate.Type,
        elementName:String,
        parser:NSXMLParser) {/*...*/}
    func finishedChild(s:String) {/*...*/}
}
```

Here's how these properties and methods are intended to work:

name
     The name of the element we are parsing now.

text

> A place for any characters to accumulate as we parse our element.

parent

> A reference to the MyXMLParserDelegate who created us and whose child we are.

child

> If we encounter a child element, we'll create a MyXMLParserDelegate and retain it here, making it the delegate and making ourselves its parent.

makeChild:elementName:parser:

> If we encounter a child element, there's a standard dance to do: instantiate some subclass of MyXMLParserDelegate, make ourself its parent, make it our child, and make it the parser's delegate. This is a utility method that embodies that dance.

finishedChild:

> When a child receives parser:didEndElement..., it should send this message to its parent before making its parent the delegate. The parameter is the text, but the parent can use this signal to obtain any information it expects from the child before the child goes out of existence.

Now we can sketch in the default implementations for the methods I just described:

```
required init(name:String, parent:MyXMLParserDelegate?) {
    self.name = name
    self.parent = parent
    super.init()
}
func makeChild(klass:MyXMLParserDelegate.Type,
    elementName:String,
    parser:NSXMLParser) {
        let del = klass.init(name:elementName, parent:self)
        self.child = del
        parser.delegate = del
}
func finishedChild(s:String) { // subclasses must override!
    fatalError("Subclass must implement finishedChild:!")
}
```

But that's only half the story. MyXMLParserDelegate is also an NSXMLParserDelegate — that's the point! Thus, I now extend MyXMLParserDelegate to adopt NSXMLParserDelegate:

```
extension MyXMLParserDelegate : NSXMLParserDelegate {
    func parser(parser: NSXMLParser, foundCharacters string: String) {
        self.text = self.text + string
    }
    func parser(parser: NSXMLParser, didEndElement elementName: String,
        namespaceURI: String?, qualifiedName qName: String?) {
            if self.parent != nil {
                self.parent!.finishedChild(self.text)
```

```
            parser.delegate = self.parent
        }
    }
}
```

That completes the picture, and we can now proceed to create specialized subclasses of MyXMLParserDelegate, one for each kind of element we expect to parse. Each subclass has very little work to do:

- In `parser:didStartElement...`, if a child element is encountered, it should call the utility method `makeChild:elementName:parser:` to create the appropriate child parser.

- The reverse process is already built into the default implementation of `parser:did-EndElement...`: we call the parent's `finishedChild:` and make the parent the delegate. Each subclass should implement `finishedChild:` in order to receive whatever data the child hands back.

We can now parse our sample XML into an array of Person objects very easily. We start by obtaining the URL of the XML file, handing it to an NSXMLParser, creating our first delegate parser and making it the delegate, and telling the NSXMLParser to start parsing:

```
if let url = NSBundle.mainBundle().URLForResource(
    "folks", withExtension: "xml") {
        if let parser = NSXMLParser(contentsOfURL: url) {
            let people = MyPeopleParser(name:"", parent:nil)
            parser.delegate = people
            parser.parse()
            // all done! do something with people.people here
        }
}
```

MyPeopleParser is the top-level parser. It has a `people` property that starts out as an empty Person array; as it encounters a `<person>` element, it creates a `<person>` parser — a MyPersonParser, whose `person` property is expected, when it finishes parsing and `finishedChild:` is called, to be a Person object, suitable for appending to `people`:

```
var people = [Person]()
func parser(parser: NSXMLParser, didStartElement elementName: String,
    namespaceURI: String?, qualifiedName qName: String?,
    attributes attributeDict: [NSObject : AnyObject]) {
        if elementName == "person" {
            self.makeChild(
                MyPersonParser.self, elementName: elementName,
                parser: parser)
        }
}
override func finishedChild(s: String) {
    self.people.append((self.child as! MyPersonParser).person)
}
```

MyPersonParser does the same child-making dance when it encounters a `<firstName>` or a `<lastName>` element; it uses a plain vanilla MyXMLParserDelegate to parse these children, because the built-in ability to accumulate text and hand it back is all that's needed. In `finishedChild:`, key–value coding is elegantly used to match the name of the element with the name of the Person property to be set:

```
var person = Person(firstName: "", lastName: "")
func parser(parser: NSXMLParser, didStartElement elementName: String,
    namespaceURI: String?, qualifiedName qName: String?,
    attributes attributeDict: [NSObject : AnyObject]) {
        self.makeChild(MyXMLParserDelegate.self,
            elementName: elementName, parser: parser)
}
override func finishedChild(s: String) {
    self.person.setValue(s, forKey:self.child.name)
}
```

This may seem like a lot of work to parse such a simple bit of XML, but it is neatly object-oriented and requires very little new code once we've established the MyXMLParser-Delegate superclass, which is of course reusable in many other situations.

A Foundation class for constructing and parsing JSON strings is also provided — NSJSONSerialization. It's a very simple class: all its methods are class methods, and eligible structures are required to be an array or dictionary (corresponding to what JSON calls an *object*) whose elements must be a string, number, array, dictionary, or null. NSData is used as the medium of exchange; you'll archive or unarchive as appropriate. JSON arises often as a lightweight way of communicating structured data across the network; for more information, see *http://www.json.org/*.

SQLite

SQLite (*http://www.sqlite.org/docs.html*) is a lightweight, full-featured relational database that you can talk to using SQL, the universal language of databases. This can be an appropriate storage format when your data comes in rows and columns (records and fields) and needs to be rapidly searchable. Also, the database as a whole is never loaded into memory; the data is accessed only as needed. This is valuable in an environment like an iOS device, where memory is at a premium.

To use SQLite, set the Other Linker Flags build setting to `-lsqlite3`. Talking to `sqlite3` involves an elaborate C interface which may prove annoying; there are, however, a number of lightweight Objective-C front ends. In this example, I use `fmdb` (*https://github.com/ccgus/fmdb*) to read the names of people out of a previously created database (this requires a bridging header in which we `#import "FMDB.h"`):

```
let db = FMDatabase(path:self.dbpath)
if !db.open() {
    return
}
if let rs = db.executeQuery("select * from people") {
    while rs.next() {
        print(rs["firstname"], rs["lastname"])
    }
}
db.close()
/*
Matt Neuburg
Snidely Whiplash
Dudley Doright
*/
```

You can include a previously constructed SQLite file in your app bundle, but you can't write to it there; the solution is to copy it from your app bundle into another location, such as the Documents directory, before you start working with it.

Core Data

The Core Data framework provides a generalized way of expressing objects and properties that form a relational graph; moreover, it has built-in facilities for persisting those objects to disk — typically using SQLite as a storage format — and reading them from disk only when they are needed, thus making efficient use of memory. For example, a person might have not only multiple addresses but also multiple friends who are also persons; expressing persons and addresses as explicit object types, working out how to link them and how to translate between objects in memory and data in storage, and tracking the effects of changes, such as when a person is deleted, can be tedious. Core Data can help.

It is important to stress, however, that Core Data is *not* a beginner-level technology. It is difficult to use and extremely difficult to debug. It expresses itself in a highly verbose, rigid, arcane way. It has its own elaborate way of doing things — everything you already know about how to create, access, alter, or delete an object within an object collection becomes completely irrelevant! — and trying to bend it to your particular needs can be tricky and can have unintended side effects. Nor should Core Data be seen as a substitute for a true relational database.

Therefore, I have no intention of explaining Core Data; that would require an entire book. Indeed, such books exist, and if Core Data interests you, you should read some of them. See also Apple's *Core Data Programming Guide* and the other resources referred to there. I will, however, illustrate what it's like to work with Core Data.

I will rewrite the People Groups example from earlier in this chapter as a Core Data app. We will no longer have multiple documents, each representing a single group of people;

instead, we will now have a single document, maintained for us by Core Data, containing all of our groups and all of their people.

A Core Data project must `import CoreData`. To construct a Core Data project from scratch, it is simplest to specify the Master–Detail Application template (or the Single View Application template) and check Use Core Data in the second screen. This gives you template code in the app delegate implementation file for constructing the Core Data *persistence stack*, a set of objects that work together to fetch and save your data; in most cases there will no reason to alter this template code, and I have not done so for this example.

The app delegate template code gives the app delegate three properties representing the important singleton objects constituting the persistence stack: `managedObject-Context`, `managedObjectModel`, and `persistentStoreCoordinator`. It also supplies `lazy` initializers to give these properties their values when first needed. Of these, the `managedObjectContext` is the most important for other classes to have access to. The managed object context is the world in which your data objects live and move and have their being: to obtain an object, you fetch it from the managed object context; to create an object, you insert it into the managed object context; to save your data, you save the managed object context.

The Master–Detail Application template also gives the master view controller a `managed-ObjectContext` property, and the app delegate sets its value. My master view controller is called GroupLister, so the app delegate's `application:didFinishLaunchingWith-Options:` contains these lines:

```
let navigationController =
    self.window!.rootViewController as! UINavigationController
let controller = navigationController.topViewController as! GroupLister
controller.managedObjectContext = self.managedObjectContext
```

To describe the structure and relationships of the objects constituting your data model, you design an object graph in a data model document. Our object graph is very simple: a Group can have multiple Persons (Figure 23-9). The attributes, analogous to object properties, are all strings, except for the timestamps which are dates. (The timestamps will be used for determining the sort order in which groups and people will be displayed in the interface.)

Core Data attributes are not quite object properties. Group and Person are not classes; they are entity names. All Core Data model objects are instances of NSManagedObject, and therefore they do not, of themselves, have a `name` property, a `firstName` property, a `lastName` property, and so on. Instead, Core Data model objects make themselves dynamically KVC compliant for attribute names. For example, Core Data knows, thanks to our object graph, that a Person entity is to have a `firstName` attribute, so you can set a Person's `firstName` attribute using KVC (`setValue:forKey:`). I find this maddening,

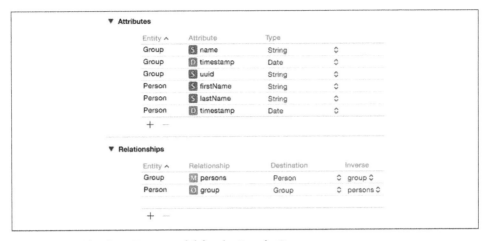

Figure 23-9. The Core Data model for the People Groups app

so, at the very least, I like to give NSManagedObject the necessary properties through an extension:

```
extension NSManagedObject {
    @NSManaged var firstName : String
    @NSManaged var lastName : String
    @NSManaged var name : String
    @NSManaged var uuid : String
    @NSManaged var timestamp : NSDate
    @NSManaged var group : NSManagedObject
}
```

Now we'll be able to use firstName and the rest as properties, and Core Data will generate the corresponding accessors for us.

Now let's talk about the first view controller, GroupLister. Its job is to list groups and to allow the user to create a new group (Figure 23-6). The way you ask Core Data for a model object is with a fetch request. In iOS, where Core Data model objects are often the data source for a UITableView, fetch requests are conveniently managed through an NSFetchedResultsController. The template code gives us an NSFetchedResults-Controller private property with a corresponding public computed property that generates an NSFetchedResultsController if the private property is nil; this seems overblown, and in my implementation I've replaced it with a single lazy NSFetchedResults-Controller property, which I've called frc. My entity name is "Group" and my cache name is "Groups"; apart from that, and some shortened variable names, this is pure template code:

```
lazy var frc : NSFetchedResultsController = {
    let req = NSFetchRequest()
    let entity = NSEntityDescription.entityForName("Group",
        inManagedObjectContext:self.managedObjectContext)
    req.entity = entity
    req.fetchBatchSize = 20
    let sortDescriptor = NSSortDescriptor(key:"timestamp", ascending:true)
    req.sortDescriptors = [sortDescriptor]
    let afrc = NSFetchedResultsController(fetchRequest:req,
        managedObjectContext:self.managedObjectContext,
        sectionNameKeyPath:nil, cacheName:"Groups")
    afrc.delegate = self
    do {
        try afrc.performFetch()
    } catch {
        print("Unresolved error \(error)")
        fatalError("Aborting with unresolved error")
    }
    return afrc
}()
```

The result is that self.frc is the data model, analogous to an array of Group objects.
The implementation of the table view's Three Big Questions to the data source, all pretty
much straight from the template code, looks like this:

```
override func numberOfSectionsInTableView(
    tableView: UITableView) -> Int {
        return self.frc.sections!.count
}
override func tableView(tableView: UITableView,
    numberOfRowsInSection section: Int) -> Int {
        let sectionInfo = self.frc.sections![section]
        return sectionInfo.numberOfObjects
}
override func tableView(tableView: UITableView,
    cellForRowAtIndexPath indexPath: NSIndexPath) -> UITableViewCell {
        let cell = tableView.dequeueReusableCellWithIdentifier(
            "Cell", forIndexPath:indexPath)
        cell.accessoryType = .DisclosureIndicator
        let object =
            self.frc.objectAtIndexPath(indexPath) as! NSManagedObject
        cell.textLabel!.text = object.name
        return cell
}
```

Now let's talk about object creation. GroupLister's table is initially empty because our
app starts life with no data. When the user asks to create a group, I put up an alert asking
for the name of the new group. In the handler for its OK button, if the user provides a
valid name, I create a new Group entity and save the managed object context. Again,
this is almost boilerplate code, copied from the template's insertNewObject: method:

```
av.addAction(UIAlertAction(title: "OK", style: .Default) {
    _ in
    guard let name = av.textFields![0].text where !name.isEmpty else {
        return
    }
    let context = self.frc.managedObjectContext
    let entity = self.frc.fetchRequest.entity!
    let mo = NSEntityDescription.insertNewObjectForEntityForName(
        entity.name!, inManagedObjectContext: context)
    mo.name = name
    mo.uuid = NSUUID().UUIDString
    mo.timestamp = NSDate()
    do {
        try context.save()
    } catch {
        print(error)
        return
    }
    let pl = PeopleLister(groupManagedObject: mo)
    self.navigationController!.pushViewController(pl, animated: true)
})
```

The second view controller class is PeopleLister. It lists all the people in a particular
Group, so I don't want PeopleLister to be instantiated without a Group; therefore, its
designated initializer is init(groupManagedObject:). To navigate from the Group-
Lister view to the PeopleLister view, I instantiate PeopleLister and push it onto the
navigation controller's stack, as the preceding code shows; I do the same sort of thing
when the user taps an existing Group name in the GroupLister table view:

```
override func tableView(tableView: UITableView,
    didSelectRowAtIndexPath indexPath: NSIndexPath) {
        let pl = PeopleLister(groupManagedObject:
            self.frc.objectAtIndexPath(indexPath) as! NSManagedObject)
        self.navigationController!.pushViewController(pl, animated: true)
}
```

PeopleLister, too, has an frc property, along with a lazy initializer that is almost identical to the template code for generating an NSFetchedResultsController — almost, but
not quite. In the case of GroupLister, we wanted *every* group; but a PeopleLister instance
should list only the People belonging to *one particular group*, which has been stored as
the groupObject property. So PeopleLister's implementation of the frc initializer contains these lines:

```
let pred = NSPredicate(format:"group = %@", self.groupObject)
req.predicate = pred // req is the fetch request we're configuring
```

As you can see from Figure 23-6, the PeopleLister interface consists of a table of text
fields. Populating the table is easy enough:

```
override func tableView(tableView: UITableView,
    cellForRowAtIndexPath indexPath: NSIndexPath) -> UITableViewCell {
        let cell = tableView.dequeueReusableCellWithIdentifier(
            "Person", forIndexPath:indexPath)
        let object =
            self.frc.objectAtIndexPath(indexPath) as! NSManagedObject
        let first = cell.viewWithTag(1) as! UITextField
        let last = cell.viewWithTag(2) as! UITextField
        first.text = object.firstName
        last.text = object.lastName
        first.delegate = self; last.delegate = self
        return cell
}
```

When the user edits a text field (the first or last name of a Person), I update the data model and save the managed object context; the first part of this code should be familiar from Chapter 8:

```
func textFieldDidEndEditing(textField: UITextField) {
    var v = textField.superview!
    while !(v is UITableViewCell) {v = v.superview!}
    let cell = v as! UITableViewCell
    let ip = self.tableView.indexPathForCell(cell)!
    let object = self.frc.objectAtIndexPath(ip) as! NSManagedObject
    object.setValue(textField.text, forKey: (
        (textField.tag == 1) ? "firstName" : "lastName"))
    do {
        try object.managedObjectContext!.save()
    } catch {
        print(error)
    }
}
```

The trickiest part is what happens when the user asks to make a new Person. It starts out analogously to making a new Group: I make a new Person entity, configure its attributes with an empty first name and last name, and save the context. But we must also make this empty Person appear in the table! To do so, we act as the NSFetched-ResultsController's delegate (NSFetchedResultsControllerDelegate); the delegate methods are triggered by the change in the managed object context:

```
func doAdd(_:AnyObject) {
    self.tableView.endEditing(true)
    let context = self.frc.managedObjectContext
    let entity = self.frc.fetchRequest.entity!
    let mo = NSEntityDescription.insertNewObjectForEntityForName(
        entity.name!, inManagedObjectContext:context)
    mo.group = self.groupObject
    mo.lastName = ""
    mo.firstName = ""
    mo.timestamp = NSDate()
    do {
        try context.save()
```

```
        } catch {
            print(error)
        }
    }
    // ================= delegate methods =====================
    func controllerWillChangeContent(controller: NSFetchedResultsController) {
        self.tableView.beginUpdates()
    }
    func controllerDidChangeContent(controller: NSFetchedResultsController) {
        self.tableView.endUpdates()
    }
    func controller(controller: NSFetchedResultsController,
        didChangeObject anObject: AnyObject,
        atIndexPath indexPath: NSIndexPath?,
        forChangeType type: NSFetchedResultsChangeType,
        newIndexPath: NSIndexPath?) {
            if type == .Insert {
                self.tableView.insertRowsAtIndexPaths(
                    [newIndexPath!], withRowAnimation: .Automatic)
                dispatch_async(dispatch_get_main_queue()) {
                    let cell =
                        self.tableView.cellForRowAtIndexPath(newIndexPath!)!
                    let tf = cell.viewWithTag(1) as! UITextField
                    tf.becomeFirstResponder()
                }
            }
    }
}
```

Image File Formats

The Image I/O framework provides a simple, unified way to open image files (from disk or downloaded from the network, as described in Chapter 24), to save image files, to convert between image file formats, and to read metadata from standard image file formats, including EXIF and GPS information from a digital camera. You'll need to import ImageIO.

Obviously, such features were not entirely missing from iOS before the Image I/O framework was introduced (starting in iOS 4). UIImage can read the data from most standard image formats, and you can convert formats with functions such as UIImage-JPEGRepresentation and UIImagePNGRepresentation. But you could not, for example, save an image as a TIFF without the Image I/O framework.

The Image I/O framework introduces the notion of an *image source* (CGImageSource). This can be created from the URL of a file on disk or from an NSData object (actually CFData, to which NSData is toll-free bridged). You can use this to obtain a CGImage of the source's image (or, if the source format contains multiple images, a particular image). But you can also obtain metadata from the source *without* transforming the source into a CGImage, thus conserving memory. For example:

```
let url = NSBundle.mainBundle().URLForResource(
    "colson", withExtension: "jpg")!
let src = CGImageSourceCreateWithURL(url, nil)!
let result = CGImageSourceCopyPropertiesAtIndex(src, 0, nil)!
    as [NSObject:AnyObject]
// ... do something with result ...
```

Without having opened the image file as an image, we now have a dictionary full of information about it, including its pixel dimensions (kCGImagePropertyPixelWidth and kCGImagePropertyPixelHeight), its resolution, its color model, its color depth, and its orientation — plus, because this picture originally comes from a digital camera, the EXIF data such as the aperture and exposure at which it was taken, plus the make and model of the camera.

We can obtain the image as a CGImage, with CGImageSourceCreateImageAtIndex. Alternatively, we can request a thumbnail version of the image. This is a very useful thing to do, and the name "thumbnail" doesn't really do justice to its importance and power. If your purpose in opening this image is to display it in your interface, you don't care about the original image data; a thumbnail is *precisely* what you want, especially because you can specify any size for this "thumbnail" all the way up to the original size of the image! This is tremendously convenient, because to assign a large image to a small image view wastes all the memory reflected by the size difference.

To generate a thumbnail at a given size, you start with a dictionary specifying the size along with other instructions, and pass that, together with the image source, to CGImage-SourceCreateThumbnailAtIndex. The only pitfall is that, because we are working with a CGImage and specifying actual pixels, we must remember to take account of the scale of our device's screen. So, for example, let's say we want to scale our image so that its largest dimension is no larger than the width of the UIImageView (self.iv) into which we intend to place it:

```
let url = NSBundle.mainBundle().URLForResource(
    "colson", withExtension: "jpg")!
let src = CGImageSourceCreateWithURL(url, nil)!
let scale = UIScreen.mainScreen().scale
let w = self.iv.bounds.width * scale
let d : [NSObject:AnyObject] = [
    kCGImageSourceShouldAllowFloat : true,
    kCGImageSourceCreateThumbnailWithTransform : true,
    kCGImageSourceCreateThumbnailFromImageAlways : true,
    kCGImageSourceThumbnailMaxPixelSize : w
]
let imref = CGImageSourceCreateThumbnailAtIndex(src, 0, d)!
let im = UIImage(CGImage: imref, scale: scale, orientation: .Up)
self.iv.image = im
```

The Image I/O framework also introduces the notion of an *image destination*, used for saving an image into a specified file format. As a final example, I'll show how to save our image as a TIFF. We never open the image as an image! We save directly from the image source to the image destination:

```
let url = NSBundle.mainBundle().URLForResource(
    "colson", withExtension: "jpg")!
let src = CGImageSourceCreateWithURL(url, nil)!
let fm = NSFileManager()
let suppurl = try! fm.URLForDirectory(.ApplicationSupportDirectory,
    inDomain: .UserDomainMask, appropriateForURL: nil, create: true)
let tiff = suppurl.URLByAppendingPathComponent("mytiff.tiff")
let dest = CGImageDestinationCreateWithURL(tiff, kUTTypeTIFF, 1, nil)!
CGImageDestinationAddImageFromSource(dest, src, 0, nil)
let ok = CGImageDestinationFinalize(dest)
```

CHAPTER 24

Basic Networking

Networking is difficult and complicated, chiefly because it's ultimately out of your control. My motto with regard to the network is, "There's many a slip 'twixt the cup and the lip." You can ask for a resource from across the network, but at that point anything can happen: the resource might not be found (the server is down, perhaps), it might take a while to arrive, it might never arrive, the network itself might vanish after the resource has partially arrived. iOS, however, makes at least the *basics* of networking very easy, so that's what this chapter will deal with.

To go further into networking than this chapter takes you, start with Apple's *URL Loading System Programming Guide*. To go even deeper under the hood, see the *CFNetwork Programming Guide*. Apple also provides a generous amount of sample code. See in particular SimpleURLConnections, AdvancedURLConnections, SimpleNetwork-Streams, SimpleFTPSample, and MVCNetworking.

Many earlier chapters have described interface and frameworks that network for you automatically. Put a web view in your interface (Chapter 11) and poof, you're networking; the web view does all the grunt work, and it does it a lot better than you'd be likely to do it from scratch. The same is true of AVPlayer (Chapter 15), MKMapView (Chapter 24), and so on.

 New in iOS 9, App Transport Security is enforced, meaning that HTTP requests must be HTTPS requests and that the server must be using TLS 1.2 or higher. To tweak the behavior of App Transport Security, you must make an entry in the *Info.plist*. For example, to allow arbitrary HTTP downloads, the NSAppTransport-Security dictionary must contain an NSAllowsArbitraryLoads Bool set to <true/> (and the examples in this chapter assume that this has been done). See Apple's *App Transport Security Technote*.

HTTP Requests

An HTTP request is made through an NSURLSession object. An NSURLSession is a kind of grand overarching environment in which network-related tasks are to take place. You will often need only one NSURLSession object:

- For very simple, occasional use, this object might be the singleton `shared-Session` object.
- More generally, you'll create your own NSURLSession by calling an initializer:
  - `init(configuration:)`
  - `init(configuration:delegate:delegateQueue:)`

  You'll hand these initializers an NSURLSessionConfiguration object describing the desired environment.

To use the NSURLSession object to perform a request across the network, you ask it for a new NSURLSessionTask object. This is the object that actually performs (and represents) one upload or download process. NSURLSessionTask is an abstract superclass, embodying various properties, such as:

- A `taskDescription` and `taskIdentifier`; the former is up to you, while the latter is a unique identifier within the NSURLSession
- The `originalRequest` and `currentRequest` (the request can change because there might be a redirect)
- An initial `response` from the server
- Various `countOfBytes...` properties allowing you to track progress
- A `state`, which might be (NSURLSessionTaskState):
  - `.Running`
  - `.Suspended`
  - `.Canceling`
  - `.Completed`
- An `error` if the task failed

In addition, you can tell a task to `resume`, `suspend`, or `cancel`. A task is *born suspended*; it does *not* start until it is told to `resume` for the first time.

You can also set an NSURLSessionTask's `priority` to a Float between 0 and 1; this is just a hint to the system, and may be used to rank the relative importance of your tasks. For convenience, three constant values are also provided:

- NSURLSessionTaskPriorityLow (0.25)

- NSURLSessionTaskPriorityDefault (0.5)

- NSURLSessionTaskPriorityHigh (0.75)

There are four kinds of actual session task:

NSURLSessionDataTask
> An NSURLSessionTask subclass. With a data task, the data is provided incrementally to your app as it arrives across the network.

NSURLSessionDownloadTask
> An NSURLSessionTask subclass. With a download task, the data is stored as a file, and the saved file URL is handed to you at the end of the process. The file is outside your sandbox and will be destroyed, so preserving it (or its contents) is up to you.

NSURLSessionUploadTask
> An NSURLSessionDataTask subclass. With an upload task, you can provide a file to be uploaded and stand back, though you can also hear about the upload progress if you wish.

NSURLStreamTask
> An NSURLSessionTask subclass. New in iOS 9, this type of task makes it possible to deal with streams without having to drop down to the level of NSStream.

Once you've obtained a new session task from the NSURLSession, the session retains it; you can keep a reference to the task if you wish, but you don't have to. The session will provide you with a list of its tasks in progress; call `getAllTasksWithCompletion-Handler:`. The completion handler is handed an array of tasks. The session releases a task after it is cancelled or completed; thus, if an NSURLSession has no running or suspended tasks, the task array is empty.

There are two ways to ask your NSURLSession for a new NSURLSessionTask:

Call a convenience method
> The convenience methods all take a `completionHandler:` parameter. This completion handler is called when the task process ends.

Call a delegate-based method
> You give the NSURLSession a delegate when you create it, and the delegate is called back at various stages of a task's progress.

The two ways of asking for an NSURLSessionTask entail two different ways of working with it. I'll demonstrate both.

Simple HTTP Request

I'll start by illustrating the utmost in simplicity:

- We use the shared NSURLSession.
- We obtain a download task, handing it a URL and a completion handler.

The structure of the resulting code is indeed extremely simple. To kick things off, we call `resume` to start the task, and our code then finishes:

```
let s = "http://www.someserver.com/somefolder/someimage.jpg"
let url = NSURL(string:s)!
let session = NSURLSession.sharedSession()
let task = session.downloadTaskWithURL(url) {
    (loc:NSURL?, response:NSURLResponse?, error:NSError?) in // ...
}
task.resume()
```

All that remains is to write the contents of the completion handler. Observe that our code has finished running, and the completion handler will be called *later*. That's what asynchronous means! The download proceeds asynchronously on a background thread; thus, the interface is not blocked, and the user can tap buttons and so forth. The completion handler won't be called until the download finishes, whenever that may be.

When the completion handler *is* called, we can do something with the downloaded data (here, an image file). We must make no assumptions about what thread the completion handler will be called on; indeed, unless we take steps to the contrary, it will be a background thread. In this particular example, the URL is that of an image that I intend to display in my interface; therefore, I step out to the main thread (Chapter 25) in order to talk to the interface:

```
let s = "http://www.someserver.com/somefolder/someimage.jpg"
let url = NSURL(string:s)!
let session = NSURLSession.sharedSession()
let task = session.downloadTaskWithURL(url) {
    (loc:NSURL?, response:NSURLResponse?, error:NSError?) in
    let d = NSData(contentsOfURL:loc!)!
    let im = UIImage(data:d)
    dispatch_async(dispatch_get_main_queue()) {
        self.iv.image = im
    }
}
task.resume()
```

There's many a slip, as I've already mentioned, so in real life I would probably hedge my bets a little more by checking for errors along the way; but the skeleton of the structure remains exactly the same:

```
let s = "http://www.someserver.com/somefolder/someimage.jpg"
let url = NSURL(string:s)!
let session = NSURLSession.sharedSession()
let task = session.downloadTaskWithURL(url) {
    (loc:NSURL?, response:NSURLResponse?, error:NSError?) in
    if error != nil {
        print(error)
        return
    }
    let status = (response as! NSHTTPURLResponse).statusCode
    if status != 200 {
        print("response status: \(status)")
        return
    }
    let d = NSData(contentsOfURL:loc!)!
    let im = UIImage(data:d)
    dispatch_async(dispatch_get_main_queue()) {
        self.iv.image = im
    }
}
task.resume()
```

Formal HTTP Request

Now let's go to the other extreme and be very formal:

- We'll create and retain our own NSURLSession.
- We'll configure the NSURLSession with an NSURLSessionConfiguration object.
- We'll give the session a delegate.
- Instead of a mere URL, we'll start with an NSURLRequest.

The NSURLSession initializers permit us to supply an NSURLSessionConfiguration object dictating various options to be applied to the session. Possible options include:

- Whether to permit cell data use, or to require Wi-Fi
- The maximum number of simultaneous connections to the remote server
- Timeout values:

    timeoutIntervalForRequest
        The maximum time you're willing to wait *between* pieces of data.

    timeoutIntervalForResource
        The maximum time for the *entire* download to arrive.

- Cookie, caching, and credential policies

We're going to call init(configuration:delegate:delegateQueue:), so we'll also specify a delegate, as well as stating the queue (roughly, the thread — see Chapter 25) on which the delegate methods are to be called. For each type of task, there's a delegate protocol, which is itself often a composite of multiple protocols.

For example, for a data task, we would want a data delegate — an object conforming to the NSURLSessionDataDelegate protocol, which itself conforms to the NSURLSession-TaskDelegate protocol, which in turn conforms to the NSURLSessionDelegate protocol, resulting in about a dozen delegate methods we could implement, though only a few are crucial:

`URLSession:dataTask:didReceiveData:`
> Some data has arrived, as an NSData object. The data will arrive piecemeal, so this method may be called many times during the download process, supplying new data each time. Our job is to accumulate all those chunks of data; this involves maintaining state between calls.

`URLSession:task:didCompleteWithError:`
> If there is an error, we'll find out about it here. If there's no error, this is our signal that the download is over; we can now do something with the accumulated data.

Similarly, for a download task, we need a download delegate, conforming to NSURL-SessionDownloadDelegate, which conforms to NSURLSessionTaskDelegate, which conforms to NSURLSessionDelegate. Here are some useful delegate methods:

`URLSession:downloadTask:didResumeAtOffset:expectedTotalBytes:`
> This method is of interest only in the case of a resumable download that has in fact been paused and resumed.

`URLSession:downloadTask:didWriteData:totalBytesWritten:totalBytes-`
`ExpectedToWrite:`
> Called periodically, to keep us apprised of the download's progress.

`URLSession:downloadTask:didFinishDownloadingToURL:`
> Called at the end of the process; we must grab the downloaded file immediately, as it will be destroyed. This is the only required delegate method.

It's also a good idea to implement `URLSession:task:didCompleteWithError:`; if there was a communication problem, the `error:` parameter will tell you about it.

Here, then, is my recasting of the same image file download as in the previous example. I'm going to keep a reference both to the NSURLSession (`self.session`) and to the current download task (`self.task`). In this particular example, I'll perform just one task at a time, so I can use the task instance variable as a flag to indicate that the task is in progress. Since one NSURLSession can perform multiple tasks, there will typically be just one NSURLSession; so I'll make a `lazy` initializer that creates and configures it:

```
var task : NSURLSessionTask!
lazy var session : NSURLSession = {
    let config = NSURLSessionConfiguration.ephemeralSessionConfiguration()
    config.allowsCellularAccess = false
    let session = NSURLSession(configuration: config,
        delegate: self, delegateQueue: NSOperationQueue.mainQueue())
    return session
}()
```

I've specified, for purposes of the example, that no caching is to take place and that data downloading via cell is forbidden; you could configure the NSURLSession much more heavily and meaningfully, of course. I have specified self as the delegate, and I have requested delegate callbacks on the main thread.

Here we go. I blank out the image view, to make the progress of the task more obvious for test purposes, and I create, retain, and start the download task:

```
let s = "http://www.someserver.com/somefolder/someimage.jpg"
let url = NSURL(string:s)!
let req = NSMutableURLRequest(URL:url)
let task = self.session.downloadTaskWithRequest(req)
self.task = task
self.iv.image = nil
task.resume()
```

In this particular example, there is very little merit in using an NSURLRequest instead of an NSURL to form our task. Still, an NSURLRequest can come in handy (as I'll demonstrate later in this chapter), and an upload task requires one.

 Do *not* use the NSURLRequest to configure properties of the request that are configurable through the NSURLSession. Those properties are left over from the era before NSURLSession existed. For example, there is no point setting the NSURLRequest's timeoutInterval, as it is the NSURLSession's timeout properties that are significant.

Here are some delegate methods for responding to the download:

```
func URLSession(session: NSURLSession,
    downloadTask: NSURLSessionDownloadTask,
    didWriteData bytesWritten: Int64,
    totalBytesWritten writ: Int64,
    totalBytesExpectedToWrite exp: Int64) {
        print("downloaded \(100*writ/exp)%")
}
func URLSession(session: NSURLSession,
    task: NSURLSessionTask,
    didCompleteWithError error: NSError?) {
        print("completed: error: \(error)")
}
```

```
func URLSession(session: NSURLSession,
    downloadTask: NSURLSessionDownloadTask,
    didFinishDownloadingToURL location: NSURL) {
        self.task = nil
        let response = downloadTask.response as! NSHTTPURLResponse
        let stat = response.statusCode
        print("status \(stat)")
        if stat != 200 {
            return
        }
        let d = NSData(contentsOfURL:location)!
        let im = UIImage(data:d)
        dispatch_async(dispatch_get_main_queue()) {
            self.iv.image = im
        }
}
```

That was a download task; now I'll describe a data task. A data task is a little more elaborate than a download task, but not much; the chief difference is that it's up to you to accumulate the data as it arrives in chunks. For this purpose, you'll want to keep an NSMutableData object on hand; I'll use a property:

```
var data = NSMutableData()
```

When I create the data task, I am careful to prepare self.data (by giving it a zero length):

```
let s = "http://www.someserver.com/somefolder/someimage.jpg"
let url = NSURL(string:s)!
let req = NSMutableURLRequest(URL:url)
let task = self.session.dataTaskWithRequest(req) // *
self.task = task
self.iv.image = nil
self.data.length = 0 // *
task.resume()
```

As the chunks of data arrive, I keep appending them to self.data. When all the data has arrived, it is ready for use:

```
func URLSession(session: NSURLSession,
    dataTask: NSURLSessionDataTask,
    didReceiveData data: NSData) {
        self.data.appendData(data)
}
func URLSession(session: NSURLSession,
    task: NSURLSessionTask,
    didCompleteWithError error: NSError?) {
        self.task = nil
        if error == nil {
            self.iv.image = UIImage(data:self.data)
        }
}
```

Some delegate methods provide a `completionHandler:` parameter. These are delegate methods that require a response from you. For example, in the case of a data task, `URLSession:dataTask:didReceiveResponse:completionHandler:` arrives when we first connect to the server. Here, we could check the status code of the initial NSHTTPURLResponse. We must also return a response saying whether or not to proceed (or whether to convert the data task to a download task, which could certainly come in handy). But because of the multithreaded, asynchronous nature of networking, we do this, not by returning a value directly, but by calling the `completionHandler:` that we're handed as a parameter and passing our response into it. Several of the delegate methods are constructed in this way.

There is one final and extremely important consideration when using NSURLSession with a delegate — memory management. The NSURLSession *retains its delegate*. This is understandable, as it would be disastrous if the delegate could simply vanish out from the middle of an asynchronous time-consuming process; but it is also unusual, and requires special measures on our part. In the examples I've been describing in this section, we have a retain cycle! That's because we have an NSURLSession instance variable `self.session`, but that NSURLSession is retaining `self` as its delegate.

As with an NSTimer, the solution is to invalidate the NSURLSession at some appropriate moment. There are two ways to do this:

`finishTasksAndInvalidate`

Allows any existing tasks to run to completion. Afterward, the NSURLSession releases the delegate and cannot be used for anything further.

`invalidateAndCancel`

Interrupts any existing tasks immediately. The NSURLSession releases the delegate and cannot be used for anything further.

Let's suppose that `self` is a view controller. Then `viewWillDisappear:` could be a good place to invalidate the NSURLSession. (We cannot use `deinit`, because `deinit` won't be called until *after* we have invalidated the NSURLSession; that's what it means to have a retain cycle.) So, for example:

```
override func viewWillDisappear(animated: Bool) {
    super.viewWillDisappear(animated)
    self.session.finishTasksAndInvalidate()
}
```

Encapsulating the Session, Task, and Delegate

The little memory-management dance at the end of the preceding section reveals a weakness in our architecture. I've been implementing all this code directly in a view controller subclass: the NSURLSession is a property of the view controller, and the view controller is the NSURLSession's delegate. This is a misuse of a view controller. Things would be better if we had an instance of some *separate class* whose job is to hold the NSURLSession in a property and to serve as its delegate. There would still be a retain cycle until the NSURLSession was invalidated, but at least the management of this object's memory would not be entangled with that of a view controller.

To illustrate, I'll design a class MyDownloader, which holds an NSURLSession and serves as its delegate, and which has a public method cancelAllTasks. I imagine that our view controller will then create and maintain an instance of MyDownloader early in its lifetime, and can invalidate it in deinit:

```
lazy var downloader : MyDownloader = {
    let d : MyDownloader = // ??
    return d
}()
deinit {
    self.downloader.cancelAllTasks()
}
```

In that code, I omitted the initialization of MyDownloader. How should this work? The MyDownloader object will create its own NSURLSession, but I think the client should be allowed to configure the session; fortunately, that's extremely convenient, because the NSURLSessionConfiguration is a separate object! So the missing initialization should look like this:

```
let config : NSURLSessionConfiguration = // ...
let d = MyDownloader(configuration:config)
```

Now let's decide how a client will communicate with a MyDownloader object. The client will presumably hand a MyDownloader a URL string; the MyDownloader will generate the NSURLSessionDownloadTask and tell it to resume. Acting as the NSURLSession's delegate, the MyDownloader will be told when the download is over. At that point, the MyDownloader has a file URL for the downloaded object, which it needs to hand back to the client immediately. How should *this* work?

One solution might be for MyDownloader to define a delegate protocol; the client would then be the delegate, and the MyDownloader could call the client back using a method defined by the protocol. But that's far too rigid and restrictive. One NSURLSession can have many simultaneous tasks; I want a MyDownloader to be able to serve as a central locus for lots of downloading activity. I'm imagining, for example, that a MyDownloader might have multiple clients, or that a single client might initiate multiple downloads from various different contexts. All that downloading takes place asynchronously, and perhaps simultaneously. When a download ends, how is the MyDownloader to know which client to hand the downloaded file URL to? When the MyDownloader hands a downloaded file's URL to a client, how is that client to know which download request this file URL corresponds to?

My solution, which I think is rather elegant, is that the client, when it hands the MyDownloader object a URL string to initiate a download, should also hand the

MyDownloader *a completion handler*. To return the file URL at the end of a download, the MyDownloader calls that handler, handing it the URL as a parameter. I can even define a `typealias` naming my completion handler type:

```
typealias MyDownloaderCompletion = (NSURL!) -> ()
```

From the client's point of view, then, the process will look something like this:

```
let s = "http://www.someserver.com/somefolder/someimage.jpg"
self.downloader.download(s) {
    url in
    if url == nil {
        return
    }
    if let d = NSData(contentsOfURL: url) {
        let im = UIImage(data:d)
        dispatch_async(dispatch_get_main_queue()) {
            self.iv.image = im
        }
    }
}
```

That looks excellent, so now let's implement this architecture within MyDownloader. We have posited a method `download:completionHandler:`. When that method is called, MyDownloader stores the completion handler; it then asks for a new download task and sets it going:

```
func download(s:String,
    completionHandler ch : MyDownloaderCompletion)
    -> NSURLSessionTask {
        let url = NSURL(string:s)!
        let req = NSMutableURLRequest(URL:url)
        // ... store the completion handler somehow ...
        let task = self.session.downloadTaskWithRequest(req)
        task.resume()
        return task
}
```

(I return to the client a reference to the task, so that the client can subsequently cancel the task if need be. I'll give an example later.)

When the download finishes, MyDownloader hears about it (as session delegate) and calls the completion handler:

```
func URLSession(session: NSURLSession,
    downloadTask: NSURLSessionDownloadTask,
    didFinishDownloadingToURL location: NSURL) {
        let response = downloadTask.response as! NSHTTPURLResponse
        let stat = response.statusCode
        var url : NSURL! = nil
        if stat == 200 {
            url = location
```

```
            }
            let ch = // ... retrieve the completion handler somehow ...
            ch(url)
    }
```

In my carefree speculative coding design, I have repeatedly postponed grappling with the heart of the matter. It is now time to face the problem (signified by the word "somehow" in the preceding two code snippets). I reason as follows:

- The completion handler arrives in one method (`download:completionHandler:`) but is called in another (`URLSession:downloadTask:didFinishDownloadingTo-URL:`). The completion handler clearly needs to be stored, in the first method, in such a way that it can be retrieved, in the second method.

- You might respond: So put it in a property. But a simple property won't do here. In my design, there can be *multiple* download tasks — and each one has a *different* completion handler associated with it. Thus we need a way to implement this association between task and completion handler. Clearly, we want to store each completion handler *together with* its download task.

- But wait! We are guaranteed that the *same* download task instance makes its appearance in *both* methods, because the download task we create in the first method is handed back to the delegate in the second method. Thus, the problem would be completely solved if we could store the completion handler *in* its download task!

At first glance, it appears that this is impossible, because we can't subclass NSURLSession-DownloadTask (and even if we could, we can't ask NSURLSession to generate an instance of our subclass). But there is, in fact, a way to do this. It turns out that we are allowed to *attach an arbitrary property* to an NSURLRequest, as long as we start with its mutable subclass, NSMutableURLRequest. The mechanism for doing this is a little weird — we actually call an NSURLProtocol class method — but that doesn't matter. The NSURLRequest is attached to the download task as its `originalRequest`, and we can retrieve it, and hence the arbitrary property, at the end of the download.

Doing this in Swift is a bit tricky. The methods for attaching a property to an NSMutable-URLRequest and retrieving it again later are:

- `setProperty:forKey:inRequest:`

- `propertyForKey:inRequest:`

The `property:` in the first method, and the result returned by the second method, is an AnyObject. But a Swift function is *not* an AnyObject. A simple solution (see also Appendix B) is a generic wrapper class:

```
class Wrapper<T> {
    let p:T
    init(_ p:T){self.p = p}
}
```

We can hand anything to a Wrapper, which will store it in its p property; and a Wrapper *is* an AnyObject, so it can travel anywhere.

At long last we are ready to write MyDownloader for real. Here it is:

```
let config : NSURLSessionConfiguration
lazy var session : NSURLSession = {
    let queue = NSOperationQueue.mainQueue()
    return NSURLSession(configuration:self.config,
        delegate:self, delegateQueue:queue)
}()
init(configuration config:NSURLSessionConfiguration) {
    self.config = config
    super.init()
}
func download(s:String, completionHandler ch : MyDownloaderCompletion)
    -> NSURLSessionTask {
        let url = NSURL(string:s)!
        let req = NSMutableURLRequest(URL:url)
        NSURLProtocol.setProperty(Wrapper(ch), forKey:"ch", inRequest:req)
        let task = self.session.downloadTaskWithRequest(req)
        task.resume()
        return task
}
func URLSession(session: NSURLSession,
    downloadTask: NSURLSessionDownloadTask,
    didFinishDownloadingToURL location: NSURL) {
        let req = downloadTask.originalRequest!
        let ch : AnyObject =
            NSURLProtocol.propertyForKey("ch", inRequest:req)!
        let response = downloadTask.response as! NSHTTPURLResponse
        let stat = response.statusCode
        var url : NSURL! = nil
        if stat == 200 {
            url = location
        }
        let ch2 = (ch as! Wrapper).p as MyDownloaderCompletion
        ch2(url)
}
func cancelAllTasks() {
    self.session.invalidateAndCancel()
}
```

(As written, MyDownloader's delegate methods are being called on the main thread. It may be preferable to run that code on a background thread. I'll describe in Chapter 25 how to do that.)

Downloading Table View Data

To exercise MyDownloader, I'll show how to solve a pesky problem that arises quite often in real life: we have a UITableView where each cell displays text and a picture, and the picture needs to be downloaded in real time. We'll supply each picture lazily, on demand, downloading a picture only when its cell becomes visible. As you know, however, we must not gum up the works in our implementation of `tableView:cellForRow-AtIndexPath:`; this method needs to return a cell *immediately*, so we must not wait around for the picture to arrive. The idea, therefore, is to put a placeholder (or no image at all) in the cell at first, and then go back for a second bite of the apple: we perform the download *after* having supplied the cell, and when we have the image, we *reload* that row of the table. As you'll see, MyDownloader is perfect for getting this job done.

The model object for our table data could be an array of dictionaries, but it is better to design a dedicated model object, even if it is nothing but a value class (a bundle of properties):

```
class Model {
    var text : String!
    var im : UIImage!
    var picurl : String!
}
```

Our model is now an array of Model:

```
array
    Model
        text: @"Manny"
        im: initially nil
        picurl: String URL for a downloadable image of Manny
    Model
        text: @"Moe"
        im: initially nil
        picurl: String URL for a downloadable image of Moe
    Model
        text: @"Jack"
        im: initially nil
        picurl: String URL for a downloadable image of Jack
    ....
```

When the table turns to the data source for a cell (`tableView:cellForRowAtIndex-Path:`), the data source will turn to the model and consult the Model object corresponding to the requested row, asking for its `im` property, which is supposed to be its image. Initially, this will be `nil`. In that case, the data source will display no image in this cell, and will immediately return a cell without an image. Meanwhile, however, the data source also turns to the downloader and asks for the image to be downloaded from this Model object's `picurl`.

When the downloader succeeds in downloading an image, it calls the table's data source back through the completion block. Here we come to the *Insanely Cool Part* (pat. pend.). This completion block has captured the contextual environment from inside `table-View:cellForRowAtIndexPath:`, where it was defined. In effect, therefore, we are back in the very same call to `tableView:cellForRowAtIndexPath:`, accessing the very same Model object as before! We can thus set that Model object's `im` property, and tell the table to reload this row. The table thus calls `tableView:cellForRowAtIndexPath:` *again*, for the very same row, and the data source turns to the same Model object and asks for its `im` property *again* — and finds it, and displays the image in the cell:

```
override func tableView(tableView: UITableView,
    cellForRowAtIndexPath indexPath: NSIndexPath) -> UITableViewCell {
        let cell = tableView.dequeueReusableCellWithIdentifier(
            "Cell", forIndexPath:indexPath)
        let m = self.model[indexPath.row]
        cell.textLabel!.text = m.text
        // have we got a picture?
        if let im = m.im {
            cell.imageView!.image = im
        } else {
            cell.imageView!.image = nil
            self.downloader.download(m.picurl) {
                url in
                if url == nil {
                    return
                }
                let data = NSData(contentsOfURL: url)!
                let im = UIImage(data:data)
                m.im = im
                dispatch_async(dispatch_get_main_queue()) {
                    self.tableView.reloadRowsAtIndexPaths(
                        [indexPath], withRowAnimation: .None)
                }
            }
        }
        return cell
}
```

A further refinement is to make it possible to cancel a download. Recall that MyDownloader's `download:completionHandler:` returns a reference to the download task exactly so that this will be possible. Why would we want to do this? Well, consider what happens when the user scrolls quickly through the entire table, possibly passing through hundreds of rows. The downloads for all of those rows, if they do not already have their pictures, will be initiated. If a row is scrolled out of sight before it has its picture, it doesn't *need* its picture after all. So to continue to download the picture is wasteful.

To prevent such waste, we can implement `tableView:didEndDisplayingCell:forRow-AtIndexPath:` to send `cancel` to the NSURLSessionTask. To make that possible, we need to capture the task when calling the downloader's download:completionHandler: and store it somewhere. Obviously, the place to store it is in the Model object for this row, which now looks like this:

```
class Model {
    var text : String!
    var im : UIImage!
    var picurl : String!
    var task : NSURLSessionTask!
}
```

Our tableView:cellForRowAtIndexPath: is now a little more complicated. We store in our Model object's task property the value returned from download:completion-Handler:, but we should also set that task property to nil as soon as we no longer need it. Moreover, each task is retaining a closure that refers to self; that's a potential retain cycle, which we break through a weak reference to self:

```
override func tableView(tableView: UITableView,
    cellForRowAtIndexPath indexPath: NSIndexPath) -> UITableViewCell {
        let cell = tableView.dequeueReusableCellWithIdentifier(
            "Cell", forIndexPath:indexPath)
        let m = self.model[indexPath.row]
        cell.textLabel!.text = m.text
        // have we got a picture?
        if let im = m.im {
            cell.imageView!.image = im
        } else {
            if m.task == nil { // no task? start one!
                cell.imageView!.image = nil
                m.task = self.downloader.download(m.picurl) { // *
                    [weak self] url in // *
                    m.task == nil // *
                    if url == nil {
                        return
                    }
                    let data = NSData(contentsOfURL: url)!
                    let im = UIImage(data:data)
                    m.im = im
                    dispatch_async(dispatch_get_main_queue()) {
                        self!.tableView.reloadRowsAtIndexPaths(
                            [indexPath], withRowAnimation: .None)
                    }
                }
            }
        }
        return cell
}
```

Now when a row scrolls out of view its download task can be cancelled:

```
override func tableView(tableView: UITableView,
    didEndDisplayingCell cell: UITableViewCell,
    forRowAtIndexPath indexPath: NSIndexPath) {
        let m = self.model[indexPath.row]
        if let task = m.task {
            if task.state == .Running {
                task.cancel()
                m.task = nil
            }
        }
}
```

Further details are merely a matter of refinement. For example, if these are large images, I'm going to end up retaining many large images in my Model array; that's bad, as we're probably doomed to run out of memory. One solution could be to reduce each image, as it arrives, to the size needed for display. If that's *still* too much memory, we'll have to modify `tableView:didEndDisplayingCell:forRowAtIndexPath:` to expunge each image from its Model when the cell scrolls out of sight; if the cell comes back into view, we'll just have to download the image again.

Another question is what should happen when a picture download fails. If you believe that the download might succeed later, you will want to try again later, rather than letting the row sit there devoid of an image forever. If the user scrolls the failed cell out of view and later scrolls it back into view, the table will ask the data source for that cell and the downloader will try again to download its image. But that won't happen for a failed cell that's *never* scrolled out of view. How you deal with this is up to you; it's a matter of providing the best user experience without having an undue impact upon performance, battery, and so forth. In this instance, because these images are fairly unimportant, I might arrange that when an NSTimer with a fairly large interval fires (every 60 seconds, say), we reload the visible rows; this will cause any visible row without an image to try again to download its image.

Finally, I have avoided a rather tricky problem by implementing MyDownloader to perform an NSURLSessionDownloadTask. If there are multiple downloads, the runtime keeps their data separate and gives each completed download its own file URL. But suppose we were to perform an NSURLSessionDataTask instead. Now we must maintain the accumulated data ourselves — and in a world where multiple downloads can happen simultaneously, that's not going to be simple. A single NSMutableData property won't do: different data tasks must not share the same NSMutableData! One possible solution is to make our property a dictionary of NSMutableData buffers, keyed by the data task's unique identifier (`taskIdentifier`).

Background Downloads

If your app goes into the background while in the middle of a download, the download might be completed coherently, or it might not. To ensure that an NSURLSession-

DownloadTask (or an NSURLSessionUploadTask) is carried out regardless, even if your app isn't frontmost — indeed, even if your app isn't running! — make your NSURL-SessionConfiguration a background configuration (call `backgroundSession-ConfigurationWithIdentifier:` to create it).

A background configuration hands the work of downloading over to the system. Your app is not actually involved. You still need an NSURLSession, but this serves primarily as a gateway for putting your app in touch with the download process; in particular, you need to operate as the NSURLSession's delegate.

The argument that you pass to `backgroundSessionConfigurationWithIdentifier:` is a string identifier. It is arbitrary, but it will distinguish your background session from all the other background sessions that other apps have requested from the system. Therefore, it should be unique to your app; a good approach is to use your app's bundle ID as its basis.

You may also want to set your configuration's `discretionary` to `true`. This will permit the system to postpone network communications to some moment that will conserve bandwidth and battery — for example, when Wi-Fi is available, and the device is plugged into a power socket. Of course, that might be days from now! But this is part of the beauty of background downloads.

There are three possibilities for how a background download will conclude, depending on the state of your app at that moment:

Your app is frontmost
> The download is treated normally: your session delegate will get the standard delegate messages, such as `URLSession:downloadTask:didWriteData:...` and `URLSession:downloadTask:didFinishDownloadingToURL:`, just as you would expect.

Your app is suspended in the background
> Your app is awakened, still in the background, long enough to receive `URLSession:downloadTask:didFinishDownloadingToURL:` and deal with it.

Your app is not running
> Your app is launched in the background. You have no NSURLSession, because your app has just launched from scratch. You will need to create one, calling `background-SessionConfigurationWithIdentifier:` with the *same identifier* as before; you will then be able to receive delegate messages, including `URLSession:download-Task:didFinishDownloadingToURL:`.

As with location monitoring (Chapter 22), your app does not formally run in the background, so you do *not* have to set the `UIBackgroundModes` of your *Info.plist*.

You do have to implement two extra methods, to be called if your app is not frontmost at the time the download is completed:

`application:handleEventsForBackgroundURLSession:completionHandler:`
This message is sent *to the app delegate*. The `session:` parameter is the string identifier you handed earlier to the configuration object; you might use this to identify the session, or even as a prompt to create and configure the session if you haven't done so already. The app delegate must store the `completionHandler:` parameter as a property, because it will be needed later.

`URLSessionDidFinishEventsForBackgroundURLSession:`
This message is sent *to the session delegate*. The session delegate must call the previously stored completion handler. This is how the system knows that your app has finished updating its interface. The system will thereupon take a new snapshot of your app's interface, still in the background, to serve as your app's thumbnail in the app switcher interface — and your app will then be suspended.

All of this is much easier if the app delegate and the session delegate are one and the same object. In this example, the app delegate holds the NSURLSession property, as well as the completion handler property that will be needed if the download completes when we are not frontmost:

```
lazy var session : NSURLSession = {
    let config =
        NSURLSessionConfiguration
            .backgroundSessionConfigurationWithIdentifier(
                "com.neuburg.matt.ch37backgroundDownload")
    config.allowsCellularAccess = false
    // could set config.discretionary here
    let sess = NSURLSession(
        configuration: config, delegate: self,
        delegateQueue: NSOperationQueue.mainQueue())
    return sess
}()
var ch : (() -> ())!
```

The NSURLSessionDownloadDelegate methods are as before, plus we have two extra methods in case the download completes when we are not frontmost:

```
func application(application: UIApplication,
    handleEventsForBackgroundURLSession identifier: String,
    completionHandler: () -> Void) {
        self.ch = completionHandler
        let _ = self.session // make sure we have one
}
func URLSessionDidFinishEventsForBackgroundURLSession(sess: NSURLSession) {
    if self.ch != nil {
        self.ch()
    }
}
```

The last line of `application:handleEventsForBackgroundURLSession:completion-Handler:` will "tickle" the `session` lazy initializer and bring the background session to life. Thus, if we were not running when the download completed, the session delegate's `URLSession:downloadTask:didFinishDownloadingToURL:` can be called immediately and will pick up the downloaded data.

 If the user kills your app in the background by way of the app switcher interface, pending background downloads will *not* be completed. The system assumes that the user doesn't want your app coming magically back to life in the background.

Background App Refresh

The idea of background app refresh is that if your app has a periodic network download to perform — because, for example, it is a news app — you can ask the system to wake or launch your app in the background from time to time so that it can perform that download in the background. That way, the next time the user brings your app to the front, it has already been refreshed with recent downloaded content.

 The user can disable your app's ability to use background app refresh, in the Settings app, under General → Background App Refresh.

This feature is a background mode; in the Capabilities tab for your app target, switch on Background Modes and check "Background fetch." Your code must also set the shared application's `minimumBackgroundFetchInterval` property; you can supply an actual number here, but in most cases you'll want to use `UIApplicationBackground-FetchIntervalMinimum`, which lets the system work out the best moments for your app to refresh its content, based on the user's behavior.

When it's time to perform a background fetch, the app delegate will be sent `application:performFetchWithCompletionHandler:`. At that moment, a clock starts counting down; your job is to do whatever needs doing, just as fast as possible, and then call the `completionHandler:` parameter to stop the clock, passing in one of these values (UIBackgroundFetchResult):

- `.NewData`
- `.NoData`
- `.Failed`

If you don't do that fast enough, the clock will time out and your app will be suspended; and the longer you take, the less willing the system will be to send you

Figure 24-1. An on-demand resource

`application:performFetchWithCompletionHandler:` in the first place. If the value you return is `.NewData`, a new snapshot will be taken, still with your app in the background, so that the thumbnail in the app switcher matches your updated app.

On-Demand Resources

New in iOS 9, your app can store resources, such as images and sound files, on Apple's server (or your own server) instead of including them in the app bundle that the user initially installs on the device, and can then download those resources as needed when the app runs. This doesn't require any conscious networking on your part. In Xcode, you assign tags to your resources; in code, you instantiate an NSBundleResourceRequest by giving it some tags, and ask it for the corresponding resources. See Apple's *On-Demand Resources Guide* for more information.

In this simple example, my app contains a lot of JPG images. To save space when installing the app, it includes only a handful of these images, and stores the rest on Apple's server. This is configured by marking the *images* folder in my app bundle with the `"pix"` tag; this marking is performed in, and is visible in, the Resource Tags pane of the target editor (Figure 24-1).

When my app needs an image, I check to see whether I've already downloaded the bulk of the images. If not, I download them and copy them into the Application Support directory:

```
func kickOffRequest() {
    if self.request != nil {
        return // request already in progress
    }
    self.request = NSBundleResourceRequest(tags: ["pix"])
    self.request?.beginAccessingResourcesWithCompletionHandler {
        (err:NSError?) in
        defer {
            self.request?.endAccessingResources()
            self.request = nil
```

```
        }
        if let err = err {
            print(err)
            return
        }
        do {
            let fm = NSFileManager()
            let f = NSBundle.mainBundle().URLForResource(
                "images", withExtension: nil)!
            let arr = try fm.contentsOfDirectoryAtURL(
                f, includingPropertiesForKeys: nil,
                options: .SkipsHiddenFiles)
            try arr.forEach {
                pic in
                if pic.pathExtension?.lowercaseString == "jpg" {
                    let newpic = self.pixFolder!
                        .URLByAppendingPathComponent(pic.lastPathComponent!)
                    try fm.copyItemAtURL(pic, toURL: newpic)
                }
            }
        } catch {
            print(error)
        }
    }
}
```

In-App Purchases

An in-app purchase is a specialized form of network communication: your app communicates with the App Store to permit the user to buy something there, or to confirm that something has already been bought there. For example, your app might be free, but the user could then be offered the opportunity to pay to unlock additional functionality. In-app purchases are made possible through the Store Kit framework; you'll need to `import StoreKit`.

There are various kinds of in-app purchase; you'll want to read the relevant chapter in Apple's *iTunes Connect Developer Guide* and the *In-App Purchase Programming Guide*, along with the PDF *Getting Started* guide available at *https://developer.apple.com/in-app-purchase/In-App-Purchase-Guidelines.pdf*.

I'll describe the simplest possible in-app purchase: my app offers a single one-time purchase, which unlocks additional functionality, allowing the user to choose a photo from the photo library (Chapter 17). (This is what Apple calls a *non-consumable* purchase.) When the user taps the Choose button, if the in-app purchase has not been made, a pair of dialogs appear, offering and describing the purchase (Figure 24-2); if the in-app purchase *has* been made, a UIImagePickerController's view appears instead.

To configure an in-app purchase, you need first to use iTunes Connect to create, in connection with your app, something that the user can purchase; this is easiest to do if

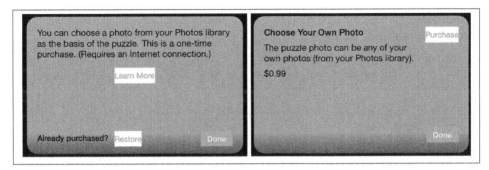

Figure 24-2. Interface for an in-app purchase

your app is already available through the App Store. For a simple non-consumable purchase like mine, you are associating your app's bundle ID with a name and arbitrary product ID representing your in-app purchase, along with a price. You'll also want to create a special Apple ID, called a *sandbox* ID, for testing purposes; you can't test your in-app purchase interface without such a sandbox ID. When testing, test on a device only, and be sure to sign out of your real Apple ID and sign in to the sandbox ID. (If you accidentally perform the in-app purchase later when logged into the App Store with your *real* Apple ID, you'll be charged for the purchase and you won't be able to get your money back. Can you guess how I know that?)

Let's skip merrily past all that and proceed to your app's interface and inner workings. For a non-consumable in-app purchase, your app must provide the following interface (all of which is visible in Figure 24-2):

- A place where the in-app purchase is described. You do not hard-code the description into your app; rather, it is downloaded in real time from the App Store, using the Display Name and Description (and price) that you entered at iTunes Connect.

- A button that launches the purchase process.

- A button that *restores* an existing purchase. The idea here is that the user has performed the purchase, but is now on a different device or has deleted and reinstalled your app, so that the NSUserDefaults entry stating that the purchase has been performed is missing. The user needs to be able to contact the App Store to get your app to recognize that the purchase has been performed and turn on the purchased functionality.

Both the purchase process and the restore process are performed through dialogs presented by the system; the purpose of the interface shown in Figure 24-2 is to give the user a way to initiate those processes.

In my app, the purchase process proceeds in two stages. When the user taps the Learn More button (StoreViewController), I first confirm that the user has not been restricted from making purchases, and I then create an SKProductsRequest, which will attempt to download an SKProductsResponse object embodying the in-app purchase corresponding to my single product ID:

```
if !SKPaymentQueue.canMakePayments() {
    // ... put up alert saying we can't do it ...
    return
}
let req = SKProductsRequest(productIdentifiers: ["DiabelliChoose"])
req.delegate = self
req.start()
```

This kicks off some network activity, and eventually the delegate of this SKProducts-Request, namely `self` (conforming to SKProductsRequestDelegate), is called back with one of two delegate messages. If we get `request:didFailWithError:`, I put up an apologetic alert, and that's the end. But if we get `productsRequest:didReceiveResponse:`, the request has succeeded, and we can proceed to the second stage.

The response from the App Store arrives as an SKProductsResponse object containing an SKProduct representing the proposed purchase. I create the second view controller, give it a reference to the SKProduct, and present it:

```
func productsRequest(request: SKProductsRequest,
    didReceiveResponse response: SKProductsResponse) {
        let p = response.products[0]
        let s = StoreViewController2(product:p)
        // and on to the next view controller
        if let presenter = self.presentingViewController {
            self.dismissViewControllerAnimated(true, completion: {
                presenter.presentViewController(
                    s, animated: true, completion: nil)
            })
        }
    }
}
```

We are now in my second view controller (StoreViewController2). It has a `product` property, and in its `viewDidLoad` it populates its interface based on the information that the `product` contains (for my `lend` utility, see Appendix B):

```
self.titleLabel.text = self.product.localizedTitle
self.descriptionLabel.text = self.product.localizedDescription
self.priceLabel.text = lend {
    (numberFormatter : NSNumberFormatter) in
    numberFormatter.formatterBehavior = .Behavior10_4
    numberFormatter.numberStyle = .CurrencyStyle
    numberFormatter.locale = self.product.priceLocale
}.stringFromNumber(self.product.price)
```

If the user taps the Purchase button, I dismiss the presented view controller, load the SKProduct into the default SKPaymentQueue, and stand back:

```
self.dismissViewControllerAnimated(true, completion: {
    let p = SKPayment(product:self.product)
    let q = SKPaymentQueue.defaultQueue()
    q.addPayment(p)
})
```

The system is now in charge of presenting a sequence of dialogs, confirming the purchase, asking for the user's App Store password, and so forth. My app knows nothing about that. If the user performs the purchase, however, my transaction observer will be sent paymentQueue:updatedTransactions:. I'll return in a moment to the implementation of this method.

Now let's talk about what happens when the user taps the Restore button (back in the first view controller, StoreViewController). It's very simple; I just tell the default SKPaymentQueue to restore any existing purchases:

```
self.dismissViewControllerAnimated(true, completion: {
    _ in
    SKPaymentQueue.defaultQueue().restoreCompletedTransactions()
})
```

Again, what happens now in the interface is out of my hands; the system will present the necessary dialogs. If the purchase is restored, however, my transaction observer will be sent paymentQueue:updatedTransactions:.

All the rest of the action, then, takes place in my transaction observer. But how does the runtime know who that is? When my app launches, it must *register a transaction observer*, that is, some object whose job it will be to receive transactions from the payment queue:

```
func application(application: UIApplication,
    didFinishLaunchingWithOptions launchOptions: [NSObject : AnyObject]?)
    -> Bool {
        SKPaymentQueue.defaultQueue().addTransactionObserver(
            self.window!.rootViewController as! SKPaymentTransactionObserver)
        return true
}
```

As you can see, I've made my root view controller the transaction observer. It adopts the SKPaymentTransactionObserver protocol. There is only one required method — paymentQueue:updatedTransactions:. This arrives with a reference to the payment queue and an array of SKPaymentTransaction objects. My job is to cycle through these transactions and, for each one, do whatever it requires, and then, if there was an actual transaction (or an error), send finishTransaction: to the payment queue, to clear the queue.

My implementation is extremely simple, because I have only one purchasable product, and because I'm not maintaining any separate record of receipts. For each transaction, I check its transactionState (SKPaymentTransactionState). If this is .Purchased or `.Restored`, I pull out its `payment`, confirm that the payment's `productIdentifier` is my product identifier (it had darned well better be, since I have only the one product), and, if so, I throw the NSUserDefaults switch that indicates to my app that the user has performed the purchase:

```
func paymentQueue(queue: SKPaymentQueue,
    updatedTransactions transactions: [SKPaymentTransaction]) {
        for t in transactions {
            switch t.transactionState {
            case .Purchasing, .Deferred: break // do nothing
            case .Purchased, .Restored:
                let p = t.payment
                if p.productIdentifier == "DiabelliChoose" {
                    NSUserDefaults.standardUserDefaults().setBool(
                        true, forKey: CHOOSE)
                    // ... present "thank you" alert to the user ...
                    queue.finishTransaction(t)
                }
            case .Failed:
                queue.finishTransaction(t)
            }
        }
}
```

CHAPTER 25

Threads

A *thread* is, simply put, a subprocess of your app that can execute even while other subprocesses are also executing. Such simultaneous execution is called *concurrency*. The iOS frameworks use threads all the time; if they didn't, your app would be less responsive to the user — perhaps even completely unresponsive. The genius of the frameworks, though, is that, for the most part, they use threads precisely so that you don't have to.

For example, suppose your app is downloading something from the network (Chapter 24). This download doesn't happen all by itself; somewhere, someone is running code that interacts with the network and obtains data. Yet none of that interferes with your code, or prevents the user from tapping and swiping things in your interface. That's concurrency in action.

This chapter discusses concurrency that involves *your* code in deliberate use of threading. It would have been nice to dispense with this topic altogether. Threads can be difficult and are always potentially dangerous, and should be avoided if possible. But sometimes that *isn't* possible. So this chapter introduces threads, along with a warning: threads entail complications and subtle pitfalls, and can make your code hard to debug. There is much more to threading, and especially to making your threaded code safe, than this chapter can possibly touch on. For detailed information about the topics introduced in this chapter, read Apple's *Concurrency Programming Guide* and *Threading Programming Guide*.

Main Thread

You are always using *some* thread. All your code must run somewhere; "somewhere" means a thread. When code calls a method, that method normally runs on the same thread as the code that called it. Your code is called through events generated by Cocoa; those events normally call your code on the *main* thread.

The main thread is the interface thread. When the *user* interacts with the interface, those interactions are reported as events — on the main thread. When *your code* interacts with the interface, it *must* do so on the main thread. Of course that will usually happen automatically, because your code normally runs on the main thread. But when you are involved with multiple threads, you must be careful.

 Trying to touch the interface with your code in any way other than on the main thread is a huge mistake (and a very common beginner mistake). A typical sign of it is an unaccountable delay of several seconds. In some cases, the console will also help with a warning.

The main thread thus has a very great deal of work to do. Here's how life goes in your app:

1. An event arrives on the main thread; the user has tapped a button, for example, and this is reported to your app as a UIEvent and to the button through the touch delivery mechanism (Chapter 5) — on the main thread.

2. The control event causes your code (the action handler) to be called — on the main thread. Your code now runs — on the main thread. *While your code runs, nothing else can happen on the main thread.* Your code might command some changes in the interface; this is safe, because your code is running on the main thread.

3. Your code finishes. The main thread's run loop is now free to report more events, and the user is free to interact with the interface once again.

The bottleneck here is obviously step 2, the running of your code. Your code runs on the main thread. That means the main thread can't do anything else while your code is running. No events can arrive while your code is running. The user can't interact with the interface while your code is running. But this is usually no problem, because:

- Your code executes really fast. It's true that the user can't interact with the interface while your code runs, but this is such a tiny interval of time that the user will probably never even notice.

- Your code, as it runs, blocks the user from interacting with the interface. But that's not bad: it's good! Your code, in response to what the user does, might update the interface; it would be insane if the user could do something else in the interface while you're in the middle of updating it.

On the other hand, as I've already mentioned, the frameworks operate in secondary threads all the time. The reason this doesn't affect you is that they usually talk to *your* code on the *main* thread. You have seen many examples of this in the preceding chapters:

- During an animation (Chapter 4), the interface remains responsive to the user, and it is possible for your code to run. The Core Animation framework is running the animation and updating the presentation layer on a background thread. But your delegate methods or completion blocks are called on the main thread.

- A web view's fetching and loading of its content is asynchronous (Chapter 11); that means the work is done in a background thread. But your delegate methods are called on the main thread.

- Sounds are played asynchronously (Chapters 14 and 16). But your delegate methods are called on the main thread. Similarly, loading, preparation, and playing of movies happens asynchronously (Chapter 15). But your delegate methods are called on the main thread.

- Saving a movie file takes time (Chapters 15 and 17). So the saving takes place on a background thread. Similarly, UIDocument saves and reads on a background thread (Chapter 23). But your delegate methods or completion blocks are called on the main thread.

Thus, you can (and should) usually ignore threads and just keep plugging away on the main thread. However, there are two kinds of situation in which your code will need to be explicitly aware of threading issues:

Your code is called back, but not on the main thread.
Some frameworks explicitly inform you in their documentation that callbacks are not guaranteed to take place on the main thread. For example, the documentation on CATiledLayer (Chapter 7) warns that `drawLayer:inContext:` is called in a background thread. By implication, our `drawRect:` code, triggered by CATiled-Layer to update tiles, is running in a background thread. (Fortunately, drawing into the current context is thread-safe.)

Similarly, the documentation on AV Foundation (Chapters 15 and 17) warns that its completion handlers and notifications can arrive on a background thread. So if you intend to update the user interface, or use a value that might also be used by your main-thread code, you'll need to be thread-conscious.

Your code takes significant time.
If your code takes significant time to run, you might need to run that code on a background thread, rather than letting it block the main thread and prevent anything else from happening there. For example:

During startup
You want your app to launch as quickly as possible. In Chapter 23, I called `URLForUbiquityContainerIdentifier:` during app launch. The documentation told me to call this method on a background thread, because it can take some time to return; we don't want to block the main thread waiting for it,

because the app is trying to launch on the main thread, and the user won't see our interface until the launch process is over.

When the user can see or interact with the app

In Chapter 19, I called `enumerateEventsMatchingPredicate:` on a background thread in order to prevent the user interface from freezing up in case the enumeration took a long time. If I hadn't done this, then when the user taps the button that triggers this call, the button will stay highlighted for a significant amount of time, during which the interface will be completely frozen.

Similarly, when your app is in the process of being suspended into the background, or resumed from the background, your app should not block the main thread for too long; it must act quickly and get out of the way.

 Moving time-consuming code off the main thread, so that the main thread is not blocked, isn't just a matter of aesthetics or politeness: the system "watchdog" will summarily *kill your app* if it discovers that the main thread is blocked for too long.

Why Threading Is Hard

The one certain thing about computer code is that it just clunks along the path of execution, one statement at a time. Lines of code, in effect, are performed in the order in which they appear. With threading, that certainty goes right out the window. If you have code that can be performed on a background thread, then you don't know when it will be performed in relation to the code being performed on any other thread. Any line of your background-thread code could be interleaved between any two lines of your main-thread code.

You also might not know *how many times* a piece of your background-thread code might be running simultaneously. Unless you take steps to prevent it, the same code could be spawned off as a thread even while it's already running in a thread. So any line of your background-thread code could be interleaved between any two lines of *itself*. (I'll discuss later in this chapter a situation in which this very thing does happen.)

This situation is particularly threatening with regard to *shared data*. Suppose two threads were to get hold of the same object and change it. Who knows what horrors might result? Objects in general have state, adding up to the state of your app as a whole. If multiple threads are permitted to access your objects, they and your entire app can be put into an indeterminate or nonsensical state.

This problem cannot be solved by simple logic. For example, suppose you try to make data access safe with a condition, as in this pseudocode:

```
if no other thread is touching this data {
    ... do something to the data ...
}
```

Such logic is utterly specious. Suppose the condition succeeds: no other thread is touching this data. But between the time when that condition is evaluated and the time when the next line executes and you start to do something to the data, another thread can still come along and start touching the data!

It is possible to request assistance at a deeper level to ensure that a section of code is not run by two threads simultaneously. For example, you can implement a *lock* around a section of code. But locks generate an entirely new level of potential pitfalls. In general, a lock is an invitation to forget to use the lock, or to forget to remove the lock after you've set it. And threads can end up contending for a lock in a way that permits neither thread to proceed.

Another problem is that the lifetime of a thread is independent of the lifetimes of other objects in your app. When an object is about to go out of existence and its `deinit` has been called and executed, you are guaranteed that none of your code in that object will ever run again. But a thread might still be running, and might try to talk to your object, even after your object has gone out of existence.

Not only is threaded code hard to get right; it's also hard to test and hard to debug. It introduces indeterminacy, so you can easily make a mistake that never appears in your testing, but that does appear for some user. The real danger is that the user's experience will consist only of distant consequences of your mistake, long after the point where you made it, making the true cause of the problem extraordinarily difficult to track down.

Perhaps you think I'm trying to scare you away from using threads. You're right! For an excellent (and suitably frightening) account of some of the dangers and considerations that threading involves, see Apple's technical note *Simple and Reliable Threading with NSOperation*. If terms like *race condition* and *deadlock* don't strike fear into your veins, look them up on Wikipedia.

 Xcode's Debug navigator distinguishes threads; you can even see pending calls and learn when a call was enqueued. Also, when you call `NSLog` in your multithreaded code, the output in the console displays a number (in square brackets, after the colon) identifying the thread on which it was called — a simple but unbelievably helpful way of distinguishing threads.

Blocking the Main Thread

To illustrate making your code multithreaded, I need some code that is worth making multithreaded. I'll use as my example an app that draws the Mandelbrot set. (This code is adapted from a small open source project I downloaded from the Internet.) All it does is draw the basic Mandelbrot set in black and white, but that's a sufficiently elaborate calculation to introduce a significant delay, especially on an older, slower device. The idea is then to see how we can safely get that delay off the main thread.

The app contains a UIView subclass, MyMandelbrotView, which has one property, a CGContext called `bitmapContext`. Here's the structure of MyMandelbrotView's implementation:

```
let MANDELBROT_STEPS = 200 // determines how long the calculation takes
var bitmapContext: CGContext!
// jumping-off point: draw the Mandelbrot set
func drawThatPuppy () {
    self.makeBitmapContext(self.bounds.size)
    let center = CGPointMake(self.bounds.midX, self.bounds.midY)
    self.drawAtCenter(center, zoom:1)
    self.setNeedsDisplay()
}
// create bitmap context
func makeBitmapContext(size:CGSize) {
    var bitmapBytesPerRow = Int(size.width * 4)
    bitmapBytesPerRow += (16 - (bitmapBytesPerRow % 16)) % 16
    let colorSpace = CGColorSpaceCreateDeviceRGB()
    let prem = CGImageAlphaInfo.PremultipliedLast.rawValue
    let context = CGBitmapContextCreate(
        nil, Int(size.width), Int(size.height), 8,
        bitmapBytesPerRow, colorSpace, prem)
    self.bitmapContext = context
}
// draw pixels of bitmap context
func drawAtCenter(center:CGPoint, zoom:CGFloat) {
    func isInMandelbrotSet(re:Float, _ im:Float) -> Bool {
        var fl = true
        var (x, y, nx, ny) : (Float,Float,Float,Float) = (0,0,0,0)
        for _ in 0 ..< MANDELBROT_STEPS {
            nx = x*x - y*y + re
            ny = 2*x*y + im
            if nx*nx + ny*ny > 4 {
                fl = false
                break
            }
            x = nx
            y = ny
        }
        return fl
    }
    CGContextSetAllowsAntialiasing(self.bitmapContext, false)
    CGContextSetRGBFillColor(self.bitmapContext, 0, 0, 0, 1)
    var re : CGFloat
    var im : CGFloat
    let maxi = Int(self.bounds.size.width)
```

```
        let maxj = Int(self.bounds.size.height)
        for i in 0 ..< maxi {
            for j in 0 ..< maxj {
                re = (CGFloat(i) - 1.33 * center.x) / 160
                im = (CGFloat(j) - 1.0 * center.y) / 160
                re /= zoom
                im /= zoom
                if (isInMandelbrotSet(Float(re), Float(im))) {
                    CGContextFillRect (
                        self.bitmapContext, CGRectMake(CGFloat(i),
                        CGFloat(j), 1.0, 1.0))
                }
            }
        }
    }
    // turn pixels of bitmap context into CGImage, draw into ourselves
    override func drawRect(rect: CGRect) {
        if self.bitmapContext != nil {
            let context = UIGraphicsGetCurrentContext()!
            let im = CGBitmapContextCreateImage(self.bitmapContext)
            CGContextDrawImage(context, self.bounds, im)
        }
    }
}
```

The `drawAtCenter:zoom:` method, which calculates the pixels of `self.bitmap-Context`, is time-consuming, and we can see this by running the app on a device. If the entire process is kicked off by tapping a button whose action handler calls `drawThat-Puppy`, there is a significant delay before the Mandelbrot graphic appears in the interface, during which time *the button remains highlighted*. This is a sure sign that we are blocking the main thread.

We need to move the calculation-intensive part of this code onto a background thread, so that the main thread is not blocked by the calculation. In doing so, we have two chief concerns:

Synchronization of threads

The button is tapped, and `drawThatPuppy` is called, on the main thread. Thus, `set-NeedsDisplay` is called on the main thread — and rightly so, since this affects the interface. Therefore, `drawRect:` is called on the main thread. In between, however, the calculation-intensive `drawAtCenter:zoom:` is to be called on a background thread. Yet these three methods must still be called in order: `drawThatPuppy`, then `drawAtCenter:zoom:`, then `drawRect:`. How is this going to work? Clearly it can't work as we have things structured now; if `drawThatPuppy` calls `drawAt-Center:zoom:` and immediately calls `setNeedsDisplay`, the former on a background thread and the latter on the main thread, the view will be redrawn too soon, before `drawAtCenter:zoom:` has had a chance to update the bitmap.

Shared data

The property `self.bitmapContext` is referred to in three different methods — in `makeBitmapContext:`, which is called by `drawThatPuppy`; in `drawAtCenter:zoom:`; and in `drawRect:`. But we have just said that those three methods involve two different threads; they must not be permitted to touch the same property in a way that might conflict or clash. A further danger is that `drawAtCenter:zoom:` is run on a background thread, and we have no way of knowing how many such background threads there may be; the user might tap the button several times in quick succession, kicking off several simultaneous calculations. The access to `self.bitmap-Context` by `drawAtCenter:zoom:` must thus not be permitted to conflict or clash *with itself.* (This problem, mercifully, does not arise in connection with the main thread; there is only one main thread, so it *can't* conflict with itself.)

Manual Threading

A naïve solution would involve spawning off a background thread as we reach the calculation-intensive part of the procedure, by calling `performSelectorIn-Background:withObject:`. This is a very bad idea, and you should *not* imitate the code in this section. I'm showing it to you only to demonstrate how horrible it is.

It is not at all simple to adapt your code to use `performSelectorInBackground:with-Object:`. There is additional work to do:

Pack the arguments

The method designated by the selector argument to `performSelectorIn-Background:withObject:` can take only one parameter, whose value you supply as the second argument. So if you want to pass more than one piece of information into the thread, or if the information you want to pass isn't an object, you'll need to pack it into a single object. Typically, this will be a dictionary.

Set up an autorelease pool

Secondary threads don't participate in the global autorelease pool. So the first thing you must do in your threaded code is to wrap everything in an autorelease pool. Otherwise, you'll probably leak memory as autoreleased objects are created behind the scenes and are never released.

We'll rewrite MyMandelbrotView to use manual threading. Our `drawAtCenter:zoom:` method takes two parameters (and neither is an object), so the argument that we pass into the thread will have to pack that information into a dictionary. Once inside the thread, we'll set up our autorelease pool and unpack the dictionary. This will all be made much easier if we interpose a trampoline method between `drawThatPuppy` and `drawAt-Center:zoom:`. So our implementation now starts like this:

```
func drawThatPuppy () {
    self.makeBitmapContext(self.bounds.size)
    let center = CGPointMake(self.bounds.midX, self.bounds.midY)
    let d = ["center":NSValue(CGPoint: center), "zoom":CGFloat(1)]
    self.performSelectorInBackground("reallyDraw:", withObject: d)
}
// trampoline, background thread entry point
func reallyDraw(d:[NSObject:AnyObject]) {
    autoreleasepool {
        self.drawAtCenter(
            (d["center"] as! NSValue).CGPointValue(),
            zoom: d["zoom"] as! CGFloat)
        // ... ??? ...
    }
}
```

The comment with the question marks indicates a missing piece of functionality: we have yet to call setNeedsDisplay, which will cause the actual drawing to take place. This call used to be in drawThatPuppy, but that is now too soon; the call to perform-SelectorInBackground:withObject: launches the thread and returns immediately, so our bitmapContext property isn't ready yet. Clearly, we need to call setNeedsDisplay *after* drawAtCenter:zoom: finishes generating the pixels of the graphics context. We can do this at the end of our trampoline method reallyDraw:, but we must remember that we're now in a background thread. Because setNeedsDisplay is a form of communication with the interface, we should call it on the main thread, with perform-SelectorOnMainThread:withObject:waitUntilDone:. For maximum flexibility, it will probably be best to implement a second trampoline method:

```
// trampoline, background thread entry point
func reallyDraw(d:[NSObject:AnyObject]) {
    autoreleasepool {
        self.drawAtCenter(
            (d["center"] as! NSValue).CGPointValue(),
            zoom: d["zoom"] as! CGFloat)
        self.performSelectorOnMainThread("allDone",
            withObject: nil, waitUntilDone: false)
    }
}
// called on main thread! background thread exit point
func allDone() {
    self.setNeedsDisplay()
}
```

This works, in the sense that when we tap the button, it is highlighted momentarily and then immediately unhighlighted; the time-consuming calculation is taking place on a background thread. But the code is specious; the seeds of nightmare are already sown. We now have a single object, MyMandelbrotView, some of whose methods are to be called on the main thread and some on a background thread; this invites us to become confused at some later time. Even worse, the main thread and the background thread are constantly sharing a piece of data, the instance property `self.bitmapContext`; what's to stop some other code from coming along and triggering `drawRect:` while `drawAt-Center:zoom:` is in the middle of manipulating this bitmap context? To solve these problems, we might need to use locks, and we would probably have to manage the thread more explicitly. Such code can become quite elaborate and difficult to understand; guaranteeing its integrity is even more difficult. There are much better ways, and I will now demonstrate two of them.

NSOperation

The essence of NSOperation is that it encapsulates a task, not a thread. The operation described by an NSOperation object may be performed on a background thread, but you don't have to concern yourself with that directly. You describe the operation and add the NSOperation to an NSOperationQueue to set it going. You arrange to be notified when the operation ends, typically by the NSOperation posting a notification. You can query both the queue and its operations from outside with regard to their state.

We'll rewrite MyMandelbrotView to use NSOperation. We need a property, an NSOperationQueue; we'll call it `queue`, and we'll create and configure it in its initializer:

```
let queue : NSOperationQueue = {
    let q = NSOperationQueue()
    // ... further configurations can go here ...
    return q
}()
```

We also have a new class, MyMandelbrotOperation, an NSOperation subclass. (It is possible to take advantage of a built-in NSOperation subclass such as NSBlockOperation, but I'm deliberately illustrating the more general case by subclassing NSOperation itself.) Our implementation of `drawThatPuppy` thus creates an instance of MyMandelbrotOperation, configures it, registers for its notification, and adds it to the queue:

```
func drawThatPuppy () {
    let center = CGPointMake(self.bounds.midX, self.bounds.midY)
    let op = MyMandelbrotOperation(
        size: self.bounds.size, center: center, zoom: 1)
    NSNotificationCenter.defaultCenter().addObserver(
        self, selector: "operationFinished:",
        name: "MyMandelbrotOperationFinished", object: op)
    self.queue.addOperation(op)
}
```

Our time-consuming calculations are performed by MyMandelbrotOperation. An NSOperation subclass, such as MyMandelbrotOperation, will typically have at least two methods:

A designated initializer

The NSOperation may need some configuration data. Once the NSOperation is added to a queue, it's too late to talk to it, so you'll usually hand it this configuration data as you create it, in its designated initializer.

A main *method*

This method will be called (with no parameters) automatically by the NSOperation-Queue when it's time for the NSOperation to start.

MyMandelbrotOperation has three private properties for configuration (size, center, and zoom), to be set in its initializer; it must be told MyMandelbrotView's geometry explicitly because it is completely separate from MyMandelbrotView. MyMandelbrotOperation also has its own CGContext property, bitmapContext; it must be publicly gettable so that MyMandelbrotView can retrieve a reference to this graphics context when the operation has finished. Note that this is different from MyMandelbrot-View's bitmapContext, thus helping to solve the problem of sharing data promiscuously between threads:

```
private let size : CGSize
private let center : CGPoint
private let zoom : CGFloat
private(set) var bitmapContext : CGContext!
init(size sz:CGSize, center c:CGPoint, zoom z:CGFloat) {
    self.size = sz
    self.center = c
    self.zoom = z
    super.init()
}
```

All the calculation work has been transferred from MyMandelbrotView to MyMandelbrotOperation without change; the only difference is that self.bitmap-Context now means MyMandelbrotOperation's property. The only method of real interest is main. First, we call the NSOperation method isCancelled to make sure we haven't been cancelled while sitting in the queue; this is good practice. Then, we do exactly what drawThatPuppy used to do, initializing our graphics context and drawing into its pixels:

```
let MANDELBROT_STEPS = 200
// create instance variable
func makeBitmapContext(size:CGSize) {
    // ... same as before
}
func drawAtCenter(center:CGPoint, zoom:CGFloat) {
    // ... same as before
}
override func main() {
    if self.cancelled {
        return
    }
```

```
    self.makeBitmapContext(self.size)
    self.drawAtCenter(self.center, zoom: self.zoom)
    if !self.cancelled {
        NSNotificationCenter.defaultCenter().postNotificationName(
            "MyMandelbrotOperationFinished", object: self)
    }
}
```

The last line of main is our signal to MyMandelbrotView that the calculation is over and
it's time to come and fetch our data. There are two ways to do this; either main can post
a notification through the NSNotificationCenter, or MyMandelbrotView can use key-
value observing to be notified when our isFinished property changes. We've chosen
the former approach; observe that we check one more time to make sure we haven't
been cancelled.

Now we are back in MyMandelbrotView, hearing through the notification that
MyMandelbrotOperation has finished. We must immediately pick up any required data,
because the NSOperationQueue is about to release this NSOperation. However, we must
be careful; the notification may have been posted on a background thread, in which case
our method for responding to it will also be called on a background thread. We are about
to set our own graphics context and tell ourselves to redraw; those are things we want
to do on the main thread. So we immediately step out to the main thread (using Grand
Central Dispatch, described more fully in the next section). We remove ourselves as
notification observer for this operation instance, copy the operation's bitmapContext
into our own bitmapContext, and now we're ready for the last step, drawing ourselves:

```
// warning! called on background thread
func operationFinished(n:NSNotification) {
    if let op = n.object as? MyMandelbrotOperation {
        dispatch_async(dispatch_get_main_queue()) {
            NSNotificationCenter.defaultCenter().removeObserver(
                self, name: "MyMandelbrotOperationFinished", object: op)
            self.bitmapContext = op.bitmapContext
            self.setNeedsDisplay()
        }
    }
}
```

Adapting our code to use NSOperation involves some work, but the result has many
advantages that help to ensure that our use of multiple threads is coherent and safe:

The operation is encapsulated.

   Because MyMandelbrotOperation is an object, we've been able to move all the code
   having to do with drawing the pixels of the Mandelbrot set into it. The *only*
   MyMandelbrotView method that can be called in the background is operation-
   Finished:, and that's a method we'd never call explicitly ourselves, so we won't
   misuse it accidentally — and it immediately steps out to the main thread in any
   case.

The data sharing is rationalized.

Because MyMandelbrotOperation is an object, it has its own `bitmapContext` property. The only moment of data sharing comes in `operationFinished:`, when we must set MyMandelbrotView's `bitmapContext` to MyMandelbrotOperation's `bitmapContext`. Even if multiple MyMandelbrotOperation objects are added to the queue, the moments when we set MyMandelbrotView's `bitmapContext` and then redraw ourselves using that bitmap context all occur on the main thread, so they cannot conflict with one another.

The threads are synchronized.

The calculation-intensive operation doesn't start until MyMandelbrotView tells it to start (`self.queue.addOperation(op)`). MyMandelbrotView then takes its hands off the steering wheel and makes *no* attempt to draw itself. If `drawRect:` is called by the runtime, `self.bitmapContext` will be `nil` (or will contain the results of an earlier calculation operation) and no harm done. Nothing else happens until the operation ends and the notification arrives (`operationFinished:`); then and only then does MyMandelbrotView update the interface — on the main thread.

If we are concerned with the possibility that more than one instance of MyMandelbrotOperation might be added to the queue and executed concurrently, we have a further line of defense — we can set the NSOperationQueue's maximum concurrency level to 1:

```
let q = NSOperationQueue()
q.maxConcurrentOperationCount = 1
return q
```

This turns the NSOperationQueue into a true serial queue; every operation on the queue must be completely executed before the next can begin. This might cause an operation added to the queue to take longer to execute, if it must wait for another operation to finish before it can even get started; however, this delay might not be important. What *is* important is that by executing the operations on this queue separately from one another, we guarantee that only one operation at a time can do any data sharing. A serial queue is thus a form of data locking.

Because MyMandelbrotView can be destroyed (if, for example, its view controller is destroyed), there is still a risk that it will create an operation that will outlive it and will try to access it after it has been destroyed. We can reduce that risk by canceling all operations in our queue before releasing it:

```
deinit {
    self.queue.cancelAllOperations()
}
```

Operation queues are good to know about for other reasons as well. A number of useful methods mentioned earlier in this book expect an NSOperationQueue argument; see, for example, Chapter 22 (`startDeviceMotionUpdatesToQueue:withHandler:`, and similarly for the other sensors) and Chapter 24 (`sessionWithConfiguration:delegate:delegateQueue:`).

There is more to NSOperation as well. One NSOperation can have another NSOperation as a *dependency*, meaning that the former cannot start until the latter has finished, even if they are in different NSOperationQueues. Moreover, the behavior of an NSOperation can be customized; an NSOperation subclass can redefine what it means to be `ready` and capable of execution. Thus, NSOperations can be combined to express your app's logic, guaranteeing that one thing happens before another (as is cogently argued in a WWDC 2015 video).

Grand Central Dispatch

Grand Central Dispatch, or *GCD*, is a sort of low-level analogue to NSOperation and NSOperationQueue (in fact, NSOperationQueue uses GCD under the hood). When I say GCD is low-level, I'm not kidding; it is effectively baked into the operating system kernel. Thus it can be used by any code whatsoever and is tremendously efficient.

GCD is like NSOperationQueue in that it uses queues: you express a task and add it to a queue, and the task is executed on a thread as needed. Moreover, by default these queues are serial queues, with each task on a queue finishing before the next is started, which, as I've already said, is a form of data locking. However, it has the advantage over NSOperationQueue that there is no need to create any extra objects; GCD uses blocks — in Swift, these will usually be anonymous functions — so all your code to be executed on different threads can appear in the same place. Also, GCD is about much more than threading, as I'll discuss at the end of this section.

We'll rewrite MyMandelbrotView to use GCD. Remarkably, the structure is only very slightly changed from the original, nonthreaded version. We have a new property to hold our queue, which is a *dispatch queue*; a dispatch queue is a lightweight opaque pseudo-object consisting essentially of a list of functions to be executed:

```
let MANDELBROT_STEPS = 200
var bitmapContext: CGContext!
let draw_queue : dispatch_queue_t = {
    let q = dispatch_queue_create("com.neuburg.mandeldraw", nil)
    return q
}()
```

(A call to `dispatch_queue_create` must be balanced by a call to `dispatch_release`. However, Swift memory management understands GCD pseudo-objects and will take care of this for us — in fact, calling `dispatch_release` explicitly is forbidden.)

Our `makeBitmapContext:` method now returns a graphics context rather than setting a property directly:

```
func makeBitmapContext(size:CGSize) -> CGContext {
    // ... as before ...
    let context = CGBitmapContextCreate(
        nil, Int(size.width), Int(size.height), 8,
        bitmapBytesPerRow, colorSpace, prem)
    return context!
}
```

Also, our drawAtCenter:zoom: method now takes an additional parameter, the graphics context to draw into:

```
func drawAtCenter(center:CGPoint, zoom:CGFloat, context:CGContext) {
    // ... as before, but we refer to local context, not self.bitmapContext
}
```

Now for the implementation of drawThatPuppy. This is where all the action is! Here it is:

```
func drawThatPuppy () {
    let center = CGPointMake(self.bounds.midX, self.bounds.midY) ❶
    dispatch_async(self.draw_queue) { ❷
        let bitmap = self.makeBitmapContext(self.bounds.size) ❸
        self.drawAtCenter(center, zoom:1, context:bitmap)
        dispatch_async(dispatch_get_main_queue()) { ❹
            self.bitmapContext = bitmap ❺
            self.setNeedsDisplay()
        }
    }
}
```

That's all there is to it: *all* our app's multithreading is concentrated in those few lines. There are no notifications; there is no sharing of data between threads; and the entire sequential synchronization of our threads is completely handled and expressed with startling clarity. Here's how drawThatPuppy works:

❶ We begin by calculating our center, as before. This value will be visible within the subsequent anonymous functions, because the rules of scope say that function body code can see its surrounding context.

❷ Now comes our task to be performed in a background thread on our queue, self.draw_queue. We specify this task with the dispatch_async function. GCD has a lot of functions, but this is the one you'll use 99 percent of the time; it's the most important thing you need to know about GCD. We specify a queue and we provide a function saying what we'd like to do on that queue.

❸ In the function, we begin by declaring bitmap as a variable *local to the function*. We then call makeBitmapContext: to create the graphics context bitmap, and then call drawAtCenter:zoom:context: to set its pixels. Bear in mind that those calls are made on a background thread, because self.draw_queue is a background queue.

❹ Now we need to step back out to the main thread. How do we do that? With dispatch_async again! This time, we specify the main queue (which is effectively the main thread) by calling dispatch_get_main_queue, and describe what we want to do on the main queue in *another* anonymous function.

❺ This second call to dispatch_async is the last line of the first anonymous function; therefore, *its* anonymous function isn't enqueued, and thus isn't performed, until the preceding commands in the first function have finished. Moreover, because the first function is part of the second function's surrounding context, the second function can see our local bitmap variable! We set our bitmap-Context property and call setNeedsDisplay — on the main thread! — and we're done.

The benefits and elegance of GCD as a form of concurrency management are simply stunning. There is no data sharing, because the bitmap variable is not shared; it is local to each specific call to drawThatPuppy. The threads are synchronized, because the nested anonymous functions are executed in succession, so any instance of bitmap must be completely filled with pixels before being used to set the bitmapContext property. Moreover, the background operation is performed on a serial queue, and bitmap-Context is touched only from code running on the main thread; thus there is no possibility of conflict. Our code is also highly maintainable, because the entire task on all threads is expressed within the single drawThatPuppy method; indeed, the code is only very slightly modified from the original, nonthreaded version.

You might object that we still have methods makeBitmapContext: and drawAt-Center:zoom:context: hanging around MyMandelbrotView, and that we must therefore still be careful not to call them on the main thread, or indeed from anywhere except from within drawThatPuppy. If that were true, we could at this point destroy makeBitmap-Context: and drawAtCenter:zoom:context: and move their functionality completely into drawThatPuppy. But it *isn't* true, because these methods are now *thread-safe*: they are self-contained utilities that touch no properties or persistent objects, so it doesn't matter what thread they are called on. Still, I'll demonstrate in a moment how we can intercept an accidental attempt to call a method on the wrong thread.

The two most important GCD functions are:

dispatch_async

> Push a function onto the end of a queue for later execution, and proceed immediately with our own code. Thus, we can finish our own execution without waiting for the function to execute.

> Examples of using dispatch_async to execute code in a background thread (dispatch_get_global_queue(0,0)) appeared in Chapters 19 and 23. Examples of using dispatch_async as a way of stepping back onto the main thread

(`dispatch_get_main_queue`) in order to talk to the interface from inside code that might be executed on a background thread appeared in Chapters 10, 15, 16, 17, and 24 (and elsewhere).

Also, it can be useful to call `dispatch_async` to step out to the main thread even though you're *already* on the main thread, as a way of waiting for the run loop to complete and for the interface to settle down — a minimal form of delayed performance. I used that technique in Chapters 12 and 23.

`dispatch_sync`

Push a function onto the end of a queue for later execution, and wait until the function has executed before proceeding with our own code — because, for example, you intend to use a result that the function is to provide. The purpose of the queue would be, once again, as a lightweight, reliable version of a lock, mediating access to a shared resource. Here's a case in point, adapted from Apple's own code:

```
func asset() -> AVAsset? {
    var theAsset : AVAsset!
    dispatch_sync(self.assetQueue) {
        theAsset = self.getAssetInternal().copy() as! AVAsset
    }
    return theAsset
}
```

Any thread might call the `asset` method; to avoid problems with shared data, we require that only functions that are executed from a particular queue (`self.asset-Queue`) may touch an AVAsset. But we need the result that this function returns; hence the call to `dispatch_sync`.

In Chapter 7 I encountered a problem where I discovered that the runtime was calling my CATiledLayer's `drawRect:` simultaneously on multiple threads — a rare example of Apple's code involving me in unexpected complications of threading. To close the door to this sort of behavior, it suffices to wrap the interior of my `drawRect:` implementation in a call to `dispatch_sync`. This is a safe and reliable mode of locking: once any thread has started to run my `drawRect:`, no other thread can start to run it until the first thread has finished with it. Thus my `drawRect:`, though it can be (and will be) run on a background thread, is immune to being run on *simultaneous* background threads. I have defined a property to hold a dedicated serial queue:

```
let drawQueue = dispatch_queue_create(nil, DISPATCH_QUEUE_SERIAL)
```

And here's how `drawRect:` is structured:

```
override func drawRect(r: CGRect) {
    dispatch_sync(drawQueue, {
        // ... draw here ...
    })
}
```

An interesting and useful exercise is to revise the MyDownloader class from Chapter 24 so that the delegate methods are run on a background thread, thus taking some strain off the main thread (and hence the user interface) while these messages are flying around behind the scenes. This looks like a reasonable and safe thing to do, because the NSURL-Session and the delegate methods are all packaged inside the MyDownloader object, isolated from our view controller.

To do so, the first step is to declare our completion handler `typealias` using the `@convention(block)` attribute; otherwise, we won't get proper Objective-C memory management of our stored handler:

```
typealias MyDownloaderCompletion = @convention(block) (NSURL!) -> ()
```

We'll also need our own background NSOperationQueue, which we can maintain as a property:

```
let q = NSOperationQueue()
```

Our session is now configured and created using this background queue:

```
lazy var session : NSURLSession = {
    let queue = self.q
    return NSURLSession(configuration:self.config,
        delegate:self, delegateQueue:queue)
}()
```

We must now give some thought to what will happen in `URLSession:downloadTask:did-FinishDownloadingToURL:` when we call back into the client through the completion handler (the one that we received in `download:completionHandler:` and stored in the NSURLRequest). It would not be very nice to involve the client in threading issues; our entire goal is to isolate such issues within MyDownloader itself. Therefore we must step out to the main thread as we call the completion handler. But we cannot do this by calling `dispatch_async`:

```
let ch2 = (ch as! Wrapper).p as MyDownloaderCompletion
dispatch_async(dispatch_get_main_queue()) { // bad idea!
    ch2(url)
}
```

The reason is that the downloaded file is slated to be destroyed as soon as we return from `URLSession:downloadTask:didFinishDownloadingToURL:` — and if we call `dispatch_async`, we will return *immediately*. Thus the downloaded file *will* be destroyed, and `url` will end up pointing at nothing by the time the client receives it. The solution is to use `dispatch_sync` instead:

```
let ch2 = (ch as! Wrapper).p as MyDownloaderCompletion
dispatch_sync(dispatch_get_main_queue()) {
    ch2(url)
}
```

That code steps out to the main thread and also postpones returning from URLSession:downloadTask:didFinishDownloadingToURL: until the client has had an opportunity to do something with the file pointed to by url. We are blocking our background NSOperationQueue, but only very briefly. Again, our real purpose in using dispatch_sync is to lock down some shared data — in this case, the downloaded file.

It is also good to know about the GCD function dispatch_after; many examples in this book have made use of it, by way of my utility method delay (see Appendix B) — see, for instance, Chapters 2, 7, and 10.

Another useful GCD function is dispatch_once, a thread-safe way of ensuring that code is run only once; I probably could have used this instead of the Bool property flags scattered throughout my example code (such as self.viewInitializationDone in Chapter 6). Your call to this function must be accompanied by a reference to an already defined variable which serves as a *token* (a dispatch_once_t); the scope of the notion "once" is determined by the scope and lifetime at which this token is declared. Thus, in the following example, the code in question will run just once *per instance of this class*, because the token is declared as a property, at the level of the instance:

```
class SomeClass {
    var once_token : dispatch_once_t = 0
    func test() {
        dispatch_once(&once_token) {
            // this code will run just once in the life of this object
        }
    }
}
```

In Objective-C, dispatch_once is often used to vend a singleton; in Swift, however, you are more likely to use the built-in lazy initialization feature.

Besides serial dispatch queues, there are also *concurrent* dispatch queues. A concurrent queue's functions are started in the order in which they were submitted to the queue, but a function is allowed to start while another function is still executing. Obviously, you wouldn't want to submit to a concurrent queue a task that touches a shared resource! The advantage of concurrent queues is a possible speed boost when you don't care about the order in which multiple tasks are finished — for example, when you want to do something with regard to every element of an array.

The built-in global queues (available by calling dispatch_get_global_queue) are concurrent; you can also create a concurrent queue yourself, by passing DISPATCH_QUEUE_CONCURRENT as the second argument to dispatch_queue_create.

A frequent use of concurrent queues is with dispatch_apply. This function is like dispatch_sync (the caller pauses until everything has finished executing), but the function that you supply is called multiple times with an iterator argument. Thus, dispatch_apply on a concurrent queue is like a for loop whose iterations are multithreaded; on a device with multiple cores, this could result in a speed improvement. (Of course, this technique is applicable only if the iterations do not depend on one another.)

Arbitrary context data can be attached to a queue in the form of key–value pairs (`dispatch_queue_set_specific`) and retrieved by key. There are two ways to retrieve the context data:

`dispatch_queue_get_specific`
Retrieves a key's value for a queue to which we already have a valid reference.

`dispatch_get_specific`
Retrieves a key's value for the *current* queue, the one in whose thread we are actually running. In fact, `dispatch_get_specific` is the *only* valid way to identify the current queue. (`dispatch_get_current_queue`, a function formerly used for this purpose, has been shown to be potentially unsafe and is now deprecated.)

We can use this technique, for example, to make certain that a method is called only on the correct queue. Recall that in our Mandelbrot-drawing example, we may be concerned that a method such as `makeBitmapContext:` might be called on some other queue than the background queue that we created for this purpose. If this is really a worry, we can attach an identifying key–value pair to that queue when we create it. The value should be a pointer; to make this possible, I'll configure some global variables beforehand:

```
let qkeyString = "label" as NSString
let QKEY = qkeyString.UTF8String
let qvalString = "com.neuburg.mandeldraw" as NSString
var QVAL = qvalString.UTF8String
```

We then create and configure the queue like this:

```
let q = dispatch_queue_create(QVAL, nil)
dispatch_queue_set_specific(q, QKEY, &QVAL, nil)
```

Later, we can examine that identifying key–value pair for the queue on which a particular method is called:

```
func assertOnBackgroundThread() {
    let s = dispatch_get_specific(QKEY)
    assert(s == &QVAL)
}
```

Threads and App Backgrounding

When your app is backgrounded and suspended, a problem arises if your code is running. The system doesn't want to stop your code while it's executing; on the other hand, some other app may need to be given the bulk of the device's resources now. So as your app goes into the background, the system waits a very short time for your app to finish doing whatever it may be doing, and it then suspends your app.

This shouldn't be a problem from your main thread's point of view, because your app shouldn't have any time-consuming code on the main thread in the first place; you now know that you can avoid this by using a background thread. On the other hand, it could be a problem for lengthy background operations, including asynchronous tasks performed by the frameworks. You can request extra time to complete a lengthy task (or at to least abort it yourself, coherently) in case your app is backgrounded, by wrapping it in calls to UIApplication's `beginBackgroundTaskWithExpirationHandler:` and `endBackgroundTask:`. Here's how you do it:

1. You call `beginBackgroundTaskWithExpirationHandler:` to announce that a lengthy task is beginning; it returns an identification number. This tells the system that if your app is backgrounded, you'd like to be woken from suspension in the background now and then in order to complete the task.

2. At the end of your lengthy task, you call `endBackgroundTask:`, passing in the same identification number that you got from your call to `beginBackgroundTaskWithExpirationHandler:`. This tells the system that your lengthy task is over and that there is no need to grant you any more background time.

The function that you pass as argument to `beginBackgroundTaskWithExpirationHandler:` does *not* express the lengthy task. It expresses what you will do *if your extra time expires* before you finish your lengthy task. This is a chance for you to clean up. At the very least, your expiration handler must call `endBackgroundTask:`! Otherwise, the runtime won't know that you've run your expiration handler, and your app may be killed, as a punishment for trying to use too much background time. If your expiration handler *is* called, you should make no assumptions about what thread it is running on.

Let's use MyMandelbrotView as an example. Let's say that if `drawThatPuppy` is started, we'd like it to be allowed to finish, even if the app is suspended in the middle of it, so that our `bitmapContext` property is updated as requested. To try to ensure this, we call `beginBackgroundTaskWithExpirationHandler:` beforehand and call `endBackgroundTask:` at the end of the innermost anonymous function:

```
func drawThatPuppy () {
    let center = CGPointMake(self.bounds.midX, self.bounds.midY)
    // === configure background task
    var bti : UIBackgroundTaskIdentifier = 0
    bti = UIApplication.sharedApplication()
        .beginBackgroundTaskWithExpirationHandler({
            UIApplication.sharedApplication().endBackgroundTask(bti)
        })
    if bti == UIBackgroundTaskInvalid {
        return
    }
    // ===
    dispatch_async(self.draw_queue) {
```

```
        let bitmap = self.makeBitmapContext(self.bounds.size)
        self.drawAtCenter(center, zoom:1, context:bitmap)
        dispatch_async(dispatch_get_main_queue()) {
            self.bitmapContext = bitmap
            self.setNeedsDisplay()
            UIApplication.sharedApplication().endBackgroundTask(bti) // *
        }
    }
}
```

If our app is backgrounded while `drawThatPuppy` is in progress, it will (we hope) be given enough background time to run that it can eventually proceed all the way to the end. Thus, the property `bitmapContext` will be updated, and `setNeedsDisplay` will be called, while we are still in the background. Our `drawRect:` will not be called until our app is brought back to the front, but there's nothing wrong with that.

It's good policy to use a similar technique when you're notified that your app is being backgrounded. You might respond to the app delegate message `applicationDid-EnterBackground:` (or the corresponding `UIApplicationDidEnterBackground-Notification`) by saving data and reducing memory usage, but this can take time, whereas you'd like to return from `applicationDidEnterBackground:` as quickly as possible. A reasonable solution is to implement `applicationDidEnterBackground:` very much like `drawThatPuppy` in the example I just gave: call `beginBackgroundTask-WithExpirationHandler:`, and then call `dispatch_async` to get off the main thread and do your saving and so forth.

CHAPTER 26

Undo

The ability to undo the most recent action is familiar from OS X. The idea is that, provided the user realizes soon enough that a mistake has been made, that mistake can be reversed. Typically, a Mac application will maintain an internal stack of undoable actions; choosing Edit → Undo or pressing Command-Z will reverse the action at the top of the stack, and will also make that action available for redo.

Some iOS apps, too, may benefit from at least a limited undo facility, and this is not difficult to implement. Some built-in views — in particular, those that involve text entry, UITextField and UITextView (Chapter 10) — implement undo already. And you can add it in other areas of your app.

Undo is provided through an instance of NSUndoManager, which basically just maintains a stack of undoable actions, along with a secondary stack of redoable actions. The goal in general is to work with the NSUndoManager so as to handle both undo and redo in the standard manner: when the user chooses to undo the most recent action, the action at the top of the undo stack is popped off and reversed and is pushed onto the top of the redo stack.

In this chapter, I'll illustrate an NSUndoManager for a simple app that has just one kind of undoable action. More complicated apps, obviously, will be more complicated! On the other hand, iOS apps, unlike OS X apps, do not generally need deep or pervasive undo functionality. For more about the NSUndoManager class and how to use it, read Apple's *Undo Architecture* as well as the documentation for the class itself. Also, UIDocument (see Chapter 23) has an undo manager (its undoManager property), which automatically and appropriately updates the document's "dirty" state for you.

Undo Manager

In our artificially simple app, the user can drag a small square around the screen. We'll start with an instance of a UIView subclass, MyView, to which has been attached a

UIPanGestureRecognizer to make it draggable, as described in Chapter 5. The gesture recognizer's action target is the MyView instance itself:

```
func dragging (p : UIPanGestureRecognizer) {
    switch p.state {
    case .Began, .Changed:
        let delta = p.translationInView(self.superview!)
        var c = self.center
        c.x += delta.x; c.y += delta.y
        self.center = c
        p.setTranslation(CGPointZero, inView: self.superview!)
    default:break
    }
}
```

To make dragging of this view undoable, we need an NSUndoManager instance. Let's store this in a property of MyView itself, `self.undoer`:

```
let undoer = NSUndoManager()
```

Target–Action Undo

There are three ways to register an action as undoable. I'll start with the NSUndo-Manager method `registerUndoWithTarget:selector:object:`. This method uses a target–action architecture: you provide a target, a selector for a method that takes one parameter, and the object value to be passed as argument when the method is called. Then, later, if the NSUndoManager is sent the undo message, it simply sends that action to that target with that argument. The job of the action method is to undo whatever it is that needs undoing.

What we want to undo here is the setting of our `center` property. This can't be expressed directly using a target–action architecture, because the parameter of `setCenter:` needs to be a CGPoint; we can't use a CGPoint as the `object:` in `registerUndoWith-Target:selector:object:`, because it isn't an Objective-C object (Swift will complain that it doesn't conform to AnyObject). Therefore we're going to have to provide, as our action method, a secondary method that *does* take an object parameter. This is neither bad nor unusual; it is quite common for actions to have a special representation just for the purpose of making them undoable.

So, in our `dragging:` method, instead of setting `self.center` to c directly, we now call a secondary method (let's call it `setCenterUndoably:`):

```
var c = self.center
c.x += delta.x; c.y += delta.y
self.setCenterUndoably(NSValue(CGPoint:c))
```

At a minimum, `setCenterUndoably:` should do the job that setting `self.center` used to do:

```
func setCenterUndoably (newCenter:NSValue) {
    self.center = newCenter.CGPointValue()
}
```

This works in the sense that the view is draggable exactly as before, but we have not yet made this action undoable. To do so, we must ask ourselves what message the NSUndo-Manager would need to send in order to undo the action we are about to perform. We would want the NSUndoManager to set self.center back to the value it has *now*, before we change it as we are about to do. And what method would NSUndoManager call in order to do that? It would call setCenterUndoably:, the very method we are implementing now! So:

```
func setCenterUndoably (newCenter:NSValue) {
    self.undoer.registerUndoWithTarget(
        self, selector: "setCenterUndoably:",
        object: NSValue(CGPoint:self.center))
    self.center = newCenter.CGPointValue()
}
```

That code has a remarkable effect: it makes our action not only undoable but also redo-able! The reason is that NSUndoManager has an internal state, and responds differently to registerUndoWithTarget:selector:object: depending on its state. If the NSUndoManager is sent registerUndoWithTarget:selector:object: *while it is undoing*, it puts the target–action information on the redo stack instead of the undo stack (because redo *is* the undo of an undo, if you see what I mean).

Here's how our code works to undo and then redo an action:

1. We perform an action by way of setCenterUndoably:, which calls registerUndo-WithTarget:selector:object: with the *old* value of self.center. The NSUndo-Manager adds this to its undo stack.

2. Now suppose we want to undo that action. We send undo to the NSUndoManager.

3. The NSUndoManager calls setCenterUndoably: with the old value that we passed in earlier when we called registerUndoWithTarget:selector:object:. Thus, we are going to set the center back to that old value. But before we do that, we send registerUndoWithTarget:selector:object: to the NSUndoManager with the *current* value of self.center. The NSUndoManager knows that it is currently undoing, so it understands this registration as something to be added to its redo stack.

4. Now suppose we want to redo that undo. We send redo to the NSUndoManager, and sure enough, the NSUndoManager calls setCenterUndoably: with the value that we previously undid. (And, once again, we call registerUndoWith-Target:selector:object: with an action that goes onto the NSUndoManager's undo stack.)

Undo Grouping

So far, so good. But our implementation of undo is very annoying, because we are adding a single object to the undo stack every time `dragging:` is called — and it is called many times during the course of a single drag. Thus, undoing merely undoes the tiny increment corresponding to one individual `dragging:` call. What we'd like is for undoing to undo an *entire* dragging gesture. We can implement this through *undo grouping*. As the gesture begins, we start a group; when the gesture ends, we end the group:

```
func dragging (p : UIPanGestureRecognizer) {
    switch p.state {
    case .Began:
        self.undoer.beginUndoGrouping()
        fallthrough
    case .Began, .Changed:
        let delta = p.translationInView(self.superview!)
        var c = self.center
        c.x += delta.x; c.y += delta.y
        self.setCenterUndoably(NSValue(CGPoint:c))
        p.setTranslation(CGPointZero, inView: self.superview!)
    case .Ended, .Cancelled:
        self.undoer.endUndoGrouping()
    default: break
    }
}
```

This works: each complete gesture of dragging MyView, from the time the user's finger contacts the view to the time it leaves, is now undoable (and redoable) as a single unit.

A further refinement would be to animate the "drag" that the NSUndoManager performs when it undoes or redoes a user drag gesture. To do so, we take advantage of the fact that we, too, can examine the NSUndoManager's state by way of its `isUndoing` and `isRedoing` properties; we animate the `center` change when the NSUndoManager is "dragging," but not when the user is dragging:

```
func setCenterUndoably (newCenter:NSValue) {
    self.undoer.registerUndoWithTarget(
        self, selector: "setCenterUndoably:",
        object: NSValue(CGPoint:self.center))
    if self.undoer.undoing || self.undoer.redoing {
        UIView.animateWithDuration(
            0.4, delay: 0.1, options: [], animations: {
                self.center = newCenter.CGPointValue()
            }, completion: nil)
    } else {
        // just do it
        self.center = newCenter.CGPointValue()
    }
}
```

Invocation Undo

Earlier I said that `registerUndoWithTarget:selector:object:` was one of three ways to register an action as undoable. The second way is `prepareWithInvocationTarget:`. In general, the advantage of `prepareWithInvocationTarget:` is that it lets you specify a method with any number of parameters, and those parameters needn't be objects. You provide the target and, *in the same line of code*, send to the object returned from this call the message and arguments you want sent when the NSUndoManager is sent `undo` or `redo`. So, in our example, instead of this line:

```
self.undoer.registerUndoWithTarget(
    self, selector: "setCenterUndoably:",
    object: NSValue(CGPoint:self.center))
```

You'd say this:

```
self.undoer.prepareWithInvocationTarget(self)
    .setCenterUndoably(self.center)
```

That code seems impossible: how can we send `setCenterUndoably:` without *calling* `setCenterUndoably:`? Either we are sending it to `self`, in which case it should actually be called at this moment, or we are sending it to some other object that doesn't implement `setCenterUndoably:`, in which case our app should crash. However, under the hood, the NSUndoManager is cleverly using dynamism (similarly to the message-forwarding example in Chapter 12) to capture this call as an NSInvocation object, which it can use later to send the same message with the same arguments to the specified target.

If we're going to use `prepareWithInvocationTarget:`, there's no need to wrap the CGPoint value representing the old and new `center` of our view as an NSValue. So our complete implementation now looks like this:

```
func setCenterUndoably (newCenter:CGPoint) { // *
    self.undoer.prepareWithInvocationTarget(self)
        .setCenterUndoably(self.center) // *
    if self.undoer.undoing || self.undoer.redoing {
        UIView.animateWithDuration(
            0.4, delay: 0.1, options: [], animations: {
                self.center = newCenter // *
            }, completion: nil)
    } else {
        // just do it
        self.center = newCenter // *
    }
}
func dragging (p : UIPanGestureRecognizer) {
    switch p.state {
    case .Began:
        self.undoer.beginUndoGrouping()
        fallthrough
    case .Began, .Changed:
```

```
        let delta = p.translationInView(self.superview!)
        var c = self.center
        c.x += delta.x; c.y += delta.y
        self.setCenterUndoably(c) // *
        p.setTranslation(CGPointZero, inView: self.superview!)
    case .Ended, .Cancelled:
        self.undoer.endUndoGrouping()
    default: break
    }
}
```

Functional Undo

New in iOS 9, there's a third way to register an action as undoable: `registerUndoWith-Target:handler:`. The `handler:` is a function that will take one parameter, namely whatever you pass as the `target:` argument, and will be called when undoing (or, if we register while undoing, when redoing). This gives us a more idiomatic way to do what `prepareWithInvocationTarget:` does:

```
func setCenterUndoably (newCenter:CGPoint) {
    let oldCenter = self.center
    self.undoer.registerUndoWithTarget(self) {
        v in
        v.setCenterUndoably(oldCenter)
    }
    if self.undoer.undoing || self.undoer.redoing {
        UIView.animateWithDuration(
            0.4, delay: 0.1, options: [], animations: {
                self.center = newCenter // *
            }, completion: nil)
    } else {
        // just do it
        self.center = newCenter // *
    }
}
```

My handler code refers to `v`, rather than to `self`, even though `self` and `v` are the same object, so that I don't accidentally capture `self` strongly in the closure. The reason for setting `oldCenter` before calling `registerUndoWithTarget:handler:` is to capture the value of `self.center` as it is *now*; if our handler function were to call `setCenter-Undoably(v.center)`, we'd be using the value that `v.center` will have *at undo time*, and we would be setting the center to the value it already has, which would be pointless.

Our code works, but we are failing to take full advantage of the fact that we now have the ability to register with the undo manager a full-fledged function rather than a mere function call. This means that we can move into the `handler:` function everything that should happen when undoing. This includes the animation! So our `setCenter-Undoably:` implementation now looks like this:

```
func setCenterUndoably (newCenter:CGPoint) {
    let oldCenter = self.center
    self.undoer.registerUndoWithTarget(self) {
        v in
        UIView.animateWithDuration(
            0.4, delay: 0.1, options: [], animations: {
                v.center = oldCenter
            }, completion: nil)
        v.setCenterUndoably(oldCenter)
    }
    if !(self.undoer.undoing || self.undoer.redoing) {
        // just do it
        self.center = newCenter
    }
}
```

That's much cleaner. Our `handler:` function still needs to call `setCenterUndoably:`, because otherwise we won't get redo registration during undo. But if we are undoing or redoing, our `registerUndoWithTarget:` call is the *only* thing that happens; we set `self.center` to `newCenter` only if we were called by the `dragging:` gesture recognizer handler.

But wait! In that case, why are we setting `self.center` here at all? We can do it back in the `dragging:` gesture recognizer handler, just we were doing before we added undo to this app! The result is, I think, the cleanest and clearest implementation of all:

```
func registerForUndo() {
    let oldCenter = self.center
    self.undoer.registerUndoWithTarget(self) {
        v in
        UIView.animateWithDuration(
            0.4, delay: 0.1, options: [], animations: {
                v.center = oldCenter
            }, completion: nil)
        v.registerForUndo()
    }
}
func dragging (p : UIPanGestureRecognizer) {
    switch p.state {
    case .Began:
        self.undoer.beginUndoGrouping()
        fallthrough
    case .Began, .Changed:
        let delta = p.translationInView(self.superview!)
        var c = self.center
        c.x += delta.x; c.y += delta.y
        self.registerForUndo() // *
        self.center = c // *
        p.setTranslation(CGPointZero, inView: self.superview!)
    case .Ended, .Cancelled:
```

```
        self.undoer.endUndoGrouping()
    default: break
    }
}
```

(A further refinement might be to move `registerForUndo` *inside* the `dragging:` gesture recognizer handler as a local function.)

Undo Interface

We must also decide how to let the user *request* undo and redo. In developing the code from the preceding section, I used two buttons: an Undo button that sent `undo` to the NSUndoManager, and a Redo button that sent `redo` to the NSUndoManager. This can be a perfectly reasonable interface, but let's talk about some others.

Shake-To-Edit

By default, your app supports *shake-to-edit*. This means the user can shake the device to bring up an undo/redo interface. We discussed this briefly in Chapter 22. If you don't turn off this feature by setting the shared UIApplication's `applicationSupportsShakeToEdit` property to `false`, then when the user shakes the device, the runtime walks up the responder chain, starting with the first responder, looking for a responder whose inherited `undoManager` property returns an actual NSUndoManager instance. If it finds one, it puts up an undo/redo interface, allowing the user to communicate with that NSUndoManager.

You will recall what it takes for a UIResponder to be first responder in this sense: it must return `true` from `canBecomeFirstResponder`, and it must actually be made first responder through a call to `becomeFirstResponder`. Let's make MyView satisfy these requirements. For example, we might call `becomeFirstResponder` at the end of `dragging:`, like this:

```
override func canBecomeFirstResponder() -> Bool {
    return true
}
func dragging (p : UIPanGestureRecognizer) {
    switch p.state {
    // ... the rest as before ...
    case .Ended, .Cancelled:
        self.undoer.endUndoGrouping()
        self.becomeFirstResponder()
    default: break
    }
}
```

Then, to make shake-to-edit work, we have only to provide a getter for the `undoManager` property that returns our undo manager, `self.undoer`:

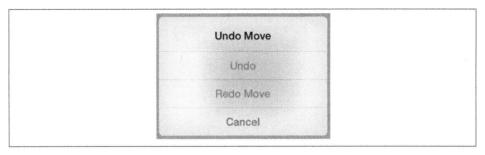

Figure 26-1. The shake-to-edit undo/redo interface

```
let undoer = NSUndoManager()
override var undoManager : NSUndoManager? {
    return self.undoer
}
```

This works: shaking the device now brings up the undo/redo interface, and its buttons work correctly. However, I don't like the way the buttons are labeled; they just say Undo and Redo. To make this interface more expressive, we should provide a string describing each undoable action by calling `setActionName:`. We can appropriately and conveniently do this at the same time that we register our undo action:

```
self.undoer.setActionName("Move")
```

Now the undo/redo interface has more informative labels, as shown in Figure 26-1.

Undo Menu

Another possible interface is through a menu (Figure 26-2). Personally, I prefer this approach, as I am not fond of shake-to-edit (it seems both violent and unreliable). This is the same menu used by a UITextField or UITextView for displaying the Copy and Paste menu items (Chapter 10). The requirements for summoning this menu are effectively the same as those for shake-to-edit: we need a responder chain with a first responder at the bottom of it. So the code we've just supplied for making MyView first responder remains applicable.

We can make a menu appear, for example, in response to a long press on our MyView instance. So let's attach another gesture recognizer to MyView. This will be a UILongPressGestureRecognizer, whose action handler is called `longPress:`. Recall from Chapter 10 how to implement the menu: we get the singleton global UIMenuController object and specify an array of custom UIMenuItems as its `menuItems` property. We can make the menu appear by sending the UIMenuController the `setMenuVisible:animated:` message. But a particular menu item will appear in the menu only if we also return `true` from `canPerformAction:withSender:` for that menu item's action. Delightfully, the NSUndoManager's `canUndo` and `canRedo` properties tell us what value `canPerform-`

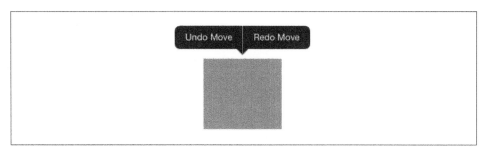

Figure 26-2. The shared menu as an undo/redo interface

`Action:withSender:` should return. We can also get the titles for our custom menu items from the NSUndoManager itself, through its `undoMenuItemTitle` property:

```
func longPress (g : UIGestureRecognizer) {
    if g.state == .Began {
        let m = UIMenuController.sharedMenuController()
        m.setTargetRect(self.bounds, inView: self)
        let mi1 = UIMenuItem(
            title: self.undoer.undoMenuItemTitle, action: "undo:")
        let mi2 = UIMenuItem(
            title: self.undoer.redoMenuItemTitle, action: "redo:")
        m.menuItems = [mi1, mi2]
        m.setMenuVisible(true, animated:true)
    }
}
override func canPerformAction(
    action: Selector, withSender sender: AnyObject!) -> Bool {
        if action == Selector("undo:") {
            return self.undoer.canUndo
        }
        if action == Selector("redo:") {
            return self.undoer.canRedo
        }
        return super.canPerformAction(action, withSender: sender)
}
func undo(_:AnyObject?) {
    self.undoer.undo()
}
func redo(_:AnyObject?) {
    self.undoer.redo()
}
```

Application Lifetime Events

Your app's one and only application object (a UIApplication instance, or on rare occasions a UIApplication subclass instance) is created for you as the shared application object by UIApplicationMain, along with its delegate; in the Xcode project templates, this delegate is an instance of the AppDelegate class. The application reports lifetime events through method calls to its delegate; other instances can also register to receive most of these events as notifications.

These events, notifying you of stages in the lifetime of your app as a whole and giving your code an opportunity to run in response, are extraordinarily important and fundamental. This appendix is devoted to a survey of them, along with some typical scenarios in which they will arrive.

Application States

In the early days of iOS — before iOS 4 — the lifetime of an app was extremely simple: either it was running or it wasn't. The user tapped your app's icon in the springboard, and your app was launched and began to run. The user used your app for a while. Eventually, the user pressed the Home button (the physical button next to the screen) and your app was terminated — it was no longer running. The user had *quit* your app. Launch, run, quit: that was the entire life cycle of an app. If the user decided to use your app again, the whole cycle started again.

The reason for this simplicity was that, before iOS 4, an iOS device, with its slow processor and its almost brutal paucity of memory and other resources, compensated for its own shortcomings by a simple rule: it could run *only one app at a time*. While your app was running, it occupied not only the entire screen but the vast majority of the device's resources, leaving room only for the system and some hidden built-in processes to support it; it had, in effect, sole and complete control of the device.

Starting in iOS 4, that changed. Apple devised an ingenious architecture whereby, despite the device's limited resources, more than one app could run simultaneously — sort of. The Home button changed its meaning and its effect upon your app: contrary to the naïve perception of some users, the Home button was no longer a Quit button. Nowadays, when the user presses the Home button to leave your app, your app does not die; technically, the Home button does not terminate your app. When your app occupies the entire screen, it is *in the foreground* (or *frontmost*); when some other app proceeds to occupy the entire screen, your app is *backgrounded and suspended*. This means that your app is essentially freeze-dried; its process still exists, but it isn't actively running, and it isn't getting any events — though notifications can be stored by the system for later delivery if your app comes to the front once again.

The cleverness of this arrangement is that your app, when the user returns to it after having left it to use some other app for a while, is found in the *very same state* as when the user left it. The app was not terminated; it simply stopped and froze, and waited in suspended animation. Returning to your app no longer means that your app is *launched*, but merely that it is *resumed*.

All of this is not to say, however, that your app *can't* be terminated. It can be — though not by the user pressing the Home button. The most common scenario is that the system quietly kills your app while it is suspended. This undermines the app's ability to resume; when the user returns to your app, it *will* have to launch from scratch, just as in the pre–iOS 4 days. The death of your app is rather like that of the scientists killed by HAL 9000 in *2001: A Space Odyssey* — they went to sleep expecting to wake up later, but instead their life-support systems were turned off while they slept. The iOS system's reasons for killing your app are not quite as paranoid as HAL's, but they do have a certain Darwinian ruthlessness: your app, while suspended, continues to occupy a chunk of the device's memory, and the system needs to reclaim that memory so some *other* app can use it. It is also possible, of course, that the user will switch off the device while your app is asleep.

 Your app can opt out of background suspension: you set the "Application does not run in background" key (UIApplicationExitsOnSuspend) in your *Info.plist*, and now the Home button *does* terminate your app, just as in the pre–iOS 4 days. It's improbable that you would want to do this, but it could make sense for some apps.

When the user leaves your app, therefore, one of two things might happen later. It could be woken and resumed from suspended animation, in the very state that it was in when the user left it, or it could be launched from scratch because it was terminated in the background. It is this bifurcation of your app's possible fates that state saving and restoration, discussed at the end of Chapter 6, is intended to cope with. The idea, in theory, is that your app should behave the same way when it comes to the front, regardless of whether it was terminated or merely suspended. We all know from experience, however, that this goal is difficult to achieve, and Apple's own apps are noteworthy for failing to achieve it; for example, it is perfectly obvious whether iBooks was suspended or terminated, as it behaves completely differently when it comes to the front.

A further complication is that your app can be backgrounded *without* being suspended. This is a special privilege, accorded in order that your app may perform a limited range of highly focussed activities. For example, an app that is playing music or tracking the device's location when it goes into the background may be permitted to continue doing so in the background. In addition, an app that has been suspended can be woken briefly, *remaining in the background*, in order to receive and respond to a message — in order to update its data via the network, for example, or to be told that the user has crossed a geofence. (See Chapters 14, 22, and 24.)

There is also an intermediate state in which your app can find itself, where it is neither frontmost nor backgrounded. This happens, for example, when the user summons the control center or notification center in front of your app — or, new in iOS 9, during iPad multitasking. In such situations, your app may be *inactive* without actually being backgrounded.

Your app's code can thus, in fact, be running even though the app is not frontmost. If your code needs to know the app's state in this regard, it can ask the shared UIApplication object for its `applicationState` (UIApplicationState), which will be one of these:

- `.Active`
- `.Inactive`
- `.Background`

App Delegate Events

The suite of basic application lifetime events that may be sent to your app delegate is surprisingly limited; indeed, in my opinion, the information your app is given is unfortunately rather too coarse-grained. The events are as follows:

`application:didFinishLaunchingWithOptions:`
> The app has started up from scratch. You'll typically perform initializations here. If an app doesn't have a main storyboard, this code must also create the app's window and show it.
>
> (Another event, `application:willFinishLaunchingWithOptions:`, arrives even earlier. Its purpose is to allow your app to participate in the state saving and restoration mechanism discussed in Chapter 6.)

`applicationDidBecomeActive:`

> Received after `application:didFinishLaunchingWithOptions:`. Also received after the end of the situation that caused the app delegate to receive `application-WillResignActive:`.

`applicationWillResignActive:`

> One possibility is that something has blocked the app's interface — for example, the screen has been locked. A local notification alert or an incoming phone call could also cause this event. So too, in iOS 9, can an iPad multitasking situation.
>
> When this situation ends, the app delegate will receive `applicationDidBecome-Active:`. Alternatively, the app may be about to go into the background (and will then probably be suspended); in that case, the next event will be `applicationDid-EnterBackground:`.

`applicationDidEnterBackground:`

> The application has been backgrounded. Always preceded by `applicationWill-ResignActive:`.
>
> Your app will then probably be suspended; before that happens, you have a little time to finish up last-minute tasks, such as relinquishing unneeded memory (see Chapter 6), and if you need more time for a lengthy task, you can ask for it (see Chapter 25).

`applicationWillEnterForeground:`

> The application was backgrounded, and is now coming back to the front. Always followed by `applicationDidBecomeActive:`. Note that this message is *not* sent on launch, because the app wasn't previously in the background.

`applicationWillTerminate:`

> The application is about to be killed dead. Surprisingly, however, even though every running app will eventually be terminated, it is extremely unlikely that your app will *ever* receive this event (unless it has opted out of background suspension, with `UIApplicationExitsOnSuspend`). The reason is that, by the time your app is terminated by the system, it is usually already suspended and incapable of receiving events. (I'll mention some exceptional cases, though, in a moment; and see Chapter 14 for another.)

App Lifetime Scenarios

The application lifetime events are best understood through some typical scenarios:

The app launches from scratch

> Your app delegate receives these messages:
>
> - `application:didFinishLaunchingWithOptions:`

- `applicationDidBecomeActive:`

The user clicks the Home button
Your app delegate receives these messages:

- `applicationWillResignActive:`
- `applicationDidEnterBackground:`

The user summons your backgrounded app to the front
Your app delegate receives these messages:

- `applicationWillEnterForeground:`
- `applicationDidBecomeActive:`

If the user summons your backgrounded app to the front indirectly, another delegate message may be sent between these two calls. For example, if the user asks another app to hand a file over to your app (Chapter 23), your app receives `application:openURL:options:` between `applicationWillEnterForeground:` and `applicationDidBecomeActive:`.

The user double-clicks the Home button
The user can now work in the app switcher interface. If your app is frontmost, your app delegate receives this message:

- `applicationWillResignActive:`

The user, in the app switcher, chooses another app
If your app was frontmost, your app delegate receives this message:

- `applicationDidEnterBackground:`

The user, in the app switcher, chooses your app
If your app was the most recently frontmost app, then it was never backgrounded, so your app delegate receives this message:

- `applicationDidBecomeActive:`

The user, in the app switcher, terminates your app
If your app was the most recently frontmost app, your app delegate receives these messages:

- `applicationDidEnterBackground:`
- `applicationWillTerminate:`

This is one of the few extraordinary circumstances under which your app can receive `applicationWillTerminate:`, because it was never backgrounded long enough to be suspended.

The user summons the control center or notification center
    If your app is frontmost, your app delegate receives this message:

- `applicationWillResignActive:`

The user dismisses the control center or notification center
    If your app is frontmost, your app delegate receives this message:

- `applicationDidBecomeActive:`

A local notification alert from another app appears
    If your app is frontmost, your app delegate receives this message:

- `applicationWillResignActive:`

From a local notification alert, the user launches the other app
    Your app delegate receives this message:

- `applicationDidEnterBackground:`

On a multitasking iPad, the user splits the screen to show the app switcher
    Your app delegate receives this message:

- `applicationWillResignActive:`

On a multitasking iPad, the user splits the screen to show two apps
    Your app delegate, if it received `applicationWillResignActive:`, receives this message:

- `applicationDidBecomeActive:` (both apps are active when they share the screen)

On a multitasking iPad, the user toggles between split sizes
    Your app delegate receives these messages:

- `applicationWillResignActive:`
- `applicationDidBecomeActive:` (the app is inactive while the user is dragging the divider)

The screen is locked
    If your app is frontmost, your app delegate receives these messages:

- `applicationWillResignActive:`
- `applicationDidEnterBackground:`

The screen is unlocked
    If your app is frontmost, your app delegate receives these messages:

- `applicationWillEnterForeground:`

- `applicationDidBecomeActive:`

The user holds the screen-lock button down
The device offers to shut itself off. If your app is frontmost, your app delegate receives this message:

- `applicationWillResignActive:`

The user, as the device offers to shut itself off, cancels
If your app is frontmost, your app delegate receives this message:

- `applicationDidBecomeActive:`

The user, as the device offers to shut itself off, accepts
If your app is frontmost, the app delegate receives these messages:

- `applicationDidEnterBackground:`

- `applicationWillTerminate:`

Bear in mind that you can't make any assumptions about the *timing* of the app delegate messages with respect to lifetime events received by other objects. They may well be interwoven in surprising ways. For example, there are circumstances where the root view controller may receive its initial lifetime events, such as `viewDidLoad:` and `view-WillAppear:`, before `application:didFinishLaunchingWithOptions:` has even finished running.

Different systems can also introduce changes in timing. iOS 8 brought with it a momentous change: the app delegate receives `applicationDidBecomeActive:` *after* the root view controller's interface has appeared and the root view controller has received `view-DidAppear:`, so that the opening sequence of events in iOS 8 is like this:

- `application:didFinishLaunchingWithOptions:`

- `viewDidLoad`

- `viewWillAppear:`

- `viewDidAppear:`

- `applicationDidBecomeActive:`

This was a disaster for many of my apps. I very typically register for `UIApplicationDid-BecomeActiveNotification` in the view controller's `viewDidAppear:` in order to be notified of *subsequent* activations of the app; but if I do that in iOS 8, the notification I just registered for arrives *immediately*. In iOS 9, however, the order returns to what it was in iOS 7 and before:

- `application:didFinishLaunchingWithOptions:`

- `viewDidLoad`

- `viewWillAppear:`

- `applicationDidBecomeActive:`

- `viewDidAppear:`

Needless to say, this difference alone can make writing an app compatible with both iOS 8 and iOS 9 a fairly daunting proposition.

Some Useful Utility Functions

As you work with iOS and Swift, you'll doubtless develop a personal library of frequently used convenience functions. Here are some that have come in handy in my own life, to which I've referred in the course of this book.

Delayed Performance

Delayed performance is of paramount importance in iOS programming, where it is often the case that the interface must be given a moment to settle down before we proceed to the next command in a sequence. Calling `dispatch_after` is particularly tedious in Swift, because its strict numeric typing necessitates a lot of casting, so here's a utility function:

```swift
func delay(delay:Double, closure:()->()) {
    dispatch_after(
        dispatch_time(
            DISPATCH_TIME_NOW,
            Int64(delay * Double(NSEC_PER_SEC))
        ),
        dispatch_get_main_queue(), closure)
}
```

And call it like this:

```swift
delay(0.4) {
    // do something here
}
```

In my world, this is far and away the most important utility function; I use it in every single app.

Center of a CGRect

One so frequently wants the center point of a CGRect that even the Swift shorthand `CGPointMake(rect.midX, rect.midY)` becomes tedious. You can extend CGRect to do the work for you:

```
extension CGRect {
    var center : CGPoint {
        return CGPointMake(self.midX, self.midY)
    }
}
```

Adjust a CGSize

There's a CGRect `insetBy`, but there's no comparable method for changing an existing CGSize by a width delta and a height delta. Let's make one:

```
extension CGSize {
    func sizeByDelta(dw dw:CGFloat, dh:CGFloat) -> CGSize {
        return CGSizeMake(self.width + dw, self.height + dh)
    }
}
```

Dictionary of Views

There are no Swift macros (because there's no Swift preprocessor), so you can't write the equivalent of Objective-C's `NSDictionaryOfVariableBindings`, which turns a literal list of view names into a dictionary of string names and view references for use in connection with NSLayoutConstraint's `constraintsWithVisualFormat`. You can, however, generate such a dictionary with fixed string names, like this:

```
func dictionaryOfNames(arr:UIView...) -> [String:UIView] {
    var d = [String:UIView]()
    for (ix,v) in arr.enumerate() {
        d["v\(ix+1)"] = v
    }
    return d
}
```

This utility function takes a list of views and simply makes up new string names for them, of the form `"v1"`, `"v2"`, and so on, in order. Knowing the rule by which the string names are generated, you then use those string names in your visual format strings. For example, if you generate the dictionary by calling `dictionaryOfNames(mainView, myLabel)`, then in any visual format string that uses this dictionary, you will refer to `mainView` by the name `v1` and `myLabel` by the name `v2`.

Constraint Issues

These are NSLayoutConstraint class methods, added in an extension, aimed at helping to detect and analyze constraint issues (referred to in Chapter 1):

```
extension NSLayoutConstraint {
    class func reportAmbiguity (var v:UIView?) {
        if v == nil {
            v = UIApplication.sharedApplication().keyWindow
        }
        for vv in v!.subviews {
            print("\(vv) \(vv.hasAmbiguousLayout())")
            if vv.subviews.count > 0 {
                self.reportAmbiguity(vv)
            }
        }
    }
    class func listConstraints (var v:UIView?) {
        if v == nil {
            v = UIApplication.sharedApplication().keyWindow
        }
        for vv in v!.subviews {
            let arr1 = vv.constraintsAffectingLayoutForAxis(.Horizontal)
            let arr2 = vv.constraintsAffectingLayoutForAxis(.Vertical)
            NSLog("\n\n%@\nH: %@\nV:%@", vv, arr1, arr2)
            if vv.subviews.count > 0 {
                self.listConstraints(vv)
            }
        }
    }
}
```

Drawing Into an Image Context

Our goal here is to encapsulate the boring, repetitive, clunky, imperative-programming dance of beginning a UIGraphics image context, drawing into it, extracting the image, and ending the context. This utility function expresses everything but the drawing; you hand it a function describing the drawing, and you get back an image:

```
func imageOfSize(size:CGSize, _ opaque:Bool = false,
    @noescape _ closure:() -> ()) -> UIImage {
        UIGraphicsBeginImageContextWithOptions(size, opaque, 0)
        closure()
        let result = UIGraphicsGetImageFromCurrentImageContext()
        UIGraphicsEndImageContext()
        return result
}
```

You call it like this:

```
let im = imageOfSize(CGSizeMake(100,100)) {
    let con = UIGraphicsGetCurrentContext()!
    CGContextAddEllipseInRect(con, CGRectMake(0,0,100,100))
    CGContextSetFillColorWithColor(con, UIColor.blueColor().CGColor)
    CGContextFillPath(con)
}
```

Finite Repetition of an Animation

This is a solution to the problem, posed in Chapter 4, of how to repeat a view animation
a small fixed number of times without using "begin/commit" syntax. My approach is to
employ tail recursion and a counter to chain the individual animations. The delay call
unwinds the call stack and works around possible drawing glitches:

```
extension UIView {
    class func animateWithTimes(times:Int,
        duration dur: NSTimeInterval,
        delay del: NSTimeInterval,
        options opts: UIViewAnimationOptions,
        animations anim: () -> Void,
        completion comp: ((Bool) -> Void)?) {
            func helper(t:Int,
                _ dur: NSTimeInterval,
                _ del: NSTimeInterval,
                _ opt: UIViewAnimationOptions,
                _ anim: () -> Void,
                _ com: ((Bool) -> Void)?) {
                    UIView.animateWithDuration(dur,
                        delay: del, options: opt,
                        animations: anim, completion: {
                            done in
                            if com != nil {
                                com!(done)
                            }
                            if t > 0 {
                                delay(0) {
                                    helper(t-1, dur, del, opt, anim, com)
                                }
                            }
                    })
            }
            helper(times-1, dur, del, opts, anim, comp)
    }
}
```

The calling syntax is exactly like ordering a UIView animation in its full form, except
that there's an initial times parameter:

```
let opts = UIViewAnimationOptions.Autoreverse
let xorig = self.v.center.x
UIView.animateWithTimes(3, duration:1, delay:0, options:opts, animations:{
    self.v.center.x += 100
    }, completion:{
        _ in
        self.v.center.x = xorig
})
```

Remove Multiple Indexes From Array

It is often convenient to collect the indexes of items to be deleted from an array, and then to delete those items. An Array extension can be helpful here. We must be careful to sort the indexes in decreasing numeric order first, because array indexes will be off by one after an item at a lower index is removed:

```
extension Array {
    mutating func removeAtIndexes (ixs:[Int]) -> () {
        for i in ixs.sort(>) {
            self.removeAtIndex(i)
        }
    }
}
```

Configure a Value Class At the Point of Use

A recurring pattern in Cocoa is that a value class is instantiated and that instance is configured beforehand for a one-time use:

```
let para = NSMutableParagraphStyle()
para.headIndent = 10
para.firstLineHeadIndent = 10
para.tailIndent = -10
para.lineBreakMode = .ByWordWrapping
para.alignment = .Center
para.paragraphSpacing = 15
content.addAttribute(
    NSParagraphStyleAttributeName,
    value:para, range:NSMakeRange(0,1))
```

This has a clunky, procedural feel. It would be clearer and more functional, as well as reflecting the natural order of thought, if all of that could happen at the actual point of use. Here's a generic function that permits us to do that:

```
func lend<T where T:NSObject> (@noescape closure:(T)->()) -> T {
    let orig = T()
    closure(orig)
    return orig
}
```

Now we can express ourselves like this:

```
content.addAttribute(NSParagraphStyleAttributeName,
    value:lend {
        (para:NSMutableParagraphStyle) in
        para.headIndent = 10
        para.firstLineHeadIndent = 10
        para.tailIndent = -10
        para.lineBreakMode = .ByWordWrapping
        para.alignment = .Center
        para.paragraphSpacing = 15
    }, range:NSMakeRange(0,1))
```

Cancelable Closure-Based Timer

The Objective-C methods performSelector:withObject:afterDelay: and cancel-
PreviousPerformRequestsWithTarget: were unavailable in Swift 1.2 and before, so I
created an alternative. They became available in Swift 2.0, but I still like my alternative
better! It is also a nice functional replacement for NSTimer.

My replacement is a class, CancelableTimer; it revolves around a GCD timer dispatch
source, along with Swift's ability to receive a function as a parameter. The initializer is
init(once:handler:). The handler: is called when the timer fires. If once: is false,
this will be a repeating timer. It obeys two methods, startWithInterval: and cancel:

```
class CancelableTimer: NSObject {
    private var q = dispatch_queue_create("timer",nil)
    private var timer : dispatch_source_t!
    private var firsttime = true
    private var once : Bool
    private var handler : () -> ()
    init(once:Bool, handler:()->()) {
        self.once = once
        self.handler = handler
        super.init()
    }
    func startWithInterval(interval:Double) {
        self.firsttime = true
        self.cancel()
        self.timer = dispatch_source_create(
            DISPATCH_SOURCE_TYPE_TIMER,
            0, 0, self.q)
        dispatch_source_set_timer(self.timer,
            dispatch_walltime(nil, 0),
            UInt64(interval * Double(NSEC_PER_SEC)),
            UInt64(0.05 * Double(NSEC_PER_SEC)))
        dispatch_source_set_event_handler(self.timer, {
            if self.firsttime {
                self.firsttime = false
                return
            }
            self.handler()
```

```
            if self.once {
                self.cancel()
            }
        })
        dispatch_resume(self.timer)
    }
    func cancel() {
        if self.timer != nil {
            dispatch_source_cancel(timer)
        }
    }
}
```

For an example of its use, see Chapter 22.

Generic Wrapper

This is the generic wrapper class used in Chapter 24. I didn't think of this; the idea comes from a Stack Overflow post (*http://stackoverflow.com/a/24760061/341994*):

```
class Wrapper<T> {
    let p:T
    init(_ p:T){self.p = p}
}
```

This is useful because it is an AnyObject and can therefore be passed into an Objective-C API wherever an AnyObject is expected. Making a Wrapper object is easy:

```
let w = Wrapper(anything)
```

Retrieving the anything when a Wrapper returns to you as an AnyObject requires that you discover, or know in advance, the type of its p and that you cast to that type:

```
let thing : AnyObject = // some kind of Wrapper
let realthing = (thing as! Wrapper).p as SomeType
```

Index

We'd like to hear your suggestions for improving our indexes. Send email to index@oreilly.com.

gravity, 874
groups, undo, 978
GUI (see interface)
guides, layout, 40, 271
gyroscope, 879

H

header, 431, 445
heading, 868
hierarchy, layer, 113
hierarchy, view, 8
hierarchy, view controller, 251
    message percolation, 534
high-resolution image files, 66
high-resolution layers, 123
highlighted table view cells, 460
hit-testing drawings, 236
hit-testing during animation, 238
hit-testing layers, 235
hit-testing views, 233
Home button, 986
HTML files, 601
HTTP requests, 930
HTTP, and App Transport Security, 927

I

IBDesignable, 61
IBInspectable, 61
iCloud, 909
identifier path, 377
image context, 76
image files, 66, 923
Image I/O framework, 923
imageOfSize, 995
images, animated, 142
images, drawing, 76, 79
images, inline, 558
images, resizable, 70
images, reversing, 75
images, small, 924
images, template, 74
implicit constraints, 32
in-app purchase, 948
initial view controller, 269
initialization of nib-based instances, 267
Instruments, 136, 420
interaction controller, 321
interactive view controller transitions, 320

interface and threads, 954
interface for calendar, 825
interface for contacts, 808
interface for mail, 829
interface for map, 835
interface for messages, 829
interface for music library, 769
interface for photos, 773
interface for playing video or audio, 738
interface for posting, 829
interface for searching, 467
interface for taking pictures, 794
interface for trimming video, 753
interface for undoing, 982
interface that differs on iPad, 264, 297, 523
interface, resizing, 273, 539
interface, reversing, 48, 75
interface, rotating, 22, 273, 299
Internet, displaying resources from, 601
intrinsic content size, 44
iPad multitasking, 278, 539, 742
iPad, interface that differs on, 264, 297, 523
iPad, presented view controllers on, 295
iPad, resources that differ on, 67
iPod app (see Music app)
iPod library (see music library)
iTunes Match (see cloud-based music)
iTunes, sharing files through, 897

J

JavaScript, 608
JSON, 916

K

keyboard, 570–577, 585–586
    customizing, 576
    dismissing, 571, 579, 585
    language, 577
    scrolling in response, 571
    table views, 574

L

labels, 563–567
    built-in cell styles, 428
    line breaking vs. attributed strings, 564
    number of lines, 563
    sizing to fit content, 564

System Sound Services, 711

About the Author

Matt Neuburg started programming computers in 1968, when he was 14 years old, as a member of a literally underground high school club, which met once a week to do timesharing on a bank of PDP-10s by way of primitive teletype machines. He also occasionally used Princeton University's IBM-360/67, but gave it up in frustration when one day he dropped his punch cards. He majored in Greek at Swarthmore College, and received his PhD from Cornell University in 1981, writing his doctoral dissertation (about Aeschylus) on a mainframe. He proceeded to teach Classical languages, literature, and culture at many well-known institutions of higher learning, most of which now disavow knowledge of his existence, and to publish numerous scholarly articles unlikely to interest anyone. Meanwhile he obtained an Apple IIc and became hopelessly hooked on computers again, migrating to a Macintosh in 1990. He wrote some educational and utility freeware, became an early regular contributor to the online journal *TidBITS*, and in 1995 left academe to edit *MacTech* magazine. In August 1996 he became a freelancer, which means he has been looking for work ever since. He is the author of *Frontier: The Definitive Guide*, *REALbasic: The Definitive Guide*, and *AppleScript: The Definitive Guide*.

Colophon

The animal on the cover of *Programming iOS 9* is a kingbird, one of the 13 species of North American songbirds making up the genus *Tyrannus*. A group of kingbirds is called a "coronation," a "court," or a "tyranny."

Kingbirds eat insects, which they often catch in flight, swooping from a perch to grab the insect midair. They may also supplement their diets with berries and fruits. They have long, pointed wings, and males perform elaborate aerial courtship displays.

Both the genus name (meaning "tyrant" or "despot") and the common name ("kingbird") refer to these birds' aggressive defense of their territories, breeding areas, and mates. They have been documented attacking red-tailed hawks (which are more than twenty times their size), knocking bluejays out of trees, and driving away crows and ravens. (For its habit of standing up to much larger birds, the gray kingbird has been adopted as a Puerto Rican nationalist symbol.)

"Kingbird" most often refers to the Eastern kingbird (*T. tyrannus*), an average-size kingbird (7.5–9 inches long, wingspan 13–15 inches) found all across North America. This common and widespread bird has a dark head and back, with a white throat, chest, and belly. Its red crown patch is rarely seen. Its high-pitched, buzzing, stuttering sounds have been described as resembling "sparks jumping between wires" or an electric fence.

The cover image is from *Cassell's Natural History*. The cover fonts are URW Typewriter and Guardian Sans. The text font is Adobe Minion Pro; the heading font is Adobe Myriad Condensed; and the code font is Dalton Maag's Ubuntu Mono.

Get even more for your money.

Join the O'Reilly Community, and register the O'Reilly books you own. It's free, and you'll get:

- $4.99 ebook upgrade offer
- 40% upgrade offer on O'Reilly print books
- Membership discounts on books and events
- Free lifetime updates to ebooks and videos
- Multiple ebook formats, DRM FREE
- Participation in the O'Reilly community
- Newsletters
- Account management
- 100% Satisfaction Guarantee

Signing up is easy:

1. Go to: oreilly.com/go/register
2. Create an O'Reilly login.
3. Provide your address.
4. Register your books.

Note: English-language books only

To order books online:
oreilly.com/store

For questions about products or an order:
orders@oreilly.com

To sign up to get topic-specific email announcements and/or news about upcoming books, conferences, special offers, and new technologies:
elists@oreilly.com

For technical questions about book content:
booktech@oreilly.com

To submit new book proposals to our editors:
proposals@oreilly.com

O'Reilly books are available in multiple DRM-free ebook formats. For more information:
oreilly.com/ebooks

Lightning Source UK Ltd.
Milton Keynes UK
UKOW05f1058100216

268056UK00004B/5/P